# BASIC DOCUMENT
# ON HUMAN RIGHTS

# BASIC DOCUMENTS ON HUMAN RIGHTS

FOURTH EDITION

Edited by

IAN BROWNLIE, CBE, QC

and

GUY S. GOODWIN-GILL

OXFORD

UNIVERSITY PRESS

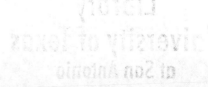

# OXFORD

UNIVERSITY PRESS

Great Clarendon Street, Oxford OX2 6DP

Oxford University Press is a department of the University of Oxford.
It furthers the University's objective of excellence in research, scholarship,
and education by publishing worldwide in

Oxford New York

Auckland Bangkok Buenos Aires Cape Town Chennai
Dar es Salaam Delhi Hong Kong Istanbul Karachi Kolkata
Kuala Lumpur Madrid Melbourne Mexico City Mumbai Nairobi
São Paulo Shanghai Singapore Taipei Tokyo Toronto

with an associated company in Berlin

Oxford is a registered trade mark of Oxford University Press
in the UK and in certain other countries

Published in the United States
by Oxford University Press Inc., New York

British Library Cataloguing in Publication Data

Data available

Library of Congress Cataloging in Publication Data

Data applied for

ISBN 0-19-924944-X

Typeset in Baskerville
by RefineCatch Limited, Bungay, Suffolk
Printed in Great Britain by
TJ International Ltd
Padstow, Cornwall

# CONTENTS

PART ONE

## STANDARD-SETTING BY THE UNITED
## NATIONS ORGANIZATION

## PART TWO

## IMPLEMENTATION AND STANDARD-SETTING IN
## CONVENTIONS SPONSORED BY THE UNITED NATIONS

PART THREE

# CONTRIBUTION OF THE INTERNATIONAL LABOUR ORGANIZATION

PART FOUR

# CONTRIBUTION OF THE UNITED NATIONS EDUCATIONAL, SCIENTIFIC, AND CULTURAL ORGANIZATION

PART FIVE

# EUROPEAN INSTITUTIONS AND CONVENTIONS

## PART SIX

## LATIN AMERICAN DEVELOPMENTS

PART SEVEN

# DEVELOPMENTS IN AFRICA

PART EIGHT

# DEVELOPMENTS IN THE ARAB WORLD

PART NINE

# THE CONCEPT OF EQUALITY

PART TEN

## HUMAN RIGHTS AND THE HUMAN GENOME

PART ELEVEN

## TRADE AND DEVELOPMENT

# PREFACE TO THE FOURTH EDITION

THE object of this work continues to be to provide a useful collection of sources on human rights in the form of a handbook. Inevitably, the size of that handbook increases with each new edition, and the editors are particularly conscious both of the need for care in selection, and of the desirability of not duplicating other discrete collections. We have therefore omitted from this volume the instruments relating to international humanitarian law and international criminal law, although there are obvious overlapping areas of interest, particularly in regard to the protection of human rights. One minor exception is the inclusion of the Optional Protocol to the Convention on the Rights of the Child on the involvement of Children in Armed Conflict, which has been placed together with its parent document.

We have used the opportunity provided by this new edition to re-order some of the earlier material, in addition to providing new sources. This will be most evident in Part One, which now concentrates exclusively on non-treaty instruments adopted within the United Nations Organization, with UN-sponsored treaties now brought together in Part Three. We have chosen, in general, to reproduce material chronologically within each Part, save that additional or amending protocols are grouped for the sake of convenience and ease of use with the principal instrument; within Part Five, material emanating from the Council of Europe, the European Union, and the CSCE/OSCE is also grouped together.

This edition incorporates some forty-eight new items. Among these are protocols additional to existing treaties, but also the text of new or revised instruments, including the European Convention on Human Rights in its amended and consolidated form. Additional documents from Latin America and Africa have also been added, together with a new Part on developments among Arab States. In view of its rapidly increasing importance, a further new Part has been included on human rights and the human genome. Finally, the section on trade and development has been brought up to date; the Declaration on the Right to Development has been brought in, together with extracts from the Secretary General's 1995 *Agenda for Development* and the Copenhagen Declaration of 1995.

The growth in available sources has necessitated some deletions. Besides superseded texts, these include, from the work of the International Labour Organization, the Equality of Treatment (Social Security) Convention 1962, the Social Policy (Basic Aims and Standards Convention) 1962, and the Employment Policy Convention 1964. Developments in the ILO's approach to standard-setting through conventions are summarized in Part Three.

The extensive documentation from the CSCE (now the OSCE) has been pruned in order to maintain the focus on the human dimension, with the same selectivity applying to the choice of new items.

Some of the early material relating to Africa has also been deleted, namely, that dealing with the First and Second Conferences of Independent African States in 1958 and 1960, and certain resolutions of the First Assembly of the Heads of State and Government of the Organization of African States. Three new or additional treaties have been substituted.

Readers will often need to access up-to-date information on ratifications or other details. Given the nature of this handbook, it has not been possible to provide information, among others, on reservations and objections to reservations, while details of States parties will change with some frequency. We have therefore added a new Chart of ratifications and official sources, providing web addresses (URLs) wherever possible. The information on numbers of States parties which was available on 31 January 2002 is now to be found in this section, rather than in the introductory material to each instrument.

Both editors have once again enjoyed the courtesy and co-operation of Oxford University Press, and are particularly grateful to Jane Kavanagh, Christina White and Katy Plowright for their assistance.

IAN BROWNLIE
BLACKSTONE CHAMBERS
TEMPLE, LONDON

GUY S. GOODWIN-GILL
FACULTY OF LAW
UNIVERSITY OF OXFORD

# TABLE OF RATIFICATIONS AND SOURCES

This Table shows ratifications and status at 31 January 2002. The treaties are numbered by reference to their order in this work. The source (treaty series, documentary) also includes the URL (or Universal Resource Locator)—a website providing details of ratifications, reservations, declarations, etc. The resources listed include the United Nations (subscription service) treaty database: http://untreaty.un.org, as well as those of other UN agencies, and of regional and non-governmental organizations.

| Number | Treaty | Date of signature | Date of entry into force | Number of States party | Source |
|---|---|---|---|---|---|
| 19 | Convention on the Prevention and Punishment of the Crime of Genocide, 1948 | 09/12/48 | 12/01/51 | 133 | 78 UNTS 277 http://untreaty.un.org |
| 20 | Convention relating to the Status of Refugees, 1951 | 25/07/51 | 22/04/54 | 140 | 189 UNTS 137 |
|  | [Protocol relating to the Status of Refugees, 1967] | 31/1/67 | 04/10/67 | 138 | 660 UNTS 267 www.unhcr.ch http://untreaty.un.org |
| 21 | Convention on the Political Rights of Women, 1953 | 31/03/53 | 07/07/54 | 115 | 193 UNTS 135 http://untreaty.un.org |
| 22 | Slavery Convention, 1926, amended by Protocol, 1953 | 25/09/26 07/12/53 | 09/03/27 07/07/55 | 43 95 | 60 LNTS 253 212 UNTS 17 http://untreaty.un.org |
| 23 | Supplementary Convention on the Abolition of Slavery, the Slave Trade, and Institutions and Practices Similar to Slavery, 1956 | 07/09/56 | 30/04/57 | 119 | 266 UNTS 3 http://untreaty.un.org |
| 24 | Convention relating to the Status of Stateless Persons, 1954 | 23/09/54 | 06/06/60 | 54 | 360 UNTS 117 http://untreaty.un.org |
| 25 | Convention on the Reduction of Statelessness, 1961 | 28/08/61 | 13/12/75 | 26 | 989 UNTS 175 http://untreaty.un.org |

| Number | Treaty | Date of signature | Date of entry into force | Number of States party | Source |
|---|---|---|---|---|---|
| 26 | International Convention on the Elimination of All Forms of Racial Discrimination, 1966 | 07/03/66 | 04/01/69 | 161 | 660 UNTS 195 http://untreaty.un.org |
| 27 | International Covenant on Economic, Social and Cultural Rights, 1966 | 16/12/66 | 03/01/76 | 145 | 993 UNTS 3 http://untreaty.un.org |
| 28 | International Covenant on Civil and Political Rights, 1966 | 16/12/66 | 23/03/76 | 148 | 999 UNTS 171 http://untreaty.un.org |
| 29 | Optional Protocol to the International Covenant on Civil and Political Rights, 1966 | 16/12/66 | 23/03/76 | 101 | 999 UNTS 171 http://untreaty.un.org |
| 30 | Second Optional Protocol to the International Covenant on Civil and Political Rights, aiming at the abolition of the death penalty, 1990 | 15/12/89 | 11/07/91 | 46 | UNGA Res. 44/128, annex http://untreaty.un.org |
| 31 | International Convention on the Suppression and Punishment of the Crime of Apartheid, 1973 | 30/11/73 | 18/07/76 | 101 | 1015 UNTS 243 http://untreaty.un.org |
| 32 | Convention on the Elimination of All Forms of Discrimination against Women, 1979 | 18/12/79 | 03/09/81 | 168 | 1249 UNTS 13 http://untreaty.un.org |
| 33 | Optional Protocol to the Convention on the Elimination of Discrimination against Women, 1999 | 10/12/99 | 22/12/00 | 31 | UNGA Res. 54/4, 6 October 1999 http://untreaty.un.org |
| 34 | Convention against Torture and Other Cruel, Inhuman or Degrading Treatment or Punishment, 1984 | 10/12/84 | 26/06/87 | 128 | 1465 UNTS 85 http://untreaty.un.org |
| 35 | Convention on the Rights of the Child, 1989 | 20/11/89 | 02/09/90 | 191 | 1577 UNTS 3 http://untreaty.un.org |

| Number | Treaty | Date of signature | Date of entry into force | Number of States party | Source |
|---|---|---|---|---|---|
| 36 | Optional Protocol to the Convention on the Rights of the Child on the Involvement of Children in Armed Conflicts, 2000 | 25/05/00 | 12/02/02 | 14 | UNGA Res. 54/263, 25 May 2000 http://untreaty.un.org |
| 37 | Optional Protocol to the Convention on the Rights of the Child on the Sale of Children, Child Prostitution and Child Pornography, 2000 | 25/05/00 | 18/01/02 | 17 | UNGA Res. 54/263, 25 May 2000 http://untreaty.un.org |
| 38 | International Convention on the Protection of the Rights of All Migrant Workers and Their Families, 1990 | 18/12/90 | [3 months after 20th ratification: Art. 86] | 19 | UNGA Res. 45/158, 18 December 1990 http://untreaty.un.org |
| 40 | Forced Labour Convention, 1930 | 10/06/30 | 01/05/32 | 160 | ILO No. C29 39 UNTS 55 http://ilolex.ilo.ch:1567/english |
| 41 | Freedom of Association and Protection of the Right to Organize Convention, 1948 | 09/07/48 | 04/07/50 | 139 | ILO No. C87 68 UNTS 17 http://ilolex.ilo.ch:1567/english |
| 42 | Right to Organize and Collective Bargaining Convention, 1949 | 01/07/49 | 18/07/51 | 151 | ILO No. C98 96 UNTS 257 http://ilolex.ilo.ch:1567/english |
| 43 | Equal Remuneration Convention, 1951 | 29/06/51 | 23/05/53 | 156 | ILO No. C100 165 UNTS 304 http://ilolex.ilo.ch:1567/english |
| 44 | Abolition of Forced Labour Convention, 1957 | 25/06/57 | 17/01/59 | 157 | ILO No. C105 320 UNTS 291 http://ilolex.ilo.ch:1567/english |
| 45 | Discrimination (Employment and Occupation) Convention, 1958 | 25/06/58 | 15/06/60 | 154 | ILO No. C111 363 UNTS 31 http://ilolex.ilo.ch:1567/english |

| Number | Treaty | Date of signature | Date of entry into force | Number of States party | Source |
|---|---|---|---|---|---|
| 47 | Minimum Age Convention, 1973 | 26/06/73 | 19/06/76 | 116 | ILO No. C138 1015 UNTS No. 14862 http://ilolex.ilo.ch:1567/ english |
| 48 | Employment Promotion and Protection against Unemployment Convention, 1988 | 21/06/88 | 17/10/91 | 6 | ILO No. C168 http://ilolex.ilo.ch:1567/ english |
| 49 | Indigenous abd Tribal Peoples Convention, 1989 | 27/06/89 | 05/09/91 | 14 | ILO No. C169 http://ilolex.ilo.ch:1567/ english |
| 51 | Worst Forms of Child Labour Convention, 1999 | 17/06/99 | 19/11/00 | 115 | ILO No. C182 http://ilolex.ilo.ch:1567/ english |
| 52 | Convention Against Discrimination in Education, 1960 | 14/12/60 | 22/05/62 | 89 | 429 UNTS 93 http://www.unesco.org |
| 54 | European Convention for the Protection of Human Rights and Fundamental Freedoms, 1950, together with its Protocols, as amended by Protocol No. 11     Protocol No. 1     Protocol No. 4     Protocol No. 6     Protocol No. 7 | 04/11/50 | 03/09/53 01/11/98 18/05/54 02/05/68 01/03/85 01/11/88 | 41 41 38 33 39 30 | ETS No. 5 http://conventions.coe.int ETS No. 155 ETS No. 9 ETS No. 46 ETS No. 114 ETS No. 117 http://conventions.coe.int |
| 55 | Protocol No. 12 to the European Convention for the Protection of Human Rights and Fundamental Freedoms, on a General Prohibition of Discrimination, 2000 | 04/11/00 | [3 months after 10th ratification: Art. 5] | 1 | ETS No. 177 http://conventions.coe.int |
| 56 | European Social Charter, 1961 | 18/10/61 | 26/02/65 | 25 | ETS No. 35 http://conventions.coe.int |
| 57 | Additional Protocol to the European Social Charter, 1988 | 05/05/88 | 04/09/92 | 10 | ETS No. 128 http://conventions.coe.int |

| Number | Treaty | Date of signature | Date of entry into force | Number of States party | Source |
|--------|--------|-------------------|--------------------------|------------------------|--------|
| 58 | Protocol amending the European Social Charter, 1991 | 21/10/91 | [After ratification by all States party to the Charter: Art. 8] | 17 | ETS No. 142 http://conventions.coe.int |
| 59 | Additional Protocol to the European Social Charter Providing for a System of Collective Complaints, 1995 | 09/11/95 | 01/07/98 | 9 | ETS No. 158 http://conventions.coe.int |
| 60 | European Social Charter (Revised), 1996 | 03/05/96 | 01/07/99 | 12 | ETS No. 163 http://conventions.coe.int |
| 61 | European Convention on the Legal Status of Migrant Workers, 1977 | 24/11/77 | 01/05/93 | 8 | ETS No. 93 http://conventions.coe.int |
| 62 | European Convention for the Prevention of Torture and Inhuman or Degrading Treatment or Punishment, 1987 | 26/11/87 | 01/02/89 | 41 | ETS No. 126 http://conventions.coe.int |
| 63 | Protocol No. 1 to the European Convention for the Prevention of Torture and Inhuman or Degrading Treatment or Punishment, 1993 | 04/11/93 | 01/03/02 | 41 | ETS No. 151 http://conventions.coe.int |
| 64 | Protocol No. 2 to the European Convention for the Prevention of Torture and Inhuman or Degrading Treatment or Punishment, 1993 | 04/11/93 | 01/03/02 | 41 | ETS No. 152 http://conventions.coe.int |
| 65 | European Charter for Regional or Minority Languages, 1992 | 05/11/92 | 01/03/98 | 16 | ETS No. 148 http://conventions.coe.int |

| Number | Treaty | Date of signature | Date of entry into force | Number of States party | Source |
|---|---|---|---|---|---|
| 66 | European Framework Convention for the Protection of National Minorities, 1995 | 01/02/95 | 01/02/98 | 34 | ETS No. 157 http://conventions.coe.int |
| 67 | European Convention on the Exercise of Children's Rights, 1996 | 25/01/96 | 01/07/00 | 5 | ETS No. 160 http://conventions.coe.int |
| 68 | European Convention on Nationality, 1997 | 06/11/97 | 01/03/00 | 7 | ETS No. 166 http://conventions.coe.int |
| 79 | American Convention on Human Rights, 1969 | 22/11/69 | 18/07/78 | 25 | OAS *Treaty Series*, No. 36 (1969) http://www.oas.org |
| 80 | Additional Protocol to the American Convention on Human Rights in the Area of Economic, Social and Cultural Rights, 1988 | 14/11/88 | 16/11/99 | 12 | OAS *Treaty Series* No. 69 (1988) http://www.oas.org |
| 81 | Protocol to the American Convention on Human Rights to Abolish the Death Penalty, 1990 | 08/06/90 | [Among ratifying States on ratification] | 8 | OAS *Treaty Series* No. 73 (1990) http://www.oas.org |
| 82 | Inter-American Convention to Prevent and Punish Torture, 1985 | 09/12/95 | 28/02/87 | 16 | OAS *Treaty Series*, No. 67 (1985) http://www.oas.org |
| 83 | Inter-American Convention on the Prevention, Punishment and Eradication of Violence against Women, 1994 | 09/06/94 | 05/03/95 | 30 | 33 ILM 1534 (1994) http://www.oas.org |
| 84 | Inter-American Convention on Forced Disappearance of Persons, 1994 | 09/06/94 | 28/03/96 | 8 | 33 ILM 1529 (1994) http://www.oas.org |
| 85 | Convention governing the Specific Aspects of Refugee Problems in Africa, 1969 | 10/09/69 | 20/06/74 | 45 | 1000 UNTS 46 http://untreaty.un.org |

| Number | Treaty | Date of signature | Date of entry into force | Number of States party | Source |
|---|---|---|---|---|---|
| 86 | African Charter on Human and Peoples' Rights, 1981 | 17/06/81 | 21/10/86 | 52 | 1520 UNTS No. 26, 363 OAU doc. CAB/LEG/ 67/3 rev. 5; 21 ILM 58 (1982) http://www.up.ac.za/ chr/ahrdb/ |
| 87 | Protocol to the African Charter on Human and Peoples' Rights on the Establishment of an African Court on Human and Peoples' Rights, 1998 | 08/06/98 | [30 days after 15th ratification or accession: Art. 34] | 4 | http://www.up.ac.za/ chr/ahrdb/ |
| 88 | African Charter on the Rights and Welfare of the Child, 1990 | 11/07/90 | 29/11/99 | 21 | OAU doc. CAB/LEG/ 24.9/49 (1990) http://www.up.ac.za/ chr/ahrdb/ |
| 91 | Arab Charter on Human Rights, 1994 | 15/09/94 | [2 months after 7th ratification or accession: Art. 42] | | 8 *Human Rights Law Journal* 151 (1997) |
| 94 | European Convention for the Protection of Human Rights and Dignity of the Human Being with Regard to the Application of Biology and Medicine (Convention on Human Rights and Biomedicine), 1997 | 04/04/97 | 01/12/99 | 11 | ETS No. 164 http://conventions.coe.int |
| 95 | Additional Protocol to the Convention for the Protection of Human Rights and Dignity of the Human Being with Regard to the Application of Biology and Medicine on the Prohibition of Cloning Human Beings, 1998 | 12/01/98 | 01/03/01 | 9 | ETS No. 168 http://conventions.coe.int |

# SELECTED ABBREVIATIONS

| | |
|---|---|
| *AJIL* | *American Journal of International Law* |
| *BYIL* | *British Yearbook of International Law* |
| CSCE | Conference on Security and Co-operation in Europe |
| ECOWAS | Economic Community of West African States |
| *EJIL* | *European Journal of International Law* |
| ETS | European Treaty Series |
| ICJ | International Court of Justice |
| *ICLQ* | *International and Comparative Law Quarterly* |
| *IJRL* | *International Journal of Refugee Law* |
| ILM | International Legal Materials |
| LNTS | League of Nations Treaty Series |
| NGO | Non-Governmental Organization |
| OAS | Organization of American States |
| OAU | Organization of African Unity |
| OSCE | Organization for Security and Co-operation in Europe |
| UN | United Nations |
| UNGA | United Nations General Assembly |
| United Kingdom TS | United Kingdom Treaty Series |
| UNTS | United Nations Treaty Series |

# STANDARD-SETTING BY THE UNITED NATIONS ORGANIZATION

## INTRODUCTION

A MAJOR achievement of the drafters of the Charter of the United Nations was the emphasis of the provisions on the importance of social justice and human rights as the foundation for a stable international order. The Organization, and especially the General Assembly and the Economic and Social Council, has given impetus to the development of standards concerning human rights. The United Nations has undertaken both general propaganda work and the burden of drafting legal instruments containing detailed provisions.

The bodies most closely concerned with questions of human rights have been the Commission on Human Rights created by the Economic and Social Council and the Office of the High Commissioner for Human Rights, which has taken over responsibility from the Division of Human Rights of the United Nations Secretariat. In addition, there is a Commission on the Status of Women, and the Human Rights Commission has created two Sub-Commissions: The Sub-Commission on Freedom of Information and of the Press, and the Sub-Commission on the Promotion and Protection of Human Rights (formerly known as the Sub-Commission on the Prevention of Discrimination and the Protection of Minorities).

For further reference, see Alston, P. (ed.), *The United Nations and Human Rights: A Critical Appraisal*, 1992, particularly chapters 1–8.

Certain of the specialized agencies associated with the United Nations are also concerned with human rights, the International Labour Organization being the most prominent in this respect. On the I.L.O. and UNESCO see further below. The specialized agencies make periodic reports on human rights, which are forwarded to the Commission on Human Rights and other bodies by the Secretary-General of the United Nations.

The instruments reproduced in this section reflect in particular the work of United Nations Charter-based organs, including the General Assembly, the Economic and Social Council, and the 'functional commissions'. Where their standard-setting activities have resulted in specific treaties, these are now included in Part Two.

# 1. RELEVANT PROVISIONS OF THE UNITED NATIONS CHARTER, 1945

The Charter of the United Nations was signed on 26 June 1945, in San Francisco, at the conclusion of the United Nations Conference on International Organization, and came into force on 24 October 1945. The Statute of the International Court of Justice is an integral part of the Charter. Of the articles included below, Article 61 has been amended twice, increasing membership of the Economic and Social Council from eighteen to twenty-seven (General Assembly Resolution 1991 (XVIII), 17 December 1963; in force 31 August 1965); and from twenty-seven to fifty-four (General Assembly Resolution 2847 (XXVI), 20 December 1971 (105–2–15); in force 24 September 1973).

See Simma, B., ed., *The Charter of the United Nations: A Commentary*, 1995.

## TEXT

## WE THE PEOPLES OF THE UNITED NATIONS DETERMINED

to save succeeding generations from the scourge of war, which twice in our lifetime has brought untold sorrow to mankind, and

to reaffirm faith in fundamental human rights, in the dignity and worth of the human person, in the equal rights of men and women and of nations large and small, and

to establish conditions under which justice and respect for the obligations arising from treaties and other sources of international law can be maintained, and

to promote social progress and better standards of life in larger freedom,

## AND FOR THESE ENDS

to practise tolerance and live together in peace with one another as good neighbours, and

to unite our strength to maintain international peace and security, and

to ensure by the acceptance of principles and the institution of methods, that armed force shall not be used, save in the common interest, and

to employ international machinery for the promotion of the economic and social advancement of all peoples,

## HAVE RESOLVED TO COMBINE OUR EFFORTS TO ACCOMPLISH THESE AIMS

Accordingly, our respective Governments, through representatives assembled in the City of San Francisco, who have exhibited their full powers found to be in good and due form, have agreed to the present Charter of the United Nations and do hereby establish an international organization to be known as the United Nations.

# CHAPTER I
## Purposes and Principles

*Article* 1

The Purposes of the United Nations are:

1. To maintain international peace and security, and to that end: to take effective collective measures for the prevention and removal of threats to the peace, and for the suppression of acts of aggression or other breaches of the peace, and to bring about by peaceful means, and in conformity with the principles of justice and international law, adjustment or settlement of international disputes or situations which might lead to a breach of the peace;

2. To develop friendly relations among nations based on respect for the principle of equal rights and self-determination of peoples, and to take other appropriate measures to strengthen universal peace;

3. To achieve international co-operation in solving international problems of an economic, social, cultural, or humanitarian character, and in promoting and encouraging respect for human rights and for fundamental freedoms for all without distinction as to race, sex, language, or religion; and

4. To be a centre for harmonizing the actions of nations in the attainment of these common ends.

*Article* 2

The Organization and its Members, in pursuit of the Purposes stated in Article 1, shall act in accordance with the following Principles.

1. The Organization is based on the principle of the sovereign equality of all its Members.

2. All Members, in order to ensure to all of them the rights and benefits resulting from membership, shall fulfill in good faith the obligations assumed by them in accordance with the present Charter.

3. All Members shall settle their international disputes by peaceful means in such a manner that international peace and security, and justice, are not endangered.

4. All Members shall refrain in their international relations from the threat or use of force against the territorial integrity or political independence of any State, or in any other manner inconsistent with the Purposes of the United Nations.

5. All Members shall give the United Nations every assistance in any action it takes in accordance with the present Charter, and shall refrain from giving assistance to any State against which the United Nations is taking preventive or enforcement action.

6. The Organization shall ensure that States which are not Members of the United Nations act in accordance with these Principles so far as may be necessary for the maintenance of international peace and security.

7. Nothing contained in the present Charter shall authorize the United Nations to intervene in matters which are essentially within the domestic jurisdiction of any State or shall require the Members to submit such matters to settlement under

the present Charter; but this principle shall not prejudice the application of enforcement measures under Chapter VII.

*Article* 10

The General Assembly may discuss any questions or any matters within the scope of the present Charter or relating to the powers and functions of any organs provided for in the present Charter, and, except as provided in Article 12, may make recommendations to the Members of the United Nations or to the Security Council or to both on any such questions or matters.

*Article* 13

1. The General Assembly shall initiate studies and make recommendations for the purpose of:

   *(a)* promoting international cooperation in the political field and encouraging the progressive development of international law and its codification;

   *(b)* promoting international cooperation in the economic, social, cultural, educational, and health fields, and assisting in the realization of human rights and fundamental freedoms for all without distinction as to race, sex, language, or religion.

2. The further responsibilities, functions and powers of the General Assembly with respect to matters mentioned in paragraph 1(b) above are set forth in Chapters IX and X.

*Article* 16

The General Assembly shall perform such functions with respect to the international trusteeship system as are assigned to it under Chapters XII and XIII, including the approval of the trusteeship agreements for areas not designated as strategic.

# CHAPTER IX
## International Economic and Social Co-operation

*Article* 55

With a view to the creation of conditions of stability and well-being which are necessary for peaceful and friendly relations among nations based on respect for the principle of equal rights and self-determination of peoples, the United Nations shall promote:

   *(a)* higher standards of living, full employment, and conditions of economic and social progress and development;

   *(b)* solutions of international economic, social, health, and related problems; and international cultural and educational co-operation; and

   *(c)* universal respect for, and observance of, human rights and fundamental freedoms for all without distinction as to race, sex, language, or religion.

*Article 56*

All Members pledge themselves to take joint and separate action in co-operation with the Organization for the achievement of the purposes set forth in Article 55.

*Article 57*

1. The various specialized agencies, established by intergovernmental agreement and having wide international responsibilities, as defined in their basic instruments, in economic, social, cultural, educational, health, and related fields, shall be brought into relationship with the United Nations in accordance with the provisions of Article 63.

2. Such agencies thus brought into relationship with the United Nations are hereinafter referred to as specialized agencies.

*Article 58*

The Organization shall make recommendations for the coordination of the policies and activities of the specialized agencies.

*Article 59*

The Organization shall, where appropriate, initiate negotiations among the States concerned for the creation of any new specialized agencies required for the accomplishment of the purposes set forth in Article 55.

*Article 60*

Responsibility for the discharge of the functions of the Organization set forth in this Chapter shall be vested in the General Assembly and, under the authority of the General Assembly, in the Economic and Social Council, which shall have for this purpose the powers set forth in Chapter X.

# CHAPTER X
## The Economic and Social Council

*Composition*

*Article 61*

1. The Economic and Social Council shall consist of fifty-four Members of the United Nations elected by the General Assembly.

2. Subject to the provisions of paragraph 3, eighteen members of the Economic and Social Council shall be elected each year for a term of three years. A retiring member shall be eligible for immediate re-election.

3. At the first election after the increase in the membership of the Economic and Social Council from twenty-seven to fifty-four members, in addition to the members elected in place of the nine members whose term of office expires at the end of that year, twenty-seven additional members shall be elected. Of these twenty-seven additional members, the term of office of nine members so elected shall

expire at the end of one year, and of nine other members at the end of two years, in accordance with arrangements made by the General Assembly.

4. Each member of the Economic and Social Council shall have one representative.

*Functions and Powers*

*Article 62*

1. The Economic and Social Council may make or initiate studies and reports with respect to international economic, social, cultural, educational, health, and related matters and may make recommendations with respect to any such matters to the General Assembly, to the Members of the United Nations, and to the specialized agencies concerned.

2. It may make recommendations for the purpose of promoting respect for, and observance of, human rights and fundamental freedoms for all.

3. It may prepare draft conventions for submission to the General Assembly, with respect to matters falling within its competence.

4. It may call, in accordance with the rules prescribed by the United Nations, international conferences on matters falling within its competence.

*Article 63*

1. The Economic and Social Council may enter into agreements with any of the agencies referred to in Article 57, defining the terms on which the agency concerned shall be brought into relationship with the United Nations. Such agreements shall be subject to approval by the General Assembly.

2. It may coordinate the activities of the specialized agencies through consultation with and recommendations to such agencies and through recommendations to the General Assembly and to the Members of the United Nations.

*Article 64*

1. The Economic and Social Council may take appropriate steps to obtain regular reports from the specialized agencies. It may make arrangements with the Members of the United Nations and with the specialized agencies to obtain reports on the steps taken to give effect to its own recommendations and to recommendations on matters falling within its competence made by the General Assembly.

2. It may communicate its observations on these reports to the General Assembly.

*Article 65*

The Economic and Social Council may furnish information to the Security Council and shall assist the Security Council upon its request.

*Article 66*

1. The Economic and Social Council shall perform such functions as fall within its competence in connection with the carrying out of the recommendations of the General Assembly.

2. It may, with the approval of the General Assembly, perform services at the request of Members of the United Nations and at the request of specialized agencies.

3. It shall perform such other functions as are specified elsewhere in the present Charter or as may be assigned to it by the General Assembly.

*Voting*

*Article* 67

1. Each member of the Economic and Social Council shall have one vote.

2. Decisions of the Economic and Social Council shall be made by a majority of the members present and voting.

*Procedure*

*Article* 68

The Economic and Social Council shall set up commissions in economic and social fields and for the promotion of human rights, and such other commissions as may be required for the performance of its functions.

*Article* 69

The Economic and Social Council shall invite any Member of the United Nations to participate, without vote, in its deliberations on any matter of particular concern to that Member.

*Article* 70

The Economic and Social Council may make arrangements for representatives of the specialized agencies to participate, without vote, in its deliberations and in those of the commissions established by it, and for its representatives to participate in the deliberations of the specialized agencies.

*Article* 71

The Economic and Social Council may make suitable arrangements for consultation with non-governmental organizations which are concerned with matters within its competence. Such arrangements may be made with international organizations and, where appropriate, with national organizations after consultation with the Member of the United Nations concerned.

*Article* 72

1. The Economic and Social Council shall adopt its own rules of procedure, including the method of selecting its President.

2. The Economic and Social Council shall meet as required in accordance with its rules, which shall include provision for the convening of meetings on the request of a majority of its members.

## CHAPTER XI
### Declaration Regarding Non-Self-Governing Territories

*Article* 73

Members of the United Nations which have or assume responsibilities for the administration of territories whose peoples have not yet attained a full measure of self-government recognize the principle that the interests of the inhabitants of these territories are paramount, and accept as a sacred trust the obligation to promote to the utmost, within the system of international peace and security established by the present Charter, the well-being of the inhabitants of these territories, and, to this end:

*(a)* to ensure, with due respect for the culture of the peoples concerned, their political, economic, social, and educational advancement, their just treatment, and their protection against abuses;

*(b)* to develop self-government, to take due account of the political aspirations of the peoples, and to assist them in the progressive development of their free political institutions, according to the particular circumstances of each territory and its peoples and their varying stages of advancement;

*(c)* to further international peace and security;

*(d)* to promote constructive measures of development, to encourage research, and to co-operate with one another and, when and where appropriate, with specialized international bodies with a view to the practical achievement of the social, economic, and scientific purposes set forth in this Article; and

*(e)* to transmit regularly to the Secretary-General for information purposes, subject to such limitation as security and constitutional considerations may require, statistical and other information of a technical nature relating to economic, social, and educational conditions in the territories for which they are respectively responsible other than those territories to which Chapter XII and XIII apply.

*Article* 74

Members of the United Nations also agree that their policy in respect of the territories to which this Chapter applies, no less than in respect of their metropolitan areas, must be based on the general principle of good-neighbourliness, due account being taken of the interests and well-being of the rest of the world, in social, economic, and commercial matters.

## CHAPTER XII
### International Trusteeship System

*Article* 75

The United Nations shall establish under its authority an international trusteeship system for the administration and supervision of such territories as may be placed thereunder by subsequent individual agreements. These territories are hereinafter referred to as trust territories.

*Article* 76

The basic objectives of the trusteeship system, in accordance with the Purposes of the United Nations laid down in Article 1 of the present Charter, shall be:

*(a)* to further international peace and security;

*(b)* to promote the political, economic, social, and educational advancement of the inhabitants of the trust territories, and their progressive development towards self-government or independence as may be appropriate to the particular circumstances of each territory and its peoples and the freely expressed wishes of the peoples concerned, and as may be provided by the terms of each trusteeship agreement;

*(c)* to encourage respect for human rights and for fundamental freedoms for all without distinction as to race, sex, language, or religion, and to encourage recognition of the interdependence of the peoples of the world; and

*(d)* to ensure equal treatment in social, economic, and commercial matters for all Members of the United Nations and their nationals and also equal treatment for the latter in the administration of justice without prejudice to the attainment of the foregoing objectives and subject to the provisions of Article 80.

*Article* 77

1. The trusteeship system shall apply to such territories in the following categories as may be placed thereunder by means of trusteeship agreements:

*(a)* territories now held under mandate;

*(b)* territories which may be detached from enemy States as a result of the Second World War; and

*(c)* territories voluntarily placed under the system by States responsible for their administration.

2. It will be a matter for subsequent agreement as to which territories in the foregoing categories will be brought under the trusteeship system and upon what terms.

*Article* 78

The trusteeship system shall not apply to territories which have become Members of the United Nations, relationship among which shall be based on respect for the principle of sovereign equality.

*Article* 79

The terms of trusteeship for each territory to be placed under the trusteeship system, including any alteration or amendment, shall be agreed upon by the States directly concerned, including the mandatory power in the case of territories held under mandate by a Member of the United Nations, and shall be approved as provided for in Articles 83 and 85.

*Article* 80

1. Except as may be agreed upon in individual trusteeship agreements, made under Articles 77, 79, and 81, placing each territory under the trusteeship system,

and until such agreements have been concluded, nothing in this Chapter shall be construed in or of itself to alter in any manner the rights whatsoever of any States or any peoples or the terms of existing international instruments to which Members of the United Nations may respectively be parties.

2. Paragraph 1 of this Article shall not be interpreted as giving grounds for delay or postponement of the negotiation and conclusion of agreements for placing mandated and other territories under the trusteeship system as provided for in Article 77.

*Article* 81

The trusteeship agreement shall in each case include the terms under which the trust territory will be administered and designate the authority which will exercise the administration of the trust territory. Such authority, hereinafter called the administering authority, may be one or more States or the Organization itself.

*Article* 82

There may be designated, in any trusteeship agreement, a strategic area or areas which may include part or all of the trust territory to which the agreement applies, without prejudice to any special agreement or agreements made under Article 43.

*Article* 83

1. All functions of the United Nations relating to strategic areas, including the approval of the terms of the trusteeship agreements and of their alteration or amendment, shall be exercised by the Security Council.

2. The basic objectives set forth in Article 76 shall be applicable to the people of each strategic area.

3. The Security Council shall, subject to the provisions of the trusteeship agreements and without prejudice to security considerations, avail itself of the assistance of the Trusteeship Council to perform those functions of the United Nations under the trusteeship system relating to political. economic, social, and educational matters in the strategic areas.

*Article* 84

It shall be the duty of the administering authority to ensure that the trust territory shall play its part in the maintenance of international peace and security. To this end the administering authority may make use of volunteer forces, facilities, and assistance from the trust territory in carrying out the obligations towards the Security Council undertaken in this regard by the administering authority, as well as for local defence and the maintenance of law and order within the trust territory.

*Article* 85

1. The functions of the United Nations with regard to trusteeship agreements for all areas not designated as strategic, including the approval of the terms of the trusteeship agreements and of their alteration or amendment, shall be exercised by the General Assembly.

2. The Trusteeship Council, operating under the authority of the General Assembly, shall assist the General Assembly in carrying out these functions.

# CHAPTER XIII
## The Trusteeship Council

*Composition*

*Article 86*

1. The Trusteeship Council shall consist of the following Members of the United Nations:

   *(a)* those Members administering trust territories;
   *(b)* such of those Members mentioned by name in Article 23 as are not administering trust territories; and
   *(c)* as many other Members elected for three-year terms by the General Assembly as may be necessary to ensure that the total number of members of the Trusteeship Council is equally divided between those Members of the United Nations which administer trust territories and those which do not.

2. Each member of the Trusteeship Council shall designate one specially qualified person to represent it therein.

*Functions and Powers*

*Article 87*

The General Assembly and, under its authority, the Trusteeship Council, in carrying out their functions, may:

   *(a)* consider reports submitted by the administering authority;
   *(b)* accept petitions and examine them in consultation with the administering authority;
   *(c)* provide for periodic visits to the respective trust territories at times agreed upon with the administering authority; and
   *(d)* take these and other actions in conformity with the terms of the trusteeship agreements.

*Article 88*

The Trusteeship Council shall formulate a questionnaire on the political, economic, social, and educational advancement of the inhabitants of each trust territory, and the administering authority for each trust territory within the competence of the General Assembly shall make an annual report to the General Assembly upon the basis of such questionnaire.

*Voting*

*Article 89*

1. Each member of the Trusteeship Council shall have one vote.
2. Decisions of the Trusteeship Council shall be made by a majority of the members present and voting.

*Procedure*

*Article* 90

1. The Trusteeship Council shall adopt its own rules of procedure, including the method of selecting its President.

2. The Trusteeship Council shall meet as required in accordance with its rules, which shall include provision for the convening of meetings on the request of a majority of its members.

## 2. PROCEDURE IN THE COMMISSION ON HUMAN RIGHTS OF THE ECONOMIC AND SOCIAL COUNCIL

The role of the Human Rights Commission in respect of complaints of human rights violations was minimal before 1967. Since that year three functions have been exercised:

(a) In 1967 ECOSOC adopted Resolution 1235 (XLII) which authorized the Human
Rights Commission and its Sub-Commission on Prevention of Discrimination and
Protection of Minorities 'to examine information relevant to gross violations of
human rights and fundamental freedoms, as exemplified by the policy of apartheid as
practised in the Republic of South Africa and racial discrimination as practised notably in Southern Rhodesia, contained in the communications listed by the Secretary-
General to [ECOSOC] resolution 728 F' and to 'make a thorough study of situations
which reveal a consistent pattern of violations of human rights, and report, with
recommendations thereon, to the Economic and Social Council'.

The 'communications listed by the Secretary-General' consist of the list of individual petitions (complaints concerning human rights) which is distributed to
Commission members before each session.

The powers given by ECOSOC Resolution 1235 (XLII) have been exercised in
limited circumstances, that is, gross violations linked to general political situations in
which a large number of United Nations Members were concerned, such as the
policies of South Africa.

(b) After 1967 the Commission on Human Rights began to carry out regular operational
fact-finding activities, with particular reference to South Africa, the territories occupied by Israel and the situation in Chile. Latterly, it has turned its attention to, among
others, East Timor, Haiti, Myanmar, Nigeria, Rwanda, and the former Yugoslavia.

(c) In 1970 the Economic and Social Council devised a greatly improved procedure for
handling communications (complaints) from individuals and non-governmental
organizations relating to violations of human rights. The new procedure was established by ECOSOC Resolution 1503 (XLVIII), and calls for special examination.

The text of Resolution 1503 is set out below, together with the Resolution adopted
by the Sub-Commission on 13 August 1971 on matters of procedure. The machinery
set up by Resolution 1503 is complex. The object is to secure further examination
(during the screening of communications) of those communications which 'appear to
reveal a consistent pattern of gross and reliably attested violations of human rights
and fundamental freedoms'. The procedure is in several stages, involving a working
group of the Sub-Commission on Prevention of Discrimination (since renamed the
Sub-Commission on the Promotion and Protection of Human Rights), the Sub-
Commission itself, the Commission on Human Rights and eventually an *ad hoc*
investigatory committee appointed by the Commission.

Whilst the Resolution 1503 Procedure is a great improvement on what went on
before 1970, the procedure still has many drawbacks. A leading U.N. official (not
writing in his official capacity) commented: 'The procedure appeared to be very
promising but due to many procedural technicalities, its time-consuming character
and above all the inability or unwillingness of the Commission on Human Rights to
act effectively, high expectations made way for strong disappointment. Although
official United Nations documentation is silent on this score as a result of the rule of
confidentiality, press reports reveal that the Commission on Human Rights saw fit to
drop all cases (with the exception of the situations relating to the occupied territories

in the Middle East and Chile, which were on the public agenda anyway), referred to it by the Sub-Commission': see Van Boven, T., in Cassese, A. (ed.), *U.N. Law: Fundamental Rights* (1979), 119 at 124.

For further reference see Alston, P., *The United Nations and Human Rights: A Critical Appraisal* (1992): Van Boven, T., 15 *Netherlands International Law Review* 374–93 (1968); Humphrey, J., 62 *AJIL* 869–88 (1968); International Law Association, *Report of the Fifty-Fifth Conference*, 1972, 539–624 (especially the reports of Humphrey and Schwelb). See generally also: http://www.unhchr.ch.

## Resolution 1503 (XLVIII), 27 May 1970, ECOSOC

*The Economic and Social Council*

*Noting* resolutions 7 (**XXVI**) and 17 (**XXV**) of the Commission on Human Rights and resolution 2 (**XXI**) of the Sub-Commission on Prevention of Discrimination and Protection of Minorities.

1. *Authorizes* the Sub-Commission on Prevention of Discrimination and Protection of Minorities to appoint a working group consisting of not more than five of its members, with due regard to geographical distribution, to meet once a year in private meetings for a period not exceeding ten days immediately before the sessions of the Sub-Commission to consider all communications, including replies of Governments thereon, received by the Secretary-General under Council resolution 738 F (**XXVIII**) of 30 July 1959 with a view to bringing to the attention of the Sub-Commission those communications, together with replies of Governments, if any, which appear to reveal a consistent pattern of gross and reliably attested violations of human rights and fundamental freedoms within the terms of reference of the Sub-Commission.

2. *Decides* that the Sub-Commission on Prevention of Discrimination and Protection of Minorities should, as the first stage in the implementation of the present resolution, devise at its twenty-third session appropriate procedures for dealing with the question of admissibility of communications received by the Secretary-General under Council resolution 728 F (**XXVIII**) and in accordance with Council resolution 1235 (**XLII**) of 6 June 1967.

3. *Requests* the Secretary-General to prepare a document on the question of admissibility of communications for the Sub-Commission's consideration at its twenty-third session.

4. *Further requests* the Secretary-General:

   *(a)* To furnish to the members of the Sub-Commission every month a list of communications prepared by him in accordance with Council resolution 728 F (**XXVIII**) and a brief description of them, together with the text of any replies received from Governments;

   *(b)* To make available to the members of the working group at their meetings the originals of such communications listed as they may request, having due regard to the provisions of paragraph 2 (b) of Council resolution 728 F

(XXVIII) concerning the divulging of the identity of the authors of communications;

(c) To circulate to the members of the Sub-Commission, in the working languages, the originals of such communications as are referred to the Sub-Commission by the working group.

5. *Requests* the Sub-Commission on Prevention of Discrimination and Protection of Minorities to consider in private meetings, in accordance with paragraph 1 above, the communications brought before it in accordance with the decision of a majority of the members of the working group and any replies of Governments relating thereto and other relevant information, with a view to determining whether to refer to the Commission on Human Rights particular situations which appear to reveal a consistent pattern of gross and reliably attested violations of human rights requiring consideration by the Commission.

6. *Requests* the Commission on Human Rights after it has examined any situation referred to it by the Sub-Commission to determine:

(a) Whether it requires a thorough study by the Commission and a report and recommendations thereon to the Council in accordance with paragraph 3 of Council resolution 1235 (XLII);

(b) Whether it may be a subject of an investigation by an *ad hoc* committee to be appointed by the Commission which shall be undertaken only with the express consent of the State concerned and shall be conducted in constant co-operation with that State and under conditions determined by agreement with it. In any event, the investigation may be undertaken only if:

(i) All available means at the national level have been resorted to and exhausted;

(ii) The situation does not relate to a matter which is being dealt with under other procedures prescribed in the constituent instruments of, or conventions adopted by, the United Nations and the specialized agencies, or in regional conventions, or which the State concerned wishes to submit to other procedures in accordance with general or special international agreements to which it is a party.

7. *Decides* that if the Commission on Human Rights appoints an *ad hoc* committee to carry on an investigation with the consent of the State concerned:

(a) The composition of the committee shall be determined by the Commission. The members of the committee shall be independent persons whose competence and impartiality is beyond question. Their appointment shall be subject to the consent of the Government concerned;

(b) The committee shall establish its own rules of procedure. It shall be subject to the quorum rule. It shall have authority to receive communications and hear witnesses, as necessary. The investigation shall be conducted in co-operation with the Government concerned;

(c) The committee's procedure shall be confidential, its proceedings shall be conducted in private meetings and its communications shall not be publicized in any way;

(d) The committee shall strive for friendly solutions before, during and even after the investigation;

*(e)* The committee shall report to the Commission on Human Rights with such observations and suggestions as it may deem appropriate.

8. *Decides* that all actions envisaged in the implementation of the present resolution by the Sub-Commission on Prevention of Discrimination and Protection of Minorities or the Commission on Human Rights shall remain confidential until such time as the Commission may decide to make recommendations to the Economic and Social Council.

9. *Decides* to authorize the Secretary-General to provide all facilities which may be required to carry out the present resolution, making use of the existing staff of the Division of Human Rights of the United Nations Secretariat.

10. *Decides* that the procedure set out in the present resolution for dealing with communications relating to violations of human rights and fundamental freedoms should be reviewed if any new organ entitled to deal with such communications should be established within the United Nations or by international agreement.

### Resolution of the Sub-Commission on Prevention of Discrimination and Protection of Minorities, 13 August 1971

*The Sub-Commission on Prevention of Discrimination and Protection of Minorities,*

*Considering* that the Economic and Social Council, by its resolution 1503 (XLVIII), decided that the Sub-Commission should devise appropriate procedures for dealing with the question of admissibility of communications received by the Secretary-General under Council resolution 728 F (XXVIII) of 30 July 1959 and in accordance with Council resolution 1235 (XLII) of 6 June 1967,

*Adopts* the following provisional procedures for dealing with the question of admissibility of communications referred to above:

(1) *Standards and criteria*

   *(a)* The object of the communication must not be inconsistent with the relevant principles of the Charter, of the Universal Declaration of Human Rights and of the other applicable instruments in the field of human rights.

   *(b)* Communications shall be admissible only if, after consideration thereof, together with the replies of any of the Governments concerned, there are reasonable grounds to believe that they may reveal a consistent pattern of gross and reliably attested violations of human rights and fundamental freedoms, including policies of racial discrimination and segregation and of *apartheid*, in any country, including colonial and other dependent countries and peoples.

(2) *Source of communications*

   *(a)* Admissible communications may originate from a person or group of persons who, it can be reasonably presumed, are victims of the violations referred to in subparagraph (1) (b) above, any person or group of persons who have direct and reliable knowledge of those violations, or non-governmental organizations acting in good faith in accordance with recognized principles of human rights, not resorting to politically motivated

stands contrary to the provisions of the Charter of the United Nations and having direct and reliable knowledge of such violations.

(b) Anonymous communications shall be inadmissible, subject to the requirements of subparagraph 2(b) of resolution 728 F (XXVIII) of the Economic and Social Council, the author of a communication, whether an individual, a group of individuals or an organization, must be clearly identified.

(c) Communications shall not be inadmissible solely because the knowledge of the individual authors is second-hand, provided that they are accompanied by clear evidence.

(3) *Contents of communications and nature of allegations*

(a) The communication must contain a description of the facts and must indicate the purpose of the petition and the rights that have been violated.

(b) Communications shall be inadmissible if their language is essentially abusive and in particular if they contain insulting references to the State against which the complaint is directed. Such communications may be considered if they meet the other criteria for admissibility after deletion of the abusive language.

(c) A communication shall be inadmissible if it has manifestly political motivations and its subject is contrary to the provisions of the Charter of the United Nations.

(d) A communication shall be inadmissible if it appears that it is based exclusively on reports disseminated by mass media.

(4) *Existence of other remedies*

(a) Communications shall be inadmissible if their admission would prejudice the functions of the specialized agencies of the United Nations system.

(b) Communications shall be inadmissible if domestic remedies have not been exhausted, unless it appears that such remedies would be ineffective or unreasonably prolonged. Any failure to exhaust remedies should be satisfactorily established.

(c) Communications relating to cases which have been settled by the State concerned in accordance with the principles set forth in the Universal Declaration of Human Rights and other applicable documents in the field of human rights will not be considered.

(5) *Timeliness*

A communication shall be inadmissible if it is not submitted to the United Nations within a reasonable time after the exhaustion of the domestic remedies as provided above.

## 3. UNIVERSAL DECLARATION OF HUMAN RIGHTS, 1948

The references to human rights in the Charter of the United Nations (see preamble, Articles 1, 55, 56, 62, 68, and 76) have provided the basis for elaboration of the content of standards and of the machinery for implementing protection of human rights. On 10 December 1948 the General Assembly of the United Nations adopted a Universal Declaration of Human Rights: UN doc. A/811. The voting was forty-eight for and none against. The following eight States abstained: Byelorussian S.S.R., Czechoslovakia, Poland, Saudi Arabia, Ukrainian S.S.R., U.S.S.R., Union of South Africa, and Yugoslavia. The Declaration is not a legally binding instrument as such, and certain of its provisions depart, or departed, from then existing and generally accepted rules. Nevertheless some of its provisions either constitute general principles of law (see the Statute of the International Court of Justice, Article 38(1)(c)), or represent elementary considerations of humanity. More important is its status as an authoritative guide, produced by the General Assembly, to the interpretation of the Charter. In this capacity the Declaration has considerable indirect legal effect, and it is regarded by the Assembly and by some jurists as a part of the 'law of the United Nations'. On the Declaration, see Oppenheim, *International Law* (Lauterpacht, H., ed., 8th edn) I, 744–6; (Jennings, R. Y. A., & Watts, A., eds., 9th edn., 1992), I, 1000–5; Waldock, H., 106 *Recueil des cours* (Hague Academy of International Law), 1962–II, 198–9.

The Declaration has its own importance and cannot be regarded as having merely a historical significance. In particular, many States are not yet parties to the International Covenants (see below). The Universal Declaration is also given prominence in, among others, the Proclamation of Tehran, adopted by the United Nations Conference on Human Rights: see the Final Act of the International Conference on Human Rights, Tehran, 22 April–13 May 1968: UN doc. A/CONF. 32/41; the Vienna Declaration and Programme of Action, adopted by the World Conference on Human Rights on 25 June 1993: UN doc. A/CONF.157/23 12 July 1993; and the Beijing Declaration and Platform of Action adopted by the Fourth UN World Conference on Women, Beijing, 4–15 September 1995: UN doc. A/CONF.177/20, 17 October 1995.

*TEXT*

### Preamble

*Whereas* recognition of the inherent dignity and of the equal and inalienable rights of all members of the human family is the foundation of freedom, justice and peace in the world,

*Whereas* disregard and contempt for human rights have resulted in barbarous acts which have outraged the conscience of mankind, and the advent of a world in which human beings shall enjoy freedom of speech and belief and freedom from fear and want has been proclaimed as the highest aspiration of the common people,

*Whereas* it is essential, if man is not to be compelled to have recourse, as a last resort, to rebellion against tyranny and oppression, that human rights should be protected by the rule of law,

*Whereas* it is essential to promote the development of friendly relations between nations,

*Whereas* the peoples of the United Nations have in the Charter reaffirmed their faith in fundamental human rights, in the dignity and worth of the human person and in the equal rights of men and women and have determined to promote social progress and better standards of life in larger freedom,

*Whereas* Member States have pledged themselves to achieve, in cooperation with the United Nations, the promotion of universal respect for and observance of human rights and fundamental freedoms,

*Whereas* a common understanding of these rights and freedoms is of the greatest importance for the full realization of this pledge,

*Now, therefore,*

## The General Assembly

*Proclaims this Universal Declaration of Human Rights* as a common standard of achievement for all peoples and all nations, to the end that every individual and every organ of society, keeping this Declaration constantly in mind, shall strive by teaching and education to promote respect for these rights and freedoms and by progressive measures, national and international, to secure their universal and effective recognition and observance, both among the peoples of Member States themselves and among the peoples of territories under their jurisdiction.

*Article* 1

All human beings are born free and equal in dignity and rights. They are endowed with reason and conscience and should act towards one another in a spirit of brotherhood.

*Article* 2

Everyone is entitled to all the rights and freedoms set forth in this Declaration, without distinction of any kind, such as race, colour, sex, language, religion, political or other opinion, national or social origin, property, birth or other status.

Furthermore, no distinction shall be made on the basis of the political, jurisdictional or international status of the country or territory to which a person belongs, whether it be independent, trust, non-self-governing or under any other limitation of sovereignty.

*Article* 3

Everyone has the right to life, liberty and security of person.

*Article* 4

No one shall be held in slavery or servitude; slavery and the slave trade shall be prohibited in all their forms.

*Article* 5

No one shall be subjected to torture or to cruel, inhuman or degrading treatment or punishment.

*Article* 6

Everyone has the right to recognition everywhere as a person before the law.

*Article* 7

All are equal before the law and are entitled without any discrimination to equal protection of the law. All are entitled to equal protection against any discrimination in violation of this Declaration and against any incitement to such discrimination.

*Article* 8

Everyone has the right to an effective remedy by the competent national tribunals for acts violating the fundamental rights granted him by the constitution or by law.

*Article* 9

No one shall be subjected to arbitrary arrest, detention or exile.

*Article* 10

Everyone is entitled in full equality to a fair and public hearing by an independent and impartial tribunal, in the determination of his rights and obligations and of any criminal charge against him.

*Article* 11

1. Everyone charged with a penal offence has the right to be presumed innocent until proved guilty according to law in a public trial at which he has had all the guarantees necessary for his defence.

2. No one shall be held guilty of any penal offence on account of any act or omission which did not constitute a penal offence, under national or international law, at the time when it was committed. Nor shall a heavier penalty be imposed than the one that was applicable at the time the penal offence was committed.

*Article* 12

No one shall be subjected to arbitrary interference with his privacy, family, home or correspondence, nor to attacks upon his honour and reputation.

Everyone has the right to the protection of the law against such interference or attacks.

*Article* 13

1. Everyone has the right to freedom of movement and residence within the borders of each State.

2. Everyone has the right to leave any country, including his own, and to return to his country.

*Article* 14

1. Everyone has the right to seek and to enjoy in other countries asylum from persecution.

2. This right may not be invoked in the case of prosecutions genuinely arising from non-political crimes or from acts contrary to the purposes and principles of the United Nations.

*Article* 15

1. Everyone has the right to a nationality.

2. No one shall be arbitrarily deprived of his nationality nor denied the right to change his nationality.

*Article* 16

1. Men and women of full age, without any limitation due to race, nationality or religion, have the right to marry and to found a family. They are entitled to equal rights as to marriage, during marriage and at its dissolution.

2. Marriage shall be entered into only with the free and full consent of the intending spouses.

3. The family is the natural and fundamental group unit of society and is entitled to protection by society and the State.

*Article* 17

1. Everyone has the right to own property alone as well as in association with others.

2. No one shall be arbitrarily deprived of his property.

*Article* 18

Everyone has the right to freedom of thought, conscience and religion; this right includes freedom to change his religion or belief, and freedom, either alone or in community with others and in public or private, to manifest his religion or belief in teaching, practice, worship and observance.

*Article* 19

Everyone has the right to freedom of opinion and expression; this right includes freedom to hold opinions without interference and to seek, receive and impart information and ideas through any media and regardless of frontiers.

*Article* 20

1. Everyone has the right to freedom of peaceful assembly and association.

2. No one may be compelled to belong to an association.

*Article* 21

1. Everyone has the right to take part in the government of his country, directly or through freely chosen representatives.

2. Everyone has the right to equal access to public service in his country.

3. The will of the people shall be the basis of the authority of government; this will shall be expressed in periodic and genuine elections which shall be by universal and equal suffrage and shall be held by secret vote or by equivalent free voting procedures.

*Article* 22

Everyone, as a member of society, has the right to social security and is entitled to realization, through national effort and international co-operation and in accordance with the organization and resources of each State, of the economic, social and cultural rights indispensable for his dignity and the free development of his personality.

*Article* 23

1. Everyone has the right to work, to free choice of employment, to just and favourable conditions of work and to protection against unemployment.

2. Everyone, without any discrimination, has the right to equal pay for equal work.

3. Everyone who works has the right to just and favourable remuneration ensuring for himself and his family an existence worthy of human dignity, and supplemented, if necessary, by other means of social protection.

4. Everyone has the right to form and to join trade unions for the protection of his interests.

*Article* 24

Everyone has the right to rest and leisure, including reasonable limitation of working hours and periodic holidays with pay.

*Article* 25

1. Everyone has the right to a standard of living adequate for the health and well-being of himself and of his family, including food, clothing, housing and medical care and necessary social services, and the right to security in the event of unemployment, sickness, disability, widowhood, old age or other lack of livelihood in circumstances beyond his control.

2. Motherhood and childhood are entitled to special care and assistance. All children, whether born in or out of wedlock, shall enjoy the same social protection.

*Article* 26

1. Everyone has the right to education. Education shall be free, at least in the elementary and fundamental stages. Elementary education shall be compulsory. Technical and professional education shall be made generally available and higher education shall be equally accessible to all on the basis of merit.

2. Education shall be directed to the full development of the human personality and to the strengthening of respect for human rights and fundamental freedoms. It shall promote understanding, tolerance and friendship among all nations, racial or religious groups, and shall further the activities of the United Nations for the maintenance of peace.

3. Parents have a prior right to choose the kind of education that shall be given to their children.

*Article* 27

1. Everyone has the right freely to participate in the cultural life of the community, to enjoy the arts and to share in scientific advancement and its benefits.

2. Everyone has the right to the protection of the moral and material interests resulting from any scientific, literary or artistic production of which he is the author.

*Article* 28

Everyone is entitled to a social and international order in which the rights and freedoms set forth in this Declaration can be fully realized.

*Article* 29

1. Everyone has duties to the community in which alone the free and full development of his personality is possible.

2. In the exercise of his rights and freedoms, everyone shall be subject only to such limitations as are determined by law solely for the purpose of securing due recognition and respect for the rights and freedoms of others and of meeting the just requirements of morality, public order and the general welfare in a democratic society.

3. These rights and freedoms may in no case be exercised contrary to the purposes and principles of the United Nations.

*Article* 30

Nothing in this Declaration may be interpreted as implying for any State, group or person any right to engage in any activity or to perform any act aimed at the destruction of any of the rights and freedoms set forth herein.

## 4. DECLARATION ON THE GRANTING OF INDEPENDENCE TO COLONIAL COUNTRIES AND PEOPLES, 1960

The Declaration below was adopted by the United Nations General Assembly in Resolution 1514 (XV) on 14 December 1960. Eighty-nine States voted for the resolution and none against, but there were nine abstentions: Portugal, Spain, Union of South Africa, United Kingdom, United States, Australia, Belgium, Dominican Republic, and France. The Declaration relates the normative development in the field of human rights to the rights of national groups, and, in particular, the right of self-determination. The Declaration, in conjunction with the United Nations Charter, supports the view that self-determination is now a legal principle, and, although its precise ramifications are still to be finally determined, the principle has great significance as a root of particular legal developments. See also the Declaration on the Inadmissibility of Intervention in Resolution 2131 (XX) of 14 January 1966. Generally on self-determination, see Whiteman, M. M., 5 *Digest of International Law*, 38–87; Brownlie, I., *Principles of Public International Law* (5th edn., 1998), 599–602; Rigo Sureda, A., *The Evolution of the Right of Self-determination: A Study of United Nations Practice* (1973). Resolution 1514 (XV) is in the form of an authoritative interpretation of the Charter rather than a recommendation. For comment see Waldock, H., 106 *Recueil des cours de l'Académie de droit international*, 1962–II, 29–34; and Jennings, R. Y., *The Acquisition of Territory in International Law* (1963), 78–87. For earlier resolutions see Resolutions 637 A (VII) of 16 December 1952 and 1314 (XIII) of 12 December 1958.

The General Assembly established as a subsidiary organ a Special Committee on the Situation with regard to the Implementation of the Declaration on the Granting of Independence by Resolution 1654 (XVI) of 27 November 1961 This consisted at first of seventeen and later of twenty-four States. In 1964 the Special Committee examined situations and made recommendations in respect of fifty-five territories. In 1963 the General Assembly decided to discontinue the Committee on information from non-self-governing territories and to transfer its functions to the Special Committee. As a result, apart from the Trusteeship Council, the Special Committee is the only body responsible for matters relating to dependent territories. See 'Report of the Special Committee on the Situation with regard to the Implementation of the Declaration on the Granting of Independence to Colonial Countries and Peoples on its work during 2001': UN doc. A/56/23, 16 July 2001.

Cassese, A., *Self-Determination of Peoples. A Legal Reappraisal* (1995); Koskenniemi, M., 'National Self-Determination Today: Problems of Legal Theory and Practice' (1994) 43 *ICLQ* 241–69; McCorquodale, R., 'Self-Determination: A Human Rights Approach' (1994) 43 *ICLQ* 857–85; Higgins, R., *Problems and Process: International Law and How We Use it* (1994), 111–28.

*TEXT*

*The General Assembly,*

*Mindful* of the determination proclaimed by the peoples of the world in the Charter of the United Nations to reaffirm faith in fundamental human rights, in the dignity and worth of the human person, in the equal rights of men and women and of nations large and small and to promote social progress and better standards of life in larger freedom,

*Conscious* of the need for the creation of conditions of stability and well-being and peaceful and friendly relations based on respect for the principles of equal rights and self-determination of all peoples, and of universal respect for, and observance of, human rights and fundamental freedoms for all without distinction as to race, sex, language or religion,

*Recognizing* the passionate yearning for freedom in all dependent peoples and the decisive role of such peoples in the attainment of their independence,

*Aware* of the increasing conflicts resulting from the denial of or impediments in the way of the freedom of such peoples, which constitute a serious threat to world peace,

*Considering* the important role of the United Nations in assisting the movement for independence in Trust and Non-Self-Governing Territories,

*Recognizing* that the peoples of the world ardently desire the end of colonialism in all its manifestations,

*Convinced* that the continued existence of colonialism prevents the development of international economic co-operation, impedes the social, cultural and economic development of dependent peoples and militates against the United Nations ideal of universal peace,

*Affirming* that peoples may, for their own ends, freely dispose of their natural wealth and resources without prejudice to any obligations arising out of international economic co-operation, based upon the principle of mutual benefit, and international law,

*Believing* that the process of liberation is irresistible and irreversible and that, in order to avoid serious crises, an end must be put to colonialism and all practices of segregation and discrimination associated therewith,

*Welcoming* the emergence in recent years of a large number of dependent territories into freedom and independence, and recognizing the increasingly powerful trends towards freedom in such territories which have not yet attained independence,

*Convinced* that all peoples have an inalienable right to complete freedom, the exercise of their sovereignty and the integrity of their national territory,

*Solemnly proclaims* the necessity of bringing to a speedy and unconditional end colonialism in all its forms and manifestations;

And to this end

*Declares* that:

1. The subjection of peoples to alien subjugation, domination and exploitation constitutes a denial of fundamental human rights, is contrary to the Charter of the United Nations and is an impediment to the promotion of world peace and co-operation.

2. All peoples have the right to self-determination; by virtue of that right they freely determine their political status and freely pursue their economic, social and cultural development.

3. Inadequacy of political, economic, social or educational preparedness should never serve as a pretext for delaying independence.

4. All armed action or repressive measures of all kinds directed against dependent peoples shall cease in order to enable them to exercise peacefully and freely their right to complete independence, and the integrity of their national territory shall be respected.

5. Immediate steps shall be taken, in Trust and Non-Self-Governing Territories or all other territories which have not yet attained independence, to transfer all powers to the peoples of those territories, without any conditions or reservations, in accordance with their freely expressed will and desire, without any distinction as to race, creed or colour, in order to enable them to enjoy complete independence and freedom.

6. Any attempt aimed at the partial or total disruption of the national unity and the territorial integrity of a country is incompatible with the purposes and principles of the Charter of the United Nations.

7. All States shall observe faithfully and strictly the provisions of the Charter of the United Nations, the Universal Declaration of Human Rights and the present Declaration on the basis of equality, non-interference in the internal affairs of all States, and respect for the sovereign rights of all peoples and their territorial integrity.

# 5. DECLARATION ON THE PROTECTION OF ALL PERSONS FROM BEING SUBJECTED TO TORTURE AND OTHER CRUEL, INHUMAN OR DEGRADING TREATMENT OR PUNISHMENT, 1975

This Declaration is annexed to General Assembly Resolution 3452 (XXX), UN doc. A/10034 (1975), adopted by consensus on 9 December 1975. While General Assembly resolutions are not legislative in effect, they provide evidence of the evolution of principles of general international law. The Declaration annexed to the resolution constitutes evidence for the view that the prohibition of torture is an existing principle of international law: see the consideranda in the preamble and note the terms of Article 2. On the relation between human rights and general international law, see the *Barcelona Traction Case*, ICJ Reports 1970, 3, at 32, and Brownlie, I., *Principles of Public International Law* (5th edn., 1998), 528–31.

Further reference should be made to Resolutions 3448 and 3453 adopted by the General Assembly on the same date; and to Resolution 31/85 adopted on 13 December 1976.

The adoption of the declaration was the prelude to the drafting of a Convention against torture (see further below). However, it must be emphasized that the Declaration is declaratory of existing legal norms. The prohibition of torture is enhanced by the appearance of the Convention but the legality of torture does not depend upon the existence of a Convention. The Resolution to which the Declaration is annexed refers to the 'obligation of States under the Charter'.

## TEXT

### Article 1

1. For the purpose of this Declaration, torture means any act by which severe pain or suffering, whether physical or mental, is intentionally inflicted by or at the instigation of a public official on a person for such purposes as obtaining from him or a third person information or confession, punishing him for an act he has committed or is suspected of having committed, or intimidating him or other persons. It does not include pain or suffering arising only from, inherent in or incidental to, lawful sanctions to the extent consistent with the Standard Minimum Rules for the Treatment of Prisoners.

2. Torture constitutes an aggravated and deliberate form of cruel, inhuman or degrading treatment or punishment.

### Article 2

Any act of torture or other cruel, inhuman or degrading treatment or punishment is an offence to human dignity and shall be condemned as a denial of the purposes of the Charter of the United Nations and as a violation of the human rights and fundamental freedoms proclaimed in the Universal Declaration of Human Rights.

### Article 3

No State may permit or tolerate torture or other cruel, inhuman or degrading treatment or punishment. Exceptional circumstances such as a state of war or a threat of war, internal political instability or any other public emergency may not be invoked as a justification of torture or other cruel, inhuman or degrading treatment or punishment.

*Article* 4

Each State shall, in accordance with the provisions of this Declaration, take effective measures to prevent torture and other cruel, inhuman or degrading treatment or punishment from being practised within its jurisdiction.

*Article* 5

The training of law enforcement personnel and of other public officials who may be responsible for persons deprived of their liberty shall ensure that full account is taken of the prohibition against torture and other cruel, inhuman or degrading treatment or punishment. This prohibition shall also, where appropriate, be included in such general rules or instructions as are issued in regard to the duties and functions of anyone who may be involved in the custody or treatment of such persons.

*Article* 6

Each State shall keep under systematic review interrogation methods and practices as well as arrangements for the custody and treatment of persons deprived of their liberty in its territory, with a view to preventing any cases of torture or other cruel, inhuman or degrading treatment or punishment.

*Article* 7

Each State shall ensure that all acts of torture as defined in Article 1 are offences under its criminal law. The same shall apply in regard to acts which constitute participation in, complicity in, incitement to or an attempt to commit torture.

*Article* 8

Any person who alleges that he has been subjected to torture or other cruel, inhuman or degrading treatment or punishment by or at the instigation of a public official shall have the right to complain to, and to have his case impartially examined by, the competent authorities of the State concerned.

*Article* 9

Wherever there is reasonable ground to believe that an act of torture as defined in Article 1 has been committed, the competent authorities of the State concerned shall promptly proceed to an impartial investigation even if there has been no formal complaint.

*Article* 10

If an investigation under Article 8 or Article 9 establishes that an act of torture as defined in Article 1 appears to have been committed, criminal proceedings shall be instituted against the alleged offender or offenders in accordance with national law. If an allegation of other forms of cruel, inhuman or degrading treatment or punishment is considered to be well founded, the alleged offender or offenders shall be subject to criminal, disciplinary or other appropriate proceedings.

*Article* 11

Where it is proved that an act of torture or other cruel, inhuman or degrading treatment or punishment has been committed by or at the instigation of a public official, the victim shall be afforded redress and compensation in accordance with national law.

*Article* 12

Any statement which is established to have been made as a result of torture or other cruel, inhuman or degrading treatment or punishment may not be invoked as evidence against the person concerned or against any other person in any proceedings.

## 6. DECLARATION ON THE RIGHTS OF DISABLED PERSONS, 1975

This Declaration was adopted by General Assembly Resolution 3447 (XXX), 9 December 1975, UN doc. A/10034 (1975). See also General Assembly Resolution 48/96, 20 December 1993, 'Standard Rules on the Equalization of Opportunities for Persons with Disabilities', UN doc. A/48/49 (1993); General Assembly Resolution 48/99, 20 December 1993, 'Towards full integration of persons with disabilities into society: a continuing world programme of action': UN doc. A/48/49 (1993); General Assembly Resolution 49/153, 23 December 1994, UN doc. A/49/49 (1994); Committee on Economic, Social and Cultural Rights, General Comment No. 5, Persons with disabilities (Eleventh session, 1994), UN doc. E/C.12/1994/13 (1994); Commission on Human Rights Resolution 1998/31, 'Human rights of persons with disabilities', UN doc. E/CN.4/1998/31 (1998).

*TEXT*

*The General Assembly,*

*Mindful* of the pledge made by Member States, under the Charter of the United Nations to take joint and separate action in co-operation with the Organization to promote higher standards of living, full employment and conditions of economic and social progress and development,

*Reaffirming* its faith in human rights and fundamental freedoms and in the principles of peace, of the dignity and worth of the human person and of social justice proclaimed in the Charter,

*Recalling* the principles of the Universal Declaration of Human Rights, the International Covenants on Human Rights, the Declaration of the Rights of the Child and the Declaration on the Rights of Mentally Retarded Persons, as well as the standards already set for social progress in the constitutions, conventions, recommendations and resolutions of the International Labour Organisation, the United Nations Educational, Scientific and Cultural Organization, the World Health Organization, the United Nations Children's Fund and other organizations concerned,

*Recalling also* Economic and Social Council resolution 1921 (LVIII) of 6 May 1975 on the prevention of disability and the rehabilitation of disabled persons,

*Emphasizing* that the Declaration on Social Progress and Development has proclaimed the necessity of protecting the rights and assuring the welfare and rehabilitation of the physically and mentally disadvantaged,

*Bearing in mind* the necessity of preventing physical and mental disabilities and of assisting disabled persons to develop their abilities in the most varied fields of activities and of promoting their integration as far as possible in normal life,

*Aware* that certain countries, at their present stage of development, can devote only limited efforts to this end,

*Proclaims* this Declaration on the Rights of Disabled Persons and calls for national and international action to ensure that it will be used as a common basis and frame of reference for the protection of these rights:

1. The term 'disabled person' means any person unable to ensure by himself or herself, wholly or partly, the necessities of a normal individual and/or social life, as a result of deficiency, either congenital or not, in his or her physical or mental capabilities.

2. Disabled persons shall enjoy all the rights set forth in this Declaration. These rights shall be granted to all disabled persons without any exception whatsoever and without distinction or discrimination on the basis of race, colour, sex, language, religion, political or other opinions, national or social origin, state of wealth, birth or any other situation applying either to the disabled person himself or herself or to his or her family.

3. Disabled persons have the inherent right to respect for their human dignity. Disabled persons, whatever the origin, nature and seriousness of their handicaps and disabilities, have the same fundamental rights as their fellow-citizens of the same age, which implies first and foremost the right to enjoy a decent life, as normal and full as possible.

4. Disabled persons have the same civil and political rights as other human beings; paragraph 7 of the Declaration on the Rights of Mentally Retarded Persons applies to any possible limitation or suppression of those rights for mentally disabled persons.

5. Disabled persons are entitled to the measures designed to enable them to become as self-reliant as possible.

6. Disabled persons have the right to medical, psychological and functional treatment, including prosthetic and orthetic appliances, to medical and social rehabilitation, education, vocational training and rehabilitation, aid, counselling, placement services and other services which will enable them to develop their capabilities and skills to the maximum and will hasten the processes of their social integration or reintegration.

7. Disabled persons have the right to economic and social security and to a decent level of living. They have the right, according to their capabilities, to secure and retain employment or to engage in a useful, productive and remunerative occupation and to join trade unions.

8. Disabled persons are entitled to have their special needs taken into consideration at all stages of economic and social planning.

9. Disabled persons have the right to live with their families or with foster parents and to participate in all social, creative or recreational activities. No disabled person shall be subjected, as far as his or her residence is concerned, to differential treatment other than that required by his or her condition or by the improvement which he or she may derive therefrom. If the stay of a disabled person in a specialized establishment is indispensable, the environment and living conditions therein shall be as close as possible to those of the normal life of a person of his or her age.

10. Disabled persons shall be protected against all exploitation, all regulations and all treatment of a discriminatory, abusive or degrading nature.

11. Disabled persons shall be able to avail themselves of qualified legal aid when such aid proves indispensable for the protection of their persons and property. If

judicial proceedings are instituted against them, the legal procedure applied shall take their physical and mental condition fully into account.

12. Organizations of disabled persons may be usefully consulted in all matters regarding the rights of disabled persons.

13. Disabled persons, their families and communities shall be fully informed, by all appropriate means, of the rights contained in this Declaration.

## 7. DECLARATION ON THE ELIMINATION OF ALL FORMS OF INTOLERANCE AND OF DISCRIMINATION BASED ON RELIGION OR BELIEF, 1981

This Declaration was adopted without a vote by the General Assembly in Resolution 36/55 on 25 November 1981: UN doc. A/36/684 (1981). For the background, see *Yearbook of the United Nations*, 1981, 879–83. The Declaration was prepared by the Human Rights Commission of the Economic and Social Council. For an earlier proposal of a draft Convention on the subject, see the second edition of this work, at 111.

Janis, M. W., & Evans, C., *Religion and International Law* (1999); Dickson, B., 'The United Nations and Freedom of Religion' (1995) 44 *ICLQ* 327–57.

## TEXT

*The General Assembly,*

*Considering* that one of the basic principles of the Charter of the United Nations is that of the dignity and equality inherent in all human beings, and that all Member States have pledged themselves to take joint and separate action in co-operation with the Organization to promote and encourage universal respect for and observance of human rights and fundamental freedoms for all, without distinction as to race, sex, language or religion,

*Considering* that the Universal Declaration of Human Rights and the International Covenants on Human Rights proclaim the principles of non-discrimination and equality before the law and the right to freedom of thought, conscience, religion and belief,

*Considering* that the disregard and infringement of human rights and fundamental freedoms, in particular of the right to freedom of thought, conscience, religion or whatever belief, have brought, directly or indirectly, wars and great suffering to mankind, especially where they serve as a means of foreign interference in the internal affairs of other States and amount to kindling hatred between peoples and nations,

*Considering* that religion or belief, for anyone who professes either, is one of the fundamental elements in his conception of life and that freedom of religion or belief should be fully respected and guaranteed,

*Considering* that it is essential to promote understanding, tolerance and respect in matters relating to freedom of religion and belief and to ensure that the use of religion or belief for ends inconsistent with the Charter of the United Nations, other relevant instruments of the United Nations and the purposes and principles of the present Declaration is inadmissible,

*Convinced* that freedom of religion and belief should also contribute to the attainment of the goals of world peace, social justice and friendship among peoples and to the elimination of ideologies or practices of colonialism and racial discrimination,

*Noting* with satisfaction the adoption of several, and the coming into force of some, conventions, under the aegis of the United Nations and of the specialized agencies, for the elimination of various forms of discrimination,

*Concerned* by manifestations of intolerance and by the existence of discrimination in matters of religion or belief still in evidence in some areas of the world,

*Resolved* to adopt all necessary measures for the speedy elimination of such intolerance in all its forms and manifestations and to prevent and combat discrimination on the ground of religion or belief,

*Proclaims* this Declaration on the Elimination of All Forms of Intolerance and of Discrimination Based on Religion or Belief:

*Article* 1

1. Everyone shall have the right to freedom of thought, conscience and religion. This right shall include freedom to have a religion or whatever belief of his choice, and freedom, either individually or in community with others and in public or private, to manifest his religion or belief in worship, observance, practice and teaching.

2. No one shall be subject to coercion which would impair his freedom to have a religion or belief of his choice.

3. Freedom to manifest one's religion or belief may be subject only to such limitations as are prescribed by law and are necessary to protect public safety, order, health or morals or the fundamental rights and freedoms of others.

*Article* 2

1. No one shall be subject to discrimination by any State, institution, group of persons, or person on the grounds of religion or other belief.

2. For the purposes of the present Declaration, the expression 'intolerance and discrimination based on religion or belief' means any distinction, exclusion, restriction or preference based on religion or belief and having as its purpose or as its effect nullification or impairment of the recognition, enjoyment or exercise of human rights and fundamental freedoms on an equal basis.

*Article* 3

Discrimination between human being on the grounds of religion or belief constitutes an affront to human dignity and a disavowal of the principles of the Charter of the United Nations, and shall be condemned as a violation of the human rights and fundamental freedoms proclaimed in the Universal Declaration of Human Rights and enunciated in detail in the International Covenants on Human Rights, and as an obstacle to friendly and peaceful relations between nations.

*Article* 4

1. All States shall take effective measures to prevent and eliminate discrimination on the grounds of religion or belief in the recognition, exercise and enjoyment of human rights and fundamental freedoms in all fields of civil, economic, political, social and cultural life.

2. All States shall make all efforts to enact or rescind legislation where necessary to prohibit any such discrimination, and to take all appropriate measures to combat intolerance on the grounds of religion or other beliefs in this matter.

*Article* 5

1. The parents or, as the case may be, the legal guardians of the child have the right to organize the life within the family in accordance with their religion or belief and bearing in mind the moral education in which they believe the child should be brought up.

2. Every child shall enjoy the right to have access to education in the matter of religion or belief in accordance with the wishes of his parents or, as the case may be, legal guardians, and shall not be compelled to receive teaching on religion or belief against the wishes of his parents or legal guardians, the best interests of the child being the guiding principle.

3. The child shall be protected from any form of discrimination on the ground of religion or belief. He shall be brought up in a spirit of understanding, tolerance, friendship among peoples, peace and universal brotherhood, respect for freedom of religion or belief of others, and in full consciousness that his energy and talents should be devoted to the service of his fellow men.

4. In the case of a child who is not under the care either of his parents or of legal guardians, due account shall be taken of their expressed wishes or of any other proof of their wishes in the matter of religion or belief, the best interests of the child being the guiding principle.

5. Practices of a religion or belief in which a child is brought up must not be injurious to his physical or mental health or to his full development, taking into account Article 1, paragraph 3, of the present Declaration.

*Article* 6

In accordance with Article 1 of the present Declaration, and subject to the provisions of Article 1, paragraph 3, the right to freedom of thought, conscience, religion or belief shall include, inter alia, the following freedoms:

(a) To worship or assemble in connection with a religion or belief, and to establish and maintain places for these purposes;

(b) To establish and maintain appropriate charitable or humanitarian institutions;

(c) To make, acquire and use to an adequate extent the necessary articles and materials related to the rites or customs of a religion or belief;

(d) To write, issue and disseminate relevant publications in these areas;

(e) To teach a religion or belief in places suitable for these purposes;

(f) To solicit and receive voluntary financial and other contributions from individuals and institutions;

(g) To train, appoint, elect or designate by succession appropriate leaders called for by the requirements and standards of any religion or belief;

(h) To observe days of rest and to celebrate holidays and ceremonies in accordance with the precepts of one's religion or belief;

(i) To establish and maintain communications with individuals and communities in matters of religion and belief at the national and international levels.

*Article* 7

The rights and freedoms set forth in the present Declaration shall be accorded in national legislation in such a manner that everyone shall be able to avail himself of such rights and freedoms in practice.

*Article* 8

Nothing in the present Declaration shall be construed as restricting or derogating from any right defined in the Universal Declaration of Human Rights and the International Covenants on Human Rights.

## 8. DECLARATION ON THE HUMAN RIGHTS OF INDIVIDUALS WHO ARE NOT NATIONALS OF THE COUNTRY IN WHICH THEY LIVE, 1985

This Declaration was adopted by General Assembly Resolution 40/144 without a vote on 13 December 1985; UN doc. A/40/53 (1985).

Lillich, R. B., *The Human Rights of Aliens in Contemporary International Law*,1984; Cholewinski, R., *Migrant Workers in International Human Rights Law: Their Protection in Countries of Employment*, 1997.

*TEXT*

*The General Assembly,*

*Considering* that the Charter of the United Nations encourages universal respect for and observance of the human rights and fundamental freedoms of all human beings, without distinction as to race, sex, language or religion,

*Considering* that the Universal Declaration of Human Rights proclaims that all human beings are born free and equal in dignity and rights and that everyone is entitled to all the rights and freedoms set forth in that Declaration, without distinction of any kind, such as race, colour, sex, language, religion, political or other opinion, national or social origin, property, birth or other status,

*Considering* that the Universal Declaration of Human Rights proclaims further that everyone has the right to recognition everywhere as a person before the law, that all are equal before the law and entitled without any discrimination to equal protection of the law, and that all are entitled to equal protection against any discrimination in violation of that Declaration and against any incitement to such discrimination,

*Being aware* that the States Parties to the International Covenants on Human Rights undertake to guarantee that the rights enunciated in these Covenants will be exercised without discrimination of any kind as to race, colour, sex, language, religion, political or other opinion, national or social origin, property, birth or other status,

*Conscious* that, with improving communications and the development of peaceful and friendly relations among countries, individuals increasingly live in countries of which they are not nationals

*Reaffirming* the purposes and principles of the Charter of the United Nations,

*Recognizing* that the protection of human rights and fundamental freedoms provided for in international instruments should also be ensured for individuals who are not nationals of the country in which they live,

*Proclaims* this Declaration:

*Article 1*

For the purposes of this Declaration, the term 'alien' shall apply, with due regard to qualifications made in subsequent articles, to any individual who is not a national of the State in which he or she is present.

*Article 2*

1. Nothing in this Declaration shall be interpreted as legitimizing the illegal entry into and presence in a State of any alien, nor shall any provision be interpreted as restricting the right of any State to promulgate laws and regulations concerning the entry of aliens and the terms and conditions of their stay or to establish differences between nationals and aliens. However, such laws and regulations shall not be incompatible with the international legal obligations of that State, including those in the field of human rights.

2. This Declaration shall not prejudice the enjoyment of the rights accorded by domestic law and of the rights which under international law a State is obliged to accord to aliens, even where this Declaration does not recognize such rights or recognizes them to a lesser extent.

*Article 3*

Every State shall make public its national legislation or regulations affecting aliens.

*Article 4*

Aliens shall observe the laws of the State in which they reside or are present and regard with respect the customs and traditions of the people of that State.

*Article 5*

1. Aliens shall enjoy, in accordance with domestic law and subject to the relevant international obligation of the State in which they are present, in particular the following rights:

> (a) The right to life and security of person; no alien shall be subjected to arbitrary arrest or detention; no alien shall be deprived of his or her liberty except on such grounds and in accordance with such procedures as are established by law;
>
> (b) The right to protection against arbitrary or unlawful interference with privacy, family, home or correspondence;
>
> (c) The right to be equal before the courts, tribunals and all other organs and authorities administering justice and, when necessary, to free assistance of an interpreter in criminal proceedings and, when prescribed by law, other proceedings;
>
> (d) The right to choose a spouse, to marry, to found a family;
>
> (e) The right to freedom of thought, opinion, conscience and religion; the right to manifest their religion or beliefs, subject only to such limitations as are prescribed by law and are necessary to protect public safety, order, health or morals or the fundamental rights and freedoms of others;
>
> (f) The right to retain their own language, culture and tradition;
>
> (g) The right to transfer abroad earnings, savings or other personal monetary assets, subject to domestic currency regulations.

2. Subject to such restrictions as are prescribed by law and which are necessary in a democratic society to protect national security, public safety, public order, public health or morals or the rights and freedoms of others, and which are consistent

with the other rights recognized in the relevant international instruments and those set forth in this Declaration, aliens shall enjoy the following rights:

*(a)* The right to leave the country;

*(b)* The right to freedom of expression;

*(c)* The right to peaceful assembly;

*(d)* The right to own property alone as well as in association with others, subject to domestic law.

3. Subject to the provisions referred to in paragraph 2, aliens lawfully in the territory of a State shall enjoy the right to liberty of movement and freedom to choose their residence within the borders of the State.

4. Subject to national legislation and due authorization, the spouse and minor or dependent children of an alien lawfully residing in the territory of a State shall be admitted to accompany, join and stay with the alien.

*Article* 6

No alien shall be subjected to torture or to cruel, inhuman or degrading treatment or punishment and, in particular, no alien shall be subjected without his or her free consent to medical or scientific experimentation.

*Article* 7

An alien lawfully in the territory of a State may be expelled therefrom only in pursuance of a decision reached in accordance with law and shall, except where compelling reasons of national security otherwise require, be allowed to submit the reasons why he or she should not be expelled and to have the case reviewed by, and be represented for the purpose before, the competent authority or a person or persons specially designated by the competent authority. Individual or collective expulsion of such aliens on grounds of race, colour, religion, culture, descent or national or ethnic origin is prohibited.

*Article* 8

1. Aliens lawfully residing in the territory of a State shall also enjoy, in accordance with the national laws, the following rights, subject to their obligations under Article 4:

*(a)* The right to safe and healthy working conditions, to fair wages and equal remuneration for work of equal value without distinction of any kind, in particular, women being guaranteed conditions of work not inferior to those enjoyed by men, with equal pay for equal work;

*(b)* The right to join trade unions and other organizations or associations of their choice and to participate in their activities. No restrictions may be placed on the exercise of this right other than those prescribed by law and which are necessary, in a democratic society, in the interests of national security or public order or for the protection of the rights and freedoms of others;

*(c)* The right to health protection, medical care, social security, social services, education, rest and leisure, provided that they fulfil the requirements under

the relevant regulations for participation and that undue strain is not placed on the resources of the State.

2. With a view to protecting the rights of aliens carrying on lawful paid activities in the country in which they are present, such rights may be specified by the Governments concerned in multilateral or bilateral conventions.

*Article* 9

No alien shall be arbitrarily deprived of his or her lawfully acquired assets.

*Article* 10

Any alien shall be free at any time to communicate with the consulate or diplomatic mission of the State of which he or she is a national or, in the absence thereof, with the consulate or diplomatic mission of any other State entrusted with the protection of the interests of the State of which he or she is a national in the State where he or she resides.

## 9. BODY OF PRINCIPLES FOR THE PROTECTION OF ALL PERSONS UNDER ANY FORM OF DETENTION OR IMPRISONMENT, 1988

These principles are annexed to General Assembly Resolution 43/173, adopted without a vote on 9 December 1988.

### TEXT

*The General Assembly,*

*Recalling* its resolution 35/177 of 15 December 1980, in which it referred the task of elaborating the draft Body of Principles for the Protection of All Persons under Any Form of Detention or Imprisonment to the Sixth Committee and decided to establish an open-ended working group for that purpose,

*Taking note* of the report of the Working Group on the Draft Body of Principles for the Protection of All Persons under Any Form of Detention or Imprisonment, which met during the forty-third session of the General Assembly and completed the elaboration of the draft Body of Principles,

*Considering* that the Working Group decided to submit the text of the draft Body of Principles to the Sixth Committee for its consideration and adoption,

*Convinced* that the adoption of the draft Body of Principles would make an important contribution to the protection of human rights,

*Considering* the need to ensure the wide dissemination of the text of the Body of Principles,

1. *Approves* the Body of Principles for the Protection of All Persons under Any Form of Detention or Imprisonment, the text of which is annexed to the present resolution;

2. *Expresses* its appreciation to the Working Group on the Draft Body of Principles for the Protection of All Persons under Any Form of Detention or Imprisonment for its important contribution to the elaboration of the Body of Principles;

3. *Requests* the Secretary-General to inform the States Members of the United Nations or members of specialized agencies of the adoption of the Body of Principles;

4. *Urges* that every effort be made so that the Body of Principles becomes generally known and respected.

### ANNEX

Body of Principles for the Protection of All Persons under
Any Form of Detention or Imprisonment

Scope of the Body of Principles

These principles apply for the protection of all persons under any form of detention or imprisonment.

*Use of terms*

For the purposes of the Body of Principles:

*(a)* 'Arrest' means the act of apprehending a person for the alleged commission of an offence or by the action of an authority;

*(b)* 'Detained person' means any person deprived of personal liberty except as a result of conviction for an offence;

*(c)* 'Imprisoned person' means any person deprived of personal liberty as a result of conviction for an offence;

*(d)* 'Detention' means the condition of detained persons as defined above;

*(e)* 'Imprisonment' means the condition of imprisoned persons as defined above;

*(f)* The words 'a judicial or other authority' mean a judicial or other authority under the law whose status and tenure should afford the strongest possible guarantees of competence, impartiality and independence.

*Principle* 1

All persons under any form of detention or imprisonment shall be treated in a humane manner and with respect for the inherent dignity of the human person.

*Principle* 2

Arrest, detention or imprisonment shall only be carried out strictly in accordance with the provisions of the law and by competent officials or persons authorized for that purpose.

*Principle* 3

There shall be no restriction upon or derogation from any of the human rights of persons under any form of detention or imprisonment recognized or existing in any State pursuant to law, conventions, regulations or custom on the pretext that this Body of Principles does not recognize such rights or that it recognizes them to a lesser extent.

*Principle* 4

Any form of detention or imprisonment and all measures affecting the human rights of a person under any form of detention or imprisonment shall be ordered by, or be subject to the effective control of, a judicial or other authority.

*Principle* 5

1. These principles shall be applied to all persons within the territory of any given State, without distinction of any kind, such as race, colour, sex, language, religion or religious belief, political or other opinion, national, ethnic or social origin, property, birth or other status.

2. Measures applied under the law and designed solely to protect the rights and special status of women, especially pregnant women and nursing mothers, children and juveniles, aged, sick or handicapped persons shall not be deemed to be discriminatory. The need for, and the application of, such measures shall always be subject to review by a judicial or other authority.

*Principle* 6

No person under any form of detention or imprisonment shall be subjected to torture or to cruel, inhuman or degrading treatment or punishment.* No circumstance whatever may be invoked as a justification for torture or other cruel, inhuman or degrading treatment or punishment.

* The term 'cruel, inhuman or degrading treatment or punishment' should be interpreted so as to extend the widest possible protection against abuses, whether physical or mental, including the holding of a detained or imprisoned person in conditions which deprive him, temporarily or permanently, of the use of any of his natural senses, such as sight or hearing, or of his awareness of place and the passing of time.

*Principle* 7

1. States should prohibit by law any act contrary to the rights and duties contained in these principles, make any such act subject to appropriate sanctions and conduct impartial investigations upon complaints.
2. Officials who have reason to believe that a violation of this Body of Principles has occurred or is about to occur shall report the matter to their superior authorities and, where necessary, to other appropriate authorities or organs vested with reviewing or remedial powers.
3. Any other person who has ground to believe that a violation of this Body of Principles has occurred or is about to occur shall have the right to report the matter to the superiors of the officials involved as well as to other appropriate authorities or organs vested with reviewing or remedial powers.

*Principle* 8

Persons in detention shall be subject to treatment appropriate to their unconvicted status. Accordingly, they shall, whenever possible, be kept separate from imprisoned persons.

*Principle* 9

The authorities which arrest a person, keep him under detention or investigate the case shall exercise only the powers granted to them under the law and the exercise of these powers shall be subject to recourse to a judicial or other authority.

*Principle* 10

Anyone who is arrested shall be informed at the time of his arrest of the reason for his arrest and shall be promptly informed of any charges against him.

*Principle* 11

1. A person shall not be kept in detention without being given an effective opportunity to be heard promptly by a judicial or other authority. A detained person shall have the right to defend himself or to be assisted by counsel as prescribed by law.
2. A detained person and his counsel, if any, shall receive prompt and full communication of any order of detention, together with the reasons therefor.

3. A judicial or other authority shall be empowered to review as appropriate the continuance of detention.

*Principle* 12

1. There shall be duly recorded:

    *(a)* The reasons for the arrest;

    *(b)* The time of the arrest and the taking of the arrested person to a place of custody as well as that of his first appearance before a judicial or other authority;

    *(c)* The identity of the law enforcement officials concerned;

    *(d)* Precise information concerning the place of custody.

2. Such records shall be communicated to the detained person, or his counsel, if any, in the form prescribed by law.

*Principle* 13

Any person shall, at the moment of arrest and at the commencement of detention or imprisonment, or promptly thereafter, be provided by the authority responsible for his arrest, detention or imprisonment, respectively, with information on and an explanation of his rights and how to avail himself of such rights.

*Principle* 14

A person who does not adequately understand or speak the language used by the authorities responsible for his arrest, detention or imprisonment is entitled to receive promptly in a language which he understands the information referred to in principle 10, principle 11, paragraph 2, principle 12, paragraph 1, and principle 13 and to have the assistance, free of charge, if necessary, of an interpreter in connection with legal proceedings subsequent to his arrest.

*Principle* 15

Notwithstanding the exceptions contained in principle 16, paragraph 4, and principle 18, paragraph 3, communication of the detained or imprisoned person with the outside world, and in particular his family or counsel, shall not be denied for more than a matter of days.

*Principle* 16

1. Promptly after arrest and after each transfer from one place of detention or imprisonment to another, a detained or imprisoned person shall be entitled to notify or to require the competent authority to notify members of his family or other appropriate persons of his choice of his arrest, detention or imprisonment or of the transfer and of the place where he is kept in custody.

2. If a detained or imprisoned person is a foreigner, he shall also be promptly informed of his right to communicate by appropriate means with a consular post or the diplomatic mission of the State of which he is a national or which is otherwise entitled to receive such communication in accordance with international law or with the representative of the competent international organization, if he is a refugee or is otherwise under the protection of an intergovernmental organization.

3. If a detained or imprisoned person is a juvenile or is incapable of understanding his entitlement, the competent authority shall on its own initiative undertake the notification referred to in the present principle. Special attention shall be given to notifying parents or guardians.

4. Any notification referred to in the present principle shall be made or permitted to be made without delay. The competent authority may however delay a notification for a reasonable period where exceptional needs of the investigation so require.

*Principle* 17

1. A detained person shall be entitled to have the assistance of a legal counsel. He shall be informed of his right by the competent authority promptly after arrest and shall be provided with reasonable facilities for exercising it.

2. If a detained person does not have a legal counsel of his own choice, he shall be entitled to have a legal counsel assigned to him by a judicial or other authority in all cases where the interests of justice so require and without payment by him if he does not have sufficient means to pay.

*Principle* 18

1. A detained or imprisoned person shall be entitled to communicate and consult with his legal counsel.

2. A detained or imprisoned person shall be allowed adequate time and facilities for consultations with his legal counsel.

3. The right of a detained or imprisoned person to be visited by and to consult and communicate, without delay or censorship and in full confidentiality, with his legal counsel may not be suspended or restricted save in exceptional circumstances, to be specified by law or lawful regulations, when it is considered indispensable by a judicial or other authority in order to maintain security and good order.

4. Interviews between a detained or imprisoned person and his legal counsel may be within sight, but not within the hearing, of a law enforcement official.

5. Communications between a detained or imprisoned person and his legal counsel mentioned in the present principle shall be inadmissible as evidence against the detained or imprisoned person unless they are connected with a continuing or contemplated crime.

*Principle* 19

A detained or imprisoned person shall have the right to be visited by and to correspond with, in particular, members of his family and shall be given adequate opportunity to communicate with the outside world, subject to reasonable conditions and restrictions as specified by law or lawful regulations.

*Principle* 20

If a detained or imprisoned person so requests, he shall if possible be kept in a place of detention or imprisonment reasonably near his usual place of residence.

*Principle* 21

1. It shall be prohibited to take undue advantage of the situation of a detained or

imprisoned person for the purpose of compelling him to confess, to incriminate himself otherwise or to testify against any other person.

2. No detained person while being interrogated shall be subject to violence, threats or methods of interrogation which impair his capacity of decision or his judgement.

*Principle 22*

No detained or imprisoned person shall, even with his consent, be subjected to any medical or scientific experimentation which may be detrimental to his health.

*Principle 23*

1. The duration of any interrogation of a detained or imprisoned person and of the intervals between interrogations as well as the identity of the officials who conducted the interrogations and other persons present shall be recorded and certified in such form as may be prescribed by law.

2. A detained or imprisoned person, or his counsel when provided by law, shall have access to the information described in paragraph 1 of the present principle.

*Principle 24*

A proper medical examination shall be offered to a detained or imprisoned person as promptly as possible after his admission to the place of detention or imprisonment, and thereafter medical care and treatment shall be provided whenever necessary. This care and treatment shall be provided free of charge.

*Principle 25*

A detained or imprisoned person or his counsel shall, subject only to reasonable conditions to ensure security and good order in the place of detention or imprisonment, have the right to request or petition a judicial or other authority for a second medical examination or opinion.

*Principle 26*

The fact that a detained or imprisoned person underwent a medical examination, the name of the physician and the results of such an examination shall be duly recorded. Access to such records shall be ensured. Modalities therefor shall be in accordance with relevant rules of domestic law.

*Principle 27*

Non-compliance with these principles in obtaining evidence shall be taken into account in determining the admissibility of such evidence against a detained or imprisoned person.

*Principle 28*

A detained or imprisoned person shall have the right to obtain within the limits of available resources, if from public sources, reasonable quantities of educational, cultural and informational material, subject to reasonable conditions to ensure security and good order in the place of detention or imprisonment.

*Principle* 29

1. In order to supervise the strict observance of relevant laws and regulations, places of detention shall be visited regularly by qualified and experienced persons appointed by, and responsible to, a competent authority distinct from the authority directly in charge of the administration of the place of detention or imprisonment.

2. A detained or imprisoned person shall have the right to communicate freely and in full confidentiality with the persons who visit the places of detention or imprisonment in accordance with paragraph 1 of the present principle, subject to reasonable conditions to ensure security and good order in such places.

*Principle* 30

1. The types of conduct of the detained or imprisoned person that constitute disciplinary offences during detention or imprisonment, the description and duration of disciplinary punishment that may be inflicted and the authorities competent to impose such punishment shall be specified by law or lawful regulations and duly published.

2. A detained or imprisoned person shall have the right to be heard before disciplinary action is taken. He shall have the right to bring such action to higher authorities for review.

*Principle* 31

The appropriate authorities shall endeavour to ensure, according to domestic law, assistance when needed to dependent and, in particular, minor members of the families of detained or imprisoned persons and shall devote a particular measure of care to the appropriate custody of children left without supervision.

*Principle* 32

1. A detained person or his counsel shall be entitled at any time to take proceedings according to domestic law before a judicial or other authority to challenge the lawfulness of his detention in order to obtain his release without delay, if it is unlawful.

2. The proceedings referred to in paragraph 1 of the present principle shall be simple and expeditious and at no cost for detained persons without adequate means. The detaining authority shall produce without unreasonable delay the detained person before the reviewing authority.

*Principle* 33

1. A detained or imprisoned person or his counsel shall have the right to make a request or complaint regarding his treatment, in particular in case of torture or other cruel, inhuman or degrading treatment, to the authorities responsible for the administration of the place of detention and to higher authorities and, when necessary, to appropriate authorities vested with reviewing or remedial powers.

2. In those cases where neither the detained or imprisoned person nor his counsel has the possibility to exercise his rights under paragraph 1 of the present principle, a member of the family of the detained or imprisoned person or any other person who has knowledge of the case may exercise such rights.

3. Confidentiality concerning the request or complaint shall be maintained if so requested by the complainant.

4. Every request or complaint shall be promptly dealt with and replied to without undue delay. If the request or complaint is rejected or, in case of inordinate delay, the complainant shall be entitled to bring it before a judicial or other authority. Neither the detained or imprisoned person nor any complainant under paragraph 1 of the present principle shall suffer prejudice for making a request or complaint.

*Principle* 34

Whenever the death or disappearance of a detained or imprisoned person occurs during his detention or imprisonment, an inquiry into the cause of death or disappearance shall be held by a judicial or other authority, either on its own motion or at the instance of a member of the family of such a person or any person who has knowledge of the case. When circumstances so warrant, such an inquiry shall be held on the same procedural basis whenever the death or disappearance occurs shortly after the termination of the detention or imprisonment. The findings of such inquiry or a report thereon shall be made available upon request, unless doing so would jeopardize an ongoing criminal investigation.

*Principle* 35

1. Damage incurred because of acts or omissions by a public official contrary to the rights contained in these principles shall be compensated according to the applicable rules on liability provided by domestic law.

2. Information required to be recorded under these principles shall be available in accordance with procedures provided by domestic law for use in claiming compensation under the present principle.

*Principle* 36

1. A detained person suspected of or charged with a criminal offence shall be presumed innocent and shall be treated as such until proved guilty according to law in a public trial at which he has had all the guarantees necessary for his defence.

2. The arrest or detention of such a person pending investigation and trial shall be carried out only for the purposes of the administration of justice on grounds and under conditions and procedures specified by law. The imposition of restrictions upon such a person which are not strictly required for the purpose of the detention or to prevent hindrance to the process of investigation or the administration of justice, or for the maintenance of security and good order in the place of detention shall be forbidden.

*Principle* 37

A person detained on a criminal charge shall be brought before a judicial or other authority provided by law promptly after his arrest. Such authority shall decide without delay upon the lawfulness and necessity of detention. No person may be kept under detention pending investigation or trial except upon the written order of such an authority. A detained person shall, when brought before such an authority, have the right to make a statement on the treatment received by him while in custody.

*Principle* 38

A person detained on a criminal charge shall be entitled to trial within a reasonable time or to release pending trial.

*Principle* 39

Except in special cases provided for by law, a person detained on a criminal charge shall be entitled, unless a judicial or other authority decides otherwise in the interest of the administration of justice, to release pending trial subject to the conditions that may be imposed in accordance with the law. Such authority shall keep the necessity of detention under review.

*General clause*

Nothing in this Body of Principles shall be construed as restricting or derogating from any right defined in the International Covenant on Civil and Political Rights.

## 10. BASIC PRINCIPLES FOR THE TREATMENT OF PRISONERS, 1990

These principles are annexed to General Assembly Resolution 45/111, adopted without a vote on 14 December 1990.

Nigel S. Rodley, *The Treatment of Prisoners under International Law* (2nd edn., 1999).

## TEXT

*The General Assembly,*

*Bearing in mind* the long-standing concern of the United Nations for the humanization of criminal justice and the protection of human rights,

*Bearing in mind* also that sound policies of crime prevention and control are essential to viable planning for economic and social development,

*Recognizing* that the Standard Minimum Rules for the Treatment of Prisoners, adopted by the First United Nations Congress on the Prevention of Crime and the Treatment of Offenders, are of great value and influence in the development of penal policy and practice,

*Considering* the concern of previous United Nations congresses on the prevention of crime and the treatment of offenders, regarding the obstacles of various kinds that prevent the full implementation of the Standard Minimum Rules,

*Believing* that the full implementation of the Standard Minimum Rules would be facilitated by the articulation of the basic principles underlying them,

*Recalling* resolution 10 on the status of prisoners and resolution 17 on the human rights of prisoners, adopted by the Seventh United Nations Congress on the Prevention of Crime and the Treatment of Offenders,

*Recalling also* the statement submitted at the tenth session of the Committee on Crime Prevention and Control by Caritas Internationalis, the Commission of the Churches on International Affairs of the World Council of Churches, the International Association of Educators for World Peace, the International Council for Adult Education, the International Federation of Human Rights, the International Prisoners' Aid Association, the International Union of Students, the World Alliance of Young Men's Christian Associations and the World Council of Indigenous Peoples, which are non-governmental organizations in consultative status with the Economic and Social Council, category II,

*Recalling further* the relevant recommendations contained in the report of the Interregional Preparatory Meeting for the Eighth United Nations Congress on the Prevention of Crime and the Treatment of Offenders on topic II, 'Criminal justice policies in relation to problems of imprisonment, other penal sanctions and alternative measures',

*Aware* that the Eighth Congress coincided with International Literacy Year, proclaimed by the General Assembly in its resolution 42/104 of 7 December 1987,

*Desiring* to reflect the perspective noted by the Seventh Congress, namely, that the function of the criminal justice system is to contribute to safeguarding the basic values and norms of society,

*Recognizing* the usefulness of drafting a declaration on the human rights of prisoners,

*Affirms* the Basic Principles for the Treatment of Prisoners, contained in the annex to the present resolution, and requests the Secretary-General to bring it to the attention of Member States.

## ANNEX

Basic Principles for the Treatment of Prisoners

1. All prisoners shall be treated with the respect due to their inherent dignity and value as human beings.

2. There shall be no discrimination on the grounds of race, colour, sex, language, religion, political or other opinion, national or social origin, property, birth or other status.

3. It is, however, desirable to respect the religious beliefs and cultural precepts of the group to which prisoners belong, whenever local conditions so require.

4. The responsibility of prisons for the custody of prisoners and for the protection of society against crime shall be discharged in keeping with a State's other social objectives and its fundamental responsibilities for promoting the well-being and development of all members of society.

5. Except for those limitations that are demonstrably necessitated by the fact of incarceration, all prisoners shall retain the human rights and fundamental free-doms set out in the Universal Declaration of Human Rights, and, where the State concerned is a party, the International Covenant on Economic, Social and Cul-tural Rights, and the International Covenant on Civil and Political Rights and the Optional Protocol thereto, as well as such other rights as are set out in other United Nations covenants.

6. All prisoners shall have the right to take part in cultural activities and education aimed at the full development of the human personality.

7. Efforts addressed to the abolition of solitary confinement as a punishment, or to the restriction of its use, should be undertaken and encouraged.

8. Conditions shall be created enabling prisoners to undertake meaningful remunerated employment which will facilitate their reintegration into the country's labour market and permit them to contribute to their own financial support and to that of their families.

9. Prisoners shall have access to the health services available in the country without discrimination on the grounds of their legal situation.

10. With the participation and help of the community and social institution, and with due regard to the interests of victims, favourable conditions shall be created for the reintegration of the ex-prisoner into society under the best possible conditions.

11. The above Principles shall be applied impartially.

## 11. DECLARATION ON THE PROTECTION OF ALL PERSONS FROM ENFORCED DISAPPEARANCE, 1992

This Declaration is annexed to General Assembly Resolution 47/133, adopted without a vote on 18 December 1992; see also the Inter-American Convention on Forced Disappearance of Persons, 1994, below, 715–19.

### TEXT

*The General Assembly,*

*Considering* that, in accordance with the principles proclaimed in the Charter of the United Nations and other international instruments, recognition of the inherent dignity and of the equal and inalienable rights of all members of the human family is the foundation of freedom, justice and peace in the world,

*Bearing in mind* the obligation of States under the Charter, in particular Article 55, to promote universal respect for, and observance of, human rights and fundamental freedoms,

*Deeply concerned* that in many countries, often in a persistent manner, enforced disappearances occur, in the sense that persons are arrested, detained or abducted against their will or otherwise deprived of their liberty by officials of different branches or levels of Government, or by organized groups or private individuals acting on behalf of, or with the support, direct or indirect, consent or acquiescence of the Government, followed by a refusal to disclose the fate or whereabouts of the persons concerned or a refusal to acknowledge the deprivation of their liberty, which places such persons outside the protection of the law,

*Considering* that enforced disappearance undermines the deepest values of any society committed to respect for the rule of law, human rights and fundamental freedoms, and that the systematic practice of such acts is of the nature of a crime against humanity,

*Recalling* its resolution 33/173 of 20 December 1978, in which it expressed concern about the reports from various parts of the world relating to enforced or involuntary disappearances, as well as about the anguish and sorrow caused by those disappearances, and called upon Governments to hold law enforcement and security forces legally responsible for excesses which might lead to enforced or involuntary disappearances of persons,

*Recalling* also the protection afforded to victims of armed conflicts by the Geneva Conventions of 12 August 1949 and the Additional Protocols thereto, of 1977,

*Having regard* in particular to the relevant articles of the Universal Declaration of Human Rights and the International Covenant on Civil and Political Rights, which protect the right to life, the right to liberty and security of the person, the right not to be subjected to torture and the right to recognition as a person before the law,

*Having regard also* to the Convention against Torture and Other Cruel, Inhuman or Degrading Treatment or Punishment, which provides that States parties shall take effective measures to prevent and punish acts of torture,

*Bearing in mind* the Code of Conduct for Law Enforcement Officials, the Basic Principles on the Use of Force and Firearms by Law Enforcement Officials, the Declaration of Basic Principles of Justice for Victims of Crime and Abuse of Power and the Standard Minimum Rules for the Treatment of Prisoners,

*Affirming* that, in order to prevent enforced disappearances, it is necessary to ensure strict compliance with the Body of Principles for the Protection of All Persons under Any Form of Detention or Imprisonment contained in the annex to its resolution 43/173 of 9 December 1988, and with the Principles on the Effective Prevention and Investigation of Extra-legal, Arbitrary and Summary Executions, set forth in the annex to Economic and Social Council resolution 1989/65 of 24 May 1989 and endorsed by the General Assembly in its resolution 44/162 of 15 December 1989,

*Bearing in mind* that, while the acts which comprise enforced disappearance constitute a violation of the prohibitions found in the aforementioned international instruments, it is none the less important to devise an instrument which characterizes all acts of enforced disappearance of persons as very serious offences and sets forth standards designed to punish and prevent their commission,

1. *Proclaims* the present Declaration on the Protection of All Persons from Enforced Disappearance, as a body of principles for all States;

2. *Urges* that all efforts be made so that the Declaration becomes generally known and respected;

*Article* 1

1. Any act of enforced disappearance is an offence to human dignity. It is condemned as a denial of the purposes of the Charter of the United Nations and as a grave and flagrant violation of the human rights and fundamental freedoms proclaimed in the Universal Declaration of Human Rights and reaffirmed and developed in international instruments in this field.

2. Any act of enforced disappearance places the persons subjected thereto outside the protection of the law and inflicts severe suffering on them and their families. It constitutes a violation of the rules of international law guaranteeing, inter alia, the right to recognition as a person before the law, the right to liberty and security of the person and the right not to be subjected to torture and other cruel, inhuman or degrading treatment or punishment. It also violates or constitutes a grave threat to the right to life.

*Article* 2

1. No State shall practise, permit or tolerate enforced disappearances.

2. States shall act at the national and regional levels and in cooperation with the United Nations to contribute by all means to the prevention and eradication of enforced disappearance.

*Article* 3

Each State shall take effective legislative, administrative, judicial or other measures to prevent and terminate acts of enforced disappearance in any territory under its jurisdiction.

*Article* 4

1. All acts of enforced disappearance shall be offences under criminal law punishable by appropriate penalties which shall take into account their extreme seriousness.

2. Mitigating circumstances may be established in national legislation for persons who, having participated in enforced disappearances, are instrumental in bringing the victims forward alive or in providing voluntarily information which would contribute to clarifying cases of enforced disappearance.

*Article* 5

In addition to such criminal penalties as are applicable, enforced disappearances render their perpetrators and the State or State authorities which organize, acquiesce in or tolerate such disappearances liable under civil law, without prejudice to the international responsibility of the State concerned in accordance with the principles of international law.

*Article* 6

1. No order or instruction of any public authority, civilian, military or other, may be invoked to justify an enforced disappearance. Any person receiving such an order or instruction shall have the right and duty not to obey it.

2. Each State shall ensure that orders or instructions directing, authorizing or encouraging any enforced disappearance are prohibited.

3. Training of law enforcement officials shall emphasize the provisions in paragraphs 1 and 2 of the present article.

*Article* 7

No circumstances whatsoever, whether a threat of war, a state of war, internal political instability or any other public emergency, may be invoked to justify enforced disappearances.

*Article* 8

1. No State shall expel, return (*refouler*) or extradite a person to another State where there are substantial grounds to believe that he would be in danger of enforced disappearance.

2. For the purpose of determining whether there are such grounds, the competent authorities shall take into account all relevant considerations including, where applicable, the existence in the State concerned of a consistent pattern of gross, flagrant or mass violations of human rights.

*Article* 9

1. The right to a prompt and effective judicial remedy as a means of determining the whereabouts or state of health of persons deprived of their liberty and/or identifying the authority ordering or carrying out the deprivation of liberty is required to prevent enforced disappearances under all circumstances, including those referred to in Article 7 above.

2. In such proceedings, competent national authorities shall have access to all places where persons deprived of their liberty are being held and to each part of

those places, as well as to any place in which there are grounds to believe that such persons may be found.

3. Any other competent authority entitled under the law of the State or by any international legal instrument to which the State is a party may also have access to such places.

*Article* 10

1. Any person deprived of liberty shall be held in an officially recognized place of detention and, in conformity with national law, be brought before a judicial authority promptly after detention.

2. Accurate information on the detention of such persons and their place or places of detention, including transfers, shall be made promptly available to their family members, their counsel or to any other persons having a legitimate interest in the information unless a wish to the contrary has been manifested by the persons concerned.

3. An official up-to-date register of all persons deprived of their liberty shall be maintained in every place of detention. Additionally, each State shall take steps to maintain similar centralized registers. The information contained in these registers shall be made available to the persons mentioned in the preceding paragraph, to any judicial or other competent and independent national authority and to any other competent authority entitled under the law of the State concerned or any international legal instrument to which a State concerned is a party, seeking to trace the whereabouts of a detained person.

*Article* 11

All persons deprived of liberty must be released in a manner permitting reliable verification that they have actually been released and, further, have been released in conditions in which their physical integrity and ability fully to exercise their rights are assured.

*Article* 12

1. Each State shall establish rules under its national law indicating those officials authorized to order deprivation of liberty, establishing the conditions under which such orders may be given, and stipulating penalties for officials who, without legal justification, refuse to provide information on any detention.

2. Each State shall likewise ensure strict supervision, including a clear chain of command, of all law enforcement officials responsible for apprehensions, arrests, detentions, custody, transfers and imprisonment, and of other officials authorized by law to use force and firearms.

*Article* 13

1. Each State shall ensure that any person having knowledge or a legitimate interest who alleges that a person has been subjected to enforced disappearance has the right to complain to a competent and independent State authority and to have that complaint promptly, thoroughly and impartially investigated by that authority. Whenever there are reasonable grounds to believe that an enforced disappearance has been committed, the State shall promptly refer the matter to that authority for

such an investigation, even if there has been no formal complaint. No measure shall be taken to curtail or impede the investigation.

2. Each State shall ensure that the competent authority shall have the necessary powers and resources to conduct the investigation effectively, including powers to compel attendance of witnesses and production of relevant documents and to make immediate on-site visits.

3. Steps shall be taken to ensure that all involved in the investigation, including the complainant, counsel, witnesses and those conducting the investigation, are protected against ill-treatment, intimidation or reprisal.

4. The findings of such an investigation shall be made available upon request to all persons concerned, unless doing so would jeopardize an ongoing criminal investigation.

5. Steps shall be taken to ensure that any ill-treatment, intimidation or reprisal or any other form of interference on the occasion of the lodging of a complaint or during the investigation procedure is appropriately punished.

6. An investigation, in accordance with the procedures described above, should be able to be conducted for as long as the fate of the victim of enforced disappearance remains unclarified.

*Article* 14

Any person alleged to have perpetrated an act of enforced disappearance in a particular State shall, when the facts disclosed by an official investigation so warrant, be brought before the competent civil authorities of that State for the purpose of prosecution and trial unless he has been extradited to another State wishing to exercise jurisdiction in accordance with the relevant international agreements in force. All States should take any lawful and appropriate action available to them to bring to justice all persons presumed responsible for an act of enforced disappearance, who are found to be within their jurisdiction or under their control.

*Article* 15

The fact that there are grounds to believe that a person has participated in acts of an extremely serious nature such as those referred to in Article 4, paragraph 1, above, regardless of the motives, shall be taken into account when the competent authorities of the State decide whether or not to grant asylum.

*Article* 16

1. Persons alleged to have committed any of the acts referred to in Article 4, paragraph 1, above, shall be suspended from any official duties during the investigation referred to in Article 13 above.

2. They shall be tried only by the competent ordinary courts in each State, and not by any other special tribunal, in particular military courts.

3. No privileges, immunities or special exemptions shall be admitted in such trials, without prejudice to the provisions contained in the Vienna Convention on Diplomatic Relations.

4. The persons presumed responsible for such acts shall be guaranteed fair treatment in accordance with the relevant provisions of the Universal Declaration of

Human Rights and other relevant international agreements in force at all stages of the investigation and eventual prosecution and trial.

*Article* 17

1. Acts constituting enforced disappearance shall be considered a continuing offence as long as the perpetrators continue to conceal the fate and the whereabouts of persons who have disappeared and these facts remain unclarified.

2. When the remedies provided for in Article 2 of the International Covenant on Civil and Political Rights are no longer effective, the statute of limitations relating to acts of enforced disappearance shall be suspended until these remedies are re-established.

3. Statutes of limitations, where they exist, relating to acts of enforced disappearance shall be substantial and commensurate with the extreme seriousness of the offence.

*Article* 18

1. Persons who have or are alleged to have committed offences referred to in Article 4, paragraph 1, above, shall not benefit from any special amnesty law or similar measures that might have the effect of exempting them from any criminal proceedings or sanction.

2. In the exercise of the right of pardon, the extreme seriousness of acts of enforced disappearance shall be taken into account.

*Article* 19

The victims of acts of enforced disappearance and their family shall obtain redress and shall have the right to adequate compensation, including the means for as complete a rehabilitation as possible. In the event of the death of the victim as a result of an act of enforced disappearance, their dependants shall also be entitled to compensation.

*Article* 20

1. States shall prevent and suppress the abduction of children of parents subjected to enforced disappearance and of children born during their mother's enforced disappearance, and shall devote their efforts to the search for and identification of such children and to the restitution of the children to their families of origin.

2. Considering the need to protect the best interests of children referred to in the preceding paragraph, there shall be an opportunity, in States which recognize a system of adoption, for a review of the adoption of such children and, in particular, for annulment of any adoption which originated in enforced disappearance. Such adoption should, however, continue to be in force if consent is given, at the time of the review, by the child's closest relatives.

3. The abduction of children of parents subjected to enforced disappearance or of children born during their mother's enforced disappearance, and the act of altering or suppressing documents attesting to their true identity, shall constitute an extremely serious offence, which shall be punished as such.

4. For these purposes, States shall, where appropriate, conclude bilateral and multilateral agreements.

*Article* 21

The provisions of the present Declaration are without prejudice to the provisions enunciated in the Universal Declaration of Human Rights or in any other international instrument, and shall not be construed as restricting or derogating from any of those provisions.

## 12. DECLARATION ON THE RIGHTS OF PERSONS BELONGING TO NATIONAL OR ETHNIC, RELIGIOUS AND LINGUISTIC MINORITIES, 1992

This Declaration was adopted without a vote by General Assembly Resolution 47/135, 18 December 1992.

Thornberry, P., *International Law and the Rights of Minorities* (1991); Dunbar, R., 'Minority Language Rights under International Law' (2001) 50 *ICLQ* 90–120.

### TEXT

*The General Assembly,*

*Reaffirming* that one of the basic aims of the United Nations, as proclaimed in the Charter, is to promote and encourage respect for human rights and for fundamental freedoms for all, without distinction as to race, sex, language or religion,

*Reaffirming* faith in fundamental human rights, in the dignity and worth of the human person, in the equal rights of men and women and of nations large and small,

*Desiring* to promote the realization of the principles contained in the Charter, the Universal Declaration of Human Rights, the Convention on the Prevention and Punishment of the Crime of Genocide, the International Convention on the Elimination of All Forms of Racial Discrimination, the International Covenant on Civil and Political Rights, the International Covenant on Economic, Social and Cultural Rights, the Declaration on the Elimination of All Forms of Intolerance and of Discrimination Based on Religion or Belief, and the Convention on the Rights of the Child, as well as other relevant international instruments that have been adopted at the universal or regional level and those concluded between individual States Members of the United Nations,

*Inspired* by the provisions of article 27 of the International Covenant on Civil and Political Rights concerning the rights of persons belonging to ethnic, religious or linguistic minorities,

*Considering* that the promotion and protection of the rights of persons belonging to national or ethnic, religious and linguistic minorities contribute to the political and social stability of States in which they live,

*Emphasizing* that the constant promotion and realization of the rights of persons belonging to national or ethnic, religious and linguistic minorities, as an integral part of the development of society as a whole and within a democratic framework based on the rule of law, would contribute to the strengthening of friendship and cooperation among peoples and States,

*Considering* that the United Nations has an important role to play regarding the protection of minorities,

*Bearing in mind* the work done so far within the United Nations system, in particular by the Commission on Human Rights, the Sub-Commission on Prevention of Discrimination and Protection of Minorities and the bodies established pursuant to the International Covenants on Human Rights and other relevant international human rights instruments in promoting and protecting the rights of persons belonging to national or ethnic, religious and linguistic minorities,

*Taking into account* the important work which is done by intergovernmental and non-governmental organizations in protecting minorities and in promoting and protecting the rights of persons belonging to national or ethnic, religious and linguistic minorities,

*Recognizing* the need to ensure even more effective implementation of international human rights instruments with regard to the rights of persons belonging to national or ethnic, religious and linguistic minorities,

*Proclaims* this Declaration on the Rights of Persons Belonging to National or Ethnic, Religious and Linguistic Minorities:

*Article* 1

1. States shall protect the existence and the national or ethnic, cultural, religious and linguistic identity of minorities within their respective territories and shall encourage conditions for the promotion of that identity.

2. States shall adopt appropriate legislative and other measures to achieve those ends.

*Article* 2

1. Persons belonging to national or ethnic, religious and linguistic minorities (hereinafter referred to as persons belonging to minorities) have the right to enjoy their own culture, to profess and practise their own religion, and to use their own language, in private and in public, freely and without interference or any form of discrimination.

2. Persons belonging to minorities have the right to participate effectively in cultural, religious, social, economic and public life.

3. Persons belonging to minorities have the right to participate effectively in decisions on the national and, where appropriate, regional level concerning the minority to which they belong or the regions in which they live, in a manner not incompatible with national legislation.

4. Persons belonging to minorities have the right to establish and maintain their own associations.

5. Persons belonging to minorities have the right to establish and maintain, without any discrimination, free and peaceful contacts with other members of their group and with persons belonging to other minorities, as well as contacts across frontiers with citizens of other States to whom they are related by national or ethnic, religious or linguistic ties.

*Article* 3

1. Persons belonging to minorities may exercise their rights, including those set forth in the present Declaration, individually as well as in community with other members of their group, without any discrimination.

2. No disadvantage shall result for any person belonging to a minority as the consequence of the exercise or non-exercise of the rights set forth in the present Declaration.

*Article* 4

1. States shall take measures where required to ensure that persons belonging to minorities may exercise fully and effectively all their human rights and fundamental freedoms without any discrimination and in full equality before the law.

2. States shall take measures to create favourable conditions to enable persons belonging to minorities to express their characteristics and to develop their culture, language, religion, traditions and customs, except where specific practices are in violation of national law and contrary to international standards.

3. States should take appropriate measures so that, wherever possible, persons belonging to minorities may have adequate opportunities to learn their mother tongue or to have instruction in their mother tongue.

4. States should, where appropriate, take measures in the field of education, in order to encourage knowledge of the history, traditions, language and culture of the minorities existing within their territory. Persons belonging to minorities should have adequate opportunities to gain knowledge of the society as a whole.

5. States should consider appropriate measures so that persons belonging to minorities may participate fully in the economic progress and development in their country.

*Article* 5

1. National policies and programmes shall be planned and implemented with due regard for the legitimate interests of persons belonging to minorities.

2. Programmes of co-operation and assistance among States should be planned and implemented with due regard for the legitimate interests of persons belonging to minorities.

*Article* 6

States should co-operate on questions relating to persons belonging to minorities, *inter alia*, exchanging information and experiences, in order to promote mutual understanding and confidence.

*Article* 7

States should co-operate in order to promote respect for the rights set forth in the present Declaration.

*Article* 8

1. Nothing in the present Declaration shall prevent the fulfilment of international obligations of States in relation to persons belonging to minorities. In particular, States shall fulfil in good faith the obligations and commitments they have assumed under international treaties and agreements to which they are parties.

2. The exercise of the rights set forth in the present Declaration shall not prejudice the enjoyment by all persons of universally recognized human rights and fundamental freedoms.

3. Measures taken by States to ensure the effective enjoyment of the rights set forth in the present Declaration shall not prima facie be considered contrary to the principle of equality contained in the Universal Declaration of Human Rights.

4. Nothing in the present Declaration may be construed as permitting any activity contrary to the purposes and principles of the United Nations, including sovereign equality, territorial integrity and political independence of States.

*Article* 9

The specialized agencies and other organizations of the United Nations system shall contribute to the full realization of the rights and principles set forth in the present Declaration, within their respective fields of competence.

## 13. DECLARATION ON THE ELIMINATION OF VIOLENCE AGAINST WOMEN, 1993

This Declaration was adopted without a vote in General Assembly Resolution 48/104, 20 December 1993; see also the Inter-American Convention on the Prevention, Punishment and Eradication of Violence against Women, 1994, below, 708–14.

*TEXT*

*The General Assembly,*

*Recognizing* the urgent need for the universal application to women of the rights and principles with regard to equality, security, liberty, integrity and dignity of all human beings,

*Noting* that those rights and principles are enshrined in international instruments, including the Universal Declaration of Human Rights, the International Covenant on Civil and Political Rights, the International Covenant on Economic, Social and Cultural Rights, the Convention on the Elimination of All Forms of Discrimination against Women and the Convention against Torture and Other Cruel, Inhuman or Degrading Treatment or Punishment,

*Recognizing* that effective implementation of the Convention on the Elimination of All Forms of Discrimination against Women would contribute to the elimination of violence against women and that the Declaration on the Elimination of Violence against Women, set forth in the present resolution, will strengthen and complement that process,

*Concerned* that violence against women is an obstacle to the achievement of equality, development and peace, as recognized in the Nairobi Forward-looking Strategies for the Advancement of Women, in which a set of measures to combat violence against women was recommended, and to the full implementation of the Convention on the Elimination of All Forms of Discrimination against Women,

*Affirming* that violence against women constitutes a violation of the rights and fundamental freedoms of women and impairs or nullifies their enjoyment of those rights and freedoms, and concerned about the long-standing failure to protect and promote those rights and freedoms in the case of violence against women,

*Recognizing* that violence against women is a manifestation of historically unequal power relations between men and women, which have led to domination over and discrimination against women by men and to the prevention of the full advancement of women, and that violence against women is one of the crucial social mechanisms by which women are forced into a subordinate position compared with men,

*Concerned* that some groups of women, such as women belonging to minority groups, indigenous women, refugee women, migrant women, women living in rural or remote communities, destitute women, women in institutions or in detention, female children, women with disabilities, elderly women and women in situations of armed conflict, are especially vulnerable to violence,

*Recalling* the conclusion in paragraph 23 of the annex to Economic and Social Council resolution 1990/15 of 24 May 1990 that the recognition that violence against women in the family and society was pervasive and cut across lines of income, class and culture had to be matched by urgent and effective steps to eliminate its incidence,

*Recalling also* Economic and Social Council resolution 1991/18 of 30 May 1991, in which the Council recommended the development of a framework for an international instrument that would address explicitly the issue of violence against women,

*Welcoming* the role that women's movements are playing in drawing increasing attention to the nature, severity and magnitude of the problem of violence against women,

*Alarmed* that opportunities for women to achieve legal, social, political and economic equality in society are limited, inter alia, by continuing and endemic violence,

*Convinced* that in the light of the above there is a need for a clear and comprehensive definition of violence against women, a clear statement of the rights to be applied to ensure the elimination of violence against women in all its forms, a commitment by States in respect of their responsibilities, and a commitment by the international community at large to the elimination of violence against women,

*Solemnly* proclaims the following Declaration on the Elimination of Violence against Women and urges that every effort be made so that it becomes generally known and respected:

*Article* 1

For the purposes of this Declaration, the term 'violence against women' means any act of gender-based violence that results in, or is likely to result in, physical, sexual or psychological harm or suffering to women, including threats of such acts, coercion or arbitrary deprivation of liberty, whether occurring in public or in private life.

*Article* 2

Violence against women shall be understood to encompass, but not be limited to, the following:

(a) Physical, sexual and psychological violence occurring in the family, including battering, sexual abuse of female children in the household, dowry-related violence, marital rape, female genital mutilation and other traditional practices harmful to women, non-spousal violence and violence related to exploitation;

(b) Physical, sexual and psychological violence occurring within the general community, including rape, sexual abuse, sexual harassment and intimidation at work, in educational institutions and elsewhere, trafficking in women and forced prostitution;

(c) Physical, sexual and psychological violence perpetrated or condoned by the State, wherever it occurs.

*Article* 3

Women are entitled to the equal enjoyment and protection of all human rights and fundamental freedoms in the political, economic, social, cultural, civil or any other field. These rights include, inter alia:

(a)  The right to life;

(b)  The right to equality;

(c)  The right to liberty and security of person;

(d)  The right to equal protection under the law;

(e)  The right to be free from all forms of discrimination;

(f)  The right to the highest standard attainable of physical and mental health;

(g)  The right to just and favourable conditions of work;

(h)  The right not to be subjected to torture, or other cruel, inhuman or degrading treatment or punishment.

*Article* 4

States should condemn violence against women and should not invoke any custom, tradition or religious consideration to avoid their obligations with respect to its elimination. States should pursue by all appropriate means and without delay a policy of eliminating violence against women and, to this end, should:

(a)  Consider, where they have not yet done so, ratifying or acceding to the Convention on the Elimination of All Forms of Discrimination against Women or withdrawing reservations to that Convention;

(b)  Refrain from engaging in violence against women;

(c)  Exercise due diligence to prevent, investigate and, in accordance with national legislation, punish acts of violence against women, whether those acts are perpetrated by the State or by private persons;

(d)  Develop penal, civil, labour and administrative sanctions in domestic legislation to punish and redress the wrongs caused to women who are subjected to violence; women who are subjected to violence should be provided with access to the mechanisms of justice and, as provided for by national legislation, to just and effective remedies for the harm that they have suffered; States should also inform women of their rights in seeking redress through such mechanisms;

(e)  Consider the possibility of developing national plans of action to promote the protection of women against any form of violence, or to include provisions for that purpose in plans already existing, taking into account, as appropriate, such cooperation as can be provided by non-governmental organizations, particularly those concerned with the issue of violence against women;

(f)  Develop, in a comprehensive way, preventive approaches and all those measures of a legal, political, administrative and cultural nature that promote the protection of women against any form of violence, and ensure that the re-victimization of women does not occur because of laws insensitive to gender considerations, enforcement practices or other interventions;

(g)  Work to ensure, to the maximum extent feasible in the light of their

available resources and, where needed, within the framework of international cooperation, that women subjected to violence and, where
appropriate, their children have specialized assistance, such as rehabilitation, assistance in child care and maintenance, treatment, counselling, and
health and social services, facilities and programmes, as well as support
structures, and should take all other appropriate measures to promote their
safety and physical and psychological rehabilitation;

(h) Include in government budgets adequate resources for their activities
related to the elimination of violence against women;

(i) Take measures to ensure that law enforcement officers and public officials
responsible for implementing policies to prevent, investigate and punish
violence against women receive training to sensitize them to the needs of
women;

(j) Adopt all appropriate measures, especially in the field of education, to
modify the social and cultural patterns of conduct of men and women and
to eliminate prejudices, customary practices and all other practices based on
the idea of the inferiority or superiority of either of the sexes and on
stereotyped roles for men and women;

(k) Promote research, collect data and compile statistics, especially concerning
domestic violence, relating to the prevalence of different forms of violence
against women and encourage research on the causes, nature, seriousness
and consequences of violence against women and on the effectiveness of
measures implemented to prevent and redress violence against women;
those statistics and findings of the research will be made public;

(l) Adopt measures directed towards the elimination of violence against
women who are especially vulnerable to violence;

(m) Include, in submitting reports as required under relevant human rights
instruments of the United Nations, information pertaining to violence
against women and measures taken to implement the present Declaration;

(n) Encourage the development of appropriate guidelines to assist in the
implementation of the principles set forth in the present Declaration;

(o) Recognize the important role of the women's movement and non-
governmental organizations world wide in raising awareness and alleviating
the problem of violence against women;

(p) Facilitate and enhance the work of the women's movement and non-
governmental organizations and cooperate with them at local, national and
regional levels;

(q) Encourage intergovernmental regional organizations of which they are
members to include the elimination of violence against women in their
programmes, as appropriate.

*Article* 5

The organs and specialized agencies of the United Nations system should, within
their respective fields of competence, contribute to the recognition and realization
of the rights and the principles set forth in the present Declaration and, to this end,
should, inter alia:

*(a)* Foster international and regional cooperation with a view to defining regional strategies for combating violence, exchanging experiences and financing programmes relating to the elimination of violence against women;

*(b)* Promote meetings and seminars with the aim of creating and raising awareness among all persons of the issue of the elimination of violence against women;

*(c)* Foster coordination and exchange within the United Nations system between human rights treaty bodies to address the issue of violence against women effectively;

*(d)* Include in analyses prepared by organizations and bodies of the United Nations system of social trends and problems, such as the periodic reports on the world social situation, examination of trends in violence against women;

*(e)* Encourage coordination between organizations and bodies of the United Nations system to incorporate the issue of violence against women into ongoing programmes, especially with reference to groups of women particularly vulnerable to violence;

*(f)* Promote the formulation of guidelines or manuals relating to violence against women, taking into account the measures referred to in the present Declaration;

*(g)* Consider the issue of the elimination of violence against women, as appropriate, in fulfilling their mandates with respect to the implementation of human rights instruments;

*(h)* Cooperate with non-governmental organizations in addressing the issue of violence against women.

*Article* 6

Nothing in the present Declaration shall affect any provision that is more conducive to the elimination of violence against women that may be contained in the legislation of a State or in any international convention, treaty or other instrument in force in a State.

## 14. APPOINTMENT OF A UNITED NATIONS HIGH COMMISSIONER FOR HUMAN RIGHTS, 1993

After many years of discussion, the General Assembly decided in 1993 to appoint a 'High Commissioner for the Promotion and Protection of All Human Rights': UNGA Resolution 48/141, adopted without a vote on 20 December 1993. The first holder of the post was Ayala Lasso, an Ecuadorian diplomat. He was succeeded by Mary Robinson, former President of Ireland, in 1997.

Clapham, A., 'Creating the High Commissioner for Human Rights: The Outside Story', 5 *EJIL* 556–68 (1994).

*TEXT*

*The General Assembly,*

*Reaffirming* its commitment to the purposes and principles of the Charter of the United Nations,

*Emphasizing* the responsibilities of all States, in conformity with the Charter, to promote and encourage respect for all human rights and fundamental freedoms for all, without distinction as to race, sex, language or religion,

*Emphasizing* the need to observe the Universal Declaration of Human Rights and for the full implementation of the human rights instruments, including the International Covenant on Civil and Political Rights, the International Covenant on Economic, Social and Cultural Rights, as well as the Declaration on the Right to Development,

*Reaffirming* that the right to development is a universal and inalienable right which is a fundamental part of the rights of the human person,

*Considering* that the promotion and the protection of all human rights is one of the priorities of the international community,

*Recalling* that one of the purposes of the United Nations enshrined in the Charter is to achieve international cooperation in promoting and encouraging respect for human rights,

*Reaffirming* the commitment made under Article 56 of the Charter to take joint and separate action in cooperation with the United Nations for the achievement of the purposes set forth in Article 55 of the Charter,

*Emphasizing* the need for the promotion and protection of all human rights to be guided by the principles of impartiality, objectivity and non-selectivity, in the spirit of constructive international dialogue and cooperation,

*Aware* that all human rights are universal, indivisible, interdependent and interrelated and that as such they should be given the same emphasis,

*Affirming* its commitment to the Vienna Declaration and Programme of Action, adopted by the World Conference on Human Rights, held at Vienna from 14 to 25 June 1993,

*Convinced* that the World Conference on Human Rights made an important contribution to the cause of human rights and that its recommendations should be implemented through effective action by all States, the competent organs of the United Nations and the specialized agencies, in cooperation with non-governmental organizations,

*Acknowledging* the importance of strengthening the provision of advisory services and technical assistance by the Centre for Human Rights of the Secretariat and other relevant programmes and bodies of the United Nations system for the purpose of the promotion and protection of all human rights,

*Determined* to adapt, strengthen and streamline the existing mechanisms to promote and protect all human rights and fundamental freedoms while avoiding unnecessary duplication,

*Recognizing* that the activities of the United Nations in the field of human rights should be rationalized and enhanced in order to strengthen the United Nations machinery in this field and to further the objectives of universal respect for observance of international human rights standards,

*Reaffirming* that the General Assembly, the Economic and Social Council and the Commission on Human Rights are the responsible organs for decision- and policy-making for the promotion and protection of all human rights,

*Reaffirming* the necessity for a continued adaptation of the United Nations human rights machinery to the current and future needs in the promotion and protection of human rights and the need to improve its coordination, efficiency and effectiveness, as reflected in the Vienna Declaration and Programme of Action and within the framework of a balanced and sustainable development for all people,

*Having considered* the recommendation contained in paragraph 18 of section II of the Vienna Declaration and Programme of Action,

1. Decides to create the post of the High Commissioner for Human Rights;

2. Decides that the High Commissioner for Human Rights shall:

    *(a)* Be a person of high moral standing and personal integrity and shall possess expertise, including in the field of human rights, and the general knowledge and understanding of diverse cultures necessary for impartial, objective, non-selective and effective performance of the duties of the High Commissioner;

    *(b)* Be appointed by the Secretary-General of the United Nations and approved by the General Assembly, with due regard to geographical rotation, and have a fixed term of four years with a possibility of one renewal for another fixed term of four years;

    *(c)* Be of the rank of Under-Secretary-General;

3. Decides that the High Commissioner for Human Rights shall:

    *(a)* Function within the framework of the Charter of the United Nations, the Universal Declaration of Human Rights, other international instruments of human rights and international law, including the obligations, within this framework, to respect the sovereignty, territorial integrity and domestic jurisdiction of States and to promote the universal respect for and observance of all human rights, in the recognition that, in the framework of the purposes and principles of the Charter, the promotion and protection of all human rights is a legitimate concern of the international community;

*(b)* Be guided by the recognition that all human rights—civil, cultural, economic, political and social—are universal, indivisible, interdependent and interrelated and that, while the significance of national and regional particularities and various historical, cultural and religious backgrounds must be borne in mind, it is the duty of States, regardless of their political, economic and cultural systems, to promote and protect all human rights and fundamental freedoms;

*(c)* Recognize the importance of promoting a balanced and sustainable development for all people and of ensuring realization of the right to development, as established in the Declaration on the Right to Development;

4. Decides that the High Commissioner for Human Rights shall be the United Nations official with principal responsibility for United Nations human rights activities under the direction and authority of the Secretary-General; within the framework of the overall competence, authority and decisions of the General Assembly, the Economic and Social Council and the Commission on Human Rights, the High Commissioner's responsibilities shall be:

*(a)* To promote and protect the effective enjoyment by all of all civil, cultural, economic, political and social rights;

*(b)* To carry out the tasks assigned to him/her by the competent bodies of the United Nations system in the field of human rights and to make recommendations to them with a view to improving the promotion and protection of all human rights;

*(c)* To promote and protect the realization of the right to development and to enhance support from relevant bodies of the United Nations system for this purpose;

*(d)* To provide, through the Centre for Human Rights of the Secretariat and other appropriate institutions, advisory services and technical and financial assistance, at the request of the State concerned and, where appropriate, the regional human rights organizations, with a view to supporting actions and programmes in the field of human rights;

*(e)* To coordinate relevant United Nations education and public information programmes in the field of human rights;

*(f)* To play an active role in removing the current obstacles and in meeting the challenges to the full realization of all human rights and in preventing the continuation of human rights violations throughout the world, as reflected in the Vienna Declaration and Programme of Action;

*(g)* To engage in a dialogue with all Governments in the implementation of his/her mandate with a view to securing respect for all human rights;

*(h)* To enhance international cooperation for the promotion and protection of all human rights;

*(i)* To coordinate the human rights promotion and protection activities throughout the United Nations system;

*(j)* To rationalize, adapt, strengthen and streamline the United Nations machinery in the field of human rights with a view to improving its efficiency and effectiveness;

*(k)* To carry out overall supervision of the Centre for Human Rights;

5. Requests the High Commissioner for Human Rights to report annually on his/her activities, in accordance with his/her mandate, to the Commission on Human Rights and, through the Economic and Social Council, to the General Assembly;

6. Decides that the Office of the High Commissioner for Human Rights shall be located at Geneva and shall have a liaison office in New York;

7. Requests the Secretary-General to provide appropriate staff and resources, within the existing and future regular budgets of the United Nations, to enable the High Commissioner to fulfil his/her mandate, without diverting resources from the development programmes and activities of the United Nations;

8. Also requests the Secretary-General to report to the General Assembly at its forty-ninth session on the implementation of the present resolution.

## 15. DRAFT UNITED NATIONS DECLARATION ON THE RIGHTS OF INDIGENOUS PEOPLES, 1994

In 1994, the Sub-Commission on Prevention of Discrimination and Protection of Minorities adopted the draft declaration on the rights of indigenous peoples (Resolution 1994/45, 26 August 1994), which had been completed by the Working Group on Indigenous Populations, chaired by Erica-Irene Daes (Report of the Working Group: UN doc. E/CN.4/Sub.2/1994/30 and Corr.1). The draft was duly submitted to the Commission on Human Rights and the Secretary-General was requested to transmit the text to indigenous peoples and organizations, governments and intergovernmental organizations.

The Commission on Human Rights established an open-ended inter-sessional Working Group on the draft declaration in 1995, in accordance with Commission on Human Rights Resolution 1995/32 and Economic and Social Council Resolution 1995/32. The sole purpose of the Working Group is to elaborate a draft declaration on the rights of indigenous peoples, considering the draft adopted by the Sub-Commission, reproduced below without its accompanying resolution, with a view to its being considered and adopted by the General Assembly during the International Decade of the World's Indigenous People. See also Sub-Commission on the Promotion and Protection of Human Rights, 'Working paper on the relationship and distinction between the rights of persons belonging to minorities and those of indigenous peoples': UN doc. E/CN.4/Sub.2/2000/10, 19 July 2000 (prepared by Asbjørn Eide and Erica-Irene Daes).

The Working Group, which is a subsidiary organ of the Commission on Human Rights, is composed of representatives of Member States. Non-governmental and indigenous organizations with consultative status with the Economic and Social Council are able to take part in the proceedings, and Commission on Human Rights Resolution 1995/32 makes provision also for participation by indigenous organizations without consultative status.

The sixth session of the Working Group was held in Geneva from 20 November–1 December 2000 (UN doc. E/CN.4/2001/85), and confirmed the continuing lack of consensus on certain key issues, including the term 'indigenous peoples', on which certain States maintain reservations, partly because of its possible implications with respect to self-determination and individual and collective rights. See also Commission on Human Rights Resolution 2001/58, 24 April 2001.

### TEXT

*Affirming* that indigenous peoples are equal in dignity and rights to all other peoples, while recognizing the right of all peoples to be different, to consider themselves different, and to be respected as such,

*Affirming* also that all peoples contribute to the diversity and richness of civilizations and cultures, which constitute the common heritage of humankind,

*Affirming further* that all doctrines, policies and practices based on or advocating superiority of peoples or individuals on the basis of national origin, racial, religious, ethnic or cultural differences are racist, scientifically false, legally invalid, morally condemnable and socially unjust,

*Reaffirming also* that indigenous peoples, in the exercise of their rights, should be free from discrimination of any kind,

*Concerned* that indigenous peoples have been deprived of their human rights and fundamental freedoms, resulting, inter alia, in their colonization and dispossession of their lands, territories and resources, thus preventing them from exercising, in particular, their right to development in accordance with their own needs and interests,

*Recognizing* the urgent need to respect and promote the inherent rights and characteristics of indigenous peoples, especially their rights to their lands, territories and resources, which derive from their political, economic and social structures and from their cultures, spiritual traditions, histories and philosophies,

*Welcoming* the fact that indigenous peoples are organizing themselves for political, economic, social and cultural enhancement and in order to bring an end to all forms of discrimination and oppression wherever they occur,

*Convinced* that control by indigenous peoples over developments affecting them and their lands, territories and resources will enable them to maintain and strengthen their institutions, cultures and traditions, and to promote their development in accordance with their aspirations and needs,

*Recognizing also* that respect for indigenous knowledge, cultures and traditional practices contributes to sustainable and equitable development and proper management of the environment,

*Emphasizing* the need for demilitarization of the lands and territories of indigenous peoples, which will contribute to peace, economic and social progress and development, understanding and friendly relations among nations and peoples of the world,

*Recognizing* in particular the right of indigenous families and communities to retain shared responsibility for the upbringing, training, education and well-being of their children,

*Recognizing also* that indigenous peoples have the right freely to determine their relationships with States in a spirit of coexistence, mutual benefit and full respect,

*Considering* that treaties, agreements and other arrangements between States and indigenous peoples are properly matters of international concern and responsibility,

*Acknowledging* that the Charter of the United Nations, the International Covenant on Economic, Social and Cultural Rights and the International Covenant on Civil and Political Rights affirm the fundamental importance of the right of self-determination of all peoples, by virtue of which they freely determine their political status and freely pursue their economic, social and cultural development,

*Bearing in mind* that nothing in this Declaration may be used to deny any peoples their right of self-determination,

*Encouraging* States to comply with and effectively implement all international instruments, in particular those related to human rights, as they apply to indigenous peoples, in consultation and cooperation with the peoples concerned,

*Emphasizing* that the United Nations has an important and continuing role to play in promoting and protecting the rights of indigenous peoples,

*Believing* that this Declaration is a further important step forward for the recognition, promotion and protection of the rights and freedoms of indigenous peoples and in the development of relevant activities of the United Nations system in this field,

*Solemnly proclaims* the following United Nations Declaration on the Rights of Indigenous Peoples:

# PART I

*Article* 1

Indigenous peoples have the right to the full and effective enjoyment of all human rights and fundamental freedoms recognized in the Charter of the United Nations, the Universal Declaration of Human Rights and international human rights law.

*Article* 2

Indigenous individuals and peoples are free and equal to all other individuals and peoples in dignity and rights, and have the right to be free from any kind of adverse discrimination, in particular that based on their indigenous origin or identity.

*Article* 3

Indigenous peoples have the right of self-determination. By virtue of that right they freely determine their political status and freely pursue their economic, social and cultural development.

*Article* 4

Indigenous peoples have the right to maintain and strengthen their distinct political, economic, social and cultural characteristics, as well as their legal systems, while retaining their rights to participate fully, if they so choose, in the political, economic, social and cultural life of the State.

*Article* 5

Every indigenous individual has the right to a nationality.

# PART II

*Article* 6

Indigenous peoples have the collective right to live in freedom, peace and security as distinct peoples and to full guarantees against genocide or any other act of violence, including the removal of indigenous children from their families and communities under any pretext.

In addition, they have the individual rights to life, physical and mental integrity, liberty and security of person.

*Article* 7

Indigenous peoples have the collective and individual right not to be subjected to ethnocide and cultural genocide, including prevention of and redress for:

(a) Any action which has the aim or effect of depriving them of their integrity as distinct peoples, or of their cultural values or ethnic identities;

(b)  Any action which has the aim or effect of dispossessing them of their lands, territories or resources;

(c)  Any form of population transfer which has the aim or effect of violating or undermining any of their rights;

(d)  Any form of assimilation or integration by other cultures or ways of life imposed on them by legislative, administrative or other measures;

(e)  Any form of propaganda directed against them.

*Article* 8

Indigenous peoples have the collective and individual right to maintain and develop their distinct identities and characteristics, including the right to identify themselves as indigenous and to be recognized as such.

*Article* 9

Indigenous peoples and individuals have the right to belong to an indigenous community or nation, in accordance with the traditions and customs of the community or nation concerned. No disadvantage of any kind may arise from the exercise of such a right.

*Article* 10

Indigenous peoples shall not be forcibly removed from their lands or territories. No relocation shall take place without the free and informed consent of the indigenous peoples concerned and after agreement on just and fair compensation and, where possible, with the option of return.

*Article* 11

Indigenous peoples have the right to special protection and security in periods of armed conflict.

States shall observe international standards, in particular the Fourth Geneva Convention of 1949, for the protection of civilian populations in circumstances of emergency and armed conflict, and shall not:

(a)  Recruit indigenous individuals against their will into the armed forces and, in particular, for use against other indigenous peoples;

(b)  Recruit indigenous children into the armed forces under any circumstances;

(c)  Force indigenous individuals to abandon their lands, territories or means of subsistence, or relocate them in special centres for military purposes;

(d)  Force indigenous individuals to work for military purposes under any discriminatory conditions.

# PART III

*Article* 12

Indigenous peoples have the right to practise and revitalize their cultural traditions and customs. This includes the right to maintain, protect and develop the past, present and future manifestations of their cultures, such as archaeological and historical sites, artifacts, designs, ceremonies, technologies and visual and performing arts and literature, as well as the right to the restitution of cultural, intellectual, religious and spiritual property taken without their free and informed consent or in violation of their laws, traditions and customs.

*Article* 13

Indigenous peoples have the right to manifest, practise, develop and teach their spiritual and religious traditions, customs and ceremonies; the right to maintain, protect, and have access in privacy to their religious and cultural sites; the right to the use and control of ceremonial objects; and the right to the repatriation of human remains.

States shall take effective measures, in conjunction with the indigenous peoples concerned, to ensure that indigenous sacred places, including burial sites, be preserved, respected and protected.

*Article* 14

Indigenous peoples have the right to revitalize, use, develop and transmit to future generations their histories, languages, oral traditions, philosophies, writing systems and literatures, and to designate and retain their own names for communities, places and persons.

States shall take effective measures, whenever any right of indigenous peoples may be threatened, to ensure this right is protected and also to ensure that they can understand and be understood in political, legal and administrative proceedings, where necessary through the provision of interpretation or by other appropriate means.

## PART IV

*Article* 15

Indigenous children have the right to all levels and forms of education of the State. All indigenous peoples also have this right and the right to establish and control their educational systems and institutions providing education in their own languages, in a manner appropriate to their cultural methods of teaching and learning.

Indigenous children living outside their communities have the right to be provided access to education in their own culture and language.

States shall take effective measures to provide appropriate resources for these purposes.

*Article* 16

Indigenous peoples have the right to have the dignity and diversity of their cultures, traditions, histories and aspirations appropriately reflected in all forms of education and public information.

States shall take effective measures, in consultation with the indigenous peoples concerned, to eliminate prejudice and discrimination and to promote tolerance, understanding and good relations among indigenous peoples and all segments of society.

*Article* 17

Indigenous peoples have the right to establish their own media in their own languages. They also have the right to equal access to all forms of non-indigenous media.

States shall take effective measures to ensure that State-owned media duly reflect indigenous cultural diversity.

*Article* 18

Indigenous peoples have the right to enjoy fully all rights established under international labour law and national labour legislation.

Indigenous individuals have the right not to be subjected to any discriminatory conditions of labour, employment or salary.

## PART V

*Article* 19

Indigenous peoples have the right to participate fully, if they so choose, at all levels of decision-making in matters which may affect their rights, lives and destinies through representatives chosen by themselves in accordance with their own procedures, as well as to maintain and develop their own indigenous decision-making institutions.

*Article* 20

Indigenous peoples have the right to participate fully, if they so choose, through procedures determined by them, in devising legislative or administrative measures that may affect them.

States shall obtain the free and informed consent of the peoples concerned before adopting and implementing such measures.

*Article* 21

Indigenous peoples have the right to maintain and develop their political, economic and social systems, to be secure in the enjoyment of their own means of subsistence and development, and to engage freely in all their traditional and other economic activities. Indigenous peoples who have been deprived of their means of subsistence and development are entitled to just and fair compensation.

*Article* 22

Indigenous peoples have the right to special measures for the immediate, effective and continuing improvement of their economic and social conditions, including in the areas of employment, vocational training and retraining, housing, sanitation, health and social security.

Particular attention shall be paid to the rights and special needs of indigenous elders, women, youth, children and disabled persons.

*Article* 23

Indigenous peoples have the right to determine and develop priorities and strategies for exercising their right to development. In particular, indigenous peoples have the right to determine and develop all health, housing and other economic and social programmes affecting them and, as far as possible, to administer such programmes through their own institutions.

*Article* 24

Indigenous peoples have the right to their traditional medicines and health practices, including the right to the protection of vital medicinal plants, animals and minerals.

They also have the right to access, without any discrimination, to all medical institutions, health services and medical care.

# PART VI

*Article* 25

Indigenous peoples have the right to maintain and strengthen their distinctive spiritual and material relationship with the lands, territories, waters and coastal seas and other resources which they have traditionally owned or otherwise occupied or used, and to uphold their responsibilities to future generations in this regard.

*Article* 26

Indigenous peoples have the right to own, develop, control and use the lands and territories, including the total environment of the lands, air, waters, coastal seas, sea-ice, flora and fauna and other resources which they have traditionally owned or otherwise occupied or used. This includes the right to the full recognition of their laws, traditions and customs, land-tenure systems and institutions for the development and management of resources, and the right to effective measures by States to prevent any interference with, alienation of or encroachment upon these rights.

*Article* 27

Indigenous peoples have the right to the restitution of the lands, territories and resources which they have traditionally owned or otherwise occupied or used, and which have been confiscated, occupied, used or damaged without their free and informed consent. Where this is not possible, they have the right to just and fair compensation. Unless otherwise freely agreed upon by the peoples concerned, compensation shall take the form of lands, territories and resources equal in quality, size and legal status.

*Article* 28

Indigenous peoples have the right to the conservation, restoration and protection of the total environment and the productive capacity of their lands, territories and resources, as well as to assistance for this purpose from States and through international cooperation. Military activities shall not take place in the lands and territories of indigenous peoples, unless otherwise freely agreed upon by the peoples concerned.

States shall take effective measures to ensure that no storage or disposal of hazardous materials shall take place in the lands and territories of indigenous peoples.

States shall also take effective measures to ensure, as needed, that programmes for monitoring, maintaining and restoring the health of indigenous peoples, as developed and implemented by the peoples affected by such materials, are duly implemented.

*Article* 29

Indigenous peoples are entitled to the recognition of the full ownership, control and protection of their cultural and intellectual property.

They have the right to special measures to control, develop and protect their sciences, technologies and cultural manifestations, including human and other genetic resources, seeds, medicines, knowledge of the properties of fauna and flora, oral traditions, literatures, designs and visual and performing arts.

*Article* 30

Indigenous peoples have the right to determine and develop priorities and strategies for the development or use of their lands, territories and other resources, including the right to require that States obtain their free and informed consent prior to the approval of any project affecting their lands, territories and other resources, particularly in connection with the development, utilization or exploitation of mineral, water or other resources. Pursuant to agreement with the indigenous peoples concerned, just and fair compensation shall be provided for any such activities and measures taken to mitigate adverse environmental, economic, social, cultural or spiritual impact.

## PART VII

*Article* 31

Indigenous peoples, as a specific form of exercising their right to self-determination, have the right to autonomy or self-government in matters relating to their internal and local affairs, including culture, religion, education, information, media, health, housing, employment, social welfare, economic activities, land and resources management, environment and entry by non-members, as well as ways and means for financing these autonomous functions.

*Article* 32

Indigenous peoples have the collective right to determine their own citizenship in accordance with their customs and traditions. Indigenous citizenship does not impair the right of indigenous individuals to obtain citizenship of the States in which they live.

Indigenous peoples have the right to determine the structures and to select the membership of their institutions in accordance with their own procedures.

*Article 33*

Indigenous peoples have the right to promote, develop and maintain their institutional structures and their distinctive juridical customs, traditions, procedures and practices, in accordance with internationally recognized human rights standards.

*Article 34*

Indigenous peoples have the collective right to determine the responsibilities of individuals to their communities.

*Article 35*

Indigenous peoples, in particular those divided by international borders, have the right to maintain and develop contacts, relations and cooperation, including activities for spiritual, cultural, political, economic and social purposes, with other peoples across borders.

    States shall take effective measures to ensure the exercise and implementation of this right.

*Article 36*

Indigenous peoples have the right to the recognition, observance and enforcement of treaties, agreements and other constructive arrangements concluded with States or their successors, according to their original spirit and intent, and to have States honour and respect such treaties, agreements and other constructive arrangements.

    Conflicts and disputes which cannot otherwise be settled should be submitted to competent international bodies agreed to by all parties concerned.

## PART VIII

*Article 37*

States shall take effective and appropriate measures, in consultation with the indigenous peoples concerned, to give full effect to the provisions of this Declaration. The rights recognized herein shall be adopted and included in national legislation in such a manner that indigenous peoples can avail themselves of such rights in practice.

*Article 38*

Indigenous peoples have the right to have access to adequate financial and technical assistance, from States and through international cooperation, to pursue freely their political, economic, social, cultural and spiritual development and for the enjoyment of the rights and freedoms recognized in this Declaration.

*Article 39*

Indigenous peoples have the right to have access to and prompt decision through mutually acceptable and fair procedures for the resolution of conflicts and disputes with States, as well as to effective remedies for all infringements of their individual and collective rights. Such a decision shall take into consideration the customs, traditions, rules and legal systems of the indigenous peoples concerned.

*Article* 40

The organs and specialized agencies of the United Nations system and other intergovernmental organizations shall contribute to the full realization of the provisions of this Declaration through the mobilization, inter alia, of financial co-operation and technical assistance. Ways and means of ensuring participation of indigenous peoples on issues affecting them shall be established.

*Article* 41

The United Nations shall take the necessary steps to ensure the implementation of this Declaration including the creation of a body at the highest level with special competence in this field and with the direct participation of indigenous peoples. All United Nations bodies shall promote respect for and full application of the provisions of this Declaration.

# PART IX

*Article* 42

The rights recognized herein constitute the minimum standards for the survival, dignity and well-being of the indigenous peoples of the world.

*Article* 43

All the rights and freedoms recognized herein are equally guaranteed to male and female indigenous individuals.

*Article* 44

Nothing in this Declaration may be construed as diminishing or extinguishing existing or future rights indigenous peoples may have or acquire.

*Article* 45

Nothing in this Declaration may be interpreted as implying for any State, group or person any right to engage in any activity or to perform any act contrary to the Charter of the United Nations.

## 16. GUIDING PRINCIPLES ON INTERNAL DISPLACEMENT, 1997

These principles are published in the 'Report of the Representative of the Secretary-General, Mr. Francis M. Deng, submitted to the United Nations Commission on Human Rights, pursuant to Commission resolution 1997/39, Addendum': UN doc. E/CN.4/1998/53/Add.2. The introductory note has been omitted.

For further reference, see Bagshaw, S., 'Internally Displaced Persons at the Fifty-Fourth Session of the United Nations Commission on Human Rights, 16 March–24 April 1998', 10 *IJRL* 548 (1998); Kälin, W., 'Introduction to the 'Guiding Principles on Internal Displacement' submitted by Francis Deng, Special Representative of the Secretary-General, to the UN Commission on Human Rights', 10 *IJRL* 557 (1998); Kälin, W., *Guiding Principles on Internal Displacement: Annotations*, American Society of International Law, Brookings Institution, 2000; Cohen, R., and Deng, F. M., *Masses in Flight. The Global Crisis of Internal Displacement*. Washington, DC: Brookings Institution Press (1998).

The Guiding Principles were 'noted' by the Commission on Human Rights and have been referred to in various General Assembly resolutions. Although many of the principles are based in treaties and customary international law, the precise status of the 'collection' and the process of 'adoption' continues to excite some controversy among Governments; for comment, see Goodwin-Gill, G. S., 'Note on paragraph 20 of General Assembly resolution 55/74', 13 *IJRL* 255–8 (2001).

*TEXT*

### INTRODUCTION: SCOPE AND PURPOSE

1. These Guiding Principles address the specific needs of internally displaced persons worldwide. They identify rights and guarantees relevant to the protection of persons from forced displacement and to their protection and assistance during displacement as well as during return or resettlement and reintegration.

2. For the purposes of these Principles, internally displaced persons are persons or groups of persons who have been forced or obliged to flee or to leave their homes or places of habitual residence, in particular as a result of or in order to avoid the effects of armed conflict, situations of generalized violence, violations of human rights or natural or human-made disasters, and who have not crossed an internationally recognized State border.

3. These Principles reflect and are consistent with international human rights law and international humanitarian law. They provide guidance to:

   (a) The Representative of the Secretary-General on internally displaced persons in carrying out his mandate;

   (b) States when faced with the phenomenon of internal displacement;

   (c) All other authorities, groups and persons in their relations with internally displaced persons; and

   (d) Intergovernmental and non-governmental organizations when addressing internal displacement.

4. These Guiding Principles should be disseminated and applied as widely as possible.

# SECTION I
## General Principles

*Principle* 1

1. Internally displaced persons shall enjoy, in full equality, the same rights and freedoms under international and domestic law as do other persons in their country. They shall not be discriminated against in the enjoyment of any rights and freedoms on the ground that they are internally displaced.

2. These Principles are without prejudice to individual criminal responsibility under international law, in particular relating to genocide, crimes against humanity and war crimes.

*Principle* 2

1. These Principles shall be observed by all authorities, groups and persons irrespective of their legal status and applied without any adverse distinction. The observance of these Principles shall not affect the legal status of any authorities, groups or persons involved.

2. These Principles shall not be interpreted as restricting, modifying or impairing the provisions of any international human rights or international humanitarian law instrument or rights granted to persons under domestic law. In particular, these Principles are without prejudice to the right to seek and enjoy asylum in other countries.

*Principle* 3

1. National authorities have the primary duty and responsibility to provide protection and humanitarian assistance to internally displaced persons within their jurisdiction.

2. Internally displaced persons have the right to request and to receive protection and humanitarian assistance from these authorities. They shall not be persecuted or punished for making such a request.

*Principle* 4

1. These Principles shall be applied without discrimination of any kind, such as race, colour, sex, language, religion or belief, political or other opinion, national, ethnic or social origin, legal or social status, age, disability, property, birth, or on any other similar criteria.

2. Certain internally displaced persons, such as children, especially unaccompanied minors, expectant mothers, mothers with young children, female heads of household, persons with disabilities and elderly persons, shall be entitled to protection and assistance required by their condition and to treatment which takes into account their special needs.

## SECTION II
### Principles Relating to Protection From Displacement

*Principle* 5

All authorities and international actors shall respect and ensure respect for their obligations under international law, including human rights and humanitarian law, in all circumstances, so as to prevent and avoid conditions that might lead to displacement of persons.

*Principle* 6

1. Every human being shall have the right to be protected against being arbitrarily displaced from his or her home or place of habitual residence.

2. The prohibition of arbitrary displacement includes displacement:

   *(a)* When it is based on policies of apartheid, 'ethnic cleansing' or similar practices aimed at/or resulting in altering the ethnic, religious or racial composition of the affected population;

   *(b)* In situations of armed conflict, unless the security of the civilians involved or imperative military reasons so demand;

   *(c)* In cases of large-scale development projects, which are not justified by compelling and overriding public interests;

   *(d)* In cases of disasters, unless the safety and health of those affected requires their evacuation; and

   *(e)* When it is used as a collective punishment.

3. Displacement shall last no longer than required by the circumstances.

*Principle* 7

1. Prior to any decision requiring the displacement of persons, the authorities concerned shall ensure that all feasible alternatives are explored in order to avoid displacement altogether. Where no alternatives exist, all measures shall be taken to minimize displacement and its adverse effects.

2. The authorities undertaking such displacement shall ensure, to the greatest practicable extent, that proper accommodation is provided to the displaced persons, that such displacements are effected in satisfactory conditions of safety, nutrition, health and hygiene, and that members of the same family are not separated.

3. If displacement occurs in situations other than during the emergency stages of armed conflicts and disasters, the following guarantees shall be complied with:

   *(a)* A specific decision shall be taken by a State authority empowered by law to order such measures;

   *(b)* Adequate measures shall be taken to guarantee to those to be displaced full information on the reasons and procedures for their displacement and, where applicable, on compensation and relocation;

   *(c)* The free and informed consent of those to be displaced shall be sought;

   *(d)* The authorities concerned shall endeavour to involve those affected, particularly women, in the planning and management of their relocation;

*(e)* Law enforcement measures, where required, shall be carried out by competent legal authorities; and

*(f)* The right to an effective remedy, including the review of such decisions by appropriate judicial authorities, shall be respected.

*Principle* 8

Displacement shall not be carried out in a manner that violates the rights to life, dignity, liberty and security of those affected.

*Principle* 9

States are under a particular obligation to protect against the displacement of indigenous peoples, minorities, peasants, pastoralists and other groups with a special dependency on and attachment to their lands.

## SECTION III
### Principles Relating to Protection During Displacement

*Principle* 10

1. Every human being has the inherent right to life which shall be protected by law. No one shall be arbitrarily deprived of his or her life. Internally displaced persons shall be protected in particular against:

*(a)* Genocide;

*(b)* Murder;

*(c)* Summary or arbitrary executions; and

*(d)* Enforced disappearances, including abduction or unacknowledged detention, threatening or resulting in death.

Threats and incitement to commit any of the foregoing acts shall be prohibited.

2. Attacks or other acts of violence against internally displaced persons who do not or no longer participate in hostilities are prohibited in all circumstances. Internally displaced persons shall be protected, in particular, against:

*(a)* Direct or indiscriminate attacks or other acts of violence, including the creation of areas wherein attacks on civilians are permitted;

*(b)* Starvation as a method of combat;

*(c)* Their use to shield military objectives from attack or to shield, favour or impede military operations;

*(d)* Attacks against their camps or settlements; and

*(e)* The use of anti-personnel landmines.

*Principle* 11

1. Every human being has the right to dignity and physical, mental and moral integrity.

2. Internally displaced persons, whether or not their liberty has been restricted, shall be protected in particular against:

(a) Rape, mutilation, torture, cruel, inhuman or degrading treatment or punishment, and other outrages upon personal dignity, such as acts of gender-specific violence, forced prostitution and any form of indecent assault;

(b) Slavery or any contemporary form of slavery, such as sale into marriage, sexual exploitation, or forced labour of children; and

(c) Acts of violence intended to spread terror among internally displaced persons.

Threats and incitement to commit any of the foregoing acts shall be prohibited.

*Principle* 12

1. Every human being has the right to liberty and security of person. No one shall be subjected to arbitrary arrest or detention.

2. To give effect to this right for internally displaced persons, they shall not be interned in or confined to a camp. If in exceptional circumstances such internment or confinement is absolutely necessary, it shall not last longer than required by the circumstances.

3. Internally displaced persons shall be protected from discriminatory arrest and detention as a result of their displacement.

4. In no case shall internally displaced persons be taken hostage.

*Principle* 13

1. In no circumstances shall displaced children be recruited nor be required or permitted to take part in hostilities.

2. Internally displaced persons shall be protected against discriminatory practices of recruitment into any armed forces or groups as a result of their displacement. In particular any cruel, inhuman or degrading practices that compel compliance or punish non-compliance with recruitment are prohibited in all circumstances.

*Principle* 14

1. Every internally displaced person has the right to liberty of movement and freedom to choose his or her residence.

2. In particular, internally displaced persons have the right to move freely in and out of camps or other settlements.

*Principle* 15

Internally displaced persons have:

(a) The right to seek safety in another part of the country;

(b) The right to leave their country;

(c) The right to seek asylum in another country; and

(d) The right to be protected against forcible return to or resettlement in any place where their life, safety, liberty and/or health would be at risk.

*Principle* 16

1. All internally displaced persons have the right to know the fate and whereabouts of missing relatives.

2. The authorities concerned shall endeavour to establish the fate and where-abouts of internally displaced persons reported missing, and cooperate with relevant international organizations engaged in this task. They shall inform the next of kin on the progress of the investigation and notify them of any result.

3. The authorities concerned shall endeavour to collect and identify the mortal remains of those deceased, prevent their despoliation or mutilation, and facilitate the return of those remains to the next of kin or dispose of them respectfully.

4. Grave sites of internally displaced persons should be protected and respected in all circumstances. Internally displaced persons should have the right of access to the grave sites of their deceased relatives.

*Principle* 17

1. Every human being has the right to respect of his or her family life.

2. To give effect to this right for internally displaced persons, family members who wish to remain together shall be allowed to do so.

3. Families which are separated by displacement should be reunited as quickly as possible. All appropriate steps shall be taken to expedite the reunion of such families, particularly when children are involved. The responsible authorities shall facilitate inquiries made by family members and encourage and cooperate with the work of humanitarian organizations engaged in the task of family reunification.

4. Members of internally displaced families whose personal liberty has been restricted by internment or confinement in camps shall have the right to remain together.

*Principle* 18

1. All internally displaced persons have the right to an adequate standard of living.

2. At the minimum, regardless of the circumstances, and without discrimination, competent authorities shall provide internally displaced persons with and ensure safe access to:

   *(a)* Essential food and potable water;
   *(b)* Basic shelter and housing;
   *(c)* Appropriate clothing; and
   *(d)* Essential medical services and sanitation.

3. Special efforts should be made to ensure the full participation of women in the planning and distribution of these basic supplies.

*Principle* 19

1. All wounded and sick internally displaced persons as well as those with disabilities shall receive to the fullest extent practicable and with the least possible delay, the medical care and attention they require, without distinction on any grounds other than medical ones. When necessary, internally displaced persons shall have access to psychological and social services.

2. Special attention should be paid to the health needs of women, including access to female health care providers and services, such as reproductive health care, as well as appropriate counselling for victims of sexual and other abuses.

3. Special attention should also be given to the prevention of contagious and infectious diseases, including AIDS, among internally displaced persons.

*Principle* 20

1. Every human being has the right to recognition everywhere as a person before the law.

2. To give effect to this right for internally displaced persons, the authorities concerned shall issue to them all documents necessary for the enjoyment and exercise of their legal rights, such as passports, personal identification documents, birth certificates and marriage certificates. In particular, the authorities shall facilitate the issuance of new documents or the replacement of documents lost in the course of displacement, without imposing unreasonable conditions, such as requiring the return to one's area of habitual residence in order to obtain these or other required documents.

3. Women and men shall have equal rights to obtain such necessary documents and shall have the right to have such documentation issued in their own names.

*Principle* 21

1. No one shall be arbitrarily deprived of property and possessions.

2. The property and possessions of internally displaced persons shall in all circumstances be protected, in particular, against the following acts:

  (a) Pillage;
  (b) Direct or indiscriminate attacks or other acts of violence;
  (c) Being used to shield military operations or objectives;
  (d) Being made the object of reprisal; and
  (e) Being destroyed or appropriated as a form of collective punishment.

3. Property and possessions left behind by internally displaced persons should be protected against destruction and arbitrary and illegal appropriation, occupation or use.

*Principle* 22

1. Internally displaced persons, whether or not they are living in camps, shall not be discriminated against as a result of their displacement in the enjoyment of the following rights:

  (a) The rights to freedom of thought, conscience, religion or belief, opinion and expression;
  (b) The right to seek freely opportunities for employment and to participate in economic activities;
  (c) The right to associate freely and participate equally in community affairs;
  (d) The right to vote and to participate in governmental and public affairs, including the right to have access to the means necessary to exercise this right; and
  (e) The right to communicate in a language they understand.

*Principle* 23

1. Every human being has the right to education.

2. To give effect to this right for internally displaced persons, the authorities concerned shall ensure that such persons, in particular displaced children, receive education which shall be free and compulsory at the primary level. Education should respect their cultural identity, language and religion.

3. Special efforts should be made to ensure the full and equal participation of women and girls in educational programmes.

4. Education and training facilities shall be made available to internally displaced persons, in particular adolescents and women, whether or not living in camps, as soon as conditions permit.


# SECTION IV
## Principles Relating to Humanitarian Assistance

*Principle* 24

1. All humanitarian assistance shall be carried out in accordance with the principles of humanity and impartiality and without discrimination.

2. Humanitarian assistance to internally displaced persons shall not be diverted, in particular for political or military reasons.

*Principle* 25

1. The primary duty and responsibility for providing humanitarian assistance to internally displaced persons lies with national authorities.

2. International humanitarian organizations and other appropriate actors have the right to offer their services in support of the internally displaced. Such an offer shall not be regarded as an unfriendly act or an interference in a State's internal affairs and shall be considered in good faith. Consent thereto shall not be arbitrarily withheld, particularly when authorities concerned are unable or unwilling to provide the required humanitarian assistance.

3. All authorities concerned shall grant and facilitate the free passage of humanitarian assistance and grant persons engaged in the provision of such assistance rapid and unimpeded access to the internally displaced.

*Principle* 26

Persons engaged in humanitarian assistance, their transport and supplies shall be respected and protected. They shall not be the object of attack or other acts of violence.

*Principle* 27

1. International humanitarian organizations and other appropriate actors when providing assistance should give due regard to the protection needs and human rights of internally displaced persons and take appropriate measures in this regard. In so doing, these organizations and actors should respect relevant international standards and codes of conduct.

2. The preceding paragraph is without prejudice to the protection responsibilities of international organizations mandated for this purpose, whose services may be offered or requested by States.

# SECTION V
## Principles Relating to Return, Resettlement and Reintegration

*Principle* 28

1. Competent authorities have the primary duty and responsibility to establish conditions, as well as provide the means, which allow internally displaced persons to return voluntarily, in safety and with dignity, to their homes or places of habitual residence, or to resettle voluntarily in another part of the country. Such authorities shall endeavour to facilitate the reintegration of returned or resettled internally displaced persons.

2. Special efforts should be made to ensure the full participation of internally displaced persons in the planning and management of their return or resettlement and reintegration.

*Principle* 29

1. Internally displaced persons who have returned to their homes or places of habitual residence or who have resettled in another part of the country shall not be discriminated against as a result of their having been displaced. They shall have the right to participate fully and equally in public affairs at all levels and have equal access to public services.

2. Competent authorities have the duty and responsibility to assist returned and/or resettled internally displaced persons to recover, to the extent possible, their property and possessions which they left behind or were dispossessed of upon their displacement. When recovery of such property and possessions is not possible, competent authorities shall provide or assist these persons in obtaining appropriate compensation or another form of just reparation.

*Principle* 30

All authorities concerned shall grant and facilitate for international humanitarian organizations and other appropriate actors, in the exercise of their respective mandates, rapid and unimpeded access to internally displaced persons to assist in their return or resettlement and reintegration.

## 17. DECLARATION ON THE RIGHT AND RESPONSIBILITY OF INDIVIDUALS, GROUPS AND ORGANS OF SOCIETY TO PROMOTE AND PROTECT UNIVERSALLY RECOGNIZED HUMAN RIGHTS AND FUNDAMENTAL FREEDOMS, 1998

This Declaration was adopted by the General Assembly in Resolution 53/144 on 9 December 1998, without a vote. While reaffirming many of the rights already established by treaty, the Declaration also emphasizes responsibilities in promoting and protecting the environment in which human rights are to be enjoyed. It recognizes the primary responsibility of States in this regard, but also underlines the role and duties of individuals and non-governmental organizations.

*TEXT*

*The General Assembly,*

*Reaffirming* the importance of the observance of the purposes and principles of the Charter of the United Nations for the promotion and protection of all human rights and fundamental freedoms for all persons in all countries of the world,

*Taking note* of Commission on Human Rights resolution 1998/7 of 3 April 1998, in which the Commission approved the text of the draft declaration on the right and responsibility of individuals, groups and organs of society to promote and protect universally recognized human rights and fundamental freedoms,

*Taking note also* of Economic and Social Council resolution 1998/33 of 30 July 1998, in which the Council recommended the draft declaration to the General Assembly for adoption,

*Conscious* of the importance of the adoption of the draft declaration in the context of the fiftieth anniversary of the Universal Declaration of Human Rights,

1. *Adopts* the Declaration on the Right and Responsibility of Individuals, Groups and Organs of Society to Promote and Protect Universally Recognized Human Rights and Fundamental Freedoms, annexed to the present resolution;

2. *Invites* Governments, agencies and organizations of the United Nations system and intergovernmental and non-governmental organizations to intensify their efforts to disseminate the Declaration and to promote universal respect and understanding thereof, and requests the Secretary-General to include the text of the Declaration in the next edition of *Human Rights: A Compilation of International Instruments.*

ANNEX

DECLARATION ON THE RIGHT AND RESPONSIBILITY OF INDIVIDUALS, GROUPS
AND ORGANS OF SOCIETY TO PROMOTE AND PROTECT UNIVERSALLY
RECOGNIZED HUMAN RIGHTS AND FUNDAMENTAL FREEDOMS

*The General Assembly,*

*Reaffirming* the importance of the observance of the purposes and principles of
the Charter of the United Nations for the promotion and protection of all human
rights and fundamental freedoms for all persons in all countries of the world,

*Reaffirming also* the importance of the Universal Declaration of Human Rights
and the International Covenants on Human Rights as basic elements of international efforts to promote universal respect for and observance of human rights
and fundamental freedoms and the importance of other human rights instruments adopted within the United Nations system, as well as those at the regional
level,

*Stressing* that all members of the international community shall fulfil, jointly and
separately, their solemn obligation to promote and encourage respect for human
rights and fundamental freedoms for all without distinction of any kind, including
distinctions based on race, colour, sex, language, religion, political or other opinion, national or social origin, property, birth or other status, and reaffirming the
particular importance of achieving international cooperation to fulfil this
obligation according to the Charter,

*Acknowledging* the important role of international cooperation for, and the valuable work of individuals, groups and associations in contributing to, the effective
elimination of all violations of human rights and fundamental freedoms of peoples
and individuals, including in relation to mass, flagrant or systematic violations such
as those resulting from apartheid, all forms of racial discrimination, colonialism,
foreign domination or occupation, aggression or threats to national sovereignty,
national unity or territorial integrity and from the refusal to recognize the right of
peoples to self-determination and the right of every people to exercise full sovereignty over its wealth and natural resources,

*Recognizing* the relationship between international peace and security and the
enjoyment of human rights and fundamental freedoms, and mindful that the
absence of international peace and security does not excuse non-compliance,

*Reiterating* that all human rights and fundamental freedoms are universal, indivisible, interdependent and interrelated and should be promoted and implemented in
a fair and equitable manner, without prejudice to the implementation of each of
those rights and freedoms,

*Stressing* that the prime responsibility and duty to promote and protect human
rights and fundamental freedoms lie with the State,

*Recognizing* the right and the responsibility of individuals, groups and
associations to promote respect for and foster knowledge of human rights and
fundamental freedoms at the national and international levels,

*Declares*:

*Article* 1

Everyone has the right, individually and in association with others, to promote and to strive for the protection and realization of human rights and fundamental freedoms at the national and international levels.

## Article 2

1. Each State has a prime responsibility and duty to protect, promote and implement all human rights and fundamental freedoms, *inter alia*, by adopting such steps as may be necessary to create all conditions necessary in the social, economic, political and other fields, as well as the legal guarantees required to ensure that all persons under its jurisdiction, individually and in association with others, are able to enjoy all those rights and freedoms in practice.

2. Each State shall adopt such legislative, administrative and other steps as may be necessary to ensure that the rights and freedoms referred to in the present Declaration are effectively guaranteed.

## Article 3

Domestic law consistent with the Charter of the United Nations and other international obligations of the State in the field of human rights and fundamental freedoms is the juridical framework within which human rights and fundamental freedoms should be implemented and enjoyed and within which all activities referred to in the present Declaration for the promotion, protection and effective realization of those rights and freedoms should be conducted.

## Article 4

Nothing in the present Declaration shall be construed as impairing or contradicting the purposes and principles of the Charter of the United Nations or as restricting or derogating from the provisions of the Universal Declaration of Human Rights, the International Covenants on Human Rights and other international instruments and commitments applicable in this field.

## Article 5

For the purpose of promoting and protecting human rights and fundamental freedoms, everyone has the right, individually and in association with others, at the national and international levels:

(a) To meet or assemble peacefully;

(b) To form, join and participate in non-governmental organizations, associations or groups;

(c) To communicate with non-governmental or intergovernmental organizations.

## Article 6

Everyone has the right, individually and in association with others:

(a) To know, seek, obtain, receive and hold information about all human rights and fundamental freedoms, including having access to information as to how those rights and freedoms are given effect in domestic legislative, judicial or administrative systems;

(b) As provided for in human rights and other applicable international instruments, freely to publish, impart or disseminate to others views, information and knowledge on all human rights and fundamental freedoms;

(c) To study, discuss, form and hold opinions on the observance, both in law and in practice, of all human rights and fundamental freedoms and, through these and other appropriate means, to draw public attention to those matters.

*Article* 7

Everyone has the right, individually and in association with others, to develop and discuss new human rights ideas and principles and to advocate their acceptance.

*Article* 8

1. Everyone has the right, individually and in association with others, to have effective access, on a non-discriminatory basis, to participation in the government of his or her country and in the conduct of public affairs.

2. This includes, *inter alia*, the right, individually and in association with others, to submit to governmental bodies and agencies and organizations concerned with public affairs criticism and proposals for improving their functioning and to draw attention to any aspect of their work that may hinder or impede the promotion, protection and realization of human rights and fundamental freedoms.

*Article* 9

1. In the exercise of human rights and fundamental freedoms, including the promotion and protection of human rights as referred to in the present Declaration, everyone has the right, individually and in association with others, to benefit from an effective remedy and to be protected in the event of the violation of those rights.

2. To this end, everyone whose rights or freedoms are allegedly violated has the right, either in person or through legally authorized representation, to complain to and have that complaint promptly reviewed in a public hearing before an independent, impartial and competent judicial or other authority established by law and to obtain from such an authority a decision, in accordance with law, providing redress, including any compensation due, where there has been a violation of that person's rights or freedoms, as well as enforcement of the eventual decision and award, all without undue delay.

3. To the same end, everyone has the right, individually and in association with others, *inter alia*:

(a) To complain about the policies and actions of individual officials and governmental bodies with regard to violations of human rights and fundamental freedoms, by petition or other appropriate means, to competent domestic judicial, administrative or legislative authorities or any other competent authority provided for by the legal system of the State, which should render their decision on the complaint without undue delay;

(b) To attend public hearings, proceedings and trials so as to form an opinion on their compliance with national law and applicable international obligations and commitments;

(c) To offer and provide professionally qualified legal assistance or other relevant advice and assistance in defending human rights and fundamental freedoms.

4. To the same end, and in accordance with applicable international instruments and procedures, everyone has the right, individually and in association with others, to unhindered access to and communication with international bodies with general or special competence to receive and consider communications on matters of human rights and fundamental freedoms.

5. The State shall conduct a prompt and impartial investigation or ensure that an inquiry takes place whenever there is reasonable ground to believe that a violation of human rights and fundamental freedoms has occurred in any territory under its jurisdiction.

*Article* 10

No one shall participate, by act or by failure to act where required, in violating human rights and fundamental freedoms and no one shall be subjected to punishment or adverse action of any kind for refusing to do so.

*Article* 11

Everyone has the right, individually and in association with others, to the lawful exercise of his or her occupation or profession. Everyone who, as a result of his or her profession, can affect the human dignity, human rights and fundamental freedoms of others should respect those rights and freedoms and comply with relevant national and international standards of occupational and professional conduct or ethics.

*Article* 12

1. Everyone has the right, individually and in association with others, to participate in peaceful activities against violations of human rights and fundamental freedoms.

2. The State shall take all necessary measures to ensure the protection by the competent authorities of everyone, individually and in association with others, against any violence, threats, retaliation, *de facto* or *de jure* adverse discrimination, pressure or any other arbitrary action as a consequence of his or her legitimate exercise of the rights referred to in the present Declaration.

3. In this connection, everyone is entitled, individually and in association with others, to be protected effectively under national law in reacting against or opposing, through peaceful means, activities and acts, including those by omission, attributable to States that result in violations of human rights and fundamental freedoms, as well as acts of violence perpetrated by groups or individuals that affect the enjoyment of human rights and fundamental freedoms.

*Article* 13

Everyone has the right, individually and in association with others, to solicit, receive and utilize resources for the express purpose of promoting and protecting human rights and fundamental freedoms through peaceful means, in accordance with article 3 of the present Declaration.

*Article* 14

1. The State has the responsibility to take legislative, judicial, administrative or other appropriate measures to promote the understanding by all persons under its jurisdiction of their civil, political, economic, social and cultural rights.

2. Such measures shall include, *inter alia*:

   (a)  The publication and widespread availability of national laws and regulations and of applicable basic international human rights instruments;

   (b)  Full and equal access to international documents in the field of human rights, including the periodic reports by the State to the bodies established by the international human rights treaties to which it is a party, as well as the summary records of discussions and the official reports of these bodies.

3. The State shall ensure and support, where appropriate, the creation and development of further independent national institutions for the promotion and protection of human rights and fundamental freedoms in all territory under its jurisdiction, whether they be ombudsmen, human rights commissions or any other form of national institution.

*Article* 15

The State has the responsibility to promote and facilitate the teaching of human rights and fundamental freedoms at all levels of education and to ensure that all those responsible for training lawyers, law enforcement officers, the personnel of the armed forces and public officials include appropriate elements of human rights teaching in their training programme.

*Article* 16

Individuals, non-governmental organizations and relevant institutions have an important role to play in contributing to making the public more aware of questions relating to all human rights and fundamental freedoms through activities such as education, training and research in these areas to strengthen further, *inter alia*, understanding, tolerance, peace and friendly relations among nations and among all racial and religious groups, bearing in mind the various backgrounds of the societies and communities in which they carry out their activities.

*Article* 17

In the exercise of the rights and freedoms referred to in the present Declaration, everyone, acting individually and in association with others, shall be subject only to such limitations as are in accordance with applicable international obligations and are determined by law solely for the purpose of securing due recognition and respect for the rights and freedoms of others and of meeting the just requirements of morality, public order and the general welfare in a democratic society.

*Article* 18

1. Everyone has duties towards and within the community, in which alone the free and full development of his or her personality is possible.

2. Individuals, groups, institutions and non-governmental organizations have an important role to play and a responsibility in safeguarding democracy, promoting

human rights and fundamental freedoms and contributing to the promotion and advancement of democratic societies, institutions and processes.

3. Individuals, groups, institutions and non-governmental organizations also have an important role and a responsibility in contributing, as appropriate, to the promotion of the right of everyone to a social and international order in which the rights and freedoms set forth in the Universal Declaration of Human Rights and other human rights instruments can be fully realized.

*Article* 19

Nothing in the present Declaration shall be interpreted as implying for any individual, group or organ of society or any State the right to engage in any activity or to perform any act aimed at the destruction of the rights and freedoms referred to in the present Declaration.

*Article* 20

Nothing in the present Declaration shall be interpreted as permitting States to support and promote activities of individuals, groups of individuals, institutions or non-governmental organizations contrary to the provisions of the Charter of the United Nations.

## 18. NATIONALITY OF NATURAL PERSONS IN RELATION TO THE SUCCESSION OF STATES, 2000

The Declaration of articles is annexed to General Assembly Resolution 55/153, 12 December 2000, adopted without a vote on the report of the Sixth Committee: UN doc. A/55/610. It makes a significant contribution to resolving problems of statelessness, which continue to emerge, particularly with the fragmentation of previously existing federations, such as the USSR and the former Yugoslavia. The Declaration is the culmination of the mandate given to the International Law Commission in 1993; see UNGA Resolution 48/31, 9 December 1993. Besides the annual reports of the ILC from 1993–1999, see the reports of the Special Rapporteur: UN docs. A/CN.4/467, A/CN.4/474. A/CN.4/480 and A/CN.4/489.

### TEXT

*The General Assembly,*

*Having considered* chapter IV of the report of the International Law Commission on the work of its fifty-first session, which contains final draft articles on nationality of natural persons in relation to the succession of States,

*Noting* that the International Law Commission decided to recommend the draft articles to the General Assembly for their adoption in the form of a declaration,

*Recalling* its resolution 54/112 of 9 December 1999, in which it decided to consider at its fifty-fifth session the draft articles on nationality of natural persons in relation to the succession of States with a view to their adoption as a declaration,

*Considering* that the work of the International Law Commission on nationality of natural persons in relation to the succession of States would provide a useful guide for practice in dealing with this issue,

*Acknowledging* that the work of the International Law Commission on this topic could contribute to the elaboration of a convention or other appropriate instrument in the future, and reiterating its invitation, contained in its resolution 54/112, for Governments to submit comments and observations on the question of a convention on nationality of natural persons in relation to the succession of States,

1. *Expresses* its appreciation to the International Law Commission for its valuable work on nationality of natural persons in relation to the succession of States;

2. *Takes note* of the articles on nationality of natural persons in relation to the succession of States, presented by the International Law Commission in the form of a declaration, the text of which is annexed to the present resolution;

3. *Invites* Governments to take into account, as appropriate, the provisions contained in the articles in dealing with issues of nationality of natural persons in relation to the succession of States;

4. *Recommends* that all efforts be made for the wide dissemination of the text of the articles;

5. *Decides* to include in the provisional agenda of its fifty-ninth session an item entitled 'Nationality of natural persons in relation to the succession of States'.

## ANNEX
Nationality of natural persons in relation to the succession of States

### Preamble

*Considering* that problems of nationality arising from succession of States concern the international community,

*Emphasizing* that nationality is essentially governed by internal law within the limits set by international law,

*Recognizing* that in matters concerning nationality, due account should be taken both of the legitimate interests of States and those of individuals,

*Recalling* that the Universal Declaration of Human Rights of 1948 proclaimed the right of every person to a nationality,

*Recalling also* that the International Covenant on Civil and Political Rights of 1966 and the Convention on the Rights of the Child of 1989 recognize the right of every child to acquire a nationality,

*Emphasizing* that the human rights and fundamental freedoms of persons whose nationality may be affected by a succession of States must be fully respected,

*Bearing in mind* the provisions of the Convention on the Reduction of Statelessness of 1961, the Vienna Convention on Succession of States in Respect of Treaties of 1978 and the Vienna Convention on Succession of States in Respect of State Property, Archives and Debts of 1983,

*Convinced* of the need for the codification and progressive development of the rules of international law concerning nationality in relation to the succession of States as a means for ensuring greater juridical security for States and for individuals,

## PART I
### General provisions

*Article 1—Right to a nationality*

Every individual who, on the date of the succession of States, had the nationality of the predecessor State, irrespective of the mode of acquisition of that nationality, has the right to the nationality of at least one of the States concerned, in accordance with the present articles.

*Article 2—Use of terms*

For the purposes of the present articles:

  (a) 'Succession of States' means the replacement of one State by another in the responsibility for the international relations of territory;

  (b) 'Predecessor State' means the State which has been replaced by another State on the occurrence of a succession of States;

  (c) 'Successor State' means the State which has replaced another State on the occurrence of a succession of States;

(d) 'State concerned' means the predecessor State or the successor State, as the case may be;

(e) 'Third State' means any State other than the predecessor State or the successor State;

(f) 'Person concerned' means every individual who, on the date of the succession of States, had the nationality of the predecessor State and whose nationality may be affected by such succession;

(g) 'Date of the succession of States' means the date upon which the successor State replaced the predecessor State in the responsibility for the international relations of the territory to which the succession of States relates.

### Article 3—Cases of succession of States covered by the present articles

The present articles apply only to the effects of a succession of States occurring in conformity with international law and, in particular, with the principles of international law embodied in the Charter of the United Nations.

### Article 4—Prevention of statelessness

States concerned shall take all appropriate measures to prevent persons who, on the date of the succession of States, had the nationality of the predecessor State from becoming stateless as a result of such succession.

### Article 5—Presumption of nationality

Subject to the provisions of the present articles, persons concerned having their habitual residence in the territory affected by the succession of States are presumed to acquire the nationality of the successor State on the date of such succession.

### Article 6—Legislation on nationality and other connected issues

Each State concerned should, without undue delay, enact legislation on nationality and other connected issues arising in relation to the succession of States consistent with the provisions of the present articles. It should take all appropriate measures to ensure that persons concerned will be apprised, within a reasonable time period, of the effect of its legislation on their nationality, of any choices they may have thereunder, as well as of the consequences that the exercise of such choices will have on their status.

### Article 7—Effective date

The attribution of nationality in relation to the succession of States, as well as the acquisition of nationality following the exercise of an option, shall take effect on the date of such succession, if persons concerned would otherwise be stateless during the period between the date of the succession of States and such attribution or acquisition of nationality.

### Article 8—Persons concerned having their habitual residence in another State

1. A successor State does not have the obligation to attribute its nationality to persons concerned who have their habitual residence in another State and also have the nationality of that or any other State.

2. A successor State shall not attribute its nationality to persons concerned who

have their habitual residence in another State against the will of the persons concerned unless they would otherwise become stateless.

*Article 9—Renunciation of the nationality of another State as a condition for attribution of nationality*

When a person concerned who is qualified to acquire the nationality of a successor State has the nationality of another State concerned, the former State may make the attribution of its nationality dependent on the renunciation by such person of the nationality of the latter State. However, such requirement shall not be applied in a manner which would result in rendering the person concerned stateless, even if only temporarily.

*Article 10—Loss of nationality upon the voluntary acquisition of the nationality of another State*

1. A predecessor State may provide that persons concerned who, in relation to the succession of States, voluntarily acquire the nationality of a successor State shall lose its nationality.

2. A successor State may provide that persons concerned who, in relation to the succession of States, voluntarily acquire the nationality of another successor State or, as the case may be, retain the nationality of the predecessor State shall lose its nationality acquired in relation to such succession.

*Article 11—Respect for the will of persons concerned*

1. States concerned shall give consideration to the will of persons concerned whenever those persons are qualified to acquire the nationality of two or more States concerned.

2. Each State concerned shall grant a right to opt for its nationality to persons concerned who have appropriate connection with that State if those persons would otherwise become stateless as a result of the succession of States.

3. When persons entitled to the right of option have exercised such right, the State whose nationality they have opted for shall attribute its nationality to such persons.

4. When persons entitled to the right of option have exercised such right, the State whose nationality they have renounced shall withdraw its nationality from such persons, unless they would thereby become stateless.

5. States concerned should provide a reasonable time limit for the exercise of the right of option.

*Article 12—Unity of a family*

Where the acquisition or loss of nationality in relation to the succession of States would impair the unity of a family, States concerned shall take all appropriate measures to allow that family to remain together or to be reunited.

*Article 13—Child born after the succession of States*

A child of a person concerned, born after the date of the succession of States, who has not acquired any nationality, has the right to the nationality of the State concerned on whose territory that child was born.

*Article* 14—*Status of habitual residents*

1. The status of persons concerned as habitual residents shall not be affected by the succession of States.

2. A State concerned shall take all necessary measures to allow persons concerned who, because of events connected with the succession of States, were forced to leave their habitual residence on its territory to return thereto.

*Article* 15—*Non-discrimination*

States concerned shall not deny persons concerned the right to retain or acquire a nationality or the right of option upon the succession of States by discriminating on any ground.

*Article* 16—*Prohibition of arbitrary decisions concerning nationality issues*

Persons concerned shall not be arbitrarily deprived of the nationality of the predecessor State, or arbitrarily denied the right to acquire the nationality of the successor State or any right of option, to which they are entitled in relation to the succession of States.

*Article* 17—*Procedures relating to nationality issues*

Applications relating to the acquisition, retention or renunciation of nationality or to the exercise of the right of option, in relation to the succession of States, shall be processed without undue delay. Relevant decisions shall be issued in writing and shall be open to effective administrative or judicial review.

*Article* 18—*Exchange of information, consultation and negotiation*

1. States concerned shall exchange information and consult in order to identify any detrimental effects on persons concerned with respect to their nationality and other connected issues regarding their status as a result of the succession of States.

2. States concerned shall, when necessary, seek a solution to eliminate or mitigate such detrimental effects by negotiation and, as appropriate, through agreement.

*Article* 19—*Other States*

1. Nothing in the present articles requires States to treat persons concerned having no effective link with a State concerned as nationals of that State, unless this would result in treating those persons as if they were stateless.

2. Nothing in the present articles precludes States from treating persons concerned, who have become stateless as a result of the succession of States, as nationals of the State concerned whose nationality they would be entitled to acquire or retain, if such treatment is beneficial to those persons.

## PART II
Provisions relating to specific categories of succession of States

### Section 1

### Transfer of part of the territory

*Article 20—Attribution of the nationality of the successor State and withdrawal of the nationality of the predecessor State*

When part of the territory of a State is transferred by that State to another State, the successor State shall attribute its nationality to the persons concerned who have their habitual residence in the transferred territory and the predecessor State shall withdraw its nationality from such persons, unless otherwise indicated by the exercise of the right of option which such persons shall be granted. The predecessor State shall not, however, withdraw its nationality before such persons acquire the nationality of the successor State.

### Section 2

### Unification of States

*Article 21—Attribution of the nationality of the successor State*

Subject to the provisions of Article 8, when two or more States unite and so form one successor State, irrespective of whether the successor State is a new State or whether its personality is identical to that of one of the States which have united, the successor State shall attribute its nationality to all persons who, on the date of the succession of States, had the nationality of a predecessor State.

### Section 3

### Dissolution of a State

*Article 22—Attribution of the nationality of the successor States*

When a State dissolves and ceases to exist and the various parts of the territory of the predecessor State form two or more successor States, each successor State shall, unless otherwise indicated by the exercise of a right of option, attribute its nationality to:

(a) Persons concerned having their habitual residence in its territory; and

(b) Subject to the provisions of Article 8:

    (i) Persons concerned not covered by subparagraph (a) having an appropriate legal connection with a constituent unit of the predecessor State that has become part of that successor State;

    (ii) Persons concerned not entitled to a nationality of any State concerned under subparagraphs (a) and (b) (i) having their habitual residence in a third State, who were born in or, before leaving the predecessor State, had their last habitual residence in what has become the territory of that successor State or having any other appropriate connection with that successor State.

*Article 23—Granting of the right of option by the successor States*

1. Successor States shall grant a right of option to persons concerned covered by the provisions of Article 22 who are qualified to acquire the nationality of two or more successor States.

2. Each successor State shall grant a right to opt for its nationality to persons concerned who are not covered by the provisions of Article 22.

## SECTION 4

### Separation of part or parts of the territory

*Article 24—Attribution of the nationality of the successor State*

When part or parts of the territory of a State separate from that State and form one or more successor States while the predecessor State continues to exist, a successor State shall, unless otherwise indicated by the exercise of a right of option, attribute its nationality to:

(a)  Persons concerned having their habitual residence in its territory; and

(b)  Subject to the provisions of Article 8:

(i)   Persons concerned not covered by subparagraph (a) having an appropriate legal connection with a constituent unit of the predecessor State that has become part of that successor State;

(ii)  Persons concerned not entitled to a nationality of any State concerned under subparagraphs (a) and (b) (i) having their habitual residence in a third State, who were born in or, before leaving the predecessor State, had their last habitual residence in what has become the territory of that successor State or having any other appropriate connection with that successor State.

*Article 25—Withdrawal of the nationality of the predecessor State*

1. The predecessor State shall withdraw its nationality from persons concerned qualified to acquire the nationality of the successor State in accordance with Article 24. It shall not, however, withdraw its nationality before such persons acquire the nationality of the successor State.

2. Unless otherwise indicated by the exercise of a right of option, the predecessor State shall not, however, withdraw its nationality from persons referred to in paragraph 1 who:

(a)  Have their habitual residence in its territory;

(b)  Are not covered by subparagraph (a) and have an appropriate legal connection with a constituent unit of the predecessor State that has remained part of the predecessor State;

(c)  Have their habitual residence in a third State, and were born in or, before leaving the predecessor State, had their last habitual residence in what has remained part of the territory of the predecessor State or have any other appropriate connection with that State.

*Article 26—Granting of the right of option by the predecessor and the successor States*

Predecessor and successor States shall grant a right of option to all persons concerned covered by the provisions of Article 24 and paragraph 2 of Article 25 who are qualified to have the nationality of both the predecessor and successor States or of two or more successor States.

PART TWO

# IMPLEMENTATION AND STANDARD-SETTING IN CONVENTIONS SPONSORED BY THE UNITED NATIONS

## INTRODUCTION

THE DOCUMENTS that follow are concerned with standard-setting, and at the same time provide for measures of implementation apart from the ordinary working of the national legal systems of individual States parties to the Conventions. The two International Covenants of 1966 are intended to supersede the Universal Declaration of Human Rights, with their undoubted legal force as treaties for the parties to them.

## 19. CONVENTION ON THE PREVENTION AND PUNISHMENT OF THE CRIME OF GENOCIDE, 1948

This agreement was adopted and proposed for signature and ratification or accession by General Assembly Resolution 260 A (III) of 9 December 1948; it entered into force on 12 January 1951, in accordance with Article XIII. The United Kingdom has ratified it: see the Genocide Act 1969, in force 30 April 1970, now repealed and replaced by the International Criminal Court Act 2001.

For the text in various languages, see 78 UNTS 277; HMSO, Misc. No. 2 (1966), Cmnd. 2904.

For further reference, see Robinson, N., *The Genocide Convention: A Commentary* (1960); Lemkin, R., *Axis Rule in Occupied Europe: Laws of Occupation, Analysis of Government, Proposals for Redress* (1944); Anon., 58 *Yale Law Journal* 1142 (1949); Whiteman, M. M., 11 *Digest of International Law* 848–74; Shaw, M. N., 'Genocide and International Law', in Dinstein, Y. (ed.), *International Law at a Time of Perplexity: Essays in Honour of Shabtai Rosenne* (1989), 797–820.

## *TEXT*

*The Contracting Parties,*

*Having considered* the declaration made by the General Assembly of the United Nations in its resolution 96 (I) dated 11 December 1946 that genocide is a crime under international law, contrary to the spirit and aims of the United Nations and condemned by the civilized world,

*Recognizing* that at all periods of history genocide has inflicted great losses on humanity, and

*Being convinced* that, in order to liberate mankind from such an odious scourge, international co-operation is required,

*Hereby agree* as hereinafter provided:

### *Article* I

The Contracting Parties confirm that genocide, whether committed in time of peace or in time of war, is a crime under international law which they undertake to prevent and to punish.

### *Article* II

In the present Convention, genocide means any of the following acts committed with intent to destroy, in whole or in part, a national, ethnical, racial or religious group, as such:

- *(a)* Killing members of the group;
- *(b)* Causing serious bodily or mental harm to members of the group;
- *(c)* Deliberately inflicting on the group conditions of life calculated to bring about its physical destruction in whole or in part;
- *(d)* Imposing measures intended to prevent births within the group;
- *(e)* Forcibly transferring children of the group to another group.

*Article* III

The following acts shall be punishable:

- *(a)* Genocide;
- *(b)* Conspiracy to commit genocide;
- *(c)* Direct and public incitement to commit genocide;
- *(d)* Attempt to commit genocide;
- *(e)* Complicity in genocide.

*Article* IV

Persons committing genocide or any of the other acts enumerated in Article III shall be punished, whether they are constitutionally responsible rulers, public officials or private individuals.

*Article* V

The Contracting Parties undertake to enact, in accordance with their respective Constitutions, the necessary legislation to give effect to the provisions of the present Convention, and, in particular, to provide effective penalties for persons guilty of genocide or any of the other acts enumerated in Article III.

*Article* VI

Persons charged with genocide or any of the other acts enumerated in Article III shall be tried by a competent tribunal of the State in the territory of which the act was committed, or by such international penal tribunal as may have jurisdiction with respect to those Contracting Parties which shall have accepted its jurisdiction.

*Article* VII

Genocide and the other acts enumerated in Article III shall not be considered as political crimes for the purpose of extradition.

The Contracting Parties pledge themselves in such cases to grant extradition in accordance with their laws and treaties in force.

*Article* VIII

Any Contracting Party may call upon the competent organs of the United Nations to take such action under the Charter of the United Nations as they consider appropriate for the prevention and suppression of acts of genocide or any of the other acts enumerated in Article III.

*Article* IX

Disputes between the Contracting Parties relating to the interpretation, application or fulfilment of the present Convention, including those relating to the responsibility of a State for genocide or for any of the other acts enumerated in Article III, shall be submitted to the International Court of Justice at the request of any of the parties to the dispute.

*Article* X

The present Convention, of which the Chinese, English, French, Russian and Spanish texts are equally authentic, shall bear the date of 9 December 1948.

*Article* XI

The present Convention shall be open until 31 December 1949 for signature on behalf of any Member of the United Nations and of any non-member State to which an invitation to sign has been addressed by the General Assembly.

The present Convention shall be ratified, and the instruments of ratification shall be deposited with the Secretary-General of the United Nations.

After 1 January 1950, the present Convention may be acceded to on behalf of any Member of the United Nations and of any non-member State which has received an invitation as aforesaid. Instruments of accession shall be deposited with the Secretary-General of the United Nations.

*Article* XII

Any Contracting Party may at any time, by notification addressed to the Secretary-General of the United Nations, extend the application of the present Convention to all or any of the territories for the conduct of whose foreign relations that Contracting Party is responsible.

*Article* XIII

On the day when the first twenty instruments of ratification or accession have been deposited, the Secretary-General shall draw up a *procès-verbal* and transmit a copy thereof to each Member of the United Nations and to each of the non-member States contemplated in Article XI.

The present Convention shall come into force on the ninetieth day following the date of deposit of the twentieth instrument of ratification or accession.

Any ratification or accession effected, subsequent to the latter date shall become effective on the ninetieth day following the deposit of the instrument of ratification or accession.

*Article* XIV

The present Convention shall remain in effect for a period of ten years as from the date of its coming into force.

It shall thereafter remain in force for successive periods of five years for such Contracting Parties as have not denounced it at least six months before the expiration of the current period.

Denunciation shall be effected by a written notification addressed to the Secretary-General of the United Nations.

*Article* XV

If, as a result of denunciations, the number of Parties to the present Convention should become less than sixteen, the Convention shall cease to be in force as from the date on which the last of these denunciations shall become effective.

*Article* XVI

A request for the revision of the present Convention may be made at any time by any Contracting Party by means of a notification in writing addressed to the Secretary-General.

The General Assembly shall decide upon the steps, if any, to be taken in respect of such request.

*Article* XVII

The Secretary-General of the United Nations shall notify all Members of the United Nations and the non-member States contemplated in Article XI of the following:

    *(a)* Signatures, ratifications and accessions received in accordance with Article XI;

    *(b)* Notifications received in accordance with Article XII;

    *(c)* The date upon which the present Convention comes into force in accordance with Article XIII;

    *(d)* Denunciations received in accordance with Article XIV;

    *(e)* The abrogation of the Convention in accordance with Article XV;

    *(f)* Notifications received in accordance with Article XVI.

*Article* XVIII

The original of the present Convention shall be deposited in the archives of the United Nations.

A certified copy of the Convention shall be transmitted to each Member of the United Nations and to each of the non-member States contemplated in Article XI.

*Article* XIX

The present Convention shall be registered by the Secretary-General of the United Nations on the date of its coming into force.

## 20. CONVENTION RELATING TO THE STATUS OF REFUGEES, 1951

The Convention was adopted by the UN Conference on the Status of Refugees and Stateless Persons at Geneva on 25 July 1951, by twenty-four votes to none with no abstentions, and opened for signature at the European Office of the United Nations from 28 July to 31 August 1951. It was re-opened for signature at United Nations Headquarters in New York from 17 September 1951 to 31 December 1952. The Final Act of the Conference included five recommendations, adopted unanimously, which are not included below; see further, Goodwin-Gill, G. S., *The Refugee in International Law* (2nd edn., 1996), 389–93. The Convention entered into force on 22 April 1954. For the text in various languages, see 189 UNTS 137; UK Treaty Series, No. 39 (1954), Cmd. 9171.

For further reference, see Weis, P., 30 *BYIL* 478 (1953); 48 *AJIL* 193 (1954); 87 *Journal de droit international* 928 (1960); Grahl-Madsen, A., *The Status of Refugees in International Law*, 2 vols. (1966, 1972); Goodwin-Gill, G. S., *The Refugee in International Law* (2nd edn., 1996).

The definition of 'refugee' in the Convention which follows is confined to those who became refugees 'as a result of events occurring before 1 January 1951'. This limitation is removed by the Protocol relating to the Status of Refugees adopted by the UN General Assembly on 16 December 1966; see Weis, P., 42 *BYIL* 39 (1967); Goodwin-Gill, G. S., *The Refugee in International Law*, 296–8 (text of Protocol at 409–12). The Protocol came into force on 4 October 1967. For the text in various languages, see 606 UNTS 267; UK Treaty Series, No. 15 (1969), Cmnd. 3906. The Protocol is not reproduced here; the changes it makes in Article 1A(2) of the Convention are indicated by square brackets, and States parties to the Protocol undertake to apply Articles 2 to 34 inclusive of the Convention, as if the bracketed words were omitted.

### TEXT

### Preamble

*The High Contracting Parties,*

*Considering* that the Charter of the United Nations and the Universal Declaration of Human Rights approved on 10 December 1948 by the General Assembly have affirmed the principle that human beings shall enjoy fundamental rights and freedoms without discrimination,

*Considering* that the United Nations has, on various occasions, manifested its profound concern for refugees and endeavoured to assure refugees the widest possible exercise of these fundamental rights and freedoms,

*Considering* that it is desirable to revise and consolidate previous international agreements relating to the status of refugees and to extend the scope of and protection accorded by such instruments by means of a new agreement,

*Considering* that the grant of asylum may place unduly heavy burdens on certain countries, and that a satisfactory solution of a problem of which the United Nations has recognized the international scope and nature cannot therefore be achieved without international co-operation,

*Expressing* the wish that all States, recognizing the social and humanitarian nature of the problem of refugees will do everything within their power to prevent this problem from becoming a cause of tension between States,

*Noting* that the United Nations High Commissioner for Refugees is charged with the task of supervising international conventions providing for the protection of refugees, and recognizing that the effective co-ordination of measures taken to deal with this problem will depend upon the co-operation of States with the High Commissioner,

*Have agreed* as follows:

## CHAPTER I—GENERAL PROVISIONS

*Article 1—Definition of the term 'Refugee'*

A. For the purposes of the present Convention, the term 'refugee' shall apply to any person who:

(1) Has been considered a refugee under the Arrangements of 12 May 1926 and 30 June 1928 or under the Conventions of 28 October 1933 and 10 February 1938, the Protocol of 14 September 1939 or the Constitution of the International Refugee Organization;

Decisions of non-eligibility taken by the International Refugee Organization during the period of its activities shall not prevent the status of refugee being accorded to persons who fulfil the conditions of paragraph 2 of this section;

(2) [As a result of events occurring before 1 January 1951 and] owing to a well-founded fear of being persecuted for reasons of race, religion, nationality, membership of a particular social group or political opinion, is outside the country of his nationality and is unable or, owing to such fear, is unwilling to avail himself of the protection of that country; or who, not having a nationality and being outside the country of his former habitual residence [as a result of such events], is unable or, owing to such fear, is unwilling to return to it.

In the case of a person who has more than one nationality, the term 'the country of his nationality' shall mean each of the countries of which he is a national, and a person shall not be deemed to be lacking the protection of the country of his nationality if, without any valid reason based on well-founded fear, he has not availed himself of the protection of one of the countries of which he is a national.

B. (1) For the purposes of this Convention, the words 'events occurring before 1 January 1951' in Article 1, Section A, shall be understood to mean either

  (a) 'events occurring in Europe before 1 January 1951'; or

  (b) 'events occurring in Europe or elsewhere before 1 January 1951', and each Contracting State shall make a declaration at the time of signature, ratification or accession, specifying which of these meanings it applies for the purpose of its obligations under this Convention.

(2) Any Contracting State which has adopted alternative (a) may at any time extend its obligations by adopting alternative (b) by means of a notification addressed to the Secretary-General of the United Nations.

C. This Convention shall cease to apply to any person falling under the terms of

Section A if:

(1) He has voluntarily re-availed himself of the protection of the country of his nationality; or

(2) Having lost his nationality, he has voluntarily re-acquired it, or

(3) He has acquired a new nationality, and enjoys the protection of the country of his new nationality; or

(4) He has voluntarily re-established himself in the country which he left or outside which he remained owing to fear of persecution; or

(5) He can no longer, because the circumstances in connection with which he has been recognized as a refugee have ceased to exist, continue to refuse to avail himself of the protection of the country of his nationality;

Provided that this paragraph shall not apply to a refugee falling under Section A(1) of this Article who is able to invoke compelling reasons arising out of previous persecution for refusing to avail himself of the protection of the country of nationality;

(6) Being a person who has no nationality he is, because of the circumstances in connection with which he has been recognized as a refugee have ceased to exist, able to return to the country of his former habitual residence;

Provided that this paragraph shall not apply to a refugee falling under section A(1) of this Article who is able to invoke compelling reasons arising out of previous persecution for refusing to return to the country of his former habitual residence.

D. This Convention shall not apply to persons who are at present receiving from organs or agencies of the United Nations other than the United Nations High Commissioner for Refugees protection or assistance.

When such protection or assistance has ceased for any reason, without the position of such persons being definitively settled in accordance with the relevant resolutions adopted by the General Assembly of the United Nations, these persons shall *ipso facto* be entitled to the benefits of this Convention.

E. This Convention shall not apply to a person who is recognized by the competent authorities of the country in which he has taken residence as having the rights and obligations which are attached to the possession of the nationality of that country.

F. The provisions of this Convention shall not apply to any person with respect to whom there are serious reasons for considering that:

   *(a)* he has committed a crime against peace, a war crime, or a crime against humanity, as defined in the international instruments drawn up to make provision in respect of such crimes;

   *(b)* he has committed a serious non-political crime outside the country of refuge prior to his admission to that country as a refugee;

   *(c)* he has been guilty of acts contrary to the purposes and principles of the United Nations.

*Article 2—General obligations*

Every refugee has duties to the country in which he finds himself, which require in particular that he conform to its laws and regulations as well as to measures taken for the maintenance of public order.

*Article 3—Non-discrimination*

The Contracting States shall apply the provisions of this Convention to refugees without discrimination as to race, religion or country of origin.

*Article 4—Religion*

The Contracting States shall accord to refugees within their territories treatment at least as favourable as that accorded to their nationals with respect to freedom to practise their religion and freedom as regards the religious education of their children.

*Article 5—Rights granted apart from this Convention*

Nothing in this Convention shall be deemed to impair any rights and benefits granted by a Contracting State to refugees apart from this Convention.

*Article 6—The term 'in the same circumstances'*

For the purposes of this Convention, the term 'in the same circumstances' implies that any requirements (including requirements as to length and conditions of sojourn or residence) which the particular individual would have to fulfil for the enjoyment of the right in question, if he were not a refugee, must be fulfilled by him, with the exception of requirements which by their nature a refugee is incapable of fulfilling.

*Article 7—Exemption from reciprocity*

1. Except where this Convention contains more favourable provisions, a Contracting State shall accord to refugees the same treatment as is accorded to aliens generally.

2. After a period of three years' residence, all refugees shall enjoy exemption from legislative reciprocity in the territory of the Contracting States.

3. Each Contracting State shall continue to accord to refugees the rights and benefits to which they were already entitled, in the absence of reciprocity, at the date of entry into force of this Convention for that State.

4. The Contracting States shall consider favourably the possibility of according to refugees, in the absence of reciprocity, rights and benefits beyond those to which they are entitled according to paragraphs 2 and 3, and to extending exemption from reciprocity to refugees who do not fulfil the conditions provided for in paragraphs 2 and 3.

5. The provisions of paragraphs 2 and 3 apply both to the rights and benefits referred to in Articles 13, 18, 19, 21 and 22 of this Convention and to rights and benefits for which this Convention does not provide.

*Article 8—Exemption from exceptional measures*

With regard to exceptional measures which may be taken against the person, property or interests of nationals of a foreign State, the Contracting States shall not apply such measures to a refugee who is formally a national of the said State solely on account of such nationality. Contracting States which, under their legislation, are prevented from applying the general principle expressed in this Article, shall, in appropriate cases, grant exemptions in favour of such refugees.

*Article 9—Provisional measures*

Nothing in this Convention shall prevent a Contracting State, in time of war or other grave and exceptional circumstances, from taking provisionally measures which it considers to be essential to the national security in the case of a particular person, pending a determination by the Contracting State that that person is in fact a refugee and that the continuance of such measures is necessary in his case in the interests of national security.

*Article 10—Continuity of residence*

1. Where a refugee has been forcibly displaced during the Second World War and removed to the territory of a Contracting State, and is resident there, the period of such enforced sojourn shall be considered to have been lawful residence within that territory.

2. Where a refugee has been forcibly displaced during the Second World War from the territory of a Contracting State and has, prior to the date of entry into force of this Convention, returned there for the purpose of taking up residence, the period of residence before and after such enforced displacement shall be regarded as one uninterrupted period for any purposes for which uninterrupted residence is required.

*Article 11—Refugee seamen*

In the case of refugees regularly serving as crew members on board a ship flying the flag of a Contracting State, that State shall give sympathetic consideration to their establishment on its territory and the issue of travel documents to them or their temporary admission to its territory particularly with a view to facilitating their establishment in another country.


# CHAPTER II—JURIDICAL STATUS

*Article 12—Personal status*

1. The personal status of a refugee shall be governed by the law of the country of his domicile or, if he has no domicile, by the law of the country of his residence.

2. Rights previously acquired by a refugee and dependent on personal status, more particularly rights attaching to marriage, shall be respected by a Contracting State, subject to compliance, if this be necessary, with the formalities required by the law of that State, provided that the right in question is one which would have been recognized by the law of that State had he not become a refugee.

*Article 13—Movable and immovable property*

The Contracting States shall accord to a refugee treatment as favourable as possible and, in any event, not less favourable than that accorded to aliens generally in the same circumstances, as regards the acquisition of movable and immovable property and other rights pertaining thereto, and to leases and other contracts relating to movable and immovable property.

*Article* 14—*Artistic rights and industrial property*

In respect of the protection of industrial property, such as inventions, designs or models, trade marks, trade names, and of rights in literary, artistic, and scientific works, a refugee shall be accorded in the country in which he has his habitual residence the same protection as is accorded to nationals of that country. In the territory of any other Contracting State, he shall be accorded the same protection as is accorded in that territory to nationals of the country in which he has his habitual residence.

*Article* 15—*Right of association*

As regards non-political and non-profit making associations and trade unions the Contracting States shall accord to refugees lawfully staying in their territory the most favourable treatment accorded to nationals of a foreign country, in the same circumstances.

*Article* 16—*Access to courts*

1. A refugee shall have free access to the courts of law on the territory of all Contracting States.

2. A refugee shall enjoy in the Contracting State in which he has his habitual residence the same treatment as a national in matters pertaining to access to the courts, including legal assistance and exemption from *cautio judicatum solvi*.

3. A refugee shall be accorded in the matters referred to in paragraph 2 in countries other than that in which he has his habitual residence the treatment granted to a national of the country of his habitual residence.

## CHAPTER III—GAINFUL EMPLOYMENT

*Article* 17—*Wage-earning employment*

1. The Contracting States shall accord to refugees lawfully staying in their territory the most favourable treatment accorded to nationals of a foreign country in the same circumstances, as regards the right to engage in wage-earning employment.

2. In any case, restrictive measures imposed on aliens or the employment of aliens for the protection of the national labour market shall not be applied to a refugee who was already exempt from them at the date of entry into force of this Convention for the Contracting State concerned, or who fulfils one of the following conditions:

   *(a)* He has completed three years' residence in the country;

   *(b)* He has a spouse possessing the nationality of the country of residence. A refugee may not invoke the benefits of this provision if he has abandoned his spouse;

   *(c)* He has one or more children possessing the nationality of the country of residence.

3. The Contracting States shall give sympathetic consideration to assimilating the rights of all refugees with regard to wage-earning employment to those of

nationals, and in particular of those refugees who have entered their territory pursuant to programmes of labour recruitment or under immigration schemes.

### Article 18—Self-employment

The Contracting States shall accord to a refugee lawfully in their territory treatment as favourable as possible and, in any event, not less favourable that that accorded to aliens generally in the same circumstances, as regards the right to engage on his own account in agriculture, industry, handicrafts and commerce and to establish commercial and industrial companies.

### Article 19—Liberal professions

1. Each Contracting State shall accord to refugees lawfully staying in their territory who hold diplomas recognized by the competent authorities of that State, and who are desirous of practising a liberal profession, treatment as favourable as possible and, in any event, not less favourable than that accorded to aliens generally in the same circumstances.

2. The Contracting States shall use their best endeavours consistently with their laws and constitutions to secure the settlement of such refugees in the territories, other than the metropolitan territory, for whose international relations they are responsible.

## CHAPTER IV—WELFARE

### Article 20—Rationing

Where a rationing system exists, which applies to the population at large and regulates the general distribution of products in short supply, refugees shall be accorded the same treatment as nationals.

### Article 21—Housing

As regards housing, the Contracting States, in so far as the matter is regulated by laws or regulations or is subject to the control of public authorities, shall accord to refugees lawfully staying in their territory treatment as favourable as possible and, in any event, not less favourable than that accorded to aliens generally in the same circumstances.

### Article 22—Public education

1. The Contracting States shall accord to refugees the same treatment as is accorded to nationals with respect to elementary education.

2. The Contracting States shall accord to refugees treatment as favourable as possible, and, in any event, not less favourable than that accorded to aliens generally in the same circumstances, with respect to education other than elementary education and, in particular, as regards access to studies, the recognition of foreign school certificates, diplomas and degrees, the remission of fees and charges and the award of scholarships.

*Article 23—Public relief*

The Contracting States shall accord to refugees lawfully staying in their territory the same treatment with respect to public relief and assistance as is accorded to their nationals.

*Article 24—Labour legislation and social security*

1. The Contracting States shall accord to refugees lawfully staying in their territory the same treatment as is accorded to nationals in respect of the following matters:

   *(a)* In so far as such matters are governed by laws or regulations or are subject to the control of administrative authorities: remuneration, including family allowances where these form part of remuneration, hours of work, overtime arrangements, holidays with pay, restrictions on home work, minimum age of employment, apprenticeship and training, women's work and the work of young persons, and the enjoyment of the benefits of collective bargaining;

   *(b)* Social security (legal provisions in respect of employment injury, occupational diseases, maternity, sickness, disability, old age, death, unemployment, family responsibilities and any other contingency which, according to national laws or regulations, is covered by a social security scheme), subject to the following limitations:

       (i) There may be appropriate arrangements for the maintenance of acquired rights and rights in course of acquisition;

       (ii) National laws or regulations of the country of residence may prescribe special arrangements concerning benefits or portions of benefits which are payable wholly out of public funds, and concerning allowances paid to persons who do not fulfil the contribution conditions prescribed for the award of a normal pension.

2. The right to compensation for the death of a refugee resulting from employment injury or from occupational disease shall not be affected by the fact that the residence of the beneficiary is outside the territory of the Contracting State.

3. The Contracting States shall extend to refugees the benefits of agreements concluded between them, or which may be concluded between them in the future, concerning the maintenance of acquired rights and rights in the process of acquisition in regard to social security, subject only to the conditions which apply to nationals of the States signatory to the agreements in question.

4. The Contracting States will give sympathetic consideration to extending to refugees so far as possible the benefits of similar agreements which may at any time be in force between such Contracting States and non-contracting States.


## CHAPTER V—ADMINISTRATIVE MEASURES

*Article 25—Administrative assistance*

1. When the exercise of a right by a refugee would normally require the assistance of authorities of a foreign country to whom he cannot have recourse, the

Contracting States in whose territory he is residing shall arrange that such assist-ance be afforded to him by their own authorities or by an international authority.

2. The authority or authorities mentioned in paragraph 1 shall deliver or cause to be delivered under their supervision to refugees such documents or certifications as would normally be delivered to aliens by or through their national authorities.

3. Documents or certifications so delivered shall stand in the stead of the official instruments delivered to aliens by or through their national authorities, and shall be given credence in the absence of proof to the contrary.

4. Subject to such exceptional treatment as may be granted to indigent persons, fees may be charged for the services mentioned herein, but such fees shall be moderate and commensurate with those charged to nationals for similar services.

5. The provisions of this Article shall be without prejudice to Articles 27 and 28.

*Article 26—Freedom of movement*

Each Contracting State shall accord to refugees lawfully in its territory the right to choose their place of residence and to move freely within its territory, subject to any regulations applicable to aliens generally in the same circumstances.

*Article 27—Identity papers*

The Contracting States shall issue identity papers to any refugee in their territory who does not possess a valid travel document.

*Article 28—Travel documents*

1. The Contracting States shall issue to refugees lawfully staying in their territory travel documents for the purpose of travel outside their territory unless compelling reasons of national security or public order otherwise require, and the provisions of the Schedule to this Convention shall apply with respect to such documents. The Contracting States may issue such a travel document to any other refugee in their territory; they shall in particular give sympathetic consideration to the issue of such a travel document to refugees in their territory who are unable to obtain a travel document from the country of their lawful residence.

2. Travel documents issued to refugees under previous international agreements by parties thereto shall be recognized and treated by the Contracting States in the same way as if they had been issued pursuant to this article.

*Article 29—Fiscal charges*

1. The Contracting States shall not impose upon refugee duties, charges or taxes, of any description whatsoever, other or higher than those which are or may be levied on their nationals in similar situations.

2. Nothing in the above paragraph shall prevent the application to refugees of the laws and regulations concerning charges in respect of the issue to aliens of administrative documents including identity papers.

*Article 30—Transfer of assets*

1. A Contracting State shall, in conformity with its laws and regulations, permit refugees to transfer assets which they have brought into its territory, to another country where they have been admitted for the purposes of resettlement.

2. A Contracting State shall give sympathetic consideration to the application of refugees for permission to transfer assets wherever they may be and which are necessary for their resettlement in another country to which they have been admitted.

### Article 31—*Refugees unlawfully in the country of refuge*

1. The Contracting States shall not impose penalties, on account of their illegal entry or presence, on refugees who, coming directly from a territory where their life or freedom was threatened in the sense of Article 1, enter or are present in their territory without authorization, provided they present themselves without delay to the authorities and show good cause for their illegal entry or presence.

2. The Contracting States shall not apply to the movements of such refugees restrictions other than those which are necessary and such restrictions shall only be applied until their status in the country is regularized or they obtain admission into another country. The Contracting States shall allow such refugees a reasonable period and all the necessary facilities to obtain admission into another country.

### Article 32—*Expulsion*

1. The Contracting States shall not expel a refugee lawfully in their territory save on grounds of national security or public order.

2. The expulsion of such a refugee shall be only in pursuance of a decision reached in accordance with due process of law. Except where compelling reasons of national security otherwise require, the refugee shall be allowed to submit evidence to clear himself, and to appeal to and be represented for the purpose before competent authority or a person or persons specially designated by the competent authority.

3. The Contracting States shall allow such a refugee a reasonable period within which to seek legal admission into another country. The Contracting States reserve the right to apply during that period such internal measures as they may deem necessary.

### Article 33—*Prohibition of expulsion or return ('refoulement')*

1. No Contracting State shall expel or return ('refouler') a refugee in any manner whatsoever to the frontiers of territories where his life or freedom would be threatened on account of his race, religion, nationality, membership of a particular social group or political opinion.

2. The benefit of the present provision may not, however, be claimed by a refugee whom there are reasonable grounds for regarding as a danger to the security of the country in which he is, or who, having been convicted by a final judgment of a particularly serious crime, constitutes a danger to the community of that country.

### Article 34—*Naturalization*

The Contracting States shall as far as possible facilitate the assimilation and naturalization of refugees. They shall in particular make every effort to expedite naturalization proceedings and to reduce as far as possible the charges and costs of such proceedings.

## CHAPTER VI—EXECUTORY AND TRANSITORY PROVISIONS

*Article 35—Co-operation of the national authorities with the United Nations*

1. The Contracting States undertake to co-operate with the Office of the United Nations High Commissioner for Refugees, or any other agency of the United Nations which may succeed it, in the exercise of its functions, and shall in particular facilitate its duty of supervising the application of the provisions of this Convention.

2. In order to enable the Office of the High Commissioner or any other agency of the United Nations which may succeed it, to make reports to the competent organs of the United Nations, the Contracting States undertake to provide them in the appropriate form with information and statistical data requested concerning:

   *(a)* the condition of refugees,

   *(b)* the implementation of this Convention, and

   *(c)* laws, regulations and decrees which are, or may hereafter be, in force relating to refugees.

*Article 36—Information on national legislation*

The Contracting States shall communicate to the Secretary-General of the United Nations the laws and regulations which they may adopt to ensure the application of this Convention.

*Article 37—Relation to previous Conventions*

Without prejudice to Article 28, paragraph 2, of this Convention, this Convention replaces, as between parties to it, the Arrangements of 5 July 1922, 31 May 1924, 12 May 1926, 30 June 1928 and 30 July 1935, the Conventions of 28 October 1933 and 10 February 1938, the Protocol of 14 September 1939 and the Agreement of 15 October 1946.

## CHAPTER VII—FINAL CLAUSES

*Article 38—Settlement of disputes*

Any dispute between parties to this Convention relating to its interpretation or application, which cannot be settled by other means, shall be referred to the International Court of Justice at the request of any one of the parties to the dispute.

*Article 39—Signature, ratification and accession*

1. This Convention shall be opened for signature at Geneva on 28 July 1951 and shall hereafter be deposited with the Secretary-General of the United Nations. It shall be open for signature at the European Office of the United Nations from 28 July to 31 August 1951 and shall be re-opened for signature at the Headquarters of the United Nations from 17 September 1951 to 31 December 1952.

2. This Convention shall be open for signature on behalf of all States Members of the United Nations, and also on behalf of any other State invited to attend the Conference of Plenipotentiaries on the Status of Refugees and Stateless Persons or

to which an invitation to sign will have been addressed by the General Assembly. It shall be ratified and the instruments of ratification shall be deposited with the Secretary-General of the United Nations.

3. This Convention shall be open from 28 July 1951 for accession by the States referred to in paragraph 2 of this Article. Accession shall be effected by the deposit of an instrument of accession with the Secretary-General of the United Nations.

*Article 40—Territorial application clause*

1. Any State may, at the time of signature, ratification or accession, declare that this Convention shall extend to all or any of the territories for the international relations of which it is responsible. Such a declaration shall take effect when the Convention enters into force for the State concerned.

2. At any time thereafter any such extension shall be made by notification addressed to the Secretary-General of the United Nations and shall take effect as from the ninetieth day after the day of receipt by the Secretary-General of the United Nations of this notification, or as from the date of entry into force of the Convention for the State concerned, whichever is the later.

3. With respect to those territories to which this Convention is not extended at the time of signature, ratification or accession, each State concerned shall consider the possibility of taking the necessary steps in order to extend the application of this Convention to such territories, subject, where necessary for constitutional reasons, to the consent of the governments of such territories.

*Article 41—Federal clause*

In the case of a Federal or non-unitary State, the following provisions shall apply:

   *(a)* With respect to those Articles of this Convention that come within the legislative jurisdiction of the federal legislative authority, the obligations of the Federal Government shall to this extent be the same as those of Parties which are not Federal States,

   *(b)* With respect to those Articles of this Convention that come within the legislative jurisdiction of constituent States, provinces or cantons which are not, under the constitutional system of the federation, bound to take legislative action, the Federal Government shall bring such Articles with a favourable recommendation to the notice of the appropriate authorities of States, provinces or cantons at the earliest possible moment.

   *(c)* A Federal State Party to this Convention shall, at the request of any other Contracting State transmitted through the Secretary-General of the United Nations, supply a statement of the law and practice of the Federation and its constituent units in regard to any particular provision of the Convention showing the extent to which effect has been given to that provision by legislative or other action.

*Article 42—Reservations*

1. At the time of signature, ratification or accession, any State may make reservations to articles of the Convention other than to Articles 1, 3, 4, 16(1), 33, 36–46 inclusive.

2. Any State making a reservation in accordance with paragraph 1 of this article may at any time withdraw the reservation by a communication to that effect addressed to the Secretary-General of the United Nations.

*Article 43—Entry into force*

1. This Convention shall come into force on the ninetieth day following the day of deposit of the sixth instrument of ratification or accession.

2. For each State ratifying or acceding to the Convention after the deposit of the sixth instrument of ratification or accession, the Convention shall enter into force on the ninetieth day following the date of deposit by such State of its instrument of ratification or accession.

*Article 44—Denunciation*

1. Any Contracting State may denounce this Convention at any time by a notification addressed to the Secretary-General of the United Nations.

2. Such denunciation shall take effect for the Contracting State concerned one year from the date upon which it is received by the Secretary-General of the United Nations.

3. Any State which has made a declaration or notification under Article 40 may, at any time thereafter, by a notification to the Secretary-General of the United Nations, declare that the Convention shall cease to extend to such territory one year after the date of receipt of the notification by the Secretary-General.

*Article 45—Revision*

1. Any Contracting State may request revision of this Convention at any time by a notification addressed to the Secretary-General of the United Nations.

2. The General Assembly of the United Nations shall recommend the steps, if any, to be taken in respect of such request.

*Article 46—Notifications by the Secretary-General of the United Nations*

The Secretary-General of the United Nations shall inform all Members of the United Nations and non-member States referred to in Article 39:

*(a)* of declarations and notifications in accordance with Section B of Article 1;

*(b)* of signatures, ratifications and accessions in accordance with Article 39;

*(c)* of declarations and notifications in accordance with Article 40;

*(d)* of reservations and withdrawals in accordance with Article 42;

*(e)* of the date on which this Convention will come into force in accordance with Article 43;

*(f)* of denunciations and notifications in accordance with Article 44;

*(g)* of requests for revision in accordance with Article 45.

*In faith whereof* the undersigned, duly authorized, have signed this Convention on behalf of their respective Governments,

*Done at Geneva*, this twenty-eighth day of July, one thousand nine hundred and fifty-one, in a single copy, of which the English and French texts are equally authentic and which shall remain deposited in the archives of the United Nations, and certified true copies of which shall be delivered to all Members of the United Nations and to the non-member States referred to in Article 39.

## SCHEDULE

### *Paragraph 1*

1. The travel document referred to in Article 28 of this Convention shall be similar to the specimen annexed hereto.

2. The document shall be made out in at least two languages, one of which shall be English or French.

### *Paragraph 2*

Subject to the regulations obtaining in the country of issue, children may be included in the travel document of a parent or, in exceptional circumstances, of another adult refugee.

### *Paragraph 3*

The fees charged for issue of the document shall not exceed the lowest scale of charges for national passports.

### *Paragraph 4*

Save in special or exceptional cases, the document shall be made valid for the largest possible number of countries.

### *Paragraph 5*

The document shall have a validity of either one or two years, at the discretion of the issuing authority.

### *Paragraph 6*

1. The renewal or extension of the validity of the document is a matter for the authority which issued it, so long as the holder has not established lawful residence in another territory and resides lawfully in the territory of the said authority. The issue of a new document is, under the same conditions, a matter for the authority which issued the former document.

2. Diplomatic or consular authorities, specially authorized for the purpose, shall be empowered to extend, for a period not exceeding six months, the validity of travel documents issued by their Governments.

3. The Contracting States shall give sympathetic consideration to renewing or extending the validity of travel documents or issuing new documents to refugees no longer lawfully resident in their territory who are unable to obtain a travel document from the country of their lawful residence.

### *Paragraph 7*

The Contracting States shall recognize the validity of the documents issued in accordance with the provisions of Article 28 of this Convention.

*Paragraph* 8

The competent authorities of the country to which the refugee desires to proceed shall, if they are prepared to admit him and if a visa is required, affix a visa on the document of which he is the holder.

*Paragraph* 9

1. The Contracting States undertake to issue transit visas to refugees who have obtained visas for a territory of final destination.

2. The issue of such visas may be refused on grounds which would justify refusal of a visa to any alien.

*Paragraph* 10

The fees for the issue of exit, entry or transit visas shall not exceed the lowest scale of charges for visas on foreign passports.

*Paragraph* 11

When a refugee has lawfully taken up residence in the territory of another Contracting State, the responsibility for the issue of a new document, under the terms and conditions of Article 28, shall be that of the competent authority of that territory, to which the refugee shall be entitled to apply.

*Paragraph* 12

The authority issuing a new document shall withdraw the old document and shall return it to the country of issue, if it is stated in the document that it should be so returned; otherwise it shall withdraw and cancel the document.

*Paragraph* 13

1. Each Contracting State undertakes that the holder of a travel document issued by it in accordance with Article 28 of this Convention shall be re-admitted to its territory at any time during the period of its validity.

2. Subject to the provisions of the preceding sub-paragraph, a Contracting State may require the holder of the document to comply with such formalities as may be prescribed in regard to exit from or return to its territory.

3. The Contracting States reserve the right, in exceptional cases, or in cases where the refugee's stay is authorized for a specific period, when issuing the document, to limit the period during which the refugee may return to a period of not less than three months.

*Paragraph* 14

Subject only to the terms of paragraph 13, the provisions of this Schedule in no way affect the laws and regulations governing the conditions of admission to, transit through, residence and establishment in, and departure from, the territories of the Contracting States.

*Paragraph* 15

Neither the issue of the document nor the entries made thereon determine or affect the status of the holder, particularly as regards nationality.

*Paragraph* 16

The issue of the document does not in any way entitle the holder to the protection of the diplomatic or consular authorities of the country of issue, and does not confer on these authorities a right of protection.

[The Annex with details of the Specimen Travel Document is omitted]

## 21. CONVENTION ON THE POLITICAL RIGHTS OF WOMEN, 1953

The Convention was adopted by General Assembly Resolution 640 (VII) of 20 December 1952, opened for signature on 31 March 1953, and entered into force on 7 July 1954. For the text in various languages, see 193 UNTS 135; UK Treaty Series, No. 101 (1967), Cmnd. 3449.

See further, *Convention on the Political Rights of Women: History and Commentary*, ST/SOA/27, UN Sales No. 1955, IV, 17; *Yearbook on Human Rights*, 1948, 439 (Bogotá Convention).

### TEXT

*The Contracting Parties,*

*Desiring* to implement the principle of equality of rights for men and women contained in the Charter of the United Nations,

*Recognizing* that everyone has the right to take part in the government of his country directly or indirectly through freely chosen representatives, and has the right to equal access to public service in his country, and desiring to equalize the status of men and women in the enjoyment and exercise of political rights, in accordance with the provisions of the Charter of the United Nations and of the Universal Declaration of Human Rights,

*Having resolved* to conclude a Convention for this purpose,

*Hereby agree* as hereinafter provided:

*Article* I

Women shall be entitled to vote in all elections on equal terms with men, without any discrimination.

*Article* II

Women shall be eligible for election to all publicly elected bodies, established by national law, on equal terms with men, without any discrimination.

*Article* III

Women shall be entitled to hold public office and to exercise all public functions, established by national law, on equal terms with men, without any discrimination.

*Article* IV

1. This Convention shall be open for signature on behalf of any Member of the United Nations and also on behalf of any other State to which an invitation has been addressed by the General Assembly.

2. This Convention shall be ratified and the instruments of ratification shall be deposited with the Secretary-General of the United Nations.

*Article* V

1. This Convention shall be open for accession to all States referred to in paragraph 1 of Article IV.

2. Accession shall be effected by the deposit of an instrument of accession with the Secretary-General of the United Nations.

*Article* VI

1. This Convention shall come into force on the ninetieth day following the date of deposit of the sixth instrument of ratification or accession.

2. For each State ratifying or acceding to the Convention after the deposit of the sixth instrument of ratification or accession the Convention shall enter into force on the ninetieth day after deposit by such State of its instrument of ratification or accession.

*Article* VII

In the event that any State submits a reservation to any of the articles of this Convention at the time of signature, ratification or accession, the Secretary-General shall communicate the text of the reservation to all States which are or may become Parties to this Convention. Any State which objects to the reservation may, within a period of ninety days from the date of the said communication (or upon the date of its becoming a Party to the Convention), notify the Secretary-General that it does not accept it. In such case, the Convention shall not enter into force as between such State and the State making the reservation.

*Article* VIII

1. Any State may denounce this Convention by written notification to the Secretary-General of the United Nations. Denunciation shall take effect one year after the date of receipt of the notification by the Secretary-General.

2. This Convention shall cease to be in force as from the date when the denunciation which reduces the number of Parties to less than six becomes effective.

*Article* IX

Any dispute which may arise between any two or more Contracting States concerning the interpretation or application of this Convention, which is not settled by negotiation, shall at the request of any one of the parties to the dispute be referred to the International Court of Justice for decision, unless they agree to another mode of settlement.

*Article* X

The Secretary-General of the United Nations shall notify all Members of the United Nations and the non-member States contemplated in paragraph 1 of Article IV of this Convention of the following:

*(a)* Signatures and instruments of ratification received in accordance with Article IV;

*(b)* Instruments of accession received in accordance with Article V;

*(c)* The date upon which this Convention enters into force in accordance with Article VI;

*(d)* Communications and notifications received in accordance with Article VII;

*(e)* Notifications of denunciation received in accordance with paragraph 1 of Article VIII;

(f)   Abrogation in accordance with paragraph 2 of Article VIII.

*Article* XI

1. This Convention, of which the Chinese, English, French, Russian and Spanish texts shall be equally authentic, shall be deposited in the archives of the United Nations.

2. The Secretary-General of the United Nations shall transmit a certified copy to all Members of the United Nations and to the non-member States contemplated in paragraph 1 of Article IV.

## 22. SLAVERY CONVENTION, 1926, AMENDED BY PROTOCOL, 1953

The Slavery Convention was signed on 25 September 1926 and entered into force on 9 March 1927. For the text in various languages, see 60 LNTS 253; UK Treaty Series, No. 24 (1956), Cmd. 9797. The Protocol of Amendment was approved by General Assembly Resolution 794 (VIII) of 23 October 1953, opened for signature on 7 December 1953, and the Slavery Convention as amended by the Protocol entered into force on 7 July 1955. For the text in various languages, see 212 UNTS 17; UK Treaty Series, No. 24 (1956), Cmd. 9797; the Preamble has been omitted from the text below.

There have been problems in defining slavery and associated practices, and the position has been improved by the Supplementary Convention, below, 136–41. See also the ILO Conventions on forced labour, below, 310, 334.

*TEXT*

*Article* 1

For the purpose of the present Convention, the following definitions are agreed upon:

(1) Slavery is the status or condition of a person over whom any or all of the powers attaching to the right of ownership are exercised.

(2) The slave trade includes all acts involved in the capture, acquisition or disposal of a person with intent to reduce him to slavery; all acts involved in the acquisition of a slave with a view to selling or exchanging him; all acts of disposal by sale or exchange of a slave acquired with a view to being sold or exchanged, and, in general, every act of trade or transport in slaves.

*Article* 2

The High Contracting Parties undertake, each in respect of the territories placed under its sovereignty, jurisdiction, protection, suzerainty or tutelage, so far as they have not already taken the necessary steps:

(a) To prevent and suppress the slave trade;

(b) To bring about, progressively and as soon as possible, the complete abolition of slavery in all its forms.

*Article* 3

The High Contracting Parties undertake to adopt all appropriate measures with a view to preventing and suppressing the embarkation, disembarkation and transport of slaves in their territorial waters and upon all vessels flying their respective flags.

The High Contracting Parties undertake to negotiate as soon as possible a general Convention with regard to the slave trade which will give them rights and impose upon them duties of the same nature as those provided for in the Convention of June 17th, 1925, relative to the International Trade in Arms (Articles 12, 20, 21, 22, 23, 24, and paragraphs 3, 4 and 5 of Section II of Annex II), with the necessary adaptations, it being understood that this general Convention will not place the ships (even of small tonnage) of any High Contracting Parties in a position different from that of the other High Contracting Parties.

It is also understood that, before or after the coming into force of this general Convention the High Contracting Parties are entirely free to conclude between themselves, without, however, derogating from the principles laid down in the preceding paragraph, such special agreements as, by reason of their peculiar situation, might appear to be suitable in order to bring about as soon as possible the complete disappearance of the slave trade.

### Article 4

The High Contracting Parties shall give to one another every assistance with the object of securing the abolition of slavery and the slave trade.

### Article 5

The High Contracting Parties recognize that recourse to compulsory or forced labour may have grave consequences and undertake, each in respect of the territories placed under its sovereignty, jurisdiction, protection, suzerainty or tutelage, to take all necessary measures to prevent compulsory or forced labour from developing into conditions analogous to slavery.

It is agreed that:

(1) Subject to the transitional provisions laid down in paragraph (2) below, compulsory or forced labour may only be exacted for public purposes.

(2) In territories in which compulsory or forced labour for other than public purposes still survives, the High Contracting Parties shall endeavour progressively and as soon as possible to put an end to the practice. So long as such forced or compulsory labour exists, this labour shall invariably be of an exceptional character, shall always receive adequate remuneration, and shall not involve the removal of the labourers from their usual place of residence.

(3) In all cases, the responsibility for any recourse to compulsory or forced labour shall rest with the competent central authorities of the territory concerned.

### Article 6

Those of the High Contracting Parties whose laws do not at present make adequate provision for the punishment of infractions of laws and regulations enacted with a view to giving effect to the purposes of the present Convention undertake to adopt the necessary measures in order that severe penalties may be imposed in respect of such infractions.

### Article 7

The High Contracting Parties undertake to communicate to each other and to the Secretary-General of the League of Nations any laws and regulations which they may enact with a view to the application of the provisions of the present Convention.

### Article 8

The High Contracting Parties agree that disputes arising between them relating to the interpretation or application of this Convention shall, if they cannot be settled by direct negotiation, be referred for decision to the Permanent Court of International Justice. In case either or both of the States Parties to such a dispute should not be parties to the Protocol of December 16th, 1920 relating to the Permanent Court of International Justice, the dispute shall be referred, at the choice of the Parties and in accordance with the constitutional procedure of each State either to the Permanent Court of International Justice or to a court of arbitration constituted in accordance with the Convention of October 18th, 1907, for the Pacific Settlement of International Disputes, or to some other court of arbitration.

*Article* 9

At the time of signature or of ratification or of accession, any High Contracting Party may declare that its acceptance of the present Convention does not bind some or all of the territories placed under its sovereignty, jurisdiction, protection, suzerainty or tutelage in respect of all or any provisions of the Convention; it may subsequently accede separately on behalf of any one of them or in respect of any provision to which any one of them is not a party.

*Article* 10

In the event of a High Contracting Party wishing to denounce the present Convention, the denunciation shall be notified in writing to the Secretary-General of the League of Nations, who will at once communicate a certified true copy of the notification to all the other High Contracting Parties, informing them of the date on which it was received.

The denunciation shall only have effect in regard to the notifying State, and one year after the notification has reached the Secretary-General of the League of Nations.

Denunciation may also be made separately in respect of any territory placed under its sovereignty, jurisdiction, protection, suzerainty or tutelage.

*Article* 11

The present Convention, which will bear this day's date and of which the French and English texts are both authentic, will remain open for signature by the States Members of the League of Nations until April 1st, 1927.

The Secretary-General of the League of Nations will subsequently bring the present Convention to the notice of States which have not signed it, including States which are not Members of the League of Nations, and invite them to accede thereto.

A State desiring to accede to the Convention shall notify its intention in writing to the Secretary-General of the League of Nations and transmit to him the instrument of accession, which shall be deposited in the archives of the League.

The Secretary-General shall immediately transmit to all the other High Contracting Parties a certified true copy of the notification and of the instrument of accession, informing them of the date on which he received them.

*Article* 12

The present Convention will be ratified and the instruments of ratification shall be deposited in the office of the Secretary-General of the League of Nations. The Secretary-General will inform all the High Contracting Parties of such deposit.

The Convention will come into operation for each State on the date of the deposit of its ratification or of its accession.

In faith whereof the Plenipotentiaries have signed the present Convention.

DONE at Geneva the twenty-fifth day of September, One thousand nine hundred and twenty-six, in one copy, which will be deposited in the archives of the League of Nations. A certified copy shall be forwarded to each signatory State.

## PROTOCOL AMENDING THE SLAVERY CONVENTION, 1953

The States Parties to the present Protocol,

*Considering* that under the Slavery Convention signed at Geneva on 25 September 1926 (hereinafter called 'the Convention') the League of Nations was invested with certain duties and functions, and

*Considering* that it is expedient that these duties and functions should be continued by the United Nations,

*Have agreed* as follows:

*Article* I

The States Parties to the present Protocol undertake that as between themselves they will, in accordance with the provisions of the Protocol, attribute full legal force and effect to and duly apply the amendments to the Convention set forth in the annex to the Protocol.

*Article* II

1. The present Protocol shall be open for signature or acceptance by any of the States Parties to the Convention to which the Secretary-General has communicated for this purpose a copy of the Protocol.

2. States may become Parties to the present Protocol by:

  *(a)* Signature without reservation as to acceptance;

  *(b)* Signature with reservation as to acceptance, followed by acceptance;

  *(c)* Acceptance.

3. Acceptance shall be effected by the deposit of a formal instrument with the Secretary-General of the United Nations.

*Article* III

1. The present Protocol shall come into force on the date on which two States shall have become Parties thereto, and shall thereafter come into force in respect of each State upon the date on which it becomes a Party to the Protocol.

2. The amendments set forth in the annex to the present Protocol shall come into force when twenty-three States shall have become Parties to the Protocol, and consequently any State becoming a Party to the Convention, after the amendments thereto have come into force, shall become a Party to the Convention as so amended.

*Article* IV

In accordance with paragraph 1 of Article 102 of the Charter of the United Nations and the regulations pursuant thereto adopted by the General Assembly, the Secretary-General of the United Nations is authorized to effect registration of the present Protocol and of the amendments made in the Convention by the Protocol on the respective dates of their entry into force and to publish the Protocol and the amended text of the Convention as soon as possible after registration.

*Article* V

The present Protocol, of which the Chinese, English, French, Russian and Spanish texts are equally authentic, shall be deposited in the archives of the United Nations Secretariat. The texts of the Convention to be amended in accordance with the annex being authentic in the English and French languages only, the English and French texts of the annex shall be equally authentic, and the Chinese, Russian and Spanish texts shall be translations. The Secretary-General shall prepare certified copies of the Protocol, including the annex, for communication to States Parties to the Convention, as well as to all other States Members of the United Nations. He shall likewise prepare for communication to States, including States not Members of the United Nations, upon the entry into force of the amendments as provided in article III, certified copies of the Convention as so amended.

## ANNEX

In article 7 'the Secretary-General of the United Nations' *shall be substituted for* 'the Secretary-General of the League of Nations'.

In article 8 'the International Court of Justice' *shall be substituted for* 'the Permanent Court of International Justice', and 'the Statute of the International Court of Justice' *shall be substituted for* 'the Protocol of December 16th, 1920, relating to the Permanent Court of International Justice'.

In the first and second paragraphs of article 10 'the United Nations' *shall be substituted for* 'the League of Nations'.

The last three paragraphs of article 11 shall be *deleted* and the following *substituted*:

'The present Convention shall be open to accession by all States, including States which are not Members of the United Nations, to which the Secretary-General of the United Nations shall have communicated a certified copy of the Convention.

'Accession shall be effected by the deposit of a formal instrument with the Secretary-General of the United Nations, who shall give notice thereof to all States Parties to the Convention and to all other States contemplated in the present article, informing them of the date on which each such instrument of accession was received in deposit.'

In article 12 'the United Nations' *shall be substituted for* 'the League of Nations'.

## 23. SUPPLEMENTARY CONVENTION ON THE ABOLITION OF SLAVERY, THE SLAVE TRADE, AND INSTITUTIONS AND PRACTICES SIMILAR TO SLAVERY, 1956

The Supplementary Convention was adopted on 7 September 1956 by a United Nations Conference, convened by Economic and Social Council resolution 608(XXI) of 30 April 1956; it entered into force on 30 April 1957. For the text in various languages, see 266 UNTS 3; UK Treaty Series, No. 59 (1957), Cmnd. 257.

For further reference, see Gutteridge, J., 'Supplementary Slavery Convention, 1956', (1957) 6 *ICLQ* 449; Schreiber, M., 'Convention supplémentaire des Nations Unies relative à l'abolition de l'esclavage, la traite des esclaves et des institutions et pratiques analogues à l'esclavage', (1956) 3 *Annuaire français de droit international* 547–57.

*TEXT*

### Preamble

The States Parties to the present Convention
   *Considering* that freedom is the birthright of every human being;
   *Mindful* that the peoples of the United Nations reaffirmed in the Charter their faith in the dignity and worth of the human person;
   *Considering* that the Universal Declaration of Human Rights, proclaimed by the General Assembly of the United Nations as a common standard of achievement for all peoples and all nations, states that no one shall be held in slavery or servitude and that slavery and the slave trade shall be prohibited in all their forms;
   *Recognizing* that, since the conclusion of the Slavery Convention signed at Geneva on 25 September 1926, which was designed to secure the abolition of slavery and of the slave trade, further progress has been made towards this end;
   *Having regard* to the Forced Labour Convention of 1930 and to subsequent action by the International Labour Organization in regard to forced or compulsory labour;
   *Being aware*, however, that slavery, the slave trade and institutions and practices similar to slavery have not yet been eliminated in all parts of the world;
   *Having decided*, therefore, that the Convention of 1926, which remains operative, should now be augmented by the conclusion of a supplementary convention designed to intensify national as well as international efforts towards the abolition of slavery, the slave trade and institutions and practices similar to slavery;
   *Have agreed* as follows:

## SECTION I

## INSTITUTIONS AND PRACTICES SIMILAR TO SLAVERY

*Article* 1

Each of the States Parties to this Convention shall take all practicable and necessary legislative and other measures to bring about progressively and as soon as
possible the complete abolition or abandonment of the following institutions and
practices, where they still exist and whether or not they are covered by the definition of slavery contained in article 1 of the Slavery Convention signed at Geneva
on 25 September 1926:

(a) Debt bondage, that is to say, the status or condition arising from a pledge by
a debtor of his personal services or of those of a person under his control as
security for a debt, if the value of those services as reasonably assessed is not
applied towards the liquidation of the debt or the length and nature of
those services are not respectively limited and defined;

(b) Serfdom, that is to say, the condition or status of a tenant who is by law,
custom or agreement bound to live and labour on land belonging to
another person and to render some determinate service to such other
person, whether for reward or not, and is not free to change his status;

(c) Any institution or practice whereby:

(i) A woman, without the right to refuse, is promised or given in marriage
on payment of a consideration in money or in kind to her parents,
guardian, family or any other person or group; or

(ii) The husband of a woman, his family, or his clan, has the right to
transfer her to another person for value received or otherwise; or

(iii) A woman on the death of her husband is liable to be inherited by
another person;

(d) Any institution or practice whereby a child or young person under the age
of 18 years is delivered by either or both of his natural parents or by his
guardian to another person, whether for reward or not, with a view to the
exploitation of the child or young person or of his labour.

*Article* 2

With a view to bringing to an end the institutions and practices mentioned in
Article 1 (c) of this Convention, the States Parties undertake to prescribe, where
appropriate, suitable minimum ages of marriage, to encourage the use of facilities
whereby the consent of both parties to a marriage may be freely expressed in
the presence of a competent civil or religious authority, and to encourage the
registration of marriages.

## SECTION II

## THE SLAVE TRADE

*Article 3*

1. The act of conveying or attempting to convey slaves from one country to another by whatever means of transport, or of being accessory thereto, shall be a criminal offence under the laws of the States Parties to this Convention and persons convicted thereof shall be liable to very severe penalties.

2. *(a)* The States Parties shall take all effective measures to prevent ships and aircraft authorized to fly their flags from conveying slaves and to punish persons guilty of such acts or of using national flags for that purpose.

   *(b)* The States Parties shall take all effective measures to ensure that their ports, airfields and coasts are not used for the conveyance of slaves.

3. The States Parties to this Convention shall exchange information in order to ensure the practical co-ordination of the measures taken by them in combating the slave trade and shall inform each other of every case of the slave trade, and of every attempt to commit this criminal offence, which comes to their notice.

*Article 4*

Any slave who takes refuge on board any vessel of a State Party to this Convention shall *ipso facto* be free.

## SECTION III

## SLAVERY AND INSTITUTIONS AND PRACTICES SIMILAR TO SLAVERY

*Article 5*

In a country where the abolition or abandonment of slavery, or of the institutions or practices mentioned in Article 1 of this Convention, is not yet complete, the act of mutilating, branding or otherwise marking a slave or a person of servile status in order to indicate his status, or as a punishment, or for any other reason, or of being accessory thereto, shall be a criminal offence under the laws of the States Parties to this Convention and persons convicted thereof shall be liable to punishment.

*Article 6*

1. The act of enslaving another person or of inducing another person to give himself or a person dependent upon him into slavery, or of attempting these acts, or being accessory thereto, or being a party to a conspiracy to accomplish any such acts, shall be a criminal offence under the laws of the States Parties to this Convention and persons convicted thereof shall be liable to punishment.

2. Subject to the provisions of the introductory paragraph of Article 1 of this Convention, the provisions of paragraph 1 of the present article shall also apply to the act of inducing another person to place himself or a person dependent upon him into the servile status resulting from any of the institutions or practices

mentioned in Article 1, to any attempt to perform such acts, to bring accessory thereto, and to being a party to a conspiracy to accomplish any such acts.

## SECTION IV

## DEFINITIONS

*Article* 7

For the purposes of the present Convention:

(a) 'Slavery' means, as defined in the Slavery Convention of 1926, the status or condition of a person over whom any or all of the powers attaching to the right of ownership are exercised, and 'slave' means a person in such condition or status;

(b) 'A person of servile status' means a person in the condition or status resulting from any of the institutions or practices mentioned in Article 1 of this Convention;

(c) 'Slave trade' means and includes all acts involved in the capture, acquisition or disposal of a person with intent to reduce him to slavery; all acts involved in the acquisition of a slave with a view to selling or exchanging him; all acts of disposal by sale of exchange of a person acquired with a view to being sold or exchanged; and, in general, every act of trade or transport in slaves by whatever means of conveyance.

## SECTION V

## CO-OPERATION BETWEEN STATES PARTIES AND COMMUNICATION OF INFORMATION

*Article* 8

1. The States Parties to this Convention undertake to co-operate with each other and with the United Nations to give effect to the foregoing provisions.

2. The Parties undertake to communicate to the Secretary-General of the United Nations copies of any laws, regulations and administrative measures enacted or put into effect to implement the provisions of this Convention.

3. The Secretary-General shall communicate the information received under paragraph 2 of this article to the other Parties and to the Economic and Social Council as part of the documentation for any discussion which the Council might undertake with a view to making further recommendations for the abolition of slavery, the slave trade or the institutions and practices which are the subject of this Convention.

## SECTION VI

## FINAL CLAUSES

*Article* 9

No reservations may be made to this Convention.

*Article* 10

Any dispute between States Parties to this Convention relating to its interpretation or application, which is not settled by negotiation, shall be referred to the International Court of Justice at the request of any one of the parties to the dispute, unless the parties concerned agree on another mode of settlement.

*Article* 11

1. This Convention shall be open until 1 July 1957 for signature by any State Member of the United Nations or of a specialized agency. It shall be subject to ratification by the signatory States, and the instruments of ratification shall be deposited with the Secretary-General of the United Nations, who shall inform each signatory and acceding State.

2. After 1 July 1957 this Convention shall be open for accession by any State Member of the United Nations or of a specialized agency, or by any other State to which an invitation to accede has been addressed by the General Assembly of the United Nations. Accession shall be effected by the deposit of a formal instrument with the Secretary-General of the United Nations, who shall inform each signatory and acceding State.

*Article* 12

1. This Convention shall apply to all non-self-governing, trust, colonial and other non-metropolitan territories for the international relations of which any State Party is responsible; the Party concerned shall, subject to the provisions of paragraph 2 of this article, at the time of signature, ratification or accession declare the non-metropolitan territory or territories to which the Convention shall apply *ipso facto* as a result of such signature, ratification or accession.

2. In any case in which the previous consent of a non-metropolitan territory is required by the constitutional laws or practices of the Party or of the non-metropolitan territory, the Party concerned shall endeavour to secure the needed consent of the non-metropolitan territory within the period of twelve months from the date of signature of the Convention by the metropolitan State, and when such consent has been obtained the Party shall notify the Secretary-General. This Convention shall apply to the territory or territories named in such notification from the date of its receipt by the Secretary-General.

3. After the expiry of the twelve month period mentioned in the preceding paragraph, the States Parties concerned shall inform the Secretary-General of the results of the consultations with those non-metropolitan territories for whose international relations they are responsible and whose consent to the application of this Convention may have been withheld.

*Article* 13

1. This Convention shall enter into force on the date on which two States have become Parties thereto.

2. It shall thereafter enter into force with respect to each State and territory on the date of deposit of the instrument of ratification or accession of that State or notification of application to that territory.

*Article* 14

1. The application of this Convention shall be divided into successive periods of three years, of which the first shall begin on the date of entry into force of the Convention in accordance with paragraph 1 of Article 13.

2. Any State Party may denounce this Convention by a notice addressed by that State to the Secretary-General not less than six months before the expiration of the current three-year period. The Secretary-General shall notify all other Parties of each such notice and the date of the receipt thereof.

3. Denunciations shall take effect at the expiration of the current three-year period.

4. In cases where, in accordance with the provisions of Article 12, this Convention has become applicable to a non-metropolitan territory of a Party, that Party may at any time thereafter, with the consent of the territory concerned, give notice to the Secretary-General of the United Nations denouncing this Convention separately in respect of that territory. The denunciation shall take effect one year after the date of the receipt of such notice by the Secretary-General, who shall notify all other Parties of such notice and the date of the receipt thereof.

*Article* 15

This Convention, of which the Chinese, English, French, Russian and Spanish texts are equally authentic, shall be deposited in the archives of the United Nations Secretariat. The Secretary-General shall prepare a certified copy thereof for communication to States Parties to this Convention, as well as to all other States Members of the United Nations and of the specialized agencies.

In witness whereof the undersigned, being duly authorized thereto by their respective Governments, have signed this Convention on the date appearing opposite their respective signatures.

*Done* at the European Office of the United Nations at Geneva, this seventh day of September one thousand nine hundred and fifty-six.

## 24. CONVENTION RELATING TO THE STATUS OF STATELESS PERSONS, 1960

Statelessness continues to be a very serious problem, but measures to reduce its incidence have not readily found favour with States. The persistence of statelessness has necessitated the creation of a regime which will give stateless persons a stable basis of life in host countries. A Protocol relating to the Status of Stateless Persons was intended also to be adopted by the Conference of Plenipotentiaries which agreed the 1951 Convention relating to the Status of Refugees (above, 112–27), but the matter was deferred to a later conference which met in New York from 13–23 September 1954. The Stateless Persons Convention came into force on 6 June 1960. For the text in various languages, see 360 UNTS 117; UK Treaty Series, Misc. No. 41, 1960, Cmnd. 1098. The text below does not include the Schedule on the issue of travel documents to stateless persons under Article 28, which is similar in many details to that included in the 1951 Convention relating to the Status of Refugees, above 125–7.

For background and further reference, see United Nations, *A Study of Statelessness*, 1949; Weis, P., 'The Status of Stateless Persons', (1961) 10 *ICLQ* 255; Batchelor, C., 'Stateless Persons: Some Gaps in International Protection', (1995) 7 *IJRL* 232; Batchelor, C., 'Statelessness and the Problem of Resolving Nationality Status', 10 *IJRL* 156 (1998). See also the Convention on the Reduction of Statelessness, 1961 (below, 153–9); the European Convention on Nationality, 1997, (below 535–46); and the Declaration of Articles on Nationality of Natural Persons in relation to the Succession of States, 2000 (above, 98–105).

*TEXT*

Preamble

*The High Contracting Parties,*

   *Considering* that the Charter of the United Nations and the Universal Declaration of Human Rights approved on 10 December 1948 by the General Assembly of the United Nations have affirmed the principle that human beings shall enjoy fundamental rights and freedoms without discrimination,

   *Considering* that the United Nations has, on various occasions, manifested its profound concern for stateless persons and endeavoured to assure stateless persons the widest possible exercise of these fundamental rights and freedoms,

   *Considering* that only those stateless persons who are also refugees are covered by the Convention relating to the Status of Refugees of 28 July 1951, and that there are many stateless persons who are not covered by that Convention,

   *Considering* that it is desirable to regulate and improve the status of stateless persons by an international agreement,

   *Have agreed* as follows:

# CHAPTER I

## GENERAL PROVISIONS

*Article 1—Definition of the term 'stateless person'*

1. For the purpose of this Convention, the term 'stateless person' means a person who is not considered as a national by any State under the operation of its law.

2. This Convention shall not apply:

(i) To persons who are at present receiving from organs or agencies of the United Nations other than the United Nations High Commissioner for Refugees protection or assistance so long as they are receiving such protection or assistance;

(ii) To persons who are recognized by the competent authorities of the country in which they have taken residence as having the rights and obligations which are attached to the possession of the nationality of that country;

(iii) To persons with respect to whom there are serious reasons for considering that:

(a) They have committed a crime against peace, a war crime, or a crime against humanity, as defined in the international instruments drawn up to make provisions in respect of such crimes;

(b) They have committed a serious non-political crime outside the country of their residence prior to their admission to that country;

(c) They have been guilty of acts contrary to the purposes and principles of the United Nations.

*Article 2—General obligations*

Every stateless person has duties to the country in which he finds himself, which require in particular that he conform to its laws and regulations as well as to measures taken for the maintenance of public order.

*Article 3—Non-discrimination*

The Contracting States shall apply the provisions of this Convention to stateless persons without discrimination as to race, religion or country of origin.

*Article 4—Religion*

The Contracting States shall accord to stateless persons within their territories treatment at least as favourable as that accorded to their nationals with respect to freedom to practise their religion and freedom as regards the religious education of their children.

*Article 5—Rights granted apart from this Convention*

Nothing in this Convention shall be deemed to impair any rights and benefits granted by a Contracting State to stateless persons apart from this Convention.

*Article 6—The term 'in the same circumstances'*

For the purpose of this Convention, the term ' in the same circumstances' implies that any requirements (including requirements as to length and conditions of sojourn or residence) which the particular individual would have to fulfil for the enjoyment of the right in question, if he were not a stateless person, must be fulfilled by him, with the exception of requirements which by their nature a stateless person is incapable of fulfilling.

*Article 7—Exemption from reciprocity*

1. Except where this Convention contains more favourable provisions, a Contracting State shall accord to stateless persons the same treatment as is accorded to aliens generally.

2. After a period of three years' residence, all stateless persons shall enjoy exemption from legislative reciprocity in the territory of the Contracting States.

3. Each Contracting State shall continue to accord to stateless persons the rights and benefits to which they were already entitled, in the absence of reciprocity, at the date of entry into force of this Convention for that State.

4. The Contracting States shall consider favourably the possibility of according to stateless persons, in the absence of reciprocity, rights and benefits beyond those to which they are entitled according to paragraphs 2 and 3, and to extending exemption from reciprocity to stateless persons who do not fulfil the conditions provided for in paragraphs 2 and 3.

5. The provisions of paragraphs 2 and 3 apply both to the rights and benefits referred to in Articles 13, 18, 19, 21 and 22 of this Convention and to rights and benefits for which this Convention does not provide.

*Article 8—Exemption from exceptional measures*

With regard to exceptional measures which may be taken against the person, property or interests of nationals or former nationals of a foreign State, the Contracting States shall not apply such measures to a stateless person solely on account of his having previously possessed the nationality of the foreign State in question. Contracting States which, under their legislation, are prevented from applying the general principle expressed in this article shall, in appropriate cases, grant exemptions in favour of such stateless persons.

*Article 9—Provisional measures*

Nothing in this Convention shall prevent a Contracting State, in time of war or other grave and exceptional circumstances, from taking provisionally measures which it considers to be essential to the national security in the case of a particular person, pending a determination by the Contracting State that that person is in fact a stateless person and that the continuance of such measures is necessary in his case in the interests of national security.

*Article 10—Continuity of residence*

1. Where a stateless person has been forcibly displaced during the Second World War and removed to the territory of a Contracting State, and is resident there, the period of such enforced sojourn shall be considered to have been lawful residence within that territory.

2. Where a stateless person has been forcibly displaced during the Second World War from the territory of a Contracting State and has, prior to the date of entry

into force of this Convention, returned there for the purpose of taking up residence, the period of residence before and after such enforced displacement shall be regarded as one uninterrupted period for any purposes for which uninterrupted residence is required.

*Article* 11—*Stateless seamen*

In the case of stateless persons regularly serving as crew members on board a ship flying the flag of a Contracting State, that State shall give sympathetic consideration to their establishment on its territory and the issue of travel documents to them or their temporary admission to its territory particularly with a view to facilitating their establishment in another country.


# CHAPTER II

## JURIDICAL STATUS

*Article* 12—*Personal status*

1. The personal status of a stateless person shall be governed by the law of the country of his domicile or, if he has no domicile, by the law of the country of his residence.

2. Rights previously acquired by a stateless person and dependent on personal status, more particularly rights attaching to marriage, shall be respected by a Contracting State, subject to compliance, if this be necessary, with the formalities required by the law of that State, provided that the right in question is one which would have been recognized by the law of that State had he not become stateless.

*Article* 13—*Movable and immovable property*

The Contracting States shall accord to a stateless person treatment as favourable as possible and, in any event, not less favourable than that accorded to aliens generally in the same circumstances, as regards the acquisition of movable and immovable property and other rights pertaining thereto, and to leases and other contracts relating to movable and immovable property.

*Article* 14—*Artistic rights and industrial property*

In respect of the protection of industrial property, such as inventions, designs or models, trade marks, trade names, and of rights in literary, artistic and scientific works, a stateless person shall be accorded in the country in which he has his habitual residence the same protection as is accorded to nationals of that country. In the territory of any other Contracting State, he shall be accorded the same protection as is accorded in that territory to nationals of the country in which he has his habitual residence.

*Article* 15—*Right of association*

As regards non-political and non-profit-making associations and trade unions the Contracting States shall accord to stateless persons lawfully staying in their territory treatment as favourable as possible, and in any event, not less favourable than that accorded to aliens generally in the same circumstances.

*Article 16—Access to courts*

1. A stateless person shall have free access to the courts of law on the territory of all Contracting States.

2. A stateless person shall enjoy in the Contracting State in which he has his habitual residence the same treatment as a national in matters pertaining to access to the courts, including legal assistance and exemption from *cautio judicatum solvi*.

3. A stateless person shall be accorded in the matters referred to in paragraph 2 in countries other than that in which he has his habitual residence the treatment granted to a national of the country of his habitual residence.

## CHAPTER III

## GAINFUL EMPLOYMENT

*Article 17—Wage-earning employment*

1. The Contracting States shall accord to stateless persons lawfully staying in their territory treatment as favourable as possible and, in any event, not less favourable that that accorded to aliens generally in the same circumstances, as regards the right to engage in wage-earning employment.

2. The Contracting States shall give sympathetic consideration to assimilating the rights of all stateless persons with regard to wage-earning employment to those of nationals, and in particular of those stateless persons who have entered their territory pursuant to programmes of labour recruitment or under immigration schemes.

*Article 18—Self-employment*

The Contracting States shall accord to a stateless person lawfully in their territory treatment as favourable as possible and, in any event, not less favourable than that accorded to aliens generally in the same circumstances, as regards the right to engage on his own account in agriculture, industry, handicrafts and commerce and to establish commercial and industrial companies.

*Article 19—Liberal professions*

Each Contracting State shall accord to stateless persons lawfully staying in their territory who hold diplomas recognized by the competent authorities of that State, and who are desirous of practising a liberal profession, treatment as favourable as possible and, in any event, not less favourable than that accorded to aliens generally in the same circumstances.

## CHAPTER IV

## WELFARE

*Article 20—Rationing*

Where a rationing system exists, which applies to the population at large and regulates the general distribution of products in short supply, stateless persons shall be accorded the same treatment as nationals.

*Article 21—Housing*

As regards housing, the Contracting States, in so far as the matter is regulated by laws or regulations or is subject to the control of public authorities, shall accord to stateless persons lawfully staying in their territory treatment as favourable as possible and, in any event, not less favourable than that accorded to aliens generally in the same circumstances.

*Article 22—Public education*

1. The Contracting States shall accord to stateless persons the same treatment as is accorded to nationals with respect to elementary education.

2. The Contracting States shall accord to stateless persons treatment as favourable as possible and, in any event, not less favourable than that accorded to aliens generally in the same circumstances, with respect to education other than elementary education and, in particular, as regards access to studies, the recognition of foreign school certificates, diplomas and degrees, the remission of fees and charges and the award of scholarships.

*Article 23—Public relief*

The Contracting States shall accord to stateless persons lawfully staying in their territory the same treatment with respect to public relief and assistance as is accorded to their nationals.

*Article 24—Labour legislation and social security*

1. The Contracting States shall accord to stateless persons lawfully staying in their territory the same treatment as is accorded to nationals in respect of the following matters:

    *(a)* In so far as such matters are governed by laws or regulations or are subject to the control of administrative authorities; remuneration, including family allowances where these form part of remuneration, hours of work, overtime arrangements, holidays with pay, restrictions on home work, minimum age of employment, apprenticeship and training, women's work and the work of young persons, and the enjoyment of the benefits of collective bargaining;

    *(b)* Social security (legal provisions in respect of employment injury, occupational diseases, maternity, sickness, disability, old age, death, unemployment, family responsibilities and any other contingency which, according to national laws or regulations, is covered by a social security scheme), subject to the following limitations:

(i) There may be appropriate arrangements for the maintenance of acquired rights and rights in course of acquisition;

(ii) National laws or regulations of the country of residence may prescribe special arrangements concerning benefits or portions of benefits which are payable wholly out of public funds, and concerning allowances paid to persons who do not fulfil the contribution conditions prescribed for the award of a normal pension.

2. The right to compensation for the death of a stateless person resulting from employment injury or from occupational disease shall not be affected by the fact that the residence of the beneficiary is outside the territory of the Contracting State.

3. The Contracting States shall extend to stateless persons the benefits of agreements concluded between them, or which may be concluded between them in the future, concerning the maintenance of acquired rights and rights in the process of acquisition in regard to social security, subject only to the conditions which apply to nationals of the States signatory to the agreements in question.

4. The Contracting States will give sympathetic consideration to extending to stateless persons so far as possible the benefits of similar agreements which may at any time be in force between such Contracting States and non-contracting States.

## CHAPTER V

## ADMINISTRATIVE MEASURES

*Article 25—Administrative assistance*

1. When the exercise of a right by a stateless person would normally require the assistance of authorities of a foreign country to whom he cannot have recourse, the Contracting State in whose territory he is residing shall arrange that such assistance be afforded to him by their own authorities.

2. The authority or authorities mentioned in paragraph 1 shall deliver or cause to be delivered under their supervision to stateless persons such documents or certifications as would normally be delivered to aliens by or through their national authorities.

3. Documents or certifications so delivered shall stand in the stead of the official instruments delivered to aliens by or through their national authorities and shall be given credence in the absence of proof to the contrary.

4. Subject to such exceptional treatment as may be granted to indigent persons, fees may be charged for the services mentioned herein, but such fees shall be moderate and commensurate with those charged to nationals for similar services.

5. The provisions of this article shall be without prejudice to Articles 27 and 28.

*Article 26—Freedom of movement*

Each Contracting State shall accord to stateless persons lawfully in its territory the right to choose their place of residence and to move freely within its territory, subject to any regulations applicable to aliens generally in the same circumstances.

*Article 27—Identity papers*

The Contracting States shall issue identity papers to any stateless person in their territory who does not possess a valid travel document.

*Article 28—Travel documents*

The Contracting States shall issue to stateless persons lawfully staying in their territory travel documents for the purpose of travel outside their territory, unless compelling reasons of national security or public order otherwise require, and the provisions of the Schedule to this Convention shall apply with respect to such documents. The Contracting States may issue such a travel document to any other stateless person in their territory; they shall in particular give sympathetic consideration to the issue of such a travel document to stateless persons in their territory who are unable to obtain a travel document from the country of their lawful residence.

*Article 29—Fiscal charges*

1. The Contracting States shall not impose upon stateless persons duties, charges or taxes, of any description whatsoever, other or higher than those which are or may be levied on their nationals in similar situations.

2. Nothing in the above paragraph shall prevent the application to stateless persons of the laws and regulations concerning charges in respect of the issue to aliens of administrative documents including identity papers.

*Article 30—Transfer of assets*

1. A Contracting State shall, in conformity with its laws and regulations, permit stateless persons to transfer assets which they have brought into its territory, to another country where they have been admitted for the purposes of resettlement.

2. A Contracting State shall give sympathetic consideration to the application of stateless persons for permission to transfer assets wherever they may be and which are necessary for their resettlement in another country to which they have been admitted.

*Article 31—Expulsion*

1. The Contracting States shall not expel a stateless person lawfully in their territory save on grounds of national security or public order.

2. The expulsion of such a stateless person shall be only in pursuance of a decision reached in accordance with due process of law. Except where compelling reasons of national security otherwise require, the stateless person shall be allowed to submit evidence to clear himself, and to appeal to and be represented for the purpose before competent authority or a person or persons specially designated by the competent authority.

3. The Contracting States shall allow such a stateless person a reasonable period within which to seek legal admission into another country. The Contracting States reserve the right to apply during that period such internal measures as they may deem necessary.

*Article 32—Naturalization*

The Contracting States shall as far as possible facilitate the assimilation and naturalization of stateless persons. They shall in particular make every effort to expedite naturalization proceedings and to reduce as far as possible the charges and costs of such proceedings.

## CHAPTER VI

## FINAL CLAUSES

*Article 33—Information on national legislation*

The Contracting States shall communicate to the Secretary-General of the United Nations the laws and regulations which they may adopt to ensure the application of this Convention.

*Article 34—Settlement of disputes*

Any dispute between Parties to this Convention relating to its interpretation or application, which cannot be settled by other means, shall be referred to the International Court of Justice at the request of any one of the parties to the dispute.

*Article 35—Signature, ratification and accession*

1. This Convention shall be open for signature at the Headquarters of the United Nations until 31 December 1955.

2. It shall be open for signature on behalf of:

   *(a)* Any State Member of the United Nations;

   *(b)* Any other State invited to attend the United Nations Conference on the Status of Stateless Persons; and

   *(c)* Any State to which an invitation to sign or to accede may be addressed by the General Assembly of the United Nations.

3. It shall be ratified and the instruments of ratification shall be deposited with the Secretary-General of the United Nations.

4. It shall be open for accession by the States referred to in paragraph 2 of this article. Accession shall be effected by the deposit of an instrument of accession with the Secretary-General of the United Nations.

*Article 36—Territorial application clause*

1. Any State may, at the time of signature, ratification or accession, declare that this Convention shall extend to all or any of the territories for the international relations of which it is responsible. Such a declaration shall take effect when the Convention enters into force for the State concerned.

2. At any time thereafter any such extension shall be made by notification addressed to the Secretary-General of the United Nations and shall take effect as from the ninetieth day after the day of receipt by the Secretary-General of the

United Nations of this notification, or as from the date of entry into force of the Convention for the State concerned, whichever is the later.

3. With respect to those territories to which this Convention is not extended at the time of signature, ratification or accession, each State concerned shall consider the possibility of taking the necessary steps in order to extend the application of this Convention to such territories, subject, where necessary for constitutional reasons, to the consent of the Governments of such territories.

## Article 37—Federal clause

In the case of a Federal or non-unitary State, the following provisions shall apply

   (a) With respect to those articles of this Convention that come within the legislative jurisdiction of the federal legislative authority, the obligations of the Federal Government shall to this extent be the same as those of Parties which are not Federal States;

   (b) With respect to those articles of this Convention that come within the legislative jurisdiction of constituent States, provinces or cantons which are not, under the constitutional system of the Federation, bound to take legislative action, the Federal Government shall bring such articles with a favourable recommendation to the notice of the appropriate authorities of States, provinces or cantons at the earliest possible moment;

   (c) A Federal State Party to this Convention shall, at the request of any other Contracting State transmitted through the Secretary-General of the United Nations, supply a statement of the law and practice of the Federation and its constituent units in regard to any particular provision of the Convention showing the extent to which effect has been given to that provision by legislative or other action.

## Article 38—Reservations

1. At the time of signature, ratification or accession, any State may make reservations to articles of the Convention other than to Articles 1, 3, 4, 16 (1) and 33 to 42 inclusive.

2. Any State making a reservation in accordance with paragraph 1 of this article may at any time withdraw the reservation by a communication to that effect addressed to the Secretary-General of the United Nations.

## Article 39—Entry into force

1. This Convention shall come into force on the ninetieth day following the day of deposit of the sixth instrument of ratification or accession.

2. For each State ratifying or acceding to the Convention after the deposit of the sixth instrument of ratification or accession, the Convention shall enter into force on the ninetieth day following the date of deposit by such State of its instrument of ratification or accession.

## Article 40—Denunciation

1. Any Contracting State may denounce this Convention at any time by a notification addressed to the Secretary-General of the United Nations.

2. Such denunciation shall take effect for the Contracting State concerned one

year from the date upon which it is received by the Secretary-General of the United Nations.

3. Any State which has made a declaration or notification under Article 36 may, at any time thereafter, by a notification to the Secretary-General of the United Nations, declare that the Convention shall cease to extend to such territory one year after the date of receipt of the notification by the Secretary-General.

*Article 41—Revision*

1. Any Contracting State may request revision of this Convention at any time by a notification addressed to the Secretary-General of the United Nations.

2. The General Assembly of the United Nations shall recommend the steps, if any, to be taken in respect of such request.

*Article 42—Notifications by the Secretary-General of the United Nations*

The Secretary-General of the United Nations shall inform all Members of the United Nations and non-member States referred to in Article 35:

  *(a)*  Of signatures, ratifications and accessions in accordance with Article 35;

  *(b)*  Of declarations and notifications in accordance with Article 36;

  *(c)*  Of reservations and withdrawals in accordance with Article 38;

  *(d)*  Of the date on which this Convention will come into force in accordance with Article 39;

  *(e)*  Of denunciations and notifications in accordance with Article 40;

  *(f)*  Of request for revision in accordance with Article 41.

*In faith whereof* the undersigned, duly authorized, have signed this Convention on behalf of their respective Governments.

*Done* at New York, this twenty-eighth day of September, one thousand nine hundred and fifty-four, in a single copy, of which the English, French and Spanish texts are equally authentic and which shall remain deposited in the archives of the United Nations, and certified true copies of which shall be delivered to all Members of the United Nations and to the non-member States referred to in Article 35.

[Schedule on travel documents omitted]

## 25. CONVENTION ON THE REDUCTION OF STATELESSNESS, 1961

The Convention was adopted by the UN Conference on the Elimination or Reduction of Future Statelessness, 24 March–18 April 1959 and 15–28 August 1961; it entered into force on 13 December 1975. For the text, see 989 UNTS 175. The Office of the United Nations High Commissioner for Refugees has been appointed to undertake the functions foreseen under Article 11; see General Assembly Resolution 3274 (XXIX), 10 December 1974.

*TEXT*

*The Contracting States,*

*Acting* in pursuance of resolution 896 (IX), adopted by the General Assembly of the United Nations on 4 December 1954,

*Considering* it desirable to reduce statelessness by international agreement,

*Have agreed* as follows:

*Article* 1

1. A Contracting State shall grant its nationality to a person born in its territory who would otherwise be stateless. Such nationality shall be granted:

   (a) At birth, by operation of law, or

   (b) Upon an application being lodged with the appropriate authority, by or on behalf of the person concerned, in the manner prescribed by the national law. Subject to the provisions of paragraph 2 of this article, no such application may be rejected.

A Contracting State which provides for the grant of its nationality in accordance with subparagraph (b) of this paragraph may also provide for the grant of its nationality by operation of law at such age and subject to such conditions as may be prescribed by the national law.

2. A Contracting State may make the grant of its nationality in accordance with subparagraph (b) of paragraph 1 of this article subject to one or more of the following conditions:

   (a) That the application is lodged during a period, fixed by the Contracting State, beginning not later than at the age of eighteen years and ending not earlier than at the age of twenty-one years, so, however, that the person concerned shall be allowed at least one year during which he may himself make the application without having to obtain legal authorization to do so;

   (b) That the person concerned has habitually resided in the territory of the Contracting State for such period as may be fixed by that State, not exceeding five years immediately preceding the lodging of the application nor ten years in all;

   (c) That the person concerned has neither been convicted of an offence against national security nor has been sentenced to imprisonment for a term of five years or more on a criminal charge;

(d)  That the person concerned has always been stateless.

3. Notwithstanding the provisions of paragraphs 1 (b) and 2 of this article, a child born in wedlock in the territory of a Contracting State, whose mother has the nationality of that State, shall acquire at birth that nationality if it otherwise would be stateless.

4. A Contracting State shall grant its nationality to a person who would other-wise be stateless and who is unable to acquire the nationality of the Contracting State in whose territory he was born because he has passed the age for lodging his application or has not fulfilled the required residence conditions, if the nationality of one of his parents at the time of the person's birth was that of the Contracting State first above-mentioned. If his parents did not possess the same nationality at the time of his birth, the question whether the nationality of the person concerned should follow that of the father or that of the mother shall be determined by the national law of such Contracting State. If application for such nationality is required, the application shall be made to the appropriate authority by or on behalf of the applicant in the manner prescribed by the national law. Subject to the provisions of paragraph 5 of this article, such application shall not be refused.

5. The Contracting State may make the grant of its nationality in accordance with the provisions of paragraph 4 of this article subject to one or more of the following conditions:

(a)  That the application is lodged before the applicant reaches an age, being not less than twenty-three years, fixed by the Contracting State;

(b)  That the person concerned has habitually resided in the territory of the Contracting State for such period immediately preceding the lodging of the application, not exceeding three years, as may be fixed by that State;

(c)  That the person concerned has always been stateless.

*Article 2*

A foundling found in the territory of a Contracting State shall, in the absence of proof to the contrary, be considered to have been born within that territory of parents possessing the nationality of that State.

*Article 3*

For the purpose of determining the obligations of Contracting States under this Convention, birth on a ship or in an aircraft shall be deemed to have taken place in the territory of the State whose flag the ship flies or in the territory of the State in which the aircraft is registered, as the case may be.

*Article 4*

1. A Contracting State shall grant its nationality to a person, not born in the territory of a Contracting State, who would otherwise be stateless, if the national-ity of one of his parents at the time of the person's birth was that of that State. If his parents did not possess the same nationality at the time of his birth, the ques-tion whether the nationality of the person concerned should follow that of the father or that of the mother shall be determined by the national law of such

Contracting State. Nationality granted in accordance with the provisions of this paragraph shall be granted:

    *(a)*  At birth, by operation of law, or

    *(b)*  Upon an application being lodged with the appropriate authority, by or on behalf of the person concerned, in the manner prescribed by the national law. Subject to the provisions of paragraph 2 of this article, no such application may be rejected.

2. A Contracting State may make the grant of its nationality in accordance with the provisions of paragraph 1 of this article subject to one or more of the following conditions:

    *(a)*  That the application is lodged before the applicant reaches an age, being not less than twenty-three years, fixed by the Contracting State;

    *(b)*  That the person concerned has habitually resided in the territory of the Contracting State for such period immediately preceding the lodging of the application, not exceeding three years, as may be fixed by that State;

    *(c)*  That the person concerned has not been convicted of an offence against national security;

    *(d)*  That the person concerned has always been stateless.

## Article 5

1. If the law of a Contracting State entails loss of nationality as a consequence of any change in the personal status of a person such as marriage, termination of marriage, legitimation, recognition or adoption, such loss shall be conditional upon possession or acquisition of another nationality.

2. If, under the law of a Contracting State, a child born out of wedlock loses the nationality of that State in consequence of a recognition of affiliation, he shall be given an opportunity to recover that nationality by written application to the appropriate authority, and the conditions governing such application shall not be more rigorous than those laid down in paragraph 2 of Article 1 of this Convention.

## Article 6

If the law of a Contracting State provides for loss of its nationality by a person's spouse or children as a consequence of that person losing or being deprived of that nationality, such loss shall be conditional upon their possession or acquisition of another nationality.

## Article 7

1. *(a)* If the law of a Contracting State entails loss or renunciation of nationality, such renunciation shall not result in loss of nationality unless the person concerned possesses or acquires another nationality;

    *(b)* The provisions of subparagraph (a) of this paragraph shall not apply where their application would be inconsistent with the principles stated in Articles 13 and 14 of the Universal Declaration of Human Rights approved on 10 December 1948 by the General Assembly of the United Nations.

2. A national of a Contracting State who seeks naturalization in a foreign country

shall not lose his nationality unless he acquires or has been accorded assurance of acquiring the nationality of that foreign country.

3. Subject to the provisions of paragraphs 4 and 5 of this article, a national of a Contracting State shall not lose his nationality, so as to become stateless, on the ground of departure, residence abroad, failure to register or on any similar ground.

4. A naturalized person may lose his nationality on account of residence abroad for a period, not less than seven consecutive years, specified by the law of the Contracting State concerned if he fails to declare to the appropriate authority his intention to retain his nationality.

5. In the case of a national of a Contracting State, born outside its territory, the law of that State may make the retention of its nationality after the expiry of one year from his attaining his majority conditional upon residence at that time in the territory of the State or registration with the appropriate authority.

6. Except in the circumstances mentioned in this article, a person shall not lose the nationality of a Contracting State, if such loss would render him stateless, notwithstanding that such loss is not expressly prohibited by any other provision of this Convention.

*Article* 8

1. A Contracting State shall not deprive a person of his nationality if such deprivation would render him stateless.

2. Notwithstanding the provisions of paragraph 1 of this article, a person may be deprived of the nationality of a Contracting State:

> *(a)* In the circumstances in which, under paragraphs 4 and 5 of Article 7, it is permissible that a person should lose his nationality;
>
> *(b)* Where the nationality has been obtained by misrepresentation or fraud.

3. Notwithstanding the provisions of paragraph 1 of this article, a Contracting State may retain the right to deprive a person of his nationality, if at the time of signature, ratification or accession it specifies its retention of such right on one or more of the following grounds, being grounds existing in its national law at that time:

> *(a)* That, inconsistently with his duty of loyalty to the Contracting State, the person:
>> (i) Has, in disregard of an express prohibition by the Contracting State rendered or continued to render services to, or received or continued to receive emoluments from, another State, or
>> (ii) Has conducted himself in a manner seriously prejudicial to the vital interests of the State;
>
> *(b)* That the person has taken an oath, or made a formal declaration, of allegiance to another State, or given definite evidence of his determination to repudiate his allegiance to the Contracting State.

4. A Contracting State shall not exercise a power of deprivation permitted by paragraphs 2 or 3 of this article except in accordance with law, which shall provide for the person concerned the right to a fair hearing by a court or other independent body.

*Article* 9

A Contracting State may not deprive any person or group of persons of their nationality on racial, ethnic, religious or political grounds.

*Article* 10

1. Every treaty between Contracting States providing for the transfer of territory shall include provisions designed to secure that no person shall become stateless as a result of the transfer. A Contracting State shall use its best endeavours to secure that any such treaty made by it with a State which is not a Party to this Convention includes such provisions.

2. In the absence of such provisions a Contracting State to which territory is transferred or which otherwise acquires territory shall confer its nationality on such persons as would otherwise become stateless as a result of the transfer or acquisition.

*Article* 11

The Contracting States shall promote the establishment within the framework of the United Nations, as soon as may be after the deposit of the sixth instrument of ratification or accession, of a body to which a person claiming the benefit of this Convention may apply for the examination of his claim and for assistance in presenting it to the appropriate authority.

*Article* 12

1. In relation to a Contracting State which does not, in accordance with the provisions of paragraph 1 of Article 1 or of Article 4 of this Convention, grant its nationality at birth by operation of law, the provisions of paragraph 1 of Article 1 or of Article 4, as the case may be, shall apply to persons born before as well as to persons born after the entry into force of this Convention.

2. The provisions of paragraph 4 of Article 1 of this Convention shall apply to persons born before as well as to persons born after its entry into force.

3. The provisions of Article 2 of this Convention shall apply only to foundlings found in the territory of a Contracting State after the entry into force of the Convention for that State.

*Article* 13

This Convention shall not be construed as affecting any provisions more conducive to the reduction of statelessness which may be contained in the law of any Contracting State now or hereafter in force, or may be contained in any other convention, treaty or agreement now or hereafter in force between two or more Contracting States.

*Article* 14

Any dispute between Contracting States concerning the interpretation or application of this Convention which cannot be settled by other means shall be submitted to the International Court of Justice at the request of any one of the parties to the dispute.

*Article* 15

1. This Convention shall apply to all non-self-governing, trust, colonial and other non-metropolitan territories for the international relations of which any Contracting State is responsible; the Contracting State concerned shall, subject to the provisions of paragraph 2 of this article, at the time of signature, ratification or accession, declare the non-metropolitan territory or territories to which the Convention shall apply *ipso facto* as a result of such signature, ratification or accession.

2. In any case in which, for the purpose of nationality, a non-metropolitan territory is not treated as one with the metropolitan territory, or in any case in which the previous consent of a non-metropolitan territory is required by the constitutional laws or practices of the Contracting State or of the non-metropolitan territory for the application of the Convention to that territory, that Contracting State shall endeavour to secure the needed consent of the non-metropolitan territory within the period of twelve months from the date of signature of the Convention by that Contracting State, and when such consent has been obtained the Contracting State shall notify the Secretary General of the United Nations. This Convention shall apply to the territory or territories named in such notification from the date of its receipt by the Secretary-General.

3. After the expiry of the twelve-month period mentioned in paragraph 2 of this article, the Contracting States concerned shall inform the Secretary-General of the results of the consultations with those non-metropolitan territories for whose international relations they are responsible and whose consent to the application of this Convention may have been withheld.

*Article* 16

1. This Convention shall be open for signature at the Headquarters of the United Nations from 30 August 1961 to 31 May 1962.

2. This Convention shall be open for signature on behalf of:

   *(a)* Any State Member of the United Nations;
   *(b)* Any other State invited to attend the United Nations Conference on the Elimination or Reduction of Future Statelessness;
   *(c)* Any State to which an invitation to sign or to accede may be addressed by the General Assembly of the United Nations.

3. This Convention shall be ratified and the instruments of ratification shall be deposited with the Secretary-General of the United Nations.

4. This Convention shall be open for accession by the States referred to in paragraph 2 of this article. Accession shall be effected by the deposit of an instrument of accession with the Secretary-General of the United Nations.

*Article* 17

1. At the time of signature, ratification or accession any State may make a reservation in respect of Articles 11, 14 or 15.

2. No other reservations to this Convention shall be admissible.

*Article* 18

1. This Convention shall enter into force two years after the date of the deposit of the sixth instrument of ratification or accession.

2. For each State ratifying or acceding to this Convention after the deposit of the sixth instrument of ratification or accession, it shall enter into force on the ninetieth day after the deposit by such State of its instrument of ratification or accession or on the date on which this Convention enters into force in accordance with the provisions of paragraph 1 of this article, whichever is the later.

*Article* 19

1. Any Contracting State may denounce this Convention at any time by a written notification addressed to the Secretary-General of the United Nations. Such denunciation shall take effect for the Contracting State concerned one year after the date of its receipt by the Secretary-General.

2. In cases where, in accordance with the provisions of Article 15, this Convention has become applicable to a non-metropolitan territory of a Contracting State, that State may at any time thereafter, with the consent of the territory concerned, give notice to the Secretary-General of the United Nations denouncing this Convention separately in respect to that territory. The denunciation shall take effect one year after the date of the receipt of such notice by the Secretary-General, who shall notify all other Contracting States of such notice and the date of receipt thereof.

*Article* 20

1. The Secretary-General of the United Nations shall notify all Members of the United Nations and the non-member States referred to in Article 16 of the following particulars:

   *(a)* Signatures, ratifications and accessions under Article 16;
   *(b)* Reservations under Article 17;
   *(c)* The date upon which this Convention enters into force in pursuance of Article 18;
   *(d)* Denunciations under Article 19.

2. The Secretary-General of the United Nations shall, after the deposit of the sixth instrument of ratification or accession at the latest, bring to the attention of the General Assembly the question of the establishment, in accordance with Article 11, of such a body as therein mentioned.

*Article* 21

This Convention shall be registered by the Secretary-General of the United Nations on the date of its entry into force.

*In witness whereof* the undersigned Plenipotentiaries have signed this Convention.

*Done* at New York, this thirtieth day of August, one thousand nine hundred and sixty-one, in a single copy, of which the Chinese, English, French, Russian and Spanish texts are equally authentic and which shall be deposited in the archives of the United Nations, and certified copies of which shall be delivered by the Secretary-General of the United Nations to all Members of the United Nations and to the non-member States referred to in Article 16 of this Convention.

## 26. INTERNATIONAL CONVENTION ON THE ELIMINATION OF ALL FORMS OF RACIAL DISCRIMINATION, 1966

The great theme which pervades the provisions of the UN Charter and other instruments, both national and international, concerned with human rights and civil liberties, is that of equality. It slowly came to be recognized that racial discrimination and resulting conflict are major issues in world affairs. The Convention, opened for signature on 7 March 1966, was adopted by the General Assembly Resolution 2106 (XX) of 21 December 1965; it entered into force on 4 January 1969. For the text in various languages see 660 UNTS 195; UK Treaty Series, Misc. No. 77, 1969, Cmnd. 4108. The individual complaints procedure under Article 14 is not yet operative.

For further reference see Mason, P., *Patterns of Dominance* (1970); Schwelb, E., 'The International Convention on the Elimination of All Forms of Racial Discrimination' (1966) 15 *ICLQ* 996; Brownlie, I., *Principles of Public International Law* (5th edn, 1998), 602–5; Meron, T., 'The Meaning and Reach of the International Convention on the Elimination of All Forms of Racial Discrimination', 79 *AJIL* 283 (1985); Partsch, K. J., 'The Committee on the Elimination of Racial Discrimination', in Alston, P. (ed.), *The United Nations and Human Rights* (1992), 339–68.

The link between the issue of racial equality and decolonization is established in Resolution 2106 (XX), B, associated with the adoption by the General Assembly of the Convention itself and printed as an annex below. See further Resolution 2547 (XXIV) adopted by the General Assembly on 15 December 1969.

*TEXT*

*The States Parties to this Convention,*

*Considering* that the Charter of the United Nations is based on the principles of the dignity and equality inherent in all human beings, and that all Member States have pledged themselves to take joint and separate action, in co-operation with the Organization, for the achievement of one of the purposes of the United Nations which is to promote and encourage universal respect for and observance of human rights and fundamental freedoms for all, without distinction as to race, sex, language or religion,

*Considering* that the Universal Declaration of Human Rights proclaims that all human beings are born free and equal in dignity and rights and that everyone is entitled to all the rights and freedoms set out therein, without distinction of any kind, in particular as to race, colour or national origin,

*Considering* that all human beings are equal before the law and are entitled to equal protection of the law against any discrimination and against any incitement to discrimination,

*Considering* that the United Nations has condemned colonialism and all practices of segregation and discrimination associated therewith, in whatever form and wherever they exist, and that the Declaration on the Granting of Independence to Colonial Countries and Peoples of 14 December 1960 (General Assembly resolution 1514 (XV)) has affirmed and solemnly proclaimed the necessity of bringing them to a speedy and unconditional end,

*Considering* that the United Nations Declaration on the Elimination of All Forms of Racial Discrimination of 20 November 1963 (General Assembly resolution 1904 (XVIII)) solemnly affirms the necessity of speedily eliminating racial discrimination throughout the world in all its forms and manifestations and of securing understanding of and respect for the dignity of the human person,

*Convinced* that any doctrine of superiority based on racial differentiation is scientifically false, morally condemnable, socially unjust and dangerous, and that there is no justification for racial discrimination, in theory or in practice, anywhere,

*Reaffirming* that discrimination between human beings on the grounds of race, colour or ethnic origin is an obstacle to friendly and peaceful relations among nations and is capable of disturbing peace and security among peoples and the harmony of persons living side by side even within one and the same State,

*Convinced* that the existence of racial barriers is repugnant to the ideals of any human society,

*Alarmed* by manifestations of racial discrimination still in evidence in some areas of the world and by governmental policies based on racial superiority or hatred, such as policies of apartheid, segregation or separation,

*Resolved* to adopt all necessary measures for speedily eliminating racial discrimination in all its forms and manifestations, and to prevent and combat racist doctrines and practices in order to promote understanding between races and to build an international community free from all forms of racial segregation and racial discrimination,

*Bearing in mind* the Convention concerning Discrimination in respect of Employment and Occupation adopted by the International Labour Organization in 1958, and the Convention against Discrimination in Education adopted by the United Nations Educational, Scientific and Cultural Organization in 1960,

*Desiring* to implement the principles embodied in the United Nations Declaration on the Elimination of All Forms of Racial Discrimination and to secure the earliest adoption of practical measures to that end,

*Have agreed* as follows:

## PART I

*Article* 1

1. In this Convention, the term 'racial discrimination' shall mean any distinction, exclusion, restriction or preference based on race, colour, descent, or national or ethnic origin which has the purpose or effect of nullifying or impairing the recognition, enjoyment or exercise, on an equal footing, of human rights and fundamental freedoms in the political, economic, social, cultural or any other field of public life.

2. This Convention shall not apply to distinctions, exclusions, restrictions or preferences made by a State Party to this Convention between citizens and non-citizens.

3. Nothing in this Convention may be interpreted as affecting in any way the legal provisions of States Parties concerning nationality, citizenship or

naturalization, provided that such provisions do not discriminate against any particular nationality.

4. Special measures taken for the sole purpose of securing adequate advancement of certain racial or ethnic groups or individuals requiring such protection as may be necessary in order to ensure such groups or individuals equal enjoyment or exercise of human rights and fundamental freedoms shall not be deemed racial discrimination, provided, however, that such measures do not, as a consequence, lead to the maintenance of separate rights for different racial groups and that they shall not be continued after the objectives for which they were taken have been achieved.

*Article 2*

1. States Parties condemn racial discrimination and undertake to pursue by all appropriate means and without delay a policy of eliminating racial discrimination in all its forms and promoting understanding among all races, and, to this end:

  *(a)* Each State Party undertakes to engage in no act or practice of racial discrimination against persons, groups of persons or institutions and to ensure that all public authorities and public institutions, national and local, shall act in conformity with this obligation;

  *(b)* Each State Party undertakes not to sponsor, defend or support racial discrimination by any persons or organizations;

  *(c)* Each State Party shall take effective measures to review governmental, national and local policies, and to amend, rescind or nullify any laws and regulations which have the effect of creating or perpetuating racial discrimination wherever it exists;

  *(d)* Each State Party shall prohibit and bring to an end, by all appropriate means, including legislation as required by circumstances, racial discrimination by any persons, group or organization;

  *(e)* Each State Party undertakes to encourage, where appropriate, integrationist multiracial organizations and movements and other means of eliminating barriers between races, and to discourage anything which tends to strengthen racial division.

2. States Parties shall, when the circumstances so warrant, take, in the social, economic, cultural and other fields, special and concrete measures to ensure the adequate development and protection of certain racial groups or individuals belonging to them, for the purpose of guaranteeing them the full and equal enjoyment of human rights and fundamental freedoms. These measures shall in no case entail as a consequence the maintenance of unequal or separate rights for different racial groups after the objectives for which they were taken have been achieved.

*Article 3*

States Parties particularly condemn racial segregation and apartheid and undertake to prevent, prohibit and eradicate all practices of this nature in territories under their jurisdiction.

*Article 4*

States Parties condemn all propaganda and all organizations which are based on ideas or theories of superiority of one race or group of persons of one colour or ethnic origin, or which attempt to justify or promote racial hatred and discrimination in any form, and undertake to adopt immediate and positive measures designed to eradicate all incitement to, or acts of, such discrimination and, to this end, with due regard to the principles embodied in the Universal Declaration of Human Rights and the rights expressly set forth in Article 5 of this Convention, *inter alia:*

(a) Shall declare an offence punishable by law all dissemination of ideas based on racial superiority or hatred, incitement to racial discrimination, as well as all acts of violence or incitement to such acts against any race or group of persons of another colour or ethnic origin, and also the provision of any assistance to racist activities, including the financing thereof;

(b) Shall declare illegal and prohibit organizations, and also organized and all other propaganda activities, which promote and incite racial discrimination, and shall recognize participation in such organizations or activities as an offence punishable by law;

(c) Shall not permit public authorities or public institutions, national or local, to promote or incite racial discrimination.

*Article* 5

In compliance with the fundamental obligations laid down in Article 2 of this Convention, States Parties undertake to prohibit and to eliminate racial discrimination in all its forms and to guarantee the right of everyone, without distinction as to race, colour, or national or ethnic origin, to equality before the law, notably in the enjoyment of the following rights:

(a) The right to equal treatment before the tribunals and all other organs administering justice;

(b) The right to security of person and protection by the State against violence or bodily harm, whether inflicted by government officials or by any individual group or institution;

(c) Political rights, in particular the right to participate in elections—to vote and to stand for election—on the basis of universal and equal suffrage, to take part in the Government as well as in the conduct of public affairs at any level and to have equal access to public service;

(d) Other civil rights, in particular:

(i) The right to freedom of movement and residence within the border of the State;

(ii) The right to leave any country, including one's own, and to return to one's country;

(iii) The right to nationality;

(iv) The right to marriage and choice of spouse;

(v) The right to own property alone as well as in association with others;

(vi) The right to inherit;

(vii) The right to freedom of thought, conscience and religion;

(viii) The right to freedom of opinion and expression;

(ix) The right to freedom of peaceful assembly and association;

*(e)* Economic, social and cultural rights, in particular:

(i)   The rights to work, to free choice of employment, to just and favourable conditions of work, to protection against unemployment, to equal
pay for equal work, to just and favourable remuneration;

(ii)  The right to form and join trade unions;

(iii) The right to housing;

(iv)  The right to public health, medical care, social security and social
services;

(v)   The right to education and training;

(vi)  The right to equal participation in cultural activities;

*(f)* The right of access to any place or service intended for use by the general
public, such as transport, hotels, restaurants, cafés, theatres and parks.

*Article* 6

States Parties shall assure to everyone within their jurisdiction effective protection
and remedies, through the competent national tribunals and other State institutions, against any acts of racial discrimination which violate his human rights and
fundamental freedoms contrary to this Convention, as well as the right to seek from
such tribunals just and adequate reparation or satisfaction for any damage suffered
as a result of such discrimination.

*Article* 7

States Parties undertake to adopt immediate and effective measures, particularly in
the fields of teaching, education, culture and information, with a view to combatting prejudices which lead to racial discrimination and to promoting understanding, tolerance and friendship among nations and racial or ethnical groups, as well
as to propagating the purposes and principles of the Charter of the United
Nations, the Universal Declaration of Human Rights, the United Nations
Declaration on the Elimination of All Forms of Racial Discrimination, and this
Convention.

# PART II

*Article* 8

1. There shall be established a Committee on the Elimination of Racial Discrimination (hereinafter referred to as the Committee) consisting of eighteen
experts of high moral standing and acknowledged impartiality elected by States
Parties from among their nationals, who shall serve in their personal capacity,
consideration being given to equitable geographical distribution and to the representation of the different forms of civilization as well as of the principal legal
systems.

2. The members of the Committee shall be elected by secret ballot from a list of
persons nominated by the States Parties. Each State Party may nominate one
person from among its own nationals.

3. The initial election shall be held six months after the date of the entry into force

of this Convention. At least three months before the date of each election the Secretary-General of the United Nations shall address a letter to the States Parties inviting them to submit their nominations within two months. The Secretary-General shall prepare a list in alphabetical order of all persons thus nominated, indicating the States Parties which have nominated them, and shall submit it to the States Parties.

4. Elections of the members of the Committee shall be held at a meeting of States Parties convened by the Secretary-General at United Nations Headquarters. At that meeting, for which two thirds of the States Parties shall constitute a quorum, the persons elected to the Committee shall be nominees who obtain the largest number of votes and an absolute majority of the votes of the representatives of States Parties present and voting.

5. *(a)* The members of the Committee shall be elected for a term of four years. However, the terms of nine of the members elected at the first election shall expire at the end of two years; immediately after the first election the names of these nine members shall be chosen by lot by the Chairman of the Committee;

*(b)* For the filling of casual vacancies, the State Party whose expert has ceased to function as a member of the Committee shall appoint another expert from among its nationals, subject to the approval of the Committee.

6. States Parties shall be responsible for the expenses of the members of the Committee while they are in performance of Committee duties.

*Article* 9

1. States Parties undertake to submit to the Secretary-General of the United Nations, for consideration by the Committee, a report on the legislative, judicial, administrative or other measures which they have adopted and which give effect to the provisions of this Convention:

(a) within one year after the entry into force of the Convention for the State concerned; and

(b) thereafter every two years and whenever the Committee so requests. The Committee may request further information from the States Parties.

2. The Committee shall report annually, through the Secretary-General, to the General Assembly of the United Nations on its activities and may make suggestions and general recommendations based on the examination of the reports and information received from the States Parties. Such suggestions and general recommendations shall be reported to the General Assembly together with comments, if any, from States Parties.

*Article* 10

1. The Committee shall adopt its own rules of procedure.

2. The Committee shall elect its officers for a term of two years.

3. The secretariat of the Committee shall be provided by the Secretary-General of the United Nations.

4. The meetings of the Committee shall normally be held at United Nations Headquarters.

*Article* 11

1. If a State Party considers that another State Party is not giving effect to the provisions of this Convention, it may bring the matter to the attention of the Committee. The Committee shall then transmit the communication to the State Party concerned. Within three months, the receiving State shall submit to the Committee written explanations or statements clarifying the matter and the remedy, if any, that may have been taken by that State.

2. If the matter is not adjusted to the satisfaction of both parties, either by bilateral negotiations or by any other procedure open to them, within six months after the receipt by the receiving State of the initial communication, either State shall have the right to refer the matter again to the Committee by notifying the Committee and also the other State.

3. The Committee shall deal with a matter referred to it in accordance with paragraph 2 of this article after it has ascertained that all available domestic remedies have been invoked and exhausted in the case, in conformity with the generally recognized principles of international law. This shall not be the rule where the application of the remedies is unreasonably prolonged.

4. In any matter referred to it, the Committee may call upon the States Parties concerned to supply any other relevant information.

5. When any matter arising out of this article is being considered by the Committee, the States Parties concerned shall be entitled to send a representative to take part in the proceedings of the Committee, without voting rights, while the matter is under consideration.

*Article* 12

1. *(a)* After the Committee has obtained and collated all the information it deems necessary, the Chairman shall appoint an ad hoc Conciliation Commission (hereinafter referred to as the Commission) comprising five persons who may or may not be members of the Committee. The members of the Commission shall be appointed with the unanimous consent of the parties to the dispute, and its good offices shall be made available to the States concerned with a view to an amicable solution of the matter on the basis of respect for this Convention;

*(b)* If the States parties to the dispute fail to reach agreement within three months on all or part of the composition of the Commission, the members of the Commission not agreed upon by the States parties to the dispute shall be elected by secret ballot by a two-thirds majority vote of the Committee from among its own members.

2. The members of the Commission shall serve in their personal capacity. They shall not be nationals of the States parties to the dispute or of a State not Party to this Convention.

3. The Commission shall elect its own Chairman and adopt its own rules of procedure.

4. The meetings of the Commission shall normally be held at United Nations Headquarters or at any other convenient place as determined by the Commission.

5. The secretariat provided in accordance with Article 10, paragraph 3, of this

Convention shall also service the Commission whenever a dispute among States Parties brings the Commission into being.

6. The States parties to the dispute shall share equally all the expenses of the members of the Commission in accordance with estimates to be provided by the Secretary-General of the United Nations.

7. The Secretary-General shall be empowered to pay the expenses of the members of the Commission, if necessary, before reimbursement by the States parties to the dispute in accordance with paragraph 6 of this article.

8. The information obtained and collated by the Committee shall be made available to the Commission, and the Commission may call upon the States concerned to supply any other relevant information.

*Article* 13

1. When the Commission has fully considered the matter, it shall prepare and submit to the Chairman of the Committee a report embodying its findings on all questions of fact relevant to the issue between the parties and containing such recommendations as it may think proper for the amicable solution of the dispute.

2. The Chairman of the Committee shall communicate the report of the Commission to each of the States parties to the dispute. These States shall, within three months, inform the Chairman of the Committee whether or not they accept the recommendations contained in the report of the Commission.

3. After the period provided for in paragraph 2 of this article, the Chairman of the Committee shall communicate the report of the Commission and the declarations of the States Parties concerned to the other States Parties to this Convention.

*Article* 14

1. A State Party may at any time declare that it recognizes the competence of the Committee to receive and consider communications from individuals or groups of individuals within its jurisdiction claiming to be victims of a violation by that State Party of any of the rights set forth in this Convention. No communication shall be received by the Committee if it concerns a State Party which has not made such a declaration.

2. Any State Party which makes a declaration as provided for in paragraph 1 of this article may establish or indicate a body within its national legal order which shall be competent to receive and consider petitions from individuals and groups of individuals within its jurisdiction who claim to be victims of a violation of any of the rights set forth in this Convention and who have exhausted other available local remedies.

3. A declaration made in accordance with paragraph 1 of this article and the name of any body established or indicated in accordance with paragraph 2 of this article shall be deposited by the State Party concerned with the Secretary-General of the United Nations, who shall transmit copies thereof to the other States Parties. A declaration may be withdrawn at any time by notification to the Secretary-General, but such a withdrawal shall not affect communications pending before the Committee.

4. A register of petitions shall be kept by the body established or indicated in accordance with paragraph 2 of this article, and certified copies of the register

shall be filed annually through appropriate channels with the Secretary-General on the understanding that the contents shall not be publicly disclosed.

5. In the event of failure to obtain satisfaction from the body established or indicated in accordance with paragraph 2 of this article, the petitioner shall have the right to communicate the matter to the Committee within six months.

6. *(a)* The Committee shall confidentially bring any communication referred to it to the attention of the State Party alleged to be violating any provision of this Convention, but the identity of the individual or groups of individuals concerned shall not be revealed without his or their express consent. The Committee shall not receive anonymous communications;

*(b)* Within three months, the receiving State shall submit to the Committee written explanations or statements clarifying the matter and the remedy, if any, that may have been taken by that State.

7. *(a)* The Committee shall consider communications in the light of all information made available to it by the State Party concerned and by the petitioner. The Committee shall not consider any communication from a petitioner unless it has ascertained that the petitioner has exhausted all available domestic remedies. However, this shall not be the rule where the application of the remedies is unreasonably prolonged;

*(b)* The Committee shall forward its suggestions and recommendations, if any, to the State Party concerned and to the petitioner.

8. The Committee shall include in its annual report a summary of such communications and, where appropriate, a summary of the explanations and statements of the States Parties concerned and of its own suggestions and recommendations.

9. The Committee shall be competent to exercise the functions provided for in this article only when at least ten States Parties to this Convention are bound by declarations in accordance with paragraph 1 of this article.

*Article* 15

1. Pending the achievement of the objectives of the Declaration on the Granting of Independence to Colonial Countries and Peoples, contained in General Assembly resolution 1514 (XV) of 14 December 1960, the provisions of this Convention shall in no way limit the right of petition granted to these peoples by other international instruments or by the United Nations and its specialized agencies.

2. *(a)* The Committee established under Article 8, paragraph 1, of this Convention shall receive copies of the petitions from, and submit expressions of opinion and recommendations on these petitions to, the bodies of the United Nations which deal with matters directly related to the principles and objectives of this Convention in their consideration of petitions from the inhabitants of Trust and Non-Self-Governing Territories and all other territories to which General Assembly resolution 1514 (XV) applies, relating to matters covered by this Convention which are before these bodies;

*(b)* The Committee shall receive from the competent bodies of the United Nations copies of the reports concerning the legislative, judicial, administrative or other measures directly related to the principles and objectives of this Convention applied by the administering Powers within the Territories mentioned in subpara-

graph (a) of this paragraph, and shall express opinions and make recommendations to these bodies.

3. The Committee shall include in its report to the General Assembly a summary of the petitions and reports it has received from United Nations bodies, and the expressions of opinion and recommendations of the Committee relating to the said petitions and reports.

4. The Committee shall request from the Secretary-General of the United Nations all information relevant to the objectives of this Convention and available to him regarding the Territories mentioned in paragraph 2 (a) of this article.

*Article* 16

The provisions of this Convention concerning the settlement of disputes or complaints shall be applied without prejudice to other procedures for settling disputes or complaints in the field of discrimination laid down in the constituent instruments of, or conventions adopted by, the United Nations and its specialized agencies, and shall not prevent the States Parties from having recourse to other procedures for settling a dispute in accordance with general or special international agreements in force between them.

## PART III

*Article* 17

1. This Convention is open for signature by any State Member of the United Nations or member of any of its specialized agencies, by any State Party to the Statute of the International Court of Justice, and by any other State which has been invited by the General Assembly of the United Nations to become a Party to this Convention.

2. This Convention is subject to ratification. Instruments of ratification shall be deposited with the Secretary-General of the United Nations.

*Article* 18

1. This Convention shall be open to accession by any State referred to in Article 17, paragraph 1, of the Convention.

2. Accession shall be effected by the deposit of an instrument of accession with the Secretary-General of the United Nations.

*Article* 19

1. This Convention shall enter into force on the thirtieth day after the date of the deposit with the Secretary-General of the United Nations of the twenty-seventh instrument of ratification or instrument of accession.

2. For each State ratifying this Convention or acceding to it after the deposit of the twenty-seventh instrument of ratification or instrument of accession, the Convention shall enter into force on the thirtieth day after the date of the deposit of its own instrument of ratification or instrument of accession.

*Article* 20

1. The Secretary-General of the United Nations shall receive and circulate to all States which are or may become Parties to this Convention reservations made by States at the time of ratification or accession. Any State which objects to the reservation shall, within a period of ninety days from the date of the said communication, notify the Secretary-General that it does not accept it.

2. A reservation incompatible with the object and purpose of this Convention shall not be permitted, nor shall a reservation the effect of which would inhibit the operation of any of the bodies established by this Convention be allowed. A reservation shall be considered incompatible or inhibitive if at least two thirds of the States Parties to this Convention object to it.

3. Reservations may be withdrawn at any time by notification to this effect addressed to the Secretary-General. Such notification shall take effect on the date on which it is received.

*Article* 21

A State Party may denounce this Convention by written notification to the Secretary-General of the United Nations. Denunciation shall take effect one year after the date of receipt of the notification by the Secretary General.

*Article* 22

Any dispute between two or more States Parties with respect to the interpretation or application of this Convention, which is not settled by negotiation or by the procedures expressly provided for in this Convention, shall, at the request of any of the parties to the dispute, be referred to the International Court of Justice for decision, unless the disputants agree to another mode of settlement.

*Article* 23

1. A request for the revision of this Convention may be made at any time by any State Party by means of a notification in writing addressed to the Secretary-General of the United Nations.

2. The General Assembly of the United Nations shall decide upon the steps, if any, to be taken in respect of such a request.

*Article* 24

The Secretary-General of the United Nations shall inform all States referred to in Article 17, paragraph 1, of this Convention of the following particulars:

    *(a)* Signatures, ratifications and accessions under Articles 17 and 18;

    *(b)* The date of entry into force of this Convention under Article 19;

    *(c)* Communications and declarations received under Articles 14, 20 and 23;

    *(d)* Denunciations under Article 21.

*Article* 25

1. This Convention, of which the Chinese, English, French, Russian and Spanish texts are equally authentic, shall be deposited in the archives of the United Nations.

2. The Secretary-General of the United Nations shall transmit certified copies of this Convention to all States belonging to any of the categories mentioned in Article 17, paragraph 1, of the Convention.

## 27. INTERNATIONAL COVENANT ON ECONOMIC, SOCIAL AND CULTURAL RIGHTS, 1966

This appears in the annex to General Assembly Resolution 2200 A (XXI) of 16 December 1966, UN doc. A/6316 (1966). For text in various languages, see 993 UNTS 3; UK Treaty Series No. 6 (1977); Cmnd. 6702. The Covenant entered into force on 3 January 1976, in accordance with Article 27. See generally on the Covenants, Schreiber, M., 'La pratique récente des Nations Unies dans le domaine de la protection des droits de l'homme', 145 *Recueil des cours* (Hague Academy of International Law), 1975–II, 299–398; Alston, P., 'The Committee on Economic and Social Rights', in Alston, P. (ed.), *The United Nations and Human Rights*, 473–508; Craven, M., *The International Covenant on Economic, Social and Cultural Rights* (1995); 1986 Limburg Principles on the Implementation of the International Covenant on Economic, Social and Cultural Rights (1987) 9 *Human Rights Quarterly* 121.

*TEXT*

### Preamble

*The States Parties to the present Covenant,*

*Considering* that, in accordance with the principles proclaimed in the Charter of the United Nations, recognition of the inherent dignity and of the equal and inalienable rights of all members of the human family is the foundation of freedom, justice and peace in the world,

*Recognizing* that these rights derive from the inherent dignity of the human person,

*Recognizing* that, in accordance with the Universal Declaration of Human Rights, the ideal of free human beings enjoying freedom from fear and want can only be achieved if conditions are created whereby everyone may enjoy his economic, social and cultural rights, as well as his civil and political rights,

*Considering* the obligation of States under the Charter of the United Nations to promote universal respect for, and observance of, human rights and freedoms,

*Realizing* that the individual, having duties to other individuals and to the community to which he belongs, is under a responsibility to strive for the promotion and observance of the rights recognized in the present Covenant,

*Agree* upon the following articles:

### PART I

*Article 1*

1. All peoples have the right of self-determination. By virtue of that right they freely determine their political status and freely pursue their economic, social and cultural development.

2. All peoples may, for their own ends, freely dispose of their natural wealth and

resources without prejudice to any obligations arising out of international economic co-operation, based upon the principle of mutual benefit, and international law. In no case may a people be deprived of its own means of subsistence.

3. The States Parties to the present Covenant, including those having responsibility for the administration of Non-Self-Governing and Trust Territories, shall promote the realization of the right of self-determination, and shall respect that right, in conformity with the provisions of the Charter of the United Nations.

# PART II

*Article 2*

1. Each State Party to the present Covenant undertakes to take steps, individually and through international assistance and co-operation, especially economic and technical, to the maximum of its available resources, with a view to achieving progressively the full realization of the rights recognized in the present Covenant by all appropriate means, including particularly the adoption of legislative measures.

2. The States Parties to the present Covenant undertake to guarantee that the rights enunciated in the present Covenant will be exercised without discrimination of any kind as to race, colour, sex, language, religion, political or other opinion, national or social origin, property, birth or other status.

3. Developing countries, with due regard to human rights and their national economy, may determine to what extent they would guarantee the economic rights recognized in the present Covenant to non-nationals.

*Article 3*

The States Parties to the present Covenant undertake to ensure the equal right of men and women to the enjoyment of all economic, social and cultural rights set forth in the present Covenant.

*Article 4*

The States Parties to the present Covenant recognize that, in the enjoyment of those rights provided by the State in conformity with the present Covenant, the State may subject such rights only to such limitations as are determined by law only in so far as this may be compatible with the nature of these rights and solely for the purpose of promoting the general welfare in a democratic society.

*Article 5*

1. Nothing in the present Covenant may be interpreted as implying for any State, group or person any right to engage in any activity or to perform any act aimed at the destruction of any of the rights or freedoms recognized herein, or at their limitation to a greater extent than is provided for in the present Covenant.

2. No restriction upon or derogation from any of the fundamental human rights recognized or existing in any country in virtue of law, conventions, regulations

or custom shall be admitted on the pretext that the present Covenant does not recognize such rights or that it recognizes them to a lesser extent.

# PART III

*Article* 6

1. The States Parties to the present Covenant recognize the right to work, which includes the right of everyone to the opportunity to gain his living by work which he freely chooses or accepts, and will take appropriate steps to safeguard this right.

2. The steps to be taken by a State Party to the present Covenant to achieve the full realization of this right shall include technical and vocational guidance and training programmes, policies and techniques to achieve steady economic, social and cultural development and full and productive employment under conditions safeguarding fundamental political and economic freedoms to the individual.

*Article* 7

The States Parties to the present Covenant recognize the right of everyone to the enjoyment of just and favourable conditions of work which ensure, in particular:

(a) Remuneration which provides all workers, as a minimum, with:
  (i) Fair wages and equal remuneration for work of equal value without distinction of any kind, in particular women being guaranteed conditions of work not inferior to those enjoyed by men, with equal pay for equal work;
  (ii) A decent living for themselves and their families in accordance with the provisions of the present Covenant;

(b) Safe and healthy working conditions;

(c) Equal opportunity for everyone to be promoted in his employment to an appropriate higher level, subject to no considerations other than those of seniority and competence;

(d) Rest, leisure and reasonable limitation of working hours and periodic holidays with pay, as well as remuneration for public holidays.

*Article* 8

1. The States Parties to the present Covenant undertake to ensure:

(a) The right of everyone to form trade unions and join the trade union of his choice, subject only to the rules of the organization concerned, for the promotion and protection of his economic and social interests. No restrictions may be placed on the exercise of this right other than those prescribed by law and which are necessary in a democratic society in the interests of national security or public order or for the protection of the rights and freedoms of others;

(b) The right of trade unions to establish national federations or confederations and the right of the latter to form or join international trade-union organizations;

*(c)* The right of trade unions to function freely subject to no limitations other than those prescribed by law and which are necessary in a democratic society in the interests of national security or public order or for the protection of the rights and freedoms of others;

*(d)* The right to strike, provided that it is exercised in conformity with the laws of the particular country.

2. This article shall not prevent the imposition of lawful restrictions on the exercise of these rights by members of the armed forces or of the police or of the administration of the State.

3. Nothing in this article shall authorize States Parties to the International Labour Organization Convention of 1948 concerning Freedom of Association and Protection of the Right to Organize to take legislative measures which would prejudice, or apply the law in such a manner as would prejudice, the guarantees provided for in that Convention.

*Article* 9

The States Parties to the present Covenant recognize the right of everyone to social security, including social insurance.

*Article* 10

The States Parties to the present Covenant recognize that:

1. The widest possible protection and assistance should be accorded to the family, which is the natural and fundamental group unit of society, particularly for its establishment and while it is responsible for the care and education of dependent children. Marriage must be entered into with the free consent of the intending spouses.

2. Special protection should be accorded to mothers during a reasonable period before and after childbirth. During such period working mothers should be accorded paid leave or leave with adequate social security benefits.

3. Special measures of protection and assistance should be taken on behalf of all children and young persons without any discrimination for reasons of parentage or other conditions. Children and young persons should be protected from economic and social exploitation. Their employment in work harmful to their morals or health or dangerous to life or likely to hamper their normal development should be punishable by law. States should also set age limits below which the paid employment of child labour should be prohibited and punishable by law.

*Article* 11

1. The States Parties to the present Covenant recognize the right of everyone to an adequate standard of living for himself and his family, including adequate food, clothing and housing, and to the continuous improvement of living conditions. The States Parties will take appropriate steps to ensure the realization of this right, recognizing to this effect the essential importance of international co-operation based on free consent.

2. The States Parties to the present Covenant, recognizing the fundamental right of everyone to be free from hunger, shall take, individually and through

international co-operation, the measures, including specific programmes, which are needed:

  (a)  To improve methods of production, conservation and distribution of food by making full use of technical and scientific knowledge, by disseminating knowledge of the principles of nutrition and by developing or reforming agrarian systems in such a way as to achieve the most efficient development and utilization of natural resources;

  (b)  Taking into account the problems of both food-importing and food-exporting countries, to ensure an equitable distribution of world food supplies in relation to need.

*Article* 12

1. The States Parties to the present Covenant recognize the right of everyone to the enjoyment of the highest attainable standard of physical and mental health.

2. The steps to be taken by the States Parties to the present Covenant to achieve the full realization of this right shall include those necessary for:

  (a)  The provision for the reduction of the stillbirth-rate and of infant mortality and for the healthy development of the child;

  (b)  The improvement of all aspects of environmental and industrial hygiene;

  (c)  The prevention, treatment and control of epidemic, endemic, occupational and other diseases;

  (d)  The creation of conditions which would assure to all medical service and medical attention in the event of sickness.

*Article* 13

1. The States Parties to the present Covenant recognize the right of everyone to education. They agree that education shall be directed to the full development of the human personality and the sense of its dignity, and shall strengthen the respect for human rights and fundamental freedoms. They further agree that education shall enable all persons to participate effectively in a free society, promote understanding, tolerance and friendship among all nations and all racial, ethnic or religious groups, and further the activities of the United Nations for the maintenance of peace.

2. The States Parties to the present Covenant recognize that, with a view to achieving the full realization of this right:

  (a)  Primary education shall be compulsory and available free to all;

  (b)  Secondary education in its different forms, including technical and vocational secondary education, shall be made generally available and accessible to all by every appropriate means, and in particular by the progressive introduction of free education;

  (c)  Higher education shall be made equally accessible to all, on the basis of capacity, by every appropriate means, and in particular by the progressive introduction of free education;

  (d)  Fundamental education shall be encouraged or intensified as far as possible for those persons who have not received or completed the whole period of their primary education;

*(e)* The development of a system of schools at all levels shall be actively pursued, an adequate fellowship system shall be established, and the material conditions of teaching staff shall be continuously improved.

3. The States Parties to the present Covenant undertake to have respect for the liberty of parents and, when applicable, legal guardians to choose for their children schools, other than those established by the public authorities, which conform to such minimum educational standards as may be laid down or approved by the State and to ensure the religious and moral education of their children in conformity with their own convictions.

4. No part of this article shall be construed so as to interfere with the liberty of individuals and bodies to establish and direct educational institutions, subject always to the observance of the principles set forth in paragraph 1 of this article and to the requirement that the education given in such institutions shall conform to such minimum standards as may be laid down by the State.

*Article* 14

Each State Party to the present Covenant which, at the time of becoming a Party, has not been able to secure in its metropolitan territory or other territories under its jurisdiction compulsory primary education, free of charge, undertakes, within two years, to work out and adopt a detailed plan of action for the progressive implementation, within a reasonable number of years, to be fixed in the plan, of the principle of compulsory education free of charge for all.

*Article* 15

1. The States Parties to the present Covenant recognize the right of everyone:

*(a)* To take part in cultural life;

*(b)* To enjoy the benefits of scientific progress and its applications;

*(c)* To benefit from the protection of the moral and material interests resulting from any scientific, literary or artistic production of which he is the author.

2. The steps to be taken by the States Parties to the present Covenant to achieve the full realization of this right shall include those necessary for the conservation, the development and the diffusion of science and culture.

3. The States Parties to the present Covenant undertake to respect the freedom indispensable for scientific research and creative activity.

4. The States Parties to the present Covenant recognize the benefits to be derived from the encouragement and development of international contacts and co-operation in the scientific and cultural fields.

## PART IV

*Article* 16

1. The States Parties to the present Covenant undertake to submit in conformity with this part of the Covenant reports on the measures which they have adopted and the progress made in achieving the observance of the rights recognized herein.

2. *(a)* All reports shall be submitted to the Secretary-General of the United Nations, who shall transmit copies to the Economic and Social Council for consideration in accordance with the provisions of the present Covenant;

*(b)* The Secretary-General of the United Nations shall also transmit to the specialized agencies copies of the reports, or any relevant parts therefrom, from States Parties to the present Covenant which are also members of these specialized agencies in so far as these reports, or parts therefrom, relate to any matters which fall within the responsibilities of the said agencies in accordance with their constitutional instruments.

*Article* 17

1. The States Parties to the present Covenant shall furnish their reports in stages, in accordance with a programme to be established by the Economic and Social Council within one year of the entry into force of the present Covenant after consultation with the States Parties and the specialized agencies concerned.

2. Reports may indicate factors and difficulties affecting the degree of fulfilment of obligations under the present Covenant.

3. Where relevant information has previously been furnished to the United Nations or to any specialized agency by any State Party to the present Covenant, it will not be necessary to reproduce that information, but a precise reference to the information so furnished will suffice.

*Article* 18

Pursuant to its responsibilities under the Charter of the United Nations in the field of human rights and fundamental freedoms, the Economic and Social Council may make arrangements with the specialized agencies in respect of their reporting to it on the progress made in achieving the observance of the provisions of the present Covenant falling within the scope of their activities. These reports may include particulars of decisions and recommendations on such implementation adopted by their competent organs.

*Article* 19

The Economic and Social Council may transmit to the Commission on Human Rights for study and general recommendation or, as appropriate, for information the reports concerning human rights submitted by States in accordance with Articles 16 and 17, and those concerning human rights submitted by the specialized agencies in accordance with Article 18.

*Article* 20

The States Parties to the present Covenant and the specialized agencies concerned may submit comments to the Economic and Social Council on any general recommendation under Article 19 or reference to such general recommendation in any report of the Commission on Human Rights or any documentation referred to therein.

*Article* 21

The Economic and Social Council may submit from time to time to the General

Assembly reports with recommendations of a general nature and a summary of the information received from the States Parties to the present Covenant and the specialized agencies on the measures taken and the progress made in achieving general observance of the rights recognized in the present Covenant.

*Article* 22

The Economic and Social Council may bring to the attention of other organs of the United Nations, their subsidiary organs and specialized agencies concerned with furnishing technical assistance any matters arising out of the reports referred to in this part of the present Covenant which may assist such bodies in deciding, each within its field of competence, on the advisability of international measures likely to contribute to the effective progressive implementation of the present Covenant.

*Article* 23

The States Parties to the present Covenant agree that international action for the achievement of the rights recognized in the present Covenant includes such methods as the conclusion of conventions, the adoption of recommendations, the furnishing of technical assistance and the holding of regional meetings and technical meetings for the purpose of consultation and study organized in conjunction with the Governments concerned.

*Article* 24

Nothing in the present Covenant shall be interpreted as impairing the provisions of the Charter of the United Nations and of the constitutions of the specialized agencies which define the respective responsibilities of the various organs of the United Nations and of the specialized agencies in regard to the matters dealt with in the present Covenant.

*Article* 25

Nothing in the present Covenant shall be interpreted as impairing the inherent right of all peoples to enjoy and utilize fully and freely their natural wealth and resources.

# PART V

*Article* 26

1. The present Covenant is open for signature by any State Member of the United Nations or member of any of its specialized agencies, by any State Party to the Statute of the International Court of Justice, and by any other State which has been invited by the General Assembly of the United Nations to become a party to the present Covenant.

2. The present Covenant is subject to ratification. Instruments of ratification shall be deposited with the Secretary-General of the United Nations.

3. The present Covenant shall be open to accession by any State referred to in paragraph 1 of this article.

4. Accession shall be effected by the deposit of an instrument of accession with the Secretary-General of the United Nations.

5. The Secretary-General of the United Nations shall inform all States which have signed the present Covenant or acceded to it of the deposit of each instrument of ratification or accession.

*Article* 27

1. The present Covenant shall enter into force three months after the date of the deposit with the Secretary-General of the United Nations of the thirty-fifth instrument of ratification or instrument of accession.

2. For each State ratifying the present Covenant or acceding to it after the deposit of the thirty-fifth instrument of ratification or instrument of accession, the present Covenant shall enter into force three months after the date of the deposit of its own instrument of ratification or instrument of accession.

*Article* 28

The provisions of the present Covenant shall extend to all parts of federal States without any limitations or exceptions.

*Article* 29

1. Any State Party to the present Covenant may propose an amendment and file it with the Secretary-General of the United Nations. The Secretary-General shall thereupon communicate any proposed amendments to the States Parties to the present Covenant with a request that they notify him whether they favour a conference of States Parties for the purpose of considering and voting upon the proposals. In the event that at least one third of the States Parties favours such a conference, the Secretary-General shall convene the conference under the auspices of the United Nations. Any amendment adopted by a majority of the States Parties present and voting at the conference shall be submitted to the General Assembly of the United Nations for approval.

2. Amendments shall come into force when they have been approved by the General Assembly of the United Nations and accepted by a two-thirds majority of the States Parties to the present Covenant in accordance with their respective constitutional processes.

3. When amendments come into force they shall be binding on those States Parties which have accepted them, other States Parties still being bound by the provisions of the present Covenant and any earlier amendment which they have accepted.

*Article* 30

Irrespective of the notifications made under Article 26, paragraph 5, the Secretary-General of the United Nations shall inform all States referred to in paragraph 1 of the same article of the following particulars:

    *(a)* Signatures, ratifications and accessions under Article 26;

    *(b)* The date of the entry into force of the present Covenant under Article 27 and the date of the entry into force of any amendments under Article 29.

*Article* 31

1. The present Covenant, of which the Chinese, English, French, Russian and Spanish texts are equally authentic, shall be deposited in the archives of the United Nations.

2. The Secretary-General of the United Nations shall transmit certified copies of the present Covenant to all States referred to in Article 26.

# 28. INTERNATIONAL COVENANT ON CIVIL AND POLITICAL RIGHTS, 1966

This was adopted at the same time as the last Covenant, and entered into force on 23 March 1976; see General Assembly Resolution 2200A (XXI), UN doc. A/6316 (1966). For the text in various languages, see 999 UNTS 171; UK Treaty Series No. 6 (1977); Cmnd. 6702.

With respect to inter-State complaints under the optional procedure provided for in Article 41, there is an overlap with the procedure under the European Convention on Human Rights, below. However, unlike its European counterpart, the Covenant provision has not so far been employed.

Generally, see Joseph, S., Schultz, J., & Castan, M., *The International Covenant on Civil and Political Rights, Cases, Materials, and Commentary* (2000); Nowak, M., *UN Covenant on Civil and Political Rights, CCPR Commentary* (1990); Opsahl, T. 'The Human Rights Committee,' in Alston, P. (ed.), *The United Nations and Human Rights* (1992), 369–443; Schwelb, E., 'Civil and Political Rights: The International Measures of Implementation', 62 *AJIL* 827–68 (1968).

## TEXT

## Preamble

*The States Parties to the present Covenant,*

*Considering* that, in accordance with the principles proclaimed in the Charter of the United Nations, recognition of the inherent dignity and of the equal and inalienable rights of all members of the human family is the foundation of freedom, justice and peace in the world,

*Recognizing* that these rights derive from the inherent dignity of the human person,

*Recognizing* that, in accordance with the Universal Declaration of Human Rights, the ideal of free human beings enjoying civil and political freedom and freedom from fear and want can only be achieved if conditions are created whereby everyone may enjoy his civil and political rights, as well as his economic, social and cultural rights,

*Considering* the obligation of States under the Charter of the United Nations to promote universal respect for, and observance of, human rights and freedoms,

*Realizing* that the individual, having duties to other individuals and to the community to which he belongs, is under a responsibility to strive for the promotion and observance of the rights recognized in the present Covenant,

*Agree* upon the following articles:

## PART I

*Article 1*

1. All peoples have the right of self-determination. By virtue of that right they freely determine their political status and freely pursue their economic, social and cultural development.

2. All peoples may, for their own ends, freely dispose of their natural wealth and resources without prejudice to any obligations arising out of international economic co-operation, based upon the principle of mutual benefit, and international law. In no case may a people be deprived of its own means of subsistence.

3. The States Parties to the present Covenant, including those having responsibility for the administration of Non-Self-Governing and Trust Territories, shall promote the realization of the right of self-determination, and shall respect that right, in conformity with the provisions of the Charter of the United Nations.

# PART II

*Article 2*

1. Each State Party to the present Covenant undertakes to respect and to ensure to all individuals within its territory and subject to its jurisdiction the rights recognized in the present Covenant, without distinction of any kind, such as race, colour, sex, language, religion, political or other opinion, national or social origin, property, birth or other status.

2. Where not already provided for by existing legislative or other measures, each State Party to the present Covenant undertakes to take the necessary steps, in accordance with its constitutional processes and with the provisions of the present Covenant, to adopt such legislative or other measures as may be necessary to give effect to the rights recognized in the present Covenant.

3. Each State Party to the present Covenant undertakes:

   *(a)* To ensure that any person whose rights or freedoms as herein recognized are violated shall have an effective remedy, notwithstanding that the violation has been committed by persons acting in an official capacity;

   *(b)* To ensure that any person claiming such a remedy shall have his right thereto determined by competent judicial, administrative or legislative authorities, or by any other competent authority provided for by the legal system of the State, and to develop the possibilities of judicial remedy;

   *(c)* To ensure that the competent authorities shall enforce such remedies when granted.

*Article 3*

The States Parties to the present Covenant undertake to ensure the equal right of men and women to the enjoyment of all civil and political rights set forth in the present Covenant.

*Article 4*

1. In time of public emergency which threatens the life of the nation and the existence of which is officially proclaimed, the States Parties to the present Covenant may take measures derogating from their obligations under the present Covenant to the extent strictly required by the exigencies of the situation, provided that such measures are not inconsistent with their other obligations under

international law and do not involve discrimination solely on the ground of race, colour, sex, language, religion or social origin.

2. No derogation from Articles 6, 7, 8 (paragraphs 1 and 2), 11, 15, 16 and 18 may be made under this provision.

3. Any State Party to the present Covenant availing itself of the right of deroga-tion shall immediately inform the other States Parties to the present Covenant, through the intermediary of the Secretary-General of the United Nations, of the provisions from which it has derogated and of the reasons by which it was actuated. A further communication shall be made, through the same intermediary, on the date on which it terminates such derogation.

*Article 5*

1. Nothing in the present Covenant may be interpreted as implying for any State, group or person any right to engage in any activity or perform any act aimed at the destruction of any of the rights and freedoms recognized herein or at their limitation to a greater extent than is provided for in the present Covenant.

2. There shall be no restriction upon or derogation from any of the fundamental human rights recognized or existing in any State Party to the present Covenant pursuant to law, conventions, regulations or custom on the pretext that the present Covenant does not recognize such rights or that it recognizes them to a lesser extent.

# PART III

*Article 6*

1. Every human being has the inherent right to life. This right shall be protected by law. No one shall be arbitrarily deprived of his life.

2. In countries which have not abolished the death penalty, sentence of death may be imposed only for the most serious crimes in accordance with the law in force at the time of the commission of the crime and not contrary to the provisions of the present Covenant and to the Convention on the Prevention and Punishment of the Crime of Genocide. This penalty can only be carried out pursuant to a final judgment rendered by a competent court.

3. When deprivation of life constitutes the crime of genocide, it is understood that nothing in this article shall authorize any State Party to the present Covenant to derogate in any way from any obligation assumed under the provisions of the Convention on the Prevention and Punishment of the Crime of Genocide.

4. Anyone sentenced to death shall have the right to seek pardon or commutation of the sentence. Amnesty, pardon or commutation of the sentence of death may be granted in all cases.

5. Sentence of death shall not be imposed for crimes committed by persons below eighteen years of age and shall not be carried out on pregnant women.

6. Nothing in this article shall be invoked to delay or to prevent the abolition of capital punishment by any State Party to the present Covenant.

*Article* 7

No one shall be subjected to torture or to cruel, inhuman or degrading treatment or punishment. In particular, no one shall be subjected without his free consent to medical or scientific experimentation.

*Article* 8

1. No one shall be held in slavery; slavery and the slave-trade in all their forms shall be prohibited.

2. No one shall be held in servitude.

3. *(a)* No one shall be required to perform forced or compulsory labour;

    *(b)* Paragraph 3 *(a)* shall not be held to preclude, in countries where imprisonment with hard labour may be imposed as a punishment for a crime, the performance of hard labour in pursuance of a sentence to such punishment by a competent court;

    *(c)* For the purpose of this paragraph the term 'forced or compulsory labour' shall not include:

        (i) Any work or service, not referred to in subparagraph (b), normally required of a person who is under detention in consequence of a lawful order of a court, or of a person during conditional release from such detention;

        (ii) Any service of a military character and, in countries where conscientious objection is recognized, any national service required by law of conscientious objectors;

        (iii) Any service exacted in cases of emergency or calamity threatening the life or well-being of the community;

        (iv) Any work or service which forms part of normal civil obligations.

*Article* 9

1. Everyone has the right to liberty and security of person. No one shall be subjected to arbitrary arrest or detention. No one shall be deprived of his liberty except on such grounds and in accordance with such procedure as are established by law.

2. Anyone who is arrested shall be informed, at the time of arrest, of the reasons for his arrest and shall be promptly informed of any charges against him.

3. Anyone arrested or detained on a criminal charge shall be brought promptly before a judge or other officer authorized by law to exercise judicial power and shall be entitled to trial within a reasonable time or to release. It shall not be the general rule that persons awaiting trial shall be detained in custody, but release may be subject to guarantees to appear for trial, at any other stage of the judicial proceedings, and, should occasion arise, for execution of the judgment.

4. Anyone who is deprived of his liberty by arrest or detention shall be entitled to take proceedings before a court, in order that court may decide without delay on the lawfulness of his detention and order his release if the detention is not lawful.

5. Anyone who has been the victim of unlawful arrest or detention shall have an enforceable right to compensation.

*Article* 10

1. All persons deprived of their liberty shall be treated with humanity and with respect for the inherent dignity of the human person.

2. *(a)* Accused persons shall, save in exceptional circumstances, be segregated from convicted persons and shall be subject to separate treatment appropriate to their status as unconvicted persons;

*(b)* Accused juvenile persons shall be separated from adults and brought as speedily as possible for adjudication.

3. The penitentiary system shall comprise treatment of prisoners the essential aim of which shall be their reformation and social rehabilitation. Juvenile offenders shall be segregated from adults and be accorded treatment appropriate to their age and legal status.

*Article* 11

No one shall be imprisoned merely on the ground of inability to fulfil a contractual obligation.

*Article* 12

1. Everyone lawfully within the territory of a State shall, within that territory, have the right to liberty of movement and freedom to choose his residence.

2. Everyone shall be free to leave any country, including his own.

3. The above-mentioned rights shall not be subject to any restrictions except those which are provided by law, are necessary to protect national security, public order (*ordre public*), public health or morals or the rights and freedoms of others, and are consistent with the other rights recognized in the present Covenant.

4. No one shall be arbitrarily deprived of the right to enter his own country.

*Article* 13

An alien lawfully in the territory of a State Party to the present Covenant may be expelled therefrom only in pursuance of a decision reached in accordance with law and shall, except where compelling reasons of national security otherwise require, be allowed to submit the reasons against his expulsion and to have his case reviewed by, and be represented for the purpose before, the competent authority or a person or persons especially designated by the competent authority.

*Article* 14

1. All persons shall be equal before the courts and tribunals. In the determination of any criminal charge against him, or of his rights and obligations in a suit at law, everyone shall be entitled to a fair and public hearing by a competent, independent and impartial tribunal established by law. The press and the public may be excluded from all or part of a trial for reasons of morals, public order (*ordre public*) or national security in a democratic society, or when the interest of the private lives of the parties so requires, or to the extent strictly necessary in the opinion of the court in special circumstances where publicity would prejudice the interests of justice; but any judgment rendered in a criminal case or in a suit at law shall be made public except where the interest of juvenile persons otherwise requires or the proceedings concern matrimonial disputes or the guardianship of children.

2. Everyone charged with a criminal offence shall have the right to be presumed innocent until proved guilty according to law.

3. In the determination of any criminal charge against him, everyone shall be entitled to the following minimum guarantees, in full equality:

(a) To be informed promptly and in detail in a language which he understands of the nature and cause of the charge against him;

(b) To have adequate time and facilities for the preparation of his defence and to communicate with counsel of his own choosing;

(c) To be tried without undue delay;

(d) To be tried in his presence, and to defend himself in person or through legal assistance of his own choosing; to be informed, if he does not have legal assistance, of this right; and to have legal assistance assigned to him, in any case where the interests of justice so require, and without payment by him in any such case if he does not have sufficient means to pay for it;

(e) To examine, or have examined, the witnesses against him and to obtain the attendance and examination of witnesses on his behalf under the same conditions as witnesses against him;

(f) To have the free assistance of an interpreter if he cannot understand or speak the language used in court;

(g) Not to be compelled to testify against himself or to confess guilt.

4. In the case of juvenile persons, the procedure shall be such as will take account of their age and the desirability of promoting their rehabilitation.

5. Everyone convicted of a crime shall have the right to his conviction and sentence being reviewed by a higher tribunal according to law.

6. When a person has by a final decision been convicted of a criminal offence and when subsequently his conviction has been reversed or he has been pardoned on the ground that a new or newly discovered fact shows conclusively that there has been a miscarriage of justice, the person who has suffered punishment as a result of such conviction shall be compensated according to law, unless it is proved that the non-disclosure of the unknown fact in time is wholly or partly attributable to him.

7. No one shall be liable to be tried or punished again for an offence for which he has already been finally convicted or acquitted in accordance with the law and penal procedure of each country.

*Article* 15

1. No one shall be held guilty of any criminal offence on account of any act or omission which did not constitute a criminal offence, under national or international law, at the time when it was committed. Nor shall a heavier penalty be imposed than the one that was applicable at the time when the criminal offence was committed. If, subsequent to the commission of the offence, provision is made by law for the imposition of the lighter penalty, the offender shall benefit thereby.

2. Nothing in this article shall prejudice the trial and punishment of any person for any act or omission which, at the time when it was committed, was criminal according to the general principles of law recognized by the community of nations.

*Article* 16

Everyone shall have the right to recognition everywhere as a person before the law.

*Article* 17

1. No one shall be subjected to arbitrary or unlawful interference with his privacy, family, home or correspondence, nor to unlawful attacks on his honour and reputation.

2. Everyone has the right to the protection of the law against such interference or attacks.

*Article* 18

1. Everyone shall have the right to freedom of thought, conscience and religion. This right shall include freedom to have or to adopt a religion or belief of his choice, and freedom, either individually or in community with others and in public or private, to manifest his religion or belief in worship, observance, practice and teaching.

2. No one shall be subject to coercion which would impair his freedom to have or to adopt a religion or belief of his choice.

3. Freedom to manifest one's religion or beliefs may be subject only to such limitations as are prescribed by law and are necessary to protect public safety, order, health, or morals or the fundamental rights and freedoms of others.

4. The States Parties to the present Covenant undertake to have respect for the liberty of parents and, when applicable, legal guardians to ensure the religious and moral education of their children in conformity with their own convictions.

*Article* 19

1. Everyone shall have the right to hold opinions without interference.

2. Everyone shall have the right to freedom of expression; this right shall include freedom to seek, receive and impart information and ideas of all kinds, regardless of frontiers, either orally, in writing or in print, in the form of art, or through any other media of his choice.

3. The exercise of the rights provided for in paragraph 2 of this article carries with it special duties and responsibilities. It may therefore be subject to certain restrictions, but these shall only be such as are provided by law and are necessary:

    *(a)* For respect of the rights or reputations of others;

    *(b)* For the protection of national security or of public order (*ordre public*), or of public health or morals.

*Article* 20

1. Any propaganda for war shall be prohibited by law.

2. Any advocacy of national, racial or religious hatred that constitutes incitement to discrimination, hostility or violence shall be prohibited by law.

*Article* 21

The right of peaceful assembly shall be recognized. No restrictions may be placed on the exercise of this right other than those imposed in conformity with the law and which are necessary in a democratic society in the interests of national security or public safety, public order (*ordre public*), the protection of public health or morals or the protection of the rights and freedoms of others.

*Article 22*

1. Everyone shall have the right to freedom of association with others, including the right to form and join trade unions for the protection of his interests.

2. No restrictions may be placed on the exercise of this right other than those which are prescribed by law and which are necessary in a democratic society in the interests of national security or public safety, public order (*ordre public*), the protection of public health or morals or the protection of the rights and freedoms of others. This article shall not prevent the imposition of lawful restrictions on members of the armed forces and of the police in their exercise of this right.

3. Nothing in this article shall authorize States Parties to the International Labour Organization Convention of 1948 concerning Freedom of Association and Protection of the Right to Organize to take legislative measures which would prejudice, or to apply the law in such a manner as to prejudice, the guarantees provided for in that Convention.

*Article 23*

1. The family is the natural and fundamental group unit of society and is entitled to protection by society and the State.

2. The right of men and women of marriageable age to marry and to found a family shall be recognized.

3. No marriage shall be entered into without the free and full consent of the intending spouses.

4. States Parties to the present Covenant shall take appropriate steps to ensure equality of rights and responsibilities of spouses as to marriage, during marriage and at its dissolution. In the case of dissolution, provision shall be made for the necessary protection of any children.

*Article 24*

1. Every child shall have, without any discrimination as to race, colour, sex, language, religion, national or social origin, property or birth, the right to such measures of protection as are required by his status as a minor, on the part of his family, society and the State.

2. Every child shall be registered immediately after birth and shall have a name.

3. Every child has the right to acquire a nationality.

*Article 25*

Every citizen shall have the right and the opportunity, without any of the distinctions mentioned in Article 2 and without unreasonable restrictions:

   (a) To take part in the conduct of public affairs, directly or through freely chosen representatives;

   (b) To vote and to be elected at genuine periodic elections which shall be by universal and equal suffrage and shall be held by secret ballot, guaranteeing the free expression of the will of the electors;

(c)  To have access, on general terms of equality, to public service in his country.

*Article* 26

All persons are equal before the law and are entitled without any discrimination to the equal protection of the law. In this respect, the law shall prohibit any discrimination and guarantee to all persons equal and effective protection against discrimination on any ground such as race, colour, sex, language, religion, political or other opinion, national or social origin, property, birth or other status.

*Article* 27

In those States in which ethnic, religious or linguistic minorities exist, persons belonging to such minorities shall not be denied the right, in community with the other members of their group, to enjoy their own culture, to profess and practise their own religion, or to use their own language.

# PART IV

*Article* 28

1.  There shall be established a Human Rights Committee (hereafter referred to in the present Covenant as the Committee). It shall consist of eighteen members and shall carry out the functions hereinafter provided.

2.  The Committee shall be composed of nationals of the States Parties to the present Covenant who shall be persons of high moral character and recognized competence in the field of human rights, consideration being given to the usefulness of the participation of some persons having legal experience.

3.  The members of the Committee shall be elected and shall serve in their personal capacity.

*Article* 29

1.  The members of the Committee shall be elected by secret ballot from a list of persons possessing the qualifications prescribed in Article 28 and nominated for the purpose by the States Parties to the present Covenant.

2.  Each State Party to the present Covenant may nominate not more than two persons. These persons shall be nationals of the nominating State.

3.  A person shall be eligible for renomination.

*Article* 30

1.  The initial election shall be held no later than six months after the date of the entry into force of the present Covenant.

2.  At least four months before the date of each election to the Committee, other than an election to fill a vacancy declared in accordance with Article 34, the Secretary-General of the United Nations shall address a written invitation to the

States Parties to the present Covenant to submit their nominations for membership of the Committee within three months.

3. The Secretary-General of the United Nations shall prepare a list in alphabetical order of all the persons thus nominated, with an indication of the States Parties which have nominated them, and shall submit it to the States Parties to the present Covenant no later than one month before the date of each election.

4. Elections of the members of the Committee shall be held at a meeting of the States Parties to the present Covenant convened by the Secretary-General of the United Nations at the Headquarters of the United Nations. At that meeting, for which two thirds of the States Parties to the present Covenant shall constitute a quorum, the persons elected to the Committee shall be those nominees who obtain the largest number of votes and an absolute majority of the votes of the representatives of States Parties present and voting.

*Article* 31

1. The Committee may not include more than one national of the same State.

2. In the election of the Committee, consideration shall be given to equitable geographical distribution of membership and to the representation of the different forms of civilization and of the principal legal systems.

*Article* 32

1. The members of the Committee shall be elected for a term of four years. They shall be eligible for re-election if renominated. However, the terms of nine of the members elected at the first election shall expire at the end of two years; immediately after the first election, the names of these nine members shall be chosen by lot by the Chairman of the meeting referred to in Article 30, paragraph 4.

2. Elections at the expiry of office shall be held in accordance with the preceding articles of this part of the present Covenant.

*Article* 33

1. If, in the unanimous opinion of the other members, a member of the Committee has ceased to carry out his functions for any cause other than absence of a temporary character, the Chairman of the Committee shall notify the Secretary-General of the United Nations, who shall then declare the seat of that member to be vacant.

2. In the event of the death or the resignation of a member of the Committee, the Chairman shall immediately notify the Secretary-General of the United Nations, who shall declare the seat vacant from the date of death or the date on which the resignation takes effect.

*Article* 34

1. When a vacancy is declared in accordance with Article 33 and if the term of office of the member to be replaced does not expire within six months of the declaration of the vacancy, the Secretary-General of the United Nations shall notify each of the States Parties to the present Covenant, which may within two months submit nominations in accordance with Article 29 for the purpose of filling the vacancy.

2. The Secretary-General of the United Nations shall prepare a list in alphabetical order of the persons thus nominated and shall submit it to the States Parties to the present Covenant. The election to fill the vacancy shall then take place in accordance with the relevant provisions of this part of the present Covenant.

3. A member of the Committee elected to fill a vacancy declared in accordance with Article 33 shall hold office for the remainder of the term of the member who vacated the seat on the Committee under the provisions of that article.

*Article* 35

The members of the Committee shall, with the approval of the General Assembly of the United Nations, receive emoluments from United Nations resources on such terms and conditions as the General Assembly may decide, having regard to the importance of the Committee's responsibilities.

*Article* 36

The Secretary-General of the United Nations shall provide the necessary staff and facilities for the effective performance of the functions of the Committee under the present Covenant.

*Article* 37

1. The Secretary-General of the United Nations shall convene the initial meeting of the Committee at the Headquarters of the United Nations.

2. After its initial meeting, the Committee shall meet at such times as shall be provided in its rules of procedure.

3. The Committee shall normally meet at the Headquarters of the United Nations or at the United Nations Office at Geneva.

*Article* 38

Every member of the Committee shall, before taking up his duties, make a solemn declaration in open committee that he will perform his functions impartially and conscientiously.

*Article* 39

1. The Committee shall elect its officers for a term of two years. They may be re-elected.

2. The Committee shall establish its own rules of procedure, but these rules shall provide, *inter alia*, that:

    *(a)* Twelve members shall constitute a quorum;
    *(b)* Decisions of the Committee shall be made by a majority vote of the members present.

*Article* 40

1. The States Parties to the present Covenant undertake to submit reports on the measures they have adopted which give effect to the rights recognized herein and on the progress made in the enjoyment of those rights:

    *(a)* Within one year of the entry into force of the present Covenant for the States Parties concerned;

(b) Thereafter whenever the Committee so requests.

2. All reports shall be submitted to the Secretary-General of the United Nations, who shall transmit them to the Committee for consideration. Reports shall indicate the factors and difficulties, if any, affecting the implementation of the present Covenant.

3. The Secretary-General of the United Nations may, after consultation with the Committee, transmit to the specialized agencies concerned copies of such parts of the reports as may fall within their field of competence.

4. The Committee shall study the reports submitted by the States Parties to the present Covenant. It shall transmit its reports, and such general comments as it may consider appropriate, to the States Parties. The Committee may also transmit to the Economic and Social Council these comments along with the copies of the reports it has received from States Parties to the present Covenant.

5. The States Parties to the present Covenant may submit to the Committee observations on any comments that may be made in accordance with paragraph 4 of this article.

*Article* 41

1. A State Party to the present Covenant may at any time declare under this article that it recognizes the competence of the Committee to receive and consider communications to the effect that a State Party claims that another State Party is not fulfilling its obligations under the present Covenant. Communications under this article may be received and considered only if submitted by a State Party which has made a declaration recognizing in regard to itself the competence of the Committee. No communication shall be received by the Committee if it concerns a State Party which has not made such a declaration. Communications received under this article shall be dealt with in accordance with the following procedure:

(a) If a State Party to the present Covenant considers that another State Party is not giving effect to the provisions of the present Covenant, it may, by written communication, bring the matter to the attention of that State Party. Within three months after the receipt of the communication the receiving State shall afford the State which sent the communication an explanation, or any other statement in writing clarifying the matter which should include, to the extent possible and pertinent, reference to domestic procedures and remedies taken, pending, or available in the matter;

(b) If the matter is not adjusted to the satisfaction of both States Parties concerned within six months after the receipt by the receiving State of the initial communication, either State shall have the right to refer the matter to the Committee, by notice given to the Committee and to the other State;

(c) The Committee shall deal with a matter referred to it only after it has ascertained that all available domestic remedies have been invoked and exhausted in the matter, in conformity with the generally recognized principles of international law. This shall not be the rule where the application of the remedies is unreasonably prolonged;

(d) The Committee shall hold closed meetings when examining communications under this article;

*(e)* Subject to the provisions of subparagraph (c), the Committee shall make available its good offices to the States Parties concerned with a view to a friendly solution of the matter on the basis of respect for human rights and fundamental freedoms as recognized in the present Covenant;

*(f)* In any matter referred to it, the Committee may call upon the States Parties concerned, referred to in subparagraph (b), to supply any relevant information;

*(g)* The States Parties concerned, referred to in subparagraph (b), shall have the right to be represented when the matter is being considered in the Committee and to make submissions orally and/or in writing;

*(h)* The Committee shall, within twelve months after the date of receipt of notice under subparagraph (b), submit a report:

(i) If a solution within the terms of subparagraph (e) is reached, the Committee shall confine its report to a brief statement of the facts and of the solution reached;

(ii) If a solution within the terms of subparagraph (e) is not reached, the Committee shall confine its report to a brief statement of the facts; the written submissions and record of the oral submissions made by the States Parties concerned shall be attached to the report. In every matter, the report shall be communicated to the States Parties concerned.

2. The provisions of this article shall come into force when ten States Parties to the present Covenant have made declarations under paragraph 1 of this article. Such declarations shall be deposited by the States Parties with the Secretary-General of the United Nations, who shall transmit copies thereof to the other States Parties. A declaration may be withdrawn at any time by notification to the Secretary-General. Such a withdrawal shall not prejudice the consideration of any matter which is the subject of a communication already transmitted under this article; no further communication by any State Party shall be received after the notification of withdrawal of the declaration has been received by the Secretary-General, unless the State Party concerned has made a new declaration.

*Article* 42

1. *(a)* If a matter referred to the Committee in accordance with Article 41 is not resolved to the satisfaction of the States Parties concerned, the Committee may, with the prior consent of the States Parties concerned, appoint an ad hoc Conciliation Commission (hereinafter referred to as the Commission). The good offices of the Commission shall be made available to the States Parties concerned with a view to an amicable solution of the matter on the basis of respect for the present Covenant;

*(b)* The Commission shall consist of five persons acceptable to the States Parties concerned. If the States Parties concerned fail to reach agreement within three months on all or part of the composition of the Commission, the members of the Commission concerning whom no agreement has been reached shall be elected by secret ballot by a two-thirds majority vote of the Committee from among its members.

2. The members of the Commission shall serve in their personal capacity. They

shall not be nationals of the States Parties concerned, or of a State not Party to the present Covenant, or of a State Party which has not made a declaration under Article 41.

3. The Commission shall elect its own Chairman and adopt its own rules of procedure.

4. The meetings of the Commission shall normally be held at the Headquarters of the United Nations or at the United Nations Office at Geneva. However, they may be held at such other convenient places as the Commission may determine in consultation with the Secretary-General of the United Nations and the States Parties concerned.

5. The secretariat provided in accordance with Article 36 shall also service the commissions appointed under this article.

6. The information received and collated by the Committee shall be made available to the Commission and the Commission may call upon the States Parties concerned to supply any other relevant information.

7. When the Commission has fully considered the matter, but in any event not later than twelve months after having been seized of the matter, it shall submit to the Chairman of the Committee a report for communication to the States Parties concerned:

(a) If the Commission is unable to complete its consideration of the matter within twelve months, it shall confine its report to a brief statement of the status of its consideration of the matter;

(b) If an amicable solution to the matter on the basis of respect for human rights as recognized in the present Covenant is reached, the Commission shall confine its report to a brief statement of the facts and of the solution reached;

(c) If a solution within the terms of subparagraph (b) is not reached, the Commission's report shall embody its findings on all questions of fact relevant to the issues between the States Parties concerned, and its views on the possibilities of an amicable solution of the matter. This report shall also contain the written submissions and a record of the oral submissions made by the States Parties concerned;

(d) If the Commission's report is submitted under subparagraph (c), the States Parties concerned shall, within three months of the receipt of the report, notify the Chairman of the Committee whether or not they accept the contents of the report of the Commission.

8. The provisions of this article are without prejudice to the responsibilities of the Committee under Article 41.

9. The States Parties concerned shall share equally all the expenses of the members of the Commission in accordance with estimates to be provided by the Secretary-General of the United Nations.

10. The Secretary-General of the United Nations shall be empowered to pay the expenses of the members of the Commission, if necessary, before reimbursement by the States Parties concerned, in accordance with paragraph 9 of this article.

*Article* 43

The members of the Committee, and of the ad hoc conciliation commissions which may be appointed under Article 42, shall be entitled to the facilities, privileges and immunities of experts on mission for the United Nations as laid down in the relevant sections of the Convention on the Privileges and Immunities of the United Nations.

*Article* 44

The provisions for the implementation of the present Covenant shall apply without prejudice to the procedures prescribed in the field of human rights by or under the constituent instruments and the conventions of the United Nations and of the specialized agencies and shall not prevent the States Parties to the present Covenant from having recourse to other procedures for settling a dispute in accordance with general or special international agreements in force between them.

*Article* 45

The Committee shall submit to the General Assembly of the United Nations, through the Economic and Social Council, an annual report on its activities.


# PART V

*Article* 46

Nothing in the present Covenant shall be interpreted as impairing the provisions of the Charter of the United Nations and of the constitutions of the specialized agencies which define the respective responsibilities of the various organs of the United Nations and of the specialized agencies in regard to the matters dealt with in the present Covenant.

*Article* 47

Nothing in the present Covenant shall be interpreted as impairing the inherent right of all peoples to enjoy and utilize fully and freely their natural wealth and resources.


# PART VI

*Article* 48

1. The present Covenant is open for signature by any State Member of the United Nations or member of any of its specialized agencies, by any State Party to the Statute of the International Court of Justice, and by any other State which has been invited by the General Assembly of the United Nations to become a Party to the present Covenant.

2. The present Covenant is subject to ratification. Instruments of ratification shall be deposited with the Secretary-General of the United Nations.

3. The present Covenant shall be open to accession by any State referred to in paragraph 1 of this article.

4. Accession shall be effected by the deposit of an instrument of accession with the Secretary-General of the United Nations.

5. The Secretary-General of the United Nations shall inform all States which have signed this Covenant or acceded to it of the deposit of each instrument of ratification or accession.

*Article* 49

1. The present Covenant shall enter into force three months after the date of the deposit with the Secretary-General of the United Nations of the thirty-fifth instrument of ratification or instrument of accession.

2. For each State ratifying the present Covenant or acceding to it after the deposit of the thirty-fifth instrument of ratification or instrument of accession, the present Covenant shall enter into force three months after the date of the deposit of its own instrument of ratification or instrument of accession.

*Article* 50

The provisions of the present Covenant shall extend to all parts of federal States without any limitations or exceptions.

*Article* 51

1. Any State Party to the present Covenant may propose an amendment and file it with the Secretary-General of the United Nations. The Secretary-General of the United Nations shall thereupon communicate any proposed amendments to the States Parties to the present Covenant with a request that they notify him whether they favour a conference of States Parties for the purpose of considering and voting upon the proposals. In the event that at least one third of the States Parties favours such a conference, the Secretary-General shall convene the conference under the auspices of the United Nations. Any amendment adopted by a majority of the States Parties present and voting at the conference shall be submitted to the General Assembly of the United Nations for approval.

2. Amendments shall come into force when they have been approved by the General Assembly of the United Nations and accepted by a two-thirds majority of the States Parties to the present Covenant in accordance with their respective constitutional processes.

3. When amendments come into force, they shall be binding on those States Parties which have accepted them, other States Parties still being bound by the provisions of the present Covenant and any earlier amendment which they have accepted.

*Article* 52

Irrespective of the notifications made under Article 48, paragraph 5, the Secretary-General of the United Nations shall inform all States referred to in paragraph 1 of the same article of the following particulars:

  (a)  Signatures, ratifications and accessions under Article 48;
  (b)  The date of the entry into force of the present Covenant under Article 49 and the date of the entry into force of any amendments under Article 51.

*Article* 53

1. The present Covenant, of which the Chinese, English, French, Russian and Spanish texts are equally authentic, shall be deposited in the archives of the United Nations.

2. The Secretary-General of the United Nations shall transmit certified copies of the present Covenant to all States referred to in Article 48.

## 29. OPTIONAL PROTOCOL TO THE INTERNATIONAL COVENANT ON CIVIL AND POLITICAL RIGHTS, 1966

The Protocol entered into force on 23 March 1976. On the Human Rights Committee, see McGoldrick, D., *The Human Rights Committee: Its Role in the Development of the International Covenant on Civil and Political Rights* (1991). For the jurisprudence and General Comments of the Committee, see http://www.unhchr.ch.

### *TEXT*

*The States Parties to the present Protocol,*

*Considering* that in order further to achieve the purposes of the International Covenant on Civil and Political Rights (hereinafter referred to as the Covenant) and the implementation of its provisions it would be appropriate to enable the Human Rights Committee set up in part IV of the Covenant (hereinafter referred to as the Committee) to receive and consider, as provided in the present Protocol, communications from individuals claiming to be victims of violations of any of the rights set forth in the Covenant,

Have *agreed* as follows:

### *Article* 1

A State Party to the Covenant that becomes a Party to the present Protocol recognizes the competence of the Committee to receive and consider communications from individuals subject to its jurisdiction who claim to be victims of a violation by that State Party of any of the rights set forth in the Covenant. No communication shall be received by the Committee if it concerns a State Party to the Covenant which is not a Party to the present Protocol.

### *Article* 2

Subject to the provisions of Article 1, individuals who claim that any of their rights enumerated in the Covenant have been violated and who have exhausted all available domestic remedies may submit a written communication to the Committee for consideration.

### *Article* 3

The Committee shall consider inadmissible any communication under the present Protocol which is anonymous, or which it considers to be an abuse of the right of submission of such communications or to be incompatible with the provisions of the Covenant.

### *Article* 4

1. Subject to the provisions of Article 3, the Committee shall bring any communications submitted to it under the present Protocol to the attention of the State Party to the present Protocol alleged to be violating any provision of the Covenant.

2. Within six months, the receiving State shall submit to the Committee written explanations or statements clarifying the matter and the remedy, if any, that may have been taken by that State.

*Article 5*

1. The Committee shall consider communications received under the present Protocol in the light of all written information made available to it by the individual and by the State Party concerned.

2. The Committee shall not consider any communication from an individual unless it has ascertained that:

    *(a)* The same matter is not being examined under another procedure of international investigation or settlement;

    *(b)* The individual has exhausted all available domestic remedies. This shall not be the rule where the application of the remedies is unreasonably prolonged.

3. The Committee shall hold closed meetings when examining communications under the present Protocol.

4. The Committee shall forward its views to the State Party concerned and to the individual.

*Article 6*

The Committee shall include in its annual report under Article 45 of the Covenant a summary of its activities under the present Protocol.

*Article 7*

Pending the achievement of the objectives of resolution 1514(XV) adopted by the General Assembly of the United Nations on 14 December 1960 concerning the Declaration on the Granting of Independence to Colonial Countries and Peoples, the provisions of the present Protocol shall in no way limit the right of petition granted to these peoples by the Charter of the United Nations and other international conventions and instruments under the United Nations and its specialized agencies.

*Article 8*

1. The present Protocol is open for signature by any State which has signed the Covenant.

2. The present Protocol is subject to ratification by any State which has ratified or acceded to the Covenant. Instruments of ratification shall be deposited with the Secretary-General of the United Nations.

3. The present Protocol shall be open to accession by any State which has ratified or acceded to the Covenant.

4. Accession shall be effected by the deposit of an instrument of accession with the Secretary-General of the United Nations.

5. The Secretary-General of the United Nations shall inform all States which have signed the present Protocol or acceded to it of the deposit of each instrument of ratification or accession.

*Article* 9

1. Subject to the entry into force of the Covenant, the present Protocol shall enter into force three months after the date of the deposit with the Secretary-General of the United Nations of the tenth instrument of ratification or instrument of accession.

2. For each State ratifying the present Protocol or acceding to it after the deposit of the tenth instrument of ratification or instrument of accession, the present Protocol shall enter into force three months after the date of the deposit of its own instrument of ratification or instrument of accession.

*Article* 10

The provisions of the present Protocol shall extend to all parts of federal States without any limitations or exceptions.

*Article* 11

1. Any State Party to the present Protocol may propose an amendment and file it with the Secretary-General of the United Nations. The Secretary-General shall thereupon communicate any proposed amendments to the States Parties to the present Protocol with a request that they notify him whether they favour a conference of States Parties for the purpose of considering and voting upon the proposal. In the event that at least one third of the States Parties favours such a conference, the Secretary-General shall convene the conference under the auspices of the United Nations. Any amendment adopted by a majority of the States Parties present and voting at the conference shall be submitted to the General Assembly of the United Nations for approval.

2. Amendments shall come into force when they have been approved by the General Assembly of the United Nations and accepted by a two-thirds majority of the States Parties to the present Protocol in accordance with their respective constitutional processes.

3. When amendments come into force, they shall be binding on those States Parties which have accepted them, other States Parties still being bound by the provisions of the present Protocol and any earlier amendment which they have accepted.

*Article* 12

1. Any State Party may denounce the present Protocol at any time by written notification addressed to the Secretary-General of the United Nations. Denunciation shall take effect three months after the date of receipt of the notification by the Secretary-General.

2. Denunciation shall be without prejudice to the continued application of the provisions of the present Protocol to any communication submitted under Article 2 before the effective date of denunciation.

*Article* 13

Irrespective of the notifications made under Article 8, paragraph 5, of the present Protocol, the Secretary-General of the United Nations shall inform all States referred to in Article 48, paragraph 1, of the Covenant of the following particulars:

(a) Signatures, ratifications and accessions under Article 8;

(b) The date of the entry into force of the present Protocol under Article 9 and the date of the entry into force of any amendments under Article 11;

(c) Denunciations under Article 12.

*Article* 14

1. The present Protocol, of which the Chinese, English, French, Russian and Spanish texts are equally authentic, shall be deposited in the archives of the United Nations.

2. The Secretary-General of the United Nations shall transmit certified copies of the present Protocol to all States referred to in Article 48 of the Covenant.

## 30. SECOND OPTIONAL PROTOCOL TO THE INTERNATIONAL COVENANT ON CIVIL AND POLITICAL RIGHTS, 1990

The second optional protocol, aiming at the abolition of the death penalty, was adopted by General Assembly Resolution 44/128, 15 December 1989, on a recorded vote of 59–26–48; UN doc. A/44/49 (1989); it entered into force on 11 July 1991.

Hood, R., *The Death Penalty: A World Wide Perspective* (2nd edn., 1996); Schabas, W. A., *The Abolition of the Death Penalty in International Law* (2nd edn., 1997).

*TEXT*

*The States Parties to the present Protocol,*

*Believing* that abolition of the death penalty contributes to enhancement of human dignity and progressive development of human rights,

*Recalling* Article 3 of the Universal Declaration of Human Rights, adopted on 10 December 1948, and Article 6 of the International Covenant on Civil and Political Rights, adopted on 16 December 1966,

*Noting* that Article 6 of the International Covenant on Civil and Political Rights refers to abolition of the death penalty in terms that strongly suggest that abolition is desirable,

*Convinced* that all measures of abolition of the death penalty should be considered as progress in the enjoyment of the right to life,

*Desirous* to undertake hereby an international commitment to abolish the death penalty,

*Have agreed* as follows:

*Article 1*

1. No one within the jurisdiction of a State Party to the present Protocol shall be executed.

2. Each State Party shall take all necessary measures to abolish the death penalty within its jurisdiction.

*Article 2*

1. No reservation is admissible to the present Protocol, except for a reservation made at the time of ratification or accession that provides for the application of the death penalty in time of war pursuant to a conviction for a most serious crime of a military nature committed during wartime.

2. The State Party making such a reservation shall at the time of ratification or accession communicate to the Secretary-General of the United Nations the relevant provisions of its national legislation applicable during wartime.

3. The State Party having made such a reservation shall notify the Secretary-General of the United Nations of any beginning or ending of a state of war applicable to its territory.

*Article* 3

The States Parties to the present Protocol shall include in the reports they submit to the Human Rights Committee, in accordance with Article 40 of the Covenant, information on the measures that they have adopted to give effect to the present Protocol.

*Article* 4

With respect to the States Parties to the Covenant that have made a declaration under Article 41, the competence of the Human Rights Committee to receive and consider communications when a State Party claims that another State Party is not fulfilling its obligations shall extend to the provisions of the present Protocol, unless the State Party concerned has made a statement to the contrary at the moment of ratification or accession.

*Article* 5

With respect to the States Parties to the first Optional Protocol to the International Covenant on Civil and Political Rights adopted on 16 December 1966, the competence of the Human Rights Committee to receive and consider communications from individuals subject to its jurisdiction shall extend to the provisions of the present Protocol, unless the State Party concerned has made a statement to the contrary at the moment of ratification or accession.

*Article* 6

1. The provisions of the present Protocol shall apply as additional provisions to the Covenant.

2. Without prejudice to the possibility of a reservation under Article 2 of the present Protocol, the right guaranteed in Article 1, paragraph 1, of the present Protocol shall not be subject to any derogation under Article 4 of the Covenant.

*Article* 7

1. The present Protocol is open for signature by any State that has signed the Covenant.

2. The present Protocol is subject to ratification by any State that has ratified the Covenant or acceded to it. Instruments of ratification shall be deposited with the Secretary-General of the United Nations.

3. The present Protocol shall be open to accession by any State that has ratified the Covenant or acceded to it.

4. Accession shall be effected by the deposit of an instrument of accession with the Secretary-General of the United Nations.

5. The Secretary-General of the United Nations shall inform all States that have signed the present Protocol or acceded to it of the deposit of each instrument of ratification or accession.

*Article* 8

1. The present Protocol shall enter into force three months after the date of the deposit with the Secretary-General of the United Nations of the tenth instrument of ratification or accession.

2. For each State ratifying the present Protocol or acceding to it after the deposit of the tenth instrument of ratification or accession, the present Protocol shall enter into force three months after the date of the deposit of its own instrument of ratification or accession.

*Article* 9

The provisions of the present Protocol shall extend to all parts of federal States without any limitations or exceptions.

*Article* 10

The Secretary-General of the United Nations shall inform all States referred to in Article 48, paragraph 1, of the Covenant of the following particulars:

- *(a)* Reservations, communications and notifications under Article 2 of the present Protocol;
- *(b)* Statements made under Articles 4 or 5 of the present Protocol;
- *(c)* Signatures, ratifications and accessions under Article 7 of the present Protocol:
- *(d)* The date of the entry into force of the present Protocol under Article 8 thereof.

*Article* 11

1. The present Protocol, of which the Arabic, Chinese, English, French, Russian and Spanish texts are equally authentic, shall be deposited in the archives of the United Nations.

2. The Secretary-General of the United Nations shall transmit certified copies of the present Protocol to all States referred to in Article 48 of the Covenant.

## 31. INTERNATIONAL CONVENTION ON THE SUPPRESSION AND PUNISHMENT OF THE CRIME OF APARTHEID, 1973

This Convention was adopted and opened for signature by General Assembly Resolution 3068 (XXVIII) of 30 November 1973. The Resolution was adopted by ninety-one votes in favour, and with twenty-six abstentions. Portugal, South Africa, the United Kingdom, and the United States voted against the Resolution. The basis of the opposition of the United States is set forth in *Digest of United States Practice in International Law* (1973), 130–2, where it is pointed out that the Convention was 'not necessary in view of the broad, all-inclusive provisions of the International Convention on the Elimination of All Forms of Racial Discrimination'.

The Convention entered into force on 18 July 1976. Western States have avoided signature, ratification, or accession. For text, see 1015 UNTS 243.

### TEXT

*The States Parties to the present Convention,*

*Recalling* the provisions of the Charter of the United Nations, in which all Members pledged themselves to take joint and separate action in co-operation with the Organization for the achievement of universal respect for, and observance of, human rights and fundamental freedoms for all without distinction as to race, sex, language or religion,

*Considering* the Universal Declaration of Human Rights, which states that all human beings are born free and equal in dignity and rights and that everyone is entitled to all the rights and freedoms set forth in the Declaration, without distinction of any kind, such as race, colour or national origin,

*Considering* the Declaration on the Granting of Independence to Colonial Countries and Peoples, in which the General Assembly stated that the process of liberation is irresistible and irreversible and that, in the interests of human dignity, progress and justice, an end must be put to colonialism and all practices of segregation and discrimination associated therewith,

*Observing* that, in accordance with the International Convention on the Elimination of All Forms of Racial Discrimination, States particularly condemn racial segregation and apartheid and undertake to prevent, prohibit and eradicate all practices of this nature in territories under their jurisdiction,

*Observing* that, in the Convention on the Prevention and Punishment of the Crime of Genocide, certain acts which may also be qualified as acts of apartheid constitute a crime under international law,

*Observing* that, in the Convention on the Non-Applicability of Statutory Limitations to War Crimes and Crimes against Humanity, 'inhuman acts resulting from the policy of apartheid' are qualified as crimes against humanity,

*Observing* that the General Assembly of the United Nations has adopted a number of resolutions in which the policies and practices of apartheid are condemned as a crime against humanity,

*Observing* that the Security Council has emphasized that apartheid and its continued intensification and expansion seriously disturb and threaten international peace and security,

*Convinced* that an International Convention on the Suppression and Punishment of the Crime of Apartheid would make it possible to take more effective measures at the international and national levels with a view to the suppression and punishment of the crime of apartheid,

*Have agreed* as follows:

*Article* I

1. The States Parties to the present Convention declare that apartheid is a crime against humanity and that inhuman acts resulting from the policies and practices of apartheid and similar policies and practices of racial segregation and discrimination, as defined in article II of the Convention, are crimes violating the principles of international law, in particular the purposes and principles of the Charter of the United Nations, and constituting a serious threat to international peace and security.

2. The States Parties to the present Convention declare criminal those organizations, institutions and individuals committing the crime of apartheid.

*Article* II

For the purpose of the present Convention, the term 'the crime of apartheid', which shall include similar policies and practices of racial segregation and discrimination as practised in southern Africa, shall apply to the following inhuman acts committed for the purpose of establishing and maintaining domination by one racial group of persons over any other racial group of persons and systematically oppressing them:

 (a) Denial to a member or members of a racial group or groups of the right to life and liberty of person:
   (i) By murder of members of a racial group or groups;
   (ii) By the infliction upon the members of a racial group or groups of serious bodily or mental harm, by the infringement of their freedom or dignity, or by subjecting them to torture or to cruel, inhuman or degrading treatment or punishment;
   (iii) By arbitrary arrest and illegal imprisonment of the members of a racial group or groups;
 (b) Deliberate imposition on a racial group or groups of living conditions calculated to cause its or their physical destruction in whole or in part;
 (c) Any legislative measures and other measures calculated to prevent a racial group or groups from participation in the political, social, economic and cultural life of the country and the deliberate creation of conditions preventing the full development of such a group or groups, in particular by denying to members of a racial group or groups basic human rights and freedoms, including the right to work, the right to form recognized trade unions, the right to education, the right to leave and to return to their country, the right to a nationality, the right to freedom of movement and residence, the right to freedom of opinion and expression, and the right to freedom of peaceful assembly and association;

(d)  Any measures, including legislative measures, designed to divide the population along racial lines by the creation of separate reserves and ghettos for the
members of a racial group or groups, the prohibition of mixed marriages
among members of various racial groups, the expropriation of landed
property belonging to a racial group or groups or to members thereof;

(e)  Exploitation of the labour of the members of a racial group or groups, in
particular by submitting them to forced labour;

(f)  Persecution of organizations and persons, by depriving them of
fundamental rights and freedoms, because they oppose apartheid.

*Article* III

International criminal responsibility shall apply, irrespective of the motive
involved, to individuals, members of organizations and institutions and representatives of the State, whether residing in the territory of the State in which the acts are
perpetrated or in some other State, whenever they:

(a)  Commit, participate in, directly incite or conspire in the commission of the
acts mentioned in Article II of the present Convention;

(b)  Directly abet, encourage or co-operate in the commission of the crime of
apartheid.

*Article* IV

The States Parties to the present Convention undertake:

(a)  To adopt any legislative or other measures necessary to suppress as well as
to prevent any encouragement of the crime of apartheid and similar segre-
gationist policies or their manifestations and to punish persons guilty of that
crime;

(b)  To adopt legislative, judicial and administrative measures to prosecute,
bring to trial and punish in accordance with their jurisdiction persons
responsible for, or accused of, the acts defined in Article II of the present
Convention, whether or not such persons reside in the territory of the State
in which the acts are committed or are nationals of that State or of some
other State or are stateless persons.

*Article* V

Persons charged with the acts enumerated in Article II of the present Convention
may be tried by a competent tribunal of any State Party to the Convention which
may acquire jurisdiction over the person of the accused or by an international
penal tribunal having jurisdiction with respect to those States Parties which shall
have accepted its jurisdiction.

*Article* VI

The States Parties to the present Convention undertake to accept and carry out in
accordance with the Charter of the United Nations the decisions taken by the
Security Council aimed at the prevention, suppression and punishment of the
crime of apartheid, and to co-operate in the implementation of decisions adopted
by other competent organs of the United Nations with a view to achieving the
purposes of the Convention.

*Article* VII

1. The States Parties to the present Convention undertake to submit periodic reports to the group established under Article IX on the legislative, judicial, administrative or other measures that they have adopted and that give effect to the provisions of the Convention.

2. Copies of the reports shall be transmitted through the Secretary-General of the United Nations to the Special Committee on Apartheid.

*Article* VIII

Any State Party to the present Convention may call upon any competent organ of the United Nations to take such action under the Charter of the United Nations as it considers appropriate for the prevention and suppression of the crime of apartheid.

*Article* IX

1. The Chairman of the Commission on Human Rights shall appoint a group consisting of three members of the Commission on Human Rights, who are also representatives of States Parties to the present Convention, to consider reports submitted by States Parties in accordance with Article VII.

2. If, among the members of the Commission on Human Rights, there are no representatives of States Parties to the present Convention or if there are fewer than three such representatives, the Secretary-General of the United Nations shall, after consulting all States Parties to the Convention, designate a representative of the State Party or representatives of the States Parties which are not members of the Commission on Human Rights to take part in the work of the group established in accordance with paragraph 1 of this article, until such time as representatives of the States Parties to the Convention are elected to the Commission on Human Rights.

3. The group may meet for a period of not more than five days, either before the opening or after the closing of the session of the Commission on Human Rights, to consider the reports submitted in accordance with Article VII.

*Article* X

1. The States Parties to the present Convention empower the Commission on Human Rights:

   (a) To request United Nations organs, when transmitting copies of petitions under Article 15 of the International Convention on the Elimination of All Forms of Racial Discrimination, to draw its attention to complaints concerning acts which are enumerated in Article II of the present Convention;

   (b) To prepare, on the basis of reports from competent organs of the United Nations and periodic reports from States Parties to the present Convention, a list of individuals, organizations, institutions and representatives of States which are alleged to be responsible for the crimes enumerated in Article II of the Convention, as well as those against whom legal proceedings have been undertaken by States Parties to the Convention;

   (c) To request information from the competent United Nations organs

concerning measures taken by the authorities responsible for the administration of Trust and Non-Self-Governing Territories, and all other Territories to which General Assembly resolution 1514 (XV) of 14 December 1960
applies, with regard to such individuals alleged to be responsible for crimes
under Article II of the Convention who are believed to be under their
territorial and administrative jurisdiction.

2. Pending the achievement of the objectives of the Declaration on the Granting
of Independence to Colonial Countries and Peoples, contained in General
Assembly resolution 1514 (XV), the provisions of the present Convention shall in
no way limit the right of petition granted to those peoples by other international
instruments or by the United Nations and its specialized agencies.

*Article* XI

1. Acts enumerated in Article II of the present Convention shall not be considered
political crimes for the purpose of extradition.

2. The States Parties to the present Convention undertake in such cases to grant
extradition in accordance with their legislation and with the treaties in force.

*Article* XII

Disputes between States Parties arising out of the interpretation, application or
implementation of the present Convention which have not been settled by negotiation shall, at the request of the States parties to the dispute, be brought before the
International Court of Justice, save where the parties to the dispute have agreed on
some other form of settlement.

*Article* XIII

The present Convention is open for signature by all States. Any State which does
not sign the Convention before its entry into force may accede to it.

*Article* XIV

1. The present Convention is subject to ratification. Instruments of ratification
shall be deposited with the Secretary-General of the United Nations.

2. Accession shall be effected by the deposit of an instrument of accession with the
Secretary-General of the United Nations.

*Article* XV

1. The present Convention shall enter into force on the thirtieth day after the date
of the deposit with the Secretary-General of the United Nations of the twentieth
instrument of ratification or accession.

2. For each State ratifying the present Convention or acceding to it after the
deposit of the twentieth instrument of ratification or instrument of accession, the
Convention shall enter into force on the thirtieth day after the date of the deposit
of its own instrument of ratification or instrument of accession.

*Article* XVI

A State Party may denounce the present Convention by written notification to the
Secretary-General of the United Nations. Denunciation shall take effect one year
after the date of receipt of the notification by the Secretary-General.

*Article* XVII

1. A request for the revision of the present Convention may be made at any time by any State Party by means of a notification in writing addressed to the Secretary-General of the United Nations.

2. The General Assembly of the United Nations shall decide upon the steps, if any, to be taken in respect of such request.

*Article* XVIII

The Secretary-General of the United Nations shall inform all States of the following particulars:

    *(a)*  Signatures, ratifications and accessions under Articles XIII and XIV;

    *(b)*  The date of entry into force of the present Convention under Article XV;

    *(c)*  Denunciations under Article XVI;

    *(d)*  Notifications under Article XVII.

*Article* XIX

1. The present Convention, of which the Chinese, English, French, Russian and Spanish texts are equally authentic, shall be deposited in the archives of the United Nations.

2. The Secretary-General of the United Nations shall transmit certified copies of the present Convention to all States.

## 32. CONVENTION ON THE ELIMINATION OF ALL FORMS OF DISCRIMINATION AGAINST WOMEN, 1979

The text which follows was adopted by General Assembly Resolution 34/180 on 18 December 1979: UN doc. A/34/46; there were 130 votes in favour, none against, and ten abstentions. The Convention came into force on 3 September 1981; for text see 1249 UNTS 13. The precursor to the Convention was the Declaration on Elimination of Discrimination against Women, adopted unanimously by the General Assembly on 7 December 1967; for the text, see the first edition of the present work, at 183.

Reference should also be made to the ILO Convention concerning equal remuneration for men and women workers for work of equal value, (see below, 330–3).

Generally, see Jacobson, R., 'The Committee on the Elimination of Discrimination against Women', in Alston, P. (ed.), *The United Nations and Human Rights* (1992), 444–72. On the standard of non-discrimination in general international law see Brownlie, I., *Principles of Public International Law* (5th edn., 1998), 602–5. On sexual equality, see McDougall, M. S., Lasswell, H. D., & Lung-Chu Chen, 'Human Rights for Women and World Public Order: The Outlawing of Sex-based Discrimination', 69 *AJIL* 497–533 (1975).

*TEXT*

*The States Parties to the present Convention,*

*Noting* that the Charter of the United Nations reaffirms faith in fundamental human rights, in the dignity and worth of the human person and in the equal rights of men and women,

*Noting* that the Universal Declaration of Human Rights affirms the principle of the inadmissibility of discrimination and proclaims that all human beings are born free and equal in dignity and rights and that everyone is entitled to all the rights and freedoms set forth therein, without distinction of any kind, including distinction based on sex,

*Noting* that the States Parties to the International Covenants on Human Rights have the obligation to ensure the equal rights of men and women to enjoy all economic, social, cultural, civil and political rights,

*Considering* the international conventions concluded under the auspices of the United Nations and the specialized agencies promoting equality of rights of men and women,

*Noting* also the resolutions, declarations and recommendations adopted by the United Nations and the specialized agencies promoting equality of rights of men and women,

*Concerned,* however, that despite these various instruments extensive discrimination against women continues to exist,

*Recalling* that discrimination against women violates the principles of equality of rights and respect for human dignity, is an obstacle to the participation of women, on equal terms with men, in the political, social, economic and cultural life of their countries, hampers the growth of the prosperity of society and the family and makes more difficult the full development of the potentialities of women in the service of their countries and of humanity,

*Concerned* that in situations of poverty women have the least access to food, health, education, training and opportunities for employment and other needs,

*Convinced* that the establishment of the new international economic order based on equity and justice will contribute significantly towards the promotion of equality between men and women,

*Emphasizing* that the eradication of apartheid, all forms of racism, racial discrimination, colonialism, neo-colonialism, aggression, foreign occupation and domination and interference in the internal affairs of States is essential to the full enjoyment of the rights of men and women,

*Affirming* that the strengthening of international peace and security, the relaxation of international tension, mutual co-operation among all States irrespective of their social and economic systems, general and complete disarmament, in particular nuclear disarmament under strict and effective international control, the affirmation of the principles of justice, equality and mutual benefit in relations among countries and the realization of the right of peoples under alien and colonial domination and foreign occupation to self-determination and independence, as well as respect for national sovereignty and territorial integrity, will promote social progress and development and as a consequence will contribute to the attainment of full equality between men and women,

*Convinced* that the full and complete development of a country, the welfare of the world and the cause of peace require the maximum participation of women on equal terms with men in all fields,

*Bearing in mind* the great contribution of women to the welfare of the family and to the development of society, so far not fully recognized, the social significance of maternity and the role of both parents in the family and in the upbringing of children, and aware that the role of women in procreation should not be a basis for discrimination but that the upbringing of children requires a sharing of responsibility between men and women and society as a whole,

*Aware* that a change in the traditional role of men as well as the role of women in society and in the family is needed to achieve full equality between men and women,

*Determined* to implement the principles set forth in the Declaration on the Elimination of Discrimination against Women and, for that purpose, to adopt the measures required for the elimination of such discrimination in all its forms and manifestations,

*Have agreed* on the following:

## PART I

*Article* 1

For the purposes of the present Convention, the term 'discrimination against women' shall mean any distinction, exclusion or restriction made on the basis of sex which has the effect or purpose of impairing or nullifying the recognition, enjoyment or exercise by women, irrespective of their marital status, on a basis of

equality of men and women, of human rights and fundamental freedoms in the
political, economic, social, cultural, civil or any other field.

*Article 2*

States Parties condemn discrimination against women in all its forms, agree to
pursue by all appropriate means and without delay a policy of eliminating discrimination against women and, to this end, undertake:

(a) To embody the principle of the equality of men and women in their
national constitutions or other appropriate legislation if not yet incorporated therein and to ensure, through law and other appropriate means, the
practical realization of this principle;

(b) To adopt appropriate legislative and other measures, including sanctions
where appropriate, prohibiting all discrimination against women;

(c) To establish legal protection of the rights of women on an equal basis with
men and to ensure through competent national tribunals and other public
institutions the effective protection of women against any act of
discrimination;

(d) To refrain from engaging in any act or practice of discrimination against
women and to ensure that public authorities and institutions shall act in
conformity with this obligation;

(e) To take all appropriate measures to eliminate discrimination against women
by any person, organization or enterprise;

(f) To take all appropriate measures, including legislation, to modify or
abolish existing laws, regulations, customs and practices which constitute
discrimination against women;

(g) To repeal all national penal provisions which constitute discrimination
against women.

*Article 3*

States Parties shall take in all fields, in particular in the political, social, economic
and cultural fields, all appropriate measures, including legislation, to ensure the
full development and advancement of women, for the purpose of guaranteeing
them the exercise and enjoyment of human rights and fundamental freedoms on a
basis of equality with men.

*Article 4*

1. Adoption by States Parties of temporary special measures aimed at accelerating
de facto equality between men and women shall not be considered discrimination
as defined in the present Convention, but shall in no way entail as a consequence
the maintenance of unequal or separate standards; these measures shall be dis-
continued when the objectives of equality of opportunity and treatment have been
achieved.

2. Adoption by States Parties of special measures, including those measures contained in the present Convention, aimed at protecting maternity shall not be
considered discriminatory.

*Article* 5

States Parties shall take all appropriate measures:

(a) To modify the social and cultural patterns of conduct of men and women, with a view to achieving the elimination of prejudices and customary and all other practices which are based on the idea of the inferiority or the superiority of either of the sexes or on stereotyped roles for men and women;

(b) To ensure that family education includes a proper understanding of maternity as a social function and the recognition of the common responsibility of men and women in the upbringing and development of their children, it being understood that the interest of the children is the primordial consideration in all cases.

*Article* 6

States Parties shall take all appropriate measures, including legislation, to suppress all forms of traffic in women and exploitation of prostitution of women.

## PART II

*Article* 7

States Parties shall take all appropriate measures to eliminate discrimination against women in the political and public life of the country and, in particular, shall ensure to women, on equal terms with men, the right:

(a) To vote in all elections and public referenda and to be eligible for election to all publicly elected bodies;

(b) To participate in the formulation of government policy and the implementation thereof and to hold public office and perform all public functions at all levels of government;

(c) To participate in non-governmental organizations and associations concerned with the public and political life of the country.

*Article* 8

States Parties shall take all appropriate measures to ensure to women, on equal terms with men and without any discrimination, the opportunity to represent their Governments at the international level and to participate in the work of international organizations.

*Article* 9

1. States Parties shall grant women equal rights with men to acquire, change or retain their nationality. They shall ensure in particular that neither marriage to an alien nor change of nationality by the husband during marriage shall automatically change the nationality of the wife, render her stateless or force upon her the nationality of the husband.

2. States Parties shall grant women equal rights with men with respect to the nationality of their children.

## PART III

*Article* 10

States Parties shall take all appropriate measures to eliminate discrimination against women in order to ensure to them equal rights with men in the field of education and in particular to ensure, on a basis of equality of men and women:

*(a)* The same conditions for career and vocational guidance, for access to studies and for the achievement of diplomas in educational establishments of all categories in rural as well as in urban areas; this equality shall be ensured in pre-school, general, technical, professional and higher technical education, as well as in all types of vocational training;

*(b)* Access to the same curricula, the same examinations, teaching staff with qualifications of the same standard and school premises and equipment of the same quality;

*(c)* The elimination of any stereotyped concept of the roles of men and women at all levels and in all forms of education by encouraging coeducation and other types of education which will help to achieve this aim and, in particular, by the revision of textbooks and school programmes and the adaptation of teaching methods;

*(d)* The same opportunities to benefit from scholarships and other study grants;

*(e)* The same opportunities for access to programmes of continuing education, including adult and functional literacy programmes, particularly those aimed at reducing, at the earliest possible time, any gap in education existing between men and women;

*(f)* The reduction of female student drop-out rates and the organization of programmes for girls and women who have left school prematurely;

*(g)* The same opportunities to participate actively in sports and physical education;

*(h)* Access to specific educational information to help to ensure the health and well-being of families, including information and advice on family planning.

*Article* 11

1. States Parties shall take all appropriate measures to eliminate discrimination against women in the field of employment in order to ensure, on a basis of equality of men and women, the same rights, in particular:

*(a)* The right to work as an inalienable right of all human beings;

*(b)* The right to the same employment opportunities, including the application of the same criteria for selection in matters of employment;

*(c)* The right to free choice of profession and employment, the right to promotion, job security and all benefits and conditions of service and the right to receive vocational training and retraining, including apprenticeships, advanced vocational training and recurrent training;

*(d)* The right to equal remuneration, including benefits, and to equal treatment in respect of work of equal value, as well as equality of treatment in the evaluation of the quality of work;

*(e)* The right to social security, particularly in cases of retirement, unemployment, sickness, invalidity and old age and other incapacity to work, as well as the right to paid leave;

*(f)* The right to protection of health and to safety in working conditions, including the safeguarding of the function of reproduction.

2. In order to prevent discrimination against women on the grounds of marriage or maternity and to ensure their effective right to work, States Parties shall take appropriate measures:

*(a)* To prohibit, subject to the imposition of sanctions, dismissal on the grounds of pregnancy or of maternity leave and discrimination in dismissals on the basis of marital status;

*(b)* To introduce maternity leave with pay or with comparable social benefits without loss of former employment, seniority or social allowances;

*(c)* To encourage the provision of the necessary supporting social services to enable parents to combine family obligations with work responsibilities and participation in public life, in particular through promoting the establishment and development of a network of child-care facilities;

*(d)* To provide special protection to women during pregnancy in types of work proved to be harmful to them.

3. Protective legislation relating to matters covered in this article shall be reviewed periodically in the light of scientific and technological knowledge and shall be revised, repealed or extended as necessary.

*Article* 12

1. States Parties shall take all appropriate measures to eliminate discrimination against women in the field of health care in order to ensure, on a basis of equality of men and women, access to health care services, including those related to family planning.

2. Notwithstanding the provisions of paragraph 1 of this article, States Parties shall ensure to women appropriate services in connection with pregnancy, confinement and the post-natal period, granting free services where necessary, as well as adequate nutrition during pregnancy and lactation.

*Article* 13

States Parties shall take all appropriate measures to eliminate discrimination against women in other areas of economic and social life in order to ensure, on a basis of equality of men and women, the same rights, in particular:

*(a)* The right to family benefits;

*(b)* The right to bank loans, mortgages and other forms of financial credit;

*(c)* The right to participate in recreational activities, sports and all aspects of cultural life.

*Article* 14

1. States Parties shall take into account the particular problems faced by rural women and the significant roles which rural women play in the economic survival of their families, including their work in the non-monetized sectors of the

economy, and shall take all appropriate measures to ensure the application of the provisions of the present Convention to women in rural areas.

2. States Parties shall take all appropriate measures to eliminate discrimination against women in rural areas in order to ensure, on a basis of equality of men and women, that they participate in and benefit from rural development and, in particular, shall ensure to such women the right:

(a) To participate in the elaboration and implementation of development planning at all levels;

(b) To have access to adequate health care facilities, including information, counselling and services in family planning;

(c) To benefit directly from social security programmes;

(d) To obtain all types of training and education, formal and non-formal, including that relating to functional literacy, as well as, *inter alia*, the benefit of all community and extension services, in order to increase their technical proficiency;

(e) To organize self-help groups and co-operatives in order to obtain equal access to economic opportunities through employment or self employment;

(f) To participate in all community activities;

(g) To have access to agricultural credit and loans, marketing facilities, appropriate technology and equal treatment in land and agrarian reform as well as in land resettlement schemes;

(h) To enjoy adequate living conditions, particularly in relation to housing, sanitation, electricity and water supply, transport and communications.

# PART IV

*Article* 15

1. States Parties shall accord to women equality with men before the law.

2. States Parties shall accord to women, in civil matters, a legal capacity identical to that of men and the same opportunities to exercise that capacity. In particular, they shall give women equal rights to conclude contracts and to administer property and shall treat them equally in all stages of procedure in courts and tribunals.

3. States Parties agree that all contracts and all other private instruments of any kind with a legal effect which is directed at restricting the legal capacity of women shall be deemed null and void.

4. States Parties shall accord to men and women the same rights with regard to the law relating to the movement of persons and the freedom to choose their residence and domicile.

*Article* 16

1. States Parties shall take all appropriate measures to eliminate discrimination against women in all matters relating to marriage and family relations and in particular shall ensure, on a basis of equality of men and women:

*(a)* The same right to enter into marriage;

*(b)* The same right freely to choose a spouse and to enter into marriage only with their free and full consent;

*(c)* The same rights and responsibilities during marriage and at its dissolution;

*(d)* The same rights and responsibilities as parents, irrespective of their marital status, in matters relating to their children; in all cases the interests of the children shall be paramount;

*(e)* The same rights to decide freely and responsibly on the number and spacing of their children and to have access to the information, education and means to enable them to exercise these rights;

*(f)* The same rights and responsibilities with regard to guardianship, wardship, trusteeship and adoption of children, or similar institutions where these concepts exist in national legislation; in all cases the interests of the children shall be paramount;

*(g)* The same personal rights as husband and wife, including the right to choose a family name, a profession and an occupation;

*(h)* The same rights for both spouses in respect of the ownership, acquisition, management, administration, enjoyment and disposition of property, whether free of charge or for a valuable consideration.

2. The betrothal and the marriage of a child shall have no legal effect, and all necessary action, including legislation, shall be taken to specify a minimum age for marriage and to make the registration of marriages in an official registry compulsory.


# PART V

*Article* 17

1. For the purpose of considering the progress made in the implementation of the present Convention, there shall be established a Committee on the Elimination of Discrimination against Women (hereinafter referred to as the Committee) consisting, at the time of entry into force of the Convention, of eighteen and, after ratification of or accession to the Convention by the thirty-fifth State Party, of twenty-three experts of high moral standing and competence in the field covered by the Convention. The experts shall be elected by States Parties from among their nationals and shall serve in their personal capacity, consideration being given to equitable geographical distribution and to the representation of the different forms of civilization as well as the principal legal systems.

2. The members of the Committee shall be elected by secret ballot from a list of persons nominated by States Parties. Each State Party may nominate one person from among its own nationals.

3. The initial election shall be held six months after the date of the entry into force of the present Convention. At least three months before the date of each election the Secretary-General of the United Nations shall address a letter to the States Parties inviting them to submit their nominations within two months. The

Secretary-General shall prepare a list in alphabetical order of all persons thus nominated, indicating the States Parties which have nominated them, and shall submit it to the States Parties.

4. Elections of the members of the Committee shall be held at a meeting of States Parties convened by the Secretary-General at United Nations Headquarters. At that meeting, for which two thirds of the States Parties shall constitute a quorum, the persons elected to the Committee shall be those nominees who obtain the largest number of votes and an absolute majority of the votes of the representatives of States Parties present and voting.

5. The members of the Committee shall be elected for a term of four years. However, the terms of nine of the members elected at the first election shall expire at the end of two years; immediately after the first election the names of these nine members shall be chosen by lot by the Chairman of the Committee.

6. The election of the five additional members of the Committee shall be held in accordance with the provisions of paragraphs 2, 3 and 4 of this article, following the thirty-fifth ratification or accession. The terms of two of the additional members elected on this occasion shall expire at the end of two years, the names of these two members having been chosen by lot by the Chairman of the Committee.

7. For the filling of casual vacancies, the State Party whose expert has ceased to function as a member of the Committee shall appoint another expert from among its nationals, subject to the approval of the Committee.

8. The members of the Committee shall, with the approval of the General Assembly, receive emoluments from United Nations resources on such terms and conditions as the Assembly may decide, having regard to the importance of the Committee's responsibilities.

9. The Secretary-General of the United Nations shall provide the necessary staff and facilities for the effective performance of the functions of the Committee under the present Convention.

*Article* 18

1. States Parties undertake to submit to the Secretary-General of the United Nations, for consideration by the Committee, a report on the legislative, judicial, administrative or other measures which they have adopted to give effect to the provisions of the present Convention and on the progress made in this respect:

   *(a)* Within one year after the entry into force for the State concerned;

   *(b)* Thereafter at least every four years and further whenever the Committee so requests.

2. Reports may indicate factors and difficulties affecting the degree of fulfilment of obligations under the present Convention.

*Article* 19

1. The Committee shall adopt its own rules of procedure.

2. The Committee shall elect its officers for a term of two years.

*Article* 20

1. The Committee shall normally meet for a period of not more than two weeks

annually in order to consider the reports submitted in accordance with Article 18 of the present Convention.

2. The meetings of the Committee shall normally be held at United Nations Headquarters or at any other convenient place as determined by the Committee.

*Article* 21

1. The Committee shall, through the Economic and Social Council, report annually to the General Assembly of the United Nations on its activities and may make suggestions and general recommendations based on the examination of reports and information received from the States Parties. Such suggestions and general recommendations shall be included in the report of the Committee together with comments, if any, from States Parties.

2. The Secretary-General of the United Nations shall transmit the reports of the Committee to the Commission on the Status of Women for its information.

*Article* 22

The specialized agencies shall be entitled to be represented at the consideration of the implementation of such provisions of the present Convention as fall within the scope of their activities. The Committee may invite the specialized agencies to submit reports on the implementation of the Convention in areas falling within the scope of their activities.


# PART VI

*Article* 23

Nothing in the present Convention shall affect any provisions that are more conducive to the achievement of equality between men and women which may be contained:

   *(a)* In the legislation of a State Party; or

   *(b)* In any other international convention, treaty or agreement in force for that State.

*Article* 24

States Parties undertake to adopt all necessary measures at the national level aimed at achieving the full realization of the rights recognized in the present Convention.

*Article* 25

1. The present Convention shall be open for signature by all States.

2. The Secretary-General of the United Nations is designated as the depositary of the present Convention.

3. The present Convention is subject to ratification. Instruments of ratification shall be deposited with the Secretary-General of the United Nations.

4. The present Convention shall be open to accession by all States. Accession shall be effected by the deposit of an instrument of accession with the Secretary-General of the United Nations.

*Article* 26

1. A request for the revision of the present Convention may be made at any time by any State Party by means of a notification in writing addressed to the Secretary-General of the United Nations.

2. The General Assembly of the United Nations shall decide upon the steps, if any, to be taken in respect of such a request.

*Article* 27

1. The present Convention shall enter into force on the thirtieth day after the date of deposit with the Secretary-General of the United Nations of the twentieth instrument of ratification or accession.

2. For each State ratifying the present Convention or acceding to it after the deposit of the twentieth instrument of ratification or accession, the Convention shall enter into force on the thirtieth day after the date of the deposit of its own instrument of ratification or accession.

*Article* 28

1. The Secretary-General of the United Nations shall receive and circulate to all States the text of reservations made by States at the time of ratification or accession.

2. A reservation incompatible with the object and purpose of the present Convention shall not be permitted.

3. Reservations may be withdrawn at any time by notification to this effect addressed to the Secretary-General of the United Nations, who shall then inform all States thereof. Such notification shall take effect on the date on which it is received.

*Article* 29

1. Any dispute between two or more States Parties concerning the interpretation or application of the present Convention which is not settled by negotiation shall, at the request of one of them, be submitted to arbitration. If within six months from the date of the request for arbitration the parties are unable to agree on the organization of the arbitration, any one of those parties may refer the dispute to the International Court of Justice by request in conformity with the Statute of the Court.

2. Each State Party may at the time of signature or ratification of the present Convention or accession thereto declare that it does not consider itself bound by paragraph 1 of this article. The other States Parties shall not be bound by that paragraph with respect to any State Party which has made such a reservation.

3. Any State Party which has made a reservation in accordance with paragraph 2 of this article may at any time withdraw that reservation by notification to the Secretary-General of the United Nations.

*Article* 30

The present Convention, the Arabic, Chinese, English, French, Russian and

Spanish texts of which are equally authentic, shall be deposited with the Secretary-General of the United Nations.

*In witness whereof* the undersigned, duly authorized, have signed the present Convention.

## 33. OPTIONAL PROTOCOL TO THE CONVENTION ON THE ELIMINATION OF DISCRIMINATION AGAINST WOMEN, 1999

This protocol was adopted and opened for signature by General Assembly Resolution 54/49 on 6 October 1999, without a vote; UN doc. A/54/49 (Vol. I) (2000); it entered into force on 22 December 2000.

### TEXT

*The States Parties to the present Protocol,*

*Noting* that the Charter of the United Nations reaffirms faith in fundamental human rights, in the dignity and worth of the human person and in the equal rights of men and women,

*Also noting* that the Universal Declaration of Human Rights proclaims that all human beings are born free and equal in dignity and rights and that everyone is entitled to all the rights and freedoms set forth therein, without distinction of any kind, including distinction based on sex,

*Recalling* that the International Covenants on Human Rights and other international human rights instruments prohibit discrimination on the basis of sex,

*Also recalling* the Convention on the Elimination of All Forms of Discrimination against Women ('the Convention'), in which the States Parties thereto condemn discrimination against women in all its forms and agree to pursue by all appropriate means and without delay a policy of eliminating discrimination against women,

*Reaffirming* their determination to ensure the full and equal enjoyment by women of all human rights and fundamental freedoms and to take effective action to prevent violations of these rights and freedoms,

*Have agreed* as follows:

### Article 1

A State Party to the present Protocol ('State Party') recognizes the competence of the Committee on the Elimination of Discrimination against Women ('the Committee') to receive and consider communications submitted in accordance with Article 2.

### Article 2

Communications may be submitted by or on behalf of individuals or groups of individuals, under the jurisdiction of a State Party, claiming to be victims of a violation of any of the rights set forth in the Convention by that State Party. Where a communication is submitted on behalf of individuals or groups of individuals, this shall be with their consent unless the author can justify acting on their behalf without such consent.

*Article 3*

Communications shall be in writing and shall not be anonymous. No communication shall be received by the Committee if it concerns a State Party to the Convention that is not a party to the present Protocol.

*Article 4*

1. The Committee shall not consider a communication unless it has ascertained that all available domestic remedies have been exhausted unless the application of such remedies is unreasonably prolonged or unlikely to bring effective relief.

2. The Committee shall declare a communication inadmissible where:

   (a) The same matter has already been examined by the Committee or has been or is being examined under another procedure of international investigation or settlement;

   (b) It is incompatible with the provisions of the Convention;

   (c) It is manifestly ill-founded or not sufficiently substantiated;

   (d) It is an abuse of the right to submit a communication;

   (e) The facts that are the subject of the communication occurred prior to the entry into force of the present Protocol for the State Party concerned unless those facts continued after that date.

*Article 5*

1. At any time after the receipt of a communication and before a determination on the merits has been reached, the Committee may transmit to the State Party concerned for its urgent consideration a request that the State Party take such interim measures as may be necessary to avoid possible irreparable damage to the victim or victims of the alleged violation.

2. Where the Committee exercises its discretion under paragraph 1 of the present article, this does not imply a determination on admissibility or on the merits of the communication.

*Article 6*

1. Unless the Committee considers a communication inadmissible without reference to the State Party concerned, and provided that the individual or individuals consent to the disclosure of their identity to that State Party, the Committee shall bring any communication submitted to it under the present Protocol confidentially to the attention of the State Party concerned.

2. Within six months, the receiving State Party shall submit to the Committee written explanations or statements clarifying the matter and the remedy, if any, that may have been provided by that State Party.

*Article 7*

1. The Committee shall consider communications received under the present Protocol in the light of all information made available to it by or on behalf of individuals or groups of individuals and by the State Party concerned, provided that this information is transmitted to the parties concerned.

2. The Committee shall hold closed meetings when examining communications under the present Protocol.

3. After examining a communication, the Committee shall transmit its views on the communication, together with its recommendations, if any, to the parties concerned.

4. The State Party shall give due consideration to the views of the Committee, together with its recommendations, if any, and shall submit to the Committee, within six months, a written response, including information on any action taken in the light of the views and recommendations of the Committee.

5. The Committee may invite the State Party to submit further information about any measures the State Party has taken in response to its views or recommendations, if any, including as deemed appropriate by the Committee, in the State Party's subsequent reports under Article 18 of the Convention.

*Article* 8

1. If the Committee receives reliable information indicating grave or systematic violations by a State Party of rights set forth in the Convention, the Committee shall invite that State Party to cooperate in the examination of the information and to this end to submit observations with regard to the information concerned.

2. Taking into account any observations that may have been submitted by the State Party concerned as well as any other reliable information available to it, the Committee may designate one or more of its members to conduct an inquiry and to report urgently to the Committee. Where warranted and with the consent of the State Party, the inquiry may include a visit to its territory.

3. After examining the findings of such an inquiry, the Committee shall transmit these findings to the State Party concerned together with any comments and recommendations.

4. The State Party concerned shall, within six months of receiving the findings, comments and recommendations transmitted by the Committee, submit its observations to the Committee.

5. Such an inquiry shall be conducted confidentially and the cooperation of the State Party shall be sought at all stages of the proceedings.

*Article* 9

1. The Committee may invite the State Party concerned to include in its report under Article 18 of the Convention details of any measures taken in response to an inquiry conducted under Article 8 of the present Protocol.

2. The Committee may, if necessary, after the end of the period of six months referred to in Article 8.4, invite the State Party concerned to inform it of the measures taken in response to such an inquiry.

*Article* 10

1. Each State Party may, at the time of signature or ratification of the present Protocol or accession thereto, declare that it does not recognize the competence of the Committee provided for in Articles 8 and 9.

2. Any State Party having made a declaration in accordance with paragraph 1 of

the present article may, at any time, withdraw this declaration by notification to the Secretary-General.

## Article 11

A State Party shall take all appropriate steps to ensure that individuals under its jurisdiction are not subjected to ill-treatment or intimidation as a consequence of communicating with the Committee pursuant to the present Protocol.

## Article 12

The Committee shall include in its annual report under Article 21 of the Convention a summary of its activities under the present Protocol.

## Article 13

Each State Party undertakes to make widely known and to give publicity to the Convention and the present Protocol and to facilitate access to information about the views and recommendations of the Committee, in particular, on matters involving that State Party.

## Article 14

The Committee shall develop its own rules of procedure to be followed when exercising the functions conferred on it by the present Protocol.

## Article 15

1. The present Protocol shall be open for signature by any State that has signed, ratified or acceded to the Convention.

2. The present Protocol shall be subject to ratification by any State that has ratified or acceded to the Convention. Instruments of ratification shall be deposited with the Secretary-General of the United Nations.

3. The present Protocol shall be open to accession by any State that has ratified or acceded to the Convention.

4. Accession shall be effected by the deposit of an instrument of accession with the Secretary-General of the United Nations.

## Article 16

1. The present Protocol shall enter into force three months after the date of the deposit with the Secretary-General of the United Nations of the tenth instrument of ratification or accession.

2. For each State ratifying the present Protocol or acceding to it after its entry into force, the present Protocol shall enter into force three months after the date of the deposit of its own instrument of ratification or accession.

## Article 17

No reservations to the present Protocol shall be permitted.

## Article 18

1. Any State Party may propose an amendment to the present Protocol and file it with the Secretary-General of the United Nations. The Secretary-General shall

thereupon communicate any proposed amendments to the States Parties with a request that they notify her or him whether they favour a conference of States Parties for the purpose of considering and voting on the proposal. In the event that at least one third of the States Parties favour such a conference, the Secretary-General shall convene the conference under the auspices of the United Nations. Any amendment adopted by a majority of the States Parties present and voting at the conference shall be submitted to the General Assembly of the United Nations for approval.

2. Amendments shall come into force when they have been approved by the General Assembly of the United Nations and accepted by a two-thirds majority of the States Parties to the present Protocol in accordance with their respective constitutional processes.

3. When amendments come into force, they shall be binding on those States Parties that have accepted them, other States Parties still being bound by the provisions of the present Protocol and any earlier amendments that they have accepted.

*Article* 19

1. Any State Party may denounce the present Protocol at any time by written notification addressed to the Secretary-General of the United Nations. Denunciation shall take effect six months after the date of receipt of the notification by the Secretary-General.

2. Denunciation shall be without prejudice to the continued application of the provisions of the present Protocol to any communication submitted under Article 2 or any inquiry initiated under Article 8 before the effective date of denunciation.

*Article* 20

The Secretary-General of the United Nations shall inform all States of:

  *(a)*  Signatures, ratifications and accessions under the present Protocol;
  *(b)*  The date of entry into force of the present Protocol and of any amendment under Article 18;
  *(c)*  Any denunciation under Article 19.

*Article* 21

1. The present Protocol, of which the Arabic, Chinese, English, French, Russian and Spanish texts are equally authentic, shall be deposited in the archives of the United Nations.

2. The Secretary-General of the United Nations shall transmit certified copies of the present Protocol to all States referred to in Article 25 of the Convention.

## 34. CONVENTION AGAINST TORTURE AND OTHER CRUEL, INHUMAN OR DEGRADING TREATMENT OR PUNISHMENT, 1984

This Convention was the sequel to the Declaration on Protection from Torture (see above, 27–9). The Convention was adopted by General Assembly Resolution 39/46, 10 December 1984, UN doc. A/39/51 (1984), and entered into force on 26 June 1987; for text, see 1465 UNTS 85. See also the European Convention on the Prevention of Torture, 1987 and Protocols (below, 493–503); and the Inter-American Convention to Prevent and Punish Torture, 1985 (below, 703–7).

Burgers, H. and Danelius, H. *The United Nations Convention against Torture* (1988); Byrnes, A., 'The Committee against Torture', in Alston, P. (ed.), *The United Nations and Human Rights* (1992), 509–46; Scott, C. (ed.), *Torture as Tort* (2001).

*TEXT*

*The States Parties to this Convention,*

*Considering* that, in accordance with the principles proclaimed in the Charter of the United Nations, recognition of the equal and inalienable rights of all members of the human family is the foundation of freedom, justice and peace in the world,

*Recognizing* that those rights derive from the inherent dignity of the human person,

*Considering* the obligation of States under the Charter, in particular Article 55, to promote universal respect for, and observance of, human rights and fundamental freedoms,

*Having regard* to Article 5 of the Universal Declaration of Human Rights and Article 7 of the International Covenant on Civil and Political Rights, both of which provide that no one shall be subjected to torture or to cruel, inhuman or degrading treatment or punishment,

*Having regard also* to the Declaration on the Protection of All Persons from Being Subjected to Torture and Other Cruel, Inhuman or Degrading Treatment or Punishment, adopted by the General Assembly on 9 December 1975,

*Desiring* to make more effective the struggle against torture and other cruel, inhuman or degrading treatment or punishment throughout the world,

*Have agreed* as follows:

## PART I

*Article 1*

1. For the purposes of this Convention, the term 'torture' means any act by which severe pain or suffering, whether physical or mental, is intentionally inflicted on a person for such purposes as obtaining from him or a third person information or a

confession, punishing him for an act he or a third person has committed or is suspected of having committed, or intimidating or coercing him or a third person, or for any reason based on discrimination of any kind, when such pain or suffering is inflicted by or at the instigation of or with the consent or acquiescence of a public official or other person acting in an official capacity. It does not include pain or suffering arising only from, inherent in or incidental to lawful sanctions.

2. This article is without prejudice to any international instrument or national legislation which does or may contain provisions of wider application.

*Article* 2

1. Each State Party shall take effective legislative, administrative, judicial or other measures to prevent acts of torture in any territory under its jurisdiction.

2. No exceptional circumstances whatsoever, whether a state of war or a threat of war, internal political instability or any other public emergency, may be invoked as a justification of torture.

3. An order from a superior officer or a public authority may not be invoked as a justification of torture.

*Article* 3

1. No State Party shall expel, return ('refouler') or extradite a person to another State where there are substantial grounds for believing that he would be in danger of being subjected to torture.

2. For the purpose of determining whether there are such grounds, the competent authorities shall take into account all relevant considerations including, where applicable, the existence in the State concerned of a consistent pattern of gross, flagrant or mass violations of human rights.

*Article* 4

1. Each State Party shall ensure that all acts of torture are offences under its criminal law. The same shall apply to an attempt to commit torture and to an act by any person which constitutes complicity or participation in torture.

2. Each State Party shall make these offences punishable by appropriate penalties which take into account their grave nature.

*Article* 5

1. Each State Party shall take such measures as may be necessary to establish its jurisdiction over the offences referred to in Article 4 in the following cases:

- *(a)* When the offences are committed in any territory under its jurisdiction or on board a ship or aircraft registered in that State;
- *(b)* When the alleged offender is a national of that State;
- *(c)* When the victim is a national of that State if that State considers it appropriate.

2. Each State Party shall likewise take such measures as may be necessary to establish its jurisdiction over such offences in cases where the alleged offender is present in any territory under its jurisdiction and it does not extradite him pursuant to Article 8 to any of the States mentioned in paragraph 1 of this article.

3. This Convention does not exclude any criminal jurisdiction exercised in accordance with internal law.

*Article* 6

1. Upon being satisfied, after an examination of information available to it, that the circumstances so warrant, any State Party in whose territory a person alleged to have committed any offence referred to in Article 4 is present shall take him into custody or take other legal measures to ensure his presence. The custody and other legal measures shall be as provided in the law of that State but may be continued only for such time as is necessary to enable any criminal or extradition proceedings to be instituted.

2. Such State shall immediately make a preliminary inquiry into the facts.

3. Any person in custody pursuant to paragraph 1 of this article shall be assisted in communicating immediately with the nearest appropriate representative of the State of which he is a national, or, if he is a stateless person, with the representative of the State where he usually resides.

4. When a State, pursuant to this article, has taken a person into custody, it shall immediately notify the States referred to in Article 5, paragraph 1, of the fact that such person is in custody and of the circumstances which warrant his detention. The State which makes the preliminary inquiry contemplated in paragraph 2 of this article shall promptly report its findings to the said States and shall indicate whether it intends to exercise jurisdiction.

*Article* 7

1. The State Party in the territory under whose jurisdiction a person alleged to have committed any offence referred to in Article 4 is found shall in the cases contemplated in Article 5, if it does not extradite him, submit the case to its competent authorities for the purpose of prosecution.

2. These authorities shall take their decision in the same manner as in the case of any ordinary offence of a serious nature under the law of that State. In the cases referred to in Article 5, paragraph 2, the standards of evidence required for prosecution and conviction shall in no way be less stringent than those which apply in the cases referred to in Article 5, paragraph 1.

3. Any person regarding whom proceedings are brought in connection with any of the offences referred to in Article 4 shall be guaranteed fair treatment at all stages of the proceedings.

*Article* 8

1. The offences referred to in Article 4 shall be deemed to be included as extraditable offences in any extradition treaty existing between States Parties. States Parties undertake to include such offences as extraditable offences in every extradition treaty to be concluded between them.

2. If a State Party which makes extradition conditional on the existence of a treaty receives a request for extradition from another State Party with which it has no extradition treaty, it may consider this Convention as the legal basis for extradition in respect of such offences. Extradition shall be subject to the other conditions provided by the law of the requested State.

3. States Parties which do not make extradition conditional on the existence of a treaty shall recognize such offences as extraditable offences between themselves subject to the conditions provided by the law of the requested State.

4. Such offences shall be treated, for the purpose of extradition between States Parties, as if they had been committed not only in the place in which they occurred but also in the territories of the States required to establish their jurisdiction in accordance with Article 5, paragraph 1.

*Article* 9

1. States Parties shall afford one another the greatest measure of assistance in connection with criminal proceedings brought in respect of any of the offences referred to in Article 4, including the supply of all evidence at their disposal necessary for the proceedings.

2. States Parties shall carry out their obligations under paragraph 1 of this article in conformity with any treaties on mutual judicial assistance that may exist between them.

*Article* 10

1. Each State Party shall ensure that education and information regarding the prohibition against torture are fully included in the training of law enforcement personnel, civil or military, medical personnel, public officials and other persons who may be involved in the custody, interrogation or treatment of any individual subjected to any form of arrest, detention or imprisonment.

2. Each State Party shall include this prohibition in the rules or instructions issued in regard to the duties and functions of any such person.

*Article* 11

Each State Party shall keep under systematic review interrogation rules, instructions, methods and practices as well as arrangements for the custody and treatment of persons subjected to any form of arrest, detention or imprisonment in any territory under its jurisdiction, with a view to preventing any cases of torture.

*Article* 12

Each State Party shall ensure that its competent authorities proceed to a prompt and impartial investigation, wherever there is reasonable ground to believe that an act of torture has been committed in any territory under its jurisdiction.

*Article* 13

Each State Party shall ensure that any individual who alleges he has been subjected to torture in any territory under its jurisdiction has the right to complain to, and to have his case promptly and impartially examined by, its competent authorities. Steps shall be taken to ensure that the complainant and witnesses are protected against all ill-treatment or intimidation as a consequence of his complaint or any evidence given.

*Article* 14

1. Each State Party shall ensure in its legal system that the victim of an act of

torture obtains redress and has an enforceable right to fair and adequate compensation, including the means for as full rehabilitation as possible. In the event of the death of the victim as a result of an act of torture, his dependants shall be entitled to compensation.

2. Nothing in this article shall affect any right of the victim or other persons to compensation which may exist under national law.

*Article* 15

Each State Party shall ensure that any statement which is established to have been made as a result of torture shall not be invoked as evidence in any proceedings, except against a person accused of torture as evidence that the statement was made.

*Article* 16

1. Each State Party shall undertake to prevent in any territory under its jurisdiction other acts of cruel, inhuman or degrading treatment or punishment which do not amount to torture as defined in Article 1, when such acts are committed by or at the instigation of or with the consent or acquiescence of a public official or other person acting in an official capacity. In particular, the obligations contained in Articles 10, 11, 12 and 13 shall apply with the substitution for references to torture of references to other forms of cruel, inhuman or degrading treatment or punishment.

2. The provisions of this Convention are without prejudice to the provisions of any other international instrument or national law which prohibits cruel, inhuman or degrading treatment or punishment or which relates to extradition or expulsion.

## PART II

*Article* 17

1. There shall be established a Committee against Torture (hereinafter referred to as the Committee) which shall carry out the functions hereinafter provided. The Committee shall consist of ten experts of high moral standing and recognized competence in the field of human rights, who shall serve in their personal capacity. The experts shall be elected by the States Parties, consideration being given to equitable geographical distribution and to the usefulness of the participation of some persons having legal experience.

2. The members of the Committee shall be elected by secret ballot from a list of persons nominated by States Parties. Each State Party may nominate one person from among its own nationals. States Parties shall bear in mind the usefulness of nominating persons who are also members of the Human Rights Committee established under the International Covenant on Civil and Political Rights and who are willing to serve on the Committee against Torture.

3. Elections of the members of the Committee shall be held at biennial meetings of States Parties convened by the Secretary-General of the United Nations. At those meetings, for which two thirds of the States Parties shall constitute a quorum,

the persons elected to the Committee shall be those who obtain the largest number of votes and an absolute majority of the votes of the representatives of States Parties present and voting.

4. The initial election shall be held no later than six months after the date of the entry into force of this Convention. At least four months before the date of each election, the Secretary-General of the United Nations shall address a letter to the States Parties inviting them to submit their nominations within three months. The Secretary-General shall prepare a list in alphabetical order of all persons thus nominated, indicating the States Parties which have nominated them, and shall submit it to the States Parties.

5. The members of the Committee shall be elected for a term of four years. They shall be eligible for re-election if renominated. However, the term of five of the members elected at the first election shall expire at the end of two years; immediately after the first election the names of these five members shall be chosen by lot by the Chairman of the meeting referred to in paragraph 3 of this article.

6. If a member of the Committee dies or resigns or for any other cause can no longer perform his Committee duties, the State Party which nominated him shall appoint another expert from among its nationals to serve for the remainder of his term, subject to the approval of the majority of the States Parties. The approval shall be considered given unless half or more of the States Parties respond negatively within six weeks after having been informed by the Secretary-General of the United Nations of the proposed appointment.

7. States Parties shall be responsible for the expenses of the members of the Committee while they are in performance of Committee duties.

*Article* 18

1. The Committee shall elect its officers for a term of two years. They may be re-elected.

2. The Committee shall establish its own rules of procedure, but these rules shall provide, *inter alia*, that:

 *(a)* Six members shall constitute a quorum;

 *(b)* Decisions of the Committee shall be made by a majority vote of the members present.

3. The Secretary-General of the United Nations shall provide the necessary staff and facilities for the effective performance of the functions of the Committee under this Convention.

4. The Secretary-General of the United Nations shall convene the initial meeting of the Committee. After its initial meeting, the Committee shall meet at such times as shall be provided in its rules of procedure.

5. The States Parties shall be responsible for expenses incurred in connection with the holding of meetings of the States Parties and of the Committee, including reimbursement to the United Nations for any expenses, such as the cost of staff and facilities, incurred by the United Nations pursuant to paragraph 3 of this article.

*Article* 19

1. The States Parties shall submit to the Committee, through the Secretary-General of the United Nations, reports on the measures they have taken to give effect to their undertakings under this Convention, within one year after the entry into force of the Convention for the State Party concerned. Thereafter the States Parties shall submit supplementary reports every four years on any new measures taken and such other reports as the Committee may request.

2. The Secretary-General of the United Nations shall transmit the reports to all States Parties.

3. Each report shall be considered by the Committee which may make such general comments on the report as it may consider appropriate and shall forward these to the State Party concerned. That State Party may respond with any observations it chooses to the Committee.

4. The Committee may, at its discretion, decide to include any comments made by it in accordance with paragraph 3 of this article, together with the observations thereon received from the State Party concerned, in its annual report made in accordance with Article 24. If so requested by the State Party concerned, the Committee may also include a copy of the report submitted under paragraph 1 of this article.

*Article* 20

1. If the Committee receives reliable information which appears to it to contain well-founded indications that torture is being systematically practised in the territory of a State Party, the Committee shall invite that State Party to co-operate in the examination of the information and to this end to submit observations with regard to the information concerned.

2. Taking into account any observations which may have been submitted by the State Party concerned, as well as any other relevant information available to it, the Committee may, if it decides that this is warranted, designate one or more of its members to make a confidential inquiry and to report to the Committee urgently.

3. If an inquiry is made in accordance with paragraph 2 of this article, the Committee shall seek the co-operation of the State Party concerned. In agreement with that State Party, such an inquiry may include a visit to its territory.

4. After examining the findings of its member or members submitted in accordance with paragraph 2 of this article, the Commission shall transmit these findings to the State Party concerned together with any comments or suggestions which seem appropriate in view of the situation.

5. All the proceedings of the Committee referred to in paragraphs 1 to 4 of this article shall be confidential, and at all stages of the proceedings the co-operation of the State Party shall be sought. After such proceedings have been completed with regard to an inquiry made in accordance with paragraph 2, the Committee may, after consultations with the State Party concerned, decide to include a summary account of the results of the proceedings in its annual report made in accordance with Article 24.

*Article* 21

1. A State Party to this Convention may at any time declare under this article that

it recognizes the competence of the Committee to receive and consider communications to the effect that a State Party claims that another State Party is not
fulfilling its obligations under this Convention. Such communications may be
received and considered according to the procedures laid down in this article only
if submitted by a State Party which has made a declaration recognizing in regard
to itself the competence of the Committee. No communication shall be dealt with
by the Committee under this article if it concerns a State Party which has not made
such a declaration. Communications received under this article shall be dealt with
in accordance with the following procedure;

(a) If a State Party considers that another State Party is not giving effect to the
provisions of this Convention, it may, by written communication, bring
the matter to the attention of that State Party. Within three months after the
receipt of the communication the receiving State shall afford the State
which sent the communication an explanation or any other statement in
writing clarifying the matter, which should include, to the extent possible
and pertinent, reference to domestic procedures and remedies taken,
pending or available in the matter;

(b) If the matter is not adjusted to the satisfaction of both States Parties concerned within six months after the receipt by the receiving State of the
initial communication, either State shall have the right to refer the matter to
the Committee, by notice given to the Committee and to the other State;

(c) The Committee shall deal with a matter referred to it under this article only
after it has ascertained that all domestic remedies have been invoked and
exhausted in the matter, in conformity with the generally recognized principles of international law. This shall not be the rule where the application
of the remedies is unreasonably prolonged or is unlikely to bring effective
relief to the person who is the victim of the violation of this Convention;

(d) The Committee shall hold closed meetings when examining communications under this article;

(e) Subject to the provisions of subparagraph (c), the Committee shall make
available its good offices to the States Parties concerned with a view to a
friendly solution of the matter on the basis of respect for the obligations
provided for in this Convention. For this purpose, the Committee may,
when appropriate, set up an ad hoc conciliation commission;

(f) In any matter referred to it under this article, the Committee may call upon
the States Parties concerned, referred to in subparagraph (b), to supply any
relevant information;

(g) The States Parties concerned, referred to in subparagraph (b), shall have
the right to be represented when the matter is being considered by the
Committee and to make submissions orally and/or in writing;

(h) The Committee shall, within twelve months after the date of receipt of
notice under subparagraph (b), submit a report:

(i) If a solution within the terms of subparagraph (e) is reached, the
Committee shall confine its report to a brief statement of the facts and
of the solution reached;

(ii) If a solution within the terms of subparagraph (e) is not reached, the

Committee shall confine its report to a brief statement of the facts; the written submissions and record of the oral submissions made by the States Parties concerned shall be attached to the report. In every matter, the report shall be communicated to the States Parties concerned.

2. The provisions of this article shall come into force when five States Parties to this Convention have made declarations under paragraph 1 of this article. Such declarations shall be deposited by the States Parties with the Secretary-General of the United Nations, who shall transmit copies thereof to the other States Parties. A declaration may be withdrawn at any time by notification to the Secretary-General. Such a withdrawal shall not prejudice the consideration of any matter which is the subject of a communication already transmitted under this article; no further communication by any State Party shall be received under this article after the notification of withdrawal of the declaration has been received by the Secretary-General, unless the State Party concerned has made a new declaration.

*Article 22*

1. A State Party to this Convention may at any time declare under this article that it recognizes the competence of the Committee to receive and consider communications from or on behalf of individuals subject to its jurisdiction who claim to be victims of a violation by a State Party of the provisions of the Convention. No communication shall be received by the Committee if it concerns a State Party which has not made such a declaration.

2. The Committee shall consider inadmissible any communication under this article which is anonymous or which it considers to be an abuse of the right of submission of such communications or to be incompatible with the provisions of this Convention.

3. Subject to the provisions of paragraph 2, the Committee shall bring any communications submitted to it under this article to the attention of the State Party to this Convention which has made a declaration under paragraph 1 and is alleged to be violating any provisions of the Convention. Within six months, the receiving State shall submit to the Committee written explanations or statements clarifying the matter and the remedy, if any, that may have been taken by that State.

4. The Committee shall consider communications received under this article in the light of all information made available to it by or on behalf of the individual and by the State Party concerned.

5. The Committee shall not consider any communications from an individual under this article unless it has ascertained that:

(a) The same matter has not been, and is not being, examined under another procedure of international investigation or settlement;

(b) The individual has exhausted all available domestic remedies; this shall not be the rule where the application of the remedies is unreasonably prolonged or is unlikely to bring effective relief to the person who is the victim of the violation of this Convention.

6. The Committee shall hold closed meetings when examining communications under this article.

7. The Committee shall forward its views to the State Party concerned and to the individual.

8. The provisions of this article shall come into force when five States Parties to this Convention have made declarations under paragraph 1 of this article. Such declarations shall be deposited by the States Parties with the Secretary-General of the United Nations, who shall transmit copies thereof to the other States Parties. A declaration may be withdrawn at any time by notification to the Secretary-General. Such a withdrawal shall not prejudice the consideration of any matter which is the subject of a communication already transmitted under this article; no further communication by or on behalf of an individual shall be received under this article after the notification of withdrawal of the declaration has been received by the Secretary General, unless the State Party has made a new declaration.

*Article* 23

The members of the Committee and of the ad hoc conciliation commissions which may be appointed under Article 21, paragraph 1 (e), shall be entitled to the facilities, privileges and immunities of experts on mission for the United Nations as laid down in the relevant sections of the Convention on the Privileges and Immunities of the United Nations.

*Article* 24

The Committee shall submit an annual report on its activities under this Convention to the States Parties and to the General Assembly of the United Nations.

## PART III

*Article* 25

1. This Convention is open for signature by all States.

2. This Convention is subject to ratification. Instruments of ratification shall be deposited with the Secretary-General of the United Nations.

*Article* 26

This Convention is open to accession by all States. Accession shall be effected by the deposit of an instrument of accession with the Secretary-General of the United Nations.

*Article* 27

1. This Convention shall enter into force on the thirtieth day after the date of the deposit with the Secretary-General of the United Nations of the twentieth instrument of ratification or accession.

2. For each State ratifying this Convention or acceding to it after the deposit of the twentieth instrument of ratification or accession, the Convention shall enter into force on the thirtieth day after the date of the deposit of its own instrument of ratification or accession.

*Article* 28

1. Each State may, at the time of signature or ratification of this Convention or accession thereto, declare that it does not recognize the competence of the Committee provided for in Article 20.

2. Any State Party having made a reservation in accordance with paragraph 1 of this article may, at any time, withdraw this reservation by notification to the Secretary-General of the United Nations.

*Article* 29

1. Any State Party to this Convention may propose an amendment and file it with the Secretary-General of the United Nations. The Secretary-General shall thereupon communicate the proposed amendment to the States Parties with a request that they notify him whether they favour a conference of States Parties for the purpose of considering and voting upon the proposal. In the event that within four months from the date of such communication at least one third of the States Parties favours such a conference, the Secretary-General shall convene the conference under the auspices of the United Nations. Any amendment adopted by a majority of the States Parties present and voting at the conference shall be submitted by the Secretary-General to all the States Parties for acceptance.

2. An amendment adopted in accordance with paragraph 1 of this article shall enter into force when two thirds of the States Parties to this Convention have notified the Secretary-General of the United Nations that they have accepted it in accordance with their respective constitutional processes.

3. When amendments enter into force, they shall be binding on those States Parties which have accepted them, other States Parties still being bound by the provisions of this Convention and any earlier amendments which they have accepted.

*Article* 30

1. Any dispute between two or more States Parties concerning the interpretation or application of this Convention which cannot be settled through negotiation shall, at the request of one of them, be submitted to arbitration. If within six months from the date of the request for arbitration the Parties are unable to agree on the organization of the arbitration, any one of those Parties may refer the dispute to the International Court of Justice by request in conformity with the Statute of the Court.

2. Each State may, at the time of signature or ratification of this Convention or accession thereto, declare that it does not consider itself bound by paragraph 1 of this article. The other States Parties shall not be bound by paragraph 1 of this article with respect to any State Party having made such a reservation.

3. Any State Party having made a reservation in accordance with paragraph 2 of this article may at any time withdraw this reservation by notification to the Secretary-General of the United Nations.

*Article* 31

1. A State Party may denounce this Convention by written notification to the Secretary-General of the United Nations. Denunciation becomes effective one year after the date of receipt of the notification by the Secretary-General .

2. Such a denunciation shall not have the effect of releasing the State Party from its obligations under this Convention in regard to any act or omission which occurs prior to the date at which the denunciation becomes effective, nor shall denunciation prejudice in any way the continued consideration of any matter which is already under consideration by the Committee prior to the date at which the denunciation becomes effective.

3. Following the date at which the denunciation of a State Party becomes effective, the Committee shall not commence consideration of any new matter regarding that State.

*Article* 32

The Secretary-General of the United Nations shall inform all States Members of the United Nations and all States which have signed this Convention or acceded to it of the following:

   *(a)* Signatures, ratifications and accessions under Articles 25 and 26;
   *(b)* The date of entry into force of this Convention under Article 27 and the date of the entry into force of any amendments under Article 29;
   *(c)* Denunciations under Article 31.

*Article* 33

1. This Convention, of which the Arabic, Chinese, English, French, Russian and Spanish texts are equally authentic, shall be deposited with the Secretary-General of the United Nations.

2. The Secretary-General of the United Nations shall transmit certified copies of this Convention to all States.

## 35. CONVENTION ON THE RIGHTS OF THE CHILD, 1989

The Convention was adopted by General Assembly Resolution 44/25 without vote on 20 November 1989. The text appears in the Annex to the Resolution: UN doc. A/44/49 (1989). The Convention entered into force on 2 September 1990, one month after the twentieth State ratified it, in accordance with Article 49(1). For text see 1577 UNTS 3.

The Convention is an elaboration of human rights standards in respect of the child. However, human rights standards were applicable to the child (as an individual) independently of the new instrument by virtue of the principles of general international law. The rights of the child are also the subject of Article 24 of the International Covenant on Civil and Political Rights (see above).

In 1979 the United Nations Human Rights Commission began consideration of a Polish proposal for a draft Convention on the Rights of the Child. The precursors of the Convention of 1989 include the Universal Declaration of Human Rights, Articles 2 and 25(2) (see above, 18–23), and the Declaration of the Rights of the Child adopted by the General Assembly on 20 December 1959 (for the text, see the second edition of this work, p. 108)

For comment on the Convention, see Cohen, C. P., (1989) 28 *ILM* 1448; McGoldrick, D., (1991) 5 *International Journal of Law and the Family*, 132. See also Alston, P., *The Best Interests of the Child: Reconciling Culture and Human Rights* (1994); Van Bueren, G., *The International Law on the Rights of the Child* (1995).

*TEXT*

### Preamble

*The States Parties to the present Convention,*

*Considering* that, in accordance with the principles proclaimed in the Charter of the United Nations, recognition of the inherent dignity and of the equal and inalienable rights of all members of the human family is the foundation of freedom, justice and peace in the world,

*Bearing in mind* that the peoples of the United Nations have, in the Charter, reaffirmed their faith in fundamental human rights and in the dignity and worth of the human person, and have determined to promote social progress and better standards of life in larger freedom,

*Recognizing* that the United Nations has, in the Universal Declaration of Human Rights and in the International Covenants on Human Rights, proclaimed and agreed that everyone is entitled to all the rights and freedoms set forth therein, without distinction of any kind, such as race, colour, sex, language, religion, political or other opinion, national or social origin, property, birth or other status,

*Recalling* that, in the Universal Declaration of Human Rights, the United Nations has proclaimed that childhood is entitled to special care and assistance,

*Convinced* that the family, as the fundamental group of society and the natural environment for the growth and well-being of all its members and particularly children, should be afforded the necessary protection and assistance so that it can fully assume its responsibilities within the community,

*Recognizing* that the child, for the full and harmonious development of his or her personality, should grow up in a family environment, in an atmosphere of happiness, love and understanding,

*Considering* that the child should be fully prepared to live an individual life in society, and brought up in the spirit of the ideals proclaimed in the Charter of the United Nations, and in particular in the spirit of peace, dignity, tolerance, freedom, equality and solidarity,

*Bearing in mind* that the need to extend particular care to the child has been stated in the Geneva Declaration of the Rights of the Child of 1924 and in the Declaration of the Rights of the Child adopted by the General Assembly on 20 November 1959 and recognized in the Universal Declaration of Human Rights, in the International Covenant on Civil and Political Rights (in particular in Articles 23 and 24), in the International Covenant on Economic, Social and Cultural Rights (in particular in Article 10) and in the statutes and relevant instruments of specialized agencies and international organizations concerned with the welfare of children,

*Bearing in mind* that, as indicated in the Declaration of the Rights of the Child, 'the child, by reason of his physical and mental immaturity, needs special safeguards and care, including appropriate legal protection, before as well as after birth',

*Recalling* the provisions of the Declaration on Social and Legal Principles relating to the Protection and Welfare of Children, with Special Reference to Foster Placement and Adoption Nationally and Internationally; the United Nations Standard Minimum Rules for the Administration of Juvenile Justice (The Beijing Rules); and the Declaration on the Protection of Women and Children in Emergency and Armed Conflict,

*Recognizing* that, in all countries in the world, there are children living in exceptionally difficult conditions, and that such children need special consideration,

*Taking due account* of the importance of the traditions and cultural values of each people for the protection and harmonious development of the child,

*Recognizing* the importance of international co-operation for improving the living conditions of children in every country, in particular in the developing countries,

*Have agreed* as follows:

# PART I

*Article* 1

For the purposes of the present Convention, a child means every human being below the age of eighteen years unless under the law applicable to the child, majority is attained earlier.

*Article* 2

1. States Parties shall respect and ensure the rights set forth in the present Convention to each child within their jurisdiction without discrimination of any kind, irrespective of the child's or his or her parent's or legal guardian's race, colour, sex,

language, religion, political or other opinion, national, ethnic or social origin, property, disability, birth or other status.

2. States Parties shall take all appropriate measures to ensure that the child is protected against all forms of discrimination or punishment on the basis of the status, activities, expressed opinions, or beliefs of the child's parents, legal guardians, or family members.

## Article 3

1. In all actions concerning children, whether undertaken by public or private social welfare institutions, courts of law, administrative authorities or legislative bodies, the best interests of the child shall be a primary consideration.

2. States Parties undertake to ensure the child such protection and care as is necessary for his or her well-being, taking into account the rights and duties of his or her parents, legal guardians, or other individuals legally responsible for him or her, and, to this end, shall take all appropriate legislative and administrative measures.

3. States Parties shall ensure that the institutions, services and facilities responsible for the care or protection of children shall conform with the standards established by competent authorities, particularly in the areas of safety, health, in the number and suitability of their staff, as well as competent supervision.

## Article 4

States Parties shall undertake all appropriate legislative, administrative, and other measures for the implementation of the rights recognized in the present Convention. With regard to economic, social and cultural rights, States Parties shall undertake such measures to the maximum extent of their available resources and, where needed, within the framework of international co-operation.

## Article 5

States Parties shall respect the responsibilities, rights and duties of parents or, where applicable, the members of the extended family or community as provided for by local custom, legal guardians or other persons legally responsible for the child, to provide, in a manner consistent with the evolving capacities of the child, appropriate direction and guidance in the exercise by the child of the rights recognized in the present Convention.

## Article 6

1. States Parties recognize that every child has the inherent right to life.

2. States Parties shall ensure to the maximum extent possible the survival and development of the child.

## Article 7

1. The child shall be registered immediately after birth and shall have the right from birth to a name, the right to acquire a nationality and, as far as possible, the right to know and be cared for by his or her parents.

2. States Parties shall ensure the implementation of these rights in accordance with their national law and their obligations under the relevant international instruments in this field, in particular where the child would otherwise be stateless.

*Article* 8

1. States Parties undertake to respect the right of the child to preserve his or her identity, including nationality, name and family relations as recognized by law without unlawful interference.

2. Where a child is illegally deprived of some or all of the elements of his or her identity, States Parties shall provide appropriate assistance and protection, with a view to re-establishing speedily his or her identity.

*Article* 9

1. States Parties shall ensure that a child shall not be separated from his or her parents against their will, except when competent authorities subject to judicial review determine, in accordance with applicable law and procedures, that such separation is necessary for the best interests of the child. Such determination may be necessary in a particular case such as one involving abuse or neglect of the child by the parents, or one where the parents are living separately and a decision must be made as to the child's place of residence.

2. In any proceedings pursuant to paragraph 1 of the present article, all interested parties shall be given an opportunity to participate in the proceedings and make their views known.

3. States Parties shall respect the right of the child who is separated from one or both parents to maintain personal relations and direct contact with both parents on a regular basis, except if it is contrary to the child's best interests.

4. Where such separation results from any action initiated by a State Party, such as the detention, imprisonment, exile, deportation or death (including death arising from any cause while the person is in the custody of the State) of one or both parents or of the child, that State Party shall, upon request, provide the parents, the child or, if appropriate, another member of the family with the essential information concerning the whereabouts of the absent member(s) of the family unless the provision of the information would be detrimental to the well-being of the child. States Parties shall further ensure that the submission of such a request shall of itself entail no adverse consequences for the person(s) concerned.

*Article* 10

1. In accordance with the obligation of States Parties under Article 9, paragraph 1, applications by a child or his or her parents to enter or leave a State Party for the purpose of family reunification shall be dealt with by States Parties in a positive, humane and expeditious manner. States Parties shall further ensure that the submission of such a request shall entail no adverse consequences for the applicants and for the members of their family.

2. A child whose parents reside in different States shall have the right to maintain on a regular basis, save in exceptional circumstances personal relations and direct contacts with both parents. Towards that end and in accordance with the obligation of States Parties under Article 9, paragraph 1, States Parties shall respect the right of the child and his or her parents to leave any country, including their own, and to enter their own country. The right to leave any country shall be subject only to such restrictions as are prescribed by law and which are necessary to protect the national security, public order (*ordre public*), public health or morals or the rights

and freedoms of others and are consistent with the other rights recognized in the present Convention.

*Article* 11

1. States Parties shall take measures to combat the illicit transfer and non-return of children abroad.

2. To this end, States Parties shall promote the conclusion of bilateral or multilateral agreements or accession to existing agreements.

*Article* 12

1. States Parties shall assure to the child who is capable of forming his or her own views the right to express those views freely in all matters affecting the child, the views of the child being given due weight in accordance with the age and maturity of the child.

2. For this purpose, the child shall in particular be provided the opportunity to be heard in any judicial and administrative proceedings affecting the child, either directly, or through a representative or an appropriate body, in a manner consistent with the procedural rules of national law.

*Article* 13

1. The child shall have the right to freedom of expression; this right shall include freedom to seek, receive and impart information and ideas of all kinds, regardless of frontiers, either orally, in writing or in print, in the form of art, or through any other media of the child's choice.

2. The exercise of this right may be subject to certain restrictions, but these shall only be such as are provided by law and are necessary:

    *(a)*  For respect of the rights or reputations of others; or

    *(b)*  For the protection of national security or of public order (*ordre public*), or of public health or morals.

*Article* 14

1. States Parties shall respect the right of the child to freedom of thought, conscience and religion.

2. States Parties shall respect the rights and duties of the parents and, when applicable, legal guardians, to provide direction to the child in the exercise of his or her right in a manner consistent with the evolving capacities of the child.

3. Freedom to manifest one's religion or beliefs may be subject only to such limitations as are prescribed by law and are necessary to protect public safety, order, health or morals, or the fundamental rights and freedoms of others.

*Article* 15

1. States Parties recognize the rights of the child to freedom of association and to freedom of peaceful assembly.

2. No restrictions may be placed on the exercise of these rights other than those imposed in conformity with the law and which are necessary in a democratic society in the interests of national security or public safety, public order (*ordre*

*public*), the protection of public health or morals or the protection of the rights and freedoms of others.

*Article* 16

1. No child shall be subjected to arbitrary or unlawful interference with his or her privacy, family, home or correspondence, nor to unlawful attacks on his or her honour and reputation.

2. The child has the right to the protection of the law against such interference or attacks.

*Article* 17

States Parties recognize the important function performed by the mass media and shall ensure that the child has access to information and material from a diversity of national and international sources, especially those aimed at the promotion of his or her social, spiritual and moral well-being and physical and mental health. To this end, States Parties shall:

> *(a)* Encourage the mass media to disseminate information and material of social and cultural benefit to the child and in accordance with the spirit of Article 29;
>
> *(b)* Encourage international co-operation in the production, exchange and dissemination of such information and material from a diversity of cultural, national and international sources;
>
> *(c)* Encourage the production and dissemination of children's books;
>
> *(d)* Encourage the mass media to have particular regard to the linguistic needs of the child who belongs to a minority group or who is indigenous;
>
> *(e)* Encourage the development of appropriate guidelines for the protection of the child from information and material injurious to his or her well-being, bearing in mind the provisions of Articles 13 and 18.

*Article* 18

1. States Parties shall use their best efforts to ensure recognition of the principle that both parents have common responsibilities for the upbringing and development of the child. Parents or, as the case may be, legal guardians, have the primary responsibility for the upbringing and development of the child. The best interests of the child will be their basic concern.

2. For the purpose of guaranteeing and promoting the rights set forth in the present Convention, States Parties shall render appropriate assistance to parents and legal guardians in the performance of their child-rearing responsibilities and shall ensure the development of institutions, facilities and services for the care of children.

3. States Parties shall take all appropriate measures to ensure that children of working parents have the right to benefit from child-care services and facilities for which they are eligible.

*Article* 19

1. States Parties shall take all appropriate legislative, administrative, social and

educational measures to protect the child from all forms of physical or mental violence, injury or abuse, neglect or negligent treatment, maltreatment or exploitation, including sexual abuse, while in the care of parent(s), legal guardian(s) or any other person who has the care of the child.

2. Such protective measures should, as appropriate, include effective procedures for the establishment of social programmes to provide necessary support for the child and for those who have the care of the child, as well as for other forms of prevention and for identification, reporting, referral, investigation, treatment and follow-up of instances of child maltreatment described heretofore, and, as appropriate, for judicial involvement.

*Article* 20

1. A child temporarily or permanently deprived of his or her family environment, or in whose own best interests cannot be allowed to remain in that environment, shall be entitled to special protection and assistance provided by the State.

2. States Parties shall in accordance with their national laws ensure alternative care for such a child.

3. Such care could include, *inter alia*, foster placement, kafalah of Islamic law, adoption or if necessary placement in suitable institutions for the care of children. When considering solutions, due regard shall be paid to the desirability of continuity in a child's upbringing and to the child's ethnic, religious, cultural and linguistic background.

*Article* 21

States Parties that recognize and/or permit the system of adoption shall ensure that the best interests of the child shall be the paramount consideration and they shall:

(a) Ensure that the adoption of a child is authorized only by competent authorities who determine, in accordance with applicable law and procedures and on the basis of all pertinent and reliable information, that the adoption is permissible in view of the child's status concerning parents, relatives and legal guardians and that, if required, the persons concerned have given their informed consent to the adoption on the basis of such counselling as may be necessary;

(b) Recognize that inter-country adoption may be considered as an alternative means of child's care, if the child cannot be placed in a foster or an adoptive family or cannot in any suitable manner be cared for in the child's country of origin;

(c) Ensure that the child concerned by inter-country adoption enjoys safeguards and standards equivalent to those existing in the case of national adoption;

(d) Take all appropriate measures to ensure that, in inter-country adoption, the placement does not result in improper financial gain for those involved in it;

(e) Promote, where appropriate, the objectives of the present article by concluding bilateral or multilateral arrangements or agreements, and endeavour, within this framework, to ensure that the placement of the child in another country is carried out by competent authorities or organs.

*Article 22*

1. States Parties shall take appropriate measures to ensure that a child who is seeking refugee status or who is considered a refugee in accordance with applicable international or domestic law and procedures shall, whether unaccompanied or accompanied by his or her parents or by any other person, receive appropriate protection and humanitarian assistance in the enjoyment of applicable rights set forth in the present Convention and in other international human rights or humanitarian instruments to which the said States are Parties.

2. For this purpose, States Parties shall provide, as they consider appropriate, co-operation in any efforts by the United Nations and other competent intergovernmental organizations or non-governmental organizations co-operating with the United Nations to protect and assist such a child and to trace the parents or other members of the family of any refugee child in order to obtain information necessary for reunification with his or her family. In cases where no parents or other members of the family can be found, the child shall be accorded the same protection as any other child permanently or temporarily deprived of his or her family environment for any reason, as set forth in the present Convention.

*Article 23*

1. States Parties recognize that a mentally or physically disabled child should enjoy a full and decent life, in conditions which ensure dignity, promote self-reliance and facilitate the child's active participation in the community.

2. States Parties recognize the right of the disabled child to special care and shall encourage and ensure the extension, subject to available resources, to the eligible child and those responsible for his or her care, of assistance for which application is made and which is appropriate to the child's condition and to the circumstances of the parents or others caring for the child.

3. Recognizing the special needs of a disabled child, assistance extended in accordance with paragraph 2 of the present article shall be provided free of charge, whenever possible, taking into account the financial resources of the parents or others caring for the child, and shall be designed to ensure that the disabled child has effective access to and receives education, training, health care services, rehabilitation services, preparation for employment and recreation opportunities in a manner conducive to the child's achieving the fullest possible social integration and individual development, including his or her cultural and spiritual development

4. States Parties shall promote, in the spirit of international cooperation, the exchange of appropriate information in the field of preventive health care and of medical, psychological and functional treatment of disabled children, including dissemination of and access to information concerning methods of rehabilitation, education and vocational services, with the aim of enabling States Parties to improve their capabilities and skills and to widen their experience in these areas. In this regard, particular account shall be taken of the needs of developing countries.

*Article 24*

1. States Parties recognize the right of the child to the enjoyment of the highest attainable standard of health and to facilities for the treatment of illness and

rehabilitation of health. States Parties shall strive to ensure that no child is deprived of his or her right of access to such health care services.

2. States Parties shall pursue full implementation of this right and, in particular, shall take appropriate measures:

(a)  To diminish infant and child mortality;

(b)  To ensure the provision of necessary medical assistance and health care to all children with emphasis on the development of primary health care;

(c)  To combat disease and malnutrition, including within the framework of primary health care, through, *inter alia*, the application of readily available technology and through the provision of adequate nutritious foods and clean drinking-water, taking into consideration the dangers and risks of environmental pollution;

(d)  To ensure appropriate pre-natal and post-natal health care for mothers;

(e)  To ensure that all segments of society, in particular parents and children, are informed, have access to education and are supported in the use of basic knowledge of child health and nutrition, the advantages of breastfeeding, hygiene and environmental sanitation and the prevention of accidents;

(f)  To develop preventive health care, guidance for parents and family planning education and services.

3. States Parties shall take all effective and appropriate measures with a view to abolishing traditional practices prejudicial to the health of children.

4. States Parties undertake to promote and encourage international co-operation with a view to achieving progressively the full realization of the right recognized in the present article. In this regard, particular account shall be taken of the needs of developing countries.

*Article* 25

States Parties recognize the right of a child who has been placed by the competent authorities for the purposes of care, protection or treatment of his or her physical or mental health, to a periodic review of the treatment provided to the child and all other circumstances relevant to his or her placement.

*Article* 26

1. States Parties shall recognize for every child the right to benefit from social security, including social insurance, and shall take the necessary measures to achieve the full realization of this right in accordance with their national law.

2. The benefits should, where appropriate, be granted, taking into account the resources and the circumstances of the child and persons having responsibility for the maintenance of the child, as well as any other consideration relevant to an application for benefits made by or on behalf of the child.

*Article* 27

1. States Parties recognize the right of every child to a standard of living adequate for the child's physical, mental, spiritual, moral and social development.

2. The parent(s) or others responsible for the child have the primary responsibility

to secure, within their abilities and financial capacities, the conditions of living necessary for the child's development.

3. States Parties, in accordance with national conditions and within their means, shall take appropriate measures to assist parents and others responsible for the child to implement this right and shall in case of need provide material assistance and support programmes, particularly with regard to nutrition, clothing and housing.

4. States Parties shall take all appropriate measures to secure the recovery of maintenance for the child from the parents or other persons having financial responsibility for the child, both within the State Party and from abroad. In particular, where the person having financial responsibility for the child lives in a State different from that of the child, States Parties shall promote the accession to international agreements or the conclusion of such agreements, as well as the making of other appropriate arrangements.

*Article* 28

1. States Parties recognize the right of the child to education, and with a view to achieving this right progressively and on the basis of equal opportunity, they shall, in particular:

 (a) Make primary education compulsory and available free to all;

 (b) Encourage the development of different forms of secondary education, including general and vocational education, make them available and accessible to every child, and take appropriate measures such as the introduction of free education and offering financial assistance in case of need;

 (c) Make higher education accessible to all on the basis of capacity by every appropriate means;

 (d) Make educational and vocational information and guidance available and accessible to all children;

 (e) Take measures to encourage regular attendance at schools and the reduction of drop-out rates.

2. States Parties shall take all appropriate measures to ensure that school discipline is administered in a manner consistent with the child's human dignity and in conformity with the present Convention.

3. States Parties shall promote and encourage international cooperation in matters relating to education, in particular with a view to contributing to the elimination of ignorance and illiteracy throughout the world and facilitating access to scientific and technical knowledge and modern teaching methods. In this regard, particular account shall be taken of the needs of developing countries.

*Article* 29

1. States Parties agree that the education of the child shall be directed to:

 (a) The development of the child's personality, talents and mental and physical abilities to their fullest potential;

 (b) The development of respect for human rights and fundamental freedoms, and for the principles enshrined in the Charter of the United Nations;

(c) The development of respect for the child's parents, his or her own cultural identity, language and values, for the national values of the country in which the child is living, the country from which he or she may originate, and for civilizations different from his or her own;

(d) The preparation of the child for responsible life in a free society, in the spirit of understanding, peace, tolerance, equality of sexes, and friendship among all peoples, ethnic, national and religious groups and persons of indigenous origin;

(e) The development of respect for the natural environment.

2. No part of the present article or Article 28 shall be construed so as to interfere with the liberty of individuals and bodies to establish and direct educational institutions, subject always to the observance of the principle set forth in paragraph 1 of the present article and to the requirements that the education given in such institutions shall conform to such minimum standards as may be laid down by the State.

### Article 30

In those States in which ethnic, religious or linguistic minorities or persons of indigenous origin exist, a child belonging to such a minority or who is indigenous shall not be denied the right, in community with other members of his or her group, to enjoy his or her own culture, to profess and practise his or her own religion, or to use his or her own language.

### Article 31

1. States Parties recognize the right of the child to rest and leisure, to engage in play and recreational activities appropriate to the age of the child and to participate freely in cultural life and the arts.

2. States Parties shall respect and promote the right of the child to participate fully in cultural and artistic life and shall encourage the provision of appropriate and equal opportunities for cultural, artistic, recreational and leisure activity.

### Article 32

1. States Parties recognize the right of the child to be protected from economic exploitation and from performing any work that is likely to be hazardous or to interfere with the child's education, or to be harmful to the child's health or physical, mental, spiritual, moral or social development.

2. States Parties shall take legislative, administrative, social and educational measures to ensure the implementation of the present article. To this end, and having regard to the relevant provisions of other international instruments, States Parties shall in particular:

(a) Provide for a minimum age or minimum ages for admission to employment;

(b) Provide for appropriate regulation of the hours and conditions of employment;

(c) Provide for appropriate penalties or other sanctions to ensure the effective enforcement of the present article.

*Article* 33

States Parties shall take all appropriate measures, including legislative, administrative, social and educational measures, to protect children from the illicit use of narcotic drugs and psychotropic substances as defined in the relevant international treaties, and to prevent the use of children in the illicit production and trafficking of such substances.

*Article* 34

States Parties undertake to protect the child from all forms of sexual exploitation and sexual abuse. For these purposes, States Parties shall in particular take all appropriate national, bilateral and multilateral measures to prevent:

(a) The inducement or coercion of a child to engage in any unlawful sexual activity;

(b) The exploitative use of children in prostitution or other unlawful sexual practices;

(c) The exploitative use of children in pornographic performances and materials.

*Article* 35

States Parties shall take all appropriate national, bilateral and multilateral measures to prevent the abduction of, the sale of or traffic in children for any purpose or in any form.

*Article* 36

States Parties shall protect the child against all other forms of exploitation prejudicial to any aspects of the child's welfare.

*Article* 37

States Parties shall ensure that:

(a) No child shall be subjected to torture or other cruel, inhuman or degrading treatment or punishment. Neither capital punishment nor life imprisonment without possibility of release shall be imposed for offences committed by persons below eighteen years of age;

(b) No child shall be deprived of his or her liberty unlawfully or arbitrarily. The arrest, detention or imprisonment of a child shall be in conformity with the law and shall be used only as a measure of last resort and for the shortest appropriate period of time;

(c) Every child deprived of liberty shall be treated with humanity and respect for the inherent dignity of the human person, and in a manner which takes into account the needs of persons of his or her age. In particular, every child deprived of liberty shall be separated from adults unless it is considered in the child's best interest not to do so and shall have the right to maintain contact with his or her family through correspondence and visits, save in exceptional circumstances;

(d) Every child deprived of his or her liberty shall have the right to prompt access to legal and other appropriate assistance, as well as the right to challenge the legality of the deprivation of his or her liberty before a court or other competent, independent and impartial authority, and to a prompt decision on any such action.

## Article 38

1. States Parties undertake to respect and to ensure respect for rules of international humanitarian law applicable to them in armed conflicts which are relevant to the child.

2. States Parties shall take all feasible measures to ensure that persons who have not attained the age of fifteen years do not take a direct part in hostilities.

3. States Parties shall refrain from recruiting any person who has not attained the age of fifteen years into their armed forces. In recruiting among those persons who have attained the age of fifteen years but who have not attained the age of eighteen years, States Parties shall endeavour to give priority to those who are oldest.

4. In accordance with their obligations under international humanitarian law to protect the civilian population in armed conflicts, States Parties shall take all feasible measures to ensure protection and care of children who are affected by an armed conflict.

## Article 39

States Parties shall take all appropriate measures to promote physical and psychological recovery and social reintegration of a child victim of: any form of neglect, exploitation, or abuse; torture or any other form of cruel, inhuman or degrading treatment or punishment; or armed conflicts. Such recovery and reintegration shall take place in an environment which fosters the health, self-respect and dignity of the child.

## Article 40

1. States Parties recognize the right of every child alleged as, accused of, or recognized as having infringed the penal law to be treated in a manner consistent with the promotion of the child's sense of dignity and worth, which reinforces the child's respect for the human rights and fundamental freedoms of others and which takes into account the child's age and the desirability of promoting the child's reintegration and the child's assuming a constructive role in society.

2. To this end, and having regard to the relevant provisions of international instruments, States Parties shall, in particular, ensure that:

(a) No child shall be alleged as, be accused of, or recognized as having infringed the penal law by reason of acts or omissions that were not prohibited by national or international law at the time they were committed;

(b) Every child alleged as or accused of having infringed the penal law has at least the following guarantees:

(i) To be presumed innocent until proven guilty according to law;

(ii) To be informed promptly and directly of the charges against him or her, and, if appropriate, through his or her parents or legal guardians, and to have legal or other appropriate assistance in the preparation and presentation of his or her defence;

(iii) To have the matter determined without delay by a competent, independent and impartial authority or judicial body in a fair hearing according to law, in the presence of legal or other appropriate assistance and, unless it is considered not to be in the best interest of the child, in particular, taking into account his or her age or situation, his or her parents or legal guardians;

(iv) Not to be compelled to give testimony or to confess guilt; to examine or have examined adverse witnesses and to obtain the participation and examination of witnesses on his or her behalf under conditions of equality;

(v) If considered to have infringed the penal law, to have this decision and any measures imposed in consequence thereof reviewed by a higher competent, independent and impartial authority or judicial body according to law;

(vi) To have the free assistance of an interpreter if the child cannot understand or speak the language used;

(vii) To have his or her privacy fully respected at all stages of the proceedings.

3. States Parties shall seek to promote the establishment of laws, procedures, authorities and institutions specifically applicable to children alleged as, accused of, or recognized as having infringed the penal law, and, in particular:

(a) The establishment of a minimum age below which children shall be presumed not to have the capacity to infringe the penal law;

(b) Whenever appropriate and desirable, measures for dealing with such children without resorting to judicial proceedings, providing that human rights and legal safeguards are fully respected.

4. A variety of dispositions, such as care, guidance and supervision orders; counselling; probation; foster care; education and vocational training programmes and other alternatives to institutional care shall be available to ensure that children are dealt with in a manner appropriate to their well-being and proportionate both to their circumstances and the offence.

*Article* 41

Nothing in the present Convention shall affect any provisions which are more conducive to the realization of the rights of the child and which may be contained in:

(a) The law of a State party; or

(b) International law in force for that State.


# PART II

*Article* 42

States Parties undertake to make the principles and provisions of the Convention widely known, by appropriate and active means, to adults and children alike.

*Article* 43

1. For the purpose of examining the progress made by States Parties in achieving the realization of the obligations undertaken in the present Convention, there shall be established a Committee on the Rights of the Child, which shall carry out the functions hereinafter provided.

2. The Committee shall consist of ten experts of high moral standing and recognized competence in the field covered by this Convention. The members of the Committee shall be elected by States Parties from among their nationals and shall serve in their personal capacity, consideration being given to equitable geographical distribution, as well as to the principal legal systems.

3. The members of the Committee shall be elected by secret ballot from a list of persons nominated by States Parties. Each State Party may nominate one person from among its own nationals.

4. The initial election to the Committee shall be held no later than six months after the date of the entry into force of the present Convention and thereafter every second year. At least four months before the date of each election, the Secretary-General of the United Nations shall address a letter to States Parties inviting them to submit their nominations within two months. The Secretary-General shall subsequently prepare a list in alphabetical order of all persons thus nominated, indicating States Parties which have nominated them, and shall submit it to the States Parties to the present Convention.

5. The elections shall be held at meetings of States Parties convened by the Secretary-General at United Nations Headquarters. At those meetings, for which two thirds of States Parties shall constitute a quorum, the persons elected to the Committee shall be those who obtain the largest number of votes and an absolute majority of the votes of the representatives of States Parties present and voting.

6. The members of the Committee shall be elected for a term of four years. They shall be eligible for re-election if renominated. The term of five of the members elected at the first election shall expire at the end of two years; immediately after the first election, the names of these five members shall be chosen by lot by the Chairman of the meeting.

7. If a member of the Committee dies or resigns or declares that for any other cause he or she can no longer perform the duties of the Committee, the State Party which nominated the member shall appoint another expert from among its nationals to serve for the remainder of the term, subject to the approval of the Committee.

8. The Committee shall establish its own rules of procedure.

9. The Committee shall elect its officers for a period of two years.

10. The meetings of the Committee shall normally be held at United Nations Headquarters or at any other convenient place as determined by the Committee. The Committee shall normally meet annually. The duration of the meetings of the Committee shall be determined, and reviewed, if necessary, by a meeting of the States Parties to the present Convention, subject to the approval of the General Assembly.

11. The Secretary-General of the United Nations shall provide the necessary staff

and facilities for the effective performance of the functions of the Committee under the present Convention.

12. With the approval of the General Assembly, the members of the Committee established under the present Convention shall receive emoluments from United Nations resources on such terms and conditions as the Assembly may decide.

*Article* 44

1. States Parties undertake to submit to the Committee, through the Secretary-General of the United Nations, reports on the measures they have adopted which give effect to the rights recognized herein and on the progress made on the enjoyment of those rights:

> (a) Within two years of the entry into force of the Convention for the State Party concerned;
>
> (b) Thereafter every five years.

2. Reports made under the present article shall indicate factors and difficulties, if any, affecting the degree of fulfilment of the obligations under the present Convention. Reports shall also contain sufficient information to provide the Committee with a comprehensive understanding of the implementation of the Convention in the country concerned.

3. A State Party which has submitted a comprehensive initial report to the Committee need not, in its subsequent reports submitted in accordance with paragraph 1 (b) of the present article, repeat basic information previously provided.

4. The Committee may request from States Parties further information relevant to the implementation of the Convention.

5. The Committee shall submit to the General Assembly, through the Economic and Social Council, every two years, reports on its activities.

6. States Parties shall make their reports widely available to the public in their own countries.

*Article* 45

In order to foster the effective implementation of the Convention and to encourage international co-operation in the field covered by the Convention:

> (a) The specialized agencies, the United Nations Children's Fund, and other United Nations organs shall be entitled to be represented at the consideration of the implementation of such provisions of the present Convention as fall within the scope of their mandate. The Committee may invite the specialized agencies, the United Nations Children's Fund and other competent bodies as it may consider appropriate to provide expert advice on the implementation of the Convention in areas falling within the scope of their respective mandates. The Committee may invite the specialized agencies, the United Nations Children's Fund, and other United Nations organs to submit reports on the implementation of the Convention in areas falling within the scope of their activities;
>
> (b) The Committee shall transmit, as it may consider appropriate, to the specialized agencies, the United Nations Children's Fund and other competent bodies, any reports from States Parties that contain a request, or indicate a

need, for technical advice or assistance, along with the Committee's observations and suggestions, if any, on these requests or indications;

*(c)*  The Committee may recommend to the General Assembly to request the Secretary-General to undertake on its behalf studies on specific issues relating to the rights of the child;

*(d)*  The Committee may make suggestions and general recommendations based on information received pursuant to Articles 44 and 45 of the present Convention. Such suggestions and general recommendations shall be transmitted to any State Party concerned and reported to the General Assembly, together with comments, if any, from States Parties.

## PART III

*Article* 46

The present Convention shall be open for signature by all States.

*Article* 47

The present Convention is subject to ratification. Instruments of ratification shall be deposited with the Secretary-General of the United Nations.

*Article* 48

The present Convention shall remain open for accession by any State. The instruments of accession shall be deposited with the Secretary-General of the United Nations.

*Article* 49

1. The present Convention shall enter into force on the thirtieth day following the date of deposit with the Secretary-General of the United Nations of the twentieth instrument of ratification or accession.

2. For each State ratifying or acceding to the Convention after the deposit of the twentieth instrument of ratification or accession, the Convention shall enter into force on the thirtieth day after the deposit by such State of its instrument of ratification or accession.

*Article* 50

1. Any State Party may propose an amendment and file it with the Secretary-General of the United Nations. The Secretary-General shall thereupon communicate the proposed amendment to States Parties, with a request that they indicate whether they favour a conference of States Parties for the purpose of considering and voting upon the proposals. In the event that, within four months from the date of such communication, at least one third of the States Parties favour such a conference, the Secretary-General shall convene the conference under the auspices of the United Nations. Any amendment adopted by a majority of States Parties present and voting at the conference shall be submitted to the General Assembly for approval.

2. An amendment adopted in accordance with paragraph 1 of the present article shall enter into force when it has been approved by the General Assembly of the United Nations and accepted by a two-thirds majority of States Parties.

3. When an amendment enters into force, it shall be binding on those States Parties which have accepted it, other States Parties still being bound by the provisions of the present Convention and any earlier amendments which they have accepted.

*Article* 51

1. The Secretary-General of the United Nations shall receive and circulate to all States the text of reservations made by States at the time of ratification or accession.

2. A reservation incompatible with the object and purpose of the present Convention shall not be permitted.

3. Reservations may be withdrawn at any time by notification to that effect addressed to the Secretary-General of the United Nations, who shall then inform all States. Such notification shall take effect on the date on which it is received by the Secretary-General

*Article* 52

A State Party may denounce the present Convention by written notification to the Secretary-General of the United Nations. Denunciation becomes effective one year after the date of receipt of the notification by the Secretary-General.

*Article* 53

The Secretary-General of the United Nations is designated as the depositary of the present Convention.

*Article* 54

The original of the present Convention, of which the Arabic, Chinese, English, French, Russian and Spanish texts are equally authentic, shall be deposited with the Secretary-General of the United Nations.

*In witness thereof* the undersigned plenipotentiaries, being duly authorized thereto by their respective governments, have signed the present Convention.

## 36. OPTIONAL PROTOCOL TO THE CONVENTION ON THE RIGHTS OF THE CHILD ON THE INVOLVEMENT OF CHILDREN IN ARMED CONFLICTS, 2000

Annexed to General Assembly Resolution 54/263, adopted without a vote on 25 May 2000. The Protocol entered into force on 12 February 2002.

For background, see Cohn, I., & Goodwin-Gill, G. S., *Child Soldiers: The Role of Children in Armed Conflict* (1994).

*TEXT*

*The States Parties to the present Protocol,*

*Encouraged* by the overwhelming support for the Convention on the Rights of the Child, demonstrating the widespread commitment that exists to strive for the promotion and protection of the rights of the child,

*Reaffirming* that the rights of children require special protection, and calling for continuous improvement of the situation of children without distinction, as well as for their development and education in conditions of peace and security,

*Disturbed* by the harmful and widespread impact of armed conflict on children and the long-term consequences it has for durable peace, security and development,

*Condemning* the targeting of children in situations of armed conflict and direct attacks on objects protected under international law, including places that generally have a significant presence of children, such as schools and hospitals,

*Noting* the adoption of the Rome Statute of the International Criminal Court, in particular, the inclusion therein as a war crime, of conscripting or enlisting children under the age of 15 years or using them to participate actively in hostilities in both international and non-international armed conflicts,

*Considering* therefore that to strengthen further the implementation of rights recognized in the Convention on the Rights of the Child there is a need to increase the protection of children from involvement in armed conflict,

*Noting* that Article 1 of the Convention on the Rights of the Child specifies that, for the purposes of that Convention, a child means every human being below the age of 18 years unless, under the law applicable to the child, majority is attained earlier,

*Convinced* that an optional protocol to the Convention that raises the age of possible recruitment of persons into armed forces and their participation in hostilities will contribute effectively to the implementation of the principle that the best interests of the child are to be a primary consideration in all actions concerning children,

*Noting* that the twenty-sixth International Conference of the Red Cross and Red Crescent in December 1995 recommended, *inter alia*, that parties to conflict take every feasible step to ensure that children below the age of 18 years do not take part in hostilities,

*Welcoming* the unanimous adoption, in June 1999, of International Labour Organization Convention No. 182 on the Prohibition and Immediate Action for the Elimination of the Worst Forms of Child Labour, which prohibits, *inter alia*, forced or compulsory recruitment of children for use in armed conflict,

*Condemning* with the gravest concern the recruitment, training and use within and across national borders of children in hostilities by armed groups distinct from the armed forces of a State, and recognizing the responsibility of those who recruit, train and use children in this regard,

*Recalling* the obligation of each party to an armed conflict to abide by the provisions of international humanitarian law,

*Stressing* that the present Protocol is without prejudice to the purposes and principles contained in the Charter of the United Nations, including Article 51, and relevant norms of humanitarian law,

*Bearing in mind* that conditions of peace and security based on full respect of the purposes and principles contained in the Charter and observance of applicable human rights instruments are indispensable for the full protection of children, in particular during armed conflicts and foreign occupation,

*Recognizing* the special needs of those children who are particularly vulnerable to recruitment or use in hostilities contrary to the present Protocol owing to their economic or social status or gender,

*Mindful* of the necessity of taking into consideration the economic, social and political root causes of the involvement of children in armed conflicts,

*Convinced* of the need to strengthen international cooperation in the implementation of the present Protocol, as well as the physical and psychosocial rehabilitation and social reintegration of children who are victims of armed conflict,

*Encouraging* the participation of the community and, in particular, children and child victims in the dissemination of informational and educational programmes concerning the implementation of the Protocol,

*Have agreed* as follows:

*Article* 1

States Parties shall take all feasible measures to ensure that members of their armed forces who have not attained the age of 18 years do not take a direct part in hostilities.

*Article* 2

States Parties shall ensure that persons who have not attained the age of 18 years are not compulsorily recruited into their armed forces.

*Article* 3

1. States Parties shall raise the minimum age for the voluntary recruitment of persons into their national armed forces from that set out in Article 38, paragraph 3, of the Convention on the Rights of the Child, taking account of the principles contained in that article and recognizing that under the Convention persons under the age of 18 years are entitled to special protection.

2. Each State Party shall deposit a binding declaration upon ratification of or accession to the present Protocol that sets forth the minimum age at which it will

permit voluntary recruitment into its national armed forces and a description of the safeguards it has adopted to ensure that such recruitment is not forced or coerced.

3. States Parties that permit voluntary recruitment into their national armed forces under the age of 18 years shall maintain safeguards to ensure, as a minimum, that:

(a) Such recruitment is genuinely voluntary;

(b) Such recruitment is carried out with the informed consent of the person's parents or legal guardians;

(c) Such persons are fully informed of the duties involved in such military service;

(d) Such persons provide reliable proof of age prior to acceptance into national military service.

4. Each State Party may strengthen its declaration at any time by notification to that effect addressed to the Secretary-General of the United Nations, who shall inform all States Parties. Such notification shall take effect on the date on which it is received by the Secretary-General.

5. The requirement to raise the age in paragraph 1 of the present article does not apply to schools operated by or under the control of the armed forces of the States Parties, in keeping with Articles 28 and 29 of the Convention on the Rights of the Child.

*Article 4*

1. Armed groups that are distinct from the armed forces of a State should not, under any circumstances, recruit or use in hostilities persons under the age of 18 years.

2. States Parties shall take all feasible measures to prevent such recruitment and use, including the adoption of legal measures necessary to prohibit and criminalize such practices.

3. The application of the present article shall not affect the legal status of any party to an armed conflict.

*Article 5*

Nothing in the present Protocol shall be construed as precluding provisions in the law of a State Party or in international instruments and international humanitarian law that are more conducive to the realization of the rights of the child.

*Article 6*

1. Each State Party shall take all necessary legal, administrative and other measures to ensure the effective implementation and enforcement of the provisions of the present Protocol within its jurisdiction.

2. States Parties undertake to make the principles and provisions of the present Protocol widely known and promoted by appropriate means, to adults and children alike.

3. States Parties shall take all feasible measures to ensure that persons within their jurisdiction recruited or used in hostilities contrary to the present Protocol

are demobilized or otherwise released from service. States Parties shall, when necessary, accord to such persons all appropriate assistance for their physical and psychological recovery and their social reintegration.

*Article 7*

1. States Parties shall cooperate in the implementation of the present Protocol, including in the prevention of any activity contrary thereto and in the rehabilitation and social reintegration of persons who are victims of acts contrary thereto, including through technical cooperation and financial assistance. Such assistance and cooperation will be undertaken in consultation with the States Parties concerned and the relevant international organizations.

2. States Parties in a position to do so shall provide such assistance through existing multilateral, bilateral or other programmes or, *inter alia*, through a voluntary fund established in accordance with the rules of the General Assembly.

*Article 8*

1. Each State Party shall, within two years following the entry into force of the present Protocol for that State Party, submit a report to the Committee on the Rights of the Child providing comprehensive information on the measures it has taken to implement the provisions of the Protocol, including the measures taken to implement the provisions on participation and recruitment.

2. Following the submission of the comprehensive report, each State Party shall include in the reports it submits to the Committee on the Rights of the Child, in accordance with Article 44 of the Convention, any further information with respect to the implementation of the Protocol. Other States Parties to the Protocol shall submit a report every five years.

3. The Committee on the Rights of the Child may request from States Parties further information relevant to the implementation of the present Protocol.

*Article 9*

1. The present Protocol is open for signature by any State that is a party to the Convention or has signed it.

2. The present Protocol is subject to ratification and is open to accession by any State. Instruments of ratification or accession shall be deposited with the Secretary-General of the United Nations.

3. The Secretary-General, in his capacity as depositary of the Convention and the Protocol, shall inform all States Parties to the Convention and all States that have signed the Convention of each instrument of declaration pursuant to Article 3.

*Article 10*

1. The present Protocol shall enter into force three months after the deposit of the tenth instrument of ratification or accession.

2. For each State ratifying the present Protocol or acceding to it after its entry into force, the Protocol shall enter into force one month after the date of the deposit of its own instrument of ratification or accession.

*Article* 11

1. Any State Party may denounce the present Protocol at any time by written notification to the Secretary-General of the United Nations, who shall thereafter inform the other States Parties to the Convention and all States that have signed the Convention. The denunciation shall take effect one year after the date of receipt of the notification by the Secretary-General. If, however, on the expiry of that year the denouncing State Party is engaged in armed conflict, the denunciation shall not take effect before the end of the armed conflict.

2. Such a denunciation shall not have the effect of releasing the State Party from its obligations under the present Protocol in regard to any act that occurs prior to the date on which the denunciation becomes effective. Nor shall such a denunciation prejudice in any way the continued consideration of any matter that is already under consideration by the Committee on the Rights of the Child prior to the date on which the denunciation becomes effective.

*Article* 12

1. Any State Party may propose an amendment and file it with the Secretary-General of the United Nations. The Secretary-General shall thereupon communicate the proposed amendment to States Parties with a request that they indicate whether they favour a conference of States Parties for the purpose of considering and voting upon the proposals. In the event that, within four months from the date of such communication, at least one third of the States Parties favour such a conference, the Secretary-General shall convene the conference under the auspices of the United Nations. Any amendment adopted by a majority of States Parties present and voting at the conference shall be submitted to the General Assembly of the United Nations for approval.

2. An amendment adopted in accordance with paragraph 1 of the present article shall enter into force when it has been approved by the General Assembly and accepted by a two-thirds majority of States Parties.

3. When an amendment enters into force, it shall be binding on those States Parties that have accepted it, other States Parties still being bound by the provisions of the present Protocol and any earlier amendments they have accepted.

*Article* 13

1. The present Protocol, of which the Arabic, Chinese, English, French, Russian and Spanish texts are equally authentic, shall be deposited in the archives of the United Nations.

2. The Secretary-General of the United Nations shall transmit certified copies of the present Protocol to all States Parties to the Convention and all States that have signed the Convention.

## 37. OPTIONAL PROTOCOL TO THE CONVENTION ON THE RIGHTS OF THE CHILD ON THE SALE OF CHILDREN, CHILD PROSTITUTION AND CHILD PORNOGRAPHY, 2000

Annexed to General Assembly Resolution 54/263, adopted without a vote on 25 May 2000. The Protocol entered into force on 18 January 2002.

*TEXT*

*The States Parties to the present Protocol,*

*Considering* that, in order further to achieve the purposes of the Convention on the Rights of the Child and the implementation of its provisions, especially Articles 1, 11, 21, 32, 33, 34, 35 and 36, it would be appropriate to extend the measures that States Parties should undertake in order to guarantee the protection of the child from the sale of children, child prostitution and child pornography,

*Considering* also that the Convention on the Rights of the Child recognizes the right of the child to be protected from economic exploitation and from performing any work that is likely to be hazardous or to interfere with the child's education, or to be harmful to the child's health or physical, mental, spiritual, moral or social development,

*Gravely concerned* at the significant and increasing international traffic in children for the purpose of the sale of children, child prostitution and child pornography,

*Deeply concerned* at the widespread and continuing practice of sex tourism, to which children are especially vulnerable, as it directly promotes the sale of children, child prostitution and child pornography,

*Recognizing* that a number of particularly vulnerable groups, including girl children, are at greater risk of sexual exploitation and that girl children are disproportionately represented among the sexually exploited,

*Concerned* about the growing availability of child pornography on the Internet and other evolving technologies, and recalling the International Conference on Combatting Child Pornography on the Internet, held in Vienna in 1999, in particular its conclusion calling for the worldwide criminalization of the production, distribution, exportation, transmission, importation, intentional possession and advertising of child pornography, and stressing the importance of closer cooperation and partnership between Governments and the Internet industry,

*Believing* that the elimination of the sale of children, child prostitution and child pornography will be facilitated by adopting a holistic approach, addressing the contributing factors, including underdevelopment, poverty, economic disparities, inequitable socio-economic structure, dysfunctioning families, lack of education, urban-rural migration, gender discrimination, irresponsible adult sexual behaviour, harmful traditional practices, armed conflicts and trafficking in children,

*Believing* also that efforts to raise public awareness are needed to reduce consumer demand for the sale of children, child prostitution and child pornography, and believing further in the importance of strengthening global partnership among all actors and of improving law enforcement at the national level,

*Noting* the provisions of international legal instruments relevant to the protection of children, including the Hague Convention on Protection of Children and Cooperation in Respect of Intercountry Adoption, the Hague Convention on the Civil Aspects of International Child Abduction, the Hague Convention on Jurisdiction, Applicable Law, Recognition, Enforcement and Cooperation in Respect of Parental Responsibility and Measures for the Protection of Children, and International Labour Organization Convention No. 182 on the Prohibition and Immediate Action for the Elimination of the Worst Forms of Child Labour,

*Encouraged* by the overwhelming support for the Convention on the Rights of the Child, demonstrating the widespread commitment that exists for the promotion and protection of the rights of the child,

*Recognizing* the importance of the implementation of the provisions of the Programme of Action for the Prevention of the Sale of Children, Child Prostitution and Child Pornography and the Declaration and Agenda for Action adopted at the World Congress against Commercial Sexual Exploitation of Children, held in Stockholm from 27 to 31 August 1996, and the other relevant decisions and recommendations of pertinent international bodies,

*Taking due account* of the importance of the traditions and cultural values of each people for the protection and harmonious development of the child,

*Have agreed* as follows:

*Article 1*

States Parties shall prohibit the sale of children, child prostitution and child pornography as provided for by the present Protocol.

*Article 2*

For the purposes of the present Protocol:

    *(a)* Sale of children means any act or transaction whereby a child is transferred by any person or group of persons to another for remuneration or any other consideration;

    *(b)* Child prostitution means the use of a child in sexual activities for remuneration or any other form of consideration;

    *(c)* Child pornography means any representation, by whatever means, of a child engaged in real or simulated explicit sexual activities or any representation of the sexual parts of a child for primarily sexual purposes.

*Article 3*

1. Each State Party shall ensure that, as a minimum, the following acts and activities are fully covered under its criminal or penal law, whether such offences are committed domestically or transnationally or on an individual or organized basis:

    *(a)* In the context of sale of children as defined in Article 2:

        (i) Offering, delivering or accepting, by whatever means, a child for the purpose of:

    a.   Sexual exploitation of the child;

    b.   Transfer of organs of the child for profit;

    c.   Engagement of the child in forced labour;

   (ii)  Improperly inducing consent, as an intermediary, for the adoption of a child in violation of applicable international legal instruments on adoption;

  *(b)*  Offering, obtaining, procuring or providing a child for child prostitution, as defined in Article 2;

  *(c)*  Producing, distributing, disseminating, importing, exporting, offering, selling or possessing for the above purposes child pornography as defined in Article 2.

2. Subject to the provisions of the national law of a State Party, the same shall apply to an attempt to commit any of the said acts and to complicity or participation in any of the said acts.

3. Each State Party shall make such offences punishable by appropriate penalties that take into account their grave nature.

4. Subject to the provisions of its national law, each State Party shall take measures, where appropriate, to establish the liability of legal persons for offences established in paragraph 1 of the present article. Subject to the legal principles of the State Party, such liability of legal persons may be criminal, civil or administrative.

5. States Parties shall take all appropriate legal and administrative measures to ensure that all persons involved in the adoption of a child act in conformity with applicable international legal instruments.

*Article* 4

1. Each State Party shall take such measures as may be necessary to establish its jurisdiction over the offences referred to in Article 3, paragraph 1, when the offences are committed in its territory or on board a ship or aircraft registered in that State.

2. Each State Party may take such measures as may be necessary to establish its jurisdiction over the offences referred to in Article 3, paragraph 1, in the following cases:

  *(a)*  When the alleged offender is a national of that State or a person who has his habitual residence in its territory;

  *(b)*  When the victim is a national of that State.

3. Each State Party shall also take such measures as may be necessary to establish its jurisdiction over the aforementioned offences when the alleged offender is present in its territory and it does not extradite him or her to another State Party on the ground that the offence has been committed by one of its nationals.

4. The present Protocol does not exclude any criminal jurisdiction exercised in accordance with internal law.

*Article* 5

1. The offences referred to in Article 3, paragraph 1, shall be deemed to be included as extraditable offences in any extradition treaty existing between States Parties and shall be included as extraditable offences in every extradition treaty subsequently concluded between them, in accordance with the conditions set forth in such treaties.

2. If a State Party that makes extradition conditional on the existence of a treaty receives a request for extradition from another State Party with which it has no extradition treaty, it may consider the present Protocol to be a legal basis for extradition in respect of such offences. Extradition shall be subject to the conditions provided by the law of the requested State.

3. States Parties that do not make extradition conditional on the existence of a treaty shall recognize such offences as extraditable offences between themselves subject to the conditions provided by the law of the requested State.

4. Such offences shall be treated, for the purpose of extradition between States Parties, as if they had been committed not only in the place in which they occurred but also in the territories of the States required to establish their jurisdiction in accordance with Article 4.

5. If an extradition request is made with respect to an offence described in Article 3, paragraph 1, and the requested State Party does not or will not extradite on the basis of the nationality of the offender, that State shall take suitable measures to submit the case to its competent authorities for the purpose of prosecution.

*Article 6*

1. States Parties shall afford one another the greatest measure of assistance in connection with investigations or criminal or extradition proceedings brought in respect of the offences set forth in Article 3, paragraph 1, including assistance in obtaining evidence at their disposal necessary for the proceedings.

2. States Parties shall carry out their obligations under paragraph 1 of the present article in conformity with any treaties or other arrangements on mutual legal assistance that may exist between them. In the absence of such treaties or arrangements, States Parties shall afford one another assistance in accordance with their domestic law.

*Article 7*

States Parties shall, subject to the provisions of their national law:

(a) Take measures to provide for the seizure and confiscation, as appropriate, of:
   (i) Goods, such as materials, assets and other instrumentalities used to commit or facilitate offences under the present protocol;
   (ii) Proceeds derived from such offences;
(b) Execute requests from another State Party for seizure or confiscation of goods or proceeds referred to in subparagraph (a) (i) and (ii);
(c) Take measures aimed at closing, on a temporary or definitive basis, premises used to commit such offences.

*Article 8*

1. States Parties shall adopt appropriate measures to protect the rights and interests of child victims of the practices prohibited under the present Protocol at all stages of the criminal justice process, in particular by:

(a) Recognizing the vulnerability of child victims and adapting procedures to recognize their special needs, including their special needs as witnesses;

*(b)* Informing child victims of their rights, their role and the scope, timing and progress of the proceedings and of the disposition of their cases;

*(c)* Allowing the views, needs and concerns of child victims to be presented and considered in proceedings where their personal interests are affected, in a manner consistent with the procedural rules of national law;

*(d)* Providing appropriate support services to child victims throughout the legal process;

*(e)* Protecting, as appropriate, the privacy and identity of child victims and taking measures in accordance with national law to avoid the inappropriate dissemination of information that could lead to the identification of child victims;

*(f)* Providing, in appropriate cases, for the safety of child victims, as well as that of their families and witnesses on their behalf, from intimidation and retaliation;

*(g)* Avoiding unnecessary delay in the disposition of cases and the execution of orders or decrees granting compensation to child victims.

2. States Parties shall ensure that uncertainty as to the actual age of the victim shall not prevent the initiation of criminal investigations, including investigations aimed at establishing the age of the victim.

3. States Parties shall ensure that, in the treatment by the criminal justice system of children who are victims of the offences described in the present Protocol, the best interest of the child shall be a primary consideration.

4. States Parties shall take measures to ensure appropriate training, in particular legal and psychological training, for the persons who work with victims of the offences prohibited under the present Protocol.

5. States Parties shall, in appropriate cases, adopt measures in order to protect the safety and integrity of those persons and/or organizations involved in the prevention and/or protection and rehabilitation of victims of such offences.

6. Nothing in the present article shall be construed to be prejudicial to or inconsistent with the rights of the accused to a fair and impartial trial.

*Article* 9

1. States Parties shall adopt or strengthen, implement and disseminate laws, administrative measures, social policies and programmes to prevent the offences referred to in the present Protocol. Particular attention shall be given to protect children who are especially vulnerable to such practices.

2. States Parties shall promote awareness in the public at large, including children, through information by all appropriate means, education and training, about the preventive measures and harmful effects of the offences referred to in the present Protocol. In fulfilling their obligations under this article, States Parties shall encourage the participation of the community and, in particular, children and child victims, in such information and education and training programmes, including at the international level.

3. States Parties shall take all feasible measures with the aim of ensuring all appropriate assistance to victims of such offences, including their full social reintegration and their full physical and psychological recovery.

4. States Parties shall ensure that all child victims of the offences described in the present Protocol have access to adequate procedures to seek, without discrimination, compensation for damages from those legally responsible.

5. States Parties shall take appropriate measures aimed at effectively prohibiting the production and dissemination of material advertising the offences described in the present Protocol.

*Article* 10

1. States Parties shall take all necessary steps to strengthen international co-operation by multilateral, regional and bilateral arrangements for the prevention, detection, investigation, prosecution and punishment of those responsible for acts involving the sale of children, child prostitution, child pornography and child sex tourism. States Parties shall also promote international cooperation and coordination between their authorities, national and international non-governmental organizations and international organizations.

2. States Parties shall promote international cooperation to assist child victims in their physical and psychological recovery, social reintegration and repatriation.

3. States Parties shall promote the strengthening of international cooperation in order to address the root causes, such as poverty and underdevelopment, contributing to the vulnerability of children to the sale of children, child prostitution, child pornography and child sex tourism.

4. States Parties in a position to do so shall provide financial, technical or other assistance through existing multilateral, regional, bilateral or other programmes.

*Article* 11

Nothing in the present Protocol shall affect any provisions that are more conducive to the realization of the rights of the child and that may be contained in:

*(a)* The law of a State Party;

*(b)* International law in force for that State.

*Article* 12

1. Each State Party shall, within two years following the entry into force of the present Protocol for that State Party, submit a report to the Committee on the Rights of the Child providing comprehensive information on the measures it has taken to implement the provisions of the Protocol.

2. Following the submission of the comprehensive report, each State Party shall include in the reports they submit to the Committee on the Rights of the Child, in accordance with Article 44 of the Convention, any further information with respect to the implementation of the present Protocol. Other States Parties to the Protocol shall submit a report every five years.

3. The Committee on the Rights of the Child may request from States Parties further information relevant to the implementation of the present Protocol.

*Article* 13

1. The present Protocol is open for signature by any State that is a party to the Convention or has signed it.

2. The present Protocol is subject to ratification and is open to accession by any State that is a party to the Convention or has signed it. Instruments of ratification or accession shall be deposited with the Secretary-General of the United Nations.

### Article 14

1. The present Protocol shall enter into force three months after the deposit of the tenth instrument of ratification or accession.

2. For each State ratifying the present Protocol or acceding to it after its entry into force, the Protocol shall enter into force one month after the date of the deposit of its own instrument of ratification or accession.

### Article 15

1. Any State Party may denounce the present Protocol at any time by written notification to the Secretary-General of the United Nations, who shall thereafter inform the other States Parties to the Convention and all States that have signed the Convention. The denunciation shall take effect one year after the date of receipt of the notification by the Secretary-General.

2. Such a denunciation shall not have the effect of releasing the State Party from its obligations under the present Protocol in regard to any offence that occurs prior to the date on which the denunciation becomes effective. Nor shall such a denunciation prejudice in any way the continued consideration of any matter that is already under consideration by the Committee on the Rights of the Child prior to the date on which the denunciation becomes effective.

### Article 16

1. Any State Party may propose an amendment and file it with the Secretary-General of the United Nations. The Secretary-General shall thereupon communicate the proposed amendment to States Parties with a request that they indicate whether they favour a conference of States Parties for the purpose of considering and voting upon the proposals. In the event that, within four months from the date of such communication, at least one third of the States Parties favour such a conference, the Secretary-General shall convene the conference under the auspices of the United Nations. Any amendment adopted by a majority of States Parties present and voting at the conference shall be submitted to the General Assembly of the United Nations for approval.

2. An amendment adopted in accordance with paragraph 1 of the present article shall enter into force when it has been approved by the General Assembly and accepted by a two-thirds majority of States Parties.

3. When an amendment enters into force, it shall be binding on those States Parties that have accepted it, other States Parties still being bound by the provisions of the present Protocol and any earlier amendments they have accepted.

### Article 17

1. The present Protocol, of which the Arabic, Chinese, English, French, Russian and Spanish texts are equally authentic, shall be deposited in the archives of the United Nations.

2. The Secretary-General of the United Nations shall transmit certified copies of the present Protocol to all States Parties to the Convention and all States that have signed the Convention.

## 38. INTERNATIONAL CONVENTION ON THE PROTECTION OF THE RIGHTS OF ALL MIGRANT WORKERS AND MEMBERS OF THEIR FAMILIES, 1990

The Convention was adopted without a vote by General Assembly Resolution 45/158 of 18 December 1990. It constitutes an elaboration of human rights standards, and consequently migrant workers will remain protected by human rights standards even in States which do not become parties to the Convention. The Convention provides for the establishment of a committee to monitor its implementation, together with optional procedures for the examination and determination of complaints on behalf of States parties to the Convention, and on behalf of individuals, concerning breaches of the obligations created by the Convention by a State party.

However, both the negotiating history leading to the adoption of the final text and events since 1990 confirm the major divisions separating migrant-sending from migrant-receiving countries.

Cholewinski, R., *Migrant Workers in International Human Rights Law: Their Protection in Countries of Employment* (1997); Goodwin-Gill, G. S., 'Migration—International Law and Human Rights', in Ghosh, B. (ed.), *Managing Migration: Time for a New International Regime?* (2000), 160–89.

*TEXT*

### Preamble

*The States Parties to the present Convention,*

*Taking into account* the principles embodied in the basic instruments of the United Nations concerning human rights, in particular the Universal Declaration of Human Rights, the International Covenant on Economic, Social and Cultural Rights, the International Covenant on Civil and Political Rights, the International Convention on the Elimination of All Forms of Racial Discrimination, the Convention on the Elimination of All Forms of Discrimination against Women and the Convention on the Rights of the Child,

*Taking into account also* the principles and standards set forth in the relevant instruments elaborated within the framework of the International Labour Organisation, especially the Convention concerning Migration for Employment (No. 97), the Convention concerning Migrations in Abusive Conditions and the Promotion of Equality of Opportunity and Treatment of Migrant Workers (No. 143), the Recommendation concerning Migration for Employment (No. 86), the Recommendation concerning Migrant Workers (No. 151), the Convention concerning Forced or Compulsory Labour (No. 29) and the Convention concerning Abolition of Forced Labour (No. 105),

*Reaffirming* the importance of the principles contained in the Convention against Discrimination in Education of the United Nations Educational, Scientific and Cultural Organization,

*Recalling* the Convention against Torture and Other Cruel, Inhuman or

Degrading Treatment or Punishment, the Declaration of the Fourth United Nations Congress on the Prevention of Crime and the Treatment of Offenders, the Code of Conduct for Law Enforcement Officials, and the Slavery Conventions,

*Recalling* that one of the objectives of the International Labour Organization, as stated in its Constitution, is the protection of the interests of workers when employed in countries other than their own, and bearing in mind the expertise and experience of that organization in matters related to migrant workers and members of their families,

*Recognizing* the importance of the work done in connection with migrant workers and members of their families in various organs of the United Nations, in particular in the Commission on Human Rights and the Commission for Social Development, and in the Food and Agriculture Organization of the United Nations, the United Nations Educational, Scientific and Cultural Organization and the World Health Organization, as well as in other international organizations,

*Recognizing also* the progress made by certain States on a regional or bilateral basis towards the protection of the rights of migrant workers and members of their families, as well as the importance and usefulness of bilateral and multilateral agreements in this field,

*Realizing* the importance and extent of the migration phenomenon, which involves millions of people and affects a large number of States in the international community,

*Aware* of the impact of the flows of migrant workers on States and people concerned, and desiring to establish norms which may contribute to the harmonization of the attitudes of States through the acceptance of basic principles concerning the treatment of migrant workers and members of their families,

*Considering* the situation of vulnerability in which migrant workers and members of their families frequently find themselves owing, among other things, to their absence from their State of origin and to the difficulties they may encounter arising from their presence in the State of employment,

*Convinced* that the rights of migrant workers and members of their families have not been sufficiently recognized everywhere and therefore require appropriate international protection,

*Taking into account* the fact that migration is often the cause of serious problems for the members of the families of migrant workers as well as for the workers themselves, in particular because of the scattering of the family,

*Bearing in mind* that the human problems involved in migration are even more serious in the case of irregular migration and convinced therefore that appropriate action should be encouraged in order to prevent and eliminate clandestine movements and trafficking in migrant workers, while at the same time assuring the protection of their fundamental human rights,

*Considering* that workers who are non-documented or in an irregular situation are frequently employed under less favourable conditions of work than other workers and that certain employers find this an inducement to seek such labour in order to reap the benefits of unfair competition,

*Considering also* that recourse to the employment of migrant workers who are in an irregular situation will be discouraged if the fundamental human rights of all migrant workers are more widely recognized and, moreover, that granting certain additional rights to migrant workers and members of their families in a regular situation will encourage all migrants and employers to respect and comply with the laws and procedures established by the States concerned,

*Convinced*, therefore, of the need to bring about the international protection of the rights of all migrant workers and members of their families, reaffirming and establishing basic norms in a comprehensive convention which could be applied universally,

*Have agreed* as follows:

# PART I

## SCOPE AND DEFINITIONS

*Article* 1

1. The present Convention is applicable, except as otherwise provided hereafter, to all migrant workers and members of their families without distinction of any kind such as sex, race, colour, language, religion or conviction, political or other opinion, national, ethnic or social origin, nationality, age, economic position, property, marital status, birth or other status.

2. The present Convention shall apply during the entire migration process of migrant workers and members of their families, which comprises preparation for migration, departure, transit and the entire period of stay and remunerated activity in the State of employment as well as return to the State of origin or the State of habitual residence.

*Article* 2

For the purposes of the present Convention:

1. The term 'migrant worker' refers to a person who is to be engaged, is engaged or has been engaged in a remunerated activity in a State of which he or she is not a national.

2. *(a)* The term 'frontier worker' refers to a migrant worker who retains his or her habitual residence in a neighbouring State to which he or she normally returns every day or at least once a week;

     *(b)* The term 'seasonal worker' refers to a migrant worker whose work by its character is dependent on seasonal conditions and is performed only during part of the year;

     *(c)* The term 'seafarer', which includes a fisherman, refers to a migrant worker employed on board a vessel registered in a State of which he or she is not a national;

     *(d)* The term 'worker on an offshore installation' refers to a migrant worker employed on an offshore installation that is under the jurisdiction of a State of which he or she is not a national;

     *(e)* The term 'itinerant worker' refers to a migrant worker who, having his or her habitual residence in one State, has to travel to another State or States for short periods, owing to the nature of his or her occupation;

(f) The term 'project-tied worker' refers to a migrant worker admitted to a State of employment for a defined period to work solely on a specific project being carried out in that State by his or her employer;

(g) The term 'specified-employment worker' refers to a migrant worker:

(i) Who has been sent by his or her employer for a restricted and defined period of time to a State of employment to undertake a specific assignment or duty; or

(ii) Who engages for a restricted and defined period of time in work that requires professional, commercial, technical or other highly specialized skill; or

(iii) Who, upon the request of his or her employer in the State of employment, engages for a restricted and defined period of time in work whose nature is transitory or brief; and who is required to depart from the State of employment either at the expiration of his or her authorized period of stay, or earlier if he or she no longer undertakes that specific assignment or duty or engages in that work;

(h) The term 'self-employed worker' refers to a migrant worker who is engaged in a remunerated activity otherwise than under a contract of employment and who earns his or her living through this activity normally working alone or together with members of his or her family, and to any other migrant worker recognized as self-employed by applicable legislation of the State of employment or bilateral or multilateral agreements.

*Article* 3

The present Convention shall not apply to:

(a) Persons sent or employed by international organizations and agencies or persons sent or employed by a State outside its territory to perform official functions, whose admission and status are regulated by general international law or by specific international agreements or conventions;

(b) Persons sent or employed by a State or on its behalf outside its territory who participate in development programmes and other co-operation programmes, whose admission and status are regulated by agreement with the State of employment and who, in accordance with that agreement, are not considered migrant workers;

(c) Persons taking up residence in a State different from their State of origin as investors;

(d) Refugees and stateless persons, unless such application is provided for in the relevant national legislation of, or international instruments in force for, the State Party concerned;

(e) Students and trainees;

(f) Seafarers and workers on an offshore installation who have not been admitted to take up residence and engage in a remunerated activity in the State of employment.

*Article* 4

For the purposes of the present Convention the term 'members of the family' refers to persons married to migrant workers or having with them a relationship that, according to applicable law, produces effects equivalent to marriage, as well as their dependent children and other dependent persons who are recognized as members of the family by applicable legislation or applicable bilateral or multilateral agreements between the States concerned.

*Article 5*

For the purposes of the present Convention, migrant workers and members of their families:

   *(a)*  Are considered as documented or in a regular situation if they are authorized to enter, to stay and to engage in a remunerated activity in the State of employment pursuant to the law of that State and to international agreements to which that State is a party;

   *(b)*  Are considered as non-documented or in an irregular situation if they do not comply with the conditions provided for in subparagraph (a) of the present article.

*Article 6*

For the purposes of the present Convention:

   *(a)*  The term 'State of origin' means the State of which the person concerned is a national;

   *(b)*  The term 'State of employment' means a State where the migrant worker is to be engaged, is engaged or has been engaged in a remunerated activity, as the case may be;

   *(c)*  The term 'State of transit' means any State through which the person concerned passes on any journey to the State of employment or from the State of employment to the State of origin or the State of habitual residence.


# PART II

## NON-DISCRIMINATION WITH RESPECT TO RIGHTS

*Article 7*

States Parties undertake, in accordance with the international instruments concerning human rights, to respect and to ensure to all migrant workers and members of their families within their territory or subject to their jurisdiction the rights provided for in the present Convention without distinction of any kind such as to sex, race, colour, language, religion or conviction, political or other opinion, national, ethnic or social origin, nationality, age, economic position, property, marital status, birth or other status.

## PART III

## HUMAN RIGHTS OF ALL MIGRANT WORKERS AND MEMBERS OF THEIR FAMILIES

*Article* 8

1. Migrant workers and members of their families shall be free to leave any State, including their State of origin. This right shall not be subject to any restrictions except those that are provided by law, are necessary to protect national security, public order (*ordre public*), public health or morals or the rights and freedoms of others and are consistent with the other rights recognized in the present part of the Convention.

2. Migrant workers and members of their families shall have the right at any time to enter and remain in their State of origin.

*Article* 9

The right to life of migrant workers and members of their families shall be protected by law.

*Article* 10

No migrant worker or member of his or her family shall be subjected to torture or to cruel, inhuman or degrading treatment or punishment.

*Article* 11

1. No migrant worker or member of his or her family shall be held in slavery or servitude.

2. No migrant worker or member of his or her family shall be required to perform forced or compulsory labour.

3. Paragraph 2 of the present article shall not be held to preclude, in States where imprisonment with hard labour may be imposed as a punishment for a crime, the performance of hard labour in pursuance of a sentence to such punishment by a competent court.

4. For the purpose of the present article the term 'forced or compulsory labour' shall not include:

   (a) Any work or service not referred to in paragraph 3 of the present article normally required of a person who is under detention in consequence of a lawful order of a court or of a person during conditional release from such detention;

   (b) Any service exacted in cases of emergency or calamity threatening the life or well-being of the community;

   (c) Any work or service that forms part of normal civil obligations so far as it is imposed also on citizens of the State concerned.

*Article* 12

1. Migrant workers and members of their families shall have the right to freedom of thought, conscience and religion. This right shall include freedom to have or to adopt a religion or belief of their choice and freedom either individually or in community with others and in public or private to manifest their religion or belief in worship, observance, practice and teaching.

2. Migrant workers and members of their families shall not be subject to coercion that would impair their freedom to have or to adopt a religion or belief of their choice.

3. Freedom to manifest one's religion or belief may be subject only to such limitations as are prescribed by law and are necessary to protect public safety, order, health or morals or the fundamental rights and freedoms of others.

4. States Parties to the present Convention undertake to have respect for the liberty of parents, at least one of whom is a migrant worker, and, when applicable, legal guardians to ensure the religious and moral education of their children in conformity with their own convictions.

*Article* 13

1. Migrant workers and members of their families shall have the right to hold opinions without interference.

2. Migrant workers and members of their families shall have the right to freedom of expression; this right shall include freedom to seek, receive and impart information and ideas of all kinds, regardless of frontiers, either orally, in writing or in print, in the form of art or through any other media of their choice.

3. The exercise of the right provided for in paragraph 2 of the present article carries with it special duties and responsibilities. It may therefore be subject to certain restrictions, but these shall only be such as are provided by law and are necessary:

　　*(a)* For respect of the rights or reputation of others;

　　*(b)* For the protection of the national security of the States concerned or of public order (*ordre public*) or of public health or morals;

　　*(c)* For the purpose of preventing any propaganda for war;

　　*(d)* For the purpose of preventing any advocacy of national, racial or religious hatred that constitutes incitement to discrimination, hostility or violence.

*Article* 14

No migrant worker or member of his or her family shall be subjected to arbitrary or unlawful interference with his or her privacy, family, home, correspondence or other communications, or to unlawful attacks on his or her honour and reputation. Each migrant worker and member of his or her family shall have the right to the protection of the law against such interference or attacks.

*Article* 15

No migrant worker or member of his or her family shall be arbitrarily deprived of property, whether owned individually or in association with others. Where, under the legislation in force in the State of employment, the assets of a migrant worker or a member of his or her family are expropriated in whole or in part, the person concerned shall have the right to fair and adequate compensation.

*Article* 16

1. Migrant workers and members of their families shall have the right to liberty and security of person.

2. Migrant workers and members of their families shall be entitled to effective protection by the State against violence, physical injury, threats and intimidation, whether by public officials or by private individuals, groups or institutions.

3. Any verification by law enforcement officials of the identity of migrant workers or members of their families shall be carried out in accordance with procedure established by law.

4. Migrant workers and members of their families shall not be subjected individually or collectively to arbitrary arrest or detention; they shall not be deprived of their liberty except on such grounds and in accordance with such procedures as are established by law.

5. Migrant workers and members of their families who are arrested shall be informed at the time of arrest as far as possible in a language they understand of the reasons for their arrest and they shall be promptly informed in a language they understand of any charges against them.

6. Migrant workers and members of their families who are arrested or detained on a criminal charge shall be brought promptly before a judge or other officer authorized by law to exercise judicial power and shall be entitled to trial within a reasonable time or to release. It shall not be the general rule that while awaiting trial they shall be detained in custody, but release may be subject to guarantees to appear for trial, at any other stage of the judicial proceedings and, should the occasion arise, for the execution of the judgment.

7. When a migrant worker or a member of his or her family is arrested or committed to prison or custody pending trial or is detained in any other manner:

   *(a)* The consular or diplomatic authorities of his or her State of origin or of a State representing the interests of that State shall, if he or she so requests, be informed without delay of his or her arrest or detention and of the reasons therefor;

   *(b)* The person concerned shall have the right to communicate with the said authorities. Any communication by the person concerned to the said authorities shall be forwarded without delay, and he or she shall also have the right to receive communications sent by the said authorities without delay;

   *(c)* The person concerned shall be informed without delay of this right and of rights deriving from relevant treaties, if any, applicable between the States concerned, to correspond and to meet with representatives of the said authorities and to make arrangements with them for his or her legal representation.

8. Migrant workers and members of their families who are deprived of their liberty by arrest or detention shall be entitled to take proceedings before a court, in order that that court may decide without delay on the lawfulness of their detention and order their release if the detention is not lawful. When they attend such proceedings, they shall have the assistance, if necessary without cost to them, of an interpreter, if they cannot understand or speak the language used.

9. Migrant workers and members of their families who have been victims of unlawful arrest or detention shall have an enforceable right to compensation.

*Article* 17

1. Migrant workers and members of their families who are deprived of their liberty shall be treated with humanity and with respect for the inherent dignity of the human person and for their cultural identity.

2. Accused migrant workers and members of their families shall, save in exceptional circumstances, be separated from convicted persons and shall be subject to separate treatment appropriate to their status as unconvicted persons. Accused juvenile persons shall be separated from adults and brought as speedily as possible for adjudication.

3. Any migrant worker or member of his or her family who is detained in a State of transit or in a State of employment for violation of provisions relating to migration shall be held, in so far as practicable, separately from convicted persons or persons detained pending trial.

4. During any period of imprisonment in pursuance of a sentence imposed by a court of law, the essential aim of the treatment of a migrant worker or a member of his or her family shall be his or her reformation and social rehabilitation. Juvenile offenders shall be separated from adults and be accorded treatment appropriate to their age and legal status.

5. During detention or imprisonment, migrant workers and members of their families shall enjoy the same rights as nationals to visits by members of their families.

6. Whenever a migrant worker is deprived of his or her liberty, the competent authorities of the State concerned shall pay attention to the problems that may be posed for members of his or her family, in particular for spouses and minor children.

7. Migrant workers and members of their families who are subjected to any form of detention or imprisonment in accordance with the law in force in the State of employment or in the State of transit shall enjoy the same rights as nationals of those States who are in the same situation.

8. If a migrant worker or a member of his or her family is detained for the purpose of verifying any infraction of provisions related to migration, he or she shall not bear any costs arising therefrom.

*Article* 18

1. Migrant workers and members of their families shall have the right to equality with nationals of the State concerned before the courts and tribunals. In the determination of any criminal charge against them or of their rights and obligations in a suit of law, they shall be entitled to a fair and public hearing by a competent, independent and impartial tribunal established by law.

2. Migrant workers and members of their families who are charged with a criminal offence shall have the right to be presumed innocent until proven guilty according to law.

3. In the determination of any criminal charge against them, migrant workers and members of their families shall be entitled to the following minimum guarantees:

    *(a)* To be informed promptly and in detail in a language they understand of the nature and cause of the charge against them;

*(b)* To have adequate time and facilities for the preparation of their defence and to communicate with counsel of their own choosing;

*(c)* To be tried without undue delay;

*(d)* To be tried in their presence and to defend themselves in person or through legal assistance of their own choosing; to be informed, if they do not have legal assistance, of this right; and to have legal assistance assigned to them, in any case where the interests of justice so require and without payment by them in any such case if they do not have sufficient means to pay;

*(e)* To examine or have examined the witnesses against them and to obtain the attendance and examination of witnesses on their behalf under the same conditions as witnesses against them;

*(f)* To have the free assistance of an interpreter if they cannot understand or speak the language used in court;

*(g)* Not to be compelled to testify against themselves or to confess guilt.

4. In the case of juvenile persons, the procedure shall be such as will take account of their age and the desirability of promoting their rehabilitation.

5. Migrant workers and members of their families convicted of a crime shall have the right to their conviction and sentence being reviewed by a higher tribunal according to law.

6. When a migrant worker or a member of his or her family has, by a final decision, been convicted of a criminal offence and when subsequently his or her conviction has been reversed or he or she has been pardoned on the ground that a new or newly discovered fact shows conclusively that there has been a miscarriage of justice, the person who has suffered punishment as a result of such conviction shall be compensated according to law, unless it is proved that the non-disclosure of the unknown fact in time is wholly or partly attributable to that person.

7. No migrant worker or member of his or her family shall be liable to be tried or punished again for an offence for which he or she has already been finally convicted or acquitted in accordance with the law and penal procedure of the State concerned.

*Article* 19

1. No migrant worker or member of his or her family shall be held guilty of any criminal offence on account of any act or omission that did not constitute a criminal offence under national or international law at the time when the criminal offence was committed, nor shall a heavier penalty be imposed than the one that was applicable at the time when it was committed. If, subsequent to the commission of the offence, provision is made by law for the imposition of a lighter penalty, he or she shall benefit thereby.

2. Humanitarian considerations related to the status of a migrant worker, in particular with respect to his or her right of residence or work, should be taken into account in imposing a sentence for a criminal offence committed by a migrant worker or a member of his or her family.

*Article* 20

1. No migrant worker or member of his or her family shall be imprisoned merely on the ground of failure to fulfil a contractual obligation.

2. No migrant worker or member of his or her family shall be deprived of his or her authorization of residence or work permit or expelled merely on the ground of failure to fulfil an obligation arising out of a work contract unless fulfilment of that obligation constitutes a condition for such authorization or permit.

## Article 21

It shall be unlawful for anyone, other than a public official duly authorized by law, to confiscate, destroy or attempt to destroy identity documents, documents authorizing entry to or stay, residence or establishment in the national territory or work permits. No authorized confiscation of such documents shall take place without delivery of a detailed receipt. In no case shall it be permitted to destroy the passport or equivalent document of a migrant worker or a member of his or her family.

## Article 22

1. Migrant workers and members of their families shall not be subject to measures of collective expulsion. Each case of expulsion shall be examined and decided individually.

2. Migrant workers and members of their families may be expelled from the territory of a State Party only in pursuance of a decision taken by the competent authority in accordance with law.

3. The decision shall be communicated to them in a language they understand. Upon their request where not otherwise mandatory, the decision shall be communicated to them in writing and, save in exceptional circumstances on account of national security, the reasons for the decision likewise stated. The persons concerned shall be informed of these rights before or at the latest at the time the decision is rendered.

4. Except where a final decision is pronounced by a judicial authority, the person concerned shall have the right to submit the reason he or she should not be expelled and to have his or her case reviewed by the competent authority, unless compelling reasons of national security require otherwise. Pending such review, the person concerned shall have the right to seek a stay of the decision of expulsion.

5. If a decision of expulsion that has already been executed is subsequently annulled, the person concerned shall have the right to seek compensation according to law and the earlier decision shall not be used to prevent him or her from re-entering the State concerned.

6. In case of expulsion, the person concerned shall have a reasonable opportunity before or after departure to settle any claims for wages and other entitlements due to him or her and any pending liabilities.

7. Without prejudice to the execution of a decision of expulsion, a migrant worker or a member of his or her family who is subject to such a decision may seek entry into a State other than his or her State of origin.

8. In case of expulsion of a migrant worker or a member of his or her family the costs of expulsion shall not be borne by him or her. The person concerned may be required to pay his or her own travel costs.

9. Expulsion from the State of employment shall not in itself prejudice any rights

of a migrant worker or a member of his or her family acquired in accordance with the law of that State, including the right to receive wages and other entitlements due to him or her.

## Article 23

Migrant workers and members of their families shall have the right to have recourse to the protection and assistance of the consular or diplomatic authorities of their State of origin or of a State representing the interests of that State whenever the rights recognized in the present Convention are impaired. In particular, in case of expulsion, the person concerned shall be informed of this right without delay and the authorities of the expelling State shall facilitate the exercise of such right.

## Article 24

Every migrant worker and every member of his or her family shall have the right to recognition everywhere as a person before the law.

## Article 25

1. Migrant workers shall enjoy treatment not less favourable than that which applies to nationals of the State of employment in respect of remuneration and:

   (a) Other conditions of work, that is to say, overtime, hours of work, weekly rest, holidays with pay, safety, health, termination of the employment relationship and any other conditions of work which, according to national law and practice, are covered by these terms;

   (b) Other terms of employment, that is to say, minimum age of employment, restriction on home work and any other matters which, according to national law and practice, are considered a term of employment.

2. It shall not be lawful to derogate in private contracts of employment from the principle of equality of treatment referred to in paragraph 1 of the present article.

3. States Parties shall take all appropriate measures to ensure that migrant workers are not deprived of any rights derived from this principle by reason of any irregularity in their stay or employment. In particular, employers shall not be relieved of any legal or contractual obligations, nor shall their obligations be limited in any manner by reason of such irregularity.

## Article 26

1. States Parties recognize the right of migrant workers and members of their families:

   (a) To take part in meetings and activities of trade unions and of any other associations established in accordance with law, with a view to protecting their economic, social, cultural and other interests, subject only to the rules of the organization concerned;

   (b) To join freely any trade union and any such association as aforesaid, subject only to the rules of the organization concerned;

   (c) To seek the aid and assistance of any trade union and of any such association as aforesaid.

2. No restrictions may be placed on the exercise of these rights other than those that are prescribed by law and which are necessary in a democratic society in the interests of national security, public order (*ordre public*) or the protection of the rights and freedoms of others.

*Article 27*

1. With respect to social security, migrant workers and members of their families shall enjoy in the State of employment the same treatment granted to nationals in so far as they fulfil the requirements provided for by the applicable legislation of that State and the applicable bilateral and multilateral treaties. The competent authorities of the State of origin and the State of employment can at any time establish the necessary arrangements to determine the modalities of application of this norm.

2. Where the applicable legislation does not allow migrant workers and members of their families a benefit, the States concerned shall examine the possibility of reimbursing interested persons the amount of contributions made by them with respect to that benefit on the basis of the treatment granted to nationals who are in similar circumstances.

*Article 28*

Migrant workers and members of their families shall have the right to receive any medical care that is urgently required for the preservation of their life or the avoidance of irreparable harm to their health on the basis of equality of treatment with nationals of the State concerned. Such emergency medical care shall not be refused them by reason of any irregularity with regard to stay or employment.

*Article 29*

Each child of a migrant worker shall have the right to a name, to registration of birth and to a nationality.

*Article 30*

Each child of a migrant worker shall have the basic right of access to education on the basis of equality of treatment with nationals of the State concerned. Access to public pre-school educational institutions or schools shall not be refused or limited by reason of the irregular situation with respect to stay or employment of either parent or by reason of the irregularity of the child's stay in the State of employment.

*Article 31*

1. States Parties shall ensure respect for the cultural identity of migrant workers and members of their families and shall not prevent them from maintaining their cultural links with their State of origin.

2. States Parties may take appropriate measures to assist and encourage efforts in this respect.

*Article 32*

Upon the termination of their stay in the State of employment, migrant workers and members of their families shall have the right to transfer their earnings and savings and, in accordance with the applicable legislation of the States concerned, their personal effects and belongings.

*Article 33*

1. Migrant workers and members of their families shall have the right to be informed by the State of origin, the State of employment or the State of transit as the case may be concerning:

   *(a)* Their rights arising out of the present Convention;

   *(b)* The conditions of their admission, their rights and obligations under the law and practice of the State concerned and such other matters as will enable them to comply with administrative or other formalities in that State.

2. States Parties shall take all measures they deem appropriate to disseminate the said information or to ensure that it is provided by employers, trade unions or other appropriate bodies or institutions. As appropriate, they shall co-operate with other States concerned.

3. Such adequate information shall be provided upon request to migrant workers and members of their families, free of charge, and, as far as possible, in a language they are able to understand.

*Article 34*

Nothing in the present part of the Convention shall have the effect of relieving migrant workers and the members of their families from either the obligation to comply with the laws and regulations of any State of transit and the State of employment or the obligation to respect the cultural identity of the inhabitants of such States.

*Article 35*

Nothing in the present part of the Convention shall be interpreted as implying the regularization of the situation of migrant workers or members of their families who are non-documented or in an irregular situation or any right to such regularization of their situation, nor shall it prejudice the measures intended to ensure sound and equitable conditions for international migration as provided in Part VI of the present Convention.

## PART IV

### OTHER RIGHTS OF MIGRANT WORKERS AND MEMBERS OF THEIR FAMILIES WHO ARE DOCUMENTED OR IN A REGULAR SITUATION

*Article 36*

Migrant workers and members of their families who are documented or in a regular situation in the State of employment shall enjoy the rights set forth in the present part of the Convention in addition to those set forth in Part III.

*Article* 37

Before their departure, or at the latest at the time of their admission to the State of employment, migrant workers and members of their families shall have the right to be fully informed by the State of origin or the State of employment, as appropriate, of all conditions applicable to their admission and particularly those concerning their stay and the remunerated activities in which they may engage as well as of the requirements they must satisfy in the State of employment and the authority to which they must address themselves for any modification of those conditions.

*Article* 38

1. States of employment shall make every effort to authorize migrant workers and members of the families to be temporarily absent without effect upon their authorization to stay or to work, as the case may be. In doing so, States of employment shall take into account the special needs and obligations of migrant workers and members of their families, in particular in their States of origin.

2. Migrant workers and members of their families shall have the right to be fully informed of the terms on which such temporary absences are authorized.

*Article* 39

1. Migrant workers and members of their families shall have the right to liberty of movement in the territory of the State of employment and freedom to choose their residence there.

2. The rights mentioned in paragraph 1 of the present article shall not be subject to any restrictions except those that are provided by law, are necessary to protect national security, public order (*ordre public*), public health or morals, or the rights and freedoms of others and are consistent with the other rights recognized in the present Convention.

*Article* 40

1. Migrant workers and members of their families shall have the right to form associations and trade unions in the State of employment for the promotion and protection of their economic, social, cultural and other interests.

2. No restrictions may be placed on the exercise of this right other than those that are prescribed by law and are necessary in a democratic society in the interests of national security, public order (*ordre public*) or the protection of the rights and freedoms of others.

*Article* 41

1. Migrant workers and members of their families shall have the right to participate in public affairs of their State of origin and to vote and to be elected at elections of that State, in accordance with its legislation.

2. The States concerned shall, as appropriate and in accordance with their legislation, facilitate the exercise of these rights.

*Article* 42

1. States Parties shall consider the establishment of procedures or institutions through which account may be taken, both in States of origin and in States of

employment, of special needs, aspirations and obligations of migrant workers and members of their families and shall envisage, as appropriate, the possibility for migrant workers and members of their families to have their freely chosen representatives in those institutions.

2. States of employment shall facilitate, in accordance with their national legislation, the consultation or participation of migrant workers and members of their families in decisions concerning the life and administration of local communities.

3. Migrant workers may enjoy political rights in the State of employment if that State, in the exercise of its sovereignty, grants them such rights.

*Article* 43

1. Migrant workers shall enjoy equality of treatment with nationals of the State of employment in relation to:

   *(a)* Access to educational institutions and services subject to the admission requirements and other regulations of the institutions and services concerned;

   *(b)* Access to vocational guidance and placement services;

   *(c)* Access to vocational training and retraining facilities and institutions;

   *(d)* Access to housing, including social housing schemes, and protection against exploitation in respect of rents;

   *(e)* Access to social and health services, provided that the requirements for participation in the respective schemes are met;

   *(f)* Access to co-operatives and self-managed enterprises, which shall not imply a change of their migration status and shall be subject to the rules and regulations of the bodies concerned;

   *(g)* Access to and participation in cultural life.

2. States Parties shall promote conditions to ensure effective equality of treatment to enable migrant workers to enjoy the rights mentioned in paragraph 1 of the present article whenever the terms of their stay, as authorized by the State of employment, meet the appropriate requirements.

3. States of employment shall not prevent an employer of migrant workers from establishing housing or social or cultural facilities for them. Subject to Article 70 of the present Convention, a State of employment may make the establishment of such facilities subject to the requirements generally applied in that State concerning their installation.

*Article* 44

1. States Parties, recognizing that the family is the natural and fundamental group unit of society and is entitled to protection by society and the State, shall take appropriate measures to ensure the protection of the unity of the families of migrant workers.

2. States Parties shall take measures that they deem appropriate and that fall within their competence to facilitate the reunification of migrant workers with their spouses or persons who have with the migrant worker a relationship that, according to applicable law, produces effects equivalent to marriage, as well as with their minor dependent unmarried children.

3. States of employment, on humanitarian grounds, shall favourably consider granting equal treatment, as set forth in paragraph 2 of the present article, to other family members of migrant workers.

*Article* 45

1. Members of the families of migrant workers shall, in the State of employment, enjoy equality of treatment with nationals of that State in relation to:

    *(a)* Access to educational institutions and services, subject to the admission requirements and other regulations of the institutions and services concerned;

    *(b)* Access to vocational guidance and training institutions and services, provided that requirements for participation are met;

    *(c)* Access to social and health services, provided that requirements for participation in the respective schemes are met;

    *(d)* Access to and participation in cultural life.

2. States of employment shall pursue a policy, where appropriate in collaboration with the States of origin, aimed at facilitating the integration of children of migrant workers in the local school system, particularly in respect of teaching them the local language.

3. States of employment shall endeavour to facilitate for the children of migrant workers the teaching of their mother tongue and culture and, in this regard, States of origin shall collaborate whenever appropriate.

4. States of employment may provide special schemes of education in the mother tongue of children of migrant workers, if necessary in collaboration with the States of origin.

*Article* 46

Migrant workers and members of their families shall, subject to the applicable legislation of the States concerned, as well as relevant international agreements and the obligations of the States concerned arising out of their participation in customs unions, enjoy exemption from import and export duties and taxes in respect of their personal and household effects as well as the equipment necessary to engage in the remunerated activity for which they were admitted to the State of employment:

    *(a)* Upon departure from the State of origin or State of habitual residence;

    *(b)* Upon initial admission to the State of employment;

    *(c)* Upon final departure from the State of employment;

    *(d)* Upon final return to the State of origin or State of habitual residence.

*Article* 47

1. Migrant workers shall have the right to transfer their earnings and savings, in particular those funds necessary for the support of their families, from the State of employment to their State of origin or any other State. Such transfers shall be made in conformity with procedures established by applicable legislation of the State concerned and in conformity with applicable international agreements.

2. States concerned shall take appropriate measures to facilitate such transfers.

*Article* 48

1. Without prejudice to applicable double taxation agreements, migrant workers and members of their families shall, in the matter of earnings in the State of employment:

   *(a)* Not be liable to taxes, duties or charges of any description higher or more onerous than those imposed on nationals in similar circumstances;

   *(b)* Be entitled to deductions or exemptions from taxes of any description and to any tax allowances applicable to nationals in similar circumstances, including tax allowances for dependent members of their families.

2. States Parties shall endeavour to adopt appropriate measures to avoid double taxation of the earnings and savings of migrant workers and members of their families.

*Article* 49

1. Where separate authorizations to reside and to engage in employment are required by national legislation, the States of employment shall issue to migrant workers authorization of residence for at least the same period of time as their authorization to engage in remunerated activity.

2. Migrant workers who in the State of employment are allowed freely to choose their remunerated activity shall neither be regarded as in an irregular situation nor shall they lose their authorization of residence by the mere fact of the termination of their remunerated activity prior to the expiration of their work permits or similar authorizations.

3. In order to allow migrant workers referred to in paragraph 2 of the present article sufficient time to find alternative remunerated activities, the authorization of residence shall not be withdrawn at least for a period corresponding to that during which they may be entitled to unemployment benefits.

*Article* 50

1. In the case of death of a migrant worker or dissolution of marriage, the State of employment shall favourably consider granting family members of that migrant worker residing in that State on the basis of family reunion an authorization to stay; the State of employment shall take into account the length of time they have already resided in that State.

2. Members of the family to whom such authorization is not granted shall be allowed before departure a reasonable period of time in order to enable them to settle their affairs in the State of employment.

3. The provisions of paragraphs 1 and 2 of the present article may not be interpreted as adversely affecting any right to stay and work otherwise granted to such family members by the legislation of the State of employment or by bilateral and multilateral treaties applicable to that State.

*Article* 51

Migrant workers who in the State of employment are not permitted freely to choose their remunerated activity shall neither be regarded as in an irregular situation nor shall they lose their authorization of residence by the mere fact of the termination of their remunerated activity prior to the expiration of their work permit, except where the authorization of residence is expressly dependent upon the specific remunerated activity for which they were admitted. Such migrant workers shall have the right to seek alternative employment, participation in public work schemes and retraining during the remaining period of their author-ization to work, subject to such conditions and limitations as are specified in the authorization to work.

*Article* 52

1. Migrant workers in the State of employment shall have the right freely to choose their remunerated activity, subject to the following restrictions or conditions.

2. For any migrant worker a State of employment may:

   *(a)* Restrict access to limited categories of employment, functions, services or activities where this is necessary in the interests of this State and provided for by national legislation;

   *(b)* Restrict free choice of remunerated activity in accordance with its legisla-tion concerning recognition of occupational qualifications acquired outside its territory. However, States Parties concerned shall endeavour to provide for recognition of such qualifications.

3. For migrant workers whose permission to work is limited in time, a State of employment may also:

   *(a)* Make the right freely to choose their remunerated activities subject to the condition that the migrant worker has resided lawfully in its territory for the purpose of remunerated activity for a period of time prescribed in its national legislation that should not exceed two years;

   *(b)* Limit access by a migrant worker to remunerated activities in pursuance of a policy of granting priority to its nationals or to persons who are assimi-lated to them for these purposes by virtue of legislation or bilateral or multilateral agreements. Any such limitation shall cease to apply to a migrant worker who has resided lawfully in its territory for the purpose of remunerated activity for a period of time prescribed in its national legislation that should not exceed five years.

4. States of employment shall prescribe the conditions under which a migrant worker who has been admitted to take up employment may be authorized to engage in work on his or her own account. Account shall be taken of the period during which the worker has already been lawfully in the State of employment.

*Article* 53

1. Members of a migrant worker's family who have themselves an authorization of residence or admission that is without limit of time or is automatically renewable shall be permitted freely to choose their remunerated activity under the same conditions as are applicable to the said migrant worker in accordance with Article 52 of the present Convention.

2. With respect to members of a migrant worker's family who are not permitted

freely to choose their remunerated activity, States Parties shall consider favourably granting them priority in obtaining permission to engage in a remunerated activity over other workers who seek admission to the State of employment, subject to applicable bilateral and multilateral agreements.

*Article* 54

1. Without prejudice to the terms of their authorization of residence or their permission to work and the rights provided for in Articles 25 and 27 of the present Convention, migrant workers shall enjoy equality of treatment with nationals of the State of employment in respect of:

   *(a)*  Protection against dismissal;

   *(b)*  Unemployment benefits;

   *(c)*  Access to public work schemes intended to combat unemployment;

   *(d)*  Access to alternative employment in the event of loss of work or termination of other remunerated activity, subject to Article 52 of the present Convention.

2. If a migrant worker claims that the terms of his or her work contract have been violated by his or her employer, he or she shall have the right to address his or her case to the competent authorities of the State of employment, on terms provided for in Article 18, paragraph 1, of the present Convention.

*Article* 55

Migrant workers who have been granted permission to engage in a remunerated activity, subject to the conditions attached to such permission, shall be entitled to equality of treatment with nationals of the State of employment in the exercise of that remunerated activity.

*Article* 56

1. Migrant workers and members of their families referred to in the present part of the Convention may not be expelled from a State of employment, except for reasons defined in the national legislation of that State, and subject to the safeguards established in Part III.

2. Expulsion shall not be resorted to for the purpose of depriving a migrant worker or a member of his or her family of the rights arising out of the authorization of residence and the work permit.

3. In considering whether to expel a migrant worker or a member of his or her family, account should be taken of humanitarian considerations and of the length of time that the person concerned has already resided in the State of employment.

## PART V

## PROVISIONS APPLICABLE TO PARTICULAR CATEGORIES OF MIGRANT WORKERS AND OF THEIR FAMILIES

*Article* 57

The particular categories of migrant workers and members of their families specified in the present part of the Convention who are documented or in a regular situation shall enjoy the rights set forth in part m and, except as modified below, the rights set forth in Part IV.

*Article* 58

1. Frontier workers, as defined in Article 2, paragraph 2 (a), of the present Convention, shall be entitled to the rights provided for in Part IV that can be applied to them by reason of their presence and work in the territory of the State of employment, taking into account that they do not have their habitual residence in that State.

2. States of employment shall consider favourably granting frontier workers the right freely to choose their remunerated activity after a specified period of time. The granting of that right shall not affect their status as frontier workers.

*Article* 59

1. Seasonal workers, as defined in Article 2, paragraph 2 (b), of the present Convention, shall be entitled to the rights provided for in Part IV that can be applied to them by reason of their presence and work in the territory of the State of employment and that are compatible with their status in that State as seasonal workers, taking into account the fact that they are present in that State for only part of the year.

2. The State of employment shall, subject to paragraph 1 of the present article, consider granting seasonal workers who have been employed in its territory for a significant period of time the possibility of taking up other remunerated activities and giving them priority over other workers who seek admission to that State, subject to applicable bilateral and multilateral agreements.

*Article* 60

Itinerant workers, as defined in Article 2, paragraph 2 (a), of the present Convention, shall be entitled to the rights provided for in Part IV that can be granted to them by reason of their presence and work in the territory of the State of employment and that are compatible with their status as itinerant workers in that State.

*Article* 61

1. Project-tied workers, as defined in Article 2, paragraph 2 (of the present Convention, and members of their families shall be entitled to the rights provided for in Part IV except the provisions of Article 43, paragraphs 1 (b) and (c), Article 43, paragraph 1 (d), as it pertains to social housing schemes, Article 45, paragraph 1 (b), and Articles 52 to 55.

2. If a project-tied worker claims that the terms of his or her work contract have been violated by his or her employer, he or she shall have the right to address his or her case to the competent authorities of the State which has jurisdiction over that employer, on terms provided for in Article 18, paragraph 1, of the present Convention.

3. Subject to bilateral or multilateral agreements in force for them, the States Parties concerned shall endeavour to enable project-tied workers to remain adequately protected by the social security systems of their States of origin or habitual residence during their engagement in the project. States Parties concerned shall take appropriate measures with the aim of avoiding any denial of rights or duplication of payments in this respect.

4. Without prejudice to the provisions of Article 47 of the present Convention and to relevant bilateral or multilateral agreements, States Parties concerned shall permit payment of the earnings of project-tied workers in their State of origin or habitual residence.

*Article* 62

1. Specified-employment workers as defined in Article 2, paragraph 2 (g), of the present Convention, shall be entitled to the rights provided for in Part IV, except the provisions of Article 43, paragraphs 1 (b) and (c), Article 43, paragraph 1 (d), as it pertains to social housing schemes, Article 52, and Article 54, paragraph 1 (d).

2. Members of the families of specified-employment workers shall be entitled to the rights relating to family members of migrant workers provided for in Part IV of the present Convention, except the provisions of Article 53.

*Article* 63

1. Self-employed workers, as defined in Article 2, paragraph 2 (h), of the present Convention, shall be entitled to the rights provided for in Part IV with the exception of those rights which are exclusively applicable to workers having a contract of employment.

2. Without prejudice to Articles 52 and 79 of the present Convention, the termination of the economic activity of the self-employed workers shall not in itself imply the withdrawal of the authorization for them or for the members of their families to stay or to engage in a remunerated activity in the State of employment except where the authorization of residence is expressly dependent upon the specific remunerated activity for which they were admitted.


PART VI

PROMOTION OF SOUND, EQUITABLE, HUMANE AND LAWFUL CONDITIONS IN CONNECTION WITH INTERNATIONAL MIGRATION OF WORKERS AND MEMBERS OF THEIR FAMILIES

*Article* 64

1. Without prejudice to Article 79 of the present Convention, the States Parties

concerned shall as appropriate consult and co-operate with a view to promoting sound, equitable and humane conditions in connection with international migration of workers and members of their families.

2. In this respect, due regard shall be paid not only to labour needs and resources, but also to the social, economic, cultural and other needs of migrant workers and members of their families involved, as well as to the consequences of such migration for the communities concerned.

*Article* 65

1. States Parties shall maintain appropriate services to deal with questions concerning international migration of workers and members of their families. Their functions shall include, *inter alia:*

   (a) The formulation and implementation of policies regarding such migration;

   (b) An exchange of information. consultation and co-operation with the competent authorities of other States Parties involved in such migration;

   (c) The provision of appropriate information, particularly to employers, workers and their organizations on policies, laws and regulations relating to migration and employment, on agreements concluded with other States concerning migration and on other relevant matters;

   (d) The provision of information and appropriate assistance to migrant workers and members of their families regarding requisite authorizations and formalities and arrangements for departure, travel, arrival, stay, remunerated activities, exit and return, as well as on conditions of work and life in the State of employment and on customs, currency, tax and other relevant laws and regulations.

2. States Parties shall facilitate as appropriate the provision of adequate consular and other services that are necessary to meet the social, cultural and other needs of migrant workers and members of their families.

*Article* 66

1. Subject to paragraph 2 of the present article, the right to undertake operations with a view to the recruitment of workers for employment in another State shall be restricted to:

   (a) Public services or bodies of the State in which such operations take place;

   (b) Public services or bodies of the State of employment on the basis of agreement between the States concerned;

   (c) A body established by virtue of a bilateral or multilateral agreement.

2. Subject to any authorization, approval and supervision by the public authorities of the States Parties concerned as may be established pursuant to the legislation and practice of those States, agencies, prospective employers or persons acting on their behalf may also be permitted to undertake the said operations.

*Article* 67

1. States Parties concerned shall co-operate as appropriate in the adoption of measures regarding the orderly return of migrant workers and members of their families to the State of origin when they decide to return or their authorization of

residence or employment expires or when they are in the State of employment in an irregular situation.

2. Concerning migrant workers and members of their families in a regular situation, States Parties concerned shall co-operate as appropriate, on terms agreed upon by those States, with a view to promoting adequate economic conditions for their resettlement and to facilitating their durable social and cultural reintegration in the State of origin.

*Article* 68

1. States Parties, including States of transit, shall collaborate with a view to preventing and eliminating illegal or clandestine movements and employment of migrant workers in an irregular situation. The measures to be taken to this end within the jurisdiction of each State concerned shall include:

(a) Appropriate measures against the dissemination of misleading information relating to emigration and immigration;

(b) Measures to detect and eradicate illegal or clandestine movements of migrant workers and members of their families and to impose effective sanctions on persons, groups or entities which organize, operate or assist in organizing or operating such movements;

(c) Measures to impose effective sanctions on persons, groups or entities which use violence, threats or intimidation against migrant workers or members of their families in an irregular situation.

2. States of employment shall take all adequate and effective measures to eliminate employment in their territory of migrant workers in an irregular situation, including, whenever appropriate, sanctions on employers of such workers. The rights of migrant workers vis-à-vis their employer arising from employment shall not be impaired by these measures.

*Article* 69

1. States Parties shall, when there are migrant workers and members of their families within their territory in an irregular situation, take appropriate measures to ensure that such a situation does not persist.

2. Whenever States Parties concerned consider the possibility of regularizing the situation of such persons in accordance with applicable national legislation and bilateral or multilateral agreements, appropriate account shall be taken of the circumstances of their entry, the duration of their stay in the States of employment and other relevant considerations, in particular those relating to their family situation.

*Article* 70

States Parties shall take measures not less favourable than those applied to nationals to ensure that working and living conditions of migrant workers and members of their families in a regular situation are in keeping with the standards of fitness, safety, health and principles of human dignity.

*Article* 71

1. States Parties shall facilitate, whenever necessary, the repatriation to the State of origin of the bodies of deceased migrant workers or members of their families.

2. As regards compensation matters relating to the death of a migrant worker or a member of his or her family, States Parties shall, as appropriate, provide assistance to the persons concerned with a view to the prompt settlement of such matters. Settlement of these matters shall be carried out on the basis of applicable national law in accordance with the provisions of the present Convention and any relevant bilateral or multilateral agreements.

## PART VII

## APPLICATION OF THE CONVENTION

*Article* 72

1. *(a)* For the purpose of reviewing the application of the present Convention, there shall be established a Committee on the Protection of the Rights of All Migrant Workers and Members of Their Families (hereinafter referred to as 'the Committee');

*(b)* The Committee shall consist, at the time of entry into force of the present Convention, of ten and, after the entry into force of the Convention for the forty-first State Party, of fourteen experts of high moral standing, impartiality and recognized competence in the field covered by the Convention.

2. *(a)* Members of the Committee shall be elected by secret ballot by the States Parties from a list of persons nominated by the States Parties, due consideration being given to equitable geographical distribution, including both States of origin and States of employment, and to the representation of the principal legal system. Each State Party may nominate one person from among its own nationals;

*(b)* Members shall be elected and shall serve in their personal capacity.

3. The initial election shall be held no later than six months after the date of the entry into force of the present Convention and subsequent elections every second year. At least four months before the date of each election, the Secretary-General of the United Nations shall address a letter to all States Parties inviting them to submit their nominations within two months. The Secretary-General shall prepare a list in alphabetical order of all persons thus nominated, indicating the States Parties that have nominated them, and shall submit it to the States Parties not later than one month before the date of the corresponding election, together with the curricula vitae of the persons thus nominated.

4. Elections of members of the Committee shall be held at a meeting of States Parties convened by the Secretary-General at United Nations Headquarters. At that meeting, for which two thirds of the States Parties shall constitute a quorum, the persons elected to the Committee shall be those nominees who obtain the largest number of votes and an absolute majority of the votes of the States Parties present and voting.

5. *(a)* The members of the Committee shall serve for a term of four years. However, the terms of five of the members elected in the first election shall expire at the end of two years; immediately after the first election, the names of these five members shall be chosen by lot by the Chairman of the meeting of States Parties;

*(b)* The election of the four additional members of the Committee shall be held in accordance with the provisions of paragraphs 2, 3 and 4 of the present article, following the entry into force of the Convention for the forty-first State Party. The term of two of the additional members elected on this occasion shall expire at the end of two years; the names of these members shall be chosen by lot by the Chairman of the meeting of States Parties;

*(c)* The members of the Committee shall be eligible for re-election if renominated.

6. If a member of the Committee dies or resigns or declares that for any other cause he or she can no longer perform the duties of the Committee, the State Party that nominated the expert shall appoint another expert from among its own nationals for the remaining part of the term. The new appointment is subject to the approval of the Committee.

7. The Secretary-General of the United Nations shall provide the necessary staff and facilities for the effective performance of the functions of the Committee.

8. The members of the Committee shall receive emoluments from United Nations resources on such terms and conditions as the General Assembly may decide.

9. The members of the Committee shall be entitled to the facilities, privileges and immunities of experts on mission for the United Nations as laid down in the relevant sections of the Convention on the Privileges and Immunities of the United Nations.

*Article 73*

1. States Parties undertake to submit to the Secretary-General of the United Nations for consideration by the Committee a report on the legislative, judicial, administrative and other measures they have taken to give effect to the provisions of the present Convention:

   *(a)* Within one year after the entry into force of the Convention for the State Party concerned;

   *(b)* Thereafter every five years and whenever the Committee so requests.

2. Reports prepared under the present article shall also indicate factors and difficulties, if any, affecting the implementation of the Convention and shall include information on the characteristics of migration flows in which the State Party concerned is involved.

3. The Committee shall decide any further guidelines applicable to the content of the reports.

4. States Parties shall make their reports widely available to the public in their own countries.

*Article* 74

1. The Committee shall examine the reports submitted by each State Party and shall transmit such comments as it may consider appropriate to the State Party concerned. This State Party may submit to the Committee observations on any comment made by the Committee in accordance with the present article. The Committee may request supplementary information from States Parties when considering these reports.

2. The Secretary-General of the United Nations shall, in due time before the opening of each regular session of the Committee, transmit to the Director-General of the International Labour Office copies of the reports submitted by States Parties concerned and information relevant to the consideration of these reports, in order to enable the Office to assist the Committee with the expertise the Office may provide regarding those matters dealt with by the present Convention that fall within the sphere of competence of the International Labour Organization. The Committee shall consider in its deliberations such comments and materials as the Office may provide.

3. The Secretary-General of the United Nations may also, after consultation with the Committee, transmit to other specialized agencies as well as to intergovernmental organizations, copies of such parts of these reports as may fall within their competence.

4. The Committee may invite the specialized agencies and organs of the United Nations, as well as intergovernmental organizations and other concerned bodies to submit, for consideration by the Committee, written information on such matters dealt with in the present Convention as fall within the scope of their activities.

5. The International Labour Office shall be invited by the Committee to appoint representatives to participate, in a consultative capacity, in the meetings of the Committee.

6. The Committee may invite representatives of other specialized agencies and organs of the United Nations, as well as of intergovernmental organizations, to be present and to be heard in its meetings whenever matters falling within their field of competence are considered.

7. The Committee shall present an annual report to the General Assembly of the United Nations on the implementation of the present Convention, containing its own considerations and recommendations, based, in particular, on the examination of the reports and any observations presented by States Parties.

8. The Secretary-General of the United Nations shall transmit the annual reports of the Committee to the States Parties to the present Convention, the Economic and Social Council, the Commission on Human Rights of the United Nations, the Director-General of the International Labour Office and other relevant organizations.

*Article* 75

1. The Committee shall adopt its own rules of procedure.

2. The Committee shall elect its officers for a term of two years.

3. The Committee shall normally meet annually.

4. The meetings of the Committee shall normally be held at United Nations Headquarters.

*Article* 76

1. A State Party to the present Convention may at any time declare under this article that it recognizes the competence of the Committee to receive and consider communications to the effect that a State Party claims that another State Party is not fulfilling its obligations under the present Convention. Communications under this article may be received and considered only if submitted by a State Party that has made a declaration recognizing in regard to itself the competence of the Committee. No communication shall be received by the Committee if it concerns a State Party which has not made such a declaration. Communications received under this article shall be dealt with in accordance with the following procedure:

(a)  If a State Party to the present Convention considers that another State Party is not fulfilling its obligations under the present Convention, it may, by written communication, bring the matter to the attention of that State Party. The State Party may also inform the Committee of the matter. Within three months after the receipt of the communication the receiving State shall afford the State that sent the communication an explanation, or any other statement in writing clarifying the matter which should include, to the extent possible and pertinent, reference to domestic procedures and remedies taken, pending or available in the matter;

(b)  If the matter is not adjusted to the satisfaction of both States Parties concerned within six months after the receipt by the receiving State of the initial communication, either State shall have the right to refer the matter to the Committee, by notice given to the Committee and to the other State;

(c)  The Committee shall deal with a matter referred to it only after it has ascertained that all available domestic remedies have been invoked and exhausted in the matter, in conformity with the generally recognized principles of international law. This shall not be the rule where, in the view of the Committee, the application of the remedies is unreasonably prolonged;

(d)  Subject to the provisions of subparagraph (c) of the present paragraph, the Committee shall make available its good offices to the States Parties concerned with a view to a friendly solution of the matter on the basis of the respect for the obligations set forth in the present Convention;

(e)  The Committee shall hold closed meetings when examining communications under the present article;

(f)  In any matter referred to it in accordance with subparagraph (b) of the present paragraph, the Committee may call upon the States Parties concerned, referred to in subparagraph (b), to supply any relevant information;

(g)  The States Parties concerned, referred to in subparagraph (b) of the present paragraph, shall have the right to be represented when the matter is being considered by the Committee and to make submissions orally and/or in writing;

(h)  The Committee shall, within twelve months after the date of receipt of notice under subparagraph (b) of the present paragraph, submit a report, as follows:

(i)  If a solution within the terms of subparagraph (d) of the present paragraph is reached, the Committee shall confine its report to a brief statement of the facts and of the solution reached;

(ii) If a solution within the terms of subparagraph (d) is not reached, the Committee shall, in its report, set forth the relevant facts concerning the issue between the States Parties concerned. The written submissions and record of the oral submissions made by the States Parties concerned shall be attached to the report. The Committee may also communicate only to the States Parties concerned any views that it may consider relevant to the issue between them. In every matter, the report shall be communicated to the States Parties concerned.

2. The provisions of the present article shall come into force when ten States Parties to the present Convention have made a declaration under paragraph 1 of the present article. Such declarations shall be deposited by the States Parties with the Secretary-General of the United Nations, who shall transmit copies thereof to the other States Parties. A declaration may be withdrawn at any time by notification to the Secretary-General. Such a withdrawal shall not prejudice the consideration of any matter that is the subject of a communication already transmitted under the present article; no further communication by any State Party shall be received under the present article after the notification of withdrawal of the declaration has been received by the Secretary-General, unless the State Party concerned has made a new declaration.

*Article 77*

1. A State Party to the present Convention may at any time declare under the present article that it recognizes the competence of the Committee to receive and consider communications from or on behalf of individuals subject to its jurisdiction who claim that their individual rights as established by the present Convention have been violated by that State Party. No communication shall be received by the Committee if it concerns a State Party that has not made such a declaration.

2. The Committee shall consider inadmissible any communication under the present article which is anonymous or which it considers to be an abuse of the right of submission of such communications or to be incompatible with the provisions of the present Convention.

3. The Committee shall not consider any communication from an individual under the present article unless it has ascertained that:

(a) The same matter has not been, and is not being, examined under another procedure of international investigation or settlement;

(b) The individual has exhausted all available domestic remedies; this shall not be the rule where, in the view of the Committee, the application of the remedies is unreasonably prolonged or is unlikely to bring effective relief to that individual.

4. Subject to the provisions of paragraph 2 of the present article, the Committee shall bring any communications submitted to it under this article to the attention of the State Party to the present Convention that has made a declaration under paragraph 1 and is alleged to be violating any provisions of the Convention. Within six months, the receiving State shall submit to the Committee written explanations

or statements clarifying the matter and the remedy, if any, that may have been taken by that State.

5. The Committee shall consider communications received under the present article in the light of all information made available to it by or on behalf of the individual and by the State Party concerned.

6. The Committee shall hold closed meetings when examining communications under the present article.

7. The Committee shall forward its views to the State Party concerned and to the individual.

8. The provisions of the present article shall come into force when ten States Parties to the present Convention have made declarations under paragraph 1 of the present article. Such declarations shall be deposited by the States Parties with the Secretary-General of the United Nations, who shall transmit copies thereof to the other States Parties. A declaration may be withdrawn at any time by notification to the Secretary-General. Such a withdrawal shall not prejudice the consideration of any matter that is the subject of a communication already transmitted under the present article; no further communication by or on behalf of an individual shall be received under the present article after the notification of withdrawal of the declaration has been received by the Secretary-General, unless the State Party has made a new declaration.

*Article 78*

The provisions of Article 76 of the present Convention shall be applied without prejudice to any procedures for settling disputes or complaints in the field covered by the present Convention laid down in the constituent instruments of, or in conventions adopted by, the United Nations and the specialized agencies and shall not prevent the States Parties from having recourse to any procedures for settling a dispute in accordance with international agreements in force between them.

## PART VIII

## GENERAL PROVISIONS

*Article 79*

Nothing in the present Convention shall affect the right of each State Party to establish the criteria governing admission of migrant workers and members of their families. Concerning other matters related to their legal situation and treatment as migrant workers and members of their families, States Parties shall be subject to the limitations set forth in the present Convention.

*Article 80*

Nothing in the present Convention shall be interpreted as impairing the provisions of the Charter of the United Nations and of the constitutions of the specialized agencies which define the respective responsibilities of the various organs of the United Nations and of the specialized agencies in regard to the matters dealt with in the present Convention.

*Article* 81

1. Nothing in the present Convention shall affect more favourable rights or free-doms granted to migrant workers and members of their families by virtue of:

    *(a)*  The law or practice of a State Party; or

    *(b)*  Any bilateral or multilateral treaty in force for the State Party concerned.

2. Nothing in the present Convention may be interpreted as implying for any State, group or person any right to engage in any activity or perform any act that would impair any of the rights and freedoms as set forth in the present Convention.

*Article* 82

The rights of migrant workers and members of their families provided for in the present Convention may not be renounced. It shall not be permissible to exert any form of pressure upon migrant workers and members of their families with a view to their relinquishing or foregoing any of the said rights. It shall not be possible to derogate by contract from rights recognized in the present Convention. States Parties shall take appropriate measures to ensure that these principles are respected.

*Article* 83

Each State Party to the present Convention undertakes:

    *(a)*  To ensure that any person whose rights or freedoms as herein recognized are violated shall have an effective remedy, notwithstanding that the violation has been committed by persons acting in an official capacity;

    *(b)*  To ensure that any persons seeking such a remedy shall have his or her claim reviewed and decided by competent judicial, administrative or legisla-tive authorities, or by any other competent authority provided for by the legal system of the State, and to develop the possibilities of judicial remedy;

    *(c)*  To ensure that the competent authorities shall enforce such remedies when granted.

*Article* 84

Each State Party undertakes to adopt the legislative and other measures that are necessary to implement the provisions of the present Convention.


# PART IX

## FINAL PROVISIONS

*Article* 85

The Secretary-General of the United Nations is designated as the depositary of the present Convention.

*Article* 86

1. The present Convention shall be open for signature by all States. It is subject to ratification.

2. The present Convention shall be open to accession by any State.

3. Instruments of ratification or accession shall be deposited with the Secretary-General of the United Nations.

*Article* 87

1. The present Convention shall enter into force on the first day of the month following a period of three months after the date of the deposit of the twentieth instrument of ratification or accession.

2. For each State ratifying or acceding to the present Convention after its entry into force, the Convention shall enter into force on the first day of the month following a period of three months after the date of the deposit of its own instrument of ratification or accession.

*Article* 88

A State ratifying or acceding to the present Convention may not exclude the application of any Part of it, or, without prejudice to Article 3, exclude any particular category of migrant workers from its application.

*Article* 89

1. Any State Party may denounce the present Convention, not earlier than five years after the Convention has entered into force for the State concerned, by means of a notification writing addressed to the Secretary-General of the United Nations.

2. Such denunciation shall become effective on the first day of the month following the expiration of a period of twelve months after the date of the receipt of the notification by the Secretary-General of the United Nations.

3. Such a denunciation shall not have the effect of releasing the State Party from its obligations under the present Convention in regard to any act or omission which occurs prior to the date at which the denunciation becomes effective, nor shall denunciation prejudice in any way the continued consideration of any matter which is already under consideration by the Committee prior to the date at which the denunciation becomes effective.

4. Following the date at which the denunciation of a State Party becomes effective, the Committee shall not commence consideration of any new matter regarding that State.

*Article* 90

1. After five years from the entry into force of the Convention a request for the revision of the Convention may be made at any time by any State Party by means of a notification in writing addressed to the Secretary-General of the United Nations. The Secretary-General shall thereupon communicate any proposed amendments to the States Parties with a request that they notify him whether the favour a conference of States Parties for the purpose of considering and voting upon the proposals. In the event that within four months from the date of such communication at least one third of the States Parties favours such a conference, the Secretary-General shall convene the conference under the auspices of the United Nations. Any amendment adopted by a majority of the States Parties

present and voting shall be submitted to the General Assembly for approval.

2. Amendments shall come into force when they have been approved by the General Assembly of the United Nations and accepted by a two-thirds majority of the States Parties in accordance with their respective constitutional processes.

3. When amendments come into force, they shall be binding on those States Parties that have accepted them, other States Parties still being bound by the provisions of the present Convention and any earlier amendment that they have accepted.

*Article* 91

1. The Secretary-General of the United Nations shall receive and circulate to all States the text of reservations made by States at the time of signature, ratification or accession.

2. A reservation incompatible with the object and purpose of the present Convention shall not be permitted.

3. Reservations may be withdrawn at any time by notification to this effect addressed to the Secretary-General of the United Nations, who shall then inform all States thereof. Such notification shall take effect on the date on which it is received.

*Article* 92

1. Any dispute between two or more States Parties concerning the interpretation or application of the present Convention that is not settled by negotiation shall, at the request of one of them, be submitted to arbitration. If within six months from the date of the request for arbitration the Parties are unable to agree on the organization of the arbitration, any one of those Parties may refer the dispute to the International Court of Justice by request in conformity with the Statute of the Court.

2. Each State Party may at the time of signature or ratification of the present Convention or accession thereto declare that it does not consider itself bound by paragraph 1 of the present article. The other States Parties shall not be bound by that paragraph with respect to any State Party that has made such a declaration.

3. Any State Party that has made a declaration in accordance with paragraph 2 of the present article may at any time withdraw that declaration by notification to the Secretary-General of the United Nations.

*Article* 93

1. The present Convention, of which the Arabic, Chinese, English, French, Russian and Spanish texts are equally authentic, shall be deposited with the Secretary-General of the United Nations.

2. The Secretary-General of the United Nations shall transmit certified copies of the present Convention to all States.

*In witness whereof* the undersigned plenipotentiaries, being duly authorized thereto by their respective Governments, have signed the present Convention.

PART THREE

# CONTRIBUTION OF THE INTERNATIONAL LABOUR ORGANIZATION

## INTRODUCTION

THE International Labour Organization is one of twelve Specialized Agencies brought into relationship with the United Nations under Articles 57 and 63 of the United Nations Charter. The Organization started its life in 1919, and it has the distinction of being in advance of other international institutions in that its major concern is social justice. The preamble to the Constitution begins: 'Whereas universal and lasting peace can be established only if it is based upon social justice'. Now, in the era of the United Nations, there is more emphasis on the attainment of social justice as an aim of international co-operation and action. The Constitution of the I.L.O., with various amendments of 1964 indicated (these are not yet in force), is contained in Brownlie, I., *Basic Documents in International Law* (4th edn., 1995), 50. The aims of the I.L.O. are set out in the Declaration adopted by the General Conference of the I.L.O. in 1944, printed below.

The I.L.O. has played a prominent and pioneer role in standard-setting in carefully drafted conventions dealing with specific subject matters. The I.L.O.'s Governing Body has now identified eight conventions as being fundamental to the rights of human beings at work, irrespective of the level of development of individual member States. These rights are seen as a precondition for all the others, and can be grouped under the following four rubrics: (a) Freedom of association: Freedom of Association and Protection of the Right to Organize Convention, 1948; and Right to Organize and Collective Bargaining Convention, 1949; (b) Abolition of forced labour: Forced Labour Convention, 1939; and Abolition of Forced Labour Convention, 1957; (c) Equality: Discrimination (Employment and Occupation) Convention, 1958; and Equal Remuneration Convention, 1951; (d) Elimination of child labour: Minimum Age Convention, 1973; and Worst Forms of Child Labour Convention, 1999. Those fundamental conventions and other relevant instruments are included in this Part.

The I.L.O., along with other Specialized Agencies, submits periodic reports to the Commission on Human Rights of the Economic and Social Council of the United Nations.

On the work of the I.L.O., see Jenks, C. W., *Social Justice in the Law of Nations* (1970); the same, *Human Rights and International Labour Standards* (1960); McNair, A.D., *The Expansion of International Law* (1962), 29–52; Landy, E. A., *The Effectiveness of International Supervision: Thirty Years of ILO Experience* (1966); *The Impact of International Labour Conventions and Recommendations* (I.L.O., Geneva, 1976); Valticos, N., *International Labour Law* (1979); Leary, V., 'Lessons from the Experience of the International Labour Organisation', in Alston, P. (ed.), *The United Nations and Human Rights* (1992), 580–619; Leary, V., *International Labour Conventions and National Law* (1982); International Labour Office, 'Possible improvements in the standard-setting activities of the ILO', doc. GB.277/LILS/2, Geneva, March 2000.

On the protection of the rights of migrant workers under the I.L.O. instruments of 1949 and 1975 see Cholewinski, R., *Migrant Workers in International Human Rights Law: Their Protection in Countries of Employment* (1997), ch. 3.

## 39. DECLARATION CONCERNING THE AIMS AND PURPOSES OF THE INTERNATIONAL LABOUR ORGANIZATION, 1944

*TEXT*

The General Conference of the International Labour Organization meeting in its Twenty-sixth Session in Philadelphia, hereby adopts this tenth day of May in the year nineteen hundred and forty-four, the present Declaration of the aims and purposes of the International Labour Organization and of the principles which should inspire the policy of its Members.

I

The Conference reaffirms the fundamental principles on which the Organization is based and, in particular, that:

*(a)* labour is not a commodity;

*(b)* freedom of expression and of association are essential to sustained progress;

*(c)* poverty anywhere constitutes a danger to prosperity everywhere;

*(d)* the war against want required to be carried on with unrelenting vigour within each nation, and by continuous and concerted international effort in which the representatives of workers and employers, enjoying equal status with those of Governments, loin with them in free discussion and democratic decision with a view to the promotion of the common welfare.

II

Believing that experience has fully demonstrated the truth of the statement in the Constitution of the International Labour Organization that lasting peace can be established only if it is based on social justice, the Conference affirms that:

*(a)* all human beings, irrespective of race, creed or sex, have the right to pursue both their material well-being and their spiritual development in conditions of freedom and dignity, of economic security and equal opportunity;

*(b)* the attainment of the conditions in which this shall be possible must constitute the central aim of national and international policy;

*(c)* all national and international policies and measures, in particular those of an economic and financial character, should be judged in this light and accepted only in so far as they may be held to promote and not to hinder the achievement of this fundamental objective;

(d) it is a responsibility of the International Labour Organization to examine and consider all international economic and financial policies and measures in the light of this fundamental objective;

(e) in discharging the tasks entrusted to it the International Labour Organization, having considered all relevant economic and financial factors, may include in its decisions and recommendations any provisions which it considers appropriate.

## III

The Conference recognizes the solemn obligation of the International Labour Organization to further among the nations of the world programmes which will achieve:

(a) full employment and the raising of standards of living;

(b) the employment of workers in the occupations in which they can have the satisfaction of giving the fullest measure of their skill and attainments and make their greatest contribution to the common well-being;

(c) the provision, as a means to the attainment of this end and under adequate guarantees for all concerned, of facilities for training and the transfer of labour, including migration for employment and settlement;

(d) policies in regard to wages and earnings, hours and other conditions of work calculated to ensure a just share of the fruits of progress to all, and a minimum living wage to all employed and in need of such protection;

(e) the effective recognition of the right of collective bargaining, the co-operation of management and labour in the continuous improvement of productive efficiency, and the collaboration of workers and employers in the preparation and application of social and economic measures;

(f) the extension of social security measures to provide a basic income to all in need of such protection and comprehensive medical care;

(g) adequate protection for the life and health of workers in all occupations;

(h) provision for child welfare and maternity protection;

(i) the provision of adequate nutrition, housing and facilities for recreation and culture;

(j) the assurance of equality of educational and vocational opportunity.

## IV

Confident that the fuller and broader utilization of the world's productive resources necessary for the achievement of the objectives set forth in this Declaration can be secured by effective international and national action, including measures to expand production and consumption, to avoid severe economic fluctuations, to promote the economic and social advancement of the less developed regions of the world, to assure greater stability in world prices of primary products, and to promote a high and steady volume of international trade, the Conference pledges the full co-operation of the International Labour Organization with such international bodies as may be entrusted with a share of the responsibility for this great task and for the promotion of the health, education and well-being of all peoples.

## V

The Conference affirms that the principles set forth in this Declaration are fully applicable to all peoples everywhere and that, while the manner of their application must be determined with due regard to the stage of social and economic development reached by each people, their progressive application to peoples who are still dependent, as well as to those who have already achieved self-government, is a matter of concern to the whole civilized world.

## 40.  FORCED LABOUR CONVENTION, 1930

The Convention (C29) was adopted by the General Conference of the I.L.O. on 10 June 1930, and entered into force on 1 May 1932. The Convention is aimed at practices in colonial countries and certain independent States at a certain stage of development. The focus is thus on forced labour as a form of economic exploitation. For the text in English and French, see 39 UNTS 55. The following version is the authentic text of the Convention, as modified by the Final Articles Revision Convention, 1946. The original text of the Convention was authenticated on 25 July 1930 by the signatures of E. Mahaim, President of the Conference, and Albert Thomas, Director of the International Labour Office. The Convention first came into force on 1 May 1932.

The definition of forced labour is not an easy matter. The technical difficulties are discussed by Fawcett, J., *The Application of the European Convention on Human Rights* (2nd edn., 1987), 56–63. Fawcett comments (at 48): 'the margin between the planned use of labour and the direction of labour, between free and compulsory employment, can become almost indiscernibly narrow'.

For further reference, see Avins, A., 'Involuntary Servitude in British Commonwealth Law' (1967) 16 *ICLQ* 29–55.

*TEXT*

*The General Conference of the International Labour Organization,*

*Having been convened* at Geneva by the Governing Body of the International Labour Office, and having met in its Fourteenth Session on 10 June 1930, and

*Having decided* upon the adoption of certain proposals with regard to forced or compulsory labour, which is included in the first item on the agenda of the Session, and

*Having determined* that these proposals shall take the form of an international Convention,

*Adopts* this twenty-eighth day of June of the year one thousand nine hundred and thirty the following Convention, which may be cited as the Forced Labour Convention, 1930, for ratification by the Members of the International Labour Organization in accordance with the provisions of the Constitution of the International Labour Organization:

*Article* 1

1. Each Member of the International Labour Organization which ratifies this Convention undertakes to suppress the use of forced or compulsory labour in all its forms within the shortest possible period.

2. With a view to this complete suppression, recourse to forced or compulsory labour may be had, during the transitional period, for public purposes only and as an exceptional measure, subject to the conditions and guarantees hereinafter provided.

3. At the expiration of a period of five years after the coming into force of this Convention, and when the Governing Body of the International Labour Office prepares the report provided for in Article 31 below, the said Governing Body shall consider the possibility of the suppression of forced or compulsory labour in all its forms without a further transitional period and the desirability of placing this question on the agenda of the Conference.

*Article* 2

1. For the purposes of this Convention the term 'forced or compulsory labour' shall mean all work or service which is exacted from any person under the menace of any penalty and for which the said person has not offered himself voluntarily.

2. Nevertheless, for the purposes of this Convention, the term 'forced or compulsory labour' shall not include—

   *(a)* any work or service exacted in virtue of compulsory military service laws for work of a purely military character;

   *(b)* any work or service which forms part of the normal civic obligations of the citizens of a fully self-governing country;

   *(c)* any work or service exacted from any person as a consequence of a conviction in a court of law, provided that the said work or service is carried out under the supervision and control of a public authority and that the said person is not hired to or placed at the disposal of private individuals, companies or associations;

   *(d)* any work or service exacted in cases of emergency, that is to say, in the event of war or of a calamity or threatened calamity, such as fire, flood, famine, earthquake, violent epidemic or epizootic diseases, invasion by animal, insect or vegetable pests, and in general any circumstance that would endanger the existence or the well-being of the whole or part of the population;

   *(e)* minor communal services of a kind which, being performed by the members of the community in the direct interest of the said community, can therefore be considered as normal civic obligations incumbent upon the members of the community, provided that the members of the community or their direct representatives shall have the right to be consulted in regard to the need for such services.

*Article* 3

For the purposes of this Convention the term 'competent authority' shall mean either an authority of the metropolitan country or the highest central authority in the territory concerned.

*Article* 4

1. The competent authority shall not impose or permit the imposition of forced or compulsory labour for the benefit of private individuals, companies or associations.

2. Where such forced or compulsory labour for the benefit of private individuals, companies or associations exists at the date on which a Member's ratification of this Convention is registered by the Director-General of the International Labour

Office, the Member shall completely suppress such forced or compulsory labour from the date on which this Convention comes into force for that Member.

*Article* 5

1. No concession granted to private individuals, companies or associations shall involve any form of forced or compulsory labour for the production or the collection of products which such private individuals, companies or associations utilise or in which they trade.

2. Where concessions exist containing provisions involving such forced or compulsory labour, such provisions shall be rescinded as soon as possible, in order to comply with Article 1 of this Convention.

*Article* 6

Officials of the administration, even when they have the duty of encouraging the populations under their charge to engage in some form of labour, shall not put constraint upon the said populations or upon any individual members thereof to work for private individuals, companies or associations.

*Article* 7

1. Chiefs who do not exercise administrative functions shall not have recourse to forced or compulsory labour.

2. Chiefs who exercise administrative functions may, with the express permission of the competent authority, have recourse to forced or compulsory labour, subject to the provisions of Article 10 of this Convention.

3. Chiefs who are duly recognised and who do not receive adequate remuneration in other forms may have the enjoyment of personal services, subject to due regulation and provided that all necessary measures are taken to prevent abuses.

*Article* 8

1. The responsibility for every decision to have recourse to forced or compulsory labour shall rest with the highest civil authority in the territory concerned.

2. Nevertheless, that authority may delegate powers to the highest local authorities to exact forced or compulsory labour which does not involve the removal of the workers from their place of habitual residence. That authority may also delegate, for such periods and subject to such conditions as may be laid down in the regulations provided for in Article 23 of this Convention, powers to the highest local authorities to exact forced or compulsory labour which involves the removal of the workers from their place of habitual residence for the purpose of facilitating the movement of officials of the administration, when on duty, and for the transport of Government stores.

*Article* 9

Except as otherwise provided for in Article 10 of this Convention, any authority competent to exact forced or compulsory labour shall, before deciding to have recourse to such labour, satisfy itself—

    *(a)* that the work to be done or the service to be rendered is of important direct interest for the community called upon to do the work or render the service;

(b)  that the work or service is of present or imminent necessity;

(c)  that it has been impossible to obtain voluntary labour for carrying out the work or rendering the service by the offer of rates of wages and conditions of labour not less favourable than those prevailing in the area concerned for similar work or service; and

(d)  that the work or service will not lay too heavy a burden upon the present population, having regard to the labour available and its capacity to undertake the work.

*Article* 10

1.  Forced or compulsory labour exacted as a tax and forced or compulsory labour to which recourse is had for the execution of public works by chiefs who exercise administrative functions shall be progressively abolished.

2.  Meanwhile, where forced or compulsory labour is exacted as a tax, and where recourse is had to forced or compulsory labour for the execution of public works by chiefs who exercise administrative functions, the authority concerned shall first satisfy itself—

(a)  that the work to be done or the service to be rendered is of important direct interest for the community called upon to do the work or render the service;

(b)  that the work or the service is of present or imminent necessity;

(c)  that the work or service will not lay too heavy a burden upon the present population, having regard to the labour available and its capacity to undertake the work;

(d)  that the work or service will not entail the removal of the workers from their place of habitual residence;

(e)  that the execution of the work or the rendering of the service will be directed in accordance with the exigencies of religion, social life and agriculture.

*Article* 11

1.  Only adult able-bodied males who are of an apparent age of not less than 18 and not more than 45 years may be called upon for forced or compulsory labour. Except in respect of the kinds of labour provided for in Article 10 of this Convention, the following limitations and conditions shall apply:

(a)  whenever possible prior determination by a medical officer appointed by the administration that the persons concerned are not suffering from any infectious or contagious disease and that they are physically fit for the work required and for the conditions under which it is to be carried out;

(b)  exemption of school teachers and pupils and of officials of the administration in general;

(c)  the maintenance in each community of the number of adult able-bodied men indispensable for family and social life;

(d)  respect for conjugal and family ties.

2.  For the purposes of sub-paragraph (c) of the preceding paragraph, the regulations provided for in Article 23 of this Convention shall fix the proportion of the

resident adult able-bodied males who may be taken at any one time for forced or compulsory labour, provided always that this proportion shall in no case exceed 25 per cent. In fixing this proportion the competent authority shall take account of the density of the population, of its social and physical development, of the seasons, and of the work which must be done by the persons concerned on their own behalf in their locality, and, generally, shall have regard to the economic and social necessities of the normal life of the community concerned.

*Article* 12

1. The maximum period for which any person may be taken for forced or compulsory labour of all kinds in any one period of twelve months shall not exceed sixty days, including the time spent in going to and from the place of work.

2. Every person from whom forced or compulsory labour is exacted shall be furnished with a certificate indicating the periods of such labour which he has completed.

*Article* 13

1. The normal working hours of any person from whom forced or compulsory labour is exacted shall be the same as those prevailing in the case of voluntary labour, and the hours worked in excess of the normal working hours shall be remunerated at the rates prevailing in the case of overtime for voluntary labour.

2. A weekly day of rest shall be granted to all persons from whom forced or compulsory labour of any kind is exacted and this day shall coincide as far as possible with the day fixed by tradition or custom in the territories or regions concerned.

*Article* 14

1. With the exception of the forced or compulsory labour provided for in Article 10 of this Convention, forced or compulsory labour of all kinds shall be remunerated in cash at rates not less than those prevailing for similar kinds of work either in the district in which the labour is employed or in the district from which the labour is recruited, whichever may be the higher.

2. In the case of labour to which recourse is had by chiefs in the exercise of their administrative functions, payment of wages in accordance with the provisions of the preceding paragraph shall be introduced as soon as possible.

3. The wages shall be paid to each worker individually and not to his tribal chief or to any other authority.

4. For the purpose of payment of wages the days spent in travelling to and from the place of work shall be counted as working days.

5. Nothing in this Article shall prevent ordinary rations being given as a part of wages, such rations to be at least equivalent in value to the money payment they are taken to represent, but deductions from wages shall not be made either for the payment of taxes or for special food, clothing or accommodation supplied to a worker for the purpose of maintaining him in a fit condition to carry on his work under the special conditions of any employment, or for the supply of tools.

*Article* 15

1. Any laws or regulations relating to workmen's compensation for accidents or sickness arising out of the employment of the worker and any laws or regulations providing compensation for the dependants of deceased or incapacitated workers which are or shall be in force in the territory concerned shall be equally applicable to persons from whom forced or compulsory labour is exacted and to voluntary workers.

2. In any case it shall be an obligation on any authority employing any worker on forced or compulsory labour to ensure the subsistence of any such worker who, by accident or sickness arising out of his employment, is rendered wholly or partially incapable of providing for himself, and to take measures to ensure the maintenance of any persons actually dependent upon such a worker in the event of his incapacity or decease arising out of his employment.

*Article* 16

1. Except in cases of special necessity, persons from whom forced or compulsory labour is exacted shall not be transferred to districts where the food and climate differ so considerably from those to which they have been accustomed as to endanger their health.

2. In no case shall the transfer of such workers be permitted unless all measures relating to hygiene and accommodation which are necessary to adapt such workers to the conditions and to safeguard their health can be strictly applied.

3. When such transfer cannot be avoided, measures of gradual habituation to the new conditions of diet and of climate shall be adopted on competent medical advice.

4. In cases where such workers are required to perform regular work to which they are not accustomed, measures shall be taken to ensure their habituation to it, especially as regards progressive training, the hours of work and the provision of rest intervals, and any increase or amelioration of diet which may be necessary.

*Article* 17

Before permitting recourse to forced or compulsory labour for works of construction or maintenance which entail the workers remaining at the workplaces for considerable periods, the competent authority shall satisfy itself—

(1) that all necessary measures are taken to safeguard the health of the workers and to guarantee the necessary medical care, and, in particular, (a) that the workers are medically examined before commencing the work and at fixed intervals during the period of service, (b) that there is an adequate medical staff, provided with the dispensaries, infirmaries, hospitals and equipment necessary to meet all requirements, and (c) that the sanitary conditions of the workplaces, the supply of drinking water, food, fuel, and cooking utensils, and, where necessary, of housing and clothing, are satisfactory;

(2) that definite arrangements are made to ensure the subsistence of the families of the workers, in particular by facilitating the remittance, by a safe method, of part of the wages to the family, at the request or with the consent of the workers;

(3)  that the journeys of the workers to and from the workplaces are made at the expense and under the responsibility of the administration, which shall facilitate such journeys by making the fullest use of all available means of transport;

(4)  that, in case of illness or accident causing incapacity to work of a certain duration, the worker is repatriated at the expense of the administration;

(5)  that any worker who may wish to remain as a voluntary worker at the end of his period of forced or compulsory labour is permitted to do so without, for a period of two years, losing his right to repatriation free of expense to himself.

*Article* 18

1.  Forced or compulsory labour for the transport of persons or goods, such as the labour of porters or boatmen, shall be abolished within the shortest possible period. Meanwhile the competent authority shall promulgate regulations determining, *inter alia*, (a) that such labour shall only be employed for the purpose of facilitating the movement of officials of the administration, when on duty, or for the transport of Government stores, or, in cases of very urgent necessity, the transport of persons other than officials, (b) that the workers so employed shall be medically certified to be physically fit, where medical examination is possible, and that where such medical examination is not practicable the person employing such workers shall be held responsible for ensuring that they are physically fit and not suffering from any infectious or contagious disease, (c) the maximum load which these workers may carry, (d) the maximum distance from their homes to which they may be taken, (e) the maximum number of days per month or other period for which they may be taken, including the days spent in returning to their homes, and (f) the persons entitled to demand this form of forced or compulsory labour and the extent to which they are entitled to demand it.

2.  In fixing the maxima referred to under (c), (d) and (e) in the foregoing paragraph, the competent authority shall have regard to all relevant factors, including the physical development of the population from which the workers are recruited, the nature of the country through which they must travel and the climatic conditions.

3.  The competent authority shall further provide that the normal daily journey of such workers shall not exceed a distance corresponding to an average working day of eight hours, it being understood that account shall be taken not only of the weight to be carried and the distance to be covered, but also of the nature of the road, the season and all other relevant factors, and that, where hours of journey in excess of the normal daily journey are exacted, they shall be remunerated at rates higher than the normal rates.

*Article* 19

1.  The competent authority shall only authorise recourse to compulsory cultivation as a method of precaution against famine or a deficiency of food supplies and always under the condition that the food or produce shall remain the property of the individuals or the community producing it.

2.  Nothing in this Article shall be construed as abrogating the obligation on

members of a community, where production is organised on a communal basis by virtue of law or custom and where the produce or any profit accruing from the sale thereof remain the property of the community, to perform the work demanded by the community by virtue of law or custom.

*Article* 20

Collective punishment laws under which a community may be punished for crimes committed by any of its members shall not contain provisions for forced or compulsory labour by the community as one of the methods of punishment.

*Article* 21

Forced or compulsory labour shall not be used for work underground in mines.

*Article* 22

The annual reports that Members which ratify this Convention agree to make to the International Labour Office, pursuant to the provisions of Article 22 of the Constitution of the International Labour Organization, on the measures they have taken to give effect to the provisions of this Convention, shall contain as full information as possible, in respect of each territory concerned, regarding the extent to which recourse has been had to forced or compulsory labour in that territory, the purposes for which it has been employed, the sickness and death rates, hours of work, methods of payment of wages and rates of wages, and any other relevant information.

*Article* 23

1. To give effect to the provisions of this Convention the competent authority shall issue complete and precise regulations governing the use of forced or compulsory labour.

2. These regulations shall contain, inter alia, rules permitting any person from whom forced or compulsory labour is exacted to forward all complaints relative to the conditions of labour to the authorities and ensuring that such complaints will be examined and taken into consideration.

*Article* 24

Adequate measures shall in all cases be taken to ensure that the regulations governing the employment of forced or compulsory labour are strictly applied, either by extending the duties of any existing labour inspectorate which has been established for the inspection of voluntary labour to cover the inspection of forced or compulsory labour or in some other appropriate manner. Measures shall also be taken to ensure that the regulations are brought to the knowledge of persons from whom such labour is exacted.

*Article* 25

The illegal exaction of forced or compulsory labour shall be punishable as a penal offence, and it shall be an obligation on any Member ratifying this Convention to ensure that the penalties imposed by law are really adequate and are strictly enforced.

*Article* 26

1. Each Member of the International Labour Organization which ratifies this Convention undertakes to apply it to the territories placed under its sovereignty, jurisdiction, protection, suzerainty, tutelage or authority, so far as it has the right to accept obligations affecting matters of internal jurisdiction; provided that, if such Member may desire to take advantage of the provisions of Article 35 of the Constitution of the International Labour Organization, it shall append to its ratification a declaration stating—

    (1)  the territories to which it intends to apply the provisions of this Convention without modification;

    (2)  the territories to which it intends to apply the provisions of this Convention with modifications, together with details of the said modifications:

    (3)  the territories in respect of which it reserves its decision.

2. The aforesaid declaration shall be deemed to be an integral part of the ratification and shall have the force of ratification. It shall be open to any Member, by a subsequent declaration, to cancel in whole or in part the reservations made, in pursuance of the provisions of subparagraphs (2) and (3) of this Article, in the original declaration.

*Article* 27

The formal ratifications of this Convention under the conditions set forth in the Constitution of the International Labour Organization shall be communicated to the Director-General of the International Labour Office for registration.

*Article* 28

1. This Convention shall be binding only upon those Members whose ratifications have been registered with the International Labour Office.

2. It shall come into force twelve months after the date on which the ratifications of two Members of the International Labour Organization have been registered with the Director-General.

3. Thereafter, this Convention shall come into force for any Member twelve months after the date on which the ratification has been registered.

*Article* 29

As soon as the ratifications of two Members of the International Labour Organization have been registered with the International Labour Office, the Director-General of the International Labour Office shall so notify all the Members of the International Labour Organization. He shall likewise notify them of the registration of ratifications which may be communicated subsequently by other Members of the Organization.

*Article* 30

1. A Member which has ratified this Convention may denounce it after the expiration of ten years from the date on which the Convention first comes into force, by an act communicated to the Director-General of the International Labour Office for registration. Such denunciation shall not take effect until one year after the date on which it is registered with the International Labour Office.

2. Each Member which has ratified this Convention and which does not, within the year following the expiration of the period of ten years mentioned in the preceding paragraph, exercise the right of denunciation provided for in this Article, will be bound for another period of five years and, thereafter, may denounce this Convention at the expiration of each period of five years under the terms provided for in this Article.

*Article 31*

At the expiration of each period of five years after the coming into force of this Convention, the Governing Body of the International Labour Office shall present to the General Conference a report on the working of this Convention and shall consider the desirability of placing on the agenda of the Conference the question of its revision in whole or in part.

*Article 32*

1. Should the Conference adopt a new Convention revising this Convention in whole or in part, the ratification by a Member of the new revising Convention shall ipso jure involve denunciation of this Convention without any requirement of delay, notwithstanding the provisions of Article 30 above, if and when the new revising Convention shall have come into force.

2. As from the date of the coming into force of the new revising Convention, the present Convention shall cease to be open to ratification by the Members.

3. Nevertheless, this Convention shall remain in force in its actual form and content for those Members which have ratified it but have not ratified the revising Convention.

*Article 33*

The French and English texts of this Convention shall both be authentic.

## 41. FREEDOM OF ASSOCIATION AND PROTECTION OF THE RIGHT TO ORGANIZE CONVENTION, 1948

This convention (C87) was adopted by the General Conference of the I.L.O. on 9 July 1948, and entered into force on 4 July 1950. For the text in various languages, see 68 UNTS 17. This Convention and the one which follows (below) protect the major points of trade union activity and power: freedom to organize and freedom to engage in collective bargaining. Similar freedom is provided for employers. See also the Right of Association (Agriculture) Convention, 1921 and the Right of Association (Non-Metropolitan Territories) Convention, 1947; 171 UNTS 329; [1948] *Yearbook on Human Rights* 420. It has been pointed out that none of the Conventions recognizes in terms the right to strike. For further reference, see *The I.L.O. and Human Rights* (1968) 32–41; and the Collective Agreements Recommendation adopted by the I.L.O. General Conference on 29 June 1951: [1951] *Yearbook on Human Rights* 472.

In 1950 the I.L.O. Governing Body decided to establish a Fact-finding and Conciliation Commission on Freedom of Association: see [1949] *Yearbook on Human Rights* 293. This needs the consent of governments before it can act. However, in the case of a ratified convention the complaints procedure under Article 26 of the Constitution of the I.L.O. applies. A Committee on Freedom of Information was established in 1951. On the various procedures, see Wolf, F., 'Human Rights and the International Labour Organization', in Meron, T. (ed.) *Human Rights in International Law* (1984) ii, 273–305, 290–3.

### TEXT

*The General Conference of the International Labour Organization,*

*Having* been convened at San Francisco by the Governing Body of the International Labour Office, and having met in its Thirty-first Session on 17 June 1948;

*Having decided* to adopt, in the form of a Convention, certain proposals concerning freedom of association and protection of the right to organize, which is the seventh item on the agenda of the session;

*Considering* that the Preamble to the Constitution of the International Labour Organization declares recognition of the principle of freedom of association to be a means of improving conditions of labour and of establishing peace;

*Considering* that the Declaration of Philadelphia reaffirms that freedom of expression and of association are essential to sustained progress;

*Considering* that the International Labour Conference, at its Thirtieth Session, unanimously adopted the principles which should form the basis for international regulation;

*Considering* that the General Assembly of the United Nations, at its Second Session, endorsed these principles and requested the International Labour Organization to continue every effort in order that it may be possible to adopt one or several international Conventions;

*Adopts* the ninth day of July of the year one thousand nine hundred and forty-eight, the following Convention, which may be cited as the Freedom of Association and Protection of the Right to Organize Convention, 1948:

## PART I

## FREEDOM OF ASSOCIATION

*Article* 1

Each Member of the International Labour Organization for which this Convention is in force undertakes to give effect to the following provisions.

*Article* 2

Workers and employers, without distinction whatsoever, shall have the right to establish and, subject only to the rules of the organization concerned, to join organizations of their own choosing without previous authorisation.

*Article* 3

1. Workers' and employers' organizations shall have the right to draw up their constitutions and rules, to elect their representatives in full freedom, to organize their administration and activities and to formulate their programmes.
2. The public authorities shall refrain from any interference which would restrict this right or impede the lawful exercise thereof.

*Article* 4

Workers' and employers' organizations shall not be liable to be dissolved or suspended by administrative authority.

*Article* 5

Workers' and employers' organizations shall have the right to establish and join federations and confederations and any such organization, federation or confederation shall have the right to affiliate with international organizations of workers and employers.

*Article* 6

The provisions of Articles 2, 3 and 4 hereof apply to federations and confederations of workers' and employers' organizations.

*Article* 7

The acquisition of legal personality by workers' and employers' organizations, federations and confederations shall not be made subject to conditions of such a character as to restrict the application of the provisions of Articles 2, 3 and 4 hereof.

*Article* 8

1. In exercising the rights provided for in this Convention workers and employers and their respective organizations, like other persons or organized collectivities, shall respect the law of the land.
2. The law of the land shall not be such as to impair, nor shall it be so applied as to impair, the guarantees provided for in this Convention.

*Article* 9

1. The extent to which the guarantees provided for in this Convention shall apply to the armed forces and the police shall be determined by national laws or regulations.

2. In accordance with the principle set forth in paragraph 8 of Article 19 of the Constitution of the International Labour Organization the ratification of this Convention by any Member shall not be deemed to affect any existing law, award, custom or agreement in virtue of which members of the armed forces or the police enjoy any right guaranteed by this Convention.

*Article* 10

In this Convention the term 'organization' means any organization of workers or of employers for furthering and defending the interests of workers or of employers.


# PART II

## PROTECTION OF THE RIGHT TO ORGANIZE

*Article* 11

Each Member of the International Labour Organization for which this Convention is in force undertakes to take all necessary and appropriate measures to ensure that workers and employers may exercise freely the right to organize.


# PART III

## MISCELLANEOUS PROVISIONS

*Article* 12

1. In respect of the territories referred to in Article 35 of the Constitution of the International Labour Organization as amended by the Constitution of the International Labour Organization Instrument of Amendment 1946, other than the territories referred to in paragraphs 4 and 5 of the said article as so amended, each Member of the Organization which ratifies this Convention shall communicate to the Director-General of the International Labour Office as soon as possible after ratification a declaration stating:

   *(a)*  the territories in respect of which it undertakes that the provisions of the Convention shall be applied without modification;

   *(b)*  the territories in respect of which it undertakes that the provisions of the Convention shall be applied subject to modifications, together with details of the said modifications;

   *(c)*  the territories in respect of which the Convention is inapplicable and in such cases the grounds on which it is inapplicable;

   *(d)*  the territories in respect of which it reserves its decision.

2. The undertakings referred to in subparagraphs (a) and (b) of paragraph 1 of this Article shall be deemed to be an integral part of the ratification and shall have the force of ratification.

3. Any Member may at any time by a subsequent declaration cancel in whole or in part any reservations made in its original declaration in virtue of subparagraphs (b), (c) or (d) of paragraph 1 of this Article.

4. Any Member may, at any time at which the Convention is subject to denunciation in accordance with the provisions of Article 16, communicate to the Director-General a declaration modifying in any other respect the terms of any former declaration and stating the present position in respect of such territories as it may specify.

*Article* 13

1. Where the subject matter of this Convention is within the self-governing powers of any non-metropolitan territory, the Member responsible for the international relations of that territory may, in agreement with the Government of the territory, communicate to the Director-General of the International Labour Office a declaration accepting on behalf of the territory the obligations of this Convention.

2. A declaration accepting the obligations of this Convention may be communicated to the Director-General of the International Labour Office:

   *(a)* by two or more Members of the Organization in respect of any territory which is under their joint authority; or

   *(b)* by any international authority responsible for the administration of any territory, in virtue of the Charter of the United Nations or otherwise, in respect of any such territory.

3. Declarations communicated to the Director-General of the International Labour Office in accordance with the preceding paragraphs of this Article shall indicate whether the provisions of the Convention will be applied in the territory concerned without modifications or subject to modification; when the declaration indicates that the provisions of the Convention will be applied subject to modifications it shall give details of the said modifications.

4. The Member, Members or international authority concerned may at any time by a subsequent declaration renounce in whole or in part the right to have recourse to any modification indicated in any former declaration.

5. The Member, Members or international authority concerned may, at any time at which this Convention is subject to denunciation in accordance with the provisions of Article 16, communicate to the Director-General a declaration modifying in any other respect the terms of any former declaration and stating the present position in respect of the application of the Convention.

## PART IV

## FINAL PROVISIONS

*Article* 14

The formal ratifications of this Convention shall be communicated to the Director-General of the International Labour Office for registration.

*Article* 15

1. This Convention shall be binding only upon those Members of the International Labour Organization whose ratifications have been registered with the Director-General.

2. It shall come into force twelve months after the date on which the ratifications of two Members have been registered with the Director-General.

3. Thereafter, this Convention shall come into force for any Member twelve months after the date on which its ratifications has been registered.

*Article* 16

1. A Member which has ratified this Convention may denounce it after the expiration of ten years from the date on which the Convention first comes into force, by an Act communicated to the Director-General of the International Labour Office for registration. Such denunciation should not take effect until one year after the date on which it is registered.

2. Each Member which has ratified this Convention and which does not, within the year following the expiration of the period of ten years mentioned in the preceding paragraph, exercise the right of denunciation provided for in this Article, will be bound for another period of ten years and, thereafter, may denounce this Convention at the expiration of each period of ten years under the terms provided for in this Article.

*Article* 17

1. The Director-General of the International Labour Office shall notify all Members of the International Labour Organization of the registration of all ratifications, declarations and denunciations communicated to him by the Members of the Organization.

2. When notifying the Members of the Organization of the registration of the second ratification communicated to him, the Director-General shall draw the attention of the Members of the Organization to the date upon which the Convention will come into force.

*Article* 18

The Director-General of the International Labour Office shall communicate to the Secretary-General of the United Nations for registration in accordance with Article 102 of the Charter of the United Nations full particulars of all ratifications and acts of denunciation registered by him in accordance with the provisions of the preceding Articles.

*Article* 19

At the expiration of each period of ten years after the coming into force of this Convention, the Governing Body of the International Labour Office shall present to the General Conference a report on the working of this Convention and shall examine the desirability of placing on the agenda of the Conference the question of its revision in whole or in part.

*Article* 20

1. Should the Conference adopt a new Convention revising this Convention in whole or in part, then, unless the new Convention otherwise provides:

 *(a)* the ratification by a Member of the new revising Convention shall *ipso jure* involve the immediate denunciation of this Convention, notwithstanding the provisions of Article 16 above, if and when the new revising Convention shall have come into force;

 *(b)* as from the date when the new revising Convention comes into force this Convention shall cease to be open to ratification by the Members.

2. This Convention shall in any case remain in force in its actual form and content for those Members which have ratified it but have not ratified the revising Convention.

*Article* 21

The English and French versions of the text of this Convention are equally authoritative.

## 42. RIGHT TO ORGANIZE AND COLLECTIVE BARGAINING CONVENTION, 1949

The Convention concerning the Application of the Principles of the Right to Organize and to Bargain Collectively (C98) was adopted by the General Conference of the I.L.O. on 1 July 1949, and entered into force on 18 July 1951. For the text in various languages, see 96 UNTS 257. See also the note above at 320.

### TEXT

*The General Conference of the International Labour Organization,*

*Having been convened* at Geneva by the Governing Body of the International Labour Office, and having met in its Thirty-second Session on 8 June 1949, and

*Having decided* upon the adoption of certain proposals concerning the application of the principles of the right to organize and to bargain collectively, which is the fourth item on the agenda of the session, and

*Having determined* that these proposals shall take the form of an international Convention,

*Adopts* the first day of July of the year one thousand nine hundred and forty-nine, the following Convention, which may be cited as the Right to Organize and Collective Bargaining Convention, 1949:

*Article* 1

1. Workers shall enjoy adequate protection against acts of anti-union discrimination in respect of their employment.

2. Such protection shall apply more particularly in respect of acts calculated to—

   *(a)* make the employment of a worker subject to the condition that he shall not join a union or shall relinquish trade union membership;

   *(b)* cause the dismissal of or otherwise prejudice a worker by reason of union membership or because of participation in union activities outside working hours or, with the consent of the employer, within working hours.

*Article* 2

1. Workers' and employers' organizations shall enjoy adequate protection against any acts of interference by each other or each other's agents or members in their establishment, functioning or administration.

2. In particular, acts which are designed to promote the establishment of workers' organizations under the domination of employers or employers' organizations, or to support workers' organizations by financial or other means, with the object of placing such organizations under the control of employers or employers' organizations, shall be deemed to constitute acts of interference within the meaning of this Article.

*Article* 3

Machinery appropriate to national conditions shall be established, where necessary, for the purpose of ensuring respect for the right to organize as defined in the preceding Articles.

*Article* 4

Measures appropriate to national conditions shall be taken, where necessary, to encourage and promote the full development and utilisation of machinery for voluntary negotiation between employers or employers' organizations and workers' organizations, with a view to the regulation of terms and conditions of employment by means of collective agreements.

*Article* 5

1. The extent to which the guarantees provided for in this Convention shall apply to the armed forces and the police shall be determined by national laws or regulations.

2. In accordance with the principle set forth in paragraph 8 of Article 19 of the Constitution of the International Labour Organization the ratification of this Convention by any Member shall not be deemed to affect any existing law, award, custom or agreement in virtue of which members of the armed forces or the police enjoy any right guaranteed by this Convention.

*Article* 6

This Convention does not deal with the position of public servants engaged in the administration of the State, nor shall it be construed as prejudicing their rights or status in any way.

*Article* 7

The formal ratifications of this Convention shall be communicated to the Director-General of the International Labour Office for registration.

*Article* 8

1. This Convention shall be binding only upon those Members of the International Labour Organization whose ratifications have been registered with the Director-General.

2. It shall come into force twelve months after the date on which the ratifications of two Members have been registered with the Director-General.

3. Thereafter, this Convention shall come into force for any Member twelve months after the date on which its ratifications has been registered.

*Article* 9

1. Declarations communicated to the Director-General of the International Labour Office in accordance with paragraph 2 of Article 35 of the Constitution of the International Labour Organization shall indicate—

  (*a*) the territories in respect of which the Member concerned undertakes that the provisions of the Convention shall be applied without modification;

*(b)* the territories in respect of which it undertakes that the provisions of the Convention shall be applied subject to modifications, together with details of the said modifications;

*(c)* the territories in respect of which the Convention is inapplicable and in such cases the grounds on which it is inapplicable;

*(d)* the territories in respect of which it reserves its decision pending further consideration of the position.

2. The undertakings referred to in subparagraphs (a) and (b) of paragraph 1 of this Article shall be deemed to be an integral part of the ratification and shall have the force of ratification.

3. Any Member may at any time by a subsequent declaration cancel in whole or in part any reservation made in its original declaration in virtue of subparagraph (b), (c) or (d) of paragraph 1 of this Article.

4. Any Member may, at any time at which the Convention is subject to denunciation in accordance with the provisions of Article 11, communicate to the Director-General a declaration modifying in any other respect the terms of any former declaration and stating the present position in respect of such territories as it may specify.

*Article* 10

1. Declarations communicated to the Director-General of the International Labour Office in accordance with paragraph 4 or 5 of Article 35 of the Constitution of the International Labour Organization shall indicate whether the provisions of the Convention will be applied in the territory concerned without modification or subject to modifications; when the declaration indicates that the provisions of the Convention will be applied subject to modifications, it shall give details of the said modifications.

2. The Member, Members or international authority concerned may at any time by a subsequent declaration renounce in whole or in part the right to have recourse to any modification indicated in any former declaration.

3. The Member, Members or international authority concerned may, at any time at which the Convention is subject to denunciation in accordance with the provisions of Article 11, communicate to the Director-General a declaration modifying in any other respect the terms of any former declaration and stating the present position in respect of the application of the Convention.

*Article* 11

1. A Member which has ratified this Convention may denounce it after the expiration of ten years from the date on which the Convention first comes into force, by an Act communicated to the Director-General of the International Labour Office for registration. Such denunciation should not take effect until one year after the date on which it is registered.

2. Each Member which has ratified this Convention and which does not, within the year following the expiration of the period of ten years mentioned in the preceding paragraph, exercise the right of denunciation provided for in this Article, will be bound for another period of ten years and, thereafter, may

denounce this Convention at the expiration of each period of ten years under the terms provided for in this Article.

*Article* 12

1. The Director-General of the International Labour Office shall notify all Members of the International Labour Organization of the registration of all ratifications and denunciations communicated to him by the Members of the Organization.

2. When notifying the Members of the Organization of the registration of the second ratification communicated to him, the Director-General shall draw the attention of the Members of the Organization to the date upon which the Convention will come into force.

*Article* 13

The Director-General of the International Labour Office shall communicate to the Secretary-General of the United Nations for registration in accordance with Article 102 of the Charter of the United Nations full particulars of all ratifications and acts of denunciation registered by him in accordance with the provisions of the preceding Articles.

*Article* 14

At such times as may consider necessary the Governing Body of the International Labour Office shall present to the General Conference a report on the working of this Convention and shall examine the desirability of placing on the agenda of the Conference the question of its revision in whole or in part.

*Article* 15

1. Should the Conference adopt a new Convention revising this Convention in whole or in part, then, unless the new Convention otherwise provides:

  *(a)*  the ratification by a Member of the new revising Convention shall ipso jure involve the immediate denunciation of this Convention, notwithstanding the provisions of Article 11 above, if and when the new revising Convention shall have come into force;

  *(b)*  as from the date when the new revising Convention comes into force this Convention shall cease to be open to ratification by the Members.

2. This Convention shall in any case remain in force in its actual form and content for those Members which have ratified it but have not ratified the revising Convention.

*Article* 16

The English and French versions of the text of this Convention are equally authoritative.

## 43. EQUAL REMUNERATION CONVENTION, 1951

The full title is the Convention concerning Equal Remuneration for Men and Women Workers for Work of Equal Value. The Convention (C100) was adopted by the General Conference of the I.L.O. on 29 June 1951, and entered into force on 23 May 1953. For the text in various languages, see 165 UNTS 304. See also the Equal Remuneration Recommendation, 1951, adopted at the same time.

Equality as between the sexes in the matter of wages and salaries has achieved but slow and reluctant recognition, even in the more advanced societies.

### TEXT

*The General Conference of the International Labour Organization,*

*Having been convened* at Geneva by the Governing Body of the International Labour Office, and having met in its Thirty-fourth Session on 6 June 1951, and

*Having decided* upon the adoption of certain proposals with regard to the principle of equal remuneration for men and women workers for work of equal value, which is the seventh item on the agenda of the session, and

*Having determined* that these proposals shall take the form of an international Convention,

*Adopts* the twenty-ninth day of June of the year one thousand nine hundred and fifty-one, the following Convention, which may be cited as the Equal Remuneration Convention, 1951:

*Article* 1

For the purpose of this Convention:

    *(a)* the term 'remuneration' includes the ordinary, basic or minimum wage or salary and any additional emoluments whatsoever payable directly or indirectly, whether in cash or in kind, by the employer to the worker and arising out of the worker's employment;

    *(b)* the term 'equal remuneration for men and women workers for work of equal value' refers to rates of remuneration established without discrimination based on sex.

*Article* 2

1. Each Member shall, by means appropriate to the methods in operation for determining rates of remuneration, promote and, in so far as is consistent with such methods, ensure the application to all workers of the principle of equal remuneration for men and women workers for work of equal value.

2. This principle may be applied by means of:

    *(a)* national laws or regulations;

    *(b)* legally established or recognised machinery for wage determination;

    *(c)* collective agreements between employers and workers; or

(d)  a combination of these various means.

## Article 3

1. Where such action will assist in giving effect to the provisions of this Convention measures shall be taken to promote objective appraisal of jobs on the basis of the work to be performed.

2. The methods to be followed in this appraisal may be decided upon by the authorities responsible for the determination of rates of remuneration, or, where such rates are determined by collective agreements, by the parties thereto.

3. Differential rates between workers which correspond, without regard to sex, to differences, as determined by such objective appraisal, in the work to be performed shall not be considered as being contrary to the principle of equal remuneration for men and women workers for work of equal value.

## Article 4

Each Member shall co-operate as appropriate with the employers' and workers' organizations concerned for the purpose of giving effect to the provisions of this Convention.

## Article 5

The formal ratifications of this Convention shall be communicated to the Director-General of the International Labour Office for registration.

## Article 6

1. This Convention shall be binding only upon those Members of the International Labour Organization whose ratifications have been registered with the Director-General.

2. It shall come into force twelve months after the date on which the ratifications of two Members have been registered with the Director-General.

3. Thereafter, this Convention shall come into force for any Member twelve months after the date on which its ratifications has been registered.

## Article 7

1. Declarations communicated to the Director-General of the International Labour Office in accordance with paragraph 2 of article 35 of the Constitution of the International Labour Organization shall indicate:

(a)  the territories in respect of which the Member concerned undertakes that the provisions of the Convention shall be applied without modification;

(b)  the territories in respect of which it undertakes that the provisions of the Convention shall be applied subject to modifications, together with details of the said modifications;

(c)  the territories in respect of which the Convention is inapplicable and in such cases the grounds on which it is inapplicable;

(d)  the territories in respect of which it reserves its decision pending further consideration of the position.

2. The undertakings referred to in subparagraphs (a) and (b) of paragraph 1 of this

Article shall be deemed to be an integral part of the ratification and shall have the force of ratification.

3. Any Member may at any time by a subsequent declaration cancel in whole or in part any reservation made in its original declaration in virtue of subparagraph (b), (c) or (d) of paragraph 1 of this Article.

4. Any Member may, at any time at which the Convention is subject to denunciation in accordance with the provisions of Article 9, communicate to the Director-General a declaration modifying in any other respect the terms of any former declaration and stating the present position in respect of such territories as it may specify.

*Article* 8

1. Declarations communicated to the Director-General of the International Labour Office in accordance with paragraph 4 or 5 of Article 35 of the Constitution of the International Labour Organization shall indicate whether the provisions of the Convention will be applied in the territory concerned without modification or subject to modifications; when the declaration indicates that the provisions of the Convention will be applied subject to modifications, it shall give details of the said modifications.

2. The Member, Members or international authority concerned may at any time by a subsequent declaration renounce in whole or in part the right to have recourse to any modification indicated in any former declaration.

3. The Member, Members or international authority concerned may, at any time at which the Convention is subject to denunciation in accordance with the provisions of Article 9, communicate to the Director-General a declaration modifying in any other respect the terms of any former declaration and stating the present position in respect of the application of the Convention.

*Article* 9

1. A Member which has ratified this Convention may denounce it after the expiration of ten years from the date on which the Convention first comes into force, by an Act communicated to the Director-General of the International Labour Office for registration. Such denunciation should not take effect until one year after the date on which it is registered.

2. Each Member which has ratified this Convention and which does not, within the year following the expiration of the period of ten years mentioned in the preceding paragraph, exercise the right of denunciation provided for in this Article, will be bound for another period of ten years and, thereafter, may denounce this Convention at the expiration of each period of ten years under the terms provided for in this Article.

*Article* 10

1. The Director-General of the International Labour Office shall notify all Members of the International Labour Organization of the registration of all ratifications and denunciations communicated to him by the Members of the Organization.

2. When notifying the Members of the Organization of the registration of the

second ratification communicated to him, the Director-General shall draw the attention of the Members of the Organization to the date upon which the Convention will come into force.

*Article* 11

The Director-General of the International Labour Office shall communicate to the Secretary-General of the United Nations for registration in accordance with Article 102 of the Charter of the United Nations full particulars of all ratifications and acts of denunciation registered by him in accordance with the provisions of the preceding Articles.

*Article* 12

At such times as may consider necessary the Governing Body of the International Labour Office shall present to the General Conference a report on the working of this Convention and shall examine the desirability of placing on the agenda of the Conference the question of its revision in whole or in part.

*Article* 13

1. Should the Conference adopt a new Convention revising this Convention in whole or in part, then, unless the new Convention otherwise provides:

   (a)  the ratification by a Member of the new revising Convention shall *ipso jure* involve the immediate denunciation of this Convention, notwithstanding the provisions of Article 9 above, if and when the new revising Convention shall have come into force;

   (b)  as from the date when the new revising Convention comes into force this Convention shall cease to be open to ratification by the Members.

2. This Convention shall in any case remain in force in its actual form and content for those Members which have ratified it but have not ratified the revising Convention.

*Article* 14

The English and French versions of the text of this Convention are equally authoritative.

## 44. ABOLITION OF FORCED LABOUR CONVENTION, 1957

This convention (C105) complements other conventions, including the Slavery Convention, 1926 (above, 131–5), the Supplementary Convention on Abolition of Slavery, etc, 1956 (above, 136–41), and the Forced Labour Convention, 1930 (above, 310–19). It was adopted by the General Conference of the I.L.O. on 25 June 1957, and entered into force on 17 January 1959. For the text in various languages, see 320 UNTS 291.

The present Convention is concerned especially with forced labour as a means of political coercion.

### TEXT

*The General Conference of the International Labour Organization,*

*Having been convened* at Geneva by the Governing Body of the International Labour Office, and having met in its Fortieth Session on 5 June 1957, and

*Having considered* the question of forced labour, which is the fourth item on the agenda of the session, and

*Having noted* the provisions of the Forced Labour Convention, 1930, and

*Having noted* that the Slavery Convention, 1926, provides that all necessary measures shall be taken to prevent compulsory or forced labour from developing into conditions analogous to slavery and that the Supplementary Convention on the Abolition of Slavery, the Slave Trade and Institutions and Practices Similar to Slavery, 1956, provides for the complete abolition of debt bondage and serfdom, and

*Having noted* that the Protection of Wages Convention, 1949, provides that wages shall be paid regularly and prohibits methods of payment which deprive the worker of a genuine possibility of terminating his employment, and

*Having decided* upon the adoption of further proposals with regard to the abolition of certain forms of forced or compulsory labour constituting a violation of the rights of man referred to in the Charter of the United Nations and enunciated by the Universal Declaration of Human Rights, and

*Having determined* that these proposals shall take the form of an international Convention,

*Adopts* the twenty-fifth day of June of the year one thousand nine hundred and fifty-seven, the following Convention, which may be cited as the Abolition of Forced Labour Convention, 1957:

*Article 1*

Each Member of the International Labour Organization which ratifies this Convention undertakes to suppress and not to make use of any form of forced or compulsory labour:

*(a)* as a means of political coercion or education or as a punishment for

holding or expressing political views or views ideologically opposed to the established political, social or economic system;

(b) as a method of mobilising and using labour for purposes of economic development;

(c) as a means of labour discipline;

(d) as a punishment for having participated in strikes;

(e) as a means of racial, social, national or religious discrimination.

*Article* 2

Each Member of the International Labour Organization which ratifies this Convention undertakes to take effective measures to secure the immediate and complete abolition of forced or compulsory labour as specified in Article 1 of this Convention.

*Article* 3

The formal ratifications of this Convention shall be communicated to the Director-General of the International Labour Office for registration.

*Article* 4

1. This Convention shall be binding only upon those Members of the International Labour Organization whose ratifications have been registered with the Director-General.

2. It shall come into force twelve months after the date on which the ratifications of two Members have been registered with the Director-General.

3. Thereafter, this Convention shall come into force for any Member twelve months after the date on which its ratifications has been registered.

*Article* 5

1. A Member which has ratified this Convention may denounce it after the expiration of ten years from the date on which the Convention first comes into force, by an Act communicated to the Director-General of the International Labour Office for registration. Such denunciation should not take effect until one year after the date on which it is registered.

2. Each Member which has ratified this Convention and which does not, within the year following the expiration of the period of ten years mentioned in the preceding paragraph, exercise the right of denunciation provided for in this Article, will be bound for another period of ten years and, thereafter, may denounce this Convention at the expiration of each period of ten years under the terms provided for in this Article.

*Article* 6

1. The Director-General of the International Labour Office shall notify all Members of the International Labour Organization of the registration of all ratifications and denunciations communicated to him by the Members of the Organization.

2. When notifying the Members of the Organization of the registration of the

second ratification communicated to him, the Director-General shall draw the attention of the Members of the Organization to the date upon which the Convention will come into force.

*Article 7*

The Director-General of the International Labour Office shall communicate to the Secretary-General of the United Nations for registration in accordance with Article 102 of the Charter of the United Nations full particulars of all ratifications and acts of denunciation registered by him in accordance with the provisions of the preceding Articles.

*Article 8*

At such times as it may consider necessary the Governing Body of the International Labour Office shall present to the General Conference a report on the working of this Convention and shall examine the desirability of placing on the agenda of the Conference the question of its revision in whole or in part.

*Article 9*

1. Should the Conference adopt a new Convention revising this Convention in whole or in part, then, unless the new Convention otherwise provides:

   *(a)* the ratification by a Member of the new revising Convention shall ipso jure involve the immediate denunciation of this Convention, notwithstanding the provisions of Article 5 above, if and when the new revising Convention shall have come into force;

   *(b)* as from the date when the new revising Convention comes into force this Convention shall cease to be open to ratification by the Members.

2. This Convention shall in any case remain in force in its actual form and content for those Members which have ratified it but have not ratified the revising Convention.

*Article 10*

The English and French versions of the text of this Convention are equally authoritative.

## 45. DISCRIMINATION (EMPLOYMENT AND OCCUPATION) CONVENTION, 1958

The most important aspect of this convention (C111) is its application to racial matters, but it is also aimed at other forms of discrimination. The convention was adopted by the General Conference of the I.L.O. on 25 June 1958 and entered into force on 15 June 1960. For the text in various languages, see 363 UNTS 31. The relevant Recommendation of the International Labour Conference is reproduced after the text of the convention, below at 341-4.

See further Nielsen, H. K., 'The Concept of Discrimination in I.L.O. Convention No. 111' (1994) 43 *ICLQ* 827–56.

### TEXT

*The General Conference of the International Labour Organization,*

*Having been convened* at Geneva by the Governing Body of the International Labour Office, and having met in its Forty-second Session on 4 June 1958, and

*Having decided* upon the adoption of certain proposals with regard to discrimination in the field of employment and occupation, which is the fourth item on the agenda of the session, and

*Having determined* that these proposals shall take the form of an international Convention, and

*Considering* that the Declaration of Philadelphia affirms that all human beings, irrespective of race, creed or sex, have the right to pursue both their material well-being and their spiritual development in conditions of freedom and dignity, of economic security and equal opportunity, and

*Considering* further that discrimination constitutes a violation of rights enunciated by the Universal Declaration of Human Rights,

*Adopts* the twenty-fifth day of June of the year one thousand nine hundred and fifty-eight, the following Convention, which may be cited as the Discrimination (Employment and Occupation) Convention, 1958:

### Article 1

1. For the purpose of this Convention the term 'discrimination' includes:

    *(a)* any distinction, exclusion or preference made on the basis of race, colour sex, religion, political opinion, national extraction or social origin, which has the effect of nullifying or impairing equality of opportunity or treatment in employment or occupation;

    *(b)* such other distinction, exclusion or preference which has the effect of nullifying or impairing equality of opportunity or treatment in employment or occupation as may be determined by the Member concerned after consultation with representative employers' and workers' organizations, where such exist, and with other appropriate bodies.

2. Any distinction, exclusion or preference in respect of a particular job based on the inherent requirements thereof shall not be deemed to be discrimination.

3. For the purpose of this Convention the terms 'employment' and 'occupation' include access to vocational training, access to employment and to particular occupations, and terms and conditions of employment.

*Article 2*

Each Member for which this Convention is in force undertakes to declare and pursue a national policy designed to promote, by methods appropriate to national conditions and practice, equality of opportunity and treatment in respect of employment and occupation, with a view to eliminating any discrimination in respect thereof.

*Article 3*

Each Member for which this Convention is in force undertakes, by methods appropriate to national conditions and practice:

  (a) to seek the co-operation of employers' and workers' organizations and other appropriate bodies in promoting the acceptance and observance of this policy;

  (b) to enact such legislation and to promote such educational programmes as may be calculated to secure the acceptance and observance of the policy;

  (c) to repeal any statutory provisions and modify any administrative instructions or practices which are inconsistent with the policy;

  (d) to pursue the policy in respect of employment under the direct control of a national authority;

  (e) to ensure observance of the policy in the activities of vocational guidance, vocational training and placement services under the direction of a national authority;

  (f) to indicate in its annual reports on the application of the Convention the action taken in pursuance of the policy and the results secured by such action.

*Article 4*

Any measures affecting an individual who is justifiably suspected of, or engaged in, activities prejudicial to the security of the State shall not be deemed to be discrimination, provided that the individual concerned shall have the right to appeal to a competent body established in accordance with national practice.

*Article 5*

1. Special measures of protection or assistance provided for in other Conventions or Recommendations adopted by the International Labour Conference shall not be deemed to be discrimination.

2. Any Member may, after consultation with representative employers' and workers' organizations, where such exist, determine that other special measures designed to meet the particular requirements of persons who, for reasons such as sex, age, disablement, family responsibilities or social or cultural status, are generally recognized to require special protection or assistance, shall not be deemed to be discrimination.

*Article* 6

Each Member which ratifies this Convention undertakes to apply it to non-metropolitan territories in accordance with the provisions of the Constitution of the International Labour Organization.

*Article* 7

The formal ratifications of this Convention shall be communicated to the Director-General of the International Labour Office for registration.

*Article* 8

1. This Convention shall be binding only upon those Members of the International Labour Organization whose ratifications have been registered with the Director-General.

2. It shall come into force twelve months after the date on which the ratifications of two Members have been registered with the Director-General.

3. Thereafter, this Convention shall come into force for any Member twelve months after the date on which its ratifications has been registered.

*Article* 9

1. A Member which has ratified this Convention may denounce it after the expiration of ten years from the date on which the Convention first comes into force, by an Act communicated to the Director-General of the International Labour Office for registration. Such denunciation should not take effect until one year after the date on which it is registered.

2. Each Member which has ratified this Convention and which does not, within the year following the expiration of the period of ten years mentioned in the preceding paragraph, exercise the right of denunciation provided for in this Article, will be bound for another period of ten years and, thereafter, may denounce this Convention at the expiration of each period of ten years under the terms provided for in this Article.

*Article* 10

1. The Director-General of the International Labour Office shall notify all Members of the International Labour Organization of the registration of all ratifications and denunciations communicated to him by the Members of the Organization.

2. When notifying the Members of the Organization of the registration of the second ratification communicated to him, the Director-General shall draw the attention of the Members of the Organization to the date upon which the Convention will come into force.

*Article* 11

The Director-General of the International Labour Office shall communicate to the Secretary-General of the United Nations for registration in accordance with Article 102 of the Charter of the United Nations full particulars of all ratifications and acts of denunciation registered by him in accordance with the provisions of the preceding Articles.

*Article* 12

At such times as it may consider necessary the Governing Body of the International Labour Office shall present to the General Conference a report on the working of this Convention and shall examine the desirability of placing on the agenda of the Conference the question of its revision in whole or in part.

*Article* 13

1. Should the Conference adopt a new Convention revising this Convention in whole or in part, then, unless the new Convention otherwise provides:

   (a) the ratification by a Member of the new revising Convention shall *ipso jure* involve the immediate denunciation of this Convention, notwithstanding the provisions of Article 9 above, if and when the new revising Convention shall have come into force;

   (b) as from the date when the new revising Convention comes into force this Convention shall cease to be open to ratification by the Members.

2. This Convention shall in any case remain in force in its actual form and content for those Members which have ratified it but have not ratified the revising Convention.

*Article* 14

The English and French versions of the text of this Convention are equally authoritative.

## 46. DISCRIMINATION (EMPLOYMENT AND OCCUPATION) RECOMMENDATION, 1958

Adopted 25 June 1958.

*TEXT*

*The General Conference of the International Labour Organization,*

*Having been convened* at Geneva by the Governing Body of the International Labour Office, and having met in its Forty-second Session on 4 June 1958, and

*Having decided* upon the adoption of certain proposals with regard to discrimination in the field of employment and occupation, which is the fourth item on the agenda of the session, and

*Having determined* that these proposals shall take the form of a Recommendation supplementing the Discrimination (Employment and Occupation) Convention, 1958,

*Adopts* this twenty-fifth day of June of the year one thousand nine hundred and fifty-eight, the following Recommendation, which may be cited as the Discrimination (Employment and Occupation) Recommendation, 1958:

The Conference recommends that each Member should apply the following provisions:

## I. DEFINITIONS

1. (1) For the purpose of this Recommendation the term 'discrimination' includes:

   *(a)* Any distinction, exclusion or preference made on the basis of race, colour, sex, religion, political opinion, national extraction or social origin, which has the effect of nullifying or impairing equality of opportunity or treatment in employment or occupation;

   *(b)* Such other distinction, exclusion or preference which has the effect of nullifying or impairing equality of opportunity or treatment in employment or occupation as may be determined by the Member concerned after consultation with representative employers' and workers' organizations, where such exist, and with other appropriate bodies.

   (2) Any distinction, exclusion or preference in respect of a particular job based on the inherent requirements thereof is not deemed to be discrimination.

   (3) For the purpose of this Recommendation the terms 'employment' and 'occupation' include access to vocational training, access to employment and to particular occupations, and terms and conditions of employment.

## II. FORMULATION AND APPLICATION OF POLICY

2. Each Member should formulate a national policy for the prevention of discrimination in employment and occupation. This policy should be applied by means of legislative measures, collective agreements between representative employers' and workers' organizations or in any other manner consistent with national conditions and practice, and should have regard to the following principles:

    *(a)* The promotion of equality of opportunity and treatment in employment and occupation is a matter of public concern;

    *(b)* All persons should, without discrimination, enjoy equality of opportunity and treatment in respect of:

        (i)   Access to vocational guidance and placement services;

        (ii)  Access to training and employment of their own choice on the basis of individual suitability for such training or employment;

        (iii) Advancement in accordance with their individual character, experience, ability and diligence;

        (iv) Security of tenure of employment;

        (v)  Remuneration for work of equal value;

        (vi) Conditions of work including hours of work, rest periods, annual holidays with pay, occupational safety and occupational health measures, as well as social security measures and welfare facilities and benefits provided in connection with employment;

    *(c)* Government agencies should apply non-discriminatory employment policies in all their activities;

    *(d)* Employers should not practise or countenance discrimination in engaging or training any person for employment, in advancing or retaining such person in employment, or in fixing terms and conditions of employment; nor should any person or organization obstruct or interfere, either directly or indirectly, with employers in pursuing this principle;

    *(e)* In collective negotiations and industrial relations the parties should respect the principle of equality of opportunity and treatment in employment and occupation, and should ensure that collective agreements contain no provisions of a discriminatory character in respect of access to, training for, advancement in or retention of employment or in respect of the terms and conditions of employment;

    *(f)* Employers' and workers' organizations should not practise or countenance discrimination in respect of admission, retention of membership or participation in their affairs.

3. Each Member should:

    *(a)* Ensure application of the principles of non-discrimination:

        (i)   In respect of employment under the direct control of a national authority;

        (ii)  In the activities of vocational guidance, vocational training and placement services under the direction of a national authority;

*(b)* Promote their observance, where practicable and necessary, in respect of other employment and other vocational guidance, vocational training and placement services by such methods as:

(i)   Encouraging state, provincial or local government departments or agencies and industries and undertakings operated under public owner-ship or control to ensure the application of the principles;

(ii)  Making eligibility for contracts involving the expenditure of public funds dependent on observance of the principles;

(iii) Making eligibility for grants to training establishments and for a licence to operate a private employment agency or a private vocational guid-ance office dependent on observance of the principles.

4. Appropriate agencies, to be assisted where practicable by advisory committees composed of representatives of employers' and workers' organizations, where such exist, and of other interested bodies, should be established for the purpose of promoting application of the policy in all fields of public and private employment, and in particular:

*(a)*   To take all practicable measures to foster public understanding and accept-ance of the principles of non-discrimination;

*(b)*   To receive, examine and investigate complaints that the policy is not being observed and, if necessary by conciliation, to secure the correction of any practices regarded as in conflict with the policy; and

*(c)*   To consider further any complaints which cannot be effectively settled by conciliation and to render opinions or issue decisions concerning the man-ner in which discriminatory practices revealed should be corrected.

5. Each Member should repeal any statutory provisions and modify any adminis-trative instructions or practices which are inconsistent with the policy.

6. Application of the policy should not adversely affect special measures designed to meet the particular requirements of persons who, for reasons such as sex, age, disablement, family responsibilities or social or cultural status are generally recog-nised to require special protection or assistance.

7. Any measures affecting an individual who is justifiably suspected of, or engaged in, activities prejudicial to the security of the State should not be deemed to be discrimination, provided that the individual concerned has the right to appeal to a competent body established in accordance with national practice.

8. With respect to immigrant workers of foreign nationality and the members of their families, regard should be had to the provisions of the Migration for Employment Convention (Revised), 1949, relating to equality of treatment and the provisions of the Migration for Employment Recommendation (Revised), 1949, relating to the lifting of restrictions on access to employment.

9. There should be continuing co-operation between the competent authorities, representatives of employers and workers and appropriate bodies to consider what further positive measures may be necessary in the light of national conditions to put the principles of non-discrimination into effect.

### III. CO-ORDINATION OF MEASURES FOR THE PREVENTION OF DISCRIMINATION IN ALL FIELDS

10. The authorities responsible for action against discrimination in employment and occupation should co-operate closely and continuously with the authorities responsible for action against discrimination in other fields in order that measures taken in all fields may be co-ordinated.

# 47. MINIMUM AGE CONVENTION, 1973

The Convention concerning Minimum Age for Admission to Employment (C138) was adopted in Geneva on 26 June 1973 and came into force on 19 June 1976.

## TEXT

*The General Conference of the International Labour Organization,*

*Having been convened* at Geneva by the Governing Body of the International Labour Office, and having met in its Fifty-eighth Session on 6 June 1973, and

*Having decided* upon the adoption of certain proposals with regard to minimum age for admission to employment, which is the fourth item on the agenda of the session, and

*Noting* the terms of the Minimum Age (Industry) Convention, 1919, the Minimum Age (Sea) Convention, 1920, the Minimum Age (Agriculture) Convention, 1921, the Minimum Age (Trimmers and Stokers) Convention, 1921, the Minimum Age (Non-Industrial Employment) Convention, 1932, the Minimum Age (Sea) Convention (Revised), 1936, the Minimum Age (Industry) Convention (Revised), 1937, the Minimum Age (Non-Industrial Employment) Convention (Revised), 1937, the Minimum Age (Fishermen) Convention, 1959, and the Minimum Age (Underground Work) Convention, 1965, and

*Considering* that the time has come to establish a general instrument on the subject, which would gradually replace the existing ones applicable to limited economic sectors, with a view to achieving the total abolition of child labour, and

*Having determined* that these proposals shall take the form of an international Convention,

*Adopts* the twenty-sixth day of June of the year one thousand nine hundred and seventy-three, the following Convention, which may be cited as the Minimum Age Convention, 1973:

### Article 1

Each Member for which this Convention is in force undertakes to pursue a national policy designed to ensure the effective abolition of child labour and to raise progressively the minimum age for admission to employment or work to a level consistent with the fullest physical and mental development of young persons.

### Article 2

1. Each Member which ratifies this Convention shall specify, in a declaration appended to its ratification, a minimum age for admission to employment or work within its territory and on means of transport registered in its territory; subject to Articles 4 to 8 of this Convention, no one under that age shall be admitted to employment or work in any occupation.

2. Each Member which has ratified this Convention may subsequently notify the

Director-General of the International Labour Office, by further declarations, that it specifies a minimum age higher than that previously specified.

3. The minimum age specified in pursuance of paragraph 1 of this Article shall not be less than the age of completion of compulsory schooling and, in any case, shall not be less than 15 years.

4. Notwithstanding the provisions of paragraph 3 of this Article, a Member whose economy and educational facilities are insufficiently developed may, after consultation with the organizations of employers and workers concerned, where such exist, initially specify a minimum age of 14 years.

5. Each Member which has specified a minimum age of 14 years in pursuance of the provisions of the preceding paragraph shall include in its reports on the application of this Convention submitted under Article 22 of the constitution of the International Labour Organization a statement:

> *(a)*  that its reason for doing so subsists; or
>
> *(b)*  that it renounces its right to avail itself of the provisions in question as from a stated date.

## Article 3

1. The minimum age for admission to any type of employment or work which by its nature or the circumstances in which it is carried out is likely to jeopardise the health, safety or morals of young persons shall not be less than 18 years.

2. The types of employment or work to which paragraph 1 of this Article applies shall be determined by national laws or regulations or by the competent authority, after consultation with the organizations of employers and workers concerned, where such exist.

3. Notwithstanding the provisions of paragraph 1 of this Article, national laws or regulations or the competent authority may, after consultation with the organizations of employers and workers concerned, where such exist, authorise employment or work as from the age of 16 years on condition that the health, safety and morals of the young persons concerned are fully protected and that the young persons have received adequate specific instruction or vocational training in the relevant branch of activity.

## Article 4

1. In so far as necessary, the competent authority, after consultation with the organizations of employers and workers concerned, where such exist, may exclude from the application of this Convention limited categories of employment or work in respect of which special and substantial problems of application arise.

2. Each Member which ratifies this Convention shall list in its first report on the application of the Convention submitted under Article 22 of the Constitution of the International Labour Organization any categories which may have been excluded in pursuance of paragraph 1 of this Article, giving the reasons for such exclusion, and shall state in subsequent reports the position of its law and practice in respect of the categories excluded and the extent to which effect has been given or is proposed to be given to the Convention in respect of such categories.

3. Employment or work covered by Article 3 of this Convention shall not be excluded from the application of the Convention in pursuance of this Article.

*Article 5*

1. A Member whose economy and administrative facilities are insufficiently developed may, after consultation with the organizations of employers and workers concerned, where such exist, initially limit the scope of application of this Convention.

2. Each Member which avails itself of the provisions of paragraph 1 of this Article shall specify, in a declaration appended to its ratification, the branches of economic activity or types of undertakings to which it will apply the provisions of the Convention.

3. The provisions of the Convention shall be applicable as a minimum to the following: mining and quarrying; manufacturing; construction; electricity, gas and water; sanitary services; transport, storage and communication; and plantations and other agricultural undertakings mainly producing for commercial purposes, but excluding family and small-scale holdings producing for local consumption and not regularly employing hired workers.

4. Any Member which has limited the scope of application of this Convention in pursuance of this Article:

(a) shall indicate in its reports under Article 22 of the Constitution of the International Labour Organization the general position as regards the employment or work of young persons and children in the branches of activity which are excluded from the scope of application of this Convention and any progress which may have been made towards wider application of the provisions of the Convention;

(b) may at any time formally extend the scope of application by a declaration addressed to the Director-General of the International Labour Office.

*Article 6*

This Convention does not apply to work done by children and young persons in schools for general, vocational or technical education or in other training institutions, or to work done by persons at least 14 years of age in undertakings, where such work is carried out in accordance with conditions prescribed by the competent authority, after consultation with the organizations of employers and workers concerned, where such exist, and is an integral part of:

(a) a course of education or training for which a school or training institution is primarily responsible;

(b) a programme of training mainly or entirely in an undertaking, which programme has been approved by the competent authority; or

(c) a programme of guidance or orientation designed to facilitate the choice of an occupation or of a line of training.

*Article 7*

1. National laws or regulations may permit the employment or work of persons 13 to 15 years of age on light work which is:

*(a)* not likely to be harmful to their health or development; and

*(b)* not such as to prejudice their attendance at school, their participation in vocational orientation or training programmes approved by the competent authority or their capacity to benefit from the instruction received.

2. National laws or regulations may also permit the employment or work of persons who are at least 15 years of age but have not yet completed their compulsory schooling on work which meets the requirements set forth in sub-paragraphs (a) and (b) of paragraph 1 of this Article.

3. The competent authority shall determine the activities in which employment or work may be permitted under paragraphs 1 and 2 of this Article and shall prescribe the number of hours during which and the conditions in which such employment or work may be undertaken.

4. Notwithstanding the provisions of paragraphs 1 and 2 of this Article, a Member which has availed itself of the provisions of paragraph 4 of Article 2 may, for as long as it continues to do so, substitute the ages 12 and 14 for the ages 13 and 15 in paragraph 1 and the age 14 for the age 15 in paragraph 2 of this Article.

*Article* 8

1. After consultation with the organizations of employers and workers concerned, where such exist, the competent authority may, by permits granted in individual cases, allow exceptions to the prohibition of employment or work provided for in Article 2 of this Convention, for such purposes as participation in artistic performances.

2. Permits so granted shall limit the number of hours during which and prescribe the conditions in which employment or work is allowed.

*Article* 9

1. All necessary measures, including the provision of appropriate penalties, shall be taken by the competent authority to ensure the effective enforcement of the provisions of this Convention.

2. National laws or regulations or the competent authority shall define the persons responsible for compliance with the provisions giving effect to the Convention.

3. National laws or regulations or the competent authority shall prescribe the registers or other documents which shall be kept and made available by the employer; such registers or documents shall contain the names and ages or dates of birth, duly certified wherever possible, of persons whom he employs or who work for him and who are less than 18 years of age.

*Article* 10

1. This Convention revises, on the terms set forth in this Article, the Minimum Age (Industry) Convention, 1919, the Minimum Age (Sea) Convention, 1920, the Minimum Age (Agriculture) Convention, 1921, the Minimum Age (Trimmers and Stokers) Convention, 1921, the Minimum Age (Non-Industrial Employment) Convention, 1932, the Minimum Age (Sea) Convention (Revised), 1936, the Minimum Age (Industry) Convention (Revised), 1937, the Minimum Age (Non-Industrial Employment) Convention (Revised), 1937, the Minimum Age (Fishermen) Convention, 1959, and the Minimum Age (Underground Work) Convention, 1965.

2. The coming into force of this Convention shall not close the Minimum Age (Sea) Convention (Revised), 1936, the Minimum Age (Industry) Convention (Revised), 1937, the Minimum Age (Non-Industrial Employment) Convention (Revised), 1937, the Minimum Age (Fishermen) Convention, 1959, or the Minimum Age (Underground Work) Convention, 1965, to further ratification.

3. The Minimum Age (Industry) Convention, 1919, the Minimum Age (Sea) Convention, 1920, the Minimum Age (Agriculture) Convention, 1921, and the Minimum Age (Trimmers and Stokers) Convention, 1921, shall be closed to further ratification when all the parties thereto have consented to such closing by ratification of this Convention or by a declaration communicated to the Director-General of the International Labour Office.

4. When the obligations of this Convention are accepted:

(a) by a Member which is a party to the Minimum Age (Industry) Convention (Revised), 1937, and a minimum age of not less than 15 years is specified in pursuance of Article 2 of this Convention, this shall *ipso jure* involve the immediate denunciation of that Convention,

(b) in respect of non-industrial employment as defined in the Minimum Age (Non-Industrial Employment) Convention, 1932, by a Member which is a party to that Convention, this shall *ipso jure* involve the immediate denunciation of that Convention,

(c) in respect of non-industrial employment as defined in the Minimum Age (Non-Industrial Employment) Convention (Revised), 1937, by a Member which is a party to that Convention, and a minimum age of not less than 15 years is specified in pursuance of Article 2 of this Convention, this shall *ipso jure* involve the immediate denunciation of that Convention,

(d) in respect of maritime employment, by a Member which is a party to the Minimum Age (Sea) Convention (Revised), 1936, and a minimum age of not less than 15 years is specified in pursuance of Article 2 of this Convention or the Member specifies that Article 3 of this Convention applies to maritime employment, this shall *ipso jure* involve the immediate denunciation of that Convention,

(e) in respect of employment in maritime fishing, by a Member which is a party to the Minimum Age (Fishermen) Convention, 1959, and a minimum age of not less than 15 years is specified in pursuance of Article 2 of this Convention or the Member specifies that Article 3 of this Convention applies to employment in maritime fishing, this shall *ipso jure* involve the immediate denunciation of that Convention,

(f) by a Member which is a party to the Minimum Age (Underground Work) Convention, 1965, and a minimum age of not less than the age specified in pursuance of that Convention is specified in pursuance of Article 2 of this Convention or the Member specifies that such an age applies to employment underground in mines in virtue of Article 3 of this Convention, this shall *ipso jure* involve the immediate denunciation of that Convention, if and when this Convention shall have come into force.

5. Acceptance of the obligations of this Convention:

(a) shall involve the denunciation of the Minimum Age (Industry) Convention, 1919, in accordance with Article 12 thereof,

(b) in respect of agriculture shall involve the denunciation of the Minimum Age (Agriculture) Convention, 1921, in accordance with Article 9 thereof,

(c) in respect of maritime employment shall involve the denunciation of the Minimum Age (Sea) Convention, 1920, in accordance with Article 10 thereof, and of the Minimum Age (Trimmers and Stokers) Convention, 1921, in accordance with Article 12 thereof, if and when this Convention shall have come into force.

*Article* 11

The formal ratifications of this Convention shall be communicated to the Director-General of the International Labour Office for registration.

*Article* 12

1. This Convention shall be binding only upon those Members of the International Labour Organization whose ratifications have been registered with the Director-General.

2. It shall come into force twelve months after the date on which the ratifications of two Members have been registered with the Director-General.

3. Thereafter, this Convention shall come into force for any Member twelve months after the date on which its ratifications has been registered.

*Article* 13

1. A Member which has ratified this Convention may denounce it after the expiration of ten years from the date on which the Convention first comes into force, by an Act communicated to the Director-General of the International Labour Office for registration. Such denunciation should not take effect until one year after the date on which it is registered.

2. Each Member which has ratified this Convention and which does not, within the year following the expiration of the period of ten years mentioned in the preceding paragraph, exercise the right of denunciation provided for in this Article, will be bound for another period of ten years and, thereafter, may denounce this Convention at the expiration of each period of ten years under the terms provided for in this Article.

*Article* 14

1. The Director-General of the International Labour Office shall notify all Members of the International Labour Organization of the registration of all ratifications and denunciations communicated to him by the Members of the Organization.

2. When notifying the Members of the Organization of the registration of the second ratification communicated to him, the Director-General shall draw the attention of the Members of the Organization to the date upon which the Convention will come into force.

*Article* 15

The Director-General of the International Labour Office shall communicate to the Secretary-General of the United Nations for registration in accordance with Article 102 of the Charter of the United Nations full particulars of all ratifications and acts of denunciation registered by him in accordance with the provisions of the preceding Articles.

*Article* 16

At such times as it may consider necessary the Governing Body of the International Labour Office shall present to the General Conference a report on the working of this Convention and shall examine the desirability of placing on the agenda of the Conference the question of its revision in whole or in part.

*Article* 17

1. Should the Conference adopt a new Convention revising this Convention in whole or in part, then, unless the new Convention otherwise provides:

   *(a)* the ratification by a Member of the new revising Convention shall *ipso jure* involve the immediate denunciation of this Convention, notwithstanding the provisions of Article 13 above, if and when the new revising Convention shall have come into force;

   *(b)* as from the date when the new revising Convention comes into force this Convention shall cease to be open to ratification by the Members.

2. This Convention shall in any case remain in force in its actual form and content for those Members which have ratified it but have not ratified the revising Convention.

*Article* 18

The English and French versions of the text of this Convention are equally authoritative.

## 48. EMPLOYMENT PROMOTION AND PROTECTION AGAINST UNEMPLOYMENT CONVENTION, 1988

This Convention (C168) was adopted on 21 June 1988 and came into force on 17 October 1991.

*TEXT*

*The General Conference of the International Labour Organization,*

*Having been convened* at Geneva by the Governing Body of the International Labour Office, and having met in its Seventy-fifth Session on 1 June 1988, and

*Emphasising* the importance of work and productive employment in any society not only because of the resources which they create for the community, but also because of the income which they bring to workers, the social role which they confer and the feeling of self-esteem which workers derive from them, and

*Recalling* the existing international standards in the field of employment and unemployment protection the Unemployment Provision Convention and Recommendation, 1934, the Unemployment (Young Persons) Recommendation, 1935, the Income Security Recommendation, 1944, the Social Security (Minimum Standards) Convention, 1952, the Employment Policy Convention and Recommendation, 1964, the Human Resources Development Convention and Recommendation, 1975, the Labour Administration Convention and Recommendation, 1978, and the Employment Policy (Supplementary Provisions) Recommendation, 1984, and

*Considering* the widespread unemployment and underemployment affecting various countries throughout the world at all stages of development and in particular the problems of young people, many of whom are seeking their first employment, and

*Considering* that, since the adoption of the international instruments concerning protection against unemployment referred to above, there have been important new developments in the law and practice of many Members necessitating the revision of existing standards, in particular the Unemployment Provision Convention, 1934, and the adoption of new international standards concerning the promotion of full, productive and freely chosen employment by all appropriate means, including social security, and

*Noting* that the provisions concerning unemployment benefit in the Social Security (Minimum Standards) Convention, 1952, lay down a level of protection that has now been surpassed by most of the existing compensation schemes in the industrialised countries and, unlike standards concerning other benefits, have not been followed by higher standards, but that the standards in question can still constitute a target for developing countries that are in a position to set up an unemployment compensation scheme, and

*Recognising* that policies leading to stable, sustained, non-inflationary economic growth and a flexible response to change, as well as to creation and promotion of all forms of productive and freely chosen employment including small undertakings, co-operatives, self-employment and local initiatives for employment, even through the re-distribution of resources currently devoted to the financing of purely assistance-oriented activities towards activities which promote employment especially vocational guidance, training and rehabilitation, offer the best protection against the adverse effects of involuntary unemployment, but that involuntary unemployment nevertheless exists and that it is therefore important to ensure that social security systems should provide employment assistance and economic support to those who are involuntarily unemployed, and

*Having decided* upon the adoption of certain proposals with regard to employment promotion and social security which is the fifth item on the agenda of the session with a view, in particular, to revising the Unemployment Provision Convention, 1934, and

*Having determined* that these proposals shall take the form of an international Convention,

*Adopts* the twenty-first day of June of the year one thousand nine hundred and eighty-eight, the following Convention, which may be cited as the Employment Promotion and Protection against Unemployment Convention, 1988:

## I. GENERAL PROVISIONS

*Article* 1

In this Convention:

  (a) the term 'legislation' includes any social security rules as well as laws and regulations;

  (b) the term 'prescribed' means determined by or in virtue of national legislation.

*Article* 2

Each Member shall take appropriate steps to co-ordinate its system of protection against unemployment and its employment policy. To this end, it shall seek to ensure that its system of protection against unemployment, and in particular the methods of providing unemployment benefit, contribute to the promotion of full, productive and freely chosen employment, and are not such as to discourage employers from offering and workers from seeking productive employment.

*Article* 3

The provisions of this Convention shall be implemented in consultation and co-operation with the organizations of employers and workers, in accordance with national practice.

*Article* 4

1. Each Member which ratifies this Convention may, by a declaration accompanying its ratification, exclude the provisions of Part VII from the obligations accepted by ratification.

2. Each Member which has made a declaration under paragraph 1 above may withdraw it at any time by a subsequent declaration.

*Article* 5

1. Each Member may avail itself, by a declaration accompanying its ratification, of at most two of the temporary exceptions provided for in Article 10, paragraph 4, Article 11, paragraph 3, Article 15, paragraph 2, Article 18, paragraph 2, Article 19, paragraph 4, Article 23, paragraph 2, Article 24, paragraph 2, and Article 25, paragraph 2. Such a declaration shall state the reasons which justify these exceptions.

2. Notwithstanding the provisions of paragraph 1 above, a Member, where it is justified by the extent of protection of its social security system, may avail itself, by a declaration accompanying its ratification, of the temporary exceptions provided for in Article 10, paragraph 4, Article 11, paragraph 3, Article 15, paragraph 2, Article 18, paragraph 2, Article 19, paragraph 4, Article 23, paragraph 2, Article 24, paragraph 2 and Article 25, paragraph 2. Such a declaration shall state the reasons which justify these exceptions.

3. Each Member which has made a declaration under paragraph 1 or paragraph 2 shall include in its reports on the application of this Convention submitted under Article 22 of the Constitution of the International Labour Organization a statement in respect of each exception of which it avails itself:

  *(a)*  that its reason for doing so subsists; or

  *(b)*  that it renounces its right to avail itself of the exception in question as from a stated date.

4. Each Member which has made a declaration under paragraph 1 or paragraph 2 shall, as appropriate to the terms of such declaration and as circumstances permit:

  *(a)*  cover the contingency of partial unemployment;

  *(b)*  increase the number of persons protected;

  *(c)*  increase the amount of the benefits;

  *(d)*  reduce the length of the waiting period;

  *(e)*  extend the duration of payment of benefits;

  *(f)*  adapt statutory social security schemes to the occupational circumstances of part-time workers;

  *(g)*  endeavour to ensure the provision of medical care to persons in receipt of unemployment benefit and their dependants;

  *(h)*  endeavour to guarantee that the periods during which such benefit is paid will be taken into account for the acquisition of the right to social security benefits and, where appropriate, the calculation of disability, old-age and survivors' benefit.

*Article* 6

1. Each Member shall ensure equality of treatment for all persons protected, without discrimination on the basis of race, colour, sex, religion, political opinion, national extraction, nationality, ethnic or social origin, disability or age.

2. The provisions of paragraph 1 shall not prevent the adoption of special

measures which are justified by the circumstances of identified groups under the schemes referred to in Article 12, paragraph 2, or are designed to meet the specific needs of categories of persons who have particular problems in the labour market, in particular disadvantaged groups, or the conclusion between States of bilateral or multilateral agreements relating to unemployment benefits on the basis of reciprocity.

## II. PROMOTION OF PRODUCTIVE EMPLOYMENT

*Article* 7

Each Member shall declare as a priority objective a policy designed to promote full, productive and freely chosen employment by all appropriate means, including social security. Such means should include, inter alia, employment services, vocational training and vocational guidance.

*Article* 8

1. Each Member shall endeavour to establish, subject to national law and practice, special programmes to promote additional job opportunities and employment assistance and to encourage freely chosen and productive employment for identified categories of disadvantaged persons having or liable to have difficulties in finding lasting employment such as women, young workers, disabled persons, older workers, the long-term unemployed, migrant workers lawfully resident in the country and workers affected by structural change.

2. Each Member shall specify, in its reports under Article 22 of the Constitution of the International Labour Organization, the categories of persons for whom it undertakes to promote employment programmes.

3. Each Member shall endeavour to extend the promotion of productive employment progressively to a greater number of categories than the number initially covered.

*Article* 9

The measures envisaged in this Part shall be taken in the light of the Human Resources Development Convention and Recommendation, 1975, and the Employment Policy (supplementary Provisions) Recommendation, 1984.

## III. CONTINGENCIES COVERED

*Article* 10

1. The contingencies covered shall include, under prescribed conditions, full unemployment defined as the loss of earnings due to inability to obtain suitable employment with due regard to the provisions of Article 21, paragraph 2, in the case of a person capable of working, available for work and actually seeking work.

2. Each Member shall endeavour to extend the protection of the Convention, under prescribed conditions, to the following contingencies:

(a) loss of earnings due to partial unemployment, defined as a temporary reduction in the normal or statutory hours of work; and

(b) suspension or reduction of earnings due to a temporary suspension of work, without any break in the employment relationship for reasons of, in particular, an economic, technological, structural or similar nature.

3. Each Member shall in addition endeavour to provide the payment of benefits to part-time workers who are actually seeking full-time work. The total of benefits and earnings from their part-time work may be such as to maintain incentives to take up full-time work.

4. Where a declaration made in virtue of Article 5 is in force, the implementation of paragraphs 2 and 3 above may be deferred.


## IV. PERSONS PROTECTED

*Article* 11

1. The persons protected shall comprise prescribed classes of employees, constituting not less than 85 per cent of all employees, including public employees and apprentices.

2. Notwithstanding the provisions of paragraph 1 above, public employees whose employment up to normal retiring age is guaranteed by national laws or regulations may be excluded from protection.

3. Where a declaration made in virtue of Article 5 is in force, the persons protected shall comprise:

(a) prescribed classes of employees constituting not less than 50 per cent of all employees; or

(b) where specifically justified by the level of development, prescribed classes of employees constituting not less than 50 per cent of all employees in industrial workplaces employing 20 persons or more.


## V. METHODS OF PROTECTION

*Article* 12

1. Unless it is otherwise provided in this Convention, each Member may determine the method or methods of protection by which it chooses to put into effect the provisions of the Convention, whether by a contributory or non-contributory system, or by a combination of such systems.

2. Nevertheless, if the legislation of a Member protects all residents whose resources, during the contingency, do not exceed prescribed limits, the protection afforded may be limited, in the light of the resources of the beneficiary and his or her family, in accordance with the provisions of Article 16.

## VI. BENEFIT TO BE PROVIDED

*Article* 13

Benefits provided in the form of periodical payments to the unemployed may be related to the methods of protection.

*Article* 14

In cases of full unemployment, benefits shall be provided in the form of periodical payments calculated in such a way as to provide the beneficiary with partial and transitional wage replacement and, at the same time, to avoid creating disincentives either to work or to employment creation.

*Article* 15

1. In cases of full unemployment and suspension of earnings due to a temporary suspension of work without any break in the employment relationship, when this contingency is covered, benefits shall be provided in the form of periodical payments, calculated as follows:

   (a) where these benefits are based on the contributions of or on behalf of the person protected or on previous earnings, they shall be fixed at not less than 50 per cent of previous earnings, it being permitted to fix a maximum for the amount of the benefit or for the earnings to be taken into account, which may be related, for example, to the wage of a skilled manual employee or to the average wage of workers in the region concerned;

   (b) where such benefits are not based on contributions or previous earnings, they shall be fixed at not less than 50 per cent of the statutory minimum wage or of the wage of an ordinary labourer, or at a level which provides the minimum essential for basic living expenses, whichever is the highest;

2. Where a declaration made in virtue of Article 5 is in force, the amount of the benefits shall be equal:

   (a) to not less than 45 per cent of the previous earnings; or

   (b) to not less than 45 per cent of the statutory minimum wage or of the wage of an ordinary labourer but no less than a level which provides the minimum essential for basic living expenses.

3. If appropriate, the percentages specified in paragraphs 1 and 2 may be reached by comparing net periodical payments after tax and contributions with net earnings after tax and contributions.

*Article* 16

Notwithstanding the provisions of Article 15, the benefit provided beyond the initial period specified in Article 19, paragraph 2 (a), as well as benefits paid by a Member in accordance with Article 12, paragraph 2, may be fixed after taking account of other resources, beyond a prescribed limit, available to the beneficiary and his or her family, in accordance with a prescribed scale. In any case, these benefits, in combination with any other benefits to which they may be entitled, shall guarantee them healthy and reasonable living conditions in accordance with national standards.

*Article* 17

1. Where the legislation of a Member makes the right to unemployment benefit conditional upon the completion of a qualifying period, this period shall not exceed the length deemed necessary to prevent abuse.

2. Each Member shall endeavour to adapt the qualifying period to the occupational circumstances of seasonal workers.

*Article* 18

1. If the legislation of a Member provides that the payment of benefit in cases of full unemployment should begin only after the expiry of a waiting period, such period shall not exceed seven days.

2. Where a declaration made in virtue of Article 5 is in force, the length of the waiting period shall not exceed ten days.

3. In the case of seasonal workers the waiting period specified in paragraph 1 above may be adapted to their occupational circumstances.

*Article* 19

1. The benefits provided in cases of full unemployment and suspension of earnings due to a temporary suspension of work without any break in the employment relationship shall be paid throughout these contingencies.

2. Nevertheless, in the case of full unemployment:

  (a)  the initial duration of payment of the benefit provided for in Article 15 may be limited to 26 weeks in each spell of unemployment, or to 39 weeks over any period of 24 months;

  (b)  in the event of unemployment continuing beyond this initial period of benefit, the duration of payment of benefit, which may be calculated in the light of the resources of the beneficiary and his or her family in accordance with the provisions of Article 16, may be limited to a prescribed period.

3. If the legislation of a Member provides that the initial duration of payment of the benefit provided for in Article 15 shall vary with the length of the qualifying period, the average duration fixed for the payment of benefits shall be at least 26 weeks.

4. Where a declaration made in virtue of Article 5 is in force, the duration of payment of benefit may be limited to 13 weeks over any periods of 12 months or to an average of 13 weeks if the legislation provides that the initial duration of payment shall vary with the length of the qualifying period.

5. In the cases envisaged in paragraph 2 (b) above each Member shall endeavour to grant appropriate additional assistance to the persons concerned with a view to permitting them to find productive and freely chosen employment, having recourse in particular to the measures specified in Part II.

6. The duration of payment of benefit to seasonal workers may be adapted to their occupational circumstances, without prejudice to the provisions of paragraph 2 (b) above.

*Article* 20

The benefit to which a protected person would have been entitled in the cases of full or partial unemployment or suspension of earnings due to a temporary suspension of work without any break in the employment relationship may be refused, withdrawn, suspended or reduced to the extent prescribed:

(a) for as long as the person concerned is absent from the territory of the Member;

(b) when it has been determined by the competent authority that the person concerned had deliberately contributed to his or her own dismissal;

(c) when it has been determined by the competent authority that the person concerned has left employment voluntarily without just cause;

(d) during the period of a labour dispute, when the person concerned has stopped work to take part in a labour dispute or when he or she is prevented from working as a direct result of a stoppage of work due to this labour dispute;

(e) when the person concerned has attempted to obtain or has obtained benefits fraudulently;

(f) when the person concerned has failed without just cause to use the facilities available for placement, vocational guidance, training, retraining or redeployment in suitable work;

(g) as long as the person concerned is in receipt of another income maintenance benefit provided for in the legislation of the Member concerned, except a family benefit, provided that the part of the benefit which is suspended does not exceed that other benefit.

*Article* 21

1. The benefit to which a protected person would have been entitled in the case of full unemployment may be refused, withdrawn, suspended or reduced, to the extent prescribed, when the person concerned refuses to accept suitable employment.

2. In assessing the suitability of employment, account shall be taken, in particular, under prescribed conditions and to an appropriate extent, of the age of unemployed persons, their length of service in their former occupation, their acquired experience, the length of their period of unemployment, the labour market situation, the impact of the employment in question on their personal and family situation and whether the employment is vacant as a direct result of a stoppage of work due to an on-going labour dispute.

*Article* 22

When protected persons have received directly from their employer or from any other source under national laws or regulations or collective agreements, severance pay, the principal purpose of which is to contribute towards compensating them for the loss of earnings suffered in the event of full unemployment:

(a) the unemployment benefit to which the persons concerned would be entitled may be suspended for a period corresponding to that during which the severance pay compensates for the loss of earnings suffered; or

(b) the severance pay may be reduced by an amount corresponding to the value converted into a lump sum of the unemployment benefit to which the persons concerned are entitled for a period corresponding to that during which the severance pay compensates for the loss of earnings suffered, as each Member may decide.

*Article* 23

1. Each Member whose legislation provides for the right to medical care and makes it directly or indirectly conditional upon occupational activity shall endeavour to ensure, under prescribed conditions, the provision of medical care to persons in receipt of unemployment benefit and to their dependants.

2. Where a declaration made in virtue of Article 5 is in force, the implementation of paragraph 1 above may be deferred.

*Article* 24

1. Each Member shall endeavour to guarantee to persons in receipt of unemployment benefit, under prescribed conditions, that the periods during which benefits are paid will be taken into consideration:

(a) for acquisition of the right to and, where appropriate, calculation of disability, old-age and survivors' benefit, and

(b) for acquisition of the right to medical care and sickness, maternity and family benefit after the end of unemployment, when the legislation of the Member concerned provides for such benefits and makes them directly or indirectly conditional upon occupational activity.

2. Where a declaration made in virtue of Article 5 is in force, the implementation of paragraph 1 above may be deferred.

*Article* 25

1. Each Member shall ensure that statutory social security schemes which are based on occupational activity are adjusted to the occupational circumstances of part-time workers, unless their hours of work or earnings can be considered, under prescribed conditions, as negligible.

2. Where a declaration made in virtue of Article 5 is in force, the implementation of paragraph 1 above may be deferred.

## VII. SPECIAL PROVISIONS FOR NEW APPLICANTS FOR EMPLOYMENT

*Article* 26

1. Members shall take account of the fact that there are many categories of persons seeking work who have never been, or have ceased to be, recognised as unemployed or have never been, or have ceased to be, covered by schemes for the protection of the unemployed. Consequently, at least three of the following ten categories of persons seeking work shall receive social benefits, in accordance with prescribed terms and conditions:

(a) young persons who have completed their vocational training;

*(b)*   young persons who have completed their studies;

*(c)*   young persons who have completed their compulsory military service;

*(d)*   persons after a period devoted to bringing up a child or caring for someone who is sick, disabled or elderly;

*(e)*   persons whose spouse had died, when they are not entitled to a survivor's benefit;

*(f)*   divorced or separated persons;

*(g)*   released prisoners;

*(h)*   adults, including disabled persons, who have completed a period of training;

*(i)*   migrant workers on return to their home country, except in so far as they have acquired rights under the legislation of the country where they last worked;

*(j)*   previously self-employed persons.

2. Each Member shall specify, in its reports under article 22 of the Constitution of the International Labour Organization, the categories of persons listed in paragraph 1 above which it undertakes to protect.

3. Each Member shall endeavour to extend protection progressively to a greater number of categories than the number initially protected.


## VIII. LEGAL, ADMINISTRATIVE AND FINANCIAL GUARANTEES

*Article* 27

1. In the event of refusal, withdrawal, suspension or reduction of benefit or dispute as to its amount, claimants shall have the right to present a complaint to the body administering the benefit scheme and to appeal thereafter to an independent body. They shall be informed in writing of the procedures available, which shall be simple and rapid.

2. The appeal procedure shall enable the claimant, in accordance with national law and practice, to be represented or assisted by a qualified person of the claimant's choice or by a delegate of a representative workers' organization or by a delegate of an organization representative of protected persons.

*Article* 28

Each Member shall assume general responsibility for the sound administration of the institutions and services entrusted with the application of the Convention.

*Article* 29

1. When the administration is directly entrusted to a government department responsible to Parliament, representatives of the protected persons and of the employers shall be associated in the administration in an advisory capacity, under prescribed conditions.

2. When the administration is not entrusted to a government department responsible to Parliament:

(a) representatives of the protected persons shall participate in the administration or be associated therewith in an advisory capacity under prescribed conditions;

(b) national laws or regulations may also provide for the participation of employers' representatives;

(c) the laws or regulations may further provide for the participation of representatives of the public authorities.

*Article 30*

In cases where subsidies are granted by the State or the social security system in order to safeguard employment, Members shall take the necessary steps to ensure that the payments are expended only for the intended purpose and to prevent fraud or abuse by those who receive such payments.

*Article 31*

This Convention revises the Unemployment Provision Convention, 1934.

*Article 32*

The formal ratifications of this Convention shall be communicated to the Director-General of the International Labour Office for registration.

*Article 33*

1. This Convention shall be binding only upon those Members of the International Labour Organization whose ratifications have been registered with the Director-General.

2. It shall come into force twelve months after the date on which the ratifications of two Members have been registered with the Director-General.

3. Thereafter, this Convention shall come into force for any Member twelve months after the date on which its ratification has been registered.

*Article 34*

1. A Member which has ratified this Convention may denounce it after the expiration of ten years from the date on which the Convention first comes into force, by an act communicated to the Director-General of the International Labour Office for registration. Such denunciation shall not take effect until one year after the date on which it is registered.

2. Each Member which has ratified this Convention and which does not, within the year following the expiration of the period of ten years mentioned in the preceding paragraph, exercise the right of denunciation provided for in this Article, will be bound for another period of ten years and, thereafter, may denounce this Convention at the expiration of each period of ten years under the terms provided for in this Article.

*Article 35*

1. The Director-General of the International Labour Office shall notify all Members of the International Labour Organization of the registration of all ratifications and denunciations communicated to him by the Members of the Organization.

2. When notifying the members of the Organization of the registration of the second ratification communicated to him, the Director-General shall draw the attention of the Members of the Organization to the date upon which the Convention will come into force.

*Article 36*

The Director-General of the International Labour Office shall communicate to the Secretary-General of the United Nations for registration in accordance with Article 102 of the Charter of the United Nations full particulars of all ratifications and acts of denunciation registered by him in accordance with the provisions of the preceding Articles.

*Article 37*

At such times as it may consider necessary the Governing Body of the International Labour Office shall present to the General Conference a report on the working of this Convention and shall examine the desirability of placing on the agenda of the Conference the question of its revision in whole or in part.

*Article 38*

1. Should the Conference adopt a new Convention revising this Convention in whole or in part, then, unless the new Convention otherwise provides:

   (a) the ratification by a Member of the new revising Convention shall *ipso jure* involve the immediate denunciation of this Convention, notwithstanding the provisions of Article 34 above, if and when the new revising Convention shall have come into force;

   (b) as from the date when the new revising Convention comes into force this Convention shall cease to be open to ratification by the Members.

2. This Convention shall in any case remain in force in its actual form and content for those Members which have ratified it but have not ratified the revising Convention.

*Article 39*

The English and French versions of the text of this Convention are equally authoritative.

## 49. INDIGENOUS AND TRIBAL PEOPLES
## CONVENTION, 1989

The Convention (C169) was adopted during the 1989 Session of the I.L.O. It revises the provisions of the Indigenous and Tribal Populations Convention, 1957 (No. 107), and came into force on 5 September 1991.

See also the UN Draft Declaration on the Rights of Indigenous Peoples, 1994, above 72–81. Bennett, G. I., 'The ILO Convention on Indigenous and Tribal Populations: The Resolution of a Problem of *Vires*' (1972–73) 46 *BYIL* 382–92.

*TEXT*

*The General Conference of the International Labour Organization,*

*Having been convened* at Geneva by the Governing Body of the International Labour Office, and having met in its 76th Session on 7 June 1989, and

*Noting* the international standards contained in the Indigenous and Tribal Populations Convention and Recommendation, 1957, and

*Recalling* the terms of the Universal Declaration of Human Rights, the International Covenant on Economic, Social and Cultural Rights, the International Covenant on Civil and Political Rights, and the many international instruments on the prevention of discrimination, and

*Considering* that the developments which have taken place in international law since 1957, as well as developments in the situation of indigenous and tribal peoples in all regions of the world, have made it appropriate to adopt new international standards on the subject with a view to removing the assimilationist orientation of the earlier standards, and

*Recognising* the aspirations of these peoples to exercise control over their own institutions, ways of life and economic development and to maintain and develop their identities, languages and religions, within the framework of the States in which they live, and

*Noting* that in many parts of the world these peoples are unable to enjoy their fundamental human rights to the same degree as the rest of the population of the States within which they live, and that their laws, values, customs and perspectives have often been eroded, and

*Calling* attention to the distinctive contributions of indigenous and tribal peoples to the cultural diversity and social and ecological harmony of humankind and to international co-operation and understanding, and

*Noting* that the following provisions have been framed with the co-operation of the United Nations, the Food and Agriculture Organization of the United Nations, the United Nations Educational, Scientific and Cultural Organization and the World Health Organization, as well as of the Inter-American Indian Institute, at appropriate levels and in their respective fields, and that it is proposed to continue this co-operation in promoting and securing the application of these provisions, and

*Having decided* upon the adoption of certain proposals with regard to the partial revision of the Indigenous and Tribal Populations Convention, 1957 (No. 107), which is the fourth item on the agenda of the session, and

*Having determined* that these proposals shall take the form of an international Convention revising the Indigenous and Tribal Populations Convention, 1957;

*Adopts* the twenty-seventh day of June of the year one thousand nine hundred and eighty-nine, the following Convention, which may be cited as the Indigenous and Tribal Peoples Convention, 1989;

# PART I

## GENERAL POLICY

*Article* 1

1. This Convention applies to:

   (a) tribal peoples in independent countries whose social, cultural and economic conditions distinguish them from other sections of the national community, and whose status is regulated wholly or partially by their own customs or traditions or by special laws or regulations;

   (b) peoples in independent countries who are regarded as indigenous on account of their descent from the populations which inhabited the country, or a geographical region to which the country belongs, at the time of conquest or colonisation or the establishment of present state boundaries and who, irrespective of their legal status, retain some or all of their own social, economic, cultural and political institutions.

2. Self-identification as indigenous or tribal shall be regarded as a fundamental criterion for determining the groups to which the provisions of this Convention apply.

3. The use of the term 'peoples' in this Convention shall not be construed as having any implications as regards the rights which may attach to the term under international law.

*Article* 2

1. Governments shall have the responsibility for developing, with the participation of the peoples concerned, co-ordinated and systematic action to protect the rights of these peoples and to guarantee respect for their integrity.

2. Such action shall include measures for:

   (a) ensuring that members of these peoples benefit on an equal footing from the rights and opportunities which national laws and regulations grant to other members of the population;

   (b) promoting the full realisation of the social, economic and cultural rights of these peoples with respect for their social and cultural identity, their customs and traditions and their institutions;

   (c) assisting the members of the peoples concerned to eliminate socioeconomic gaps that may exist between indigenous and other members of the national community, in a manner compatible with their aspirations and ways of life.

*Article* 3

1. Indigenous and tribal peoples shall enjoy the full measure of human rights and fundamental freedoms without hindrance or discrimination. The provisions of the Convention shall be applied without discrimination to male and female members of these peoples.

2. No form of force or coercion shall be used in violation of the human rights and fundamental freedoms of the peoples concerned, including the rights contained in this Convention.

*Article* 4

1. Special measures shall be adopted as appropriate for safeguarding the persons, institutions, property, labour, cultures and environment of the peoples concerned.

2. Such special measures shall not be contrary to the freely-expressed wishes of the peoples concerned.

3. Enjoyment of the general rights of citizenship, without discrimination, shall not be prejudiced in any way by such special measures.

*Article* 5

In applying the provisions of this Convention:

(a) the social, cultural, religious and spiritual values and practices of these peoples shall be recognised and protected, and due account shall be taken of the nature of the problems which face them both as groups and as individuals;

(b) the integrity of the values, practices and institutions of these peoples shall be respected;

(c) policies aimed at mitigating the difficulties experienced by these peoples in facing new conditions of life and work shall be adopted, with the participation and co-operation of the peoples affected.

*Article* 6

1. In applying the provisions of this Convention, governments shall:

(a) consult the peoples concerned, through appropriate procedures and in particular through their representative institutions, whenever consideration is being given to legislative or administrative measures which may affect them directly;

(b) establish means by which these peoples can freely participate, to at least the same extent as other sectors of the population, at all levels of decision-making in elective institutions and administrative and other bodies responsible for policies and programmes which concern them;

(c) establish means for the full development of these peoples' own institutions and initiatives, and in appropriate cases provide the resources necessary for this purpose.

2. The consultations carried out in application of this Convention shall be undertaken, in good faith and in a form appropriate to the circumstances, with the objective of achieving agreement or consent to the proposed measures.

*Article 7*

1. The peoples concerned shall have the right to decide their own priorities for the process of development as it affects their lives, beliefs, institutions and spiritual well-being and the lands they occupy or otherwise use, and to exercise control, to the extent possible, over their own economic, social and cultural development. In addition, they shall participate in the formulation, implementation and evaluation of plans and programmes for national and regional development which may affect them directly.

2. The improvement of the conditions of life and work and levels of health and education of the peoples concerned, with their participation and co-operation, shall be a matter of priority in plans for the overall economic development of areas they inhabit. Special projects for development of the areas in question shall also be so designed as to promote such improvement.

3. Governments shall ensure that, whenever appropriate, studies are carried out, in co-operation with the peoples concerned, to assess the social, spiritual, cultural and environmental impact on them of planned development activities. The results of these studies shall be considered as fundamental criteria for the implementation of these activities.

4. Governments shall take measures, in co-operation with the peoples concerned, to protect and preserve the environment of the territories they inhabit.

*Article 8*

1. In applying national laws and regulations to the peoples concerned, due regard shall be had to their customs or customary laws.

2. These peoples shall have the right to retain their own customs and institutions, where these are not incompatible with fundamental rights defined by the national legal system and with internationally recognised human rights. Procedures shall be established, whenever necessary, to resolve conflicts which may arise in the application of this principle.

3. The application of paragraphs 1 and 2 of this Article shall not prevent members of these peoples from exercising the rights granted to all citizens and from assuming the corresponding duties.

*Article 9*

1. To the extent compatible with the national legal system and internationally recognised human rights, the methods customarily practised by the peoples concerned for dealing with offences committed by their members shall be respected.

2. The customs of these peoples in regard to penal matters shall be taken into consideration by the authorities and courts dealing with such cases.

*Article 10*

1. In imposing penalties laid down by general law on members of these peoples account shall be taken of their economic, social and cultural characteristics.

2. Preference shall be given to methods of punishment other than confinement in prison.

*Article* 11

The exaction from members of the peoples concerned of compulsory personal services in any form, whether paid or unpaid, shall be prohibited and punishable by law, except in cases prescribed by law for all citizens.

*Article* 12

The peoples concerned shall be safeguarded against the abuse of their rights and shall be able to take legal proceedings, either individually or through their representative bodies, for the effective protection of these rights. Measures shall be taken to ensure that members of these peoples can understand and be understood in legal proceedings, where necessary through the provision of interpretation or by other effective means.

# PART II

## LAND

*Article* 13

1. In applying the provisions of this Part of the Convention governments shall respect the special importance for the cultures and spiritual values of the peoples concerned of their relationship with the lands or territories, or both as applicable, which they occupy or otherwise use, and in particular the collective aspects of this relationship.

2. The use of the term 'lands' in Articles 15 and 16 shall include the concept of territories, which covers the total environment of the areas which the peoples concerned occupy or otherwise use.

*Article* 14

1. The rights of ownership and possession of the peoples concerned over the lands which they traditionally occupy shall be recognised. In addition, measures shall be taken in appropriate cases to safeguard the right of the peoples concerned to use lands not exclusively occupied by them, but to which they have traditionally had access for their subsistence and traditional activities. Particular attention shall be paid to the situation of nomadic peoples and shifting cultivators in this respect.

2. Governments shall take steps as necessary to identify the lands which the peoples concerned traditionally occupy, and to guarantee effective protection of their rights of ownership and possession.

3. Adequate procedures shall be established within the national legal system to resolve land claims by the peoples concerned.

*Article* 15

1. The rights of the peoples concerned to the natural resources pertaining to their

lands shall be specially safeguarded. These rights include the right of these peoples to participate in the use, management and conservation of these resources.

2. In cases in which the State retains the ownership of mineral or sub-surface resources or rights to other resources pertaining to lands, governments shall establish or maintain procedures through which they shall consult these peoples, with a view to ascertaining whether and to what degree their interests would be prejudiced, before undertaking or permitting any programmes for the exploration or exploitation of such resources pertaining to their lands. The peoples concerned shall wherever possible participate in the benefits of such activities, and shall receive fair compensation for any damages which they may sustain as a result of such activities.

*Article* 16

1. Subject to the following paragraphs of this Article, the peoples concerned shall not be removed from the lands which they occupy.

2. Where the relocation of these peoples is considered necessary as an exceptional measure, such relocation shall take place only with their free and informed consent. Where their consent cannot be obtained, such relocation shall take place only following appropriate procedures established by national laws and regulations, including public inquiries where appropriate, which provide the opportunity for effective representation of the peoples concerned.

3. Whenever possible, these peoples shall have the right to return to their traditional lands, as soon as the grounds for relocation cease to exist.

4. When such return is not possible, as determined by agreement or, in the absence of such agreement, through appropriate procedures, these peoples shall be provided in all possible cases with lands of quality and legal status at least equal to that of the lands previously occupied by them, suitable to provide for their present needs and future development. Where the peoples concerned express a preference for compensation in money or in kind, they shall be so compensated under appropriate guarantees.

5. Persons thus relocated shall be fully compensated for any resulting loss or injury.

*Article* 17

1. Procedures established by the peoples concerned for the transmission of land rights among members of these peoples shall be respected.

2. The peoples concerned shall be consulted whenever consideration is being given to their capacity to alienate their lands or otherwise transmit their rights outside their own community.

3. Persons not belonging to these peoples shall be prevented from taking advantage of their customs or of lack of understanding of the laws on the part of their members to secure the ownership, possession or use of land belonging to them.

*Article* 18

Adequate penalties shall be established by law for unauthorised intrusion upon, or use of, the lands of the peoples concerned, and governments shall take measures to prevent such offences.

*Article* 19

National agrarian programmes shall secure to the peoples concerned treatment equivalent to that accorded to other sectors of the population with regard to:

(a) the provision of more land for these peoples when they have not the area necessary for providing the essentials of a normal existence, or for any possible increase in their numbers;

(b) the provision of the means required to promote the development of the lands which these peoples already possess.

# PART III

## RECRUITMENT AND CONDITIONS OF EMPLOYMENT

*Article* 20

1. Governments shall, within the framework of national laws and regulations, and in co-operation with the peoples concerned, adopt special measures to ensure the effective protection with regard to recruitment and conditions of employment of workers belonging to these peoples, to the extent that they are not effectively protected by laws applicable to workers in general.

2. Governments shall do everything possible to prevent any discrimination between workers belonging to the peoples concerned and other workers, in particular as regards:

(a) admission to employment, including skilled employment, as well as measures for promotion and advancement;

(b) equal remuneration for work of equal value;

(c) medical and social assistance, occupational safety and health, all social security benefits and any other occupationally related benefits, and housing;

(d) the right of association and freedom for all lawful trade union activities, and the right to conclude collective agreements with employers or employers' organizations.

3. The measures taken shall include measures to ensure:

(a) that workers belonging to the peoples concerned, including seasonal, casual and migrant workers in agricultural and other employment, as well as those employed by labour contractors, enjoy the protection afforded by national law and practice to other such workers in the same sectors, and that they are fully informed of their rights under labour legislation and of the means of redress available to them;

(b) that workers belonging to these peoples are not subjected to working conditions hazardous to their health, in particular through exposure to pesticides or other toxic substances;

(c) that workers belonging to these peoples are not subjected to coercive recruitment systems, including bonded labour and other forms of debt servitude;

(d) that workers belonging to these peoples enjoy equal opportunities and equal treatment in employment for men and women, and protection from sexual harassment.

4. Particular attention shall be paid to the establishment of adequate labour inspection services in areas where workers belonging to the peoples concerned undertake wage employment, in order to ensure compliance with the provisions of this Part of this Convention.

## PART IV

## VOCATIONAL TRAINING, HANDICRAFTS AND RURAL INDUSTRIES

*Article 21*

Members of the peoples concerned shall enjoy opportunities at least equal to those of other citizens in respect of vocational training measures.

*Article 22*

1. Measures shall be taken to promote the voluntary participation of members of the peoples concerned in vocational training programmes of general application.

2. Whenever existing programmes of vocational training of general application do not meet the special needs of the peoples concerned, governments shall, with the participation of these peoples, ensure the provision of special training programmes and facilities.

3. Any special training programmes shall be based on the economic environment, social and cultural conditions and practical needs of the peoples concerned. Any studies made in this connection shall be carried out in co-operation with these peoples, who shall be consulted on the organization and operation of such programmes. Where feasible, these peoples shall progressively assume responsibility for the organization and operation of such special training programmes, if they so decide.

*Article 23*

1. Handicrafts, rural and community-based industries, and subsistence economy and traditional activities of the peoples concerned, such as hunting, fishing, trapping and gathering, shall be recognised as important factors in the maintenance of their cultures and in their economic self-reliance and development. Governments shall, with the participation of these people and whenever appropriate, ensure that these activities are strengthened and promoted.

2. Upon the request of the peoples concerned, appropriate technical and financial assistance shall be provided wherever possible, taking into account the traditional technologies and cultural characteristics of these peoples, as well as the importance of sustainable and equitable development.

## PART V

## SOCIAL SECURITY AND HEALTH

*Article* 24

Social security schemes shall be extended progressively to cover the peoples concerned, and applied without discrimination against them.

*Article* 25

1. Governments shall ensure that adequate health services are made available to the peoples concerned, or shall provide them with resources to allow them to design and deliver such services under their own responsibility and control, so that they may enjoy the highest attainable standard of physical and mental health.

2. Health services shall, to the extent possible, be community-based. These services shall be planned and administered in co-operation with the peoples concerned and take into account their economic, geographic, social and cultural conditions as well as their traditional preventive care, healing practices and medicines.

3. The health care system shall give preference to the training and employment of local community health workers, and focus on primary health care while maintaining strong links with other levels of health care services.

4. The provision of such health services shall be co-ordinated with other social, economic and cultural measures in the country.

## PART VI

## EDUCATION AND MEANS OF COMMUNICATION

*Article* 26

Measures shall be taken to ensure that members of the peoples concerned have the opportunity to acquire education at all levels on at least an equal footing with the rest of the national community.

*Article* 27

1. Education programmes and services for the peoples concerned shall be developed and implemented in co-operation with them to address their special needs, and shall incorporate their histories, their knowledge and technologies, their value systems and their further social, economic and cultural aspirations.

2. The competent authority shall ensure the training of members of these peoples and their involvement in the formulation and implementation of education programmes, with a view to the progressive transfer of responsibility for the conduct of these programmes to these peoples as appropriate.

3. In addition, governments shall recognise the right of these peoples to establish their own educational institutions and facilities, provided that such institutions meet minimum standards established by the competent authority in consultation with these peoples. Appropriate resources shall be provided for this purpose.

*Article* 28

1. Children belonging to the peoples concerned shall, wherever practicable, be taught to read and write in their own indigenous language or in the language most commonly used by the group to which they belong. When this is not practicable, the competent authorities shall undertake consultations with these peoples with a view to the adoption of measures to achieve this objective.

2. Adequate measures shall be taken to ensure that these peoples have the opportunity to attain fluency in the national language or in one of the official languages of the country.

3. Measures shall be taken to preserve and promote the development and practice of the indigenous languages of the peoples concerned.

*Article* 29

The imparting of general knowledge and skills that will help children belonging to the peoples concerned to participate fully and on an equal footing in their own community and in the national community shall be an aim of education for these peoples.

*Article* 30

1. Governments shall adopt measures appropriate to the traditions and cultures of the peoples concerned, to make known to them their rights and duties, especially in regard to labour, economic opportunities, education and health matters, social welfare and their rights deriving from this Convention.

2. If necessary, this shall be done by means of written translations and through the use of mass communications in the languages of these peoples.

*Article* 31

Educational measures shall be taken among all sections of the national community, and particularly among those that are in most direct contact with the peoples concerned, with the object of eliminating prejudices that they may harbour in respect of these peoples. To this end, efforts shall be made to ensure that history textbooks and other educational materials provide a fair, accurate and informative portrayal of the societies and cultures of these peoples.

## PART VII

## CONTACTS AND CO-OPERATION ACROSS BORDERS

*Article* 32

Governments shall take appropriate measures, including by means of international agreements, to facilitate contacts and co-operation between indigenous and tribal peoples across borders, including activities in the economic, social, cultural, spiritual and environmental fields.

# PART VIII

## ADMINISTRATION

*Article 33*

1. The governmental authority responsible for the matters covered in this Convention shall ensure that agencies or other appropriate mechanisms exist to administer the programmes affecting the peoples concerned, and shall ensure that they have the means necessary for the proper fulfilment of the functions assigned to them.

2. These programmes shall include:

    *(a)* the planning, co-ordination, execution and evaluation, in co-operation with the peoples concerned, of the measures provided for in this Convention;

    *(b)* the proposing of legislative and other measures to the competent authorities and supervision of the application of the measures taken, in co-operation with the peoples concerned.

# PART IX

## GENERAL PROVISIONS

*Article 34*

The nature and scope of the measures to be taken to give effect to this Convention shall be determined in a flexible manner, having regard to the conditions characteristic of each country.

*Article 35*

The application of the provisions of this Convention shall not adversely affect rights and benefits of the peoples concerned pursuant to other Conventions and Recommendations, international instruments, treaties, or national laws, awards, custom or agreements.

# PART X

## FINAL PROVISIONS

*Article 36*

This Convention revises the Indigenous and Tribal Populations Convention, 1957.

*Article 37*

The formal ratifications of this Convention shall be communicated to the Director-General of the International Labour Office for registration.

*Article* 38

1. This Convention shall be binding only upon those Members of the International Labour Organization whose ratifications have been registered with the Director-General.

2. It shall come into force twelve months after the date on which the ratifications of two Members have been registered with the Director-General.

3. Thereafter, this Convention shall come into force for any Member twelve months after the date on which its ratification has been registered.

*Article* 39

1. A Member which has ratified this Convention may denounce it after the expiration of ten years from the date on which the Convention first comes into force, by an act communicated to the Director-General of the International Labour Office for registration. Such denunciation shall not take effect until one year after the date on which it is registered.

2. Each Member which has ratified this Convention and which does not, within the year following the expiration of the period of ten years mentioned in the preceding paragraph, exercise the right of denunciation provided for in this Article, will be bound for another period of ten years and, thereafter, may denounce this Convention at the expiration of each period of ten years under the terms provided for in this Article.

*Article* 40

1. The Director-General of the International Labour Office shall notify all Members of the International Labour Organization of the registration of all ratifications and denunciations communicated to him by the Members of the Organization.

2. When notifying the Members of the Organization of the registration of the second ratification communicated to him, the Director-General shall draw the attention of the Members of the Organization to the date upon which the Convention will come into force.

*Article* 41

The Director-General of the International Labour Office shall communicate to the Secretary-General of the United Nations for registration in accordance with Article 102 of the Charter of the United Nations full particulars of all ratifications and acts of denunciation registered by him in accordance with the provisions of the preceding Articles.

*Article* 42

At such times as it may consider necessary the Governing Body of the International Labour Office shall present to the General Conference a report on the working of this Convention and shall examine the desirability of placing on the agenda of the Conference the question of its revision in whole or in part.

*Article* 43

1. Should the Conference adopt a new Convention revising this Convention in whole or in part, then, unless the new Convention otherwise provides:

*(a)* the ratification by a Member of the new revising Convention shall *ipso jure* involve the immediate denunciation of this Convention, notwithstanding the provisions of Article 39 above, if and when the new revising Convention shall have come into force;

*(b)* as from the date when the new revising Convention comes into force this Convention shall cease to be open to ratification by the Members.

*(b)* as from the date when the new revising Convention comes into force this Convention shall cease to be open to ratification by the Members.

2. This Convention shall in any case remain in force in its actual form and content for those Members which have ratified it but have not ratified the revising Convention.

*Article* 44

The English and French versions of the text of this Convention are equally authoritative.

## 50. DECLARATION ON FUNDAMENTAL PRINCIPLES AND RIGHTS AT WORK, 1988

This Declaration was adopted by the I.L.O. at its 86th Session in Geneva on 18 June 1998, in large measure in response to the challenges of globalization; for text see 37 ILM 1233 (1998). See also the Copenhagen Declaration on Social Development, 1995, below 869–90, in which Heads of State and Government undertook specific commitments to safeguard and promote respect for basic workers' rights; see paragraph 54(b) of the Copenhagen Declaration.

In the case of States party to the various I.L.O. conventions, the existing supervisory machinery already provides the means to assure their application. For non-parties, however, this Declaration breaks new ground, first, by recognizing that I.L.O. Members generally have an obligation to respect 'in good faith and in accordance with the Constitution, the principles concerning the fundamental rights which are the subject of those Conventions'; and secondly, as means of follow-up, by invoking the I.L.O's Constitutional procedure under which States which have not ratified the 'fundamental conventions' will be asked to report on progress made implementing the principles they contain.

*TEXT*

*Whereas* the ILO was founded in the conviction that social justice is essential to universal and lasting peace;

*Whereas* economic growth is essential but not sufficient to ensure equity, social progress and the eradication of poverty, confirming the need for the ILO to promote strong social policies, justice and democratic institutions;

*Whereas* the ILO should, now more than ever, draw upon all its standard-setting, technical cooperation and research resources in all its areas of competence, in particular employment, vocational training and working conditions, to ensure that, in the context of a global strategy for economic and social development, economic and social policies are mutually reinforcing components in order to create broad-based sustainable development;

*Whereas* the ILO should give special attention to the problems of persons with special social needs, particularly the unemployed and migrant workers, and mobilize and encourage international, regional and national efforts aimed at resolving their problems, and promote effective policies aimed at job creation;

*Whereas*, in seeking to maintain the link between social progress and economic growth, the guarantee of Fundamental Principles and Rights at Work is of particular significance in that it enables the persons concerned, to claim freely and on the basis of equality of opportunity, their fair share of the wealth which they have helped to generate, and to achieve fully their human potential;

*Whereas* the ILO is the constitutionally mandated international organization and the competent body to set and deal with international labour standards, and enjoys universal support and acknowledgement in promoting Fundamental Rights at Work as the expression of its constitutional principles;

*Whereas* it is urgent, in a situation of growing economic interdependence, to reaffirm the immutable nature of the Fundamental Principles and Rights embodied in the Constitution of the Organization and to promote their universal application;

*The International Labour Conference*

1. Recalls:

    *(a)* that in freely joining the ILO, all Members have endorsed the principles and rights set out in its Constitution and in the Declaration of Philadelphia, and have undertaken to work towards attaining the overall objectives of the Organization to the best of their resources and fully in line with their specific circumstances;

    *(b)* that these principles and rights have been expressed and developed in the form of specific rights and obligations in Conventions recognized as fundamental both inside and outside the Organization.

2. Declares that all Members, even if they have not ratified the Conventions in question, have an obligation arising from the very fact of membership in the Organization to respect, to promote and to realize, in good faith and in accordance with the Constitution, the principles concerning the fundamental rights which are the subject of those Conventions, namely:

    *(a)* freedom of association and the effective recognition of the right to collective bargaining;

    *(b)* the elimination of all forms of forced or compulsory labour;

    *(c)* the effective abolition of child labour; and

    *(d)* the elimination of discrimination in respect of employment and occupation.

3. Recognizes the obligation on the Organization to assist its Members, in response to their established and expressed needs, in order to attain these objectives by making full use of its constitutional, operational and budgetary resources, including, by the mobilization of external resources and support, as well as by encouraging other international organizations with which the ILO has established relations, pursuant to Article 12 of its Constitution, to support these efforts:

    *(a)* by offering technical cooperation and advisory services to promote the ratification and implementation of the fundamental Conventions;

    *(b)* by assisting those Members not yet in a position to ratify some or all of these Conventions in their efforts to respect, to promote and to realize the principles concerning fundamental rights which are the subject of these Conventions; and

    *(c)* by helping the Members in their efforts to create a climate for economic and social development.

4. Decides that, to give full effect to this Declaration, a promotional follow-up, which is meaningful and effective, shall be implemented in accordance with the measures specified in the annex hereto, which shall be considered as an integral part of this Declaration.

5. Stresses that labour standards should not be used for protectionist trade purposes, and that nothing in this Declaration and its follow-up shall be invoked or

otherwise used for such purposes; in addition, the comparative advantage of any country should in no way be called into question by this Declaration and its follow-up.

# ANNEX

# FOLLOW-UP TO THE DECLARATION

## I. Overall purpose

1. The aim of the follow-up described below is to encourage the efforts made by the Members of the Organization to promote the fundamental principles and rights enshrined in the Constitution of the ILO and the Declaration of Philadelphia and reaffirmed in this Declaration.

2. In line with this objective, which is of a strictly promotional nature, this follow-up will allow the identification of areas in which the assistance of the Organization through its technical cooperation activities may prove useful to its Members to help them implement these fundamental principles and rights. It is not a substitute for the established supervisory mechanisms, nor shall it impede their functioning; consequently, specific situations within the purview of those mechanisms shall not be examined or re-examined within the framework of this follow-up.

3. The two aspects of this follow-up, described below, are based on existing procedures: the annual follow-up concerning non-ratified fundamental Conventions will entail merely some adaptation of the present modalities of application of Article 19, paragraph 5(e) of the Constitution; and the global report will serve to obtain the best results from the procedures carried out pursuant to the Constitution.

## II. Annual follow-up concerning non-ratified fundamental Conventions

### A. Purpose and scope

1. The purpose is to provide an opportunity to review each year, by means of simplified procedures to replace the four-year review introduced by the Governing Body in 1995, the efforts made in accordance with the Declaration by Members which have not yet ratified all the fundamental Conventions.

2. The follow-up will cover each year the four areas of fundamental principles and rights specified in the Declaration.

### B. Modalities

1. The follow-up will be based on reports requested from Members under Article 19, paragraph 5(e) of the Constitution. The report forms will be drawn up so as to obtain information from governments which have not ratified one or more of the fundamental Conventions, on any changes which may have taken place in their law and practice, taking due account of Article 23 of the Constitution and established practice.

2. These reports, as compiled by the Office, will be reviewed by the Governing Body.

3. With a view to presenting an introduction to the reports thus compiled, drawing attention to any aspects which might call for a more in-depth discussion, the Office may call upon a group of experts appointed for this purpose by the Governing Body.

4. Adjustments to the Governing Body's existing procedures should be examined to allow Members which are not represented on the Governing Body to provide, in the most appropriate way, clarifications which might prove necessary or useful during Governing Body discussions to supplement the information contained in their reports.

III.  Global report

A.  Purpose and scope

1. The purpose of this report is to provide a dynamic global picture relating to each category of fundamental principles and rights noted during the preceding four-year period, and to serve as a basis for assessing the effectiveness of the assistance provided by the Organization, and for determining priorities for the following period, in the form of action plans for technical cooperation designed in particular to mobilize the internal and external resources necessary to carry them out.

2. The report will cover, each year, one of the four categories of fundamental principles and rights in turn.

B.  Modalities

1. The report will be drawn up under the responsibility of the Director-General on the basis of official information, or information gathered and assessed in accordance with established procedures. In the case of States which have not ratified the fundamental Conventions, it will be based in particular on the findings of the aforementioned annual follow-up. In the case of Members which have ratified the Conventions concerned, the report will be based in particular on reports as dealt with pursuant to Article 22 of the Constitution.

2. This report will be submitted to the Conference for tripartite discussion as a report of the Director-General. The Conference may deal with this report separately from reports under Article 12 of its Standing Orders, and may discuss it during a sitting devoted entirely to this report, or in any other appropriate way. It will then be for the Governing Body, at an early session, to draw conclusions from this discussion concerning the priorities and plans of action for technical cooperation to be implemented for the following four-year period.

IV.  It is understood that:

1. Proposals shall be made for amendments to the Standing Orders of the Governing Body and the Conference which are required to implement the preceding provisions.

2. The Conference shall, in due course, review the operation of this follow-up in the light of the experience acquired to assess whether it has adequately fulfilled the overall purpose articulated in Part I.

## 51. WORST FORMS OF CHILD LABOUR
## CONVENTION, 1999

The Convention concerning the Prohibition and Immediate Action for the Elimination of the Worst Forms of Child Labour (C182) was adopted on 17 June 1999 and came into force on 19 November 2000. It focuses on the prohibition and elimination of slavery, debt bondage, prostitution, pornography and other forms of abusive child labour. See also the 'Report of the Committee on Child Labour', I.L.O., Geneva, 87th Session, June 1999.

*TEXT*

*The General Conference of the International Labour Organization,*

   *Having been convened* at Geneva by the Governing Body of the International Labour Office, and having met in its 87th Session on 1 June 1999, and

   *Considering* the need to adopt new instruments for the prohibition and elimination of the worst forms of child labour, as the main priority for national and international action, including international cooperation and assistance, to complement the Convention and the Recommendation concerning Minimum Age for Admission to Employment, 1973, which remain fundamental instruments on child labour, and

   *Considering* that the effective elimination of the worst forms of child labour requires immediate and comprehensive action, taking into account the importance of free basic education and the need to remove the children concerned from all such work and to provide for their rehabilitation and social integration while addressing the needs of their families, and

   *Recalling* the resolution concerning the elimination of child labour adopted by the International Labour Conference at its 83rd Session in 1996, and

   *Recognizing* that child labour is to a great extent caused by poverty and that the long-term solution lies in sustained economic growth leading to social progress, in particular poverty alleviation and universal education, and

   *Recalling* the Convention on the Rights of the Child adopted by the United Nations General Assembly on 20 November 1989, and

   *Recalling* the ILO Declaration on Fundamental Principles and Rights at Work and its Follow-up, adopted by the International Labour Conference at its 86th Session in 1998, and

   *Recalling* that some of the worst forms of child labour are covered by other international instruments, in particular the Forced Labour Convention, 1930, and the United Nations Supplementary Convention on the Abolition of Slavery, the Slave Trade, and Institutions and Practices Similar to Slavery, 1956, and

   *Having decided* upon the adoption of certain proposals with regard to child labour, which is the fourth item on the agenda of the session, and

   *Having determined* that these proposals shall take the form of an international Convention;

   *Adopts* this seventeenth day of June of the year one thousand nine hundred and ninety-nine the following Convention, which may be cited as the Worst Forms of Child Labour Convention, 1999.

*Article* 1

Each Member which ratifies this Convention shall take immediate and effective measures to secure the prohibition and elimination of the worst forms of child labour as a matter of urgency.

*Article* 2

For the purposes of this Convention, the term 'child' shall apply to all persons under the age of 18.

*Article* 3

For the purposes of this Convention, the term 'the worst forms of child labour' comprises:

(a) all forms of slavery or practices similar to slavery, such as the sale and trafficking of children, debt bondage and serfdom and forced or compulsory labour, including forced or compulsory recruitment of children for use in armed conflict;

(b) the use, procuring or offering of a child for prostitution, for the production of pornography or for pornographic performances;

(c) the use, procuring or offering of a child for illicit activities, in particular for the production and trafficking of drugs as defined in the relevant international treaties;

(d) work which, by its nature or the circumstances in which it is carried out, is likely to harm the health, safety or morals of children.

*Article* 4

1. The types of work referred to under Article 3(d) shall be determined by national laws or regulations or by the competent authority, after consultation with the organizations of employers and workers concerned, taking into consideration relevant international standards, in particular Paragraphs 3 and 4 of the Worst Forms of Child Labour Recommendation, 1999.

2. The competent authority, after consultation with the organizations of employers and workers concerned, shall identify where the types of work so determined exist.

3. The list of the types of work determined under paragraph 1 of this Article shall be periodically examined and revised as necessary, in consultation with the organizations of employers and workers concerned.

*Article* 5

Each Member shall, after consultation with employers' and workers' organizations, establish or designate appropriate mechanisms to monitor the implementation of the provisions giving effect to this Convention.

*Article* 6

1. Each Member shall design and implement programmes of action to eliminate as a priority the worst forms of child labour.

2. Such programmes of action shall be designed and implemented in consultation with relevant government institutions and employers' and workers' organizations, taking into consideration the views of other concerned groups as appropriate.

*Article* 7

1. Each Member shall take all necessary measures to ensure the effective implementation and enforcement of the provisions giving effect to this Convention including the provision and application of penal sanctions or, as appropriate, other sanctions.

2. Each Member shall, taking into account the importance of education in eliminating child labour, take effective and time-bound measures to:

   *(a)*  prevent the engagement of children in the worst forms of child labour;

   *(b)*  provide the necessary and appropriate direct assistance for the removal of children from the worst forms of child labour and for their rehabilitation and social integration;

   *(c)*  ensure access to free basic education, and, wherever possible and appropriate, vocational training, for all children removed from the worst forms of child labour;

   *(d)*  identify and reach out to children at special risk; and

   *(e)*  take account of the special situation of girls.

3. Each Member shall designate the competent authority responsible for the implementation of the provisions giving effect to this Convention.

*Article* 8

Members shall take appropriate steps to assist one another in giving effect to the provisions of this Convention through enhanced international cooperation and/or assistance including support for social and economic development, poverty eradication programmes and universal education.

*Article* 9

The formal ratifications of this Convention shall be communicated to the Director-General of the International Labour Office for registration.

*Article* 10

1. This Convention shall be binding only upon those Members of the International Labour Organization whose ratifications have been registered with the Director-General of the International Labour Office.

2. It shall come into force 12 months after the date on which the ratifications of two Members have been registered with the Director-General.

3. Thereafter, this Convention shall come into force for any Member 12 months after the date on which its ratification has been registered.

*Article* 11

1. A Member which has ratified this Convention may denounce it after the expiration of ten years from the date on which the Convention first comes into force, by an act communicated to the Director-General of the International Labour Office

for registration. Such denunciation shall not take effect until one year after the date on which it is registered.

2. Each Member which has ratified this Convention and which does not, within the year following the expiration of the period of ten years mentioned in the preceding paragraph, exercise the right of denunciation provided for in this Article, will be bound for another period of ten years and, thereafter, may denounce this Convention at the expiration of each period of ten years under the terms provided for in this Article.

*Article* 12

1. The Director-General of the International Labour Office shall notify all Members of the International Labour Organization of the registration of all ratifications and acts of denunciation communicated by the Members of the Organization.

2. When notifying the Members of the Organization of the registration of the second ratification, the Director-General shall draw the attention of the Members of the Organization to the date upon which the Convention shall come into force.

*Article* 13

The Director-General of the International Labour Office shall communicate to the Secretary-General of the United Nations, for registration in accordance with article 102 of the Charter of the United Nations, full particulars of all ratifications and acts of denunciation registered by the Director-General in accordance with the provisions of the preceding Articles.

*Article* 14

At such times as it may consider necessary, the Governing Body of the International Labour Office shall present to the General Conference a report on the working of this Convention and shall examine the desirability of placing on the agenda of the Conference the question of its revision in whole or in part.

*Article* 15

1. Should the Conference adopt a new Convention revising this Convention in whole or in part, then, unless the new Convention otherwise provides:

   (a) the ratification by a Member of the new revising Convention shall ipso jure involve the immediate denunciation of this Convention, notwithstanding the provisions of Article 11 above, if and when the new revising Convention shall have come into force;

   (b) as from the date when the new revising Convention comes into force, this Convention shall cease to be open to ratification by the Members.

2. This Convention shall in any case remain in force in its actual form and content for those Members which have ratified it but have not ratified the revising Convention.

*Article* 16

The English and French versions of the text of this Convention are equally authoritative.

PART FOUR

# CONTRIBUTION OF THE UNITED NATIONS EDUCATIONAL, SCIENTIFIC, AND CULTURAL ORGANIZATION

## INTRODUCTION

UNESCO is a Specialized Agency associated with the United Nations. Several aspects of its work concern human rights, in particular, problems of illiteracy in many countries and the production and dissemination of studies which combat racial prejudice.

See, further, Symonides, J., *Human Rights: Concepts and Standards* (UNESCO, 2000); Humphrey J., *No Distant Millennium: The International Law of Human Rights* (UNESCO, 1989).

In 1978 the Executive Board of UNESCO adopted the procedure for examining communications concerning violations of human rights in relation to education, science, culture and information: see further Robertson, A. H., & Merrills, J. G. (eds), *Human Rights in the World* (4th edn., 1996), 288–92; Marks, S. P., 'The Complaint Procedure of the United Nations Educational, Scientific and Cultural Organization', in Hannum, H. (ed.), *Guide to International Human Rights Practice.* (3rd edn., 1999), 86–97.

See also below, 810–16, the Universal Declaration on the Human Genome and Human Rights, adopted by the UNESCO General Conference in 1997.

## 52. CONVENTION AGAINST DISCRIMINATION IN EDUCATION, 1960

Adopted by the UNESCO General Conference at its eleventh session in Paris on 14 December 1960, this Convention can be compared with the I.L.O. Convention concerning discrimination in respect of employment and occupation, above, 337–40. The United Nations Sub-Commission on Prevention of Discrimination and Protection of Minorities initiated a study of discrimination in education, and in due course it was decided to ask UNESCO to consider the possibility of drafting and adopting a convention on the subject. The General Conference of UNESCO duly adopted the Convention, which entered into force on 22 May 1962.

For the text in various languages, see 429 UNTS 93; UK Treaty Series, No. 44 (1962), Cmnd. 1760. See also the Protocol instituting a Conciliation and Good Offices Commission to be responsible for seeking the Settlement of any Disputes which may arise between States parties to the Convention against Discrimination in Education, adopted in Paris, 10 December 1962: UK Treaty Series No. 23 (1969), Cmnd. 3894. The Protocol entered into force on 24 October 1968.

*TEXT*

*The General Conference of the United Nations Educational, Scientific and Cultural Organization, meeting in Paris from 14 November to 15 December 1960, at its eleventh session,*

*Recalling* that the Universal Declaration of Human Rights asserts the principle of non-discrimination and proclaims that every person has the right to education,

*Considering* that discrimination in education is a violation of rights enunciated in that Declaration,

*Considering* that, under the terms of its Constitution, the United Nations Educational, Scientific and Cultural Organization has the purpose of instituting collaboration among the nations with a view to furthering for all universal respect for human rights and equality of educational opportunity,

*Recognizing* that, consequently, the United Nations Educational, Scientific and Cultural Organization, while respecting the diversity of national educational systems, has the duty not only to proscribe any form of discrimination in education but also to promote equality of opportunity and treatment for all in education,

*Having before it* proposals concerning the different aspects of discrimination in education, constituting item 17.1.4 of the agenda of the session,

*Having decided* at its tenth session that this question should be made the subject of an international convention as well as of recommendations to Member States,

*Adopts* this Convention on the fourteenth day of December 1960.

*Article* 1

1. For the purposes of this Convention, the term 'discrimination' includes any distinction, exclusion, limitation or preference which, being based on race, colour, sex, language, religion, political or other opinion, national or social origin,

economic condition or birth, has the purpose or effect of nullifying or impairing equality of treatment in education and in particular:

    *(a)* Of depriving any person or group of persons of access to education of any type or at any level;

    *(b)* Of limiting any person or group of persons to education of an inferior standard;

    *(c)* Subject to the provisions of Article 2 of this Convention, of establishing or maintaining separate educational systems or institutions for persons or groups of persons; or

    *(d)* Of inflicting on any person or group of persons conditions which are incompatible with the dignity of man.

2. For the purposes of this Convention, the term 'education' refers to all types and levels of education, and includes access to education, the standard and quality of education, and the conditions under which it is given.

*Article* 2

When permitted in a State, the following situations shall not be deemed to constitute discrimination, within the meaning of Article 1 of this Convention:

    *(a)* The establishment or maintenance of separate educational systems or institutions for pupils of the two sexes, if these systems or institutions offer equivalent access to education, provide a teaching staff with qualifications of the same standard as well as school premises and equipment of the same quality, and afford the opportunity to take the same or equivalent courses of study;

    *(b)* The establishment or maintenance, for religious or linguistic reasons, of separate educational systems or institutions offering an education which is in keeping with the wishes of the pupil's parents or legal guardians, if participation in such systems or attendance at such institutions is optional and if the education provided conforms to such standards as may be laid down or approved by the competent authorities, in particular for education of the same level;

    *(c)* The establishment or maintenance of private educational institutions, if the object of the institutions is not to secure the exclusion of any group but to provide educational facilities in addition to those provided by the public authorities, if the institutions are conducted in accordance with that object, and if the education provided conforms with such standards as may be laid down or approved by the competent authorities, in particular for education of the same level.

*Article* 3

In order to eliminate and prevent discrimination within the meaning of this Convention, the States Parties thereto undertake:

    *(a)* To abrogate any statutory provisions and any administrative instructions and to discontinue any administrative practices which involve discrimination in education;

(b)  To ensure, by legislation where necessary, that there is no discrimination in the admission of pupils to educational institutions;

(c)  Not to allow any differences of treatment by the public authorities between nationals, except on the basis of merit or need, in the matter of school fees and the grant of scholarships or other forms of assistance to pupils and necessary permits and facilities for the pursuit of studies in foreign countries;

(d)  Not to allow, in any form of assistance granted by the public authorities to educational institutions, any restrictions or preference based solely on the ground that pupils belong to a particular group;

(e)  To give foreign nationals resident within their territory the same access to education as that given to their own nationals.

*Article* 4

The States Parties to this Convention undertake furthermore to formulate, develop and apply a national policy which, by methods appropriate to the circumstances and to national usage, will tend to promote equality of opportunity and of treatment in the matter of education and in particular:

(a)  To make primary education free and compulsory; make secondary education in its different forms generally available and accessible to all; make higher education equally accessible to all on the basis of individual capacity; assure compliance by all with the obligation to attend school prescribed by law;

(b)  To ensure that the standards of education are equivalent in all public educational institutions of the same level, and that the conditions relating to the quality of the education provided are also equivalent;

(c)  To encourage and intensify by appropriate methods the education of persons who have not received any primary education or who have not completed the entire primary education course and the continuation of their education on the basis of individual capacity;

(d)  To provide training for the teaching profession without discrimination.

*Article* 5

1.  The States Parties to this Convention agree that:

(a)  Education shall be directed to the full development of the human personality and to the strengthening of respect for human rights and fundamental freedoms; it shall promote understanding, tolerance and friendship among all nations, racial or religious groups, and shall further the activities of the United Nations for the maintenance of peace;

(b)  It is essential to respect the liberty of parents and, where applicable, of legal guardians, firstly to choose for their children institutions other than those maintained by the public authorities but conforming to such minimum educational standards as may be laid down or approved by the competent authorities and, secondly, to ensure in a manner consistent with the procedures followed in the State for the application of its legislation, the religious and moral education of the children in conformity with their own convictions; and no person or group of persons should be compelled to receive religious instruction inconsistent with his or their convictions;

(c) It is essential to recognize the right of members of national minorities to carry on their own educational activities, including the maintenance of schools and, depending on the educational policy of each State, the use or the teaching of their own language, provided however:

   (i)   That this right is not exercised in a manner which prevents the members of these minorities from understanding the culture and language of the community as a whole and from participating in its activities, or which prejudices national sovereignty;

   (ii)  That the standard of education is not lower than the general standard laid down or approved by the competent authorities; and

   (iii) That attendance at such schools is optional.

2. The States Parties to this Convention undertake to take all necessary measures to ensure the application of the principles enunciated in paragraph 1 of this Article.

*Article* 6

In the application of this Convention, the States Parties to it undertake to pay the greatest attention to any recommendations hereafter adopted by the General Conference of the United Nations Educational, Scientific and Cultural Organization defining the measures to be taken against the different forms of discrimination in education and for the purpose of ensuring equality of opportunity and treatment in education.

*Article* 7

The States Parties to this Convention shall in their periodic reports submitted to the General Conference of the United Nations Educational, Scientific and Cultural Organization on dates and in a manner to be determined by it, give information on the legislative and administrative provisions which they have adopted and other action which they have taken for the application of this Convention, including that taken for the formulation and the development of the national policy defined in Article 4 as well as the results achieved and the obstacles encountered in the application of that policy.

*Article* 8

Any dispute which may arise between any two or more States Parties to this Convention concerning the interpretation or application of this Convention, which is not settled by negotiation shall at the request of the parties to the dispute be referred, failing other means of settling the dispute, to the International Court of Justice for decision.

*Article* 9

Reservations to this Convention shall not be permitted.

*Article* 10

This Convention shall not have the effect of diminishing the rights which individuals or groups may enjoy by virtue of agreements concluded between two or more States, where such rights are not contrary to the letter or spirit of this Convention.

*Article* 11

This Convention is drawn up in English, French, Russian and Spanish, the four texts being equally authoritative.

*Article* 12

1. This Convention shall be subject to ratification or acceptance by States Members of the United Nations Educational, Scientific and Cultural Organization in accordance with their respective constitutional procedures.

2. The instruments of ratification or acceptance shall be deposited with the Director-General of the United Nations Educational, Scientific and Cultural Organization.

*Article* 13

1. This Convention shall be open to accession by all States not Members of the United Nations Educational, Scientific and Cultural Organization which are invited to do so by the Executive Board of the Organization.

2. Accession shall be effected by the deposit of an instrument of accession with the Director-General of the United Nations Educational, Scientific and Cultural Organization.

*Article* 14

This Convention shall enter into force three months after the date of the deposit of the third instrument of ratification, acceptance or accession, but only with respect to those States which have deposited their respective instruments on or before that date. It shall enter into force with respect to any other State three months after the deposit of its instrument of ratification, acceptance or accession.

*Article* 15

The States Parties to this Convention recognize that the Convention is applicable not only to their metropolitan territory but also to all non-self-governing, trust, colonial and other territories for the international relations of which they are responsible; they undertake to consult, if necessary, the governments or other competent authorities of these territories on or before ratification, acceptance or accession with a view to securing the application of the Convention to those territories, and to notify the Director-General of the United Nations Educational, Scientific and Cultural Organization of the territories to which it is accordingly applied, the notification to take effect three months after the date of its receipt.

*Article* 16

1. Each State Party to this Convention may denounce the Convention on its own behalf or on behalf of any territory for whose international relations it is responsible.

2. The denunciation shall be notified by an instrument in writing, deposited with

the Director-General of the United Nations Educational, Scientific and Cultural Organization.

3. The denunciation shall take effect twelve months after the receipt of the instrument of denunciation.

*Article* 17

The Director-General of the United Nations Educational, Scientific and Cultural Organization shall inform the States Members of the Organization, the States not members of the Organization which are referred to in Article 13, as well as the United Nations, of the deposit of all the instruments of ratification, acceptance and accession provided for in Articles 12 and 13, and of the notifications and denunciations provided for in Articles 15 and 16 respectively.

*Article* 18

1. This Convention may be revised by the General Conference of the United Nations Educational, Scientific and Cultural Organization. Any such revision shall, however, bind only the States which shall become Parties to the revising convention.

2. If the General Conference should adopt a new convention revising this Convention in whole or in part, then, unless the new convention otherwise provides, this Convention shall cease to be open to ratification, acceptance or accession as from the date on which the new revising convention enters into force.

*Article* 19

In conformity with Article 102 of the Charter of the United Nations, this Convention shall be registered with the Secretariat of the United Nations at the request of the Director-General of the United Nations Educational, Scientific and Cultural Organization.

## 53. DECLARATION OF THE PRINCIPLES OF INTERNATIONAL CULTURAL CO-OPERATION, 1966

Proclaimed by the General Conference of the United Nations Educational, Scientific and Cultural Organization at its fourteenth session on 4 November 1966.

### TEXT

The General Conference of the United Nations Educational, Scientific and Cultural Organization, met in Paris for its fourteenth session, this fourth day of November 1966, being the twentieth anniversary of the foundation of the Organization,

*Recalling* that the Constitution of the Organization declares that 'since wars begin in the minds of men, it is in the minds of men that the defences of peace must be constructed' and that the peace must be founded, if it is not to fail, upon the intellectual and moral solidarity of mankind,

*Recalling* that the Constitution also states that the wide diffusion of culture and the education of humanity for justice and liberty and peace are indispensable to the dignity of man and constitute a sacred duty which all the nations must fulfil in a spirit of mutual assistance and concern,

*Considering* that the Organization's Member States, believing in the pursuit of truth and the free exchange of ideas and knowledge, have agreed and determined to develop and to increase the means of communication between their peoples,

*Considering* that, despite the technical advances which facilitate the development and dissemination of knowledge and ideas, ignorance of the way of life and customs of peoples still presents an obstacle to friendship among the nations, to peaceful co-operation and to the progress of mankind,

*Taking account* of the Universal Declaration of Human Rights, the Declaration of the Rights of the Child, the Declaration on the Granting of Independence to Colonial Countries and Peoples, the United Nations Declaration on the Elimination of All Forms of Racial Discrimination, the Declaration on the Promotion among Youth of the Ideals of Peace, Mutual Respect and Understanding between Peoples, and the Declaration on the Inadmissibility of Intervention in the Domestic Affairs of States and the Protection of their Independence and Sovereignty, proclaimed successively by the General Assembly of the United Nations,

*Convinced* by the experience of the Organization's first twenty years that, if international cultural co-operation is to be strengthened, its principles require to be affirmed,

*Proclaims* this Declaration of the principles of international cultural co-operation, to the end that governments, authorities, organizations, associations and institutions responsible for cultural activities may constantly be guided by these principles; and for the purpose, as set out in the Constitution of the Organization, of advancing, through the educational, scientific and cultural relations of the peoples of the world, the objectives of peace and welfare that are defined in the Charter of the United Nations:

*Article* 1

1. Each culture has a dignity and value which must be respected and preserved.

2. Every people has the right and the duty to develop its culture.

3. In their rich variety and diversity, and in the reciprocal influences they exert on one another, all cultures form part of the common heritage belonging to all mankind.

*Article* 2

Nations shall endeavour to develop the various branches of culture side by side and, as far as possible, simultaneously, so as to establish a harmonious balance between technical progress and the intellectual and moral advancement of mankind.

*Article* 3

International cultural co-operation shall cover all aspects of intellectual and creative activities relating to education, science and culture.

*Article* 4

The aims of international cultural co-operation in its various forms, bilateral or multilateral, regional or universal, shall be:

  (1)  To spread knowledge, to stimulate talent and to enrich cultures;

  (2)  To develop peaceful relations and friendship among the peoples and bring about a better understanding of each other's way of life;

  (3)  To contribute to the application of the principles set out in the United Nations Declarations that are recalled in the Preamble to this Declaration;

  (4)  To enable everyone to have access to knowledge, to enjoy the arts and literature of all peoples, to share in advances made in science in all parts of the world and in the resulting benefits, and to contribute to the enrichment of cultural life;

  (5)  To raise the level of the spiritual and material life of man in all parts of the world.

*Article* 5

Cultural co-operation is a right and a duty for all peoples and all nations, which should share with one another their knowledge and skills.

*Article* 6

International co-operation, while promoting the enrichment of all cultures through its beneficent action, shall respect the distinctive character of each.

*Article* 7

1. Broad dissemination of ideas and knowledge, based on the freest exchange and

discussion, is essential to creative activity, the pursuit of truth and the development of the personality.

2. In cultural co-operation, stress shall be laid on ideas and values conducive to the creation of a climate of friendship and peace. Any mark of hostility in attitudes and in expression of opinion shall be avoided. Every effort shall be made, in presenting and disseminating information, to ensure its authenticity.

*Article* 8

Cultural co-operation shall be carried on for the mutual benefit of all the nations practising it. Exchanges to which it gives rise shall be arranged in a spirit of broad reciprocity.

*Article* 9

Cultural co-operation shall contribute to the establishment of stable, long-term relations between peoples, which should be subjected as little as possible to the strains which may arise in international life.

*Article* 10

Cultural co-operation shall be specially concerned with the moral and intellectual education of young people in a spirit of friendship, international understanding and peace and shall foster awareness among States of the need to stimulate talent and promote the training of the rising generations in the most varied sectors.

*Article* 11

1. In their cultural relations, States shall bear in mind the principles of the United Nations. In seeking to achieve international co-operation, they shall respect the sovereign equality of States and shall refrain from intervention in matters which are essentially within the domestic jurisdiction of any State.

2. The principles of this Declaration shall be applied with due regard for human rights and fundamental freedoms.

# PART FIVE

# EUROPEAN INSTITUTIONS
# AND CONVENTIONS

---

## INTRODUCTION

THE instruments in this Part derive, among others, from the work of the Council of Europe, an organization created in 1949 as a sort of social and ideological counterpart to the military aspects of European co-operation represented in the North Atlantic Treaty Organization. The Council of Europe was inspired partly by interest in the promotion of European unity, and partly by the political desire for solidarity in the face of the ideology of Communism.

The membership of the Council of Europe has expanded considerably; the original ten signatories of the Statute of the Council of Europe were Belgium, Denmark, France, Ireland, Italy, Luxembourg, the Netherlands, Norway, Sweden, and the United Kingdom, later joined by Greece, Turkey, Iceland, the Federal Republic of Germany, Austria, Cyprus, Switzerland, Malta, Portugal, Spain, Liechtenstein, San Marino, and Finland. Following the end of the Cold War, the membership has further grown to forty-three States (at 31 January 2002), with two other European States (Bosnia and Herzegovina and the Federal Republic of Yugoslavia) as 'special guests' to the Parliamentary Assembly.

The promotion of human rights has also figured prominently in the work of the Conference on (later the 'Organization for') Security and Co-operation in Europe (CSCE/OSCE), which emerged after 1975. On a more limited regional level, and after many years of debate, the Member States of the European Union adopted a Charter of Fundamental Rights in December 2000; it remains to be seen to what extent this will serve to introduce human rights thinking into the economic, social and political work of the Community.

## 54. THE EUROPEAN CONVENTION FOR THE PROTECTION OF HUMAN RIGHTS AND FUNDAMENTAL FREEDOMS, 1950, TOGETHER WITH PROTOCOLS NOS. 1, 4, 6 AND 7, AS AMENDED BY PROTOCOL NO. 11

The European Convention was the first essay in giving specific legal content to human rights in an international agreement, and combining this with the establishment of machinery for supervision and enforcement. It was signed in Rome on 4 November 1950 and entered into force on 3 September 1953. for the text, see ETS No. 5. A central feature of this regime is the right of individual and inter-State petition, and at the request of the Committee of Ministers, the European Court of Human Rights may also give advisory opinions on the interpretation of the Convention and the Protocols. However, the role of the Court (and of the European Commission and Court in the arrangements preceding the entry into force of Protocol No. 11 in 1998) and the Committee of Ministers is that of review, and not that of an appeal court from the decisions of national tribunals. Their task is to ensure that the standards of the Convention and its Protocols are observed by the administrations of the States concerned. The work of these institutions has had important consequences: valuable material has been provided for the elaboration of the provisions on civil liberties; and anomalies have been exposed in national systems of law, often with the result that the relevant national legislation has been changed for the better. Several individual cases have also served effectively as test cases, and/or have raised issues affecting a whole class of persons, for example, a linguistic minority.

Following the entry into force of Protocol No. 11 (ETS No. 155) on 1 November 1998, the control machinery was substantially restructured. All alleged violations of human rights are referred directly to the Court. In most cases, the Court sits in Chambers of seven judges. It decides on the admissibility and merits of applications and, if necessary, undertakes an investigation. The Court will also make itself available to the parties with a view to securing a friendly settlement on the basis of human rights as defined in the Convention and Protocols.

Over the years, the Convention was supplemented and/or amended by some eleven Protocols, many of which have now been effectively superseded following the entry into force of Protocol No. 11 on 1 November 1998. Of the four remaining Protocols, the first entered into force on 18 May 1954; the fourth on 2 May 1968; the sixth on 1 March 1985; and the seventh on 1 November 1988. A twelfth Protocol (on non-discrimination) has been opened for signature but is not yet in force. The texts of the Protocols follow that of the principal Convention below.

See generally Harris, D., O'Boyle, K. & Warbrick, C. *The Law of the European Convention on Human Rights* (1995); van Dijk, P., van Hoof, G. J. H., & Heringa, A. W., *Theory and Practice of the European Convention on Human Rights*, (3rd edn., 1998); Janis, M., Kay, R., & Bradley, A. *European Human Rights Law*, (2nd edn., 2000); Gomien, D., Harris, D. & Zwaak, L., *Law and Practice of the European Convention on Human Rights and the European Social Charter* (1996); Jacobs, F., & White, R. C. A., *The European Convention on Human Rights* (2nd edn., 1996); Fawcett, J. E. S., *The Application of the European Convention on Human Rights* (2nd edn., 1987); Higgins, R., 'The European Convention on Human Rights', in Meron, T., (ed.), *Human Rights in International Law* (1984), ii, 495–549.

The text of the Convention was amended by Protocol No. 3 (ETS No. 45), which entered into force on 21 September 1970, Protocol No. 5 (ETS No. 55), which entered into force on 20 December 1971, and Protocol No. 8 (ETS No. 118), which entered into force on 1 January 1990. It also comprised the text of Protocol No. 2 (ETS No. 44) which, in accordance with

Article 5, paragraph 3 thereof, had been an integral part of the Convention since its entry into force on 21 September 1970. All those provisions which had been amended or added by the above Protocols are now replaced by Protocol No. 11. As from its entry into force on 1 November 1998, Protocol No. 9 (ETS No. 140), which entered into force on 1 October 1994, is repealed, and Protocol No. 10 (ETS No. 146) has lost its purpose.

The text below reflects these changes. Protocol 11 added the headings to articles 1–18 and 52–59, added Section II, renumbered Section III, and amended the text of Articles 56(1), 56(2), and 58(4). It also added the headings of articles and amended the text of Protocol No. 1 (ETS No. 9), Protocol No. 4 (ETS No. 46), Protocol No. 6 (ETS No. 114), and Protocol No. 7 (ETS No. 117).

## TEXT

The Governments signatory hereto, being members of the Council of Europe,

*Considering* the Universal Declaration of Human Rights proclaimed by the General Assembly of the United Nations on 10th December 1948;

*Considering* that this Declaration aims at securing the universal and effective recognition and observance of the Rights therein declared;

*Considering* that the aim of the Council of Europe is the achievement of greater unity between its members and that one of the methods by which that aim is to be pursued is the maintenance and further realization of human rights and fundamental freedoms;

*Reaffirming* their profound belief in those fundamental freedoms which are the foundation of justice and peace in the world and are best maintained on the one hand by an effective political democracy and on the other by a common understanding and observance of the human rights upon which they depend;

*Being resolved*, as the governments of European countries which are like-minded and have a common heritage of political traditions, ideals, freedom and the rule of law, to take the first steps for the collective enforcement of certain of the rights stated in the Universal Declaration,

*Have agreed* as follows:

### Article 1—*Obligation to respect human rights*

The High Contracting Parties shall secure to everyone within their jurisdiction the rights and freedoms defined in Section I of this Convention.

## SECTION I—RIGHTS AND FREEDOMS

### Article 2—*Right to life*

1. Everyone's right to life shall be protected by law. No one shall be deprived of his life intentionally save in the execution of a sentence of a court following his conviction of a crime for which this penalty is provided by law.

2. Deprivation of life shall not be regarded as inflicted in contravention of this article when it results from the use of force which is no more than absolutely necessary:

(a) in defence of any person from unlawful violence;

(b) in order to effect a lawful arrest or to prevent the escape of a person lawfully detained;

(c) in action lawfully taken for the purpose of quelling a riot or insurrection.

### Article 3—Prohibition of torture

No one shall be subjected to torture or to inhuman or degrading treatment or punishment.

### Article 4—Prohibition of slavery and forced labour

1. No one shall be held in slavery or servitude.

2. No one shall be required to perform forced or compulsory labour.

3. For the purpose of this article the term 'forced or compulsory labour' shall not include:

(a) any work required to be done in the ordinary course of detention imposed according to the provisions of Article 5 of this Convention or during conditional release from such detention;

(b) any service of a military character or, in case of conscientious objectors in countries where they are recognized, service exacted instead of compulsory military service;

(c) any service exacted in case of an emergency or calamity threatening the life or well-being of the community;

(d) any work or service which forms part of normal civic obligations.

### Article 5—Right to liberty and security

1. Everyone has the right to liberty and security of person. No one shall be deprived of his liberty save in the following cases and in accordance with a procedure prescribed by law:

(a) the lawful detention of a person after conviction by a competent court;

(b) the lawful arrest or detention of a person for non-compliance with the lawful order of a court or in order to secure the fulfilment of any obligation prescribed by law;

(c) the lawful arrest or detention of a person effected for the purpose of bringing him before the competent legal authority on reasonable suspicion of having committed an offence or when it is reasonably considered necessary to prevent his committing an offence or fleeing after having done so;

(d) the detention of a minor by lawful order for the purpose of educational supervision or his lawful detention for the purpose of bringing him before the competent legal authority;

(e) the lawful detention of persons for the prevention of the spreading of infectious diseases, of persons of unsound mind, alcoholics or drug addicts or vagrants;

(f) the lawful arrest or detention of a person to prevent his effecting an unauthorized entry into the country or of a person against whom action is being taken with a view to deportation or extradition.

2. Everyone who is arrested shall be informed promptly, in a language which he understands, of the reasons for his arrest and of any charge against him.

3. Everyone arrested or detained in accordance with the provisions of paragraph 1.c of this article shall be brought promptly before a judge or other officer authorized by law to exercise judicial power and shall be entitled to trial within a reasonable time or to release pending trial. Release may be conditioned by guarantees to appear for trial.

4. Everyone who is deprived of his liberty by arrest or detention shall be entitled to take proceedings by which the lawfulness of his detention shall be decided speedily by a court and his release ordered if the detention is not lawful.

5. Everyone who has been the victim of arrest or detention in contravention of the provisions of this article shall have an enforceable right to compensation.

*Article 6—Right to a fair trial*

1. In the determination of his civil rights and obligations or of any criminal charge against him, everyone is entitled to a fair and public hearing within a reasonable time by an independent and impartial tribunal established by law. Judgment shall be pronounced publicly but the press and public may be excluded from all or part of the trial in the interests of morals, public order or national security in a democratic society, where the interests of juveniles or the protection of the private life of the parties so require, or to the extent strictly necessary in the opinion of the court in special circumstances where publicity would prejudice the interests of justice.

2. Everyone charged with a criminal offence shall be presumed innocent until proved guilty according to law.

3. Everyone charged with a criminal offence has the following minimum rights:

- *(a)* to be informed promptly, in a language which he understands and in detail, of the nature and cause of the accusation against him;
- *(b)* to have adequate time and facilities for the preparation of his defence;
- *(c)* to defend himself in person or through legal assistance of his own choosing or, if he has not sufficient means to pay for legal assistance, to be given it free when the interests of justice so require;
- *(d)* to examine or have examined witnesses against him and to obtain the attendance and examination of witnesses on his behalf under the same conditions as witnesses against him;
- *(e)* to have the free assistance of an interpreter if he cannot understand or speak the language used in court.

*Article 7—No punishment without law*

1. No one shall be held guilty of any criminal offence on account of any act or omission which did not constitute a criminal offence under national or international law at the time when it was committed. Nor shall a heavier penalty be imposed than the one that was applicable at the time the criminal offence was committed.

2. This article shall not prejudice the trial and punishment of any person for any act or omission which, at the time when it was committed, was criminal according to the general principles of law recognized by civilised nations.

*Article 8—Right to respect for private and family life*

1. Everyone has the right to respect for his private and family life, his home and his correspondence.

2. There shall be no interference by a public authority with the exercise of this right except such as is in accordance with the law and is necessary in a democratic society in the interests of national security, public safety or the economic well-being of the country, for the prevention of disorder or crime, for the protection of health or morals, or for the protection of the rights and freedoms of others.

*Article 9—Freedom of thought, conscience and religion*

1. Everyone has the right to freedom of thought, conscience and religion; this right includes freedom to change his religion or belief and freedom, either alone or in community with others and in public or private, to manifest his religion or belief, in worship, teaching, practice and observance.

2. Freedom to manifest one's religion or beliefs shall be subject only to such limitations as are prescribed by law and are necessary in a democratic society in the interests of public safety, for the protection of public order, health or morals, or for the protection of the rights and freedoms of others.

*Article 10—Freedom of expression*

1. Everyone has the right to freedom of expression. This right shall include freedom to hold opinions and to receive and impart information and ideas without interference by public authority and regardless of frontiers. This article shall not prevent States from requiring the licensing of broadcasting, television or cinema enterprises.

2. The exercise of these freedoms, since it carries with it duties and responsibilities, may be subject to such formalities, conditions, restrictions or penalties as are prescribed by law and are necessary in a democratic society, in the interests of national security, territorial integrity or public safety, for the prevention of disorder or crime, for the protection of health or morals, for the protection of the reputation or rights of others, for preventing the disclosure of information received in confidence, or for maintaining the authority and impartiality of the judiciary.

*Article 11—Freedom of assembly and association*

1. Everyone has the right to freedom of peaceful assembly and to freedom of association with others, including the right to form and to join trade unions for the protection of his interests.

2. No restrictions shall be placed on the exercise of these rights other than such as are prescribed by law and are necessary in a democratic society in the interests of national security or public safety, for the prevention of disorder or crime, for the protection of health or morals or for the protection of the rights and freedoms of others. This article shall not prevent the imposition of lawful restrictions on the exercise of these rights by members of the armed forces, of the police or of the administration of the State.

*Article* 12—*Right to marry*

Men and women of marriageable age have the right to marry and to found a family, according to the national laws governing the exercise of this right.

*Article* 13—*Right to an effective remedy*

Everyone whose rights and freedoms as set forth in this Convention are violated shall have an effective remedy before a national authority notwithstanding that the violation has been committed by persons acting in an official capacity.

*Article* 14—*Prohibition of discrimination*

The enjoyment of the rights and freedoms set forth in this Convention shall be secured without discrimination on any ground such as sex, race, colour, language, religion, political or other opinion, national or social origin, association with a national minority, property, birth or other status.

*Article* 15—*Derogation in time of emergency*

1. In time of war or other public emergency threatening the life of the nation any High Contracting Party may take measures derogating from its obligations under this Convention to the extent strictly required by the exigencies of the situation, provided that such measures are not inconsistent with its other obligations under international law.

2. No derogation from Article 2, except in respect of deaths resulting from lawful acts of war, or from Articles 3, 4 (paragraph 1) and 7 shall be made under this provision.

3. Any High Contracting Party availing itself of this right of derogation shall keep the Secretary General of the Council of Europe fully informed of the measures which it has taken and the reasons therefor. It shall also inform the Secretary General of the Council of Europe when such measures have ceased to operate and the provisions of the Convention are again being fully executed.

*Article* 16—*Restrictions on political activity of aliens*

Nothing in Articles 10, 11 and 14 shall be regarded as preventing the High Contracting Parties from imposing restrictions on the political activity of aliens.

*Article* 17—*Prohibition of abuse of rights*

Nothing in this Convention may be interpreted as implying for any State, group or person any right to engage in any activity or perform any act aimed at the destruction of any of the rights and freedoms set forth herein or at their limitation to a greater extent than is provided for in the Convention.

*Article* 18—*Limitation on use of restrictions on rights*

The restrictions permitted under this Convention to the said rights and freedoms shall not be applied for any purpose other than those for which they have been prescribed.

## SECTION II—EUROPEAN COURT OF HUMAN RIGHTS

*Article 19—Establishment of the Court*

To ensure the observance of the engagements undertaken by the High Contracting Parties in the Convention and the Protocols thereto, there shall be set up a European Court of Human Rights, hereinafter referred to as 'the Court'. It shall function on a permanent basis.

*Article 20—Number of judges*

The Court shall consist of a number of judges equal to that of the High Contracting Parties.

*Article 21—Criteria for office*

1. The judges shall be of high moral character and must either possess the qualifications required for appointment to high judicial office or be jurisconsults of recognised competence.

2. The judges shall sit on the Court in their individual capacity.

3. During their term of office the judges shall not engage in any activity which is incompatible with their independence, impartiality or with the demands of a full-time office; all questions arising from the application of this paragraph shall be decided by the Court.

*Article 22—Election of judges*

1. The judges shall be elected by the Parliamentary Assembly with respect to each High Contracting Party by a majority of votes cast from a list of three candidates nominated by the High Contracting Party.

2. The same procedure shall be followed to complete the Court in the event of the accession of new High Contracting Parties and in filling casual vacancies.

*Article 23—Terms of office*

1. The judges shall be elected for a period of six years. They may be re-elected. However, the terms of office of one-half of the judges elected at the first election shall expire at the end of three years.

2. The judges whose terms of office are to expire at the end of the initial period of three years shall be chosen by lot by the Secretary General of the Council of Europe immediately after their election.

3. In order to ensure that, as far as possible, the terms of office of one-half of the judges are renewed every three years, the Parliamentary Assembly may decide, before proceeding to any subsequent election, that the term or terms of office of one or more judges to be elected shall be for a period other than six years but not more than nine and not less than three years.

4. In cases where more than one term of office is involved and where the Parliamentary Assembly applies the preceding paragraph, the allocation of the terms of office shall be effected by a drawing of lots by the Secretary General of the Council of Europe immediately after the election.

5. A judge elected to replace a judge whose term of office has not expired shall hold office for the remainder of his predecessor's term.

6. The terms of office of judges shall expire when they reach the age of 70.

7. The judges shall hold office until replaced. They shall, however, continue to deal with such cases as they already have under consideration.

### Article 24—Dismissal

No judge may be dismissed from his office unless the other judges decide by a majority of two-thirds that he has ceased to fulfil the required conditions.

### Article 25—Registry and legal secretaries

The Court shall have a registry, the functions and organization of which shall be laid down in the rules of the Court. The Court shall be assisted by legal secretaries.

### Article 26—Plenary Court

The plenary Court shall

(a) elect its President and one or two Vice-Presidents for a period of three years; they may be re-elected;

(b) set up Chambers, constituted for a fixed period of time;

(c) elect the Presidents of the Chambers of the Court; they may be re-elected;

(d) adopt the rules of the Court, and

(e) elect the Registrar and one or more Deputy Registrars.

### Article 27—Committees, Chambers and Grand Chamber

1. To consider cases brought before it, the Court shall sit in committees of three judges, in Chambers of seven judges and in a Grand Chamber of seventeen judges. The Court's Chambers shall set up committees for a fixed period of time.

2. There shall sit as an *ex officio* member of the Chamber and the Grand Chamber the judge elected in respect of the State Party concerned or, if there is none or if he is unable to sit, a person of its choice who shall sit in the capacity of judge.

3. The Grand Chamber shall also include the President of the Court, the Vice-Presidents, the Presidents of the Chambers and other judges chosen in accordance with the rules of the Court. When a case is referred to the Grand Chamber under Article 43, no judge from the Chamber which rendered the judgment shall sit in the Grand Chamber, with the exception of the President of the Chamber and the judge who sat in respect of the State Party concerned.

### Article 28—Declarations of inadmissibility by committees

A committee may, by a unanimous vote, declare inadmissible or strike out of its list of cases an application submitted under Article 34 where such a decision can be taken without further examination. The decision shall be final.

### Article 29—Decisions by Chambers on admissibility and merits

1. If no decision is taken under Article 28, a Chamber shall decide on the admissibility and merits of individual applications submitted under Article 34.

2. A Chamber shall decide on the admissibility and merits of inter-State applications submitted under Article 33.

3. The decision on admissibility shall be taken separately unless the Court, in exceptional cases, decides otherwise.

*Article 30—Relinquishment of jurisdiction to the Grand Chamber*

Where a case pending before a Chamber raises a serious question affecting the interpretation of the Convention or the protocols thereto, or where the resolution of a question before the Chamber might have a result inconsistent with a judgment previously delivered by the Court, the Chamber may, at any time before it has rendered its judgment, relinquish jurisdiction in favour of the Grand Chamber, unless one of the parties to the case objects.

*Article 31—Powers of the Grand Chamber*

The Grand Chamber shall

(a) determine applications submitted either under Article 33 or Article 34 when a Chamber has relinquished jurisdiction under Article 30 or when the case has been referred to it under Article 43; and

(b) consider requests for advisory opinions submitted under Article 47.

*Article 32—Jurisdiction of the Court*

1. The jurisdiction of the Court shall extend to all matters concerning the interpretation and application of the Convention and the protocols thereto which are referred to it as provided in Articles 33, 34 and 47.

2. In the event of dispute as to whether the Court has jurisdiction, the Court shall decide.

*Article 33—Inter-State cases*

Any High Contracting Party may refer to the Court any alleged breach of the provisions of the Convention and the protocols thereto by another High Contracting Party.

*Article 34—Individual applications*

The Court may receive applications from any person, non-governmental organization or group of individuals claiming to be the victim of a violation by one of the High Contracting Parties of the rights set forth in the Convention or the protocols thereto. The High Contracting Parties undertake not to hinder in any way the effective exercise of this right.

*Article 35—Admissibility criteria*

1. The Court may only deal with the matter after all domestic remedies have been exhausted, according to the generally recognised rules of international law, and within a period of six months from the date on which the final decision was taken.

2. The Court shall not deal with any application submitted under Article 34 that

(a) is anonymous; or

(b) is substantially the same as a matter that has already been examined by the Court or has already been submitted to another procedure of international investigation or settlement and contains no relevant new information.

3. The Court shall declare inadmissible any individual application submitted under Article 34 which it considers incompatible with the provisions of the Convention or the protocols thereto, manifestly ill-founded, or an abuse of the right of application.

4. The Court shall reject any application which it considers inadmissible under this Article. It may do so at any stage of the proceedings.

### Article 36—*Third party intervention*

1. In all cases before a Chamber or the Grand Chamber, a High Contracting Party one of whose nationals is an applicant shall have the right to submit written comments and to take part in hearings.

2. The President of the Court may, in the interest of the proper administration of justice, invite any High Contracting Party which is not a party to the proceedings or any person concerned who is not the applicant to submit written comments or take part in hearings.

### Article 37—*Striking out applications*

1. The Court may at any stage of the proceedings decide to strike an application out of its list of cases where the circumstances lead to the conclusion that

   *(a)* the applicant does not intend to pursue his application; or

   *(b)* the matter has been resolved; or

   *(c)* for any other reason established by the Court, it is no longer justified to continue the examination of the application.

   However, the Court shall continue the examination of the application if respect for human rights as defined in the Convention and the protocols thereto so requires.

2. The Court may decide to restore an application to its list of cases if it considers that the circumstances justify such a course.

### Article 38—*Examination of the case and friendly settlement proceedings*

1. If the Court declares the application admissible, it shall

   *(a)* pursue the examination of the case, together with the representatives of the parties, and if need be, undertake an investigation, for the effective conduct of which the States concerned shall furnish all necessary facilities;

   *(b)* place itself at the disposal of the parties concerned with a view to securing a friendly settlement of the matter on the basis of respect for human rights as defined in the Convention and the protocols thereto.

2. Proceedings conducted under paragraph 1(b) shall be confidential.

### Article 39—*Finding of a friendly settlement*

If a friendly settlement is effected, the Court shall strike the case out of its list by means of a decision which shall be confined to a brief statement of the facts and of the solution reached.

*Article 40—Public hearings and access to documents*

1. Hearings shall be in public unless the Court in exceptional circumstances decides otherwise.

2. Documents deposited with the Registrar shall be accessible to the public unless the President of the Court decides otherwise.

*Article 41—Just satisfaction*

If the Court finds that there has been a violation of the Convention or the protocols thereto, and if the internal law of the High Contracting Party concerned allows only partial reparation to be made, the Court shall, if necessary, afford just satisfaction to the injured party.

*Article 42—Judgments of Chambers*

Judgments of Chambers shall become final in accordance with the provisions of Article 44, paragraph 2.

*Article 43—Referral to the Grand Chamber*

1. Within a period of three months from the date of the judgment of the Chamber, any party to the case may, in exceptional cases, request that the case be referred to the Grand Chamber.

2. A panel of five judges of the Grand Chamber shall accept the request if the case raises a serious question affecting the interpretation or application of the Convention or the protocols thereto, or a serious issue of general importance.

3. If the panel accepts the request, the Grand Chamber shall decide the case by means of a judgment.

*Article 44—Final judgments*

1. The judgment of the Grand Chamber shall be final.

2. The judgment of a Chamber shall become final

   *(a)* when the parties declare that they will not request that the case be referred to the Grand Chamber; or

   *(b)* three months after the date of the judgment, if reference of the case to the Grand Chamber has not been requested; or

   *(c)* when the panel of the Grand Chamber rejects the request to refer under Article 43.

3. The final judgment shall be published.

*Article 45—Reasons for judgments and decisions*

1. Reasons shall be given for judgments as well as for decisions declaring applications admissible or inadmissible.

2. If a judgment does not represent, in whole or in part, the unanimous opinion of the judges, any judge shall be entitled to deliver a separate opinion.

*Article 46—Binding force and execution of judgments*

1. The High Contracting Parties undertake to abide by the final judgment of the Court in any case to which they are parties.

2. The final judgment of the Court shall be transmitted to the Committee of Ministers, which shall supervise its execution.

*Article 47—Advisory opinions*

1. The Court may, at the request of the Committee of Ministers, give advisory opinions on legal questions concerning the interpretation of the Convention and the protocols thereto.

2. Such opinions shall not deal with any question relating to the content or scope of the rights or freedoms defined in Section I of the Convention and the protocols thereto, or with any other question which the Court or the Committee of Ministers might have to consider in consequence of any such proceedings as could be instituted in accordance with the Convention.

3. Decisions of the Committee of Ministers to request an advisory opinion of the Court shall require a majority vote of the representatives entitled to sit on the Committee.

*Article 48—Advisory jurisdiction of the Court*

The Court shall decide whether a request for an advisory opinion submitted by the Committee of Ministers is within its competence as defined in Article 47.

*Article 49—Reasons for advisory opinions*

1. Reasons shall be given for advisory opinions of the Court.

2. If the advisory opinion does not represent, in whole or in part, the unanimous opinion of the judges, any judge shall be entitled to deliver a separate opinion.

3. Advisory opinions of the Court shall be communicated to the Committee of Ministers.

*Article 50—Expenditure on the Court*

The expenditure on the Court shall be borne by the Council of Europe.

*Article 51—Privileges and immunities of judges*

The judges shall be entitled, during the exercise of their functions, to the privileges and immunities provided for in Article 40 of the Statute of the Council of Europe and in the agreements made thereunder.

## SECTION III—MISCELLANEOUS PROVISIONS

*Article 52—Inquiries by the Secretary General*

On receipt of a request from the Secretary General of the Council of Europe any High Contracting Party shall furnish an explanation of the manner in which its internal law ensures the effective implementation of any of the provisions of the Convention.

*Article 53—Safeguard for existing human rights*

Nothing in this Convention shall be construed as limiting or derogating from any of the human rights and fundamental freedoms which may be ensured under the laws of any High Contracting Party or under any other agreement to which it is a Party.

### Article 54—*Powers of the Committee of Ministers*

Nothing in this Convention shall prejudice the powers conferred on the Committee of Ministers by the Statute of the Council of Europe.

### Article 55—*Exclusion of other means of dispute settlement*

The High Contracting Parties agree that, except by special agreement, they will not avail themselves of treaties, conventions or declarations in force between them for the purpose of submitting, by way of petition, a dispute arising out of the interpretation or application of this Convention to a means of settlement other than those provided for in this Convention.

### Article 56—*Territorial application*

1. Any State may at the time of its ratification or at any time thereafter declare by notification addressed to the Secretary General of the Council of Europe that the present Convention shall, subject to paragraph 4 of this Article, extend to all or any of the territories for whose international relations it is responsible.

2. The Convention shall extend to the territory or territories named in the notification as from the thirtieth day after the receipt of this notification by the Secretary General of the Council of Europe.

3. The provisions of this Convention shall be applied in such territories with due regard, however, to local requirements.

4. Any State which has made a declaration in accordance with paragraph 1 of this article may at any time thereafter declare on behalf of one or more of the territories to which the declaration relates that it accepts the competence of the Court to receive applications from individuals, non-governmental organizations or groups of individuals as provided by Article 34 of the Convention.

### Article 57—*Reservations*

1. Any State may, when signing this Convention or when depositing its instrument of ratification, make a reservation in respect of any particular provision of the Convention to the extent that any law then in force in its territory is not in conformity with the provision. Reservations of a general character shall not be permitted under this article.

2. Any reservation made under this article shall contain a brief statement of the law concerned.

### Article 58—*Denunciation*

1. A High Contracting Party may denounce the present Convention only after the expiry of five years from the date on which it became a party to it and after six months' notice contained in a notification addressed to the Secretary General of the Council of Europe, who shall inform the other High Contracting Parties.

2. Such a denunciation shall not have the effect of releasing the High Contracting Party concerned from its obligations under this Convention in respect of any act which, being capable of constituting a violation of such obligations, may

have been performed by it before the date at which the denunciation became effective.

3. Any High Contracting Party which shall cease to be a member of the Council of Europe shall cease to be a Party to this Convention under the same conditions.

4. The Convention may be denounced in accordance with the provisions of the preceding paragraphs in respect of any territory to which it has been declared to extend under the terms of Article 56.

*Article 59—Signature and ratification*

1. This Convention shall be open to the signature of the members of the Council of Europe. It shall be ratified. Ratifications shall be deposited with the Secretary General of the Council of Europe.

2. The present Convention shall come into force after the deposit of ten instruments of ratification.

3. As regards any signatory ratifying subsequently, the Convention shall come into force at the date of the deposit of its instrument of ratification.

4. The Secretary General of the Council of Europe shall notify all the members of the Council of Europe of the entry into force of the Convention, the names of the High Contracting Parties who have ratified it, and the deposit of all instruments of ratification which may be effected subsequently.

*Done* at Rome this 4th day of November 1950, in English and French, both texts being equally authentic, in a single copy which shall remain deposited in the archives of the Council of Europe. The Secretary General shall transmit certified copies to each of the signatories.

# PROTOCOLS

## PROTOCOL NO. 1, AS AMENDED BY PROTOCOL NO. 11

The Governments signatory hereto, being Members of the Council of Europe,

*Being resolved* to take steps to ensure the collective enforcement of certain rights and freedoms other than those already included in Section I of the Convention for the Protection of Human Rights and Fundamental Freedoms signed at Rome on 4 November 1950 (hereinafter referred to as 'the Convention'),

*Have agreed* as follows:

*Article 1—Protection of property*

Every natural or legal person is entitled to the peaceful enjoyment of his possessions. No one shall be deprived of his possessions except in the public interest and subject to the conditions provided for by law and by the general principles of international law.

The preceding provisions shall not, however, in any way impair the right of a State to enforce such laws as it deems necessary to control the use of property in accordance with the general interest or to secure the payment of taxes or other contributions or penalties.

*Article 2—Right to education*

No person shall be denied the right to education. In the exercise of any functions which it assumes in relation to education and to teaching, the State shall respect the right of parents to ensure such education and teaching in conformity with their own religious and philosophical convictions.

*Article 3—Right to free elections*

The High Contracting Parties undertake to hold free elections at reasonable intervals by secret ballot, under conditions which will ensure the free expression of the opinion of the people in the choice of the legislature.

*Article 4—Territorial application*

Any High Contracting Party may at the time of signature or ratification or at any time thereafter communicate to the Secretary General of the Council of Europe a declaration stating the extent to which it undertakes that the provisions of the present Protocol shall apply to such of the territories for the international relations of which it is responsible as are named therein.

Any High Contracting Party which has communicated a declaration in virtue of the preceding paragraph may from time to time communicate a further declaration modifying the terms of any former declaration or terminating the application of the provisions of this Protocol in respect of any territory.

A declaration made in accordance with this article shall be deemed to have been made in accordance with paragraph 1 of Article 56 of the Convention.

*Article 5—Relationship to the Convention*

As between the High Contracting Parties the provisions of Articles 1, 2, 3 and 4 of this Protocol shall be regarded as additional articles to the Convention and all the provisions of the Convention shall apply accordingly.

*Article 6—Signature and ratification*

This Protocol shall be open for signature by the Members of the Council of Europe, who are the signatories of the Convention; it shall be ratified at the same time as or after the ratification of the Convention. It shall enter into force after the deposit of ten instruments of ratification. As regards any signatory ratifying subsequently, the Protocol shall enter into force at the date of the deposit of its instrument of ratification.

The instruments of ratification shall be deposited with the Secretary General of the Council of Europe, who will notify all members of the names of those who have ratified.

*Done* at Paris on the 20th day of March 1952, in English and French, both texts being equally authentic, in a single copy which shall remain deposited in the archives of the Council of Europe. The Secretary General shall transmit certified copies to each of the signatory Governments.

# PROTOCOL NO. 4, AS AMENDED BY PROTOCOL NO. 11

The Governments signatory hereto, being Members of the Council of Europe,

*Being resolved* to take steps to ensure the collective enforcement of certain rights and freedoms other than those already included in Section 1 of the Convention for the Protection of Human Rights and Fundamental Freedoms signed at Rome on 4th November 1950 (hereinafter referred to as the 'Convention') and in Articles 1 to 3 of the First Protocol to the Convention , signed at Paris on 20th March 1952,

*Have agreed* as follows:

### Article 1—*Prohibition of imprisonment for debt*

No one shall be deprived of his liberty merely on the ground of inability to fulfil a contractual obligation.

### Article 2—*Freedom of movement*

1. Everyone lawfully within the territory of a State shall, within that territory, have the right to liberty of movement and freedom to choose his residence.

2. Everyone shall be free to leave any country, including his own.

3. No restrictions shall be placed on the exercise of these rights other than such as are in accordance with law and are necessary in a democratic society in the interests of national security or public safety, for the maintenance of *ordre public*, for the prevention of crime, for the protection of health or morals, or for the protection of the rights and freedoms of others.

4. The rights set forth in paragraph 1 may also be subject, in particular areas, to restrictions imposed in accordance with law and justified by the public interest in a democratic society.

### Article 3—*Prohibition of expulsion of nationals*

1. No one shall be expelled, by means either of an individual or of a collective measure, from the territory of the State of which he is a national.

2. No one shall be deprived of the right to enter the territory of the State of which he is a national.

### Article 4—*Prohibition of collective expulsion of aliens*

Collective expulsion of aliens is prohibited.

### Article 5—*Territorial application*

1. Any High Contracting Party may, at the time of signature or ratification of this Protocol, or at any time thereafter, communicate to the Secretary General of the Council of Europe a declaration stating the extent to which it undertakes that the provisions of this Protocol shall apply to such of the territories for the international relations of which it is responsible as are named therein.

2. Any High Contracting Party which has communicated a declaration in virtue of the preceding paragraph may, from time to time, communicate a further declaration modifying the terms of any former declaration or terminating the application of the provisions of this Protocol in respect of any territory.

3. A declaration made in accordance with this article shall be deemed to have been made in accordance with paragraph 1 of Article 56 of the Convention.

4. The territory of any State to which this Protocol applies by virtue of ratification or acceptance by that State, and each territory to which this Protocol is applied by virtue of a declaration by that State under this article, shall be treated as separate territories for the purpose of the references in Articles 2 and 3 to the territory of a State.

5. Any State which has made a declaration in accordance with paragraph 1 or 2 of this Article may at any time thereafter declare on behalf of one or more of the territories to which the declaration relates that it accepts the competence of the Court to receive applications from individuals, non-governmental organizations or groups of individuals as provided in Article 34 of the Convention in respect of all or any of Articles 1 to 4 of this Protocol.

### Article 6—*Relationship to the Convention*

As between the High Contracting Parties the provisions of Articles 1 to 5 of this Protocol shall be regarded as additional articles to the Convention, and all the provisions of the Convention shall apply accordingly.

### Article 7—*Signature and ratification*

1. This Protocol shall be open for signature by the members of the Council of Europe who are the signatories of the Convention; it shall be ratified at the same time as or after the ratification of the Convention. It shall enter into force after the deposit of five instruments of ratification. As regards any signatory ratifying subsequently, the Protocol shall enter into force at the date of the deposit of its instrument of ratification.

2. The instruments of ratification shall be deposited with the Secretary General of the Council of Europe, who will notify all Members of the names of those who have ratified.

In witness whereof the undersigned, being duly authorized thereto, have signed this Protocol.

*Done* at Strasbourg, this 16th day of September 1963, in English and in French, both texts being equally authoritative, in a single copy which shall remain deposited in the archives of the Council of Europe. The Secretary General shall transmit certified copies to each of the signatory States.


## PROTOCOL NO. 6, AS AMENDED BY PROTOCOL NO. 11

The member States of the Council of Europe, signatory to this Protocol to the Convention for the Protection of Human Rights and Fundamental Freedoms, signed at Rome on 4 November 1950 (hereinafter referred to as 'the Convention'),

*Considering* that the evolution that has occurred in several member States of the Council of Europe expresses a general tendency in favour of abolition of the death penalty,

*Have agreed* as follows:

*Article 1—Abolition of the death penalty*

The death penalty shall be abolished. No-one shall be condemned to such penalty or executed.

*Article 2—Death penalty in time of war*

A State may make provision in its law for the death penalty in respect of acts committed in time of war or of imminent threat of war; such penalty shall be applied only in the instances laid down in the law and in accordance with its provisions. The State shall communicate to the Secretary General of the Council of Europe the relevant provisions of that law.

*Article 3—Prohibition of derogations*

No derogation from the provisions of this Protocol shall be made under Article 15 of the Convention.

*Article 4—Prohibition of reservations*

No reservation may be made under Article 57 of the Convention in respect of the provisions of this Protocol.

*Article 5—Territorial application*

1. Any State may at the time of signature or when depositing its instrument of ratification, acceptance or approval, specify the territory or territories to which this Protocol shall apply.

2. Any State may at any later date, by a declaration addressed to the Secretary General of the Council of Europe, extend the application of this Protocol to any other territory specified in the declaration. In respect of such territory the Protocol shall enter into force on the first day of the month following the date of receipt of such declaration by the Secretary General.

3. Any declaration made under the two preceding paragraphs may, in respect of any territory specified in such declaration, be withdrawn by a notification addressed to the Secretary General. The withdrawal shall become effective on the first day of the month following the date of receipt of such notification by the Secretary General.

*Article 6—Relationship to the Convention*

As between the States Parties the provisions of Articles 1 and 5 of this Protocol shall be regarded as additional articles to the Convention and all the provisions of the Convention shall apply accordingly.

*Article 7—Signature and ratification*

The Protocol shall be open for signature by the member States of the Council of Europe, signatories to the Convention. It shall be subject to ratification, acceptance or approval. A member State of the Council of Europe may not ratify, accept or approve this Protocol unless it has, simultaneously or previously, ratified the Convention. Instruments of ratification, acceptance or approval shall be deposited with the Secretary General of the Council of Europe.

*Article 8—Entry into force*

1. This Protocol shall enter into force on the first day of the month following the date on which five member States of the Council of Europe have expressed their consent to be bound by the Protocol in accordance with the provisions of Article 7.

2. In respect of any member State which subsequently expresses its consent to be bound by it, the Protocol shall enter into force on the first day of the month following the date of the deposit of the instrument of ratification, acceptance or approval.

*Article 9—Depositary functions*

The Secretary General of the Council of Europe shall notify the member States of the Council of:

*(a)*  any signature;

*(b)*  the deposit of any instrument of ratification, acceptance or approval;

*(c)*  any date of entry into force of this Protocol in accordance with Articles 5 and 8;

*(d)*  any other act, notification or communication relating to this Protocol.

In witness whereof the undersigned, being duly authorized thereto, have signed this Protocol.

*Done* at Strasbourg, this 28th day of April 1983, in English and in French, both texts being equally authentic, in a single copy which shall be deposited in the archives of the Council of Europe. The Secretary General of the Council of Europe shall transmit certified copies to each member State of the Council of Europe.

## PROTOCOL NO. 7, AS AMENDED BY PROTOCOL NO. 11

The member States of the Council of Europe signatory hereto,

*Being resolved* to take further steps to ensure the collective enforcement of certain rights and freedoms by means of the Convention for the Protection of Human Rights and Fundamental Freedoms signed at Rome on 4 November 1950 (hereinafter referred to as 'the Convention'),

*Have agreed* as follows:

*Article 1—Procedural safeguards relating to expulsion of aliens*

1. An alien lawfully resident in the territory of a State shall not be expelled therefrom except in pursuance of a decision reached in accordance with law and shall be allowed:

*(a)*  to submit reasons against his expulsion,

*(b)*  to have his case reviewed, and

*(c)*  to be represented for these purposes before the competent authority or a person or persons designated by that authority.

2. An alien may be expelled before the exercise of his rights under paragraph 1.a, b

and c of this Article, when such expulsion is necessary in the interests of public order or is grounded on reasons of national security.

### Article 2—*Right of appeal in criminal matters*

1. Everyone convicted of a criminal offence by a tribunal shall have the right to have his conviction or sentence reviewed by a higher tribunal. The exercise of this right, including the grounds on which it may be exercised, shall be governed by law.

2. This right may be subject to exceptions in regard to offences of a minor character, as prescribed by law, or in cases in which the person concerned was tried in the first instance by the highest tribunal or was convicted following an appeal against acquittal.

### Article 3—*Compensation for wrongful conviction*

When a person has by a final decision been convicted of a criminal offence and when subsequently his conviction has been reversed, or he has been pardoned, on the ground that a new or newly discovered fact shows conclusively that there has been a miscarriage of justice, the person who has suffered punishment as a result of such conviction shall be compensated according to the law or the practice of the State concerned, unless it is proved that the non-disclosure of the unknown fact in time is wholly or partly attributable to him.

### Article 4—*Right not to be tried or punished twice*

1. No one shall be liable to be tried or punished again in criminal proceedings under the jurisdiction of the same State for an offence for which he has already been finally acquitted or convicted in accordance with the law and penal procedure of that State.

2. The provisions of the preceding paragraph shall not prevent the reopening of the case in accordance with the law and penal procedure of the State concerned, if there is evidence of new or newly discovered facts, or if there has been a fundamental defect in the previous proceedings, which could affect the outcome of the case.

3. No derogation from this Article shall be made under Article 15 of the Convention.

### Article 5—*Equality between spouses*

Spouses shall enjoy equality of rights and responsibilities of a private law character between them, and in their relations with their children, as to marriage, during marriage and in the event of its dissolution. This Article shall not prevent States from taking such measures as are necessary in the interests of the children.

### Article 6—*Territorial application*

1. Any State may at the time of signature or when depositing its instrument of ratification, acceptance or approval, specify the territory or territories to which the Protocol shall apply and state the extent to which it undertakes that the provisions of this Protocol shall apply to such territory or territories.

2. Any State may at any later date, by a declaration addressed to the Secretary General of the Council of Europe, extend the application of this Protocol to any

other territory specified in the declaration. In respect of such territory the Protocol shall enter into force on the first day of the month following the expiration of a period of two months after the date of receipt by the Secretary General of such declaration.

3. Any declaration made under the two preceding paragraphs may, in respect of any territory specified in such declaration, be withdrawn or modified by a notification addressed to the Secretary General. The withdrawal or modification shall become effective on the first day of the month following the expiration of a period of two months after the date of receipt of such notification by the Secretary General.

4. A declaration made in accordance with this Article shall be deemed to have been made in accordance with paragraph 1 of Article 56 of the Convention.

5. The territory of any State to which this Protocol applies by virtue of ratification, acceptance or approval by that State, and each territory to which this Protocol is applied by virtue of a declaration by that State under this Article, may be treated as separate territories for the purpose of the reference in Article 1 to the territory of a State.

6. Any State which has made a declaration in accordance with paragraph 1 or 2 of this Article may at any time thereafter declare on behalf of one or more of the territories to which the declaration relates that it accepts the competence of the Court to receive applications from individuals, non-governmental organizations or groups of individuals as provided in Article 34 of the Convention in respect of Articles 1 to 5 of this Protocol.

*Article 7—Relationship to the Convention*

As between the States Parties, the provisions of Articles 1 to 6 of this Protocol shall be regarded as additional Articles to the Convention, and all the provisions of the Convention shall apply accordingly.

*Article 8—Signature and ratification*

This Protocol shall be open for signature by member States of the Council of Europe which have signed the Convention. It is subject to ratification, acceptance or approval. A member State of the Council of Europe may not ratify, accept or approve this Protocol without previously or simultaneously ratifying the Convention. Instruments of ratification, acceptance or approval shall be deposited with the Secretary General of the Council of Europe.

*Article 9—Entry into force*

1. This Protocol shall enter into force on the first day of the month following the expiration of a period of two months after the date on which seven member States of the Council of Europe have expressed their consent to be bound by the Protocol in accordance with the provisions of Article 8.

2. In respect of any member State which subsequently expresses its consent to be bound by it, the Protocol shall enter into force on the first day of the month following the expiration of a period of two months after the date of the deposit of the instrument of ratification, acceptance or approval.

*Article* 10—*Depositary functions*

The Secretary General of the Council of Europe shall notify all the member States of the Council of Europe of:

   *(a)* any signature;

   *(b)* the deposit of any instrument of ratification, acceptance or approval;

   *(c)* any date of entry into force of this Protocol in accordance with Articles 6 and 9;

   *(d)* any other act, notification or declaration relating to this Protocol.

In witness whereof the undersigned, being duly authorized thereto, have signed this Protocol.

*Done* at Strasbourg, this 22nd day of November 1984, in English and French, both texts being equally authentic, in a single copy which shall be deposited in the archives of the Council of Europe. The Secretary General of the Council of Europe shall transmit certified copies to each member State of the Council of Europe.

## 55. PROTOCOL NO. 12 TO THE EUROPEAN CONVENTION FOR THE PROTECTION OF HUMAN RIGHTS AND FUNDAMENTAL FREEDOMS

This protocol was opened for signature on 4 November 2000, and will enter into force after receiving ten ratifications. It provides for a general prohibition of discrimination. For text, see ETS No. 177.

*TEXT*

The member States of the Council of Europe signatory hereto,

*Having regard* to the fundamental principle according to which all persons are equal before the law and are entitled to the equal protection of the law;

*Being resolved* to take further steps to promote the equality of all persons through the collective enforcement of a general prohibition of discrimination by means of the Convention for the Protection of Human Rights and Fundamental Freedoms signed at Rome on 4 November 1950 (hereinafter referred to as 'the Convention');

*Reaffirming* that the principle of non-discrimination does not prevent States Parties from taking measures in order to promote full and effective equality, provided that there is an objective and reasonable justification for those measures,

*Have agreed* as follows:

*Article 1—General prohibition of discrimination*

1. The enjoyment of any right set forth by law shall be secured without discrimination on any ground such as sex, race, colour, language, religion, political or other opinion, national or social origin, association with a national minority, property, birth or other status.

2. No one shall be discriminated against by any public authority on any ground such as those mentioned in paragraph 1.

*Article 2—Territorial application*

1. Any State may, at the time of signature or when depositing its instrument of ratification, acceptance or approval, specify the territory or territories to which this Protocol shall apply.

2. Any State may at any later date, by a declaration addressed to the Secretary General of the Council of Europe, extend the application of this Protocol to any other territory specified in the declaration. In respect of such territory the Protocol shall enter into force on the first day of the month following the expiration of a period of three months after the date of receipt by the Secretary General of such declaration.

3. Any declaration made under the two preceding paragraphs may, in respect of any territory specified in such declaration, be withdrawn or modified by a notification addressed to the Secretary General of the Council of Europe. The withdrawal

or modification shall become effective on the first day of the month following the expiration of a period of three months after the date of receipt of such notification by the Secretary General.

4. A declaration made in accordance with this article shall be deemed to have been made in accordance with paragraph 1 of Article 56 of the Convention.

5. Any State which has made a declaration in accordance with paragraph 1 or 2 of this article may at any time thereafter declare on behalf of one or more of the territories to which the declaration relates that it accepts the competence of the Court to receive applications from individuals, non-governmental organizations or groups of individuals as provided by Article 34 of the Convention in respect of Article 1 of this Protocol.

## Article 3—*Relationship to the Convention*

As between the States Parties, the provisions of Articles 1 and 2 of this Protocol shall be regarded as additional articles to the Convention, and all the provisions of the Convention shall apply accordingly.

## Article 4—*Signature and ratification*

This Protocol shall be open for signature by member States of the Council of Europe which have signed the Convention. It is subject to ratification, acceptance or approval. A member State of the Council of Europe may not ratify, accept or approve this Protocol without previously or simultaneously ratifying the Convention. Instruments of ratification, acceptance or approval shall be deposited with the Secretary General of the Council of Europe.

## Article 5—*Entry into force*

1. This Protocol shall enter into force on the first day of the month following the expiration of a period of three months after the date on which ten member States of the Council of Europe have expressed their consent to be bound by the Protocol in accordance with the provisions of Article 4.

2. In respect of any member State which subsequently expresses its consent to be bound by it, the Protocol shall enter into force on the first day of the month following the expiration of a period of three months after the date of the deposit of the instrument of ratification, acceptance or approval.

## Article 6—*Depositary functions*

The Secretary General of the Council of Europe shall notify all the member States of the Council of Europe of:

(a) any signature;

(b) the deposit of any instrument of ratification, acceptance or approval;

(c) any date of entry into force of this Protocol in accordance with Articles 2 and 5;

(d) any other act, notification or communication relating to this Protocol.

In witness whereof the undersigned, being duly authorized thereto, have signed this Protocol.

*Done* at Rome, this 4th day of November 2000, in English and in French, both texts being equally authentic, in a single copy which shall be deposited in the archives of the Council of Europe. The Secretary General of the Council of Europe shall transmit certified copies to each member State of the Council of Europe.

# 56. EUROPEAN SOCIAL CHARTER, 1961

This was intended to be complementary to the European Convention on Human Rights. The Charter is concerned to develop and protect social and economic rights, while the Convention is concerned with political and civil rights, although this division is by no means exact.

The Charter was signed at Turin on 18 October 1961, and came into force on 26 February 1965; for text see ETS No. 35; 529 UNTS 89; UK Treaty Series, No. 38 (1965), Cmnd. 2643 (English and French texts, declarations made on ratification). See further the European Code of Social Security, signed at Strasbourg on 16 April 1964, in force in 1968: ETS No. 48; UK Treaty Series, No. 10 (1969), Cmnd. 3871 (does not include the Protocol).

For extended commentary, see Harris, D., *The European Social Charter* (1984); Robertson, A.H. & Merrills, J.G., *Human Rights in the World* (4th edn., 1996), 168–79.

## TEXT

### Preamble

*The Governments signatory hereto, being Members of the Council of Europe,*

*Considering* that the aim of the Council of Europe is the achievement of greater unity between its members for the purpose of safeguarding and realizing the ideals and principles which are their common heritage and of facilitating their economic and social progress, in particular by the maintenance and further realization of human rights and fundamental freedoms;

*Considering* that in the European Convention for the Protection of Human Rights and Fundamental Freedoms signed at Rome on 4th November 1950, and the Protocol thereto signed at Paris on 20th March 1952, the member States of the Council of Europe agreed to secure to their populations the civil and political rights and freedoms therein specified;

*Considering* that the enjoyment of social rights should be secured without discrimination on grounds of race, colour, sex, religion, political opinion, national extraction or social origin;

*Being resolved* to make every effort in common to improve the standard of living and to promote the social well-being of both their urban and rural populations by means of appropriate institutions and action,

*Have agreed* as follows:

## PART I

The Contracting Parties accept as the aim of their policy, to be pursued by all appropriate means, both national and international in character, the attainment of conditions in which the following rights and principles may be effectively realised:

(1) Everyone shall have the opportunity to earn his living in an occupation freely entered upon.

(2) All workers have the right to just conditions of work.

(3) All workers have the right to safe and healthy working conditions.

(4) All workers have the right to a fair remuneration sufficient for a decent standard of living for themselves and their families.

(5) All workers and employers have the right to freedom of association in national or international organisations for the protection of their economic and social interests.

(6) All workers and employers have the right to bargain collectively.

(7) Children and young persons have the right to a special protection against the physical and moral hazards to which they are exposed.

(8) Employed women, in case of maternity, and other employed women as appropriate, have the right to a special protection in their work.

(9) Everyone has the right to appropriate facilities for vocational guidance with a view to helping him choose an occupation suited to his personal aptitude and interests.

(10) Everyone has the right to appropriate facilities for vocational training.

(11) Everyone has the right to benefit from any measures enabling him to enjoy the highest possible standard of health attainable.

(12) All workers and their dependents have the right to social security.

(13) Anyone without adequate resources has the right to social and medical assistance.

(14) Everyone has the right to benefit from social welfare services.

(15) Disabled persons have the right to vocational training, rehabilitation and resettlement, whatever the origin and nature of their disability.

(16) The family as a fundamental unit of society has the right to appropriate social, legal and economic protection to ensure its full development.

(17) Mothers and children, irrespective of marital status and family relations, have the right to appropriate social and economic protection.

(18) The nationals of any one of the Contracting Parties have the right to engage in any gainful occupation in the territory of any one of the others on a footing of equality with the nationals of the latter, subject to restrictions based on cogent economic or social reasons.

(19) Migrant workers who are nationals of a Contracting Party and their families have the right to protection and assistance in the territory of any other Contracting Party.

## PART II

The Contracting Parties undertake, as provided for in Part III, to consider themselves bound by the obligations laid down in the following articles and paragraphs.

*Article 1—The right to work*

With a view to ensuring the effective exercise of the right to work, the Contracting Parties undertake:

(1) To accept as one of their primary aims and responsibilities the achievement and maintenance of as high and stable a level of employment as possible, with a view to the attainment of full employment;

(2) To protect effectively the right of the worker to earn his living in an occupation freely entered upon;

(3) To establish or maintain free employment services for all workers;

(4) To provide or promote appropriate vocational guidance, training and rehabilitation.

*Article 2—The right to just conditions of work*

With a view to ensuring the effective exercise of the right to just conditions of work, the Contracting Parties undertake:

(1) To provide for reasonable daily and weekly working hours, the working week to be progressively reduced to the extent that the increase of productivity and other relevant factors permit;

(2) To provide for public holidays with pay;

(3) To provide for a minimum of two weeks annual holiday with pay;

(4) To provide for additional paid holidays or reduced working hours for workers engaged in dangerous or unhealthy occupations as prescribed;

(5) To ensure a weekly rest period which shall, as far as possible, coincide with the day recognised by tradition or custom in the country or region concerned as a day of rest.

*Article 3 The right to safe and healthy working conditions*

With a view to ensuring the effective exercise of the right to safe and healthy working conditions, the Contracting Parties undertake:

(1) To issue safety and health regulations;

(2) To provide for the enforcement of such regulations by measures of supervision;

(3) To consult, as appropriate, employers' and workers' organizations on measures intended to improve industrial safety and health.

*Article 4—The right to a fair remuneration*

With a view to ensuring the effective exercise of the right to a fair remuneration, the Contracting Parties undertake:

(1) To recognize the right of workers to a remuneration such as will give them and their families a decent standard of living;

(2) To recognize the right of workers to an increased rate of remuneration for overtime work, subject to exceptions in particular cases;

(3) To recognize the right of men and women workers to equal pay for work of equal value;

(4) To recognize the right of all workers to a reasonable period of notice for termination of employment;

(5) To permit deductions from wages only under conditions and to the extent

prescribed by national laws or regulations or fixed by collective agreements or arbitration awards.

The exercise of these rights shall be achieved by freely concluded collective agreements, by statutory wage-fixing machinery, or by other means appropriate to national conditions.

### Article 5—*The right to organize*

With a view to ensuring or promoting the freedom of workers and employers to form local, national or international organisations for the protection of their economic and social interests and to join those organizations, the Contracting Parties undertake that national law shall not be such as to impair, nor shall it be so applied as to impair, this freedom. The extent to which the guarantees provided for in this article shall apply to the police shall be determined by national laws or regulations. The principle governing the application to the members of the armed forces of these guarantees and the extent to which they shall apply to persons in this category shall equally be determined by national laws or regulations.

### Article 6—*The right to bargain collectively*

With a view to ensuring the effective exercise of the right to bargain collectively, the Contracting Parties undertake:

(1) To promote joint consultation between workers and employers;

(2) To promote, where necessary and appropriate, machinery for voluntary negotiations between employers or employers' organisations and workers' organisations, with a view to the regulation of terms and conditions of employment by means of collective agreements;

(3) To promote the establishment and use of appropriate machinery for conciliation and voluntary arbitration for the settlement of labour disputes;

and recognize:

(4) The right of workers and employers to collective action in cases of conflicts of interest, including the right to strike, subject to obligations that might arise out of collective agreements previously entered into.

### Article 7—*The right of children and young persons to protection*

With a view to ensuring the effective exercise of the right of children and young persons to protection, the Contracting Parties undertake:

(1) To provide that the minimum age of admission to employment shall be 15 years, subject to exceptions for children employed in prescribed light work without harm to their health, morals or education;

(2) To provide that a higher minimum age of admission to employment shall be fixed with respect to prescribed occupations regarded as dangerous or unhealthy;

(3) To provide that persons who are still subject to compulsory education shall not be employed in such work as would deprive them of the full benefit of their education;

(4) To provide that the working hours of persons under 16 years of age shall be

limited in accordance with the needs of their development, and particularly with their need for vocational training;

(5) To recognize the right of young workers and apprentices to a fair wage or other appropriate allowances;

(6) To provide that the time spent by young persons in vocational training during the normal working hours with the consent of the employer shall be treated as forming part of the working day;

(7) To provide that employed persons of under 18 years of age shall be entitled to not less than three weeks' annual holiday with pay;

(8) To provide that persons under 18 years of age shall not be employed in night work with the exception of certain occupations provided for by national laws or regulations;

(9) To provide that persons under 18 years of age employed in occupations prescribed by national laws or regulations shall be subject to regular medical control;

(10) To ensure special protection against physical and moral dangers to which children and young persons are exposed, and particularly against those resulting directly or indirectly from their work.

*Article 8—The right of employed women to protection*

With a view to ensuring the effective exercise of the right of employed women to protection, the Contracting Parties undertake:

(1) To provide either by paid leave, by adequate social security benefits or by benefits from public funds for women to take leave before and after childbirth up to a total of at least 12 weeks;

(2) To consider it as unlawful for an employer to give a woman notice of dismissal during her absence on maternity leave or to give her notice of dismissal at such a time that the notice would expire during such absence;

(3) To provide that mothers who are nursing their infants shall be entitled to sufficient time off for this purpose;

(4) *(a)* To regulate the employment of women workers on night work in industrial employment;

  *(b)* To prohibit the employment of women workers in underground mining, and, as appropriate, on all other work which is unsuitable for them by reason of its dangerous, unhealthy, or arduous nature.

*Article 9—The right to vocational guidance*

With a view to ensuring the effective exercise of the right to vocational guidance, the Contracting Parties undertake to provide or promote, as necessary, a service which will assist all persons, including the handicapped, to solve problems related to occupational choice and progress, with due regard to the individual's characteristics and their relation to occupational opportunity: this assistance should be available free of charge, both to young persons, including school children, and to adults.

*Article* 10—*The right to vocational training*

With a view to ensuring the effective exercise of the right to vocational training, the Contracting Parties undertake:

(1) To provide or promote, as necessary, the technical and vocational training of all persons, including the handicapped, in consultation with employers' and workers' organizations, and to grant facilities for access to higher technical and university education, based solely on individual aptitude;

(2) To provide or promote a system of apprenticeship and other systematic arrangements for training young boys and girls in their various employments;

(3) To provide or promote, as necessary:

    *(a)* adequate and readily available training facilities for adult workers;

    *(b)* special facilities for the re-training of adult workers needed as a result of technological development or new trends in employment;

(4) To encourage the full utilisation of the facilities provided by appropriate measures such as:

    *(a)* reducing or abolishing any fees or charges;

    *(b)* granting financial assistance in appropriate cases;

    *(c)* including in the normal working hours time spent on supplementary training taken by the worker, at the request of his employer, during employment;

    *(d)* ensuring, through adequate supervision, in consultation with the employers' and workers' organizations, the efficiency of apprenticeship and other training arrangements for young workers, and the adequate protection of young workers generally.

*Article* 11—*The right to protection of health*

With a view to ensuring the effective exercise of the right to protection of health, the Contracting Parties undertake, either directly or in co-operation with public or private organizations, to take appropriate measures designed *inter alia*:

(1) To remove as far as possible the causes of ill-health;

(2) To provide advisory and educational facilities for the promotion of health and the encouragement of individual responsibility in matters of health;

(3) To prevent as far as possible epidemic, endemic and other diseases.

*Article* 12—*The right to social security*

With a view to ensuring the effective exercise of the right to social security, the Contracting Parties undertake:

(1) To establish or maintain a system of social security;

(2) To maintain the social security system at a satisfactory level at least equal to that required for ratification of International Labour Convention (No. 102) Concerning Minimum Standards of Social Security;

(3) To endeavour to raise progressively the system of social security to a higher level;

(4) To take steps, by the conclusion of appropriate bilateral and multilateral agreements, or by other means, and subject to the conditions laid down in such agreements, in order to ensure:

(a) equal treatment with their own nationals of the nationals of other Contracting Parties in respect of social security rights, including the retention of benefits arising out of social security legislation, whatever movements the persons protected may undertake between the territories of the Contracting Parties;

(b) the granting, maintenance and resumption of social security rights by such means as the accumulation of insurance or employment periods completed under the legislation of each of the Contracting Parties.

*Article 13—The right to social and medical assistance*

With a view to ensuring the effective exercise of the right to social and medical assistance, the Contracting Parties undertake:

(1) To ensure that any person who is without adequate resources and who is unable to secure such resources either by his own efforts or from other sources, in particular by benefits under a social security scheme, be granted adequate assistance, and, in case of sickness, the care necessitated by his condition;

(2) To ensure that persons receiving such assistance shall not, for that reason, suffer from a diminution of their political or social rights;

(3) To provide that everyone may receive by appropriate public or private services such advice and personal help as may be required to prevent, to remove, or to alleviate personal or family want;

(4) To apply the provisions referred to in paragraphs 1, 2 and 3 of this article on an equal footing with their nationals to nationals of other Contracting Parties lawfully within their territories, in accordance with their obligations under the European Convention on Social and Medical Assistance, signed at Paris on 11th December 1953.

*Article 14—The right to benefit from social welfare services*

With a view to ensuring the effective exercise of the right to benefit from social welfare services, the Contracting Parties undertake:

(1) To promote or provide services which, by using methods of social work, would contribute to the welfare and development of both individuals and groups in the community, and to their adjustment to the social environment;

(2) To encourage the participation of individuals and voluntary or other organizations in the establishment and maintenance of such services.

*Article 15—The right of physically or mentally disabled persons to vocational training, rehabilitation and social resettlement*

With a view to ensuring the effective exercise of the right of the physically or mentally disabled to vocational training, rehabilitation and resettlement, the Contracting Parties undertake:

(1) To take adequate measures for the provision of training facilities, including, where necessary, specialised institutions, public or private;

(2) To take adequate measures for the placing of disabled persons in employment, such as specialised placing services, facilities for sheltered employment and measures to encourage employers to admit disabled persons
to employment.

*Article 16—The right of the family to social, legal and economic protection*

With a view to ensuring the necessary conditions for the full development of the
family, which is a fundamental unit of society, the Contracting Parties undertake to
promote the economic, legal and social protection of family life by such means as
social and family benefits, fiscal arrangements, provision of family housing, benefits
for the newly married, and other appropriate means.

*Article 17—The right of mothers and children to social and economic protection*

With a view to ensuring the effective exercise of the right of mothers and children
to social and economic protection, the Contracting Parties will take all appropriate
and necessary measures to that end, including the establishment or maintenance of
appropriate institutions or services.

*Article 18—The right to engage in a gainful occupation in the territory of
other Contracting Parties*

With a view to ensuring the effective exercise of the right to engage in a gainful
occupation in the territory of any other Contracting Party, the Contracting Parties
undertake:

(1) To apply existing regulations in a spirit of liberality;

(2) To simplify existing formalities and to reduce or abolish chancery dues and
other charges payable by foreign workers or their employers;

(3) To liberalise, individually or collectively, regulations governing the
employment of foreign workers;

and recognize:

(4) The right of their nationals to leave the country to engage in a gainful
occupation in the territories of the other Contracting Parties.

*Article 19—The right of migrant workers and their families to protection and assistance*

With a view to ensuring the effective exercise of the right of migrant workers and
their families to protection and assistance in the territory of any other Contracting
Party, the Contracting Parties undertake:

(1) To maintain or to satisfy themselves that there are maintained adequate and
free services to assist such workers, particularly in obtaining accurate information, and to take all appropriate steps, so far as national laws and regulations permit, against misleading propaganda relating to emigration and
immigration;

(2) To adopt appropriate measures within their own jurisdiction to facilitate
the departure, journey and reception of such workers and their families,
and to provide, within their own jurisdiction, appropriate services for
health, medical attention and good hygienic conditions during the
journey;

(3) To promote co-operation, as appropriate, between social services, public and private, in emigration and immigration countries;

(4) To secure for such workers lawfully within their territories, insofar as such matters are regulated by law or regulations or are subject to the control of administrative authorities, treatment not less favourable than that of their own nationals in respect of the following matters:

   *(a)* remuneration and other employment and working conditions;

   *(b)* membership of trade unions and enjoyment of the benefits of collective bargaining;

   *(c)* accommodation;

(5) To secure for such workers lawfully within their territories treatment not less favourable than that of their own nationals with regard to employment taxes, dues or contributions payable in respect of employed persons;

(6) To facilitate as far as possible the reunion of the family of a foreign worker permitted to establish himself in the territory;

(7) To secure for such workers lawfully within their territories treatment not less favourable than that of their own nationals in respect of legal proceedings relating to matters referred to in this article;

(8) To secure that such workers lawfully residing within their territories are not expelled unless they endanger national security or offend against public interest or morality;

(9) To permit, within legal limits, the transfer of such parts of the earnings and savings of such workers as they may desire;

(10) To extend the protection and assistance provided for in this article to self-employed migrants insofar as such measures apply.


# PART III

*Article 20    Undertakings*

1. Each of the Contracting Parties undertakes:

   *(a)* To consider Part I of this Charter as a declaration of the aims which it will pursue by all appropriate means, as stated in the introductory paragraph of that Part;

   *(b)* To consider itself bound by at least five of the following articles of Part II of this Charter: Articles 1, 5, 6, 12, 13, 16 and 19;

   *(c)* In addition to the articles selected by it in accordance with the preceding sub-paragraph, to consider itself bound by such a number of articles or numbered paragraphs of Part II of the Charter as it may select, provided that the total number of articles or numbered paragraphs by which it is bound is not less than 10 articles or 45 numbered paragraphs.

2. The articles or paragraphs selected in accordance with sub-paragraphs (b) and (c) of paragraph 1 of this article shall be notified to the Secretary General of the Council of Europe at the time when the instrument of ratification or approval of the Contracting Party concerned is deposited.

3. Any Contracting Party may, at a later date, declare by notification to the Secretary General that it considers itself bound by any articles or any numbered paragraphs of Part II of the Charter which it has not already accepted under the terms of paragraph 1 of this article. Such undertakings subsequently given shall be deemed to be an integral part of the ratification or approval, and shall have the same effect as from the thirtieth day after the date of the notification.

4. The Secretary General shall communicate to all the signatory governments and to the Director General of the International Labour Office any notification which he shall have received pursuant to this part of the Charter.

5. Each Contracting Party shall maintain a system of labour inspection appropriate to national conditions.

## PART IV

*Article 21—Reports concerning accepted provisions*

The Contracting Parties shall send to the Secretary General of the Council of Europe a report at two-yearly intervals, in a form to be determined by the Committee of Ministers, concerning the application of such provisions of Part II of the Charter as they have accepted.

*Article 22—Reports concerning provisions which are not accepted*

The Contracting Parties shall send to the Secretary General, at appropriate intervals as requested by the Committee of Ministers, reports relating to the provisions of Part II of the Charter which they did not accept at the time of their ratification or approval or in a subsequent notification. The Committee of Ministers shall determine from time to time in respect of which provisions such reports shall be requested and the form of the reports to be provided.

*Article 23—Communication of copies*

1. Each Contracting Party shall communicate copies of its reports referred to in Articles 21 and 22 to such of its national organizations as are members of the international organizations of employers and trade unions to be invited under Article 27, paragraph 2, to be represented at meetings of the Sub-committee of the Governmental Social Committee.

2. The Contracting Parties shall forward to the Secretary General any comments on the said reports received from these national organizations, if so requested by them.

*Article 24—Examination of the reports*

The reports sent to the Secretary General in accordance with Articles 21 and 22 shall be examined by a Committee of Experts, who shall have also before them any comments forwarded to the Secretary General in accordance with paragraph 2 of Article 23.

*Article 25—Committee of Experts*

1. The Committee of Experts shall consist of not more than seven members appointed by the Committee of Ministers from a list of independent experts of the highest integrity and of recognised competence in international social questions, nominated by the Contracting Parties.

2. The members of the committee shall be appointed for a period of six years. They may be reappointed. However, of the members first appointed, the terms of office of two members shall expire at the end of four years.

3. The members whose terms of office are to expire at the end of the initial period of four years shall be chosen by lot by the Committee of Ministers immediately after the first appointment has been made.

4. A member of the Committee of Experts appointed to replace a member whose term of office has not expired shall hold office for the remainder of his predecessor's term.

*Article 26—Participation of the International Labour Organization*

The International Labour Organization shall be invited to nominate a representative to participate in a consultative capacity in the deliberations of the Committee of Experts.

*Article 27—Sub-committee of the Governmental Social Committee*

1. The reports of the Contracting Parties and the conclusions of the Committee of Experts shall be submitted for examination to a sub-committee of the Governmental Social Committee of the Council of Europe.

2. The sub-committee shall be composed of one representative of each of the Contracting Parties. It shall invite no more than two international organizations of employers and no more than two international trade union organizations as it may designate to be represented as observers in a consultative capacity at its meetings. Moreover, it may consult no more than two representatives of international non-governmental organizations having consultative status with the Council of Europe, in respect of questions with which the organizations are particularly qualified to deal, such as social welfare, and the economic and social protection of the family.

3. The sub-committee shall present to the Committee of Ministers a report containing its conclusions and append the report of the Committee of Experts.

*Article 28—Consultative Assembly*

The Secretary General of the Council of Europe shall transmit to the Consultative Assembly the conclusions of the Committee of Experts. The Consultative Assembly shall communicate its views on these conclusions to the Committee of Ministers.

*Article 29—Committee of Ministers*

By a majority of two-thirds of the members entitled to sit on the Committee, the Committee of Ministers may, on the basis of the report of the sub-committee, and after consultation with the Consultative Assembly, make to each Contracting Party any necessary recommendations.

## PART V

*Article 30—Derogations in time of war or public emergency*

1. In time of war or other public emergency threatening the life of the nation any Contracting Party may take measures derogating from its obligations under this Charter to the extent strictly required by the exigencies of the situation, provided that such measures are not inconsistent with its other obligations under international law.

2. Any Contracting Party which has availed itself of this right of derogation shall, within a reasonable lapse of time, keep the Secretary General of the Council of Europe fully informed of the measures taken and of the reasons therefor. It shall likewise inform the Secretary General when such measures have ceased to operate and the provisions of the Charter which it has accepted are again being fully executed.

3. The Secretary General shall in turn inform other Contracting Parties and the Director-General of the International Labour Office of all communications received in accordance with paragraph 2 of this article.

*Article 31—Restrictions*

1. The rights and principles set forth in Part I when effectively realized, and their effective exercise as provided for in Part II, shall not be subject to any restrictions or limitations not specified in those parts, except such as are prescribed by law and are necessary in a democratic society for the protection of the rights and freedoms of others or for the protection of public interest, national security, public health, or morals.

2. The restrictions permitted under this Charter to the rights and obligations set forth herein shall not be applied for any purpose other than that for which they have been prescribed.

*Article 32—Relations between the Charter and domestic law or international agreements*

The provisions of this Charter shall not prejudice the provisions of domestic law or of any bilateral or multilateral treaties, conventions or agreements which are already in force, or may come into force, under which more favourable treatment would be accorded to the persons protected.

*Article 33—Implementation by collective agreements*

1. In member States where the provisions of paragraphs 1, 2, 3, 4 and 5 of Article 2, paragraphs 4, 6 and 7 of Article 7 and paragraphs 1, 2, 3 and 4 of Article 10 of Part II of this Charter are matters normally left to agreements between employers or employers' organizations and workers' organizations, or are normally carried out otherwise than by law, the undertakings of those paragraphs may be given and compliance with them shall be treated as effective if their provisions are applied through such agreements or other means to the great majority of the workers concerned.

2. In member States where these provisions are normally the subject of legislation, the undertakings concerned may likewise be given, and compliance with them shall be regarded as effective if the provisions are applied by law to the great majority of the workers concerned.

*Article 34—Territorial application*

1. This Charter shall apply to the metropolitan territory of each Contracting Party. Each signatory government may, at the time of signature or of the deposit of its instrument of ratification or approval, specify, by declaration addressed to the Secretary General of the Council of Europe, the territory which shall be considered to be its metropolitan territory for this purpose.

2. Any Contracting Party may, at the time of ratification or approval of this Charter or at any time thereafter, declare by notification addressed to the Secretary General of the Council of Europe, that the Charter shall extend in whole or in part to a non-metropolitan territory or territories specified in the said declaration for whose international relations it is responsible or for which it assumes international responsibility. It shall specify in the declaration the articles or paragraphs of Part II of the Charter which it accepts as binding in respect of the territories named in the declaration.

3. The Charter shall extend to the territory or territories named in the aforesaid declaration as from the thirtieth day after the date on which the Secretary General shall have received notification of such declaration.

4. Any Contracting Party may declare at a later date, by notification addressed to the Secretary General of the Council of Europe, that, in respect of one or more of the territories to which the Charter has been extended in accordance with paragraph 2 of this article, it accepts as binding any articles or any numbered paragraphs which it has not already accepted in respect of that territory or territories. Such undertakings subsequently given shall be deemed to be an integral part of the original declaration in respect of the territory concerned, and shall have the same effect as from the thirtieth day after the date of the notification.

5. The Secretary General shall communicate to the other signatory governments and to the Director-General of the International Labour Office any notification transmitted to him in accordance with this article.

*Article 35—Signature, ratification and entry into force*

1. This Charter shall be open for signature by the members of the Council of Europe. It shall be ratified or approved. Instruments of ratification or approval shall be deposited with the Secretary General of the Council of Europe.

2. This Charter shall come into force as from the thirtieth day after the date of deposit of the fifth instrument of ratification or approval.

3. In respect of any signatory government ratifying subsequently, the Charter shall come into force as from the thirtieth day after the date of deposit of its instrument of ratification or approval.

4. The Secretary General shall notify all the members of the Council of Europe and the Director-General of the International Labour Office of the entry into force of the Charter, the names of the Contracting Parties which have ratified or approved it and the subsequent deposit of any instruments of ratification or approval.

*Article 36—Amendments*

Any member of the Council of Europe may propose amendments to this Charter in a communication addressed to the Secretary General of the Council of Europe.

The Secretary General shall transmit to the other members of the Council of Europe any amendments so proposed, which shall then be considered by the Committee of Ministers and submitted to the Consultative Assembly for opinion. Any amendments approved by the Committee of Ministers shall enter into force as from the thirtieth day after all the Contracting Parties have informed the Secretary General of their acceptance. The Secretary General shall notify all the members of the Council of Europe and the Director-General of the International Labour Office of the entry into force of such amendments.

*Article 37—Denunciation*

1. Any Contracting Party may denounce this Charter only at the end of a period of five years from the date on which the Charter entered into force for it, or at the end of any successive period of two years, and, in each case, after giving six months notice to the Secretary General of the Council of Europe who shall inform the other Parties and the Director-General of the International Labour Office accordingly. Such denunciation shall not affect the validity of the Charter in respect of the other Contracting Parties provided that at all times there are not less than five such Contracting Parties.

2. Any Contracting Party may, in accordance with the provisions set out in the preceding paragraph, denounce any article or paragraph of Part II of the Charter accepted by it provided that the number of articles or paragraphs by which this Contracting Party is bound shall never be less than 10 in the former case and 45 in the latter and that this number of articles or paragraphs shall continue to include the articles selected by the Contracting Party among those to which special reference is made in Article 20, paragraph 1, sub-paragraph (b).

3. Any Contracting Party may denounce the present Charter or any of the articles or paragraphs of Part II of the Charter, under the conditions specified in paragraph 1 of this article in respect of any territory to which the said Charter is applicable by virtue of a declaration made in accordance with paragraph 2 of Article 34.

*Article 38—Appendix*

The Appendix to this Charter shall form an integral part of it.

In witness whereof, the undersigned, being duly authorized thereto, have signed this Charter.

*Done* at Turin, this 18th day of October 1961, in English and French, both texts being equally authoritative, in a single copy which shall be deposited within the archives of the Council of Europe. The Secretary General shall transmit certified copies to each of the Signatories.


# APPENDIX TO THE SOCIAL CHARTER

Scope of the Social Charter in terms of persons protected

1. Without prejudice to Article 12, paragraph 4, and Article 13, paragraph 4, the persons covered by Articles 1 to 17 include foreigners only insofar as they are

nationals of other Contracting Parties lawfully resident or working regularly within the territory of the Contracting Party concerned, subject to the understanding that these articles are to be interpreted in the light of the provisions of Articles 18 and 19. This interpretation would not prejudice the extension of similar facilities to other persons by any of the Contracting Parties.

2. Each Contracting Party will grant to refugees as defined in the Convention relating to the Status of Refugees, signed at Geneva on 28th July 1951, and lawfully staying in its territory, treatment as favourable as possible, and in any case not less favourable than under the obligations accepted by the Contracting Party under the said Convention and under any other existing international instruments applicable to those refugees.

## PART I, PARAGRAPH 18, AND PART II, ARTICLE 18, PARAGRAPH 1

It is understood that these provisions are not concerned with the question of entry into the territories of the Contracting Parties and do not prejudice the provisions of the European Convention on Establishment, signed at Paris on 13th December 1955.

## PART II

*Article* 1, *paragraph* 2

This provision shall not be interpreted as prohibiting or authorizing any union security clause or practice.

*Article* 4, *paragraph* 4

This provision shall be so understood as not to prohibit immediate dismissal for any serious offence.

*Article* 4, *paragraph* 5

It is understood that a Contracting Party may give the undertaking required in this paragraph if the great majority of workers are not permitted to suffer deductions from wages either by law or through collective agreements or arbitration awards, the exceptions being those persons not so covered.

*Article* 6, *paragraph* 4

It is understood that each Contracting Party may, insofar as it is concerned, regulate the exercise of the right to strike by law, provided that any further restriction that this might place on the right can be justified under the terms of Article 31.

*Article* 7, *paragraph* 8

It is understood that a Contracting Party may give the undertaking required in this paragraph if it fulfils the spirit of the undertaking by providing by law that the great majority of persons under 18 years of age shall not be employed in night work.

*Article* 12, *paragraph* 4

The words 'and subject to the conditions laid down in such agreements' in the introduction to this paragraph are taken to imply *inter alia* that with regard to benefits which are available independently of any insurance contribution a Contracting Party may require the completion of a prescribed period of residence before granting such benefits to nationals of other Contracting Parties.

*Article* 13, *paragraph* 4

Governments not Parties to the European Convention on Social and Medical Assistance may ratify the Social Charter in respect of this paragraph provided that they grant to nationals of other Contracting Parties a treatment which is in conformity with the provisions of the said Convention.

*Article* 19, *paragraph* 6

For the purpose of this provision, the term 'family of a foreign worker' is understood to mean at least his wife and dependent children under the age of 21 years.

# PART III

It is understood that the Charter contains legal obligations of an international character, the application of which is submitted solely to the supervision provided for in Part IV thereof.

*Article* 20, *paragraph* 1

It is understood that the 'numbered paragraphs' may include articles consisting of only one paragraph.

# PART V

*Article* 30

The term 'in time of war or other public emergency' shall be so understood as to cover also the threat of war.

## 57. ADDITIONAL PROTOCOL TO THE EUROPEAN SOCIAL CHARTER, 1988

This first Additional Protocol to the European Social Charter (ETS No. 128) was opened for signature by the Member States of the Council of Europe who are signatories to the Charter on 5 May 1988; it entered into force on 4 September 1992.

The Additional Protocol aims at extending the protection of the social and economic rights guaranteed by the European Social Charter, particularly the right for workers to equal opportunities and equal treatment in matters of employment and occupation without discrimination on the ground of sex; the right for workers to be informed and consulted within the undertaking; the right for workers to take part in the determination of working conditions and the working environment in the undertaking; and the right for elderly persons to social protection.

*TEXT*

### Preamble

The member States of the Council of Europe signatory hereto,

*Resolved* to take new measures to extend the protection of the social and economic rights guaranteed by the European Social Charter, opened for signature in Turin on 18 October 1961 (hereinafter referred to as 'the Charter'),

*Have agreed* as follows:

### PART I

The Parties accept as the aim of their policy to be pursued by all appropriate means, both national and international in character, the attainment of conditions in which the following rights and principles may be effectively realised:

1. All workers have the right to equal opportunities and equal treatment in matters of employment and occupation without discrimination on the grounds of sex.

2. Workers have the right to be informed and to be consulted within the undertaking.

3. Workers have the right to take part in the determination and improvement of the working conditions and working environment in the undertaking.

4. Every elderly person has the right to social protection.

### PART II

The Parties undertake, as provided for in Part III, to consider themselves bound by the obligations laid down in the following articles:

*Article* 1—*Right to equal opportunities and equal treatment in matters of employment and occupation without discrimination on the grounds of sex*

1. With a view to ensuring the effective exercise of the right to equal opportunities and equal treatment in matters of employment and occupation without discrimination on the grounds of sex, the Parties undertake to recognize that right and to take appropriate measures to ensure or promote its application in the following fields:

— access to employment, protection against dismissal and occupational resettlement;

— vocational guidance, training, retraining and rehabilitation;

— terms of employment and working conditions including remuneration;

— career development including promotion.

2. Provisions concerning the protection of women, particularly as regards pregnancy, confinement and the post-natal period, shall not be deemed to be discrimination as referred to in paragraph 1 of this article.

3. Paragraph 1 of this article shall not prevent the adoption of specific measures aimed at removing *de facto* inequalities.

4. Occupational activities which, by reason of their nature or the context in which they are carried out, can be entrusted only to persons of a particular sex may be excluded from the scope of this article or some of its provisions.

*Article* 2—*Right to information and consultation*

1. With a view to ensuring the effective exercise of the right of workers to be informed and consulted within the undertaking, the Parties undertake to adopt or encourage measures enabling workers or their representatives, in accordance with national legislation and practice:

(a) to be informed regularly or at the appropriate time and in a comprehensible way about the economic and financial situation of the undertaking employing them, on the understanding that the disclosure of certain information which could be prejudicial to the undertaking may be refused or subject to confidentiality; and

(b) to be consulted in good time on proposed decisions which could substantially affect the interests of workers, particularly on those decisions which could have an important impact on the employment situation in the undertaking.

2. The Parties may exclude from the field of application of paragraph 1 of this article, those undertakings employing less than a certain number of workers to be determined by national legislation or practice.

*Article* 3—*Right to take part in the determination and improvement of the working conditions and working environment*

1. With a view to ensuring the effective exercise of the right of workers to take part in the determination and improvement of the working conditions and working environment in the undertaking, the Parties undertake to adopt or encourage measures enabling workers or their representatives, in accordance with national legislation and practice, to contribute:

(a) to the determination and the improvement of the working conditions, work organization and working environment;

(b) to the protection of health and safety within the undertaking;

(c) to the organization of social and socio-cultural services and facilities within the undertaking;

(d) to the supervision of the observance of regulations on these matters.

2. The Parties may exclude from the field of application of paragraph 1 of this article, those undertakings employing less than a certain number of workers to be determined by national legislation or practice.

*Article 4—Right of elderly persons to social protection*

With a view to ensuring the effective exercise of the right of elderly persons to social protection, the Parties undertake to adopt or encourage, either directly or in co-operation with public or private organizations, appropriate measures designed in particular:

1. to enable elderly persons to remain full members of society for as long as possible, by means of:

(a) adequate resources enabling them to lead a decent life and play an active part in public, social and cultural life;

(b) provision of information about services and facilities available for elderly persons and their opportunities to make use of them;

2. to enable elderly persons to choose their life-style freely and to lead independent lives in their familiar surroundings for as long as they wish and are able, by means of:

(a) provision of housing suited to their needs and their state of health or of adequate support for adapting their housing;

(b) the health care and the services necessitated by their state;

3. to guarantee elderly persons living in institutions appropriate support, while respecting their privacy, and participation in decisions concerning living conditions in the institution.

## PART III

*Article 5—Undertakings*

1. Each of the Parties undertakes:

(a) to consider Part I of this Protocol as a declaration of the aims which it will pursue by all appropriate means, as stated in the introductory paragraph of that part;

(b) to consider itself bound by one or more articles of Part II of this Protocol.

2. The article or articles selected in accordance with sub-paragraph (b) of paragraph 1 of this article, shall be notified to the Secretary-General of the Council of Europe at the time when the instrument of ratification, acceptance or approval of the Contracting State concerned is deposited.

3. Any Party may, at a later date, declare by notification to the Secretary General that it considers itself bound by any articles of Part II of this Protocol which it has not already accepted under the terms of paragraph 1 of this article. Such undertakings subsequently given shall be deemed to be an integral part of the ratification, acceptance or approval, and shall have the same effect as from the thirtieth day after the date of the notification.


## PART IV

*Article 6—Supervision of compliance with the undertakings given*

The Parties shall submit reports on the application of those provisions of Part II of this Protocol which they have accepted in the reports submitted by virtue of Article 21 of the Charter.


## PART V

*Article 7—Implementation of the undertakings given*

1. The relevant provisions of Articles 1 to 4 of Part II of this Protocol may be implemented by:

   (a)  laws or regulations;

   (b)  agreements between employers or employers' organizations and workers' organizations;

   (c)  a combination of those two methods; or

   (d)  other appropriate means.

2. Compliance with the undertakings deriving from Articles 2 and 3 of Part II of this Protocol shall be regarded as effective if the provisions are applied, in accordance with paragraph 1 of this article, to the great majority of the workers concerned.

*Article 8—Relations between the Charter and this Protocol*

1. The provisions of this Protocol shall not prejudice the provisions of the Charter.

2. Articles 22 to 32 and Article 36 of the Charter shall apply, *mutatis mutandis*, to this Protocol.

*Article 9—Territorial application*

1. This Protocol shall apply to the metropolitan territory of each Party. Any State may, at the time of signature or when depositing its instrument of ratification, acceptance or approval, specify by declaration addressed to the Secretary General of the Council of Europe, the territory which shall be considered to be its metropolitan territory for this purpose.

2. Any Contracting State may, at the time of ratification, acceptance or approval of this Protocol or at any time thereafter, declare by notification addressed to the

Secretary General of the Council of Europe that the Protocol shall extend in whole or in part to a non-metropolitan territory or territories specified in the said declaration for whose international relations it is responsible or for which it assumes international responsibility. It shall specify in the declaration the article or articles of Part II of this Protocol which it accepts as binding in respect of the territories named in the declaration.

3. This Protocol shall enter into force in respect of the territory or territories named in the aforesaid declaration as from the thirtieth day after the date on which the Secretary General shall have notification of such declaration.

4. Any Party may declare at a later date by notification addressed to the Secretary General of the Council of Europe, that, in respect of one or more of the territories to which this Protocol has been extended in accordance with paragraph 2 of this article, it accepts as binding any articles which it has not already accepted in respect of that territory or territories. Such undertakings subsequently given shall be deemed to be an integral part of the original declaration in respect of the territory concerned, and shall have the same effect as from the thirtieth day after the date on which the Secretary General shall have notification of such declaration.

*Article 10—Signature, ratification, acceptance, approval and entry into force*

1. This Protocol shall be open for signature by member States of the Council of Europe who are signatories to the Charter. It is subject to ratification, acceptance or approval. No member State of the Council of Europe shall ratify, accept or approve this Protocol except at the same time as or after ratification of the Charter. Instruments of ratification, acceptance or approval shall be deposited with the Secretary General of the Council of Europe.

2. This Protocol shall enter into force on the thirtieth day after the date of deposit of the third instrument of ratification, acceptance or approval.

3. In respect of any signatory State ratifying subsequently, this Protocol shall come into force as from the thirtieth day after the date of deposit of its instrument of ratification, acceptance or approval.

*Article 11—Denunciation*

1. Any Party may denounce this Protocol only at the end of a period of five years from the date on which the Protocol entered into force for it, or at the end of any successive period of two years, and, in each case, after giving six months' notice to the Secretary General of the Council of Europe. Such denunciation shall not affect the validity of the Protocol in respect of the other Parties provided that at all times there are not less than three such Parties.

2. Any Party may, in accordance with the provisions set out in the preceding paragraph, denounce any article of Part II of this Protocol accepted by it, provided that the number of articles by which this Party is bound shall never be less than one.

3. Any Party may denounce this Protocol or any of the articles of Part II of the Protocol, under the conditions specified in paragraph 1 of this article, in respect of any territory to which the Protocol is applicable by virtue of a declaration made in accordance with paragraphs 2 and 4 of Article 9.

4. Any Party bound by the Charter and this Protocol which denounces the Charter in accordance with the provisions of paragraph 1 of Article 37 thereof, will be considered to have denounced the Protocol likewise.

*Article 12—Notifications*

The Secretary General of the Council of Europe shall notify the member States of the Council and the Director-General of the International Labour Office of:

    (a)   any signature;

    (b)   the deposit of any instrument of ratification, acceptance or approval;

    (c)   any date of entry into force of this Protocol in accordance with Articles 9 and 10;

    (d)   any other act, notification or communication relating to this Protocol.

*Article 13—Appendix*

The appendix to this Protocol shall form an integral part of it.

In witness whereof the undersigned, being duly authorized thereto, have signed this Protocol.

*Done* at Strasbourg, this 5th day of May, 1988, in English and French, both texts being equally authentic, in a single copy which shall be deposited in the archives of the Council of Europe. The Secretary General of the Council in Europe shall transmit certified copies to each member State of the Council of Europe.

# APPENDIX TO THE PROTOCOL

### *Scope of the Protocol in terms of persons protected*

1. The persons covered by Articles 1 to 4 include foreigners only insofar as they are nationals of other Parties lawfully resident or working regularly within the territory of the Party concerned subject to the understanding that these articles are to be interpreted in the light of the provisions of Articles 18 and 19 of the Charter. This interpretation would not prejudice the extension of similar facilities to other persons by any of the Parties.

2. Each Party will grant to refugees as defined in the Convention relating to the Status of Refugees, signed at Geneva on 28 July 1951 and in the Protocol of 31 January 1967, and lawfully staying in its territory, treatment as favourable as possible and in any case not less favourable than under the obligations accepted by the Party under the said instruments and under any other existing international instruments applicable to those refugees.

3. Each Party will grant to stateless persons as defined in the Convention on the Status of Stateless Persons done at New York on 28 September 1954 and lawfully staying in its territory, treatment as favourable as possible and in any case not less favourable than under the obligations accepted by the Party under the said instrument and under any other existing international instruments applicable to those stateless persons.

*Article* 1

It is understood that social security matters, as well as other provisions relating to unemployment benefit, old age benefit and survivor's benefit, may be excluded from the scope of this article.

*Article* 1, *paragraph* 4

This provision is not to be interpreted as requiring the Parties to embody in laws or regulations a list of occupations which, by reason of their nature or the context in which they are carried out, may be reserved to persons of a particular sex.

*Articles* 2 *and* 3

1. For the purpose of the application of these articles, the term 'workers' representatives' means persons who are recognised as such under national legislation or practice.

2. The term 'national legislation and practice' embraces as the case may be, in addition to laws and regulations, collective agreements, other agreements between employers and workers' representatives, customs, as well as relevant case law.

3. For the purpose of the application of these articles, the term 'undertaking' is understood as referring to a set of tangible and intangible components, with or without legal personality, formed to produce or provide services for financial gain and with power to determine its own market policy.

4. It is understood that religious communities and their institutions may be excluded from the application of these articles, even if these institutions are 'undertakings' within the meaning of paragraph 3. Establishments pursuing activities which are inspired by certain ideals or guided by certain moral concepts, ideals and concepts which are protected by national legislation, may be excluded from the application of these articles to such an extent as is necessary to protect the orientation of the undertaking.

5. It is understood that where in a State the rights set out in Articles 2 and 3 are exercised in the various establishments of the undertaking, the Party concerned is to be considered as fulfilling the obligations deriving from these provisions.

*Article* 3

This provision affects neither the powers and obligations of States as regards the adoption of health and safety regulations for workplaces, nor the powers and responsibilities of the bodies in charge of monitoring their application. The terms 'social and socio-cultural services and facilities' are understood as referring to the social and/or cultural facilities for workers provided by some undertakings such as welfare assistance, sports fields, rooms for nursing mothers, libraries, children's holiday camps, etc.

*Article* 4, *paragraph* 1

For the purpose of the application of this paragraph, the term 'for as long as possible' refers to the elderly person's physical, psychological and intellectual capacities.

*Article* 7

It is understood that workers excluded in accordance with paragraph 2 of Article 2 and paragraph 2 of Article 3 are not taken into account in establishing the number of workers concerned.

## 58. PROTOCOL AMENDING THE EUROPEAN SOCIAL CHARTER, 1991

This Protocol (ETS No. 142) was opened for signature by the Member States of the Council of Europe signatories to the Charter on 21 October 1991, and will enter into force once it has been ratified by all Parties to the Charter. It seeks to improve the Charter's control machinery, to clarify the functions of two principal organs (the Committee of Independent Experts and the Governmental Committee), and to strengthen the political role of the Committee of Ministers and the Parliamentary Assembly of the Council of Europe.

*TEXT*

The member States of the Council of Europe, signatory to this Protocol to the European Social Charter, opened for signature in Turin on 18 October 1961 (hereinafter referred to as 'the Charter'),

*Being resolved* to take some measures to improve the effectiveness of the Charter, and particularly the functioning of its supervisory machinery;

*Considering* therefore that it is desirable to amend certain provisions of the Charter,

*Have agreed* as follows:

*Article* 1

Article 23 of the Charter shall read as follows:

'*Article 23—Communication of copies of reports and comments*

1. When sending to the Secretary General a report pursuant to Articles 21 and 22, each Contracting Party shall forward a copy of that report to such of its national organizations as are members of the international organizations of employers and trade unions invited, under Article 27, paragraph 2, to be represented at meetings of the Governmental Committee. Those organizations shall send to the Secretary General any comments on the reports of the Contracting Parties. The Secretary General shall send a copy of those comments to the Contracting Parties concerned, who might wish to respond.

2. The Secretary General shall forward a copy of the reports of the Contracting Parties to the international non-governmental organizations which have consultative status with the Council of Europe and have particular competence in the matters governed by the present Charter.

3. The reports and comments referred to in Articles 21 and 22 and in the present article shall be made available to the public on request.'

*Article* 2

Article 24 of the Charter shall read as follows:

'*Article 24—Examination of the reports*

1. The reports sent to the Secretary General in accordance with Articles 21 and 22 shall be examined by a Committee of Independent Experts constituted pursuant to Article 25. The committee shall also have before it any comments forwarded to the Secretary General in accordance with paragraph 1 of Article 23. On completion of its examination, the Committee of Independent Experts shall draw up a report containing its conclusions.

2. With regard to the reports referred to in Article 21, the Committee of Independent Experts shall assess from a legal standpoint the compliance of national law and practice with the obligations arising from the Charter for the Contracting Parties concerned.

3. The Committee of Independent Experts may address requests for additional information and clarification directly to Contracting Parties. In this connection the Committee of Independent Experts may also hold, if necessary, a meeting with the representatives of a Contracting Party, either on its own initiative or at the request of the Contracting Party concerned. The organizations referred to in paragraph 1 of Article 23 shall be kept informed.

4. The conclusions of the Committee of Independent Experts shall be made public and communicated by the Secretary General to the Governmental Committee, to the Parliamentary Assembly and to the organizations which are mentioned in paragraph 1 of Article 23 and paragraph 2 of Article 27.'

## Article 3

Article 25 of the Charter shall read as follows:

'*Article 25—Committee of Independent Experts*

1. The Committee of Independent Experts shall consist of at least nine members elected by the Parliamentary Assembly by a majority of votes cast from a list of experts of the highest integrity and of recognised competence in national and international social questions, nominated by the Contracting Parties. The exact number of members shall be determined by the Committee of Ministers.

2. The members of the committee shall be elected for a period of six years. They may stand for re-election once.

3. A member of the Committee of Independent Experts elected to replace a member whose term of office has not expired shall hold office for the remainder of his predecessor's term.

4. The members of the committee shall sit in their individual capacity. Throughout their term of office, they may not perform any function incompatible with the requirements of independence, impartiality and availability inherent in their office.'

## Article 4

Article 27 of the Charter shall read as follows:

'*Article 27—Governmental Committee*

1. The reports of the Contracting Parties, the comments and information

communicated in accordance with paragraphs 1 of Article 23 and 3 of Article 24, and the reports of the Committee of Independent Experts shall be submitted to a Governmental Committee.

2. The committee shall be composed of one representative of each of the Contracting Parties. It shall invite no more than two international organizations of employers and no more than two international trade union organizations to send observers in a consultative capacity to its meetings. Moreover, it may consult representatives of international non-governmental organizations which have consultative status with the Council of Europe and have particular competence in the matters governed by the present Charter.

3. The Governmental Committee shall prepare the decisions of the Committee of Ministers. In particular, in the light of the reports of the Committee of Independent Experts and of the Contracting Parties, it shall select, giving reasons for its choice, on the basis of social, economic and other policy considerations the situations which should, in its view, be the subject of recommendations to each Contracting Party concerned, in accordance with Article 28 of the Charter. It shall present to the Committee of Ministers a report which shall be made public.

4. On the basis of its findings on the implementation of the Social Charter in general, the Governmental Committee may submit proposals to the Committee of Ministers aiming at studies to be carried out on social issues and on articles of the Charter which possibly might be updated.'

*Article 5*

Article 28 of the Charter shall read as follows:

'*Article 28—Committee of Ministers*

1. The Committee of Ministers shall adopt, by a majority of two-thirds of those voting, with entitlement to voting limited to the Contracting Parties, on the basis of the report of the Governmental Committee, a resolution covering the entire supervision cycle and containing individual recommendations to the Contracting Parties concerned.

2. Having regard to the proposals made by the Governmental Committee pursuant to paragraph 4 of Article 27, the Committee of Ministers shall take such decisions as it deems appropriate.'

*Article 6*

Article 29 of the Charter shall read as follows:

'*Article 29—Parliamentary Assembly*

The Secretary General of the Council of Europe shall transmit to the Parliamentary Assembly, with a view to the holding of periodical plenary debates, the reports of the Committee of Independent Experts and of the Governmental Committee, as well as the resolutions of the Committee of Ministers.'

*Article 7*

1. This Protocol shall be open for signature by member States of the Council of

Europe signatories to the Charter, which may express their consent to be bound by:

(a) signature without reservation as to ratification, acceptance or approval; or

(b) signature subject to ratification, acceptance or approval, followed by ratification, acceptance or approval.

2. Instruments of ratification, acceptance or approval shall be deposited with the Secretary General of the Council of Europe.

*Article* 8

This Protocol shall enter into force on the thirtieth day after the date on which all Contracting Parties to the Charter have expressed their consent to be bound by the Protocol in accordance with the provisions of Article 7.

*Article* 9

The Secretary General of the Council of Europe shall notify the member States of the Council of:

(a) any signature;

(b) the deposit of any instrument of ratification, acceptance or approval;

(c) the date of entry into force of this Protocol in accordance with Article 8;

(d) any other act, notification or communication relating to this Protocol.

In witness whereof the undersigned, being duly authorized thereto, have signed this Protocol.

*Done* at Turin, this 21st day of October 1991, in English and French, both texts being equally authentic, in a single copy which shall be deposited in the archives of the Council of Europe. The Secretary General of the Council of Europe shall transmit certified copies to each member State of the Council of Europe.

## 59. ADDITIONAL PROTOCOL TO THE EUROPEAN SOCIAL CHARTER PROVIDING FOR A SYSTEM OF COLLECTIVE COMPLAINTS, 1995

This Protocol was opened for signature on 9 November 1995 and entered into force on 1 July 1998. It is intended to improve effective enforcement of the Charter, and allows social partners and NGOs to submit collective complaints alleging unsatisfactory performance on the part of a State party, with a view to its examination first by a Committee of Independent Experts and then by the Committee of Ministers. The Protocol also seeks to increase the interest in the Charter of social partners and of non-governmental organizations. For text, see ETS No. 158.

*TEXT*

Preamble

The member States of the Council of Europe, signatories to this Protocol to the European Social Charter, opened for signature in Turin on 18 October 1961 (hereinafter referred to as 'the Charter'),

*Resolved* to take new measures to improve the effective enforcement of the social rights guaranteed by the Charter;

*Considering* that this aim could be achieved in particular by the establishment of a collective complaints procedure, which, *inter alia*, would strengthen the participation of management and labour and of non-governmental organizations,

*Have agreed* as follows:

*Article* 1

The Contracting Parties to this Protocol recognize the right of the following organizations to submit complaints alleging unsatisfactory application of the Charter:

(1) international organizations of employers and trade unions referred to in paragraph 2 of Article 27 of the Charter;

(2) other international non-governmental organizations which have consultative status with the Council of Europe and have been put on a list established for this purpose by the Governmental Committee;

(3) representative national organizations of employers and trade unions within the jurisdiction of the Contracting Party against which they have lodged a complaint.

*Article* 2

1. Any Contracting State may also, when it expresses its consent to be bound by this Protocol, in accordance with the provisions of Article 13, or at any moment thereafter, declare that it recognizes the right of any other representative national non-governmental organization within its jurisdiction which has particular

competence in the matters governed by the Charter, to lodge complaints against it.

2. Such declarations may be made for a specific period.

3. The declarations shall be deposited with the Secretary General of the Council of Europe who shall transmit copies thereof to the Contracting Parties and publish them.

*Article 3*

The international non-governmental organizations and the national non-governmental organizations referred to in Article 1.b and Article 2 respectively may submit complaints in accordance with the procedure prescribed by the aforesaid provisions only in respect of those matters regarding which they have been recognized as having particular competence.

*Article 4*

The complaint shall be lodged in writing, relate to a provision of the Charter accepted by the Contracting Party concerned and indicate in what respect the latter has not ensured the satisfactory application of this provision.

*Article 5*

Any complaint shall be addressed to the Secretary General who shall acknowledge receipt of it, notify it to the Contracting Party concerned and immediately transmit it to the Committee of Independent Experts.

*Article 6*

The Committee of Independent Experts may request the Contracting Party concerned and the organization which lodged the complaint to submit written information and observations on the admissibility of the complaint within such time-limit as it shall prescribe.

*Article 7*

1. If it decides that a complaint is admissible, the Committee of Independent Experts shall notify the Contracting Parties to the Charter through the Secretary General. It shall request the Contracting Party concerned and the organization which lodged the complaint to submit, within such time-limit as it shall prescribe, all relevant written explanations or information, and the other Contracting Parties to this Protocol, the comments they wish to submit, within the same time-limit.

2. If the complaint has been lodged by a national organization of employers or a national trade union or by another national or international non-governmental organization, the Committee of Independent Experts shall notify the international organizations of employers or trade unions referred to in paragraph 2 of Article 27 of the Charter, through the Secretary General, and invite them to submit observations within such time-limit as it shall prescribe.

3. On the basis of the explanations, information or observations submitted under paragraphs 1 and 2 above, the Contracting Party concerned and the organization which lodged the complaint may submit any additional written information or observations within such time-limit as the Committee of Independent Experts shall prescribe.

4. In the course of the examination of the complaint, the Committee of Independent Experts may organize a hearing with the representatives of the parties.

*Article* 8

1. The Committee of Independent Experts shall draw up a report in which it shall describe the steps taken by it to examine the complaint and present its conclusions as to whether or not the Contracting Party concerned has ensured the satisfactory application of the provision of the Charter referred to in the complaint.

2. The report shall be transmitted to the Committee of Ministers. It shall also be transmitted to the organization that lodged the complaint and to the Contracting Parties to the Charter, which shall not be at liberty to publish it. It shall be transmitted to the Parliamentary Assembly and made public at the same time as the resolution referred to in Article 9 or no later than four months after it has been transmitted to the Committee of Ministers.

*Article* 9

1. On the basis of the report of the Committee of Independent Experts, the Committee of Ministers shall adopt a resolution by a majority of those voting. If the Committee of Independent Experts finds that the Charter has not been applied in a satisfactory manner, the Committee of Ministers shall adopt, by a majority of two-thirds of those voting, a recommendation addressed to the Contracting Party concerned. In both cases, entitlement to voting shall be limited to the Contracting Parties to the Charter.

2. At the request of the Contracting Party concerned, the Committee of Ministers may decide, where the report of the Committee of Independent Experts raises new issues, by a two-thirds majority of the Contracting Parties to the Charter, to consult the Governmental Committee.

*Article* 10

The Contracting Party concerned shall provide information on the measures it has taken to give effect to the Committee of Ministers' recommendation, in the next report which it submits to the Secretary General under Article 21 of the Charter.

*Article* 11

Articles 1 to 10 of this Protocol shall apply also to the articles of Part II of the first Additional Protocol to the Charter in respect of the States Parties to that Protocol, to the extent that these articles have been accepted.

*Article* 12

The States Parties to this Protocol consider that the first paragraph of the appendix to the Charter, relating to Part III, reads as follows:

'It is understood that the Charter contains legal obligations of an international character, the application of which is submitted solely to the supervision provided for in Part IV thereof and in the provisions of this Protocol.'

*Article* 13

1. This Protocol shall be open for signature by member States of the Council of

Europe signatories to the Charter, which may express their consent to be bound by:

(1)  signature without reservation as to ratification, acceptance or approval; or

(2)  signature subject to ratification, acceptance or approval, followed by ratification, acceptance or approval.

2. A member State of the Council of Europe may not express its consent to be bound by this Protocol without previously or simultaneously ratifying the Charter.

3. Instruments of ratification, acceptance or approval shall be deposited with the Secretary General of the Council of Europe.

*Article* 14

1. This Protocol shall enter into force on the first day of the month following the expiration of a period of one month after the date on which five member States of the Council of Europe have expressed their consent to be bound by the Protocol in accordance with the provisions of Article 13.

2. In respect of any member State which subsequently expresses its consent to be bound by it, the Protocol shall enter into force on the first day of the month following the expiration of a period of one month after the date of the deposit of the instrument of ratification, acceptance or approval.

*Article* 15

1. Any Party may at any time denounce this Protocol by means of a notification addressed to the Secretary General of the Council of Europe.

2. Such denunciation shall become effective on the first day of the month following the expiration of a period of twelve months after the date of receipt of such notification by the Secretary General.

*Article* 16

The Secretary General of the Council of Europe shall notify all the member States of the Council of:

*(a)*  any signature;

*(b)*  the deposit of any instrument of ratification, acceptance or approval;

*(c)*  the date of entry into force of this Protocol in accordance with Article 14;

*(d)*  any other act, notification or declaration relating to this Protocol.

In witness whereof the undersigned, being duly authorised thereto, have signed this Protocol.

*Done* at Strasbourg, this 9th day of November 1995, in English and French, both texts being equally authentic, in a single copy which shall be deposited in the archives of the Council of Europe. The Secretary General of the Council of Europe shall transmit certified copies to each member State of the Council of Europe.

# 60. EUROPEAN SOCIAL CHARTER (REVISED), 1996

The revised European Social Charter was opened for signature by the member States of the Council of Europe, in Strasbourg, on 3 May 1996, and it entered into force on 1 July 1999. It co-exists with and runs in parallel to the regime established under the 1961 Charter, which it is intended ultimately to replace. The revised Charter does not provide for denunciation of the earlier one, but if a Contracting State accepts the provisions of the revised Charter, the corresponding provisions of the 1961 Charter and its Protocol cease to apply to that State. In this way, States are not simultaneously bound by undertakings at different levels.

The new Charter takes account of the evolution in the understanding and content of social and economic rights since 1961, contains all the rights guaranteed by the original Charter and the 1988 Protocol, and adds the following new rights: right to protection against poverty and social exclusion; right to housing; right to protection in cases of termination of employment; right to protection against sexual harassment in the workplace and other forms of harassment; rights of workers with family responsibilities to equal opportunities and equal treatment; rights of workers' representatives. It also reinforces the principle of non-discrimination, improves gender equality in all fields within the treaty; provides better protection in matters of maternity and social protection of mothers, better social, legal and economic protection of employed children, and better protection of handicapped people.

Enforcement of the new Charter is submitted to the same system of control as the 1961 Charter, as developed by the 1991 Protocol and by the 1995 Protocol, providing a system of collective complaints. For text see ETS No. 163.

*TEXT*

## Preamble

The Governments signatory hereto, being Members of the Council of Europe,

*Considering* that the aim of the Council of Europe is the achievement of greater unity between its members for the purpose of safeguarding and realising the ideals and principles which are their common heritage and of facilitating their economic and social progress, in particular by the maintenance and further realisation of human rights and fundamental freedoms;

*Considering* that in the Convention for the Protection of Human Rights and Fundamental Freedoms signed at Rome on 4 November 1950, and the Protocols thereto, the member States of the Council of Europe agreed to secure to their populations the civil and political rights and freedoms therein specified;

*Considering* that in the European Social Charter opened for signature in Turin on 18 October 1961 and the Protocols thereto, the member States of the Council of Europe agreed to secure to their populations the social rights specified therein in order to improve their standard of living and their social well-being;

*Recalling* that the Ministerial Conference on Human Rights held in Rome on 5 November 1990 stressed the need, on the one hand, to preserve the indivisible nature of all human rights, be they civil, political, economic, social or cultural and, on the other hand, to give the European Social Charter fresh impetus;

*Resolved,* as was decided during the Ministerial Conference held in Turin on 21 and 22 October 1991, to update and adapt the substantive contents of the Charter in order to take account in particular of the fundamental social changes which have occurred since the text was adopted;

*Recognising* the advantage of embodying in a Revised Charter, designed progressively to take the place of the European Social Charter, the rights guaranteed by the Charter as amended, the rights guaranteed by the Additional Protocol of 1988 and to add new rights,

*Have agreed* as follows:

## PART I

The Parties accept as the aim of their policy, to be pursued by all appropriate means both national and international in character, the attainment of conditions in which the following rights and principles may be effectively realised:

(1) Everyone shall have the opportunity to earn his living in an occupation freely entered upon.

(2) All workers have the right to just conditions of work.

(3) All workers have the right to safe and healthy working conditions.

(4) All workers have the right to a fair remuneration sufficient for a decent standard of living for themselves and their families.

(5) All workers and employers have the right to freedom of association in national or international organizations for the protection of their economic and social interests.

(6) All workers and employers have the right to bargain collectively.

(7) Children and young persons have the right to a special protection against the physical and moral hazards to which they are exposed.

(8) Employed women, in case of maternity, have the right to a special protection.

(9) Everyone has the right to appropriate facilities for vocational guidance with a view to helping him choose an occupation suited to his personal aptitude and interests.

(10) Everyone has the right to appropriate facilities for vocational training.

(11) Everyone has the right to benefit from any measures enabling him to enjoy the highest possible standard of health attainable.

(12) All workers and their dependents have the right to social security.

(13) Anyone without adequate resources has the right to social and medical assistance.

(14) Everyone has the right to benefit from social welfare services.

(15) Disabled persons have the right to independence, social integration and participation in the life of the community.

(16) The family as a fundamental unit of society has the right to appropriate social, legal and economic protection to ensure its full development.

(17) Children and young persons have the right to appropriate social, legal and economic protection.

(18) The nationals of any one of the Parties have the right to engage in any gainful occupation in the territory of any one of the others on a footing of equality with the nationals of the latter, subject to restrictions based on cogent economic or social reasons.

(19) Migrant workers who are nationals of a Party and their families have the right to protection and assistance in the territory of any other Party.

(20) All workers have the right to equal opportunities and equal treatment in matters of employment and occupation without discrimination on the grounds of sex.

(21) Workers have the right to be informed and to be consulted within the undertaking.

(22) Workers have the right to take part in the determination and improvement of the working conditions and working environment in the undertaking.

(23) Every elderly person has the right to social protection.

(24) All workers have the right to protection in cases of termination of employment.

(25) All workers have the right to protection of their claims in the event of the insolvency of their employer.

(26) All workers have the right to dignity at work.

(27) All persons with family responsibilities and who are engaged or wish to engage in employment have a right to do so without being subject to discrimination and as far as possible without conflict between their employment and family responsibilities.

(28) Workers' representatives in undertakings have the right to protection against acts prejudicial to them and should be afforded appropriate facilities to carry out their functions.

(29) All workers have the right to be informed and consulted in collective redundancy procedures.

(30) Everyone has the right to protection against poverty and social exclusion.

(31) Everyone has the right to housing.


# PART II

The Parties undertake, as provided for in Part III, to consider themselves bound by the obligations laid down in the following articles and paragraphs.

*Article 1—The right to work*

With a view to ensuring the effective exercise of the right to work, the Parties undertake:

(1) to accept as one of their primary aims and responsibilities the achievement and maintenance of as high and stable a level of employment as possible, with a view to the attainment of full employment;

(2)  to protect effectively the right of the worker to earn his living in an occupa-tion freely entered upon;

(3)  to establish or maintain free employment services for all workers;

(4)  to provide or promote appropriate vocational guidance, training and rehabilitation.

*Article 2—The right to just conditions of work*

With a view to ensuring the effective exercise of the right to just conditions of work, the Parties undertake:

(1)  to provide for reasonable daily and weekly working hours, the working week to be progressively reduced to the extent that the increase of productivity and other relevant factors permit;

(2)  to provide for public holidays with pay;

(3)  to provide for a minimum of four weeks' annual holiday with pay;

(4)  to eliminate risks in inherently dangerous or unhealthy occupations, and where it has not yet been possible to eliminate or reduce sufficiently these risks, to provide for either a reduction of working hours or additional paid holidays for workers engaged in such occupations;

(5)  to ensure a weekly rest period which shall, as far as possible, coincide with the day recognised by tradition or custom in the country or region concerned as a day of rest;

(6)  to ensure that workers are informed in written form, as soon as possible, and in any event not later than two months after the date of commencing their employment, of the essential aspects of the contract or employment relationship;

(7)  to ensure that workers performing night work benefit from measures which take account of the special nature of the work.

*Article 3—The right to safe and healthy working conditions*

With a view to ensuring the effective exercise of the right to safe and healthy working conditions, the Parties undertake, in consultation with employers' and workers' organizations:

(1)  to formulate, implement and periodically review a coherent national policy on occupational safety, occupational health and the working environment. The primary aim of this policy shall be to improve occupational safety and health and to prevent accidents and injury to health arising out of, linked with or occurring in the course of work, particularly by minimising the causes of hazards inherent in the working environment;

(2)  to issue safety and health regulations;

(3)  to provide for the enforcement of such regulations by measures of supervision;

(4)  to promote the progressive development of occupational health services for all workers with essentially preventive and advisory functions.

*Article 4—The right to a fair remuneration*

With a view to ensuring the effective exercise of the right to a fair remuneration, the Parties undertake:

(1)  to recognize the right of workers to a remuneration such as will give them and their families a decent standard of living;

(2)  to recognize the right of workers to an increased rate of remuneration for overtime work, subject to exceptions in particular cases;

(3)  to recognize the right of men and women workers to equal pay for work of equal value;

(4)  to recognize the right of all workers to a reasonable period of notice for termination of employment;

(5)  to permit deductions from wages only under conditions and to the extent prescribed by national laws or regulations or fixed by collective agreements or arbitration awards.

The exercise of these rights shall be achieved by freely concluded collective agreements, by statutory wage-fixing machinery, or by other means appropriate to national conditions.

*Article 5—The right to organize*

With a view to ensuring or promoting the freedom of workers and employers to form local, national or international organizations for the protection of their economic and social interests and to join those organizations, the Parties undertake that national law shall not be such as to impair, nor shall it be so applied as to impair, this freedom. The extent to which the guarantees provided for in this article shall apply to the police shall be determined by national laws or regulations. The principle governing the application to the members of the armed forces of these guarantees and the extent to which they shall apply to persons in this category shall equally be determined by national laws or regulations.

*Article 6—The right to bargain collectively*

With a view to ensuring the effective exercise of the right to bargain collectively, the Parties undertake:

(1)  to promote joint consultation between workers and employers;

(2)  to promote, where necessary and appropriate, machinery for voluntary negotiations between employers or employers' organizations and workers' organizations, with a view to the regulation of terms and conditions of employment by means of collective agreements;

(3)  to promote the establishment and use of appropriate machinery for conciliation and voluntary arbitration for the settlement of labour disputes;

and recognize:

(4)  the right of workers and employers to collective action in cases of conflicts of interest, including the right to strike, subject to obligations that might arise out of collective agreements previously entered into.

*Article 7—The right of children and young persons to protection*

With a view to ensuring the effective exercise of the right of children and young persons to protection, the Parties undertake:

(1)  to provide that the minimum age of admission to employment shall be 15 years, subject to exceptions for children employed in prescribed light work without harm to their health, morals or education;

(2)  to provide that the minimum age of admission to employment shall be 18 years with respect to prescribed occupations regarded as dangerous or unhealthy;

(3)  to provide that persons who are still subject to compulsory education shall not be employed in such work as would deprive them of the full benefit of their education;

(4)  to provide that the working hours of persons under 18 years of age shall be limited in accordance with the needs of their development, and particularly with their need for vocational training;

(5)  to recognize the right of young workers and apprentices to a fair wage or other appropriate allowances;

(6)  to provide that the time spent by young persons in vocational training during the normal working hours with the consent of the employer shall be treated as forming part of the working day;

(7)  to provide that employed persons of under 18 years of age shall be entitled to a minimum of four weeks' annual holiday with pay;

(8)  to provide that persons under 18 years of age shall not be employed in night work with the exception of certain occupations provided for by national laws or regulations;

(9)  to provide that persons under 18 years of age employed in occupations prescribed by national laws or regulations shall be subject to regular medical control;

(10) to ensure special protection against physical and moral dangers to which children and young persons are exposed, and particularly against those resulting directly or indirectly from their work.

*Article 8—The right of employed women to protection of maternity*

With a view to ensuring the effective exercise of the right of employed women to the protection of maternity, the Parties undertake:

(1)  to provide either by paid leave, by adequate social security benefits or by benefits from public funds for employed women to take leave before and after childbirth up to a total of at least fourteen weeks;

(2)  to consider it as unlawful for an employer to give a woman notice of dismissal during the period from the time she notifies her employer that she is pregnant until the end of her maternity leave, or to give her notice of dismissal at such a time that the notice would expire during such a period;

(3)  to provide that mothers who are nursing their infants shall be entitled to sufficient time off for this purpose;

(4) to regulate the employment in night work of pregnant women, women who have recently given birth and women nursing their infants;

(5) to prohibit the employment of pregnant women, women who have recently given birth or who are nursing their infants in underground mining and all other work which is unsuitable by reason of its dangerous, unhealthy or arduous nature and to take appropriate measures to protect the employment rights of these women.

*Article 9—The right to vocational guidance*

With a view to ensuring the effective exercise of the right to vocational guidance, the Parties undertake to provide or promote, as necessary, a service which will assist all persons, including the handicapped, to solve problems related to occupational choice and progress, with due regard to the individual's characteristics and their relation to occupational opportunity: this assistance should be available free of charge, both to young persons, including schoolchildren, and to adults.

*Article 10—The right to vocational training*

With a view to ensuring the effective exercise of the right to vocational training, the Parties undertake:

(1) to provide or promote, as necessary, the technical and vocational training of all persons, including the handicapped, in consultation with employers' and workers' organizations, and to grant facilities for access to higher technical and university education, based solely on individual aptitude;

(2) to provide or promote a system of apprenticeship and other systematic arrangements for training young boys and girls in their various employments;

(3) to provide or promote, as necessary:
   *(a)* adequate and readily available training facilities for adult workers;
   *(b)* special facilities for the retraining of adult workers needed as a result of technological development or new trends in employment;

(4) to provide or promote, as necessary, special measures for the retraining and reintegration of the long-term unemployed;

(5) to encourage the full utilisation of the facilities provided by appropriate measures such as:
   *(a)* reducing or abolishing any fees or charges;
   *(b)* granting financial assistance in appropriate cases;
   *(c)* including in the normal working hours time spent on supplementary training taken by the worker, at the request of his employer, during employment;
   *(d)* ensuring, through adequate supervision, in consultation with the employers' and workers' organizations, the efficiency of apprenticeship and other training arrangements for young workers, and the adequate protection of young workers generally.

*Article 11—The right to protection of health*

With a view to ensuring the effective exercise of the right to protection of health, the Parties undertake, either directly or in cooperation with public or private organizations, to take appropriate measures designed *inter alia*:

(1) to remove as far as possible the causes of ill-health;

(2) to provide advisory and educational facilities for the promotion of health and the encouragement of individual responsibility in matters of health;

(3) to prevent as far as possible epidemic, endemic and other diseases, as well as accidents.

*Article 12—The right to social security*

With a view to ensuring the effective exercise of the right to social security, the Parties undertake:

(1) to establish or maintain a system of social security;

(2) to maintain the social security system at a satisfactory level at least equal to that necessary for the ratification of the European Code of Social Security;

(3) to endeavour to raise progressively the system of social security to a higher level;

(4) to take steps, by the conclusion of appropriate bilateral and multilateral agreements or by other means, and subject to the conditions laid down in such agreements, in order to ensure:

    *(a)* equal treatment with their own nationals of the nationals of other Parties in respect of social security rights, including the retention of benefits arising out of social security legislation, whatever movements the persons protected may undertake between the territories of the Parties;

    *(b)* the granting, maintenance and resumption of social security rights by such means as the accumulation of insurance or employment periods completed under the legislation of each of the Parties.

*Article 13—The right to social and medical assistance*

With a view to ensuring the effective exercise of the right to social and medical assistance, the Parties undertake:

(1) to ensure that any person who is without adequate resources and who is unable to secure such resources either by his own efforts or from other sources, in particular by benefits under a social security scheme, be granted adequate assistance, and, in case of sickness, the care necessitated by his condition;

(2) to ensure that persons receiving such assistance shall not, for that reason, suffer from a diminution of their political or social rights;

(3) to provide that everyone may receive by appropriate public or private services such advice and personal help as may be required to prevent, to remove, or to alleviate personal or family want;

(4) to apply the provisions referred to in paragraphs 1, 2 and 3 of this article on an equal footing with their nationals to nationals of other Parties lawfully within their territories, in accordance with their obligations under the European Convention on Social and Medical Assistance, signed at Paris on 11 December 1953.

*Article 14—The right to benefit from social welfare services*

With a view to ensuring the effective exercise of the right to benefit from social welfare services, the Parties undertake:

(1) to promote or provide services which, by using methods of social work, would contribute to the welfare and development of both individuals and groups in the community, and to their adjustment to the social environment;

(2) to encourage the participation of individuals and voluntary or other organizations in the establishment and maintenance of such services.

*Article 15—The right of persons with disabilities to independence, social integration and participation in the life of the community*

With a view to ensuring to persons with disabilities, irrespective of age and the nature and origin of their disabilities, the effective exercise of the right to independence, social integration and participation in the life of the community, the Parties undertake, in particular:

(1) to take the necessary measures to provide persons with disabilities with guidance, education and vocational training in the framework of general schemes wherever possible or, where this is not possible, through specialised bodies, public or private;

(2) to promote their access to employment through all measures tending to encourage employers to hire and keep in employment persons with disabilities in the ordinary working environment and to adjust the working conditions to the needs of the disabled or, where this is not possible by reason of the disability, by arranging for or creating sheltered employment according to the level of disability. In certain cases, such measures may require recourse to specialised placement and support services;

(3) to promote their full social integration and participation in the life of the community in particular through measures, including technical aids, aiming to overcome barriers to communication and mobility and enabling access to transport, housing, cultural activities and leisure.

*Article 16—The right of the family to social, legal and economic protection*

With a view to ensuring the necessary conditions for the full development of the family, which is a fundamental unit of society, the Parties undertake to promote the economic, legal and social protection of family life by such means as social and family benefits, fiscal arrangements, provision of family housing, benefits for the newly married and other appropriate means.

*Article 17—The right of children and young persons to social, legal and economic protection*

With a view to ensuring the effective exercise of the right of children and young persons to grow up in an environment which encourages the full development of their personality and of their physical and mental capacities, the Parties undertake, either directly or in co-operation with public and private organizations, to take all appropriate and necessary measures designed:

(1) *(a)* to ensure that children and young persons, taking account of the rights and duties of their parents, have the care, the assistance, the education

and the training they need, in particular by providing for the establishment or maintenance of institutions and services sufficient and
adequate for this purpose;

(b) to protect children and young persons against negligence, violence or
exploitation;

(c) to provide protection and special aid from the state for children and
young persons temporarily or definitively deprived of their family's
support;

(2) to provide to children and young persons a free primary and secondary
education as well as to encourage regular attendance at schools.

*Article* 18—*The right to engage in a gainful occupation in the territory of other Parties*

With a view to ensuring the effective exercise of the right to engage in a gainful
occupation in the territory of any other Party, the Parties undertake:

(1) to apply existing regulations in a spirit of liberality;

(2) to simplify existing formalities and to reduce or abolish chancery dues and
other charges payable by foreign workers or their employers;

(3) to liberalise, individually or collectively, regulations governing the employment of foreign workers;

and recognize:

(4) the right of their nationals to leave the country to engage in a gainful
occupation in the territories of the other Parties.

*Article* 19—*The right of migrant workers and their families to protection and assistance*

With a view to ensuring the effective exercise of the right of migrant workers and
their families to protection and assistance in the territory of any other Party, the
Parties undertake:

(1) to maintain or to satisfy themselves that there are maintained adequate and
free services to assist such workers, particularly in obtaining accurate
information, and to take all appropriate steps, so far as national laws and
regulations permit, against misleading propaganda relating to emigration
and immigration;

(2) to adopt appropriate measures within their own jurisdiction to facilitate the
departure, journey and reception of such workers and their families, and
to provide, within their own jurisdiction, appropriate services for health,
medical attention and good hygienic conditions during the journey;

(3) to promote co-operation, as appropriate, between social services, public
and private, in emigration and immigration countries;

(4) to secure for such workers lawfully within their territories, insofar as such
matters are regulated by law or regulations or are subject to the control of
administrative authorities, treatment not less favourable than that of their
own nationals in respect of the following matters:

(a) remuneration and other employment and working conditions;

(b) membership of trade unions and enjoyment of the benefits of collective
bargaining;

    *(c)* accommodation;

(5) to secure for such workers lawfully within their territories treatment not less favourable than that of their own nationals with regard to employment taxes, dues or contributions payable in respect of employed persons;

(6) to facilitate as far as possible the reunion of the family of a foreign worker permitted to establish himself in the territory;

(7) to secure for such workers lawfully within their territories treatment not less favourable than that of their own nationals in respect of legal proceedings relating to matters referred to in this article;

(8) to secure that such workers lawfully residing within their territories are not expelled unless they endanger national security or offend against public interest or morality;

(9) to permit, within legal limits, the transfer of such parts of the earnings and savings of such workers as they may desire;

(10) to extend the protection and assistance provided for in this article to self-employed migrants insofar as such measures apply;

(11) to promote and facilitate the teaching of the national language of the receiving state or, if there are several, one of these languages, to migrant workers and members of their families;

(12) to promote and facilitate, as far as practicable, the teaching of the migrant worker's mother tongue to the children of the migrant worker.

*Article 20—The right to equal opportunities and equal treatment in matters of employment and occupation without discrimination on the grounds of sex*

With a view to ensuring the effective exercise of the right to equal opportunities and equal treatment in matters of employment and occupation without discrimination on the grounds of sex, the Parties undertake to recognize that right and to take appropriate measures to ensure or promote its application in the following fields:

    *(a)* access to employment, protection against dismissal and occupational reintegration;

    *(b)* vocational guidance, training, retraining and rehabilitation;

    *(c)* terms of employment and working conditions, including remuneration;

    *(d)* career development, including promotion.

*Article 21—The right to information and consultation*

With a view to ensuring the effective exercise of the right of workers to be informed and consulted within the undertaking, the Parties undertake to adopt or encourage measures enabling workers or their representatives, in accordance with national legislation and practice:

    *(a)* to be informed regularly or at the appropriate time and in a comprehensible way about the economic and financial situation of the undertaking employing them, on the understanding that the disclosure of certain information which could be prejudicial to the undertaking may be refused or subject to confidentiality; and

*(b)* to be consulted in good time on proposed decisions which could substantially affect the interests of workers, particularly on those decisions which could have an important impact on the employment situation in the undertaking.

*Article 22—The right to take part in the determination and improvement of the working conditions and working environment*

With a view to ensuring the effective exercise of the right of workers to take part in the determination and improvement of the working conditions and working environment in the undertaking, the Parties undertake to adopt or encourage measures enabling workers or their representatives, in accordance with national legislation and practice, to contribute:

*(a)* to the determination and the improvement of the working conditions, work organization and working environment;

*(b)* to the protection of health and safety within the undertaking;

*(c)* to the organization of social and socio-cultural services and facilities within the undertaking;

*(d)* to the supervision of the observance of regulations on these matters.

*Article 23—The right of elderly persons to social protection*

With a view to ensuring the effective exercise of the right of elderly persons to social protection, the Parties undertake to adopt or encourage, either directly or in co-operation with public or private organizations, appropriate measures designed in particular:

— to enable elderly persons to remain full members of society for as long as possible, by means of:

*(a)* adequate resources enabling them to lead a decent life and play an active part in public, social and cultural life;

*(b)* provision of information about services and facilities available for elderly persons and their opportunities to make use of them;

— to enable elderly persons to choose their life-style freely and to lead independent lives in their familiar surroundings for as long as they wish and are able, by means of:

*(a)* provision of housing suited to their needs and their state of health or of adequate support for adapting their housing;

*(b)* the health care and the services necessitated by their state;

— to guarantee elderly persons living in institutions appropriate support, while respecting their privacy, and participation in decisions concerning living conditions in the institution.

*Article 24—The right to protection in cases of termination of employment*

With a view to ensuring the effective exercise of the right of workers to protection in cases of termination of employment, the Parties undertake to recognize:

*(a)* the right of all workers not to have their employment terminated without valid reasons for such termination connected with their capacity or conduct

or based on the operational requirements of the undertaking, establishment or service;

*(b)* the right of workers whose employment is terminated without a valid reason to adequate compensation or other appropriate relief.

To this end the Parties undertake to ensure that a worker who considers that his employment has been terminated without a valid reason shall have the right to appeal to an impartial body.

*Article 25—The right of workers to the protection of their claims in the event of the insolvency of their employer*

With a view to ensuring the effective exercise of the right of workers to the protection of their claims in the event of the insolvency of their employer, the Parties undertake to provide that workers' claims arising from contracts of employment or employment relationships be guaranteed by a guarantee institution or by any other effective form of protection.

*Article 26—The right to dignity at work*

With a view to ensuring the effective exercise of the right of all workers to protection of their dignity at work, the Parties undertake, in consultation with employers' and workers' organizations:

(1) to promote awareness, information and prevention of sexual harassment in the workplace or in relation to work and to take all appropriate measures to protect workers from such conduct;

(2) to promote awareness, information and prevention of recurrent reprehensible or distinctly negative and offensive actions directed against individual workers in the workplace or in relation to work and to take all appropriate measures to protect workers from such conduct.

*Article 27—The right of workers with family responsibilities to equal opportunities and equal treatment*

With a view to ensuring the exercise of the right to equality of opportunity and treatment for men and women workers with family responsibilities and between such workers and other workers, the Parties undertake:

(1) to take appropriate measures:

*(a)* to enable workers with family responsibilities to enter and remain in employment, as well as to reenter employment after an absence due to those responsibilities, including measures in the field of vocational guidance and training;

*(b)* to take account of their needs in terms of conditions of employment and social security;

*(c)* to develop or promote services, public or private, in particular child daycare services and other childcare arrangements;

(2) to provide a possibility for either parent to obtain, during a period after maternity leave, parental leave to take care of a child, the duration and conditions of which should be determined by national legislation, collective agreements or practice;

(3)  to ensure that family responsibilities shall not, as such, constitute a valid reason for termination of employment.

*Article 28—The right of workers' representatives to protection in the undertaking and facilities to be accorded to them*

With a view to ensuring the effective exercise of the right of workers' representatives to carry out their functions, the Parties undertake to ensure that in the undertaking:

> *(a)*  they enjoy effective protection against acts prejudicial to them, including dismissal, based on their status or activities as workers' representatives within the undertaking;
>
> *(b)*  they are afforded such facilities as may be appropriate in order to enable them to carry out their functions promptly and efficiently, account being taken of the industrial relations system of the country and the needs, size and capabilities of the undertaking concerned.

*Article 29—The right to information and consultation in collective redundancy procedures*

With a view to ensuring the effective exercise of the right of workers to be informed and consulted in situations of collective redundancies, the Parties undertake to ensure that employers shall inform and consult workers' representatives, in good time prior to such collective redundancies, on ways and means of avoiding collective redundancies or limiting their occurrence and mitigating their consequences, for example by recourse to accompanying social measures aimed, in particular, at aid for the redeployment or retraining of the workers concerned.

*Article 30—The right to protection against poverty and social exclusion*

With a view to ensuring the effective exercise of the right to protection against poverty and social exclusion, the Parties undertake:

> *(a)*  to take measures within the framework of an overall and co-ordinated approach to promote the effective access of persons who live or risk living in a situation of social exclusion or poverty, as well as their families, to, in particular, employment, housing, training, education, culture and social and medical assistance;
>
> *(b)*  to review these measures with a view to their adaptation if necessary.

*Article 31—The right to housing*

With a view to ensuring the effective exercise of the right to housing, the Parties undertake to take measures designed:

> (1)  to promote access to housing of an adequate standard;
> (2)  to prevent and reduce homelessness with a view to its gradual elimination;
> (3)  to make the price of housing accessible to those without adequate resources.

# PART III

*Article A—Undertakings*

1. Subject to the provisions of Article B below, each of the Parties undertakes:

    *(a)* to consider Part I of this Charter as a declaration of the aims which it will pursue by all appropriate means, as stated in the introductory paragraph of that part;

    *(b)* to consider itself bound by at least six of the following nine articles of Part II of this Charter: Articles 1, 5, 6, 7, 12, 13, 16, 19 and 20;

    *(c)* to consider itself bound by an additional number of articles or numbered paragraphs of Part II of the Charter which it may select, provided that the total number of articles or numbered paragraphs by which it is bound is not less than sixteen articles or sixty-three numbered paragraphs.

2. The articles or paragraphs selected in accordance with sub-paragraphs b and c of paragraph 1 of this article shall be notified to the Secretary General of the Council of Europe at the time when the instrument of ratification, acceptance or approval is deposited.

3. Any Party may, at a later date, declare by notification addressed to the Secretary General that it considers itself bound by any articles or any numbered paragraphs of Part II of the Charter which it has not already accepted under the terms of paragraph 1 of this article. Such undertakings subsequently given shall be deemed to be an integral part of the ratification, acceptance or approval and shall have the same effect as from the first day of the month following the expiration of a period of one month after the date of the notification.

4. Each Party shall maintain a system of labour inspection appropriate to national conditions.

*Article B—Links with the European Social Charter and the 1988 Additional Protocol*

1. No Contracting Party to the European Social Charter or Party to the Additional Protocol of 5 May 1988 may ratify, accept or approve this Charter without considering itself bound by at least the provisions corresponding to the provisions of the European Social Charter and, where appropriate, of the Additional Protocol, to which it was bound.

2. Acceptance of the obligations of any provision of this Charter shall, from the date of entry into force of those obligations for the Party concerned, result in the corresponding provision of the European Social Charter and, where appropriate, of its Additional Protocol of 1988 ceasing to apply to the Party concerned in the event of that Party being bound by the first of those instruments or by both instruments.

# PART IV

*Article C—Supervision of the implementation of the undertakings contained in this Charter*

The implementation of the legal obligations contained in this Charter shall be submitted to the same supervision as the European Social Charter.

*Article D—Collective complaints*

1. The provisions of the Additional Protocol to the European Social Charter providing for a system of collective complaints shall apply to the undertakings given in this Charter for the States which have ratified the said Protocol.

2. Any State which is not bound by the Additional Protocol to the European Social Charter providing for a system of collective complaints may when depositing its instrument of ratification, acceptance or approval of this Charter or at any time thereafter, declare by notification addressed to the Secretary General of the Council of Europe, that it accepts the supervision of its obligations under this Charter following the procedure provided for in the said Protocol.

# PART V

*Article E—Non-discrimination*

The enjoyment of the rights set forth in this Charter shall be secured without discrimination on any ground such as race, colour, sex, language, religion, political or other opinion, national extraction or social origin, health, association with a national minority, birth or other status.

*Article F—Derogations in time of war or public emergency*

1. In time of war or other public emergency threatening the life of the nation any Party may take measures derogating from its obligations under this Charter to the extent strictly required by the exigencies of the situation, provided that such measures are not inconsistent with its other obligations under international law.

2. Any Party which has availed itself of this right of derogation shall, within a reasonable lapse of time, keep the Secretary General of the Council of Europe fully informed of the measures taken and of the reasons therefor. It shall likewise inform the Secretary General when such measures have ceased to operate and the provisions of the Charter which it has accepted are again being fully executed.

*Article G—Restrictions*

1. The rights and principles set forth in Part I when effectively realized, and their effective exercise as provided for in Part II, shall not be subject to any restrictions or limitations not specified in those parts, except such as are prescribed by law and are necessary in a democratic society for the protection of the rights and freedoms of others or for the protection of public interest, national security, public health, or morals.

2. The restrictions permitted under this Charter to the rights and obligations set forth herein shall not be applied for any purpose other than that for which they have been prescribed.

*Article H—Relations between the Charter and domestic law or international agreements*

The provisions of this Charter shall not prejudice the provisions of domestic law or of any bilateral or multilateral treaties, conventions or agreements which are already in force, or may come into force, under which more favourable treatment would be accorded to the persons protected.

*Article I—Implementation of the undertakings given*

1. Without prejudice to the methods of implementation foreseen in these articles the relevant provisions of Articles 1 to 31 of Part II of this Charter shall be implemented by:

    *(a)* laws or regulations;

    *(b)* agreements between employers or employers' organizations and workers' organizations;

    *(c)* a combination of those two methods;

    *(d)* other appropriate means.

2. Compliance with the undertakings deriving from the provisions of paragraphs 1, 2, 3, 4, 5 and 7 of Article 2, paragraphs 4, 6 and 7 of Article 7, paragraphs 1, 2, 3 and 5 of Article 10 and Articles 21 and 22 of Part II of this Charter shall be regarded as effective if the provisions are applied, in accordance with paragraph 1 of this article, to the great majority of the workers concerned.

*Article J—Amendments*

1. Any amendment to Parts I and II of this Charter with the purpose of extending the rights guaranteed in this Charter as well as any amendment to Parts III to VI, proposed by a Party or by the Governmental Committee, shall be communicated to the Secretary General of the Council of Europe and forwarded by the Secretary General to the Parties to this Charter.

2. Any amendment proposed in accordance with the provisions of the preceding paragraph shall be examined by the Governmental Committee which shall submit the text adopted to the Committee of Ministers for approval after consultation with the Parliamentary Assembly. After its approval by the Committee of Ministers this text shall be forwarded to the Parties for acceptance.

3. Any amendment to Part I and to Part II of this Charter shall enter into force, in respect of those Parties which have accepted it, on the first day of the month following the expiration of a period of one month after the date on which three Parties have informed the Secretary General that they have accepted it.

In respect of any Party which subsequently accepts it, the amendment shall enter into force on the first day of the month following the expiration of a period of one month after the date on which that Party has informed the Secretary General of its acceptance.

4. Any amendment to Parts III to VI of this Charter shall enter into force on the first day of the month following the expiration of a period of one month after the date on which all Parties have informed the Secretary General that they have accepted it.

## PART VI

*Article K—Signature, ratification and entry into force*

1. This Charter shall be open for signature by the member States of the Council of

Europe. It shall be subject to ratification, acceptance or approval. Instruments of ratification, acceptance or approval shall be deposited with the Secretary General of the Council of Europe.

2. This Charter shall enter into force on the first day of the month following the expiration of a period of one month after the date on which three member States of the Council of Europe have expressed their consent to be bound by this Charter in accordance with the preceding paragraph.

3. In respect of any member State which subsequently expresses its consent to be bound by this Charter, it shall enter into force on the first day of the month following the expiration of a period of one month after the date of the deposit of the instrument of ratification, acceptance or approval.

*Article L—Territorial application*

1. This Charter shall apply to the metropolitan territory of each Party. Each signatory may, at the time of signature or of the deposit of its instrument of ratification, acceptance or approval, specify, by declaration addressed to the Secretary General of the Council of Europe, the territory which shall be considered to be its metropolitan territory for this purpose.

2. Any signatory may, at the time of signature or of the deposit of its instrument of ratification, acceptance or approval, or at any time thereafter, declare by notification addressed to the Secretary General of the Council of Europe, that the Charter shall extend in whole or in part to a non-metropolitan territory or territories specified in the said declaration for whose international relations it is responsible or for which it assumes international responsibility. It shall specify in the declaration the articles or paragraphs of Part II of the Charter which it accepts as binding in respect of the territories named in the declaration.

3. The Charter shall extend its application to the territory or territories named in the aforesaid declaration as from the first day of the month following the expiration of a period of one month after the date of receipt of the notification of such declaration by the Secretary General.

4. Any Party may declare at a later date by notification addressed to the Secretary General of the Council of Europe that, in respect of one or more of the territories to which the Charter has been applied in accordance with paragraph 2 of this article, it accepts as binding any articles or any numbered paragraphs which it has not already accepted in respect of that territory or territories. Such undertakings subsequently given shall be deemed to be an integral part of the original declaration in respect of the territory concerned, and shall have the same effect as from the first day of the month following the expiration of a period of one month after the date of receipt of such notification by the Secretary General.

*Article M—Denunciation*

1. Any Party may denounce this Charter only at the end of a period of five years from the date on which the Charter entered into force for it, or at the end of any subsequent period of two years, and in either case after giving six months' notice to the Secretary General of the Council of Europe who shall inform the other Parties accordingly.

2. Any Party may, in accordance with the provisions set out in the preceding

paragraph, denounce any article or paragraph of Part II of the Charter accepted by it provided that the number of articles or paragraphs by which this Party is bound shall never be less than sixteen in the former case and sixty-three in the latter and that this number of articles or paragraphs shall continue to include the articles selected by the Party among those to which special reference is made in Article A, paragraph 1, sub-paragraph b.

3. Any Party may denounce the present Charter or any of the articles or paragraphs of Part II of the Charter under the conditions specified in paragraph 1 of this article in respect of any territory to which the said Charter is applicable, by virtue of a declaration made in accordance with paragraph 2 of Article L.

*Article N—Appendix*

The appendix to this Charter shall form an integral part of it.

*Article O—Notifications*

The Secretary General of the Council of Europe shall notify the member States of the Council and the Director-General of the International Labour Office of:

*(a)* any signature;

*(b)* the deposit of any instrument of ratification, acceptance or approval;

*(c)* any date of entry into force of this Charter in accordance with Article K;

*(d)* any declaration made in application of Articles A, paragraphs 2 and 3, D, paragraphs 1 and 2, F, paragraph 2, L, paragraphs 1, 2, 3 and 4;

*(e)* any amendment in accordance with Article J;

*(f)* any denunciation in accordance with Article M;

*(g)* any other act, notification or communication relating to this Charter.

In witness whereof, the undersigned, being duly authorized thereto, have signed this revised Charter.

*Done* at Strasbourg, this 3rd day of May 1996, in English and French, both texts being equally authentic, in a single copy which shall be deposited in the archives of the Council of Europe. The Secretary General of the Council of Europe shall transmit certified copies to each member State of the Council of Europe and to the Director-General of the International Labour Office.

## APPENDIX TO THE REVISED EUROPEAN SOCIAL CHARTER
### Scope of the Revised European Social Charter in terms of persons protected

1. Without prejudice to Article 12, paragraph 4, and Article 13, paragraph 4, the persons covered by Articles 1 to 17 and 20 to 31 include foreigners only in so far as they are nationals of other Parties lawfully resident or working regularly within the territory of the Party concerned, subject to the understanding that these articles are to be interpreted in the light of the provisions of Articles 18 and 19.

This interpretation would not prejudice the extension of similar facilities to other persons by any of the Parties.

2. Each Party will grant to refugees as defined in the Convention relating to the

Status of Refugees, signed in Geneva on 28 July 1951 and in the Protocol of 31 January 1967, and lawfully staying in its territory, treatment as favourable as possible, and in any case not less favourable than under the obligations accepted by the Party under the said convention and under any other existing international instruments applicable to those refugees.

3. Each Party will grant to stateless persons as defined in the Convention on the Status of Stateless Persons done in New York on 28 September 1954 and lawfully staying in its territory, treatment as favourable as possible and in any case not less favourable than under the obligations accepted by the Party under the said instrument and under any other existing international instruments applicable to those stateless persons.

## PART I, PARAGRAPH 18, AND PART II, ARTICLE 18, PARAGRAPH 1

It is understood that these provisions are not concerned with the question of entry into the territories of the Parties and do not prejudice the provisions of the European Convention on Establishment, signed in Paris on 13 December 1955.

## PART II

*Article* 1, *paragraph* 2

This provision shall not be interpreted as prohibiting or authorizing any union security clause or practice.

*Article* 2, *paragraph* 6

Parties may provide that this provision shall not apply:

  *(a)*  to workers having a contract or employment relationship with a total dura-
        tion not exceeding one month and/or with a working week not exceeding
        eight hours;
  *(b)*  where the contract or employment relationship is of a casual and/or
        specific nature, provided, in these cases, that its non-application is justified
        by objective considerations.

*Article* 3, *paragraph* 4

It is understood that for the purposes of this provision the functions, organization and conditions of operation of these services shall be determined by national laws or regulations, collective agreements or other means appropriate to national conditions.

*Article* 4, *paragraph* 4

This provision shall be so understood as not to prohibit immediate dismissal for any serious offence.

*Article* 4, *paragraph* 5

It is understood that a Party may give the undertaking required in this paragraph if the great majority of workers are not permitted to suffer deductions from wages either by law or through collective agreements or arbitration awards, the exceptions being those persons not so covered.

*Article* 6, *paragraph* 4

It is understood that each Party may, insofar as it is concerned, regulate the exercise of the right to strike by law, provided that any further restriction that this might place on the right can be justified under the terms of Article G.

*Article* 7, *paragraph* 2

This provision does not prevent Parties from providing in their legislation that young persons not having reached the minimum age laid down may perform work in so far as it is absolutely necessary for their vocational training where such work is carried out in accordance with conditions prescribed by the competent authority and measures are taken to protect the health and safety of these young persons.

*Article* 7, *paragraph* 8

It is understood that a Party may give the undertaking required in this paragraph if it fulfils the spirit of the undertaking by providing by law that the great majority of persons under eighteen years of age shall not be employed in night work.

*Article* 8, *paragraph* 2

This provision shall not be interpreted as laying down an absolute prohibition. Exceptions could be made, for instance, in the following cases:

*(a)* if an employed woman has been guilty of misconduct which justifies breaking off the employment relationship;

*(b)* if the undertaking concerned ceases to operate;

*(c)* if the period prescribed in the employment contract has expired.

*Article* 12, *paragraph* 4

The words 'and subject to the conditions laid down in such agreements' in the introduction to this paragraph are taken to imply *inter alia* that with regard to benefits which are available independently of any insurance contribution, a Party may require the completion of a prescribed period of residence before granting such benefits to nationals of other Parties.

*Article* 13, *paragraph* 4

Governments not Parties to the European Convention on Social and Medical Assistance may ratify the Charter in respect of this paragraph provided that they grant to nationals of other Parties a treatment which is in conformity with the provisions of the said convention.

*Article* 16

It is understood that the protection afforded in this provision covers single-parent families.

*Article* 17

It is understood that this provision covers all persons below the age of 18 years, unless under the law applicable to the child majority is attained earlier, without prejudice to the other specific provisions provided by the Charter, particularly Article 7.

This does not imply an obligation to provide compulsory education up to the above-mentioned age.

*Article* 19, *paragraph* 6

For the purpose of applying this provision, the term 'family of a foreign worker' is understood to mean at least the worker's spouse and unmarried children, as long as the latter are considered to be minors by the receiving State and are dependent on the migrant worker.

*Article* 20

1. It is understood that social security matters, as well as other provisions relating to unemployment benefit, old age benefit and survivor's benefit, may be excluded from the scope of this article.

2. Provisions concerning the protection of women, particularly as regards pregnancy, confinement and the post-natal period, shall not be deemed to be discrimination as referred to in this article.

3. This article shall not prevent the adoption of specific measures aimed at removing *de facto* inequalities.

4. Occupational activities which, by reason of their nature or the context in which they are carried out, can be entrusted only to persons of a particular sex may be excluded from the scope of this article or some of its provisions. This provision is not to be interpreted as requiring the Parties to embody in laws or regulations a list of occupations which, by reason of their nature or the context in which they are carried out, may be reserved to persons of a particular sex.

*Articles* 21 *and* 22

1. For the purpose of the application of these articles, the term 'workers' representatives' means persons who are recognized as such under national legislation or practice.

2. The terms 'national legislation and practice' embrace as the case may be, in addition to laws and regulations, collective agreements, other agreements between employers and workers' representatives, customs as well as relevant case law.

3. For the purpose of the application of these articles, the term 'undertaking' is understood as referring to a set of tangible and intangible components, with or without legal personality, formed to produce goods or provide services for financial gain and with power to determine its own market policy.

4. It is understood that religious communities and their institutions may be excluded from the application of these articles, even if these institutions are 'undertakings' within the meaning of paragraph 3. Establishments pursuing activities which are inspired by certain ideals or guided by certain moral concepts, ideals and concepts which are protected by national legislation, may be excluded from the

application of these articles to such an extent as is necessary to protect the orientation of the undertaking.

5. It is understood that where in a state the rights set out in these articles are exercised in the various establishments of the undertaking, the Party concerned is to be considered as fulfilling the obligations deriving from these provisions.

6. The Parties may exclude from the field of application of these articles, those undertakings employing less than a certain number of workers, to be determined by national legislation or practice.

### Article 22

1. This provision affects neither the powers and obligations of States as regards the adoption of health and safety regulations for workplaces, nor the powers and responsibilities of the bodies in charge of monitoring their application.

2. The terms 'social and socio-cultural services and facilities' are understood as referring to the social and/or cultural facilities for workers provided by some undertakings such as welfare assistance, sports fields, rooms for nursing mothers, libraries, children's holiday camps, etc.

### Article 23, paragraph 1

For the purpose of the application of this paragraph, the term 'for as long as possible' refers to the elderly person's physical, psychological and intellectual capacities.

### Article 24

1. It is understood that for the purposes of this article the terms 'termination of employment' and 'terminated' mean termination of employment at the initiative of the employer.

2. It is understood that this article covers all workers but that a Party may exclude from some or all of its protection the following categories of employed persons:

   (a) workers engaged under a contract of employment for a specified period of time or a specified task;

   (b) workers undergoing a period of probation or a qualifying period of employment, provided that this is determined in advance and is of a reasonable duration;

   (c) workers engaged on a casual basis for a short period.

3. For the purpose of this article the following, in particular, shall not constitute valid reasons for termination of employment:

   (a) trade union membership or participation in union activities outside working hours, or, with the consent of the employer, within working hours;

   (b) seeking office as, acting or having acted in the capacity of a workers' representative;

   (c) the filing of a complaint or the participation in proceedings against an employer involving alleged violation of laws or regulations or recourse to competent administrative authorities;

   (d) race, colour, sex, marital status, family responsibilities, pregnancy, religion, political opinion, national extraction or social origin;

    *(e)*   maternity or parental leave;

    *(f)*   temporary absence from work due to illness or injury.

4. It is understood that compensation or other appropriate relief in case of termination of employment without valid reasons shall be determined by national laws or regulations, collective agreements or other means appropriate to national conditions.

*Article* 25

1. It is understood that the competent national authority may, by way of exemption and after consulting organizations of employers and workers, exclude certain categories of workers from the protection provided in this provision by reason of the special nature of their employment relationship.

2. It is understood that the definition of the term 'insolvency' must be determined by national law and practice.

3. The workers' claims covered by this provision shall include at least:

    *(a)*   the workers' claims for wages relating to a prescribed period, which shall not be less than three months under a privilege system and eight weeks under a guarantee system, prior to the insolvency or to the termination of employment;

    *(b)*   the workers' claims for holiday pay due as a result of work performed during the year in which the insolvency or the termination of employment occurred;

    *(c)*   the workers' claims for amounts due in respect of other types of paid absence relating to a prescribed period, which shall not be less than three months under a privilege system and eight weeks under a guarantee system, prior to the insolvency or the termination of the employment.

4. National laws or regulations may limit the protection of workers' claims to a prescribed amount, which shall be of a socially acceptable level.

*Article* 26

It is understood that this article does not require that legislation be enacted by the Parties. It is understood that paragraph 2 does not cover sexual harassment.

*Article* 27

It is understood that this article applies to men and women workers with family responsibilities in relation to their dependent children as well as in relation to other members of their immediate family who clearly need their care or support where such responsibilities restrict their possibilities of preparing for, entering, participating in or advancing in economic activity. The terms 'dependent children' and 'other members of their immediate family who clearly need their care and support' mean persons defined as such by the national legislation of the Party concerned.

*Articles* 28 *and* 29

For the purpose of the application of this article, the term 'workers' representatives' means persons who are recognized as such under national legislation or practice.

## PART III

It is understood that the Charter contains legal obligations of an international character, the application of which is submitted solely to the supervision provided for in Part IV thereof.

### Article A, paragraph 1

It is understood that the numbered paragraphs may include articles consisting of only one paragraph.

### Article B, paragraph 2

For the purpose of paragraph 2 of Article B, the provisions of the revised Charter correspond to the provisions of the Charter with the same article or paragraph number with the exception of:

(a) Article 3, paragraph 2, of the revised Charter which corresponds to Article 3, paragraphs 1 and 3, of the Charter;

(b) Article 3, paragraph 3, of the revised Charter which corresponds to Article 3, paragraphs 2 and 3, of the Charter;

(c) Article 10, paragraph 5, of the revised Charter which corresponds to Article 10, paragraph 4, of the Charter;

(d) Article 17, paragraph 1, of the revised Charter which corresponds to Article 17 of the Charter.

## PART V

### Article E

A differential treatment based on an objective and reasonable justification shall not be deemed discriminatory.

### Article F

The terms 'in time of war or other public emergency' shall be so understood as to cover also the threat of war.

### Article I

It is understood that workers excluded in accordance with the appendix to Articles 21 and 22 are not taken into account in establishing the number of workers concerned.

### Article J

The term 'amendment' shall be extended so as to cover also the addition of new articles to the Charter.

# 61. EUROPEAN CONVENTION ON THE LEGAL STATUS OF MIGRANT WORKERS, 1977

This convention (ETS No. 93) was opened for signature on 24 November 1977 and entered into force on 1 May 1993. It deals with some of the principal aspects of the legal situation of migrant workers, including recruitment, occupational tests, residence permits, work permits, family reunion, working conditions, transfer of social security benefits, and so forth. It does not deal with migration as such, however, and leaves State rights in the matter of admission and expulsion largely unaffected.

## TEXT

The member States of the Council of Europe, signatory hereto,

*Considering* that the aim of the Council of Europe is to achieve a greater unity between its members for the purpose of safeguarding and realizing the ideals and principles which are their common heritage and facilitating their economic and social progress while respecting human rights and fundamental freedoms;

*Considering* that the legal status of migrant workers who are nationals of Council of Europe member States should be regulated so as to ensure that as far as possible they are treated no less favourably than workers who are nationals of the receiving State in all aspects of living and working conditions;

*Being resolved* to facilitate the social advancement of migrant workers and members of their families;

*Affirming* that the rights and privileges which they grant to each other's nationals are conceded by virtue of the close association uniting the member States of the Council of Europe by means of its Statute,

*Have agreed* as follows:

## CHAPTER I

*Article 1—Definition*

1. For the purpose of this Convention, the term 'migrant worker' shall mean a national of a Contracting Party who has been authorized by another Contracting Party to reside in its territory in order to take up paid employment.

2. This Convention shall not apply to:

    *(a)* frontier workers;

    *(b)* artists, other entertainers and sportsmen engaged for a short period and members of a liberal profession;

    *(c)* seamen;

    *(d)* persons undergoing training;

    *(e)* seasonal workers; seasonal migrant workers are those who, being nationals

of a Contracting Party, are employed on the territory of another Contracting Party in an activity dependent on the rhythm of the seasons, on the basis of a contract for a specified period or for specified employment;

(f) workers, who are nationals of a Contracting Party, carrying out specific work in the territory of another Contracting Party on behalf of an undertaking having its registered office outside the territory of that Contracting Party.

## CHAPTER II

*Article 2—Forms of recruitment*

1. The recruitment of prospective migrant workers may be carried out either by named or by unnamed request and in the latter case shall be effected through the intermediary of the official authority in the State of origin if such an authority exists and, where appropriate, through the intermediary of the official authority of the receiving State.

2. The administrative costs of recruitment, introduction and placing, when these operations are carried out by an official authority, shall not be borne by the prospective migrant worker.

*Article 3—Medical examinations and vocational test*

1. Recruitment of prospective migrant workers may be preceded by a medical examination and a vocational test.

2. The medical examination and the vocational test are intended to establish whether the prospective migrant worker is physically and mentally fit and technically qualified for the job offered to him and to make certain that his state of health does not endanger public health.

3. Arrangements for the reimbursement of expenses connected with medical examination and vocational test shall be laid down when appropriate by bilateral agreements, so as to ensure that such expenses do not fall upon the prospective migrant worker.

4. A migrant worker to whom an individual offer of employment is made shall not be required, otherwise than on grounds of fraud, to undergo a vocational test except at the employer's request.

*Article 4—Right of exit—Right to admission—Administrative formalities*

1. Each Contracting Party shall guarantee the following rights to migrant workers:
— the right to leave the territory of the Contracting Party of which they are nationals;
— the right to admission to the territory of a Contracting Party in order to take up paid employment after being authorised to do so and obtaining the necessary papers.

2. These rights shall be subject to such limitations as are prescribed by legislation and are necessary for the protection of national security, public order, public health or morals.

3. The papers required of the migrant worker for emigration and immigration shall be issued as expeditiously as possible free of charge or on payment of an amount not exceeding their administrative cost.

*Article 5—Formalities and procedure relating to the work contract*

Every migrant worker accepted for employment shall be provided prior to departure for the receiving State with a contract of employment or a definite offer of employment, either of which may be drawn up in one or more of the languages in use in the State of origin and in one or more of the languages in use in the receiving State. The use of at least one language of the State of origin and one language of the receiving State shall be compulsory in the case of recruitment by an official authority or an officially recognised employment bureau.

*Article 6—Information*

1. The Contracting Parties shall exchange and provide for prospective migrants appropriate information on their residence, conditions of and opportunities for family reunion, the nature of the job, the possibility of a new work contract being concluded after the first has lapsed, the qualifications required, working and living conditions (including the cost of living), remuneration, social security, housing, food, the transfer of savings, travel, and on deductions made from wages in respect of contributions for social protection and social security, taxes and other charges. Information may also be provided on the cultural and religious conditions in the receiving State.

2. In the case of recruitment through an official authority of the receiving State, such information shall be provided, before his departure, in a language which the prospective migrant worker can understand, to enable him to take a decision in full knowledge of the facts. The translation, where necessary, of such information into a language that the prospective migrant worker can understand shall be provided as a general rule by the State of origin.

3. Each Contracting Party undertakes to adopt the appropriate steps to prevent misleading propaganda relating to emigration and immigration.

*Article 7—Travel*

1. Each Contracting Party undertakes to ensure, in the case of official collective recruitment, that the cost of travel to the receiving State shall never be borne by the migrant worker. The arrangements for payment shall be determined under bilateral agreements, which may also extend these measures to families and to workers recruited individually.

2. In the case of migrant workers and their families in transit through the territory of one Contracting Party en route to the receiving State, or on their return journey to the State of origin, all steps shall be taken by the competent authorities of the transit State to expedite their journey and prevent administrative delays and difficulties.

3. Each Contracting Party shall exempt from import duties and taxes at the time of entry into the receiving State and of the final return to the State of origin and in transit:

(a) the personal effects and movable property of migrant workers and members of their family belonging to their household;

(b) a reasonable quantity of hand-tools and portable equipment necessary for the occupation to be engaged in.

The exemptions referred to above shall be granted in accordance with the laws or regulations in force in the States concerned.

# CHAPTER III

*Article 8—Work permit*

1. Each Contracting Party which allows a migrant worker to enter its territory to take up paid employment shall issue or renew a work permit for him (unless he is exempt from this requirement), subject to the conditions laid down in its legislation.

2. However, a work permit issued for the first time may not as a rule bind the worker to the same employer or the same locality for a period longer than one year.

3. In case of renewal of the migrant worker's work permit, this should as a general rule be for a period of at least one year, in so far as the current state and development of the employment situation permits.

*Article 9—Residence permit*

1. Where required by national legislation, each Contracting Party shall issue residence permits to migrant workers who have been authorised to take up paid employment on their territory under conditions laid down in this Convention.

2. The residence permit shall in accordance with the provisions of national legislation be issued and, if necessary, renewed for a period as a general rule at least as long as that of the work permit. When the work permit is valid indefinitely, the residence permit shall as a general rule be issued and, if necessary, renewed for a period of at least one year. It shall be issued and renewed free of charge or for a sum covering administrative costs only.

3. The provisions of this Article shall also apply to members of the migrant worker's family who are authorized to join him in accordance with Article 12 of this Convention.

4. If a migrant worker is no longer in employment, either because he is temporarily incapable of work as a result of illness or accident or because he is involuntarily unemployed, this being duly confirmed by the competent authorities, he shall be allowed for the purpose of the application of Article 25 of this Convention to remain on the territory of the receiving State for a period which should not be less than five months. Nevertheless, no Contracting Party shall be bound, in the case provided for in the above sub-paragraph, to allow a migrant worker to remain for a period exceeding the period of payment of the unemployment allowance.

5. The residence permit, issued in accordance with the provisions of paragraphs 1 to 3 of this Article, may be withdrawn:

(a) for reasons of national security, public policy or morals;

(b) if the holder refuses, after having been duly informed of the consequences of such refusal, to comply with the measures prescribed for him by an official medical authority with a view to the protection of public health;

(c)   if a condition essential to its issue or validity is not fulfilled. Each Contracting Party nevertheless undertakes to grant to migrant workers whose residence permits have been withdrawn, an effective right to appeal, in accordance with the procedure for which provision is made in its legislation, to a judicial or administrative authority.

### Article 10—Reception

1. After arrival in the receiving State, migrant workers and members of their families shall be given all appropriate information and advice as well as all necessary assistance for their settlement and adaption.

2. For this purpose, migrant workers and members of their families shall be entitled to help and assistance from the social services of the receiving State or from bodies working in the public interest in the receiving State and to help from the consular authorities of their State or origin. Moreover, migrant workers shall be entitled, on the same basis as national workers, to help and assistance from the employment services. However, each Contracting Party shall endeavour to ensure that special social services are available, whenever the situation so demands, to facilitate or co-ordinate the reception of migrant workers and their families.

3. Each Contracting Party undertakes to ensure that migrant workers and members of their families can worship freely, in accordance with their faith; each Contracting Party shall facilitate such worship, within the limit of available means.

### Article 11—Recovery of sums due in respect of maintenance

1. The status of migrant workers must not interfere with the recovery of sums due in respect of maintenance to persons in the State of origin to whom they have maintenance obligations arising from a family relationship, parentage, marriage or affinity, including a maintenance obligation in respect of a child who is not legitimate.

2. Each Contracting Party shall take the steps necessary to ensure the recovery of sums due in respect of such maintenance, making use as far as possible of the form adopted by the Committee of Ministers of the Council of Europe.

3. As far as possible, each Contracting Party shall take steps to appoint a single national or regional authority to receive and despatch applications for sums due in respect of maintenance provided for in paragraph1 above.

4. This Article shall not affect existing or future bilateral or multilateral agreements.

### Article 12—Family reunion

1. The spouse of a migrant worker who is lawfully employed in the territory of a Contracting Party and the unmarried children thereof, as long as they are considered to be minors by the relevant law of the receiving State, who are dependent on the migrant worker, are authorised on conditions analogous to those which this Convention applies to the admission of migrant workers and according to the admission procedure prescribed by such law or by international agreements to join the migrant worker in the territory of a Contracting Party, provided that the latter

has available for the family housing considered as normal for national workers in the region where the migrant worker is employed. Each Contracting Party may make the giving of authorisation conditional upon a waiting period which shall not exceed twelve months.

2. Any State may, at any time, by declaration addressed to the Secretary General of the Council of Europe, which shall take effect one month after the date of receipt, make the family reunion referred to in paragraph 1 above further conditional upon the migrant worker having steady resources sufficient to meet the needs of his family.

3. Any State may, at any time, by declaration addressed to the Secretary General of the Council of Europe, which shall take effect one month after the date of its receipt, derogate temporarily from the obligation to give the authorisation provided for in paragraph 1 above, for one or more parts of its territory which it shall designate in its declaration, on the condition that these measures do not conflict with obligations under other international instruments. The declarations shall state the special reasons justifying the derogation with regard to receiving capacity.

Any State availing itself of this possibility of derogation shall keep the Secretary General of the Council of Europe fully informed of the measures which it has taken and shall ensure that these measures are published as soon as possible. It shall also inform the Secretary General of the Council of Europe when such measures cease to operate and the provisions of the Convention are again being fully executed.

The derogation shall not, as a general rule, affect requests for family reunion submitted to the competent authorities, before the declaration is addressed to the Secretary General, by migrant workers already established in the part of the territory concerned.

*Article* 13—*Housing*

1. Each Contracting Party shall accord to migrant workers, with regard to access to housing and rents, treatment not less favourable than that accorded to its own nationals, insofar as this matter is covered by domestic laws and regulations.

2. Each Contracting Party shall ensure that the competent national authorities carry out inspections in appropriate cases in collaboration with the respective consular authorities, acting within their competence, to ensure that standards of fitness of accommodation are kept up for migrant workers as for its own nationals.

3. Each Contracting Party undertakes to protect migrant workers against exploitation in respect of rents, in accordance with its laws and regulations on the matter.

4. Each Contracting Party shall ensure, by the means available to the competent national authorities, that the housing of the migrant worker shall be suitable.

*Article* 14—*Pretraining—Schooling—Linguistic training—Vocational training and retraining*

1. Migrant workers and members of their families officially admitted to the territory of a Contracting Party shall be entitled, on the same basis and under the same conditions as national workers, to general education and vocation training and retraining and shall be granted access to higher education according to the general regulations governing admission to respective institutions in the receiving State.

2. To promote access to general and vocational schools and to vocational training centres, the receiving State shall facilitate the teaching of its language or, if there are several, one of its languages to migrant workers and members of their families.

3. For the purpose of the application of paragraphs 1 and 2 above, the granting of scholarships shall be left to the discretion of each Contracting Party which shall make efforts to grant the children of migrant workers living with their families in the receiving State—in accordance with the provisions of Article 12 of this Convention—the same facilities in this respect as the receiving State's nationals.

4. The workers' previous attainments, as well as diplomas and vocational qualifications acquired in the State of origin, shall be recognised by each Contracting Party in accordance with arrangements laid down in bilateral and multilateral agreements.

5. The Contracting Parties concerned, acting in close co-operation shall endeavour to ensure that the vocational training and retraining schemes, within the meaning of this Article, cater as far as possible for the needs of migrant workers with a view to their return to their State of origin.

### Article 15—Teaching of the migrant worker's mother tongue

The Contracting Parties concerned shall take actions by common accord to arrange, so far as practicable, for the migrant worker's children, special courses for the teaching of the migrant worker's mother tongue, to facilitate, *inter alia*, their return to their State of origin.

### Article 16—Conditions of work

1. In the matter of conditions of work, migrant workers authorized to take up employment shall enjoy treatment not less favourable than that which applies to national workers by virtue of legislative or administrative provisions, collective labour agreement or custom.

2. It shall not be possible to derogate by individual contract from the principle of equal treatment referred to in the foregoing paragraph.

### Article 17—Transfer of savings

1. Each Contracting Party shall permit, according to the agreements laid down by its legislation, the transfer of all or such parts of the earnings and savings of migrant workers as the latter may wish to transfer.

2. This provision shall apply also to the transfer of sums due by migrant workers in respect of maintenance. The transfer of sums due by migrant workers in respect of maintenance shall on no account be hindered or prevented.

3. Each Contracting Party shall permit, under bilateral agreements or by other means, the transfer of such sums as remain due to migrant workers when they leave the territory of the receiving State.

### Article 18—Social Security

1. Each Contracting Party undertakes to grant within its territory, to migrant workers and members of their families, equality of treatment with its own nationals, in the matter of social security, subject to conditions required by national

legislation and by bilateral or multilateral agreements already concluded or to be concluded between the Contracting Parties concerned.

2. The Contracting Parties shall moreover endeavour to secure to migrant workers and members of their families the conservation of rights in course of acquisition and acquired rights, as well as provision of benefits abroad, through bilateral and multilateral agreements.

### Article 19—Social and Medical Assistance

Each Contracting Party undertakes to grant within its territory, to migrant workers and members of their families who are lawfully present in its territory, social and medical assistance on the same basis as nationals in accordance with the obligations it has assumed by virtue of other international agreements and in particular of the European Convention on Social and Medical Assistance of 1953.

### Article 20—Industrial accidents and occupational diseases—Industrial hygiene

1. With regard to the prevention of industrial accidents and occupational diseases and to industrial hygiene, migrant workers shall enjoy the same rights and protec tion as national workers, in application of the laws of a Contracting Party and collective agreements and having regard to their particular situation.

2. A migrant worker who is victim of an industrial accident or who has contracted an occupational disease in the territory of the receiving State shall benefit from occupational rehabilitation on the same basis as national workers.

### Article 21—Inspection of working conditions

Each Contracting Party shall inspect or provide for inspection of the conditions of work of migrant workers in the same manner as for national workers. Such inspection shall be carried out by the competent bodies or institutions of the receiving State and by any other authority authorised by the receiving State.

### Article 22—Death

Each Contracting Party shall take care, within the framework of its laws and, if need be, within the framework of bilateral agreements, that steps are taken to provide all help and assistance necessary for the transport to the State of origin of the bodies of migrant workers deceased as the result of an industrial accident.

### Article 23—Taxation on earnings

1. In the matter of earnings and without predjudice to the provisions on double taxation contained in agreements already concluded or which may in future be concluded between Contracting Parties, migrant workers shall not be liable, in the territory of a Contracting Party, to duties, charges, taxes or contributions of any description whatsoever either higher or more burdensome than those imposed on nationals in similar circumstances. In particular, they shall be entitled to deductions or exemptions from taxes or charges and to all allowances, including allowance for dependants.

2. The Contracting Parties shall decide between themselves, by bilateral or multilateral agreements on double taxation, what measures might be taken to avoid double taxation on the earnings of migrant workers.

*Article 24—Expiry of contract and discharge*

1. On the expiry of a work contract concluded for a special period at the end of the period agreed on and on the case of anticipated cancellation of such a contract or cancellation of a work contract for an unspecified period, migrant workers shall be accorded treatment not less favourable than that accorded to national workers under the provisions of national legislation or collective labour agreements.

2. In the event of individual or collective dismissal, migrant workers shall receive the treatment applicable to national workers under national legislation or collective labour agreements, as regards the form and period of notice, the compensation provided for in legislation or agreements or such as may be due in cases of unwarranted cancellation of their work contracts.

*Article 25—Re-employment*

1. If a migrant worker loses his job for reasons beyond his control, such as redundancy or prolonged illness, the competent authority of the receiving State shall facilitate his re-employment in accordance with the laws and regulations of that State.

2. To this end the receiving State shall promote the measures necessary to ensure, as far as possible, the vocational retraining and occupational rehabilitation of the migrant worker in question, provided that he intends to continue in employment in the State concerned afterwards.

*Article 26—Right of access to the courts and administrative authorities in the receiving State*

1. Each Contracting Party shall secure to migrant workers treatment not less favourable than that of its own nationals in respect of legal proceedings. Migrant workers shall be entitled, under the same conditions as nationals, to full legal and judicial protection of their persons property and their right and interests; in particular, they shall have, in the same manner as nationals, the right of access to the competent courts and administrative authorities, in accordance with the law of the receiving State, and the right to obtain the assistance of any person of their choice who is qualified by the law of that State, for instance in disputes with employers, members of their families or third parties. The rules of private international law of the receiving State shall not be affected by this Article.

2. Each Contracting Party shall provide migrant workers with legal assistance on the same conditions as for their own nationals and, in the case of civil or criminal proceedings, the possibility of obtaining the assistance of an interpreter where they cannot understand or speak the language used in court.

*Article 27—Use of employment services*

Each Contracting Party recognises the right of migrant workers and of the members of their families officially admitted to its territory to make use of employment services under the same conditions as national workers subject to the legal provisions and regulations and administrative practice, including conditions of access, in force in that State.

*Article 28—Exercise of the right to organize*

Each Contracting Party shall allow to migrant workers the right to organize for the protection of their economic and social interests on the conditions provided for by national legislation for its own nationals.

*Article 29—Participation in the affairs of the undertaking*

Each Contracting Party shall facilitate as far as possible the participation of migrant workers in the affairs of the undertaking on the same conditions as national workers.

## CHAPTER IV

*Article 30—Return home*

1. Each Contracting Pary shall, as far as possible, take appropriate measures to assist migrant workers and their families on the occasion of their final return to their State of origin, and in particular the steps referred to in paragraphs 2 and 3 of Article 7 of this Convention. The provision of financial assistance shall be left to the discretion of each Contracting Party.

2. To enable migrant workers to know, before they set out on their return journey, the conditions on which they will be able to resettle in their State of origin, this State shall communicate to the receiving State, which shall keep available for those who request it, information regarding in particular:

— possibilities and conditions of employment in the State of origin;
— financial aid granted for economic reintegration;
— the maintenance of social security rights aquired abroad;
— steps to be taken to facilitate the finding of accommodation;
— equivalence accorded to occupational qualifications obtained abroad and any tests to be passed to secure their official recognition;
— equivalence accorded to educational qualification, so that migrant workers' children can be admitted to schools without down-grading.

## CHAPTER V

*Article 31—Conservation of acquired rights*

No provision of this Convention may be interpreted as justifying less favourable treatment than that enjoyed by migrant workers under the national legislation of the receiving State or under bilateral and multilateral agreements to which that State is a Contracting Party.

*Article 32—Relations between this Convention and the laws of the Contracting Parties or international agreements*

The provisions of this Convention shall not prejudice the provisions of the laws of the Contracting Parties or of any bilateral or multilateral treaties, conventions, agreements or arrangements, as well as the steps taken to implement them, which are already in force, or may come into force, and under which more favourable treatment has been, or would be, accorded to the persons protected by the Convention.

*Article 33—Application of the Convention*

1. A Consultative Committee shall be set up within a year of the entry into force of this Convention.

2. Each Contracting Party shall appoint a representative to the Consultative Committee. Any other member State of the Council of Europe may be represented by an observer with the right to speak.

3. The Consultative Committee shall examine any proposals submitted to it by one of the Contracting Parties with a view to facilitating or improving the application of the Convention, as well as any proposal to amend it.

4. The opinions and recommendations of the Consultative Committee shall be adopted by a majority of the members of the Committee; however, proposals to amend the Convention shall be adopted unanimously by the members of the Committee.

5. The opinions, recommendations and proposals of the Consultative Committee referred to above shall be addressed to the Committee of Ministers of the Council of Europe, which shall decide on the action to be taken.

6. The Consultative Committee shall be convened by the Secretary General of the Council of Europe and shall meet, as a general rule, at least once every two years and, in addition, whenever at least two Contracting Parties or the Committee of Ministers so requests. The committee shall also meet at the request of one Contracting Party whenever the provisions of paragraph 3 of Article 12 are applied.

7. The Consultative Committee shall draw up periodically, for the attention of the Committee of Ministers, a report containing information regarding the laws and regulations in force in the territory of the Contracting Parties in respect of matters provided for in this Convention.

# CHAPTER VI

*Article 34—Signature, ratification and entry into force*

1. This Convention shall be open to signature by the member States of the Council of Europe. It shall be subject to ratification, acceptance or approval. Instruments of ratification, acceptance or approval shall be deposited with the Secretary General of the Council of Europe.

2. This Convention shall enter into force on the first day of the third month following the date of the deposit of the fifth instrument of ratification, acceptance or approval.

3. In respect of a signatory State ratifying, approving or accepting subsequently, the Convention shall enter into force on the first day of the third month following the date of the deposit of its instrument of ratification, acceptance or approval.

*Article 35—Territorial scope*

1. Any State may, at the time of signature or when depositing its instrument of ratification, acceptance or approval or at any later date, by declaration to the Secretary General of the Council of Europe, extend the application of this Convention to all or any of the territories for whose international relations it is responsible or on whose behalf it is authorized to give undertakings.

2. Any declaration made in pursuance of the preceding paragraph may, in respect of any territory mentioned in such declaration, be withdrawn. Such withdrawal shall take effect six months after receipt by the Secretary General of the Council of Europe of the declaration of withdrawal.

*Article 36—Reservations*

1. Any Contracting Party may, at the time of signature or when depositing its instrument of ratification, acceptance or approval, make one or more reservations which may relate to no more than nine articles of Chapters II to IV inclusive, other than Articles 4, 8, 9, 12, 16, 17, 20, 25, 26.

2. Any Contracting Party may, at any time, wholly or partly withdraw a reservation it has made in accordance with the foregoing paragraph by means of a declaration addressed to the Secretary General of the Council of Europe, which shall become effective as from the date of its receipt.

*Article 37—Denunciation of the Convention*

1. Each Contracting Party may denounce this Convention by notification addressed to the Secretary General of the Council of Europe, which shall take effect six months after the date of its receipt.

2. No denunciation may be made within five years of the date of the entry into force of the Convention in respect of the Contracting Party concerned.

3. Each Contracting Party which ceases to be a member of the Council of Europe shall cease to be a Party to this Convention six months after the date on which it loses its quality as a member of the Council of Europe.

*Article 38—Notifications*

The Secretary General of the Council of Europe shall notify the member States of the Council of:

(a) any signature;

(b) the deposit of any instrument of ratification, acceptance or approval;

(c) any notification received in respect of paragraphs 2 and 3 of Article 12;

(d) any date of entry into force of this Convention in accordance with Article 34 thereof;

(e) any declaration received in pursuance of the provisions of Article 35;

(f) any reservation made in pursuance of the provisions of paragraph 1 of Article 36;

(g) withdrawal of any reservation carried out in pursuance of the provisions of paragraph 2 of Article 36;

(h) any notification received in pursuance of the provisions of Article 37 and the date on which denunciation takes place.

In witness whereof, the undersigned, being duly authorized thereto, have signed this Convention.

*Done* at Strasbourg, this 24th day of November 1977, in English and in French, both texts being equally authoritative, in a single copy which shall remain deposited in the archives of the Council of Europe. The Secretary General of the Council of Europe shall transmit certified copies to each of the signatory States.

# 62. EUROPEAN CONVENTION FOR THE PREVENTION OF TORTURE AND INHUMAN OR DEGRADING TREATMENT OR PUNISHMENT, 1987

The Convention entered into force on 1 February 1989; for text see ETS No. 126. It originated in the Legal Affairs Committee of the Council of Europe and parallels the Convention on the same subject adopted by the UN General Assembly in 1984 (see above, 229). However, the regional Convention has a distinctive feature, the constitution of the European Committee for the Prevention of Torture and Inhuman or Degrading Treatment or Punishment. Each party to the Convention is obliged to permit visits by the Committee to any place within its jurisdiction where persons are deprived of their liberty by a public authority (Article 2). For an example of a report under Article 10, see the report to the United Kingdom Government on the Visit to Northern Ireland in 1999, doc. CPT/Inf.(2001) 6; for the Government's response, see doc. CPT/Inf.(2001) 7. Evans, M. D., & Morgan, R., *Preventing Torture* (1998); Evans, M., & Morgan, R., 'The European Convention for the Prevention of Torture: Operational Practice' (1992) 41 *ICLQ* 590–614. The Committee has issued annual reports since 1990; see generally, www.cpt.coe.int/en/.

## TEXT

The member States of the Council of Europe, signatory hereto,

*Having regard* to the provisions of the Convention for the Protection of Human Rights and Fundamental Freedoms,

*Recalling* that, under Article 3 of the same Convention, 'no one shall be subjected to torture or to inhuman or degrading treatment or punishment';

*Noting* that the machinery provided for in that Convention operates in relation to persons who allege that they are victims of violations of Article 3;

*Convinced* that the protection of persons deprived of their liberty against torture and inhuman or degrading treatment or punishment could be strengthened by non-judicial means of a preventive character based on visits,

*Have agreed* as follows:

## CHAPTER I

*Article* 1

There shall be established a European Committee for the Prevention of Torture and Inhuman or Degrading Treatment or Punishment (hereinafter referred to as the 'Committee'). The Committee shall, by means of visits, examine the treatment of persons deprived of their liberty with a view to strengthening, if necessary, the protection of such persons from torture and from inhuman or degrading treatment or punishment.

*Article* 2

Each party shall permit visits, in accordance with this Convention, to any place within its jurisdiction where persons are deprived of their liberty by a public authority.

*Article* 3

In the application of this Convention, the Committee and the competent national authorities of the party concerned shall co-operate with each other.

## CHAPTER II

*Article* 4

1. The Committee shall consist of a number of members equal to that of the Parties.

2. The members of the Committee shall be chosen from among persons of high moral and character, known for their competence in the field of human rights or having professional experiences in the areas covered by this Convention.

3. No two members of the Committee may be nationals of the same State.

4. The members shall serve in their individual capacity, shall be independent and impartial, and shall be available to serve the Committee effectively.

*Article* 5

1. The members of the Committee shall be elected by the Committee of Ministers of the Council of Europe by an absolute majority of votes, from a list of names drawn up by the Bureau of the Consultative Assembly of the Council of Europe; each national delegation of the Parties in the Consultative Assembly shall put forward three candidates, of whom two at least shall be its nationals.

2. The same procedure shall be followed in filling casual vacancies.

3. The members of the Committee shall be elected for a period of four years. They may only be re-elected once. However, among the members elected at the first election, the terms of three members shall expire at the end of two years. The members whose terms are to expire at the end of the initial period of two years shall be chosen by lot by the Secretary General of the Council of Europe immediately after the first election has been completed.

*Article* 6

1. The Committee shall meet in camera. A quorum shall be equal to the majority of its members. The decisions of the Committee shall be taken by a majority of the members present, subject to the provisions of Article 10, paragraph 2.

2. The Committee shall draw up its own rules of procedure.

3. The Secretariat of the Committee shall be provided by the Secretary General of the Council of Europe.

# CHAPTER III

*Article 7*

1. The Committee shall organize visits to places referred to in Article 2. Apart from periodic visits, the Committee may organize such other visits as appear to it to be required in the circumstances.

2. As a general rule, the visits shall be carried out by at least two members of the Committee. The Committee may, if it considers it necessary, be assisted by experts and interpreters.

*Article 8*

1. The Committee shall notify the Government of the Party concerned of its intention to carry out a visit. After such notification, it may at any time visit any place referred to in Article 2.

2. A Party shall provide the Committee with the following facilities to carry out its task:

   *(a)* access to its territory and the right to travel without restriction;
   *(b)* full information on the place where persons deprived of their liberty are being held;
   *(c)* unlimited access to any place where persons are deprived of their liberty, including the right to move inside such places without restriction;
   *(d)* other information available to the Party which is necessary for the Committee to carry out its task. In seeking such information, the Committee shall have regard to applicable rules of national law and professional ethics.

3. The Committee may interview in private persons deprived of their liberty.

4. The Committee may communicate freely with any person whom it believes can supply relevant information.

5. If necessary, the Committee may immediately communicate observations to the competent authorities of the Party concerned.

*Article 9*

1. In exceptional circumstances, the competent authorities of the Party concerned may make representations to the Committee against a visit at the time or to the particular place proposed by the Committee. Such representations may only be made on grounds of national defence, public safety, serious disorder in places where persons are deprived of their liberty, the medical condition of a person or that an urgent interrogation relating to a serious crime is in progress.

2. Following such representations, the Committee and the Party shall immediately enter into consultations in order to clarify the situation and seek agreement on arrangements to enable the Committee to exercise its functions expeditiously. Such arrangements may include the transfer to another place of any person whom the Committee proposed to visit. Until the visit takes place, the Party shall provide information to the Committee about any person concerned.

*Article 10*

1. After each visit, the Committee shall draw a report on the facts found during the

visit, taking account of any observations which may have been submitted by the Party concerned. It shall transmit to the latter its report containing any recommendations it considers necessary. The Committee may consult with the Party with a view to suggesting, if necessary, improvements in the protection of persons deprived of their liberty.

2. If the Party fails to co-operate or refuses to improve the situation in the light of the Committee's recommendations, the Committee may decide, after the Party has had an opportunity to make known its views, by a majority of two-thirds of its members to make a public statement on the matter.

*Article* 11

1. The information gathered by the Committee in relation to a visit, its report and its consultations with the Party concerned shall be confidential.

2. The Committee shall publish its report, together with any comments of the Party concerned, whenever requested to do so by that Party.

3. However, no personal data shall be published without the express consent of the person concerned.

*Article* 12

Subject to the rules of confidentiality in Article 11, the Committee shall every year submit to the Committee of Ministers a general report on its activities which shall be transmitted to the Consultative Assembly and made public.

*Article* 13

The members of the Committee, experts and other persons assisting the Committee are required, during and after their terms of office, to maintain the confidentiality of the facts or information of which they have become aware during the discharge of their functions.

*Article* 14

1. The names of persons assisting the Committee shall be specified in the notification under Article 8, paragraph 1.

2. Experts shall act on the instructions and under the authority of the Committee. They shall have particular knowledge and experience in the areas covered by this Convention and shall be bound by the same duties and independence, impartiality and availability as the members of the Committee.

3. A Party may exceptionally declare that an expert or other person assisting the Committee may not be allowed to take part in a visit to a place within its jurisdiction.

## CHAPTER IV

*Article* 15

Each Party shall inform the Committee of the name and address of the authority competent to receive notifications to its Government, and of any liaison officer it may appoint.

*Article* 16

The Committee, its members and experts referred to in Article 7, paragraph 2 shall enjoy the privileges and immunities set out in the Annex to this Convention.

*Article* 17

1. This Convention shall not prejudice the provisions of domestic law or any international agreement which provide greater protection for persons deprived of their liberty.

2. Nothing in this Convention shall be construed as limiting or derogating from the competence of the organs of the European Convention on Human Rights or from the obligations assumed by the Parties under that Convention.

3. The Committee shall not visit places which representatives or delegates of Protecting Powers or the International Committee of the Red Cross effectively visit on a regular basis by virtue of the Geneva Conventions of 12 August 1949 and the Additional Protocols of 8 June 1977 thereto.

## CHAPTER V

*Article* 18

The Convention shall be open for signature by the member States of the Council of Europe. It is subject to ratification, acceptance or approval. Instruments of ratification, acceptance or approval shall be deposited with the Secretary General of the Council of Europe.

*Article* 19

1. This Convention shall enter into force on the first day of the month following the expiration of a period of three months after the date on which seven member States of the Council of Europe have expressed their consent to be bound by the Convention in accordance with the provisions of Article 18.

2. In respect of any member State which subsequently expresses its consent to be bound by it, the Convention shall enter into force on the first day of the month following the expiration of a period of three months after the date of the deposit of the instrument of ratification, acceptance or approval.

*Article* 20

1. Any State may at the time of the signature or when depositing its instrument of ratification, acceptance or approval, specify the territory or territories to which this Convention shall apply.

2. Any State may at any later date, by a declaration addressed to the Secretary General of the Council of Europe, extend the application of this Convention to any other territory specified in the declaration. In respect of such territory the Convention shall enter into force on the first day of the month following the expiration of a period of three months after the date of receipt of such declaration by the Secretary General.

3. Any declaration made under the two preceding paragraphs may, in respect of any territory specified in such declaration, be withdrawn by a notification addressed to the Secretary General. The withdrawal shall become effective on the first day of the month following the expiration of a period of three months after the date of receipt of such notification by the Secretary General.

*Article* 21

No reservation may be made in respect of the provisions of this Convention.

*Article* 22

1. Any Party may, at any time, denounce this Convention by means of a notification addressed to the Secretary General of the Council of Europe.

2. Such denunciation shall become effective on the first day of the month following the expiration of a period of twelve months after the date of receipt of the notification by the Secretary General.

*Article* 23

The Secretary General of the Council of Europe shall notify the member States of the Council of Europe of:

    *(a)*  any signature;

    *(b)*  the deposit of any instrument of ratification, acceptance or approval;

    *(c)*  any date of entry into force of this Convention in accordance with Articles 19 and 20;

    *(d)*  any other act, notification or communication relating to this Convention, except for action taken in pursuance of Articles 8 and 10.

In witness whereof, the undersigned, being duly authorized thereto, have signed this Convention.

    *Done* at Strasbourg, the 26 November 1987, in English and French, both texts being equally authentic, in a single copy which shall be deposited in the archives of the Council of Europe. The Secretary General of the Council of Europe shall transmit certified copies to each member State of the Council of Europe.

## ANNEX
### Privileges and Immunities

(Article 16)

1. For the purpose of this annex, references to members of the Committee shall be deemed to include references to experts mentioned in Article 7, paragraph 2.

2. The members of the Committee shall, while exercising their functions and during journeys made in the exercise of their functions, enjoy the following privileges and immunities:

    *(a)*  immunity from personal arrest or detention and from seizure of their personal baggage and, in respect of words spoken or written and all acts

done by them in their official capacity, immunity from legal process of every kind;

(b) exemption from any restrictions on their freedom of movement on exit from and return to their country of residence, and entry into and exit from the country in which they exercise their functions, and from alien registration in the country which they are visiting or through which they are passing in the exercise of their functions.

3. In the course of journeys undertaken in the exercise of their functions, the members of the Committee shall, in the matter of customs and exchange control, be accorded:

(a) by their own Government, the same facilities as those accorded to senior officials travelling abroad on temporary official duty;

(b) by the Government of other Parties, the same facilities as those accorded to representatives of foreign Governments on temporary official duty.

4. Documents and papers of the Committee, in so far as they relate to the business of the Committee, shall be inviolable.

The official correspondence and other official communications of the Committee may not be held up or subjected to censorship.

5. In order to secure for the members of the Committee complete freedom of speech and complete independence in the discharge of their duties, the immunity from legal process in respect of words spoken or written and all acts done by them in discharging their duties shall continue to be accorded, notwithstanding that the persons concerned are no longer engaged in the discharge of such duties.

6. Privileges and immunities are accorded to the members of the Committee, not for the personal benefit of the individuals themselves but in order to safeguard the independent exercise of their functions. The Committee alone shall be competent to waive the immunity of its members; it has not only the right, but is under a duty, to waive the immunity of one of its members in any case where, in its opinion, the immunity would impede the course of justice, and where it can be waived without prejudice to the purpose for which the immunity is accorded.

# 63. PROTOCOL NO. 1 TO THE EUROPEAN CONVENTION FOR THE PREVENTION OF TORTURE AND INHUMAN OR DEGRADING TREATMENT OR PUNISHMENT, 1993

The first Protocol opens up the Convention by providing that the Committee of Ministers of the Council of Europe may invite any non-member State to accede to it; for text, see ETS No. 151.

## TEXT

The member States of the Council of Europe, signatories to this Protocol to the European Convention for the Prevention of Torture and Inhuman or Degrading Treatment or Punishment, signed at Strasbourg on 26 November 1987 (hereinafter referred to as 'the Convention'),

*Considering* that non-member States of the Council of Europe should be allowed to accede to the Convention at the invitation of the Committee of Ministers,

*Have agreed* as follows:

*Article* 1

A sub-paragraph shall be added to Article 5, paragraph 1, of the Convention as follows:

'Where a member is to be elected to the Committee in respect of a non-member State of the Council of Europe, the Bureau of the Consultative Assembly shall invite the Parliament of that State to put forward three candidates, of whom two at least shall be its nationals. The election by the Committee of Ministers shall take place after consultation with the Party concerned.'

*Article* 2

Article 12 of the Convention shall read as follows:

'Subject to the rules of confidentiality in Article 11, the Committee shall every year submit to the Committee of Ministers a general report on its activities which shall be transmitted to the Consultative Assembly and to any non-member State of the Council of Europe which is a party to the Convention, and made public.'

*Article* 3

The text of Article 18 of the Convention shall become paragraph 1 of that article and shall be supplemented by the following second paragraph:

'2. The Committee of Ministers of the Council of Europe may invite any non-member State of the Council of Europe to accede to the Convention.'

*Article* 4

In paragraph 2 of Article 19 of the Convention, the word 'member' shall be deleted and the words 'or approval,' shall be replaced by 'approval or accession'.

*Article* 5

In paragraph 1 of Article 20 of the Convention, the words 'or approval' shall be replaced by 'approval or accession,'.

*Article* 6

1. The introductory sentence of Article 23 of the Convention shall read as follows:

'The Secretary General of the Council of Europe shall notify the member States and any non-member State of the Council of Europe party to the Convention of:'

2. In Article 23 (b) of the Convention, the words 'or approval;' shall be replaced by 'approval or accession;'.

*Article* 7

1. This Protocol shall be open for signature by member States of the Council of Europe signatories to the Convention, which may express their consent to be bound by:

   (1)  signature without reservation as to ratification, acceptance or approval; or
   (2)  signature subject to ratification, acceptance or approval, followed by ratification, acceptance or approval.

2. Instruments of ratification, acceptance or approval shall be deposited with the Secretary General of the Council of Europe.

*Article* 8

This Protocol shall enter into force on the first day of the month following the expiration of a period of three months after the date on which all Parties to the Convention have expressed their consent to be bound by the Protocol, in accordance with the provisions of Article 7.

*Article* 9

The Secretary General of the Council of Europe shall notify the member States of the Council of Europe of:

   (1)  any signature;
   (2)  the deposit of any instrument of ratification, acceptance or approval;
   (3)  the date of entry into force of this Protocol, in accordance with Article 8;
   (4)  any other act, notification or communication relating to this Protocol.

In witness whereof, the undersigned, being duly authorized thereto, have signed this Protocol.

*Done* at Strasbourg, this 4th day of November 1993, in English and French, both texts being equally authentic, in a single copy which shall be deposited in the archives of the Council of Europe. The Secretary General of the Council of Europe shall transmit certified copies to each member State of the Council of Europe.

# 64. PROTOCOL NO. 2 TO THE EUROPEAN CONVENTION FOR THE PREVENTION OF TORTURE AND INHUMAN OR DEGRADING TREATMENT OR PUNISHMENT, 1993

The Second Protocol introduces amendments of a technical nature. Provision is made for members of the European Committee for the Prevention of Torture and Inhuman or Degrading Treatment or Punishment (CPT) to be placed in one of two groups for election purposes, the aim being to ensure that one half of the Committee's membership is renewed every two years. The Protocol also provides that members of the CPT may be re-elected twice, instead of only once as at present. For text see ETS No. 152.

## TEXT

The States, signatories to this Protocol to the European Convention for the Prevention of Torture and Inhuman or Degrading Treatment or Punishment, signed at Strasbourg on 26 November 1987 (hereinafter referred to as 'the Convention'),

*Convinced* of the advisability of enabling members of the European Committee for the Prevention of Torture and Inhuman and Degrading Treatment (hereinafter referred to as 'the Committee') to be re-elected twice;

*Also considering* the need to guarantee an orderly renewal of the membership of the Committee,

*Have agreed* as follows:

*Article* 1

1. In Article 5, paragraph 3, the second sentence shall read as follows:

'They may be re-elected twice.'

2. Article 5 of the Convention shall be supplemented by the following paragraphs 4 and 5:

4. 'In order to ensure that, as far as possible, one half of the membership of the Committee shall be renewed every two years, the Committee of Ministers may decide, before proceeding to any subsequent election, that the term or terms of office of one or more members to be elected shall be for a period other than four years but not more than six and not less than two years.

5. In cases where more than one term of office is involved and the Committee of Ministers applies the preceding paragraph, the allocation of the terms of office shall be effected by the drawing of lots by the Secretary General, immediately after the election.'

*Article* 2

1. This Protocol shall be open for signature by States signatories to the Convention or acceding thereto, which may express their consent to be bound by:

*(a)* signature without reservation as to ratification, acceptance or approval; or

(b) signature subject to ratification, acceptance or approval, followed by ratification, acceptance or approval.

2. Instruments of ratification, acceptance or approval shall be deposited with the Secretary General of the Council of Europe.

*Article* 3

This Protocol shall enter into force on the first day of the month following the expiration of a period of three months after the date on which all Parties to the Convention have expressed their consent to be bound by the Protocol, in accordance with the provisions of Article 2.

*Article* 4

The Secretary General of the Council of Europe shall notify the member States of the Council of Europe and non-member States Parties to the Convention of:

(a) any signature;

(b) the deposit of any instrument of ratification, acceptance or approval;

(c) the date of any entry into force of this Protocol, in accordance with Article 3;

(d) any other act, notification or communication relating to this Protocol.

In witness whereof, the undersigned, being duly authorized thereto, have signed this Protocol.

*Done* at Strasbourg, this 4th day of November 1993, in English and French, both texts being equally authentic, in a single copy which shall be deposited in the archives of the Council of Europe. The Secretary General of the Council of Europe shall transmit certified copies to each member State of the Council of Europe.

# 65. EUROPEAN CHARTER FOR REGIONAL OR MINORITY LANGUAGES, 1992

The Charter was opened for signature on 5 November 1992 and entered into force on 1 March 1998; for text see ETS No. 148.

The treaty aims to protect and promote the 'historical regional or minority languages' of Europe, setting objectives and principles, but also various specific measures which States parties undertake to implement.

## TEXT

### Preamble

The member States of the Council of Europe signatory hereto,

*Considering* that the aim of the Council of Europe is to achieve a greater unity between its members, particularly for the purpose of safeguarding and realising the ideals and principles which are their common heritage;

*Considering* that the protection of the historical regional or minority languages of Europe, some of which are in danger of eventual extinction, contributes to the maintenance and development of Europe's cultural wealth and traditions;

*Considering* that the right to use a regional or minority language in private and public life is an inalienable right conforming to the principles embodied in the United Nations International Covenant on Civil and Political Rights, and according to the spirit of the Council of Europe Convention for the Protection of Human Rights and Fundamental Freedoms;

*Having regard* to the work carried out within the CSCE and in particular to the Helsinki Final Act of 1975 and the document of the Copenhagen Meeting of 1990;

*Stressing* the value of interculturalism and multilingualism and considering that the protection and encouragement of regional or minority languages should not be to the detriment of the official languages and the need to learn them;

*Realising* that the protection and promotion of regional or minority languages in the different countries and regions of Europe represent an important contribution to the building of a Europe based on the principles of democracy and cultural diversity within the framework of national sovereignty and territorial integrity;

*Taking into consideration* the specific conditions and historical traditions in the different regions of the European States,

*Have agreed* as follows:

## PART I—GENERAL PROVISIONS

*Article 1—Definitions*

For the purposes of this Charter:

(a) 'regional or minority languages' means languages that are:

> (i)   traditionally used within a given territory of a State by nationals of that State who form a group numerically smaller than the rest of the State's population; and
>
> (ii)  different from the official language(s) of that State;
>
> it does not include either dialects of the official language(s) of the State or the languages of migrants;
>
> *(b)* 'territory in which the regional or minority language is used' means the geographical area in which the said language is the mode of expression of a number of people justifying the adoption of the various protective and promotional measures provided for in this Charter;
>
> *(c)* 'non-territorial languages' means languages used by nationals of the State which differ from the language or languages used by the rest of the State's population but which, although traditionally used within the territory of the State, cannot be identified with a particular area thereof.

### Article 2—Undertakings

1. Each Party undertakes to apply the provisions of Part II to all the regional or minority languages spoken within its territory and which comply with the definition in Article 1.

2. In respect of each language specified at the time of ratification, acceptance or approval, in accordance with Article 3, each Party undertakes to apply a minimum of thirty-five paragraphs or sub-paragraphs chosen from among the provisions of Part III of the Charter, including at least three chosen from each of the Articles 8 and 12 and one from each of the Articles 9, 10, 11 and 13.

### Article 3—Practical arrangements

1. Each Contracting State shall specify in its instrument of ratification, acceptance or approval, each regional or minority language, or official language which is less widely used on the whole or part of its territory, to which the paragraphs chosen in accordance with Article 2, paragraph 2, shall apply.

2. Any Party may, at any subsequent time, notify the Secretary General that it accepts the obligations arising out of the provisions of any other paragraph of the Charter not already specified in its instrument of ratification, acceptance or approval, or that it will apply paragraph 1 of the present article to other regional or minority languages, or to other official languages which are less widely used on the whole or part of its territory.

3. The undertakings referred to in the foregoing paragraph shall be deemed to form an integral part of the ratification, acceptance or approval and will have the same effect as from their date of notification.

### Article 4—Existing regimes of protection

1. Nothing in this Charter shall be construed as limiting or derogating from any of the rights guaranteed by the European Convention on Human Rights.

2. The provisions of this Charter shall not affect any more favourable provisions concerning the status of regional or minority languages, or the legal regime of persons belonging to minorities which may exist in a Party or are provided for by relevant bilateral or multilateral international agreements.

*Article 5—Existing obligations*

Nothing in this Charter may be interpreted as implying any right to engage in any activity or perform any action in contravention of the purposes of the Charter of the United Nations or other obligations under international law, including the principle of the sovereignty and territorial integrity of States.

*Article 6—Information*

The Parties undertake to see to it that the authorities, organizations and persons concerned are informed of the rights and duties established by this Charter.

## PART II—OBJECTIVES AND PRINCIPLES PURSUED IN ACCORDANCE WITH ARTICLE 2, PARAGRAPH 1

*Article 7—Objectives and principles*

1. In respect of regional or minority languages, within the territories in which such languages are used and according to the situation of each language, the Parties shall base their policies, legislation and practice on the following objectives and principles:

   *(a)* the recognition of the regional or minority languages as an expression of cultural wealth;

   *(b)* the respect of the geographical area of each regional or minority language in order to ensure that existing or new administrative divisions do not constitute an obstacle to the promotion of the regional or minority language in question;

   *(c)* the need for resolute action to promote regional or minority languages in order to safeguard them;

   *(d)* the facilitation and/or encouragement of the use of regional or minority languages, in speech and writing, in public and private life;

   *(e)* the maintenance and development of links, in the fields covered by this Charter, between groups using a regional or minority language and other groups in the State employing a language used in identical or similar form, as well as the establishment of cultural relations with other groups in the State using different languages;

   *(f)* the provision of appropriate forms and means for the teaching and study of regional or minority languages at all appropriate stages;

   *(g)* the provision of facilities enabling non-speakers of a regional or minority language living in the area where it is used to learn it if they so desire;

   *(h)* the promotion of study and research on regional or minority languages at universities or equivalent institutions;

   *(i)* the promotion of appropriate types of transnational exchanges, in the fields covered by this Charter, for regional or minority languages used in identical or similar form in two or more States.

2. The Parties undertake to eliminate, if they have not yet done so, any unjustified distinction, exclusion, restriction or preference relating to the use of a regional or

minority language and intended to discourage or endanger the maintenance or development of it. The adoption of special measures in favour of regional or minority languages aimed at promoting equality between the users of these languages and the rest of the population or which take due account of their specific conditions is not considered to be an act of discrimination against the users of more widely-used languages.

3. The Parties undertake to promote, by appropriate measures, mutual understanding between all the linguistic groups of the country and in particular the inclusion of respect, understanding and tolerance in relation to regional or minority languages among the objectives of education and training provided within their countries and encouragement of the mass media to pursue the same objective.

4. In determining their policy with regard to regional or minority languages, the Parties shall take into consideration the needs and wishes expressed by the groups which use such languages. They are encouraged to establish bodies, if necessary, for the purpose of advising the authorities on all matters pertaining to regional or minority languages.

5. The Parties undertake to apply, *mutatis mutandis*, the principles listed in paragraphs 1 to 4 above to non-territorial languages. However, as far as these languages are concerned, the nature and scope of the measures to be taken to give effect to this Charter shall be determined in a flexible manner, bearing in mind the needs and wishes, and respecting the traditions and characteristics, of the groups which use the languages concerned.

# PART III— MEASURES TO PROMOTE THE USE OF REGIONAL OR MINORITY LANGUAGES IN PUBLIC LIFE IN ACCORDANCE WITH THE UNDERTAKINGS ENTERED INTO UNDER ARTICLE 2, PARAGRAPH 2

*Article 8—Education*

1. With regard to education, the Parties undertake, within the territory in which such languages are used, according to the situation of each of these languages, and without prejudice to the teaching of the official language(s) of the State:

  *(a)* (i)     to make available pre-school education in the relevant regional or minority languages; or

  (ii)     to make available a substantial part of pre-school education in the relevant regional or minority languages; or

  (iii)     to apply one of the measures provided for under (i) and (ii) above at least to those pupils whose families so request and whose number is considered sufficient; or

  (iv)     the public authorities have no direct competence in the field of pre-school education, to favour and/or encourage the application of the measures referred to under (i) to (iii) above;

  *(b)* (i)     to make available primary education in the relevant regional or minority languages; or

  (ii)     to make available a substantial part of primary education in the relevant regional or minority languages; or

      (iii)    to provide, within primary education, for the teaching of the relevant regional or minority languages as an integral part of the curriculum; or

      (iv)    to apply one of the measures provided for under (i) to (iii) above at least to those pupils whose families so request and whose number is considered sufficient;

*(c)* (i)    to make available secondary education in the relevant regional or minority languages; or

      (ii)    to make available a substantial part of secondary education in the relevant regional or minority languages; or

      (iii)    to provide, within secondary education, for the teaching of the relevant regional or minority languages as an integral part of the curriculum; or

      (iv)    to apply one of the measures provided for under (i) to (iii) above at least to those pupils who, or where appropriate whose families, so wish in a number considered sufficient;

*(d)* (i)    to make available technical and vocational education in the relevant regional or minority languages; or

      (ii)    to make available a substantial part of technical and vocational education in the relevant regional or minority languages; or

      (iii)    to provide, within technical and vocational education, for the teaching of the relevant regional or minority languages as an integral part of the curriculum; or

      (iv)    to apply one of the measures provided for under (i) to (iii) above at least to those pupils who, or where appropriate whose families, so wish in a number considered sufficient;

*(e)* (i)    to make available university and other higher education in regional or minority languages; or

      (ii)    to provide facilities for the study of these languages as university and higher education subjects; or

      (iii)    if, by reason of the role of the State in relation to higher education institutions, sub-paragraphs (i) and (ii) cannot be applied, to encourage and/or allow the provision of university or other forms of higher education in regional or minority languages or of facilities for the study of these languages as university or higher education subjects;

*(f)* (i)    to arrange for the provision of adult and continuing education courses which are taught mainly or wholly in the regional or minority languages; or

      (ii)    to offer such languages as subjects of adult and continuing education; or

      (iii)    if the public authorities have no direct competence in the field of adult education, to favour and/or encourage the offering of such languages as subjects of adult and continuing education;

*(g)*    to make arrangements to ensure the teaching of the history and the culture which is reflected by the regional or minority language;

*(h)*    to provide the basic and further training of the teachers required to implement those of paragraphs (a) to (g) accepted by the Party;

*(i)* to set up a supervisory body or bodies responsible for monitoring the measures taken and progress achieved in establishing or developing the teaching of regional or minority languages and for drawing up periodic reports of their findings, which will be made public.

2. With regard to education and in respect of territories other than those in which the regional or minority languages are traditionally used, the Parties undertake, if the number of users of a regional or minority language justifies it, to allow, encourage or provide teaching in or of the regional or minority language at all the appropriate stages of education.

*Article 9—Judicial authorities*

1. The Parties undertake, in respect of those judicial districts in which the number of residents using the regional or minority languages justifies the measures specified below, according to the situation of each of these languages and on condition that the use of the facilities afforded by the present paragraph is not considered by the judge to hamper the proper administration of justice:

    *(a)* in criminal proceedings:

        (i) to provide that the courts, at the request of one of the parties, shall conduct the proceedings in the regional or minority languages; and/or

        (ii) to guarantee the accused the right to use his/her regional or minority language; and/or

        (iii) to provide that requests and evidence, whether written or oral, shall not be considered inadmissible solely because they are formulated in a regional or minority language; and/or

        (iv) to produce, on request, documents connected with legal proceedings in the relevant regional or minority language,

if necessary by the use of interpreters and translations involving no extra expense for the persons concerned;

    *(b)* in civil proceedings:

        (i) to provide that the courts, at the request of one of the parties, shall conduct the proceedings in the regional or minority languages; and/or

        (ii) to allow, whenever a litigant has to appear in person before a court, that he or she may use his or her regional or minority language without thereby incurring additional expense; and/or

        (iii) to allow documents and evidence to be produced in the regional or minority languages,

if necessary by the use of interpreters and translations;

    *(c)* in proceedings before courts concerning administrative matters:

        (i) to provide that the courts, at the request of one of the parties, shall conduct the proceedings in the regional or minority languages; and/or

        (ii) to allow, whenever a litigant has to appear in person before a court, that he or she may use his or her regional or minority language without thereby incurring additional expense; and/or

        (iii) to allow documents and evidence to be produced in the regional or minority languages, if necessary by the use of interpreters and translations;

  *(d)*  to take steps to ensure that the application of sub-paragraphs (i) and (iii) of paragraphs (b) and (c) above and any necessary use of interpreters and translations does not involve extra expense for the persons concerned.

2. The Parties undertake:

  *(a)*  not to deny the validity of legal documents drawn up within the State solely because they are drafted in a regional or minority language; or

  *(b)*  not to deny the validity, as between the parties, of legal documents drawn up within the country solely because they are drafted in a regional or minority language, and to provide that they can be invoked against interested third parties who are not users of these languages on condition that the contents of the document are made known to them by the person(s) who invoke(s) it; or

  *(c)*  not to deny the validity, as between the parties, of legal documents drawn up within the country solely because they are drafted in a regional or minority language.

3. The Parties undertake to make available in the regional or minority languages the most important national statutory texts and those relating particularly to users of these languages, unless they are otherwise provided.

*Article* 10—*Administrative authorities and public services*

1. Within the administrative districts of the State in which the number of residents who are users of regional or minority languages justifies the measures specified below and according to the situation of each language, the Parties undertake, as far as this is reasonably possible:

  *(a)*  (i)    to ensure that the administrative authorities use the regional or minority languages; or

       (ii)   to ensure that such of their officers as are in contact with the public use the regional or minority languages in their relations with persons applying to them in these languages; or

       (iii)  to ensure that users of regional or minority languages may submit oral or written applications and receive a reply in these languages; or

       (iv)   to ensure that users of regional or minority languages may submit oral or written applications in these languages; or

       (v)    to ensure that users of regional or minority languages may validly submit a document in these languages;

  (b)  to make available widely used administrative texts and forms for the population in the regional or minority languages or in bilingual versions;

  (c)  to allow the administrative authorities to draft documents in a regional or minority language.

2. In respect of the local and regional authorities on whose territory the number of residents who are users of regional or minority languages is such as to justify the measures specified below, the Parties undertake to allow and/or encourage:

  *(a)*  the use of regional or minority languages within the framework of the regional or local authority;

*(b)* the possibility for users of regional or minority languages to submit oral or written applications in these languages;

*(c)* the publication by regional authorities of their official documents also in the relevant regional or minority languages;

*(d)* the publication by local authorities of their official documents also in the relevant regional or minority languages;

*(e)* the use by regional authorities of regional or minority languages in debates in their assemblies, without excluding, however, the use of the official language(s) of the State;

*(f)* the use by local authorities of regional or minority languages in debates in their assemblies, without excluding, however, the use of the official language(s) of the State;

*(g)* the use or adoption, if necessary in conjunction with the name in the official language(s), of traditional and correct forms of place-names in regional or minority languages.

3. With regard to public services provided by the administrative authorities or other persons acting on their behalf, the Parties undertake, within the territory in which regional or minority languages are used, in accordance with the situation of each language and as far as this is reasonably possible:

*(a)* to ensure that the regional or minority languages are used in the provision of the service; or

*(b)* to allow users of regional or minority languages to submit a request and receive a reply in these languages; or

*(c)* to allow users of regional or minority languages to submit a request in these languages.

4. With a view to putting into effect those provisions of paragraphs 1, 2 and 3 accepted by them, the Parties undertake to take one or more of the following measures:

*(a)* translation or interpretation as may be required;

*(b)* recruitment and, where necessary, training of the officials and other public service employees required;

*(c)* compliance as far as possible with requests from public service employees having a knowledge of a regional or minority language to be appointed in the territory in which that language is used.

5. The Parties undertake to allow the use or adoption of family names in the regional or minority languages, at the request of those concerned.

*Article* 11—*Media*

1. The Parties undertake, for the users of the regional or minority languages within the territories in which those languages are spoken, according to the situation of each language, to the extent that the public authorities, directly or indirectly, are competent, have power or play a role in this field, and respecting the principle of the independence and autonomy of the media:

*(a)* to the extent that radio and television carry out a public service mission:

       (i)     to ensure the creation of at least one radio station and one television channel in the regional or minority languages; or

       (ii)    to encourage and/or facilitate the creation of at least one radio station and one television channel in the regional or minority languages; or

       (iii)   to make adequate provision so that broadcasters offer programmes in the regional or minority languages;

*(b)* (i)     to encourage and/or facilitate the creation of at least one radio station in the regional or minority languages; or

       (ii)    to encourage and/or facilitate the broadcasting of radio programmes in the regional or minority languages on a regular basis;

*(c)* (i)     to encourage and/or facilitate the creation of at least one television channel in the regional or minority languages; or

       (ii)    to encourage and/or facilitate the broadcasting of television programmes in the regional or minority languages on a regular basis;

*(d)*   to encourage and/or facilitate the production and distribution of audio and audiovisual works in the regional or minority languages;

*(e)* (i)     to encourage and/or facilitate the creation and/or maintenance of at least one newspaper in the regional or minority languages; or

       (ii)    to encourage and/or facilitate the publication of newspaper articles in the regional or minority languages on a regular basis;

*(f)* (i)     to cover the additional costs of those media which use regional or minority languages, wherever the law provides for financial assistance in general for the media; or

       (ii)    to apply existing measures for financial assistance also to audiovisual productions in the regional or minority languages;

*(g)*   to support the training of journalists and other staff for media using regional or minority languages.

2. The Parties undertake to guarantee freedom of direct reception of radio and television broadcasts from neighbouring countries in a language used in identical or similar form to a regional or minority language, and not to oppose the retransmission of radio and television broadcasts from neighbouring countries in such a language. They further undertake to ensure that no restrictions will be placed on the freedom of expression and free circulation of information in the written press in a language used in identical or similar form to a regional or minority language. The exercise of the above-mentioned freedoms, since it carries with it duties and responsibilities, may be subject to such formalities, conditions, restrictions or penalties as are prescribed by law and are necessary in a democratic society, in the interests of national security, territorial integrity or public safety, for the prevention of disorder or crime, for the protection of health or morals, for the protection of the reputation or rights of others, for preventing disclosure of information received in confidence, or for maintaining the authority and impartiality of the judiciary.

3. The Parties undertake to ensure that the interests of the users of regional or minority languages are represented or taken into account within such bodies as

may be established in accordance with the law with responsibility for guaranteeing the freedom and pluralism of the media.

*Article 12—Cultural activities and facilities*

1. With regard to cultural activities and facilities—especially libraries, video libraries, cultural centres, museums, archives, academies, theatres and cinemas, as well as literary work and film production, vernacular forms of cultural expression, festivals and the culture industries, including *inter alia* the use of new technologies—the Parties undertake, within the territory in which such languages are used and to the extent that the public authorities are competent, have power or play a role in this field:

    *(a)* to encourage types of expression and initiative specific to regional or minority languages and foster the different means of access to works produced in these languages;

    *(b)* to foster the different means of access in other languages to works produced in regional or minority languages by aiding and developing translation, dubbing, post-synchronisation and subtitling activities;

    *(c)* to foster access in regional or minority languages to works produced in other languages by aiding and developing translation, dubbing, post-synchronisation and subtitling activities;

    *(d)* to ensure that the bodies responsible for organizing or supporting cultural activities of various kinds make appropriate allowance for incorporating the knowledge and use of regional or minority languages and cultures in the undertakings which they initiate or for which they provide backing;

    *(e)* to promote measures to ensure that the bodies responsible for organizing or supporting cultural activities have at their disposal staff who have a full command of the regional or minority language concerned, as well as of the language(s) of the rest of the population;

    *(f)* to encourage direct participation by representatives of the users of a given regional or minority language in providing facilities and planning cultural activities;

    *(g)* to encourage and/or facilitate the creation of a body or bodies responsible for collecting, keeping a copy of and presenting or publishing works produced in the regional or minority languages;

    *(h)* if necessary, to create and/or promote and finance translation and terminological research services, particularly with a view to maintaining and developing appropriate administrative, commercial, economic, social, technical or legal terminology in each regional or minority language.

2. In respect of territories other than those in which the regional or minority languages are traditionally used, the Parties undertake, if the number of users of a regional or minority language justifies it, to allow, encourage and/or provide appropriate cultural activities and facilities in accordance with the preceding paragraph.

3. The Parties undertake to make appropriate provision, in pursuing their cultural policy abroad, for regional or minority languages and the cultures they reflect.

*Article* 13—*Economic and social life*

1. With regard to economic and social activities, the Parties undertake, within the whole country:

   *(a)* to eliminate from their legislation any provision prohibiting or limiting without justifiable reasons the use of regional or minority languages in documents relating to economic or social life, particularly contracts of employment, and in technical documents such as instructions for the use of products or installations;

   *(b)* to prohibit the insertion in internal regulations of companies and private documents of any clauses excluding or restricting the use of regional or minority languages, at least between users of the same language;

   *(c)* to oppose practices designed to discourage the use of regional or minority languages in connection with economic or social activities;

   *(d)* to facilitate and/or encourage the use of regional or minority languages by means other than those specified in the above sub-paragraphs.

2. With regard to economic and social activities, the Parties undertake, in so far as the public authorities are competent, within the territory in which the regional or minority languages are used, and as far as this is reasonably possible:

   *(a)* to include in their financial and banking regulations provisions which allow, by means of procedures compatible with commercial practice, the use of regional or minority languages in drawing up payment orders (cheques, drafts, etc.) or other financial documents, or, where appropriate, to ensure the implementation of such provisions;

   *(b)* in the economic and social sectors directly under their control (public sector), to organize activities to promote the use of regional or minority languages;

   *(c)* to ensure that social care facilities such as hospitals, retirement homes and hostels offer the possibility of receiving and treating in their own language persons using a regional or minority language who are in need of care on grounds of ill-health, old age or for other reasons;

   *(d)* to ensure by appropriate means that safety instructions are also drawn up in regional or minority languages;

   *(e)* to arrange for information provided by the competent public authorities concerning the rights of consumers to be made available in regional or minority languages.

*Article* 14—*Transfrontier exchanges*

The Parties undertake:

   *(a)* to apply existing bilateral and multilateral agreements which bind them with the States in which the same language is used in identical or similar form, or if necessary to seek to conclude such agreements, in such a way as to foster contacts between the users of the same language in the States concerned in the fields of culture, education, information, vocational training and permanent education;

(b) for the benefit of regional or minority languages, to facilitate and/or promote co-operation across borders, in particular between regional or local authorities in whose territory the same language is used in identical or similar form.

## PART IV—APPLICATION OF THE CHARTER

*Article* 15—*Periodical reports*

1. The Parties shall present periodically to the Secretary General of the Council of Europe, in a form to be prescribed by the Committee of Ministers, a report on their policy pursued in accordance with Part II of this Charter and on the measures taken in application of those provisions of Part III which they have accepted. The first report shall be presented within the year following the entry into force of the Charter with respect to the Party concerned, the other reports at three-yearly intervals after the first report.

2. The Parties shall make their reports public.

*Article* 16—*Examination of the reports*

1. The reports presented to the Secretary General of the Council of Europe under Article 15 shall be examined by a committee of experts constituted in accordance with Article 17.

2. Bodies or associations legally established in a Party may draw the attention of the committee of experts to matters relating to the undertakings entered into by that Party under Part III of this Charter. After consulting the Party concerned, the committee of experts may take account of this information in the preparation of the report specified in paragraph 3 below. These bodies or associations can furthermore submit statements concerning the policy pursued by a Party in accordance with Part II.

3. On the basis of the reports specified in paragraph 1 and the information mentioned in paragraph 2, the committee of experts shall prepare a report for the Committee of Ministers. This report shall be accompanied by the comments which the Parties have been requested to make and may be made public by the Committee of Ministers.

4. The report specified in paragraph 3 shall contain in particular the proposals of the committee of experts to the Committee of Ministers for the preparation of such recommendations of the latter body to one or more of the Parties as may be required.

5. The Secretary General of the Council of Europe shall make a two-yearly detailed report to the Parliamentary Assembly on the application of the Charter.

*Article* 17—*Committee of experts*

1. The committee of experts shall be composed of one member per Party, appointed by the Committee of Ministers from a list of individuals of the highest integrity and recognised competence in the matters dealt with in the Charter, who shall be nominated by the Party concerned.

2. Members of the committee shall be appointed for a period of six years and shall be eligible for reappointment. A member who is unable to complete a term of office shall be replaced in accordance with the procedure laid down in paragraph 1, and the replacing member shall complete his predecessor's term of office.

3. The committee of experts shall adopt rules of procedure. Its secretarial services shall be provided by the Secretary General of the Council of Europe.

# PART V—FINAL PROVISIONS

*Article* 18

This Charter shall be open for signature by the member States of the Council of Europe. It is subject to ratification, acceptance or approval. Instruments of ratification, acceptance or approval shall be deposited with the Secretary General of the Council of Europe.

*Article* 19

1. This Charter shall enter into force on the first day of the month following the expiration of a period of three months after the date on which five member States of the Council of Europe have expressed their consent to be bound by the Charter in accordance with the provisions of Article 18.

2. In respect of any member State which subsequently expresses its consent to be bound by it, the Charter shall enter into force on the first day of the month following the expiration of a period of three months after the date of the deposit of the instrument of ratification, acceptance or approval.

*Article* 20

1. After the entry into force of this Charter, the Committee of Ministers of the Council of Europe may invite any State not a member of the Council of Europe to accede to this Charter.

2. In respect of any acceding State, the Charter shall enter into force on the first day of the month following the expiration of a period of three months after the date of deposit of the instrument of accession with the Secretary General of the Council of Europe.

*Article* 21

1. Any State may, at the time of signature or when depositing its instrument of ratification, acceptance, approval or accession, make one or more reservations to paragraphs 2 to 5 of Article 7 of this Charter. No other reservation may be made.

2. Any Contracting State which has made a reservation under the preceding paragraph may wholly or partly withdraw it by means of a notification addressed to the Secretary General of the Council of Europe. The withdrawal shall take effect on the date of receipt of such notification by the Secretary General.

*Article* 22

1. Any Party may at any time denounce this Charter by means of a notification addressed to the Secretary General of the Council of Europe.

2. Such denunciation shall become effective on the first day of the month following the expiration of a period of six months after the date of receipt of the notification by the Secretary General.

*Article 23*

The Secretary General of the Council of Europe shall notify the member States of the Council and any State which has acceded to this Charter of:

(a) any signature;

(b) the deposit of any instrument of ratification, acceptance, approval or accession;

(c) any date of entry into force of this Charter in accordance with Articles 19 and 20;

(d) any notification received in application of the provisions of Article 3, paragraph 2;

(e) any other act, notification or communication relating to this Charter.

In witness whereof the undersigned, being duly authorized thereto, have signed this Charter.

*Done* at Strasbourg, this 5th day of November 1992, in English and French, both texts being equally authentic, in a single copy which shall be deposited in the archives of the Council of Europe. The Secretary General of the Council of Europe shall transmit certified copies to each member State of the Council of Europe and to any State invited to accede to this Charter.

## 66. FRAMEWORK CONVENTION FOR THE
## PROTECTION OF NATIONAL MINORITIES, 1995

This Convention was opened for signature on 1 February 1995 and entered into force on 1 February 1998; for text see ETS No. 157.

## TEXT

The member States of the Council of Europe and the other States, signatories to the present framework Convention,

*Considering* that the aim of the Council of Europe is to achieve greater unity between its members for the purpose of safeguarding and realizing the ideals and principles which are their common heritage;

*Considering* that one of the methods by which that aim is to be pursued is the maintenance and further realization of human rights and fundamental freedoms;

*Wishing* to follow-up the Declaration of the Heads of State and Government of the member States of the Council of Europe adopted in Vienna on 9 October 1993;

*Being resolved* to protect within their respective territories the existence of national minorities;

*Considering* that the upheavals of European history have shown that the protection of national minorities is essential to stability, democratic security and peace in this continent;

*Considering* that a pluralist and genuinely democratic society should not only respect the ethnic, cultural, linguistic and religious identity of each person belonging to a national minority, but also create appropriate conditions enabling them to express, preserve and develop this identity;

*Considering* that the creation of a climate of tolerance and dialogue is necessary to enable cultural diversity to be a source and a factor, not of division, but of enrichment for each society;

*Considering* that the realization of a tolerant and prosperous Europe does not depend solely on co-operation between States but also requires transfrontier co-operation between local and regional authorities without prejudice to the constitution and territorial integrity of each State;

*Having regard* to the Convention for the Protection of Human Rights and Fundamental Freedoms and the Protocols thereto;

*Having regard* to the commitments concerning the protection of national minorities in United Nations conventions and declarations and in the documents of the Conference on Security and Co-operation in Europe, particularly the Copenhagen Document of 29 June 1990;

*Being resolved* to define the principles to be respected and the obligations which flow from them, in order to ensure, in the member States and such other States as may become Parties to the present instrument, the effective protection of national minorities and of the rights and freedoms of persons belonging to those minorities, within the rule of law, respecting the territorial integrity and national sovereignty of States;

*Being determined* to implement the principles set out in this framework Convention through national legislation and appropriate governmental policies,

*Have agreed* as follows:

## SECTION I

*Article 1*

The protection of national minorities and of the rights and freedoms of persons belonging to those minorities forms an integral part of the international protection of human rights, and as such falls within the scope of international co-operation.

*Article 2*

The provisions of this framework Convention shall be applied in good faith, in a spirit of understanding and tolerance and in conformity with the principles of good neighbourliness, friendly relations and co-operation between States.

*Article 3*

1. Every person belonging to a national minority shall have the right freely to choose to be treated or not to be treated as such and no disadvantage shall result from this choice or from the exercise of the rights which are connected to that choice.

2. Persons belonging to national minorities may exercise the rights and enjoy the freedoms flowing from the principles enshrined in the present framework Convention individually as well as in community with others.

## SECTION II

*Article 4*

1. The Parties undertake to guarantee to persons belonging to national minorities the right of equality before the law and of equal protection of the law. In this respect, any discrimination based on belonging to a national minority shall be prohibited.

2. The Parties undertake to adopt, where necessary, adequate measures in order to promote, in all areas of economic, social, political and cultural life, full and effective equality between persons belonging to a national minority and those belonging to the majority. In this respect, they shall take due account of the specific conditions of the persons belonging to national minorities.

3. The measures adopted in accordance with paragraph 2 shall not be considered to be an act of discrimination.

*Article 5*

1. The Parties undertake to promote the conditions necessary for persons

belonging to national minorities to maintain and develop their culture, and to preserve the essential elements of their identity, namely their religion, language, traditions and cultural heritage.

2. Without prejudice to measures taken in pursuance of their general integration policy, the Parties shall refrain from policies or practices aimed at assimilation of persons belonging to national minorities against their will and shall protect these persons from any action aimed at such assimilation.

*Article* 6

1. The Parties shall encourage a spirit of tolerance and intercultural dialogue and take effective measures to promote mutual respect and understanding and co-operation among all persons living on their territory, irrespective of those persons' ethnic, cultural, linguistic or religious identity, in particular in the fields of education, culture and the media.

2. The Parties undertake to take appropriate measures to protect persons who may be subject to threats or acts of discrimination, hostility or violence as a result of their ethnic, cultural, linguistic or religious identity.

*Article* 7

The Parties shall ensure respect for the right of every person belonging to a national minority to freedom of peaceful assembly, freedom of association, freedom of expression, and freedom of thought, conscience and religion.

*Article* 8

The Parties undertake to recognize that every person belonging to a national minority has the right to manifest his or her religion or belief and to establish religious institutions, organisations and associations.

*Article* 9

1. The Parties undertake to recognize that the right to freedom of expression of every person belonging to a national minority includes freedom to hold opinions and to receive and impart information and ideas in the minority language, without interference by public authorities and regardless of frontiers. The Parties shall ensure, within the framework of their legal systems, that persons belonging to a national minority are not discriminated against in their access to the media.

2. Paragraph 1 shall not prevent Parties from requiring the licensing, without discrimination and based on objective criteria, of sound radio and television broadcasting, or cinema enterprises.

3. The Parties shall not hinder the creation and the use of printed media by persons belonging to national minorities. In the legal framework of sound radio and television broadcasting, they shall ensure, as far as possible, and taking into account the provisions of paragraph 1, that persons belonging to national minorities are granted the possibility of creating and using their own media.

4. In the framework of their legal systems, the Parties shall adopt adequate measures in order to facilitate access to the media for persons belonging to national minorities and in order to promote tolerance and permit cultural pluralism.

*Article* 10

1. The Parties undertake to recognize that every person belonging to a national minority has the right to use freely and without interference his or her minority language, in private and in public, orally and in writing.

2. In areas inhabited by persons belonging to national minorities traditionally or in substantial numbers, if those persons so request and where such a request corresponds to a real need, the Parties shall endeavour to ensure, as far as possible, the conditions which would make it possible to use the minority language in relations between those persons and the administrative authorities.

3. The Parties undertake to guarantee the right of every person belonging to a national minority to be informed promptly, in a language which he or she understands, of the reasons for his or her arrest, and of the nature and cause of any accusation against him or her, and to defend himself or herself in this language, if necessary with the free assistance of an interpreter.

*Article* 11

1. The Parties undertake to recognize that every person belonging to a national minority has the right to use his or her surname (patronym) and first names in the minority language and the right to official recognition of them, according to modalities provided for in their legal system.

2. The Parties undertake to recognize that every person belonging to a national minority has the right to display in his or her minority language signs, inscriptions and other information of a private nature visible to the public.

3. In areas traditionally inhabited by substantial numbers of persons belonging to a national minority, the Parties shall endeavour, in the framework of their legal system, including, where appropriate, agreements with other States, and taking into account their specific conditions, to display traditional local names, street names and other topographical indications intended for the public also in the minority language when there is a sufficient demand for such indications.

*Article* 12

1. The Parties shall, where appropriate, take measures in the fields of education and research to foster knowledge of the culture, history, language and religion of their national minorities and of the majority.

2. In this context the Parties shall *inter alia* provide adequate opportunities for teacher training and access to textbooks, and facilitate contacts among students and teachers of different communities.

3. The Parties undertake to promote equal opportunities for access to education at all levels for persons belonging to national minorities.

*Article* 13

1. Within the framework of their education systems, the Parties shall recognize that persons belonging to a national minority have the right to set up and to manage their own private educational and training establishments.

2. The exercise of this right shall not entail any financial obligation for the Parties.

*Article* 14

1. The Parties undertake to recognize that every person belonging to a national minority has the right to learn his or her minority language.

2. In areas inhabited by persons belonging to national minorities traditionally or in substantial numbers, if there is sufficient demand, the Parties shall endeavour to ensure, as far as possible and within the framework of their education systems, that persons belonging to those minorities have adequate opportunities for being taught the minority language or for receiving instruction in this language.

3. Paragraph 2 of this article shall be implemented without prejudice to the learning of the official language or the teaching in this language.

*Article* 15

The Parties shall create the conditions necessary for the effective participation of persons belonging to national minorities in cultural, social and economic life and in public affairs, in particular those affecting them.

*Article* 16

The Parties shall refrain from measures which alter the proportions of the population in areas inhabited by persons belonging to national minorities and are aimed at restricting the rights and freedoms flowing from the principles enshrined in the present framework Convention.

*Article* 17

1. The Parties undertake not to interfere with the right of persons belonging to national minorities to establish and maintain free and peaceful contacts across frontiers with persons lawfully staying in other States, in particular those with whom they share an ethnic, cultural, linguistic or religious identity, or a common cultural heritage.

2. The Parties undertake not to interfere with the right of persons belonging to national minorities to participate in the activities of non-governmental organizations, both at the national and international levels.

*Article* 18

1. The Parties shall endeavour to conclude, where necessary, bilateral and multilateral agreements with other States, in particular neighbouring States, in order to ensure the protection of persons belonging to the national minorities concerned.

2. Where relevant, the Parties shall take measures to encourage transfrontier co-operation.

*Article* 19

The Parties undertake to respect and implement the principles enshrined in the present framework Convention making, where necessary, only those limitations, restrictions or derogations which are provided for in international legal instruments, in particular the Convention for the Protection of Human Rights and Fundamental Freedoms, in so far as they are relevant to the rights and freedoms flowing from the said principles.

## SECTION III

*Article* 20

In the exercise of the rights and freedoms flowing from the principles enshrined in the present framework Convention, any person belonging to a national minority shall respect the national legislation and the rights of others, in particular those of persons belonging to the majority or to other national minorities.

*Article* 21

Nothing in the present framework Convention shall be interpreted as implying any right to engage in any activity or perform any act contrary to the fundamental principles of international law and in particular of the sovereign equality, territorial integrity and political independence of States.

*Article* 22

Nothing in the present framework Convention shall be construed as limiting or derogating from any of the human rights and fundamental freedoms which may be ensured under the laws of any Contracting Party or under any other agreement to which it is a Party.

*Article* 23

The rights and freedoms flowing from the principles enshrined in the present framework Convention, in so far as they are the subject of a corresponding provision in the Convention for the Protection of Human Rights and Fundamental Freedoms or in the Protocols thereto, shall be understood so as to conform to the latter provisions.

## SECTION IV

*Article* 24

1. The Committee of Ministers of the Council of Europe shall monitor the implementation of this framework Convention by the Contracting Parties.

2. The Parties which are not members of the Council of Europe shall participate in the implementation mechanism, according to modalities to be determined.

*Article* 25

1. Within a period of one year following the entry into force of this framework Convention in respect of a Contracting Party, the latter shall transmit to the Secretary General of the Council of Europe full information on the legislative and other measures taken to give effect to the principles set out in this framework Convention.

2. Thereafter, each Party shall transmit to the Secretary General on a periodical basis and whenever the Committee of Ministers so requests any further information of relevance to the implementation of this framework Convention.

3. The Secretary General shall forward to the Committee of Ministers the information transmitted under the terms of this article.

*Article* 26

1. In evaluating the adequacy of the measures taken by the Parties to give effect to the principles set out in this framework Convention the Committee of Ministers shall be assisted by an advisory committee, the members of which shall have recognised expertise in the field of the protection of national minorities.

2. The composition of this advisory committee and its procedure shall be determined by the Committee of Ministers within a period of one year following the entry into force of this framework Convention.

## SECTION V

*Article* 27

This framework Convention shall be open for signature by the member States of the Council of Europe. Up until the date when the Convention enters into force, it shall also be open for signature by any other State so invited by the Committee of Ministers. It is subject to ratification, acceptance or approval. Instruments of ratification, acceptance or approval shall be deposited with the Secretary General of the Council of Europe.

*Article* 28

1. This framework Convention shall enter into force on the first day of the month following the expiration of a period of three months after the date on which twelve member States of the Council of Europe have expressed their consent to be bound by the Convention in accordance with the provisions of Article 27.

2. In respect of any member State which subsequently expresses its consent to be bound by it, the framework Convention shall enter into force on the first day of the month following the expiration of a period of three months after the date of the deposit of the instrument of ratification, acceptance or approval.

*Article* 29

1. After the entry into force of this framework Convention and after consulting the Contracting States, the Committee of Ministers of the Council of Europe may invite to accede to the Convention, by a decision taken by the majority provided for in Article 20.d of the Statute of the Council of Europe, any non-member State of the Council of Europe which, invited to sign in accordance with the provisions of Article 27, has not yet done so, and any other non-member State.

2. In respect of any acceding State, the framework Convention shall enter into force on the first day of the month following the expiration of a period of three months after the date of the deposit of the instrument of accession with the Secretary General of the Council of Europe.

*Article* 30

1. Any State may at the time of signature or when depositing its instrument of ratification, acceptance, approval or accession, specify the territory or territories for whose international relations it is responsible to which this framework Convention shall apply.

2. Any State may at any later date, by a declaration addressed to the Secretary General of the Council of Europe, extend the application of this framework Convention to any other territory specified in the declaration. In respect of such territory the framework Convention shall enter into force on the first day of the month following the expiration of a period of three months after the date of receipt of such declaration by the Secretary General.

3. Any declaration made under the two preceding paragraphs may, in respect of any territory specified in such declaration, be withdrawn by a notification addressed to the Secretary General. The withdrawal shall become effective on the first day of the month following the expiration of a period of three months after the date of receipt of such notification by the Secretary General.

*Article* 31

1. Any Party may at any time denounce this framework Convention by means of a notification addressed to the Secretary General of the Council of Europe.

2. Such denunciation shall become effective on the first day of the month following the expiration of a period of six months after the date of receipt of the notification by the Secretary General.

*Article* 32

The Secretary General of the Council of Europe shall notify the member States of the Council, other signatory States and any State which has acceded to this framework Convention, of:

  (a) any signature;
  (b) the deposit of any instrument of ratification, acceptance, approval or accession;
  (c) any date of entry into force of this framework Convention in accordance with Articles 28, 29 and 30;
  (d) any other act, notification or communication relating to this framework Convention.

In witness whereof the undersigned, being duly authorized thereto, have signed this framework Convention.

*Done* at Strasbourg, this 1st day of February 1995, in English and French, both texts being equally authentic, in a single copy which shall be deposited in the archives of the Council of Europe. The Secretary General of the Council of Europe shall transmit certified copies to each member State of the Council of Europe and to any State invited to sign or accede to this framework Convention.

## 67. EUROPEAN CONVENTION ON THE EXERCISE OF CHILDREN'S RIGHTS, 1996

This Convention was opened for signature on 25 January 1996 by Council of Europe Member States and non-member States which had participated in its drafting. It entered into force on 1 July 2000; for text, see ETS No. 160.

*TEXT*

### Preamble

The member States of the Council of Europe and the other States signatory hereto,

*Considering* that the aim of the Council of Europe is to achieve greater unity between its members;

*Having regard* to the United Nations Convention on the rights of the child and in particular Article 4 which requires States Parties to undertake all appropriate legislative, administrative and other measures for the implementation of the rights recognised in the said Convention;

*Noting* the contents of Recommendation 1121 (1990) of the Parliamentary Assembly on the rights of the child;

*Convinced* that the rights and best interests of children should be promoted and to that end children should have the opportunity to exercise their rights, in particular in family proceedings affecting them;

*Recognizing* that children should be provided with relevant information to enable such rights and best interests to be promoted and that due weight should be given to the views of children;

*Recognizing* the importance of the parental role in protecting and promoting the rights and best interests of children and considering that, where necessary, States should also engage in such protection and promotion;

*Considering*, however, that in the event of conflict it is desirable for families to try to reach agreement before bringing the matter before a judicial authority,

*Have agreed* as follows:

### CHAPTER I

### SCOPE AND OBJECT OF THE CONVENTION AND DEFINITIONS

*Article 1—Scope and object of the Convention*

1. This Convention shall apply to children who have not reached the age of 18 years.

2. The object of the present Convention is, in the best interests of children, to

promote their rights, to grant them procedural rights and to facilitate the exercise of these rights by ensuring that children are, themselves or through other persons or bodies, informed and allowed to participate in proceedings affecting them before a judicial authority.

3. For the purposes of this Convention proceedings before a judicial authority affecting children are family proceedings, in particular those involving the exercise of parental responsibilities such as residence and access to children.

4. Every State shall, at the time of signature or when depositing its instrument of ratification, acceptance, approval or accession, by a declaration addressed to the Secretary General of the Council of Europe, specify at least three categories of family cases before a judicial authority to which this Convention is to apply.

5. Any Party may, by further declaration, specify additional categories of family cases to which this Convention is to apply or provide information concerning the application of Article 5, paragraph 2 of Article 9, paragraph 2 of Article 10 and Article 11.

6. Nothing in this Convention shall prevent Parties from applying rules more favourable to the promotion and the exercise of children's rights.

*Article 2—Definitions*

For the purposes of this Convention:

 (a) the term 'judicial authority' means a court or an administrative authority having equivalent powers;

 (b) the term 'holders of parental responsibilities' means parents and other persons or bodies entitled to exercise some or all parental responsibilities;

 (c) the term 'representative' means a person, such as a lawyer, or a body appointed to act before a judicial authority on behalf of a child;

 (d) the term 'relevant information' means information which is appropriate to the age and understanding of the child, and which will be given to enable the child to exercise his or her rights fully unless the provision of such information were contrary to the welfare of the child.

## CHAPTER II

## PROCEDURAL MEASURES TO PROMOTE THE EXERCISE OF CHILDREN'S RIGHTS

### A. *Procedural rights of a child*

*Article 3—Right to be informed and to express his or her views in proceedings*

A child considered by internal law as having sufficient understanding, in the case of proceedings before a judicial authority affecting him or her, shall be granted, and shall be entitled to request, the following rights:

 (a) to receive all relevant information;

 (b) to be consulted and express his or her views;

*(c)* to be informed of the possible consequences of compliance with these views and the possible consequences of any decision.

### Article 4—*Right to apply for the appointment of a special representative*

1. Subject to Article 9, the child shall have the right to apply, in person or through other persons or bodies, for a special representative in proceedings before a judicial authority affecting the child where internal law precludes the holders of parental responsibilities from representing the child as a result of a conflict of interest with the latter.

2. States are free to limit the right in paragraph 1 to children who are considered by internal law to have sufficient understanding.

### Article 5—*Other possible procedural rights*

Parties shall consider granting children additional procedural rights in relation to proceedings before a judicial authority affecting them, in particular:

*(a)* the right to apply to be assisted by an appropriate person of their choice in order to help them express their views;

*(b)* the right to apply themselves, or through other persons or bodies, for the appointment of a separate representative, in appropriate cases a lawyer;

*(c)* the right to appoint their own representative;

*(d)* the right to exercise some or all of the rights of parties to such proceedings.

### B. *Role of judicial authorities*

### Article 6—*Decision-making process*

In proceedings affecting a child, the judicial authority, before taking a decision, shall:

*(a)* consider whether it has sufficient information at its disposal in order to take a decision in the best interests of the child and, where necessary, it shall obtain further information, in particular from the holders of parental responsibilities;

*(b)* in a case where the child is considered by internal law as having sufficient understanding:

(i) ensure that the child has received all relevant information;

(ii) consult the child in person in appropriate cases, if necessary privately, itself or through other persons or bodies, in a manner appropriate to his or her understanding, unless this would be manifestly contrary to the best interests of the child;

(iii) allow the child to express his or her views;

*(c)* give due weight to the views expressed by the child.

### Article 7—*Duty to act speedily*

In proceedings affecting a child the judicial authority shall act speedily to avoid any unnecessary delay and procedures shall be available to ensure that its decisions are rapidly enforced. In urgent cases the judicial authority shall have the power, where appropriate, to take decisions which are immediately enforceable.

*Article 8—Acting on own motion*

In proceedings affecting a child the judicial authority shall have the power to act on its own motion in cases determined by internal law where the welfare of a child is in serious danger.

*Article 9—Appointment of a representative*

1. In proceedings affecting a child where, by internal law, the holders of parental responsibilities are precluded from representing the child as a result of a conflict of interest between them and the child, the judicial authority shall have the power to appoint a special representative for the child in those proceedings.

2. Parties shall consider providing that, in proceedings affecting a child, the judicial authority shall have the power to appoint a separate representative, in appropriate cases a lawyer, to represent the child.

### C. *Role of representatives*

*Article 10*

1. In the case of proceedings before a judicial authority affecting a child the representative shall, unless this would be manifestly contrary to the best interests of the child:

> *(a)* provide all relevant information to the child, if the child is considered by internal law as having sufficient understanding;
>
> *(b)* provide explanations to the child if the child is considered by internal law as having sufficient understanding, concerning the possible consequences of compliance with his or her views and the possible consequences of any action by the representative;
>
> *(c)* determine the views of the child and present these views to the judicial authority.

2. Parties shall consider extending the provisions of paragraph 1 to the holders of parental responsibilities.

### D. *Extension of certain provisions*

*Article 11*

Parties shall consider extending the provisions of Articles 3, 4 and 9 to proceedings affecting children before other bodies and to matters affecting children which are not the subject of proceedings.

### E. *National bodies*

*Article 12*

1. Parties shall encourage, through bodies which perform, *inter alia*, the functions set out in paragraph 2, the promotion and the exercise of children's rights.

2. The functions are as follows:

> *(a)* to make proposals to strengthen the law relating to the exercise of children's rights;

(b) to give opinions concerning draft legislation relating to the exercise of children's rights;

(c) to provide general information concerning the exercise of children's rights to the media, the public and persons and bodies dealing with questions relating to children;

(d) to seek the views of children and provide them with relevant information.

### F. Other matters

*Article 13—Mediation or other processes to resolve disputes*

In order to prevent or resolve disputes or to avoid proceedings before a judicial authority affecting children, Parties shall encourage the provision of mediation or other processes to resolve disputes and the use of such processes to reach agreement in appropriate cases to be determined by Parties.

*Article 14—Legal aid and advice*

Where internal law provides for legal aid or advice for the representation of children in proceedings before a judicial authority affecting them, such provisions shall apply in relation to the matters covered by Articles 4 and 9.

*Article 15—Relations with other international instruments*

This Convention shall not restrict the application of any other international instrument which deals with specific issues arising in the context of the protection of children and families, and to which a Party to this Convention is, or becomes, a Party.

## CHAPTER III

## STANDING COMMITTEE

*Article 16—Establishment and functions of the Standing Committee*

1. A Standing Committee is set up for the purposes of this Convention.

2. The Standing Committee shall keep under review problems relating to this Convention. It may, in particular:

(a) consider any relevant questions concerning the interpretation or implementation of the Convention. The Standing Committee's conclusions concerning the implementation of the Convention may take the form of a recommendation; recommendations shall be adopted by a three-quarters majority of the votes cast;

(b) propose amendments to the Convention and examine those proposed in accordance with Article 20;

(c) provide advice and assistance to the national bodies having the functions under paragraph 2 of Article 12 and promote international co-operation between them.

*Article* 17—*Composition*

1. Each Party may be represented on the Standing Committee by one or more delegates. Each Party shall have one vote.

2. Any State referred to in Article 21, which is not a Party to this Convention, may be represented in the Standing Committee by an observer. The same applies to any other State or to the European Community after having been invited to accede to the Convention in accordance with the provisions of Article 22.

3. Unless a Party has informed the Secretary General of its objection, at least one month before the meeting, the Standing Committee may invite the following to attend as observers at all its meetings or at one meeting or part of a meeting:

- *(a)* any State not referred to in paragraph 2 above;
- *(b)* the United Nations Committee on the Rights of the Child;
- *(c)* the European Community;
- *(d)* any international governmental body;
- *(e)* any international non-governmental body with one or more functions mentioned under paragraph 2 of Article 12;
- *(f)* any national governmental or non-governmental body with one or more functions mentioned under paragraph 2 of Article 12.

4. The Standing Committee may exchange information with relevant organizations dealing with the exercise of children's rights.

*Article* 18—*Meetings*

1. At the end of the third year following the date of entry into force of this Convention and, on his or her own initiative, at any time after this date, the Secretary General of the Council of Europe shall invite the Standing Committee to meet.

2. Decisions may only be taken in the Standing Committee if at least one-half of the Parties are present.

3. Subject to Articles 16 and 20 the decisions of the Standing Committee shall be taken by a majority of the members present.

4. Subject to the provisions of this Convention the Standing Committee shall draw up its own rules of procedure and the rules of procedure of any working party it may set up to carry out all appropriate tasks under the Convention.

*Article* 19—*Reports of the Standing Committee*

After each meeting, the Standing Committee shall forward to the Parties and the Committee of Ministers of the Council of Europe a report on its discussions and any decisions taken.

# CHAPTER IV

# AMENDMENTS TO THE CONVENTION

*Article 20*

1. Any amendment to the articles of this Convention proposed by a Party or the Standing Committee shall be communicated to the Secretary General of the Council of Europe and forwarded by him or her, at least two months before the next meeting of the Standing Committee, to the member States of the Council of Europe, any signatory, any Party, any State invited to sign this Convention in accordance with the provisions of Article 21 and any State or the European Community invited to accede to it in accordance with the provisions of Article 22.

2. Any amendment proposed in accordance with the provisions of the preceding paragraph shall be examined by the Standing Committee which shall submit the text adopted by a three-quarters majority of the votes cast to the Committee of Ministers for approval. After its approval, this text shall be forwarded to the Parties for acceptance.

3. Any amendment shall enter into force on the first day of the month following the expiration of a period of one month after the date on which all Parties have informed the Secretary General that they have accepted it.

# CHAPTER V

# FINAL CLAUSES

*Article 21—Signature, ratification and entry into force*

1. This Convention shall be open for signature by the member States of the Council of Europe and the non-member States which have participated in its elaboration.

2. This Convention is subject to ratification, acceptance or approval. Instruments of ratification, acceptance or approval shall be deposited with the Secretary General of the Council of Europe.

3. This Convention shall enter into force on the first day of the month following the expiration of a period of three months after the date on which three States, including at least two member States of the Council of Europe, have expressed their consent to be bound by the Convention in accordance with the provisions of the preceding paragraph.

4. In respect of any signatory which subsequently expresses its consent to be bound by it, the Convention shall enter into force on the first day of the month following the expiration of a period of three months after the date of the deposit of its instrument of ratification, acceptance or approval.

*Article 22—Non-member States and the European Community*

1. After the entry into force of this Convention, the Committee of Ministers of the Council of Europe may, on its own initiative or following a proposal from the

Standing Committee and after consultation of the Parties, invite any non-member State of the Council of Europe, which has not participated in the elaboration of the Convention, as well as the European Community to accede to this Convention by a decision taken by the majority provided for in Article 20, sub-paragraph d of the Statute of the Council of Europe, and by the unanimous vote of the representatives of the contracting States entitled to sit on the Committee of Ministers.

2. In respect of any acceding State or the European Community, the Convention shall enter into force on the first day of the month following the expiration of a period of three months after the date of deposit of the instrument of accession with the Secretary General of the Council of Europe.

### Article 23—Territorial application

1. Any State may, at the time of signature or when depositing its instrument of ratification, acceptance, approval or accession, specify the territory or territories to which this Convention shall apply.

2. Any Party may, at any later date, by a declaration addressed to the Secretary General of the Council of Europe, extend the application of this Convention to any other territory specified in the declaration and for whose international relations it is responsible or on whose behalf it is authorized to give undertakings. In respect of such territory the Convention shall enter into force on the first day of the month following the expiration of a period of three months after the date of receipt of such declaration by the Secretary General.

3. Any declaration made under the two preceding paragraphs may, in respect of any territory specified in such declaration, be withdrawn by a notification addressed to the Secretary General. The withdrawal shall become effective on the first day of the month following the expiration of a period of three months after the date of receipt of such notification by the Secretary General.

### Article 24—Reservations

No reservation may be made to the Convention.

### Article 25—Denunciation

1. Any Party may at any time denounce this Convention by means of a notification addressed to the Secretary General of the Council of Europe.

2. Such denunciation shall become effective on the first day of the month following the expiration of a period of three months after the date of receipt of notification by the Secretary General.

### Article 26—Notifications

The Secretary General of the Council of Europe shall notify the member States of the Council, any signatory, any Party and any other State or the European Community which has been invited to accede to this Convention of:

- (a) any signature;
- (b) the deposit of any instrument of ratification, acceptance, approval or accession;
- (c) any date of entry into force of this Convention in accordance with Articles 21 or 22;

(d)  any amendment adopted in accordance with Article 20 and the date on which such an amendment enters into force;

(e)  any declaration made under the provisions of Articles 1 and 23;

(f)  any denunciation made in pursuance of the provisions of Article 25;

(g)  any other act, notification or communication relating to this Convention.

In witness whereof, the undersigned, being duly authorized thereto, have signed this Convention.

*Done* at Strasbourg, the 25th January 1996, in English and French, both texts being equally authentic, in a single copy which shall be deposited in the archives of the Council of Europe. The Secretary General of the Council of Europe shall transmit certified copies to each member State of the Council of Europe, to the non-member States which have participated in the elaboration of this Convention, to the European Community and to any State invited to accede to this Convention.

# 68. EUROPEAN CONVENTION ON NATIONALITY, 1997

Opened for signature by Member States of the Council of Europe and by non-member States which participated in its elaboration on 6 November 1997, this Convention entered into force on 1 March 2000; for text see ETS No. 166. It is intended to make easier the acquisition of a new nationality or the recovery of a former nationality, to ensure that nationality is not arbitrarily withdrawn, and that the risk of statelessness is reduced. See also the Convention on the Status of Stateless Persons, 1954 (above, 142–52), and the Convention on the Reduction of Statelessness, 1961 (above, 153–9); the Declaration of Articles on Nationality of Natural Persons in relation to the Succession of States, 2000 (above, 98–105); Batchelor, C., 'Stateless-ness and the Problem of Resolving Nationality Status', 10 *IJRL* 156 (1998).

*TEXT*

## Preamble

The member States of the Council of Europe and the other States signatory to this Convention,

*Considering* that the aim of the Council of Europe is to achieve greater unity between its members;

*Bearing in mind* the numerous international instruments relating to nationality, multiple nationality and statelessness;

*Recognising* that, in matters concerning nationality, account should be taken both of the legitimate interests of States and those of individuals;

*Desiring* to promote the progressive development of legal principles concerning nationality, as well as their adoption in internal law and desiring to avoid, as far as possible, cases of statelessness;

*Desiring* to avoid discrimination in matters relating to nationality;

*Aware* of the right to respect for family life as contained in Article 8 of the Convention for the Protection of Human Rights and Fundamental Freedoms;

*Noting* the varied approach of States to the question of multiple nationality and recognizing that each State is free to decide which consequences it attaches in its internal law to the fact that a national acquires or possesses another nationality;

*Agreeing* on the desirability of finding appropriate solutions to consequences of multiple nationality and in particular as regards the rights and duties of multiple nationals;

*Considering* it desirable that persons possessing the nationality of two or more States Parties should be required to fulfil their military obligations in relation to only one of those Parties;

*Considering* the need to promote international co-operation between the national authorities responsible for nationality matters,

*Have agreed* as follows:

# CHAPTER I

## GENERAL MATTERS

*Article 1—Object of the Convention*

This Convention establishes principles and rules relating to the nationality of natural persons and rules regulating military obligations in cases of multiple nationality, to which the internal law of States Parties shall conform.

*Article 2—Definitions*

For the purpose of this Convention:

   *(a)* 'nationality' means the legal bond between a person and a State and does not indicate the person's ethnic origin;

   *(b)* 'multiple nationality' means the simultaneous possession of two or more nationalities by the same person;

   *(c)* 'child' means every person below the age of 18 years unless, under the law applicable to the child, majority is attained earlier;

   *(d)* 'internal law' means all types of provisions of the national legal system, including the constitution, legislation, regulations, decrees, case-law, customary rules and practice as well as rules deriving from binding international instruments.

# CHAPTER II

## GENERAL PRINCIPLES RELATING TO NATIONALITY

*Article 3—Competence of the State*

1. Each State shall determine under its own law who are its nationals.

2. This law shall be accepted by other States in so far as it is consistent with applicable international conventions, customary international law and the principles of law generally recognized with regard to nationality.

*Article 4—Principles*

The rules on nationality of each State Party shall be based on the following principles:

   *(a)* everyone has the right to a nationality;

   *(b)* statelessness shall be avoided;

   *(c)* no one shall be arbitrarily deprived of his or her nationality;

   *(d)* neither marriage nor the dissolution of a marriage between a national of a State Party and an alien, nor the change of nationality by one of the spouses during marriage, shall automatically affect the nationality of the other spouse.

*Article 5—Non-discrimination*

1. The rules of a State Party on nationality shall not contain distinctions or include any practice which amount to discrimination on the grounds of sex, religion, race, colour or national or ethnic origin.

2. Each State Party shall be guided by the principle of non-discrimination between its nationals, whether they are nationals by birth or have acquired its nationality subsequently.

## CHAPTER III

## RULES RELATING TO NATIONALITY

*Article 6—Acquisition of nationality*

1. Each State Party shall provide in its internal law for its nationality to be acquired *ex lege* by the following persons:

    *(a)* children one of whose parents possesses, at the time of the birth of these children, the nationality of that State Party, subject to any exceptions which may be provided for by its internal law as regards children born abroad. With respect to children whose parenthood is established by recognition, court order or similar procedures, each State Party may provide that the child acquires its nationality following the procedure determined by its internal law;

    *(b)* foundlings found in its territory who would otherwise be stateless.

2. Each State Party shall provide in its internal law for its nationality to be acquired by children born on its territory who do not acquire at birth another nationality. Such nationality shall be granted:

    *(a)* at birth *ex lege*; or

    *(b)* subsequently, to children who remained stateless, upon an application being lodged with the appropriate authority, by or on behalf of the child concerned, in the manner prescribed by the internal law of the State Party. Such an application may be made subject to the lawful and habitual residence on its territory for a period not exceeding five years immediately preceding the lodging of the application.

3. Each State Party shall provide in its internal law for the possibility of naturalization of persons lawfully and habitually resident on its territory. In establishing the conditions for naturalization, it shall not provide for a period of residence exceeding ten years before the lodging of an application.

4. Each State Party shall facilitate in its internal law the acquisition of its nationality for the following persons:

    *(a)* spouses of its nationals;

    *(b)* children of one of its nationals, falling under the exception of Article 6, paragraph 1, sub-paragraph (a);

    *(c)* children one of whose parents acquires or has acquired its nationality;

> *(d)* children adopted by one of its nationals;
>
> *(e)* persons who were born on its territory and reside there lawfully and habitually;
>
> *(f)* persons who are lawfully and habitually resident on its territory for a period of time beginning before the age of 18, that period to be determined by the internal law of the State Party concerned;
>
> *(g)* stateless persons and recognized refugees lawfully and habitually resident on its territory.

*Article 7—Loss of nationality* ex lege *or at the initiative of a State Party*

1. A State Party may not provide in its internal law for the loss of its nationality *ex lege* or at the initiative of the State Party except in the following cases:

> *(a)* voluntary acquisition of another nationality;
>
> *(b)* acquisition of the nationality of the State Party by means of fraudulent conduct, false information or concealment of any relevant fact attributable to the applicant;
>
> *(c)* voluntary service in a foreign military force;
>
> *(d)* conduct seriously prejudicial to the vital interests of the State Party;
>
> *(e)* lack of a genuine link between the State Party and a national habitually residing abroad;
>
> *(f)* where it is established during the minority of a child that the preconditions laid down by internal law which led to the *ex lege* acquisition of the nationality of the State Party are no longer fulfilled;
>
> *(g)* adoption of a child if the child acquires or possesses the foreign nationality of one or both of the adopting parents.

2. A State Party may provide for the loss of its nationality by children whose parents lose that nationality except in cases covered by sub-paragraphs (c) and (d) of paragraph 1. However, children shall not lose that nationality if one of their parents retains it.

3. A State Party may not provide in its internal law for the loss of its nationality under paragraphs 1 and 2 of this article if the person concerned would thereby become stateless, with the exception of the cases mentioned in paragraph 1, sub-paragraph (b), of this article.

*Article 8—Loss of nationality at the initiative of the individual*

1. Each State Party shall permit the renunciation of its nationality provided the persons concerned do not thereby become stateless.

2. However, a State Party may provide in its internal law that renunciation may be effected only by nationals who are habitually resident abroad.

*Article 9—Recovery of nationality*

Each State Party shall facilitate, in the cases and under the conditions provided for by its internal law, the recovery of its nationality by former nationals who are lawfully and habitually resident on its territory.

# CHAPTER IV

## PROCEDURES RELATING TO NATIONALITY

*Article 10—Processing of applications*

Each State Party shall ensure that applications relating to the acquisition, retention, loss, recovery or certification of its nationality be processed within a reasonable time.

*Article 11—Decisions*

Each State Party shall ensure that decisions relating to the acquisition, retention, loss, recovery or certification of its nationality contain reasons in writing.

*Article 12—Right to a review*

Each State Party shall ensure that decisions relating to the acquisition, retention, loss, recovery or certification of its nationality be open to an administrative or judicial review in conformity with its internal law.

*Article 13—Fees*

1. Each State Party shall ensure that the fees for the acquisition, retention, loss, recovery or certification of its nationality be reasonable.

2. Each State Party shall ensure that the fees for an administrative or judicial review be not an obstacle for applicants.

# CHAPTER V

## MULTIPLE NATIONALITY

*Article 14— Cases of multiple nationality* ex lege

1. A State Party shall allow:

   (a) children having different nationalities acquired automatically at birth to retain these nationalities;

   (b) its nationals to possess another nationality where this other nationality is automatically acquired by marriage.

2. The retention of the nationalities mentioned in paragraph 1 is subject to the relevant provisions of Article 7 of this Convention.

*Article 15—Other possible cases of multiple nationality*

The provisions of this Convention shall not limit the right of a State Party to determine in its internal law whether:

   (a) its nationals who acquire or possess the nationality of another State retain its nationality or lose it;

   (b) the acquisition or retention of its nationality is subject to the renunciation or loss of another nationality.

*Article* 16—*Conservation of previous nationality*

A State Party shall not make the renunciation or loss of another nationality a condition for the acquisition or retention of its nationality where such renunciation or loss is not possible or cannot reasonably be required.

*Article* 17—*Rights and duties related to multiple nationality*

1. Nationals of a State Party in possession of another nationality shall have, in the territory of that State Party in which they reside, the same rights and duties as other nationals of that State Party.

2. The provisions of this chapter do not affect:

   *(a)* the rules of international law concerning diplomatic or consular protection by a State Party in favour of one of its nationals who simultaneously possesses another nationality;

   *(b)* the application of the rules of private international law of each State Party in cases of multiple nationality.


# CHAPTER VI

# STATE SUCCESSION AND NATIONALITY

*Article* 18—*Principles*

1. In matters of nationality in cases of State succession, each State Party concerned shall respect the principles of the rule of law, the rules concerning human rights and the principles contained in Articles 4 and 5 of this Convention and in paragraph 2 of this article, in particular in order to avoid statelessness.

2. In deciding on the granting or the retention of nationality in cases of State succession, each State Party concerned shall take account in particular of:

   *(a)* the genuine and effective link of the person concerned with the State;

   *(b)* the habitual residence of the person concerned at the time of State succession;

   *(c)* the will of the person concerned;

   *(d)* the territorial origin of the person concerned.

3. Where the acquisition of nationality is subject to the loss of a foreign nationality, the provisions of Article 16 of this Convention shall apply.

*Article* 19—*Settlement by international agreement*

In cases of State succession, States Parties concerned shall endeavour to regulate matters relating to nationality by agreement amongst themselves and, where applicable, in their relationship with other States concerned. Such agreements shall respect the principles and rules contained or referred to in this chapter.

*Article* 20—*Principles concerning non-nationals*

1. Each State Party shall respect the following principles:

(a) nationals of a predecessor State habitually resident in the territory over which sovereignty is transferred to a successor State and who have not acquired its nationality shall have the right to remain in that State;

(b) persons referred to in sub-paragraph a shall enjoy equality of treatment with nationals of the successor State in relation to social and economic rights.

2. Each State Party may exclude persons considered under paragraph 1 from employment in the public service involving the exercise of sovereign powers.

## CHAPTER VII

### MILITARY OBLIGATIONS IN CASES OF MULTIPLE NATIONALITY

*Article 21—Fulfilment of military obligations*

1. Persons possessing the nationality of two or more States Parties shall be required to fulfil their military obligations in relation to one of those States Parties only.

2. The modes of application of paragraph 1 may be determined by special agreements between any of the States Parties.

3. Except where a special agreement which has been, or may be, concluded provides otherwise, the following provisions are applicable to persons possessing the nationality of two or more States Parties:

(a) Any such person shall be subject to military obligations in relation to the State Party in whose territory they are habitually resident. Nevertheless, they shall be free to choose, up to the age of 19 years, to submit themselves to military obligations as volunteers in relation to any other State Party of which they are also nationals for a total and effective period at least equal to that of the active military service required by the former State Party;

(b) Persons who are habitually resident in the territory of a State Party of which they are not nationals or in that of a State which is not a State Party may choose to perform their military service in the territory of any State Party of which they are nationals;

(c) Persons who, in accordance with the rules laid down in paragraphs a and b, shall fulfil their military obligations in relation to one State Party, as prescribed by the law of that State Party, shall be deemed to have fulfilled their military obligations in relation to any other State Party or States Parties of which they are also nationals;

(d) Persons who, before the entry into force of this Convention between the States Parties of which they are nationals, have, in relation to one of those States Parties, fulfilled their military obligations in accordance with the law of that State Party, shall be deemed to have fulfilled the same obligations in relation to any other State Party or States Parties of which they are also nationals;

(e) Persons who, in conformity with paragraph a, have performed their active military service in relation to one of the States Parties of which they are nationals, and subsequently transfer their habitual residence to the territory of the other State Party of which they are nationals, shall be liable to military service in the reserve only in relation to the latter State Party;

(f) The application of this article shall not prejudice, in any respect, the nationality of the persons concerned;

(g) In the event of mobilisation by any State Party, the obligations arising under this article shall not be binding upon that State Party.

*Article 22—Exemption from military obligations or alternative civil service*

Except where a special agreement which has been, or may be, concluded provides otherwise, the following provisions are also applicable to persons possessing the nationality of two or more States Parties:

(a) Article 21, paragraph 3, sub-paragraph c, of this Convention shall apply to persons who have been exempted from their military obligations or have fulfilled civil service as an alternative;

(b) persons who are nationals of a State Party which does not require obligatory military service shall be considered as having satisfied their military obligations when they have their habitual residence in the territory of that State Party. Nevertheless, they should be deemed not to have satisfied their military obligations in relation to a State Party or States Parties of which they are equally nationals and where military service is required unless the said habitual residence has been maintained up to a certain age, which each State Party concerned shall notify at the time of signature or when depositing its instruments of ratification, acceptance or accession;

(c) also persons who are nationals of a State Party which does not require obligatory military service shall be considered as having satisfied their military obligations when they have enlisted voluntarily in the military forces of that Party for a total and effective period which is at least equal to that of the active military service of the State Party or States Parties of which they are also nationals without regard to where they have their habitual residence.

## CHAPTER VIII

## CO-OPERATION BETWEEN THE STATES PARTIES

*Article 23—Co-operation between the States Parties*

1. With a view to facilitating co-operation between the States Parties, their competent authorities shall:

(a) provide the Secretary General of the Council of Europe with information about their internal law relating to nationality, including instances of statelessness and multiple nationality, and about developments concerning the application of the Convention;

(b) provide each other upon request with information about their internal law relating to nationality and about developments concerning the application of the Convention.

2. States Parties shall co-operate amongst themselves and with other member States of the Council of Europe within the framework of the appropriate inter-governmental body of the Council of Europe in order to deal with all relevant problems and to promote the progressive development of legal principles and practice concerning nationality and related matters.

*Article 24—Exchange of information*

Each State Party may at any time declare that it shall inform any other State Party, having made the same declaration, of the voluntary acquisition of its nationality by nationals of the other State Party, subject to applicable laws concerning data pro-tection. Such a declaration may indicate the conditions under which the State Party will give such information. The declaration may be withdrawn at any time.

## CHAPTER IX

## APPLICATION OF THE CONVENTION

*Article 25—Declarations concerning the application of the Convention*

1. Each State may declare, at the time of signature or when depositing its instru-ment of ratification, acceptance, approval or accession, that it will exclude Chapter VII from the application of the Convention.

2 The provisions of Chapter VII shall be applicable only in the relations between States Parties for which it is in force.

3. Each State Party may, at any subsequent time, notify the Secretary General of the Council of Europe that it will apply the provisions of Chapter VII excluded at the time of signature or in its instrument of ratification, acceptance, approval or accession. This notification shall become effective as from the date of its receipt.

*Article 26—Effects of this Convention*

1. The provisions of this Convention shall not prejudice the provisions of internal law and binding international instruments which are already in force or may come into force, under which more favourable rights are or would be accorded to individuals in the field of nationality.

2. This Convention does not prejudice the application of:

(a) the 1963 Convention on the Reduction of Cases of Multiple Nationality and Military Obligations in Cases of Multiple Nationality and its Protocols;

(b) other binding international instruments in so far as such instruments are compatible with this Convention,

in the relationship between the States Parties bound by these instruments.

# CHAPTER X

## FINAL CLAUSES

*Article 27—Signature and entry into force*

1. This Convention shall be open for signature by the member States of the Council of Europe and the non-member States which have participated in its elaboration. Such States may express their consent to be bound by:

   *(a)* signature without reservation as to ratification, acceptance or approval; or

   *(b)* signature subject to ratification, acceptance or approval, followed by ratification, acceptance or approval.

Instruments of ratification, acceptance or approval shall be deposited with the Secretary General of the Council of Europe.

2. This Convention shall enter into force, for all States having expressed their consent to be bound by the Convention, on the first day of the month following the expiration of a period of three months after the date on which three member States of the Council of Europe have expressed their consent to be bound by this Convention in accordance with the provisions of the preceding paragraph.

3. In respect of any State which subsequently expresses its consent to be bound by it, the Convention shall enter into force on the first day of the month following the expiration of a period of three months after the date of signature or of the deposit of its instrument of ratification, acceptance or approval.

*Article 28—Accession*

1. After the entry into force of this Convention, the Committee of Ministers of the Council of Europe may invite any non-member State of the Council of Europe which has not participated in its elaboration to accede to this Convention.

2. In respect of any acceding State, this Convention shall enter into force on the first day of the month following the expiration of a period of three months after the date of deposit of the instrument of accession with the Secretary General of the Council of Europe.

*Article 29—Reservations*

1. No reservations may be made to any of the provisions contained in Chapters I, II and VI of this Convention. Any State may, at the time of signature or when depositing its instrument of ratification, acceptance, approval or accession, make one or more reservations to other provisions of the Convention so long as they are compatible with the object and purpose of this Convention.

2. Any State which makes one or more reservations shall notify the Secretary General of the Council of Europe of the relevant contents of its internal law or of any other relevant information.

3. A State which has made one or more reservations in accordance with paragraph 1 shall consider withdrawing them in whole or in part as soon as circumstances permit. Such withdrawal shall be made by means of a notification addressed to the Secretary General of the Council of Europe and shall become effective as from the date of its receipt.

4. Any State which extends the application of this Convention to a territory mentioned in the declaration referred to in Article 30, paragraph 2, may, in respect of the territory concerned, make one or more reservations in accordance with the provisions of the preceding paragraphs.

5. A State Party which has made reservations in respect of any of the provisions in Chapter VII of the Convention may not claim application of the said provisions by another State Party save in so far as it has itself accepted these provisions.

*Article 30—Territorial application*

1. Any State may, at the time of signature or when depositing its instrument of ratification, acceptance, approval or accession, specify the territory or territories to which this Convention shall apply.

2. Any State may, at any later date, by a declaration addressed to the Secretary General of the Council of Europe, extend the application of this Convention to any other territory specified in the declaration and for whose international relations it is responsible or on whose behalf it is authorized to give undertakings. In respect of such territory, the Convention shall enter into force on the first day of the month following the expiration of a period of three months after the date of receipt of such declaration by the Secretary General.

3. Any declaration made under the two preceding paragraphs may, in respect of any territory specified in such declaration, be withdrawn by a notification addressed to the Secretary General. The withdrawal shall become effective on the first day of the month following the expiration of a period of three months after the date of receipt of such notification by the Secretary General.

*Article 31—Denunciation*

1. Any State Party may at any time denounce the Convention as a whole or Chapter VII only by means of a notification addressed to the Secretary General of the Council of Europe.

2. Such denunciation shall become effective on the first day of the month following the expiration of a period of three months after the date of receipt of notification by the Secretary General.

*Article 32—Notifications by the Secretary General*

The Secretary General of the Council of Europe shall notify the member States of the Council of Europe, any Signatory, any Party and any other State which has acceded to this Convention of:

(a) any signature;

(b) the deposit of any instrument of ratification, acceptance, approval or accession;

(c) any date of entry into force of this Convention in accordance with Articles 27 or 28 of this Convention;

(d) any reservation and withdrawal of reservations made in pursuance of the provisions of Article 29 of this Convention;

(e) any notification or declaration made under the provisions of Articles 23, 24, 25, 27, 28, 29, 30 and 31 of this Convention;

*(f)* any other act, notification or communication relating to this Convention.

In witness whereof the undersigned, being duly authorized thereto, have signed this Convention.

*Done* at Strasbourg, this sixth day of November 1997, in English and in French, both texts being equally authentic, in a single copy which shall be deposited in the archives of the Council of Europe. The Secretary General of the Council of Europe shall transmit certified copies to each member State of the Council of Europe, to the non-member States which have participated in the elaboration of this Convention and to any State invited to accede to this Convention.

## 69. CHARTER OF FUNDAMENTAL RIGHTS OF THE EUROPEAN UNION, 2000

The place of human rights within the European Union was debated over many years. In June 1999, the European Council decided to entrust the drafting of a charter of rights to a Convention, which first met in December of that year, and adopted the draft text on 2 October 2000. This was unanimously approved by the European Council in Biarritz the same month, and forwarded to the European Parliament and the Commission. The Parliament gave its approval on 14 November 2000 and the European Commission on 6 December 2000. At a meeting in Nice on 7 December 2000, the Presidents of the European Parliament, the Council and the Commission signed and proclaimed the Charter on behalf of their institutions. For text, see [2000] OJEC C 364/1.

The rights are based, in particular, on those set out in the European Convention on Human Rights and the European Social Charter. There are some notable developments. For example, see Article 18 on the 'right to asylum' and Article 19 on 'Protection in the event of removal, expulsion or extradition'; but see Article 51 on 'Scope'. The EU Charter is not a treaty as such; it is expected to have a normative role in Community law but its exact place remains to be determined.

Alston, P., ed., *The EU and Human Rights*, 1999.

*TEXT*

### Preamble

The peoples of Europe, in creating an ever closer union among them, are resolved to share a peaceful future based on common values.

Conscious of its spiritual and moral heritage, the Union is founded on the indivisible, universal values of human dignity, freedom, equality and solidarity; it is based on the principles of democracy and the rule of law. It places the individual at the heart of its activities, by establishing the citizenship of the Union and by creating an area of freedom, security and justice.

The Union contributes to the preservation and to the development of these common values while respecting the diversity of the cultures and traditions of the peoples of Europe as well as the national identities of the Member States and the organization of their public authorities at national, regional and local levels; it seeks to promote balanced and sustainable development and ensures free movement of persons, goods, services and capital, and the freedom of establishment.

To this end, it is necessary to strengthen the protection of fundamental rights in the light of changes in society, social progress and scientific and technological developments by making those rights more visible in a Charter.

This Charter reaffirms, with due regard for the powers and tasks of the Community and the Union and the principle of subsidiarity, the rights as they result, in particular, from the constitutional traditions and international obligations common to the Member States, the Treaty on European Union, the Community Treaties, the European Convention for the Protection of Human Rights and Fundamental Freedoms, the Social Charters adopted by the Community and by the Council of

Europe and the case-law of the Court of Justice of the European Communities and of the European Court of Human Rights.

Enjoyment of these rights entails responsibilities and duties with regard to other persons, to the human community and to future generations.

The Union therefore recognizes the rights, freedoms and principles set out hereafter.

# CHAPTER I

## DIGNITY

*Article 1—Human dignity*

Human dignity is inviolable. It must be respected and protected.

*Article 2—Right to life*

1.  Everyone has the right to life.
2.  No one shall be condemned to the death penalty, or executed.

*Article 3—Right to the integrity of the person*

1.  Everyone has the right to respect for his or her physical and mental integrity.
2.  In the fields of medicine and biology, the following must be respected in particular:
— the free and informed consent of the person concerned, according to the procedures laid down by law,
— the prohibition of eugenic practices, in particular those aiming at the selection of persons,
— the prohibition on making the human body and its parts as such a source of financial gain,
— the prohibition of the reproductive cloning of human beings.

*Article 4—Prohibition of torture and inhuman or degrading treatment or punishment*

No one shall be subjected to torture or to inhuman or degrading treatment or punishment.

*Article 5—Prohibition of slavery and forced labour*

1.  No one shall be held in slavery or servitude.
2.  No one shall be required to perform forced or compulsory labour.
3.  Trafficking in human beings is prohibited.

## CHAPTER II

## FREEDOMS

### *Article 6—Right to liberty and security*

Everyone has the right to liberty and security of person.

### *Article 7—Respect for private and family life*

Everyone has the right to respect for his or her private and family life, home and communications.

### *Article 8—Protection of personal data*

1. Everyone has the right to the protection of personal data concerning him or her.

2. Such data must be processed fairly for specified purposes and on the basis of the consent of the person concerned or some other legitimate basis laid down by law. Everyone has the right of access to data which has been collected concerning him or her, and the right to have it rectified.

3. Compliance with these rules shall be subject to control by an independent authority.

### *Article 9—Right to marry and right to found a family*

The right to marry and the right to found a family shall be guaranteed in accordance with the national laws governing the exercise of these rights.

### *Article 10—Freedom of thought, conscience and religion*

1. Everyone has the right to freedom of thought, conscience and religion. This right includes freedom to change religion or belief and freedom, either alone or in community with others and in public or in private, to manifest religion or belief, in worship, teaching, practice and observance.

2. The right to conscientious objection is recognised, in accordance with the national laws governing the exercise of this right.

### *Article 11—Freedom of expression and information*

1. Everyone has the right to freedom of expression. This right shall include freedom to hold opinions and to receive and impart information and ideas without interference by public authority and regardless of frontiers.

2. The freedom and pluralism of the media shall be respected.

### *Article 12—Freedom of assembly and of association*

1. Everyone has the right to freedom of peaceful assembly and to freedom of association at all levels, in particular in political, trade union and civic matters, which implies the right of everyone to form and to join trade unions for the protection of his or her interests.

2. Political parties at Union level contribute to expressing the political will of the citizens of the Union.

*Article* 13—*Freedom of the arts and sciences*

The arts and scientific research shall be free of constraint. Academic freedom shall be respected.

*Article* 14—*Right to education*

1. Everyone has the right to education and to have access to vocational and continuing training.

2. This right includes the possibility to receive free compulsory education.

3. The freedom to found educational establishments with due respect for democratic principles and the right of parents to ensure the education and teaching of their children in conformity with their religious, philosophical and pedagogical convictions shall be respected, in accordance with the national laws governing the exercise of such freedom and right.

*Article* 15—*Freedom to choose an occupation and right to engage in work*

1. Everyone has the right to engage in work and to pursue a freely chosen or accepted occupation.

2. Every citizen of the Union has the freedom to seek employment, to work, to exercise the right of establishment and to provide services in any Member State.

3. Nationals of third countries who are authorized to work in the territories of the Member States are entitled to working conditions equivalent to those of citizens of the Union.

*Article* 16—*Freedom to conduct a business*

The freedom to conduct a business in accordance with Community law and national laws and practices is recognized.

*Article* 17—*Right to property*

1. Everyone has the right to own, use, dispose of and bequeath his or her lawfully acquired possessions. No one may be deprived of his or her possessions, except in the public interest and in the cases and under the conditions provided for by law, subject to fair compensation being paid in good time for their loss. The use of property may be regulated by law in so far as is necessary for the general interest.

2. Intellectual property shall be protected.

*Article* 18—*Right to asylum*

The right to asylum shall be guaranteed with due respect for the rules of the Geneva Convention of 28 July 1951 and the Protocol of 31 January 1967 relating to the status of refugees and in accordance with the Treaty establishing the European Community.

*Article* 19—*Protection in the event of removal, expulsion or extradition*

1. Collective expulsions are prohibited.

2. No one may be removed, expelled or extradited to a State where there is a serious risk that he or she would be subjected to the death penalty, torture or other inhuman or degrading treatment or punishment.

# CHAPTER III

## EQUALITY

*Article 20—Equality before the law*

Everyone is equal before the law.

*Article 21—Non-discrimination*

1. Any discrimination based on any ground such as sex, race, colour, ethnic or social origin, genetic features, language, religion or belief, political or any other opinion, membership of a national minority, property, birth, disability, age or sexual orientation shall be prohibited.

2. Within the scope of application of the Treaty establishing the European Community and of the Treaty on European Union, and without prejudice to the special provisions of those Treaties, any discrimination on grounds of nationality shall be prohibited.

*Article 22—Cultural, religious and linguistic diversity*

The Union shall respect cultural, religious and linguistic diversity.

*Article 23—Equality between men and women*

Equality between men and women must be ensured in all areas, including employment, work and pay.

The principle of equality shall not prevent the maintenance or adoption of measures providing for specific advantages in favour of the under-represented sex.

*Article 24—The rights of the child*

1. Children shall have the right to such protection and care as is necessary for their well-being. They may express their views freely. Such views shall be taken into consideration on matters which concern them in accordance with their age and maturity.

2. In all actions relating to children, whether taken by public authorities or private institutions, the child's best interests must be a primary consideration.

3. Every child shall have the right to maintain on a regular basis a personal relationship and direct contact with both his or her parents, unless that is contrary to his or her interests.

*Article 25—The rights of the elderly*

The Union recognizes and respects the rights of the elderly to lead a life of dignity and independence and to participate in social and cultural life.

*Article 26—Integration of persons with disabilities*

The Union recognizes and respects the right of persons with disabilities to benefit from measures designed to ensure their independence, social and occupational integration and participation in the life of the community.

# CHAPTER IV

## SOLIDARITY

*Article 27—Workers' right to information and consultation within the undertaking*

Workers or their representatives must, at the appropriate levels, be guaranteed information and consultation in good time in the cases and under the conditions provided for by Community law and national laws and practices.

*Article 28—Right of collective bargaining and action*

Workers and employers, or their respective organizations, have, in accordance with Community law and national laws and practices, the right to negotiate and conclude collective agreements at the appropriate levels and, in cases of conflicts of interest, to take collective action to defend their interests, including strike action.

*Article 29—Right of access to placement services*

Everyone has the right of access to a free placement service.

*Article 30—Protection in the event of unjustified dismissal*

Every worker has the right to protection against unjustified dismissal, in accordance with Community law and national laws and practices.

*Article 31—Fair and just working conditions*

1. Every worker has the right to working conditions which respect his or her health, safety and dignity.

2. Every worker has the right to limitation of maximum working hours, to daily and weekly rest periods and to an annual period of paid leave.

*Article 32—Prohibition of child labour and protection of young people at work*

The employment of children is prohibited. The minimum age of admission to employment may not be lower than the minimum school-leaving age, without prejudice to such rules as may be more favourable to young people and except for limited derogations.

Young people admitted to work must have working conditions appropriate to their age and be protected against economic exploitation and any work likely to harm their safety, health or physical, mental, moral or social development or to interfere with their education.

*Article 33—Family and professional life*

1. The family shall enjoy legal, economic and social protection.

2. To reconcile family and professional life, everyone shall have the right to protection from dismissal for a reason connected with maternity and the right to paid maternity leave and to parental leave following the birth or adoption of a child.

*Article 34—Social security and social assistance*

1. The Union recognizes and respects the entitlement to social security benefits and social services providing protection in cases such as maternity, illness, industrial accidents, dependency or old age, and in the case of loss of employment, in

accordance with the rules laid down by Community law and national laws and practices.

2. Everyone residing and moving legally within the European Union is entitled to social security benefits and social advantages in accordance with Community law and national laws and practices.

3. In order to combat social exclusion and poverty, the Union recognizes and respects the right to social and housing assistance so as to ensure a decent existence for all those who lack sufficient resources, in accordance with the rules laid down by Community law and national laws and practices.

*Article 35—Health care*

Everyone has the right of access to preventive health care and the right to benefit from medical treatment under the conditions established by national laws and practices. A high level of human health protection shall be ensured in the definition and implementation of all Union policies and activities.

*Article 36— Access to services of general economic interest*

The Union recognizes and respects access to services of general economic interest as provided for in national laws and practices, in accordance with the Treaty establishing the European Community, in order to promote the social and territorial cohesion of the Union.

*Article 37—Environmental protection*

A high level of environmental protection and the improvement of the quality of the environment must be integrated into the policies of the Union and ensured in accordance with the principle of sustainable development.

*Article 38—Consumer protection*

Union policies shall ensure a high level of consumer protection.

## CHAPTER V

## CITIZENS' RIGHTS

*Article 39—Right to vote and to stand as a candidate at elections to the European Parliament*

1. Every citizen of the Union has the right to vote and to stand as a candidate at elections to the European Parliament in the Member State in which he or she resides, under the same conditions as nationals of that State.

2. Members of the European Parliament shall be elected by direct universal suffrage in a free and secret ballot.

*Article 40—Right to vote and to stand as a candidate at municipal elections*

Every citizen of the Union has the right to vote and to stand as a candidate at municipal elections in the Member State in which he or she resides under the same conditions as nationals of that State.

*Article 41—Right to good administration*

1. Every person has the right to have his or her affairs handled impartially, fairly and within a reasonable time by the institutions and bodies of the Union.

2. This right includes:

— the right of every person to be heard, before any individual measure which would affect him or her adversely is taken;

— the right of every person to have access to his or her file, while respecting the legitimate interests of confidentiality and of professional and business secrecy;

—the obligation of the administration to give reasons for its decisions.

3. Every person has the right to have the Community make good any damage caused by its institutions or by its servants in the performance of their duties, in accordance with the general principles common to the laws of the Member States.

4. Every person may write to the institutions of the Union in one of the languages of the Treaties and must have an answer in the same language.

*Article 42—Right of access to documents*

Any citizen of the Union, and any natural or legal person residing or having its registered office in a Member State, has a right of access to European Parliament, Council and Commission documents.

*Article 43—Ombudsman*

Any citizen of the Union and any natural or legal person residing or having its registered office in a Member State has the right to refer to the Ombudsman of the Union cases of maladministration in the activities of the Community institutions or bodies, with the exception of the Court of Justice and the Court of First Instance acting in their judicial role.

*Article 44—Right to petition*

Any citizen of the Union and any natural or legal person residing or having its registered office in a Member State has the right to petition the European Parliament.

*Article 45—Freedom of movement and of residence*

1. Every citizen of the Union has the right to move and reside freely within the territory of the Member States.

2. Freedom of movement and residence may be granted, in accordance with the Treaty establishing the European Community, to nationals of third countries legally resident in the territory of a Member State.

*Article 46—Diplomatic and consular protection*

Every citizen of the Union shall, in the territory of a third country in which the Member State of which he or she is a national is not represented, be entitled to protection by the diplomatic or consular authorities of any Member State, on the same conditions as the nationals of that Member State.

# CHAPTER VI

## JUSTICE

*Article 47—Right to an effective remedy and to a fair trial*

Everyone whose rights and freedoms guaranteed by the law of the Union are violated has the right to an effective remedy before a tribunal in compliance with the conditions laid down in this Article.

Everyone is entitled to a fair and public hearing within a reasonable time by an independent and impartial tribunal previously established by law. Everyone shall have the possibility of being advised, defended and represented.

Legal aid shall be made available to those who lack sufficient resources in so far as such aid is necessary to ensure effective access to justice.

*Article 48—Presumption of innocence and right of defence*

1. Everyone who has been charged shall be presumed innocent until proved guilty according to law.

2. Respect for the rights of the defence of anyone who has been charged shall be guaranteed.

*Article 49—Principles of legality and proportionality of criminal offences and penalties*

1. No one shall be held guilty of any criminal offence on account of any act or omission which did not constitute a criminal offence under national law or international law at the time when it was committed. Nor shall a heavier penalty be imposed than that which was applicable at the time the criminal offence was committed. If, subsequent to the commission of a criminal offence, the law provides for a lighter penalty, that penalty shall be applicable.

2. This Article shall not prejudice the trial and punishment of any person for any act or omission which, at the time when it was committed, was criminal according to the general principles recognised by the community of nations.

3. The severity of penalties must not be disproportionate to the criminal offence.

*Article 50—Right not to be tried or punished twice in criminal proceedings for the same criminal offence*

No one shall be liable to be tried or punished again in criminal proceedings for an offence for which he or she has already been finally acquitted or convicted within the Union in accordance with the law.

# CHAPTER VII

## GENERAL PROVISIONS

*Article 51—Scope*

1. The provisions of this Charter are addressed to the institutions and bodies of the Union with due regard for the principle of subsidiarity and to the Member States only when they are implementing Union law. They shall therefore respect

the rights, observe the principles and promote the application thereof in accordance with their respective powers.

2. This Charter does not establish any new power or task for the Community or the Union, or modify powers and tasks defined by the Treaties.

*Article 52—Scope of guaranteed rights*

1. Any limitation on the exercise of the rights and freedoms recognised by this Charter must be provided for by law and respect the essence of those rights and freedoms. Subject to the principle of proportionality, limitations may be made only if they are necessary and genuinely meet objectives of general interest recognised by the Union or the need to protect the rights and freedoms of others.

2. Rights recognised by this Charter which are based on the Community Treaties or the Treaty on European Union shall be exercised under the conditions and within the limits defined by those Treaties.

3. In so far as this Charter contains rights which correspond to rights guaranteed by the Convention for the Protection of Human Rights and Fundamental Freedoms, the meaning and scope of those rights shall be the same as those laid down by the said Convention. This provision shall not prevent Union law providing more extensive protection.

*Article 53—Level of protection*

Nothing in this Charter shall be interpreted as restricting or adversely affecting human rights and fundamental freedoms as recognized, in their respective fields of application, by Union law and international law and by international agreements to which the Union, the Community or all the Member States are party, including the European Convention for the Protection of Human Rights and Fundamental Freedoms, and by the Member States' constitutions.

*Article 54—Prohibition of abuse of rights*

Nothing in this Charter shall be interpreted as implying any right to engage in any activity or to perform any act aimed at the destruction of any of the rights and freedoms recognised in this Charter or at their limitation to a greater extent than is provided for herein.

# 70. FINAL ACT OF THE HELSINKI CONFERENCE, 1975

On 1 August 1975 the Final Act of the Conference on Security and Co-operation in Europe was adopted in Helsinki. This contains a declaration of principles under the heading 'Questions relating to Security in Europe'. The Final Act was signed by representatives of thirty-five States, including the United States and the U.S.S.R. The Final Act constitutes an important statement of intent but the instrument is not a treaty and the understanding of the signatories was that it was not legally binding. See further *Digest of United States Practice in International Law* (1975), 7–12, 190–3, 236–8, 271, 325–7, 529–32, 591–4, 679–81, 688–91, 783–8; the same (1976), 141–6, 178–81; Russell, H. S., 'The Helsinki Declaration: Brobdingnag or Lilliput?'70 *AJIL* 242–72 (1976); Schachter, O., 'The Twilight Existence of Non-Binding International Agreements', 71 *AJIL* 296–304 (1977); Ruiz-Fabri, H., 'La Conférence de sécurité et de coopération europénne et le règlement des différends: l'élaboration d'une méthode' (1991) 37 *Annuaire Francais de droit international*, 297–314.

The declaration of principles includes a section entitled 'Respect for human rights and fundamental freedoms, including the freedom of thought, conscience, religion or belief'. The text contains a commitment to act in conformity with existing obligations in the field of human rights. In a technical and formal sense the Final Act is not at all innovative in respect of human rights and, indeed, the subject-matter is as much related to security and disarmament as it is to human rights, although this was not conveyed to the public in many countries. In January 1992, ten former Soviet republics joined the Conference which, as the OSCE, has since become the largest regional security organization in the world, with fifty-five participating States. For further information see **www.osce.org/general/**.

The full text of the Final Act appears in the third edition of this book at 391–449, and at **www.osce.org/docs/english/1990–1999/summits/helfa75e.htm**; the following extracts deal with the question of security in Europe and co-operation in humanitarian matters.

See also the Charter for European Security, adopted at the OSCE Istanbul Summit, November 1999: **www.osce.org/docs/english/1990–1999/summits/istachart99e.htm**; the OSCE Review Conference, Vienna and Istanbul, Consolidated Document, 1999, particularly the report of the rapporteurs on 'the review of the implementation of all OSCE principles and commitments in the human dimension': **www.osce.org/docs/english/1990–1999/rcs/istarev99e.htm**. The OSCE Parliamentary Assembly also each year adopts resolutions and declarations relevant to the human dimension: **www.osce.org/pa/annual_session**.

*TEXT*

The Conference on Security and Co-operation in Europe, which opened at Helsinki on 3 July 1973 and continued at Geneva from 18 September 1973 to 21 July 1975, was concluded at Helsinki on 1 August 1975 by the High Representatives of Austria, Belgium, Bulgaria, Canada, Cyprus, Czechoslovakia, Denmark, Finland, France, the German Democratic Republic, the Federal Republic of Germany, Greece, the Holy See, Hungary, Iceland, Ireland, Italy, Liechtenstein, Luxembourg, Malta, Monaco, the Netherlands, Norway, Poland, Portugal, Romania, San Marino, Spain, Sweden, Switzerland, Turkey, the Union of Soviet Socialist Republics, the United Kingdom, the United States of America and Yugoslavia.

During the opening and closing stages of the Conference the participants were addressed by the Secretary-General of the United Nations as their guest of honour. The Director-General of UNESCO and the Executive Secretary of the United Nations Economic Commission for Europe addressed the Conference during its second stage.

During the meetings of the second stage of the Conference, contributions were received, and statements heard, from the following non-participating Mediterranean States on various agenda items: the Democratic and Popular Republic of Algeria, the Arab Republic of Egypt, Israel, the Kingdom of Morocco, the Syrian Arab Republic, Tunisia.

Motivated by the political will, in the interest of peoples, to improve and intensify their relations and to contribute in Europe to peace, security, justice and cooperation as well as to rapprochement among themselves and with the other States of the world,

Determined, in consequence, to give full effect to the results of the Conference and to assure, among their States and throughout Europe, the benefits deriving from those results and thus to broaden, deepen and make continuing and lasting the process of détente,

The High Representatives of the participating States have solemnly adopted the following:


## QUESTIONS RELATING TO SECURITY IN EUROPE

The States participating in the Conference on Security and Co-operation in Europe,

*Reaffirming* their objective of promoting better relations among themselves and ensuring conditions in which their people can live in true and lasting peace free from any threat to or attempt against their security;

*Convinced* of the need to exert efforts to make détente both a continuing and an increasingly viable and comprehensive process, universal in scope, and that the implementation of the results of the Conference on Security and Cooperation in Europe will be a major contribution to this process;

*Considering* that solidarity among peoples, as well as the common purpose of the participating States in achieving the aims as set forth by the Conference on Security and Cooperation in Europe, should lead to the development of better and closer relations among them in all fields and thus to overcoming the confrontation stemming from the character of their past relations, and to better mutual understanding;

*Mindful* of their common history and recognizing that the existence of elements common to their traditions and values can assist them in developing their relations, and desiring to search, fully taking into account the individuality and diversity of their positions and views, for possibilities of joining their efforts with a view to overcoming distrust and increasing confidence, solving the problems that separate them and cooperating in the interest of mankind;

*Recognizing* the indivisibility of security in Europe as well as their common interest in the development of cooperation throughout Europe and among themselves and expressing their intention to pursue efforts accordingly;

*Recognizing* the close link between peace and security in Europe and in the world as a whole and conscious of the need for each of them to make its contribution to the strengthening of world peace and security and to the promotion of fundamental rights, economic and social progress and well-being for all peoples;

*Have adopted* the following:

## (a) Declaration on Principles Guiding Relations between Participating States

*The participating States,*

*Reaffirming* their commitment to peace, security and justice and the continuing development of friendly relations and co-operation;

*Recognizing* that this commitment, which reflects the interest and aspirations of peoples, constitutes for each participating State a present and future responsibility, heightened by experience of the past;

*Reaffirming*, in conformity with their membership in the United Nations and in accordance with the purposes and principles of the United Nations, their full and active support for the United Nations and for the enhancement of its role and effectiveness in strengthening international peace, security and justice, and in promoting the solution of international problems, as well as the development of friendly relations and co-operation among States;

*Expressing* their common adherence to the principles which are set forth below and are in conformity with the Charter of the United Nations, as well as their common will to act, in the application of these principles, in conformity with the purposes and principles of the Charter of the United Nations;

*Declare* their determination to respect and put into practice, each of them in its relations with all other participating States, irrespective of their political, economic or social systems as well as of their size, geographical location or level of economic development, the following principles, which all are of primary significance, guiding their mutual relations:

### I. *Sovereign Equality, Respect for the Rights Inherent in Sovereignty*

The participating States will respect each other's sovereign equality and individuality as well as all the rights inherent in and encompassed by its sovereignty, including in particular the right of every State to juridical equality, to territorial integrity and to freedom and political independence. They will also respect each other's right freely to choose and develop its political, social, economic and cultural systems as well as its right to determine its laws and regulations.

Within the framework of international law, all the participating States have equal rights and duties. They will respect each other's right to define and conduct as it wishes its relations with other States in accordance with international law and in the spirit of the present Declaration. They consider that their frontiers can be changed, in accordance with international law, by peaceful means and by agreement. They also have the right to belong or not to belong to international organizations, to be or not to be a party to bilateral or multilateral treaties including the right to be or not to be a party to treaties of alliance; they also have the right to neutrality.

## II. *Refraining from the Threat or Use of Force*

The participating States will refrain in their mutual relations, as well as in their international relations in general, from the threat or use of force against the territorial integrity or political independence of any State, or in any other manner inconsistent with the purposes of the United Nations and with the present Declaration. No consideration may be invoked to serve to warrant resort to the threat or use of force in contravention of this principle.

Accordingly, the participating States will refrain from any acts constituting a threat of force or direct or indirect use of force against another participating State.

Likewise they will refrain from any manifestation of force for the purpose of inducing another participating State to renounce the full exercise of its sovereign rights. Likewise they will also refrain in their mutual relations from any act of reprisal by force.

No such threat or use of force will be employed as a means of settling disputes, or questions likely to give rise to disputes, between them.

## III. *Inviolability of Frontiers*

The participating States regard as inviolable all one another's frontiers as well as the frontiers of all States in Europe and therefore they will refrain now and in the future from assaulting these frontiers.

Accordingly, they will also refrain from any demand for, or act of, seizure and usurpation of part or all of the territory of any participating State.

## IV. *Territorial Integrity of States*

The participating States will respect the territorial integrity of each of the participating States.

Accordingly, they will refrain from any action inconsistent with the purposes and principles of the Charter of the United Nations against the territorial integrity, political independence or the unity of any participating State, and in particular from any such action constituting a threat or use of force.

The participating States will likewise refrain from making each other's territory the object of military occupation or other direct or indirect measures of force in contravention of international law, or the object of acquisition by means of such measures or the threat of them. No such occupation or acquisition will be recognized as legal.

## V. *Peaceful Settlement of Disputes*

The participating States will settle disputes among them by peaceful means in such a manner as not to endanger international peace and security, and justice.

They will endeavour in good faith and a spirit of co-operation to reach a rapid and equitable solution on the basis of international law.

For this purpose they will use such means as negotiation, enquiry, mediation, conciliation, arbitration, judicial settlement or other peaceful means of their own choice including any settlement procedure agreed to in advance of disputes to which they are parties.

In the event of failure to reach a solution by any of the above peaceful means, the parties to a dispute will continue to seek a mutually agreed way to settle the dispute peacefully.

Participating States, parties to a dispute among them, as well as other participating States, will refrain from any action which might aggravate the situation to such a degree as to endanger the maintenance of international peace and security and thereby make a peaceful settlement of the dispute more difficult.

### VI. *Non-intervention in Internal Affairs*

The participating States will refrain from any intervention, direct or indirect, individual or collective, in the internal or external affairs falling within the domestic jurisdiction of another participating State, regardless of their mutual relations.

They will accordingly refrain from any form of armed intervention or threat of such intervention against another participating State.

They will likewise in all circumstances refrain from any other act of military, or of political, economic or other coercion designed to subordinate to their own interest the exercise by another participating State of the rights inherent in its sovereignty and thus to secure advantages of any kind.

Accordingly, they will, *inter alia,* refrain from direct or indirect assistance to terrorist activities, or to subversive or other activities directed towards the violent overthrow of the regime of another participating State.

### VII. *Respect for Human Rights and Fundamental Freedoms, including the Freedom of Thought, Conscience, Religion or Belief*

The participating States will respect human rights and fundamental freedoms, including the freedom of thought, conscience, religion or belief, for all without distinction as to race, sex, language or religion.

They will promote and encourage the effective exercise of civil, political, economic, social, cultural and other rights and freedoms all of which derive from the inherent dignity of the human person and are essential for his free and full development.

Within this framework the participating States will recognize and respect the freedom of the individual to profess and practice, alone or in community with others, religion or belief acting in accordance with the dictates of his own conscience.

The participating States on whose territory national minorities exist will respect the right of persons belonging to such minorities to equality before the law, will afford them the full opportunity for the actual enjoyment of human rights and fundamental freedoms and will, in this manner, protect their legitimate interests in this sphere.

The participating States recognize the universal significance of human rights and fundamental freedoms, respect for which is an essential factor for the peace, justice and well-being necessary to ensure the development of friendly relations and co-operation among themselves as among all States.

They will constantly respect these rights and freedoms in their mutual relations and will endeavour jointly and separately, including in co-operation with the United Nations, to promote universal and effective respect for them.

They confirm the right of the individual to know and act upon his rights and duties in this field.

In the field of human rights and fundamental freedoms, the participating States will act in conformity with the purposes and principles of the Charter of the United Nations and with the Universal Declaration of Human Rights. They will also fulfil their obligations as set forth in the international declarations and agreements in this field, including *inter alia* the International Covenants on Human Rights, by which they may be bound.

## VIII. *Equal Rights and Self-determination of Peoples*

The participating States will respect the equal rights of peoples and their right to self-determination, acting at all times in conformity with the purposes and principles of the Charter of the United Nations and with the relevant norms of international law, including those relating to territorial integrity of States.

By virtue of the principle of equal rights and self-determination of peoples, all peoples always have the right, in full freedom, to determine, when and as they wish, their internal and external political status, without external interference, and to pursue as they wish their political, economic, social and cultural development.

The participating States reaffirm the universal significance of respect for and effective exercise of equal rights and self-determination of peoples for the development of friendly relations among themselves as among all States; they also recall the importance of the elimination of any form of violation of this principle.

## IX. *Co-operation among States*

The participating States will develop their co-operation with one another and with all States in all fields in accordance with the purposes and principles of the Charter of the United Nations. In developing their co-operation the participating States will place special emphasis on the fields as set forth within the framework of the Conference on Security and Co-operation in Europe, with each of them making its contribution in conditions of full equality.

They will endeavour, in developing their co-operation as equals, to promote mutual understanding and confidence, friendly and good-neighbourly relations among themselves, international peace, security and justice. They will equally endeavour, in developing their co-operation, to improve the well-being of peoples and contribute to the fulfilment of their aspirations through, inter alia, the benefits resulting from increased mutual knowledge and from progress and achievement in the economic, scientific, technological, social, cultural and humanitarian fields. They will take steps to promote conditions favourable to making these benefits available to all; they will take into account the interest of all in the narrowing of differences in the levels of economic development, and in particular the interest of developing countries throughout the world.

They confirm that governments, institutions, organizations and persons have a relevant and positive role to play in contributing toward the achievement of these aims of their co-operation.

They will strive, in increasing their co-operation as set forth above, to develop closer relations among themselves on an improved and more enduring basis for the benefit of peoples.

### X. *Fulfilment in Good Faith of Obligations under International Law*

The participating States will fulfil in good faith their obligations under international law, both those obligations arising from the generally recognized principles and rules of international law and those obligations arising from treaties or other agreements, in conformity with international law, to which they are parties.

In exercising their sovereign rights, including the right to determine their laws and regulations, they will conform with their legal obligations under international law; they will furthermore pay due regard to and implement the provisions in the Final Act of the Conference on Security and Cooperation in Europe.

The participating States confirm that in the event of a conflict between the obligations of the members of the United Nations under the Charter of the United Nations and their obligations under any treaty or other international agreement, their obligations under the Charter will prevail, in accordance with Article 103 of the Charter of the United Nations.

All the principles set forth above are of primary significance and, accordingly, they will be equally and unreservedly applied, each of them being interpreted taking into account the others.

The participating States express their determination fully to respect and apply these principles, as set forth in the present Declaration, in all aspects, to their mutual relations and cooperation in order to ensure to each participating State the benefits resulting from the respect and application of these principles by all.

The participating States, paying due regard to the principles above and, in particular, to the first sentence of the tenth principle, 'Fulfilment in good faith of obligations under international law', note that the present Declaration does not affect their rights and obligations, nor the corresponding treaties and other agreements and arrangements.

The participating States express the conviction that respect for these principles will encourage the development of normal and friendly relations and the progress of co-operation among them in all fields. They also express the conviction that respect for these principles will encourage the development of political contacts among them which in time would contribute to better mutual understanding of their positions and views.

The participating States declare their intention to conduct their relations with all other States in the spirit of the principles contained in the present Declaration.

### (b) Matters related to giving effect to certain of the above Principles

(i) *The participating States,*

*Reaffirming* that they will respect and give effect to refraining from the threat or use of force and convinced of the necessity to make it an effective norm of international life,

*Declare* that they are resolved to respect and carry out, in their relations with one another, *inter alia*, the following provisions which are in conformity with the Declaration on Principles Guiding Relations between Participating States:

— To give effect and expression, by all the ways and forms which they consider appropriate, to the duty to refrain from the threat or use of force in their relations with one another.

— To refrain from any use of armed forces inconsistent with the purposes and principles of the Charter of the United Nations and the provisions of the Declaration on Principles Guiding Relations between Participating States, against another participating State, in particular from invasion of or attack on its territory.

— To refrain from any manifestation of force for the purpose of inducing another participating State to renounce the full exercise of its sovereign rights.

— To refrain from any act of economic coercion designed to subordinate to their own interest the exercise by another participating State of the rights inherent in its sovereignty and thus to secure advantages of any kind.

— To take effective measures which by their scope and by their nature constitute steps towards the ultimate achievement of general and complete disarmament under strict and effective international control.

— To promote, by all means which each of them considers appropriate, a climate of confidence and respect among peoples consonant with their duty to refrain from propaganda for wars of aggression or for any threat or use of force inconsistent with the purposes of the United Nations and with the Declaration on Principles Guiding Relations between Participating States, against another participating State.

— To make every effort to settle exclusively by peaceful means any dispute between them, the continuance of which is likely to endanger the maintenance of international peace and security in Europe, and to seek, first of all, a solution through the peaceful means set forth in Article 33 of the United Nations Charter.

— To refrain from any action which could hinder the peaceful settlement of disputes between the participating States.

(ii) *The participating States,*

*Reaffirming* their determination to settle their disputes as set forth in the Principle of Peaceful Settlement of Disputes;

*Convinced* that the peaceful settlement of disputes is a complement to refraining from the threat or use of force, both being essential though not exclusive factors for the maintenance and consolidation of peace and security;

*Desiring* to reinforce and to improve the methods at their disposal for the peaceful settlement of disputes;

1. Are resolved to pursue the examination and elaboration of a generally acceptable method for the peaceful settlement of disputes aimed at complementing existing methods, and to continue to this end to work upon the 'Draft Convention on a European System for the Peaceful Settlement of Disputes' submitted by Switzerland during the second stage of the Conference on Security and Co-operation

in Europe, as well as other proposals relating to it and directed towards the elaboration of such a method.

2. Decide that, on the invitation of Switzerland, a meeting of experts of all the participating States will be convoked in order to fulfil the mandate described in paragraph 1 above within the framework and under the procedures of the follow-up to the Conference laid down in the chapter 'Follow-up to the Conference'.

3. This meeting of experts will take place after the meeting of the representatives appointed by the Ministers of Foreign Affairs of the participating States, scheduled according to the chapter 'Follow-up to the Conference' for 1977; the results of the work of this meeting of experts will be submitted to Governments.

. . .

## CO-OPERATION IN HUMANITARIAN AND OTHER FIELDS

*The participating States,*

*Desiring* to contribute to the strengthening of peace and understanding among peoples and to the spiritual enrichment of the human personality without distinction as to race, sex, language or religion,

*Conscious* that increased cultural and educational exchanges, broader dissemination of information, contacts between people, and the solution of humanitarian problems will contribute to the attainment of these aims,

*Determined* therefore to co-operate among themselves, irrespective of their political, economic and social systems, in order to create better conditions in the above fields, to develop and strengthen existing forms of co-operation and to work out new ways and means appropriate to these aims,

*Convinced* that this co-operation should take place in full respect for the principles guiding relations among participating States as set forth in the relevant document,

*Have adopted* the following:

### 1. Human Contacts

*The participating States,*

*Considering* the development of contacts to be an important element in the strengthening of friendly relations and trust among peoples,

*Affirming*, in relation to their present effort to improve conditions in this area, the importance they attach to humanitarian considerations,

*Desiring* in this spirit to develop, with the continuance of détente, further efforts to achieve continuing progress in this field

*And conscious* that the questions relevant hereto must be settled by the States concerned under mutually acceptable conditions,

*Make it their aim* to facilitate freer movement and contacts, individually and collectively, whether privately or officially, among persons, institutions and organizations of the participating States, and to contribute to the solution of the humanitarian problems that arise in that connexion,

*Declare their readiness* to these ends to take measures which they consider appropriate and to conclude agreements or arrangements among themselves, as may be needed, and

*Express their intention* now to proceed to the implementation of the following:

### (a) *Contacts and Regular Meetings on the Basis of Family Ties*

In order to promote further development of contacts on the basis of family ties the participating States will favourably consider applications for travel with the purpose of allowing persons to enter or leave their territory temporarily, and on a regular basis if desired, in order to visit members of their families.

Applications for temporary visits to meet members of their families will be dealt with without distinction as to the country of origin or destination: existing requirements for travel documents and visas will be applied in this spirit. The preparation and issue of such documents and visas will be effected within reasonable time limits, cases of urgent necessity—such as serious illness or death—will be given priority treatment. They will take such steps as may be necessary to ensure that the fees for official travel documents and visas are acceptable.

They confirm that the presentation of an application concerning contacts on the basis of family ties will not modify the rights and obligations of the applicant or of members of his family.

### (b) *Reunification of Families*

The participating States will deal in a positive and humanitarian spirit with the applications of persons who wish to be reunited with members of their family, with special attention being given to requests of an urgent character—such as requests submitted by persons who are ill or old.

They will deal with applications in this field as expeditiously as possible

They will lower where necessary the fees charged in connexion with these applications to ensure that they are at a moderate level.

Applications for the purpose of family reunification which are not granted may be renewed at the appropriate level and will be reconsidered at reasonably short intervals by the authorities of the country of residence or destination, whichever is concerned, under such circumstances fees will be charged only when applications are granted.

Persons whose applications for family reunification are granted may bring with them or ship their household and personal effects; to this end the participating States will use all possibilities provided by existing regulations.

Until members of the same family are reunited meetings and contacts between them may take place in accordance with the modalities for contacts on the basis of family ties.

The participating States will support the efforts of Red Cross and Red Crescent Societies concerned with the problems of family reunification.

They confirm that the presentation of an application concerning family reunification will not modify the rights and obligations of the applicant or of members of his family.

The receiving participating State will take appropriate care with regard to employment for persons from other participating States who take up permanent residence in that State in connexion with family reunification with its citizens and see that they are afforded opportunities equal to those enjoyed by its own citizens for education, medical assistance and social security.

### (c) *Marriage between Citizens of Different States*

The participating States will examine favourably and on the basis of humanitarian considerations requests for exit or entry permits from persons who have decided to marry a citizen from another participating State.

The processing and issuing of the documents required for the above purposes and for the marriage will be in accordance with the provisions accepted for family reunification.

In dealing with requests from couples from different participating States, once married, to enable them and the minor children of their marriage to transfer their permanent residence to a State in which either one is normally a resident, the participating States will also apply the provisions accepted for family reunification.

### (d) *Travel for Personal or Professional Reasons*

The participating States intend to facilitate wider travel by their citizens for personal or professional reasons and to this end they intend in particular:

— gradually to simplify and to administer flexibly the procedures for exit and entry;

— to ease regulations concerning movement of citizens from the other participating States in their territory, with due regard to security requirements.

They will endeavour gradually to lower, where necessary, the fees for visas and official travel documents.

They intend to consider, as necessary, means—including, in so far as appropriate, the conclusion of multilateral or bilateral consular conventions or other relevant agreements or understandings—for the improvement of arrangements to provide consular services, including legal and consular assistance.

\* \* \*

They confirm that religious faiths, institutions and organizations, practising within the constitutional framework of the participating States, and their representatives can, in the field of their activities, have contacts and meetings among themselves and exchange information.

### (e) *Improvement of Conditions for Tourism on an Individual or Collective Basis*

The participating States consider that tourism contributes to a fuller knowledge of the life, culture and history of other countries, to the growth of understanding among peoples, to the improvement of contacts and to the broader use of leisure. They intend to promote the development of tourism, on an individual or collective basis, and, in particular, they intend:

— to promote visits to their respective countries by encouraging the provision of appropriate facilities and the simplification and expediting of necessary formalities relating to such visits;

— to increase, on the basis of appropriate agreements or arrangements where necessary, co-operation in the development of tourism, in particular by considering bilaterally possible ways to increase information relating to travel to other countries and to the reception and service of tourists, and other related questions of mutual interest.

### (f) *Meetings among Young People*

The participating States intend to further the development of contacts and exchanges among young people by encouraging:

— increased exchanges and contacts on a short or long term basis among young people working, training or undergoing education through bilateral or multilateral agreements or regular programmes in all cases where it is possible;

— study by their youth organizations of the question of possible agreements relating to frameworks of multilateral youth co-operation;

— agreements or regular programmes relating to the organization of exchanges of students, of international youth seminars, of courses of professional training and foreign language study;

— the further development of youth tourism and the provision to this end of appropriate facilities;

— the development, where possible, of exchanges, contacts and co-operation on a bilateral or multilateral basis between their organizations which represent wide circles of young people working, training or undergoing education;

— awareness among youth of the importance of developing mutual understanding and of strengthening friendly relations and confidence among peoples.

### (g) *Sport*

In order to expand existing links and co-operation in the field of sport the participating States will encourage contacts and exchanges of this kind, including sports meetings and competitions of all sorts, on the basis of the established international rules, regulations and practice.

### (h) *Expansion of Contacts*

By way of further developing contacts among governmental institutions and non-governmental organizations and associations, including women's organizations, the participating States will facilitate the convening of meetings as well as travel by delegations, groups and individuals.

### 2. Information

*The participating States,*

*Conscious* of the need for an ever wider knowledge and understanding of the various aspects of life in other participating States,

*Acknowledging* the contribution of this process to the growth of confidence between peoples,

*Desiring*, with the development of mutual understanding between the participating States and with the further improvement of their relations, to continue further efforts towards progress in this field,

*Recognizing* the importance of the dissemination of information from the other participating States and of a better acquaintance with such information,

*Emphasizing* therefore the essential and influential role of the press, radio, television, cinema and news agencies and of the journalists working in these fields,

*Make it their aim* to facilitate the freer and wider dissemination of information of all kinds, to encourage co-operation in the field of information and the exchange of information with other countries, and. to improve the conditions under which journalists from one participating State exercise their profession in another participating State, and

*Express their intention* in particular:

(a) *Improvement of the Circulation of, Access to, and Exchange of Information*

(i) *Oral Information*

— To facilitate the dissemination of oral information through the encouragement of lectures and lecture tours by personalities and specialists from the other participating States, as well as exchanges of opinions at round table meetings, seminars, symposia, summer schools, congresses and other bilateral and multilateral meetings.

(ii) *Printed Information*

— To facilitate the improvement of the dissemination, on their territory, of newspapers and printed publications, periodical and non-periodical, from the other participating States. For this purpose:

they will encourage their competent firms and organizations to conclude agreements and contracts designed gradually to increase the quantities and the number of titles of newspapers and publications imported from the other participating States. These agreements and contracts should in particular mention the speediest conditions of delivery and the use of the normal channels existing in each country for the distribution of its own publications and newspapers, as well as forms and means of payment agreed between the parties making it possible to achieve the objectives aimed at by these agreements and contracts;

where necessary, they will take appropriate measures to achieve the above objectives and to implement the provisions contained in the agreements and contracts.

— To contribute to the improvement of access by the public to periodical and non-periodical printed publications imported on the bases indicated above. In particular:

they will encourage an increase in the number of places where these publications are on sale,

they will facilitate the availability of these periodical publications during congresses, conferences, official visits and other international events and to tourists during the season, they will develop the possibilities for taking out subscriptions according to the modalities particular to each country;

they will improve the opportunities for reading and borrowing these publications In large public libraries and their reading rooms as well as in university libraries.

They intend to improve the possibilities for acquaintance with bulletins of official information issued by diplomatic missions and distributed by those missions on the basis of arrangements acceptable to the interested parties.

(iii)  *Filmed and Broadcast Information*

— To promote the improvement of the dissemination of filmed and broadcast information. To this end:

they will encourage the wider showing and broadcasting of a greater variety of recorded and filmed information from the other participating States, illustrating the various aspects of life in their countries and received on the basis of such agreements or arrangements as may be necessary between the organizations and firms directly concerned;

they will facilitate the import by competent organizations and firms of recorded audio-visual material from the other participating States.

The participating States note the expansion in the dissemination of information broadcast by radio, and express the hope for the continuation of this process, so as to meet the interest of mutual understanding among peoples and the aims set forth by this Conference.

(b)  *Co-operation in the Field of Information*

— To encourage co-operation in the field of information on the basis of short or long term agreements or arrangements. In particular:

they will favour increased co-operation among mass media organizations. including press agencies, as well as among publishing houses and organizations;

they will favour co-operation among public or private, national or international radio and television organizations, in particular through the exchange of both live and recorded radio and television programmes, and through the joint production and the broadcasting and distribution of such programmes;

they will encourage meetings and contacts both between journalists organizations and between journalists from the participating States;

they will view favourably the possibilities of arrangements between periodical publications as well as between newspapers from the participating States, for the purpose of exchanging and publishing articles;

they will encourage the exchange of technical information as well as the organization of joint research and meetings devoted to the exchange of experience and views between experts in the field of the press, radio and television.

(c) *Improvement of Working Conditions for Journalists*

The participating States, desiring to improve the conditions under which journalists from one participating State exercise their profession in another participating State, intend in particular to:

— examine in a favourable spirit and within a suitable and reasonable time scale requests from journalists for visas;

— grant to permanently accredited journalists of the participating States, on the basis of arrangements, multiple entry and exit visas for specified periods;

— facilitate the issue to accredited journalists of the participating States of permits for stay in their country of temporary residence and, if and when these are necessary, of other official papers which it is appropriate for them to have;

— ease, on a basis of reciprocity, procedures for arranging travel by journalists of the participating States in the country where they are exercising their profession, and to provide progressively greater opportunities for such travel, subject to the observance of regulations relating to the existence of areas closed for security reasons,

— ensure that requests by such journalists for such travel receive, in so far as possible, an expeditious response, taking into account the time scale of the request;

— increase the opportunities for journalists of the participating States to communicate personally with their sources, including organizations and official institutions;

— grant to journalists of the participating States the right to import, subject only to its being taken out again, the technical equipment (photographic, cinematographic, tape recorder, radio and television) necessary for the exercise of their profession;[1]

— enable journalists of the other participating States, whether permanently or temporarily accredited, to transmit completely, normally and rapidly by means recognized by the participating States to the information organs which they represent, the results of their professional activity, including tape recordings and undeveloped film, for the purpose of publication or of broadcasting on the radio or television.

The participating States reaffirm that the legitimate pursuit of their professional activity will neither render journalists liable to expulsion nor otherwise penalize them. If an accredited journalist is expelled, he will be informed of the reasons for this act and may submit an application for re-examination of his case.

[1] While recognizing that appropriate local personnel are employed by foreign journalists in many instances, the participating States note that the above provisions would be applied, subject to the observance of the appropriate rules, to persons from the other participating States, who are regularly and professionally engaged as technicians, photographers or cameramen of the press, radio, television or cinema.]

### 3 Co-operation and Exchanges in the Field of Culture

*The participating States*

*Considering* that cultural exchanges and co-operation contribute to a better comprehension among people and among peoples, and thus promote a lasting understanding among States,

*Confirming* the conclusions already formulated in this field at the multilateral level, particularly at the Intergovernmental Conference on Cultural Policies in Europe, organized by UNESCO in Helsinki in June 1972, where interest was manifested in the active participation of the broadest possible social groups in an increasingly diversified cultural life,

*Desiring*, with the development of mutual confidence and the further improvement of relations between the participating States, to continue further efforts toward progress in this field,

*Disposed* in this spirit to increase substantially their cultural exchanges, with regard both to persons and to cultural works, and to develop among them an active co-operation, both at the bilateral and the multilateral level, in aft the fields of culture,

*Convinced* that such a development of their mutual relations will contribute to the enrichment of the respective cultures, while respecting the originality of each, as well as to the reinforcement among them of a consciousness of common values, while continuing to develop cultural co-operation with other countries of the world,

*Declare* that they jointly set themselves the following objectives:

(*a*) to develop the mutual exchange of information with a view to a better knowledge of respective cultural achievements,

(*b*) to improve the facilities for the exchange and for the dissemination of cultural property,

(*c*) to promote access by all to respective cultural achievements,

(*d*) to develop contacts and co-operation among persons active in the field of culture,

(*e*) to seek new fields and forms of cultural co-operation,

Thus *give expression to* their common will to take progressive, coherent and long-term action in order to achieve the objectives of the present declaration; and

*Express their intention* now to proceed to the implementation of the following:

### *Extension of Relations*

To expand and improve at the various levels co-operation and links in the field of culture, in particular by:

— concluding, where appropriate, agreements on a bilateral or multilateral basis, providing for the extension of relations among competent State institutions and non-governmental organizations in the field of culture, as well as among people engaged in cultural activities, taking into account the need both for flexibility and the fullest possible use of existing agreements, and bearing in mind that agreements and also other arrangements constitute important means of developing cultural co-operation and exchanges;

— contributing to the development of direct communication and co-operation among relevant State institutions and non-governmental organizations, including, where necessary, such communication and co-operation carried out on the basis of special agreements and arrangements;

— encouraging direct contacts and communications among persons engaged in cultural activities, including, where necessary, such contacts and communications carried out on the basis of special agreements. and arrangements.

### *Mutual Knowledge*

Within their competence to adopt, on a bilateral and multilateral level, appropriate measures which would give their peoples a more comprehensive and complete mutual knowledge of their achievements in the various fields of culture, and among them:

— to examine jointly, if necessary with the assistance of appropriate international organizations, the possible creation in Europe and the structure of a bank of cultural data, which would collect information from the participating countries and make it available to its correspondents on their request, and to convene for this purpose a meeting of experts from interested States;

— to consider, if necessary in conjunction with appropriate international organizations, ways of compiling in Europe an inventory of documentary films of a cultural or scientific nature from the participating States;

— to encourage more frequent book exhibitions and to examine the possibility of organizing periodically in Europe a large-scale exhibition of books from the participating States;

— to promote the systematic exchange, between the institutions concerned and publishing houses, of catalogues of available books as well as of pre-publication material which will include, as far as possible, all forthcoming publications; and also to promote the exchange of material between firms publishing encyclopaedias, with a view to improving the presentation of each country;

— to examine jointly questions of expanding and improving exchanges of information in the various fields of culture, such as theatre, music, library work as well as the conservation and restoration of cultural property.

### *Exchanges and Dissemination*

To contribute to the improvement of facilities for exchanges and the dissemination of cultural property, by appropriate means, in particular by:

— studying the possibilities for harmonizing and reducing the charges relating to international commercial exchanges of books and other cultural materials, and also for new means of insuring works of art in foreign exhibitions and for reducing the risks of damage or loss to which these works are exposed by their movement;

— facilitating the formalities of customs clearance, in good time for programmes of artistic events, of the works of art, materials and accessories appearing on lists agreed upon by the organizers of these events;

— encouraging meetings among representatives of competent organizations and relevant firms to examine measures within their field of activity—such as the simplification of orders, time limits for sending supplies and modalities of payment—which might facilitate international commercial exchanges of books;

— promoting the loan and exchange of films among their film institutes and film libraries;

— encouraging the exchange of information among interested parties concerning events of a cultural character foreseen in the participating States, in fields where this is most appropriate, such as music, theatre and the plastic and graphic arts, with a view to contributing to the compilation and publication of a calendar of such events, with the assistance, where necessary, of the appropriate international organizations;

— encouraging a study of the impact which the foreseeable development, and a possible harmonization among interested parties, of the technical means used for the dissemination of culture might have on the development of cultural co-operation and exchanges, while keeping in view the preservation of the diversity and originality, of their respective cultures;

— encouraging, in the way they deem appropriate, within their cultural policies, the further development of interest in the cultural heritage of the other participating States, conscious of the merits and the value of each culture;

— endeavouring to ensure the full and effective application of the international agreements and conventions on copyrights and on circulation of cultural property to which they are party or to which they may decide in the future to become party.

*Access*

To promote fuller mutual access by all to the achievements—works, experiences and performing arts—in the various fields of culture of their countries, and to that end to make the best possible efforts, in accordance with their competence, more particularly:

— to promote wider dissemination of books and artistic works, in particular by such means as:

   facilitating, while taking full account of the international copyright conventions to which they are party, international contacts and communications between authors and publishing houses as well as other cultural institutions, with a view to a more complete mutual access to cultural achievements;

   recommending that, in determining the size of editions, publishing houses take into account also the demand from the other participating States, and that rights of sale in other participating States be granted, where possible, to several sales organizations of the importing countries, by agreement between interested partners;

   encouraging competent organizations and relevant firms to conclude agreements and contracts and contributing, by this means, to a gradual increase in the number and diversity of works by authors from the other participating States available in the original and in translation in their libraries and bookshops;

promoting, where deemed appropriate, an increase in the number of sales outlets where books by authors from the other participating States, imported in the original on the basis of agreements and contracts, and in translation, are for sale;

promoting, on a wider scale, the translation of works in the sphere of literature and other fields of cultural activity, produced in the languages of the other participating States, especially from the less widely-spoken languages, and the publication and dissemination of the translated works by such measures as:

> encouraging more regular contacts between interested publishing houses;
> developing their efforts in the basic and advanced training of translators;
> encouraging, by appropriate means, the publishing houses of their countries to publish translations;
> facilitating the exchange between publishers and interested institutions of lists of books which might be translated;
> promoting between their countries the professional activity and co-operation of translators;
> carrying out joint studies on ways of further promoting translations and their dissemination;
> improving and expanding exchanges of books, bibliographies and catalogue cards between libraries;

— to envisage other appropriate measures which would permit, where necessary by mutual agreement among interested parties, the facilitation of access to their respective cultural achievements, in particular in the field of books;

— to contribute by appropriate means to the wider use of the mass media in order to improve mutual acquaintance with the cultural life of each;

— to seek to develop the necessary conditions for migrant workers and their families to preserve their links with their national culture, and also to adapt themselves to their new cultural environment;

— to encourage the competent bodies and enterprises to make a wider choice and effect wider distribution of full-length and documentary films from the other participating States, and to promote more frequent non-commercial showings, such as premieres, film weeks and festivals, giving due consideration to films from countries whose cinematographic works are less well known;

— to promote, by appropriate means, the extension of opportunities for specialists from the other participating States to work with materials of a cultural character from film and audio-visual archives, within the framework of the existing rules for work on such archival materials;

— to encourage a joint study by interested bodies, where appropriate with the assistance of the competent international organizations, of the expediency and the conditions for the establishment of a repertory of their recorded television programmes of a cultural nature, as well as of the means of viewing them rapidly in order to facilitate their selection and possible acquisition.

*Contacts and Co-operation*

To contribute, by appropriate means, to the development of contacts and co-operation in the various fields of culture, especially among creative artists and people engaged in cultural activities, in particular by making efforts to:

— promote for persons active in the field of culture, travel and meetings including, where necessary, those carried out on the basis of agreements, contracts or other special arrangements and which are relevant to their cultural co-operation;

— encourage in this way contacts among creative and performing artists and artistic groups with a view to their working together, making known their works in other participating States or exchanging views on topics relevant to their common activity;

— encourage, where necessary through appropriate arrangements, exchanges of trainee and specialists and the granting of scholarships for basic and advanced training in various fields of culture such as the arts and archi-tecture, museums and libraries, literary studies and translation, and contribute to the creation of favourable conditions of reception in their respective institutions;

— encourage the exchange of experience in the training of organizers of cultural activities as well as of teachers and specialists in fields such as theatre, opera, ballet, music and fine arts;

— continue to encourage the organization of international meetings among cre-ative artists, especially young creative artists, on current questions of artistic and literary creation which are of interest for joint study;

— study other possibilities for developing exchanges and co-operation among per-sons active in the field of culture, with a view to a better mutual knowledge of the cultural fife of the participating States.

*Fields and Forms of Co-operation*

To encourage the search for new fields and forms of cultural co-operation, to these ends contributing to the conclusion among interested parties, where neces-sary, of appropriate agreements and arrangements, and in this context to promote:

— joint studies regarding cultural policies, in particular in their social aspects, and as they relate to planning, town-planning, educational and environmental policies, and the cultural aspects of tourism;

— the exchange of knowledge in the realm of cultural diversity, with a view to contributing thus to a better understanding by interested parties of such diversity where it occurs;

— the exchange of information, and as may be appropriate, meetings of experts, the elaboration and the execution of research programmes and projects, as well as their joint evaluation, and the dissemination of the results, on the subjects indicated above;

— such forms of cultural co-operation and the development of such joint projects as:

international events in the fields of the plastic and graphic arts, cinema, theatre, ballet, music, folklore, etc.; book fairs and exhibitions, joint performances of operatic and dramatic works, as well as performances given by soloists,

instrumental ensembles, orchestras, choirs and other artistic groups, including those composed of amateurs, paying due attention to the organization of international cultural youth events and the exchange of young artists;

the inclusion of works by writers and composers from the other participating States in the repertoires of soloists and artistic ensembles;

the preparation, translation and publication of articles, studies and monographs, as well as of low-cost books and of artistic and literary collections, suited to making better known respective cultural achievements, envisaging for this purpose meetings among experts and representatives of publishing houses;

the co-production and the exchange of films and of radio and television programmes, by promoting, in particular, meetings among producers, technicians and representatives of the public authorities with a view to working out favourable conditions for the execution of specific joint projects and by encouraging, in the field of co-production, the establishment of international filming teams;

the organization of competitions for architects and town-planners, bearing in mind the possible implementation of the best projects and the formation, where possible, of international teams;

the implementation of joint projects for conserving, restoring and showing to advantage works of art, historical and archaeological monuments and sites of cultural interest, with the help, in appropriate cases, of international organizations of a governmental or non-governmental character as well as of private institutions—competent and active in these fields—envisaging for this purpose:

> periodic meetings of experts of the interested parties to elaborate the necessary proposals, while bearing in mind the need to consider these questions in a wider social and economic context;
>
> the publication in appropriate periodicals of articles designed to make known and to compare, among the participating States, the most significant achievements and innovations;
>
> a joint study with a view to the improvement and possible harmonization of the different systems used to inventory and catalogue the historical monuments and places of cultural interest in their countries;
>
> the study of the possibilities for organizing international courses for the training of specialists in different disciplines relating to restoration.

* * *

*National minorities or regional cultures.* The participating States, recognizing the contribution that national minorities or regional cultures can make to co-operation among them in various fields of culture, intend, when such minorities or cultures exist within their territory, to facilitate this contribution, taking into account the legitimate interests of their members.

## 4. Co-operation and Exchanges in the Field of Education

*The participating States,*

*Conscious* that the development of relations of an international character in the fields of education and science contributes to a better mutual understanding and is to the advantage of all peoples as well as to the benefit of future generations,

*Prepared* to facilitate, between organizations, institutions and persons engaged in education and science, the further development of exchanges of knowledge and experience as well as of contacts, on the basis of special arrangements where these are necessary,

*Desiring* to strengthen the links among educational and scientific establishments and also to encourage their co-operation in sectors of common interest, particularly where the levels of knowledge and resources require efforts to be concerted internationally, and

*Convinced* that progress in these fields should be accompanied and supported by a wider knowledge of foreign languages,

*Express* to these ends their intention in particular:

### (a) *Extension of Relations*

To expand and improve at the various levels co-operation and links in the fields of education and science, in particular by:

— concluding, where appropriate, bilateral or multilateral agreements providing for co-operation and exchanges among State institutions, non-governmental bodies and persons engaged in activities in education and science, bearing in mind the need both for flexibility and the fuller use of existing agreements and arrangements;

— promoting the conclusion of direct arrangements between universities and other institutions of higher education and research, in the framework of agreements between governments where appropriate;

— encouraging among persons engaged in education and science direct contacts and communications' including those based on special agreements or arrangements where these are appropriate.

### (b) *Access and Exchanges*

To improve access, under mutually acceptable conditions, for students, teachers and scholars of the participating States to each other's educational, cultural and scientific institutions, and to intensify exchanges among these institutions in all areas of common interest, in particular by:

— increasing the exchange of information on facilities for study and courses open to foreign participants, as well as on the conditions under which they will be admitted and received;

— facilitating travel between the participating States by scholars, teachers and students for purposes of study, teaching and research as well as for improving knowledge of each other's educational, cultural and scientific achievements;

— encouraging the award of scholarships for study, teaching and research in their countries to scholars, teachers and students of other participating States;

— establishing, developing or encouraging programmes providing for the broader exchange of scholars, teachers and students, including the organization of symposia, seminars and collaborative projects, and the exchanges of educational and scholarly information such as university publications and materials from libraries;

— promoting the efficient implementation of such arrangements and programmes by providing scholars, teachers and students in good time with more detailed information about their placing in universities and institutes and the programmes envisaged for them; by granting them the opportunity to use relevant scholarly, scientific and open archival materials; and by facilitating their travel within the receiving State for the purpose of study or research as well as in the form of vacation tours on the basis of the usual procedures;

— promoting a more exact assessment of the problems of comparison and equivalence of academic degrees and diplomas by fostering the exchange of information on the organization, duration and content of studies, the comparison of methods of assessing levels of knowledge, and academic qualifications, and, where feasible, arriving at the mutual recognition of academic degrees and diplomas either through governmental agreements, where necessary, or direct arrangements between universities and other institutions of higher learning and research;

— recommending, moreover, to the appropriate international organizations that they should intensify their efforts to reach a generally acceptable solution to the problems of comparison and equivalence between academic degrees and diplomas.

(c) *Science*

Within their competence to broaden and improve co-operation and exchanges in the field of science, in particular:

To increase, on a bilateral or multilateral basis, the exchange and dissemination of scientific information and documentation by such means as:

— making this information more widely available to scientists and research workers of the other participating States through, for instance, participation in international information-sharing programmes or through other appropriate arrangements;

— broadening and facilitating the exchange of samples and other scientific materials used particularly for fundamental research in the fields of natural sciences and medicine;

— inviting scientific institutions and universities to keep each other more fully and regularly informed about their current and contemplated research work in fields of common interest.

To facilitate the extension of communications and direct contacts between universities, scientific institutions and associations as well as among scientists and research workers, including those based where necessary on special agreements or arrangements, by such means as:

— further developing exchanges of scientists and research workers and encouraging the organization of preparatory meetings or working groups on research topics of common interest;

— encouraging the creation of joint teams of scientists to pursue research projects under arrangements made by the scientific institutions of several countries;

— assisting the organization and successful functioning of international conferences and seminars and participation in them by their scientists and research workers;

— furthermore envisaging, in the near future, a 'Scientific Forum' in the form of a meeting of leading personalities in science from the participating States to discuss interrelated problems of common interest concerning current and future developments in science, and to promote the expansion of contacts, communications and the exchange of information between scientific institutions and among scientists;

— foreseeing, at an early date, a meeting of experts representing the participating States and their national scientific institutions, in order to prepare such a 'Scientific Forum' in consultation with appropriate international organizations, such as UNESCO and the EYE;

— considering in due course what further steps might be taken with respect to the 'Scientific Forum'.

To develop in the field of scientific research, on a bilateral or multilateral basis, the co-ordination of programmes carried out in the participating States and the organization of joint programmes, especially in the areas mentioned below, which may involve the combined efforts of scientists and in certain cases the use of costly or unique equipment. The list of subjects in these areas is illustrative; and specific projects would have to be determined subsequently by the potential partners in the participating States, taking account of the contribution which could be made by appropriate international organizations and scientific institutions:

— *exact and natural sciences*, in particular fundamental research in such fields as mathematics, physics, theoretical physics, geophysics, chemistry, biology, ecology and astronomy;

— *medicine*, in particular basic research into cancer and cardiovascular diseases, studies on the diseases endemic in the developing countries, as well as medico-social research with special emphasis on occupational diseases, the rehabilitation of the handicapped and the care of mothers, children and the elderly;

— *the humanities and social sciences*, such as history, geography, philosophy, psychology, pedagogical research, linguistics, sociology, the legal, political and economic sciences; comparative studies on social, socioeconomic and cultural phenomena which are of common interest to the participating States, especially the problems of human environment and urban development; and scientific studies on the methods of conserving and restoring monuments and works of art.

## (d) *Foreign Languages and Civilizations*

To encourage the study of foreign languages and civilizations as an important means of expanding communication among peoples for their better acquaintance with the culture of each country, as well as for the strengthening of international co-operation; to this end to stimulate, within their competence, the further development and improvement of foreign language teaching and the diversification of choice of languages taught at various levels, paying due attention to less widely-spread or studied languages, and in particular:

— to intensify co-operation aimed at improving the teaching of foreign languages through exchanges of information and experience concerning the development and application of effective modem teaching methods and technical aids, adapted to the needs of different categories of students, including methods of accelerated teaching; and to consider the possibility of conducting, on a bilateral or multilateral basis, studies of new methods of foreign language teaching;

— to encourage co-operation among experts in the field of lexicography with the aim of defining the necessary terminological equivalents, particularly in the scientific and technical disciplines, in order to facilitate relations among scientific institutions and specialists;

— to promote the wider spread of foreign language study among the different types of secondary education establishments and greater possibilities of choice between an increased number of European languages; and in this context to consider, wherever appropriate, the possibilities for developing the recruitment and training of teachers as well as the organization of the student groups required;

— to encourage co-operation between institutions concerned, on a bilateral or multilateral basis, aimed at exploiting more fully the resources of modem educational technology in language teaching, for example through comparative studies by their specialists and, where agreed, through exchanges or transfers of audio-visual materials, of materials used for preparing textbooks, as well as of information about new types of technical equipment used for teaching languages;

— to promote the exchange of information on the experience acquired in the training of language teachers and to intensify exchanges on a bilateral basis of language teachers and students as well as to facilitate their participation in summer courses in languages and civilizations, wherever these are organized;

— to encourage co-operation among experts in the field of lexicography with the aim of defining the necessary terminological equivalents, particularly in the scientific and technical disciplines, in order to facilitate relations among scientific institutions and specialists;

— to promote the wider spread of foreign language study among the different types of secondary education establishments and greater possibilities of choice between an increased number of European languages; and in this context to consider, wherever appropriate, the possibilities for developing the recruitment and training of teachers as well as the organization of the student groups required;

— to favour, in higher education, a wider choice in the languages offered to language students and greater opportunities for other students to study various foreign languages; also to facilitate, where desirable, the organization of courses in languages and civilizations, on the basis of special arrangements as necessary to be given by foreign lecturers, particularly from European countries having less widely-spread or studied languages;

— to promote, within the framework of adult education, the further development of specialized programmes, adapted to various needs and interests, for teaching foreign languages to their own inhabitants and the languages of host countries to interested adults from other countries; in this context to encourage interested institutions to cooperate, for example, in the elaboration of programmes for teaching by radio and television and by accelerated methods, and also, where desirable, in the definition of study objectives for such programmes, with a view to arriving at comparable levels of language proficiency;

— to encourage the association, where appropriate, of the teaching of foreign languages with the study of the corresponding civilizations and also to make further efforts to stimulate interest in the study of foreign languages, including relevant out-of-class activities.

(e)  *Teaching Methods*

To promote the exchange of experience, on a bilateral or multilateral basis, in teaching methods at all levels of education, including those used in permanent and adult education, as well as the exchange of teaching materials, in particular by:

— further developing various forms of contacts and co-operation in the different fields of pedagogical science, for example through comparative or joint studies carried out by interested institutions or through exchanges of information on the results of teaching experiments;

— intensifying exchanges of information on teaching methods used in various educational systems and on results of research into the processes by which pupils and students acquire knowledge, taking account of relevant experience in different types of specialized education;

— facilitating exchanges of experience concerning the organization and functioning of education intended for adults and recurrent education, the relationships between these and other forms and levels of education, as well as concerning the means of adapting education, including vocational and technical training, to the needs of economic and social development in their countries;

— encouraging exchanges of experience in the education of youth and adults in international understanding, with particular reference to those major problems of mankind whose solution calls for a common approach and wider international co-operation;

— encouraging exchanges of teaching materials—including school textbooks, having in mind the possibility of promoting mutual knowledge and facilitating the presentation of each country in such books—as well as exchanges of information on technical innovations in the field of education.

\* \* \*

*National minorities or regional cultures*

The participating States, recognizing the contribution that national minorities or regional cultures can make to co-operation among them in various fields of education, intend, when such minorities or cultures exist within their territory, to facilitate this contribution, taking into account the legitimate interests of their members.

## FOLLOW-UP TO THE CONFERENCE

*The participating States,*

*Having considered and evaluated* the progress made at the Conference on Security and Co-operation in Europe,

*Considering further* that, within the broader context of the world, the Conference is an important part of the process of improving security and developing co-operation in Europe and that its results will contribute significantly to this process,

*Intending* to implement the provisions of the Final Act of the Conference in order to give full effect to its results and thus to further the process of improving security and developing co-operation in Europe,

*Convinced* that, in order to achieve the aims sought by the Conference, they should make further unilateral, bilateral and multilateral efforts and continue, in the appropriate forms set forth below, the multilateral process initiated by the Conference,

1. *Declare their resolve*, in the period following the Conference, to pay due regard to and implement the provisions of the Final Act of the Conference:

   (a) unilaterally, in all cases which lend themselves to such action;

   (b) bilaterally, by negotiations with other participating States;

   (c) multilaterally, by meetings of experts of the participating States, and also within the framework of existing international organizations, such as the United Nations Economic Commission for Europe and UNESCO, with regard to educational, scientific and cultural co-operation;

2. *Declare furthermore their resolve* to continue the multilateral process initiated by the Conference:

   (a) by proceeding to a thorough exchange of views both on the implementation of the provisions of the Final Act and of the tasks defined by the Conference, as well as, in the context of the questions dealt with by the latter, on the deepening of their mutual relations, the improvement of security and the development of co-operation in Europe, and the development of the process of détente in the future;

   (b) by organizing to these ends meetings among their representatives, beginning with a meeting at the level of representatives appointed by the Ministers of foreign Affairs. This meeting will define the appropriate modalities for the holding of other meetings which could include further similar meetings and the possibility of a new Conference;

3. The first of the meetings indicated above will be held at Belgrade in 1977. A preparatory meeting to organize this meeting will be held at Belgrade on 15 June 1977. The preparatory meeting will decide on the date, duration, agenda and other modalities of the meeting of representatives appointed by the Ministers of Foreign Affairs;

4. The rules of procedure, the working methods and the scale of distribution for the expenses of the Conference will, *mutatis mutandis*, be applied to the meetings envisaged in paragraphs 1 (c), 2 and 3 above. All the above-mentioned meetings will be held in the participating States in rotation. The services of a technical secretariat will be provided by the host country.

The original of this Final Act, drawn up in English, French, German, Italian, Russian and Spanish, will be transmitted to the Government of the Republic of Finland, which will retain it in its archives. Each of the participating States will receive from the Government of the Republic of Finland a true copy of this Final Act.

The text of this Final Act will be published in each participating State, which will disseminate it and make it known as widely as possible.

The Government of the Republic of Finland is requested to transmit to the Secretary-General of the United Nations the text of this Final Act, which is not eligible for registration under Article 102 of the Charter of the United Nations, with a view to its circulation to all the members of the Organization as an official document of the United Nations.

The Government of the Republic of Finland is also requested to transmit the text of this Final Act to the Director-General of UNESCO and to the Executive Secretary of the United Nations Economic Commission for Europe.

Wherefore, the undersigned High Representatives of the participating States, mindful of the high political significance which they attach to the results of the Conference, and declaring their determination to act in accordance with the provisions contained in the above texts, have subscribed their signatures below:

*Done* at Helsinki, on 1st August 1975, in the name of . . .

## 71. CONCLUDING DOCUMENT OF THE VIENNA MEETING OF THE CSCE CONFERENCE, 1989

This document includes a significant set of principles relating to the procedure before the examination of complaints of breaches of the human rights standards set by the Helsinki Final Act (above, 557). The Vienna meetings took place from 4 November 1986 to 17 January 1989, and were convened on the basis of the provisions of the Helsinki Final Act concerning the follow up to the Conference on Security and Co-operation in Europe. It was decided that a 'Conference on the Human Dimension and the CSCE' should be convened for the purpose of reviewing developments in the human dimension. It took place in three stages, in Paris, Copenhagen and Moscow, the last two conferences producing final documents with new commitments on human dimension; see further below, 588–603, 615–30.

The full text of the following document, the official title of which is the 'Concluding Document of the Vienna Meeting (1986) of the Representatives of the Participating States of the Conference on Security and Co-operation in Europe', can be found at **www.osce.org/docs/cnglish/fupreve.htm**. The two most pertinent sections of the Vienna Concluding Document are set forth below. See also OSCE Office for Democratic Institutions and Human Rights (ODIHR), *OSCE Human Dimension Commitments: A Reference Guide*, Warsaw (2001).

*TEXT*

### HUMAN DIMENSION OF THE CSCE

*The participating States,*

*Recalling* the undertakings entered into in the Final Act and in other CSCE documents concerning respect for all human rights and fundamental freedoms, human contacts and other issues of a related humanitarian character,

*Recognizing* the need to improve the implementation of their CSCE commitments and their co-operation in these areas which are hereafter referred to as the human dimension of the CSCE,

Have, on the basis of the principles and provisions of the Final Act and of other relevant CSCE documents, decided:

1. to exchange information and respond to requests for information and to representations made to them by other participating States on questions relating to the human dimension of the CSCE. Such communications may be forwarded through diplomatic channels or be addressed to any agency designated for these purposes;

2. to hold bilateral meetings with other participating States that so request, in order to examine questions relating to the human dimension of the CSCE, including situations and specific cases, with a view to resolving them. The date and place of such meetings will be arranged by mutual agreement through diplomatic channels;

3. that any participating State which deems it necessary may bring situations and cases in the human dimension of the CSCE, including those which have been

raised in the bilateral meetings described in paragraph 2, to the attention of other participating States through diplomatic channels;

4. that any participating State which deems it necessary may provide information on the exchanges of information and the responses to its requests for information and to representations (paragraph 1) and on the results of the bilateral meetings (paragraph 2), including information concerning situations and specific cases, at the meetings of the Conference on the Human Dimension as well as at the main CSCE Follow-up Meeting.

The participating States decide further to convene a Conference on the Human Dimension of the CSCE in order to achieve further progress concerning respect for all human rights and fundamental freedoms, human contacts and other issues of a related humanitarian character. The Conference will hold three meetings before the next CSCE Follow-up Meeting.

The Conference will:

— review developments in the human dimension of the CSCE including the implementation of the relevant CSCE commitments;

— evaluate the functioning of the procedures described in paragraphs 1 to 4 and discuss the information provided according to paragraph 4,

— consider practical proposals for new measures aimed at improving the implementation of the commitments relating to the human dimension of the CSCE and enhancing the effectiveness of the procedures described in paragraphs 1 to 4.

On the basis of these proposals, the Conference will consider adopting new measures.

The first Meeting of the Conference will be held in Paris from 30 May to 23 June 1989.

The second Meeting of the Conference will be held in Copenhagen from 5 to 29 June 1990.

The third Meeting of the Conference will be held in Moscow from 10 September to 4 October 1991.

The agenda, timetable and other organizational modalities are set out in Annex X.

The next main CSCE Follow-up Meeting, to be held in Helsinki, commencing on 24 March 1992, will assess the functioning of the procedures set out in paragraphs 1 to 4 above and the progress made at the Meetings of the Conference on the Human Dimension of the CSCE. It will consider ways of further strengthening and improving these procedures and will take appropriate decisions.


## FOLLOW-UP TO THE CONFERENCE

In conformity with the relevant provisions of the Final Act and with their resolve and commitment to continue the multilateral process initiated by the CSCE, the participating States will hold further meetings regularly among their representatives.

The fourth main Follow-up Meeting will be held in Helsinki, commencing on 24 March 1992.

The agenda, work programme and modalities of the main Vienna Meeting will be applied *mutatis mutandis* to the main Helsinki Meeting, unless other decisions on these questions are taken by the preparatory meeting mentioned below.

For the purpose of making the adjustments to the agenda, work programme and modalities applied at the main Vienna Meeting, a preparatory meeting will be held in Helsinki, commencing on 10 March 1992. It is understood that in this context adjustments concern those items requiring change as a result of the change in date and place, the drawing of lots, and the mention of the other meetings held in conformity with the decisions of the Vienna Meeting 1986. The duration of the preparatory meeting shall not exceed two weeks. The agenda, work programme and modalities for CSCE follow-up meetings mentioned in this document have been prepared by the main Vienna Meeting. The results of these meetings will be taken into account, as appropriate, at the main Helsinki Meeting.

All the meetings referred to in this Chapter will be held in conformity with Paragraph 4 of the Chapter on 'Follow-up to the Conference' of the Final Act.

The participating States examined the scope for rationalizing the modalities for future CSCE follow-up meetings, for enhancing their effectiveness and for ensuring the best possible use of resources. In the light of their examination and in connection with the steps taken at the main Vienna Meeting, including the drawing up of mandates annexed to this document, they decided:

— to dispense with preparatory meetings unless otherwise agreed;
— bearing in mind the purpose of the meeting, to limit the number of subsidiary working bodies meeting simultaneously to the lowest possible;
— to limit the duration of meetings, unless otherwise agreed, to a period not exceeding four weeks;
— in the case of meetings to which non-governmental participants are invited to contribute, to make maximum use of the possibility of having informal meetings in order to allow for a more spontaneous discussion;
— to observe to the same extent as the host country its national day.

The main Helsinki Meeting will review these arrangements and other modalities in the light of experience, with a view to making any improvements which may be necessary.

The Government of Austria is requested to transmit the present document to the Secretary-General of the United Nations, to the Director General of UNESCO and to the Executive Secretary of the United Nations Economic Commission for Europe and to other international organizations mentioned in this document. The Government of Austria is also requested to transmit the present document to the Governments of the non-participating Mediterranean States.

The text of this document will be published in each participating State, which will disseminate it and make it known as widely as possible.

The representatives of the participating States express their profound gratitude to the people and Government of Austria for the excellent organization of the Vienna Meeting and the warm hospitality extended to the delegations which participated in the Meeting.

Vienna, 15 January 1989

## 72. DOCUMENT OF THE COPENHAGEN MEETING OF THE SECOND CONFERENCE ON THE HUMAN DIMENSION OF THE CSCE, 1990

This document was adopted on 29 June 1990 by the thirty-five participating States of the Conference on Security and Co-operation in Europe (CSCE). The Copenhagen meeting was the second meeting convoked in accordance with the provisions relating to the Conference on the Human Dimension of the CSCE contained in the Vienna Concluding Document (above, 585–7).

*TEXT*

The representatives of the participating States of the Conference on Security and Co-operation in Europe (CSCE), Austria, Belgium, Bulgaria, Canada, Cyprus, Czechoslovakia, Denmark, Finland, France, the German Democratic Republic, the Federal Republic of Germany, Greece, the Holy See, Hungary, Iceland, Ireland, Italy, Liechtenstein, Luxembourg, Malta, Monaco, the Netherlands, Norway, Poland, Portugal, Romania, San Marino, Spain, Sweden, Switzerland, Turkey, the Union of Soviet Socialist Republics, the United Kingdom, the United States of America and Yugoslavia, met in Copenhagen from 5 to 29 June 1990, in accordance with the provisions relating to the Conference on the Human Dimension of the CSCE contained in the Concluding Document of the Vienna Follow-up Meeting of the CSCE.

The Copenhagen Meeting was opened and closed by the Minister for Foreign Affairs of Denmark. Albania attended the Copenhagen Meeting as observer.

The first Meeting of the Conference was held in Paris from 30 May to 23 June 1989. The formal opening of the Copenhagen Meeting was attended by Her Majesty the Queen of Denmark and His Royal Highness the Prince Consort.

Opening statements were made by Ministers and Deputy Ministers of the participating States.

At a special meeting of the Ministers for Foreign Affairs of the participating States of the CSCE on 5 June 1990, convened on the invitation of the Minister for Foreign Affairs of Denmark, it was agreed to convene a Preparatory Committee in Vienna on 10 July 1990 to prepare a Summit Meeting in Paris of their Heads of State or Government.

The participating States welcome with great satisfaction the fundamental political changes that have occurred in Europe since the first Meeting of the Conference on the Human Dimension of the CSCE in Paris in 1989. They note that the CSCE process has contributed significantly to bringing about these changes and that these developments in turn have greatly advanced the implementation of the provisions of the Final Act and of the other CSCE documents.

They recognize that pluralistic democracy and the rule of law are essential for ensuring respect for all human rights and fundamental freedoms, the development of human contacts and the resolution of other issues of a related humanitarian character. They therefore welcome the commitment expressed by all participating States to the ideals of democracy and political pluralism as well as their common determination to build democratic societies based on free elections and the rule of law.

At the Copenhagen Meeting the participating States held a review of the implementation of their commitments in the field of the human dimension. They considered that the degree of compliance with the commitments contained in the relevant provisions of the CSCE documents had shown a fundamental improvement since the Paris Meeting. They also expressed the view, however, that further steps are required for the full realization of their commitments relating to the human dimension.

The participating States express their conviction that full respect for human rights and fundamental freedoms and the development of societies based on pluralistic democracy and the rule of law are prerequisites for progress in setting up the lasting order of peace, security, justice and co-operation that they seek to establish in Europe. They therefore reaffirm their commitment to implement fully all provisions of the Final Act and of the other CSCE documents relating to the human dimension and undertake to build on the progress they have made.

They recognize that co-operation among themselves, as well as the active involvement of persons, groups, organizations and institutions, will be essential to ensure continuing progress towards their shared objectives.

In order to strengthen respect for, and enjoyment of, human rights and fundamental freedoms, to develop human contacts and to resolve issues of a related humanitarian character, the participating States agree on the following:


# I


(1) The participating States express their conviction that the protection and promotion of human rights and fundamental freedoms is one of the basic purposes of government, and reaffirm that the recognition of these rights and freedoms constitutes the foundation of freedom, justice and peace.

(2) They are determined to support and advance those principles of justice which form the basis of the rule of law. They consider that the rule of law does not mean merely a formal legality which assures regularity and consistency in the achievement and enforcement of democratic order, but justice based on the recognition and full acceptance of the supreme value of the human personality and guaranteed by institutions providing a framework for its fullest expression.

(3) They reaffirm that democracy is an inherent element of the rule of law. They recognize the importance of pluralism with regard to political organizations.

(4) They confirm that they will respect each others right freely to choose and develop, in accordance with international human rights standards, their political, social, economic and cultural systems. In exercising this right, they will ensure that their laws, regulations, practices and policies conform with their obligations under international law and are brought into harmony with the provisions of the Declaration on Principles and other CSCE commitments.

(5) They solemnly declare that among those elements of justice which are essential to the full expression of the inherent dignity and of the equal and inalienable rights of all human beings are the following:

(5.1) — free elections that will be held at reasonable intervals by secret ballot or by equivalent free voting procedure, under conditions which ensure in practice the free expression of the opinion of the electors in the choice of their representatives;

(5.2) — a form of government that is representative in character, in which the executive is accountable to the elected legislature or the electorate;

(5.3) — the duty of the government and public authorities to comply with the constitution and to act in a manner consistent with law;

(5.4) — a clear separation between the State and political parties; in particular, political parties will not be merged with the State;

(5.5) — the activity of the government and the administration as well as that of the judiciary will be exercised in accordance with the system established by law. Respect for that system must be ensured;

(5.6) — military forces and the police will be under the control of, and accountable to, the civil authorities;

(5.7) — human rights and fundamental freedoms will be guaranteed by law and in accordance with their obligations under international law;

(5.8) — legislation, adopted at the end of a public procedure, and regulations will be published, that being the condition for their applicability. Those texts will be accessible to everyone;

(5.9) — all persons are equal before the law and are entitled without any discrimination to the equal protection of the law. In this respect, the law will prohibit any discrimination and guarantee to all persons equal and effective protection against discrimination on any ground;

(5.10) — everyone will have an effective means of redress against administrative decisions, so as to guarantee respect for fundamental rights and ensure legal integrity;

(5.11) — administrative decisions against a person must be fully justifiable and must as a rule indicate the usual remedies available;

(5.12) — the independence of judges and the impartial operation of the public judicial service will be ensured;

(5.13) — the independence of legal practitioners will be recognized and protected, in particular as regards conditions for recruitment and practice;

(5.14) — the rules relating to criminal procedure will contain a clear definition of powers in relation to prosecution and the measures preceding and accompanying prosecution;

(5.15) — any person arrested or detained on a criminal charge will have the right, so that the lawfulness of his arrest or detention can be decided, to be brought promptly before a judge or other officer authorized by law to exercise this function;

(5.16) — in the determination of any criminal charge against him, or of his rights and obligations in a suit at law, everyone will be entitled to a fair and public hearing by a competent, independent and impartial tribunal established by law;

(5.17) — any person prosecuted will have the right to defend himself in person or through prompt legal assistance of his own choosing or, if he does not have sufficient means to pay for legal assistance, to be given it free when the interests of justice so require;

(5.18) — no one will be charged with, tried for or convicted of any criminal offence unless the offence is provided for by a law which defines the elements of the offence with clarity and precision;

(5.19) — everyone will be presumed innocent until proved guilty according to law;

(5.20) — considering the important contribution of international instruments in the field of human rights to the rule of law at a national level, the participating States reaffirm that they will consider acceding to the International Covenant on Civil and Political Rights, the International Covenant on Economic, Social and Cultural Rights and other relevant international instruments, if they have not yet done so;

(5.21) — in order to supplement domestic remedies and better to ensure that the participating States respect the international obligations they have undertaken, the participating States will consider acceding to a regional or global international convention concerning the protection of human rights, such as the European Convention on Human Rights or the Optional Protocol to the International Covenant on Civil and Political Rights, which provide for procedures of individual recourse to international bodies.

(6) The participating States declare that the will of the people, freely and fairly expressed through periodic and genuine elections, is the basis of the authority and legitimacy of all government. The participating States will accordingly respect the right of their citizens to take part in the governing of their country, either directly or through representatives freely chosen by them through fair electoral processes. They recognize their responsibility to defend and protect, in accordance with their laws, their international human rights obligations and their international commitments, the democratic order freely established through the will of the people against the activities of persons, groups or organizations that engage in or refuse to renounce terrorism or violence aimed at the overthrow of that order or of that of another participating State.

(7) To ensure that the will of the people serves as the basis of the authority of government, the participating States will

(7.1) — hold free elections at reasonable intervals, as established by law;

(7.2) — permit all seats in at least one chamber of the national legislature to be freely contested in a popular vote;

(7.3) — guarantee universal and equal suffrage to adult citizens;

(7.4) — ensure that votes are cast by secret ballot or by equivalent free voting procedure, and that they are counted and reported honestly with the official results made public;

(7.5)   — respect the right of citizens to seek political or public office, individually or as representatives of political parties or organizations, without
discrimination;

(7.6)   — respect the right of individuals and groups to establish, in full freedom, their own political parties or other political organizations and
provide such political parties and organizations with the necessary
legal guarantees to enable them to compete with each other on a basis
of equal treatment before the law and by the authorities;

(7.7)   — ensure that law and public policy work to permit political campaign-
ing to be conducted in a fair and free atmosphere in which neither
administrative action, violence nor intimidation bars the parties and
the candidates from freely presenting their views and qualifications, or
prevents the voters from learning and discussing them or from casting
their vote free of fear of retribution;

(7.8)   — provide that no legal or administrative obstacle stands in the way of
unimpeded access to the media on a non-discriminatory basis for
all political groupings and individuals wishing to participate in the
electoral process;

(7.9)   — ensure that candidates who obtain the necessary number of votes
required by law are duly installed in office and are permitted to
remain in office until their term expires or is otherwise brought to
an end in a manner that is regulated by law in conformity with
democratic parliamentary and constitutional procedures.

(8) The participating States consider that the presence of observers, both foreign
and domestic, can enhance the electoral process for States in which elections are
taking place. They therefore invite observers from any other CSCE participating
States and any appropriate private institutions and organizations who may wish to
do so to observe the course of their national election proceedings, to the extent
permitted by law. They will also endeavour to facilitate similar access for election
proceedings held below the national level. Such observers will undertake not to
interfere in the electoral proceedings.

# II

(9) The participating States reaffirm that

(9.1)   — everyone will have the right to freedom of expression including the
right to communication. This right will include freedom to hold opinions and to receive and impart information and ideas without interference by public authority and regardless of frontiers. The exercise
of this right may be subject only to such restrictions as are prescribed
by law and are consistent with international standards. In particular,
no limitation will be imposed on access to, and use of, means of
reproducing documents of any kind, while respecting, however, rights
relating to intellectual property, including copyright;

(9.2) — everyone will have the right of peaceful assembly and demonstration. Any restrictions which may be placed on the exercise of these rights will be prescribed by law and consistent with international standards;

(9.3) — the right of association will be guaranteed. The right to form and— subject to the general right of a trade union to determine its own membership—freely to join a trade union will be guaranteed. These rights will exclude any prior control. Freedom of association for workers, including the freedom to strike, will be guaranteed, subject to limitations prescribed by law and consistent with international standards;

(9.4) — everyone will have the right to freedom of thought, conscience and religion. This right includes freedom to change ones religion or belief and freedom to manifest ones religion or belief, either alone or in community with others, in public or in private, through worship, teaching, practice and observance. The exercise of these rights may be subject only to such restrictions as are prescribed by law and are consistent with international standards;

(9.5) — they will respect the right of everyone to leave any country, including his own, and to return to his country, consistent with a States international obligations and CSCE commitments. Restrictions on this right will have the character of very rare exceptions, will be considered necessary only if they respond to a specific public need, pursue a legitimate aim and are proportionate to that aim, and will not be abused or applied in an arbitrary manner;

(9.6) — everyone has the right peacefully to enjoy his property either on his own or in common with others. No one may be deprived of his property except in the public interest and subject to the conditions provided for by law and consistent with international commitments and obligations.

(10) In reaffirming their commitment to ensure effectively the rights of the individual to know and act upon human rights and fundamental freedoms, and to contribute actively, individually or in association with others, to their promotion and protection, the participating States express their commitment to

(10.1) — respect the right of everyone, individually or in association with others, to seek, receive and impart freely views and information on human rights and fundamental freedoms, including the rights to disseminate and publish such views and information;

(10.2) — respect the rights of everyone, individually or in association with others, to study and discuss the observance of human rights and fundamental freedoms and to develop and discuss ideas for improved protection of human rights and better means for ensuring compliance with international human rights standards;

(10.3) — ensure that individuals are permitted to exercise the right to association, including the right to form, join and participate effectively in non-governmental organizations which seek the promotion and protection of human rights and fundamental freedoms, including trade unions and human rights monitoring groups;

(10.4)  — allow members of such groups and organizations to have unhindered access to and communication with similar bodies within and outside their countries and with international organizations, to engage in exchanges, contacts and co-operation with such groups and organizations and to solicit, receive and utilize for the purpose of promoting and protecting human rights and fundamental freedoms voluntary financial contributions from national and international sources as provided for by law.

(11) The participating States further affirm that, where violations of human rights and fundamental freedoms are alleged to have occurred, the effective remedies available include

(11.1)  — the right of the individual to seek and receive adequate legal assistance;

(11.2)  — the right of the individual to seek and receive assistance from others in defending human rights and fundamental freedoms, and to assist others in defending human rights and fundamental freedoms;

(11.3)  — the right of individuals or groups acting on their behalf to communicate with international bodies with competence to receive and consider information concerning allegations of human rights abuses.

(12) The participating States, wishing to ensure greater transparency in the implementation of the commitments undertaken in the Vienna Concluding Document under the heading of the human dimension of the CSCE, decide to accept as a confidence-building measure the presence of observers sent by participating States and representatives of non-governmental organizations and other interested persons at proceedings before courts as provided for in national legislation and international law; it is understood that proceedings may only be held *in camera* in the circumstances prescribed by law and consistent with obligations under international law and international commitments.

(13) The participating States decide to accord particular attention to the recognition of the rights of the child, his civil rights and his individual freedoms, his economic, social and cultural rights, and his right to special protection against all forms of violence and exploitation. They will consider acceding to the Convention on the Rights of the Child, if they have not yet done so, which was opened for signature by States on 26 January 1990. They will recognize in their domestic legislation the rights of the child as affirmed in the international agreements to which they are Parties.

(14) The participating States agree to encourage the creation, within their countries, of conditions for the training of students and trainees from other participating States, including persons taking vocational and technical courses. They also agree to promote travel by young people from their countries for the purpose of obtaining education in other participating States and to that end to encourage the conclusion, where appropriate, of bilateral and multilateral agreements between their relevant governmental institutions, organizations and educational establishments.

(15) The participating States will act in such a way as to facilitate the transfer of sentenced persons and encourage those participating States which are not Parties

to the Convention on the Transfer of Sentenced Persons, signed at Strasbourg on 21 November 1983, to consider acceding to the Convention.

(16) The participating States

(16.1) — reaffirm their commitment to prohibit torture and other cruel, inhuman or degrading treatment or punishment, to take effective legislative, administrative, judicial and other measures to prevent and punish such practices, to protect individuals from any psychiatric or other medical practices that violate human rights and fundamental freedoms and to take effective measures to prevent and punish such practices;

(16.2) — intend, as a matter of urgency, to consider acceding to the Convention against Torture and Other Cruel, Inhuman or Degrading Treatment or Punishment, if they have not yet done so, and recognizing the competences of the Committee against Torture under articles 21 and 22 of the Convention and withdrawing reservations regarding the competence of the Committee under article 20;

(16.3) — stress that no exceptional circumstances whatsoever, whether a state of war or a threat of war, internal political instability or any other public emergency, may be invoked as a justification of torture;

(16.4) — will ensure that education and information regarding the prohibition against torture are fully included in the training of law enforcement personnel, civil or military, medical personnel, public officials and other persons who may be involved in the custody, interrogation or treatment of any individual subjected to any form of arrest, detention or imprisonment;

(16.5) — will keep under systematic review interrogation rules, instructions, methods and practices as well as arrangements for the custody and treatment of persons subjected to any form of arrest, detention or imprisonment in any territory under their jurisdiction, with a view to preventing any cases of torture;

(16.6) — will take up with priority for consideration and for appropriate action, in accordance with the agreed measures and procedures for the effective implementation of the commitments relating to the human dimension of the CSCE, any cases of torture and other inhuman or degrading treatment or punishment made known to them through official channels or coming from any other reliable source of information;

(16.7) — will act upon the understanding that preserving and guaranteeing the life and security of any individual subjected to any form of torture and other inhuman or degrading treatment or punishment will be the sole criterion in determining the urgency and priorities to be accorded in taking appropriate remedial action; and, therefore, the consideration of any cases of torture and other inhuman or degrading treatment or punishment within the framework of any other international body or mechanism may not be invoked as a reason for refraining from consideration and appropriate action in accordance with the agreed measures and procedures for the effective implementation of the commitments relating to the human dimension of the CSCE.

(17)  The participating States

(17.1)  — recall the commitment undertaken in the Vienna Concluding Document to keep the question of capital punishment under consideration and to co-operate within relevant international organizations;

(17.2)  — recall, in this context, the adoption by the General Assembly of the United Nations, on 15 December 1989, of the Second Optional Protocol to the International Covenant on Civil and Political Rights, aiming at the abolition of the death penalty;

(17.3)  — note the restrictions and safeguards regarding the use of the death penalty which have been adopted by the international community, in particular article 6 of the International Covenant on Civil and Political Rights;

(17.4)  — note the provisions of the Sixth Protocol to the European Convention for the Protection of Human Rights and Fundamental Freedoms, concerning the abolition of the death penalty;

(17.5)  — note recent measures taken by a number of participating States towards the abolition of capital punishment;

(17.6)  — note the activities of several non-governmental organizations on the question of the death penalty;

(17.7)  — will exchange information within the framework of the Conference on the Human Dimension on the question of the abolition of the death penalty and keep that question under consideration;

(17.8)  — will make available to the public information regarding the use of the death penalty.

(18)  The participating States

(18.1)  — note that the United Nations Commission on Human Rights has recognized the right of everyone to have conscientious objections to military service;

(18.2)  — note recent measures taken by a number of participating States to permit exemption from compulsory military service on the basis of conscientious objections;

(18.3)  — note the activities of several non-governmental organizations on the question of conscientious objections to compulsory military service;

(18.4)  — agree to consider introducing, where this has not yet been done, various forms of alternative service, which are compatible with the reasons for conscientious objection, such forms of alternative service being in principle of a non-combatant or civilian nature, in the public interest and of a non-punitive nature;

(18.5)  — will make available to the public information on this issue;

(18.6)  — will keep under consideration, within the framework of the Conference on the Human Dimension, the relevant questions related to the exemption from compulsory military service, where it exists, of individuals on the basis of conscientious objections to armed service, and will exchange information on these questions.

(19) The participating States affirm that freer movement and contacts among their citizens are important in the context of the protection and promotion of human rights and fundamental freedoms. They will ensure that their policies concerning entry into their territories are fully consistent with the aims set out in the relevant provisions of the Final Act, the Madrid Concluding Document and the Vienna Concluding Document. While reaffirming their determination not to recede from the commitments contained in CSCE documents, they undertake to implement fully and improve present commitments in the field of human contacts, including on a bilateral and multilateral basis. In this context they will

(19.1) — strive to implement the procedures for entry into their territories, including the issuing of visas and passport and customs control, in good faith and without unjustified delay. Where necessary, they will shorten the waiting time for visa decisions, as well as simplify practices and reduce administrative requirements for visa applications;

(19.2) — ensure, in dealing with visa applications, that these are processed as expeditiously as possible in order, *inter alia*, to take due account of important family, personal or professional considerations, especially in cases of an urgent, humanitarian nature;

(19.3) — endeavour, where necessary, to reduce fees charged in connection with visa applications to the lowest possible level.

(20) The participating States concerned will consult and, where appropriate, co-operate in dealing with problems that might emerge as a result of the increased movement of persons.

(21) The participating States recommend the consideration, at the next CSCE Follow-up Meeting in Helsinki, of the advisability of holding a meeting of experts on consular matters.

(22) The participating States reaffirm that the protection and promotion of the rights of migrant workers have their human dimension. In this context, they

(22.1) — agree that the protection and promotion of the rights of migrant workers are the concern of all participating States and that as such they should be addressed within the CSCE process;

(22.2) — reaffirm their commitment to implement fully in their domestic legis-lation the rights of migrant workers provided for in international agreements to which they are parties;

(22.3) — consider that, in future international instruments concerning the rights of migrant workers, they should take into account the fact that this issue is of importance for all of them;

(22.4) — express their readiness to examine, at future CSCE meetings, the relevant aspects of the further promotion of the rights of migrant workers and their families.

(23) The participating States reaffirm their conviction expressed in the Vienna Concluding Document that the promotion of economic, social and cultural rights as well as of civil and political rights is of paramount importance for human dignity and for the attainment of the legitimate aspirations of every individual. They also reaffirm their commitment taken in the Document of the Bonn Confer-ence on Economic Co-operation in Europe to the promotion of social justice and

the improvement of living and working conditions. In the context of continuing their efforts with a view to achieving progressively the full realization of economic, social and cultural rights by all appropriate means, they will pay special attention to problems in the areas of employment, housing, social security, health, education and culture.

(24) The participating States will ensure that the exercise of all the human rights and fundamental freedoms set out above will not be subject to any restrictions except those which are provided by law and are consistent with their obligations under international law, in particular the International Covenant on Civil and Political Rights, and with their international commitments, in particular the Universal Declaration of Human Rights. These restrictions have the character of exceptions. The participating States will ensure that these restrictions are not abused and are not applied in an arbitrary manner, but in such a way that the effective exercise of these rights is ensured.

Any restriction on rights and freedoms must, in a democratic society, relate to one of the objectives of the applicable law and be strictly proportionate to the aim of that law.

(25) The participating States confirm that any derogations from obligations relating to human rights and fundamental freedoms during a state of public emergency must remain strictly within the limits provided for by international law, in particular the relevant international instruments by which they are bound, especially with respect to rights from which there can be no derogation. They also reaffirm that

(25.1) — measures derogating from such obligations must be taken in strict conformity with the procedural requirements laid down in those instruments;

(25.2) — the imposition of a state of public emergency must be proclaimed officially, publicly, and in accordance with the provisions laid down by law;

(25.3) — measures derogating from obligations will be limited to the extent strictly required by the exigencies of the situation;

(25.4) — such measures will not discriminate solely on the grounds of race, colour, sex, language, religion, social origin or of belonging to a minority.

# III

(26) The participating States recognize that vigorous democracy depends on the existence as an integral part of national life of democratic values and practices as well as an extensive range of democratic institutions. They will therefore encourage, facilitate and, where appropriate, support practical co-operative endeavours and the sharing of information, ideas and expertise among themselves and by direct contacts and co-operation between individuals, groups and organizations in areas including the following:

— constitutional law, reform and development,
— electoral legislation, administration and observation,
— establishment and management of courts and legal systems,

— the development of an impartial and effective public service where recruitment and advancement are based on a merit system,

— law enforcement,

— local government and decentralization,

— access to information and protection of privacy,

— developing political parties and their role in pluralistic societies,

— free and independent trade unions,

— co-operative movements,

— developing other forms of free associations and public interest groups,

— journalism, independent media, and intellectual and cultural life,

— the teaching of democratic values, institutions and practices in educational institutions and the fostering of an atmosphere of free enquiry.

Such endeavours may cover the range of co-operation encompassed in the human dimension of the CSCE, including training, exchange of information, books and instructional materials, co-operative programmes and projects, academic and professional exchanges and conferences, scholarships, research grants, provision of expertise and advice, business and scientific contacts and programmes.

(27) The participating States will also facilitate the establishment and strengthening of independent national institutions in the area of human rights and the rule of law, which may also serve as focal points for co-ordination and collaboration between such institutions in the participating States. They propose that co-operation be encouraged between parliamentarians from participating States, including through existing inter-parliamentary associations and, *inter alia*, through joint commissions, television debates involving parliamentarians, meetings and round-table discussions. They will also encourage existing institutions, such as organizations within the United Nations system and the Council of Europe, to continue and expand the work they have begun in this area.

(28) The participating States recognize the important expertise of the Council of Europe in the field of human rights and fundamental freedoms and agree to consider further ways and means to enable the Council of Europe to make a contribution to the human dimension of the CSCE. They agree that the nature of this contribution could be examined further in a future CSCE forum.

(29) The participating States will consider the idea of convening a meeting or seminar of experts to review and discuss co-operative measures designed to promote and sustain viable democratic institutions in participating States, including comparative studies of legislation in participating States in the area of human rights and fundamental freedoms, *inter alia* drawing upon the experience acquired in this area by the Council of Europe and the activities of the Commission 'Democracy through Law'.

# IV

(30) The participating States recognize that the questions relating to national minorities can only be satisfactorily resolved in a democratic political framework

based on the rule of law, with a functioning independent judiciary. This framework guarantees full respect for human rights and fundamental freedoms, equal rights and status for all citizens, the free expression of all their legitimate interests and aspirations, political pluralism, social tolerance and the implementation of legal rules that place effective restraints on the abuse of governmental power.

They also recognize the important role of non-governmental organizations, including political parties, trade unions, human rights organizations and religious groups, in the promotion of tolerance, cultural diversity and the resolution of questions relating to national minorities.

They further reaffirm that respect for the rights of persons belonging to national minorities as part of universally recognized human rights is an essential factor for peace, justice, stability and democracy in the participating States.

(31) Persons belonging to national minorities have the right to exercise fully and effectively their human rights and fundamental freedoms without any discrimination and in full equality before the law.

The participating States will adopt, where necessary, special measures for the purpose of ensuring to persons belonging to national minorities full equality with the other citizens in the exercise and enjoyment of human rights and fundamental freedoms.

(32) To belong to a national minority is a matter of a person's individual choice and no disadvantage may arise from the exercise of such choice.

Persons belonging to national minorities have the right freely to express, preserve and develop their ethnic, cultural, linguistic or religious identity and to maintain and develop their culture in all its aspects, free of any attempts at assimilation against their will. In particular, they have the right

(32.1)  — to use freely their mother tongue in private as well as in public;

(32.2)  — to establish and maintain their own educational, cultural and religious institutions, organizations or associations, which can seek voluntary financial and other contributions as well as public assistance, in conformity with national legislation;

(32.3)  — to profess and practise their religion, including the acquisition, possession and use of religious materials, and to conduct religious educational activities in their mother tongue;

(32.4)  — to establish and maintain unimpeded contacts among themselves within their country as well as contacts across frontiers with citizens of other States with whom they share a common ethnic or national origin, cultural heritage or religious beliefs;

(32.5)  — to disseminate, have access to and exchange information in their mother tongue;

(32.6)  — to establish and maintain organizations or associations within their country and to participate in international non-governmental organizations.

Persons belonging to national minorities can exercise and enjoy their rights individually as well as in community with other members of their group. No disadvantage may arise for a person belonging to a national minority on account of the exercise or non-exercise of any such rights.

(33) The participating States will protect the ethnic, cultural, linguistic and religious identity of national minorities on their territory and create conditions for the promotion of that identity. They will take the necessary measures to that effect after due consultations, including contacts with organizations or associations of such minorities, in accordance with the decision-making procedures of each State.

Any such measures will be in conformity with the principles of equality and non-discrimination with respect to the other citizens of the participating State concerned.

(34) The participating States will endeavour to ensure that persons belonging to national minorities, notwithstanding the need to learn the official language or languages of the State concerned, have adequate opportunities for instruction of their mother tongue or in their mother tongue, as well as, wherever possible and necessary, for its use before public authorities, in conformity with applicable national legislation.

In the context of the teaching of history and culture in educational establishments, they will also take account of the history and culture of national minorities.

(35) The participating States will respect the right of persons belonging to national minorities to effective participation in public affairs, including participation in the affairs relating to the protection and promotion of the identity of such minorities.

The participating States note the efforts undertaken to protect and create conditions for the promotion of the ethnic, cultural, linguistic and religious identity of certain national minorities by establishing, as one of the possible means to achieve these aims, appropriate local or autonomous administrations corresponding to the specific historical and territorial circumstances of such minorities and in accordance with the policies of the State concerned.

(36) The participating States recognize the particular importance of increasing constructive co-operation among themselves on questions relating to national minorities. Such co-operation seeks to promote mutual understanding and confidence, friendly and good-neighbourly relations, international peace, security and justice.

Every participating State will promote a climate of mutual respect, understanding, co-operation and solidarity among all persons living on its territory, without distinction as to ethnic or national origin or religion, and will encourage the solution of problems through dialogue based on the principles of the rule of law.

(37) None of these commitments may be interpreted as implying any right to engage in any activity or perform any action in contravention of the purposes and principles of the Charter of the United Nations, other obligations under international law or the provisions of the Final Act, including the principle of territorial integrity of States.

(38) The participating States, in their efforts to protect and promote the rights of persons belonging to national minorities, will fully respect their undertakings under existing human rights conventions and other relevant international instruments and consider adhering to the relevant conventions, if they have not yet done so, including those providing for a right of complaint by individuals.

(39) The participating States will co-operate closely in the competent international organizations to which they belong, including the United Nations and, as

appropriate, the Council of Europe, bearing in mind their on-going work with respect to questions relating to national minorities.

They will consider convening a meeting of experts for a thorough discussion of the issue of national minorities.

(40) The participating States clearly and unequivocally condemn totalitarianism, racial and ethnic hatred, anti-semitism, xenophobia and discrimination against anyone as well as persecution on religious and ideological grounds. In this context, they also recognize the particular problems of Roma (gypsies).

They declare their firm intention to intensify the efforts to combat these phenomena in all their forms and therefore will

(40.1) — take effective measures, including the adoption, in conformity with their constitutional systems and their international obligations, of such laws as may be necessary, to provide protection against any acts that constitute incitement to violence against persons or groups based on national, racial, ethnic or religious discrimination, hostility or hatred, including anti-semitism;

(40.2) — commit themselves to take appropriate and proportionate measures to protect persons or groups who may be subject to threats or acts of discrimination, hostility or violence as a result of their racial, ethnic, cultural, linguistic or religious identity, and to protect their property;

(40.3) — take effective measures, in conformity with their constitutional systems, at the national, regional and local levels to promote understanding and tolerance, particularly in the fields of education, culture and information;

(40.4) — endeavour to ensure that the objectives of education include special attention to the problem of racial prejudice and hatred and to the development of respect for different civilizations and cultures;

(40.5) — recognize the right of the individual to effective remedies and endeavour to recognize, in conformity with national legislation, the right of interested persons and groups to initiate and support complaints against acts of discrimination, including racist and xenophobic acts;

(40.6) — consider adhering, if they have not yet done so, to the international instruments which address the problem of discrimination and ensure full compliance with the obligations therein, including those relating to the submission of periodic reports;

(40.7) — consider, also, accepting those international mechanisms which allow States and individuals to bring communications relating to discrimination before international bodies.

# V

(41) The participating States reaffirm their commitment to the human dimension of the CSCE and emphasize its importance as an integral part of a balanced

approach to security and co-operation in Europe. They agree that the Conference on the Human Dimension of the CSCE and the human dimension mechanism described in the section on the human dimension of the CSCE of the Vienna Concluding Document have demonstrated their value as methods of furthering their dialogue and co-operation and assisting in the resolution of relevant specific questions. They express their conviction that these should be continued and developed as part of an expanding CSCE process.

(42) The participating States recognize the need to enhance further the effectiveness of the procedures described in paragraphs 1 to 4 of the section on the human dimension of the CSCE of the Vienna Concluding Document and with this aim decide

(42.1)  — to provide in as short a time as possible, but no later than four weeks, a written response to requests for information and to representations made to them in writing by other participating States under paragraph 1;

(42.2)  — that the bilateral meetings, as contained in paragraph 2, will take place as soon as possible, as a rule within three weeks of the date of the request;

(42.3)  — to refrain, in the course of a bilateral meeting held under paragraph 2, from raising situations and cases not connected with the subject of the meeting, unless both sides have agreed to do so.

(43) The participating States examined practical proposals for new measures aimed at improving the implementation of the commitments relating to the human dimension of the CSCE. In this regard, they considered proposals related to the sending of observers to examine situations and specific cases, the appointment of rapporteurs to investigate and suggest appropriate solutions, the setting up of a Committee on the Human Dimension of the CSCE, greater involvement of persons, organizations and institutions in the human dimension mechanism and further bilateral and multilateral efforts to promote the resolution of relevant issues.

They decide to continue to discuss thoroughly in subsequent relevant CSCE fora these and other proposals designed to strengthen the human dimension mechanism, and to consider adopting, in the context of the further development of the CSCE process, appropriate new measures. They agree that these measures should contribute to achieving further effective progress, enhance conflict prevention and confidence in the field of the human dimension of the CSCE.

\*   \*   \*

(44) The representatives of the participating States express their profound gratitude to the people and Government of Denmark for the excellent organization of the Copenhagen Meeting and the warm hospitality extended to the delegations which participated in the Meeting.

(45) In accordance with the provisions relating to the Conference on the Human Dimension of the CSCE contained in the Concluding Document of the Vienna Follow-up Meeting of the CSCE, the third Meeting of the Conference will take place in Moscow from 10 September to 4 October 1991.

## 73. THE CHARTER OF PARIS FOR A NEW EUROPE, 1990

In this declaration, adopted on 21 November 1990, the CSCE participating States (then thirty-four in number following the unification of Germany) reaffirmed their commitment to the principles of the Helsinki Final Act (above 557–84). In particular, the opening section on 'Human Rights, Democracy and the Rule of Law' relates to the protection of national minorities.

In the Helsinki Final Act, the participating States declared their resolve to continue the multilateral process initiated by the first Conference on Security and Co-operation in Europe, and decided to organize follow-up meetings and conferences. In the Charter of Paris for a New Europe (1990), it was decided that the follow-up meetings would take place every two years and would last a maximum of three months. The follow-up meetings have now been replaced by a two week Human Dimension Implementation Meeting, held in Warsaw every year in which the OSCE does not hold a Summit, and Review Conferences, which take place before Summits. The most recent 'Human Dimension Implementation Meeting' was held from 17–27 September 2001.

## TEXT

### A NEW ERA OF DEMOCRACY, PEACE AND UNITY

We, the Heads of State or Government of the States participating in the Conference on Security and Co-operation in Europe, have assembled in Paris at a time of profound change and historic expectations. The era of confrontation and division of Europe has ended. We declare that henceforth our relations will be founded on respect and co-operation.

Europe is liberating itself from the legacy of the past. The courage of men and women, the strength of the will of the peoples and the power of the ideas of the Helsinki Final Act have opened a new era of democracy, peace and unity in Europe.

Ours is a time for fulfilling the hopes and expectations our peoples have cherished for decades : steadfast commitment to democracy based on human rights and fundamental freedoms; prosperity through economic liberty and social justice; and equal security for all our countries.

The Ten Principles of the Final Act will guide us towards this ambitious future, just as they have lighted our way towards better relations for the past fifteen years. Full implementation of all CSCE commitments must form the basis for the initiatives we are now taking to enable our nations to live in accordance with their aspirations.

#### Human Rights, Democracy and Rule of Law

We undertake to build, consolidate and strengthen democracy as the only system of government of our nations. In this endeavour, we will abide by the following:

Human rights and fundamental freedoms are the birthright of all human beings, are inalienable and are guaranteed by law. Their protection and promotion is the first responsibility of government. Respect for them is an essential safeguard against an over-mighty State. Their observance and full exercise are the foundation of freedom, justice and peace.

Democratic government is based on the will of the people, expressed regularly through free and fair elections. Democracy has as its foundation respect for the human person and the rule of law. Democracy is the best safeguard of freedom of expression, tolerance of all groups of society, and equality of opportunity for each person.

Democracy, with its representative and pluralist character, entails accountability to the electorate, the obligation of public authorities to comply with the law and justice administered impartially. No one will be above the law.

We affirm that, without discrimination,
every individual has the right to

> freedom of thought, conscience and religion or belief,
> freedom of expression,
> freedom of association and peaceful assembly,
> freedom of movement,

no one will be:

> subject to arbitrary arrest or detention,
> subject to torture or other cruel, inhuman or degrading treatment or punishment;

everyone also has the right:

> to know and act upon his rights,
> to participate in free and fair elections,
> to fair and public trial if charged with an offence,
> to own property alone or in association and to exercise individual enterprise,
> to enjoy his economic, social and cultural rights.

We affirm that the ethnic, cultural, linguistic and religious identity of national minorities will be protected and that persons belonging to national minorities have the right freely to express, preserve and develop that identity without any discrimination and in full equality before the law.

We will ensure that everyone will enjoy recourse to effective remedies, national or international, against any violation of his rights.

Full respect for these precepts is the bedrock on which we will seek to construct the new Europe.

Our States will co-operate and support each other with the aim of making democratic gains irreversible.

### *Economic Liberty and Responsibility*

Economic liberty, social justice and environmental responsibility are indispensable for prosperity.

The free will of the individual, exercised in democracy and protected by the rule of law, forms the necessary basis for successful economic and social development. We will promote economic activity which respects and upholds human dignity.

Freedom and political pluralism are necessary elements in our common objective of developing market economies towards sustainable economic growth, prosperity, social justice, expanding employment and efficient use of economic resources. The success of the transition to market economy by countries making efforts to this effect is important and in the interest of us all. It will enable us to share a higher level of prosperity which is our common objective. We will co-operate to this end.

Preservation of the environment is a shared responsibility of all our nations. While supporting national and regional efforts in this field, we must also look to the pressing need for joint action on a wider scale.

### *Friendly Relations among Participating States*

Now that a new era is dawning in Europe, we are determined to expand and strengthen friendly relations and co-operation among the States of Europe, the United States of America and Canada, and to promote friendship among our peoples.

To uphold and promote democracy, peace and unity in Europe, we solemnly pledge our full commitment to the Ten Principles of the Helsinki Final Act. We affirm the continuing validity of the Ten Principles and our determination to put them into practice. All the Principles apply equally and unreservedly, each of them being interpreted taking into account the others. They form the basis for our relations.

In accordance with our obligations under the Charter of the United Nations and commitments under the Helsinki Final Act, we renew our pledge to refrain from the threat or use of force against the territorial integrity or political independence of any State, or from acting in any other manner inconsistent with the principles or purposes of those documents. We recall that non-compliance with obligations under the Charter of the United Nations constitutes a violation of international law.

We reaffirm our commitment to settle disputes by peaceful means. We decide to develop mechanisms for the prevention and resolution of conflicts among the participating States.With the ending of the division of Europe, we will strive for a new quality in our security relations while fully respecting each other's freedom of choice in that respect. Security is indivisible and the security of every participating State is inseparably linked to that of all the others. We therefore pledge to co-operate in strengthening confidence and security among us and in promoting arms control and disarmament.

We welcome the Joint Declaration of Twenty-Two States on the improvement of their relations.

Our relations will rest on our common adherence to democratic values and to human rights and fundamental freedoms. We are convinced that in order to strengthen peace and security among our States, the advancement of democracy, and respect for and effective exercise of human rights, are indispensable. We reaffirm the equal rights of peoples and their right to self-determination in con-formity with the Charter of the United Nations and with the relevant norms of international law, including those relating to territorial integrity of States.

We are determined to enhance political consultation and to widen co-operation to solve economic, social, environmental, cultural and humanitarian problems.

This common resolve and our growing interdependence will help to overcome the mistrust of decades, to increase stability and to build a united Europe.

We want Europe to be a source of peace, open to dialogue and to co-operation with other countries, welcoming exchanges and involved in the search for common responses to the challenges of the future.

### Security

Friendly relations among us will benefit from the consolidation of democracy and improved security.

We welcome the signature of the Treaty on Conventional Armed Forces in Europe by twenty-two participating States, which will lead to lower levels of armed forces. We endorse the adoption of a substantial new set of Confidence- and Security-building Measures which will lead to increased transparency and confidence among all participating States. These are important steps towards enhanced stability and security in Europe.

The unprecedented reduction in armed forces resulting from the Treaty on Conventional Armed Forces in Europe, together with new approaches to security and co-operation within the CSCE process, will lead to a new perception of security in Europe and a new dimension in our relations. In this context we fully recognize the freedom of States to choose their own security arrangements.

### Unity

Europe whole and free is calling for a new beginning. We invite our peoples to join in this great endeavour.

We note with great satisfaction the Treaty on the Final Settlement with respect to Germany signed in Moscow on 12 September 1990 and sincerely welcome the fact that the German people have united to become one State in accordance with the principles of the Final Act of the Conference on Security and Co-operation in Europe and in full accord with their neighbours. The establishment of the national unity of Germany is an important contribution to a just and lasting order of peace for a united, democratic Europe aware of its responsibility for stability, peace and co-operation.

The participation of both North American and European States is a fundamental characteristic of the CSCE; it underlies its past achievements and is essential to the future of the CSCE process. An abiding adherence to shared values and our common heritage are the ties which bind us together. With all the rich diversity of our nations, we are united in our commitment to expand our co-operation in all fields. The challenges confronting us can only be met by common action, co-operation and solidarity.

### The CSCE and the World

The destiny of our nations is linked to that of all other nations. We support fully the United Nations and the enhancement of its role in promoting international peace, security and justice. We reaffirm our commitment to the principles and purposes of the United Nations as enshrined in the Charter and condemn all violations of these principles. We recognize with satisfaction the growing role of the United Nations in world affairs and its increasing effectiveness, fostered by the improvement in relations among our States.

Aware of the dire needs of a great part of the world, we commit ourselves to solidarity with all other countries. Therefore, we issue a call from Paris today to all the nations of the world. We stand ready to join with any and all States in common efforts to protect and advance the community of fundamental human values.

## GUIDELINES FOR THE FUTURE

Proceeding from our firm commitment to the full implementation of all CSCE principles and provisions, we now resolve to give a new impetus to a balanced and comprehensive development of our co-operation in order to address the needs and aspirations of out peoples.

### Human Dimension

We declare our respect for human rights and fundamental freedoms to be irrevocable. We will fully implement and build upon the provisions relating to the human dimension of the CSCE.

Proceeding from the Document of the Copenhagen Meeting of the Conference on the Human Dimension, we will co-operate to strengthen democratic institutions and to promote the application of the rule of law. To that end, we decide to convene a seminar of experts in Oslo from 4 to 15 November 1991.

Determined to foster the rich contribution of national minorities to the life of our societies, we undertake further to improve their situation. We reaffirm our deep conviction that friendly relations among our peoples, as well as peace, justice, stability and democracy, require that the ethnic, cultural, linguistic and religious identity of national minorities be protected and conditions for the promotion of that identity be created. We declare that questions related to national minorities can only be satisfactorily resolved in a democratic political framework. We further acknowledge that the rights of persons belonging to national minorities must be fully respected as part of universal human rights. Being aware of the urgent need for increased co-operation on, as well as better protection of, national minorities, we decide to convene a meeting of experts on national minorities to be held in Geneva from 1 to 19 July 1991.

We express our determination to combat all forms of racial and ethnic hatred, antisemitism, xenophobia and discrimination against anyone as well as persecution on religious and ideological grounds.

In accordance with our CSCE commitments, we stress that free movement and contacts among our citizens as well as the free flow of information and ideas are crucial for the maintenance and development of free societies and flourishing cultures. We welcome increased tourism and visits among our countries.

The human dimension mechanism has proved its usefulness, and we are consequently determined to expand it to include new procedures involving, *inter alia*, the services of experts or a roster of eminent persons experienced in human rights issues which could be raised under the mechanism. We shall provide, in the context of the mechanism, for individuals to be involved in the protection of their rights. Therefore, we undertake to develop further our commitments in this respect, in particular at the Moscow Meeting of the Conference on the Human Dimension, without prejudice to obligations under existing international instruments to which our States may be parties.

We recognize the important contribution of the Council of Europe to the promotion of human rights and the principles of democracy and the rule of law as well as to the development of cultural co-operation. We welcome moves by several participating States to join the Council of Europe and adhere to its European Convention on Human Rights. We welcome as well the readiness of the Council of Europe to make its experience available to the CSCE.

*Security*

The changing political and military environment in Europe opens new possibilities for common efforts in the field of military security. We will build on the important achievements attained in the Treaty on Conventional Armed Forces in Europe and in the Negotiations on Confidence- and Security-building Measures. We undertake to continue the CSBM negotiations under the same mandate, and to seek to conclude them no later than the Follow-up Meeting of the CSCE to be held in Helsinki in 1992. We also welcome the decision of the participating States concerned to continue the CFE negotiation under the same mandate and to seek to conclude it no later than the Helsinki Follow-up Meeting. Following a period for national preparations, we look forward to a more structured co-operation among all participating States on security matters, and to discussions and consultations among the thirty-four participating States aimed at establishing by 1992, from the conclusion of the Helsinki Follow-up Meeting, new negotiations on disarmament and confidence and security building open to all participating States.

We call for the earliest possible conclusion of the Convention on an effectively verifiable, global and comprehensive ban on chemical weapons, and we intend to be original signatories to it.

We reaffirm the importance of the Open Skies initiative and call for the successful conclusion of the negotiations as soon as possible.

Although the threat of conflict in Europe has diminished, other dangers threaten the stability of our societies. We are determined to co-operate in defending democratic institutions against activities which violate the independence, sovereign equality or territorial integrity of the participating States. These include illegal activities involving outside pressure, coercion and subversion.

We unreservedly condemn, as criminal, all acts, methods and practices of terrorism and express our determination to work for its eradication both bilaterally and through multilateral co-operation. We will also join together in combating illicit trafficking in drugs.

Being aware that an essential complement to the duty of States to refrain from the threat or use of force is the peaceful settlement of disputes, both being essential factors for the maintenance and consolidation of international peace and security, we will not only seek effective ways of preventing, through political means, conflicts which may yet emerge, but also define, in conformity with international law, appropriate mechanisms for the peaceful resolution of any disputes which may arise. Accordingly, we undertake to seek new forms of co-operation in this area, in particular a range of methods for the peaceful settlement of disputes, including mandatory third-party involvement. We stress that full use should be made in this context of the opportunity of the Meeting on the Peaceful Settlement of Disputes which will be convened in Valletta at the beginning of 1991. The Council of Ministers for Foreign Affairs will take into account the Report of the Valletta Meeting.

### Economic Co-operation

We stress that economic co-operation based on market economy constitutes an essential element of our relations and will be instrumental in the construction of a prosperous and united Europe. Democratic institutions and economic liberty foster economic and social progress, as recognized in the Document of the Bonn Conference on Economic Co-operation, the results of which we strongly support.

We underline that co-operation in the economic field, science and technology is now an important pillar of the CSCE. The participating States should periodically review progress and give new impulses in these fields.

We are convinced that our overall economic co-operation should be expanded, free enterprise encouraged and trade increased and diversified according to GATT rules. We will promote social justice and progress and further the welfare of our peoples. We recognize in this context the importance of effective policies to address the problem of unemployment.

We reaffirm the need to continue to support democratic countries in transition towards the establishment of market economy and the creation of the basis for self-sustained economic and social growth, as already undertaken by the Group of twenty-four countries. We further underline the necessity of their increased integration, involving the acceptance of disciplines as well as benefits, into the international economic and financial system.

We consider that increased emphasis on economic co-operation within the CSCE process should take into account the interests of developing participating States.

We recall the link between respect for and promotion of human rights and fundamental freedoms and scientific progress. Co-operation in the field of science and technology will play an essential role in economic and social development. Therefore, it must evolve towards a greater sharing of appropriate scientific and technological information and knowledge with a view to overcoming the techno-logical gap which exists among the participating States. We further encourage the participating States to work together in order to develop human potential and the spirit of free enterprise.

We are determined to give the necessary impetus to co-operation among our States in the fields of energy, transport and tourism for economic and social devel-opment. We welcome, in particular, practical steps to create optimal conditions for the economic and rational development of energy resources, with due regard for environmental considerations.

We recognize the important role of the European Community in the political and economic development of Europe. International economic organizations such as the United Nations Economic Commission for Europe (ECE), the Bretton Woods Institutions, the Organization for Economic Co-operation and Development (ECD), the European Free Trade Association (EFTA) and the International Chamber of Commerce (ICC) also have a significant task in promoting economic co-operation, which will be further enhanced by the establishment of the European Bank for Reconstruction and Development (EBRD). In order to pursue our objectives, we stress the necessity for effective co-ordination of the activities of these organizations and emphasize the need to find methods for all our States to take part in these activities.

### Environment

We recognize the urgent need to tackle the problems of the environment and the importance of individual and co-operative efforts in this area. We pledge to intensify our endeavours to protect and improve our environment in order to restore and maintain a sound ecological balance in air, water and soil. Therefore, we are determined to make full use of the CSCE as a framework for the formulation of common environmental commitments and objectives, and thus to pursue the work reflected in the Report of the Sofia Meeting on the Protection of the Environment.

We emphasize the significant role of a well-informed society in enabling the public and individuals to take initiatives to improve the environment. To this end, we commit ourselves to promoting public awareness and education on the environment as well as the public reporting of the environmental impact of policies, projects and programmes.

We attach priority to the introduction of clean and low-waste technology, being aware of the need to support countries which do not yet have their own means for appropriate measures.

We underline that environmental policies should be supported by appropriate legislative measures and administrative structures to ensure their effective implementation.

We stress the need for new measures providing for the systematic evaluation of compliance with the existing commitments and, moreover, for the development of more ambitious commitments with regard to notification and exchange of information about the state of the environment and potential environmental hazards. We also welcome the creation of the European Environment Agency (EEA).

We welcome the operational activities, problem-oriented studies and policy reviews in various existing international organizations engaged in the protection of the environment, such as the United Nations Environment Programme (UNEP), the United Nations Economic Commission for Europe (ECE) and the Organization for Economic Co-operation and Development (OECD). We emphasize the need for strengthening their co-operation and for their efficient co-ordination.

### Culture

We recognize the essential contribution of our common European culture and our shared values in overcoming the division of the continent. Therefore, we underline our attachment to creative freedom and to the protection and promotion of our cultural and spiritual heritage, in all its richness and diversity.

In view of the recent changes in Europe, we stress the increased importance of the Cracow Symposium and we look forward to its consideration of guidelines for intensified co-operation in the field of culture. We invite the Council of Europe to contribute to this Symposium.

In order to promote greater familiarity amongst our peoples, we favour the establishment of cultural centres in cities of other participating States as well as increased co-operation in the audio-visual field and wider exchange in music, theatre, literature and the arts.

We resolve to make special efforts in our national policies to promote better understanding, in particular among young people, through cultural exchanges, co-operation in all fields of education and, more specifically, through teaching and training in the languages of other participating States. We intend to consider first results of this action at the Helsinki Follow-up Meeting in 1992.

## Migrant Workers

We recognize that the issues of migrant workers and their families legally residing in host countries have economic, cultural and social aspects as well as their human dimension. We reaffirm that the protection and promotion of their rights, as well as the implementation of relevant international obligations, is our common concern.

## Mediterranean

We consider that the fundamental political changes that have occurred in Europe have a positive relevance to the Mediterranean region. Thus, we will continue efforts to strengthen security and co-operation in the Mediterranean as an important factor for stability in Europe. We welcome the Report of the Palma de Mallorca Meeting on the Mediterranean, the results of which we all support.

We are concerned with the continuing tensions in the region, and renew our determination to intensify efforts towards finding just, viable and lasting solutions, through peaceful means, to outstanding crucial problems, based on respect for the principles of the Final Act.

We wish to promote favourable conditions for a harmonious development and diversification of relations with the non-participating Mediterranean States. Enhanced co-operation with these States will be pursued with the aim of promoting economic and social development and thereby enhancing stability in the region. To this end, we will strive together with these countries towards a substantial narrowing of the prosperity gap between Europe and its Mediterranean neighbours.

## Non-governmental Organizations

We recall the major role that non-governmental organizations, religious and other groups and individuals have played in the achievement of the objectives of the CSCE and will further facilitate their activities for the implementation of the CSCE commitments by the participating States. These organizations, groups and individuals must be involved in an appropriate way in the activities and new structures of the CSCE in order to fulfil their important tasks.

## NEW STRUCTURES AND INSTITUTIONS
## OF THE CSCE PROCESS

Our common efforts to consolidate respect for human rights, democracy and the rule of law, to strengthen peace and to promote unity in Europe require a new quality of political dialogue and co-operation and thus development of the structures of the CSCE.

The intensification of our consultations at all levels is of prime importance in shaping our future relations. To this end, we decide on the following:

We, the Heads of State or Government, shall meet next time in Helsinki on the occasion of the CSCE Follow-up Meeting 1992. Thereafter, we will meet on the occasion of subsequent follow-up meetings.

Our Ministers for Foreign Affairs will meet, as a Council, regularly and at least once a year. These meetings will provide the central forum for political consultations within the CSCE process. The Council will consider issues relevant to the Conference on Security and Co-operation in Europe and take appropriate decisions.

The first meeting of the Council will take place in Berlin.

A Committee of Senior Officials will prepare the meetings of the Council and carry out its decisions. The Committee will review current issues and may take appropriate decisions, including in the form of recommendations to the Council.

Additional meetings of the representatives of the participating States may be agreed upon to discuss questions of urgent concern.

The Council will examine the development of provisions for convening meetings of the Committee of Senior Officials in emergency situations.

Meetings of other Ministers may also be agreed by the participating States.

In order to provide administrative support for these consultations we establish a Secretariat in Prague.

Follow-up meetings of the participating States will be held, as a rule, every two years to allow the participating States to take stock of developments, review the implementation of their commitments and consider further steps in the CSCE process.

We decide to create a Conflict Prevention Centre in Vienna to assist the Council in reducing the risk of conflict.

We decide to establish an Office for Free Elections in Warsaw to facilitate contacts and the exchange of information on elections within participating States.

Recognizing the important role parliamentarians can play in the CSCE process, we call for greater parliamentary involvement in the CSCE, in particular through the creation of a CSCE parliamentary assembly, involving members of parliaments from all participating States. To this end, we urge that contacts be pursued at parliamentary level to discuss the field of activities, working methods and rules of procedure of such a CSCE parliamentary structure, drawing on existing experience and work already undertaken in this field.

We ask our Ministers for Foreign Affairs to review this matter on the occasion of their first meeting as a Council.

\* \* \*

Procedural and organizational modalities relating to certain provisions contained in the Charter of Paris for a New Europe are set out in the Supplementary Document which is adopted together with the Charter of Paris.

We entrust to the Council the further steps which may be required to ensure the implementation of decisions contained in the present document, as well as in the Supplementary Document, and to consider further efforts for the strengthening of security and co-operation in Europe. The Council may adopt any amendment to the supplementary document which it may deem appropriate.

*     *     *

The original of the Charter of Paris for a New Europe, drawn up in English, French, German, Italian, Russian and Spanish, will be transmitted to the Government of the French Republic, which will retain it in its archives. Each of the participating States will receive from the Government of the French Republic a true copy of the Charter of Paris.

The text of the Charter of Paris will be published in each participating State, which will disseminate it and make it known as widely as possible.

The Government of the French Republic is requested to transmit to the Secretary-General of the United Nations the text of the Charter of Paris for a New Europe which is not eligible for registration under Article 102 of the Charter of the United Nations, with a view to its circulation to all the members of the Organization as an official document of the United Nations.

The Government of the French Republic is also requested to transmit the text of the Charter of Paris to all the other international organizations mentioned in the text.

Wherefore, we, the undersigned High Representatives of the participating States, mindful of the high political significance we attach to the results of the Summit Meeting, and declaring our determination to act in accordance with the provisions we have adopted, have subscribed our signatures below:

*Done* at Paris, on 21 November 1990,
in the name of . . .

## 74. DOCUMENT OF THE MOSCOW MEETING OF THE THIRD CONFERENCE ON THE HUMAN DIMENSION OF THE CSCE, 1991

Adopted on 3 October 1991.

*TEXT*

The representatives of the participating States of the Conference on Security and Co-operation in Europe (CSCE), Albania, Austria, Belgium, Bulgaria, Canada, Cyprus, the Czech and Slovak Federal Republic, Denmark, Estonia, Finland, France, Germany, Greece, the Holy See, Hungary, Iceland, Ireland, Italy, Latvia, Liechtenstein, Lithuania, Luxembourg, Malta, Monaco, the Netherlands-European Community, Norway, Poland, Portugal, Romania, San Marino, Spain, Sweden, Switzerland, Turkey, the USSR, the United Kingdom, the United States of America and Yugoslavia, met in Moscow from 10 September to 4 October 1991, in accordance with the provisions relating to the Conference on the Human Dimension of the CSCE contained in the Concluding Document of the Vienna Follow-up Meeting of the CSCE.

They welcomed the admission as participating States of Estonia, Latvia and Lithuania decided at an additional Meeting at ministerial level of the representatives of the participating States in Moscow on 10 September 1991, convened by the Federal Minister for Foreign Affairs of the Federal Republic of Germany, Chairman-in-Office of the CSCE Council, prior to the opening of the Moscow Meeting.

The first Meeting of the Conference was held in Paris from 30 May to 23 June 1989. The second Meeting of the Conference was held in Copenhagen from 5 to 29 June 1990.

The Moscow Meeting was opened by the Minister for Foreign Affairs of the USSR. An opening address was delivered by the President of the USSR on behalf of the host country.

Opening statements were made by delegates of the participating States, among them Ministers, Deputy Ministers and the Vice-President of the Commission of the European Communities. A contribution to the Meeting was made by the Secretary General of the Council of Europe.

The participating States renew their commitment to implement fully all the principles and provisions of the Final Act of the Conference on Security and Co-operation in Europe, of the Charter of Paris for a New Europe and of the other CSCE documents relating to the human dimension, including, in particular, the Document of the Copenhagen Meeting of the Conference on the Human Dimension of the CSCE, and are determined to achieve still further progress in the implementation of these provisions, as full respect for human rights and fundamental freedoms and the development of societies based on pluralistic democracy and the rule of law are prerequisites for a lasting order of peace, security, justice and co-operation in Europe.

In this context, the participating States underlined that, in accordance with the Final Act of the Conference on Security and Co-operation in Europe and the Charter of Paris for a New Europe, the equal rights of peoples and their right to self-determination are to be respected in conformity with the Charter of the United Nations and the relevant norms of international law, including those relating to territorial integrity of States.

At the Moscow Meeting views were expressed by the participating States on the implementation of their commitments in the field of the human dimension. They considered that the degree of compliance with the commitments contained in the relevant provisions of the CSCE documents had shown further substantial improvement since the Copenhagen Meeting. They also considered that, in spite of the significant progress made, serious threats to and violations of CSCE principles and provisions continue to exist and have a sobering effect on the assessment of the overall situation in Europe. In particular, they deplored acts of discrimination, hostility and violence against persons or groups on national, ethnic or religious grounds. The participating States therefore expressed the view that, for the full realization of their commitments relating to the human dimension, continued efforts are still required which should benefit substantially from the profound political changes that have occurred.

The participating States emphasize that issues relating to human rights, fundamental freedoms, democracy and the rule of law are of international concern, as respect for these rights and freedoms constitutes one of the foundations of the international order. They categorically and irrevocably declare that the commitments undertaken in the field of the human dimension of the CSCE are matters of direct and legitimate concern to all participating States and do not belong exclusively to the internal affairs of the State concerned. They express their determination to fulfil all of their human dimension commitments and to resolve by peaceful means any related issue, individually and collectively, on the basis of mutual respect and co-operation. In this context they recognize that the active involvement of persons, groups, organizations and institutions is essential to ensure continuing progress in this direction.

The participating States express their collective determination to further safeguard human rights and fundamental freedoms and to consolidate democratic advances in their territories. They also recognize a compelling need to increase the CSCE's effectiveness in addressing human rights concerns that arise in their territories at this time of profound change in Europe.

In order to strengthen and expand the human dimension mechanism described in the section on the human dimension of the CSCE in the Concluding Document of the Vienna Meeting and to build upon and deepen the commitments set forth in the Document of the Copenhagen Meeting of the Conference on the Human Dimension of the CSCE, the participating States adopt the following:

# I

(1) The participating States emphasize that the human dimension mechanism described in paragraphs 1 to 4 of the section on the human dimension of the CSCE in the Vienna Concluding Document constitutes an essential achievement of the CSCE process, having demonstrated its value as a method of furthering respect for human rights, fundamental freedoms, democracy and the rule of law through dialogue and co-operation and assisting in the resolution of specific relevant questions. In order to improve further the implementation of the CSCE commitments in the human dimension, they decide to enhance the effectiveness of this mechanism and to strengthen and expand it as outlined in the following paragraphs.

(2) The participating States amend paragraphs 42.1 and 42.2 of the Document of the Copenhagen Meeting to the effect that they will provide in the shortest possible time, but no later than ten days, a written response to requests for information and to representations made to them in writing by other participating States under paragraph 1 of the human dimension mechanism. Bilateral meetings, as referred to in paragraph 2 of the human dimension mechanism, will take place as soon as possible, and as a rule within one week of the date of the request.

(3) A resource list comprising up to three experts appointed by each participating State will be established without delay at the CSCE Institution.[1] The experts will be eminent persons, preferably experienced in the field of the human dimension, from whom an impartial performance of their functions may be expected.

The experts will be appointed for a period of three to six years at the discretion of the appointing State, no expert serving more than two consecutive terms. Within four weeks after notification by the CSCE Institution of the appointment, any participating State may make reservations regarding no more than two experts to be appointed by another participating State. In such case, the appointing State may, within four weeks of being notified of such reservations, reconsider its decision and appoint another expert or experts; if it confirms the appointment originally intended, the expert concerned cannot take part in any procedure with respect to the State having made the reservation without the latter's express consent.

The resource list will become operational as soon as 45 experts have been appointed.

(4) A participating State may invite the assistance of a CSCE mission, consisting of up to three experts, to address or contribute to the resolution of questions in its territory relating to the human dimension of the CSCE. In such case, the State will select the person or persons concerned from the resource list. The mission of experts will not include the participating State's own nationals or residents or any of the persons it appointed to the resource list or more than one national or resident of any particular State.

The inviting State will inform without delay the CSCE Institution when a mission of experts is established, which in turn will notify all participating States. The CSCE institutions will also, whenever necessary, provide appropriate support to such a mission.

[1] The council will take the decision on the institution.

(5) The purpose of a mission of experts is to facilitate resolution of a particular question or problem relating to the human dimension of the CSCE. Such mission may gather the information necessary for carrying out its tasks and, as appropriate, use its good offices and mediation services to promote dialogue and co-operation among interested parties. The State concerned will agree with the mission on the precise terms of reference and may thus assign any further functions to the mission of experts, *inter alia*, fact-finding and advisory services, in order to suggest ways and means of facilitating the observance of CSCE commitments.

(6) The inviting State will co-operate fully with the mission of experts and facilitate its work. It will grant the mission all the facilities necessary for the independent exercise of its functions. It will, *inter alia*, allow the mission, for the purpose of carrying out its tasks, to enter its territory without delay, to hold discussions and to travel freely therein, to meet freely with officials, non-governmental organizations and any group or person from whom it wishes to receive information. The mission may also receive information in confidence from any individual, group or organization on questions it is addressing. The members of such missions will respect the confidential nature of their task.

The participating States will refrain from any action against persons, organizations or institutions on account of their contact with the mission of experts or of any publicly available information transmitted to it. The inviting State will comply with any request from a mission of experts to be accompanied by officials of that State if the mission considers this to be necessary to facilitate its work or guarantee its safety.

(7) The mission of experts will submit its observations to the inviting State as soon as possible, preferably within three weeks after the mission has been established. The inviting State will transmit the observations of the mission, together with a description of any action it has taken or intends to take upon it, to the other participating States via the CSCE Institution no later than three weeks after the submission of the observations.

These observations and any comments by the inviting State may be discussed by the Committee of Senior Officials, which may consider any possible follow-up action. The observations and comments will remain confidential until brought to the attention of the Senior Officials. Before the circulation of the observations and any comments, no other mission of experts may be appointed for the same issue.

(8) Furthermore, one or more participating States, having put into effect paragraphs 1 or 2 of the human dimension mechanism, may request that the CSCE Institution inquire of another participating State whether it would agree to invite a mission of experts to address a particular, clearly defined question on its territory relating to the human dimension of the CSCE. If the other participating State agrees to invite a mission of experts for the purpose indicated, the procedure set forth in paragraphs 4 to 7 will apply.

(9) If a participating State (a) has directed an enquiry under paragraph 8 to another participating State and that State has not established a mission of experts within a period of ten days after the enquiry has been made, or (b) judges that the issue in question has not been resolved as a result of a mission of experts, it may, with the support of at least five other participating States, initiate the establishment of a mission of up to three CSCE rapporteurs. Such a decision will be addressed to

the CSCE Institution, which will notify without delay the State concerned as well as all the other participating States.

(10) The requesting State or States may appoint one person from the resource list to serve as a CSCE rapporteur. The requested State may, if it so chooses, appoint a further rapporteur from the resource list within six days after notification by the CSCE Institution of the appointment of the rapporteur. In such case the two designated rapporteurs, who will not be nationals or residents of, or persons appointed to the resource list by any of the States concerned, will by common agreement and without delay appoint a third rapporteur from the resource list. In case they fail to reach agreement within eight days, a third rapporteur who will not be a national or resident of, or a person appointed to the resource list by any of the States concerned, will be appointed from the resource list by the ranking official of the CSCE body designated by the Council. The provisions of the second part of paragraph 4 and the whole of paragraph 6 also apply to a mission of rapporteurs.

(11) The CSCE rapporteur(s) will establish the facts, report on them and may give advice on possible solutions to the question raised. The report of the rapporteur(s), containing observations of facts, proposals or advice, will be submitted to the participating State or States concerned and, unless all the States concerned agree otherwise, to the CSCE Institution no later than three weeks after the last rapporteur has been appointed. The requested State will submit any observations on the report to the CSCE Institution, unless all the States concerned agree otherwise, no later than three weeks after the submission of the report.

The CSCE Institution will transmit the report, as well as any observations by the requested State or any other participating State, to all participating States without delay. The report may be placed on the agenda of the next regular meeting of the Committee of Senior Officials, which may decide on any possible follow-up action. The report will remain confidential until after that meeting of the Committee. Before the circulation of the report no other rapporteur may be appointed for the same issue.

(12) If a participating State considers that a particularly serious threat to the fulfilment of the provisions of the CSCE human dimension has arisen in another participating State, it may, with the support of at least nine other participating States, engage the procedure set forth in paragraph 10. The provisions of paragraph 11 will apply.

(13) Upon the request of any participating State the Committee of Senior Officials may decide to establish a mission of experts or of CSCE rapporteurs. In such case the Committee will also determine whether to apply the appropriate provisions of the preceding paragraphs.

(14) The participating State or States that have requested the establishment of a mission of experts or rapporteurs will cover the expenses of that mission. In case of the appointment of experts or rapporteurs pursuant to a decision of the Committee of Senior Officials, the expenses will be covered by the participating States in accordance with the usual scale of distribution of expenses. These procedures will be reviewed by the Helsinki Follow-up Meeting of the CSCE.

(15) Nothing in the foregoing will in any way affect the right of participating States to raise within the CSCE process any issue relating to the implementation of any

CSCE commitment, including any commitment relating to the human dimension of the CSCE.

(16) In considering whether to invoke the procedures in paragraphs 9 and 10 or 12 regarding the case of an individual, participating States should pay due regard to whether that individual's case is already sub judice in an international judicial procedure.

Any reference to the Committee of Senior Officials in this document is subject to the decision of that Committee and the Council.

# II

(17) The participating States

(17.1)   — condemn unreservedly forces which seek to take power from a representative government of a participating State against the will of the people as expressed in free and fair elections and contrary to the justly established constitutional order;

(17.2)   — will support vigorously, in accordance with the Charter of the United Nations, in case of overthrow or attempted overthrow of a legitimately elected government of a participating State by undemocratic means, the legitimate organs of that State upholding human rights, democracy and the rule of law, recognizing their common commitment to countering any attempt to curb these basic values;

(17.3)   — recognize the need to make further peaceful efforts concerning human rights, democracy and the rule of law within the context of security and co-operation in Europe, individually and collectively, to make democratic advances irreversible and prevent any falling below the standards laid down in the principles and provisions of the Final Act, the Vienna Concluding Document, the Document of the Copenhagen Meeting, the Charter of Paris for a New Europe and he present document.

(18) The participating States recall their commitment to the rule of law in the Document of the Copenhagen Meeting and affirm their dedication to supporting and advancing those principles of justice which form the basis of the rule of law. In particular, they again reaffirm that democracy is an inherent element in the rule of law and that pluralism is important in regard to political organizations.

(18.1)   Legislation will be formulated and adopted as the result of an open process reflecting the will of the people, either directly or through their elected representatives.

(18.2)   Everyone will have an effective means of redress against administrative decisions, so as to guarantee respect for fundamental rights and ensure legal integrity.

(18.3)   To the same end, there will be effective means of redress against administrative regulations for individuals affected thereby.

(18.4) The participating States will endeavour to provide for judicial review of such regulations and decisions.

(19) The participating States

(19.1) — will respect the internationally recognized standards that relate to the independence of judges and legal practitioners and the impartial operation of the public judicial service including, *inter alia*, the Universal Declaration of Human Rights and the International Covenant on Civil and Political Rights;

(19.2) — will, in implementing the relevant standards and commitments, ensure that the independence of the judiciary is guaranteed and enshrined in the constitution or the law of the country and is respected in practice, paying particular attention to the Basic Principles on the Independence of the Judiciary, which, *inter alia*, provide for

(i) prohibiting improper influence on judges;

(ii) preventing revision of judicial decisions by administrative authorities, except for the rights of the competent authorities to mitigate or commute sentences imposed by judges, in conformity with the law;

(iii) protecting the judiciary's freedom of expression and association, subject only to such restrictions as are consistent with its functions;

(iv) ensuring that judges are properly qualified, trained and selected on a non-discriminatory basis;

(v) guaranteeing tenure and appropriate conditions of service, including on the matter of promotion of judges, where applicable;

(vi) respecting conditions of immunity;

(vii) ensuring that the disciplining, suspension and removal of judges are determined according to law.

(20) For the promotion of the independence of the judiciary, the participating States will

(20.1) — recognize the important function national and international associations of judges and lawyers can perform in strengthening respect for the independence of their members and in providing education and training on the role of the judiciary and the legal profession in society;

(20.2) — promote and facilitate dialogue, exchanges and co-operation among national associations and other groups interested in ensuring respect for the independence of the judiciary and the protection of lawyers;

(20.3) — co-operate among themselves through, inter alia, dialogue, contacts and exchanges in order to identify where problem areas exist concerning the protection of the independence of judges and legal practitioners and to develop ways and means to address and resolve such problems;

(20.4) — co-operate on an ongoing basis in such areas as the education and training of judges and legal practitioners, as well as the preparation and enactment of legislation intended to strengthen respect for their independence and the impartial operation of the public judicial service.

(21) The participating States will

(21.1)  — take all necessary measures to ensure that law enforcement personnel, when enforcing public order, will act in the public interest, respond to a specific need and pursue a legitimate aim, as well as use ways and means commensurate with the circumstances, which will not exceed the needs of enforcement;

(21.2)  — ensure that law enforcement acts are subject to judicial control, that law enforcement personnel are held accountable for such acts, and that due compensation may be sought, according to domestic law, by the victims of acts found to be in violation of the above commitments.

(22) The participating States will take appropriate measures to ensure that education and information regarding the prohibition of excess force by law enforcement personnel as well as relevant international and domestic codes of conduct are included in the training of such personnel.

(23) The participating States will treat all persons deprived of their liberty with humanity and with respect for the inherent dignity of the human person and will respect the internationally recognized standards that relate to the administration of justice and the human rights of detainees.

(23.1)  The participating States will ensure that

(i)    no one will be deprived of his liberty except on such grounds and in accordance with such procedures as are established by law;

(ii)   anyone who is arrested will be informed promptly in a language which he understands of the reason for his arrest, and will be informed of any charges against him;

(iii)  any person who has been deprived of his liberty will be promptly informed about his rights according to domestic law;

(iv)   any person arrested or detained will have the right to be brought promptly before a judge or other officer authorized by law to determine the lawfulness of his arrest or detention, and will be released without delay if it is unlawful;

(v)    anyone charged with a criminal offence will have the right to defend himself in person or through legal assistance of his own choosing or, if he has not sufficient means to pay for legal assistance, to be given it free when the interests of justice so require;

(vi)   any person arrested or detained will have the right, without undue delay, to notify or to require the competent authority to notify appropriate persons of his choice of his arrest, detention, imprisonment and whereabouts; any restriction in the exercise of this right will be prescribed by law and in accordance with international standards;

(vii)  effective measures will be adopted, if this has not already been done, to provide that law enforcement bodies do not take undue advantage of the situation of a detained or imprisoned person for the purpose of compelling him to confess, or otherwise to incriminate himself, or to force him to testify against any other person;

(viii) the duration of any interrogation and the intervals between them will be recorded and certified, consistent with domestic law;

(ix)   a detained person or his counsel will have the right to make a request or complaint regarding his treatment, in particular when torture or other cruel, inhuman or degrading treatment has been applied, to the authorities responsible for the administration of the place of detention and to higher authorities, and when necessary, to appropriate authorities vested with reviewing or remedial power;

(x)   such request or complaint will be promptly dealt with and replied to without undue delay; if the request or complaint is rejected or in case of inordinate delay, the complainant will be entitled to bring it before a judicial or other authority; neither the detained or imprisoned person nor any complainant will suffer prejudice for making a request or complaint;

(xi)   anyone who has been the victim of an unlawful arrest or detention will have a legally enforceable right to seek compensation.

(23.2)   The participating States will

(i)   endeavour to take measures, as necessary, to improve the conditions of individuals in detention or imprisonment;

(ii)   pay particular attention to the question of alternatives to imprisonment.

(24) The participating States reconfirm the right to the protection of private and family life, domicile, correspondence and electronic communications. In order to avoid any improper or arbitrary intrusion by the State in the realm of the individual, which would be harmful to any democratic society, the exercise of this right will be subject only to such restrictions as are prescribed by law and are consistent with internationally recognized human rights standards. In particular, the participating States will ensure that searches and seizures of persons and private premises and property will take place only in accordance with standards that are judicially enforceable.

(25) The participating States will

(25.1)   — ensure that their military and paramilitary forces, internal security and intelligence services, and the police are subject to the effective direction and control of the appropriate civil authorities;

(25.2)   — maintain and, where necessary, strengthen executive control over the use of military and paramilitary forces as well as the activities of the internal security and intelligence services and the police;

(25.3)   — take appropriate steps to create, wherever they do not already exist, and maintain effective arrangements for legislative supervision of all such forces, services and activities.

(26) The participating States reaffirm the right to freedom of expression, including the right to communication and the right of the media to collect, report and disseminate information, news and opinions. Any restriction in the exercise of this right will be prescribed by law and in accordance with international standards. They further recognize that independent media are essential to a free and open society and accountable systems of government and are of particular importance in safeguarding human rights and fundamental freedoms.

(26.1)   They consider that the print and broadcast media in their territory should enjoy unrestricted access to foreign news and information services. The public will enjoy similar freedom to receive and impart information and ideas without interference by public authority regardless of frontiers, including through foreign publications and foreign broadcasts. Any restriction in the exercise of this right will be prescribed by law and in accordance with international standards.

(26.2)      The participating States will not discriminate against independent media with respect to affording access to information, material and facilities.

(27) The participating States

(27.1)      — express their intention to co-operate in the field of constitutional, administrative, commercial, civil and social welfare laws and their relevant areas, in order to develop, particularly in States where they do not yet exist, legal systems based on respect for human rights, the rule of law and democracy;

(27.2)      — to this end, envisage the continuation and enhancement of bilateral and multilateral legal and administrative co-operation, inter alia, in the following fields

     — development of an efficient administrative system;
     — assistance in formulating law and regulations;
     — training of administrative and legal staff;
     — exchange of legal works and periodicals.

(28) The participating States consider it important to protect human rights and fundamental freedoms during a state of public emergency, to take into account the relevant provisions of the Document of the Copenhagen Meeting, and to observer the international conventions to which they are parties.

(28.1)      The participating States reaffirm that a state of public emergency is justified only by the most exceptional and grave circumstances, consistent with the State's international obligations and CSCE commitments. A state of public emergency may not be used to subvert the democratic constitutional order, nor aim at the destruction of internationally recognized human rights and fundamental freedoms. If recourse to force cannot be avoided, its use must be reasonable and limited as far as possible.

(28.2)      A state of public emergency may be proclaimed only by a constitutionally lawful body, duly empowered to do so. In cases where the decision to impose a state of public emergency may be lawfully taken by the executive authorities, that decision should be subject to approval in the shortest possible time or to control by the legislature.

(28.3)      The decision to impose a state of public emergency will be proclaimed officially, publicly, and in accordance with provisions laid down by law. The decision will, where possible, lay down territorial limits of a state of public emergency. The State concerned will make available to its citizens information, without delay, about which measures have been taken. The state of public emergency will be lifted as soon as possible and will not remain in force longer than strictly required by the exigencies of the situation.

(28.4)      A *de facto* imposition or continuation of a state of public emergency not in accordance with provisions laid down by law is not permissible.

(28.5)      The participating States will endeavour to ensure that the normal functioning of the legislative bodies will be guaranteed to the highest possible extent during a state of public emergency.

(28.6)   The participating States confirm that any derogation from obligations relating to human rights and fundamental freedoms during a state of public emergency must remain strictly within the limits provided for by international law, in particular the relevant international instruments by which they are bound, especially with respect to rights from which there can be no derogation.

(28.7)   The participating States will endeavour to refrain from making derogations from those obligations from which, according to international conventions to which they are parties, derogation is possible under a state of public emergency. Measures derogating from such obligations must be taken in strict conformity with the procedural requirements laid down in those instruments. Such measures will neither go further nor remain in force longer than strictly required by the exigencies of the situation; they are by nature exceptional and should be interpreted and applied with restraint. Such measures will not discriminate solely on the grounds of race, colour, sex, language, religion, social origin or of belonging to a minority.

(28.8)   The participating States will endeavour to ensure that the legal guarantees necessary to uphold the rule of law will remain in force during a state of public emergency. They will endeavour to provide in their law for control over the regulations related to the state of public emergency, as well as the implementation of such regulations.

(28.9)   The participating States will endeavour to maintain freedom of expression and freedom of information, consistent with their international obligations and commitments, with a view to enabling public discussion on the observance of human rights and fundamental freedoms as well as on the lifting of the state of public emergency. They will, in conformity with international standards regarding the freedom of expression, take no measures aimed at barring journalists from the legitimate exercise of their profession other than those strictly required by the exigencies of the situation.

(28.10) When a state of public emergency is declared or lifted in a participating State, the State concerned will immediately inform the CSCE Institution[2] of this decision, as well as of any derogation made from the State's international human rights obligations. The Institution will inform the other participating States without delay.

(29) The participating States, recognizing their common interest in promoting contacts and the exchange of information amongst Ombudsmen and other institutions entrusted with similar functions of investigating individual complaints of citizens against public authorities, note with appreciation an offer by Spain to host a meeting of Ombudsmen.

(30) The participating States suggest that the appropriate CSCE fora consider expanding the functions of the Office for Free Elections to enable it to assist in strengthening democratic institutions within the participating States.

(31) The participating States acknowledge the extensive experience and expertise of the Council of Europe in the field of human rights. They welcome its contribution to strengthening democracy in Europe, including its readiness to make its experience available to the CSCE.

---

[2] The council will take the decision on the institution.

# III

(32) The participating States reaffirm their enduring commitment to the principles and provisions of the Final Act, the Vienna Concluding Document, and other relevant CSCE documents in which they undertook, inter alia, to respect human rights and fundamental freedoms and to ensure that they are guaranteed for all without distinction of any kind.

(33) The participating States will remove all legal and other restrictions with respect to travel within their territories for their own nationals and foreigners, and with respect to residence for those entitled to permanent residence, except those restrictions which may be necessary and officially declared for military, safety, ecological or other legitimate government interests, in accordance with their national laws, consistent with CSCE commitments and international human rights obligations. The participating States undertake to keep such restrictions to a minimum.

(34) The participating States will adopt, where appropriate, all feasible measures to protect journalists engaged in dangerous professional missions, particularly in cases of armed conflict, and will co-operate to that effect. These measures will include tracing mission journalists, ascertaining their fate, providing appropriate assistance and facilitating their return to their families.

(35) The participating States reaffirm that guaranteeing the freedom of artistic creation and preserving the cultural heritage form part of the human dimension of the CSCE. They consider that independent intellectual and cultural life is crucial for the maintenance of free societies and democratic institutions. They will implement their commitments in the cultural field, as laid down in the Document of the Cracow Symposium on the Cultural Heritage, and express the view that cultural issues, including cultural freedom, creativity and co-operation, should be further considered in the CSCE.

(36) The participating States recall their commitment in the Vienna Concluding Document to keep the question of capital punishment under consideration and reaffirm their undertakings in the Document of the Copenhagen Meeting to exchange information on the question of the abolition of the death penalty and to make available to the public information regarding the use of the death penalty.

(36.1) They note

(i)   that the Second Optional Protocol to the International Covenant on Civil and Political Rights aiming at the abolition of the death penalty entered into force on 11 July 1991;

(ii)  that a number of participating States have recently taken steps towards the abolition of capital punishment;

(iii) the activities of several non-governmental organizations concerning the question of the death penalty.

(37) The participating States confirm the provisions and commitments of all CSCE documents, in particular the Document of the Copenhagen Meeting of the Conference on the Human Dimension of the CSCE, concerning questions relating to national minorities and the rights of persons belonging to them, and the Report of the Geneva CSCE Meeting of Experts on National Minorities, and call for their

full and early implementation. They believe that, in particular, the use of the new and expanded CSCE mechanisms and procedures will contribute to further protection and promotion of the rights of persons belonging to national minorities.

(38) The participating States recognize the need to ensure that the rights of migrant workers and their families lawfully residing in the participating States are respected and underline their right to express freely their ethnic, cultural, religious and linguistic characteristics. The exercise of such rights may be subject to such restrictions as are prescribed by law and are consistent with international standards.

(38.1) They condemn all acts of discrimination on the ground of race, colour and ethnic origin, intolerance and xenophobia against migrant workers. They will, in conformity with domestic law and international obligations, take effective measures to promote tolerance, understanding, equality of opportunity and respect for the fundamental human rights of migrant workers and adopt, if they have not already done so, measures that would prohibit acts that constitute incitement to violence based on national, racial, ethnic or religious discrimination, hostility or hatred.

(38.2) They will adopt appropriate measures that would enable migrant workers to participate in the life of the society of the participating States.

(38.3) They note that issues which concern the human dimension of migrant workers residing on their territory could, as any other issue of the human dimension, be raised under the human dimension mechanism.

(38.4) They recommend that the CSCE in its future work on the human dimension consider appropriate means to hold focused discussions on all issues regarding migrant workers, including, inter alia, familiarization with the language and social life of the country concerned.

(39) The participating States will

(39.1) — increase their preparedness and co-operate fully to enable humanitarian relief operations to be undertaken speedily and effectively;

(39.2) — take all necessary steps to facilitate speedy and unhindered access to the affected areas for such relief operations;

(39.3) — make the necessary arrangements for those relief operations to be carried out.

(40) The participating States recognize that full and true equality between men and women is a fundamental aspect of a just and democratic society based on the rule of law. They recognize that the full development of society and the welfare of all its members require equal opportunity for full and equal participation of men and women. In this context they will

(40.1) — ensure that all CSCE commitments relating to the protection and promotion of human rights and fundamental freedoms are applied fully and without discrimination with regard to sex;

(40.2) — comply with the Convention on the Elimination of All Forms of Discrimination against Women (CEDAW), if they are parties, and, if they have not already done so, consider ratifying or acceding to this Convention; States that have ratified or acceded to this Convention with reservations will consider withdrawing them;

(40.3) — effectively implement the obligations in international instruments to which they are parties and take appropriate measures to implement the United Nations Nairobi Forward-looking Strategies for the Advancement of Women (FLS);

(40.4) — affirm that it is their goal to achieve not only *de jure* but *de facto* equality of opportunity between men and women and to promote effective measures to that end;

(40.5) — establish or strengthen national machinery, as appropriate, for the advancement of women in order to ensure that programmes and policies are assessed for their impact on women;

(40.6) — encourage measures effectively to ensure full economic opportunity for women, including non-discriminatory employment policies and practices, equal access to education and training, and measures to facilitate combining employment with family responsibilities for female and male workers; and will seek to ensure that any structural adjustment policies or programmes do not have an adversely discriminatory effect on women;

(40.7) — seek to eliminate all forms of violence against women, and all forms of traffic in women and exploitation of prostitution of women including by ensuring adequate legal prohibitions against such acts and other appropriate measures;

(40.8) — encourage and promote equal opportunity for full participation by women in all aspects of political and public life, in decision-making processes and in international co-operation in general;

(40.9) — recognize the vital role women and women's organizations play in national and international efforts to promote and enhance women's rights by providing, *inter alia*, direct services and support to women and encouraging a meaningful partnership between governments and these organizations for the purpose of advancing equality for women;

(40.10) — recognize the rich contribution of women to all aspects of political, cultural, social and economic life and promote a broad understanding of these contributions, including those made in the informal and unpaid sectors;

(40.11) — take measures to encourage that information regarding women and women's rights under international and domestic law is easily accessible;

(40.12) — develop educational policies, consistent with their constitutional systems, to support the participation of women in all areas of study and work, including non-traditional areas, and encourage and promote a greater understanding of issues relating to equality between men and women;

(40.13) — ensure the collection and analysis of data to assess adequately, monitor and improve the situation of women; these data should not contain any personal information.

(41) The participating States decide

(41.1) — to ensure protection of the human rights of persons with disabilities;

(41.2) — to take steps to ensure the equal opportunity of such persons to participate fully in the life of their society;

(41.3)  — to promote the appropriate participation of such persons in decision-making in fields concerning them;

(41.4)  — to encourage services and training of social workers for the vocational and social rehabilitation of persons with disabilities;

(41.5)  — to encourage favourable conditions for the access of persons with disabilities to public buildings and services, housing, transport, and cultural and recreational activities.

(42) The participating States

(42.1)  — affirm that human rights education is fundamental and that it is therefore essential that their citizens are educated on human rights and fundamental freedoms and the commitment to respect such rights and freedoms in domestic legislation and international instruments to which they may be parties;

(42.2)  — recognize that effective human rights education contributes to combating intolerance, religious, racial and ethnic prejudice and hatred, including against Roma, xenophobia and anti-semitism;

(42.3)  — will encourage their competent authorities responsible for education programmes to design effective human rights related curricula and courses for students at all levels, particularly students of law, administration and social sciences as well as those attending military, police and public service schools;

(42.4)  — will make information on all CSCE human dimension provisions available to their educators;

(42.5)  — will encourage organizations and educational establishments to co-operate in drawing up and exchanging human rights programmes at the national as well as the international level;

(42.6)  — will seek to ensure that activities undertaken with a view to promoting human rights education in the broader sense take into account experience, programmes and forms of co-operation within existing international governmental and non-governmental bodies, such as the United Nations and the Council of Europe.

(43) The participating States will recognize as NGOs those which declare themselves as such, according to existing national procedures, and will facilitate the ability of such organizations to conduct their national activities freely on their territories; to that effect they will

(43.1)  — endeavour to seek ways of further strengthening modalities for contacts and exchanges of views between NGOs and relevant national authorities and governmental institutions;

(43.2)  — endeavour to facilitate visits to their countries by NGOs from within any of the participating States in order to observe human dimension conditions;

(43.3)  — welcome NGO activities, including, inter alia, observing compliance with CSCE commitments in the field of the human dimension;

(43.4)  — allow NGOs, in view of their important function within the human dimension of the CSCE, to convey their views to their own governments and the governments of all the other participating States during the future work of the CSCE on the human dimension.

(43.5) During the future work of the CSCE on the human dimension, NGOs will have the opportunity to distribute written contributions on specific issues of the human dimension of the CSCE to all delegations.

(43.6) The CSCE Secretariat will, within the framework of the resources at its disposal, respond favourably to requests by NGOs for non-restricted documents of the CSCE.

(43.7) Guidelines for the participation of NGOs in the future work of the CSCE on the human dimension might, *inter alia*, include the following:

(i)   NGOs should be allotted common space at such meeting sites or in their immediate vicinity for their use as well as reasonable access, at their own expense, to technical facilities, including photocopying machines, telephones and fax machines;

(ii)  NGOs should be informed and briefed on openness and access procedures in a timely manner;

(iii) delegations to CSCE meetings should be further encouraged to include or invite NGO members.

The participating States recommend that the Helsinki Follow-up Meeting consider establishing such guidelines.

* * *

(44) The representatives of the participating States express their profound gratitude to the people and Government of the USSR for the excellent organization of the Moscow Meeting and the warm hospitality extended to the delegations which participated in the Meeting.

Moscow, 3 October 1991

# 75. DOCUMENT OF THE CSCE HELSINKI SUMMIT MEETING, 1992

Adopted on 10 July 1992. The text below contains the Summit Declaration and the decisions taken on the human dimension, including the Office for Democratic Institutions and Human Rights (ODIHR).

*TEXT*

## HELSINKI SUMMIT DECLARATION: THE CHALLENGES OF CHANGE

### *Promises and problems of change*

1. We, the Heads of State or Government of the States participating in the Conference on Security and Co-operation in Europe, have returned to the birthplace of the Helsinki process, to give new impetus to our common endeavour.

2. The Charter of Paris for a New Europe, signed at the last Summit, defined a common democratic foundation, established institutions for co-operation and set forth guidelines for realization of a community of free and democratic States from Vancouver to Vladivostok.

3. We have witnessed the end of the cold war, the fall of totalitarian regimes and the demise of the ideology on which they were based. All our countries now take democracy as the basis for their political, social and economic life. The CSCE has played a key role in these positive changes. Still, the legacy of the past remains strong. We are faced with challenges and opportunities, but also with serious difficulties and disappointments.

4. We have met here to review recent developments, to consolidate the achievements of the CSCE and to set its future direction. To meet new challenges we are approving here today a programme to enhance our capabilities for concerted action and to intensify our co-operation for democracy, prosperity and equal rights of security.

5. The aspirations of peoples freely to determine their internal and external political status have led to the spread of democracy and have recently found expression in the emergence of a number of sovereign States. Their full participation brings a new dimension to the CSCE.

6. We welcome the commitment of all participating States to our shared values. Respect for human rights and fundamental freedoms, including the rights of persons belonging to national minorities, democracy, the rule of law, economic liberty, social justice and environmental responsibility are our common aims. They are immutable. Adherence to our commitments provides the basis for participation and co-operation in the CSCE and a cornerstone for further development of our societies.

7. We reaffirm the validity of the guiding principles and common values of the Helsinki Final Act and the Charter of Paris, embodying responsibilities of States

towards each other and of governments towards their people. These are the collective conscience of our community. We recognize our accountability to each other for complying with them. We underline the democratic rights of citizens to demand from their governments respect for these values and standards.

8. We emphasize that the commitments undertaken in the field of the human dimension of the CSCE are matters of direct and legitimate concern to all participating States and do not belong exclusively to the internal affairs of the State concerned. The protection and promotion of the human rights and fundamental freedoms and the strengthening of democratic institutions continue to be a vital basis for our comprehensive security.

9. The transition to and development of democracy and market economy by the new democracies is being carried forward with determination amidst difficulties and varying conditions. We offer our support and solidarity to participating States undergoing transformation to democracy and market economy. We welcome their efforts to become fully integrated into the wider community of States. Making this transition irreversible will ensure the security and prosperity of us all.

10. Encouragement of this sense of wider community remains one of our fundamental goals. We welcome in this connection the rapid adaptation of European and transatlantic institutions and organizations which are increasingly working together to face up to the challenges before us and to provide a solid foundation for peace and prosperity.

The European Community (EC) , fulfilling its important role in the political and economic development of Europe, is moving towards a union and has decided to broaden its membership. It is closely involved in CSCE activities.

The North Atlantic Treaty Organization (NATO) , one of the essential transatlantic links, has adopted a new strategic concept and strengthened its role as an integral aspect for security in Europe. Through establishment of the North Atlantic Co-operation Council (NACC) it has established patterns of co-operation with new partners in harmony with the goals of the CSCE. It has also offered practical support for the work of the CSCE.

The Western European Union (WEU) is an integral part of the development of the European Union; it is also the means to strengthen the European pillar of the Atlantic Alliance; it is developing an operational capacity; it is opening itself to additional co-operation with new partners and has offered to provide resources in support of the CSCE.

The Council of Europe is elaborating its own programmes for new democracies, opening up to new members and is co-operating with the CSCE in the human dimension.

The Group of Seven and the Group of Twenty-Four are deeply engaged in assistance to countries in transition.

The Organisation for Economic Co-operation and Development (OECD), United Nations Economic Commission for Europe (ECE) and the European Bank for Reconstruction and Development (EBRD) have a key role to play in the construction of a new Europe.

The Commonwealth of Independent States (CIS) has stated its readiness to assist the CSCE in pursuit of its objectives.

These and the other forms of regional and sub-regional co-operation which continue to develop, such as the Council of the Baltic Sea States, the Visegrad Triangle, the Black Sea Economic Co-operation and the Central European Initiative, multiply the links uniting CSCE participating States.

11. We welcome the adoption of the Vienna 1992 Document on Confidence- and Security-building Measures and the signature of the Treaty on Open Skies, with the adoption of the Declaration on the Treaty on Open Skies. We also welcome the imminent entry into force of the Treaty on Conventional Armed Forces in Europe (CFE) and the Concluding Act of the Negotiation on Personnel Strength of Conventional Armed Forces in Europe. These agreements provide a solid foundation for our further security co-operation. We welcome the recent United States-Russian joint understanding on Strategic Offensive Arms. We reaffirm our commitment to become original signatories to the forthcoming convention on the prohibition of the development, production, stockpiling and use of chemical weapons and on their destruction, and urge other States to do so.

12. This is a time of promise but also a time of instability and insecurity. Economic decline, social tension, aggressive nationalism, intolerance, xenophobia and ethnic conflicts threaten stability in the CSCE area. Gross violations of CSCE commitments in the field of human rights and fundamental freedoms, including those related to national minorities, pose a special threat to the peaceful development of society, in particular in new democracies.

There is still much work to be done in building democratic and pluralistic societies, where diversity is fully protected and respected in practice. Consequently, we reject racial, ethnic and religious discrimination in any form. Freedom and tolerance must be taught and practised.

13. For the first time in decades we are facing warfare in the CSCE region. New armed conflicts and massive use of force to achieve hegemony and territorial expansion continue to occur. The loss of life, human misery, involving huge numbers of refugees have been the worst since the Second World War. Damage to our cultural heritage and the destruction of property have been appalling.

Our community is deeply concerned by these developments. Individually and jointly within the CSCE and the United Nations and other international organizations, we have sought to alleviate suffering and seek long term solutions to the crises which have arisen.

With the Helsinki decisions, we have put in place a comprehensive programme of co-ordinated action which will provide additional tools for the CSCE to address tensions before violence erupts and to manage crises which may regrettably develop. The Council and the Committee of Senior Officials have already established for the CSCE an important role in dealing with crises which have developed within our area.

No international effort can be successful if those engaged in conflicts do not reaffirm their will to seek peaceful solutions to their differences. We stress our determination to hold parties to conflicts accountable for their actions.

14. In times of conflict the fulfilment of basic human needs is most at risk. We will exert every effort to ensure that they are met and that humanitarian commitments are respected. We will strive to relieve suffering by humanitarian cease-fires and to facilitate the delivery of assistance under international supervision, including its safe passage. We recognize that the refugee problems resulting from these conflicts

require the co-operation of all of us. We express our support for and solidarity with those countries which bear the brunt of the refugee problems resulting from these conflicts. In this context we recognize the need for co-operation and concerted action.

15. Even where violence has been contained, the sovereignty and independence of some States still needs to be upheld. We express support for efforts by CSCE participating States to remove, in a peaceful manner and through negotiations, the problems that remain from the past, like the stationing of foreign armed forces on the territories of the Baltic States without the required consent of those countries.

Therefore, in line with basic principles of international law and in order to prevent any possible conflict, we call on the participating States concerned to conclude, without delay, appropriate bilateral agreements, including timetables, for the early, orderly and complete withdrawal of such foreign troops from the territories of the Baltic States.

16. The degradation of the environment over many years threatens us all. The danger of nuclear accidents is a pressing concern. So are, in several parts of the CSCE area, defence-related hazards for the environment.

17. The present proliferation of weapons increases the danger of conflict and is an urgent challenge. Effective export controls on nuclear materials, conventional weapons and other sensitive goods and technologies are a pressing need.

### *The CSCE and the management of change*

18. The CSCE has been instrumental in promoting changes; now it must adapt to the task of managing them. Our decisions in Helsinki are making the CSCE more operational and effective. We are determined to fully use consultations and concerted action to enable a common response to the challenges facing us.

19. In approaching these tasks, we emphasize the central role of the CSCE in fostering and managing change in our region. In this era of transition, the CSCE is crucial to our efforts to forestall aggression and violence by addressing the root causes of problems and to prevent, manage and settle conflicts peacefully by appropriate means.

20. To this end, we have further developed structures to ensure political management of crises and created new instruments of conflict prevention and crisis management. We have strengthened the Council and the Committee of Senior Officials(CSO) and devised means to assist them. The CSCE capacities in the field of early warning will be strengthened in particular by the activities of the newly established High Commissioner on National Minorities.

We have provided for CSCE peacekeeping according to agreed modalities. CSCE peacekeeping activities may be undertaken in cases of conflict within or among participating States to help maintain peace and stability in support of an ongoing effort at a political solution. In this respect, we are also prepared to seek, on a case-by-case basis, the support of international institutions and organizations, such as the EC, NATO and WEU, as well as other institutions and mechanisms, including the peacekeeping mechanism of the CIS. We welcome their readiness to support CSCE peacekeeping activities, including by making available their resources.

We are further developing our possibilities for peaceful settlement of disputes.

21. Our approach is based on our comprehensive concept of security as initiated in the Final Act. This concept relates the maintenance of peace to the respect for human rights and fundamental freedoms. It links economic and environmental solidarity and co-operation with peaceful inter-State relations. This is equally valid in managing change as it was necessary in mitigating confrontation.

22. The CSCE is a forum for dialogue, negotiation and co-operation, providing direction and giving impulse to the shaping of the new Europe. We are determined to use it to give new impetus to the process of arms control, disarmament and confidence—and security-building, to the enhancement of consultation and co-operation on security matters and to furthering the process of reducing the risk of conflict. In this context, we will also consider new steps to further strengthen norms of behaviour on politico-military aspects of security. We will ensure that our efforts in these fields are coherent, interrelated and complementary.

23. We remain convinced that security is indivisible. No State in our CSCE community will strengthen its security at the expense of the security of other States. This is our resolute message to States which resort to the threat or use of force to achieve their objectives in flagrant violation of CSCE commitments.

24. Essential to the success of our efforts to foster democratic change within the CSCE framework will be increased co-operation with other European and trans-atlantic organizations and institutions. Therefore, we are convinced that a lasting and peaceful order for our community of States will be built on mutually reinforcing institutions, each with its own area of action and responsibility.

25. Reaffirming the commitments to the Charter of the United Nations as sub-scribed to by our States, we declare our understanding that the CSCE is a regional arrangement in the sense of Chapter VIII of the Charter of the United Nations. As such, it provides an important link between European and global security. The rights and responsibilities of the Security Council remain unaffected in their entirety. The CSCE will work together closely with the United Nations especially in preventing and settling conflicts.

26. We restate our unreserved condemnation of all acts, methods and practices of terrorism. We are determined to enhance our co-operation to eliminate this threat to security, democracy and human rights. To this end, we will take measures to prevent in our territories criminal activities that support acts of terrorism in other States. We will encourage exchange of information concerning terrorist activities. We will seek further effective avenues for co-operation as appropriate. We will also take the necessary steps at a national level to fulfil our international obligations in this field.

27. Illicit trafficking in drugs represents a danger to the stability of our societies and democratic institutions. We will act together to strengthen all forms of bilateral and multilateral co-operation in the fight against illicit trafficking in drugs and other forms of international organized crime.

28. We will work to reinforce the close link which exists between political pluralism and the operation of a market economy. Enhanced co-operation in the field

of economy, science and technology has a crucial role to play in strengthening
security and stability in the CSCE region.

29. Economic co-operation remains an essential element of the CSCE. We will
continue to support the transformations under way to introduce market economies
as the means to enhance economic performance and increased integration into the
international economic and financial systems.

30. We will also facilitate expanded economic co-operation which must take
account of the prevailing political and economic conditions. We welcome the
contribution of economic, financial and technical assistance programmes of
the Group of Seven and the Group of Twenty-Four to the transition process.

In the framework of our co-operation we fully support the further development
of the European Energy Charter which is of particular importance in the period
of transition.

31. We will work together to help facilitate means of transportation and communication in order to deepen co-operation among us.

32. We renew our commitment to co-operate in protecting and improving the
environment for present and future generations. We stress in particular the importance of co-operation to effectively ensure the safety of nuclear installations and to
bring defence-related hazards for the environment under control.

We emphasize the need for greater public awareness and understanding of
environmental issues and for public involvement in the planning and decision-
making process.

We welcome the important outcome of the United Nations Conference on
Environment and Development (UNCED) held in Rio de Janeiro in June 1992. We
emphasize the need for effective and sustained implementation of UNCED
decisions.

33. Further steps must be taken to stop the proliferation of weapons. It remains
vital to ensure non-proliferation of nuclear weapons and the relevant technology
and expertise. We urge all States which have not acceded to the Treaty on Non-
proliferation of Nuclear Weapons to do so as non-nuclear weapons States and to
conclude safeguards agreements with the International Atomic Energy Agency
(IAEA). We commit ourselves to intensify our co-operation in the field of effective
export controls applicable to nuclear materials, conventional weapons and other
sensitive goods and technologies.

34. We welcome the development of regional co-operation among CSCE participating States as a valuable means of promoting pluralistic structures of stability.
Based on the CSCE principles and commitments, regional co-operative activities
serve the purpose of uniting us and promoting comprehensive security.

35. We encourage wide-ranging transfrontier co-operation, including human
contacts, involving local and regional communities and authorities. This
co-operation contributes to overcoming economic and social inequalities and
enhancing ethnic understanding, fostering good-neighbourly relations among
States and peoples.

36. In order to ensure full participation and co-operation by recently admitted
participating States we are initiating a programme of co-ordinated support.

37. We reaffirm our conviction that strengthening security and co-operation in the

Mediterranean is important for stability in the CSCE region. We recognize that the changes which have taken place in Europe are relevant to the Mediterranean region and that, conversely, economic, social, political and security developments in that region have a direct bearing on Europe.

38. We will therefore widen our co-operation and enlarge our dialogue with the non-participating Mediterranean States as a means to promote social and economic development, thereby enhancing stability in the region, in order to narrow the prosperity gap between Europe and its Mediterranean neighbours and protect the Mediterranean ecosystems. We stress the importance of intra-Mediterranean relations and the need for increased co-operation within the region.

39. We welcome and encourage the continuation of initiatives and negotiations aimed at finding just, lasting and viable solutions, through peaceful means, to the outstanding crucial problems of the Mediterranean region.

40. We have expanded dialogue with non-participating States, inviting them to take part in our activities on a selective basis when they can make a contribution.

41. We welcome the establishment of the CSCE Parliamentary Assembly which held its first meeting in Budapest on 3 to 5 July and look forward to the active participation of parliamentarians in the CSCE process.

42. We attach particular importance to the active involvement of our publics in the CSCE. We will expand the opportunities for contributions by and co-operation with individuals and non-governmental organizations in our work.

43. In order to foster our partnership, and to better manage change, we have today in Helsinki adopted an agenda for a strengthened and effective CSCE through the Helsinki Decisions. These decisions will be implemented fully and in good faith.

44. We entrust the Council with the further steps which may be required to implement them. The Council may adopt any amendment to the decisions which it may deem appropriate.

45. The full text of the Helsinki Document will be published in each participating State, which will make it known as widely as possible.

46. The Government of Finland is requested to transmit to the Secretary-General of the United Nations the text of the Helsinki Document, which is not eligible for registration under Article 102 of the Charter of the United Nations, with a view to its circulation to all the members of the Organization as an official document of the United Nations.

47. The next review conference will be held in Budapest in 1994 on the basis of modalities of the Helsinki Follow-up Meeting, *mutatis mutandis*, to be further specified by the CSO which may decide to organize a special preparatory meeting.

\*   \*   \*

## HELSINKI DECISIONS

## VI

## THE HUMAN DIMENSION

(1) The participating States conducted a useful review of implementation of CSCE commitments in the Human Dimension. They based their discussion on the new community of values established among them, as set forth by the Charter of Paris for a New Europe and developed by the new standards created within the CSCE in recent years. They noted major progress in complying with Human Dimension commitments, but recognized developments of serious concern and thus the need for further improvement.

(2) The participating States express their strong determination to ensure full respect for human rights and fundamental freedoms, to abide by the rule of law, to promote the principles of democracy and, in this regard, to build, strengthen and protect democratic institutions, as well as to promote tolerance throughout society. To these ends, they will broaden the operational framework of the CSCE, including by further enhancing the ODIHR, so that information, ideas, and concerns can be exchanged in a more concrete and meaningful way, including as an early warning of tension and potential conflict. In doing so, they will focus their attention on topics in the Human Dimension of particular importance. They will therefore keep the strengthening of the Human Dimension under constant consideration, especially in a time of change.

(3) In this regard, the participating States adopt the following:

*Framework for monitoring compliance with CSCE commitments and for promoting co-operation in the human dimension*

(4) In order to strengthen and monitor compliance with CSCE commitments as well as to promote progress in the Human Dimension, the participating States agree to enhance the framework of their co-operation and to this end decide the following:

*Enhanced role of the ODIHR*

(5) Under the general guidance of the CSO and in addition to its existing tasks as set out in the Charter of Paris for a New Europe and in the Prague Document on Further Development of CSCE Institutions and Structures, the ODIHR will, as the main institution of the Human Dimension:

(5a) assist the monitoring of implementation of commitments in the Human Dimension by:

— serving as a venue for bilateral meetings under paragraph 2 and as a channel for information under paragraph 3 of the Human Dimension Mechanism as set out in the Vienna Concluding Document;

— receiving any comments from States visited by CSCE missions of relevance to the Human Dimension other than those under the Human Dimension Mechanism; it will transmit the report of those missions as well as eventual comments to all participating States with a view to discussion at the next implementation meeting or review conference;

— participating in or undertaking missions when instructed by the Council or the CSO;

(5b) act as a clearing-house for information on:

— a state of public emergency according to paragraph 28. 10 of the Document of the Moscow Meeting of the Conference on the Human Dimension;

— resource lists, and assistance, e. g. in the field of censuses or on democracy at a local and regional level, and the holding of national seminars on such issues;

(5c) assist other activities in the field of the Human Dimension, including the building of democratic institutions by:

— fulfilling the tasks as defined in the 'Programme of co-ordinated support to recently admitted participating States';

— arranging 'Seminars on the democratic process' at the request of participating States. The same procedural provisions as set out in the 'Programme of co-ordinated support for recently admitted participating States' will also apply to these seminars;

— contributing, within the resources at its disposal, to the preparation of seminars at the request of one or more participating States;

— providing, as appropriate, facilities to the High Commissioner on National Minorities;

— communicating, as appropriate, with relevant international and non-governmental organizations;

— consulting and co-operating with relevant bodies of the Council of Europe and those associated with it, and examining how they can contribute, as appropriate, to the ODIHR's activities. The ODIHR will also, at the request of participating States, supply them with information about programmes within the framework of the Council of Europe which are open to all participating States.

(6) The activities on Human Dimension issues undertaken by the ODIHR may, *inter alia*, contribute to early warning in the prevention of conflicts.

*Human Dimension Mechanism*

(7) In order to align the Human Dimension Mechanism with present CSCE structures and institutions the participating States decide that:

Any participating State which deems it necessary may provide information on situations and cases which have been the subject of requests under paragraphs1 or 2 of the chapter entitled the 'Human Dimension of the CSCE' of the Vienna Concluding Document or on the results of those procedures, to the participating States through the ODIHR—which can equally serve as a venue for bilateral meetings under paragraph 2—or diplomatic channels. Such information may be discussed at Meetings of the CSO, at implementation meetings on Human Dimension issues and review conferences.

(8) Procedures concerning the covering of expenses of expert and rapporteur missions of the Human Dimension Mechanism may be considered by the next review conference in the light of experience gained.

# IMPLEMENTATION

## Implementation meetings on Human Dimension issues

(9) Every year in which a review conference does not take place, the ODIHR will organize a three-week meeting at expert-level of all participating States at its seat to review implementation of CSCE Human Dimension commitments. The meeting will perform the following tasks:

(9a) a thorough exchange of views on the implementation of Human Dimension commitments, including discussion on the information provided in accordance with paragraph 4 of the Human Dimension Mechanism and on the Human Dimension aspects of the reports of CSCE missions, as well as the consideration of ways and means of improving implementation;

(9b) an evaluation of the procedures for monitoring compliance with commitments.

(10) The implementation meeting may draw to the attention of the CSO measures to improve implementation which it deems necessary.

(11) The implementation meeting will not produce a negotiated document.

(12) Written contributions and information material will be of a non-restricted or restricted character as indicated by the submitting State.

(13) Implementation meetings will be organized to meet in formal and informal sessions. All formal sessions will be open. In addition, the participating States may decide, on a case-by-case basis, to open informal sessions.

(14) The Council of Europe, the European Commission for Democracy through Law and the European Bank for Reconstruction and Development (EBRD), as well as other relevant international organizations and institutions will be encouraged by the implementation meeting to attend and make contributions.

(15) Non-governmental organizations having relevant experience in the field of the Human Dimension are invited to make written presentations to the implementation meeting, e. g. through the ODIHR, and may be invited by the implementation meeting, on the basis of their written presentations, to address specific questions orally as appropriate.

(16) During two half days in the course of the implementation meeting no formal session will be scheduled in order to provide better opportunities for possible contacts with NGOs. To this purpose, a hall at the meeting site will be placed at the disposal of NGOs.

## CSCE Human Dimension seminars

(17) Under the general guidance of the CSO, the ODIHR will organize CSCE Human Dimension seminars which will address specific questions of particular relevance to the Human Dimension and of current political concern. The CSO

will establish an annual work programme including the titles and dates of such seminars. The agenda and modalities of each seminar will be approved by the CSO at the latest three months before the seminar. In doing so, the CSO will take into account views expressed by the ODIHR. Unless otherwise decided, seminars will be held at the seat of the ODIHR and will not exceed one week. The work programme will take into account work by relevant international organizations and institutions.

(18) These seminars will be organized in an open and flexible manner. Relevant international organizations and institutions may be invited to attend and to make contributions. So may NGOs with relevant experience. Independent experts attending the seminar as members of national delegations will also be free to speak in their own capacity.

(19) CSCE seminars will be organized to meet in formal and informal sessions. All formal sessions will be open. In addition, the participating States may decide, on a case-by-case basis, to open informal sessions.

(20) CSCE seminars will not produce a negotiated document or follow-up programmes.

(21) Contributions by independent experts will be of a non-restricted character.

(22) In order to launch the new CSCE Human Dimension Seminars without delay, the participating States decide now at the Helsinki Follow-up Meeting that the ODIHR will organize the following four seminars:

— Migration
— Case Studies on National Minorities Issues: Positive Results
— Tolerance
— Free Media

These seminars will be held before 31 December 1993. The agenda and modalities of the seminars will be decided by the CSO. Seminars on migrant workers and on local democracy will be included in the first annual work programme of seminars. The financial implications of the seminar programme will be kept under consideration by the CSO.


## ENHANCED COMMITMENTS AND CO-OPERATION IN THE HUMAN DIMENSION

### *National minorities*

The participating States

(23) Reaffirm in the strongest terms their determination to implement in a prompt and faithful manner all their CSCE commitments, including those contained in the Vienna Concluding Document, the Copenhagen Document and the Geneva Report, regarding questions relating to national minorities and rights of persons belonging to them;

(24) Will intensify in this context their efforts to ensure the free exercise by persons belonging to national minorities, individually or in community with others, of their human rights and fundamental freedoms, including the right to participate fully, in

accordance with the democratic decision-making procedures of each State, in the political, economic, social and cultural life of their countries including through democratic participation in decision-making and consultative bodies at the national, regional and local level, *inter alia*, through political parties and associations;

(25) Will continue through unilateral, bilateral and multilateral efforts to explore further avenues for more effective implementation of their relevant CSCE commitments, including those related to the protection and the creation of conditions for the promotion of the ethnic, cultural, linguistic and religious identity of national minorities;

(26) Will address national minority issues in a constructive manner, by peaceful means and through dialogue among all parties concerned on the basis of CSCE principles and commitments;

(27) Will refrain from resettling and condemn all attempts, by the threat or use of force, to resettle persons with the aim of changing the ethnic composition of areas within their territories;

(28) Direct the ODIHR to organize, in spring 1993, a CSCE Human Dimension Seminar on Case Studies on National Minorities Issues: Positive Results.

*Indigenous populations*

The participating States

(29) Noting that persons belonging to indigenous populations may have special problems in exercising their rights, agree that their CSCE commitments regarding human rights and fundamental freedoms apply fully and without discrimination to such persons.

*Tolerance and non-discrimination*

The participating States

(30) Express their concern over recent and flagrant manifestations of intolerance, discrimination, aggressive nationalism, xenophobia, anti-semitism and racism and stress the vital role of tolerance, understanding and co-operation in the achievement and preservation of stable democratic societies;

(31) Direct the ODIHR to organize, in autumn 1992, a CSCE Human Dimension Seminar on Tolerance;

(32) Will consider adhering to the International Convention on the Elimination of All Forms of Racial Discrimination, if they have not already done so;

(33) Will consider taking appropriate measures within their constitutional framework and in conformity with their international obligations to assure to everyone on their territory protection against discrimination on racial, ethnic and religious grounds, as well as to protect all individuals, including foreigners, against acts of violence, including on any of these grounds. Moreover, they will make full use of their domestic legal processes, including enforcement of existing laws in this regard;

(34) Will consider developing programmes to create the conditions for promoting non-discrimination and cross-cultural understanding which will focus on human rights education, grass-roots action, cross-cultural training and research;

(35) Reaffirm, in this context, the need to develop appropriate programmes addressing problems of their respective nationals belonging to Roma and other groups traditionally identified as Gypsies and to create conditions for them to have equal opportunities to participate fully in the life of society, and will consider how to co-operate to this end.

### Migrant workers

The participating States

(36) Restate that human rights and fundamental freedoms are universal, that they are also enjoyed by migrant workers wherever they live and stress the importance of implementing all CSCE commitments on migrant workers and their families lawfully residing in the participating States;

(37) Will encourage the creation of conditions to foster greater harmony in relations between migrant workers and the rest of the society of the participating State in which they lawfully reside. To this end, they will seek to offer, *inter alia*, measures to facilitate the familiarization of migrant workers and their families with the languages and social life of the respective participating State in which they lawfully reside so as to enable them to participate in the life of the society of the host country;

(38) Will, in accordance with their domestic policies, laws and international obligations seek, as appropriate, to create the conditions for promoting equality of opportunity in respect of working conditions, education, social security and health services, housing, access to trade unions as well as cultural rights for lawfully residing and working migrant workers.

### Refugees and displaced persons

The participating States

(39) Express their concern over the problem of refugees and displaced persons;

(40) Emphasize the importance of preventing situations that may result in mass flows of refugees and displaced persons and stress the need to identify and address the root causes of displacement and involuntary migration;

(41) Recognize the need for international co-operation in dealing with mass flows of refugees and displaced persons;

(42) Recognize that displacement is often a result of violations of CSCE commitments, including those relating to the Human Dimension;

(43) Reaffirm the importance of existing international standards and instruments related to the protection of and assistance to refugees and will consider acceding to the Convention relating to the Status of Refugees and the Protocol, if they have not already done so;

(44) Recognize the importance of the United Nations High Commissioner for Refugees and the International Committee of the Red Cross, as well as of non-governmental organizations involved in relief work, for the protection of and assistance to refugees and displaced persons;

(45) Welcome and support unilateral, bilateral and multilateral efforts to ensure

protection of and assistance to refugees and displaced persons with the aim of finding durable solutions;

(46) Direct the ODIHR to organize, in early 1993, a CSCE Human Dimension Seminar on Migration, Including Refugees and Displaced Persons.

### *International humanitarian law*

The participating States

(47) Recall that international humanitarian law is based upon the inherent dignity of the human person;

(48) Will in all circumstances respect and ensure respect for international humanitarian law including the protection of the civilian population;

(49) Recall that those who violate international humanitarian law are held personally accountable;

(50) Acknowledge the essential role of the International Committee of the Red Cross in promoting the implementation and development of international humanitarian law, including the Geneva Conventions and their relevant Protocols;

(51) Reaffirm their commitment to extend full support to the International Committee of the Red Cross, as well as to the Red Cross and Red Crescent Societies, and to the United Nations organizations, particularly in times of armed conflict, respect their protective emblems, prevent the misuse of these emblems and, as appropriate, exert all efforts to ensure access to the areas concerned;

(52) Commit themselves to fulfilling their obligation to teach and disseminate information about their obligations under international humanitarian law.

### *Democracy at a local and regional level*

The participating States

(53) Will endeavour, in order to strengthen democratic participation and institution building and in developing co-operation among them, to share their respective experience on the functioning of democracy at a local and regional level, and welcome against this background the Council of Europe information and education network in this field;

(54) Will facilitate contacts and encourage various forms of co-operation between bodies at a local and regional level.

### *Nationality*

The participating States

(55) Recognize that everyone has the right to a nationality and that no one should be deprived of his/her nationality arbitrarily;

(56) Underline that all aspects of nationality will be governed by the process of law. They will, as appropriate, take measures, consistent with their constitutional framework not to increase statelessness;

(57) Will continue within the CSCE the discussion on these issues.

*Capital punishment*

The participating States

(58) Confirm their commitments in the Copenhagen and Moscow Documents concerning the question of capital punishment.

*Free media*

The participating States

(59) Direct the ODIHR to organize a CSCE Human Dimension Seminar on Free Media, to be held in 1993. The goal of the Seminar will be to encourage the discussion, demonstration, establishment of contacts and exchange of information between governmental representatives and media practitioners.

*Education*

The participating States

(60) Would welcome, in view of the importance of education as to the dissemination of the ideas of democracy, human rights and democratic institutions, especially in a period of change, the organization to this end of a seminar entitled 'Education: Structures, Policies and Strategies' by the Council of Europe, open to all participating States.

*Compilation of Human Dimension commitments*

The participating States

(61) Welcome the drawing up of compilations of existing CSCE Human Dimension commitments in order to promote greater understanding for the implementation of these commitments.

*Domestic implementation guidelines*

The participating States

(62) Will promote, where appropriate, the drawing up of guidelines to assist the effective implementation of domestic legislation on human rights issues related to CSCE commitments.

## 76. DOCUMENT OF THE CSCE BUDAPEST SUMMIT MEETING, 1994

Adopted on 6 December 1994. The text below contains the Summit Declaration (which announces the change from CSCE to OSCE) and the decisions taken on the human dimension, including the Office for Democratic Institutions and Human Rights (ODIHR). It contains specific provisions also on, among others, the prevention of torture, national minorities, the Roma and Sinti, and migration.

*TEXT*

### BUDAPEST SUMMIT DECLARATION: TOWARDS A GENUINE PARTNERSHIP IN A NEW ERA

1. We, the Heads of State or Government of the States participating in the Conference on Security and Co-operation in Europe, have met in Budapest to assess together the recent past, to consider the present and to look to the future. We do so as we approach the Fiftieth Anniversary of the end of World War II and the Twentieth Anniversary of the signing of the Helsinki Final Act, and as we commemorate the Fifth Anniversary of the fall of the Berlin Wall.

2. We believe in the central role of the CSCE in building a secure and stable CSCE community, whole and free. We reaffirm the principles of the Helsinki Final Act and subsequent CSCE documents. They reflect shared values which will guide our policies, individually and collectively, in all organizations and institutions to which we belong.

3. The CSCE is the security structure embracing States from Vancouver to Vladivostok. We are determined to give a new political impetus to the CSCE, thus enabling it to play a cardinal role in meeting the challenges of the twenty-first century. To reflect this determination, the CSCE will henceforth be known as the Organization for Security and Co-operation in Europe (OSCE).

4. The CSCE has been instrumental in overcoming barriers and in managing change throughout our region. Since we last met, there have been further encouraging developments. Most vestiges of the Cold War have disappeared. Free elections have been held and the roots of democracy have spread and struck deeper. Yet the path to stable democracy, efficient market economy and social justice is a hard one.

5. The spread of freedoms has been accompanied by new conflicts and the revival of old ones. Warfare in the CSCE region to achieve hegemony and territorial expansion continues to occur. Human rights and fundamental freedoms are still flouted, intolerance persists and discrimination against minorities is practised. The plagues of aggressive nationalism, racism, chauvinism, xenophobia, anti-semitism and ethnic tension are still widespread. Along with social and economic instability, they are among the main sources of crisis, loss of life and human misery. They reflect failure to apply the CSCE principles and commitments. This situation requires our resolute action. We must work together to ensure full respect for these

principles and commitments as well as effective solidarity and co-operation to relieve suffering.

6. We recognize that societies in the CSCE region are increasingly threatened by terrorism. We reiterate our unreserved condemnation of all acts and practices of terrorism, which cannot be justified under any circumstances. We reconfirm our determination to combat terrorism and our commitment for enhanced co-operation to eliminate this threat to security, democracy and human rights.

7. The CSCE will be a forum where concerns of participating States are discussed, their security interests are heard and acted upon. We will further enhance its role as an instrument for the integration of these States in resolving security problems. Through the CSCE, we will build a genuine security partnership among all participating States, whether or not they are members of other security organizations. In doing so, we will be guided by the CSCE's comprehensive concept of security and its indivisibility, as well as by our commitment not to pursue national security interests at the expense of others. The CSCE's democratic values are fundamental to our goal of a community of nations with no divisions, old or new, in which the sovereign equality and the independence of all States are fully respected, there are no spheres of influence and the human rights and fundamental freedoms of all individuals, regardless of race, colour, sex, language, religion, social origin or of belonging to a minority, are vigorously protected.

8. The CSCE will be a primary instrument for early warning, conflict prevention and crisis management in the region. We have agreed that the participating States may in exceptional circumstances jointly decide that a dispute will be referred to the United Nations Security Council on behalf of the CSCE. We have also decided to pursue more systematic and practical co-operation between the CSCE and European and other regional and transatlantic organizations and institutions that share its values and objectives.

9. The CSCE has created new tools to deal with new challenges. In this regard, we welcome the entry into force of the Convention on Conciliation and Arbitration within the CSCE. We will further enhance the CSCE's role and capabilities in early warning, conflict prevention and crisis management, using, *inter alia*, CSCE peacekeeping operations and missions. We will provide consistent political support and adequate resources for CSCE efforts. We have agreed to strengthen the CSCE's political consultative and decision-making bodies and its executive action by the Chairman-in-Office, supported by the Troika, as well as other CSCE procedures and institutions, in particular the Secretary General and the Secretariat, the High Commissioner on National Minorities and the Office for Democratic Institutions and Human Rights. We have also decided to enhance our contacts and dialogue with the CSCE Parliamentary Assembly.

10. Continuing the CSCE's norm-setting role, we have established a 'Code of Conduct on Politico-Military Aspects of Security' that, *inter alia*, sets forth principles guiding the role of armed forces in democratic societies.

11. We welcome the adoption by the CSCE Forum for Security Co-operation of substantial measures, including a new, developed Vienna Document 1994. A compendium of related measures is annexed to Decision V of the Budapest Document. In order to provide further momentum to arms control, disarmament and confidence- and security-building that adds to earlier decisions and agreements, we

have directed it to continue its work in accordance with its mandate and to develop a framework which will serve as a basis for an agenda for establishing new measures of arms control, including in particular confidence- and security-building. We have also mandated it to address specific regional security problems, with special emphasis on longer-term stability in South-Eastern Europe.

12. In view of the new threats posed by the proliferation of weapons of mass destruction, we have agreed on basic principles to guide our national policies in support of common non-proliferation objectives. We are strongly committed to the full implementation and indefinite and unconditional extension of the Treaty on the Non-Proliferation of Nuclear Weapons. We welcome the recent statements by the four nuclear-weapon-States in the CSCE region relating to nuclear testing as being consistent with negotiation of a comprehensive nuclear test-ban treaty. We urge that all signatories to the Convention on the Prohibition of Development, Production, Stockpiling or Use of Chemical Weapons and on their Destruction complete the ratification process in the shortest possible time. We also underline the importance of an early entry into force and implementation of the Treaty on Open Skies.

13. In light of continuing rapid change, we deem it important to start discussion on a model of common and comprehensive security for our region for the twenty-first century, based on the CSCE principles and commitments. This discussion will take into account the CSCE's contribution to security, stability and co-operation. The Chairman-in-Office will present a progress report to the next Ministerial Council in 1995 in Budapest. The results of discussion on such a security model will be submitted to our next Summit Meeting in Lisbon in 1996.

14. We confirm the significance of the Human Dimension in all the activities of the CSCE. Respect for human rights and fundamental freedoms, democracy and the rule of law is an essential component of security and co-operation in the CSCE region. It must remain a primary goal of CSCE action. Periodic reviews of implementation of our commitments, fundamental throughout the CSCE, are critical in the Human Dimension. The enhanced capabilities of the Office for Democratic Institutions and Human Rights will continue to assist participating States, in particular those in transition. We underline the importance of human contacts in overcoming the legacy of old divisions.

15. We recognize that market economy and sustainable economic development are integral to the CSCE's comprehensive concept of security. We encourage the strengthening of co-operation to support the transition processes, regional co-operation and environmental responsibility. We welcome the role played by the relevant international organizations and institutions, such as the United Nations Economic Commission for Europe, OECD, EBRD and EIB, in support of the CSCE's economic dimension priorities. We are committed to enhancing the effectiveness of the Economic Forum and of the CSCE's other economic dimension activities. We ask the Chairman-in-Office to explore ways to integrate economic dimension issues into the tasks faced by the CSCE and report on progress at our next Summit Meeting.

16. We welcome the Declaration of Paris which launched the process aimed at the establishment of a Pact on Stability, as well as the intention expressed therein to entrust the CSCE with following the implementation of the Pact.

17. Strengthening security and co-operation in the Mediterranean is important for stability in the CSCE region. We welcome progress towards peace in the Middle East and its positive implications for European security. The common position adopted by Algeria, Egypt, Israel, Morocco and Tunisia on CSCE-Mediterranean relations encourages us to deepen the long-standing relationship and reinforce co-operation between the CSCE and the non-participating Mediterranean States.

18. We note with satisfaction the development of our relationship with Japan. We welcome the interest of the Republic of Korea which has attended the CSCE Summit Meeting for the first time and of other States in the CSCE's experience and activities, and express our readiness to co-operate with them in areas of mutual interest.

19. In order to move towards a genuine partnership in a new era, we have today adopted the Budapest Decisions which will be implemented fully and in good faith.

20. We entrust the Ministerial Council with the further steps which may be required to implement them. The Council may adopt any amendment to the decisions which it may deem appropriate.

21. The full text of the Budapest Document will be published in each participating State, which will make it known as widely as possible.

22. The Government of Hungary is requested to transmit to the Secretary-General of the United Nations the text of the Budapest Document, which is not eligible for registration under Article 102 of the Charter of the United Nations, with a view to its circulation to all the members of the Organization as an official document of the United Nations.

## BUDAPEST DECISIONS

## VIII

## THE HUMAN DIMENSION

*Introduction*

1. In their review of implementation of CSCE commitments in the human dimension, the participating States based their discussion on the community of values established among them, which is reflected in the high standards created within the CSCE. During the discussion, it was noted that major progress had been made in compliance with human dimension commitments. The participating States acknowledged, however, that there was a serious deterioration in some areas and a need for action against the continuing violations of human rights and manifestations of aggressive nationalism, such as territorial expansionism, as well as racism, chauvinism, xenophobia and anti-semitism, which continue to cause human suffering.

2. Human rights and fundamental freedoms, the rule of law and democratic institutions are the foundations of peace and security, representing a crucial contribution to conflict prevention, within a comprehensive concept of security. The protection of human rights, including the rights of persons belonging to national

minorities, is an essential foundation of democratic civil society. Neglect of these rights has, in severe cases, contributed to extremism, regional instability and conflict. The participating States confirmed that issues of implementation of CSCE commitments are of legitimate and common concern to all participating States, and that the raising of these problems in the co-operative and result-oriented spirit of the CSCE was therefore a positive exercise. They undertook to encourage implementation of CSCE commitments through enhanced dialogue, implementation reviews and mechanisms. They will broaden the operational framework of the CSCE, in particular by enhancing the Office for Democratic Institutions and Human Rights (ODIHR), increasing its involvement in the work of the Permanent Council and mission activity, and furthering co-operation with international organizations and institutions active in human dimension areas.

3. The participation of non-governmental organizations (NGOs) was a welcome addition to the implementation review. In their statements, these organizations contributed ideas and raised issues of concern for participating States to take into consideration. They also informed the participating States of their activities, such as in the area of conflict prevention and resolution. The experience of the Budapest Review Conference invites further consideration with regard to promoting within the CSCE the dialogue between governments and NGOs of the participating States, in addition to State-to-State dialogue.

4. Reaffirming their commitments in the human dimension, the participating States, while considering it essential to concentrate their efforts on the implementation of existing CSCE commitments, decide to enhance the framework of their co-operation and to this end adopt the following:

## ENHANCING COMPLIANCE WITH CSCE COMMITMENTS AND PROMOTING CO-OPERATION AND DIALOGUE IN THE HUMAN DIMENSION

*Enhancing implementation*

5. Building on the implementation review structures in the Helsinki Document 1992 and to improve human dimension implementation, the participating States will use the Permanent Council for an enhanced dialogue on the human dimension and for possible action in cases of non-implementation. To this end, the participating States decide that human dimension issues will be regularly dealt with by the Permanent Council. They will draw more widely on the possibilities offered by the Moscow Mechanism for examining or promoting the solution of questions relating to the human dimension on their territory.

6. They encourage the Chairman-in-Office to inform the Permanent Council of serious cases of alleged non-implementation of human dimension commitments, including on the basis of information from the ODIHR, reports and recommendations of the High Commissioner on National Minorities (HCNM), or reports of the head of a CSCE mission and information from the State concerned.

7. The participating States reconfirm their appreciation for the HCNM, who has, fully in line with his mandate, been able to focus on, and to successfully address a number of national minority issues, taking also into account specific situations of participating States and of parties directly concerned.

They encourage the HCNM to continue his present activities, and support him on taking up new and further ones, including those related to his recommendations. They will increase their efforts to implement these recommendations.

*Role of the ODIHR*

8. The ODIHR, as the main institution of the human dimension, in consultation with the Chairman-in-Office, will, acting in an advisory capacity, participate in discussions of the Senior Council and the Permanent Council, by reporting at regular intervals on its activities and providing information on implementation issues. It will provide supporting material for the annual review of implementation and, where necessary, clarify or supplement information received. Acting in close consultation with the Chairman-in-Office, the Director of the ODIHR may propose further action.

9. The participating States recognize the need for enhanced co-operation through the ODIHR with other international organizations and institutions active in the human dimension, including among others the United Nations High Commissioner for Human Rights, for the exchange of information, including reports, and for further developing of future-oriented activities, such as outlined in the present document.

10. The participating States decide to

— enhance the CSCE's co-operation with other international organizations and institutions, in particular UNHCR and IOM, with a view to contributing to UNHCR's preparation of a regional conference to address the problems of refugees, displaced persons, other forms of involuntary displacement and returnees in the countries of the Commonwealth of Independent States (CIS) and other interested neighbouring States, by establishing, after consultation in the informal Financial Committee, a temporary position, financed by voluntary contributions for a migration expert;

— task the ODIHR to act as a clearing-house for the exchange of information on media issues in the region, and encourage governments, journalists and NGOs to provide the ODIHR with information on the situation of the media.

11. The ODIHR will be consulted on a CSCE mission's mandate before adoption and will contribute to the follow-up of mission reports as decided by the Permanent Council. The ODIHR's knowledge of experts on the human dimension should be used to help to staff CSCE missions. These missions will also designate a mission member to liaise with the ODIHR and with NGOs on human dimension issues.

12. The ODIHR will play an enhanced role in election monitoring, before, during and after elections. In this context, the ODIHR should assess the conditions for the free and independent functioning of the media.

The participating States request that co-ordination between the various organizations monitoring elections be improved, and task the ODIHR to consult all relevant organizations in order to develop a framework for co-ordination in this field.

In order to enhance election monitoring preparations and procedures, the ODIHR will also devise a handbook for election monitors and set up a rolling calendar for upcoming elections.

13. The provisions mentioned in the human dimension chapter of this document do not in any way constitute a change in the mandate of either the ODIHR or the HCNM.

*ODIHR seminars*

14. The number of large-scale human dimension seminars will as a rule be reduced to two per year. They will focus on topics which are of the broadest interest.

There will be more emphasis on regional seminars. Where appropriate they will form part of the Programme of Co-ordinated Support. These seminars should seek full participation from States in the region in which they are held. The ODIHR is requested to present to the Permanent Council a report on how to increase the effectiveness of human dimension seminars. Whilst these seminars will not produce a negotiated document, particular attention should be given to improving follow-up.

15. A large number of possible subjects for seminars, both large-scale and regional, was suggested during the Review Conference. The Executive Secretariat kept a list, which will be passed on to the Permanent Council. In conformity with the relevant provisions of the Helsinki Document 1992, the Permanent Council will establish an annual work programme including the titles, dates and venues of such seminars, taking into account the advice of the ODIHR and the HCNM.

16. The participating States welcomed the offer of Romania to host an International Seminar on Tolerance in Bucharest under the auspices of the ODIHR and the Council of Europe, in co-operation with UNESCO, in the context of the 1995 International Year of Tolerance.

*Role of NGOs*

17. The participating States and CSCE institutions will provide opportunities for increased involvement of NGOs in CSCE activities as foreseen in Chapter IV of the Helsinki Document 1992. They will search for ways in which the CSCE can best make use of the work and information provided by NGOs. The Secretary General is requested to make a study on how participation of NGOs can be further enhanced.

# COMMITMENTS AND CO-OPERATION

*Rule of law*

18. The participating States emphasize that all action by public authorities must be consistent with the rule of law, thus guaranteeing legal security for the individual.

They also emphasize the need for protection of human rights defenders and look forward to the completion and adoption, in the framework of the United Nations, of the draft declaration on the 'Right and Responsibility of Individuals, Groups and Organs of Society to Promote and Protect Universally Recognized Human Rights and Fundamental Freedoms'.

*Capital punishment*

19. The participating States reconfirm their commitments in the Copenhagen and Moscow Documents concerning the question of capital punishment.

*Prevention of torture*

20. The participating States strongly condemn all forms of torture as one of the most flagrant violations of human rights and human dignity. They commit themselves to strive for its elimination. They recognize the importance in this respect of international norms as laid down in international treaties on human rights, in particular the United Nations Convention against Torture and other Cruel, Inhuman or Degrading Treatment or Punishment and the European Convention for the Prevention of Torture and Inhuman or Degrading Treatment or Punishment. They also recognize the importance of national legislation aimed at eradicating torture. They commit themselves to inquire into all alleged cases of torture and to prosecute offenders. They also commit themselves to include in their educational and training programmes for law enforcement and police forces specific provisions with a view to eradicating torture. They consider that an exchange of information on this problem is an essential prerequisite. The participating States should have the possibility to obtain such information. The CSCE should in this context also draw on the experience of the Special Rapporteur on Torture and other Cruel, Inhuman or Degrading Treatment or Punishment established by the Commission on Human Rights of the United Nations and make use of information provided by NGOs.

*National minorities*

21. The participating States confirm their determination consistently to advance the implementation of the provisions of the Final Act and all other CSCE documents relating to the protection of the rights of persons belonging to national minorities. They commend the work of the HCNM in this field.

22. The participating States welcome the international efforts to improve protection of the rights of persons belonging to national minorities. They take note of the adoption, within the Council of Europe, of a Framework Convention on the Protection of National Minorities, which builds upon CSCE standards in this context. They stressed that the Convention is also open—by invitation—to signature by States which are not members of the Council of Europe and they may consider examining the possibility of becoming parties to this Convention.

*Roma and Sinti*

23. The participating States decide to appoint within the ODIHR a contact point for Roma and Sinti (Gypsies) issues. The ODIHR will be tasked to:

— act as a clearing-house for the exchange of information on Roma and Sinti (Gypsies) issues, including information on the implementation of commitments pertaining to Roma and Sinti (Gypsies);

— facilitate contacts on Roma and Sinti (Gypsies) issues between participating States, international organizations and institutions and NGOs;

— maintain and develop contacts on these issues between CSCE institutions and other international organizations and institutions.

To fulfil these tasks, the ODIHR will make full use of existing resources. In this context they welcome the announcement made by some Roma and Sinti (Gypsies) organizations of their intention to make voluntary contributions.

24. The participating States welcome the activities related to Roma and Sinti (Gypsies) issues in other international organizations and institutions, in particular those undertaken in the Council of Europe.

*Tolerance and non-discrimination*

25. The participating States condemn manifestations of intolerance, and especially of aggressive nationalism, racism, chauvinism, xenophobia and anti-semitism, and will continue to promote effective measures aimed at their eradication. They request the ODIHR to continue to pay special attention to these phenomena, collecting information on their various manifestations in participating States. They will seek to strengthen or adopt appropriate legislation to this end and take the necessary measures to ensure that existing legislation is effectively implemented, in a way that would deter manifestations of these phenomena. They also stress that action to combat these phenomena should be seen as an integral part of integration policy and education. They condemn all crimes committed in the pursuit of so-called 'ethnic cleansing' and will continue to give their effective support to the International War Crimes Tribunal for the former Yugoslavia in The Hague.

26. They commend the Council of Europe's plan of action on racism, xenophobia, anti-semitism and intolerance. In following up the Rome Council's Declaration, CSCE institutions will explore possibilities for joint work with the Council of Europe, as well as the United Nations and other international organizations.

27. Reaffirming their commitment to ensure freedom of conscience and religion and to foster a climate of mutual tolerance and respect between believers of different communities as well as between believers and non-believers, they expressed their concern about the exploitation of religion for aggressive nationalist ends.

*Migrant workers*

28. The participating States reconfirm that human rights are universal and indivisible. They recognized that the protection and promotion of the rights of migrant workers have their human dimension. They underline the right of migrant workers to express freely their ethnic, cultural, religious and linguistic characteristics. The exercise of such rights may be subject to such restrictions as are prescribed by law and consistent with international standards.

29. They decided that appropriate measures should be taken to better prevent racist attacks and other manifestations of violent intolerance against migrant workers and their families.

30. They reconfirm their condemnation of all acts of discrimination on the ground of race, colour and ethnic origin, intolerance and xenophobia against migrant workers. They will, in conformity with domestic law and international obligations, continue to take effective measures to this end.

31. They will continue to promote the integration of migrant workers in the societies in which they are lawfully residing. They recognize that a successful process of

integration also depends on its active pursuit by the migrants themselves and decided therefore to encourage them in this regard.

*Migration*

32. The participating States express their concern at mass migratory movements in the CSCE region, including millions of refugees and displaced persons, due mainly to war, armed conflict, civil strife and grave human rights violations. Taking into account the Rome Council Decisions 1993, they decide to expand their co-operation with appropriate international bodies in this respect.

They take note of efforts undertaken by UNHCR to prepare a regional conference to address the problems of refugees, displaced persons, other forms of involuntary displacement and returnees in the countries of the CIS and other interested neighbouring States.

*International humanitarian law*

33. The participating States deeply deplore the series of flagrant violations of international humanitarian law that occurred in the CSCE region in recent years and reaffirm their commitment to respect and ensure respect for general international humanitarian law and in particular for their obligations under the relevant international instruments, including the 1949 Geneva Conventions and their additional protocols, to which they are a party.

34. They emphasize the potential significance of a declaration on minimum humanitarian standards applicable in all situations and declare their willingness to actively participate in its preparation in the framework of the United Nations. They commit themselves to ensure adequate information and training within their military services with regard to the provisions of international humanitarian law and consider that relevant information should be made available.

35. They highly value the developing co-operation between the CSCE and the International Committee of the Red Cross (ICRC), in particular in the case of CSCE missions, and welcome the readiness of the ICRC to develop this co-operation and commit themselves to further extend support to the ICRC, in particular by strengthening contacts already established between CSCE missions and the ICRC's delegations in the field.

*Freedom of expression / Free media*

36. The participating States reaffirm that freedom of expression is a fundamental human right and a basic component of a democratic society. In this respect, independent and pluralistic media are essential to a free and open society and accountable systems of government. They take as their guiding principle that they will safeguard this right.

37. They condemn all attacks on and harassment of journalists and will endeavour to hold those directly responsible for such attacks and harassment accountable.

38. They further note that fomenting hatred and ethnic tension through the media, especially by governments, can serve as an early warning of conflict.

*Freedom of movement / Human contacts / Cultural heritage*

39. The participating States will further encourage and facilitate human contacts,

cultural and educational exchanges and co-operate in accordance with CSCE provisions. They will continue to implement their commitments in the cultural field, as laid down in the Document of the Cracow Symposium on the Cultural Heritage of the CSCE Participating States and other relevant CSCE documents. They will encourage public and private efforts aimed at the preservation of the cultural heritage in their States.

40. They will encourage administrative authorities dealing with citizens of other States to fully implement the CSCE commitments concerning travel and will refrain from degrading treatment and other outrages against personal dignity. They will also consider the need for elaborating a document compiling relevant CSCE provisions.

41. The Permanent Council will explore the possibility of holding informal meetings on the issues mentioned in the two preceding paragraphs.

## PROGRAMME OF CO-ORDINATED SUPPORT

42. The participating States, taking into account the progress achieved through the implementation of the Programme of Co-ordinated Support during the past two years under the co-ordination of the ODIHR, have decided that this programme should continue. The ODIHR and the Secretary General will continue to arrange meetings and seminars on CSCE-related matters to enable interested States to fulfil their CSCE commitments more easily. The participating States will continue to include representatives of these States in government-sponsored internships, study and training programmes so that levels of experience, knowledge and expertise can be raised.

43. They agreed that the ability of the ODIHR to provide in-depth expertise on human dimension issues under the Programme of Co-ordinated Support should be further developed. In order to respond to requests for advice by newly independent States concerned on all aspects of democratization, they decided that using experts-at-large within the framework of the Programme of Co-ordinated Support would be a useful enhancement of the ODIHR's role.

## 77. DOCUMENT OF THE OSCE LISBON SUMMIT MEETING, 1996

Adopted on 3 December 1996. The text below contains the Summit Declaration.

*TEXT*

## LISBON SUMMIT DECLARATION

1. We, the Heads of State or Government of the participating States of the Organization for Security and Co-operation in Europe, have met in Lisbon to assess the
situation in the OSCE region and to establish a co-operative foundation for our
common security. As we approach the new century, it is more important than
ever that we build together a peaceful OSCE region where all our nations and
individuals feel secure.

2. We today adopt the Lisbon Declaration on a Common and Comprehensive
Security Model for Europe for the twenty-first century to strengthen security and
stability throughout the OSCE region. We welcome the historic decision of OSCE
participating States signatory to the CFE Treaty to begin negotiations in early 1997
with a view towards adapting the Treaty to the changing security environment in
Europe. We intend to realize our full potential for consolidating peace and prosperity in the entire OSCE region, as demonstrated by our combined efforts—through
the OSCE and other relevant institutions—to forge a sustainable peace in Bosnia
and Herzegovina.

3. We reaffirm the OSCE principles as set forth in the Helsinki Final Act and other
OSCE commitments. We believe that observance of all these principles and
implementation of all commitments need to be improved and constantly reviewed.
We recognize that serious risks and challenges, such as those to our security and
sovereignty, continue to be of major concern. We are committed to address them.

4. Respect for human rights remains fundamental to our concept of democracy
and to the democratization process enshrined in the Charter of Paris. We are
determined to consolidate the democratic gains of the changes that have occurred
since 1989 and peacefully manage their further development in the OSCE region.
We will co-operate in strengthening democratic institutions.

5. The OSCE has a key role to play in fostering security and stability in all their
dimensions. We decide to continue our efforts to further enhance its efficiency as a
primary instrument for early warning, conflict prevention, crisis management and
post-conflict rehabilitation capabilities. We ask the Chairman-in-Office to report
on progress achieved to the 1997 Ministerial Council.

6. The Lisbon Declaration on a Common and Comprehensive Security Model for
Europe for the twenty-first century is a comprehensive expression of our
endeavour to strengthen security and stability in the OSCE region; as such, it
complements the mutually reinforcing efforts of other European and transatlantic
institutions and organizations in this field.

7. Arms control constitutes an important element of our common security. The CFE Treaty, in particular, is and will remain key to our security and stability. The Forum for Security Co-operation (FSC), the work of which is also important to our security, has adopted two decisions defining new directions for further work, 'A Framework for Arms Control' and 'Development of the Agenda of the Forum for Security Co-operation'. As an example of co-operative security, the Open Skies Treaty, covering the territory from Vancouver to Vladivostok, aims at increased transparency among all Parties. Recalling the Budapest Decision of 1994, we once again strongly emphasize the significance of the entry into force and implementation of this Treaty. In addition, ending illegal arms supplies, in particular to zones of conflict, would make a major contribution to not only regional, but also global security.

8. We welcome the fulfilment by Kazakstan, Ukraine and Belarus of their commitment to remove from their territory all nuclear warheads. This is an historic contribution to reducing the nuclear threat and to the creation of a common security space in Europe.

9. The OSCE's comprehensive approach to security requires improvement in the implementation of all commitments in the human dimension, in particular with respect to human rights and fundamental freedoms. This will further anchor the common values of a free and democratic society in all participating States, which is an essential foundation for our common security. Among the acute problems within the human dimension, the continuing violations of human rights, such as involuntary migration, and the lack of full democratization, threats to independent media, electoral fraud, manifestations of aggressive nationalism, racism, chauvinism, xenophobia and anti-Semitism, continue to endanger stability in the OSCE region. We are committed to continuing to address these problems.

10. Against the background of recent refugee tragedies in the OSCE region and taking into account the issue of forced migration, we again condemn and pledge to refrain from any policy of 'ethnic cleansing' or mass expulsion. Our States will facilitate the return, in safety and in dignity, of refugees and internally displaced persons, according to international standards. Their reintegration into their places of origin must be pursued without discrimination. We commend the work of the ODIHR Migration Advisor and express support for his continuing activities to follow up on the Programme of Action agreed at the May 1996 Regional Conference to address the problems of refugees, displaced persons, other forms of involuntary displacement and returnees in the relevant States.

11. Freedom of the press and media are among the basic prerequisites for truly democratic and civil societies. In the Helsinki Final Act, we have pledged ourselves to respect this principle. There is a need to strengthen the implementation of OSCE commitments in the field of the media, taking into account, as appropriate, the work of other international organizations. We therefore task the Permanent Council to consider ways to increase the focus on implementation of OSCE commitments in the field of the media, as well as to elaborate a mandate for the appointment of an OSCE representative on freedom of the media to be submitted not later than to the 1997 Ministerial Council.

12. The same comprehensive approach to security requires continued efforts in the implementation of OSCE commitments in the economic dimension and an

adequate development of OSCE activities dealing with security-related economic, social and environmental issues. The OSCE should focus on identifying the risks to security arising from economic, social and environmental problems, discussing their causes and potential consequences, and draw the attention of relevant international institutions to the need to take appropriate measures to alleviate the difficulties stemming from those risks. With this aim, the OSCE should further enhance its ties to mutually-reinforcing international economic and financial institutions, including regular consultations at appropriate levels aimed at improving the ability to identify and assess at an early stage the security relevance of economic, social and environmental developments. Interaction with regional, subregional and transborder co-operative initiatives in the economic and environmental field should be enhanced, as they contribute to the promotion of good-neighbourly relations and security. We therefore task the Permanent Council to review the role of the OSCE Secretariat in the economic dimension, and to elaborate a mandate for a co-ordinator within the OSCE Secretariat on OSCE economic and environmental activities, to be submitted not later than the 1997 Ministerial Council.

13. We pay tribute to the achievements of the OSCE Mission to Bosnia and Herzegovina in helping to implement the General Framework Agreement for Peace in Bosnia and Herzegovina. Pragmatic co-operation with international institutions and IFOR, as well as the role of the High Representative, have contributed greatly to this success, thus demonstrating in a tangible way the kinds of co-operative undertakings on which security can be built through the action of mutually reinforcing institutions.

14. We welcome the agreement by the Presidency of Bosnia and Herzegovina on the establishment of the Council of Ministers, which represents an important step in forming fully effective joint institutions. Reaffirming the need for the full implementation of the Peace Agreement, we welcome the guiding principles agreed at the Meeting of the Ministerial Steering Board and the Presidency of Bosnia and Herzegovina in Paris on 14 November 1996, and the OSCE decision to extend its Mission's mandate to Bosnia and Herzegovina for 1997, noting its possible prolongation in the framework of the two-year consolidation period. We pledge ourselves to provide all necessary resources, financial and personnel, for the Mission to fulfil its mandate.

15. The OSCE will continue to play an important role in the promotion and consolidation of peace in Bosnia and Herzegovina based on OSCE principles and commitments. We confirm that we will supervise the preparation and conduct of elections for the municipal governing authorities in 1997, and welcome the agreement of the Parties to Annex 3 of the Peace Agreement in this regard. We will fully support the Mission's work and its contribution to implementation of the election results. We will assist in democracy building through concrete programmes and be active in human rights promotion and monitoring. We will continue assisting in the implementation of subregional stabilization measures among the Parties to the Peace Agreement.

16. Recalling that the prime responsibility for implementing the Peace Agreement lies with the Parties themselves, we call upon them to co-operate in good faith with the OSCE and other institutions in implementing the civilian aspects of the Peace

Agreement. The role of the High Representative will remain of particular importance in this context. We call upon the Parties to co-operate fully with the
International Criminal Tribunal for the former Yugoslavia.

17.  The Agreement on Confidence- and Security-Building Measures in Bosnia and
Herzegovina and the Sub-Regional Arms Control Agreement will continue to play
an important role in promoting and consolidating military stability in and around
Bosnia and Herzegovina. Favourable conditions for full implementation of these
Agreements should be fostered. Failure to meet the commitments under these
Agreements remains, however, a serious concern. We support the November 1996
reaffirmation in Paris by the Ministerial Steering Board and the Presidency of
Bosnia and Herzegovina of the necessity for full implementation and strict avoidance of circumvention of both Agreements. We call upon the Parties to fulfil their
commitments through co-operation in good faith. With respect to regional arms
control, and depending on satisfactory progress on the implementation of Articles
II and IV, efforts undertaken to promote the implementation of Article V of Annex
1-B of the Peace Agreement will continue.

18.  The implementation of the Peace Agreement for Bosnia and Herzegovina has
opened the way for efforts at the regional and subregional levels aimed at the
achievement of durable peace, stability and good neighbourliness in Southeastern
Europe. We welcome the development of various initiatives fostering subregional
dialogue and co-operation, such as the Stability Process initiated at Royaumont,
the Southeastern European Co-operation Initiative, the Central European Initiative and the comprehensive process of stability, security and co-operation
reactivated by the Sofia Declaration of the Ministers of Foreign Affairs of the
countries of Southeastern Europe. The OSCE could contribute to using fully the
potential of the various regional co-operative efforts in a mutually supportive and
reinforcing way.

19.  We welcome the OSCE's continuing focus on the Federal Republic of Yugoslavia. We express our expectation that the OSCE Mission of Long Duration to
Kosovo, Sandjak and Vojvodina will be able to resume its work as soon as possible.
In fulfilling its mandate, such a Mission should actively contribute, among other
things, to following developments and fostering dialogue with a view to overcoming
the existing difficulties. Other forms of OSCE involvement would also be desirable. They should include efforts to accelerate democratization, promote
independent media and ensure free and fair elections. Recalling our previous
declarations, we call for the development of a substantial dialogue between the
Federal Authorities and the Albanian representatives of Kosovo in order to solve all
pending problems there.

20.  We reaffirm our utmost support for the sovereignty and territorial integrity of
Georgia within its internationally recognized borders. We condemn the 'ethnic
cleansing' resulting in mass destruction and forcible expulsion of predominantly
Georgian population in Abkhazia. Destructive acts of separatists, including
obstruction of the return of refugees and displaced persons and the decision to
hold elections in Abkhazia and in the Tskhinvali region/South Ossetia, undermine the positive efforts undertaken to promote political settlement of these conflicts. We are convinced that the international community, in particular the
United Nations and the OSCE with participation of the Russian Federation as a

facilitator, should continue to contribute actively to the search for a peaceful settlement.

21. We note that some progress has been made towards a political settlement in Moldova. Real political will is needed now to overcome the remaining difficulties in order to achieve a solution based on the sovereignty and territorial integrity of the Republic of Moldova. We call on all sides to increase their efforts to that end. Recalling the Budapest Summit Decision, we reiterate our concern over the lack of progress in bringing into force and implementing the Moldo-Russian Agreement of 21 October 1994 on the withdrawal of Russian troops. We expect an early, orderly and complete withdrawal of the Russian troops. In fulfilment of the mandate of the Mission and other relevant OSCE decisions, we confirm the commitment of the OSCE, including through its Mission, to follow closely the implementation of this process, as well as to assist in achieving a settlement in the eastern part of Moldova, in close co-operation with the Russian and Ukrainian mediators. The Chairman-in-Office will report on progress achieved to the next meeting of the Ministerial Council.

22. We welcome the recent steps towards a peaceful settlement in Chechnya, Russian Federation. We recognize the valuable role played by the OSCE Assistance Group in facilitating dialogue towards political resolution of the crisis. We believe that the Assistance Group should continue to play its role in the future, in particular with a view towards a lasting peaceful settlement, monitoring human rights and supporting humanitarian organizations.

23. We emphasize the importance of the Central Asian States in the OSCE. We are committed to increasing OSCE efforts aimed at developing democratic structures and the rule of law, maintaining stability and preventing conflicts in this area.

24. We are committed to further developing the dialogue with our Mediterranean partners for co-operation, Japan, and the Republic of Korea. In this context, strengthening security and co-operation in the Mediterranean is important for stability in the OSCE region. We welcome the continued interest displayed by the Mediterranean partners for co-operation, Japan, and the Republic of Korea in the OSCE, and the deepening of dialogue and co-operation with them. We invite them to participate in our activities, including meetings as appropriate.

25. The next Ministerial Council will take place in Copenhagen in December 1997.

26. We take note of the invitation by Turkey to host the next OSCE Summit in Istanbul.

27. Poland will exercise the function of Chairman-in-Office in 1998.

# PART SIX

# LATIN AMERICAN DEVELOPMENTS

---

## INTRODUCTION

LATIN AMERICA provides a store of contradictions in the field of human rights. Legal and political sophistication belongs to some of the Latin American socially elite groups, and the outcome of this sophistication is a desire to adopt legal instruments such as the American Convention on Human Rights (below, 671), which is broadly similar to the European Convention (above, 398). At the same time social conditions in nearly all of Latin America entail inequalities and deprivation on such a scale that recourse to guarantees of the classical Western political and civil rights is manifestly inadequate. Moreover, with only slow movement in the direction of general social and economic development, the position relating to civil and political rights is itself precarious. The successful use of international machinery to improve standards of government must normally depend upon the existence of a certain, reasonably uniform, level of development in the States concerned.

The position in Latin America has special features. Historically, the whole question of human rights has long been bound up with the status of aliens and their property, and powerful foreign corporations will likely continue to seek to rely on human rights standards to preserve an economic *status quo* favourable to their interests. More significant is the relation of human rights to the regional security system represented by the Organization of American States. There is abundant evidence that the concept of human rights in Latin America has been employed as a weapon against revolutionary regimes, particularly Cuba. Even so, formal adherence by governments to agreements containing guarantees of human rights helps politicians striving to improve social conditions, and will improve the possibility of reporting abuses.

For general reference, see Harris, D., & Livingstone, S. (eds.), *The Inter-American System of Human Rights* (1998); Buergenthal, T., & Shelton, D. (eds.), *Protecting Human Rights in the Americas* (4th edn., 1995); Cerna, C. M., 'The Structure and Functioning of the Inter-American Court of Human Rights (1979–1992)', (1992) 63 *BYIL* 135–229; Gros Espiell, H., 145 *Recueil des cours* (Hague Academy of International Law), 1975–II, 1–55; Buergenthal, T., 'The Revised OAS Charter', 69 *AJIL* 828–36 (1975); Medina Quiroga, C., *The Battle of Human Rights: Gross, Systematic Violations and the*

*Inter-American System* (1988); Robertson, A.H., and Merrills, J.G., *Human Rights in the World* (4th edn., 1996), 197–237; Buergenthal, T., 'The Inter-American Court of Human Rights', 76 *AJIL* 231–45 (1982).

# 78. AMERICAN DECLARATION OF THE RIGHTS AND DUTIES OF MAN, 1948

The declaration is to be found in the Final Act of the Ninth International Conference of American States, Bogotá, Colombia, held in 1948: *Acta y Documentos*, 297; O.A.S. Res. XXX, adopted by the Ninth International Conference of American States (1948), reprinted in *Basic Documents Pertaining to Human Rights in the Inter-American System*, OEA/Ser.L.V/II.82 doc.6 rev.1 at 17 (1992). It was based on a revision of a draft first prepared in 1946 by the Inter-American Juridical Committee. The Declaration was not intended to be binding, and its status was that of a recommendation of the Conference. However, in their practice the organs created in accordance with the American Convention on Human Rights (below, 671) have given a certain normative effect to the Declaration; see the decision of the Commission in the case of *Roach and Pinkerton* (27 March 1987) (General Secretariat of the OAS); and the advisory opinion of the Inter-American Court of Human Rights, 14 July 1989 (OC-10/89); Inter-American Court of Human Rights, Series A, Judgments and Opinions, No. 10.

## TEXT

*Whereas:*

The American peoples have acknowledged the dignity of the individual, and their national constitutions recognize that juridical and political institutions, which regulate life in human society, have as their principal aim the protection of the essential rights of man and the creation of circumstances that will permit him to achieve spiritual and material progress and attain happiness;

The American States have on repeated occasions recognized that the essential rights of man are not derived from the fact that he is a national of a certain State, but are based upon attributes of his human personality;

The international protection of the rights of man should be the principal guide of an evolving American law;

The affirmation of essential human rights by the American States together with the guarantees given by the internal regimes of the States establish the initial system of protection considered by the American States as being suited to the present social and juridical conditions, not without a recognition on their part that they should increasingly strengthen that system in the international field as conditions become more favorable,

The Ninth International Conference of American States

*Agrees*

To adopt the following

### Preamble

All men are born free and equal, in dignity and in rights, and, being endowed by nature with reason and conscience, they should conduct themselves as brothers one to another.

The fulfilment of duty by each individual is a prerequisite to the rights of all. Rights and duties are interrelated in every social and political activity of man. While rights exalt individual liberty, duties express the dignity of that liberty.

Duties of a juridical nature presuppose others of a moral nature which support them in principle and constitute their basis.

Inasmuch as spiritual development is the supreme end of human existence and the highest expression thereof, it is the duty of man to serve that end with all his strength and resources.

Since culture is the highest social and historical expression of that spiritual development, it is the duty of man to preserve, practise and foster culture by every means within his power.

And, since moral conduct constitutes the noblest flowering of culture, it is the duty of every man always to hold it in high respect.

# CHAPTER I

## RIGHTS

*Article* I

Every human being has the right to life, liberty and the security of his person.

*Article* II

All persons are equal before the law and have the rights and duties established in this Declaration, without distinction as to race, sex, language, creed or any other factor.

*Article* III

Every person has the right freely to profess a religious faith, and to manifest and practise it both in public and in private.

*Article* IV

Every person has the right to freedom of investigation, of opinion, and of the expression and dissemination of ideas, by any medium whatsoever.

*Article* V

Every person has the right to the protection of the law against abusive attacks upon his honor, his reputation, and his private and family life.

*Article* VI

Every person has the right to establish a family, the basic element of society, and to receive protection therefor.

*Article* VII

All women, during pregnancy and the nursing period, and all children have the right to special protection, care and aid.

*Article* VIII

Every person has the right to fix his residence within the territory of the State of which he is a national, to move about freely within such territory, and not to leave it except by his own will.

*Article* IX

Every person has the right to the inviolability of his home.

*Article* X

Every person has the right to the inviolability and transmission of his correspondence.

*Article* XI

Every person has the right to the preservation of his health through sanitary and social measures relating to food, clothing, housing and medical care, to the extent permitted by public and community resources.

*Article* XII

Every person has the right to an education, which should be based on the principles of liberty, morality and human solidarity.

Likewise every person has the right to an education that will prepare him to attain a decent life, to raise his standard of living, and to be a useful member of society.

The right to an education includes the right to equality of opportunity in every case, in accordance with natural talents, merit and the desire to utilize the resources that the State or the community is in a position to provide.

Every person has the right to receive, free, at least a primary education.

*Article* XIII

Every person has the right to take part in the cultural life of the community, to enjoy the arts, and to participate in the benefits that result from intellectual progress, especially scientific discoveries.

He likewise has the right to the protection of his moral and material interests as regards his inventions or any literary, scientific or artistic works of which he is the author.

*Article* XIV

Every person has the right to work, under proper conditions, and to follow his vocation freely, insofar as existing conditions of employment permit.

Every person who works has the right to receive such remuneration as will, in proportion to his capacity and skill, assure him a standard of living suitable for himself and for his family.

*Article* XV

Every person has the right to leisure time, to wholesome recreation, and to the opportunity for advantageous use of his free time to his spiritual, cultural and physical benefit.

*Article* XVI

Every person has the right to social security which will protect him from the consequences of unemployment, old age, and any disabilities arising from causes beyond his control that make it physically or mentally impossible for him to earn a living.

*Article* XVII

Every person has the right to be recognized everywhere as a person having rights and obligations, and to enjoy the basic civil rights.

*Article* XVIII

Every person may resort to the courts to ensure respect for his legal rights. There should likewise be available to him a simple, brief procedure whereby the courts will protect him from acts of authority that, to his prejudice, violate any fundamental constitutional rights.

*Article* XIX

Every person has the right to the nationality to which he is entitled by law and to change it, if he so wishes, for the nationality of any other country that is willing to grant it to him.

*Article* XX

Every person having legal capacity is entitled to participate in the government of his country, directly or through his representatives, and to take part in popular elections, which shall be by secret ballot, and shall be honest, periodic and free.

*Article* XXI

Every person has the right to assemble peaceably with others in a formal public meeting or an informal gathering, in connection with matters of common interest of any nature.

*Article* XXII

Every person has the right to associate with others to promote, exercise and protect his legitimate interests of a political, economic, religious, social, cultural, professional, labor-union or other nature.

*Article* XXIII

Every person has a right to own such private property as meets the essential needs of decent living and helps to maintain the dignity of the individual and of the home.

*Article* XXIV

Every person has the right to submit respectful petitions to any competent authority, for reasons of either general or private interest, and the right to obtain a prompt decision thereon.

*Article* **XXV**

No person may be deprived of his liberty except in the cases and according to the procedures established by pre-existing law.

No person may be deprived of liberty for nonfulfillment of obligations of a purely civil character.

Every individual who has been deprived of his liberty has the right to have the legality of his detention ascertained without delay by a court, and the right to be tried without undue delay or, otherwise, to be released. He also has the right to humane treatment during the time he is in custody.

*Article* **XXVI**

Every accused person is presumed to be innocent until proved guilty.

Every person accused of an offense has the right to be given an impartial and public hearing, and to be tried by courts previously established in accordance with pre- existing laws, and not to receive cruel, infamous or unusual punishment.

*Article* **XXVII**

Every person has the right, in case of pursuit not resulting from ordinary crimes, to seek and receive asylum in foreign territory, in accordance with the laws of each country and with international agreements.

*Article* **XXVIII**

The rights of man are limited by the rights of others, by the security of all, and by the just demands of the general welfare and the advancement of democracy.

# CHAPTER II

## DUTIES

*Article* **XXIX**

It is the duty of the individual so to conduct himself in relation to others that each and every one may fully form and develop his personality.

*Article* **XXX**

It is the duty of every person to aid, support, educate and protect his minor children, and it is the duty of children to honor their parents always and to aid, support and protect them when they need it.

*Article* **XXXI**

It is the duty of every person to acquire at least an elementary education.

*Article* **XXXII**

It is the duty of every person to vote in the popular elections of the country of which he is a national, when he is legally capable of doing so.

*Article* XXXIII

It is the duty of every person to obey the law and other legitimate commands of the authorities of his country and those of the country in which he may be.

*Article* XXXIV

It is the duty of every able-bodied person to render whatever civil and military service his country may require for its defense and preservation, and, in case of public disaster, to render such services as may be in his power.

It is likewise his duty to hold any public office to which he may be elected by popular vote in the State of which he is a national.

*Article* XXXV

It is the duty of every person to cooperate with the State and the community with respect to social security and welfare, in accordance with his ability and with existing circumstances.

*Article* XXXVI

It is the duty of every person to pay the taxes established by law for the support of public services.

*Article* XXXVII

It is the duty of every person to work, as far as his capacity and possibilities permit, in order to obtain the means of livelihood or to benefit his community.

*Article* XXXVIII

It is the duty of every person to refrain from taking part in political activities that, according to law, are reserved exclusively to the citizens of the State in which he is an alien.

## 79. AMERICAN CONVENTION ON HUMAN RIGHTS, 1969

The Bogotá Conference of 1948 had expressed a tentative interest in a proposal that an Inter-American Court be created to guarantee the basic rights of man, but no further development occurred until the Fifth Meeting of Consultation of Ministers of Foreign Affairs at Santiago, Chile, in 1959. The meeting resolved that the Inter-American Council of Jurists should prepare a draft Convention on Human Rights and that a convention should also be prepared on the creation of an Inter-American Court for the Protection of Human Rights.

The same meeting decided that an Inter-American Commission on Human Rights should be organized. The Commission came into being in 1960 as 'an autonomous entity of the Organization of American States, the function of which is to promote respect for human rights'. For the text of the statute, see Inter-American Institute of International Legal Studies, *The Inter-American System* (1966), 372; Buergenthal, T., 'The Revised OAS Charter', 69 *AJIL* 828–36 (1975); Tardu, M. E., 'The Protocol to the United Nations Covenant on Civil and Political Rights and the Inter-American System: A Study of Co-existing Petition Procedures', 70 *AJIL* 778–800 (1976). The Inter-American Commission acquired an enhanced status after the entry into force of the revised OAS Charter in 1970.

The culmination of Latin American interest in human rights was the Inter-American Specialized Conference on Human Rights held at San José, Costa Rica, 7–22 November 1969. The American Convention on Human Rights was signed on 22 November 1969 by the following States: Chile, Colombia, Costa Rica, El Salvador, Ecuador, Guatemala, Honduras, Nicaragua, Panama, Paraguay, Uruguay, and Venezuela; for text, see OAS *Official Records*, OEA/Ser.K/XVI/1/1. The Convention provides for a Commission and a Court, and bears a general resemblance to the European Convention, above. However, there are significant differences, for example, in the powers of the Commission, which are both broad and vague in the American Convention. The Commission created by the provisions of the Convention coincides with the pre-existing Inter-American Commission except that the Commission retains its previous powers in respect of States which did not ratify the new Convention: see Robertson, A.H. and Merrills, J.G., *Human Rights in the World* (4th edn., 1996), 197–237.

The American Convention entered into force on 18 July 1978, and the Inter-American Court of Human Rights was inaugurated on 3 September 1979. The seat of the Court is at San José, Costa Rica.

## TEXT

### Preamble

*The American States signatory to the present Convention,*

*Reaffirming* their intention to consolidate in this hemisphere, within the framework of democratic institutions, a system of personal liberty and social justice based on respect for the essential rights of man;

*Recognizing* that the essential rights of man are not derived from one's being a national of a certain State, but are based upon attributes of the human personality, and that they therefore justify international protection in the form of a convention reinforcing or complementing the protection provided by the domestic law of the American States;

*Considering* that these principles have been set forth in the Charter of the Organization of American States, in the American Declaration of the Rights and Duties of Man, and in the Universal Declaration of Human Rights, and that they have been reaffirmed and refined in other international instruments, worldwide as well as regional in scope;

*Reiterating* that, in accordance with the Universal Declaration of Human Rights, the ideal of free men enjoying freedom from fear and want can be achieved only if conditions are created whereby everyone may enjoy his economic, social, and cultural rights, as well as his civil and political rights; and

*Considering* that the Third Special Inter-American Conference (Buenos Aires, 1967) approved the incorporation into the Charter of the Organization itself of broader standards with respect to economic, social, and educational rights and resolved that an inter-American convention on human rights should determine the structure, competence, and procedure of the organs responsible for these matters,

*Have agreed* upon the following:

# PART I

## STATE OBLIGATIONS AND RIGHTS PROTECTED
### Chapter I—General Obligations

*Article 1—Obligation to Respect Rights*

1. The States Parties to this Convention undertake to respect the rights and freedoms recognized herein and to ensure to all persons subject to their jurisdiction the free and full exercise of those rights and freedoms, without any discrimination for reasons of race, color, sex, language, religion, political or other opinion, national or social origin, economic status, birth, or any other social condition.

2. For the purposes of this Convention, 'person' means every human being.

*Article 2—Domestic Legal Effects*

Where the exercise of any of the rights or freedoms referred to in Article 1 is not already ensured by legislative or other provisions, the States Parties undertake to adopt, in accordance with their constitutional processes and the provisions of this Convention, such legislative or other measures as may be necessary to give effect to those rights or freedoms.

### Chapter II—Civil and Political Rights

*Article 3—Right to Juridical Personality*

Every person has the right to recognition as a person before the law.

*Article 4—Right to Life*

1. Every person has the right to have his life respected. This right shall be protected by law and, in general, from the moment of conception. No one shall be arbitrarily deprived of his life.

2. In countries that have not abolished the death penalty, it may be imposed only for the most serious crimes and pursuant to a final judgment rendered by a competent court and in accordance with a law establishing such punishment, enacted prior to the commission of the crime. The application of such punishment shall not be extended to crimes to which it does not presently apply.

3. The death penalty shall not be re-established in States that have abolished it.

4. In no case shall capital punishment be inflicted for political offenses or related common crimes.

5. Capital punishment shall not be imposed upon persons who, at the time the crime was committed, were under 18 years of age or over 70 years of age; nor shall it be applied to pregnant women.

6. Every person condemned to death shall have the right to apply for amnesty, pardon, or commutation of sentence, which may be granted in all cases. Capital punishment shall not be imposed while such a petition is pending decision by the competent authority.

### Article 5—Right to Humane Treatment

1. Every person has the right to have his physical, mental, and moral integrity respected.

2. No one shall be subjected to torture or to cruel, inhuman, or degrading punishment or treatment. All persons deprived of their liberty shall be treated with respect for the inherent dignity of the human person.

3. Punishment shall not be extended to any person other than the criminal.

4. Accused persons shall, save in exceptional circumstances, be segregated from convicted persons, and shall be subject to separate treatment appropriate to their status as unconvicted persons.

5. Minors while subject to criminal proceedings shall be separated from adults and brought before specialized tribunals, as speedily as possible, so that they may be treated in accordance with their status as minors.

6. Punishments consisting of deprivation of liberty shall have as an essential aim the reform and social readaptation of the prisoners.

### Article 6—Freedom from Slavery

1. No one shall be subject to slavery or to involuntary servitude, which are prohibited in all their forms, as are the slave trade and traffic in women.

2. No one shall be required to perform forced or compulsory labor. This provision shall not be interpreted to mean that, in those countries in which the penalty established for certain crimes is deprivation of liberty at forced labor, the carrying out of such a sentence imposed by a competent court is prohibited. Forced labor shall not adversely affect the dignity or the physical or intellectual capacity of the prisoner.

3. For the purposes of this article, the following do not constitute forced or compulsory labor:

   (a) work or service normally required of a person imprisoned in execution of a sentence or formal decision passed by the competent judicial authority. Such work or service shall be carried out under the supervision and control of public authorities, and any persons performing such work or service shall not be placed at the disposal of any private party, company, or juridical person;

*(b)* military service and, in countries in which conscientious objectors are recognized, national service that the law may provide for in lieu of military service;

*(c)* service exacted in time of danger or calamity that threatens the existence or the well-being of the community; or

*(d)* work or service that forms part of normal civic obligations.

### Article 7—*Right to Personal Liberty*

1. Every person has the right to personal liberty and security.

2. No one shall be deprived of his physical liberty except for the reasons and under the conditions established beforehand by the constitution of the State Party concerned or by a law established pursuant thereto.

3. No one shall be subject to arbitrary arrest or imprisonment.

4. Anyone who is detained shall be informed of the reasons for his detention and shall be promptly notified of the charge or charges against him.

5. Any person detained shall be brought promptly before a judge or other officer authorized by law to exercise judicial power and shall be entitled to trial within a reasonable time or to be released without prejudice to the continuation of the proceedings. His release may be subject to guarantees to assure his appearance for trial.

6. Anyone who is deprived of his liberty shall be entitled to recourse to a competent court, in order that the court may decide without delay on the lawfulness of his arrest or detention and order his release if the arrest or detention is unlawful. In States Parties whose laws provide that anyone who believes himself to be threatened with deprivation of his liberty is entitled to recourse to a competent court in order that it may decide on the lawfulness of such threat, this remedy may not be restricted or abolished. The interested party or another person in his behalf is entitled to seek these remedies.

7. No one shall be detained for debt. This principle shall not limit the orders of a competent judicial authority issued for nonfulfillment of duties of support.

### Article 8—*Right to a Fair Trial*

1. Every person has the right to a hearing, with due guarantees and within a reasonable time, by a competent, independent, and impartial tribunal, previously established by law, in the substantiation of any accusation of a criminal nature made against him or for the determination of his rights and obligations of a civil, labor, fiscal, or any other nature.

2. Every person accused of a criminal offense has the right to be presumed innocent so long as his guilt has not been proven according to law. During the proceedings, every person is entitled, with full equality, to the following minimum guarantees:

*(a)* the right of the accused to be assisted without charge by a translator or

interpreter, if he does not understand or does not speak the language of the tribunal or court;

(b) prior notification in detail to the accused of the charges against him;

(c) adequate time and means for the preparation of his defense;

(d) the right of the accused to defend himself personally or to be assisted by legal counsel of his own choosing, and to communicate freely and privately with his counsel;

(e) the inalienable right to be assisted by counsel provided by the State, paid or not as the domestic law provides, if the accused does not defend himself personally or engage his own counsel within the time period established by law;

(f) the right of the defense to examine witnesses present in the court and to obtain the appearance, as witnesses, of experts or other persons who may throw light on the facts;

(g) the right not to be compelled to be a witness against himself or to plead guilty; and

(h) the right to appeal the judgment to a higher court.

3. A confession of guilt by the accused shall be valid only if it is made without coercion of any kind.

4. An accused person acquitted by a nonappealable judgment shall not be subjected to a new trial for the same cause.

5. Criminal proceedings shall be public, except insofar as may be necessary to protect the interests of justice.

### Article 9—*Freedom from Ex Post Facto Laws*

No one shall be convicted of any act or omission that did not constitute a criminal offense, under the applicable law, at the time it was committed. A heavier penalty shall not be imposed than the one that was applicable at the time the criminal offense was committed. If subsequent to the commission of the offense the law provides for the imposition of a lighter punishment, the guilty person shall benefit therefrom.

### Article 10—*Right to Compensation*

Every person has the right to be compensated in accordance with the law in the event he has been sentenced by a final judgment through a miscarriage of justice.

### Article 11—*Right to Privacy*

1. Everyone has the right to have his honor respected and his dignity recognized.

2. No one may be the object of arbitrary or abusive interference with his private life, his family, his home, or his correspondence, or of unlawful attacks on his honor or reputation.

3. Everyone has the right to the protection of the law against such interference or attacks.

*Article* 12—*Freedom of Conscience and Religion*

1. Everyone has the right to freedom of conscience and of religion. This right includes freedom to maintain or to change one's religion or beliefs, and freedom to profess or disseminate one's religion or beliefs, either individually or together with others, in public or in private.

2. No one shall be subject to restrictions that might impair his freedom to maintain or to change his religion or beliefs.

3. Freedom to manifest one's religion and beliefs may be subject only to the limitations prescribed by law that are necessary to protect public safety, order, health, or morals, or the rights or freedoms of others.

4. Parents or guardians, as the case may be, have the right to provide for the religious and moral education of their children or wards that is in accord with their own convictions.

*Article* 13—*Freedom of Thought and Expression*

1. Everyone has the right to freedom of thought and expression. This right includes freedom to seek, receive, and impart information and ideas of all kinds, regardless of frontiers, either orally, in writing, in print, in the form of art, or through any other medium of one's choice.

2. The exercise of the right provided for in the foregoing paragraph shall not be subject to prior censorship but shall be subject to subsequent imposition of liability, which shall be expressly established by law to the extent necessary to ensure:

    *(a)* respect for the rights or reputations of others; or

    *(b)* the protection of national security, public order, or public health or morals.

3. The right of expression may not be restricted by indirect methods or means, such as the abuse of government or private controls over newsprint, radio broadcasting frequencies, or equipment used in the dissemination of information, or by any other means tending to impede the communication and circulation of ideas and opinions.

4. Notwithstanding the provisions of paragraph 2 above, public entertainments may be subject by law to prior censorship for the sole purpose of regulating access to them for the moral protection of childhood and adolescence.

5. Any propaganda for war and any advocacy of national, racial, or religious hatred that constitute incitements to lawless violence or to any other similar action against any person or group of persons on any grounds including those of race, color, religion, language, or national origin shall be considered as offenses punishable by law.

*Article* 14—*Right of Reply*

1. Anyone injured by inaccurate or offensive statements or ideas disseminated to the public in general by a legally regulated medium of communication has the right to reply or to make a correction using the same communications outlet, under such conditions as the law may establish.

2. The correction or reply shall not in any case remit other legal liabilities that may have been incurred.

3. For the effective protection of honor and reputation, every publisher, and every newspaper, motion picture, radio, and television company, shall have a person responsible who is not protected by immunities or special privileges.

### Article 15—Right of Assembly

The right of peaceful assembly, without arms, is recognized. No restrictions may be placed on the exercise of this right other than those imposed in conformity with the law and necessary in a democratic society in the interest of national security, public safety or public order, or to protect public health or morals or the rights or freedom of others.

### Article 16—Freedom of Association

1. Everyone has the right to associate freely for ideological, religious, political, economic, labor, social, cultural, sports, or other purposes.

2. The exercise of this right shall be subject only to such restrictions established by law as may be necessary in a democratic society, in the interest of national security, public safety or public order, or to protect public health or morals or the rights and freedoms of others.

3. The provisions of this article do not bar the imposition of legal restrictions, including even deprivation of the exercise of the right of association, on members of the armed forces and the police.

### Article 17—Rights of the Family

1. The family is the natural and fundamental group unit of society and is entitled to protection by society and the state.

2. The right of men and women of marriageable age to marry and to raise a family shall be recognized, if they meet the conditions required by domestic laws, insofar as such conditions do not affect the principle of nondiscrimination established in this Convention.

3. No marriage shall be entered into without the free and full consent of the intending spouses.

4. The States Parties shall take appropriate steps to ensure the equality of rights and the adequate balancing of responsibilities of the spouses as to marriage, during marriage, and in the event of its dissolution. In case of dissolution, provision shall be made for the necessary protection of any children solely on the basis of their own best interests.

5. The law shall recognize equal rights for children born out of wedlock and those born in wedlock.

### Article 18—Right to a Name

Every person has the right to a given name and to the surnames of his parents or that of one of them. The law shall regulate the manner in which this right shall be ensured for all, by the use of assumed names if necessary.

### Article 19—Rights of the Child

Every minor child has the right to the measures of protection required by his condition as a minor on the part of his family, society, and the State.

*Article 20—Right to Nationality*

1. Every person has the right to a nationality.

2. Every person has the right to the nationality of the State in whose territory he was born if he does not have the right to any other nationality.

3. No one shall be arbitrarily deprived of his nationality or of the right to change it.

*Article 21—Right to Property*

1. Everyone has the right to the use and enjoyment of his property. The law may subordinate such use and enjoyment to the interest of society.

2. No one shall be deprived of his property except upon payment of just compensation, for reasons of public utility or social interest, and in the cases and according to the forms established by law.

3. Usury and any other form of exploitation of man by man shall be prohibited by law.

*Article 22—Freedom of Movement and Residence*

1. Every person lawfully in the territory of a State Party has the right to move about in it, and to reside in it subject to the provisions of the law.

2. Every person has the right lo leave any country freely, including his own.

3. The exercise of the foregoing rights may be restricted only pursuant to a law to the extent necessary in a democratic society to prevent crime or to protect national security, public safety, public order, public morals, public health, or the rights or freedoms of others.

4. The exercise of the rights recognized in paragraph 1 may also be restricted by law in designated zones for reasons of public interest.

5. No one can be expelled from the territory of the State of which he is a national or be deprived of the right to enter it.

6. An alien lawfully in the territory of a State Party to this Convention may be expelled from it only pursuant to a decision reached in accordance with law.

7. Every person has the right to seek and be granted asylum in a foreign territory, in accordance with the legislation of the State and international conventions, in the event he is being pursued for political offenses or related common crimes.

8. In no case may an alien be deported or returned to a country, regardless of whether or not it is his country of origin, if in that country his right to life or personal freedom is in danger of being violated because of his race, nationality, religion, social status, or political opinions.

9. The collective expulsion of aliens is prohibited.

*Article 23—Right to Participate in Government*

1. Every citizen shall enjoy the following rights and opportunities:

    *(a)* to take part in the conduct of public affairs, directly or through freely chosen representatives;

    *(b)* to vote and to be elected in genuine periodic elections, which shall be by

universal and equal suffrage and by secret ballot that guarantees the free expression of the will of the voters; and

(c) to have access, under general conditions of equality, to the public service of his country.

2. The law may regulate the exercise of the rights and opportunities referred to in the preceding paragraph only on the basis of age, nationality, residence, language, education, civil and mental capacity, or sentencing by a competent court in criminal proceedings.

### Article 24—Right to Equal Protection

All persons are equal before the law. Consequently, they are entitled, without discrimination, to equal protection of the law.

### Article 25—Right to Judicial Protection

1. Everyone has the right to simple and prompt recourse, or any other effective recourse, to a competent court or tribunal for protection against acts that violate his fundamental rights recognized by the constitution or laws of the State concerned or by this Convention, even though such violation may have been committed by persons acting in the course of their official duties.

2. The States Parties undertake:

(a) to ensure that any person claiming such remedy shall have his rights determined by the competent authority provided for by the legal system of the state;

(b) to develop the possibilities of judicial remedy; and

(c) to ensure that the competent authorities shall enforce such remedies when granted.

## Chapter III—Economic, Social, and Cultural Rights

### Article 26—Progressive Development

The States Parties undertake to adopt measures, both internally and through international cooperation, especially those of an economic and technical nature, with a view to achieving progressively, by legislation or other appropriate means, the full realization of the rights implicit in the economic, social, educational, scientific, and cultural standards set forth in the Charter of the Organization of American States as amended by the Protocol of Buenos Aires.

## Chapter IV—Suspension of Guarantees, Interpretation, and Application

### Article 27—Suspension of Guarantees

1. In time of war, public danger, or other emergency that threatens the independence or security of a State Party, it may take measures derogating from its obligations under the present Convention to the extent and for the period of time strictly required by the exigencies of the situation, provided that such measures are not

inconsistent with its other obligations under international law and do not involve discrimination on the ground of race, color, sex, language, religion, or social origin.

2. The foregoing provision does not authorize any suspension of the following articles: Article 3 (Right to Juridical Personality), Article 4 (Right to Life), Article 5 (Right to Humane Treatment), Article 6 (Freedom from Slavery), Article 9 (Freedom from Ex Post Facto Laws), Article 12 (Freedom of Conscience and Religion), Article 17 (Rights of the Family), Article 18 (Right to a Name), Article 19 (Rights of the Child), Article 20 (Right to Nationality), and Article 23 (Right to Participate in Government), or of the judicial guarantees essential for the protection of such rights.

3. Any State Party availing itself of the right of suspension shall immediately inform the other States Parties, through the Secretary General of the Organization of American States, of the provisions the application of which it has suspended, the reasons that gave rise to the suspension, and the date set for the termination of such suspension.

*Article 28—Federal Clause*

1. Where a State Party is constituted as a federal State, the national government of such State Party shall implement all the provisions of the Convention over whose subject matter it exercises legislative and judicial jurisdiction.

2. With respect to the provisions over whose subject matter the constituent units of the federal State have jurisdiction, the national government shall immediately take suitable measures, in accordance with its constitution and its laws, to the end that the competent authorities of the constituent units may adopt appropriate provisions for the fulfillment of this Convention.

3. Whenever two or more States Parties agree to form a federation or other type of association, they shall take care that the resulting federal or other compact contains the provisions necessary for continuing and rendering effective the standards of this Convention in the new State that is organized.

*Article 29—Restrictions Regarding Interpretation*

No provision of this Convention shall be interpreted as:

  (a) permitting any State Party, group, or person to suppress the enjoyment or exercise of the rights and freedoms recognized in this Convention or to restrict them to a greater extent than is provided for herein;

  (b) restricting the enjoyment or exercise of any right or freedom recognized by virtue of the laws of any State Party or by virtue of another convention to which one of the said States is a party;

  (c) precluding other rights or guarantees that are inherent in the human personality or derived from representative democracy as a form of government; or

  (d) excluding or limiting the effect that the American Declaration of the Rights and Duties of Man and other international acts of the same nature may have.

*Article 30—Scope of Restrictions*

The restrictions that, pursuant to this Convention, may be placed on the enjoyment or exercise of the rights or freedoms recognized herein may not be applied except in accordance with laws enacted for reasons of general interest and in accordance with the purpose for which such restrictions have been established.

*Article 31—Recognition of Other Rights*

Other rights and freedoms recognized in accordance with the procedures established in Articles 76 and 77 may be included in the system of protection of this Convention.

## Chapter V—Personal Responsibilities

*Article 32—Relationship between Duties and Rights*

1. Every person has responsibilities to his family, his community, and mankind.

2. The rights of each person are limited by the rights of others, by the security of all, and by the just demands of the general welfare, in a democratic society.

# PART II

# MEANS OF PROTECTION
## Chapter VI—Competent Organs

*Article 33*

The following organs shall have competence with respect to matters relating to the fulfillment of the commitments made by the States Parties to this Convention:

(a) the Inter-American Commission on Human Rights, referred to as 'The Commission;' and

(b) the Inter-American Court of Human Rights, referred to as 'The Court.'

## Chapter VII—Inter-American Commission on Human Rights

*Section 1. Organization*

*Article 34*

The Inter-American Commission on Human Rights shall be composed of seven members, who shall be persons of high moral character and recognized competence in the field of human rights.

*Article 35*

The Commission shall represent all the member countries of the Organization of American States.

*Article 36*

1. The members of the Commission shall be elected in a personal capacity by the General Assembly of the Organization from a list of candidates proposed by the governments of the member States.

2. Each of those governments may propose up to three candidates, who may be nationals of the States proposing them or of any other member state of the Organization of American States. When a slate of three is proposed, at least one of the candidates shall be a national of a State other than the one proposing the slate.

*Article 37*

1. The members of the Commission shall be elected for a term of four years and may be reelected only once, but the terms of three of the members chosen in the first election shall expire at the end of two years. Immediately following that election the General Assembly shall determine the names of those three members by lot.

2. No two nationals of the same State may be members of the Commission.

*Article 38*

Vacancies that may occur on the Commission for reasons other than the normal expiration of a term shall be filled by the Permanent Council of the Organization in accordance with the provisions of the Statute of the Commission.

*Article 39*

The Commission shall prepare its Statute, which it shall submit to the General Assembly for approval. It shall establish its own Regulations.

*Article 40*

Secretariat services for the Commission shall be furnished by the appropriate specialized unit of the General Secretariat of the Organization. This unit shall be provided with the resources required to accomplish the tasks assigned to it by the Commission.

*Section 2. Functions*

*Article 41*

The main function of the Commission shall be to promote respect for and defense of human rights. In the exercise of its mandate, it shall have the following functions and powers:

   *(a)* to develop an awareness of human rights among the peoples of America;

   *(b)* to make recommendations to the governments of the member States, when it considers such action advisable, for the adoption of progressive measures in favor of human rights within the framework of their domestic law and constitutional provisions as well as appropriate measures to further the observance of those rights;

   *(c)* to prepare such studies or reports as it considers advisable in the performance of its duties;

   *(d)* to request the governments of the member States to supply it with information on the measures adopted by them in matters of human rights;

   *(e)* to respond, through the General Secretariat of the Organization of American States, to inquiries made by the member States on matters related to

human rights and, within the limits of its possibilities, to provide those States with the advisory services they request;

(f) to take action on petitions and other communications pursuant to its authority under the provisions of Articles 44 through 51 of this Convention; and

(g) to submit an annual report to the General Assembly of the Organization of American States.

### Article 42

The States Parties shall transmit to the Commission a copy of each of the reports and studies that they submit annually to the Executive Committees of the Inter-American Economic and Social Council and the Inter-American Council for Education, Science, and Culture, in their respective fields, so that the Commission may watch over the promotion of the rights implicit in the economic, social, educational, scientific, and cultural standards set forth in the Charter of the Organization of American States as amended by the Protocol of Buenos Aires.

### Article 43

The States Parties undertake to provide the Commission with such information as it may request of them as to the manner in which their domestic law ensures the effective application of any provisions of this Convention.

*Section 3. Competence*

### Article 44

Any person or group of persons, or any nongovernmental entity legally recognized in one or more member States of the Organization, may lodge petitions with the Commission containing denunciations or complaints of violation of this Convention by a State Party.

### Article 45

1. Any State Party may, when it deposits its instrument of ratification of or adherence to this Convention, or at any later time, declare that it recognizes the competence of the Commission to receive and examine communications in which a State Party alleges that another State Party has committed a violation of a human right set forth in this Convention.

2. Communications presented by virtue of this article may be admitted and examined only if they are presented by a State Party that has made a declaration recognizing the aforementioned competence of the Commission. The Commission shall not admit any communication against a State Party that has not made such a declaration.

3. A declaration concerning recognition of competence may be made to be valid for an indefinite time, for a specified period, or for a specific case.

4. Declarations shall be deposited with the General Secretariat of the Organization of American States, which shall transmit copies thereof to the member States of that Organization.

*Article* 46

1. Admission by the Commission of a petition or communication lodged in accordance with Articles 44 or 45 shall be subject to the following requirements:

    *(a)* that the remedies under domestic law have been pursued and exhausted in accordance with generally recognized principles of international law;

    *(b)* that the petition or communication is lodged within a period of six months from the date on which the party alleging violation of his rights was notified of the final judgment;

    *(c)* that the subject of the petition or communication is not pending in another international proceeding for settlement; and

    *(d)* that, in the case of Article 44, the petition contains the name, nationality, profession, domicile, and signature of the person or persons or of the legal representative of the entity lodging the petition.

2. The provisions of paragraphs 1.a and 1.b of this article shall not be applicable when:

    *(a)* the domestic legislation of the State concerned does not afford due process of law for the protection of the right or rights that have allegedly been violated;

    *(b)* the party alleging violation of his rights has been denied access to the remedies under domestic law or has been prevented from exhausting them; or

    *(c)* there has been unwarranted delay in rendering a final judgment under the aforementioned remedies.

*Article* 47

The Commission shall consider inadmissible any petition or communication submitted under Articles 44 or 45 if:

    *(a)* any of the requirements indicated in Article 46 has not been met;

    *(b)* the petition or communication does not state facts that tend to establish a violation of the rights guaranteed by this Convention;

    *(c)* the statements of the petitioner or of the State indicate that the petition or communication is manifestly groundless or obviously out of order; or

    *(d)* the petition or communication is substantially the same as one previously studied by the Commission or by another international organization.

*Section 4. Procedure*

*Article* 48

1. When the Commission receives a petition or communication alleging violation of any of the rights protected by this Convention, it shall proceed as follows:

    *(a)* If it considers the petition or communication admissible, it shall request information from the government of the State indicated as being responsible for the alleged violations and shall furnish that government a transcript of the pertinent portions of the petition or communication. This information

shall be submitted within a reasonable period to be determined by the Commission in accordance with the circumstances of each case.

(b) After the information has been received, or after the period established has elapsed and the information has not been received, the Commission shall ascertain whether the grounds for the petition or communication still exist. If they do not, the Commission shall order the record to be closed.

(c) The Commission may also declare the petition or communication inadmissible or out of order on the basis of information or evidence subsequently received.

(d) If the record has not been closed, the Commission shall, with the knowledge of the parties, examine the matter set forth in the petition or communication in order to verify the facts. If necessary and advisable, the Commission shall carry out an investigation, for the effective conduct of which it shall request, and the States concerned shall furnish to it, all necessary facilities.

(e) The Commission may request the States concerned to furnish any pertinent information and, if so requested, shall hear oral statements or receive written statements from the parties concerned.

(f) The Commission shall place itself at the disposal of the parties concerned with a view to reaching a friendly settlement of the matter on the basis of respect for the human rights recognized in this Convention.

2. However, in serious and urgent cases, only the presentation of a petition or communication that fulfills all the formal requirements of admissibility shall be necessary in order for the Commission to conduct an investigation with the prior consent of the State in whose territory a violation has allegedly been committed.

*Article* 49

If a friendly settlement has been reached in accordance with paragraph 1 (f) of Article 48, the Commission shall draw up a report, which shall be transmitted to the petitioner and to the States Parties to this Convention, and shall then be communicated to the Secretary General of the Organization of American States for publication. This report shall contain a brief statement of the facts and of the solution reached. If any party in the case so requests, the fullest possible information shall be provided to it.

*Article* 50

1. If a settlement is not reached, the Commission shall, within the time limit established by its Statute, draw up a report setting forth the facts and stating its conclusions. If the report, in whole or in part, does not represent the unanimous agreement of the members of the Commission, any member may attach to it a separate opinion. The written and oral statements made by the parties in accordance with paragraph 1 (e) of Article 48 shall also be attached to the report.

2. The report shall be transmitted to the States concerned, which shall not be at liberty to publish it.

3. In transmitting the report, the Commission may make such proposals and recommendations as it sees fit.

*Article* 51

1. If, within a period of three months from the date of the transmittal of the report of the Commission to the States concerned, the matter has not either been settled or submitted by the Commission or by the State concerned to the Court and its jurisdiction accepted, the Commission may, by the vote of an absolute majority of its members, set forth its opinion and conclusions concerning the question submitted for its consideration.

2. Where appropriate, the Commission shall make pertinent recommendations and shall prescribe a period within which the State is to take the measures that are incumbent upon it to remedy the situation examined.

3. When the prescribed period has expired, the Commission shall decide by the vote of an absolute majority of its members whether the State has taken adequate measures and whether to publish its report.

## Chapter VIII—Inter-American Court of Human Rights

### *Section 1. Organization*

*Article* 52

1. The Court shall consist of seven judges, nationals of the member States of the Organization, elected in an individual capacity from among jurists of the highest moral authority and of recognized competence in the field of human rights, who possess the qualifications required for the exercise of the highest judicial functions in conformity with the law of the State of which they are nationals or of the State that proposes them as candidates.

2. No two judges may be nationals of the same State.

*Article* 53

1. The judges of the Court shall be elected by secret ballot by an absolute majority vote of the States Parties to the Convention, in the General Assembly of the Organization, from a panel of candidates proposed by those States.

2. Each of the States Parties may propose up to three candidates, nationals of the State that proposes them or of any other member State of the Organization of American States. When a slate of three is proposed, at least one of the candidates shall be a national of a State other than the one proposing the slate.

*Article* 54

1. The judges of the Court shall be elected for a term of six years and may be reelected only once. The term of three of the judges chosen in the first election shall expire at the end of three years. Immediately after the election, the names of the three judges shall be determined by lot in the General Assembly.

2. A judge elected to replace a judge whose term has not expired shall complete the term of the latter.

3. The judges shall continue in office until the expiration of their term. However, they shall continue to serve with regard to cases that they have begun to hear and

that are still pending, for which purposes they shall not be replaced by the newly elected judges.

*Article 55*

1. If a judge is a national of any of the States Parties to a case submitted to the Court, he shall retain his right to hear that case.

2. If one of the judges called upon to hear a case should be a national of one of the States Parties to the case, any other State Party in the case may appoint a person of its choice to serve on the Court as an *ad hoc* judge.

3. If among the judges called upon to hear a case none is a national of any of the States Parties to the case, each of the latter may appoint an *ad hoc* judge.

4. An *ad hoc* judge shall possess the qualifications indicated in Article 52.

5. If several States Parties to the Convention should have the same interest in a case, they shall be considered as a single party for purposes of the above provisions. In case of doubt, the Court shall decide.

*Article 56*

Five judges shall constitute a quorum for the transaction of business by the Court.

*Article 57*

The Commission shall appear in all cases before the Court.

*Article 58*

1. The Court shall have its seat at the place determined by the States Parties to the Convention in the General Assembly of the Organization; however, it may convene in the territory of any member State of the Organization of American States when a majority of the Court considers it desirable, and with the prior consent of the State concerned. The seat of the Court may be changed by the States Parties to the Convention in the General Assembly by a two-thirds vote.

2. The Court shall appoint its own Secretary.

3. The Secretary shall have his office at the place where the Court has its seat and shall attend the meetings that the Court may hold away from its seat.

*Article 59*

The Court shall establish its Secretariat, which shall function under the direction of the Secretary of the Court, in accordance with the administrative standards of the General Secretariat of the Organization in all respects not incompatible with the independence of the Court. The staff of the Court's Secretariat shall be appointed by the Secretary General of the Organization, in consultation with the Secretary of the Court.

*Article 60*

The Court shall draw up its Statute which it shall submit to the General Assembly for approval. It shall adopt its own Rules of Procedure.

*Section 2. Jurisdiction and Functions*

*Article 61*

1. Only the States Parties and the Commission shall have the right to submit a case to the Court.

2. In order for the Court to hear a case, it is necessary that the procedures set forth in Articles 48 and 50 shall have been completed.

*Article 62*

1. A State Party may, upon depositing its instrument of ratification or adherence to this Convention, or at any subsequent time, declare that it recognizes as binding, *ipso facto*, and not requiring special agreement, the jurisdiction of the Court on all matters relating to the interpretation or application of this Convention.

2. Such declaration may be made unconditionally, on the condition of reciprocity, for a specified period, or for specific cases. It shall be presented to the Secretary General of the Organization, who shall transmit copies thereof to the other member states of the Organization and to the Secretary of the Court.

3. The jurisdiction of the Court shall comprise all cases concerning the interpretation and application of the provisions of this Convention that are submitted to it, provided that the States Parties to the case recognize or have recognized such jurisdiction, whether by special declaration pursuant to the preceding paragraphs, or by a special agreement.

*Article 63*

1. If the Court finds that there has been a violation of a right or freedom protected by this Convention, the Court shall rule that the injured party be ensured the enjoyment of his right or freedom that was violated. It shall also rule, if appropriate, that the consequences of the measure or situation that constituted the breach of such right or freedom be remedied and that fair compensation be paid to the injured party.

2. In cases of extreme gravity and urgency, and when necessary to avoid irreparable damage to persons, the Court shall adopt such provisional measures as it deems pertinent in matters it has under consideration. With respect to a case not yet submitted to the Court, it may act at the request of the Commission.

*Article 64*

1. The member States of the Organization may consult the Court regarding the interpretation of this Convention or of other treaties concerning the protection of human rights in the American States. Within their spheres of competence, the organs listed in Chapter X of the Charter of the Organization of American States, as amended by the Protocol of Buenos Aires, may in like manner consult the Court.

2. The Court, at the request of a member State of the Organization, may provide that State with opinions regarding the compatibility of any of its domestic laws with the aforesaid international instruments.

*Article* 65

To each regular session of the General Assembly of the Organization of American States the Court shall submit, for the Assembly's consideration, a report on its work during the previous year. It shall specify, in particular, the cases in which a State has not complied with its judgments, making any pertinent recommendations.

*Section 3. Procedure*

*Article* 66

1. Reasons shall be given for the judgment of the Court.

2. If the judgment does not represent in whole or in part the unanimous opinion of the judges, any judge shall be entitled to have his dissenting or separate opinion attached to the judgment.

*Article* 67

The judgment of the Court shall be final and not subject to appeal. In case of disagreement as to the meaning or scope of the judgment, the Court shall interpret it at the request of any of the parties, provided the request is made within ninety days from the date of notification of the judgment.

*Article* 68

1. The States Parties to the Convention undertake to comply with the judgment of the Court in any case to which they are parties.

2. That part of a judgment that stipulates compensatory damages may be executed in the country concerned in accordance with domestic procedure governing the execution of judgments against the State.

*Article* 69

The parties to the case shall be notified of the judgment of the Court and it shall be transmitted to the States Parties to the Convention.

Chapter IX—Common Provisions

*Article* 70

1. The judges of the Court and the members of the Commission shall enjoy, from the moment of their election and throughout their term of office, the immunities extended to diplomatic agents in accordance with international law. During the exercise of their official function they shall, in addition, enjoy the diplomatic privileges necessary for the performance of their duties.

2. At no time shall the judges of the Court or the members of the Commission be held liable for any decisions or opinions issued in the exercise of their functions.

*Article* 71

The position of judge of the Court or member of the Commission is incompatible with any other activity that might affect the independence or impartiality of such judge or member, as determined in the respective statutes.

*Article* 72

The judges of the Court and the members of the Commission shall receive emoluments and travel allowances in the form and under the conditions set forth in their statutes, with due regard for the importance and independence of their office. Such emoluments and travel allowances shall be determined in the budget of the Organization of American States, which shall also include the expenses of the Court and its Secretariat. To this end, the Court shall draw up its own budget and submit it for approval to the General Assembly through the General Secretariat. The latter may not introduce any changes in it.

*Article* 73

The General Assembly may, only at the request of the Commission or the Court, as the case may be, determine sanctions to be applied against members of the Commission or judges of the Court when there are justifiable grounds for such action as set forth in the respective statutes. A vote of a two-thirds majority of the member States of the Organization shall be required for a decision in the case of members of the Commission and, in the case of judges of the Court, a two-thirds majority vote of the States Parties to the Convention shall also be required.

# PART III

## GENERAL AND TRANSITORY PROVISIONS
Chapter X—Signature, Ratification, Reservations, Amendments, Protocols, and Denunciation

*Article* 74

1. This Convention shall be open for signature and ratification by or adherence of any member State of the Organization of American States.

2. Ratification of or adherence to this Convention shall be made by the deposit of an instrument of ratification or adherence with the General Secretariat of the Organization of American States. As soon as eleven States have deposited their instruments of ratification or adherence, the Convention shall enter into force. With respect to any State that ratifies or adheres thereafter, the Convention shall enter into force on the date of the deposit of its instrument of ratification or adherence.

3. The Secretary General shall inform all member States of the Organization of the entry into force of the Convention.

*Article* 75

This Convention shall be subject to reservations only in conformity with the provisions of the Vienna Convention on the Law of Treaties signed on May 23, 1969.

*Article 76*

1. Proposals to amend this Convention may be submitted to the General Assembly for the action it deems appropriate by any State Party directly, and by the Commission or the Court through the Secretary General.

2. Amendments shall enter into force for the States ratifying them on the date when two-thirds of the States Parties to this Convention have deposited their respective instruments of ratification. With respect to the other States Parties, the amendments shall enter into force on the dates on which they deposit their respective instruments of ratification.

*Article 77*

1. In accordance with Article 31, any State Party and the Commission may submit proposed protocols to this Convention for consideration by the States Parties at the General Assembly with a view to gradually including other rights and freedoms within its system of protection.

2. Each protocol shall determine the manner of its entry into force and shall be applied only among the States Parties to it.

*Article 78*

1. The States Parties may denounce this Convention at the expiration of a five-year period from the date of its entry into force and by means of notice given one year in advance. Notice of the denunciation shall be addressed to the Secretary General of the Organization, who shall inform the other States Parties.

2. Such a denunciation shall not have the effect of releasing the State Party concerned from the obligations contained in this Convention with respect to any act that may constitute a violation of those obligations and that has been taken by that state prior to the effective date of denunciation.

Chapter XI—Transitory Provisions

*Section 1. Inter-American Commission on Human Rights*

*Article 79*

Upon the entry into force of this Convention, the Secretary General shall, in writing, request each member State of the Organization to present, within ninety days, its candidates for membership on the Inter-American Commission on Human Rights. The Secretary General shall prepare a list in alphabetical order of the candidates presented, and transmit it to the member States of the Organization at least thirty days prior to the next session of the General Assembly.

*Article 80*

The members of the Commission shall be elected by secret ballot of the General Assembly from the list of candidates referred to in Article 79. The candidates who obtain the largest number of votes and an absolute majority of the votes of the representatives of the member States shall be declared elected. Should it become necessary to have several ballots in order to elect all the members of the Commission, the candidates who receive the smallest number of votes shall be eliminated successively, in the manner determined by the General Assembly.

### Section 2. Inter-American Court of Human Rights

*Article* 81

Upon the entry into force of this Convention, the Secretary General shall, in writing, request each State Party to present, within ninety days, its candidates for membership on the Inter-American Court of Human Rights. The Secretary General shall prepare a list in alphabetical order of the candidates presented and transmit it to the States Parties at least thirty days prior to the next session of the General Assembly.

*Article* 82

The judges of the Court shall be elected from the list of candidates referred to in Article 81, by secret ballot of the States Parties to the Convention in the General Assembly. The candidates who obtain the largest number of votes and an absolute majority of the votes of the representatives of the States Parties shall be declared elected. Should it become necessary to have several ballots in order to elect all the judges of the Court, the candidates who receive the smallest number of votes shall be eliminated successively, in the manner determined by the States Parties.

[Statements and reservations, etc., omitted]

## 80. ADDITIONAL PROTOCOL TO THE AMERICAN CONVENTION ON HUMAN RIGHTS IN THE AREA OF ECONOMIC, SOCIAL AND CULTURAL RIGHTS, 1988

The States Parties to the American Convention on Human Rights adopted this Additional Protocol (the Protocol of San Salvador) on 14 November 1988; it came into force on 16 November 1999. For text, see OAS Treaty Series No. 69 (1988), signed 17 November 1988, reprinted in *Basic Documents Pertaining to Human Rights in the Inter-American System*, OEA/Ser.L.V/II.82 doc.6 rev.1, 67 (1992).

*TEXT*

Preamble

The States Parties to the American Convention on Human Rights 'Pact San José, Costa Rica',

*Reaffirming* their intention to consolidate in this hemisphere, within the frame work of democratic institutions, a system of personal liberty and social justice based on respect for the essential rights of man;

*Recognizing* that the essential rights of man are not derived from one's being a national of a certain State, but are based upon attributes of the human person, for which reason they merit international protection in the form of a convention reinforcing or complementing the protection provided by the domestic law of the American States;

*Considering* the close relationship that exists between economic, social and cultural rights, and civil and political rights, in that the different categories of rights constitute an indivisible whole based on the recognition of the dignity of the human person, for which reason both require permanent protection and promotion if they are to be fully realized, and the violation of some rights in favor of the realization of others can never be justified;

*Recognizing* the benefits that stem from the promotion and development of cooperation among States and international relations;

*Recalling* that, in accordance with the Universal Declaration of Human Rights and the American Convention on Human Rights, the ideal of free human beings enjoying freedom from fear and want can only be achieved if conditions are created whereby everyone may enjoy his economic, social and cultural rights as well as his civil and political rights;

*Bearing in mind* that, although fundamental economic, social and cultural rights have been recognized in earlier international instruments of both world and regional scope, it is essential that those rights be reaffirmed, developed, perfected and protected in order to consolidate in America, on the basis of full respect for the rights of the individual, the democratic representative form of government as well as the right of its peoples to development, self-determination, and the free disposal of their wealth and natural resources; and

*Considering* that the American Convention on Human Rights provides that draft additional protocols to that Convention may be submitted for consideration to the States Parties, meeting together on the occasion of the General Assembly of the Organization of American States, for the purpose of gradually incorporating other rights and freedoms into the protective system thereof,

*Have agreed* upon the following Additional Protocol to the American Convention on Human Rights 'Protocol of San Salvador':

*Article 1—Obligation to Adopt Measures*

The States Parties to this Additional Protocol to the American Convention on Human Rights undertake to adopt the necessary measures, both domestically and through international cooperation, especially economic and technical, to the extent allowed by their available resources, and taking into account their degree of development, for the purpose of achieving progressively and pursuant to their internal legislations, the full observance of the rights recognized in this Protocol.

*Article 2—Obligation to Enact Domestic Legislation*

If the exercise of the rights set forth in this Protocol is not already guaranteed by legislative or other provisions, the States Parties undertake to adopt, in accordance with their constitutional processes and the provisions of this Protocol, such legislative or other measures as may be necessary for making those rights a reality.

*Article 3—Obligation of nondiscrimination*

The State Parties to this Protocol undertake to guarantee the exercise of the rights set forth herein without discrimination of any kind for reasons related to race, color, sex, language, religion, political or other opinions, national or social origin, economic status, birth or any other social condition.

*Article 4—Inadmissibility of Restrictions*

A right which is recognized or in effect in a State by virtue of its internal legislation or international conventions may not be restricted or curtailed on the pretext that this Protocol does not recognize the right or recognizes it to a lesser degree.

*Article 5—Scope of Restrictions and Limitations*

The State Parties may establish restrictions and limitations on the enjoyment and exercise of the rights established herein by means of laws promulgated for the purpose of preserving the general welfare in a democratic society only to the extent that they are not incompatible with the purpose and reason underlying those rights.

*Article 6—Right to Work*

1. Everyone has the right to work, which includes the opportunity to secure the means for living a dignified and decent existence by performing a freely elected or accepted lawful activity.

2. The State Parties undertake to adopt measures that will make the right to work fully effective, especially with regard to the achievement of full employment, vocational guidance, and the development of technical and vocational training projects, in particular those directed to the disabled. The States Parties also

undertake to implement and strengthen programs that help to ensure suitable family care, so that women may enjoy a real opportunity to exercise the right to work.

*Article 7—Just, Equitable, and Satisfactory Conditions of Work*

The States Parties to this Protocol recognize that the right to work to which the foregoing article refers presupposes that everyone shall enjoy that right under just, equitable, and satisfactory conditions, which the States Parties undertake to guarantee in their internal legislation, particularly with respect to:

(a) Remuneration which guarantees, as a minimum, to all workers dignified and decent living conditions for them and their families and fair and equal wages for equal work, without distinction;

(b) The right of every worker to follow his vocation and to devote himself to the activity that best fulfills his expectations and to change employment in accordance with the pertinent national regulations;

(c) The right of every worker to promotion or upward mobility in his employment, for which purpose account shall be taken of his qualifications, competence, integrity and seniority;

(d) Stability of employment, subject to the nature of each industry and occupation and the causes for just separation. In cases of unjustified dismissal, the worker shall have the right to indemnity or to reinstatement on the job or any other benefits provided by domestic legislation;

(e) Safety and hygiene at work;

(f) The prohibition of night work or unhealthy or dangerous working conditions and, in general, of all work which jeopardizes health, safety, or morals, for persons under 18 years of age. As regards minors under the age of 16, the work day shall be subordinated to the provisions regarding compulsory education and in no case shall work constitute an impediment to school attendance or a limitation on benefitting from education received;

(g) A reasonable limitation of working hours, both daily and weekly. The days shall be shorter in the case of dangerous or unhealthy work or of night work;

(h) Rest, leisure and paid vacations as well as remuneration for national holidays.

*Article 8—Trade Union Rights*

1. The States Parties shall ensure:

(a) The right of workers to organize trade unions and to join the union of their choice for the purpose of protecting and promoting their interests. As an extension of that right, the States Parties shall permit trade unions to establish national federations or confederations, or to affiliate with those that already exist, as well as to form international trade union organizations and to affiliate with that of their choice. The States Parties shall also permit trade unions, federations and confederations to function freely;

(b) The right to strike.

2. The exercise of the rights set forth above may be subject only to restrictions established by law, provided that such restrictions are characteristic of a democratic society and necessary for safeguarding public order or for protecting public health or morals or the rights and freedoms of others. Members of the armed forces and the police and of other essential public services shall be subject to limitations and restrictions established by law.

3. No one may be compelled to belong to a trade union.

*Article 9—Right to Social Security*

1. Everyone shall have the right to social security protecting him from the consequences of old age and of disability which prevents him, physically or mentally, from securing the means for a dignified and decent existence. In the event of the death of a beneficiary, social security benefits shall be applied to his dependents.

2. In the case of persons who are employed, the right to social security shall cover at least medical care and an allowance or retirement benefit in the case of work accidents or occupational disease and, in the case of women, paid maternity leave before and after childbirth.

*Article 10—Right to Health*

1. Everyone shall have the right to health, understood to mean the enjoyment of the highest level of physical, mental and social well-being.

2. In order to ensure the exercise of the right to health, the States Parties agree to recognize health as a public good and, particularly, to adopt the following measures to ensure that right:

   *(a)* Primary health care, that is, essential health care made available to all individuals and families in the community;

   *(b)* Extension of the benefits of health services to all individuals subject to the State's jurisdiction;

   *(c)* Universal immunization against the principal infectious diseases;

   *(d)* Prevention and treatment of endemic, occupational and other diseases;

   *(e)* Education of the population on the prevention and treatment of health problems, and

   *(f)* Satisfaction of the health needs of the highest risk groups and of those whose poverty makes them the most vulnerable.

*Article 11—Right to a Healthy Environment*

1. Everyone shall have the right to live in a healthy environment and to have access to basic public services.

2. The States Parties shall promote the protection, preservation, and improvement of the environment.

*Article 12—Right to Food*

1. Everyone has the right to adequate nutrition which guarantees the possibility of enjoying the highest level of physical, emotional and intellectual development.

2. In order to promote the exercise of this right and eradicate malnutrition, the States Parties undertake to improve methods of production, supply and

distribution of food, and to this end, agree to promote greater international cooperation in support of the relevant national policies.

*Article* 13—*Right to Education*

1. Everyone has the right to education.

2. The States Parties to this Protocol agree that education should be directed towards the full development of the human personality and human dignity and should strengthen respect for human rights, ideological pluralism, fundamental freedoms, justice and peace. They further agree that education ought to enable everyone to participate effectively in a democratic and pluralistic society and achieve a decent existence and should foster understanding, tolerance and friendship among all nations and all racial, ethnic or religious groups and promote activities for the maintenance of peace.

3. The States Parties to this Protocol recognize that in order to achieve the full exercise of the right to education:

   (a) Primary education should be compulsory and accessible to all without cost;
   (b) Secondary education in its different forms, including technical and vocational secondary education, should be made generally available and accessible to all by every appropriate means, and in particular, by the progressive introduction of free education;
   (c) Higher education should be made equally accessible to all, on the basis of individual capacity, by every appropriate means, and in particular, by the progressive introduction of free education;
   (d) Basic education should be encouraged or intensified as far as possible for those persons who have not received or completed the whole cycle of primary instruction;
   (e) Programs of special education should be established for the handicapped, so as to provide special instruction and training to persons with physical disabilities or mental deficiencies.

4. In conformity with the domestic legislation of the States Parties, parents should have the right to select the type of education to be given to their children, provided that it conforms to the principles set forth above.

5. Nothing in this Protocol shall be interpreted as a restriction of the freedom of individuals and entities to establish and direct educational institutions in accordance with the domestic legislation of the States Parties.

*Article* 14—*Right to the Benefits of Culture*

1. The States Parties to this Protocol recognize the right of everyone:

   (a) To take part in the cultural and artistic life of the community;
   (b) To enjoy the benefits of scientific and technological progress;
   (c) To benefit from the protection of moral and material interests deriving from any scientific, literary or artistic production of which he is the author.

2. The steps to be taken by the States Parties to this Protocol to ensure the full exercise of this right shall include those necessary for the conservation, development and dissemination of science, culture and art.

3. The States Parties to this Protocol undertake to respect the freedom indispensable for scientific research and creative activity.

4. The States Parties to this Protocol recognize the benefits to be derived from the encouragement and development of international cooperation and relations in the fields of science, arts and culture, and accordingly agree to foster greater international cooperation in these fields.

*Article 15—Right to the Formation and the Protection of Families*

1. The family is the natural and fundamental element of society and ought to be protected by the State, which should see to the improvement of its spiritual and material conditions.

2. Everyone has the right to form a family, which shall be exercised in accordance with the provisions of the pertinent domestic legislation.

3. The States Parties hereby undertake to accord adequate protection to the family unit and in particular:

   *(a)* To provide special care and assistance to mothers during a reasonable period before and after childbirth;

   *(b)* To guarantee adequate nutrition for children at the nursing stage and during school attendance years;

   *(c)* To adopt special measures for the protection of adolescents in order to ensure the full development of their physical, intellectual and moral capacities;

   *(d)* To undertake special programs of family training so as to help create a stable and positive environment in which children will receive and develop the values of understanding, solidarity, respect and responsibility.

*Article 16—Rights of Children*

Every child, whatever his parentage, has the right to the protection that his status as a minor requires from his family, society and the State. Every child has the right to grow under the protection and responsibility of his parents; save in exceptional, judicially-recognized circumstances, a child of young age ought not to be separated from his mother. Every child has the right to free and compulsory education, at least in the elementary phase, and to continue his training at higher levels of the educational system.

*Article 17—Protection of the Elderly*

Everyone has the right to special protection in old age. With this in view the States Parties agree to take progressively the necessary steps to make this right a reality and, particularly, to:

   *(a)* Provide suitable facilities, as well as food and specialized medical care, for elderly individuals who lack them and are unable to provide them for themselves;

   *(b)* Undertake work programs specifically designed to give the elderly the opportunity to engage in a productive activity suited to their abilities and consistent with their vocations or desires;

(c) Foster the establishment of social organizations aimed at improving the quality of life for the elderly.

*Article* 18—*Protection of the Handicapped*

Everyone affected by a diminution of his physical or mental capacities is entitled to receive special attention designed to help him achieve the greatest possible development of his personality. The States Parties agree to adopt such measures as may be necessary for this purpose and, especially, to:

(a) Undertake programs specifically aimed at providing the handicapped with the resources and environment needed for attaining this goal, including work programs consistent with their possibilities and freely accepted by them or their legal representatives, as the case may be;

(b) Provide special training to the families of the handicapped in order to help them solve the problems of coexistence and convert them into active agents in the physical, mental and emotional development of the latter;

(c) Include the consideration of solutions to specific requirements arising from needs of this group as a priority component of their urban development plans;

(d) Encourage the establishment of social groups in which the handicapped can be helped to enjoy a fuller life.

*Article* 19—*Means of Protection*

1. Pursuant to the provisions of this article and the corresponding rules to be formulated for this purpose by the General Assembly of the Organization of American States, the States Parties to this Protocol undertake to submit periodic reports on the progressive measures they have taken to ensure due respect for the rights set forth in this Protocol.

2. All reports shall be submitted to the Secretary General of the OAS, who shall transmit them to the Inter-American Economic and Social Council and the Inter-American Council for Education, Science and Culture so that they may examine them in accordance with the provisions of this article. The Secretary General shall send a copy of such reports to the Inter-American Commission on Human Rights.

3. The Secretary General of the Organization of American States shall also transmit to the specialized organizations of the inter-American system of which the States Parties to the present Protocol are members, copies or pertinent portions of the reports submitted, insofar as they relate to matters within the purview of those organizations, as established by their constituent instruments.

4. The specialized organizations of the inter-American system may submit reports to the Inter-American Economic and Social Council and the Inter-American Council for Education, Science and Culture relative to compliance with the provisions of the present Protocol in their fields of activity.

5. The annual reports submitted to the General Assembly by the Inter-American Economic and Social Council and the Inter-American Council for Education, Science and Culture shall contain a summary of the information received from the States Parties to the present Protocol and the specialized organizations concerning the progressive measures adopted in order to ensure respect for the rights

acknowledged in the Protocol itself and the general recommendations they consider to be appropriate in this respect.

6. Any instance in which the rights established in paragraph (a) of Article 8 and in Article 13 are violated by action directly attributable to a State Party to this Protocol may give rise, through participation of the Inter-American Commission on Human Rights and, when applicable, of the Inter-American Court of Human Rights, to application of the system of individual petitions governed by Article 44 through 51 and 61 through 69 of the American Convention on Human Rights.

7. Without prejudice to the provisions of the preceding paragraph, the Inter-American Commission on Human Rights may formulate such observations and recommendations as it deems pertinent concerning the status of the economic, social and cultural rights established in the present Protocol in all or some of the States Parties, which it may include in its Annual Report to the General Assembly or in a special report, whichever it considers more appropriate.

8. The Councils and the Inter-American Commission on Human Rights, in discharging the functions conferred upon them in this article, shall take into account the progressive nature of the observance of the rights subject to protection by this Protocol.

*Article 20—Reservations*

The States Parties may, at the time of approval, signature, ratification or accession, make reservations to one or more specific provisions of this Protocol, provided that such reservations are not incompatible with the object and purpose of the Protocol.

*Article 21—Signature, Ratification or Accession. Entry into Effect*

1. This Protocol shall remain open to signature and ratification or accession by any State Party to the American Convention on Human Rights.

2. Ratification of or accession to this Protocol shall be effected by depositing an instrument of ratification or accession with the General Secretariat of the Organization of American States.

3. The Protocol shall enter into effect when eleven States have deposited their respective instruments of ratification or accession.

4. The Secretary General shall notify all the member States of the Organization of American States of the entry of the Protocol into effect.

*Article 22—Inclusion of other Rights and Expansion of those Recognized*

1. Any State Party and the Inter-American Commission on Human Rights may submit for the consideration of the States Parties meeting on the occasion of the General Assembly proposed amendments to include the recognition of other rights or freedoms or to extend or expand rights or freedoms recognized in this Protocol.

2. Such amendments shall enter into effect for the States that ratify them on the date of deposit of the instrument of ratification corresponding to the number representing two thirds of the States Parties to this Protocol. For all other States Parties they shall enter into effect on the date on which they deposit their respective instrument of ratification.

# 81. PROTOCOL TO THE AMERICAN CONVENTION ON HUMAN RIGHTS TO ABOLISH THE DEATH PENALTY, 1990

OAS Treaty Series No. 73 (1990), adopted 8 June 1990, reprinted in *Basic Documents Pertaining to Human Rights in the Inter-American System*, OEA/Ser.L.V/II.82 doc.6 rev.1, 80 (1992).

*TEXT*

## Preamble

The States Parties to this Protocol,
   *Considering:*
   That Article 4 of the American Convention on Human Rights recognizes the right to life and restricts the application of the death penalty;
   That everyone has the inalienable right to respect for his life, a right that cannot be suspended for any reason;
   That the tendency among the American States is to be in favor of abolition of the death penalty;
   That application of the death penalty has irrevocable consequences, forecloses the correction of judicial error, and precludes any possibility of changing or rehabilitating those convicted;
   That the abolition of the death penalty helps to ensure more effective protection of the right to life;
   That an international agreement must be arrived at that will entail a progressive development of the American Convention on Human Rights, and
   That States Parties to the American Convention on Human Rights have expressed their intention to adopt an international agreement with a view to consolidating the practice of not applying the death penalty in the Americas,
   Have agreed to sign the following Protocol to the American Convention on Human Rights to abolish the death penalty

*Article 1*

The States Parties to this Protocol shall not apply the death penalty in their territory to any person subject to their jurisdiction.

*Article 2*

1. No reservations may be made to this Protocol. However, at the time of ratification or accession, the States Parties to this instrument may declare that they reserve the right to apply the death penalty in wartime in accordance with international law, for extremely serious crimes of a military nature.

2. The State Party making this reservation shall, upon ratification or accession, inform the Secretary General of the Organization of American States of the

pertinent provisions of its national legislation applicable in wartime, as referred to in the preceding paragraph.

3. Said State Party shall notify the Secretary General of the Organization of American States of the beginning or end of any state of war in effect in its territory.

*Article 3*

1. This Protocol shall be open for signature and ratification or accession by any State Party to the American Convention on Human Rights.

2. Ratification of this Protocol or accession thereto shall be made through the deposit of an instrument of ratification or accession with the General Secretariat of the Organization of American States.

*Article 4*

This Protocol shall enter into force among the States that ratify or accede to it when they deposit their respective instruments of ratification or accession with the General Secretariat of the Organization of American States.

# 82. INTER-AMERICAN CONVENTION TO PREVENT AND PUNISH TORTURE, 1985

The Convention was adopted as part of a resolution adopted at the third plenary session of the Organization of American States held at Cartagena de Indias on 9 December 1985. It came into force on 28 February 1987. The text appears in the OAS Treaty Series, No. 67; reprinted in *Basic Documents Pertaining to Human Rights in the Inter-American System*, OEA/Ser.L.V/II.82 doc.6 rev.1, 83 (1992).

## TEXT

The American States signatory to the present Convention,

*Aware* of the provision of the American Convention on Human Rights that no one shall be subjected to torture or to cruel, inhuman, or degrading punishment or treatment;

*Reaffirming* that all acts of torture or any other cruel, inhuman, or degrading treatment or punishment constitute an offense against human dignity and a denial of the principles set forth in the Charter of the Organization of American States and in the Charter of the United Nations and are violations of the fundamental human rights and freedoms proclaimed in the American Declaration of the Rights and Duties of Man and the Universal Declaration of Human Rights;

*Noting* that, in order for the pertinent rules contained in the aforementioned global and regional instruments to take effect, it is necessary to draft an Inter-American Convention that prevents and punishes torture;

*Reaffirming* their purpose of consolidating in this hemisphere the conditions that make for recognition of and respect for the inherent dignity of man, and ensure the full exercise of his fundamental rights and freedoms,

*Have agreed* upon the following:

*Article* 1

The State Parties undertake to prevent and punish torture in accordance with the terms of this Convention.

*Article* 2

For the purposes of this Convention, torture shall be understood to be any act intentionally performed whereby physical or mental pain or suffering is inflicted on a person for purposes of criminal investigation, as a means of intimidation, as personal punishment, as a preventive measure, as a penalty, or for any other purpose. Torture shall also be understood to be the use of methods upon a person intended to obliterate the personality of the victim or to diminish his physical or mental capacities, even if they do not cause physical pain or mental anguish.

The concept of torture shall not include physical or mental pain or suffering that is inherent in or solely the consequence of lawful measures, provided that they do not include the performance of the acts or use of the methods referred to in this article.

## Article 3

The following shall be held guilty of the crime of torture:

(a) A public servant or employee who acting in that capacity orders, instigates or induces the use of torture, or who directly commits it or who, being able to prevent it, fails to do so.

(b) A person who at the instigation of a public servant or employee mentioned in subparagraph (a) orders, instigates or induces the use of torture, directly commits it or is an accomplice thereto.

## Article 4

The fact of having acted under orders of a superior shall not provide exemption from the corresponding criminal liability.

## Article 5

The existence of circumstances such as a state of war, threat of war, state of siege or of emergency, domestic disturbance or strife, suspension of constitutional guarantees, domestic political instability, or other public emergencies or disasters shall not be invoked or admitted as justification for the crime of torture.

Neither the dangerous character of the detainee or prisoner, nor the lack of security of the prison establishment or penitentiary shall justify torture.

## Article 6

In accordance with the terms of Article 1, the States Parties shall take effective measures to prevent and punish torture within their jurisdiction.

The States Parties shall ensure that all acts of torture and attempts to commit torture are offenses under their criminal law and shall make such acts punishable by severe penalties that take into account their serious nature.

The States Parties likewise shall take effective measures to prevent and punish other cruel, inhuman, or degrading treatment or punishment within their jurisdiction.

## Article 7

The States Parties shall take measures so that, in the training of police officers and other public officials responsible for the custody of persons temporarily or definitively deprived of their freedom, special emphasis shall be put on the prohibition of the use of torture in interrogation, detention, or arrest.

The States Parties likewise shall take similar measures to prevent other cruel, inhuman, or degrading treatment or punishment.

## Article 8

The States Parties shall guarantee that any person making an accusation of having been subjected to torture within their jurisdiction shall have the right to an impartial examination of his case.

Likewise, if there is an accusation or well-grounded reason to believe that an act of torture has been committed within their jurisdiction, the States Parties shall guarantee that their respective authorities will proceed properly and immediately to conduct an investigation into the case and to initiate, whenever appropriate, the corresponding criminal process.

After all the domestic legal procedures of the respective State and the corresponding appeals have been exhausted, the case may be submitted to the international fora whose competence has been recognized by that State.

*Article* 9

The States Parties undertake to incorporate into their national laws regulations guaranteeing suitable compensation for victims of torture.

None of the provisions of this article shall affect the right to receive compensation that the victim or other persons may have by virtue of existing national legislation.

*Article* 10

No statement that is verified as having been obtained through torture shall be admissible as evidence in a legal proceeding, except in a legal action taken against a person or persons accused of having elicited it through acts of torture, and only as evidence that the accused obtained such statement by such means.

*Article* 11

The States Parties shall take the necessary steps to extradite anyone accused of having committed the crime of torture or sentenced for commission of that crime, in accordance with their respective national laws on extradition and their international commitments on this matter.

*Article* 12

Every State Party shall take the necessary measures to establish its jurisdiction over the crime described in this Convention in the following cases:

*(a)* When torture has been committed within its jurisdiction;

*(b)* When the alleged criminal is a national of that State; or

*(c)* When the victim is a national of that State and it so deems appropriate.

Every State Party shall also take the necessary measures to establish its jurisdiction over the crime described in this Convention when the alleged criminal is within the area under its jurisdiction and it is not appropriate to extradite him in accordance with Article 11.

This Convention does not exclude criminal jurisdiction exercised in accordance with domestic law.

*Article* 13

The crime referred to in Article 2 shall be deemed to be included among the extraditable crimes in every extradition treaty entered into between States Parties. The States Parties undertake to include the crime of torture as an extraditable offence in every extradition treaty to be concluded between them.

Every State Party that makes extradition conditional on the existence of a treaty may, if it receives a request for extradition from another State Party with which it has no extradition treaty, consider this Convention as the legal basis for extradition in respect of the crime of torture. Extradition shall be subject to the other conditions that may be required by the law of the requested State.

States Parties which do not make extradition conditional on the existence of a treaty shall recognize such crimes as extraditable offences between themselves, subject to the conditions required by the law of the requested State.

Extradition shall not be granted nor shall the person sought be returned when there are grounds to believe that his life is in danger, that he will be subjected to torture or to cruel, inhuman or degrading treatment, or that he will be tried by special or ad hoc courts in the requesting State.

## Article 14

When a State Party does not grant the extradition, the case shall be submitted to its competent authorities as if the crime had been committed within its jurisdiction, for the purposes of investigation, and when appropriate, for criminal action, in accordance with its national law. Any decision adopted by these authorities shall be communicated to the State that has requested the extradition.

## Article 15

No provision of this Convention may be interpreted as limiting the right of asylum, when appropriate, nor as altering the obligations of the States Parties in the matter of extradition.

## Article 16

This Convention shall not limit the provisions of the American Convention on Human Rights, other conventions on the subject, or the Statutes of the Inter-American Commission on Human Rights, with respect to the crime of torture.

## Article 17

The States Parties undertake to inform the Inter-American Commission on Human Rights of any legislative, judicial, administrative, or other measures they adopt in application of this Convention.

In keeping with its duties and responsibilities, the Inter-American Commission on Human Rights will endeavor in its annual report to analyze the existing situation in the member states of the Organization of American States in regard to the prevention and elimination of torture.

## Article 18

This Convention is open to signature by the member States of the Organization of American States.

## Article 19

This Convention is subject to ratification. The instruments of ratification shall be deposited with the General Secretariat of the Organization of American States.

## Article 20

This Convention is open to accession by any other American State. The instruments of accession shall be deposited with the General Secretariat of the Organization of American States.

*Article* 21

The States Parties may, at the time of approval, signature, ratification, or accession, make reservations to this Convention, provided that such reservations are not incompatible with the object and purpose of the Convention and concern one or more specific provisions.

*Article* 22

This Convention shall enter into force on the thirtieth day following the date on which the second instrument of ratification is deposited. For each State ratifying or acceding to the Convention after the second instrument of ratification has been deposited, the Convention shall enter into force on the thirtieth day following the date on which that State deposits its instrument of ratification or accession.

*Article* 23

This Convention shall remain in force indefinitely, but may be denounced by any State Party. The instrument of denunciation shall be deposited with the General Secretariat of the Organization of American States. After one year from the date of deposit of the instrument of denunciation, this Convention shall cease to be in effect for the denouncing State but shall remain in force for the remaining States Parties.

*Article* 24

The original instrument of this Convention, the English, French, Portuguese, and Spanish texts of which are equally authentic, shall be deposited with the General Secretariat of the Organization of American States, which shall send a certified copy to the Secretariat of the United Nations for registration and publication, in accordance with the provisions of Article 102 of the United Nations Charter. The General Secretariat of the Organization of American States shall notify the member States of the Organization and the States that have acceded to the Convention of signatures and of deposits of instruments of ratification, accession, and denunciation, as well as reservations, if any.

## 83. INTER-AMERICAN CONVENTION ON THE PREVENTION, PUNISHMENT AND ERADICATION OF VIOLENCE AGAINST WOMEN, 1994

The 'Convention of Belém Do Pará' was adopted at Belém do Pará, Brazil, on 9 June 1994, at the twenty fourth regular session of the General Assembly; it entered into force on 5 March 1995. For text see 33 ILM 1534 (1994).

## TEXT

The States Parties to this Convention,

*Recognizing* that full respect for human rights has been enshrined in the American Declaration of the Rights and Duties of Man and the Universal Declaration of Human Rights, and reaffirmed in other international and regional instruments;

*Affirming* that violence against women constitutes a violation of their human rights and fundamental freedoms, and impairs or nullifies the observance, enjoyment and exercise of such rights and freedoms;

*Concerned* that violence against women is an offense against human dignity and a manifestation of the historically unequal power relations between women and men;

*Recalling* the Declaration on the Elimination of Violence against Women, adopted by the Twenty-fifth Assembly of Delegates of the Inter-American Commission of Women, and affirming that violence against women pervades every sector of society regardless of class, race or ethnic group, income, culture, level of education, age or religion and strikes at its very foundations:

*Convinced* that the elimination of violence against women is essential for their individual and social development and their full and equal participation in all walks of life; and

*Convinced* that the adoption of a convention on the prevention, punishment and eradication of all forms of violence against women within the framework of the Organization of American States is a positive contribution to protecting the rights of women and eliminating violence against them,

*Have agreed* to the following:

### Chapter I—Definition and Scope of Application

*Article* 1

For the purposes of this Convention, violence against women shall be understood as any act or conduct, based on gender, which causes death or physical, sexual or psychological harm or suffering to women, whether in the public or the private sphere.

*Article* 2

Violence against women shall be understood to include physical, sexual and psychological violence:

    *(a)*  that occurs within the family or domestic unit or within any other inter-personal relationship, whether or not the perpetrator shares or has shared the same residence with the woman, including, among others, rape, battery and sexual abuse;

    *(b)*  that occurs in the community and is perpetrated by any person, including, among others, rape, sexual abuse, torture, trafficking in persons, forced prostitution, kidnapping and sexual harassment in the workplace, as well as in educational institutions, health facilities or any other place; and

    *(c)*  that is perpetrated or condoned by the State or its agents regardless of where it occurs.

## Chapter II—Rights Protected

*Article* 3

Every woman has the right to be free from violence in both the public and private spheres.

*Article* 4

Every woman has the right to the recognition, enjoyment, exercise and protection of all human rights and freedoms embodied in regional and international human rights instruments. These rights include, among others:

    *(a)*  The right to have her life respected;

    *(b)*  The right to have her physical, mental and moral integrity respected;

    *(c)*  The right to personal liberty and security;

    *(d)*  The right not to be subjected to torture;

    *(e)*  The rights to have the inherent dignity of her person respected and her family protected;

    *(f)*  The right to equal protection before the law and of the law;

    *(g)*  The right to simple and prompt recourse to a competent court for protection against acts that violate her rights;

    *(h)*  The right to associate freely;

    *(i)*  The right of freedom to profess her religion and beliefs within the law; and

    *(j)*  The right to have equal access to the public service of her country and to take part in the conduct of public affairs, including decision-making.

*Article* 5

Every woman is entitled to the free and full exercise of her civil, political, economic, social and cultural rights, and may rely on the full protection of those rights as embodied in regional and international instruments on human rights. The States Parties recognize that violence against women prevents and nullifies the exercise of these rights.

*Article* 6

The right of every woman to be free from violence includes, among others:

- *(a)* The right of women to be free from all forms of discrimination; and
- *(b)* The right of women to be valued and educated free of stereotyped patterns of behavior and social and cultural practices based on concepts of inferiority or subordination.

### Chapter III—Duties of the States

*Article* 7

The States Parties condemn all forms of violence against women and agree to pursue, by all appropriate means and without delay, policies to prevent, punish and eradicate such violence and undertake to:

- *(a)* refrain from engaging in any act or practice of violence against women and to ensure that their authorities, officials, personnel, agents, and institutions act in conformity with this obligation;
- *(b)* apply due diligence to prevent, investigate and impose penalties for violence against women;
- *(c)* include in their domestic legislation penal, civil, administrative and any other type of provisions that may be needed to prevent, punish and eradicate violence against women and to adopt appropriate administrative measures where necessary;
- *(d)* adopt legal measures to require the perpetrator to refrain from harassing, intimidating or threatening the woman or using any method that harms or endangers her life or integrity, or damages her property;
- *(e)* take all appropriate measures, including legislative measures, to amend or repeal existing laws and regulations or to modify legal or customary practices which sustain the persistence and tolerance of violence against women;
- *(f)* establish fair and effective legal procedures for women who have been subjected to violence which include, among others, protective measures, a timely hearing and effective access to such procedures;
- *(g)* establish the necessary legal and administrative mechanisms to ensure that women subjected to violence have effective access to restitution, reparations or other just and effective remedies; and
- *(h)* adopt such legislative or other measures as may be necessary to give effect to this Convention.

*Article* 8

The States Parties agree to undertake progressively specific measures, including programs:

- *(a)* to promote awareness and observance of the right of women to be free from violence, and the right of women to have their human rights respected and protected;

*(b)* to modify social and cultural patterns of conduct of men and women, including the development of formal and informal educational programs appropriate to every level of the educational process, to counteract prejudices, customs and all other practices which are based on the idea of the inferiority or superiority of either of the sexes or on the stereotyped roles for men and women which legitimize or exacerbate violence against women;

*(c)* to promote the education and training of all those involved in the administration of justice, police and other law enforcement officers as well as other personnel responsible for implementing policies for the prevention, punishment and eradication of violence against women;

*(d)* to provide appropriate specialized services for women who have been subjected to violence, through public and private sector agencies, including shelters, counseling services for all family members where appropriate, and care and custody of the affected children;

*(e)* to promote and support governmental and private sector education designed to raise the awareness of the public with respect to the problems of and remedies for violence against women;

*(f)* to provide women who are subjected to violence access to effective readjustment and training programs to enable them to fully participate in public, private and social life;

*(g)* to encourage the communications media to develop appropriate media guidelines in order to contribute to the eradication of violence against women in all its forms, and to enhance respect for the dignity of women;

*(h)* to ensure research and the gathering of statistics and other relevant information relating to the causes, consequences and frequency of violence against women, in order to assess the effectiveness of measures to prevent, punish and eradicate violence against women and to formulate and implement the necessary changes; and

*(i)* to foster international cooperation for the exchange of ideas and experiences and the execution of programs aimed at protecting women who are subjected to violence.

*Article* 9

With respect to the adoption of the measures in this Chapter, the States Parties shall take special account of the vulnerability of women to violence by reason of, among others, their race or ethnic background or their status as migrants, refugees or displaced persons. Similar consideration shall be given to women subjected to violence while pregnant or who are disabled, of minor age, elderly, socioeconomically disadvantaged, affected by armed conflict or deprived of their freedom.

Chapter IV—Inter-American Mechanisms of Protection

*Article* 10

In order to protect the rights of every woman to be free from violence, the States Parties shall include in their national reports to the Inter-American Commission of Women information on measures adopted to prevent and prohibit violence against women, and to assist women affected by violence, as well as on any difficulties they observe in applying those measures, and the factors that contribute to violence against women.

*Article* 11

The States Parties to this Convention and the Inter-American Commission of Women may request of the Inter-American Court of Human Rights advisory opinions on the interpretation of this Convention.

*Article* 12

Any person or group of persons, or any nongovernmental entity legally recognized in one or more member States of the Organization, may lodge petitions with the Inter-American Commission on Human Rights containing denunciations or complaints of violations of Article 7 of this Convention by a State Party, and the Commission shall consider such claims in accordance with the norms and procedures established by the American Convention on Human Rights and the Statutes and Regulations of the Inter-American Commission on Human Rights for lodging and considering petitions.

Chapter V—General Provisions

*Article* 13

No part of this Convention shall be understood to restrict or limit the domestic law of any State Party that affords equal or greater protection and guarantees of the rights of women and appropriate safeguards to prevent and eradicate violence against women.

*Article* 14

No part of this Convention shall be understood to restrict or limit the American Convention on Human Rights or any other international convention on the subject that provides for equal or greater protection in this area.

*Article* 15

This Convention is open to signature by all the member States of the Organization of American States.

*Article* 16

This Convention is subject to ratification. The instruments of ratification shall be deposited with the General Secretariat of the Organization of American States.

*Article* 17

This Convention is open to accession by any other State. Instruments of accession shall be deposited with the General Secretariat of the Organization of American States.

*Article* 18

Any State may, at the time of approval, signature, ratification, or accession, make reservations to this Convention provided that such reservations are:

*(a)* not incompatible with the object and purpose of the Convention, and

*(b)* not of a general nature and relate to one or more specific provisions.

*Article* 19

Any State Party may submit to the General Assembly, through the Inter-American Commission of Women, proposals for the amendment of this Convention.

Amendments shall enter into force for the States ratifying them on the date when two-thirds of the States Parties to this Convention have deposited their respective instruments of ratification. With respect to the other States Parties, the amendments shall enter into force on the dates on which they deposit their respective instruments of ratification.

*Article* 20

If a State Party has two or more territorial units in which the matters dealt with in this Convention are governed by different systems of law, it may, at the time of signature, ratification or accession, declare that this Convention shall extend to all its territorial units or to only one or more of them.

Such a declaration may be amended at any time by subsequent declarations, which shall expressly specify the territorial unit or units to which this Convention applies. Such subsequent declarations shall be transmitted to the General Secretariat of the Organization of American States, and shall enter into force thirty days after the date of their receipt.

*Article* 21

This Convention shall enter into force on the thirtieth day after the date of deposit of the second instrument of ratification. For each State that ratifies or accedes to the Convention after the second instrument of ratification is deposited, it shall enter into force thirty days after the date on which that State deposited its instrument of ratification or accession.

*Article* 22

The Secretary General shall inform all member States of the Organization of American States of the entry into force of this Convention.

*Article* 23

The Secretary General of the Organization of American States shall present an annual report to the member States of the Organization on the status of this Convention, including the signatures, deposits of instruments of ratification and accession, and declarations, and any reservations that may have been presented by the States Parties, accompanied by a report thereon if needed.

*Article* 24

This Convention shall remain in force indefinitely, but any of the States Parties may denounce it by depositing an instrument to that effect with the General Secretariat of the Organization of American States. One year after the date of deposit of the instrument of denunciation, this Convention shall cease to be in effect for the denouncing State but shall remain in force for the remaining States Parties.

*Article* 25

The original instrument of this Convention, the English, French, Portuguese and Spanish texts of which are equally authentic, shall be deposited with the General Secretariat of the Organization of American States, which shall send a certified copy to the Secretariat of the United Nations for registration and publication in accordance with the provisions of Article 102 of the United Nations Charter.

In witness whereof the undersigned Plenipotentiaries, being duly authorized thereto by their respective governments, have signed this Convention, which shall be called the Inter-American Convention on the Prevention, Punishment and Eradication of Violence against Women 'Convention of Belém do Pará.'

*Done* in the city of Belém do Pará, Brazil, the ninth of June in the year one thousand nine hundred and ninety-four.

## 84. INTER-AMERICAN CONVENTION ON FORCED DISAPPEARANCE OF PERSONS, 1994

Signed at Belém do Pará, Brazil, on 9 June 1994; in force 28 March 1996.

*TEXT*

### Preamble

The Member States of the Organization of American States signatory to the present Convention,

*Disturbed* by the persistence of the forced disappearance of persons;

*Reaffirming* that the true meaning of American solidarity and good neighborliness can be none other than that of consolidating in this Hemisphere, in the framework of democratic institutions, a system of individual freedom and social justice based on respect for essential human rights;

*Considering* that the forced disappearance of persons in an affront to the conscience of the Hemisphere and a grave and abominable offense against the inherent dignity of the human being, and one that contradicts the principles and purposes enshrined in the Charter of the Organization of American States;

*Considering* that the forced disappearance of persons of persons violates numerous non-derogable and essential human rights enshrined in the American Convention on Human Rights, in the American Declaration of the Rights and Duties of Man, and in the Universal Declaration of Human Rights;

*Recalling* that the international protection of human rights is in the form of a convention reinforcing or complementing the protection provided by domestic law and is based upon the attributes of the human personality;

*Reaffirming* that the systematic practice of the forced disappearance of persons constitutes a crime against humanity;

*Hoping* that this Convention may help to prevent, punish, and eliminate the forced disappearance of persons in the Hemisphere and make a decisive contribution to the protection of human rights and the rule of law,

*Resolve* to adopt the following Inter-American Convention on Forced Disappearance of Persons:

*Article* I

The States Parties to this Convention undertake:

(a) Not to practice, permit, or tolerate the forced disappearance of persons, even in states of emergency or suspension of individual guarantees;

(b) To punish within their jurisdictions, those persons who commit or attempt to commit the crime of forced disappearance of persons and their accomplices and accessories;

(c) To cooperate with one another in helping to prevent, punish, and eliminate the forced disappearance of persons;

*(d)* To take legislative, administrative, judicial, and any other measures necessary to comply with the commitments undertaken in this Convention.

## *Article* II

For the purposes of this Convention, forced disappearance is considered to be the act of depriving a person or persons of his or their freedom, in whatever way, perpetrated by agents of the State or by persons or groups of persons acting with the authorization, support, or acquiescence of the State, followed by an absence of information or a refusal to acknowledge that deprivation of freedom or to give information on the whereabouts of that person, thereby impeding his or her recourse to the applicable legal remedies and procedural guarantees.

## *Article* III

The States Parties undertake to adopt, in accordance with their constitutional procedures, the legislative measures that may be needed to define the forced disappearance of persons as an offense and to impose an appropriate punishment commensurate with its extreme gravity. This offense shall be deemed continuous or permanent as long as the fate or whereabouts of the victim has not been determined.

The States Parties may establish mitigating circumstances for persons who have participated in acts constituting forced disappearance when they help to cause the victim to reappear alive or provide information that sheds light on the forced disappearance of a person.

## *Article* IV

The acts constituting the forced disappearance of persons shall be considered offenses in every State Party. Consequently, each State Party shall take measures to establish its jurisdiction over such cases in the following instances:

*(a)* When the forced disappearance of persons or any act constituting such offense was committed within its jurisdiction;

*(b)* When the accused is a national of that State;

*(c)* When the victim is a national of that State and that State sees fit to do so.

Every State Party shall, moreover, take the necessary measures to establish its jurisdiction over the crime described in this Convention when the alleged criminal is within its territory and it does not proceed to extradite him.

This Convention does not authorize any State Party to undertake, in the territory of another State Party, the exercise of jurisdiction or the performance of functions that are placed within the exclusive purview of the authorities of that other Party by its domestic law.

## *Article* V

The forced disappearance of persons shall not be considered a political offense for purposes of extradition.

The forced disappearance of persons shall be deemed to be included among the extraditable offenses in every extradition treaty entered into between States Parties.

The States Parties undertake to include the offense of forced disappearance as one which is extraditable in every extradition treaty to be concluded between them in the future.

Every State Party that makes extradition conditional on the existence of a treaty and receives a request for extradition from another State Party with which it has no extradition treaty may consider this Convention as the necessary legal basis for extradition with respect to the offense of forced disappearance.

States Parties which do not make extradition conditional on the existence of a treaty shall recognize such offense as extraditable, subject to the conditions imposed by the law of the requested State.

Extradition shall be subject to the provisions set forth in the constitution and other laws of the requested State.

## Article VI

When a State Party does not grant the extradition, the case shall be submitted to its competent authorities as if the offense had been committed within its jurisdiction, for the purposes of investigation and when appropriate, for criminal action, in accordance with its national law. Any decision adopted by these authorities shall be communicated to the State that has requested the extradition.

## Article VII

Criminal prosecution for the forced disappearance of persons and the penalty judicially imposed on its perpetrator shall not be subject to statutes of limitations.

However, if there should be a norm of a fundamental character preventing application of the stipulation contained in the previous paragraph, the period of limitation shall be equal to that which applies to the gravest crime in the domestic laws of the corresponding State Party.

## Article VIII

The defense of due obedience to superior orders or instructions that stipulate, authorize, or encourage forced disappearance shall not be admitted. All persons who receive such orders have the right and duty not to obey them.

The States Parties shall ensure that the training of public law-enforcement personnel or officials includes the necessary education on the offense of forced disappearance of persons.

## Article IX

Persons alleged to be responsible for the acts constituting the offense of forced disappearance of persons may be tried only in the competent jurisdictions of ordinary law in each State, to the exclusion of all other special jurisdictions, particularly military jurisdictions.

The acts constituting forced disappearance shall not be deemed to have been committed in the course of military duties.

Privileges, immunities, or special dispensations shall not be admitted in such trials, without prejudice to the provisions set forth in the Vienna Convention on Diplomatic Relations.

## Article X

In no case may exceptional circumstances such as a state of war, the threat of war, internal political instability, or any other public emergency be invoked to justify the forced disappearance of persons. In such cases, the right to expeditious and effective judicial procedures and recourse shall be retained as a means of determining the whereabouts or state of health of a person who has been deprived of freedom, or of identifying the official who ordered or carried out such deprivation of freedom.

In pursuing such procedures or recourse, and in keeping with applicable domestic law, the competent judicial authorities shall have free and immediate access to all detention centers and to each of their units, and to all places where there is reason to believe the disappeared person might be found including places that are subject to military jurisdiction.

*Article* XI

Every person deprived of liberty shall be held in an officially recognized place of detention and be brought before a competent judicial authority without delay, in accordance with applicable domestic law.

The States Parties shall establish and maintain official up-to-date registries of their detainees and, in accordance with their domestic law, shall make them available to relatives, judges, attorneys, any other person having a legitimate interest, and other authorities.

*Article* XII

The States Parties shall give each other mutual assistance in the search for, identification, location, and return of minors who have been removed to another State or detained therein as a consequence of the forced disappearance of their parents or guardians.

*Article* XIII

For the purposes of this Convention, the processing of petitions or communications presented to the Inter-American Commission on Human Rights alleging the forced disappearance of persons shall be subject to the procedures established in the American Convention on Human Rights and to the Statute and Regulations of the Inter-American Commission on Human Rights and to the Statute and Rules of Procedure of the Inter-American Court of Human Rights, including the provisions on precautionary measures.

*Article* XIV

Without prejudice to the provisions of the preceding article, when the Inter-American Commission on Human Rights receives a petition or communication regarding an alleged forced disappearance, its Executive Secretariat shall urgently and confidentially address the respective government, and shall request that government to provide as soon as possible information as to the whereabouts of the allegedly disappeared person together with any other information it considers pertinent, and such request shall be without prejudice as to the admissibility of the petition.

*Article* XV

None of the provisions of this Convention shall be interpreted as limiting other bilateral or multilateral treaties or other agreements signed by the Parties.

This Convention shall not apply to the international armed conflicts governed by the 1949 Geneva Conventions and their Protocols, concerning protection of wounded, sick, and shipwrecked members of the armed forces; and prisoners of war and civilians in time of war.

*Article* XVI

This Convention is open for signature by the member States of the Organization of American States.

*Article* XVII

This Convention is subject to ratification. The instruments of ratification shall be deposited with the General Secretariat of the Organization of American States.

*Article* XVIII

This Convention shall be open to accession by any other State. The instruments of accession shall be deposited with the General Secretariat of the Organization of American States.

*Article* XIX

The States may express reservations with respect to this Convention when adopting, signing, ratifying or acceding to it, unless such reservations are incompatible with the object and purpose of the Convention and as long as they refer to one or more specific provisions.

*Article* XX

This Convention shall enter into force for the ratifying States on the thirtieth day from the date of deposit of the second instrument of ratification.

For each State ratifying or acceding to the Convention after the second instrument of ratification has been deposited, the Convention shall enter into force on the thirtieth day from the date on which that State deposited its instrument of ratification or accession.

*Article* XXI

This Convention shall remain in force indefinitely, buy may be denounced by any State Party. The instrument of denunciation shall be deposited with the General Secretariat of the Organization of American States. The Convention shall cease to be in effect for the denouncing State and shall remain in force for the other States Parties one year from the date of deposit of the instrument of denunciation.

*Article* XXII

The original instrument of this Convention, the Spanish, English, Portuguese, and French texts of which are equally authentic, shall be deposited with the General Secretariat of the Organization of American States, which shall forward certified copies thereof to the United Nations Secretariat, for registration and publication, in accordance with Article 102 of the Charter of the United Nations. The General Secretariat of the Organization of American States shall notify member States of the Organization and States acceding to the Convention of the signatures and deposit of instruments of ratification, accession or denunciation, as well as of any reservations that may be expressed.

# PART SEVEN

# DEVELOPMENTS IN AFRICA

## INTRODUCTION

IN A GENERAL way, African States have taken, or reacted to, initiatives involving human rights within the framework of the United Nations. The principle of racial equality and the principle of self-determination have been primary but not exclusive concerns. See the material from the first and second Conferences of Independent African States in 1958 and 1960, and the resolutions of the First Assembly of the Heads of State and Government of the Organization of African Unity, 1964, reproduced in the third edition of this work, at 540–50.

Within the Organization of African Unity, the trend of policy has been against forms of intervention by the Organization and the principle of non-intervention has been maintained in the face of the notoriously disastrous situations in recent years in Equatorial Guinea, Uganda, the Great Lakes region, and elsewhere. Understandably, the focus of overt concern for many decades was the powerful white minority regimes in southern Africa. On the Organization of African Unity policy concerning non-interference in internal affairs see Akinyemi, A. B., 'The Organization of African Unity and the Concept of Non-Interference in Internal Affairs', (1972–3) 46 *BYIL* 393–400; Elias, T., *Africa and the Development of International Law* (1972). In recent years, attention has focused more on internal humanitarian crises, including questions of intervention and human rights, in which sub-regional organizations, such as ECOWAS and IGAD, have played an increasing role.

The text of the Charter of the Organization of African Unity may be found in Brownlie, I., *Basic Documents in International Law* (4th edn., 1995), 77. The First Assembly of the Heads of State and Government of the OAU met in Cairo in July 1964.

## 85. ORGANIZATION OF AFRICAN UNITY CONVENTION ON THE SPECIFIC ASPECTS OF REFUGEE PROBLEMS IN AFRICA, 1969

This Convention was adopted by the Heads of State and Government at the Sixth Ordinary Session of the Organization of African Unity, Addis Ababa, 10 September 1969, and entered into force on 20 June 1974, in accordance with Article XI; for text see 1000 UNTS 46.

See Oloka-Onyango, J., 'Human Rights, the OAU Convention and the Refugee Crisis in Africa', 3 *IJRL* 453 (1991); Okoth-Obbo, G., 'Thirty Years On: A Legal Review of the 1969 OAU Convention Governing the Specific Aspects of Refugee Problems in Africa', 20 *Refugee Survey Quarterly* 79 (2001).

*TEXT*

### Preamble

We, the Heads of State and Government assembled in the city of Addis Ababa, from 6–10 September 1969,

1. *Noting with concern* the constantly increasing numbers of refugees in Africa and desirous of finding ways and means of alleviating their misery and suffering as well as providing them with a better life and future,

2. *Recognizing* the need for an essentially humanitarian approach towards solving the problems of refugees,

3. *Aware*, however, that refugee problems are a source of friction among many Member States, and desirous of eliminating the source of such discord,

4. *Anxious* to make a distinction between a refugee who seeks a peaceful and normal life and a person fleeing his country for the sole purpose of fomenting subversion from outside,

5. *Determined* that the activities of such subversive elements should be discouraged, in accordance with the Declaration on the Problem of Subversion and Resolution on the Problem of Refugees adopted at Accra in 1965,

6. *Bearing in mind* that the Charter of the United Nations and the Universal Declaration of Human Rights have affirmed the principle that human beings shall enjoy fundamental rights and freedoms without discrimination,

7. *Recalling* Resolution 2312 (XXII) of 14 December 1967 of the United Nations General Assembly, relating to the Declaration on Territorial Asylum,

8. *Convinced* that all the problems of our continent must be solved in the spirit of the Charter of the Organization of African Unity and in the African context,

9. *Recognizing* that the United Nations Convention of 28 July 1951, as modified by the Protocol of 31 January 1967, constitutes the basic and universal instrument relating to the status of refugees and reflects the deep concern of States for refugees and their desire to establish common standards for their treatment,

10. *Recalling* Resolutions 26 and 104 of the OAU Assemblies of Heads of State and

Government, calling upon Member States of the Organization who had not already done so to accede to the United Nations Convention of 1951 and to the Protocol of 1967 relating to the Status of Refugees, and meanwhile to apply their provisions to refugees in Africa,

11. *Convinced* that the efficiency of the measures recommended by the present Convention to solve the problem of refugees in Africa necessitates close and continuous collaboration between the Organization of African Unity and the Office of the United Nations High Commissioner for Refugees,

*Have agreed* as follows:

*Article* I—Definition of the term 'Refugee'

1. For the purposes of this Convention, the term 'refugee' shall mean every person who, owing to well-founded fear of being persecuted for reasons of race, religion, nationality, membership of a particular social group or political opinion, is outside the country of his nationality and is unable or, owing to such fear, is unwilling to avail himself of the protection of that country, or who, not having a nationality and being outside the country of his former habitual residence as a result of such events is unable or, owing to such fear, is unwilling to return to it.

2. The term 'refugee' shall also apply to every person who, owing to external aggression, occupation, foreign domination or events seriously disturbing public order in either part or the whole of his country of origin or nationality, is compelled to leave his place of habitual residence in order to seek refuge in another place outside his country of origin or nationality.

3. In the case of a person who has several nationalities, the term 'a country of which he is a national' shall mean each of the countries of which he is a national, and a person shall not be deemed to be lacking the protection of the country of which he is a national if, without any valid reason based on well-founded fear, he has not availed himself of the protection of one of the countries of which he is a national.

4. This Convention shall cease to apply to any refugee if:

 (a) he has voluntarily re-availed himself of the protection of the country of his nationality, or,

 (b) having lost his nationality, he has voluntarily reacquired it, or,

 (c) he has acquired a new nationality, and enjoys the protection of the country of his new nationality, or,

 (d) he has voluntarily re-established himself in the country which he left or outside which he remained owing to fear of persecution, or,

 (e) he can no longer, because the circumstances in connection with which he was recognized as a refugee have ceased to exist, continue to refuse to avail himself of the protection of the country of his nationality, or,

 (f) he has committed a serious non-political crime outside his country of refuge after his admission to that country as a refugee, or,

 (g) he has seriously infringed the purposes and objectives of this Convention.

5. The provisions of this Convention shall not apply to any person with respect to whom the country of asylum has serious reasons for considering that:

    *(a)* he has committed a crime against peace, a war crime, or a crime against humanity, as defined in the international instruments drawn up to make provision in respect of such crimes;

    *(b)* he committed a serious non-political crime outside the country of refuge prior to his admission to that country as a refugee;

    *(c)* he has been guilty of acts contrary to the purposes and principles of the Organization of African Unity;

    *(d)* he has been guilty of acts contrary to the purposes and principles of the United Nations.

6. For the purposes of this Convention, the Contracting State of asylum shall determine whether an applicant is a refugee.

*Article* II—Asylum

1. Member States of the OAU shall use their best endeavours consistent with their respective legislations to receive refugees and to secure the settlement of those refugees who, for well-founded reasons, are unable or unwilling to return to their country of origin or nationality.

2. The grant of asylum to refugees is a peaceful and humanitarian act and shall not be regarded as an unfriendly act by any Member State.

3. No person shall be subjected by a Member State to measures such as rejection at the frontier, return or expulsion, which would compel him to return to or remain in a territory where his life, physical integrity or liberty would be threatened for the reasons set out in Article I, paragraphs 1 and 2.

4. Where a Member State finds difficulty in continuing to grant asylum to refugees, such Member State may appeal directly to other Member States and through the OAU, and such other Member States shall in the spirit of African solidarity and international co-operation take appropriate measures to lighten the burden of the Member State granting asylum.

5. Where a refugee has not received the right to reside in any country of asylum, he may be granted temporary residence in any country of asylum in which he first presented himself as a refugee pending arrangement for his resettlement in accordance with the preceding paragraph.

6. For reasons of security, countries of asylum shall, as far as possible, settle refugees at a reasonable distance from the frontier of their country of origin.

*Article* III—Prohibition of Subversive Activities

1. Every refugee has duties to the country in which he finds himself, which require in particular that he conforms with its laws and regulations as well as with measures taken for the maintenance of public order. He shall also abstain from any subversive activities against any Member State of the OAU.

2. Signatory States undertake to prohibit refugees residing in their respective territories from attacking any State Member of the OAU, by any activity likely to cause tension between Member States, and in particular by use of arms, through the press, or by radio.

*Article* IV—Non-Discrimination

Member States undertake to apply the provisions of this Convention to all refugees without discrimination as to race, religion, nationality, membership of a particular social group or political opinions.

*Article* V—Voluntary Repatriation

1. The essentially voluntary character of repatriation shall be respected in all cases and no refugee shall be repatriated against his will.

2. The country of asylum, in collaboration with the country of origin, shall make adequate arrangements for the safe return of refugees who request repatriation.

3. The country of origin, on receiving back refugees, shall facilitate their resettlement and grant them the full rights and privileges of nationals of the country, and subject them to the same obligations.

4. Refugees who voluntarily return to their country shall in no way be penalized for having left it for any of the reasons giving rise to refugee situations. Whenever necessary, an appeal shall be made through national information media and through the Administrative Secretary-General of the OAU, inviting refugees to return home and giving assurance that the new circumstances prevailing in their country of origin will enable them to return without risk and to take up a normal and peaceful life without fear of being disturbed or punished, and that the text of such appeal should be given to refugees and clearly explained to them by their country of asylum.

5. Refugees who freely decide to return to their homeland, as a result of such assurances or on their own initiative, shall be given every possible assistance by the country of asylum, the country of origin, voluntary agencies and international and intergovernmental organizations, to facilitate their return.

*Article* IV—Travel Documents

1. Subject to Article III, Member States shall issue to refugees lawfully staying in their territories travel documents in accordance with the United Nations Convention relating to the Status of Refugees and the Schedule and Annex thereto, for the purpose of travel outside their territory, unless compelling reasons of national security or public order otherwise require. Member States may issue such a travel document to any other refugee in their territory.

2. Where an African country of second asylum accepts a refugee from a country of first asylum, the country of first asylum may be dispensed from issuing a document with a return clause.

3. Travel documents issued to refugees under previous international agreements by States Parties thereto shall be recognized and treated by Member States in the same way as if they had been issued to refugees pursuant to this Article.

*Article* VII—Co-operation of the National Authorities with the Organization of African Unity

In order to enable the Administrative Secretary-General of the Organization of African Unity to make reports to the competent organs of the Organization of African Unity, Member States undertake to provide the Secretariat in the appropriate form with information and statistical data requested concerning:

*(a)* the condition of refugees;

*(b)* the implementation of this Convention, and

*(c)* laws, regulations and decrees which are, or may hereafter be, in force relating to refugees.

### *Article* VIII—Co-operation with the Office of the United Nations High Commissioner for Refugees

1. Member States shall co-operate with the Office of the United Nations High Commissioner for Refugees.

2. The present Convention shall be the effective regional complement in Africa of the 1951 United Nations Convention on the Status of Refugees.

### *Article* IX—Settlement of Disputes

Any dispute between States signatories to this Convention relating to its interpretation or application, which cannot be settled by other means, shall be referred to the Commission for Mediation, Conciliation and Arbitration of the Organization of African Unity, at the request of any one of the Parties to the dispute.

### *Article* X—Signature and Ratification

1. This Convention is open for signature and accession by all Member States of the Organization of African Unity and shall be ratified by signatory States in accordance with their respective constitutional processes. The instruments of ratification shall be deposited with the Administrative Secretary-General of the Organization of African Unity.

2. The original instrument, done if possible in African languages, and in English and French, all texts being equally authentic, shall be deposited with the Administrative Secretary-General of the Organization of African Unity.

3. Any independent African State, Member of the Organization of African Unity, may at any time notify the Administrative Secretary-General of the Organization of African Unity of its accession to this Convention.

### *Article* XI—Entry into force

This Convention shall come into force upon deposit of instruments of ratification by one-third of the Member States of the Organization of African Unity.

### *Article* XII—Amendment

This Convention may be amended or revised if any Member State makes a written request to the Administrative Secretary-General to that effect, provided however that the proposed amendment shall not be submitted to the Assembly of Heads of State and Government for consideration until all Member States have been duly notified of it and a period of one year has elapsed. Such an amendment shall not be effective unless approved by at least two-thirds of the Member States Parties to the present Convention.

### *Article* XIII—Denunciation

1. Any Member State Party to this Convention may denounce its provisions by a written notification to the Administrative Secretary-General.

2. At the end of one year from the date of such notification, if not withdrawn, the Convention shall cease to apply with respect to the denouncing State.

*Article* XIV

Upon entry into force of this Convention, the Administrative Secretary-General of the OAU shall register it with the Secretary-General of the United Nations, in accordance with Article 102 of the Charter of the United Nations.

*Article* XV—Notifications by the Administrative Secretary-General
of the Organization of African Unity

The Administrative Secretary-General of the Organization of African Unity shall inform all Members of the Organization:

(a) of signatures, ratifications and accessions in accordance with Article X;

(b) of entry into force, in accordance with Article XI;

(c) of requests for amendments submitted under the terms of Article XII;

(d) of denunciations, in accordance with Article XIII.

In witness whereof we, the Heads of African State and Government, have signed this Convention.

*Done* in the City of Addis Ababa this 10th day of September 1969.

## 86. AFRICAN CHARTER ON HUMAN AND PEOPLES' RIGHTS, 1981

The Charter was adopted on 17 June 1981 by the Eighteenth Assembly of the Heads of State and Government of the Organization of African Unity. The treaty entered into force on 21 October 1986. For text see OAU doc. CAB/LEG/67/3 rev. 5, 21 ILM 58 (1982).

See generally Umozurike, U. O., *The African Charter of Human and Peoples' Rights* (1997); Ankumak, E. A., *The African Commission on Human and Peoples' Rights: Practice and Procedures* (1996); Bello, E. G., 'The African Charter of Human and Peoples' Rights: A Legal Analysis', 194 *Recueil des Cours* (Hague Academy of International Law) (1985–V), 13–268; D'Sa, R. M., 'The African Charter of Human and Peoples' Rights: Problems and Prospects for Regional Action', 10 *Aust. YIL* 101–30 (1987).

*TEXT*

Preamble

The African States members of the Organization of African Unity, parties to the present convention entitled 'African Charter on Human and Peoples' Rights',

*Recalling* Decision 115 (XVI) of the Assembly of Heads of State and Government at its Sixteenth Ordinary Session held in Monrovia, Liberia, from 17 to 20 July 1979 on the preparation of 'a preliminary draft on an African Charter on Human and Peoples' Rights providing *inter alia* for the establishment of bodies to promote and protect human and peoples' rights';

*Considering* the Charter of the Organization of African Unity, which stipulates that 'freedom, equality, justice and legitimate aspirations of the African peoples';

*Reaffirming* the pledge they solemnly made in Article 2 of the said Charter to eradicate all forms of colonialism from Africa, to coordinate and intensify their cooperation and efforts to achieve a better life for the peoples' of Africa and to promote international cooperation having due regard to the Charter of the United Nations and the Universal Declaration of Human Rights;

*Taking into consideration* the virtues of their historical tradition and the values of African civilization which should inspire and characterize their reflection on the concept of human and peoples rights;

*Recognizing* on the one hand, that fundamental human rights stem from the attributes of human beings, which justifies their international protection and on the other hand that the reality and respect of peoples rights should necessarily guarantee human rights;

*Considering* that the enjoyment of rights and freedoms also implies the performance of duties on the part of everyone;

*Convinced* that it is henceforth essential to pay a particular attention to the right to development and that civil and political rights cannot be dissociated from economic, social and cultural rights in their conception as well as universality and that the satisfaction of economic, social and cultural rights is a guarantee for the enjoyment of civil and political rights;

*Conscious* of their duty to achieve the total liberation of Africa, the peoples of which are still struggling for their dignity and genuine independence, and undertaking to eliminate colonialism, neo-colonialism apartheid, zionism and to dismantle aggressive foreign military bases and all forms of discrimination, language, religion or political opinions;

*Reaffirming* their adherence to the principles of human and peoples' rights and freedoms contained in the declarations, conventions and other instruments adopted by the Organization of African Unity, the Movement of Non-Aligned Countries and the United Nations;

*Firmly convinced* of their duty to promote and protect human and peoples' rights and freedoms taking into account the importance traditionally attached to these rights and freedoms in Africa;

*Have agreed* as follows:

## PART I

## RIGHTS AND DUTIES
### Chapter I—Human and Peoples' Rights

*Article* 1

The Member States of the Organization of African Unity parties to the present Charter shall recognize the rights, duties and freedoms enshrined in this Charter and shall undertake to adopt legislative or other measures to give effect to them.

*Article* 2

Every individual shall be entitled to the enjoyment of the rights and freedoms recognized and guaranteed in the present Charter without distinction of any kind such as race, ethnic group, colour, sex, language, religion, political or any other opinion, national and social origin, fortune, birth or other status.

*Article* 3

1. Every individual shall be equal before the law.
2. Every individual shall be entitled to equal protection of the law.

*Article* 4

Human beings are inviolable. Every human being shall be entitled to respect for his life and the integrity of his person. No one may be arbitrarily deprived of this right.

*Article* 5

Every individual shall have the right to the respect of the dignity inherent in a human being and to the recognition of his legal status. All forms of exploitation and degradation of man particularly slavery, slave trade, torture, cruel, inhuman or degrading punishment and treatment shall be prohibited.

*Article* 6

Every individual shall have the right to liberty and to the security of his person. No one may be deprived of his freedom except for reasons and conditions previously laid down by law. In particular, no one may be arbitrarily arrested or detained.

*Article* 7

1. Every individual shall have the right to have his cause heard. This comprises:

   *(a)* The right to an appeal to competent national organs against acts of violating his fundamental rights as recognized and guaranteed by conventions, laws, regulations and customs in force;

   *(b)* the right to be presumed innocent until proved guilty by a competent court or tribunal;

   *(c)* the right to defence, including the right to be defended by counsel of his choice;

   *(d)* the right to be tried within a reasonable time by an impartial court or tribunal.

2. No one may be condemned for an act or omission which did not constitute a legally punishable offence at the time it was committed. No penalty may be inflicted for an offence for which no provision was made at the time it was committed. Punishment is personal and can be imposed only on the offender.

*Article* 8

Freedom of conscience, the profession and free practice of religion shall be guaranteed. No one may, subject to law and order, be submitted to measures restricting the exercise of these freedoms.

*Article* 9

1. Every individual shall have the right to receive information.

2. Every individual shall have the right to express and disseminate his opinions within the law.

*Article* 10

1. Every individual shall have the right to free association provided that he abides by the law.

2. Subject to the obligation of solidarity provided for in Article 29 no one may be compelled to join an association.

*Article* 11

Every individual shall have the right to assemble freely with others. The exercise of this right shall be subject only to necessary restrictions provided for by law in particular those enacted in the interest of national security, the safety, health, ethics rights and freedoms of others.

*Article* 12

1. Every individual shall have the right to freedom of movement and residence within the borders of a State provided he abides by the law.

2. Every individual shall have the right to leave any country including his own, and

to return to his country. This right may only be subject to restrictions, provided for by law for the protection of national security, law and order, public health or morality.

3. Every individual shall have the right, when persecuted, to seek and obtain asylum in other countries in accordance with the law of those countries and international conventions.

4. A non-national legally admitted in a territory of a State Party to the present Charter, may only be expelled from it by virtue of a decision taken in accordance with the law.

5. The mass expulsion of non-nationals shall be prohibited. Mass expulsion shall be that which is aimed at national, racial, ethnic or religious groups.

*Article* 13

1. Every citizen shall have the right to participate freely in the government of his country, either directly or through freely chosen representatives in accordance with the provisions of the law.

2. Every citizen shall have the right of equal access to the public service of his country.

3. Every individual shall have the right of access to public property and services in strict equality of all persons before the law.

*Article* 14

The right to property shall be guaranteed. It may only be encroached upon in the interest of public need or in the general interest of the community and in accordance with the provisions of appropriate laws.

*Article* 15

Every individual shall have the right to work under equitable and satisfactory conditions, and shall receive equal pay for equal work.

*Article* 16

1. Every individual shall have the right to enjoy the best attainable state of physical and mental health.

2. States Parties to the present Charter shall take the necessary measures to protect the health of their people and to ensure that they receive medical attention when they are sick.

*Article* 17

1. Every individual shall have the right to education.

2. Every individual may freely, take part in the cultural life of his community.

3. The promotion and protection of morals and traditional values recognized by the community shall be the duty of the State.

*Article* 18

1. The family shall be the natural unit and basis of society. It shall be protected by the State which shall take care of its physical health and moral.

2. The State shall have the duty to assist the family which is the custodian of morals and traditional values recognized by the community.

3. The State shall ensure the elimination of every discrimination against women and also ensure the protection of the rights of the woman and the child as stipulated in international declarations and conventions.

4. The aged and the disabled shall also have the right to special measures of protection in keeping with their physical or moral needs.

*Article* 19

All peoples shall be equal; they shall enjoy the same respect and shall have the same rights. Nothing shall justify the domination of a people by another.

*Article* 20

1. All peoples shall have right to existence. They shall have the unquestionable and inalienable right to self-determination. They shall freely determine their political status and shall pursue their economic and social development according to the policy they have freely chosen.

2. Colonized or oppressed peoples shall have the right to free themselves from the bonds of domination by resorting to any means recognized by the international community.

3. All peoples shall have the right to the assistance of the States Parties to the present Charter in their liberation struggle against foreign domination, be it political, economic or cultural.

*Article* 21

1. All peoples shall freely dispose of their wealth and natural resources. This right shall be exercised in the exclusive interest of the people. In no case shall a people be deprived of it.

2. In case of spoliation the dispossessed people shall have the right to the lawful recovery of its property as well as to an adequate compensation.

3. The free disposal of wealth and natural resources shall be exercised without prejudice to the obligation of promoting international economic cooperation based on mutual respect, equitable exchange and the principles of international law.

4. States parties to the present Charter shall individually and collectively exercise the right to free disposal of their wealth and natural resources with a view to strengthening African unity and solidarity.

5. States Parties to the present Charter shall undertake to eliminate all forms of foreign economic exploitation particularly that practised by international monopolies so as to enable their peoples to fully benefit from the advantages derived from their national resources.

*Article* 22

1. All peoples shall have the right to their economic, social and cultural development with due regard to their freedom and identity and in the equal enjoyment of the common heritage of mankind.

2. States shall have the duty, individually or collectively to ensure the exercise of the right to development.

*Article* 23

1. All peoples shall have the right to national and international peace and security. The principles of solidarity and friendly relations implicitly affirmed by the Charter of the United Nations and reaffirmed by that of the Organization of African Unity shall govern relations between States.

2. For the purpose of strengthening peace, solidarity and friendly relations, States parties to the present Charter shall ensure that:

    *(a)* any individual enjoying the right of asylum under Article 12 of the present Charter shall not engage in subversive activities against his country of origin or any other State party to the present Charter;

    *(b)* their territories shall not be used as bases for subversive or terrorist activities against the people of any other State party to the present Charter.

*Article* 24

All peoples shall have the right to a general satisfactory environment favourable to their development.

*Article* 25

States parties to the present Charter shall have the duty to promote and ensure through teaching, education and publication, the respect of the rights and freedoms contained in the present Charter and to see to it that these freedoms and rights as well as corresponding obligations and duties are understood.

*Article* 26

States parties to the present Charter shall have the duty to guarantee the independence of the Courts and shall allow the establishment and improvement of appropriate national institutions entrusted with the promotion and protection of the rights and freedoms guaranteed by the present Charter.

## Chapter II—Duties

*Article* 27

1. Every individual shall have duties towards his family and society, the State and other legally recognised communities and the international community.

2. The rights and freedoms of each individual shall be exercised with due regard to the rights of others, collective security, morality and common interest.

*Article* 28

Every individual shall have the duty to respect and consider his fellow beings without discrimination, and to maintain relations aimed at promoting, safeguarding and reinforcing mutual respect and tolerance.

*Article* 29

The individual shall also have the duty:

1. To preserve the harmonious development of the family and to work for the cohesion and respect of the family; to respect, his parents at all times, to maintain them in case of need;

2. To serve his national community by placing his physical and intellectual abilities at its service;

3. Not to compromise the security of the State whose national or resident he is;

4. To preserve and strengthen social and national solidarity, particularly when the latter is threatened;

5. To preserve and strengthen the national independence and the territorial integrity of his country and to contribute to its defence in accordance with the law;

6. To work to the best of his abilities and competence, and to pay taxes imposed by law in the interest of the society;

7. To preserve and strengthen positive African cultural values in his relations with other members of the society, in the spirit of tolerance, dialogue and consultation and, in general, to contribute to the promotion of the moral well being of society;

8. To contribute to the best of his abilities, at all times and at all levels, to the promotion and achievement of African unity.

# PART II

## MEASURES OF SAFEGUARD

### Chapter I—Establishment and Organization of the African Commission on Human and Peoples' Rights

*Article* 30

An African Commission on Human and Peoples' Rights, hereinafter called 'the Commission', shall be established within the Organization of African Unity to promote human and peoples' rights and ensure their protection in Africa.

*Article* 31

1. The Commission shall consist of eleven members chosen from amongst African personalities of the highest reputation, known for their high morality, integrity, impartiality and competence in matters of human and peoples' rights; particular consideration being given to persons having legal experience.

2. The members of the Commission shall serve in their personal capacity.

*Article* 32

The Commission shall not include more than one national of the same State.

*Article* 33

The members of the Commission shall be elected by secret ballot by the Assembly of Heads of State and Government, from a list of persons nominated by the States parties to the present Charter.

*Article* 34

Each State party to the present Charter may not nominate more than two candidates. The candidates must have the nationality of one of the States parties to the present Charter. When two candidates are nominated by a State, one of them may not be a national of that State.

*Article* 35

1. The Secretary-General of the Organization of African Unity shall invite States parties to the present Charter at least four months before the elections to nominate candidates;

2. The Secretary-General of the Organization of African Unity shall make an alphabetical list of the persons thus nominated and communicate it to the Heads of State and Government at least one month before the elections.

*Article* 36

The members of the Commission shall be elected for a six year period and shall be eligible for re-election. However, the term of office of four of the members elected at the first election shall terminate after two years and the term of office of three others, at the end of four years.

*Article* 37

Immediately after the first election, the Chairman of the Assembly of Heads of State and Government of the Organization of African Unity shall draw lots to decide the names of those members referred to in Article 36.

*Article* 38

After their election, the members of the Commission shall make a solemn declaration to discharge their duties impartially and faithfully.

*Article* 39

1. In case of death or resignation of a member of the Commission the Chairman of the Commission shall immediately inform the Secretary-General of the Organization of African Unity, who shall declare the seat vacant from the date of death or from the date on which the resignation takes effect.

2. If, in the unanimous opinion of other members of the Commission, a member has stopped discharging his duties for any reason other than a temporary absence, the Chairman of the Commission shall inform the Secretary-General of the Organization of African Unity, who shall then declare the seat vacant.

3. In each of the cases anticipated above, the Assembly of Heads of State and Government shall replace the member whose seat became vacant for the remaining period of his term unless the period is less than six months.

*Article* 40

Every member of the Commission shall be in office until the date his successor assumes office.

*Article* 41

The Secretary-General of the Organization of African Unity shall appoint the

Secretary of the Commission. He shall provide the staff and services necessary for the effective discharge of the duties of the Commission. The Organization of African Unity shall bear cost of the staff and services.

*Article* 42

1. The Commission shall elect its Chairman and Vice Chairman for a two-year period. They shall be eligible for re-election.

2. The Commission shall lay down its rules of procedure.

3. Seven members shall form the quorum.

4. In case of an equality of votes, the Chairman shall have a casting vote.

5. The Secretary-General may attend the meetings of the Commission. He shall neither participate in deliberations nor shall he be entitled to vote. The Chairman of the Commission may, however, invite him to speak.

*Article* 43

In discharging their duties, members of the Commission shall enjoy diplomatic privileges and immunities provided for in the General Convention on the Privileges and immunities of the Organization of African Unity.

*Article* 44

Provision shall be made for the emoluments and allowances of the members of the Commission in the Regular Budget of the Organization of African Unity.

## Chapter II—Mandate of the Commission

*Article* 45

The functions of the Commission shall be:

1. To promote Human and Peoples' Rights and in particular:

    (a) to collect documents, undertake studies and researches on African problems in the field of human and peoples' rights, organize seminars, symposia and conferences, disseminate information, encourage national and local institutions concerned with human and peoples' rights, and should the case arise, give its views or make recommendations to Governments.

    (b) to formulate and lay down, principles and rules aimed at solving legal problems relating to human and peoples' rights and fundamental freedoms upon which African Governments may base their legislation.

    (c) co-operate with other African and international institutions concerned with the promotion and protection of human and peoples' Rights.

2. Ensure the protection of human and peoples' rights under conditions laid down by the present Charter.

3. Interpret all the provisions of the present Charter at the request of a State party, an institution of the OAU or an African Organization recognized by the OAU.

4. Perform any other tasks which may be entrusted to it by the Assembly of Heads of State and Government.

## Chapter III—Procedure of the Commission

*Article* 46

The Commission may resort to any appropriate method of investigation; it may hear from the Secretary-General of the Organization of African Unity or any other person capable of enlightening it.

*Article* 47

If a State party to the present Charter has good reasons to believe that another State Party to this Charter has violated the provisions of the Charter, it may draw, by written communication, the attention of that State to the matter. This communication shall also be addressed to the Secretary-General of the OAU and to the Chairman of the Commission. Within three months of the receipt of the communication, the State to which the communication is addressed shall give the enquiring State, written explanation or statement elucidating the matter. This should include as much as possible relevant information relating to the laws and rules of procedure applied and applicable and the redress already given or course of action available.

*Article* 48

If within three months from the date on which the original communication is received by the State to which it is addressed, the issue is not settled to the satisfaction of the two States involved through bilateral negotiation or by any other peaceful procedure, either State shall have the right to submit the matter to the Commission through the Chairman and shall notify the other States involved.

*Article* 49

Notwithstanding the provisions of Article 47, if a State party to the present Charter considers that another State party has violated the provisions of the Charter, it may refer the matter directly to the Commission by addressing a communication to the Chairman, to the Secretary-General of the Organization of African Unity and the State concerned.

*Article* 50

The Commission can only deal with a matter submitted to it after making sure that all local remedies, if they exist, have been exhausted, unless it is obvious to the Commission that the procedure of achieving these remedies would be unduly prolonged.

*Article* 51

1. The Commission may ask the States concerned to provide it with all relevant information.
2. When the Commission is considering the matter, States concerned may be represented before it and submit written or oral representation.

*Article* 52

After having obtained from the States concerned and from other sources all the information it deems necessary and after having tried all appropriate means to reach an amicable solution based on the respect of Human and Peoples' Rights, the Commission shall prepare, within a reasonable period of time from the notification referred to in Article 48, a report to the States concerned and communicated to the Assembly of Heads of State and Government.

*Article* 53

While transmitting its report, the Commission may make to the Assembly of Heads of State and Government such recommendations as it deems useful.

*Article* 54

The Commission shall submit to each ordinary Session of the Assembly of Heads of State and Government a report on its activities.

*Article* 55

1. Before each Session, the Secretary of the Commission shall make a list of the Communications other than those of States parties to the present Charter and transmit them to the Members of the Commission, who shall indicate which communications should be considered by the commission.

2. A communication shall be considered by the Commission if a simple majority of its members so decide.

*Article* 56

Communication relating to human and peoples' rights referred to in Article 55 received by the commission, shall be considered if they:

1. Indicate their authors even if the latter request anonymity,

2. Are compatible with the Charter of the Organization of African Unity or with the present Charter,

3. Are not written in disparaging or insulting language directed against the State concerned and its institutions or to the Organization of African Unity,

4. Are not based exclusively on news disseminated through the mass media,

5. Are sent after exhausting local remedies, if any unless it is obvious that this procedure is unduly prolonged,

6. Are submitted within a reasonable period from the time local remedies are exhausted or from the date the commission is seized with the matter, and

7. Do not deal with cases which have been settled by these States involved in accordance with the principles of the Charter of the United Nations, or the Charter of the Organization of African Unity or the provisions of the present Charter.

*Article* 57

Prior to any substantive consideration, all communications shall be brought to the knowledge of the State concerned by the Chairman of the Commission.

*Article* 58

1. When it appears after deliberations of the Commission that one or more communications apparently relate to special cases which reveal the existence of a series

of serious or massive violations of human and peoples' rights, the Commission shall draw the attention of the Assembly of Heads of State and Government to these special cases.

2. The Assembly of Heads of State and Government may then request the Commission to undertake an in-depth study of these cases and make a factual report, accompanied by its finding and recommendations.

3. A case of emergency duly noticed by the Commission shall be submitted by the latter to the Chairman of the Assembly of Heads of State and Government who may request an in-depth study.

*Article* 59

1. All measures taken within the provisions of the present Chapter shall remain confidential until such a time as the Assembly of Heads of State and Government shall otherwise decide.

2. However, the report shall be published by the Chairman of the Commission upon the decision of the Assembly of Heads of State and Government.

3. The report on the activities of the Commission shall be published by its Chairman after it has been considered by the Assembly of Heads of State and Government.

## Chapter IV—Applicable Principles

*Article* 60

The Commission shall draw inspiration from international law on human and peoples' rights, particularly from the provisions of various African instruments on human and peoples' rights, the Charter of the United Nations, the Charter of the Organization of African Unity, the Universal Declaration of Human Rights, other instruments adopted by the United Nations and by African countries in the field of human and peoples' rights as well as from the provisions of various instruments adopted within the Specialised Agencies of the United Nations of which the parties to the present Charter are members.

*Article* 61

The Commission shall also take into consideration, as subsidiary measures to determine the principles of law, other general or special international conventions, laying down rules expressly recognized by member States of the Organization of African Unity, African practices consistent with international norms on human and peoples' rights, customs generally accepted as law, general principles of law recognized by African States as well as legal precedents and doctrine.

*Article* 62

Each State party shall undertake to submit every two years, from the date the present Charter comes into force, a report on the legislative or other measures taken with a view to giving effect to the rights and freedoms recognized and guaranteed by the present Charter.

*Article* 63

1. The present Charter shall be open to signature, ratification or adherence of the member States of the Organization of African Unity.

2. The instruments of ratification or adherence to the present Charter shall be deposited with the Secretary-General of the Organization of African Unity.

3. The present Charter shall come into force three months after the reception by the Secretary-General of the instruments of ratification or adherence of a simple majority of the member States of the Organization of African Unity.

# PART III

## GENERAL PROVISIONS

*Article* 64

1. After the coming into force of the present Charter, members of the Commission shall be elected in accordance with the relevant Articles of the present Charter.

2. The Secretary-General of the Organization of African Unity shall convene the first meeting of the Commission at the Headquarters of the Organization within three months of the constitution of the Commission. Thereafter, the Commission shall be convened by its Chairman whenever necessary but at least once a year.

*Article* 65

For each of the States that will ratify or adhere to the present Charter after its coming into force, the Charter shall take effect three months after the date of the deposit by that State of its instrument of ratification or adherence.

*Article* 66

Special protocols or agreements may, if necessary, supplement the provisions of the present Charter.

*Article* 67

The Secretary-General of the Organization of African Unity shall inform member States of the Organization of the deposit of each instrument of ratification or adherence.

*Article* 68

The present Charter may be amended if a State party makes a written request to that effect to the Secretary-General of the Organization of African Unity. The Assembly of Heads of State and Government may only consider the draft amendment after all the States parties have been duly informed of it and the Commission has given its opinion on it at the request of the sponsoring State. The amendment shall be approved by a simple majority of the States parties. It shall come into force for each State which has accepted it in accordance with its constitutional procedure three months after the Secretary-General has received notice of the acceptance.

## 87. PROTOCOL TO THE AFRICAN CHARTER ON HUMAN AND PEOPLES' RIGHTS ON THE ESTABLISHMENT OF AN AFRICAN COURT ON HUMAN AND PEOPLES' RIGHTS, 1998

Experience in Europe and the Americas has shown the value of regional, judicial oversight of the human rights obligations assumed by States, but also of the importance of regional human rights commissions in building the initial basis of trust among governments and among the peoples of particular regions.

The African Commission has been engaged in that task over many years, but it is now regularly encouraging States to ratify this Protocol and support the establishment of an African Court of Human and Peoples' Rights; see Final Communiqué, 27th Ordinary Session of the African Commission on Human and Peoples' Rights, 27 April–11 May 2000, Algiers, Algeria.

*TEXT*

The Member States of the Organization of African Unity, hereinafter referred to as the OAU, States Parties to the African Charter on Human and Peoples' Rights:

*Considering* that the Charter of the Organization of African Unity recognizes that freedom, equality, justice, peace and dignity are essential objectives for the achievement of the legitimate aspirations of the African peoples;

*Noting* that the African Charter on Human and Peoples' Rights reaffirms adherence to the principles of human and peoples' rights, freedoms and duties contained in the declarations, conventions and other instruments adopted by the Organization of African Unity, and other international organizations;

*Recognizing* that the twofold objective of the African Charter on Human and Peoples' Rights is to ensure on the one hand promotion and on the other protection of human and peoples' rights, freedoms and duties;

*Recognizing further* the efforts of the African Commission on Human and Peoples' Rights in the promotion and protection of human and peoples' rights since its inception in 1987;

*Recalling* resolution AHG/Res.230 (XXX) adopted by the Assembly of Heads of State and Government in June 1994 in Tunis, Tunisia, requesting the Secretary-General to convene a Government experts' meeting to ponder, in conjunction with the African Commission, over the means to enhance the efficiency of the African Commission and to consider in particular the establishment of an African Court on Human and Peoples' Rights;

*Noting* the first and second Government legal experts' meetings held respectively in Cape Town, South Africa (September 1995) and Nouakchott, Mauritania (April 1997), and the third Government Legal Experts meeting held in Addis Ababa, Ethiopia (December 1997), which was enlarged to include Diplomats;

*Firmly convinced* that the attainment of the objectives of the African Charter on Human and Peoples' Rights requires the establishment of an African Court on

Human and Peoples' Rights to complement and reinforce the functions of the African Commission on Human and Peoples' Rights.

*Have agreed* as follows:

### Article 1—*Establishment of the Court*

There shall be established within the Organization of African Unity an African Court on Human and Peoples' Rights, hereinafter referred to as 'the Court', the organization, jurisdiction and functioning of which shall be governed by the present Protocol.

### Article 2—*Relationship Between the Court and the Commission*

The Court shall, bearing in mind the provisions of this Protocol, complement the protective mandate of the African Commission on Human and Peoples' Rights, hereinafter referred to as 'the Commission', conferred upon it by the African Charter on Human and Peoples' Rights, hereinafter referred to as 'the Charter'.

### Article 3—*Jurisdiction*

1. The jurisdiction of the Court shall extend to all cases and disputes submitted to it concerning the interpretation and application of the Charter, this Protocol and any other relevant human rights instrument ratified by the States concerned.

2. In the event of a dispute as to whether the Court has jurisdiction, the Court shall decide.

### Article 4—*Advisory Opinions*

1. At the request of a Member State of the OAU, the OAU, any of its organs, or any African organization recognized by the OAU, the Court may provide an opinion on any legal matter relating to the Charter or any other relevant human rights instruments, provided that the subject matter of the opinion is not related to a matter being examined by the Commission.

2. The Court shall give reasons for its advisory opinions provided that every judge shall be entitled to deliver a separate or dissenting decision.

### Article 5—*Access to the Court*

1. The following are entitled to submit cases to the Court:

    (a) The Commission;

    (b) The State Party which has lodged a complaint to the Commission;

    (c) The State Party against which the complaint has been lodged at the Commission;

    (d) The State Party whose citizen is a victim of human rights violation;

    (e) African Intergovernmental Organizations.

2. When a State Party has an interest in a case, it may submit a request to the Court to be permitted to join.

3. The Court may entitle relevant Non-Governmental Organizations (NGOs) with observer status before the Commission, and individuals to institute cases directly before it, in accordance with Article 34(6) of this Protocol.

*Article 6—Admissibility of Cases*

1. The Court, when deciding on the admissibility of a case instituted under Article 5(3) of this Protocol, may request the opinion of the Commission which shall give it as soon as possible.

2. The Court shall rule on the admissibility of cases taking into account the provisions of Article 56 of the Charter.

3. The Court may consider cases or transfer them to the Commission.

*Article 7—Sources of Law*

The Court shall apply the provisions of the Charter and any other relevant human rights instruments ratified by the States concerned.

*Article 8—Consideration of Cases*

The Rules of Procedure of the Court shall lay down the detailed conditions under which the Court shall consider cases brought before it, bearing in mind the complementarity between the Commission and the Court.

*Article 9—Amicable Settlement*

The Court may try to reach an amicable settlement in a case pending before it in accordance with the provisions of the Charter.

*Article 10—Hearings and Representation*

1. The Court shall conduct its proceedings in public. The Court may, however, conduct proceedings in camera as may be provided for in the Rules of Procedure.

2. Any party to a case shall be entitled to be represented by a legal representative of the party's choice. Free legal representation may be provided where the interests of justice so require.

3. Any person, witness or representative of the parties, who appears before the Court, shall enjoy protection and all facilities, in accordance with international law, necessary for the discharging of their functions, tasks and duties in relation to the Court.

*Article 11—Composition*

1. The Court shall consist of eleven judges, nationals of Member States of the OAU, elected in an individual capacity from among jurists of high moral character and of recognized practical, judicial or academic competence and experience in the field of human and peoples' rights.

2. No two judges shall be nationals of the same State.

*Article 12—Nominations*

1. States Parties to the Protocol may each propose up to three candidates, at least two of whom shall be nationals of that State.

2. Due consideration shall be given to adequate gender representation in the nomination process.

*Article 13—List of Candidates*

1. Upon entry into force of this Protocol, the Secretary-General of the OAU shall

request each State Party to the Protocol to present, within ninety (90) days of such a request, its nominees for the office of judge of the Court.

2. The Secretary-General of the OAU shall prepare a list in alphabetical order of the candidates nominated and transmit it to the Member States of the OAU at least thirty days prior to the next session of the Assembly of Heads of State and Government of the OAU, hereinafter referred to as 'the Assembly'.

*Article 14—Elections*

1. The judges of the Court shall be elected by secret ballot by the Assembly from the list referred to in Article 13(2) of the present Protocol.

2. The Assembly shall ensure that in the Court as a whole there is representation of the main regions of Africa and of their principal legal traditions.

3. In the election of the judges, the Assembly shall ensure that there is adequate gender representation.

*Article 15—Term of Office*

1. The judges of the Court shall be elected for a period of six years and may be re-elected only once. The terms of four judges elected at the first election shall expire at the end of two years, and the terms of four more judges shall expire at the end of four years.

2. The judges whose terms are to expire at the end of the initial periods of two and four years shall be chosen by lot to be drawn by the Secretary-General of the OAU immediately after the first election has been completed.

3. A judge elected to replace a judge whose term of office has not expired shall hold office for the remainder of the predecessor's term.

4. All judges except the President shall perform their functions on a part-time basis. However, the Assembly may change this arrangement as it deems appropriate.

*Article 16—Oath of Office*

After their election, the judges of the Court shall make a solemn declaration to discharge their duties impartially and faithfully.

*Article 17—Independence*

1. The independence of the judges shall be fully ensured in accordance with international law.

2. No judge may hear any case in which the same judge has previously taken part as agent, counsel or advocate for one of the parties or as a member of a national or international court or a commission of enquiry or in any other capacity. Any doubt on this point shall be settled by decision of the Court.

3. The judges of the Court shall enjoy, from the moment of their election and throughout their term of office, the immunities extended to diplomatic agents in accordance with international law.

4. At no time shall the judges of the Court be held liable for any decision or opinion issued in the exercise of their functions.

*Article* 18—*Incompatibility*

The position of judge of the Court is incompatible with any activity that might interfere with the independence or impartiality of such a judge or the demands of the office, as determined in the Rules of Procedure of the Court.

*Article* 19—*Cessation of Office*

1. A judge shall not be suspended or removed from office unless, by the unanimous decision of the other judges of the Court, the judge concerned has been found to be no longer fulfilling the required conditions to be a judge of the Court.

2. Such a decision of the Court shall become final unless it is set aside by the Assembly at its next session.

*Article* 20—*Vacancies*

1. In case of death or resignation of a judge of the Court, the President of the Court shall immediately inform the Secretary-General of the Organization of African Unity, who shall declare the seat vacant from the date of death or from the date on which the resignation takes effect.

2. The Assembly shall replace the judge whose office became vacant unless the remaining period of the term is less than one hundred and eighty (180) days.

3. The same procedure and considerations as set out in Articles 12, 13 and 14 shall be followed for the filling of vacancies.

*Article* 21—*Presidency of the Court*

1. The Court shall elect its President and one Vice-President for a period of two years. They may be re-elected only once.

2. The President shall perform judicial functions on a full-time basis and shall reside at the seat of the Court.

3. The functions of the President and the Vice-President shall be set out in the Rules of Procedure of the Court.

*Article* 22—*Exclusion*

If a judge is a national of any State which is a party to a case submitted to the Court, that judge shall not hear the case.

*Article* 23—*Quorum*

The Court shall examine cases brought before it, if it has a quorum of at least seven judges.

*Article* 24—*Registry of the Court*

1. The Court shall appoint its own Registrar and other staff of the registry from among nationals of Member States of the OAU according to the Rules of Procedure.

2. The office and residence of the Registrar shall be at the place where the Court has its seat.

*Article* 25—*Seat of the Court*

1. The Court shall have its seat at the place determined by the Assembly from

among States parties to this Protocol. However, it may convene in the territory of any Member State of the OAU when the majority of the Court considers it desirable, and with the prior consent of the State concerned.

2. The seat of the Court may be changed by the Assembly after due consultation with the Court.

### Article 26—Evidence

1. The Court shall hear submissions by all parties and if deemed necessary, hold an enquiry. The States concerned shall assist by providing relevant facilities for the efficient handling of the case.

2. The Court may receive written and oral evidence including expert testimony and shall make its decision on the basis of such evidence.

### Article 27—Findings

1. If the Court finds that there has been violation of a human or peoples' right, it shall make appropriate orders to remedy the violation, including the payment of fair compensation or reparation.

2. In cases of extreme gravity and urgency, and when necessary to avoid irreparable harm to persons, the Court shall adopt such provisional measures as it deems necessary.

### Article 28—Judgement

1. The Court shall render its judgement within ninety (90) days of having completed its deliberations.

2. The judgement of the Court decided by majority shall be final and not subject to appeal.

3. Without prejudice to sub-article 2 above, the Court may review its decision in the light of new evidence under conditions to be set out in the Rules of Procedure.

4. The Court may interpret its own decision.

5. The judgement of the Court shall be read in open court, due notice having been given to the parties.

6. Reasons shall be given for the judgement of the Court.

7. If the judgement of the Court does not represent, in whole or in part, the unanimous decision of the judges, any judge shall be entitled to deliver a separate or dissenting opinion.

### Article 29—Notification of Judgement

1. The parties to the case shall be notified of the judgement of the Court and it shall be transmitted to the Member States of the OAU and the Commission.

2. The Council of Ministers shall also be notified of the judgement and shall monitor its execution on behalf of the Assembly.

### Article 30—Execution of Judgement

The States parties to the present Protocol undertake to comply with the judgement in any case to which they are parties within the time stipulated by the Court and to guarantee its execution.

*Article 31—Report*

The Court shall submit to each regular session of the Assembly, a report on its work during the previous year. The report shall specify, in particular, the cases in which a State has not complied with the Court's judgement.

*Article 32—Budget*

Expenses of the Court, emoluments and allowances for judges and the budget of its registry, shall be determined and borne by the OAU, in accordance with criteria laid down by the OAU in consultation with the Court.

*Article 33—Rules of Procedure*

The Court shall draw up its Rules and determine its own procedures. The Court shall consult the Commission as appropriate.

*Article 34—Ratification*

1. This Protocol shall be open for signature and ratification or accession by any State Party to the Charter.

2. The instrument of ratification or accession to the present Protocol shall be deposited with the Secretary-General of the OAU.

3. The Protocol shall come into force thirty days after fifteen instruments of ratification or accession have been deposited.

4. For any State Party ratifying or acceding subsequently, the present Protocol shall come into force in respect of that State on the date of the deposit of its instrument of ratification or accession.

5. The Secretary-General of the OAU shall inform all Member States of the entry into force of the present Protocol.

6. At the time of the ratification of this Protocol or any time thereafter, the State shall make a declaration accepting the competence of the Court to receive cases under article 5(3) of this Protocol. The Court shall not receive any petition under article 5(3) involving a State Party which has not made such a declaration.

7. Declarations made under sub-article (6) above shall be deposited with the Secretary-General, who shall transmit copies thereof to the State Parties.

*Article 35—Amendments*

1. The present Protocol may be amended if a State Party to the Protocol makes a written request to that effect to the Secretary-General of the OAU. The Assembly may adopt, by simple majority, the draft amendment after all the States Parties to the present Protocol have been duly informed of it and the Court has given its opinion on the amendment.

2. The Court shall also be entitled to propose such amendments to the present Protocol as it may deem necessary, through the Secretary-General of the OAU.

3. The amendment shall come into force for each State Party which has accepted it thirty days after the Secretary-General of the OAU has received notice of the acceptance.

## 88. AFRICAN CHARTER ON THE RIGHTS AND WELFARE OF THE CHILD, 1990

This Charter, the first regional treaty on the rights of the child, was adopted and opened for signature by the Twenty-Sixth Ordinary Session of the Assembly of Heads of State and Government of the Organization of African Unity, Addis Ababa, Ethiopia, 11 July 1990; it entered into force 29 November 1999. For text see OAU doc. CAB/LEG/24.9/49 (1990).

*TEXT*

Preamble

The African Member States of the Organization of African Unity, Parties to the present Charter entitled 'African Charter on the Rights and Welfare of the Child',

*Considering* that the Charter of the Organization of African Unity recognizes the paramountcy of Human Rights and the African Charter on Human and Peoples' Rights proclaimed and agreed that everyone is entitled to all the rights and freedoms recognized and guaranteed therein, without distinction of any kind such as race, ethnic group, colour, sex, language, religion, political or any other opinion, national and social origin, fortune, birth or other status,

*Recalling* the Declaration on the Rights and Welfare of the African Child (AHG/ST.4 Rev. 1) adopted by the Assembly of Heads of State and Government of the Organization of African Unity, at its Sixteenth Ordinary Session in Monrovia, Liberia, from 17 to 20 July, 1979 recognized the need to take all appropriate measures to promote and protect the rights and welfare of the African Child,

*Noting with concern* that the situation of most African children, remains critical due to the unique factors of their socioeconomic, cultural, traditional and developmental circumstances, natural disasters, armed conflicts, exploitation and hunger, and on account of the child's physical and mental immaturity he/she needs special safeguards and care,

*Recognizing* that the child occupies a unique and privileged position in the African society and that for the full harmonious development of his personality, the child should grow up in a family environment in an atmosphere of happiness, love and understanding,

*Recognizing* that the child, due to the needs of his physical and mental development requires particular care with regard to health, physical, mental, moral and social development, and requires legal protection in conditions of freedom, dignity and security,

*Taking into consideration* the virtues of their cultural heritage historical background and the values of the African civilization which should inspire and characterize their reflection on the concept of the rights and welfare of the child,

*Considering* that the promotion and protection of the rights and welfare of the child also implies the performance of duties on the part of everyone,

*Reaffirming* adherence to the principles of the rights and welfare of the child

contained in the declaration, conventions and other instruments of the Organiza-
tion of African Unity and in the United Nations and in particular the United
Nations Convention on the Rights of the Child; and the OAU Heads of State and
Government's Declaration on the Rights and Welfare of the African Child:

*Have agreed as follows*:

## PART I

## RIGHTS AND DUTIES
### Chapter One—Rights and Welfare of the Child

*Article 1—Obligation of States Parties*

1. Member States of the Organization of African Unity Parties to the present
Charter shall recognize the rights, freedoms and duties enshrined in this Charter
and shall undertake to the necessary steps, in accordance with their Constitutional
processes and with the provisions of the present Charter, to adopt such legislative
or other measures as may be necessary to give effect to the provisions of this
Charter.

2. Nothing in this Charter shall affect any provisions that are more conductive to
the realization of the rights and welfare of the child contained in the law of a State
Party or in any other international Convention or agreement in force in that State.

3. Any custom, tradition, cultural or religious practice that is inconsistent with the
rights, duties and obligations contained in the present Charter shall to the extent of
such inconsistency be discouraged.

*Article 2—Definition of a Child*

For the purposes of this Charter, a child means every human being below the age
of 18 years.

*Article 3—Non-Discrimination*

Every child shall be entitled to the enjoyment of the rights and freedoms recognized and guaranteed in this Charter irrespective of the child's or his/her parents'
or legal guardians' race, ethnic group, colour, sex, language, religion, political or
other opinion, national and social origin, fortune, birth or other status.

*Article 4—Best Interests of the Child*

1. In all actions concerning the child undertaken by any person or authority the
best interests of the child shall be the primary consideration.

2. In all judicial or administrative proceedings affecting a child who is capable of
communicating his/her own views, and opportunity shall be provided for the views
of the child to be heard either directly or through an impartial representative as a
party to the proceedings. and those views shall be taken into consideration by the
relevant authority in accordance with the provisions of appropriate law.

*Article 5—Survival and Development*

1. Every child has an inherent right to life. This right shall be protected by law.

2. States Parties to the present Charter shall ensure, to the maximum extent possible, the survival, protection and development of the child.

3. Death sentence shall not be pronounced for crimes committed by children.

*Article 6—Name and Nationality*

1. Every child shall have the right from his birth no a name.

2. Every child shall be registered immediately after birth.

3. Every child has the right to acquire a nationality.

4. States Parties to the present Charter shall undertake to ensure that their Constitutional legislation recognize the principles according to which a child shall acquire the nationality of the State in the territory of which he has been born if, at the time of the child's birth. he is not granted nationality by any other State in accordance with its laws.

*Article 7—Freedom of Expression*

Every child who is capable of communicating his or her own views shall be assured the rights to express his opinions freely in all matters and to disseminate his opinions subject to such restrictions as are prescribed by laws.

*Article 8—Freedom of Association*

Every child shall have the right to free association and freedom of peaceful assembly in conformity with the law.

*Article 9—Freedom of Thought, Conscience and Religion*

1. Every child shall have the right to freedom of thought conscience and religion.

2. Parents, and where applicable, legal guardians shall have a duty to provide guidance and direction in the exercise of these rights having regard to the evolving capacities, and best interests of the child.

3. States Parties shall respect the duty of parents and where applicable, legal guardians to provide guidance and direction in the enjoyment of these rights subject to the national laws and policies.

*Article 10—Protection of Privacy*

No child shall be subject to arbitrary or unlawful interference with his privacy, family home or correspondence, or to the attacks upon his honour or reputation, provided that parents or legal guardians shall have the right to exercise reasonable supervision over the conduct of their children. The child has the right to the protection of the law against such interference or attacks.

*Article 11—Education*

1. Every child shall have the right to an education.

2. The education of the child shall be directed to:

   *(a)* the promotion and development of the child's personality, talents and mental and physical abilities to their fullest potential;

*(b)* fostering respect for human rights and fundamental freedoms with particular reference to those set out in the provisions of various African
instruments on human and peoples' rights and international human rights
declarations and conventions;

*(c)* the preservation and strengthening of positive African morals, traditional
values and cultures;

*(d)* the preparation of the child for responsible life in a free society, in the spirit
of understanding tolerance, dialogue, mutual respect and friendship among
all peoples ethnic, tribal and religious groups;

*(e)* the preservation of national independence and territorial integrity;

*(f)* the promotion and achievements of African Unity and Solidarity;

*(g)* the development of respect for the environment and natural resources;

*(h)* the promotion of the child's understanding of primary health care.

3. States Parties to the present Charter shall take all appropriate measures with a
view to achieving the full realization of this right and shall in particular:

*(a)* provide free and compulsory basic education:

*(b)* encourage the development of secondary education in its different forms
and to progressively make it free and accessible to all;

*(c)* make the higher education accessible to all on the basis of capacity and
ability by every appropriate means;

*(d)* take measures to encourage regular attendance at schools and the reduction
of drop-out rates;

*(e)* take special measures in respect of female, gifted and disadvantaged children, to ensure equal access to education for all sections of the community.

4. States Parties to the present Charter shall respect the rights and duties of parents, and where applicable, of legal guardians to choose for their children's schools,
other than those established by public authorities, which conform to such minimum standards may be approved by the State, to ensure the religious and moral
education of the child in a manner with the evolving capacities of the child.

5. States Parties to the present Charter shall take all appropriate measures to
ensure that a child who is subjected to schools or parental discipline shall be treated
with humanity and with respect for the inherent dignity of the child and in
conformity with the present Charter.

6. States Parties to the present Charter shall have all appropriate measures to
ensure that children who become pregnant before completing their education
shall have an opportunity to continue with their education on the basis of their
individual ability.

7. No part of this Article shall be construed as to interfere with the liberty of
individuals and bodies to establish and direct educational institutions subject to the
observance of the principles set out in paragraph 1 of this Article and the requirement teal the education given in such institutions shall conform to such minimum
standards as may be laid down by the States.

*Article 12—Leisure, Recreation and Cultural Activities*

1. States Parties recognize the right of the child to rest and leisure, to engage

in play and recreational activities appropriate to the age of the child and to participate freely in cultural life and the arts.

2. States Parties shall respect and promote the right of the child to fully participate in cultural and artistic life and shall encourage the provision of appropriate and equal opportunities for cultural, artistic, recreational and leisure activity.

*Article* 13—*Handicapped Children*

1. Every child who is mentally or physically disabled shall have the right to special measures of protection in keeping with his physical and moral needs and under conditions which ensure his dignity, promote his self-reliance and active participation in the community.

2. States Parties to the present Charter shall ensure, subject to available resources, to a disabled child and to those responsible for his care, of assistance for which application is made and which is appropriate to the child's condition and in particular shall ensure that the disabled child has effective access to training, preparation for employment and recreation opportunities in a manner conducive to the child achieving the fullest possible social integration, individual development and his cultural and moral development.

3. The States Parties to the present Charter shall use their available resources with a view to achieving progressively the full convenience of the mentally and physically disabled person to movement and access to public highway buildings and other places to which the disabled may legitimately want to have access to.

*Article* 14—*Health and Health Services*

1. Every child shall have the right to enjoy the best attainable state of physical, mental and spiritual health.

2. States Parties to the present Charter shall undertake to pursue the full implementation of this right and in particular shall take measures:

    *(a)*  to reduce infant and child morality rate;

    *(b)*  to ensure the provision of necessary medical assistance and health care to all children with emphasis on the development of primary health care;

    *(c)*  to ensure the provision of adequate nutrition and safe drinking water;

    *(d)*  to combat disease and malnutrition within the framework of primary health care through the application of appropriate technology;

    *(e)*  to ensure appropriate health care for expectant and nursing mothers;

    *(f)*  to develop preventive health care and family life education and provision of service;

    *(g)*  to integrate basic health service programmes in national development plans;

    *(h)*  to ensure that all sectors of the society, in particular, parents, children, community leaders and community workers are informed and supported in the use of basic knowledge of child health and nutrition, the advantages of breastfeeding, hygiene and environmental sanitation and the prevention of domestic and other accidents;

    *(i)*  to ensure the meaningful participation of non-governmental organizations,

local communities and the beneficiary population in the planning and management of a basic service programme for children;

(j) to support through technical and financial means, the mobilization of local community resources in the development of primary health care for children.

*Article* 15—*Child Labour*

1. Every child shall be protected from all forms of economic exploitation and from performing any work that is likely to be hazardous or to interfere with the child's physical, mental, spiritual, moral, or social development.

2. States Parties to the present Charter take all appropriate legislative and administrative measures to ensure the full implementation of this Article which covers both the formal and informal sectors of employment and having regard to the relevant provisions of the International Labour Organization's instruments relating to children, States Parties shall in particular:

(a) provide through legislation, minimum wages for admission to every employment;

(b) provide for appropriate regulation of hours and conditions of employment;

(c) provide for appropriate penalties or other sanctions to ensure the effective enforcement of this Article;

(d) promote the dissemination of information on the hazards of child labour to all sectors of the community.

*Article* 16—*Protection Against Child Abuse and Torture*

1. States Parties to the present Charter shall take specific legislative, administrative, social and educational measures to protect the child from all forms of torture, inhuman or degrading treatment and especially physical or mental injury or abuse, neglect or maltreatment including sexual abuse, while in the care of the child.

2. Protective measures under this Article shall include effective procedures for the establishment of special monitoring units to provide necessary support for the child and for those who have the care of the child, as well as other forms of prevention and for identification, reporting referral investigation, treatment, and follow-up of instances of child abuse and neglect.

*Article* 17—*Administration of Juvenile Justice*

1. Every child accused or found guilty of having infringed penal law shall have the right to special treatment in a manner consistent with the child's sense of dignity and worth and which reinforces the child's respect for human rights and fundamental freedoms of others.

2. States Parties to the present Charter shall in particular:

(a) ensure that no child who is detained or imprisoned or otherwise deprived of his/her liberty is subjected to torture, inhuman or degrading treatment or punishment;

(b) ensure that children are separated from adults in their place of detention or imprisonment;

*(c)* ensure that every child accused in infringing the penal law:

  (i) shall be presumed innocent until duly recognized guilty;

  (ii) shall be informed promptly in a language that he understands and in detail of the charge against him, and shall be entitled to the assistance of an interpreter if he or she cannot understand the language used;

  (iii) shall be afforded legal and other appropriate assistance in the preparation and presentation of his defence;

  (iv) shall have the matter determined as speedily as possible by an impartial tribunal and if found guilty, be entitled to an appeal by a higher tribunal;

*(d)* prohibit the press and the public from trial.

3. The essential aim of treatment of every child during the trial and also if found guilty of infringing the penal law shall be his or her reformation, re-integration into his or her family and social rehabilitation.

4. There shall be a minimum age below which children shall be presumed not to have the capacity to infringe the penal law.

*Article* 18—*Protection of the Family*

1. The family shall be the natural unit and basis of society. it shall enjoy the protection and support of the State for its establishment and development.

2. States Parties to the present Charter shall take appropriate steps to ensure equality of rights and responsibilities of spouses with regard to children during marriage and in the even of its dissolution. In case of the dissolution, provision shall be made for the necessary protection of the child.

3. No child shall be deprived of maintenance by reference to the parents' marital status.

*Article* 19—*Parent Care and Protection*

1. Every child shall be entitled to the enjoyment of parental care and protection and shall, whenever possible, have the right to reside with his or her parents. No child shall be separated from his parents against his will, except when a judicial authority determines in accordance with the appropriate law, that such separation is in the best interest of the child.

2. Every child who is separated from one or both parents shall have the right to maintain personal relations and direct contact with both parents on a regular basis.

3. Where separation results from the action of a State Party, the State Party shall provide the child, or if appropriate, another member of the family with essential information concerning the whereabouts of the absent member or members of the family. States Parties shall also ensure that the submission of such a request shall not entail any adverse consequences for the person or persons in whose respect it is made.

4. Where a child is apprehended by a State Party, his parents or guardians shall, as soon as possible, be notified of such apprehension by that State Party.

*Article* 20—*Parental Responsibilities*

1. Parents or other persons responsible for the child shall have the primary

responsibility of the upbringing and development the child and shall have the duty:

(a) to ensure that the best interests of the child are their basic concern at all times;

(b) to secure, within their abilities and financial capacities, conditions of living necessary to the child's development; and

(c) to ensure that domestic discipline is administered with humanity and in a manner consistent with the inherent dignity of the child.

2. States Parties to the present Charter shall in accordance with their means and national conditions take all appropriate measures;

(a) to assist parents and other persons responsible for the child and in case of need provide material assistance and support programmes particularly with regard to nutrition, health, education, clothing and housing;

(b) to assist parents and others responsible for the child in the performance of child-rearing and ensure the development of institutions responsible for providing care of children; and

(c) to ensure that the children of working parents are provided with care services and facilities.

*Article 21—Protection against Harmful Social and Cultural Practices*

1. States Parties to the present Charter shall take all appropriate measures to eliminate harmful social and cultural practices affecting the welfare, dignity, normal growth and development of the child and in particular:

(a) those customs and practices prejudicial to the health or life of the child; and

(b) those customs and practices discriminatory to the child on the grounds of sex or other status.

2. Child marriage and the betrothal of girls and boys shall be prohibited and effective action, including legislation, shall be taken to specify the minimum age of marriage to be 18 years and make registration of all marriages in an official registry compulsory.

*Article 22—Armed Conflicts*

1. States Parties to this Charter shall undertake to respect and ensure respect for rules of international humanitarian law applicable in armed conflicts which affect the child.

2. States Parties to the present Charter shall take all necessary measures to ensure that no child shall take a direct part in hostilities and refrain in particular, from recruiting any child.

3. States Parties to the present Charter shall, in accordance with their obligations under international humanitarian law, protect the civilian population in armed conflicts and shall take all feasible measures to ensure the protection and care of children who are affected by armed conflicts. Such rules shall also apply to children in situations of internal armed conflicts, tension and strife.

*Article 23—Refugee Children*

1. States Parties to the present Charter shall take all appropriate measures to ensure that a child who is seeking refugee status or who is considered a refugee in accordance with applicable international or domestic law shall, whether unaccompanied or accompanied by parents, legal guardians or close relatives, receive appropriate protection and humanitarian assistance in the enjoyment of the rights set out in this Charter and other international human rights and humanitarian instruments to which the States are Parties.

2. States Parties shall undertake to cooperate with existing international organizations which protect and assist refugees in their efforts to protect and assist such a child and to trace the parents or other close relatives or an unaccompanied refugee child in order to obtain information necessary for reunification with the family.

3. Where no parents, legal guardians or close relatives can be found, the child shall be accorded the same protection as any other child permanently or temporarily deprived of his family environment for any reason.

4. The provisions of this Article apply *mutatis mutandis* to internally displaced children whether through natural disaster, internal armed conflicts, civil strife, breakdown of economic and social order or howsoever caused.

*Article 24—Adoption*

States Parties which recognize the system of adoption shall ensure that the best interest of the child shall be the paramount consideration and they shall:

(a) establish competent authorities to determine matters of adoption and ensure that the adoption is carried out in conformity with applicable laws and procedures and on the basis of all relevant and reliable information. that the adoption is permissible in view of the child's status concerning parents, relatives and guardians and that. if necessary, the appropriate persons concerned have given their informed consent to the adoption on the basis of appropriate counselling;

(b) recognize that inter-country adoption in those States who have ratified or adhered to the International Convention on the Rights of the Child or this Charter may, as the last resort, be considered as an alternative means of a child's care, if the child cannot be placed in a foster or an adoptive family or cannot in any suitable manner be cared for in the child's country of origin;

(c) ensure that the child affected by inter-country adoption enjoys safeguards and standards equivalent to those existing in the case of national adoption;

(d) take all appropriate measures to ensure that in inter-country adoption, the placement does not result in trafficking or improper financial gain for those who try to adopt a child;

(e) promote, where appropriate, the objectives of this Article by concluding bilateral or multilateral arrangements or agreements, and endeavour, within this framework to ensure that the placement of the child in another country is carried out by competent authorities or organs;

(f) establish a machinery to monitor the well-being of the adopted child.

*Article 25—Separation from Parents*

1. Any child who is permanently or temporarily deprived of his family environment for any reason shall be entitled to special protection and assistance.

2. States Parties to the present Charter:

   *(a)* shall ensure that a child who is parentless, or who is temporarily or permanently deprived of his or her family environment, or who in his or her best
interest cannot be brought up or allowed to remain in that environment
shall be provided with alternative family care, which could include, among
others. foster placement, or placement in suitable institutions for the care of
children;

   *(b)* shall take all necessary measures to trace and re-unite children with parents
or relatives where separation is caused by internal and external displacement arising from armed conflicts or natural disasters.

3. When considering alternative family care of the child and the best interests of
the child, due regard shall be paid to the desirability of continuity in a child's
up-bringing and to the child's ethnic, religious or linguistic background.

*Article 26—Protection Against Apartheid and Discrimination*

1. States Parties to the present Charter shall individually and collectively undertake to accord the highest priority to the special needs of children living under
Apartheid and in States subject to military destabilization by the Apartheid regime.

2. States Parties to the present Charter shall individually and collectively undertake to accord the highest priority to the special needs of children living under
regimes practising racial, ethnic. religious or other forms of discrimination as well
as in States subject to military destabilization.

3. States Parties shall undertake to provide whenever possible, material assistance
to such children and to direct their efforts towards the elimination of all forms of
discrimination and Apartheid on the African Continent.

*Article 27—Sexual Exploitation*

1. States Parties to the present Charter shall undertake to protect the child from all
forms of sexual exploitation and sexual abuse and shall in particular take measures
to prevent:

   *(a)* the inducement, coercion or encouragement of a child to engage in any
sexual activity;

   *(b)* the use of children in prostitution or other sexual practices;

   *(c)* the use of children in pornographic activities, performances and materials.

*Article 28—Drug Abuse*

States Parties to the present Charter shall take all appropriate measures to protect
the child from the use of narcotics and illicit use of psychotropic substances as
defined in the relevant international treaties, and to prevent the use of children in
the production and trafficking of such substances.

*Article 29—Sale, Trafficking and Abduction*

States Parties to the present Charter shall take appropriate measures to prevent:

(a)  the abduction, the sale of, or traffic in children for any purpose or in any form, by any person including parents or legal guardians of the child;

(b)  the use of children in all forms of begging.

## Article 30—Children of Imprisoned Mothers

1. States Parties to the present Charter shall undertake to provide special treatment to expectant mothers and to mothers of infants and young children who have been accused or found guilty of infringing the penal law and shall in particular:

(a)  ensure that a non-custodial sentence will always be first considered when sentencing such mothers;

(b)  establish and promote measures alternative to institutional confinement for the treatment of such mothers;

(c)  establish special alternative institutions for holding such mothers;

(d)  ensure that a mother shall not be imprisoned with her child;

(e)  ensure that a death sentence shall not be imposed on such mothers;

(f)  the essential aim of the penitentiary system will be the reformation, the integration of the mother to the family and social rehabilitation.

## Article 31—Responsibility of the Child

Every child shall have responsibilities towards his family and society, the State and other legally recognized communities and the international community. The child, subject to his age and ability, and such limitations as may be contained in the present Charter, shall have the duty:

(a)  to work for the cohesion of the family, to respect his parents, superiors and elders at all times and to assist them in case of need;

(b)  to serve his national community by placing his physical and intellectual abilities at its service;

(c)  to preserve and strengthen social and national solidarity;

(d)  to preserve and strengthen African cultural values in his relations with other members of the society, in the spirit of tolerance, dialogue and consultation and to contribute to the moral well-being of society;

(e)  to preserve and strengthen the independence and the integrity of his country;

(f)  to contribute to the best of his abilities. at all times and at all levels, to the promotion and achievement of African Unity.

# PART II

## Chapter Two—Establishment and Organization of the Committee on the Rights and Welfare of the Child

## Article 32—The Committee

An African Committee of Experts on the Rights and Welfare of the Child hereinafter called 'the Committee' shall be established within the Organization of African Unity to promote and protect the rights and welfare of the child.

*Article 33—Composition*

1. The Committee shall consist of 11 members of high moral standing, integrity, impartiality and competence in matters of the rights and welfare of the child.

2. The members of the Committee shall serve in their personal capacity.

3. The Committee shall not include more than one national of the same State.

*Article 34—Election*

As soon as this Charter shall enter into force the members of the Committee shall be elected by secret ballot by the Assembly of Heads of State and Government from a list of persons nominated by the States Parties to the present Charter.

*Article 35—Candidates*

Each State Party to the present Charter may nominate not more than two candidates. The candidates must have one of the nationalities of the States Parties to the present Charter. When two candidates are nominated by a State, one of them shall not be a national of that State.

*Article 36*

1. The Secretary-General of the Organization of African Unity shall invite States Parties to the present Charter to nominate candidates at least six months before the elections.

2. The Secretary-General of the Organization of African Unity shall draw up in alphabetical order, a list of persons nominated and communicate it to the Heads of State and Government at least two months before the elections.

*Article 37—Term of Office*

1. The members of the Committee shall be elected for a term of five years and may not be re-elected, however. the term of four of the members elected at the first election shall expire after two years and the term of six others, after four years.

2. Immediately after the first election, the Chairman of the Assembly of Heads of State and Government of the Organization of African Unity shall draw lots to determine the names of those members referred to in sub-paragraph 1 of this Article.

3. The Secretary-General of the Organization of African Unity shall convene the first meeting of Committee at the Headquarters of the Organization within six months of the election of the members of the Committee, and thereafter the Committee shall be convened by its Chairman whenever necessary, at least once a year.

*Article 38—Bureau*

1. The Committee shall establish its own Rules of Procedure.

2. The Committee shall elect its officers for a period of two years.

3. Seven Committee members shall form the quorum.

4. In case of an equality of votes, the Chairman shall have a casting vote.

5. The working languages of the Committee shall be the official languages of the OAU.

*Article 39—Vacancy*

If a member of the Committee vacates his office for any reason other than the normal expiration of a term, the State which nominated that member shall appoint another member from among its nationals to serve for the remainder of the term—subject to the approval of the Assembly.

*Article 40—Secretariat*

The Secretary-General of the Organization of African Unity shall appoint a Secretary for the Committee.

*Article 41—Privileges and Immunities*

In discharging their duties, members of the Committee shall enjoy the privileges and immunities provided for in the General Convention on the Privileges and Immunities of the Organization of African Unity.

### Chapter Three—Mandate and Procedure of the Committee

*Article 42—Mandate*

The functions of the Committee shall be:

(a) To promote and protect the rights enshrined in this Charter and in particular to:
   (i) collect and document information, commission inter-disciplinary assessment of situations on African problems in the fields of the rights and welfare of the child, organize meetings, encourage national and local institutions concerned with the rights and welfare of the child, and where necessary give its views and make recommendations to Governments;
   (ii) formulate and lay down principles and rules aimed at protecting the rights and welfare of children in Africa;
   (iii) cooperate with other African, international and regional Institutions and organizations concerned with the promotion and protection of the rights and welfare of the child.

(b) To monitor the implementation and ensure protection of the rights enshrined in this Charter.

(c) To interpret the provisions of the present Charter at the request of a State Party, an Institution of the Organization of African Unity or any other person or Institution recognized by the Organization of African Unity, or any State Party.

(d) Perform such other task as may be entrusted to it by the Assembly of Heads of State and Government, Secretary-General of the OAU and any other organs of the OAU or the United Nations.

*Article 43—Reporting Procedure*

1. Every State Party to the present Charter shall undertake to submit to the Committee through the Secretary-General of the Organization of African Unity, reports on the measures they have adopted which give effect to the provisions of this Charter and on the progress made in the enjoyment of these rights:

*(a)* within two years of the entry into force of the Charter for the State Party concerned: and

*(b)* and thereafter, every three years.

2. Every report made under this Article shall:

*(a)* contain sufficient information on the implementation of the present Charter to provide the Committee with comprehensive understanding of the implementation of the Charter in the relevant country; and

*(b)* shall indicate factors and difficulties, if any, affecting the fulfilment of the obligations contained in the Charter.

3. A State Party which has submitted a comprehensive first report to the Committee need not, in its subsequent reports submitted in accordance with paragraph 1 (a) of this Article, repeat the basic information previously provided.

*Article 44—Communications*

1. The Committee may receive communication, from any person, group or non-governmental organization recognized by the Organization of African Unity, by a Member State, or the United Nations relating to any matter covered by this Charter.

2. Every communication to the Committee shall contain the name and address of the author and shall be treated in confidence.

*Article 45—Investigations by the Committee*

1. The Committee may, resort to any appropriate method of investigating any matter falling within the ambit of the present Charter, request from the States Parties any information relevant to the implementation of the Charter and may also resort to any appropriate method of investigating the measures the State Party has adopted to implement the Charter.

2. The Committee shall submit to each Ordinary Session of the Assembly of Heads of State and Government every two years, a report on its activities and on any communication made under Article 46 [sc. 44] of this Charter.

3. The Committee shall publish its report after it has been considered by the Assembly of Heads of State and Government.

4. States Parties shall make the Committee's reports widely available to the public in their own countries.

Chapter Four—Miscellaneous Provisions

*Article 46—Sources of Inspiration*

The Committee shall draw inspiration from International Law on Human Rights, particularly from the provisions of the African Charter on Human and Peoples' Rights, the Charter of the Organization of African Unity, the Universal Declaration on Human Rights, the International Convention on the Rights of the Child, and other instruments adopted by the United Nations and by African countries in the field of human rights. and from African values and traditions.

*Article 47—Signature, Ratification or Adherence*

1. The present Charter shall be open to signature by all the Member States of the Organization of African Unity.

2. The present Charter shall be subject to ratification or adherence by Member States of the Organization of African Unity. The instruments of ratification or adherence to the present Charter shall be deposited with the Secretary-General of the Organization of African Unity.

3. The present Charter shall come into force 30 days after the reception by the Secretary-General of the Organization of African Unity of the instruments of ratification or adherence of 15 Member States of the Organization of African Unity.

*Article 48—Amendment and Revision of the Charter*

1. The present Charter may be amended or revised if any State Party makes a written request to that effect to the Secretary-General of the Organization of African Unity, provided that the proposed amendment is not submitted to the Assembly of Heads of State and Government for consideration until all the States Parties have been duly notified of it and the Committee has given its opinion on the amendment.

2. An amendment shall be approved by a simple majority of the States Parties.

# PART EIGHT

# DEVELOPMENTS IN THE ARAB WORLD

## INTRODUCTION

Agreement on human rights instruments among Arab and Islamic States has been slow in coming. Two of the documents reproduced below are in the form of declarations, and the Arab Charter on Human Rights is not yet in force. This situation has prompted some concern, particularly among non-governmental organizations; see the 'Casablanca Declaration of the Arab Human Rights Movement', adopted by the First International Conference of the Arab Human Rights Movement, Casablanca, 23–25 April 1999. The Conference, which was organized by the Cairo Institute for Human Rights Studies and hosted by the Moroccan Organization for Human Rights, examined the human rights conditions in the Arab world, and the responsibilities, tasks and prospects of the Arab human rights movement. After extensive discussions, the Conference declared that the only source of reference is international human rights law and the United Nations instruments and declarations. It also emphasized the universality of human rights. See Abdullahi An-Na'im, 'Human Rights in the Arab World: A Regional Perspective', 23 *Human Rights Quarterly* 701–32 (2001); also, Elmadmad, K., 'An Arab Convention on Forced Migration: Desirability and Possibilities', 3 *IJRL* 461–81 (1991).

## 89. CAIRO DECLARATION ON HUMAN RIGHTS IN ISLAM, 1990

The Cairo Declaration on Human Rights in Islam was adopted by the Organization of the Islamic Conference, Cairo, 5 August 1990. Text in UN doc. A/45/421—S/21797, 200; A/CONF.157/PC/35; A/CONF.157/PC/62/Add.18, 2. See also Mayer, A. E., *Islam and Human Rights: Tradition and Politics* (3rd edn., 1998); Islamic Educational, Scientific and Cultural Organization, Morocco: **www.isesco.org.ma/pub/Eng/humanrights/page7.htm**

*TEXT*

The Member States of the Organization of the Islamic Conference,

*Reaffirming* the civilizing and historical role of the Islamic Ummah which God made the best nation that has given mankind a universal and well-balanced civilization in which harmony is established between this life and the hereafter and knowledge is combined with spiritual faith; and the role that this Ummah should play to guide a humanity confused by competing trends and ideologies and to provide solutions to the chronic problems of this materialistic civilization.

*Wishing* to contribute to the efforts of mankind to assert human rights, to protect man from exploitation and persecution, and to affirm his freedom and right to a dignified life in accordance with the Islamic Shari'ah.

*Convinced* that mankind which has reached an advanced stage in materialistic science is still, and shall remain, in dire need of faith to support its civilization and of a self motivating force to guard its rights.

*Believing* that fundamental rights and universal freedoms in Islam are an integral part of the Islamic religion and that no one as a matter of principle has the right to suspend them in whole or in part or violate or ignore them in as much as they are binding divine commandments, which are contained in the Revealed Books of God and were sent through the last of His Prophets to complete the preceding divine messages thereby making their observance and act of worship and their neglect or violation an abominable sin, and accordingly every person is individually responsible—and the Ummah collectively responsible—for their safeguard.

*Proceeding* from the above-mentioned principles,

*Declare* the following:

*Article* 1

(a) All human beings form one family whose members are united by submission to God and descent from Adam. All men are equal in terms of basic human dignity and basic obligations and responsibilities, without any discrimination on the grounds of race, colour, language, sex, religious belief, political affiliation, social status or other considerations. True faith is the guarantee for enhancing such dignity along the path to human perfection.

(b) All human beings are God's subjects, and the most loved by Him are those who are most useful to the rest of His subjects, and no one has superiority over another except on the basis of piety and good deeds.

*Article 2*

(a) Life is a God-given gift and the right to life is guaranteed to every human being. It is the duty of individuals, societies and states to protect this right from any violation, and it is prohibited to take away life except for a Shari'ah prescribed reason.

(b) It is forbidden to resort to such means as may result in the genocidal annihilation of mankind.

(c) The preservation of human life throughout the term of time willed by God is a duty prescribed by Shari'ah.

(d) Safety from bodily harm is a guaranteed right. It is the duty of the State to safeguard it, and it is prohibited to breach it without a Shari'ah prescribed reason.

*Article 3*

(a) In the event of the use of force and in case of armed conflict, it is not permissible to kill non-belligerents such as old men, women and children. The wounded and the sick shall have the right to medical treatment; and prisoners of war shall have the right to be fed, sheltered and clothed. It is prohibited to mutilate dead bodies. It is a duty to exchange prisoners of war and to arrange visits or reunions of the families separated by the circumstances of war.

(b) It is prohibited to fell trees, to damage crops or livestock, and to destroy the enemy's civilian buildings and installations by shelling, blasting or any other means.

*Article 4*

Every human being is entitled to the inviolability and the protection of his good name and honour during his life and after his death. The State and Society shall protect his remains and burial place.

*Article 5*

(a) The family is the foundation of society, and marriage is the basis of its formation. Men and women have the right to marriage, and no restrictions stemming from race, colour or nationality shall prevent them from enjoying this right.

(b) Society and the State shall remove all obstacles to marriage and shall facilitate marital procedure. They shall ensure family protection and welfare.

*Article 6*

(a) Woman is equal to man in human dignity, and has rights to enjoy as well as duties to perform; she has her own civil entity and financial independence, and the right to retain her name and lineage.

(b) The husband is responsible for the support and welfare of the family.

*Article 7*

(a) As of the moment of birth, every child has rights due from the parents, Society and the State to be accorded proper nursing, education and material, hygienic and moral care. Both the fetus and the mother must be protected and accorded special care.

(b) Parents and those in such like capacity have the right to choose the type of education they desire for their children, provided they take into consideration the interest and future of the children in accordance with ethical values and the principles of the Shari'ah.

(c) Both parents are entitled to certain rights from their children, and relatives are entitled to rights from their kin, in accordance with the tenets of the Shari'ah.

*Article* 8

Every human being has the right to enjoy his legal capacity in terms of both obligation and commitment, should this capacity be lost or impaired, he shall be represented by his guardian.

*Article* 9

(a) The question for knowledge is an obligation and the provision of education is a duty for Society and the State. The State shall ensure the availability of ways and means to acquire education and shall guarantee educational diversity in the interest of Society so as to enable man to be acquainted with the religion of Islam and the facts of the Universe for the benefit of mankind.

(b) Every human being has the right to receive both religious and worldly education from the various institutions of, education and guidance, including the family, the school, the university, the media, etc., and in such and integrated and balanced manner as to develop his personality, strengthen his faith in God and promote his respect for and defence of both rights and obligations.

*Article* 10

Islam is the religion of unspoiled nature. It is prohibited to exercise any form of compulsion on man or to exploit his poverty or ignorance in order to convert him to another religion or to atheism.

*Article* 11

(a) Human beings are born free, and no one has the right to enslave, humiliate, oppress or exploit them, and there can be no subjugation but to God the Most-High.

(b) Colonialism of all types being one of the most evil forms of enslavement is totally prohibited. Peoples suffering from colonialism have the full right to freedom and self-determination. It is the duty of all States and peoples to support the struggle of colonized peoples from the liquidation of all forms of colonialism and occupation, and all States and peoples have the right to preserve their independent identity and exercise control over their wealth and natural resources.

*Article* 12

Every man shall have the right, within the framework of Shari'ah, to free movement and to select his place of residence whether inside or outside his country and if persecuted, is entitled to seek asylum in another country. The country of refuge shall ensure his protection until he reaches safety, unless asylum is motivated by an act which Shari'ah regards as a crime.

*Article* 13

Work is a right guaranteed by the State and Society for each person able to work. Everyone shall be free to choose the work that suits him best and which serves his interests and those of Society. The employee shall have the right to safety and security as well as to all other social guarantees. He may neither be assigned work beyond his capacity nor be subjected to compulsion or exploited or harmed in any way. He shall be entitled without any discrimination between males and females to fair wages for his work without delay, as well as to the holidays allowances and promotions which he deserves. For his part, he shall be required to be dedicated and meticulous in his work. Should workers and employers disagree on any matter, the State shall intervene to settle the dispute and have the grievances redressed, the rights confirmed and justice enforced without bias.

*Article* 14

Everyone shall have the right to legitimate gains without monopolization, deceit or harm to oneself or to others. Usury (riba) is absolutely prohibited.

*Article* 15

(a) Everyone shall have the right to own property acquired in a legitimate way, and shall be entitled to the rights of ownership, without prejudice to oneself, others or to society in general. Expropriation is not permissible except for the requirements of public interest and upon payment of immediate and fair compensation.

(b) Confiscation and seizure of property is prohibited except for a necessity dictated by law.

*Article* 16

Everyone shall have the right to enjoy the fruits of his scientific, literary, artistic or technical production and the right to protect the moral and material interest stemming therefrom, provided that such production is not contrary to the principles of Shari'ah.

*Article* 17

(a) Everyone shall have the right to live in a clean environment, away from vice and moral corruption, an environment that would foster his self-development and it is incumbent upon the State and Society in general to afford that right.

(b) Everyone shall have the right to medical and social care, and to all public amenities provided by Society and the State within the limits of their available resources.

(c) The State shall ensure the right of the individual to a decent living which will enable him to meet all his requirements and those of his dependents, including food, clothing, housing, education, medical care and all other basic needs.

*Article* 18

(a) Everyone shall have the right to live in security for himself, his religion, his dependents, his honour and his property.

(b) Everyone shall have the right to privacy in the conduct of his private affairs, in his home, among his family, with regard to his property and his relationships. It is not permitted to spy on him, to place him under surveillance or to besmirch his good name. The State shall protect him from arbitrary interference.

(c) A private residence is inviolable in all cases. It will not be entered without permission from its inhabitants or in any unlawful manner, nor shall it be demolished or confiscated and its dwellers evicted.

*Article* 19

(a) All individuals are equal before the law, without distinction between ruler and ruled.

(b) The right to resort to justice is guaranteed to everyone.

(c) Liability is in essence personal.

(d) There shall be no crime or punishment except as provided for in the Shari'ah.

(e) A defendant is innocent until his guilt is proven in a fair trial in which he shall be given all the guarantees of defence.

*Article* 20

It is not permitted without legitimate reason to arrest an individual, restrict his freedom, to exile or to punish him. It is not permitted to subject him to physical or psychological torture or to any form of humiliation, cruelty or indignity. Nor is it permitted to subject an individual to medical or scientific experimentation without his consent or at the risk of his health or of his life. Nor is it permitted to promulgate emergency laws that would provide executive authority for such actions.

*Article* 21

Taking hostages under any form or for any purpose is expressly forbidden.

*Article* 22

(a) Everyone shall have the right to express his opinion freely in such manner as would not be contrary to the principles of the Shari'ah.

(b) Everyone shall have the right to advocate what is right, and propagate what is good, and warn against what is wrong and evil according to the norms of Islamic Shari'ah.

(c) Information is a vital necessity to Society. It may not be exploited or misused in such a way as may violate sanctities and the dignity of Prophets, undermine moral and ethical values or disintegrate, corrupt or harm Society or weaken its faith.

(d) It is not permitted to arouse nationalistic or doctrinal hatred or to do anything that may be an incitement to any form of racial discrimination.

*Article* 23

(a) Authority is a trust; and abuse or malicious exploitation thereof is absolutely prohibited, so that fundamental human rights may be guaranteed.

(b) Everyone shall have the right to participate directly or indirectly in the administration of his country's public affairs. He shall also have the right to assume public office in accordance with the provisions of Shari'ah.

*Article* 24

All the rights and freedoms stipulated in this Declaration are subject to the Islamic Shari'ah.

*Article* 25

The Islamic Shari'ah is the only source of reference for the explanation or clarification of any of the articles of this Declaration.

## 90. DECLARATION ON THE PROTECTION OF REFUGEES AND DISPLACED PERSONS IN THE ARAB WORLD, 1992

This Declaration was adopted by a Group of Arab Experts which met in Cairo in November 1992, at the Fourth Arab Seminar on 'Asylum and Refugee Law in the Arab World', organized by the International Institute of Humanitarian Law in collaboration with the Faculty of Law of Cairo University, and under the sponsorship of the United Nations High Commissioner for Refugees.

*TEXT*

The Group of Arab Experts, meeting in Cairo, Arab Republic of Egypt, from 16 to 19 November 1992 at the Fourth Arab Seminar on 'Asylum and Refugee Law in the Arab World', organized by the International Institute of Humanitarian Law in collaboration with the Faculty of Law of Cairo University, under the sponsorship of the United Nations High Commissioner for Refugees,

1. *Noting* with deep regret the suffering which the Arab World has endured from large-scale flows of refugees and displaced persons, and also noting with deep concern the continuing outflow of refugees and displaced persons in the Arab World and the human tragedy encountered by them,

2. *Recalling* the humanitarian principles deeply rooted in Islamic Arab traditions and values and the principles and rules of Moslem law (Islamic Sharia), particularly the principles of social solidarity and asylum, which are reflected in the universally recognized principles of international humanitarian law,

3. *Recognizing* the imperative need for a humanitarian approach in solving the problems or refugees and displaced persons, without prejudice to the political rights of the Palestinian people,

4. *Emphasizing* the need for the effective implementation of paragraph 11 of General Assembly Resolution 194 (III) of 11 December 1948, calling for the right of return or compensation for Palestinian refugees,

5. *Considering* that the required solution is the full implementation of the Resolutions of the Security Council and of the United Nations, including Resolutions 181 of 1947 and Resolution 3236 of 1973, which guarantee the right of the Palestinian people to establish its independent State on its national territory,

6. *Deeply concerned* that Palestinians are not receiving effective protection either from the competent international organizations or from the competent authorities of some Arab countries,

7. *Recognizing* that the refugees and displaced persons problems must be addressed in all their aspects, in particular those relating to their causes, means of prevention and appropriate solutions,

8. *Recalling* that the United Nations Charter and the international human rights instruments affirm the principle that human beings shall enjoy fundamental rights and freedoms without discrimination of whatever nature,

9. *Considering* that Asylum and Refugee Law constitute an integral part of Human Rights Law, respect for which should be fully ensured in the Arab World,

10. *Recognizing* that the United Nations Convention of 28 July 1951 and the Protocol of 31 January 1967 constitute the basic universal instruments governing the status of refugees,

11. *Recalling* the importance or regional legal instruments such as the 1969 OAU Convention governing the Specific Aspects of Refugee Problems in Africa and the 1984 Cartagena Declaration on Refugees,

12. *Recognizing* that the fundamental principles of human rights, international humanitarian law and international refugee law represent a common standard to be attained by all peoples and nations; that they should provide constant guidance to all individuals and organs of society; and that competent national authorities should ensure respect for these principles and should endeavour to promote them by means of education and dissemination,

13. *Recalling* the historic role of Islam and its contribution to humanity, and the fact that universal respect for human rights and fundamental freedoms for all constitute an integral part of Arab values and of the principles and rules of Moslem law (Islamic Sharia),

14. *Noting* with appreciation the humanitarian role of the Office of the United Nations High Commissioner for Refugees in providing protection and assistance to refugees and displaced persons,

15. *Recalling* with particular gratitude the efforts of the International Institute of Humanitarian Law for the developing of refugee law in the Arab World and for organizing the four Arab Seminars held for this purpose in San Remo (1984), Tunis (1989), Amman (1991) and Cairo (1992), and,

16. *Recalling* with appreciation the efforts or the International Committee or the Red Cross in protecting refugees and displaced persons in armed conflict situations,

*Adopts* the following Declaration:

*Article* 1

Reaffirms the fundamental right of every person to the free movement within his own country, or to leave it for another country and to return to his country of origin;

*Article* 2

Reaffirms the importance of the principle prohibiting the return or the expulsion of a refugee to a country where his life or his freedom will be in danger and considers this principle as an imperative rule of the international public law;

*Article* 3

Considers that the granting or asylum should not as such be regarded as an unfriendly act vis-à-vis any other State;

*Article* 4

Hopes that Arab States which have not yet acceded to the 1951 Convention and the 1967 Protocol relating to the status of refugees will do so;

*Article* 5

In situations which may not be covered by the 1951 Convention, the 1967 Protocol, or any other relevant instrument in force or United Nations General Assembly resolutions, refugees, asylum seekers and displaced persons shall nevertheless be protected by:

    *(a)* the humanitarian principles of asylum in Islamic law and Arab values,

    *(b)* the basic human rights rules, established by international and regional organizations,

    *(c)* other relevant principles or international law;

*Article* 6

Recommends that, pending the elaboration of an Arab Convention relating to refugees, Arab States adopt a broad concept of 'refugee' and 'displaced person' as well as a minimum standard for their treatment, guided by the provisions of the United Nations instruments relating to human rights and refugees as well as relevant regional instruments;

*Article* 7

Calls the League of Arab States to reinforce its efforts with a view to adopting an Arab Convention relating to refugees. These efforts will hopefully be brought to fruition within a reasonable period of time;

*Article* 8

Calls upon Arab States to provide the Secretariat of the League with relevant information and statistical data, in particular concerning:

    *(a)* the condition of refugees and displaced persons in their territories,

    *(b)* the extent of their implementation of international instruments relating to the protection of refugees,

    *(c)* national laws, regulations and decrees in force, relating to refugees and displaced persons;

This will help the League of Arab States in taking an active role in the protection or refugees and displaced persons in cooperation with the competent international organizations;

*Article* 9

(a) Strongly emphasizes the need to ensure international protection for Palestinian refugees by competent international organizations and, in particular, by the United Nations, without in any way prejudicing the inalienable national rights of the Palestinian people, especially their right to repatriation and self-determination,

(b) Requests the competent organs of the United Nations to extend with due speed the necessary protection to the Palestinian people, in application of Security Council Resolution 681 of 20 December 1990,

(c) Requests the Arab States to apply in its entirety the Protocol relating to the Treatment of Palestinians in Arab States, adopted at Casablanca on 11 September 1965;

*Article* 10

Emphasizes the need to provide special protection to women and children, as the largest category of refugees and displaced persons, and the most to suffer, as well as the importance of efforts to reunite the families of refugees and displaced persons;

*Article* 11

Calls for the necessary attention which should be given to the dissemination of refugee law and to the development of the public awareness thereof in the Arab World; and for the establishment of an Arab Institute of International Humanitarian Law, in cooperation with the United Nations High Commissioner for Refugees, the International Committee of the Red Cross and the League of Arab States.

Done at Cairo, on Thursday, the 24th of Joumada al-oula A.H. 1413, the 19th of November A.D. 1992.

## FIRST RECOMMENDATION

The Arab Experts, meeting in Cairo at their Fourth Seminar on Asylum and Refugee Law in the Arab World, wish to express their deep appreciation to the International Institute of Humanitarian Law and to the Faculty of Law of Cairo University for their valuable efforts, as well as to the Office of the United Nations High Commissioner for Refugees for its generous sponsorship, all of which led to the success of the Seminar and point to the need for periodically holding similar seminars in other parts or the Arab World in view or the benefits accruing therefrom.

The Arab Experts address their special thanks to the International Institute of Humanitarian Law for publishing the proceedings and synopsis of previous seminars. They note with deep appreciation the intended publication and large-scale dissemination by the Institute of the proceedings and results of their Fourth Seminar, including the Cairo Declaration.

## SECOND RECOMMENDATION

The Arab Experts, meeting in Cairo at their Fourth Seminar on Asylum and Refugee Law in the Arab World, express their appreciation to the General Secretariat of the League of Arab States for its effective participation in the work or the Seminar and urge it to continue its constructive efforts with a view to reaching satisfactory solutions to the problems of refugees, including moral and material sponsorship of future meetings on the subject.

They also invite the League to study the feasibility of creating an Arab organism for refugees in the Arab World, within the framework of the specialized agencies of the League, with a view to providing legal and humanitarian protection for the refugees.

## 91. ARAB CHARTER ON HUMAN RIGHTS, 1994

Adopted by the Council of the League of Arab States (Resolution 5437, 102nd regular session) on 15 September 1994; open for signature by the twenty-two members of the Arab League (Jordan, United Arab Emirates, Bahrain, Tunisia, Algeria, Djibouti, Saudi Arabia, Sudan, Syrian Arab Republic, Somalia, Iraq, Oman, Palestine, Qatar, Comoros, Kuwait, Lebanon, Libyan Arab Jamahiriya, Egypt, Morocco, Mauritania, Yemen). For text see 8 *Human Rights Law Journal* 151 (1997); 56 *ICJ Review* 57 (1996). The present translation was supplied by the Office of the United Nations High Commissioner for Human Rights, United Nations, Geneva. For comment, see **www.al-bab.com/arab/human.htm**

*TEXT*

The Governments of the member States of the League of Arab States,

### Preamble

Given the Arab nation's belief in human dignity since God honoured it by making the Arab World the cradle of religions and the birthplace of civilizations which confirmed its right to a life of dignity based on freedom, justice and peace,

Pursuant to the eternal principles of brotherhood and equality among all human beings which were firmly established by the Islamic Shari'a and the other divinely-revealed religions,

Being proud of the humanitarian values and principles which it firmly established in the course of its long history and which played a major role in disseminating centres of learning between the East and the West, thereby making it an international focal point for seekers of knowledge, culture and wisdom,

Conscious of the fact that the entire Arab World has always worked together to preserve its faith, believing in its unity, struggling to protect its freedom, defending the right of nations to self-determination and to safeguard their resources, believing in the rule of law and that every individual's enjoyment of freedom, justice and equality of opportunity is the yardstick by which the merits of any society are gauged,

Rejecting racism and zionism, which constitute a violation of human rights and pose a threat to world peace,

Acknowledging the close interrelationship between human rights and world peace,

Reaffirming the principles of the Charter of the United Nations and the Universal Declaration of Human Rights, as well as the provisions of the United Nations International Covenants on Civil and Political Rights and Economic, Social and Cultural Rights and the Cairo Declaration on Human Rights in Islam.

In confirmation of all the above, have agreed as follows :

## PART I

*Article* 1

(a) All peoples have the right of self-determination and control over their natural wealth and resources and, accordingly, have the right to freely determine the form of their political structure and to freely pursue their economic, social and cultural development.

(b) Racism, zionism, occupation and foreign domination pose a challenge to human dignity and constitute a fundamental obstacle to the realization of the basic rights of peoples. There is a need to condemn and endeavour to eliminate all such practices.

## PART II

*Article* 2

Each State Party to the present Charter undertakes to ensure to all individuals within its territory and subject to its jurisdiction the right to enjoy all the rights and freedoms recognized herein, without any distinction on grounds of race, colour, sex, language, religion, political opinion, national or social origin, property, birth or other status and without any discrimination between men and women.

*Article* 3

(a) No restriction upon or derogation from any of the fundamental human rights recognized or existing in any State Party to the present Charter in virtue of law, conventions or custom shall be admitted on the pretext that the present Charter does not recognize such rights or that it recognizes them to a lesser extent.

(b) No State Party to the present Charter shall derogate from the fundamental freedoms recognized herein and which are enjoyed by the nationals of another State that shows less respect for those freedoms.

*Article* 4

(a) No restrictions shall be placed on the rights and freedoms recognized in the present Charter except where such is provided by law and deemed necessary to protect the national security and economy, public order, health or morals or the rights and freedoms of others.

(b) In time of public emergency which threatens the life of the nation, the States Parties may take measures derogating from their obligations under the present Charter to the extent strictly required by the exigencies of the situation.

(c) Such measures or derogations shall under no circumstances affect or apply to the rights and special guarantees concerning the prohibition of torture and degrading treatment, return to one's country, political asylum, trial, the inadmissibility of retrial for the same act, and the legal status of crime and punishment.

*Article* 5

Every individual has the right to life, liberty and security of person. These rights shall be protected by law.

*Article* 6

There shall be no crime or punishment except as provided by law and there shall be no punishment in respect of an act preceding the promulgation of that provision. The accused shall benefit from subsequent legislation if it is in his favour.

*Article* 7

The accused shall be presumed innocent until proved guilty at a lawful trial in which he has enjoyed the guarantees necessary for his defence.

*Article* 8

Everyone has the right to liberty and security of person and no one shall be arrested, held in custody or detained without a legal warrant and without being brought promptly before a judge.

*Article* 9

All persons are equal before the law and everyone within the territory of the State has a guaranteed right to legal remedy.

*Article* 10

The death penalty may be imposed only for the most serious crimes and anyone sentenced to death shall have the right to seek pardon or commutation of the sentence.

*Article* 11

The death penalty shall under no circumstances be imposed for a political offence.

*Article* 12

The death penalty shall not be inflicted on a person under 18 years of age, on a pregnant woman prior to her delivery or on a nursing mother within two years from the date on which she gave birth.

*Article* 13

(a) The States parties shall protect every person in their territory from being subjected to physical or mental torture or cruel, inhuman or degrading treatment. They shall take effective measures to prevent such acts and shall regard the practice thereof, or participation therein, as a punishable offence.

(b) No medical or scientific experimentation shall be carried out on any person without his free consent.

*Article* 14

No one shall be imprisoned on the ground of his proven inability to meet a debt or fulfil any civil obligation.

*Article* 15

Persons sentenced to a penalty of deprivation of liberty shall be treated with humanity.

*Article* 16

No one shall be tried twice for the same offence.

Anyone against whom such proceedings are brought shall have the right to challenge their legality and to demand his release.

Anyone who is the victim of unlawful arrest or detention shall be entitled to compensation.

*Article* 17

Privacy shall be inviolable and any infringement thereof shall constitute an offence. This privacy includes private family affairs, the inviolability of the home and the confidentiality of correspondence and other private means of communication.

*Article* 18

Everyone shall have the inherent right to recognition as a person before the law.

*Article* 19

The people are the source of authority and every citizen of full legal age shall have the right of political participation, which he shall exercise in accordance with the law.

*Article* 20

Every individual residing within the territory of a State shall have the right to liberty of movement and freedom to choose his place of residence in any part of the said territory, within the limits of the law.

*Article* 21

No citizen shall be arbitrarily or unlawfully prevented from leaving any Arab country, including his own, nor prohibited from residing, or compelled to reside, in any part of his country.

*Article* 22

No citizen shall be expelled from his country or prevented from returning thereto.

*Article* 23

Every citizen shall have the right to seek political asylum in other countries in order to escape persecution. This right shall not be enjoyed by persons facing prosecution for an offence under the ordinary law. Political refugees shall not be extraditable.

*Article* 24

No citizen shall be arbitrarily deprived of his original nationality, nor shall his right to acquire another nationality be denied without a legally valid reason.

*Article* 25

Every citizen has a guaranteed right to own private property. No citizen shall under any circumstances be divested of all or any part of his property in an arbitrary or unlawful manner.

*Article* 26

Everyone has a guaranteed right to freedom of belief, thought and opinion.

*Article* 27

Adherents of every religion have the right to practise their religious observances and to manifest their views through expression. practice or teaching, without prejudice to the rights of others. No restrictions shall be imposed on the exercise of freedom of belief, thought and opinion except as provided by law.

*Article* 28

All citizens have the right to freedom of peaceful assembly and association. No restrictions shall be placed on the exercise of this right unless so required by the exigencies of national security, public safety or the need to protect the rights and freedoms of others.

*Article* 29

The State guarantees the right to form trade unions and the right to strike within the limits laid down by law.

*Article* 30

The State guarantees every citizen's right to work in order to secure for himself a standard of living that meets the basic requirements of life. The State also guarantees every citizen's right to comprehensive social security.

*Article* 31

Free choice of work is guaranteed and forced labour is prohibited. Compelling a person to perform work under the terms of a court judgment shall not be deemed to constitute forced labour.

*Article* 32

The State shall ensure that its citizens enjoy equality of opportunity in regard to work, as well as a fair wage and equal remuneration for work of equal value.

*Article* 33

Every citizen shall have the right of access to public office in his country.

*Article* 34

The eradication of illiteracy is a binding obligation and every citizen has a right to education. Primary education, at the very least, shall be compulsory and free and both secondary and university education shall be made easily accessible to all.

*Article* 35

Citizens have a right to live in an intellectual and cultural environment in which Arab nationalism is a source of pride, in which human rights are sanctified and in which racial, religious and other forms of discrimination are rejected and international cooperation and the cause of world peace are supported.

*Article* 36

Everyone has the right to participate in cultural life, as well as the right to enjoy literary and artistic works and to be given opportunities to develop his artistic, intellectual and creative talents.

*Article* 37

Minorities shall not be deprived of their right to enjoy their culture or to follow the teachings of their religions.

*Article* 38

(a) The family is the basic unit of society, whose protection it shall enjoy.

(b) The State undertakes to provide outstanding care and special protection for the family, mothers, children and the aged.

*Article* 39

Young persons have the right to be afforded the most ample opportunities for physical and mental development.

# PART III

*Article* 40

(a) The States members of the League's Council which are parties to the Charter shall elect a Committee of Experts on Human Rights by secret ballot.

(b) The Committee shall consist of seven members nominated by the member States Parties to the Charter. The initial elections to the Committee shall be held six months after the Charter's entry into force. The Committee shall not include more than one person from the same State.

(c) The Secretary-General shall request the member States to submit their candidates two months before the scheduled date of the elections.

(d) The candidates, who must be highly experienced and competent in the Committee's field of work, shall serve in their personal capacity with full impartiality and integrity.

(e) The Committee's members shall be elected for a three-year term which, in the case of three of them, shall be renewable for one further term, their names being selected by lot. The principle of rotation shall be observed as far as possible.

(f) The Committee shall elect its chairman and shall draw up its rules of procedure specifying its method of operation.

(g) Meetings of the Committee shall be convened by the Secretary-General at the Headquarters of the League's Secretariat. With the Secretary-General's approval, the Committee may also meet in another Arab country if the exigencies of its work so require.

*Article* 41

1. The States Parties shall submit reports to the Committee of Experts on Human Rights in the following manner :

    *(a)* An initial report one year after the date of the Charter's entry into force.

    *(b)* Periodic reports every three years.

    *(c)* Reports containing the replies of States to the Committee's questions.

2. The Committee shall consider the reports submitted by the member States Parties to the Charter in accordance with the provisions of paragraph 1 of this article.

3. The Committee shall submit a report, together with the views and comments of the States, to the Standing Committee on Human Rights at the Arab League.

## PART IV

*Article* 42

(a) The Secretary-General of the League of Arab States shall submit the present Charter, after its approval by the Council of the League, to the member States for signature and ratification or accession.

(b) The present Charter shall enter into effect two months after the date of deposit of the seventh instrument of ratification or accession with the Secretariat of the League of Arab States.

*Article* 43

Following its entry into force, the present Charter shall become binding on each State two months after the date of the deposit of its instrument of ratification or accession with the Secretariat. The Secretary-General shall notify the member States of the deposit of each instrument of ratification or accession.

# PART NINE

# THE CONCEPT OF EQUALITY

## INTRODUCTION

The substance of this Part consists of a passage from the Dissenting Opinion of Judge Tanaka, the Japanese member of the International Court of Justice, in the *South-West Africa Cases* (Second Phase), 1966. In that case the Court (by the casting vote of the President) failed to deal with the merits of the submissions of the applicant States (Ethiopia and Liberia) that South Africa had violated her international obligations. However, half the members of the Court, including Judge Tanaka, were prepared to deal with the issues of substance raised by the applications. In the circumstances and given the quality of the exposition the status of the Opinion as a Dissenting Opinion is of little relevance.

The passage reproduced is from the Reports of Judgments, Advisory Opinions and Orders of the International Court of Justice, 1966, at 284–316. It contains what is probably the best exposition of the concept of equality in existing literature. Its importance derives from two sources: first, the lack of sound analysis of the concept in the literature at large; and, secondly, the prominence of the principle of equality, or the standard of non-discrimination, in legislation and other instruments concerning human rights.

For further reference see the *Advisory Opinion on Minority Schools in Albania*, 1935; *Judgments, Orders and Advisory Opinions of the Permanent Court of International Justice*, Series A/B, No. 64; the US Supreme Court in *Brown v. Board of Education*, 347 U.S. 483 (1954); the European Court of Human Rights in the *Case relating to certain aspects of the laws on the use of languages in education in Belgium* (the *Belgian Linguistics* case), Judgment of 23 July 1968, Series A, 1968, (1979–80) 1 EHRR 252; *Ealing L.B.C. v. Race Relations Board* [1972] A.C. 342; *Ahmad v. Inner London Education Authority* [1978] 1 Q.B. 36; Brownlie, I., *Principles of Public International Law* (5th edn., 1998). 602–5.

## 92. DISSENTING OPINION OF JUDGE TANAKA, SOUTH WEST AFRICA CASES (SECOND PHASE), 1966

*TEXT*

Now we shall examine Nos. 3 and 4 of the Applicants' final submissions. Submission No. 3 reads as follows:

> 'Respondent, by laws and regulations, and official methods and measures, which are set out in the pleadings herein, has practised apartheid, i.e., has distinguished as to race, colour, national or tribal origin in establishing the rights and duties of the inhabitants of the Territory; that such practice is in violation of its obligations as stated in Article 2 of the Mandate and Article 22 of the Covenant of the League of Nations; and that Respondent has the duty forthwith to cease the practice of apartheid in the Territory;' (Applicants' final submissions, C.R. 65/35, p. 69).

At the same time, Applicants have presented another submission (Submission No. 4) which states as follows:

> 'Respondent, by virtue of economic, political, social and educational policies applied within the Territory, by means of laws and regulations, and official methods and measures, which are set out in the pleadings herein, has, in the light of applicable international standards or international legal norm, or both, failed to promote to the utmost the material and moral well-being and social progress of the inhabitants of the Territory; that its failure to do so is in violation of its obligations as stated in Article 2 of the Mandate and Article 22 of the Covenant; and that Respondent has the duty forthwith to cease its violations as aforesaid and to take all practicable action to fulfil its duties under such Articles;' (Applicants' final submissions, 19 May 1965, C.R. 65/35, pp. 69–70).

The President, Sir Percy Spender, for the purpose of clarification, addressed a question to the Applicants in relation to Submissions 3 and 4 in the Memorials at page 197, which are not fundamentally different from the above-mentioned Final Submissions Nos. 3 and 4. He asked what was the distinction between one (i.e., Submission No. 3) and the other (i.e., Submission No. 4). (C.R. 65/23, 28 April 1965, p. 31).

The response of the Applicants on this point was that the distinction between the two Submissions 3 and 4 was verbal only (19 May 1965, C.R. 65/35 p. 71). This response, being made after the amendment of the Applicants' submissions, may be considered as applicable to the amended Submissions Nos. 3 and 4.

It should be pointed out that the main difference between the original and the Final Submissions Nos. 3 and 4 is that a phrase, namely: 'in the light of applicable international standards or international legal norm, or both' is inserted between 'has' and 'failed to promote to the utmost . . .' which seems to make clear the substantive identity existing between these two submissions.

Now we shall analyse each of these submissions, which occupy the central issue of the whole of the Applicants' submissions and upon which the greater part of the arguments of the Parties has been focused. This issue is without doubt the question concerning the policy of apartheid which the Respondent as Mandatory is alleged to have practised.

First, we shall deal with the concept of apartheid. The Applicants, in defining apartheid, said: 'Respondent . . . has distinguished as to race, colour, national or tribal origin in establishing the rights and duties of the inhabitants of the Territory.'

It may be said that, as between the Parties, no divergence of opinion on the concept of apartheid itself exists, notwithstanding that the Respondent prefers to use other terminology, such as 'separate development', instead of 'apartheid'. Anyhow, it seems that there has been no argument concerning the concept of apartheid itself. Furthermore, we can also recognize that the Respondent has never denied its practice of apartheid; but it wants to establish the legality and reasonableness of this policy under the mandates system and its compatibility with the obligations of the Respondent as Mandatory, as well as its necessity to perform these obligations.

Submission No. 3 contends that such practice (i.e., the practice of apartheid) is in violation of its obligations as stated in Article 2 of the Mandate and Article 22 of the Covenant. However, the Applicants' contention is not clear as to whether the violation, by the practice of apartheid, of the Respondent's obligation is conceived from the viewpoint of politics or law. If we consider Submission No. 3, only on the basis of its literal interpretation, it may be considered to be from the viewpoint of politics; this means that the policy of apartheid is not in conformity with the objectives of the Mandate, namely the promotion of well-being and social progress of the inhabitants without regard to any conceivable legal norm or standards. If the Applicants maintain this position, the issue would be a matter of discretion and the case, so far as this point is concerned, would not be justiciable, as the Respondent has contended.

Now the Applicants do not allege the violation of obligations by the Respondent independently of any legal norm or standards. Since the Applicants amended Submission No. 4 in the Memorials and inserted a phrase 'in the light of applicable international standards or international legal norm', the violation of the obligations as stated in Article 2 of the Mandate and Article 22 of the Covenant (Submission No. 3) which is identical with the failure to promote to the utmost the material and moral well-being and social progress of the inhabitants of the Territory (Submission No. 4) has come to possess a special meaning; namely of a juridical character. Applicants' cause is no longer based directly on a violation of the well-being and progress by the practice of apartheid, but on the alleged violation of certain international standards or international legal norm and not directly on the obligation to promote the well-being and social progress of the inhabitants. There is no doubt that, if such standards and norm exist, their observance in itself may constitute a part of Respondent's general obligations to promote the well-being and social progress.

From what is said above, the relationship between the Applicants' Submissions Nos. 3 and 4 may be understood as follows. The two submissions deal with the same subject-matter, namely the illegal character of the policy and practice of apartheid. However, the contents of each submission are not quite the same, consequently the distinction between the two submissions is not verbal only, as Applicants stated in answer to the question of the President; each seems to be supplementary to the other.

Briefly, the Applicants' Submissions Nos. 3 and 4, as newly formulated, rest upon a norm and/or standard. This norm or standard has been added by the Applicants to Submission No. 4. The existence of this norm or standard to be applied to the Mandate relationships, according to the Applicants' allegation, constitutes a legal limitation of the Respondent's discretionary power and makes the practice of apartheid illegal, and accordingly a violation of the obligations incumbent on the Mandatory.

What the Applicants mean by apartheid is as follows:

> 'Under apartheid, the status, rights, duties, opportunities and burdens of the population are determined and allotted arbitrarily on the basis of race, color and tribe, in a pattern which ignores the needs and capacities of the groups and individuals affected, and subordinates the interests and rights of the great majority of the people to the preferences of a minority . . . It deals with apartheid in practice, as it actually is and as it actually has been in the life of the people of the Territory . . .' (Memorials, p. 108.)

The Applicants contend the existence of a norm or standards which prohibit the practice of apartheid. These norm or standards are nothing other than those of non-discrimination or non-separation.

The Respondent denies the existence of a norm or standard to prohibit the practice of apartheid and tries to justify this practice from the discretionary nature of the Mandatory's power. The Respondent emphasizes that the practice of apartheid is only impermissible when it is carried out in bad faith.

From the viewpoint of the Applicants, the existence, and objective validity, of a norm of non-discrimination make the question of the intention or motivation irrelevant for the purposes of determining whether there has been a violation of this norm. The principle that a legal precept, as opposed to a moral one, in so far as it is not specifically provided otherwise, shall be applied objectively, independently of motivation on the part of those concerned and independently of other individual circumstances, may be applicable to the Respondent's defence of *bona fides*.

Here we are concerned with the existence of a legal norm or standards regarding non-discrimination. It is a question which is concerned with the sources of international law, and, at the same time, with the mandate law. Furthermore, the question is intimately related to the essence and nature of fundamental human rights, the promotion and encouragement of respect for which constitute one of the purposes of the United Nations (Article 1, paragraph 3, Charter of the United Nations), in which the principle of equality before the law occupies the most important part—a principle, from the Applicants' view, antithetical to the policy of apartheid.

What is meant by 'international norm or standards' can be understood as being related to the principle of equality before the law.

The question is whether a legal norm on equality before the law exists in the international sphere and whether it has a binding power upon the Respondent's conduct in carrying out its obligations as Mandatory. The question is whether the principle of equality before the law can find its place among the sources of international law which are referred to in Article 38, paragraph 1.

Now we shall examine one by one the sources of international law enumerated by the above-mentioned provision.

First we consider the international conventions (or treaties). Here we are not concerned with 'special' or 'particular' law-making bilateral treaties, but only with law-making multilateral treaties such as the Charter of the United Nations, the Constitution of the International Labour Organization, the Genocide Convention, which have special significance as legislative methods. However, even such law-making treaties bind only signatory States and they do not bind States which are not parties to them.

The question is whether the Charter of the United Nations contains a legal norm of equality before the law and the principle of non-discrimination on account of religion, race, colour, sex, language, political creed, etc. The achievement of international co-operation in 'promoting and encouraging respect for human rights and for fundamental freedoms for all without distinction as to race, sex, language, or religion' constitutes one of the purposes of the United Nations (Article 1, paragraph 3). Next, the General Assembly shall initiate studies and made recommendations for the purpose of ' ... (b) ... and assisting in the realization of human rights and fundamental freedoms without distinction as to race, sex, language, or religion' (Article 13, paragraph 1 (b)). 'Universal respect for, and observance of, human rights and fundamental freedoms for all without distinction as to race, sex, language, or religion' is one of the items which shall be promoted by the United Nations in the field of international economic and social co-operation (Articles 55(c), 56). In this field the Economic and Social Council may make recommendations for the purpose of promoting respect for, and observance of, human rights and fundamental freedoms for all (Article 62, paragraph 2, Charter). Finally, 'to encourage respect for human rights and for fundamental freedoms for all without distinction as to race, sex, language or religion' is indicated as one of the basic objectives of the trusteeship system (Article 76 (c)).

The repeated references in the Charter to the fundamental rights and freedoms—at least four times—presents itself as one of its differences from the Covenant of the League of Nations, in which the existence of intimate relationships between peace and respect for human rights were not so keenly felt as in the Charter of the United Nations. However, the Charter did not go so far as to give the definition to the fundamental rights and freedoms, nor to provide any machinery of implementation for the protection and guarantee of these rights and freedoms. The 'Universal Declaration of Human Rights and Fundamental Freedoms' of 1948 which wanted to formulate each right and freedom and give them concrete content, is no more than a declaration adopted by the General Assembly and not a treaty binding on the member States. The goal of the codification on the matter of human rights and freedoms has until now not been reached save in very limited degree, namely with the European Convention for the Protection of Human Rights and Fundamental Freedoms of 1953, the validity of which is only regional and not universal and with a few special conventions, such as 'genocide' and political rights of women, the application of which is limited to their respective matters.

In view of these situations, can the Applicants contend, as an interpretation of the Charter, that the existence of a legal norm on equality before the law, which prescribes non-discrimination on account of religion, race, colour, etc., accordingly forbids the practice of apartheid? Is what the Charter requires limited only 'to achieve international co-operation . . . in promoting and encouraging respect for human rights and for fundamental freedoms . . .' and other matters referred to above?

Under these circumstances it seems difficult to recognize that the Charter expressly imposes on member States any legal obligation with respect to the fundamental human rights and freedoms. On the other hand, we cannot ignore the enormous importance which the Charter attaches to the realization of fundamental human rights and freedoms. Article 56 states: 'All Members pledge themselves to take joint and separate action in co-operation with the Organization for the achievement of the purposes set forth in Article 55.' (Article 55 enumerates the purposes of international economic and social co-operation, in which 'universal respect for, and observance of, human rights and fundamental freedoms' is included.) Well, those who pledge themselves to take action in co-operation with the United Nations in respect of the promotion of universal respect for, and observance of, human rights and fundamental freedoms, cannot violate, without contradiction, these rights and freedoms. How can one, on the one hand, preach respect for human rights to others and, on the other hand, disclaim for oneself the obligation to respect them? From the provisions of the Charter referring to the human rights and fundamental freedoms it can be inferred that the legal obligation to respect human rights and fundamental freedoms is imposed on member States.

Judge Spiropoulos confirmed the binding character of the human rights provisions of the Charter:

> 'As the obligation to respect human rights was placed upon Member States by the Charter, it followed that any violation of human rights was a violation of the provision of the Charter.' (G.A., O.R., 3rd Session, 6th Committee, 138th Meeting, 7 December 1948, p. 765.)

Judge Jessup also attributed the same character to the human rights provisions:

> 'Since this book is written *de lege ferenda*, the attempt is made throughout to distinguish between the existing law and the future goals of the law. It is already the law, at least for Members of the United Nations, that respect for human dignity and fundamental human rights is obligatory. The duty is imposed by the Charter.' (Philip C. Jessup, *Modern Law of Nations*, 1948, p. 91.)

Without doubt, under the present circumstances, the international protection of human rights and fundamental freedoms is very imperfect. The work of codification in this field of law has advanced little from the viewpoint of defining each human right and freedom, as well as the machinery for their realization. But there is little doubt of the existence of human rights and freedoms; if not, respect for these is logically inconceivable; the Charter presupposes the existence of human rights and freedoms which shall be respected; the existence of such rights and freedoms is unthinkable without corresponding obligations of persons concerned and a legal norm underlying them. Furthermore, there is no doubt that these obligations are not only moral ones, and that they also have a legal character by the very nature of the subject-matter.

Therefore, the legislative imperfections in the definition of human rights and freedoms and the lack of mechanism for implementation, do not constitute a reason for denying their existence and the need for their legal protection.

Furthermore, it must be pointed out that the Charter provisions, as indicated above, repeatedly emphasize the principle of equality before the law by saying, 'without distinction as to race, sex, language or religion'.

Under the hypothesis that in the United Nations Charter there exists a legal norm or standards of non-discrimination, are the Applicants, referring to this norm, entitled to have recourse to the International Court of Justice according to Article 7, paragraph 2, of the Mandate? The Respondent contends that such an alleged norm does not constitute a part of the mandate agreement, and therefore the question on this norm falls outside the dispute, which, by the compromissory clause, is placed under the jurisdiction of the International Court of Justice. The Applicants' contention would amount to the introduction of a new element into the mandate agreement which is alien to this instrument.

It is evident that, as the Respondent contends, the mandate agreement does not stipulate equality before the law clause, and that this clause does not formally constitute a part of the mandate instrument. Nevertheless, the equality principle, as an integral part of the Charter of the United Nations or as an independent source of general international law, can be directly applied to the matter of the Mandate either as constituting a kind of law of the Mandate *in sensu lato* or, at least in respect of standards, as a principle of interpretation of the mandate agreement. Accordingly, the dispute concerning the legality of apartheid comes within the field of the interpretation and application of the provisions of the Mandate stipulated in Article 7, paragraph 2, of the Mandate.

This conclusion is justified only on the presupposition that the Respondent is bound by the Charter of the United Nations not only as a member State but also as a Mandatory. The Charter, being of the nature of special international law, or the law of the organized international community, must be applied to all matters which come within the purposes and competence of the United Nations and with which member States are concerned, including the matter of the Mandate. Logic requires that, so long as we recognize the unity of personality, the same principle must govern both the conduct of a member State in the United Nations itself and also its conduct as a mandatory, particularly in the matter of the protection and guarantee of human rights and freedoms.

Concerning the Applicants' contention attributing to the norm of non-discrimination or non-separation the character of customary international law, the following points must be noted.

The Applicants enumerate resolutions and declarations of international organs which condemn racial discrimination, segregation, separation and apartheid, and contend that the said resolutions and declarations were adopted by an overwhelming majority, and therefore have binding power in regard to an opposing State, namely the Respondent. Concerning the question whether the consent of all States is required for the creation of a customary international law or not, we consider that the answer must be in the negative for the reason that Article 38, paragraph 1 (b), of the Statute does not exclude the possibility of a few dissidents for the purpose of the creation of a customary international law and that the contrary view of a particular State or States would result in the permission of obstruction by veto, which could not have been expected by the legislator who drafted the said Article.

An important question involved in the Applicants' contention is whether resolutions and declarations of international organs can be recognized as a factor in the custom-generating process in the interpretation of Article 38, paragraph 1 (b), that is to say, as 'evidence of a general practice'.

According to traditional international law, a general practice is the result of the repetition of individual acts of States constituting consensus in regard to a certain content of a rule of law. Such repetition of acts is a historical process extending over a long period of time. The process of the formation of a customary law in this case may be described as individualistic. On the contrary, this process is going to change in adapting itself to changes in the way of international life. The appearance of organizations such as the League of Nations and the United Nations, with their agencies and affiliated institutions, replacing an important part of the traditional individualistic method of international negotiation by the method of 'parliamentary diplomacy' (Judgment on the *South West Africa* cases, *ICJ Reports 1962*, p. 346), is bound to influence the mode of generation of customary international law. A State, instead of pronouncing its view to a few States directly concerned, has the opportunity, through the medium of an organization, to declare its position to all members of the organization and to know immediately their reaction on the same matter. In former days, practice, repetition and *opinio juris sive necessitatis*, which are the ingredients of customary law might be combined together in a very long and slow process extending over centuries. In the contemporary age of highly developed techniques of communication and information, the formation of a custom through the medium of international organizations is greatly facilitated and accelerated; the establishment of such a custom would require no more than one generation or even far less than that. This is one of the examples of the transformation of law inevitably produced by change in the social substratum.

Of course, we cannot admit that individual resolutions, declarations, judgments, decisions, etc., have binding force upon the members of the organization. What is required for customary international law is the repetition of the same practice; accordingly, in this case resolutions, declarations, etc., on the same matter in the same, or diverse, organizations must take place repeatedly.

Parallel with such repetition, each resolution, declaration, etc., being considered as the manifestation of the collective will of individual participant States, the will of the international community can certainly be formulated more quickly and more accurately as compared with the traditional method of the normative process. This collective, cumulative and organic process of custom-generation can be characterized as the middle way between legislation by convention and the traditional process of custom making, and can be seen to have an important role from the viewpoint of the development of international law.

In short, the accumulation of authoritative pronouncements such as resolutions, declarations, decisions, etc., concerning the interpretation of the Charter by the competent organs of the international community can be characterized as evidence of the international custom referred to in Article 38, paragraph 1 (b).

In the present case the Applicants assert the existence of the international norm and standards of non-discrimination and non-separation and refer to this source of international law. They enumerate resolutions of the General Assembly which repeatedly and strongly deny the apartheid policy of racial discrimination as an interpretation of the Charter (General Assembly resolution 1178 (XII) of 26 November 1957; resolution 1248 (XIII) of 30 October 1958; resolution 1375 (XIV) of 17 November 1959; resolution 1598 (XV) of 13 April 1961; and resolutions of the Security Council (with regard to apartheid as practised in the Republic of South Africa); resolution of 7 August 1953 which declares the inconsistency of the policy of the South African Government with the principles contained in the Charter of the United Nations and with its obligations as a member State of the United Nations; resolution of 4 December 1963 which declares '. . . the policies of apartheid and racial discrimination . . . are abhorrent to the conscience of mankind . . .'. The Applicants cite also the report of the Committee on South West Africa for 1956).

Moreover, the 11 trust territories agreements, each of them containing a provision concerning the norm of official non-discrimination or non-separation on the basis of membership in a group or race, may be considered as contributions to the development of the universal acceptance of the norm of non-discrimination, in addition to the meaning which each provision possesses in each trusteeship agreement, by virtue of Article 38, paragraph 1 (a), of the Statute.

Furthermore, the Universal Declaration of Human Rights adopted by the General Assembly in 1948, although not binding in itself, constitutes evidence of the interpretation and application of the relevant Charter provisions. The same may be said of the Draft Declaration on Rights and Duties of States adopted by the International Law Commission in 1949, the Draft Covenant on Civil and Political rights, the Draft Covenant on Economic, Social and Cultural rights, the Declaration on the Elimination of all Forms of Racial Discrimination adopted by the General Assembly of the United Nations on 20 November 1963 and of regional treaties and declarations, particularly the European Convention for the Protection of Human Rights and Fundamental Freedoms signed on 3 September 1953, the Charter of the Organization of American States signed on 30 April 1948, the American Declaration of the Rights and Duties of Man, 1948, the Draft Declaration of International Rights and Duties, 1945.

From what has been said above, we consider that the norm of non-discrimination or non-separation on the basis of race has become a rule of customary international law as is contended by the Applicants, and as a result, the Respondent's obligations as Mandatory are governed by this legal norm in its capacity as a member of the United Nations either directly or at least by way of interpretation of Article 2, paragraph 2.

One of the contentions concerning the application of the said legal norm is that, if such a legal norm exists for judging the Respondent's obligations under Article 2, paragraph 2, of the Mandate, it would be the one in existence at the time the Mandate was entrusted to the Respondent. This is evidently a question of inter-temporal law.

The Respondent's position is that of denying the application of a new law to a matter which arose under an old law, namely the negation of retroactivity of a new customary law. The Applicant's argument is based on 'the relevance of the evolving practice and views of States, growth of experience and increasing knowledge in political and social science to the determination of obligations bearing on the nature and purpose of the Mandate in general, and Article 2 paragraph 2'; briefly, it rests on the assertion of the concept of the 'continuous, dynamic and ascending growth' of the obligation of the Mandatory.

Our view on this question is substantially not very different from that of the Applicants. The reason why we recognize the retroactive application of a new customary law to a matter which started more than 40 years ago is as follows.

The matter in question is in reality not that of an old law and a new law, that is to say, it is not a question which arises out of an amendment of a law and which should be decided on the basis of the principle of the protection of *droit acquis* and therefore of non-retroactivity. In the present case, the protection of the acquired rights of the Respondent is not the issue, but its obligations, because the main purposes of the mandate system are ethical and humanitarian. The Respondent has no right to behave in an inhuman way today as well as during these 40 years. Therefore, the recognition of the generation of a new customary international law on the matter of non-discrimination is not to be regarded as detrimental to the Mandatory, but as an authentic interpretation of the already existing provisions of Article 2, paragraph 2, of the Mandate and the Covenant. It is nothing other than a simple clarification of what was not so clear 40 years ago. What ought to have been clear 40 years ago has been revealed by the creation of a new customary law which plays the role of authentic interpretation the effect of which is retroactive.

Briefly, the method of the generation of customary international law is in the stage of transformation from being an individualistic process to being a collectivistic process. This phenomenon can be said to be the adaptation of the traditional creative process of international law to the reality of the growth of the organized international community. It can be characterized, considered from the sociological viewpoint, as a transition from traditional custom-making to international legislation by treaty.

Following the reference to Article 38, paragraph 1 (b), of the Statute, the Applicants base their contention on the legal norm alternatively on Article 38, paragraph 1 (c), of the Statute, namely 'the general principles of law recognized by civilized nations'.

Applicants refer to this source of international law both as an independent ground for the justification of the norm of non-discrimination and as a supplement and reinforcement of the other arguments advanced by them to demonstrate their theory.

The question is whether the legal norm of non-discrimination or non-separation denying the practice of apartheid can be recognized as a principle enunciated in the said provision.

The wording of this provision is very broad and vague; the meaning is not clear. Multiple interpretations ranging from the most strict to the most liberal are possible.

To decide this question we must clarify the meaning of 'general principles of law'. To restrict the meaning to private law principles or principles of procedural law seems from the viewpoint of literal interpretation untenable. So far as the 'general principles of law' are not qualified, the 'law' must be understood to embrace all branches of law, including municipal law, public law, constitutional and administrative law, private law, commercial law, substantive and procedural law, etc. Nevertheless, analogies drawn from these laws should not be made mechanically, that is to say, to borrow the expression of Lord McNair, 'by means of importing private law institutions "lock, stock and barrel" ready-made and fully equipped with a set of rules'. (*ICJ Reports 1950*, p. 148.)

What international law can with advantage borrow from these sources must be from the viewpoint of underlying or guiding 'principles'. These principles, therefore, must not be limited to statutory provisions and institutions of national laws: they must be extended to the fundamental concepts of each branch of law as well as to law in general so far as these can be considered as 'recognized by civilized nations.'

Accordingly, the general principles of law in the sense of Article 38, paragraph 1 (c), are not limited to certain basic principles of law such as the limitation of State sovereignty, third-party judgment, limitation of the right of self-defence, *pacta sunt servanda*, respect for acquired rights, liability for unlawful harm to one's neighbour, the principle of good faith, etc. The word 'general' may be understood to possess the same meaning as in the case of the '*general* theory of law', 'théorie *générale* de droit', 'die *Allgemeine* Rechtslehre', namely common to all branches of law. But the principles themselves are very extensive and can be interpreted to include not only the general theory of law, but the general theories of each branch of municipal law, so far as recognized by civilized nations. They may be conceived, furthermore, as including not only legal principles but the fundamental legal concepts of which the legal norms are composed such as person, right, duty, property, juristic act, contract, tort, succession, etc.

In short, they may include what can be considered as 'juridical truth' (Bin Cheng, *General Principles of Law as Applied by International Courts and Tribunals*, 1953, p. 24).

The question is whether a legal norm of non-discrimination and non-separation has come into existence in international society, as the Applicants contend. It is beyond all doubt that the presence of laws against racial discrimination and segregation in the municipal systems of virtually every State can be established by comparative law studies. The recognition of this norm by civilized nations can be ascertained. If the condition of 'general principles' is fulfilled, namely if we can say that the general principles include the norm concerning the protection of human rights by adopting the wide interpretation of the provision of Article 38, paragraph 1 (c), the norm will find its place among the sources of international law.

In this context we have to consider the relationship between a norm of a human rights nature and international law. Originally, general principles are considered to be certain private law principles found by the comparative law method and applicable by way of analogy to matters of an international character. These principles are of a nature common to all nations, that is of the character of *jus gentium*. These principles, which originally belong to private law and have the character of *jus gentium*, can be incorporated in international law so as to be applied to matters of an international nature by way of analogy, as we see in the case of the application of some rules of contract law to the interpretation of treaties. In the case of the international protection of human rights, on the contrary, what is involved is not the application by analogy of a principle or a norm of private law to a matter of international character, but the recognition of the juridical validity of a similar legal fact without any distinction as between the municipal and the international legal sphere.

In short, human rights which require protection are the same; they are not the product of a particular juridical system in the hierarchy of the legal order, but the same human rights must be recognized, respected and protected everywhere man goes. The uniformity of national laws on the protection of human rights is not derived, as in the cases of the law of contracts and commercial and maritime transactions, from considerations of expediency by the legislative organs or from the creative power of the custom of a community, but it already exists in spite of its more-or-less vague form. This is of nature *jus naturale* in roman law.

The unified national laws of the character of *jus gentium* and of the law of human rights, which is of the character of *jus naturale* in roman law, both constituting a part of the law of the world community which may be designated as World Law, Common Law of Mankind (Jenks), Transnational Law (Jessup), etc., at the same time constitute a part of international law through the medium of Article 38, paragraph 1 (c). But there is a difference between these two cases. In the former, the general principles are presented as common elements among diverse national laws; in the latter, only one and the same law exists and this is valid through all kinds of human societies in relationships of hierarchy and co-ordination.

This distinction between the two categories of law of an international character is important in deciding the scope and extent of Article 38, paragraph 1 (c). The Respondent contends that the suggested application by the Applicants of a principle recognized by civilized nations is not a correct analogy and application as contemplated by Article 38, paragraph 1 (c). The Respondent contends that the alleged norm of non-differentiation as between individuals within a State on the basis of membership of a race, class or group could not be transferred by way of analogy to the international relationship, otherwise it would mean that all nations are to be treated equally despite the difference of race, colour, etc.—a conclusion which is absurd. (C.R. 65/47, p. 7.) If we limit the application of Article 38, paragraph 1 (c), to a strict analogical extension of certain principles of municipal law, we must recognize that the contention of the Respondent is well-founded. The said provision, however, does not limit its application to cases of analogy with municipal, or private law which has certainly been a most important instance of the application of this provision. We must include the international protection of human rights in the application of this provision. It must not be regarded as a case of analogy. In reality, there is only one human right which is valid in the international sphere as well as in the domestic sphere.

The question here is not of an 'international', that is to say, inter-State nature, but it is concerned with the question of the international validity of human rights, that is to say, the question whether a State is obliged to protect human rights in the international sphere as it is obliged in the domestic sphere.

The principle of the protection of human rights is derived from the concept of man as a *person* and his relationship with society which cannot be separated from universal human nature. Then existence of human rights does not depend on the will of a State; neither internally on its law or any other legislative measure, nor internationally on treaty or custom, in which the express or tacit will of a State constitutes the essential element.

A State or States are not capable of creating human rights by law or by convention; they can only confirm their existence and give them protection. The role of the State is no more than declaratory. It is exactly the same as the International Court of Justice ruling concerning the *Reservations to the Genocide Convention* case (*ICJ Reports 1951*, p. 23):

> 'The solution of these problems must be found in the special characteristics of the Genocide Convention . . . The origins of the Convention show that it was the intention of the United Nations to condemn and punish genocide as 'a crime under international law' involving a denial of the right of existence of entire human groups, a denial which shocks the conscience of mankind and results in great losses to humanity, and which is contrary to moral law and to the spirit and aims of the United Nations (resolution 96 (I) of the General Assembly, December 11th, 1946). The first consequence arising from this conception is that the principles underlying the Convention are principles which are recognized by civilized nations as binding on States, *even without any conventional obligation*. A second consequence is the universal character both of the condemnation of genocide and of the co-operation required 'in order to liberate mankind from such an odious scourge' (Preamble to the Convention).' (Italics added.)

Human rights have always existed with the human being. They existed independently of, and before, the State. Alien and even stateless persons must not be deprived of them. Belonging to diverse kinds of communities and societies—ranging from family, club, corporation, to State and international community, the human rights of man must be protected everywhere in this social hierarchy, just as copyright is protected domestically and internationally. There must be no legal vacuum in the protection of human rights. Who can believe, as a reasonable man, that the existence of human rights depends upon the internal or international legislative measures, etc., of the State and that accordingly they can be validly abolished or modified by the will of the State?

If a law exists independently of the will of the State and, accordingly, cannot be abolished or modified even by its constitution, because it is deeply rooted in the conscience of mankind and of any reasonable man, it may be called 'natural law' in contrast to 'positive law'.

Provisions of the constitutions of some countries characterize fundamental human rights and freedoms as 'inalienable', 'sacred', 'eternal', 'inviolate', etc. Therefore, the guarantee of fundamental human rights and freedoms possesses a super-constitutional significance.

If we can introduce in the international field a category of law, namely *jus cogens*, recently examined by the International Law Commission, a kind of imperative law which constitutes the contrast to *the jus dispositivum*, capable of being changed by way of agreement between States, surely the law concerning the protection of human rights may be considered to belong to the *jus cogens*.

As an interpretation of Article 38, paragraph 1 (c), we consider that the concept of human rights and of their protection is included in the general principles mentioned in that article.

Such an interpretation would necessarily be open to the criticism of falling into the error of natural law dogma. But it is undeniable that in Article 38, paragraph 1 (c), some natural law elements are inherent. It extends the concept of the source of international law beyond the limit of legal positivism according to which, the

States being bound only by their own will, international law is nothing but the law of the consent and auto-limitation of the State. But this viewpoint, we believe, was clearly overruled by Article 38, paragraph 1 (c), by the fact that this provision does not require the consent of States as a condition of the recognition of the general principles. States which do not recognize this principle or even deny its validity are nevertheless subject to its rule. From this kind of source international law could have the foundation of its validity extended beyond the will of States, that is to say, into the sphere of natural law and assume an aspect of its supra-national and supra-positive character.

The above-mentioned character of Article 38, paragraph 1 (c), of the Statute is proved by the process of the drafting of this article by the Committee of Jurists. The original proposal made by Baron Descamps referred to '*la conscience juridique des peuples civilisés*', a concept which clearly indicated an idea originating in natural law. This proposal met with the opposition of the positivist members of the Committee, represented by Mr. Root. The final draft, namely Article 38, paragraph 1 (c), is the product of a compromise between two schools, naturalist and positivist, and there-fore the fact that the natural law idea became incorporated therein is not difficult to discover (see particularly Jean Spiropoulos, *Die Allgemeine Rechtsgrundsätze im Völkerrecht*, 1928, pp. 6off.; Bin Cheng, *op. cit.*, pp. 24–26).

Furthermore, an important role which can be played by Article 38, paragraph 1 (c), in filling in gaps in the positive sources in order to avoid *nonliquet* decisions, can only be derived from the natural law character of this provision. Professor Brierly puts it, 'its inclusion is important as a rejection of the positivistic doctrine, accord-ing to which international law consists solely of rules to which States have given their consent' (J. L. Brierly, *The Law of Nations*, 6th ed., p. 63). Mr. Rosenne comments on the general principles of law as follows:

> 'Having independent existence, their validity as legal norms does not derive from the consent of the parties as such . . . The Statute places this element on a footing of formal equality with the two positivist elements of custom and treaty, and thus is positivist recognition of the Grotian concept of the co-existence implying no sub-ordination of positive law and the so-called natural law of nations (in the Grotian sense).' (Shabtai Rosenne, *The International Court of Justice*, 1965, Vol. II, p. 610.)

Now the question is whether the alleged norm of non-discrimination and non-separation as a kind of protection of human rights can be considered as recognized by civilized nations and included in the general principles of law.

First the recognition of a principle by civilized nations, as indicated above, does not mean recognition by all civilized nations, nor does it mean recognition by an official act such as a legislative act; therefore the recognition is of a very elastic nature. The principle of equality before the law, however, is stipulated in the list of human rights recognized by the municipal system of virtually every State no mat-ter whether the form of government be republican or monarchical and in spite of any differences in the degree of precision of the relevant provisions. This principle has become an integral part of the constitutions of most of the civilized countries in the world. Common-law countries must be included. (According to *Constitutions of Nations*, 2nd edn., by Amos J. Peaslee, 1956, Vol. I, p. 7, about 73 per cent of the national constitutions contain clauses respecting equality.)

The manifestation of the recognition of this principle does not need to be limited to the act of legislation as indicated above; it may include the attitude of delegations of member States in cases of participation in resolutions, declarations, etc., against racial discrimination adopted by the organs of the League of Nations, the United Nations and other organizations which, as we have seen above, constitute an important element in the generation of customary international law.

From what we have seen above, the alleged norm of non-discrimination and non-separation, being based on the United Nations Charter, particularly Articles 55(c), 56, and on numerous resolutions and declarations of the General Assembly and other organs of the United Nations, and owing to its nature as a general principle, can be regarded as a source of international law according to the provisions of Article 38, paragraph 1 (a)–(c). In this case three kinds of sources are cumulatively functioning to defend the above-mentioned norm: (1) international convention, (2) international custom and (3) the general principles of law.

Practically the justification of any one of these is enough, but theoretically there may be a difference in the degree of importance among the three. From a positivistic, voluntaristic viewpoint, first the convention, and next the custom, is considered important, and general principles occupy merely a supplementary position. On the contrary, if we take the supra-national objective viewpoint, the general principles would come first and the two others would follow them. If we accept the fact that convention and custom are generally the manifestation and concretization of already existing general principles, we are inclined to attribute to this third source of international law the primary position vis-à-vis the other two.

To sum up, the principle of the protection of human rights has received recognition as a legal norm under three main sources of international law, namely (1) international conventions, (2) international custom and (3) the general principles of law. Now, the principle of equality before the law or equal protection by the law presents itself as a kind of human rights norm. Therefore, what has been said on human rights in general can be applied to the principle of equality. (Cf. Wilfred Jenks, *The Common Law of Mankind*, 1958, p. 121. The author recognizes the principle of respect for human rights including equality before the law as a general principle of law.)

Here we must consider the principle of equality in relationship to the Mandate. The contention of the Applicants is based on this principle as condemning the practice of apartheid. The Applicants contend not only that this practice is in violation of the obligations of the Respondent imposed upon it by Article 2 of the Mandate and Article 22 of the Covenant (Submission No. 3), but that the Respondent, by virtue of economic, political, social and educational policies has, in the light of applicable international standards or international legal norms, or both, failed to promote to the utmost the material and moral well-being and social progress of the inhabitants of the Territory. What the Applicants seek to establish seems to be that the Respondent's practice of apartheid constitutes a violation of international standards and/or an international legal norm, namely the principle of equality and, as a result, a violation of the obligations to promote to the utmost, etc. If the violation of this principle exists, this will be necessarily followed by failure to promote the well-being, etc. The question is whether the principle of equality is applicable to the relationships of the Mandate or not. The Respondent denies that the Mandate includes in its content the principle of equality as to race, colour, etc.

Regarding this point, we would refer to our above-mentioned view concerning the Respondent's contention that the alleged norm of non-discrimination of the Charter does not constitute a part of the mandate agreement, and therefore the question of this norm falls outside the dispute under Article 7, paragraph 2, of the Mandate.

We consider that the principle of equality, although it is not expressly mentioned in the mandate instrument constitutes, by its nature, an integral part of the mandates system and therefore is embodied in the Mandate. From the natural-law character of this principle its inclusion in the Mandate must be justified.

It appears to be a paradox that the inhabitants of the mandated territories are internationally more protected than citizens of States by the application of Article 7, paragraph 2, but this interpretation falls outside the scope of the present proceedings.

Next, we shall consider the content of the principle of equality which must be applied to the question of apartheid.

# IV

As we have seen above, the objectives of the mandates system, being the material and moral well-being and social progress of the inhabitants of the territory, are in themselves of a political nature. Their achievement must be measured by the criteria of politics and the method of their realization belongs to the matter of the discretion conferred upon the Mandatory by Article 2, paragraph 1, of the Mandate, and Article 22 of the Covenant of the League.

The discretionary power of the Mandatory, however, is not unlimited. Besides the general rules which prohibit the Mandatory from abusing its power and *mala fides* in performing its obligations, and besides the individual provisions of the Mandate and the Covenant, the Mandatory is subject to the Charter of the United Nations as a member State, the customary international law, general principles of law, and other sources of international law enunciated in Article 38, paragraph 1. According to the contention of the Applicants, the norm and/or standards which prohibit the practice of apartheid, are either immediately or by way of interpretation of the Mandate binding upon the discretionary power of the Mandatory. The Respondent denies the existence of such norm and/or standards.

The divergence of views between the Parties is summarized in the following formula: whether or not the policy of racial discrimination or separate development is *per se* incompatible with the well-being and social progress of the inhabitants, or in other terms, whether the policy of apartheid is illegal (*bona fides* or *mala fides*), the result or effect. From the Respondent's standpoint apartheid is not *per se* prohibited but only a special kind of discrimination which leads to oppression is prohibited.

This divergence of fundamental standpoints between the Parties is reflected in their attitudes as to what extent their contentions depend on the evidence. Contrary to the Applicants' attitude in denying the necessity of calling witnesses and experts and of an inspection *in loco*, the Respondent abundantly utilized numerous witnesses and experts and requested the Court to visit South West Africa, South Africa and other parts of Africa to make an inspection *in loco*.

First, we shall examine the content of the norm and standards of which violation by the Respondents is alleged by the Applicants.

The Applicants contend, as set forth in the Memorials (p. 108) that the Respondent's violation of its obligations under the said paragraph 2 of Article 2 of the Mandate consists in a 'systematic course of positive action which inhibits the well-being, prevents the social progress and thwarts the development of the over-whelming majority' of the inhabitants of the Territory. In pursuit of such course of action, and as a pervasive feature thereof, the Respondent has, by governmental action, installed and maintained the policy of apartheid, or separate development. What is meant by apartheid is as follows:

> 'Under apartheid, the status, rights, duties, opportunities and burdens of the population are determined and allotted arbitrarily on the basis of race, color and tribe, in a pattern which ignores the needs and capacities of the groups and individuals affected, and subordinates the interests and rights of the great majority of the people to the preferences of a minority.' (Memorials, p. 108.)

Such policy, the Applicants contend, 'runs counter to modern conceptions of human rights, dignities and freedom, irrespective of race, colour or creed', which conclusion is denied by the Respondent.

The alleged legal norms of non-discrimination or non-separation by which, by way of interpretation of Article 2, paragraph 2, of the Mandate, apartheid becomes illegal, are defined by the Applicants as follows:

> 'In the following analysis of the relevant legal norms, the terms 'non-discrimination' or 'non-separation' are used in their prevalent and customary sense: stated negatively, the terms refer to the absence of governmental policies or actions which allot status, rights, duties, privileges or burdens on the basis of membership in a group, class or race rather than on the basis of individual merit, capacity or potential: stated affirmatively, the terms refer to governmental policies and actions the objective of which is to protect equality of opportunity and equal protection of the laws to individual persons as such.' (Reply, p. 274.)

What the Applicants want to establish, are the legal norms of 'non-discrimination' or 'non-separation' which are of a *per se*, non-qualified absolute nature, namely that the decision of observance or otherwise of the norm does not depend upon the motive, result, effect, etc. Therefore from the standpoint of the Applicants, the violation of the norm of non-discrimination is established if there exists a simple fact of discrimination without regard to the intent of oppression on the part of the Mandatory.

On the other hand, the Respondent does not recognize the existence of the norm of non-discrimination of an absolute character and seeks to prove the necessity of group differentiation in the administration of a multi-racial, multi-national, or multi-lingual community. The pleadings and verbatim records are extremely rich in examples of different treatment of diverse population groups in multi-cultural societies in the world. Many examples of different treatment quoted by the Respondent and testified to by the witnesses and experts appear to belong to the system of protection of minority groups in multi-cultural communities and cover not only the field of public law but also of private law.

The doctrine of different treatment of diverse population groups constitutes a fundamental political principle by which 'the Respondent administers not only the Republic of South Africa, but the neighbouring Territory of South West Africa. The geographical, historical, ethnological, economic and cultural differences and varieties between several population groups, according to the contention of the Respondent, have necessitated the adoption of the policy of apartheid or 'separate development'. This policy is said to be required for the purpose of the promotion of the well-being and social progress of the inhabitants of the Territory. The Respondent insists that each population group developing its own characteristics and individuality, to attain self-determination, separate development should be the best way to realize the well-being and social progress of the inhabitants. The other alternative, namely the mixed integral society in the sense of Western democracy would necessarily lead to competition, friction, struggle, chaos, bloodshed, and dictatorship as examples may be found in some other African countries. Therefore, the most appropriate method of administration of the Territory is the principle of indirect rule maintaining and utilizing the merits of tribalism.

Briefly, it seems that the idea underlying the policy of apartheid or separate development is the racial philosophy which is not entirely identical with ideological Nazism but attributes great importance to the racial or ethnological factors in the fields of politics, law, economy and culture. Next, the method of apartheid is of sociological and, therefore, strong deterministic tendency, as we can guess from the fact that at the oral proceedings the standpoint of the Respondent was energetically sustained by many witnesses-experts who were sociologists and ethnologists.

Contrary to the standpoint of the Applicants who condemn the policy of apartheid or separate development of the Respondent as illegal, the latter conceives this policy as something neutral. The Respondent says that it can be utilized as a tool to attain a particular end, good or bad, as a knife can serve a surgeon as well as a murderer.

Before we decide this question, general consideration of the content of the principle of equality before the law is required. Although the existence of this principle is universally recognized as we have seen above, its precise content is not very clear.

This principle has been recognized as one of the fundamental principles of modern democracy and government based on the rule of law. Judge Lauterpacht puts it:

> 'The claim to equality before the law is in a substantial sense the most fundamental of
> the rights of man. It occupies the first place in most written constitutions. It is the
> starting point of all other liberties.' (Sir Hersch Lauterpacht, *An International Bill of the
> Rights of Man*, 1945, p.115.)

Historically, this principle was derived from the Christian idea of the equality of all men before God. All mankind are children of God, and consequently, brothers and sisters, notwithstanding their natural and social differences, namely man and woman, husband and wife, master and slave, etc. The idea of equality of man is derived from the fact that human beings 'by the common possession of reason' distinguish themselves 'from other living beings'. (Lauterpacht, *op. cit.*, p. 116.) This idea existed already in the Stoic philosophy, and was developed by the scholastic philosophers and treated by natural law scholars and encyclopedists of the seventeenth and eighteenth centuries. It received legislative formulation, however, at the end of the eighteenth century first by the Bills of Rights of some American states, next by the Declaration of the French Revolution, and then in the course of the nineteenth century the equality clause, as we have seen above, became one of the common elements of the constitutions of modern European and other countries.

Examining the principle of equality before the law, we consider that it is philo-sophically related to the concepts of freedom and justice. The freedom of indi-vidual persons, being one of the fundamental ideas of law, is not unlimited and must be restricted by the principle of equality allotting to each individual a sphere of freedom which is due to him. In other words the freedom can exist only under the premise of the equality principle.

In what way is each individual allotted his sphere of freedom by the principle of equality? What is the content of this principle? The principle is that what is equal is to be treated equally and what is different is to be treated differently, namely proportionately to the factual difference. This is what was indicated by Aristotle as *justitia commutativa* and *justitia distributiva*.

The most fundamental point in the equality principle is that all human beings as persons have an equal value in themselves, that they are the aim itself and not means for others, and that, therefore, slavery is denied. The idea of equality of men as persons and equal treatment as such is of a metaphysical nature. It under-lies all modern, democratic and humanitarian law systems as a principle of natural law. This idea, however, does not exclude the different treatment of persons from the consideration of the differences of factual circumstances such as sex, age, language, religion, economic condition, education, etc. To treat different matters equally in a mechanical way would be as unjust as to treat equal matters differently.

We know that law serves the concrete requirements of individual human beings and societies. If individuals differ one from another and societies also, their needs will be different, and accordingly, the content of law may not be identical. Hence is derived the relativity of law to individual circumstances.

This historical development of law tells us that, parallel to the trend of general-ization the tendency of individualization or differentiation is remarkable as may be exemplified by the appearance of a system of commercial law separate from the general private law in civil law countries, creation of labour law. The acquisition of independent status by commercial and labour law can be conceived as the confer-ment of a kind of privilege or special treatment to a merchant or labour class. In the field of criminal law the recent tendency of criminal legislative policy is dir-ected towards the individualization of the penalty.

We can say accordingly that the principle of equality before the law does not mean that absolute equality, namely equal treatment of men without regard to individual, concrete circumstances, but it means the relative equality, namely the principle to treat equally what are equal and unequally what are unequal.

The question is, in what case equal treatment or different treatment should exist. If we attach importance to the fact that no man is strictly equal to another and he may have some particularities, the principle of equal treatment could be easily evaded by referring to any factual and legal differences and the existence of this principle would be virtually denied. A different treatment comes into question only when and to the extent that it corresponds to the nature of the difference. To treat unequal matters differently according to their inequality is not only permitted but required. The issue is whether the difference exists. Accordingly, not every different treatment can be justified by the existence of differences, but only such as corresponds to the differences themselves, namely that which is called for by the idea of justice—'the principle to treat equal equally and unequal according to its inequality, constitutes an essential content of the idea of justice' (Goetz Hueck, *Der Grundsatz der Gleichmässigen Behandlung in Privatrecht*, 1958, p. 106) [*translation*].

Briefly, a different treatment is permitted when it can be justified by the criterion of justice. One may replace justice by the concept of reasonableness generally referred to by the Anglo-American school of law.

Justice or reasonableness as a criterion for the different treatment logically excludes arbitrariness. The arbitrariness which is prohibited, means the purely objective fact and not the subjective condition of those concerned. Accordingly, the arbitrariness can be asserted without regard to his motive or purpose.

There is no doubt that the principle of equality is binding upon administrative organs. The discretionary power exercised on considerations of expediency by the administrative organs is restricted by the norm of equality and the infringement of this norm makes an administrative measure illegal. The judicial power also is subjected to this principle. Then, what about the legislative power? Under the constitutions which express this principle in a form such as 'all citizens are equal before the law', there may be doubt whether or not the legislators also are bound by the principle of equality. From the nature of this principle the answer must be in the affirmative. The legislators cannot be permitted to exercise their power arbitrarily and unreasonably. They are bound not only in exercising the ordinary legislative power but also the power to establish the constitution. The reason therefore is that the principle of equality being in the nature of natural law and therefore of a supra-constitutional character, is placed at the summit of hierarchy of the system of law, and that all positive laws including the constitution shall be in conformity with this principle.

The Respondent for the purpose of justifying its policy of apartheid or separate development quotes many examples of different treatment such as minorities treaties, public conveniences (between man and woman), etc. Nobody would object to the different treatment in these cases as a violation of the norm of non-discrimination or non-separation on the hypothesis that such a norm exists. The Applicants contend for the unqualified application of the norm of non-discrimination or non-separation, but even from their point of view it would be impossible to assert that the above-mentioned cases of different treatment constitute a violation of the norm of nondiscrimination.

Then, what is the criterion to distinguish a permissible discrimination from an impermissible one?

In the case of the minorities treaties the norm of non-discrimination as a reverse side of the notion of equality before the law prohibits a State to exclude members of a minority group from participating in rights, interests and opportunities which a majority population group can enjoy. On the other hand, a minority group shall be guaranteed the exercise of their own religious and education activities. This guarantee is conferred on members of a minority group, for the purpose of protection of their interests and not from the motive of discrimination itself. By reason of protection of the minority this protection cannot be imposed upon members of minority groups, and consequently they have the choice to accept it or not.

In any event, in case of a minority, members belonging to this group, enjoying the citizenship on equal terms with members of majority groups, have conferred on them the possibility of cultivating their own religious, educational or linguistic values as a recognition of their fundamental human rights and freedoms.

The spirit of the minorities treaties, therefore, is not negative and prohibitive, but positive and permissive.

Whether the spirit of the policy of apartheid or separate development is common with that of minorities treaties to which the Respondent repeatedly refers, whether the different treatment between man and woman concerning the public conveniences can be referred to for the purpose of justifying the policy of apartheid or not, that is the question.

In the case of apartheid, we cannot deny the existence of reasonableness in some matters that diverse ethnic groups should be treated in certain aspects differently from one another. As we have seen above, differentiation in law and politics is one of the most remarkable tendencies of the modern political society. This tendency is in itself derived from the concept of justice, therefore it cannot be judged as wrong. It is an adaptation of the idea of justice to social realities which, as its structure, is going to be more complicated and multiplicate from the viewpoint of economic, occupational, cultural and other elements.

Therefore, different treatment requires reasonableness to justify it as is stated above. The reason may be the protection of some fundamental human rights and freedoms as we have seen in the case of minorities treaties, or of some other nature such as incapacity of minors to conclude contracts, physical differences between man and woman.

In the case of the protection of minorities, what is protected is not the religious or linguistic group as a whole but the individuals belonging to this group, the former being nothing but a name and not a group. In the case of different treatment of minors or between man and woman, it is clear that minors, disabled persons or men or women in a country do not constitute respectively a group. But whether a racial or ethnic group can be treated in the same way as categories such as minors, disabled persons, men and women, is doubtful. Our conclusion on this point is negative. The reasons therefor are that the scientific and clear-cut definition of race is not established; that what man considers as a matter of common-sense as criteria to distinguish one race from the other, are the appearance, particularly physical characteristics such as colour, hair, etc., which do not constitute in themselves relevant factors as the basis for different political or legal treatment; and that, if there exists the necessity to treat one race differently from another, this necessity is not derived from the physical characteristics or other racial qualifications but other factors, namely religious, linguistic, educational, social, etc., which in themselves are not related to race or colour.

Briefly, in these cases it is possible that the different treatment in certain aspects is reasonably required by the differences of religion, language, education, custom, etc., not by reason of race or colour. Therefore, the Respondent tries in some cases to justify the different treatment of population groups by the concept of cultural population groups. The different treatment would be justified if there really existed the need for it by reason of cultural differences. The different treatment, however, should be condemned if cultural reasons arc referred to for the purpose of dissimulating the underlying racial intention.

In any case, as we have seen above, all human beings are equal before the law and have equal opportunities without regard to religion, race, language, sex, social groups, etc. As persons they have the dignity to be treated as such. This is the principle of equality which constitutes one of the fundamental human rights and freedoms which are universal to all mankind. On the other hand, human beings, being endowed with individuality, living in different surroundings and circumstances are not all alike, and they need in some aspects politically, legally and socially different treatment. Hence the above-mentioned examples of different treatment are derived. Equal treatment is a principle but its mechanical application ignoring all concrete factors engenders injustice. Accordingly, it requires different treatment, taken into consideration, of concrete circumstances of individual cases. The different treatment is permissible and required by the considerations of justice; it does not mean a disregard of justice.

Equality being a principle and different treatment an exception, those who refer to the different treatment must prove its *raison d'être* and its reasonableness.

The Applicants' norm of non-discrimination or non-separation, being conceived as of a *per se* nature, would appear not to permit any exception. The policy of apartheid or separate development which allots status, rights, duties, privileges or burdens on the basis of membership in a group, class or race rather than on the basis of individual merit, capacity or potential is illegal whether the motive be *bona fide* or *mala fide*, oppressive or benevolent; whether its effect or result be good or bad for the inhabitants. From this viewpoint all protective measures taken in the case of minorities treaties and other matters would be included in the illegal discrimination—a conclusion which might not be expected from the Applicants. These measures, according to the Applicants, would have nothing to do with the question of discrimination. The protection the minorities treaties intended to afford to the inhabitants is concerned with life, liberty and free exercise of religion. On the contrary, the Respondent argues the existence of the same reason in the policy of apartheid—the reason of protective measures in the case of minorities treaties.

We must recognize, on the one hand, the legality of different treatment so far as justice or reasonableness exists in it. On the other hand, we cannot recognize all measures of different treatment as legal, which have been and will be performed in the name of apartheid or separate development. The Respondent tries to prove by the pleadings and the testimony of the witnesses and experts the existence of a trend of differentiation in accordance with different religious, racial, linguistic groups. From the viewpoint of the Applicants, the abundant examples quoted by the Respondent and the testimony of witnesses and experts cannot serve as the justification of the policy of apartheid, because they belong to an entirely different plane from that of apartheid and because they are of a nature quite heterogeneous to the policy of apartheid, which is based on a particular racial philosophy and group sociology.

The important question is whether there exists, from the point of view of the requirements of justice, any necessity for establishing an exception to the principle of equality, and the Respondent must prove this necessity, namely the reasonableness of different treatment.

On the aspect of 'reasonableness' two considerations arise. The one is the consideration whether or not the individual necessity exists to establish an exception to the general principle of equality before the law and equal opportunity. In this sense the necessity may be conceived as of the same nature as in the case of minorities treaties of which the objectives are protective and beneficial. The other is the consideration whether the different treatment does or does not harm the sense of dignity of individual persons.

For instance, if we consider education, on which the Parties argued extensively, we cannot deny the value of vernacular as the medium of instruction and the result thereof would be separate schooling as between children of diverse population groups, particularly between the Whites and the Natives. In this case separate education and schooling may be recognized as reasonable. This is justified by the nature of the matter in question. But even in such a case, by reason of the matter which is related to a delicate racial and ethnic problem, the manner of dealing with this matter should be extremely careful. But, so far as the public use of such facilities as hotels, buses, etc., justification of discriminatory and separate treatment by racial groups cannot be found in the same way as separation between smokers and non-smokers in a train.

We cannot condemn all measures derived from the Respondent's policy of apartheid or separate development, particularly as proposed by the Odendaal Commission, on the ground that they are motivated by the racial concept, and therefore devoid of the reasonableness. There may be some measures which are of the same character as we see in the protection measures in the case of the minorities treaties and others. We cannot approve, however, all measures constituting a kind of different treatment of apartheid policy as reasonable.

One of the characteristics of the policy of apartheid is marked by its restrictive tendency on the basis of racial distinction. The policy includes on the one hand protective measures for the benefit of the Natives as we see in the institutions of reserves and homelands connected with restrictions on land rights; however, on the other hand, several kinds of restrictions of rights and freedoms are alleged to exist regarding those Natives who live and work in the southern sector, namely the White area outside the reserves. These restrictions, if they exist, in many cases presenting themselves as violation of respective human rights and freedoms at the same time, would constitute violation of the principle of equality before the law (particularly concerning the discrimination between the Natives and the Whites).

Here we are not required to give answers exhaustively in respect of the Applicants' allegations of violation by the Respondent of the Mandate concerning the legislation (*largo sensu*) applicable in the Territory. The items enumerated by the Applicants in the Memorials (pp. 118–66) are not included in their submissions. We are not obliged to pronounce our views thereon. By way of illustration we shall examine a few points. What is required from us is a decision on the question of whether the Respondent's policy of apartheid constitutes a violation of Article 2, paragraph 2, of the Mandate or not.

For the purpose of illustration we shall consider freedom of choice of occupations (cf. Memorials, pp. 121, 122 and 136).

In the field of civil service, participation by 'Natives' in the general administration appears, in practice, to be confined to the lowest and least skilled categories, such as messengers and cleaners. This practice of 'job-reservation' for Natives is exemplified by allusion to the territorial budget, which classifies jobs as between 'European' and 'Natives'.

In the mining industry the Natives are excluded from certain occupations, such as those of prospector for precious and base minerals, dealer in unwrought precious metals, manager, assistant manager, sectional or underground manager, etc., in mines owned by persons of 'European' descent, officer in the Police Force. Concerning these occupations, 'ceilings' are put on the promotion of the Natives. The role of the 'Native' is confined to that of unskilled labourer.

In the fishing industry, the enterprises are essentially 'European' owned and operated. The role of the 'Native' is substantially confined to unskilled labour (Memorials, p. 119).

As regards railways and harbours, all graded posts in the Railway and Harbours Administration are reserved to 'Europeans', subject to temporary exceptions. The official policy appears to be that 'non-Europeans' should not be allowed to occupy graded posts.

The question is whether these restrictions are reasonable or not, whether there is a necessity to establish exceptions to the general application of the principle of equality of non-discrimination or not.

The matter of 'ceilings' was dealt with minutely and at length in the oral proceedings by the Parties. The Respondent's defence against the condemnation of arbitrariness, injustice and unreasonableness on the part of the Applicants may be summarized in two points: the one is the reason of social security and the other is the principle of balance or reciprocity.

The Respondent contends that the Whites in general do not desire to serve under the authority of the Natives in the hierarchy of industrial or bureaucratic systems. If this fact be ignored and the Natives occupy leading positions in which they would be able to supervise Whites friction between the two groups necessarily would occur and the social peace would be disturbed. This argument of the Respondent seems to be based on a pessimistic view of the possibility of harmonious coexistence of diverse racial and ethnic elements in an integrated society.

It is not deniable that there may exist certain causes of friction, conflict and animosity between diverse racial and ethnic groups which produce obstacles to their coexistence and co-operation in a friendly political community. We may recognize this as one aspect of reality of human nature and social life. It is, however, no less true that mankind aspires and strives towards the ideal of the achievement of a harmonious society composed of racially heterogeneous elements overcoming difficulties which may result from the primitive instinctive sentiment of racial prejudice and antagonism. Such sentiment must be overcome and not approved. In modern, democratic societies we have to expect this result mainly from the progress of humanitarian education. But the mission of politics and law cannot be said to be less important in minimizing racial prejudice and antagonism and avoiding collapse and tragedy. The State is obliged to educate the people by means of legislative and administrative measures for the same purpose.

To take into consideration the psychological effect upon the Whites who would be subjected to the supervision of the Natives if a ceiling did not exist, that is nothing else but the justification or official recognition of racial prejudice or sentiment of racial superiority on the part of the White population which does harm to the dignity of man.

Furthermore, individuals who could have advanced by their personal merits if there existed no ceiling are unduly deprived of their opportunity for promotion.

It is contended by the Respondent that those who are excluded from the jobs proportionate to their capacity and ability in the White areas, can find the same jobs in their own homelands where no restriction exists in regard to them. But even if they can find jobs in their homelands the conditions may not be substantially the same and, accordingly, in most cases, they may not be inclined to go back to the northern sector, their homelands, and they cannot be forced to do so.

The Respondent probably being aware of the unreasonableness in such hard cases, tries to explain it as a necessary sacrifice which should be paid by individuals for the maintenance of social security. But it is unjust to require a sacrifice for the sake of social security when this sacrifice is of such importance as humiliation of the dignity of the personality.

The establishment of ceilings in regard to certain jobs violates human rights of the Natives in two respects: one is violation of the principle of equality before the law and equal opportunity; the other is violation of the right of free choice of employment.

The Respondent furthermost advocates the establishment of ceilings by the principle of reciprocity or balance between two legal situations, namely one existing in the White areas where certain rights and freedoms of the Natives are restricted and the other situation existing in the Native areas where the corresponding rights and freedoms of the Whites are restricted. The Respondent seeks to prove by this logic that in such circumstances the principle of equality of the Whites and the Natives is observed. Unequal treatment unfavourable to one population group in area A, however, cannot be justified by similar treatment of the other population group in area B. Each unequal treatment constitutes an independent illegal conduct; the one cannot be counter-balanced by the other, as set-off is not permitted between two obligations resulting from illegal acts.

Besides, from the viewpoint of group interest, those of the Natives living in the White area outside the reserves are, owing to the number of the Native population, far bigger than those of the Whites living in the Native areas, the idea of counter—balance is quantitatively unjust.

It is also maintained, in respect of the restrictive policy as regards study to become an engineer by a non-White person, that the underlying purpose of this policy is to prevent the frustration on the part of the individual which he might experience when he could not find White assistants willing to serve under him. The sentiment of frustration on the part of non-White individuals, however, should not be rightly referred to as a reason for establishing a restriction on the educational opportunity of non-Whites, firstly because the question is that the frustration is caused by the racial prejudice on the part of the Whites which in itself must be eliminated and secondly because a more important matter is to open to the non-Whites the future possibility of social promotion. Therefore, the reason of the frustration of non-Whites cannot be justified.

Finally, we wish to make the following conclusive and supplementary remarks on the matter of the Applicant's Submissions Nos. 3 and 4.

1. The principle of equality before the law requires that what are equal are to be treated equally and what are different are to be treated differently. The question arises: what is equal and what is different.

2. All human beings, notwithstanding the differences in their appearance and other minor points, are equal in their dignity as persons. Accordingly, from the point of view of human rights and fundamental freedoms, they must be treated equally.

3. The principle of equality does not mean absolute equality, but recognizes relative equality, namely different treatment proportionate to concrete individual circumstances. Different treatment must not be given arbitrarily; it requires reasonableness, or must be in conformity with justice, as in the treatment of minorities, different treatment of the sexes regarding public conveniences, etc. In these cases, the differentiation is aimed at the protection of those concerned, and it is not detrimental and therefore not against their will.

4. Discrimination according to the criterion of 'race, colour, national or tribal origin' in establishing the rights and duties of the inhabitants of the territory is not considered reasonable and just. Race, colour, etc., do not constitute in themselves factors which can influence the rights and duties of the inhabitants as in the case of sex, age, language, religion, etc. If differentiation be required, it would be derived from the difference of language, religion, custom, etc., not from the racial difference itself. In the policy of apartheid the necessary logical and material link between difference itself and different treatment, which can justify such treatment in the case of sex, minorities, etc., does not exist.

We cannot imagine in what case the distinction between Natives and Whites, namely racial distinction apart from linguistic, cultural or other differences, may necessarily have an influence on the establishment of the rights and duties of the inhabitants of the territory.

5. Consequently, the practice of apartheid is fundamentally unreasonable and unjust. The unreasonableness and injustice do not depend upon the intention or motive of the Mandatory, namely its *mala fides*. Distinction on a racial basis is in itself contrary to the principle of equality which is of the character of natural law, and accordingly illegal.

The above-mentioned contention of the Respondent that the policy of apartheid has a neutral character, as a tool to attain a particular end, is not right. If the policy of apartheid is a means, the axiom that the end cannot justify the means can be applied to this policy.

6. As to the alleged violation by the Respondent of the obligations incumbent upon it under Article 2, paragraph 2, of the Mandate, the policy of apartheid, including in itself elements not consistent with the principle of equality before the law, constitutes a violation of the said article, because the observance of the principle of equality before the law must be considered as a necessary condition of the promotion of the material and moral well-being and the social progress of the inhabitants of the territory.

7. As indicated above, so far as the interpretation of Article 2, paragraph 2, of the Mandate is concerned, only questions of a legal nature belong to the matter upon which the Court is competent. Diverse activities which the Respondent as Mandatory carries out as a matter of discretion, to achieve the promotion of the material and moral well-being and the social progress of the inhabitants, fall outside the scope of judicial examination as matters of a political and administrative nature.

Accordingly, questions of whether the ultimate goal of the mandates system should be independence or annexation, and in the first alternative whether a unitary or federal system in regard to the local administration is preferable, whether or in what degree the principle of indirect rule or respect for tribal custom may or must be introduced—such questions, which have been very extensively argued in the written proceedings as well as in the oral proceedings, have, despite their substantial connection with the policy of apartheid, no relevance to a decision on the question of apartheid, from the legal viewpoint.

These questions are of a purely political or administrative character, the study and examination of which might have belonged or may belong to competent organs of the League or the United Nations.

8. The Court cannot examine and pronounce the legality or illegality of the policy of apartheid as a whole; it can decide that there exist some elements in the apartheid policy which are not in conformity with the principle of equality before the law or international standard or international norm of non-discrimination and non-separation. The Court can declare if it is requested to examine the laws, proclamations, ordinances and other governmental measures enacted to implement the policy of apartheid in the light of the principle of equality. For the purpose of the present cases, the foregoing consideration of a few points as illustrations may be sufficient to establish the Respondent's violation of the principle of equality, and accordingly its obligations incumbent upon it by Article 2, paragraph 2, of the Mandate and Article 22 of the Covenant.

9. Measures complained of by the Applicants appear in themselves to be violations of some of the human rights and fundamental freedoms such as rights concerning the security of the person, rights of residence, freedom of movement, etc., but such measures, being applied to the 'Natives' only and the 'Whites' being excluded therefrom, these violations, if they exist, may constitute, at the same time, violations of the principle of equality and non-discrimination also.

In short, we interpret the Applicants' Submissions Nos. 3 and 4 in such a way that their complaints include the violation by the Respondent of two kinds of human rights, namely individual human rights and rights to equal protection of the law. There is no doubt that the Respondent as Mandatory is obliged to protect all human rights and fundamental freedoms including rights to equal protection of the law as a necessary prerequisite of the material and moral well-being and the social progress of the inhabitants of the Territory. By this reason, what has been explained above about the principle of equality in connection with Article 38, paragraph 1 (c), is applicable to human rights and fundamental freedoms in general.

10. From the procedural viewpoint, two matters must be considered. The one is concerned with the effect of the Applicants' amendment of the Submissions Nos. 3 and 4 (Memorials, 15 April 1961, pp. 197–9) by the submissions of 19 May 1965 (C.R. 65/35). Since the amendment of the submissions is allowed until the stage of oral proceedings, and the amendment was made within the scope of the claim set forth in the Applications, there is no reason to deny its effectiveness. Furthermore, we wish to mention that the Respondent raised no objection during the course of the oral proceedings regarding the amendment.

The other is concerned with the question of choice by the Court of the reasons underlying its decisions.

Concerning this question, we consider that, although the Court is bound by the submissions of the Parties, it is entirely free to choose the reasons for its decisions. The Parties may present and develop their own argument as to the interpretation of the provisions of the Mandate, the Covenant, the Charter, etc., but the Court, so far as legal questions are concerned, quite unfettered by what has been put forward by the Parties, can exercise its power of interpretation in approving or rejecting the submissions of the Parties.

For the foregoing reasons, the Applicants' Submissions Nos. 3 and 4 are well-founded.

# PART TEN

# HUMAN RIGHTS AND THE HUMAN GENOME

## INTRODUCTION

The United Nations Educational, Scientific and Cultural Organization (for UNESCO's other contributions to human rights standard-setting, see above, Part 4) recognized early on that scientific advances in human genome research had potentially significant implications for individual human rights. The need to protect human beings from intrusive biological, medical or scientific experiments had long been endorsed, of course, and express prohibitions are included in, among others, Article 7 of the 1966 International Covenant on Civil and Political Rights, Article 50 of the 1949 First Geneva Convention, Article 32 of the Fourth Geneva Convention, Article 11 of the 1977 Additional Protocol I, and Article 5 of the 1977 Additional Protocol II (for the last two-mentioned instruments, see Roberts, A. & R. Guelff, *Documents on the Laws of War*, 3rd edn., 2001).

The new instruments below recognize that, in the absence of appropriate standards, human genome research carries risks and may have a negative impact on both present and future generations, especially with regard to discrimination, health care, cloning, and other experimentation.

## 93. UNIVERSAL DECLARATION ON THE HUMAN GENOME AND HUMAN RIGHTS, 1997

In 1993, UNESCO created an International Bioethics Committee which undertook the work of elaborating an international instrument for the protection of the human genome. The Committee in turn created a Legal Commission, chaired by Héctor Gros Espiell, which duly prepared a draft 'Universal Declaration'. This was finalized by a Committee of governmental experts, and was adopted unanimously and by acclamation at the twenty-ninth session of UNESCO's General Conference on 11 November 1997. The following year, the United Nations General Assembly endorsed the Declaration: see UNGA Resolution 53/152, adopted without a vote on 9 December 1998.

At its thirtieth session, on 16 November 1999, UNESCO's General Conference endorsed 'Guidelines for the Implementation of the Universal Declaration on the Human Genome and Human Rights', prepared by the International Bioethics Committee and approved by the Intergovernmental Bioethics Committee (IGBC).

See also Commission on Human Rights Resolution 1999/63, 'Human Rights and Bioethics, adopted at its fifty-fifth session on 28 April 1999: UN doc. E/CN.4/RES/1999/63; Resolution 2001/71: UN doc. E/CN.4/RES/2001/71, 25 April 2001; Sub-Commission on Human Rights Decision 2001/113: UN doc. E/CN.4/SUB.2/DEC/2001/113, 15 August 2001.

*TEXT*

*The General Conference,*

*Recalling* that the Preamble of UNESCO's Constitution refers to 'the democratic principles of the dignity, equality and mutual respect of men', rejects any 'doctrine of the inequality of men and races', stipulates 'that the wide diffusion of culture, and the education of humanity for justice and liberty and peace are indispensable to the dignity of men and constitute a sacred duty which all the nations must fulfil in a spirit of mutual assistance and concern', proclaims that 'peace must be founded upon the intellectual and moral solidarity of mankind', and states that the Organization seeks to advance 'through the educational and scientific and cultural relations of the peoples of the world, the objectives of international peace and of the common welfare of mankind for which the United Nations Organization was established and which its Charter proclaims',

*Solemnly recalling* its attachment to the universal principles of human rights, affirmed in particular in the Universal Declaration of Human Rights of 10 December 1948 and in the two International United Nations Covenants on Economic, Social and Cultural Rights and on Civil and Political Rights of 16 December 1966, in the United Nations Convention on the Prevention and Punishment of the Crime of Genocide of 9 December 1948, the International United Nations Convention on the Elimination of All Forms of Racial Discrimination of 21 December 1965, the United Nations Declaration on the Rights of Mentally Retarded Persons of 20 December 1971, the United Nations Declaration on the Rights of Disabled Persons of 9 December 1975, the United Nations Convention on the Elimination of All Forms of Discrimination Against Women of 18 December 1979, the United Nations Declaration of Basic Principles of Justice for Victims of Crime and Abuse of Power of 29 November 1985, the United Nations Convention on the Rights of the Child of 20 November 1989, the United Nations Standard Rules on the Equalization of Opportunities for Persons with Disabilities of 20 December 1993, the Convention on the Prohibition of the Development, Production and Stockpiling of Bacteriological (Biological) and Toxin Weapons and on their Destruction of 16 December 1971, the UNESCO Convention against Discrimination in Education of 14 December 1960, the UNESCO Declaration of the Principles of International Cultural Co-operation of 4 November 1966, the UNESCO Recommendation on the Status of Scientific Researchers of 20 November 1974, the UNESCO Declaration on Race and Racial Prejudice of 27 November 1978, the ILO Convention (N° 111) concerning Discrimination in Respect of Employment and Occupation of 25 June 1958 and the ILO Convention (N° 169) concerning Indigenous and Tribal Peoples in Independent Countries of 27 June 1989,

*Bearing in mind*, and without prejudice to, the international instruments which could have a bearing on the applications of genetics in the field of intellectual property, *inter alia*, the Bern Convention for the Protection of Literary and Artistic Works of 9 September 1886 and the UNESCO Universal Copyright Convention of 6 September 1952, as last revised in Paris on 24 July 1971, the Paris Convention for the Protection of Industrial Property of 20 March 1883, as last revised at Stockholm on 14 July 1967, the Budapest Treaty of the WIPO on International Recognition of the Deposit of Micro-organisms for the Purposes of Patent Procedures of 28 April 1977, and the Trade Related Aspects of Intellectual Property Rights Agreement (TRIPs) annexed to the Agreement establishing the World Trade Organization, which entered into force on 1 January 1995,

*Bearing in mind also* the United Nations Convention on Biological Diversity of 5 June 1992 and *emphasizing* in that connection that the recognition of the genetic diversity of humanity, must not give rise to any interpretation of a social or political nature which could call into question 'the inherent dignity and (. . .) the equal and inalienable rights of all members of the human family', in accordance with the Preamble to the Universal Declaration of Human Rights,

*Recalling* 22 C/Resolution 13.1, 23 C/Resolution 13.1, 24 C/Resolution 13.1, 25 C/Resolutions 5.2 and 7.3, 27 C/Resolution 5.15 and 28 C/Resolutions 0.12, 2.1 and 2.2, urging UNESCO to promote and develop ethical studies, and the actions arising out of them, on the consequences of scientific and technological progress in the fields of biology and genetics, within the framework of respect for human rights and fundamental freedoms,

*Recognizing* that research on the human genome and the resulting applications open up vast prospects for progress in improving the health of individuals and of humankind as a whole, but *emphasizing* that such research should fully respect human dignity, freedom and human rights, as well as the prohibition of all forms of discrimination based on genetic characteristics,

*Proclaims* the principles that follow and *adopts* the present Declaration.

## A. HUMAN DIGNITY AND THE HUMAN GENOME

*Article* 1

The human genome underlies the fundamental unity of all members of the human family, as well as the recognition of their inherent dignity and diversity. In a symbolic sense, it is the heritage of humanity.

*Article* 2

(a) Everyone has a right to respect for their dignity and for their rights regardless of their genetic characteristics.

(b) That dignity makes it imperative not to reduce individuals to their genetic characteristics and to respect their uniqueness and diversity.

*Article* 3

The human genome, which by its nature evolves, is subject to mutations. It contains potentialities that are expressed differently according to each individual's natural and social environment including the individual's state of health, living conditions, nutrition and education.

*Article* 4

The human genome in its natural state shall not give rise to financial gains.


## B. RIGHTS OF THE PERSONS CONCERNED

*Article* 5

(a) Research, treatment or diagnosis affecting an individual's genome shall be undertaken only after rigorous and prior assessment of the potential risks and benefits pertaining thereto and in accordance with any other requirement of national law.

(b) In all cases, the prior, free and informed consent of the person concerned shall be obtained. If the latter is not in a position to consent, consent or authorization shall be obtained in the manner prescribed by law, guided by the person's best interest.

(c) The right of each individual to decide whether or not to be informed of the results of genetic examination and the resulting consequences should be respected.

(d) In the case of research, protocols shall, in addition, be submitted for prior review in accordance with relevant national and international research standards or guidelines.

(e) If according to the law a person does not have the capacity to consent, research affecting his or her genome may only be carried out for his or her direct health benefit, subject to the authorization and the protective conditions prescribed by law. Research which does not have an expected direct health benefit may only be undertaken by way of exception, with the utmost restraint, exposing the person only to a minimal risk and minimal burden and if the research is intended to contribute to the health benefit of other persons in the same age category or with the same genetic condition, subject to the conditions prescribed by law, and provided such research is compatible with the protection of the individual's human rights.

*Article* 6

No one shall be subjected to discrimination based on genetic characteristics that is intended to infringe or has the effect of infringing human rights, fundamental freedoms and human dignity.

*Article* 7

Genetic data associated with an identifiable person and stored or processed for the purposes of research or any other purpose must be held confidential in the conditions foreseen set by law.

*Article* 8

Every individual shall have the right, according to international and national law, to just reparation for any damage sustained as a direct and determining result of an intervention affecting his or her genome.

*Article* 9

In order to protect human rights and fundamental freedoms, limitations to the principles of consent and confidentiality may only be prescribed by law, for compelling reasons within the bounds of public international law and the international law of human rights.

## C. RESEARCH ON THE HUMAN GENOME

*Article* 10

No research or research its applications concerning the human genome, in particular in the fields of biology, genetics and medicine, should prevail over respect for the human rights, fundamental freedoms and human dignity of individuals or, where applicable, of groups of people.

*Article* 11

Practices which are contrary to human dignity, such as reproductive cloning of human beings, shall not be permitted. States and competent international organizations are invited to co-operate in identifying such practices and in taking, at national or international level, the measures necessary to ensure that the principles set out in this Declaration are respected.

*Article* 12

(a) Benefits from advances in biology, genetics and medicine, concerning the human genome, shall be made available to all, with due regard to the dignity and human rights of each individual.

(b) Freedom of research, which is necessary for the progress of knowledge, is part of freedom of thought. The applications of research, including applications in biology, genetics and medicine, concerning the human genome, shall seek to offer relief from suffering and improve the health of individuals and humankind as a whole.

# D. CONDITIONS FOR THE EXERCISE OF SCIENTIFIC ACTIVITY

*Article* 13

The responsibilities inherent in the activities of researchers, including meticulousness, caution, intellectual honesty and integrity in carrying out their research as well as in the presentation and utilization of their findings, should be the subject of particular attention in the framework of research on the human genome, because of its ethical and social implications. Public and private science policy-makers also have particular responsibilities in this respect.

*Article* 14

States should take appropriate measures to foster the intellectual and material conditions favourable to freedom in the conduct of research on the human genome and to consider the ethical, legal, social and economic implications of such research, on the basis of the principles set out in this Declaration.

*Article* 15

States should take appropriate steps to provide the framework for the free exercise of research on the human genome with due regard for the principles set out in this Declaration, in order to safeguard respect for human rights, fundamental freedoms and human dignity and to protect public health. They should seek to ensure that research results are not used for non-peaceful purposes.

*Article* 16

States should recognize the value of promoting, at various levels as appropriate, the establishment of independent, multidisciplinary and pluralist ethics committees to assess the ethical, legal and social issues raised by research on the human genome and its applications.

# E. SOLIDARITY AND INTERNATIONAL CO-OPERATION

*Article* 17

States should respect and promote the practice of solidarity towards individuals, families and population groups who are particularly vulnerable to or affected by disease or disability of a genetic character. They should foster, *inter alia*, research on the identification, prevention and treatment of genetically-based and genetically-influenced diseases, in particular rare as well as endemic diseases which affect large numbers of the world's population.

*Article* 18

States should make every effort, with due and appropriate regard for the principles set out in this Declaration, to continue fostering the international dissemination of scientific knowledge concerning the human genome, human diversity and genetic research and, in that regard, to foster scientific and cultural co-operation, particularly between industrialized and developing countries.

*Article* 19

(a) In the framework of international co-operation with developing countries, States should seek to encourage measures enabling:

(1) assessment of the risks and benefits pertaining to research on the human genome to be carried out and abuse to be prevented;

(2) the capacity of developing countries to carry out research on human biology and genetics, taking into consideration their specific problems, to be developed and strengthened;

(3) developing countries to benefit from the achievements of scientific and technological research so that their use in favour of economic and social progress can be to the benefit of all;

(4) the free exchange of scientific knowledge and information in the areas of biology, genetics and medicine to be promoted.

(b) Relevant international organizations should support and promote the initiatives taken by States for the above mentioned purposes.

## F. PROMOTION OF THE PRINCIPLES SET OUT IN THE DECLARATION

*Article* 20

States should take appropriate measures to promote the principles set out in the Declaration, through education and relevant means, *inter alia* through the conduct of research and training in interdisciplinary fields and through the promotion of education in bioethics, at all levels, in particular for those responsible for science policies.

*Article* 21

States should take appropriate measures to encourage other forms of research, training and information dissemination conducive to raising the awareness of society and all of its members of their responsibilities regarding the fundamental issues relating to the defence of human dignity which may be raised by research in biology, in genetics and in medicine, and its applications. They should also undertake to facilitate on this subject an open international discussion, ensuring the free expression of various socio-cultural, religious and philosophical opinions.

## G. IMPLEMENTATION OF THE DECLARATION

*Article* 22

States should make every effort to promote the principles set out in this

Declaration and should, by means of all appropriate measures, promote their implementation.

*Article* 23

States should take appropriate measures to promote, through education, training and information dissemination, respect for the above mentioned principles and to foster their recognition and effective application. States should also encourage exchanges and networks among independent ethics committees, as they are established, to foster full collaboration.

*Article* 24

The International Bioethics Committee of UNESCO should contribute to the dissemination of the principles set out in this Declaration and to the further examination of issues raised by their applications and by the evolution of the technologies in question. It should organize appropriate consultations with parties concerned, such as vulnerable groups. It should make recommendations, in accordance with UNESCO's statutory procedures, addressed to the General Conference and give advice concerning the follow-up of this Declaration, in particular regarding the identification of practices that could be contrary to human dignity, such as germ-line interventions.

*Article* 25

Nothing in this Declaration may be interpreted as implying for any State, group or person any claim to engage in any activity or to perform any act contrary to human rights and fundamental freedoms, including the principles set out in this Declaration.

## 94. EUROPEAN CONVENTION FOR THE PROTECTION OF HUMAN RIGHTS AND DIGNITY OF THE HUMAN BEING WITH REGARD TO THE APPLICATION OF BIOLOGY AND MEDICINE: CONVENTION ON HUMAN RIGHTS AND BIOMEDICINE, 1997

This convention was opened for signature on 4 April 1997 and entered into force on 1 December 1999; for the text see ETS No. 164. Besides the Member States of the Council of Europe, it is also open for signature by non-Member States which participated in its drafting. The convention aims to prevent the misuse of biological and medical advances. It places the interest of the human being first, prohibits the creation of human embryos for research purposes, imposes limitations on the removal of organs, and makes detailed provision generally on the principle of consent. The text is remarkable for its attempt to establish a clear ethical basis for biological and medical developments, and to place it in a legal framework.

*TEXT*

The member States of the Council of Europe, the other States and the European Community, signatories hereto,

*Bearing in mind* the Universal Declaration of Human Rights proclaimed by the General Assembly of the United Nations on 10 December 1948;

*Bearing in mind* the Convention for the Protection of Human Rights and Fundamental Freedoms of 4 November 1950;

*Bearing in mind* the European Social Charter of 18 October 1961;

*Bearing in mind* the International Covenant on Civil and Political Rights and the International Covenant on Economic, Social and Cultural Rights of 16 December 1966;

*Bearing in mind* the Convention for the Protection of Individuals with regard to Automatic Processing of Personal Data of 28 January 1981;

*Bearing also in mind* the Convention on the Rights of the Child of 20 November 1989;

*Considering* that the aim of the Council of Europe is the achievement of a greater unity between its members and that one of the methods by which that aim is to be pursued is the maintenance and further realization of human rights and fundamental freedoms;

*Conscious* of the accelerating developments in biology and medicine;

*Convinced* of the need to respect the human being both as an individual and as a member of the human species and recognizing the importance of ensuring the dignity of the human being;

*Conscious* that the misuse of biology and medicine may lead to acts endangering human dignity;

*Affirming* that progress in biology and medicine should be used for the benefit of present and future generations;

*Stressing* the need for international co-operation so that all humanity may enjoy the benefits of biology and medicine;

*Recognizing* the importance of promoting a public debate on the questions posed by the application of biology and medicine and the responses to be given thereto;

*Wishing* to remind all members of society of their rights and responsibilities;

*Taking account* of the work of the Parliamentary Assembly in this field, including Recommendation 1160 (1991) on the preparation of a convention on bioethics;

*Resolving* to take such measures as are necessary to safeguard human dignity and the fundamental rights and freedoms of the individual with regard to the application of biology and medicine,

*Have agreed* as follows:

# PART I

## GENERAL PROVISIONS

*Article 1—Purpose and object*

Parties to this Convention shall protect the dignity and identity of all human beings and guarantee everyone, without discrimination, respect for their integrity and other rights and fundamental freedoms with regard to the application of biology and medicine.

Each Party shall take in its internal law the necessary measures to give effect to the provisions of this Convention.

*Article 2—Primacy of the human being*

The interests and welfare of the human being shall prevail over the sole interest of society or science.

*Article 3—Equitable access to health care*

Parties, taking into account health needs and available resources, shall take appropriate measures with a view to providing, within their jurisdiction, equitable access to health care of appropriate quality.

*Article 4—Professional standards*

Any intervention in the health field, including research, must be carried out in accordance with relevant professional obligations and standards.

## CHAPTER II

## CONSENT

*Article 5—General rule*

An intervention in the health field may only be carried out after the person concerned has given free and informed consent to it.

This person shall beforehand be given appropriate information as to the purpose and nature of the intervention as well as on its consequences and risks.

The person concerned may freely withdraw consent at any time.

## Article 6—*Protection of persons not able to consent*

1. Subject to Articles 17 and 20 below, an intervention may only be carried out on a person who does not have the capacity to consent, for his or her direct benefit.

2. Where, according to law, a minor does not have the capacity to consent to an intervention, the intervention may only be carried out with the authorisation of his or her representative or an authority or a person or body provided for by law.

The opinion of the minor shall be taken into consideration as an increasingly determining factor in proportion to his or her age and degree of maturity.

3. Where, according to law, an adult does not have the capacity to consent to an intervention because of a mental disability, a disease or for similar reasons, the intervention may only be carried out with the authorization of his or her representative or an authority or a person or body provided for by law.

The individual concerned shall as far as possible take part in the authorization procedure.

4. The representative, the authority, the person or the body mentioned in paragraphs 2 and 3 above shall be given, under the same conditions, the information referred to in Article 5.

5. The authorization referred to in paragraphs 2 and 3 above may be withdrawn at any time in the best interests of the person concerned.

## Article 7—*Protection of persons who have a mental disorder*

Subject to protective conditions prescribed by law, including supervisory, control and appeal procedures, a person who has a mental disorder of a serious nature may be subjected, without his or her consent, to an intervention aimed at treating his or her mental disorder only where, without such treatment, serious harm is likely to result to his or her health.

## Article 8—*Emergency situation*

When because of an emergency situation the appropriate consent cannot be obtained, any medically necessary intervention may be carried out immediately for the benefit of the health of the individual concerned.

## Article 9—*Previously expressed wishes*

The previously expressed wishes relating to a medical intervention by a patient who is not, at the time of the intervention, in a state to express his or her wishes shall be taken into account.

# CHAPTER III

## PRIVATE LIFE AND RIGHT TO INFORMATION

*Article* 10—*Private life and right to information*

1. Everyone has the right to respect for private life in relation to information about his or her health.

2. Everyone is entitled to know any information collected about his or her health. However, the wishes of individuals not to be so informed shall be observed.

3. In exceptional cases, restrictions may be placed by law on the exercise of the rights contained in paragraph 2 in the interests of the patient.

# CHAPTER IV

## HUMAN GENOME

*Article* 11—*Non-discrimination*

Any form of discrimination against a person on grounds of his or her genetic heritage is prohibited.

*Article* 12—*Predictive genetic tests*

Tests which are predictive of genetic diseases or which serve either to identify the subject as a carrier of a gene responsible for a disease or to detect a genetic predisposition or susceptibility to a disease may be performed only for health purposes or for scientific research linked to health purposes, and subject to appropriate genetic counselling.

*Article* 13—*Interventions on the human genome*

An intervention seeking to modify the human genome may only be undertaken for preventive, diagnostic or therapeutic purposes and only if its aim is not to introduce any modification in the genome of any descendants.

*Article* 14—*Non-selection of sex*

The use of techniques of medically assisted procreation shall not be allowed for the purpose of choosing a future child's sex, except where serious hereditary sex-related disease is to be avoided.

# CHAPTER V

## SCIENTIFIC RESEARCH

*Article* 15—*General rule*

Scientific research in the field of biology and medicine shall be carried out freely, subject to the provisions of this Convention and the other legal provisions ensuring the protection of the human being.

*Article 16—Protection of persons undergoing research*

Research on a person may only be undertaken if all the following conditions are met:

(i) there is no alternative of comparable effectiveness to research on humans;

(ii) the risks which may be incurred by that person are not disproportionate to the potential benefits of the research;

(iii) the research project has been approved by the competent body after independent examination of its scientific merit, including assessment of the importance of the aim of the research, and multidisciplinary review of its ethical acceptability;

(iv) the persons undergoing research have been informed of their rights and the safeguards prescribed by law for their protection;

(v) the necessary consent as provided for under Article 5 has been given expressly, specifically and is documented. Such consent may be freely withdrawn at any time.

*Article 17—Protection of persons not able to consent to research*

1. Research on a person without the capacity to consent as stipulated in Article 5 may be undertaken only if all the following conditions are met:

(i) the conditions laid down in Article 16, sub-paragraphs (i) to (iv), are fulfilled;

(ii) the results of the research have the potential to produce real and direct benefit to his or her health;

(iii) research of comparable effectiveness cannot be carried out on individuals capable of giving consent;

(iv) the necessary authorization provided for under Article 6 has been given specifically and in writing; and

(v) the person concerned does not object.

2. Exceptionally and under the protective conditions prescribed by law, where the research has not the potential to produce results of direct benefit to the health of the person concerned, such research may be authorised subject to the conditions laid down in paragraph 1, sub-paragraphs (i), (iii), (iv) and (v) above, and to the following additional conditions:

(i) the research has the aim of contributing, through significant improvement in the scientific understanding of the individual's condition, disease or disorder, to the ultimate attainment of results capable of conferring benefit to the person concerned or to other persons in the same age category or afflicted with the same disease or disorder or having the same condition;

(ii) the research entails only minimal risk and minimal burden for the individual concerned.

*Article* 18—*Research on embryos in vitro*

1. Where the law allows research on embryos in vitro, it shall ensure adequate protection of the embryo.

2. The creation of human embryos for research purposes is prohibited.


# CHAPTER VI

## ORGAN AND TISSUE REMOVAL FROM LIVING DONORS FOR TRANSPLANTATION PURPOSES

*Article* 19—*General rule*

1. Removal of organs or tissue from a living person for transplantation purposes may be carried out solely for the therapeutic benefit of the recipient and where there is no suitable organ or tissue available from a deceased person and no other alternative therapeutic method of comparable effectiveness.

2. The necessary consent as provided for under Article 5 must have been given expressly and specifically either in written form or before an official body.

*Article* 20—*Protection of persons not able to consent to organ removal*

1. No organ or tissue removal may be carried out on a person who does not have the capacity to consent under Article 5.

2. Exceptionally and under the protective conditions prescribed by law, the removal of regenerative tissue from a person who does not have the capacity to consent may be authorized provided the following conditions are met:

    (i)   there is no compatible donor available who has the capacity to consent;

    (ii)  the recipient is a brother or sister of the donor;

    (iii) the donation must have the potential to be life-saving for the recipient;

    (iv) the authorization provided for under paragraphs 2 and 3 of Article 6 has been given specifically and in writing, in accordance with the law and with the approval of the competent body;

    (v)  the potential donor concerned does not object.


# CHAPTER VII

## PROHIBITION OF FINANCIAL GAIN AND DISPOSAL OF A PART OF THE HUMAN BODY

*Article* 21—*Prohibition of financial gain*

The human body and its parts shall not, as such, give rise to financial gain.

*Article* 22—*Disposal of a removed part of the human body*

When in the course of an intervention any part of a human body is removed, it may be stored and used for a purpose other than that for which it was removed, only if this is done in conformity with appropriate information and consent procedures.

## CHAPTER VIII

## INFRINGEMENTS OF THE
## PROVISIONS OF THE CONVENTION

*Article 23—Infringement of the rights or principles*

The Parties shall provide appropriate judicial protection to prevent or to put a stop to an unlawful infringement of the rights and principles set forth in this Convention at short notice.

*Article 24—Compensation for undue damage*

The person who has suffered undue damage resulting from an intervention is entitled to fair compensation according to the conditions and procedures prescribed by law.

*Article 25—Sanctions*

Parties shall provide for appropriate sanctions to be applied in the event of infringement of the provisions contained in this Convention.

## CHAPTER IX

## RELATION BETWEEN THIS
## CONVENTION AND OTHER PROVISIONS

*Article 26—Restrictions on the exercise of the rights*

1. No restrictions shall be placed on the exercise of the rights and protective provisions contained in this Convention other than such as are prescribed by law and are necessary in a democratic society in the interest of public safety, for the prevention of crime, for the protection of public health or for the protection of the rights and freedoms of others.

2. The restrictions contemplated in the preceding paragraph may not be placed on Articles 11, 13, 14, 16, 17, 19, 20 and 21.

*Article 27—Wider protection*

None of the provisions of this Convention shall be interpreted as limiting or otherwise affecting the possibility for a Party to grant a wider measure of protection with regard to the application of biology and medicine than is stipulated in this Convention.

## CHAPTER X

## PUBLIC DEBATE

*Article 28—Public debate*

Parties to this Convention shall see to it that the fundamental questions raised by the developments of biology and medicine are the subject of appropriate public discussion in the light, in particular, of relevant medical, social, economic, ethical and legal implications, and that their possible application is made the subject of appropriate consultation.

## CHAPTER XI

## INTERPRETATION AND FOLLOW-UP OF THE CONVENTION

*Article 29—Interpretation of the Convention*

The European Court of Human Rights may give, without direct reference to any specific proceedings pending in a court, advisory opinions on legal questions concerning the interpretation of the present Convention at the request of:

— the Government of a Party, after having informed the other Parties;

— the Committee set up by Article 32, with membership restricted to the Representatives of the Parties to this Convention, by a decision adopted by a two-thirds majority of votes cast.

*Article 30—Reports on the application of the Convention*

On receipt of a request from the Secretary General of the Council of Europe any Party shall furnish an explanation of the manner in which its internal law ensures the effective implementation of any of the provisions of the Convention.

## CHAPTER XII

## PROTOCOLS

*Article 31—Protocols*

Protocols may be concluded in pursuance of Article 32, with a view to developing, in specific fields, the principles contained in this Convention.

The Protocols shall be open for signature by Signatories of the Convention. They shall be subject to ratification, acceptance or approval. A Signatory may not ratify, accept or approve Protocols without previously or simultaneously ratifying accepting or approving the Convention.

## CHAPTER XIII

## AMENDMENTS TO THE CONVENTION

*Article 32—Amendments to the Convention*

1. The tasks assigned to 'the Committee' in the present article and in Article 29 shall be carried out by the Steering Committee on Bioethics (CDBI), or by any other committee designated to do so by the Committee of Ministers.

2. Without prejudice to the specific provisions of Article 29, each member State of the Council of Europe, as well as each Party to the present Convention which is not a member of the Council of Europe, may be represented and have one vote in the Committee when the Committee carries out the tasks assigned to it by the present Convention.

3. Any State referred to in Article 33 or invited to accede to the Convention in accordance with the provisions of Article 34 which is not Party to this Convention may be represented on the Committee by an observer. If the European Community is not a Party it may be represented on the Committee by an observer.

4. In order to monitor scientific developments, the present Convention shall be examined within the Committee no later than five years from its entry into force and thereafter at such intervals as the Committee may determine.

5. Any proposal for an amendment to this Convention, and any proposal for a Protocol or for an amendment to a Protocol, presented by a Party, the Committee or the Committee of Ministers shall be communicated to the Secretary General of the Council of Europe and forwarded by him to the member States of the Council of Europe, to the European Community, to any Signatory, to any Party, to any State invited to sign this Convention in accordance with the provisions of Article 33 and to any State invited to accede to it in accordance with the provisions of Article 34.

6. The Committee shall examine the proposal not earlier than two months after it has been forwarded by the Secretary General in accordance with paragraph 5. The Committee shall submit the text adopted by a two-thirds majority of the votes cast to the Committee of Ministers for approval. After its approval, this text shall be forwarded to the Parties for ratification, acceptance or approval.

7. Any amendment shall enter into force, in respect of those Parties which have accepted it, on the first day of the month following the expiration of a period of one month after the date on which five Parties, including at least four member States of the Council of Europe, have informed the Secretary General that they have accepted it.

In respect of any Party which subsequently accepts it, the amendment shall enter into force on the first day of the month following the expiration of a period of one month after the date on which that Party has informed the Secretary General of its acceptance.


## CHAPTER XIV

## FINAL CLAUSES

*Article 33—Signature, ratification and entry into force*

1. This Convention shall be open for signature by the member States of the Council of Europe, the non-member States which have participated in its elaboration and by the European Community.

2. This Convention is subject to ratification, acceptance or approval. Instruments

of ratification, acceptance or approval shall be deposited with the Secretary General of the Council of Europe.

3. This Convention shall enter into force on the first day of the month following the expiration of a period of three months after the date on which five States, including at least four member States of the Council of Europe, have expressed their consent to be bound by the Convention in accordance with the provisions of paragraph 2 of the present article.

4. In respect of any Signatory which subsequently expresses its consent to be bound by it, the Convention shall enter into force on the first day of the month following the expiration of a period of three months after the date of the deposit of its instrument of ratification, acceptance or approval.

*Article 34—Non-member States*

1. After the entry into force of this Convention, the Committee of Ministers of the Council of Europe may, after consultation of the Parties, invite any non-member State of the Council of Europe to accede to this Convention by a decision taken by the majority provided for in Article 20, paragraph d, of the Statute of the Council of Europe, and by the unanimous vote of the representatives of the Contracting States entitled to sit on the Committee of Ministers.

2. In respect of any acceding State, the Convention shall enter into force on the first day of the month following the expiration of a period of three months after the date of deposit of the instrument of accession with the Secretary General of the Council of Europe.

*Article 35—Territories*

1. Any Signatory may, at the time of signature or when depositing its instrument of ratification, acceptance or approval, specify the territory or territories to which this Convention shall apply. Any other State may formulate the same declaration when depositing its instrument of accession.

2. Any Party may, at any later date, by a declaration addressed to the Secretary General of the Council of Europe, extend the application of this Convention to any other territory specified in the declaration and for whose international relations it is responsible or on whose behalf it is authorised to give undertakings. In respect of such territory the Convention shall enter into force on the first day of the month following the expiration of a period of three months after the date of receipt of such declaration by the Secretary General.

3. Any declaration made under the two preceding paragraphs may, in respect of any territory specified in such declaration, be withdrawn by a notification addressed to the Secretary General. The withdrawal shall become effective on the first day of the month following the expiration of a period of three months after the date of receipt of such notification by the Secretary General.

*Article 36—Reservations*

1. Any State and the European Community may, when signing this Convention or when depositing the instrument of ratification, acceptance, approval or accession, make a reservation in respect of any particular provision of the Convention to the extent that any law then in force in its territory is not in conformity with the

provision. Reservations of a general character shall not be permitted under this article.

2. Any reservation made under this article shall contain a brief statement of the relevant law.

3. Any Party which extends the application of this Convention to a territory mentioned in the declaration referred to in Article 35, paragraph 2, may, in respect of the territory concerned, make a reservation in accordance with the provisions of the preceding paragraphs.

4. Any Party which has made the reservation mentioned in this article may withdraw it by means of a declaration addressed to the Secretary General of the Council of Europe. The withdrawal shall become effective on the first day of the month following the expiration of a period of one month after the date of its receipt by the Secretary General.

*Article 37—Denunciation*

1. Any Party may at any time denounce this Convention by means of a notification addressed to the Secretary General of the Council of Europe.

2. Such denunciation shall become effective on the first day of the month following the expiration of a period of three months after the date of receipt of the notification by the Secretary General.

*Article 38—Notifications*

The Secretary General of the Council of Europe shall notify the member States of the Council, the European Community, any Signatory, any Party and any other State which has been invited to accede to this Convention of:

  (a)  any signature;
  (b)  the deposit of any instrument of ratification, acceptance, approval or accession;
  (c)  any date of entry into force of this Convention in accordance with Articles 33 or 34;
  (d)  any amendment or Protocol adopted in accordance with Article 32, and the date on which such an amendment or Protocol enters into force;
  (e)  any declaration made under the provisions of Article 35;
  (f)  any reservation and withdrawal of reservation made in pursuance of the provisions of Article 36;
  (g)  any other act, notification or communication relating to this Convention.

In witness whereof the undersigned, being duly authorised thereto, have signed this Convention.

*Done* at Oviedo (Asturias), this 4th day of April 1997, in English and French, both texts being equally authentic, in a single copy which shall be deposited in the archives of the Council of Europe. The Secretary General of the Council of Europe shall transmit certified copies to each member State of the Council of Europe, to the European Community, to the non-member States which have participated in the elaboration of this Convention, and to any State invited to accede to this Convention.

## 95. ADDITIONAL PROTOCOL TO THE EUROPEAN CONVENTION FOR THE PROTECTION OF HUMAN RIGHTS AND DIGNITY OF THE HUMAN BEING WITH REGARD TO THE APPLICATION OF BIOLOGY AND MEDICINE, ON THE PROHIBITION OF CLONING HUMAN BEINGS, 1998

This protocol was opened for signature by Council of Europe Member States, non-member States which participated in its elaboration, and the European Community on 12 January 1998; it will enter into force after receiving five ratifications. It is specifically addressed to and bans human cloning, without exception. For the text see ETS No. 168

*TEXT*

The member States of the Council of Europe, the other States and the European Community Signatories to this Additional Protocol to the Convention for the Protection of Human Rights and Dignity of the Human Being with regard to the Application of Biology and Medicine,

*Noting* scientific developments in the field of mammal cloning, particularly through embryo splitting and nuclear transfer;

*Mindful* of the progress that some cloning techniques themselves may bring to scientific knowledge and its medical application;

*Considering* that the cloning of human beings may become a technical possibility;

*Having noted* that embryo splitting may occur naturally and sometimes result in the birth of genetically identical twins;

*Considering* however that the instrumentalisation of human beings through the deliberate creation of genetically identical human beings is contrary to human dignity and thus constitutes a misuse of biology and medicine;

*Considering* also the serious difficulties of a medical, psychological and social nature that such a deliberate biomedical practice might imply for all the individuals involved;

*Considering* the purpose of the Convention on Human Rights and Biomedicine, in particular the principle mentioned in Article 1 aiming to protect the dignity and identity of all human beings,

*Have agreed* as follows:

*Article 1*

1. Any intervention seeking to create a human being genetically identical to another human being, whether living or dead, is prohibited.

2. For the purpose of this article, the term human being 'genetically identical' to another human being means a human being sharing with another the same nuclear gene set.

*Article 2*

No derogation from the provisions of this Protocol shall be made under Article 26, paragraph 1, of the Convention.

*Article 3*

As between the Parties, the provisions of Articles 1 and 2 of this Protocol shall be regarded as additional articles to the Convention and all the provisions of the Convention shall apply accordingly.

*Article 4*

This Protocol shall be open for signature by Signatories to the Convention. It is subject to ratification, acceptance or approval. A Signatory may not ratify, accept or approve this Protocol unless it has previously or simultaneously ratified, accepted or approved the Convention. Instruments of ratification, acceptance or approval shall be deposited with the Secretary General of the Council of Europe.

*Article 5*

1. This Protocol shall enter into force on the first day of the month following the expiration of a period of three months after the date on which five States, including at least four member States of the Council of Europe, have expressed their consent to be bound by the Protocol in accordance with the provisions of Article 4.

2. In respect of any Signatory which subsequently expresses its consent to be bound by it, the Protocol shall enter into force on the first day of the month following the expiration of a period of three months after the date of the deposit of the instrument of ratification, acceptance or approval.

*Article 6*

1. After the entry into force of this Protocol, any State which has acceded to the Convention may also accede to this Protocol.

2. Accession shall be effected by the deposit with the Secretary General of the Council of Europe of an instrument of accession which shall take effect on the first day of the month following the expiration of a period of three months after the date of its deposit.

*Article 7*

1. Any Party may at any time denounce this Protocol by means of a notification addressed to the Secretary General of the Council of Europe.

2. Such denunciation shall become effective on the first day of the month following the expiration of a period of three months after the date of receipt of such notification by the Secretary General.

*Article 8*

The Secretary General of the Council of Europe shall notify the member States of the Council of Europe, the European Community, any Signatory, any Party and any other State which has been invited to accede to the Convention of:

  *(a)* any signature;

*(b)* the deposit of any instrument of ratification, acceptance, approval or accession;

*(c)* any date of entry into force of this Protocol in accordance with Articles 5 and 6;

*(d)* any other act, notification or communication relating to this Protocol.

In witness whereof the undersigned, being duly authorised thereto, have signed this Protocol.

*Done* at Paris, this twelfth day of January 1998, in English and in French, both texts being equally authentic, in a single copy which shall be deposited in the archives of the Council of Europe. The Secretary General of the Council of Europe shall transmit certified copies to each member State of the Council of Europe, to the non-member States which have participated in the elaboration of this Protocol, to any State invited to accede to the Convention and to the European Community.

# PART ELEVEN

# TRADE AND DEVELOPMENT

---

## INTRODUCTION

This Part is intended to present the issues relating to the economic foundations of human rights. Economic inequalities between States are severe and are a chronic feature of international relations. The formal rules and standards concerning the Rule of Law and human rights have little meaning or possibility of effective application in societies in which a substantial proportion of the population faces unemployment, malnutrition, starvation, and illiteracy. The present structure of international 'trade and development' is not producing a stable and adequate growth in the underdeveloped countries. This, together with the fact of a considerably faster growth of population in underdeveloped countries, has resulted in a progressive widening of the large gap between the average incomes of the inhabitants of the rich industrial and the poor underdeveloped countries. See, further, UN General Assembly resolutions 2158 (XXI), on Permanent Sovereignty over Natural Resources, adopted on 25 November 1966; 2542 (XXIV), Declaration on Social Progress and Development, adopted on 11 December 1969, especially Articles 7, 17, 23, 24, and 25; 3201 (S-VI), adopted on 1 May 1974, containing a Declaration on the Establishment of a New International Economic Order; and 3281 (XXIX), adopted on 12 December 1974, Charter of Economic Rights and Duties of States. For further references see Brownlie, I., *Principles of Public International Law*, (5th edn., 1998), 542–6.

## 96. SOME ECONOMIC FOUNDATIONS OF HUMAN RIGHTS: A STUDY PREPARED BY JOSE FIGUERES, 1968

This paper was published as an official document; see UN doc. A/CONF.32/L.2, 8 February 1968, of the International Conference on Human Rights, held at Tehran in 1968 under the auspices of the United Nations. The author is a specialist in economics and a former President of Costa Rica. Notwithstanding the passage of time, the elements governing trade between the developed and developing world remain relatively unchanged, save with the accentuations due to the process of globalization.

*TEXT*

## INTRODUCTION

1. The Secretary-General of the United Nations, in his statement to the Economic and Social Council at its forty-third session in 1967, declared that *faith in the dignity of man*, and in the equal rights of men and women, is the basic reason for the Organization to promote social progress and better standards of living for all (A/6703, introduction).

2. His statement affirms that *economic and social development is* an indispensable means to the full realization of human rights in the modern world.

3. This theme has been steadily and progressively elaborated by the United Nations and its organs during the twenty-two years of the Organization's growth.

4. There have been numerous pronouncements. The Universal Declaration of Human Rights, Article 22, states that everyone is entitled to the realization of the economic, social and cultural rights indispensable for the full development of his personality. This requires national and international efforts in accordance with the resources of each State.

5. Article 23 of the Declaration recognizes the right of everyone to work, to free choice of employment, to just and favourable conditions of work, to protection against unemployment and to equal pay for equal work.

6. Also affirmed is the right of everyone who works to a remuneration ensuring for his family an existence consistent with human dignity. His income being supplemented, if necessary, by other means of social protection.

7. Another right proclaimed by the Declaration, Article 25, is that of everyone to an adequate standard of health and well-being for himself and his family.

8. Of particular interest for the purposes of this study is Article 28 of the Declaration, which states that everyone is entitled to a *social and international order* in which the rights and freedoms of the Declaration can be fully realized.

9. The Declaration on Permanent Sovereignty over Natural Resources contained in General Assembly resolution 1803 (XVII) of 14 December 1962 (Article 1), provides that the rights of peoples and nations to permanent sovereignty over their natural resources must be exercised in their own interest.

10. It further states (Article 2) that the exploration, development and disposition of such resources, as well as the foreign capital required for these purposes, should conform to the rules that the nations consider to be necessary for the authorization, restriction or prohibition of such activities.

11. It stipulates (Article 6) that international co-operation for development, whether public or private investments, exchange of goods or services, technical assistance or exchange of scientific information shall be so conducted as to further the independent national life and the sovereignty of the developing nations.

12. The International Covenant on Economic, Social and Cultural Rights (a binding legal instrument adopted in 1966 by the General Assembly) not only contains the basic economic and social rights first enunciated in the Universal Declaration, but also in some cases strengthens and supplements them.

13. One right, however, which was omitted in the Declaration but is now included in the Covenant (Article 1) states that all peoples are entitled to self-determination and may therefore freely determine their political status and the pursuit of their economic, social and cultural development. In no case may a people be deprived of its means of subsistence.

14. Article 2 (1) imposes another important obligation. Each State Party shall take steps, individually and internationally, to the maximum of its available resources, to achieve progressively the full realization of the rights recognized in the Covenant. This shall be done by all appropriate means, including particularly the adoption of legislative measures.

15. Article 11 (1) of the International Covenant on Economic, Social and Cultural Rights, after recognizing the right of everyone to an adequate standard of living for himself and his family, goes beyond the Universal Declaration and adds that everyone has the right to the continuous improvement of living conditions.

16. Of interest to the present study is also Article 11 (2) of the Covenant. It provides that the States Parties, recognizing the fundamental right of everyone to be free from hunger, commit themselves to undertake the measures and programmes that may be needed to improve methods of production, conservation and distribution of *food*.

17. Among other things, agrarian systems shall be developed or reformed so as to achieve the highest utilization of natural and human resources.

18. Also, an efficient distribution of the world food supplies should be ensured, taking into account the problems of both food importing and food exporting nations.

19. Worth noting for this study is also Article 23, which stipulates that international action for the purposes of the Covenant includes such methods as conventions, agreements, recommendations, international assistance, regional meetings and technical consultations organized in conjunction with the Governments concerned.

20. The preceding paragraphs illustrate the unceasing efforts of the United Nations to ensure for everyone the fullest measure of human dignity. These efforts include setting goals and standards in the economic and social spheres, and prescribing means and methods for their attainment.

21. This paper is written by one who fully shares the objectives of the United

Nations, and is guided by them in his study. It is intended to serve a dual purpose, broadly speaking: (a) it seeks to identify the obstacles to the full enjoyment of human rights encountered in the economic and social struggles by the peoples of the less developed world; (b) it attempts to suggest some measures that should be taken if economic and social factors are to stop denying to those peoples their full range of human rights.

22. The nature of the subject may help explain why the body of this study contains some of the features of an essay in economics. Indeed, it may be described as a study in 'The Economic Foundations of Human Rights'.

## I. ENUNCIATIONS

23. We live at a time when human rights have been beautifully enunciated in numerous documents, subscribed to by many nations. These enunciations, in themselves, are no small accomplishment.

24. Ethical codes have always preceded ethical conduct. A certain time is needed for education and adaptation. Even afterwards, perfection is never attained.

25. The Universal Declaration of Human Rights and the Covenants are now in the period of education and adaptation. Actual life in many nations is still far behind the principles. Men tend to be impatient about the apparent slow progress, because they forget that the lives of nations, of institutions, of mankind, are longer than the lives of individuals.

26. The Latin American Republics organized themselves under democratic principles when they won their independence during the first quarter of the nineteenth century.

27. For a hundred and fifty years these societies have been in the process of education and adaptation.

28. Later the principles were vigorously reiterated in the Charter of the Organization of American States, and in the documents of several subsequent conferences. Whatever the remaining shortcomings, these countries are now relatively advanced towards democratic life. It would be inconceivable to adopt today a non-democratic credo, except by force.

29. If it had not been for the enunciation of principles that were difficult to fulfil, the progress that has been made by these nations would not exist, and probably the vices of dictatorship would be officially sanctioned today.

30. I do not mean that it will take a hundred and fifty years for the Declaration of Human Rights to be implemented throughout the world. All processes move faster in our time. I do mean, however, that we should not be discouraged by differences between principle and fact.

## II. SOVEREIGNTY

31. The new nations that have emerged since the Second World War, are still in a state of mind inclined to eradicate the remnants of colonialism and to consolidate

political independence or sovereignty. There is a tendency to believe that national sovereignty automatically brings personal liberties. This is not so, as Latin America has well learned through its history.

32. It takes some time to understand that independence, however costly, should really be a means to an end. The end should be the full comprehension and enjoyment of human rights by all the people.

33. Another temporary disillusion that the emerging countries find is that independence, by itself, does not bring about economic development and social well-being.

34. Some socialists of the nineteenth century thought that general welfare was only a matter of equitable distribution of existing wealth and income, not realizing how small wealth and income were. Some of the revolutionary heroes of independence in our time, and their followers, seem to have underestimated the difficulties of development. Abundance for all the people does not come automatically with sovereignty.

35. Human rights, in their economic and social aspects, can only be achieved by a combination of high production and fair distribution. In theory at least, you could even have a society juridically so constituted that everybody enjoys civil rights and everybody is poor.

36. In actual practice, however, aspirations are so high in all modern countries that you cannot maintain political stability in the unrest provoked by the lack of fulfilment of human wants.


## III. ECONOMIC RIGHTS

37. The two Covenants of the United Nations correctly equate economic and social rights with civil and political rights.

38. The dignity of man is not respected, by himself or by others, when he is not allowed to earn a decent living. By the same token, in the international field a nation is not sufficiently respected, whatever her political independence, while her work and her trade with other nations do not allow her fully to support all her citizens.

39. The provision of an adequate standard of living for all members of society requires a high degree of economic development.

40. Before the Industrial Revolution such abundance of goods and services would have been unthinkable. It was tacitly agreed, except by some reformers, that the work of the community could only produce the welfare of a privileged minority. Today, for the first time in human history, some countries are producing enough for practically all their citizens.

41. The poorer nations, which still constitute the majority of mankind, want to do likewise. They want to develop.

42. It is of common interest to all peoples, and to the harmony of the human family, that these retarded nations should develop. The economic and social rights cannot be universally fulfilled until the necessary amount of goods and services are produced by all nations.

## IV. INTERNAL OBSTACLES

43. In their development efforts, poor countries encounter two sets of difficulties: internal and international. The internal obstacles to development are, among others, the following:

44. Lack of capital, which is a consequence of insufficient savings and, in turn, of low income; deficient technology; improper land tenure and tax systems; rapid population growth; poor general education; bad health, largely caused by malnutrition.

45. It would be hard to tell which of these internal deficiencies is more serious. They all cause one another in a series of vicious circles. Some people mention political instability first. I wonder if political instability is not also the effect of the other deficiencies.

## V. INTERNATIONAL OBSTACLES

46. The international causes of under-development are less generally recognized. Small nations cannot develop without an intense trade with the advanced countries, (a) because their people want to consume the products of foreign industry or agriculture; (b) because industrialization requires capital goods produced in the developed countries; and (c) because indispensable services such as communications and transportation are largely the property of the rich countries.

47. The poor countries have to pay for all three—consumer goods, capital goods, services—with their natural resources, such as minerals, and with their agricultural labour turned into a few commodities like coffee, tea, cocoa, bananas and sugar.

48. There is a close association between human rights and the objectives of the United Nations Conference on Trade and Development, established in New York and Geneva in 1964. The Conference was convened for the purpose of studying trade between the rich and poor countries, and to try to find means of correcting the trends that are widening the gap between the two groups.

49. Trade between rich and poor nations could be an instrument of uniform world development. If economic and social rights were universally effective, one hour of human work spent in one country would be traded for one hour spent in another. This rule, still a distant goal, would give most retarded countries sufficient foreign income for their development.

## VI. PRODUCTIVITY

50. There are activities in which the product of one hour of work depends largely on the amount of capital investment behind the worker. Also, on the amount of applied technology. A trained driver with a power shovel moves a hundred times more earth than a labourer with a hand shovel.

51. When a poor nation can export products in which investment and technology

increase production per man-hour of work, it should be the common interest of both traders, the buying and the selling countries, to make such capital and such knowledge available.

52. The field for improvement of productivity through larger investment is more restricted in agriculture than in industry. Little more could be done to improve the advanced methods already applied in some areas to the production of coffee, tea, cocoa, bananas. Yet, when the coffee farmer buys a truck from an industrial country, he exchanges hours of work at the rate of ten or twenty to one.

53. Internally, in an advanced society, there are activities where productivity per man-hour has increased greatly, like the steel industry. There are other activities where there has been no increased productivity, like the work of the barber, or, for that matter, the teacher or the musician. Logically, the compensation has increased more or less uniformly for the steel worker and for the barber, thus relating wages to the productivity of the whole economy, and not of a particular activity. The barber who serves the steel worker, indirectly produces steel also. This is in accord with the aspirations of the economic and social rights.

54. In an integrated mankind, the same principles should apply internationally. Fantastic as it may sound in our time, there is no moral reason why the Colombian labourer who supplies the Detroit worker who makes his truck, with his morning cup of coffee, should earn less (sometimes twenty times less) than his northern colleague. The fair rule would be 'equal pay for equal effort'.

## VII. SLAVE LABOUR

55. The advanced societies of today abhor even the remnants of slave labour. Minimum wage legislation prevents the economically strong employer from hiring cheap labour, when labour is weak. No low wages for foreign workers are allowed. The United States, with a legal minimum wage of $1.50 an hour, could import millions and millions of labourers for one third that legal wage. Such bargain is prevented not only by the power of the trade unions, but also by the moral sense of the nation, expressed in its legislation. It would be contrary to the economic and social rights of man.

56. Yet, the toil of countless workers at cheap wages is imported to the rich countries in the form of raw materials or primary products, particularly agricultural products. 'Free trade' is allowed between private importers who bargain from the strength of a rich economy, and private exporters who are part of the weakness of a poor economy.

57. Private exporters in poor countries are not responsible for the well-being of their people. Their interest is to have a margin between what they pay to local producers and workers, and the price they get from foreign importers. They continue to do a good business, at any level of prices and wages; unintentionally retarding economic development and social improvement.

58. This shows the need of more study for reasonable regulations of international trade, at least in the relation between rich and poor nations.

59. Such trade might to some extent be entrusted to public institutions with a social

responsibility. Or it could be regulated by such means as the International Wheat Agreement which, in times of surplus, has protected the farming communities against undeliberate exploitation in international trade.

60. The goal might be: when two or more countries trade intensely, supplying each other with needed goods and services, their joint economies should provide uniformly adequate standards of living for all their people.

## VIII. SURPLUSES

61. Surpluses of certain commodities are one of the paradoxes of our time, when two thirds of mankind suffer from scarcities of nearly everything.

62. In the rich countries, agricultural surpluses are the result of market stabilization programmes, without which the development of the rural areas would have been impossible. Large though this problem is sometimes thought to be, it is really small by comparison to the problem of export surpluses in poor countries.

63. For the less developed nations, the prices of a few exports, easily depressed by overproduction, are a question of development or stagnation. And stagnation produces social and political unrest, with all the chain reaction of ill effects.

64. The anomaly is that even at the present (1967) depressed prices, the tendency continues to over-production in coffee and other tropical products. As the economic situation in the producing countries deteriorates, the prices of other crops diminish and the temptation increases to produce more coffee.

65. Furthermore, the tendency to consume imported articles is growing constantly, spurred by the variety of desirable gadgets from the industrial countries, by advertising and by instalment payment sales. All this has negative effects on developing societies.

66. Neither the balance of payments nor the economy as a whole can afford to have too many people rapidly improving their standard of living at the same time. Colour television in one family deprives several families of the bare essentials of life. This is one of the effects of trade between rich and poor nations.

## IX. DIVERSIFICATION

67. The other effect of overstimulated consumption for commercial aims in the poor countries is a tendency to further over-produce coffee, cocoa, tea, as the only possible means of payment for increasing imports. This depresses prices even more, and the vicious circle goes on.

68. It is easy to recommend crop diversification and industrialization. Yet substitute crops for coffee, for example, are extremely difficult to find. Latitude, altitude, the rain system, soil, the local culture of whole societies that have grown together with coffee culture, all these factors present great obstacles to change. There are some flat areas of Brazil where coffee can be changed for something else at a bearable cost. Over one billion trees have been uprooted there. But on the hills of Colombia,

the five Central American countries and others, nobody has found even a half-economical way of substituting crops.

69. Industrialization is going on everywhere at the slow pace permitted by the low prices of exports. It will be a long uphill effort.

## X. WAGES AND TAXATION

70. The 'natural' way to prevent disastrous over-production is, of course, to allow prices to drop. The people who starve will not produce any more coffee.

71. Until recently, this was the only prescription given by some influential groups in the developed countries. One early exception was the International Sugar Agreement, when low prices could hurt the foreign investments in Cuba, or the sugar-beet producers of California or Florida.

72. The first important step to protect the poor economies from free trade exploitation was the International Coffee Agreement of 1962. The difficulties it has encountered, both in the producing and consuming countries, are a measure of the complexity of the problem. In spite of all, the Agreement has saved the numerous coffee countries from an even more serious recession than they are suffering today.

73. In the process of world development, we may expect more trade agreements to come for important commodities. Cocoa is now being negotiated. It would help the cause of economic and social rights, if certain rules were adopted in these agreements:

I. A 'development price' should be established for each important commodity. Perhaps it is too early in human progress to speak of a 'just price'. A just price would be one that would provide equal compensation for equal effort, anywhere in the world. So far this is not realistic.

A development price is a more modest aspiration. It could be defined as a level of compensation that would provide for (a) a certain legal minimum wage for salaried workers in all areas producing the specific commodity, (b) a certain rate of taxation in the country of origin for development purposes, and (c) a reasonable rate of capitalization for the farmer.

I know from experience that a development price is not difficult to determine for each commodity.

II. The developed, importing nations, should not pay less than the development price for those amounts of the commodity that they normally consume. This could be accomplished by the import quota system, as in sugar in the United States and other countries, or by import duties returnable to the producing country, as it is done with Puerto Rican rum in the continental United States.

III. In addition to the effects of the quota system, over-production should be fought by (a) wages, and (b) taxation.

All commodity agreements should include clauses that make it compulsory for the producing countries to enact and to make effective a uniform minimum wage in all areas producing the same article. This would prevent undue competition from the less socially advanced countries, with its depressing effects on prices. It would also increase the cost of production for the individual farmers, with a consequent effect of diminishing surpluses.

The agreement should include a minimum rate of taxation on the commodity in all producing countries. This would be a source of development revenues. Also, by reducing the income left to the farmers, it would discourage over-production.

Allowing prices to drop as a means of avoiding surpluses, diminishes the national income of the developing countries, and makes world problems more complex. Increasing the farmers' costs by wages and taxes has the same effect on surpluses, at the same time maintaining a higher national income.

## XI. MORE DIFFICULTIES

74. Difficult as the commodity price inequities are to remedy, there are other forms of unintended international exploitation which may be even harder to stop.

75. Private foreign investments, even if they were available in the amounts necessary for a relatively rapid development, could create problems for both the investing and the receiving countries. If a large proportion of important decisions affecting the economy of a country are made abroad, they are bound to create frictions, even if only because of psychological reasons.

76. Foreign enterprises would be a greater help to world development, and a normal business for investors, if their ownership and their technology were eventually and gradually transferred to the host countries under honest, mutually agreed terms.

77. In mixed economy nations, some utilities and natural monopolies could be transferred to local public institutions, and some manufacturing facilities to private companies, of local or mixed capital.

78. There are already successful examples of such transactions. An oil refinery, a telephone network, can be paid for in ten or twenty years (interest and profit to the investors included) by a small surcharge on the gallon or on the call. The capital so withdrawn by the first owners can be profitably re-used for other ventures, simultaneously doing business and helping world development.

79. It is an excess of permanent ownership from abroad that should be avoided, or at least it should not be abused.

## XII. COMMUNICATIONS

80. International communications and transportation pose another problem for the developing countries. Both services are indispensable, and both constitute a heavy drain on foreign exchange.

81. Each developed country likes to own as much as possible of the airlines, the shipping companies, the cable and electronic facilities that serve the world. This is due both to commercial and to strategic reasons.

82. Many developing countries have made the effort, perhaps out of proportion to

their possibilities, to have their own 'flag airline', or to own a few steamships. As the size and price of aircraft go up, more local companies are turning out to be too small.

83. International ownership of communications and transportation facilities should be encouraged. The Governments of developed countries, which usually subsidize their own companies, could take a broader view and facilitate the proportional ownership of the poor countries, as a step towards an equitable distribution of the world income, and as a psychological satisfaction to smaller nations.

## XIII. HARD SELLING

84. Commercial advertising and instalment selling of consumer goods in the poor countries, make the difficulties of development more acute.

85. In the last half century, a country of the size and the political system of the Soviet Union was able to consume internally what it could produce internally.

86. More recently, a short effort was made by a small country, South Korea, at the beginning of General Clark's regime. Foreign 'luxuries' were publicly burnt at the market place. This came close to Plato's ideal location for his modern city: away from the sea, banning outside traders, free from debilitating foreign ideas.

87. Obviously this is not the trend of our world. Our problem is to reconcile the development effort, the need to capitalize, the need to save foreign exchange to pay for capital goods, with the inordinate consumption of non-essential articles from the developed nations, encouraged by advertising and sales promotions.

88. All consumption is now considered an economic virtue, especially since the Great Depression of the thirties, as a popularization of what people conceive as Keynes' remedy for all ills. The ancient virtue of thrift, which made possible the development of Europe and the United States, has been practically discarded from the moral code.

89. In applying the policies of developed countries, where high consumption is needed to match high production, to the under-developed countries where production is low, we are using Peter's medicine to prevent John's illness.

90. I refer, of course, to high consumption of non-indispensable foreign goods and services, which weakens the balance of payments, lessens the acquisition of capital goods, and retards development.

91. Particularly in a democracy, it is difficult to limit advertising and instalment buying of foreign goods. In spite of high customs duties and exchange restrictions, the balance of payments of poor countries continues to be one of the main obstacles to development. This is one of the most difficult disadvantages of trade with the rich nations.

## XIV. TECHNOLOGY

92. Technology, strangely enough, sometimes poses another obstacle to the retarded countries. Constant technological progress in the developed world brings about

rapid obsolescence, which is too costly for the poor nations. Ever more sophisti-
cated machines and gadgets strengthen the demand for foreign exchange, without
a corresponding increase in the means of payment.

93. Synthetic products that substitute natural products are another source of worry.
At this moment the threat of chemical fibres to abaci, sisal and jute is very serious
for many countries in Asia, Africa and Latin America.

94. Research on synthetics is carried on by the large chemical firms which, as
private business, are not responsible for world development. In the long run their
new products represent progress. But the world is still divided between developed
and under-developed nations.

95. For many areas of the world, natural fibres are the only export product, the only
means of paying for capital goods, and therefore for development. By custom and
by nature, these areas are difficult to cultivate with other crops. And they have the
land and the labour to supply any expansion of world demand.

96. Those of us who are in the firing line of the development struggle cannot help
but wonder why the admirable chemical companies do not devote their resources
instead to find new uses for natural fibres. There must be an interesting field for
research in fibre disintegration. This would be a contribution, and not a hindrance,
to the fight on poverty in the large sisal, jute and abacá areas of the world.

97. With technological progress unrelated to any plan or orientation of the world
economy, companies in the advanced countries are increasing the need for aid and
for more taxes.

98. There is even talk of synthetic coffee. If this succeeds, who is going to feed
fourteen Latin American nations and an equal number of African countries?


## XV. AID

99. There are two possible ways of meeting the various disadvantages of international trade to the development of the weak economies. One is to study case by
case (commodity prices, different kinds of foreign investments, international services, artificially stimulated consumption, advancing technology, etc.) and find the
best possible remedy for each. Another is simply to adopt an over-all compensating
policy by that modern invention, foreign aid.

100. Probably the solution will be a combination of both measures, as transitory
mechanisms until a world economic balance is attained. On the one side commodity agreements establishing development prices, with clauses concerning wages and
taxes. On the other hand direct pecuniary compensation to the developing countries, in amounts that should be much larger than at present, preferably handled by
international agencies from contributions of all developed countries, large and
small.

101. Commodity agreements will probably become unnecessary in the future, after
the poor countries develop to a certain level, because then industrialization and
higher wages and salaries will make cheap production of primary articles
impossible.

102. Foreign aid, of course, is a temporary measure. As more countries develop, they should also become contributors to the international funds.

## XVI. FOOD BANK

103. So far I have been dealing with economic and social rights in areas that are partly the concern of UNCTAD. I will now make a reference to a specific contemporary problem on which FAO has shown deep interest: the world food shortage.

104. It is my paradoxical observation that the farmers of the world (of a hungry world) live under the spectre of abundance.

105. The danger of falling food prices under any local or seasonal abundance is such, that many producers are detained by fear of losses. Especially farmers of a certain size who use bank financing for their crops.

106. The risks of nature are bad enough for the farmer: rain or drought, bumper harvests or crop failures. The risks of the market, however, should be run by society.

107. A World Food Bank should be created. Let each agricultural area have surplus buying agencies at guaranteed prices. Establish strategic reserves in the major ports of the world. Be prepared to absorb bumper crops at one end and crop failures at another.

108. Many of the practical difficulties in this plan, such as quality control and proper preservation, have already been met by the internal agricultural programmes of several nations.

109. Experience shows that when the market is guaranteed, the farmer himself goes after technical assistance, to increase production or to reduce costs. On the other hand, in the absence of a guaranteed market, it takes a great educational effort to diffuse better methods, seeds, etc.

110. We might say that the farmers of the world have a right to proper compensation for their work, and the peoples of the world have a right to be fed. A means to fulfil such rights would be a World Food Bank.

111. The World Food Bank could be an instrument of both, FAO and UNCTAD, performing two similar functions with physical reserves: (a) encourage and regulate the world's food supplies; (b) stabilize the market for important commodities that constitute the means of international payment for under-developed countries.

112. The Bank would be a sister institution of the International Monetary Fund and the World Bank. Belatedly this would implement John Maynard Keynes' ideas at the Bretton Woods Conference in 1944.

## XVII. MORE AID

113. Let me return to foreign aid, as a means of compensating for the weak bargaining position of poor countries, and as an expression of world solidarity.

114. This is the wrong time (1967) to speak about the amounts of aid that would be needed for a satisfactory rate of world development. The largest contributing country, the United States, is presently reducing its participation.

115. In 1964, UNCTAD recommended 1 per cent of the national income of developed countries to go to foreign aid. In 1966 it was found that the amount given had actually diminished, instead of approaching the goal of 1 per cent. In the meantime, independent scholars have suggested that the total needs are about 2 per cent of the income of the developed world.

116. This would mean, for the United States alone, about 17 billion dollars a year, instead of the two and one-half to three billion which the Congress is debating now. For all advanced nations together, East and West, 2 per cent might [amount] (Editorial insertion) to an outlay of about 40 billion dollars a year in aid to the whole under-developed world.

## XVIII. AID PER HEAD

117. There are different ways of estimating not only what should be given in aid, in the absence of proper trade regulations, but also what could be effectively used.

118. In 1955, in my speech at the First Conference of Western Hemispheric Presidents held in Panama, I suggested that the Latin American continent could use in the first years of an intensive development programme roughly US$10.00 per inhabitant. Today, in 1967, I doubt if Latin America could do much with less than twenty or twenty-five United States dollars per person.

119. The difference is to be found in the drop of export prices. Twelve yearly crops of coffee and cocoa have been sold at two-thirds of what may be considered as a development price. The backlog of needs has accumulated, in spite of the programmes and financial help of the Alliance for Progress. Without the Alliance, present problems of all kinds would be a great deal worse.

120. Of course, if prices had been fairer there would have been more general consumption, and even some waste, in the small privileged circles that can afford waste. But undoubtedly, capital formation would have gone on at a reasonable rate, as it did during the early fifties when export prices were better.

121. Now it seems that an outside injection of capital of say US$20.00 per inhabitant, as an average for the first few years of an intensive programme, would be needed and could be effectively used in Latin America. With a population of 200 million, this amounts to four billion dollars a year. Current development aid to the whole continent, coming almost exclusively from the United States, is between one half and one billion a year.

## XIX. AID IN KIND

122. If, and when, foreign aid is ever given in the necessary amounts to establish a sound economic world order in a few decades, probably a large proportion of it will have to be given in kind, not in money.

123. So far the developing countries have seriously objected not only to political 'strings attached', but also to policies that would force them to buy the products of the respective aid-giving nation. I do not see why such objection should continue if intensive programmes were undertaken with all the needed aid.

124. In our time, even the strong economies are suffering from balance of payments deficits. This is attributed to defects in the world monetary system. Probably the phenomenon has deeper sources. It may be related to international trade, because the strong economies are simultaneously stimulating and preventing a healthy growth of the weak economies and markets.

125. Of course troops on foreign soil tend to create a deficit at one end and inflation at the other. There may be other causes, and probably other evils, that also cannot be stopped easily.

126. If foreign aid were given in the necessary amounts in money and not in kind, the effects of the balance of payments of the aid-giving countries would be detrimental.

127. On the other hand, if a large part of the aid is given in kind, or, if the recipient nations make most of their purchases in the respective giving country, surpluses in industrial capacity could be utilized, at a low cost to the over-all economy of the developed countries.

128. Overhead costs are currently covered by present production and sales. Any addition in volume, within the capacity of the industrial system, requires relatively small outlays.

129. Aid in kind would present some difficulties to the larger retarded countries, where certain industries like tractor-building are already established. With a certain degree of flexibility in all policies, such obstacles can be surmounted.

130. Besides, if foreign aid is handled by international agencies, goods representing surpluses of industrial capacity could go to a common pool, and would be distributed according to circumstances.

131. Thus the members of the family of nations would be applying the old motto: 'From each according to his possibilities; to each according to his needs'.


## XX. WAR EXPENSES

132. What are the probabilities of an all-out effort of development of the retarded world if, in the absence of well-regulated trade, this would require an aid contribution by all developed nations, large and small, of 2 per cent of their income.

133. I am more familiar with the political situation in the United States than in other countries. And, of course, I understand that, as of today, such contribution is politically impossible, even if it is considered to be economically possible and desirable.

134. For our present purpose, we may consider that the national product of the United States is supporting three main kinds of expenditures: (a) the current standard of living; (b) war expenses; and (c) development, both international and internal. Let us not forget internal development; pollution, traffic jams, riot areas, etc.

135. In order to increase one of the three expenditures appreciably, one or the other two must be curtailed. So far it is development that has been sacrificed, because it is politically the weakest. For internal reasons it is difficult to reduce the standard of living or even its rate of growth. And for international reasons it is considered risky to reduce the war expenses.

136. No matter how trite or how unrealistic the suggestion may be, it is the war expenses that should diminish. Now that military forces are largely concentrated in two super—Powers, it ought to be less difficult than in previous centuries to establish civilized relations among the peoples of the world. The military expenses of some poor countries are, if one may use a strong word, preposterous.

137. The arithmetic involved is child's play. If we were to reduce present war expenses by one half, we would still have enough funds to maintain order, and to continue the exploration of space, the atom, the bottom of the sea and the heart of our earth.

138. Not counting the large sums appropriated for war emergencies, the permanent military budgets of the nations of the world now reach a combined total of about US$140 billion.

139. If we are allowed to dream about a better humanity; if as some anthropologists think, mankind is heading toward integration and not to extinction; if we could cut war expenses by half, the more developed countries, without sacrificing their standard of living or their rate of growth, could devote the funds thus released to development, part internal and part international.

140. And if all nations did the same, as they should, perhaps in less than half a century our planet would be embellished by the blossoming .of the Great Human Society.


## XXI. CONCLUSION

141. I have read the documents that tell the story of the accomplishments of the United Nations in the field of human rights.

142. While a long road lies ahead in this field of man's progress, those achievements, that some persons might be tempted to regard as modest, plus the undoubtable greatness and permanency of the Declaration and the Covenants, make the last two decades of initiation in human rights the best spent period in the history of mankind.

143. Much that I have said in this paper belongs to the realm of enunciations. More ideas, more time, more education, more adaptation will be needed. Yet, the rate of progress is an accelerating movement.

144. According to these views, the fulfilment of human rights requires economic and social development.

145. Development requires not only corrections to the internal causes of poverty in the retarded nations, but also a full revision of all economic relations with the advanced countries.

146. Since several of these relations are difficult to change, an over-all compensation may have to be given for a time, in the form of increased foreign aid.

147. The increase in foreign aid may be dependent on the reduction of war expenses. This is no surprise. Human rights and world peace dwell side by side in the hearts of men. United Nations is endeavouring to achieve both.

148. Peace will help development. Development will engender peace. They are both causes and effects. They strengthen each other. Their common goal is the reign of human rights.

# 97. DECLARATION ON THE RIGHT TO DEVELOPMENT, 1986

Adopted by General Assembly Resolution 41/128 on 4 December 1986, by a vote of 146 to one against (United States), with eight abstentions, including Germany, Japan, and the United Kingdom. See further the Yearbook of the United Nations (1986), 717–21; and Brownlie, I., *The Human Right to Development*, Commonwealth Secretariat, London (1989). For later developments see UNGA Resolutions 50/184, 22 December 1995, 'Right to development' (adopted without a vote); 51/240, 20 June 1997, 'Agenda for Development' (adopted without a vote); 52/136, 12 December 1997, 'Right to development' (adopted by a vote of 129–12–32); 53/155, 9 December 1998, 'Right to development' (adopted by a vote of 125–1–42); 54/175, 17 December 1999, 'The right to development' (adopted by a vote of 119–10–38); 55/108, 4 December 2000, 'The right to development', (adopted without a vote).

## TEXT

*The General Assembly,*

*Bearing in mind* the purposes and principles of the Charter of the United Nations relating to the achievement of international co-operation in solving international problems of an economic, social, cultural or humanitarian nature, and in promoting and encouraging respect for human rights and fundamental freedoms for all without distinction as to race, sex, language or religion,

*Recognizing* that development is a comprehensive economic, social, cultural and political process, which aims at the constant improvement of the well-being of the entire population and of all individuals on the basis of their active, free and meaningful participation in development and in the fair distribution of benefits resulting therefrom,

*Considering* that under the provisions of the Universal Declaration of Human Rights everyone is entitled to a social and international order in which the rights and freedoms set forth in that Declaration can be fully realized,

*Recalling* the provisions of the International Covenant on Economic, Social and Cultural Rights and of the International Covenant on Civil and Political Rights,

*Recalling further* the relevant agreements, conventions, resolutions, recommendations and other instruments of the United Nations and its specialized agencies concerning the integral development of the human being, economic and social progress and development of all peoples, including those instruments concerning decolonization, the prevention of discrimination, respect for and observance of, human rights and fundamental freedoms, the maintenance of international peace and security and the further promotion of friendly relations and co-operation among States in accordance with the Charter,

*Recalling* the right of peoples to self-determination, by virtue of which they have the right freely to determine their political status and to pursue their economic, social and cultural development,

*Recalling also* the right of peoples to exercise, subject to the relevant provisions of both International Covenants on Human Rights, full and complete sovereignty over all their natural wealth and resources,

*Mindful* of the obligation of States under the Charter to promote universal respect for and observance of human rights and fundamental freedoms for all without distinction of any kind such as race, colour, sex, language, religion, political or other opinion, national or social origin, property, birth or other status,

*Considering* that the elimination of the massive and flagrant violations of the human rights of the peoples and individuals affected by situations such as those resulting from colonialism, neo-colonialism, apartheid, all forms of racism and racial discrimination, foreign domination and occupation, aggression and threats against national sovereignty, national unity and territorial integrity and threats of war would contribute to the establishment of circumstances propitious to the development of a great part of mankind,

*Concerned* at the existence of serious obstacles to development, as well as to the complete fulfilment of human beings and of peoples, constituted, *inter alia*, by the denial of civil, political, economic, social and cultural rights, and considering that all human rights and fundamental freedoms are indivisible and interdependent and that, in order to promote development, equal attention and urgent consideration should be given to the implementation, promotion and protection of civil, political, economic, social and cultural rights and that, accordingly, the promotion of, respect for and enjoyment of certain human rights and fundamental freedoms cannot justify the denial of other human rights and fundamental freedoms,

*Considering* that international peace and security are essential elements for the realization of the right to development,

*Reaffirming* that there is a close relationship between disarmament and development and that progress in the field of disarmament would considerably promote progress in the field of development and that resources released through disarmament measures should be devoted to the economic and social development and well-being of all peoples and, in particular, those of the developing countries,

*Recognizing* that the human person is the central subject of the development process and that development policy should therefore make the human being the main participant and beneficiary of development,

*Recognizing* that the creation of conditions favourable to the development of peoples and individuals is the primary responsibility of their States,

*Aware* that efforts at the international level to promote and protect human rights should be accompanied by efforts to establish a new international economic order,

*Confirming* that the right to development is an inalienable human right and that equality of opportunity for development is a prerogative both of nations and of individuals who make up nations,

*Proclaims* the following Declaration on the Right to Development:

*Article* 1

1. The right to development is an inalienable human right by virtue of which every human person and all peoples are entitled to participate in, contribute to, and enjoy economic, social, cultural and political development, in which all human rights and fundamental freedoms can be fully realized.

2. The human right to development also implies the full realization of the right of peoples to self-determination, which includes, subject to the relevant provisions of

both International Covenants on Human Rights, the exercise of their inalienable right to full sovereignty over all their natural wealth and resources.

*Article 2*

1. The human person is the central subject of development and should be the active participant and beneficiary of the right to development.

2. All human beings have a responsibility for development, individually and collectively, taking into account the need for full respect for their human rights and fundamental freedoms as well as their duties to the community, which alone can ensure the free and complete fulfilment of the human being, and they should therefore promote and protect an appropriate political, social and economic order for development.

3. States have the right and the duty to formulate appropriate national development policies that aim at the constant improvement of the well-being of the entire population and of all individuals, on the basis of their active, free and meaningful participation in development and in the fair distribution of the benefits resulting therefrom.

*Article 3*

1. States have the primary responsibility for the creation of national and international conditions favourable to the realization of the right to development.

2. The realization of the right to development requires full respect for the principles of international law concerning friendly relations and co-operation among States in accordance with the Charter of the United Nations.

3. States have the duty to co-operate with each other in ensuring development and eliminating obstacles to development. States should realize their rights and fulfil their duties in such a manner as to promote a new international economic order based on sovereign equality, interdependence, mutual interest and co-operation among all States, as well as to encourage the observance and realization of human rights.

*Article 4*

1. States have the duty to take steps, individually and collectively, to formulate international development policies with a view to facilitating the full realization of the right to development.

2. Sustained action is required to promote more rapid development of developing countries. As a complement to the efforts of developing countries, effective international co-operation is essential in providing these countries with appropriate means and facilities to foster their comprehensive development.

*Article 5*

States shall take resolute steps to eliminate the massive and flagrant violations of the human rights of peoples and human beings affected by situations such as those resulting from apartheid, all forms of racism and racial discrimination, colonialism, foreign domination and occupation, aggression, foreign interference and threats against national sovereignty, national unity and territorial integrity, threats of war and refusal to recognize the fundamental right of peoples to self-determination.

*Article* 6

1. All States should co-operate with a view to promoting, encouraging and strengthening universal respect for and observance of all human rights and fundamental freedoms for all without any distinction as to race, sex, language or religion.

2. All human rights and fundamental freedoms are indivisible and interdependent; equal attention and urgent consideration should be given to the implementation, promotion and protection of civil, political, economic, social and cultural rights.

3. States should take steps to eliminate obstacles to development resulting from failure to observe civil and political rights, as well as economic social and cultural rights.

*Article* 7

All States should promote the establishment, maintenance and strengthening of international peace and security and, to that end, should do their utmost to achieve general and complete disarmament under effective international control, as well as to ensure that the resources released by effective disarmament measures are used for comprehensive development, in particular that of the developing countries.

*Article* 8

1. States should undertake, at the national level, all necessary measures for the realization of the right to development and shall ensure, *inter alia*, equality of opportunity for all in their access to basic resources, education, health services, food, housing, employment and the fair distribution of income. Effective measures should be undertaken to ensure that women have an active role in the development process. Appropriate economic and social reforms should be carried out with a view to eradicating all social injustices.

2. States should encourage popular participation in all spheres as an important factor in development and in the full realization of all human rights.

*Article* 9

1. All the aspects of the right to development set forth in the present Declaration are indivisible and interdependent and each of them should be considered in the context of the whole.

2. Nothing in the present Declaration shall be construed as being contrary to the purposes and principles of the United Nations, or as implying that any State, group or person has a right to engage in any activity or to perform any act aimed at the violation of the rights set forth in the Universal Declaration of Human Rights and in the International Covenants on Human Rights.

*Article* 10

Steps should be taken to ensure the full exercise and progressive enhancement of the right to development, including the formulation, adoption and implementation of policy, legislative and other measures at the national and international levels.

## 98. AN AGENDA FOR DEVELOPMENT: REPORT AND RECOMMENDATIONS OF THE UN SECRETARY-GENERAL, 1994

For text see UN doc. A/49/665, 11 November 1994. This report was also published together with other relevant documents in Boutros-Ghali, B., *An Agenda for Development*, New York: United Nations (1995), 83–106. See also UNGA Resolution 51/240, 20 June 1997, 'Agenda for Development' (adopted without a vote).

McGoldrick, D., 'Sustainable Development and Human Rights: An Integrated Conception' (1996) 45 *ICLQ* 796–818.

*TEXT*

### Preface

1. In accordance with General Assembly resolution 47/181 of 22 December 1992, I circulated on 6 May 1994 a report on an agenda for development (A/48/935) to elicit the views of all Member States, the agencies and programmes of the United Nations system, as well as a wide range of public and private sources.

2. That report was available at the World Hearings on Development organized by the President of the General Assembly in June 1994, and was discussed at the substantive session of the Economic and Social Council in July 1994. Additional comments were received from a wide variety of sources. I have considered all contributions with great care. Most recently, I have had the benefit of statements presented during the general debate of the forty-ninth session of the General Assembly, many of which addressed an agenda for development.

3. As requested in paragraph 5 of General Assembly resolution 48/166 of 21 December 1993, I am now submitting to the General Assembly at its forty-ninth session my recommendations, to follow up on my report on an agenda for development of 6 May 1994, taking into account the discussions during the substantive session of 1994 of the Economic and Social Council, as well as the views presented during the Hearings conducted by the President of the General Assembly and summarized under his own responsibility (see A/49/320, annex). In doing so, I have been mindful of the requests regarding the contents of the agenda contained in the operative paragraph of General Assembly resolution 47/181. A summary of the recommendations appears in the annex to the present report.

## I. INTRODUCTION

4. The general recommendations that have emerged can be simply stated, but they are fundamentally important. Firstly, development should be recognized as the

foremost and most far-reaching task of our time. Recognition of this imperative, commitment to achieving development, and continual, cooperative and effective action towards it are crucial for humanity's common future. It is urgent for Governments, intergovernmental institutions and the United Nations to review their priorities with the goal of elevating dramatically the attention and support given to development.

5. Secondly, development must be seen in its many dimensions. My report on an agenda for development of 6 May 1994 identified five dimensions of development: peace, the economy, environmental protection, social justice and democracy. The importance of these dimensions has been understood and supported by Member States. For most people and most countries, economic growth is the sine qua non of development. Economic growth is not an option; it is an imperative. But it is a means to an end. New development approaches should not only generate economic growth, they should make its benefits equitably available. They should enable people to participate in decisions affecting their lives. They should provide job-led growth. They must replenish the natural heritage on which all life depends. They must be based upon a comprehensive vision of development.

6. At its core, development must be about improvement of human well-being; removal of hunger, disease and ignorance; and productive employment for all. Its first goal must be to end poverty and satisfy the priority needs of all people in a way that can be productively sustained over future generations.

7. Thirdly, the emerging consensus on the priority and dimensions of development should find expression in a new framework for international cooperation. The enterprise we call international cooperation for development is needed now more than ever, but it must be revitalized in order to escape fully its Cold War past and contribute fully to the realization of development goals.

8. Fourthly, within this new framework for development cooperation, the United Nations must play a major role in both policy leadership and operations. Comments on the May 1994 report on an agenda for development have not only strengthened understanding of the dimensions of development. They have also revealed strong support for a revitalized role of the Organization and for measures to enhance the coherence and relevance of the United Nations system in development.

9. The development mission and responsibilities of the United Nations stem directly from the Charter of the United Nations and the fundamental nature of the United Nations as an international political entity and moral force; from the inseparability of peace-keeping, humanitarian and development objectives; from the contribution of development to the universal goals of peace, freedom, social justice and environmental quality—goals for which the United Nations stands and for which it works daily around the world; and from the strengths of the programmes that have developed over its 50-year life. The United Nations cannot be a strong force for peace unless it is also a strong force for development.

10. It is time for the United Nations to realize its original mandate in the social and economic fields, to make the comprehensive pursuit of development the centre of its action, and, in this new context, to assist Member States in their efforts to realize their diverse development goals.

11. The United Nations system—the United Nations itself, the specialized

agencies, and the Bretton Woods institutions—has much to bring to the development process. But the system will realize its potential only if its intergovernmental processes are strengthened and made more coherent and if the various development assistance components integrate their complementary mandates into coherent and coordinated support for countries' aspirations. There is also great room for improvement in the Organization's operations, including the linkages among peace-keeping, humanitarian assistance and development.

12. The general recommendations that have emerged from the process of forging an agenda for development have brought to the fore three key objectives: to strengthen and revitalize international development cooperation generally; to build a stronger, more effective and coherent multilateral system in support of development; and to enhance the effectiveness of the development work of the Organization itself—its departments, regional commissions, funds and programmes—in partnership with the United Nations system as a whole.

13. The recommendations presented in the following paragraphs are addressed and organized according to these three objectives, with a special focus in each case on what the United Nations can and should do. No real improvements will be possible unless the Member States are convinced of the need for, and unless nations and peoples everywhere share the fruits of, the proposed changes. Member States are challenged to grasp this opportunity and make the United Nations system a far more effective instrument of multilateralism.

## II. RECOMMENDATIONS FOR REVITALIZING INTERNATIONAL DEVELOPMENT COOPERATION

14. A new framework for international development cooperation requires mutually supporting actions at the national and international level.

### A. National policies for development

15. Development can succeed only if it is driven by national priorities and dedicated to the improvement of the well-being of the country and its people. National capacities to plan, manage and implement development programmes must be built both in government and in civil society.

16. While the individual State is no longer the sole actor in development, each State bears primary responsibility for its own development. Whether expressed as a responsibility of States or as a right of peoples, development requires competent governmental leadership, coherent national policies and strong popular commitment.

17. A strong partnership between government and civil society is an important prerequisite for sustainable development.

18. Governments have a special responsibility to protect poor and marginalized peoples and to seek policies which offer them avenues towards productive involvement in their societies and economies.

19. Non-state actors, including grass-roots people's movements and non-governmental organizations, should be strengthened and supported. These organizations of civil society give a voice to the people, and should be recognized and included in new development models.

20. The importance of private business should not be underestimated. As part of the partnership, strong private enterprise sectors, the use of market forces and market-based mechanisms, and the cultivation of entrepreneurship should be encouraged. Governments should ensure that social and environmental costs are accurately reflected in prices, and lead to macroeconomic stability.

21. Government, civil and social action must be taken to fight corruption and protect consumers, investors, workers and the environment through appropriate regulations.

## B. International setting

22. A favourable, growth-oriented international setting for development is vital. External macroeconomic forces—trade, debt management, direct investment, capital flows and access to technology—must support development objectives. International cooperation for development must include partnerships with the business community, national and international.

23. The equitable integration of the poorest and least-endowed countries into the world economy is a major requirement. The marginalization of these countries is perceptible and must be reversed.

24. It is distressing that the official development assistance target of 0.7 per cent of gross national product, which was adopted in 1970 and reaffirmed as recently as 1992 at the United Nations Conference on Environment and Development (UNCED), was achieved in 1993 by only four countries: Denmark, the Netherlands, Norway and Sweden. Development assistance must be brought closer to the agreed targets, and its diversion to non-development priorities must be reversed. New agreements should be reached on plausible interim goals for steady increases in official development assistance. A larger share should be allocated to the development work of the United Nations.

25. There is an urgent need to increase the overall level of development assistance and to ensure that funding for peace-keeping, humanitarian emergencies and the global environment is provided from new and additional resources and not from development assistance.

26. The international community must find a solution for an issue that has bedeviled development efforts for two decades: debt. Debt problems are acute among the poorest countries, particularly those in Africa.

27. Reforming countries in debt crisis require an adequate and permanent reduction in the stock of debt that will restore private sector confidence at home and abroad and facilitate their recovery, growth and development. The debts of the least developed and poorest countries should be cancelled outright. Recycling debt to finance economic, social and environmental projects should be considered.

28. Developing nations must be provided equitable access to expanding global

opportunities in trade, technology, investment and information. The fruits of the technological and informatics revolution must be more evenly available if present international economic disparities are not to deepen further and weaken the foundations of global progress.

29. Countries in transition to a market economy face special problems stemming from the need for rapid but sensitive transformation in fundamental economic organization, lack of competitiveness in international markets, economic depression and other factors. These countries should be supported by additional resources from the international community.

30. Regional economic cooperation should be recognized as an important component of many countries' development strategies. Regional integration schemes, from loose associations to free trade agreements, provide a rich experience upon which new policy initiatives can draw. Economic and technical cooperation among developing countries with similar challenges and experiences should be encouraged.

31. Economic progress and human well-being in many parts of the world are threatened by unchecked population growth and environmental deterioration. Programmes to address these issues, including the Programme of Action recently forged at the International Conference on Population and Development in Cairo and the agreements reached at UNCED in Rio de Janeiro, must be given high priority as an integral part of comprehensive development.

32. The rapid application of new technology and changes in consumption are needed to check extravagant consumption of natural and environmental resources.

33. Excessive military spending and its consequences are deeply inimical to development goals. A unique opportunity is now available for further progress on reducing military expenditures, phasing out most forms of military assistance and subsidies to arms exporters, and effectively curtailing indiscriminate international trafficking in arms. Greater transparency of military spending is needed. The United Nations Register of Conventional Arms must be strengthened. More extensive comparative analysis of military and social budgets must be undertaken. Land-mines are a major obstacle to development, shattering lives and removing land from productive use. An outright world-wide ban on the production and transfer of land-mines and their components should be declared. The holding of world hearings on the connection between disarmament and development conducted by the President of the General Assembly should be seriously considered.

34. As the success of the International Conference on Population and Development at Cairo demonstrates, a powerful international development agenda is emerging on an ongoing basis through the work of a continuum of United Nations conferences and summits. Effective and realistic mechanisms must be made available to implement goals established at these conferences.

35. A common framework should be developed to follow up major United Nations conferences, past and future. Goals and targets in the economic and social development field endorsed by past international conferences and summits should be synthesized, costed, prioritized and placed in a reasonable time perspective for implementation.

36. The fiftieth session of the General Assembly provides an appropriate opportunity for focusing the attention of the international community on forging a new

framework for development cooperation between industrialized and developing countries, in which common interests and mutual needs provide the basic rationale for a new partnership.

37. In this regard, an international conference on the financing of development should be considered by the Assembly. Such a conference could be convened in close consultation with the Bretton Woods institutions, the regional development banks and the Development Assistance Committee of the Organization for Economic Cooperation and Development.

## III. RECOMMENDATIONS FOR AN EFFECTIVE MULTILATERAL DEVELOPMENT SYSTEM

38. With increasing global interdependence, the need for multilateral cooperation will inevitably expand. A strong and effective multilateral system with the United Nations at its centre is an essential prerequisite for successful multilateral cooperation on development and international economic policy and operations.

39. The responsibility for building a new framework for development cooperation is widely shared. But the role of the United Nations is unique and indispensable. As the world Organization based on the principle of universality, and with an unmatched global network at all levels, the United Nations can promote awareness, build consensus, inform policy in every dimension affecting development, and help to rationalize and harmonize the multiplicity of public and private efforts world wide in the cause of development. Enhancing the role of the General Assembly and the Economic and Social Council, and strengthening linkages between the Organization and the Bretton Woods institutions on the one hand, and the sectoral and technical agencies on the other, are crucial requirements to these ends.

### A. General Assembly

40. In the context of the ongoing intergovernmental reform process on the restructuring and revitalization of the United Nations in the economic, social and related fields, the General Assembly must play a major role to focus the attention of the international community on forging a new framework for development cooperation.

41. The General Assembly should identify critical issues for international cooperation and policy development and serve as a forum for regular identification of gaps and inconsistencies, as well as emerging problems that are likely to fall between the purviews of more narrowly focused institutions in the fields of development, trade and finance. The Assembly should focus on the development of norms, standards and rules of the game required to manage global interdependence in a rapidly changing international environment and promote an integrated approach to economic and social development. The roles of the Second and Third Committees could be reviewed from this perspective.

42. The early part of General Assembly sessions, with high-level representatives

present, could be used to organize a focused dialogue on these issues in the plenary sessions. Consideration could be given to convening, every few years, special sessions of the Assembly on major aspects of international cooperation for development.

## B.  Economic and Social Council

43. Key to the ongoing effort to strengthen the United Nations as the centre of an effective multilateral development system is the revitalization of the Economic and Social Council to fulfil the role envisaged for it under the Charter.

44. Firstly, the Council should deliberate and decide upon the full range of development issues in accordance with that role, mindful of the Relationship Agreements with and mandates of the specialized agencies and the Bretton Woods institutions. The Council should bring the specialized agencies into a closer working relationship with the United Nations and perform the functions specified in the Charter under Chapter IV, on the General Assembly; Chapter IX, on international economic and social cooperation; and Chapter X, on the Council itself.

45. Secondly, the Council should serve as an international development assistance review committee, providing a regular opportunity for both donors and recipients to discuss and assess aid programmes and policies. As part of this role, the Council should function as a unifying governing entity to which the existing governing bodies of the United Nations funds and programmes would relate on major policy matters. It would also provide intergovernmental oversight of the relevant United Nations departments with responsibilities for operational activities for development.

46. Thirdly, the Council should identify potential or emerging humanitarian emergencies and provide policy guidelines in developing coordinated initiatives to address such situations.

47. These responsibilities and functions of the Council could be reinforced by an expanded bureau, meeting inter-sessionally to focus the work of the Council and facilitate agreement on issues for endorsement by the Council. To preserve efficiency while retaining representativeness, the expanded bureau should be limited in membership. Its working methods should provide for maximum flexibility so as to ensure timely responses. The entire Council, at a high level, would meet at specific times of the year to provide general policy guidance and to review the work of the expanded bureau.

48. To support the General Assembly and the Economic and Social Council in providing effective leadership in development, a council of international development advisers should be considered. This council would issue an independent annual or biennial report, analyse key issues concerning the global economy and their impact on development, and inform international opinion.

## C.  Bretton Woods institutions

49. Strengthening the links with the Bretton Woods institutions was one of the

dominant themes during the recent debate in the Economic and Social Council high-level session and in the World Hearings on Development. Enhancing the relationship between the United Nations and the Bretton Woods institutions is one of the mandates contained in the original General Assembly resolution 47/181 calling for an agenda for development.

50. There are many fields in which the ongoing dialogue and substantive partnerships between the Bretton Woods institutions and the United Nations may be strengthened. In particular, with the expansion of the World Bank lending into social, environmental and other sectors which require capacity building, decentralized planning and execution, small loans and more participatory development involving all institutions of civil society, there should be greater scope for collaboration with United Nations programmes and agencies working in these areas.

51. Similarly, the World Bank could utilize and support United Nations programmes in delivering grant-based technical assistance, particularly 'free standing' technical assistance unrelated to specific capital investment projects.

52. There are successful examples of country-level collaboration between the Bretton Woods institutions and the United Nations programmes in these and other areas, which should be employed as models for replication.

53. Cooperation between the Bretton Woods institutions and the United Nations could be pursued through joint initiatives in, among others, the following fields: poverty reduction strategies, including small enterprise development and microcredit availability; improvements in the productivity of the resources sector and sustainable energy development; preventive development and post-conflict peacebuilding and reconstruction; socially and environmentally responsible structural adjustment programmes; and capacity-building and improved public sector management.

54. An issue that has attracted considerable attention in the Economic and Social Council discussions and in the World Hearings on Development is the policy conditionality for structural adjustment loans designed by the World Bank and the International Monetary Fund (IMF). There is little disagreement on the need for structural adjustment and economic reform. There is, however, controversy over the policy content of structural adjustment programmes and concern that such programmes are, in and of themselves, insufficient.

55. The Organization and the Bretton Woods institutions should work together with concerned countries on the components of the policy dialogue and other complementary and compensating initiatives that must accompany structural adjustment programmes. There is considerable scope for such collaboration in the aid consortia, consultative groups and round tables organized under multilateral auspices, particularly by the World Bank and the United Nations Development Programme (UNDP). Special attention also needs to be given to making the country policy dialogue more transparent and relevant by building Governments' capacities to lead the dialogue process and in clearly detailing policy options in country documents prepared by the World Bank/IMF and the United Nations development system. The United Nations resident coordinator should be involved with such policy dialogues. Efforts now under way to promote greater complementarity between country strategy notes and policy framework papers should be pursued.

56. The revival of the United Nations/Bretton Woods Liaison Committee could also be explored with the aim of enhancing substantive consultation. In addition, the Secretary-General should convey, as appropriate, the concerns of the United Nations system as a whole to the Joint Committee on Development of the Board of Governors of the IMF and the World Bank.

## D. Sectoral and technical agencies

57. The diversity represented in the agencies of the United Nations system can be a great source of strength if the variety of constituencies and expertise which they represent is harnessed in support of comprehensive, sustainable development.

58. The contribution which the sectoral and technical agencies have been making to the preparation for, and follow-up to, major global conferences—encompassing intergovernmental policy inputs, specialized secretariat expertise, and the promotion of contributions from different sectors of civil society—represents a model which should be applied progressively to all aspects of the development work of the Organization. Initiatives for joint action, such as the new inter-agency programme on the human immunodeficiency virus/acquired immunodeficiency syndrome (HIV/AIDS), should similarly be expanded to other areas.

59. Technical contributions from these agencies, particularly the smaller technical agencies concerned with various aspects of infrastructure development, should be integrated more fully in economic and social plans and priorities promoted by the United Nations system.

60. Maintaining the integrity and comprehensive nature of the United Nations system should be a major, constant concern of the international community. In this context, the desirability of bringing new organizations such as the World Trade Organization, endowed with wide international responsibilities in fields of international economic and social cooperation, into relationship with the United Nations, deserves priority attention.

61. In line with the objectives that have guided the recent restructuring of the inter-secretariat coordination machinery, members of the Administrative Committee on Coordination, under the chairmanship of the Secretary-General, will pursue further measures to strengthen the contribution of that Committee to enhancing the coherence and impact of the work of the system. As part of this effort, it is intended to make greater use of small task forces at the executive head level focusing on critical development issues, and to develop joint programmes based on common policies for implementation at the country level.

## IV. RECOMMENDATIONS FOR MORE EFFICIENT AND EFFECTIVE UNITED NATIONS DEVELOPMENT ACTIVITIES

62. The development activities of the Organization span a wide range: long-term social, economic and political development; post-crisis reconstruction and rehabilitation; and issues such as population, the status of women, child survival, the

environment, drug control, and housing and urban management. Confidence in the United Nations depends to a large extent on the efficiency and effectiveness of these programmes.

63. The fundamental reason for improving United Nations development assistance efforts is not because these efforts are failing but because they are succeeding. The demand for the services that the United Nations provides far outstrips its capacity. In other words, the need to build on past successes, to take full advantage of proven capabilities and to respond to new demands and new opportunities, is the most compelling reason for strengthening United Nations operational activities for development.

64. Further measures to improve and strengthen governance, management, funding, the division of labour and the allocation of responsibilities, coordination and staffing, must build upon the reform initiatives undertaken to date. These include the series of changes in United Nations operations set in motion by General Assembly resolutions 44/211 of 22 December 1989 and 47/199 of 22 December 1992, in the context of its triennial policy reviews of operational activities for development, as well as by other restructuring and revitalization efforts. Enhancing coordination and effectiveness within the United Nations itself can go a long way to foster coherence in the system as a whole.

## A.  Assets and strengths

65. Efforts to make United Nations operational activities more efficient and effective must begin with careful identification of those areas where the United Nations has special assets and strengths in support of development.

66. The United Nations provides a unique forum for raising public consciousness, providing information, defining the international development agenda and building the consensus needed for action. Once forged, consensus is translated into international norms and agreements, integrated into national development priorities and supported through United Nations operational activities.

67. The neutrality of the United Nations means that it does not represent any particular national or commercial interest. The United Nations can therefore develop special relationships of trust with the countries it supports in their development efforts. It can provide stable, long-term capacity-building assistance free of short-term political or economic objectives.

68. The United Nations has an unmatched global network of regional commissions and country offices. The resulting delivery capacity of the United Nations is uniquely strong. Because of its universal presence, the United Nations can operate effectively at both the country and the inter-country and regional levels.

69. The United Nations emphasizes bottom-up, country-driven programming of development assistance resources, without conditionalities. Coupled with the participation of developing countries in United Nations governance, this ensures that United Nations development initiatives derive from national priorities and are dedicated to the progress of the countries involved and their peoples.

70. The United Nations has a comprehensive mandate, spanning social, economic and political issues. Working in partnership with the specialized agencies, the

United Nations has expertise across virtually the full range of development interests. This breadth further enhances delivery capacity.

71. United Nations programmes focus on the neediest countries and on the neediest people within those countries. The United Nations has special strengths and experience in addressing social aspects of development and integrating social and economic dimensions, working with Governments, grass-roots people's movements and other non-governmental organizations.

72. The United Nations is able to mobilize, deliver and coordinate humanitarian assistance. It can promote reconstruction, reintegration and other development in post-emergency situations. It can link peace-keeping, refugee assistance, relief efforts and development. It provides an ideal base for support for early warning and preventive development initiatives. In this area, as in others, the United Nations organizations have established close working relationships with non-governmental organizations at all levels.

## B. Common goals

73. Where there is a shared vision and common purpose, coordination and integration in the Organization's operational activities will follow. Through international conferences and in other ways, the United Nations and its Member States are seeking to articulate and promote a shared vision of development that is human-centred, equitable, and socially and environmentally sustainable. Through this process, common goals are emerging that can serve to galvanize the energies and focus the efforts of the United Nations funds and programmes, together with their agency partners.

74. A major goal in this regard is the empowerment of women. With the emerging consensus on the priority and dimensions of development has come a deeper understanding that in virtually every dimension of development—whether political, social, economic, environmental or security related—the role of women is central. Policies and institutions that suppress the real potential of half of the Earth's people must be reformed. The empowerment of women must be recognized and utilized as a powerful tool for liberating the full creative energies of a society. The visibility, coordination, programming and accountability of the United Nations in gender-related development issues must be improved.

75. The outcome of the International Conference on Population and Development, the adoption of the Declaration on the Elimination of Violence against Women by the General Assembly at its forty-eighth session, and the decision of the Commission on Human Rights to create the position of the Special Rapporteur on violence against women, are major recent achievements for the protection of women's human rights. At the Fourth World Conference on Women, further international agreement on measures to promote the advancement of women should be reached. Implementation of such agreements should proceed in a coordinated way and be fully integrated in overall development efforts.

76. Three other common goals are outlined in the paragraphs that follow: poverty eradication, preventive and curative development, and African development. Member States are urged to support United Nations leadership in these areas.

Other key goals that can unify the development work of the United Nations funds and programmes range from support for programme country priorities in food security, full employment and education for all, to protecting and regenerating the natural resource base for sustained production.

77. All countries should agree on a global compact to eliminate poverty over a specified period of time.

78. Upcoming conferences, especially the World Summit for Social Development and the Fourth World Conference on Women, can define clear, ambitious and monitorable objectives in the area of poverty eradication, supported by operational strategies adapted to each country's situation. The United Nations should play a direct role in this effort to seek to mobilize action on these objectives by the entire international community.

79. The critical elements for a poverty eradication initiative—such as basic social services, employment generation, food security, drug and transnational crime control, and access to credit, technology, training and markets—should be integrated into a comprehensive operational package.

80. Recent years have witnessed phenomenal growth in the Organization's activities in peace-keeping, refugee assistance and other humanitarian relief. These activities must be complemented by new development initiatives for preventive and curative development.

81. Preventive development is a necessary complement to preventive diplomacy. The United Nations should build state-of-the-art capabilities to act preventively for development, anticipating and responding to crises, natural and man-made, before they occur. As proposed earlier, this should be a new main focus of the work of the Economic and Social Council.

82. A global watch system should be considered to provide early detection of impending humanitarian emergencies and guidelines for preventive action for consideration by the Economic and Social Council. This system would access, build upon and seek to strengthen existing capabilities.

83. A new focus on curative development is required. When the time comes to heal the wounds of a society, demobilize soldiers and reintegrate refugees and internally displaced persons, timely, post-conflict peace-building and development—including reconstruction and rehabilitation—are essential.

84. Special initiatives to give added momentum to development efforts in Africa are urgently required. Of the 47 least developed countries in the world, 33 are in Africa. Africa accounts for just 2 per cent of world trade and only 1.4 per cent of world exports. Economic growth is hampered by external debt problems, by the decrease in external resource flows, by sharply declining terms of trade and by mounting barriers to market access. Desertification poses a severe obstacle to development. And across the continent, the persistence of poverty and widespread unemployment have undermined social confidence and social stability, fuelling conflict and unrest.

85. In the light of Economic and Social Council resolution 1994/38 of 29 July 1994 on the United Nations New Agenda for the Development of Africa in the 1990s, and as suggested in the most recent meeting of the Administrative Committee on Coordination, consideration is being given to setting up a task force of that

Committee to identify major inter-agency initiatives to be taken in support of Africa. The task force would focus on the development of country-level cooperation around specific goals and issues and define the required policy options to galvanize international support for African economic recovery and development.

## C. Operational coordination

86. The various development entities comprising the United Nations have their own organizational cultures, public name recognition and constituencies, and resource mobilization capacities. Moreover, a certain amount of organizational diversity and pluralism can be healthy. Efforts to enhance operational coordination within the United Nations should endeavour to achieve the benefits of a unified system, while preserving the strength of the current approach.

87. Such efforts should be aimed at the following objectives, among others: building a more integrated, efficient and effective framework through which the United Nations can better assist countries in realizing their development objectives, including clearer and more complementary definition of the roles and missions of the various components; eliminating duplication and fragmentation; strengthening leadership and cooperation at country, regional and headquarters levels; strengthening United Nations capabilities in the coordination and delivery of humanitarian assistance, the linking of emergency relief and development, and in the promotion of preventive and curative development; mobilizing analytical and normative capacities and strengthening the role of the Organization in interrelated areas such as trade and access to technology, in support of operational activities; defining the appropriate level—country, region or headquarters—for activity on various issues; integrating the regional commissions with the development work of the Organization as a whole; strengthening the resident coordinator and country-driven approaches; streamlining the delivery capacity of the United Nations through common premises, the programme approach and common programming cycles; and achieving more rapid and aggressive implementation of General Assembly resolutions 44/211 and 47/199, including the country strategy note and other tools, for a more integrated United Nations response to country priorities.

88. In pursuit of these objectives, I intend to convene frequent meetings of all senior officials in the economic and social sector, with the support of the Administrator of UNDP, as a main instrument to improve overall programme coordination and policy coherence within the Organization. The outcome of the work of a strengthened Joint Consultative Group on Policy, focusing on country-level coordination and related issues, should constitute an important input into these senior official meetings.

89. When operational activities for development are undertaken within the context of a peace-keeping mission, which is placed under the command of a special representative, all elements of the United Nations system at all levels that are active in the theatre of operations must come under the command and direction of the special representative. It must be recognized that the special representative has not only a political but also an essential coordinating role in this regard.

## D.  Financing for the future

90. Although better operational coordination and a top-calibre international civil service are essential, the effectiveness of the United Nations operational activities for development will ultimately depend upon financial resources. The most significant difficulty facing the United Nations entities engaged in development work is that they are unable, owing to resource constraints, to mount assistance efforts on a scale commensurate with the challenges they help Member States address.

91. The United Nations is in financial crisis. Reliance on voluntary contributions alone, in light of the expanded development mandate of the Organization, is no longer feasible. To deal with this, a number of principles and proposals have been put forward. It has been recognized that more resources are needed, that mandates and the resources provided for them must be in a sound relationship, and that predictability in funding is essential so that operations are not undermined in the midst of performance. It has been suggested that a system of assessed, negotiated and voluntary contributions provides the most logical and appropriate means of financing the United Nations as it permits Governments to maintain proper control over the United Nations' budget and its agenda. It has further been suggested that the Organization should review its voluntarily funded programmes, especially those that are financed through trust funds, to eliminate unnecessary and duplicative expenditures. Other measures that may be considered include a fee on speculative international financial transactions, a levy on fossil fuel use (or its resulting pollution) in all countries, earmarking a small portion of the anticipated decline in world military expenditures, utilizing some of the resources that could be released through the elimination of unnecessary subsidies, and utilizing resources generated from a stamp tax on international travel and travel documents.

## V.  CONCLUSION

92. The battle for people-centred and sustainable development will be won or lost not in the corridors of Governments, but in every hamlet and home, in every village and town, in the daily enterprise of every member of the global community and every institution of civil society. The Charter of the United Nations begins with a pledge by 'We, the Peoples . . .'. It is the people, on whose behalf we all act, who are the true custodians of the emerging new vision of development. It is for them that we must work to achieve a new framework for development cooperation and the revitalization of the United Nations system.

## ANNEX

### AN AGENDA FOR DEVELOPMENT:
### KEY RECOMMENDATIONS

Development must be driven by national priorities. Through a partnership involving government, civil society and strong private enterprise sectors, national capacities to plan, manage and implement development programmes must be built.

External macroeconomics forces must support development objectives. Developing countries must be provided equitable access to expanding global opportunities in trade, technology, investment and information.

Development assistance must be brought closer to the agreed targets. New agreements should be reached on plausible interim goals for steady increases in official development assistance and a larger share should be allocated to the development work of the United Nations.

An adequate and permanent reduction in the stock of debt for countries in debt crisis undertaking economic reforms should be made. The debts of the least developed and poorest countries should be cancelled outright.

Countries in transition to market economies should be supported by additional resources from the international community.

Further progress must be made on reducing military expenditures. Hearings by the President of the General Assembly on the connection between disarmament and development may be considered.

A common framework should be developed to implement goals established in United Nations conferences. Goals and targets should be synthesized, costed, prioritized and placed in a reasonable time perspective for implementation.

The fiftieth session of the General Assembly should focus the attention of the international community on forging a new framework for development co-operation. In that context, the desirability of an international conference on the financing of development should also be considered.

An effective multilateral development system requires that the unique role of the United Nations be recognized and supported: its universality, unmatched network, and capacity to build consensus, inform policy, and help rationalize public and private development efforts.

The General Assembly should identify critical issues and serve as a forum for emerging problems that fall between the purviews of more narrowly focused institutions in development, trade and finance. It should focus on requirements for a more effective management of global interdependence and the promotion of an integrated approach to economic and social development.

The early part of General Assembly sessions, with high-level representatives present, could focus dialogue on development issues in the plenary sessions. Special sessions on major aspects of international cooperation for development should be considered.

The Economic and Social Council must be revitalized to fulfil the role envisaged in the Charter. A revitalized Council should:

- bring specialized agencies into a closer working relationship with the United Nations; serve as an international development assistance review committee, and function as a unifying governing entity to which the governing bodies of the United Nations funds and programmes would relate; and identify impending humanitarian emergencies and provide policy guidelines for coordinated initiatives.

Consideration should be given to an expanded bureau of the Council, meeting intersessionally, to facilitate agreement on issues for endorsement by the Council.

Greater cooperation between the United Nations and the Bretton Woods institutions should be pursued through joint initiatives, such as:

- poverty reduction strategies, sustainable energy development, post-conflict peace-building, capacity-building and improved public sector management.

The Organization and the Bretton Woods institutions should work together with concerned countries on the components of the policy dialogue and other initiatives that must accompany structural adjustment programmes. Governments' capacities to lead the dialogue process must be reinforced, with the support of the Resident Coordinator. Greater complementarity of country documents should be pursued.

The contributions of technical and sectoral agencies should be integrated more fully in development strategies, in support of comprehensive, sustainable development.

The integrity and comprehensive nature of the United Nations system must be maintained. Bringing new organizations such as the World Trade Organization into relationship with the United Nations deserves priority attention.

Members of the Administrative Committee on Coordination, under the chairmanship of the Secretary-General, will pursue further measures to strengthen the coherence and impact of the work of the United Nations system.

Further measures to improve governance, management, funding, and allocation of responsibilities, coordination and staffing, must build upon reform initiatives undertaken to date, including changes set in motion by General Assembly resolutions 44/211 and 47/199, as well as other restructuring and revitalization efforts.

The empowerment of women, poverty eradication, preventive and curative development, and special initiatives to support African development, are crucial areas in which the United Nations should provide leadership and focus action. Other key goals which can unify the development work of the United Nations include food, security, full employment, education for all, and protecting and regenerating the natural resource base for sustained production.

Efforts to enhance operational coordination should endeavour to achieve the benefits of a unified system, while preserving the strength of the current approach. Among the objectives should be:

- a more integrated, efficient, and effective structure for United Nations development assistance; strengthening United Nations capabilities in the coordination and delivery of humanitarian assistance; mobilizing the analytical role of the Organization in interrelated areas such as trade and access to technology in support of operations; integrating the regional commissions with the development work of the Organization; strengthening the Resident Coordinator and country-driven approaches for a more integrated United Nations response to country priorities.

To these ends, the Secretary-General will convene frequent meetings of all senior officials for the economic and social sectors with the support of the Administrator of UNDP.

In peace-keeping operations, all elements of the United Nations system at all levels undertaking development activities as part of the mission must come under the command and direction of the Special Representative in command of that mission.

United Nations development efforts must be supported by adequate financial resources. Reliance on voluntary contributions alone, in light of the expanded development mandate of the Organization, is no longer feasible.

Three principles are fundamental: more resources are needed; mandates and the resources provided for them must be in a sound relationship; and predictability in funding is essential so that operations are not undermined in the midst of performance.

## 99. COPENHAGEN DECLARATION ON SOCIAL DEVELOPMENT, 1995

For text see 'Report of the World Summit for Social Development', Copenhagen, 6–12 March 1995, UN doc. A/CONF.166/9, 19 April 1995. See also UNGA Resolution 50/161, 22 December 1995, 'Implementation of the Outcome of the World Summit for Social Development' (adopted without a vote).

*TEXT*

1. For the first time in history, at the invitation of the United Nations, we gather as heads of State and Government to recognize the significance of social development and human well-being for all and to give to these goals the highest priority both now and into the twenty-first century.

2. We acknowledge that the people of the world have shown in different ways an urgent need to address profound social problems, especially poverty, unemployment and social exclusion, that affect every country. It is our task to address both their underlying and structural causes and their distressing consequences in order to reduce uncertainty and insecurity in the life of people.

3. We acknowledge that our societies must respond more effectively to the material and spiritual needs of individuals, their families and the communities in which they live throughout our diverse countries and regions. We must do so not only as a matter of urgency but also as a matter of sustained and unshakeable commitment through the years ahead.

4. We are convinced that democracy and transparent and accountable governance and administration in all sectors of society are indispensable foundations for the realization of social and people-centred sustainable development.

5. We share the conviction that social development and social justice are indispensable for the achievement and maintenance of peace and security within and among our nations. In turn, social development and social justice cannot be attained in the absence of peace and security or in the absence of respect for all human rights and fundamental freedoms. This essential interdependence was recognized 50 years ago in the Charter of the United Nations and has since grown ever stronger.

6. We are deeply convinced that economic development, social development and environmental protection are interdependent and mutually reinforcing components of sustainable development, which is the framework for our efforts to achieve a higher quality of life for all people. Equitable social development that recognizes empowering the poor to utilize environmental resources sustainably is a necessary foundation for sustainable development. We also recognize that broad-based and sustained economic growth in the context of sustainable development is necessary to sustain social development and social justice.

7. We recognize, therefore, that social development is central to the needs and

aspirations of people throughout the world and to the responsibilities of Governments and all sectors of civil society. We affirm that, in both economic and social terms, the most productive policies and investments are those that empower people to maximize their capacities, resources and opportunities. We acknowledge that social and economic development cannot be secured in a sustainable way without the full participation of women and that equality and equity between women and men is a priority for the international community and as such must be at the centre of economic and social development.

8. We acknowledge that people are at the centre of our concerns for sustainable development and that they are entitled to a healthy and productive life in harmony with the environment.

9. We gather here to commit ourselves, our Governments and our nations to enhancing social development throughout the world so that all men and women, especially those living in poverty, may exercise the rights, utilize the resources and share the responsibilities that enable them to lead satisfying lives and to contribute to the well-being of their families, their communities and humankind. To support and promote these efforts must be the overriding goals of the international community, especially with respect to people suffering from poverty, unemployment and social exclusion.

10. We make this solemn commitment on the eve of the fiftieth anniversary of the United Nations, with a determination to capture the unique possibilities offered by the end of the cold war to promote social development and social justice. We reaffirm and are guided by the principles of the Charter of the United Nations and by agreements reached at relevant international conferences, including the World Summit for Children, held at New York in 1990;[1] the United Nations Conference on Environment and Development, held at Rio de Janeiro in 1992;[2] the World Conference on Human Rights, held at Vienna in 1993;[3] the Global Conference on the Sustainable Development of Small Island Developing States, held at Bridgetown, Barbados in 1994;[4] and the International Conference on Population and Development, held at Cairo in 1994.[5] By this Summit we launch a new commitment to social development in each of our countries and a new era of international cooperation between Governments and peoples based on a spirit of partnership that puts the needs, rights and aspirations of people at the centre of our decisions and joint actions.

11. We gather here in Copenhagen in a Summit of hope, commitment and action. We gather with full awareness of the difficulty of the tasks that lie ahead but with a conviction that major progress can be achieved, must be achieved and will be achieved.

[1] See *First Call for Children*, New York, United Nations Children's Fund, 1990.

[2] See 'Report of the United Nations Conference on Environment and Development', Rio de Janeiro, 3–14 June 1992, vol. I, Resolutions adopted by the Conference (United Nations publication, Sales No. E.93.I.8 and corrigenda).

[3] See 'Report of the World Conference on Human Rights', Vienna, 14–25 June 1993: A/CONF.157/24 (Part I).

[4] See 'Report of the Global Conference on the Sustainable Development of Small Island Developing States', Bridgetown, Barbados, 25 April-6 May 1994: United Nations publication, Sales No. E.94.I.18 and corrigenda.

[5] See 'Report of the International Conference on Population and Development', Cairo, 5–13 September 1994: A/CONF.171/13 and Add.1.

12. We commit ourselves to this Declaration and Programme of Action for enhancing social development and ensuring human well-being for all throughout the world now and into the twenty-first century. We invite all people in all countries and in all walks of life, as well as the international community, to join us in our common cause.

## A. Current social situation and reasons for convening the Summit

13. We are witnessing in countries throughout the world the expansion of prosperity for some, unfortunately accompanied by an expansion of unspeakable poverty for others. This glaring contradiction is unacceptable and needs to be corrected through urgent actions.

14. Globalization, which is a consequence of increased human mobility, enhanced communications, greatly increased trade and capital flows, and technological developments, opens new opportunities for sustained economic growth and development of the world economy, particularly in developing countries. Globalization also permits countries to share experiences and to learn from one another's achievements and difficulties, and promotes a cross-fertilization of ideals, cultural values and aspirations. At the same time, the rapid processes of change and adjustment have been accompanied by intensified poverty, unemployment and social disintegration. Threats to human well-being, such as environmental risks, have also been globalized. Furthermore, the global transformations of the world economy are profoundly changing the parameters of social development in all countries. The challenge is how to manage these processes and threats so as to enhance their benefits and mitigate their negative effects upon people.

15. There has been progress in some areas of social and economic development:

(a) The global wealth of nations has multiplied sevenfold in the past 50 years and international trade has grown even more dramatically;

(b) Life expectancy, literacy and primary education, and access to basic health care, including family planning, have increased in the majority of countries and average infant mortality has been reduced, including in developing countries;

(c) Democratic pluralism, democratic institutions and fundamental civil liberties have expanded. Decolonization efforts have achieved much progress, while the elimination of apartheid is a historic achievement.

16. Yet we recognize that far too many people, particularly women and children, are vulnerable to stress and deprivation. Poverty, unemployment and social disintegration too often result in isolation, marginalization and violence. The insecurity that many people, in particular vulnerable people, face about the future—their own and their children's—is intensifying:

(a) Within many societies, both in developed and developing countries, the gap between rich and poor has increased. Furthermore, despite the fact that some developing countries are growing rapidly the gap between developed and many developing countries, particularly the least developed countries, has widened;

(b) More than one billion people in the world live in abject poverty, most of whom go hungry every day. A large proportion, the majority of whom are women, have very limited access to income, resources, education, health care or nutrition, particularly in Africa and the least developed countries;

(c) There are also serious social problems of a different nature and magnitude in countries with economies in transition and countries experiencing fundamental political, economic and social transformations;

(d) The major cause of the continued deterioration of the global environment is the unsustainable pattern of consumption and production, particularly in industrialized countries, which is a matter of grave concern, aggravating poverty and imbalances;

(e) Continued growth in the world's population, its structure and distribution, and its relationship with poverty and social and gender inequality challenge the adaptive capacities of Governments, individuals, social institutions and the natural environment;

(f) Over 120 million people world wide are officially unemployed and many more are underemployed. Too many young people, including those with formal education, have little hope of finding productive work;

(g) More women than men live in absolute poverty and the imbalance continues to grow, with serious consequences for women and their children. Women carry a disproportionate share of the problems of coping with poverty, social disintegration, unemployment, environmental degradation and the effects of war;

(h) One of the world's largest minorities, more than 1 in 10, are people with disabilities, who are too often forced into poverty, unemployment and social isolation. In addition, in all countries older persons may be particularly vulnerable to social exclusion, poverty and marginalization;

(i) Millions of people world wide are refugees or internally displaced persons. The tragic social consequences have a critical effect on the social stability and development of their home countries, their host countries and their respective regions.

17. While these problems are global in character and affect all countries, we clearly acknowledge that the situation of most developing countries, and particularly of Africa and the least developed countries, is critical and requires special attention and action. We also acknowledge that these countries, which are undergoing fundamental political, economic and social transformation, including countries in the process of consolidating peace and democracy, require the support of the international community.

18. Countries with economies in transition, which are also undergoing fundamental political, economic and social transformation, require the support of the international community as well.

19. Other countries that are undergoing fundamental political, economic and social transformation require the support of the international community as well.

20. The goals and objectives of social development require continuous efforts to reduce and eliminate major sources of social distress and instability for the family and for society. We pledge to place particular focus on and give priority attention to the fight against the world-wide conditions that pose severe threats to the health, safety, peace, security and well-being of our people. Among these conditions are

chronic hunger; malnutrition; illicit drug problems; organized crime; corruption; foreign occupation; armed conflicts; illicit arms trafficking, terrorism, intolerance and incitement to racial, ethnic, religious and other hatreds; xenophobia; and endemic, communicable and chronic diseases. To this end, coordination and cooperation at the national level and especially at the regional and international levels should be further strengthened.

21. In this context, the negative impact on development of excessive military expenditures, the arms trade, and investment for arms production and acquisition must be addressed.

22. Communicable diseases constitute a serious health problem in all countries and are a major cause of death globally; in many cases, their incidence is increasing. These diseases are a hindrance to social development and are often the cause of poverty and social exclusion. The prevention, treatment and control of these diseases, covering a spectrum from tuberculosis and malaria to the human immunodeficiency virus/acquired immunodeficiency syndrome (HIV/AIDS), must be given the highest priority.

23. We can continue to hold the trust of the people of the world only if we make their needs our priority. We know that poverty, lack of productive employment and social disintegration are an offence to human dignity. We also know that they are negatively reinforcing and represent a waste of human resources and a manifestation of ineffectiveness in the functioning of markets and economic and social institutions and processes.

24. Our challenge is to establish a people-centred framework for social development to guide us now and in the future, to build a culture of cooperation and partnership, and to respond to the immediate needs of those who are most affected by human distress. We are determined to meet this challenge and promote social development throughout the world.

## B. PRINCIPLES AND GOALS

25. We heads of State and Government are committed to a political, economic, ethical and spiritual vision for social development that is based on human dignity, human rights, equality, respect, peace, democracy, mutual responsibility and cooperation, and full respect for the various religious and ethical values and cultural backgrounds of people. Accordingly, we will give the highest priority in national, regional and international policies an actions to the promotion of social progress, justice and the betterment of the human condition, based on full participation by all.

26. To this end, we will create a framework for action to:

(a) Place people at the centre of development and direct our economies to meet human needs more effectively;

(b) Fulfil our responsibility for present and future generations by ensuring equity among generations and protecting the integrity and sustainable use of our environment;

(c) Recognize that, while social development is a national responsibility, it cannot be successfully achieved without the collective commitment and efforts of the international community;

(d) Integrate economic, cultural and social policies so that they become mutually supportive, and acknowledge the interdependence of public and private spheres of activity;

(e) Recognize that the achievement of sustained social development requires sound, broadly based economic policies;

(f) Promote democracy, human dignity, social justice and solidarity at the national, regional and international levels; ensure tolerance, non-violence, pluralism and non-discrimination, with full respect for diversity within and among societies;

(g) Promote the equitable distribution of income and greater access to resources through equity and equality of opportunity for all;

(h) Recognize the family as the basic unit of society, and acknowledge that it plays a key role in social development and as such should be strengthened, with attention to the rights, capabilities and responsibilities of its members. In different cultural, political and social systems various forms of family exist. It is entitled to receive comprehensive protection and support;

(i) Ensure that disadvantaged and vulnerable persons and groups are included in social development, and that society acknowledges and responds to the consequences of disability by securing the legal rights of the individual and by making the physical and social environment accessible;

(j) Promote universal respect for, and observance and protection of, all human rights and fundamental freedoms for all, including the right to development; promote the effective exercise of rights and the discharge of responsibilities at all levels of society; promote equality and equity between women and men; protect the rights of children and youth; and promote the strengthening of social integration and civil society;

(k) Reaffirm the right of self-determination of all peoples, in particular of peoples under colonial or other forms of alien domination or foreign occupation, and the importance of the effective realization of this right, as enunciated, inter alia, in the Vienna Declaration and Programme of Action[6] adopted at the World Conference on Human Rights;

(l) Support progress and security for people and communities whereby every member of society is enabled to satisfy his or her basic human needs and to realize his or her personal dignity, safety and creativity;

(m) Recognize and support indigenous people in their pursuit of economic and social development, with full respect for their identity, traditions, forms of social organization and cultural values;

(n) Underline the importance of transparent and accountable governance and administration in all public and private national and international institutions;

(o) Recognize that empowering people, particularly women, to strengthen their own capacities is a main objective of development and its principal resource. Empowerment requires the full participation of people in the formulation, implementation and evaluation of decisions determining the functioning and well-being of our societies;

[6] Above note 3.

(p) Assert the universality of social development and outline a new and strengthened approach to social development, with a renewed impetus for international cooperation and partnership;

(q) Improve the possibility of older persons achieving a better life;

(r) Recognize that the new information technologies and new approaches to access to and use of technologies by people living in poverty can help in fulfilling social development goals; and therefore recognize the need to facilitate access to such technologies;

(s) Strengthen policies and programmes that improve, ensure and broaden the participation of women in all spheres of political, economic, social and cultural life, as equal partners, and improve their access to all resources needed for the full exercise of their fundamental rights;

(t) Create the political, legal, material and social conditions that allow for the voluntary repatriation of refugees in safety and dignity to their countries of origin, and the voluntary and safe return of internally displaced persons to their places of origin and their smooth reintegration into their societies;

(u) Emphasize the importance of the return of all prisoners of war, persons missing in action and hostages to their families, in accordance with international conventions, in order to reach full social development.

27. We acknowledge that it is the primary responsibility of States to attain these goals. We also acknowledge that these goals cannot be achieved by States alone. The international community, the United Nations, the multilateral financial institutions, all regional organizations and local authorities, and all actors of civil society need to positively contribute their own share of efforts and resources in order to reduce inequalities among people and narrow the gap between developed and developing countries in a global effort to reduce social tensions, and to create greater social and economic stability and security. Radical political, social and economic changes in the countries with economies in transition have been accompanied by a deterioration in their economic and social situation. We invite all people to express their personal commitment to enhancing the human condition through concrete actions in their own fields of activities and through assuming specific civic responsibilities.

## C. COMMITMENTS

28. Our global drive for social development and the recommendations for action contained in the Programme of Action are made in a spirit of consensus and international cooperation, in full conformity with the purposes and principles of the Charter of the United Nations, recognizing that the formulation and implementation of strategies, policies, programmes and actions for social development are the responsibility of each country and should take into account the economic, social and environmental diversity of conditions in each country, with full respect for the various religious and ethical values, cultural backgrounds and philosophical convictions of its people, and in conformity with all human rights and fundamental freedoms. In this context, international cooperation is essential for the full implementation of social development programmes and actions.

29. On the basis of our common pursuit of social development, which aims at social justice, solidarity, harmony and equality within and among countries, with full respect for national sovereignty and territorial integrity, as well as policy objectives, development priorities and religious and cultural diversity, and full respect for all human rights and fundamental freedoms, we launch a global drive for social progress and development embodied in the following commitments.

## COMMITMENT 1

We commit ourselves to creating an economic, political, social, cultural and legal environment that will enable people to achieve social development.
     To this end, at the national level, we will:

(a) Provide a stable legal framework, in accordance with our constitutions, laws and procedures, and consistent with international law and obligations, which includes and promotes equality and equity between women and men, full respect for all human rights and fundamental freedoms and the rule of law, access to justice, the elimination of all forms of discrimination, transparent and accountable governance and administration and the encouragement of partnership with free and representative organizations of civil society;

(b) Create an enabling economic environment aimed at promoting more equitable access for all to income, resources and social services;

(c) Reinforce, as appropriate, the means and capacities for people to participate in the formulation and implementation of social and economic policies and programmes through decentralization, open management of public institutions and strengthening the abilities and opportunities of civil society and local communities to develop their own organizations, resources and activities;

(d) Reinforce peace by promoting tolerance, non-violence and respect for diversity, and by settling disputes by peaceful means;

(e) Promote dynamic, open, free markets, while recognizing the need to intervene in markets, to the extent necessary, to prevent or counteract market failure, promote stability and long-term investment, ensure fair competition and ethical conduct, and harmonize economic and social development, including the development and implementation of appropriate programmes that would entitle and enable people living in poverty and the disadvantaged, especially women, to participate fully and productively in the economy and society;

(f) Reaffirm, promote and strive to ensure the realization of the rights set out in relevant international instruments and declarations, such as the Universal Declaration of Human Rights,[7] the Covenant on Economic, Social and Cultural Rights[8] and the Declaration on the Right to Development,[9] including those relating to education, food, shelter, employment, health and information, particularly in order to assist people living in poverty;

(g) Create the comprehensive conditions to allow for the voluntary repatriation of refugees in safety and dignity to their countries of origin, and the voluntary and

[7] General Assembly resolution 217 A (III).
[8] General Assembly resolution 2200 A (XXI), annex.
[9] General Assembly resolution 41/128, annex.

safe return of internally displaced persons to their places of origin and their smooth reintegration into their societies.

At the international level, we will:

(h) Promote international peace and security and make and support all efforts to settle international disputes by peaceful means in accordance with the Charter of the United Nations;

(i) Strengthen international cooperation for achieving social development;

(j) Promote and implement policies to create a supportive external economic environment, through, inter alia, cooperation in the formulation and implementation of macroeconomic policies, trade liberalization, mobilization and/or provision of new and additional financial resources that are both adequate and predictable and mobilized in a way that maximizes the availability of such resources for sustainable development, using all available funding sources and mechanisms, enhanced financial stability, and more equitable access of developing countries to global markets, productive investments and technologies and appropriate knowledge, with due consideration to the needs of countries with economies in transition;

(k) Strive to ensure that international agreements relating to trade, investment, technology, debt and official development assistance are implemented in a manner that promotes social development;

(l) Support, particularly through technical and financial cooperation, the efforts of developing countries to achieve rapid, broadly based sustainable development. Particular consideration should be given to the special needs of small island and land-locked developing countries and the least developed countries;

(m) Support, through appropriate international cooperation, the efforts of countries with economies in transition to achieve rapid broadly based sustainable development;

(n) Reaffirm and promote all human rights, which are universal, indivisible, interdependent and interrelated, including the right to development as a universal and inalienable right and an integral part of fundamental human rights, and strive to ensure that they are respected, protected and observed.

## COMMITMENT 2

We commit ourselves to the goal of eradicating poverty in the world, through decisive national actions and international cooperation, as an ethical, social, political and economic imperative of humankind.

To this end, at the national level, in partnership with all actors of civil society and in the context of a multidimensional and integrated approach, we will:

(a) Formulate or strengthen, as a matter of urgency, and preferably by the year 1996, the International Year for the Eradication of Poverty,[10] national policies and strategies geared to substantially reducing overall poverty in the shortest possible time, reducing inequalities and eradicating absolute poverty by a target date to be specified by each country in its national context;

(b) Focus our efforts and policies to address the root causes of poverty and to

---

[10] See General Assembly resolution 48/183.

provide for the basic needs of all. These efforts should include the elimination of hunger and malnutrition; the provision of food security, education, employment and livelihood, primary health-care services including reproductive health care, safe drinking water and sanitation, and adequate shelter; and participation in social and cultural life. Special priority will be given to the needs and rights of women and children, who often bear the greatest burden of poverty, and to the needs of vulnerable and disadvantaged groups and persons;

(c) Ensure that people living in poverty have access to productive resources, including credit, land, education and training, technology, knowledge and information, as well as to public services, and participate in decision-making on a policy and regulatory environment that would enable them to benefit from expanding employment and economic opportunities;

(d) Develop and implement policies to ensure that all people have adequate economic and social protection during unemployment, ill health, maternity, child-rearing, widowhood, disability and old age;

(e) Ensure that national budgets and policies are oriented, as necessary, to meeting basic needs, reducing inequalities and targeting poverty, as a strategic objective;

(f) Seek to reduce inequalities, increase opportunities and access to resources and income, and remove any political, legal, economic and social factors and constraints that foster and sustain inequality.

At the international level, we will:

(g) Strive to ensure that the international community and international organizations, particularly the multilateral financial institutions, assist developing countries and all countries in need in their efforts to achieve our overall goal of eradicating poverty and ensuring basic social protection;

(h) Encourage all international donors and multilateral development banks to support policies and programmes for the attainment, in a sustained manner, of the specific efforts of the developing countries and all countries in need relating to people-centred sustainable development and to meeting basic needs for all; to assess their existing programmes in consultation with the concerned developing countries to ensure the achievement of the agreed programme objectives; and to seek to ensure that their own policies and programmes will advance the attainment of agreed development goals that focus on meeting basic needs for all and eradicating absolute poverty. Efforts should be made to ensure that participation by the people concerned is an integral part of such programmes;

(i) Focus attention on and support the special needs of countries and regions in which there are substantial concentrations of people living in poverty, in particular in South Asia, and which therefore face serious difficulties in achieving social and economic development.

## COMMITMENT 3

We commit ourselves to promoting the goal of full employment as a basic priority of our economic and social policies, and to enabling all men and women to attain secure and sustainable livelihoods through freely chosen productive employment and work.

To this end, at the national level, we will:

(a) Put the creation of employment, the reduction of unemployment and the promotion of appropriately and adequately remunerated employment at the centre of strategies and policies of Governments, with full respect for workers' rights and with the participation of employers, workers and their respective organizations, giving special attention to the problems of structural, long-term unemployment and underemployment of youth, women, people with disabilities, and all other disadvantaged groups and individuals;

(b) Develop policies to expand work opportunities and productivity in both rural and urban sectors by achieving economic growth, investing in human resource development, promoting technologies that generate productive employment, and encouraging self-employment, entrepreneurship, and small and medium-sized enterprises;

(c) Improve access to land, credit, information, infrastructure and other productive resources for small and micro-enterprises, including those in the informal sector, with particular emphasis on the disadvantaged sectors of society;

(d) Develop policies to ensure that workers and employers have the education, information and training needed to adapt to changing economic conditions, technologies and labour markets;

(e) Explore innovative options for employment creation and seek new approaches to generating income and purchasing power;

(f) Foster policies that enable people to combine their paid work with their family responsibilities;

(g) Pay particular attention to women's access to employment, the protection of their position in the labour market and the promotion of equal treatment of women and men, in particular with respect to pay;

(h) Take due account of the importance of the informal sector in our employment development strategies with a view to increasing its contribution to the eradication of poverty and to social integration in developing countries, and to strengthening its linkages with the formal economy;

(i) Pursue the goal of ensuring quality jobs, and safeguard the basic rights and interests of workers and to this end, freely promote respect for relevant International Labour Organization conventions, including those on the prohibition of forced and child labour, the freedom of association, the right to organize and bargain collectively, and the principle of non-discrimination.

At the international level, we will:

(j) Ensure that migrant workers benefit from the protections provided by relevant national and international instruments, take concrete and effective measures against the exploitation of migrant workers, and encourage all countries to consider the ratification and full implementation of the relevant international instruments on migrant workers;

(k) Foster international cooperation in macroeconomic policies, liberalization of trade and investment so as to promote sustained economic growth and the creation of employment, and exchange experiences on successful policies and programmes aimed at increasing employment and reducing unemployment.

## COMMITMENT 4

We commit ourselves to promoting social integration by fostering societies that are stable, safe and just and that are based on the promotion and protection of all human rights, as well as on non-discrimination, tolerance, respect for diversity, equality of opportunity, solidarity, security, and participation of all people, including disadvantaged and vulnerable groups and persons.

To this end, at the national level, we will:

(a) Promote respect for democracy, the rule of law, pluralism and diversity, tolerance and responsibility, non-violence and solidarity by encouraging educational systems, communication media and local communities and organizations to raise people's understanding and awareness of all aspects of social integration;

(b) Formulate or strengthen policies and strategies geared to the elimination of discrimination in all its forms and the achievement of social integration based on equality and respect for human dignity;

(c) Promote access for all to education, information, technology and know-how as essential means for enhancing communication and participation in civil, political, economic, social and cultural life, and ensure respect for civil, political, economic, social and cultural rights;

(d) Ensure the protection and full integration into the economy and society of disadvantaged and vulnerable groups and persons;

(e) Formulate or strengthen measures to ensure respect for and protection of the human rights of migrants, migrant workers and their families, to eliminate the increasing acts of racism and xenophobia in sectors of many societies, and to promote greater harmony and tolerance in all societies;

(f) Recognize and respect the right of indigenous people to maintain and develop their identity, culture and interests, support their aspirations for social justice and provide an environment that enables them to participate in the social, economic and political life of their country;

(g) Foster the social protection and full integration into the economy and society of veterans, including veterans and victims of the Second World War and other wars;

(h) Acknowledge and encourage the contribution of people of all age groups as equally and vitally important for the building of a harmonious society, and foster dialogue between generations in all parts of society;

(i) Recognize and respect cultural, ethnic and religious diversity, promote and protect the rights of persons belonging to national, ethnic, religious or linguistic minorities, and take measures to facilitate their full participation in all aspects of the political, economic, social, religious and cultural life of their societies and in the economic progress and social development of their countries;

(j) Strengthen the ability of local communities and groups with common concerns to develop their own organizations and resources and to propose policies relating to social development, including through the activities of non-governmental organizations;

(k) Strengthen institutions that enhance social integration, recognizing the central role of the family and providing it with an environment that assures its protection and support. In different cultural, political and social systems, various forms of the family exist;

(l) Address the problems of crime, violence and illicit drugs as factors of social disintegration.

At the international level, we will:

(m) Encourage the ratification of, the avoidance as far as possible of the resort to reservations to, and the implementation of international instruments and adherence to internationally recognized declarations relevant to the elimination of discrimination and the promotion and protection of all human rights;

(n) Further enhance international mechanisms for the provision of humanitarian and financial assistance to refugees and host countries and promote appropriate shared responsibility;

(o) Promote international cooperation and partnership on the basis of equality, mutual respect and mutual benefit.

## COMMITMENT 5

We commit ourselves to promoting full respect for human dignity and to achieving equality and equity between women and men, and to recognizing and enhancing the participation and leadership roles of women in political, civil, economic, social and cultural life and in development.

To this end, at the national level, we will:

(a) Promote changes in attitudes, structures, policies, laws and practices in order to eliminate all obstacles to human dignity, equality and equity in the family and in society, and promote full and equal participation of urban and rural women and women with disabilities in social, economic and political life, including in the formulation, implementation and follow-up of public policies and programmes;

(b) Establish structures, policies, objectives and measurable goals to ensure gender balance and equity in decision-making processes at all levels, broaden women's political, economic, social and cultural opportunities and independence, and support the empowerment of women, including through their various organizations, especially those of indigenous women, those at the grass-roots level, and those of poverty-stricken communities, including through affirmative action, where necessary, and also through measures to integrate a gender perspective in the design and implementation of economic and social policies;

(c) Promote full and equal access of women to literacy, education and training, and remove all obstacles to their access to credit and other productive resources and to their ability to buy, hold and sell property and land equally with men;

(d) Take appropriate measures to ensure, on the basis of equality of men and women, universal access to the widest range of health-care services, including those relating to reproductive health care, consistent with the Programme of Action of the International Conference on Population and Development;[11]

(e) Remove the remaining restrictions on women's rights to own land, inherit property or borrow money, and ensure women's equal right to work;

(f) Establish policies, objectives and goals that enhance the equality of status, welfare and opportunity of the girl child, especially in regard to health, nutrition, literacy and education, recognizing that gender discrimination starts at the earliest stages of life;

(g) Promote equal partnership between women and men in family and community life and society, emphasize the shared responsibility of men and women in the care

[11] Above, note 5.

of children and support for older family members, and emphasize men's shared responsibility and promote their active involvement in responsible parenthood and responsible sexual and reproductive behaviour;

(h) Take effective measures, including through the enactment and enforcement of laws, and implement policies to combat and eliminate all forms of discrimination, exploitation, abuse and violence against women and girl children, in accordance with relevant international instruments and declarations;

(i) Promote and protect the full and equal enjoyment by women of all human rights and fundamental freedoms;

(j) Formulate or strengthen policies and practices to ensure that women are enabled to participate fully in paid work and in employment through such measures as positive action, education, training, appropriate protection under labour legislation, and facilitating the provision of quality child care and other support services.

At the international level, we will:

(k) Promote and protect women's human rights and encourage the ratification of, if possible by the year 2000, the avoidance, as far as possible, of the resort to reservations to, and the implementation of the provisions of the Convention on the Elimination of All Forms of Discrimination against Women[12] and other relevant instruments, as well as the implementation of the Nairobi Forward-looking Strategies for the Advancement of Women,[13] the Geneva Declaration for Rural Women,[14] and the Programme of Action of the International Conference on Population and Development;

(l) Give specific attention to the preparations for the Fourth World Conference on Women, to be held at Beijing in September 1995, and to the implementation and follow-up of the conclusions of that Conference;

(m) Promote international cooperation to assist developing countries, at their request, in their efforts to achieve equality and equity and the empowerment of women;

(n) Devise suitable means to recognize and make visible the full extent of the work of women and all their contributions to the national economy, including contributions in the unremunerated and domestic sectors.

## COMMITMENT 6

We commit ourselves to promoting and attaining the goals of universal and equitable access to quality education, the highest attainable standard of physical and mental health, and the access of all to primary health care, making particular efforts to rectify inequalities relating to social conditions and without distinction as to race, national origin, gender, age or disability; respecting and promoting our common and particular cultures; striving to strengthen the role of culture in development; preserving the essential bases of people-centred sustainable development; and contributing to the full development of human resources and to social

[12] General Assembly resolution 34/180, annex.
[13] 'Report of the World Conference to Review and Appraise the Achievements of the United Nations Decade for Women: Equality, Development and Peace', Nairobi, 15–26 July 1985: United Nations publication, Sales No. E.85.IV.10, chap. I, sect. A.
[14] A/47/308, annex.

development. The purpose of these activities is to eradicate poverty, promote full and productive employment and foster social integration.

To this end, at the national level, we will:

(a) Formulate and strengthen time-bound national strategies for the eradication of illiteracy and universalization of basic education, which includes early childhood education, primary education and education for the illiterate, in all communities, in particular for the introduction, if possible, of national languages in the educational system and by support of the various means of non-formal education, striving to attain the highest possible standard of learning;

(b) Emphasize lifelong learning by seeking to improve the quality of education to ensure that people of all ages are provided with useful knowledge, reasoning ability, skills, and the ethical and social values required to develop their full capacities in health and dignity and to participate fully in the social, economic and political process of development. In this regard, women and girls should be considered a priority group;

(c) Ensure that children, particularly girls, enjoy their rights and promote the exercise of those rights by making education, adequate nutrition and health care accessible to them, consistent with the Convention on the Rights of the Child,[15] and recognizing the rights, duties and responsibilities of parents and other persons legally responsible for children;

(d) Take appropriate and affirmative steps to enable all children and adolescents to attend and complete school and to close the gender gap in primary, secondary, vocational and higher education;

(e) Ensure full and equal access to education for girls and women, recognizing that investing in women's education is the key element in achieving social equality, higher productivity and social returns in terms of health, lower infant mortality and the reduced need for high fertility;

(f) Ensure equal educational opportunities at all levels for children, youth and adults with disabilities, in integrated settings, taking full account of individual differences and situations;

(g) Recognize and support the right of indigenous people to education in a manner that is responsive to their specific needs, aspirations and cultures, and ensure their full access to health care;

(h) Develop specific educational policies, with gender perspective, and design appropriate mechanisms at all levels of society in order to accelerate the conversion of general and specific information available world wide into knowledge, and the conversion of that knowledge into creativity, increased productive capacity and active participation in society;

(i) Strengthen the links between labour market and education policies, realizing that education and vocational training are vital elements in job creation and in combatting unemployment and social exclusion in our societies, and emphasize the role of higher education and scientific research in all plans of social development;

(j) Develop broad-based education programmes that promote and strengthen respect for all human rights and fundamental freedoms, including the right to development, promote the values of tolerance, responsibility and respect for the

[15] General Assembly resolution 44/25, annex.

diversity and rights of others, and provide training in peaceful conflict resolution, in recognition of the United Nations Decade for Human Rights Education (1995–2005);[16]

(k) Focus on learning acquisition and outcome, broaden the means and scope of basic education, enhance the environment for learning and strengthen partnerships among Governments, non-governmental organizations, the private sector, local communities, religious groups and families to achieve the goal of education for all;

(l) Establish or strengthen both school-based and community-based health education programmes for children, adolescents and adults, with special attention to girls and women, on a whole range of health issues, as one of the prerequisites for social development, recognizing the rights, duties and responsibilities of parents and other persons legally responsible for children consistent with the Convention on the Rights of the Child;

(m) Expedite efforts to achieve the goals of national Health-for-All strategies, based on equality and social justice in line with the Alma-Ata Declaration on Primary Health Care,[17] by developing or updating country action plans or programmes to ensure universal, non-discriminatory access to basic health services, including sanitation and drinking water, to protect health, and to promote nutrition education and preventive health programmes;

(n) Strive to ensure that persons with disabilities have access to rehabilitation and other independent living services and assistive technology to enable them to maximize their well-being, independence and full participation in society;

(o) Ensure an integrated and intersectoral approach so as to provide for the protection and promotion of health for all in economic and social development, taking cognizance of the health dimensions of policies in all sectors;

(p) Seek to attain the maternal and child health objectives, especially the objectives of reducing child and maternal mortality, of the World Summit for Children, the United Nations Conference on Environment and Development and the International Conference on Population and Development;

(q) Strengthen national efforts to address more effectively the growing HIV/AIDS pandemic by providing necessary education and prevention services, working to ensure that appropriate care and support services are available and accessible to those affected by HIV/AIDS, and taking all necessary steps to eliminate every form of discrimination against and isolation of those living with HIV/AIDS;

(r) Promote, in all educational and health policies and programmes, environmental awareness, including awareness of unsustainable patterns of consumption and production.

At the international level, we will:

(s) Strive to ensure that international organizations, in particular the international financial institutions, support these objectives, integrating them into their policy programmes and operations as appropriate. This should be complemented by renewed bilateral and regional cooperation;

---

[16] See General Assembly resolution 49/184.

[17] See 'Report of the International Conference on Primary Health Care', Alma-Ata, Kazakhstan, 6–12 September 1978, Geneva, World Health Organization, 1978.

(t) Recognize the importance of the cultural dimension of development to ensure respect for cultural diversity and that of our common human cultural heritage. Creativity should be recognized and promoted;

(u) Request the specialized agencies, notably the United Nations Educational, Scientific and Cultural Organization and the World Health Organization, as well as other international organizations dedicated to the promotion of education, culture and health, to give greater emphasis to the overriding goals of eradicating poverty, promoting full and productive employment and fostering social integration;

(v) Strengthen intergovernmental organizations that utilize various forms of education to promote culture; disseminate information through education and communication media; help spread the use of technologies; and promote technical and professional training and scientific research;

(w) Provide support for stronger, better coordinated global actions against major diseases that take a heavy toll of human lives, such as malaria, tuberculosis, cholera, typhoid fever and HIV/AIDS; in this context, continue to support the joint and co-sponsored United Nations programme on HIV/AIDS;[18]

(x) Share knowledge, experience and expertise and enhance creativity, for example by promoting the transfer of technology, in the design and delivery of effective education, training and health programmes and policies, including substance-abuse awareness, prevention and rehabilitation programmes, which will result, inter alia, in endogenous capacity-building;

(y) Intensify and coordinate international support for education and health programmes based on respect for human dignity and focused on the protection of all women and children, especially against exploitation, trafficking and harmful practices, such as child prostitution, female genital mutilation and child marriages.

## COMMITMENT 7

We commit ourselves to accelerating the economic, social and human resource development of Africa and the least developed countries.

To this end, we will:

(a) Implement, at the national level, structural adjustment policies, which should include social development goals, as well as effective development strategies that establish a more favourable climate for trade and investment, give priority to human resource development and further promote the development of democratic institutions;

(b) Support the domestic efforts of Africa and the least developed countries to implement economic reforms, programmes to increase food security, and commodity diversification efforts through international cooperation, including South-South cooperation and technical and financial assistance, as well as trade and partnership;

(c) Find effective, development-oriented and durable solutions to external debt problems, through the immediate implementation of the terms of debt forgiveness agreed upon in the Paris Club in December 1994, which encompass debt reduction, including cancellation or other debt-relief measures; invite the international financial institutions to examine innovative approaches to assist low-income

---

[18] See Economic and Social Council resolution 1994/24.

countries with a high proportion of multilateral debt, with a view to alleviating their debt burdens; and develop techniques of debt conversion applied to social development programmes and projects in conformity with Summit priorities. These actions should take into account the mid-term review of the United Nations New Agenda for the Development of Africa in the 1990s[19] and the Programme of Action for the Least Developed Countries for the 1990s,[20] and should be implemented as soon as possible;

(d) Ensure the implementation of the strategies and measures for the development of Africa decided by the international community, and support the reform efforts, development strategies and programmes decided by the African countries and the least developed countries;

(e) Increase official development assistance, both overall and for social programmes, and improve its impact, consistent with countries' economic circumstances and capacities to assist, and consistent with commitments in international agreements;

(f) Consider ratifying the United Nations Convention to Combat Desertification in Those Countries Experiencing Serious Drought and/or Desertification, Particularly in Africa,[21] and support African countries in the implementation of urgent action to combat desertification and mitigate the effects of drought;

(g) Take all necessary measures to ensure that communicable diseases, particularly HIV/AIDS, malaria and tuberculosis, do not restrict or reverse the progress made in economic and social development.

## COMMITMENT 8

We commit ourselves to ensuring that when structural adjustment programmes are agreed to they include social development goals, in particular eradicating poverty, promoting full and productive employment, and enhancing social integration.

To this end, at the national level, we will:

(a) Promote basic social programmes and expenditures, in particular those affecting the poor and the vulnerable segments of society, and protect them from budget reductions, while increasing the quality and effectiveness of social expenditures;

(b) Review the impact of structural adjustment programmes on social development, including, where appropriate, by means of gender-sensitive social impact assessments and other relevant methods, in order to develop policies to reduce their negative effects and improve their positive impact; the cooperation of international financial institutions in the review could be requested by interested countries;

(c) Promote, in the countries with economies in transition, an integrated approach to the transformation process, addressing the social consequences of reforms and human resource development needs;

(d) Reinforce the social development components of all adjustment policies and programmes, including those resulting from the globalization of markets and rapid

---

[19] General Assembly resolution 46/151, annex, sect. II.
[20] 'Report of the Second United Nations Conference on the Least Developed Countries', Paris, 3–14 September 1990: A/CONF.147/18, part one.
[21] A/49/84/Add.2, annex, appendix II.

technological change, by designing policies to promote more equitable and enhanced access to income and resources;

(e) Ensure that women do not bear a disproportionate burden of the transitional costs of such processes.

At the international level, we will:

(f) Work to ensure that multilateral development banks and other donors complement adjustment lending with enhanced targeted social development investment lending;

(g) Strive to ensure that structural adjustment programmes respond to the economic and social conditions, concerns and needs of each country;

(h) Enlist the support and cooperation of regional and international organizations and the United Nations system, in particular the Bretton Woods institutions, in the design, social management and assessment of structural adjustment policies, and in implementing social development goals and integrating them into their policies, programmes and operations.

## COMMITMENT 9

We commit ourselves to increasing significantly and/or utilizing more efficiently the resources allocated to social development in order to achieve the goals of the Summit through national action and regional and international cooperation.

To this end, at the national level, we will:

(a) Develop economic policies to promote and mobilize domestic savings and attract external resources for productive investment, and seek innovative sources of funding, both public and private, for social programmes, while ensuring their effective utilization;

(b) Implement macroeconomic and micro-economic policies to ensure sustained economic growth and sustainable development to support social development;

(c) Promote increased access to credit for small and micro-enterprises, including those in the informal sector, with particular emphasis on the disadvantaged sectors of society;

(d) Ensure that reliable statistics and statistical indicators are used to develop and assess social policies and programmes so that economic and social resources are used efficiently and effectively;

(e) Ensure that, in accordance with national priorities and policies, taxation systems are fair, progressive and economically efficient, cognizant of sustainable development concerns, and ensure effective collection of tax liabilities;

(f) In the budgetary process, ensure transparency and accountability in the use of public resources, and give priority to providing and improving basic social services;

(g) Undertake to explore new ways of generating new public and private financial resources, inter alia, through the appropriate reduction of excessive military expenditures, including global military expenditures and the arms trade, and investments for arms production and acquisition, taking into consideration national security requirements, so as to allow possible allocation of additional funds for social and economic development;

(h) Utilize and develop fully the potential and contribution of cooperatives for the attainment of social development goals, in particular the eradication of poverty, the generation of full and productive employment, and the enhancement of social integration.

At the international level, we will:

(i) Seek to mobilize new and additional financial resources that are both adequate and predictable and are mobilized in a way that maximizes the availability of such resources and uses all available funding sources and mechanisms, inter alia, multilateral, bilateral and private sources, including on concessional and grant terms;

(j) Facilitate the flow to developing countries of international finance, technology and human skill in order to realize the objective of providing new and additional resources that are both adequate and predictable;

(k) Facilitate the flow of international finance, technology and human skill towards the countries with economies in transition;

(l) Strive for the fulfilment of the agreed target of 0.7 per cent of gross national product for overall official development assistance as soon as possible, and increase the share of funding for social development programmes, commensurate with the scope and scale of activities required to achieve the objectives and goals of the present Declaration and the Programme of Action of the Summit;

(m) Increase the flow of international resources to meet the needs of countries facing problems relating to refugees and displaced persons;

(n) Support South-South cooperation, which can take advantage of the experience of developing countries that have overcome similar difficulties;

(o) Ensure the urgent implementation of existing debt-relief agreements and negotiate further initiatives, in addition to existing ones, to alleviate the debts of the poorest and heavily indebted low-income countries at an early date, especially through more favourable terms of debt forgiveness, including application of the terms of debt forgiveness agreed upon in the Paris Club in December 1994, which encompass debt reduction, including cancellation or other debt-relief measures; where appropriate, these countries should be given a reduction of their bilateral official debt sufficient to enable them to exit from the rescheduling process and resume growth and development; invite the international financial institutions to examine innovative approaches to assist low-income countries with a high proportion of multilateral debt, with a view to alleviating their debt burdens; develop techniques of debt conversion applied to social development programmes and projects in conformity with Summit priorities;

(p) Fully implement the Final Act of the Uruguay Round of multilateral trade negotiations[22] as scheduled, including the complementary provisions specified in the Marrakesh Agreement establishing the World Trade Organization,[23] in recognition of the fact that broadly based growth in incomes, employment and trade are mutually reinforcing, taking into account the need to assist African countries and the least developed countries in evaluating the impact of the implementation of the Final Act so that they can benefit fully;

[22] See 'The Results of the Uruguay Round of Multilateral Trade Negotiations: The Legal Texts', Geneva, GATT Secretariat, 1994.
[23] Above note.

(q) Monitor the impact of trade liberalization on the progress made in developing countries to meet basic human needs, giving particular attention to new initiatives to expand their access to international markets;

(r) Give attention to the needs of countries with economies in transition with respect to international cooperation and financial and technical assistance, stressing the need for the full integration of economies in transition into the world economy, in particular to improve market access for exports in accordance with multilateral trade rules, taking into account the needs of developing countries;

(s) Support United Nations development efforts by a substantial increase in resources for operational activities on a predictable, continuous and assured basis, commensurate with the increasing needs of developing countries, as stated in General Assembly resolution 47/199, and strengthen the capacity of the United Nations and the specialized agencies to fulfil their responsibilities in the implementation of the outcome of the World Summit for Social Development.

## COMMITMENT 10

We commit ourselves to an improved and strengthened framework for international, regional and subregional cooperation for social development, in a spirit of partnership, through the United Nations and other multilateral institutions.

To this end, at the national level, we will:

(a) Adopt the appropriate measures and mechanisms for implementing and monitoring the outcome of the World Summit for Social Development, with the assistance, upon request, of the specialized agencies, programmes and regional commissions of the United Nations system, with broad participation of all sectors of civil society.

At the regional level, we will:

(b) Pursue such mechanisms and measures as are necessary and appropriate in particular regions or subregions. The regional commissions, in cooperation with regional intergovernmental organizations and banks, could convene, on a biennial basis, a meeting at a high political level to evaluate progress made towards fulfilling the outcome of the Summit, exchange views on their respective experiences and adopt appropriate measures. The regional commissions should report, through the appropriate mechanisms, to the Economic and Social Council on the outcome of such meetings.

At the international level, we will:

(c) Instruct our representatives to the organizations and bodies of the United Nations system, international development agencies and multilateral development banks to enlist the support and cooperation of these organizations and bodies to take appropriate and coordinated measures for continuous and sustained progress in attaining the goals and commitments agreed to by the Summit. The United Nations and the Bretton Woods institutions should establish regular and substantive dialogue, including at the field level, for more effective and efficient coordination of assistance for social development;

(d) Refrain from any unilateral measure not in accordance with international law and the Charter of the United Nations that creates obstacles to trade relations among States;

(e) Strengthen the structure, resources and processes of the Economic and Social Council and its subsidiary bodies, and other organizations within the United Nations system that are concerned with economic and socialdevelopment;

(f) Request the Economic and Social Council to review and assess, on the basis of reports of national Governments, the regional commissions, relevant functional commissions and specialized agencies, progress made by the international community towards implementing the outcome of the World Summit for Social Development, and to report to the General Assembly, accordingly, for its appropriate consideration and action;

(g) Request the General Assembly to hold a special session in the year 2000 for an overall review and appraisal of the implementation of the outcome of the Summit and to consider further actions and initiatives.

# INDEX